SECOND EDITION

NATIVE

CULTURES AND HISTORIES OF NATIVE NORTH AMERICA

NATIONS

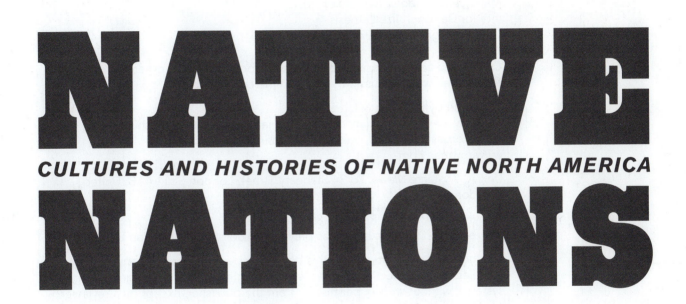

NANCY BONVILLAIN

ROWMAN & LITTLEFIELD

Lanham · Boulder · New York · London

Senior Editor: Leanne Silverman
Assistant Editor: Carli Hansen
College Marketing Manager: Karin Cholak
Marketing Manager: Deborah Hudson
Interior Designer: Ilze Lemesis
Cover Designer: Jen Huppert Design

Credits and acknowledgments for material borrowed from other sources, and reproduced with permission, appear in the credits section.

Published by Rowman & Littlefield
A wholly owned subsidiary of The Rowman & Littlefield Publishing Group, Inc.
4501 Forbes Boulevard, Suite 200, Lanham, Maryland 20706
www.rowman.com

Unit A, Whitacre Mews, 26-34 Stannary Street, London SE11 4AB, United Kingdom

British Library Cataloguing in Publication Information Available

Library of Congress Cataloging-in-Publication Data
Names: Bonvillain, Nancy, author.
Title: Native nations : cultures and histories of native North America / Nancy Bonvillain.
Description: Second edition. | Lanham, Maryland : Rowman & Littlefield, 2016. | Includes bibliographical references and index.
Identifiers: LCCN 2016032735 (print) | LCCN 2016033136 (ebook) | ISBN 9781442251441 (cloth : alk. paper) | ISBN 9781442251458 (pbk. : alk. paper) | ISBN 9781442251465 (electronic)
Subjects: LCSH: Indians of North America.
Classification: LCC E77 .B65 2016 (print) | LCC E77 (ebook) | DDC 970.004/97—dc23
LC record available at https://lccn.loc.gov/2016032735

∞™ The paper used in this publication meets the minimum requirements of American National Standard for Information Sciences—Permanence of Paper for Printed Library Materials, ANSI/NISO Z39.48-1992.

Printed in the United States of America

CONTENTS

LIST OF TABLES

THIS BOOK INCLUDES DISCUSSION of the cultures, histories, and contemporary lives of members of the First Nations of North America. Following a brief introduction, two chapters provide overviews of historical and contemporary issues. Chapter 2 is a summary of the major events that have shaped North American history, including the policies of colonial powers and of the United States and Canadian governments. Chapter 3 first presents recent social, economic, and population data from Canada and the United States and then proceeds with a discussion of contemporary issues relevant to the lives of First Nations peoples, including climate change, treaty claims, and programs to maintain and enhance cultural, environmental, economic, political, and health rights. It ends with an examination of recent decisions handed down by the Supreme Courts of the United States and Canada as they affect Native rights.

Subsequent chapters are divided into nine parts based on region (Northeast, Southeast, Plains, Great Basin, Southwest, California, Plateau, Northwest Coast, and Subarctic and Arctic). Each part begins with an overview chapter, followed by one (or in some cases, two) chapters that deal in detail with a First Nation within the region.

Each chapter (beginning with chapter 4) that explores the circumstances of Native communities starts with what is known of indigenous societies at about the time of European arrival on these shores, approximately AD 1500. Indigenous lifeways encompass economic activities, family and social life, community and political organization, and religious beliefs and practices. The chapters then turn to the histories of Native communities, focusing on the ways that historical processes affected indigenous cultures and the responses that Native peoples had to these processes. Finally, the chapters conclude with sections discussing contemporary Native life, attempting to give a picture of the strength of Native communities as they confront and respond to cultural, economic, and political changes.

This second edition includes updates in each of the chapters of social and economic data from the most recent US and Canadian government reports, as well as from information provided in First Nations websites. In most cases, data are collected from census statistics from 2010 or later, but in some cases, economic statistics (including employment, income, and poverty rates) have not been published for each nation since 1999. Chapter 3, "Native Communities Today," includes expanded coverage throughout as well as new sections dealing with the effects of climate change on indigenous communities, efforts toward safeguarding treaty rights, treatment of health and illness issues, and the aforementioned section on Supreme Court judicial rulings. This edition also includes two new chapters, a regional overview of the Plateau (chapter 19) and a separate chapter on the Nez Perce (chapter 20). Finally, the book contains a list of available websites for many Native American tribes and First Nations. In addition, a listing of all US federally recognized tribes and Canadian First Nations peoples is available at the book's webpage at www.rowman.com.

I wish to express my gratitude to Leanne Silverman, Senior Acquisitions Editor, Rowman & Littlefield, for her constant encouragement and support in the preparation of this new edition. I also want to thank Mallie Prytherch, data researcher, for her long hours of work and initiative in providing statistical data for the ethnographic chapters. And I thank reviewers whose comments and opinions helped strengthen this edition including Daniel Philip Bigman (Georgia State University), Chris Hurst-Loeffler (Irvine Valley College), Adam King (University of South Carolina), Michelle D. Stokely (Indiana University Northwest), Steven Williams (Oberlin College), Erica Cusi Wortham (George Washington University), and one anonymous reviewer. Finally, my continual appreciation goes to the people at Akwesasne for the personal and intellectual support that I have always received there. I am especially grateful to the late Gloria Thompson, the late Ernest Benedict, and Beatrice Francis and their families for the many days over many years spent in their company. My admiration goes to them and others at Akwesasne, including the teachers, staff, and students at the Akwesasne Freedom School, who have led and participated in many struggles for cultural, linguistic, and political sovereignty. It is to them that this book is dedicated.

Nancy Bonvillain
May 2016

Introduction

HUNDREDS OF DISTINCT and diverse peoples have lived in what is now called North America. Their ancestors, who lived on the continent for many thousands of years, adapted their economies to best utilize resources in their environment, developed social systems that bound families and communities together, and devised ways of integrating their communities, making group decisions and ensuring the survival of their societies. These various peoples followed ethical and religious principles that gave meaning to their lives. Chapters in this text are organized into regional divisions, usually called "culture areas" in the literature. These are essentially geographic divisions within which certain similarities, although not identities, of topography, climate, and natural flora and fauna can be found. The societies that developed within each area often shared a core of similar practices and activities, but they were not identical. Cultural or historical homogeneity did not exist. Moreover, societies were influenced by neighboring groups and were affected by continent-wide historical processes. The culture area approach is useful as an organizing principle for North America because the economies and social systems that developed here were, in general, closely related to and grew out of ecological adaptations to natural resources that were themselves adapted to existing topographical and climatic conditions. However, it is important to keep in mind that neighboring Native societies differed from one another in significant features.

Each chapter includes discussion of aboriginal or "traditional" cultures, the transformations that occurred as a result of European intrusions into North America, and the conditions of contemporary Native communities. The time frame for the discussion of aboriginal culture varies from region to region and from nation to nation depending on the time of initial European contact. The effects of Europeans' policies and actions began earliest in the Northeast, Southeast, Southwest, and coastal California, whereas they were latest in interior Subarctic and Arctic areas.

Chapter 2, "A Short History," presents an introductory analysis of historical processes begun after the appearance of Europeans on the North American continent that affected all indigenous nations to one degree or another. It reviews major federal US and Canadian legislation concerning Native peoples. It is followed, in Chapter 3, "Native Communities Today," by an overview of population, income, and employment trends in Native communities today in the United States and Canada. The chapter also reviews some contemporary economic, political, and cultural issues that may help to shape the future of Native America, focusing on significant developments as Native nations have attempted to broaden their sovereign powers and assert their political and cultural rights. Thereafter, chapters are presented in sections, each beginning with an overview of the region, followed by one (or in some cases two) chapters examining the culture and history of a nation residing within that area. The following regions and nations are included: Northeast (Mohawk, Mi'kmaq), Southeast (Choctaw), Plains (Teton Lakota, Hidatsa), Great Basin (Shoshone), Southwest (Zuni, Navajo), California (Pomo), Plateau (Nez Perce), Northwest Coast (Kwakwaka'wakw or Kwakiutl), Subarctic and Arctic (Innu or Montagnais, Inuit). The nations discussed are, of course, but a sample of the more than 500 nations indigenous to this continent.

Before proceeding, some notes on terminology are required here. The ethnic or racial category of "Native American" here refers to people whose ancestors were the indigenous inhabitants of what is now the United States and Canada. In Canada, the term "First Nations" refers to the original peoples of that country. Three additional ethnic identifications are used here: "Indian," "Inuit," and "Métis." "Inuit" is the name of Native people who live in the Arctic regions of northern Canada and parts of coastal Alaska. They are speakers of closely related languages and share many features of culture. The word "Indian" (or "American Indian") generally refers to indigenous people who are not Inuit. It has come to be general usage, but it is an unfortunate appellation both because it derives from a mistaken belief about this continent and because it lumps together people belonging to many hundreds of separate nations. It is a word of colonial invaders, not of the people being named. The term "Métis" is an ethnic identification used in Canada for people who are "mixed-bloods" or descendants of Native women and European trappers, traders, and woodsmen, especially of French, Scottish, Irish, English, and German origin. They form unique communities, principally in western Canadian provinces, and have special legal status in that country.

Finally, the terms "nation," "band," and "tribe" can be distinguished. A "nation" is a group of people who speak the same language (or dialects of the same language), who have a sense of territorial boundaries, and who share many (but not necessarily all) features of cultural practice and belief. "Tribes" and "bands" are specific types of societies having different kinds of systems of leadership, decision-making, and group cohesion. Bands are small, loosely organized groups of people that are politically autonomous and have minimal leadership. In tribes, local communities are united (with varying degrees of cohesion) within a recognized named group having some recognized leaders. Tribal social and/or political unity may be limited to the level of villages or may combine villages into networks of decision-making and cooperation.

Unknown thousands of years ago, ancestors of all of these peoples probably migrated across what is now known as the Bering Strait from Asia into North America. When these migrations began and when they ended is a subject of much debate. Numerous sources that deal extensively with this issue can be consulted. Deloria's book (1997) is recommended for its refutation of some standard archeological assumptions.

For example, Deloria suggests a counter narrative that focuses on sacred stories told by Native peoples in the Northwest Coast of Washington and British Columbia that describe vast topographic upheavals that resulted in the creation of the lakes, rivers, and coastline of the region. Although these narratives recount the adventures of mythic creatures such as Raven, Muskrat, and numerous monsters, Deloria proposes that they reflect ancient peoples' experiences and observations. In other words, they use the poetic language of tradition to transmit historical knowledge. Geologists provide evidence that corroborates Deloria's inferences. For instance, according to Dr. Eugene Kiver, "floods may have happened when people were around [many thousands of years ago]. Native Americans have myths about floods" (Robins 2004).

Although each nation is unique, there are a number of common (but not universal) features of resource utilization, production, social ethics, community cohesion, and religious beliefs. These shared features or concepts are suggestive tendencies, not absolutes. Territory and resources in Native America were owned or controlled communally rather than by individuals. Among foragers of the Plains, Subarctic, and Arctic, land and resources were owned by the community, band, or nation as a whole, while among those in the Northwest Coast and parts of California, resource sites were collectively owned by lineages. In farming nations, productive land was usually controlled by corporate kin groups such as clans or lineages. Rights to use land and exploit resource sites were inherited within the relevant unit, whether lineage, clan, or nation. When limited to kin groups, usufruct rights were conveyed either through matrilineal or patrilineal inheritance, depending upon the prevailing system of kinship and descent. Conflicts over resources rarely developed because in most areas, neighbors were permitted to obtain what they needed when foods in their own domain were scarce or supplies were exhausted.

Native economies were closely adapted to their environments. Where farming was possible (in areas of the Northeast, Southeast, Southwest, eastern Prairies, and Plains) most people grew corn, beans, and squash, the three crops that were the staples of aboriginal horticulture. Land was cleared for farming by slash-and-burn techniques, sometimes by men or sometimes by women and men working together. Women were usually responsible for the major portion of farm work once land was prepared, but in the Southwest, farming was usually (but not always) a man's task. The central diet of farm produce was supplemented by gathering wild fruits and plants and by hunting and fishing. Farming people lived in stable villages although some shifted their settlement sites every generation or so when their fields became less fertile and productive or when firewood or drinking water became scarce nearby. Village size generally varied from a few hundred to several thousand. Households were organized by kin groups, some following matrilineal descent while others were patrilineal. Bilateral kinship organization prevailed in only a few farming nations.

For other aboriginal economies, foraging constituted the primary mode of production. Nations inhabiting the northern Northeast, northern Plains, Subarctic, and Arctic were of necessity foragers because of environmental and climatic limitations. Elsewhere, foraging nations often lived side-by-side with farmers, frequently trading surpluses with one another. Most people who relied exclusively on hunting and gathering lived in small, temporary settlements. They were nomadic, attuned to the migration patterns of animals and the seasonal availability of wild plants. In the Northwest Coast and most of California, however, foraging nations were able to support a relatively dense population because of the richness of their natural environments. Unlike foragers in the rest of North America, they lived in relatively large and stable villages. Kinship and descent patterns were not the same everywhere. Some foragers were organized by bilateral descent, others were patrilineal, and some were matrilineal. Variation was attested even within a region. For example, all three types of kinship systems were found among foragers of the Northwest Coast.

Aboriginal social life centered on principles of kin-group support, cooperation, and allegiance. Families and households were the primary units of economic, social, political, and ceremonial cohesion. Social ethics stressed the importance of sharing resources, labor, and property with members of one's kin group and community. People were expected to participate in communal activities, to give economic and ceremonial support to relatives, and to respect each other's autonomy. In general, generosity, even temper, and cooperativeness were highly valued personality traits whereas anger, stinginess, pride, and acquisitiveness were considered shameful attributes. Indian and Inuit ethics valued the primacy of both individuals and communities. People's autonomy, agency, and rights to make decisions for themselves were respected. But people understood that the needs and goals of their community were also their personal needs and goals. Cooperation with others was not seen as a denial of the self but rather as an expression of one's own interest.

Most Native societies were founded on egalitarian social principles where social distinctions were based solely on age, gender, and abilities. People were esteemed because of their personalities and achievements. There were no inherent barriers to one's success or the possibility of accruing prestige. However, in some nations, particularly in the Southeast, Northwest Coast, and parts of California, systems of social stratification developed that differentiated members of the village or nation into loosely defined classes or ranks. In some of these groups, the populace was divided into an elite and a commoner status while in others a third and lowest class of slaves existed. There was usually some mobility between the elites and commoners, but slaves (typically war captives and their descendants) could not advance socially. However, even in stratified societies, an egalitarian ethic underlay people's interpersonal relations and rights to participate in their society and to have decent living conditions, including adequate food and clothing. This ethic was demonstrated in the sharing and redistribution of resources. People of high status were obligated to provide aid for members of their kin groups and communities. Indeed, generosity was an absolute requisite for anyone aspiring to prestigious positions and public renown.

The basic egalitarianism of most Native nations was demonstrated as well in gender relations. Although economic tasks were said to be the work of either men or women, in actual practice gender roles were not always rigidly demarcated. For example, given the necessity or inclination to do so, people could perform household work usually assigned to the other gender. Many tasks required the cooperative, joint, and interdependent labor of men and women. Furthermore, respect was accorded to both women and men for their economic, social, and spiritual contributions to households and communities. Although leadership was usually vested in men, women could occupy leadership positions in many nations. Women's voices were heard in household and community discussions, and their participation contributed to the formation of group consensus.

The equal treatment of women and men was reflected in generally similar attitudes toward male and female sexual activity and marital relationships in most nations. With some exceptions, violence against women in the form of beatings or rape was uncommon or even unheard of. Where such violence was tolerated, it was a reflection of some degree of male dominance in aboriginal culture (e.g., among Inuit in the Arctic) or in societies newly incorporated into European trade networks that marginalized women (e.g., among some nineteenth-century Plains nations). Although first marriages were often arranged by parents, the couple concerned usually had the right to veto a disagreeable union. And, if a marriage proved unhappy for either partner, a wife or husband was free to divorce and seek another mate. In many societies, polygamy was possible, although not of great frequency. Polygyny (marriage of a man to two or more women) was more common than polyandry (marriage of a woman to two or more men), but both forms were attested. Where polygyny existed, it seems usually to have been an indication of the high status and wealth of certain men rather than of the submissiveness of women.

Finally, both men and women participated in the religious life of their societies by engaging in ceremonial practices and by obtaining and exercising spirit power. Men and women might have different roles to play in rituals, but neither was excluded from the social recognition and spirit power attainable through religious activity. Generally, equal and balanced models of gender were symbolized in creation or transformation stories and in the pantheon of spirit beings who inhabited the universe and who offered aid and comfort to humans. Female and male deities all had important roles in the Native spirit world.

An important indication of the flexibility of gender roles and attitudes toward sex in Native cultures was the existence of a third category of gender. Documentary evidence indicates that in well over 100 nations, a person could become neither man nor woman but instead occupy a third status, now often referred to as a "Two-Spirit" (Jacobs 1997 et al.; Lang 1998). This term is translated from the Ojibwa phrase *niizh mani-doowag*, referring to people who "carry both a masculine and feminine spirit" (Murg 2011: 28). Two-Spirits were biological males and females who, for various reasons, assumed social roles other than (or sometimes in addition to) the roles usually associated with their sex. Their behavior and appearance combined features appropriate to women and men and also incorporated activities specifically assigned to them. The existence of such possibilities for males and females reflects beliefs in individual autonomy as well as underlying philosophical notions concerning the mutability of gender and of the self. Attitudes toward Two-Spirits were not everywhere the same. Although they were more often regarded as embodying acceptable alternative behaviors, in some nations they were ridiculed or feared. Of the more than 100 societies where they were documented, most were in the midwest and west, from the Mississippi Valley and Great Lakes to California, although their occurrence was also noted, with less frequency, in the east, Subarctic, and Arctic (Callender and Kochems 1983: 444). In the Plains, some women took on male roles as warriors and chiefs without necessarily identifying or being identified as a Two-Spirit.

People might become Two-Spirits as a result of either personal inclination or spiritual calling. In the first instance, a young girl or boy might take an interest in the occupations and demeanors usually displayed by members of the other sex. Parents thereafter trained the child in the subsistence skills appropriate to the child's chosen role. Among some groups, parents who had no sons might choose a daughter to learn hunting skills as a son would.

The more common mode of recruitment was to receive a spirit calling through a vision or dream. Dreaming to assume the third gender gave both spirit and social validation to a male's or female's transformation. As a consequence, Two-Spirits were often thought to have extraordinary powers as demonstrated by their ability to heal and to prophesy or foretell the future.

While the behavior of Two-Spirits differed in various societies, they typically performed economic duties usually appropriate to the opposite sex, sometimes in addition to those associated with their own biological sex. Female Two-Spirits were hunters, trappers, and occasionally warriors as well. Male Two-Spirits contributed their labor as farmers (where economies included horticulture) and were trained in domestic skills such as sewing, embroidery, and food preparation. Where warfare was a significant activity, male Two-Spirits generally refrained from battle but they might join war parties as carriers of supplies or healers for the wounded. And although female Two-Spirits did not always participate as warriors, they were not constrained from doing so, and some became famous for their military and tactical skills.

Two-Spirits were often more prosperous than other members of their community. Their ability to perform both women's and men's work gave them economic advantages. In some societies, Two-Spirits had unique sources of income because they performed ritual functions specifically assigned to them. For example, Lakota Two-Spirits received horses in return for bestowing secret, spiritually powerful names on children. In several California groups, Two-Spirits were responsible for burial and mourning rituals. In societies such as the Diné, Cheyenne, and Omaha, they were often paid for resolving conflicts between spouses or arranging liaisons and marriages (Williams 1986: 70–71).

Leadership in most Native nations was through selection and consensus rather than through automatic inheritance of position. Indeed, in most Native communities, formalized leadership was absent. Instead, people of intelligence, experience, skill, and success were looked to for advice and counsel because of their personality and proven accomplishments. Such people led by example and by exhorting their followers to proper behavior. In some nations, leadership tended to be passed in particular lineages or clans, but succession to the position was never automatic. If the eligible candidate was inappropriate because of a lack of intelligence, skill, or valued personality traits, he/she was bypassed in favor of another, more deserving candidate.

In most nations, leadership councils were also looked to for advice and direction. Such councils might be informally recognized and constituted or be highly structured and formalized. Council decisions were based on consensus and unanimity. Furthermore, the opinions of other members of a community were sought in order to arrive at a group decision. Leadership, whether individual or collective, was rarely coercive. Automatic obedience to leaders was absent. Instead, people heeded a leader's or council's advice only if they respected their opinions and intelligence.

Leadership was most typically rewarded with social prestige. Even though kin-group leaders in some Southeastern, Californian, and Northwest Coast nations might be able to amass more wealth than others because of their favored position as redistributors of resources, they were obligated to provide for their constituents' well-being through the generous giving of aid in times of need and through ceremonial giveaways hosted for all members of their communities. Only in some Southeastern and Northwest Coast nations was the standard of living of chiefs and their close kin appreciably better than those of common folk. There, chiefly families lived in more substantial and larger dwellings, and they had finer clothing and more elaborate personal ornaments. Still, nowhere did any member of the community lack adequate housing, clothing, or food. Everyone might receive aid from their kin groups and from the requisite generosity of chiefs and others of high status.

Social control was usually vested in kin groups. Wrongdoers were admonished by their families to correct errant behavior. They might be scolded, teased, or ostracized. They bore the public shame of having wronged someone else and, because of that, having wronged or dishonored their families. Rarely were formal punishments carried out. Perhaps the best counterexample comes from Plains nations where regulations concerning activities during buffalo hunts were strictly enforced by members of policing societies who might confiscate or destroy a wrongdoer's property or even mete out beatings. But such punishments were only given to people whose behavior jeopardized the success of a communal buffalo hunt, which might result in economic hardship for an entire community.

Native religions were generally based on beliefs in a spirit essence that pervaded the universe and imbued all living creatures and many inanimate objects, forces of nature, and specific locales with spirit powers. Since spirit beings could affect human activity and outcomes, their aid was sought for protection, instruction, and comfort. Fundamental to all Native belief systems, every person might acquire personal spirit power, although some people were able to obtain more power than others. Such individuals could use their extraordinary abilities to heal, foretell the future, or perform other beneficial acts on behalf of their communities.

Aboriginal religions stressed the importance of direct contact with the spirit world. People might have unsought visitations from spirit beings in dreams and spontaneous visions, or they might deliberately seek out contact through prayers, songs, intense thought, and self-sacrifice in the form of fasting and isolation. Native religions placed great significance on dreams as carriers of messages from spirit powers. Through dreams, people could learn the meanings of past or present events, foretell the future, have contact with spirit beings or with deceased kin, and obtain powerful songs and dances.

People participated in both individual and community rituals. Ceremonies were held to mark life-cycle transitions, especially birth, puberty, and death. Of these events, death usually received the most elaborate rituals and the most intense social and emotional involvement. In addition, people participated in healing rituals that combined a sophisticated knowledge of the medicinal properties of plants and animal substances with complex ritual cures based on the people's understanding of the spirit causes of illness and misfortune. Community rituals were often dedicated to resource renewal. As might be expected, nations with economies based on horticulture tended to stress calendric rites timed to planting and harvesting activities whereas nations with hunting economies tended to emphasize animal thanksgiving and renewal ceremonies.

Native nations were linked to their neighbors through trade, travel, and intermarriage. Extensive local and long-distance trading networks facilitated the exchange of raw materials and finished products from one group to another. Annual trade fairs in some regions, especially in the Plateau and the interior Northwest along the Snake and Columbia Rivers, brought together thousands of people coming from communities as distant as California, the Plains, and the Southwest. Such trading networks and fairs also helped create social and ceremonial bonds among individuals that had long-term significance for their home communities. People not only adopted new items of material culture and learned new technological skills, they also borrowed social practices, rituals, and religious and secular knowledge and literatures. Similar advantages stemmed from marriages between members of different nations as the in-marrying spouses contributed their own languages and cultural practices to the material and ideological wealth of their new homes.

The ability of Native nations to absorb foreign elements of culture had an analogy in their willingness to absorb foreign individuals, learning from them and accepting them as legitimate members of the community. Incorporation of outsiders and cultural assimilation of their descendants defined group membership and ensured stability within the context of change and adaptation.

The issue of group membership continues to be of great significance for Native people today. In both the United States and Canada, governmental policies have shaped the definition of who is an Indian or Inuit and therefore who has claim to land and resources guaranteed by treaty, official agreements, or legislation. As will be detailed in Chapter 2, federal rules that defined Indians according to legal stipulation either of blood quantum (in the United States) or patrilineal descent (in Canada) effectively denied rights to land and funds to incalculable numbers of people. In Canada, the 1876 "Indian Act" withdrew Native status from Indian and Inuit women who married non-Indians and from their descendants. The rights of women and their descendants were not restored until passage of the revised Canadian constitution in 1982 and a 1985 Supreme Court decision based on that document. In the United States, the General Allotment Act of 1887 divided reservations into allotments to be assigned to individual Indians and established tribal rolls to determine eligible membership. Although rules varied, people typically had to prove from one-quarter to one-half degree of blood in the group (Churchill 1999: 50). Regulations might even disbar people who were "full-blood" Indians but of mixed tribal parentage. Constitutions drawn up for recognized tribes in the United States after passage of the 1934 Indian Reorganization Act continued past practices by restricting membership, usually stipulating a one-quarter blood quantum requirement (52).

Results of these externally imposed policies have many repercussions today. By defining away millions of people of Native descent, they reduce the numbers of people entitled to share land, resources, and funds guaranteed by treaty and those eligible to participate in federal or tribal programs that serve Native reservations and communities. And by defining away millions of people of Native descent, they minimize the potential political strength as well as public awareness of the existence of Indians and Inuit that could be mobilized on behalf of legal, economic, and social issues of concern to Native people. Current rates of intermarriage in which an estimated two-third of people on tribal rolls marry nonmembers will mean a steady erosion of the Native population base given blood-quantum criteria. According to Churchill, "the segment of the federally recognized Native population evidencing less than one-quarter-degree blood quantum, presently about 4 percent, will have climbed to 59 percent or more by 2080" (56). In the face of this dilemma, some Indian tribes have abandoned restrictive requirements for membership in order to stave off their own "definitional and statistical extermination" (56) and have drawn up criteria more consistent with the realities of descent and cultural identification.

The government's practice of ignoring the complexity of mixed-racial and ethnic identification and instead categorizing many respondents with mixed

Indian ancestry as Whites, African Americans, or Hispanics contributes to the undercount of Native people. From a detailed analysis of racial and ancestral identification in the US census, Forbes estimates a probable Indian population of more than 15 million. As Forbes explains, a more accurate assessment of the number of people with Indian ancestry than that of the official count should include at least 7 or 8 million people with "Hispanic" identification as well as "from 30 percent to 70 percent of African-Americans who are reported to be part-Indian in various studies" (Forbes 1990: 8). Including such people would increase the number of Americans with Indian ancestry by another 7 million (18).

With some misgivings and with apologies, population and economic information and data provided in regional and tribal chapters as well as in the final chapter of this text are derived from official sources, including tribal offices, the US Bureau of the Census, the US Bureau of Indian Affairs, Canadian Statistics Canada, and the Canadian Department of Indian Affairs and Northern Development. Finally, tribal names appearing in the book follow those currently in general use in Native American journals and publications.

REFERENCES

Callender, Charles, and Lee Kochems. 1983. "The North American Berdache." *Current Anthropology* 24: 443–470.

Churchill, Ward. 1999. "The Crucible of American Indian Identity: Native Tradition Versus Colonial Imposition in Postconquest North America." *American Indian Culture and Research Journal* 23, no. 1: 39–67.

Deloria, Vine. 1997. *Red Earth, White Lies: Native Americans and the Myth of Scientific Fact.* New York: Simon & Schuster; Golden, CO: Fulcrum.

Forbes, Jack. 1990. "Undercounting Native Americans: The 1980 Census and the Manipulation of Racial Identity in the United States." *Wicazo Sa Review* 6: 2–26.

Jacobs, Sue Ellen, *et al.* 1997. *Two-Spirit People: Native American Gender Identity, Sexuality, and Spirituality.* Urbana, IL: University of Illinois Press.

Lang, Sabine. 1998. *Men as Women, Women as Men: Changing Gender in Native American Cultures.* Austin, TX: University of Texas Press.

Murg, Um. 2011. *Indian Country Today* June 6.

Robins, Jim. 2004. "Ice Age Flood Waves Leave a Walkable Trail Across the Northwest." *New York Times* August 24.

Williams, Walter. 1986. *The Spirit and the Flesh.* Boston: Beacon Press.

NATIVE NORTH AMERICA

A Short History

They made us many promises, more than I can remember, but they never kept but one. They promised to take our land and they took it.

Mahpiya Luta (Red Cloud), Lakota (1822–1909)

NATIVE PEOPLE OF NORTH AMERICA lived in societies that were continually changing from generation to generation. From their earliest origins, people adapted to the climates, ecology, and resources of their regions. As they migrated to new territories or the conditions around them changed, they adapted their economies and developed social, political, and religious practices that they felt best suited their ways of living. Some of the changes in their cultures were prompted by internal developments; others resulted from accommodations and borrowings from their neighbors or even from distant people they met as travelers and traders. Although Native societies were dynamic and continually incorporated new elements and modified their own practices as they lived in North America, the arrival of Europeans on the continent affected indigenous people in ways and to an extent unknown in previous centuries. External forces had an impact on all aspects of culture, altering economies, sociopolitical systems, and religious beliefs. Indeed, the very survival of Native nations was jeopardized as Europeans steadily took the land and either indirectly or directly exacted changes in Native ways of life. In addition, hundreds of thousands of Indians died from diseases of European origin as well as from military conflicts.

This chapter focuses on the transformations of Native societies beginning in the late fifteenth century as people responded to contact with Europeans and later with Americans and Canadians. These contacts sometimes offered opportunities that were welcomed, especially in terms of trade, but then later and more commonly led to individual and community disruption. In subsequent chapters aboriginal ways of life will be more extensively explored. This approach does not imply that Native societies were somehow static and unchanging prior to the fifteenth century. Indeed, we can learn much of earlier indigenous lifeways from archaeological studies that investigate the development of material culture to document technologies, settlements, and economies, and that suggest inferences about social and political systems. The interested reader is encouraged to consult the many sources available.

THE ARRIVAL OF EUROPEANS IN NORTH AMERICA

The first European to make an official landfall on the Northeastern coast of North America was John Cabot, who arrived in 1497 and promptly declared Newfoundland to be a possession of England. Within a few years, English, French, Portuguese, and Basque fishermen crossed the Atlantic Ocean from Europe to fish in the abundant waters off the coasts of Newfoundland, Labrador, and Nova Scotia. By 1550, approximately fifty fishing boats from each of the European countries (England, France, Portugal, Spain) were making annual visits to the Atlantic waters. By the end of the sixteenth century, the numbers doubled and tripled (Sauer 1971: 240). European fishermen and sailors began trading knives, nails, scissors, and other manufactured products with coastal Algonkian peoples in exchange for food and furs. In some cases, Indians were hired by Europeans to work as fishermen. For example, in the 1530s, Jacques Cartier reported observing a group of Montagnais who were fishing for a French captain off the Labrador coast.

Although such contacts seemed profitable for all concerned, not every encounter between Indians and Europeans was friendly. In 1501, a Portuguese explorer named Gaspar Corte-Real initiated a practice that recurred with some frequency during the next two centuries when on his return to Portugal, Corte-Real's ship bore fifty-seven Native people who had been kidnapped by his sailors. European explorers and traders often took Indians to Europe as curiosities and/or to be trained as interpreters on subsequent voyages. Many never returned to their homeland due to their early deaths from European diseases. Other Indians travelled to Europe voluntarily in order to cement economic and political alliances and to learn something of the cultures of their foreign visitors.

Soon after contact between Indians and Europeans began, commercial relations in the Northeast expanded from intermittent activities to become the focus of European concern in North America. Trade between indigenous nations and French, British, and Dutch merchants turned to fur-bearing animals, especially beaver. By 1520, Algonkians along the Atlantic coast from Newfoundland to Maine were trading furs to European fishermen and explorers. And when Cartier ventured inland along the Gulf of St. Lawrence in 1534, he was offered furs by Algonkian and Iroquoian peoples. As the wearing of beaver felt hats and collars became fashionable in Europe, the desire for animal skins accelerated. For Native people, commerce with Europeans was an extension of aboriginal trading networks. They often admired and sought new products, realizing the technological advantage of metal tools and utensils because of their durability and appreciating the novelty of luxury items such as ornaments, dried foods, and fancy articles of clothing.

While the French, British, and Dutch were establishing trading networks with aboriginal nations in the Northeast, Spanish adventurers were plundering the Southeast and Southwest. Ponce de Leon made the first historically recorded European visit to the Southeast in 1513 when he landed along the southwest coast of Florida, but he was given an unfriendly reception by members of the Calusa nation. Two decades later, Hernando de Soto led a force of more than 600 soldiers on an expedition inland from the western coast of Florida through the south to the Mississippi River to the Gulf of Mexico. During the four-year span of their invasion (1539–1543), Spanish soldiers looted stores of corn, enslaved men as guides and carriers of provisions, and raped the women. Thousands of people were murdered and their lands and resources ruined.

In the same year that de Soto began his march through the Southeast, another Spaniard, Marcos de Niza, made a brief excursion into New Mexico from Spanish bases in central Mexico. He was followed in 1540 by Francisco de Coronado, whose large expedition searched in vain for treasures of gold and silver. Failing that, they plundered Puebloan settlements in the Southwest.

The early history of North America reveals different motives stimulating European activity but their eventual impact followed similar patterns throughout the continent. Trade, conquest, and colonization spread everywhere, and within a few centuries all Native people were engulfed and their cultures forever transformed.

European assumptions about their right to claim the lands and resources of peoples in the Americas (and elsewhere) were based on what has come to be called the "Doctrine of Discovery." This "Doctrine" originates in the papal bulls of the fifteenth century. For example, in 1455 Pope Nicholas V granted rights of conquest to the king of Portugal, including the rights to "invade, search out, capture, vanquish and subdue" all peoples who were not Christian and to take their possessions and "reduce their persons to perpetual slavery." These and similar statements by subsequent popes set the stage for European colonization in North America and elsewhere. But this Doctrine was not restricted to that time period. Its underlying assumptions influenced the development of British, French, and later American and Canadian policies regarding their right to claim the lands and resources of indigenous peoples and their ability to ignore the rights and claims of the original inhabitants.

EXPANSION OF TRADE AND ITS CONSEQUENCES

Many Indians reacted positively, albeit with some distrust, to opportunities provided by foreign trade.

According to accounts given by nearly every European trader/explorer who wrote about the subject, Indians were eager to trade for tools and utensils made of iron, copper, and brass, including pots, kettles, knives, needles, and many other articles. Citing just one of many examples, Champlain described his meeting with Algonkians in Maine in 1604 that began with speeches of friendship, referring to the desire of the French to visit the country and trade with the inhabitants:

> They signified their great satisfaction, saying that no greater good could come to them than to have our friendship … and that we should dwell in their land, in order that they might in future more than ever before engage in hunting beavers, and give us a part of them in return for our providing them with things which they wanted. After he finished his discourse, I presented them with hatchets, caps, knives, and other little knickknacks. (Champlain 1907: 50)

Many people were indeed willing, even enthusiastic, to trade for European goods. Over the centuries, participation in the fur trade increased in volume and in importance in indigenous economies. The immediate consequence of trade was the addition of material and technological innovations but dependence on trade had negative effects not foreseen by most Indian participants. Since the market for beaver could not be controlled by Native trappers, they were vulnerable to changes in demand. When demand was high, men abandoned some aboriginal practices in order to keep pace. Instead of following traditional conservation principles, they over-trapped nearby territories so that they could obtain as many animals as possible. This led to the rapid depletion of beaver in some areas. As a result, men were forced to travel further from their communities to find the desired resource, often entering territories of other people who were similarly engaged in trapping and trading, resulting in conflict. When the demands of the fur market declined, people were left without the ability to procure the goods that they desired. In societies where traditional craft skills had been abandoned once people acquired manufactured tools and utensils, the loss of European goods was difficult to adjust to or even contemplate.

In some cases, the products received from European merchants had negative effects on indigenous communities, especially the commerce in guns and liquor. Although European governments were reluctant to sanction the distribution of guns to Indians, British merchants began to exchange guns for animal skins in the early years of the seventeenth century. Liquor was also given, sometimes in great quantities, although that practice also violated official European policy. Both guns and liquor wrought havoc in indigenous societies, affecting individuals and communities alike. Acquisition of guns increased the potential for violence of intertribal conflicts and the resulting numbers of casualties. Consumption of liquor increased personal disorientation, with disruption of cooperative, stable community relations. Violence perpetrated by people, usually men, under the influence of alcohol, was most often directed either at members of their families and villages or at themselves.

In addition to the acquisition of a wide range of imported goods, transformations in aboriginal societies included shifts in economic activities, changes in gender roles, development of notions of private property in goods and especially in land, emergence of, or increases in, social differences based on wealth, and intensification of warfare caused by competition over access to resources and to trade routes. These transformations were manifested more intensely in some societies than in others, but they were prevalent throughout North America at different historical periods. They occurred earliest in regions of initial European entry and settlement, that is, along the eastern coasts and nearby inland territories; but they eventually spread to the interior of the continent, leaving no nation untouched.

As early as the seventeenth century in some eastern nations, trapping and trading became men's central economic activities. Among horticultural people where farming was the responsibility of women, food supplies were maintained, but among foragers who depended more heavily on meat, fish, and fowl brought in by hunters, aboriginal food resources were not exploited as fully as had been done prior to involvement in the fur trade. Many people then traded with Europeans for food but this led to increased dependence on traders. Women, too, were involved in the fur trade because their labor was needed to prepare the pelts for the market. Since they also had to perform subsistence and household tasks, demands on their labor increased as well. As shifts in economic roles of both men and women first included and then focused on the fur trade, people grew more dependent on the trade in order to supply their needs and wants. This reliance on trade tended to intensify and solidify the productive shifts that supported it.

In addition, since European traders dealt with Native trappers as individuals, a process began that eventually resulted in a reorientation of ideology away from kin-based, community-based mutual reliance and support to one that stressed individuals rather than groups. Over the centuries, notions of personal private property developed that contrasted fundamentally with beliefs about communal ownership of resources. Although aboriginal societies had concepts of territorial rights, these rights were held by groups, not by individuals. Strangers in need were permitted to use local resources, at least temporarily, but notions of alienability of land and resources were foreign to Native cultures.

As people lost access to their own territory, competition grew for the lands and resources that remained, often leading to warfare. Wars in the Northeast and Southeast increased from the early seventeenth century until the late eighteenth. As trade and European settlement moved steadily westward in the eighteenth and nineteenth centuries, Indians along the Mississippi River and its tributaries were affected. Wars of survival pitted Native groups against one another. By mid- nineteenth century, aboriginal inhabitants of the Plains also saw their territories crowded by both Euro-American settlers and other Indians fleeing west from the sprawling conflicts in their own homelands. Conflicts were often exacerbated by Europeans who forged commercial and military alliances with Indians in opposition to other European nations and their respective indigenous allies.

Unlike most aboriginal warfare, these wars were primarily generated by economic motives and/or by the need to defend one's own community from invaders. Thousands of people were killed, and thousands more were routed from their homes and forced to flee west for safety. Native warfare changed, not only in frequency and in motive, but also in tactics. Warriors began to destroy the homes and fields of their enemies, leaving survivors with no means to sustain themselves. Death from starvation and exposure to the elements often ensued. While it is true that many of the wars involved Native antagonists, they were often encouraged by European powers who succeeded in embroiling their allies in conflicts. For example, some of the American military campaigns in the Plains in the nineteenth century found their victims with the aid of Indian scouts from other nations.

EARLY EUROPEAN SETTLEMENTS

Competition over land and resources was further intensified by European settlement. The first foreign settlement in North America was begun by the Spanish along the Atlantic coast near Cape Fear, North Carolina, in 1526, ending the following year, probably because of the antagonism of indigenous inhabitants who had heard of the Spaniards' practice of kidnapping Native people (Brasser 1978: 80). In 1585, about one hundred English would-be settlers founded a community on Roanoke Island, North Carolina. This colony, too, failed even though its leaders, Phillip Amadas and Arthur Barlowe, had first described the nearby people as "gentle, loving, and faithfull, void of all guile, and treason" (Quinn 1955, I: 108). The same description could not be applied to the English, who retaliated against an entire community because someone had stolen a silver cup. The English killed the village chief, destroyed the people's cornfields, and burned their homes before abandoning the colony. French immigrants attempted a number of settlements in the late sixteenth and early seventeenth centuries along the northern coasts of Maine, Nova Scotia, and the Gulf of St. Lawrence at Tadoussac. None of these communities lasted for more than a few years despite the encouragement of the French government.

Then in 1607, the first successful colony in the Northeast, called Jamestown, was founded by English settlers on the shores of Chesapeake Bay in Virginia. It survived with the help of the nearby Powhatans, who came to regret their cooperation because the colonists, under John Smith, soon created dissension within the Native community and ultimately took much of their territory. The English colonists' occupation of Powhatan land might be seen as an unstated response to the question posed by Wahunsonacock, the Powhatan leader, "What do you expect to gain by destroying us who provide you with food?" (Thornton 1987: 60).

In the Southeast, Spanish and French colonists attempted to establish settlements in mid- sixteenth century but none were successful. Then, in 1565 the Spanish founded the town of St. Augustine and from there tried to exert control over territory extending from southern Florida north through Georgia into South Carolina. Their authority, at least nominally, remained intact until British settlements spread from Virginia into Georgia in the seventeenth and eighteenth centuries and wrested control from the Spaniards.

Spanish presence in the Southwest began in 1539 and increased in scope by late in the century. Expeditions were sent from Mexico to explore the region and exert control over its inhabitants, demanding provisions and labor from the Indians. Resistance was answered with force. As recorded by a member of a Spanish expedition led by Antonio de Espejo into Puebloan territory in 1582:

> the corners of the pueblo were taken by four men, and four others began to seize those natives who showed themselves. And as the pueblo was large and the majority had hidden themselves, we set fire to the big pueblo, where we thought some were burned to death because of the cries they uttered. We at once took out prisoners, two at a time, and lined them up, where they were shot many times until they were dead. Sixteen were executed, not counting those who burned to death. (Hammond and Rey 1966: 204)

Spanish colonial authority expanded in 1598 when Juan de Oñate led a group of settlers into New Mexico. They built houses near Puebloan villages and, with military force, demanded provisions from the indigenous population. Oñate's tactics set the tone for the Spanish conquest of the region that extended through the next two centuries. Spanish civilians, military personnel, and priests established farms, mines, and workshops made profitable by the forced labor of Indian men and women.

In Virginia, English settlers resorted to military raids to compel Powhatans and other Native groups to abandon aboriginal territory. In at least one instance, they gave poisoned drinks to Powhatan emissaries who came to negotiate peace between the two communities. As their own statements testify, "we hold nothing injuste, that may tend to theire ruine … with these neither fayre Warr nor good quarter is ever to be held" (Washburn 1959: 21–22).

Several European governments began policies aimed at obtaining Native territory by ostensibly legal means, that is, documented sales and land cession agreements. Dutch, French, and British representatives were authorized to contact leading members of Indian nations and conclude sales and treaties that transferred land to the European Crowns. Private citizens were likewise permitted to purchase land from indigenous inhabitants. However, the degree to which Indians understood the terms of these transactions is questionable. Aside from the important issue of differences in concepts of land ownership and use-rights to resources, it is often made clear in Native complaints that borders were poorly delineated and that settlers, taking advantage of the lack of clarity, encroached on territory that Indians believed they kept in their domain. For instance, at a meeting in Albany, New York, in 1753, the Mohawk chief Hendrick presented New York's governor George Clinton with a list of colonists' illegal occupations of Mohawk lands that included:

> We have a complaint against Arent Stevens. He bought a tract of land of us, and when the surveyor came to survey it, we showed him how far to go, and then Arent Stevens came and told him he had employed him and made him go a great deal further.
>
> We have another complaint against Conradt Gunterman. We gave him a tract of land out of charity but he takes in more which we have not given or sold him.
>
> Johannes Lawyers Patent at Stonerabie to no further than the Creek. He has taken up six miles further than the Creek. (Nammack 1969: 37)

The passive acceptance of settlers' thefts of Native land reveals a consistent pattern implying collusion between government and citizen that continued from the colonial period through the nineteenth century.

MISSIONARIES AND THEIR PROGRAM OF CULTURAL CHANGE

Nearly as soon as Europeans made contact with Indians, missionaries found their way into Native communities. At first, they generally saw their role as compatible with their country's goals that included converting and civilizing pagan inhabitants of the continent while at the same time exploiting their resources. In later periods, though, missionaries sometimes came into conflict with civilian authorities, whose actions and policies toward Indians became increasingly brutal at a time when moral standards had begun to change.

Catholic priests were the earliest to establish missions in North America. In the Southwest, Spanish Franciscans dominated the field. Their actions were based on assumptions that indigenous people were subhuman and should be controlled by force if necessary. When priests entered the region in the mid-sixteenth century, they forced men to build churches, destroyed Native ceremonial kivas, and burned religious paraphernalia. They beat and tortured indigenous religious leaders into submission or at least into overt compliance. Spanish priests also compelled men and women to work on plantations or "haciendas" that they created out of aboriginal territory, producing profits for their foreign owners. Missionaries' actions sometimes came under criticism from Spanish secular authorities, although civilians' own conduct was often equally corrupt. As Captain Nicolas de Aguilar noted in 1662: "the friars are not content with a few helpers. They want … the Indians of the entire pueblo, for gathering piñon nuts, weaving, painting, and making stockings, and for other forms of service. And in all this they greatly abuse the Indians, men and women" (Simmons 1979: 183).

In the Northeast, French Jesuits applied gentler techniques. As men with formal education in philosophy and history, their approach was based on assumptions that Indians were capable of intelligent thought and reasoning (Vecsey 1997). Jesuits believed that the people's religious and intellectual errors were because they were led astray by the devil or by indigenous charlatans. The missionaries saw their role as one of enlightening misguided but sincere people. In this quest, they attempted to learn Native languages so that they could better teach and reason with the people. Overt coercion was not one of their tactics, although bribery in the form of guns and favorable trading terms with merchants was often used as a means of gaining converts. In the words of a Jesuit priest among the Huron in 1643: "The use of arquebuses [guns], refused to the Infidels by Monsieur the Governor, and granted to the Christian Neophytes, is a powerful attraction to win them; it seems that our Lord intends to use this means in order to render Christianity acceptable in these regions" (*Jesuit Relations and Allied Documents, 1610–17911896–1901*, 25: 27; hereafter *JR*). In addition, reminders of the French state's power and of the advantages of military alliance with France were frequently part of missionaries' arguments.

The number of converts that Jesuits made was initially quite small, but their impact on Native culture and history was dramatic. Policies for transforming Native ideology, social ethics, and community life were first instituted by French Jesuits in the early seventeenth century, followed later by British and American missionaries as well.

The Jesuit plan advocated changes in Native settlement patterns and systems of leadership and social control. In social and personal relations, they aimed to alter attitudes toward sexuality, marriage, and family life (Bonvillain 1986; Vecsey 1997). The priests, along with the French government, wanted to induce nomadic or seminomadic people to settle permanently, preferably near French ports and trading posts. If settled, Indians were more easily contacted for purposes of conversion as well as for deepening the state's economic and political control. The directors of the Company of New France, the major trading company operating in the Northeast, "in order to induce the Savages to settle, have granted the same favor in their store to the sedentary Christians as to the French" (*JR* 16: 33).

Aboriginal patterns of social control were also criticized since they were deemed to allow too much personal freedom and independence. Native social control was based primarily on the strength of public opinion, supported by formal acknowledgement of wrongdoing and ritualized payment of tribute or presents to victims or their families. Writing in 1645 about the Huron, Gabriel Lalemant complained that "although this form of justice restrains all these peoples, and seems more effectually to repress disorders than the personal punishment of criminals does in France … it leaves individuals in such a state of liberty that they never submit to any Laws and obey no other impulse than that of their own will" (*JR* 28: 49–51).

Along with condemnation of what they saw as lenient policies toward society's wrongdoers, priests also decried lax reactions to children's misbehavior. Instead of the patient correction and indulgence that were typical Native responses to a child's errors, missionaries advocated corporal punishment as a means of controlling a child's will.

Missionaries also condemned Native attitudes about sexuality that generally regarded premarital sexual relations as normal and natural. In most aboriginal societies, extramarital relations were tolerated, although not condoned, as long as they were not deemed excessive. For example, attitudes of the Montagnais of eastern Québec caused consternation to Jesuits who tried to alter Native behavior, as demonstrated by the following exchange between Paul LeJeune and an unnamed Montagnais man:

> I told him [a Montagnais man] that it was not honorable for a woman to love any one else except her husband, and that this evil being among them, he himself was not sure that his son, who was there present, was his son. [The man responded]: Thou hast no sense. You French people love only your own children; but we all love all the children of our tribe. (LeJeune: *JR* 6: 255)

Native marriages were ideally assumed to create enduring bonds that joined a woman and man in an economic and domestic unit. Husbands and wives were expected to cooperate with and show respect to one another. However, in practice, divorce was common, particularly in the early years of marriage. Unions became more stable after a number of children had been born to the couple. Describing the Huron, Lalemant noted that in marriage

> the faith that they pledge each other is nothing more than a conditional promise to live together so long as each shall continue to render the services that they mutually expect from each other, and shall not in any way wound the affection that they owe each other. If this fail, divorce is considered reasonable on the part of the injured one. (*JR* 28: 51–53)

French missionaries attempted to transform the basically egalitarian gender relations that they observed in most Native societies into the European system of patriarchal dominance. Although priests sometimes misinterpreted and exaggerated the actual authority of Indian women, they nevertheless admonished men to control their wives. LeJeune's remark to a Montagnais man is representative: "I told him then that he was not the master, and that in France, women do not rule their husbands" (*JR* 5: 181).

British missionaries came to convert Indians to Protestant sects, first in eastern regions of North America, emphasizing the spiritual rewards of Christianity along with the advantages of protection bestowed upon converts by the British Crown. In fact, however, little aid was ever given to the converts, and such protection as they may initially have received proved to be temporary. Even the so-called Praying Towns established in the seventeenth century in Massachusetts at Natick, Stockbridge, and elsewhere were eventually overtaken by colonists with the tacit and sometimes overt approval of the British government despite the fact that the towns had been founded under the aegis of colonial land grants.

TREATIES AND THE ESTABLISHMENT OF RESERVED LAND

The establishment of "reservations" ("reserves" in Canada) for Native people became a common technique for obtaining vast tracts of land and resettling Indians on only a portion of their former territory or removing them to new lands. Reservations consisted of land that was guaranteed by treaty for Native residence,

ownership, and control. Native leaders acceded to government demands that they cede much of their land and settle on reservations because they hoped that some measure of peace and security would result. But despite promises guaranteeing the perpetual right of Indians to reservation land, relocation often led to additional forced moves until people found themselves in territories far distant from their original homelands and often far distant from the reservations they initially accepted. In the nineteenth century, the American government quickened the pace of westward expansion, accompanied by treaty signings that transferred millions of acres of Native land to the United States and created hundreds of Indian reservations.

American officials tended to take one (or all) of several approaches when dealing with Native representatives in land-cession agreements or disputes. Intimidation and threats of military force were typical, especially when the people resisted abandoning their homelands. The words of General Edmund Gaines, speaking in 1831 to a delegation of Sauk leaders who balked at moving from their Illinois villages, are representative of this approach: "I came here neither to beg nor hire you to leave your village. My business is to remove you, peaceably if I can, but forcibly if I must. I will now give you two days to remove in, and if you do not cross the Mississippi within that time, I will adopt measures to force you away" (Jackson 1964: 111–112). And in 1851, Luke Lea, the federal Commissioner of Indian Affairs, told Santee delegates attending a treaty council that they should agree to treaty terms offered by the government to exchange valuable territory in Minnesota and South Dakota for annuities and a small reservation elsewhere because, "Suppose your Great Father wanted your lands and did not want a treaty for your good, he would come with 100,000 men and drive you off to the Rocky Mountains" (Meyer 1993: 78).

A less direct but equally effective strategy was employed in continual pressure exerted on Native nations to abandon land that had been illegally occupied by settlers in defiance of existing treaty agreements. The argument in these instances was that since the increasing numbers of settlers posed a danger to the Indians, Native people would be better off if they moved west away from the most recent American incursions.

Another strategy used from the early years of the nineteenth century until the end of the treaty period in the 1870s was collusion between government and traders to force Native representatives to sign land-cession agreements in exchange for the forgiveness of debts incurred by members of their nations. Traders were encouraged to grant credit to Indian hunters and families that amounted to more than they could repay and then officials demanded land in exchange for the debts owed. Such a policy was explained by President Thomas Jefferson in 1803: "We shall push our trading houses, and be glad to see the good and influential individuals among them [the Indians] run in debt, because we observe that when these debts get beyond what the individual can pay, they become willing to lop them off by a cession of lands" (DeRosier 1975: 86). In some cases a sizable proportion of the monies that accompanied land-cession agreements was handed over to traders who insisted on full payment of debts. For example, at a treaty signing at Traverse des Sioux between the Santee Dakota and the United States in 1851, "each Indian, as he stepped away from the treaty table, was pulled to a barrel nearby and made to sign a document prepared by the traders. By its terms, the signatories acknowledged their debts to the traders and pledged themselves to pay those obligations" (Meyer 1993: 80). By this procedure, instituted because at that time Congress had outlawed direct payment of merchants' debts, traders received $210,000, a sum that constituted approximately one-sixth of the funds Congress had set aside for the Santees as annuities for fifty years. When the Santees signed another land cession treaty in 1858, "nearly all of the payment [of $266,880] to the lower Sioux and a large part of that to the upper bands went to pay the 'just debts' of the traders" (105).

Another common tactic that government officials used in treaty negotiations was to bribe and intoxicate Indian delegates who sometimes returned to their villages still drunk. Black Hawk, a Sauk war chief of the late eighteenth and early nineteenth centuries, described events surrounding a peace council held in 1804 between the Sauk and Governor Henry Harrison of Missouri Territory to discuss the release of a Sauk prisoner who had participated in a skirmish with American settlers. Harrison demanded land as retribution while the Sauk delegates tried to obtain the freedom of their compatriot.

Quash-qua-me [leader of the delegates] and party remained a long time absent. They at length returned, and encamped a short distance below the village—but did not come up that day—nor did any person approach their camp. They appeared to be dressed in fine coats, and had medals. From these circumstances, we were in hopes that they had brought good news. Early the next morning, they came up, and gave us the following account of their mission:

On their arrival at St. Louis, they met Governor Harrison and explained to him their business, and urged the release of their friend. The American chief told them he wanted land—and they had agreed to give him some on the west side of the Mississippi, and some on the Illinois side. When the business was all arranged, they expected to have their friend released to come home with them. But about the time they were ready to start, their friend was let out of prison, who ran a short distance, and was shot dead. This is all they could recollect of what was said and done. They had been drunk the greater part of the time they were in St. Louis. (Jackson 1964: 53–54)

Treaty negotiations typically produced agreements that became legal documents compelling Indians to abandon most, if not all, of their aboriginal territory and relocate elsewhere. The negotiating process and its results had damaging effects on community stability in several ways. Of most immediate concern, people were forced away from lands to which their economies had been adapted. Their subsistence success relied on intimate knowledge of the topography, climate, and resources of their accustomed territory. Their annual cycle of productive activities was attuned to the rhythms of the natural world around them. When their aboriginal lands were taken, they had to adjust to new sets of circumstances, often many hundreds of miles from their homelands. It took many years, generations in fact, to acquire the knowledge needed to reestablish viable economies. Their task was made more difficult because the lands they were forced to accept in exchange for their own were usually less fertile and productive than the ones they lost.

In addition to economic difficulties faced by dispossessed people was the spiritual cost they bore. Traditional religious beliefs profoundly interconnected the spirit world with the natural world in which they lived. Their land was the land of spirits upon whom they depended for support and guidance. Stories of creation and transformation often told of specific locales where spirits resided or where significant primordial events had taken place. And their aboriginal territory was the resting place of ancestors whose eternal spirit essences were disturbed by Anglo settlers entering the region.

When people abandoned these lands, they lost their spiritual as well as geographical bearings.

Population shifts resulting from relocations also increased the likelihood of intertribal conflicts since displaced nations unavoidably intruded on land that was already the home or hunting territory of another group, causing competition over resources. Each incoming group of settlers caused indigenous inhabitants to either relocate or resist, both alternatives resulting in internal and intertribal turmoil.

Once Indians were settled on reservations and reserves, the federal governments began to implement policies aimed at "civilizing" Native people by transforming them into sedentary farmers who lived in nuclear-family households, wore Anglo clothing, spoke English, and attended church. Ministers, priests, and lay workers were assigned by mission organizations, with approval of the federal government, to enter Indian reservations to convert residents to a variety of Christian denominations. In many cases, they took control of local education and merged religious and secular training in farming, manual skills, and domestic duties.

In the nineteenth and twentieth centuries, the assault on Native culture in the United States and Canada centered on constructing a system of education through which children would be taught to accept Anglo values and beliefs while simultaneously shunning traditional practices. Boarding schools were preferred because they physically separated children from the influences of parents and communities. Use of Native languages was forbidden in schools. For example, an order issued in 1887 by the US Bureau of Indian Affairs Commissioner John Atkins stated: "The instruction of the Indians in the vernacular is not only of no use to them, but is detrimental to the cause of their education and civilization, and no school will be permitted on the reservation in which the English language is not exclusively taught" (Commissioner of Indian Affairs 1887: xxii). Restrictions against use of Native languages continued well into the twentieth century at schools run by the Bureau of Indian Affairs (BIA).

Participation in traditional religious ceremonies was forbidden by official policies in the United States and Canada. A federal supervisor at the Santee Reservation in Nebraska warned teachers that "No school children should be permitted to be spectators at [traditional ceremonial] dances as the Office thinks it would be better to keep their ideas away from these old-time customs" (Meyer 1993: 303). Important religious ceremonies were outlawed by federal statutes in the United States and Canada, including the Sun Dance, Ghost Dance, and socioreligious feasts called "potlatches" conducted by people of the north Pacific coast.

Many people resisted the pressure to abandon traditional practices and beliefs. The words of Big Eagle, a Mdewakantan Santee chief, are representative: "The whites are always trying to make the Indians give up their life and live like white men, and the Indians do not want to. If the Indians tried to make the whites live like them, the whites would resist, and it is the same way with many Indians" (Holcombe 1894: 384). Others literally stood in the way of federal agents and police sent to round up children and remove them from their communities to attend boarding schools. Nevertheless, despite objections and resistance, a total of 21,568 children nationwide were in boarding schools in 1900, accounting for about one-third of their age group (Churchill 1999: 51).

From the very beginning of European contact and throughout the periods of later American and Canadian administrations, communities were divided in their attitudes toward the proper course of action when dealing with the foreigners. Although the historical record indicates little if any objection to trade, there certainly was controversy concerning the wisdom of forming military alliances with European nations and becoming embroiled in their conflicts. The reasons underlying various positions were complex. Some people recognized the danger posed to aboriginal ways of life and to their very survival by extensive involvement with Europeans. Others saw short-term benefits of trade and opportunities of political or military ascendancy over neighbors. And some indigenous leaders favored alliances with Europeans as a means of enhancing their own prestige within their communities. The wealth offered by Euro-American officials in the form of gifts and bribery was no doubt an inducement as well. Finally, in the middle and late nineteenth century, when the Anglo population had grown as the indigenous population had declined precipitously, many leaders acceded to demands for aboriginal land because they believed they had no alternative. Recognizing the enormous military power of the government, they hoped that concessions would at least allow their people to survive.

Whatever the motives and means of individual decisions, debates and controversies that were stirred by the new conditions in which Native nations found themselves had serious repercussions for community stability and survival. Using the tried and true techniques of "divide and conquer," Europeans were able, sometimes with Native collusion, to turn Indians against one another, causing conflicts not only between nations but within them as well. Without a united voice, internal politics became contentious and bitter. And factions in Native communities sometimes became surrogates for Euro-American authorities. Among the stark examples of this process was the assassination of the Lakota chief and religious leader Sitting Bull in 1890, arrested and killed by Lakota members of a local police force operating on Lakota reservations at that time.

Although internal disagreements and conflicts no doubt existed before the arrival of Europeans, the new tensions resulted from both more serious cause and more serious effect. The loss of independence and autonomy experienced by Native nations, the startling decline in populations, and the rapid cultural changes taking place led to confusion as people were forced to endure conditions created by forces previously unknown to them. Given the many threats to survival that Indians faced (i.e., loss of land and continual invasions by settlers, economic insecurity, military assaults, and disease), the internal antagonisms and struggles for power that arose as the people's problems intensified often became the proverbial last straw that helped destroy a nation's ability to defend itself against external forces.

US GOVERNMENT LEGISLATION

Although the bullet and the treaty had proven effective weapons in the campaign to wrest control of Indians' land, by the late nineteenth century considerable expanses of territory, particularly in the west, still remained in the Native domain. Therefore, a novel combination of forces coalesced in support of US federal legislation that led to the loss of tens of millions of acres of land protected by treaty. Land-hungry western settlers and ranchers pressured their congressional representatives to act so that they could gain title to valuable grazing land and farmland. The legislation that resulted was also supported by missionaries, educators, and others who believed that Indians' best interests were served by leading them to "civilization" embodied in agrarian labor, nuclear-family domestic organization, and the love of private property. In 1887, Congress passed the General Allotment Act (also known as the Dawes Act) that mandated the division of reservation land into parcels of 160

acres for families and 80 acres for individuals. After all eligible people had been assigned their allotments, land remaining from the original reservation base was declared "surplus," and available for "homesteading" and sale to westerners. Thus by a mandated process, more than 60 million acres were lost (Gibson 1988: 227). Allotted land was eventually available for sale to outsiders after a protected period of 25 years had elapsed. By 1934, two-third of all allotted acreage, amounting to some 27 million acres, had been lost (227). Currently about 43 million acres of land remain in tribal trust status, and about 10 million acres are allotted to individual Indians (*American Indian Report* 1999b: 8). The Dawes Act also stipulated that Indians who accepted allotments or who had voluntarily left their reservations and "adopted the habits of civilized life" were to be granted US citizenship. It was not until 1924, however, that Congress passed the Indian Citizenship Act, bestowing citizenship on all Indians.

Federal policy toward American Indians began to change in the 1930s in the context of the New Deal promoted by President Franklin Roosevelt. At that time, the Commissioner of Indian Affairs, John Collier, developed a program aimed at changing the relations between Native people and the federal government. Collier's policies were, in part, a response to a national report issued in 1928 concerning living conditions on reservations throughout the United States. The report, called the "Meriam Report," after Lewis Meriam, director of staff, reviewed housing, health status, educational programs and achievements, and reservation governing structures. The report condemned the General Allotment Act of 1887 and the ensuing policies of the federal government. It criticized the breakup of Native territory and shrinkage of their land base. It noted the deplorable living conditions and health status that Indians endured. And it criticized the federal educational system that forced children to leave their families to be schooled in boarding schools. The Meriam Report made recommendations to significantly reorient federal policy. It urged ending the boarding school system, to be replaced with an extensive network of day schools on reservations. It also urged that tribal groups have more power to make decisions concerning programs and policies affecting their communities. Further, the Meriam Report stressed the right of Indians to maintain their language and cultural traditions if they chose to do so. However, the report also supported long-range goals of "expedit[ing] the transition and hasten[ing] the day when there will no longer be a distinctive Indian problem" because most Indians will have voluntarily chosen to leave the reservations and merge with the general population. The Meriam Report therefore can be seen as laying the foundation of both the reformist programs of John Collier and the "termination" policies of the 1950s and 1960s.

Collier's efforts to revamp government policy culminated in passage by Congress of the 1934 Indian Reorganization Act (IRA; also known as the Wheeler-Howard Act). The IRA, however, did not institute all of Collier's proposals but rather was a diluted bill that acknowledged the need for change while maintaining federal control over reservation polities. Although the Act provided for self-government on reservations, actual tribal authority was limited. Each reservation was encouraged to adopt a constitution and set up a tribal council whose members were elected by reservation constituents. The councils were given responsibilities to manage federal and local programs and to develop economic resources as tribal enterprises. They also had the task of managing efforts at improving the living standards, health, and education of their people. However, their decisions were (and in most cases still are) subject to approval by the BIA and ultimately by the Secretary of the Interior, in whose department the BIA is housed. But the IRA did move to protect Indian lands by forbidding any future allotments to individuals on reservations and outlawing the sale of already allotted land. It returned to reservations any surplus land that had not already been sold. And the Act sought to consolidate Indian landholdings through exchanges with public or private land adjacent to reservations. With Collier's urging, Congress appropriated funds for the purchase of land that had been lost through treaty violations and sales and for programs of economic development and educational improvement.

In recognition of the millions of acres lost through illegal government and private actions and in order to settle claims and clear title to claimed land, in 1946 Congress established the Indian Claims Commission. Tribes were empowered to file suit with the Commission for compensation for land that had been taken without treaty or had been lost from treaty-guaranteed territory. The Commission issued their final judgments in 1979. Under the act establishing the Commission, however, a number of crucial restrictions were mandated. First, tribes could only receive monetary awards for lost land; they could not regain their territory. Second, the amount of awards was based on the market value of the land at the time it was taken. And third, certain federal funds expended on reservations that had not been promised in treaties were deducted from the awards. In all, therefore, approximately $800 million was granted to tribes whose claims were approved (Bacheller 1997: 22).

Despite important administrative and policy changes in the 1930s and 1940s, widespread poverty continued to plague most reservations, prompting the BIA to institute a new policy aimed at encouraging Indians to leave their reservations and move to cities where jobs were supposedly available. The policy was also aimed at alleviating pressure on resources resulting from a rapidly growing Indian population with little or no financial or legal means of obtaining additional territory. Through the "Job Relocation Program," the government paid for transportation to a city and in some cases paid the fees for job-training instruction. Thousands of people, principally from

A group of Chiracahua Apaches on their first day at Carlisle Indian School.

reservations in the Plains, Southwest, and California, participated in the program and relocated to such cities as Rapid City (South Dakota), Minneapolis, Green Bay (Wisconsin), Chicago, Denver, Seattle, Portland (Oregon), San Francisco, and Los Angeles. Their efforts to improve their economic condition, however, most typically met with failure. Job-training programs either did not materialize or were inadequate. And few jobs at good wages were available in the cities to which the people relocated, resulting in their concentration in poor urban ghettos. As a consequence, most participants returned to their home communities, where they at least had the cultural and social support of their families and friends.

Federal policy shifted again in the 1950s with plans to terminate the trust status of Indian reservations and the services and funds provided by the government in fulfillment of treaty obligations. This policy, commonly referred to as "termination," was put forward in 1953 in House Concurrent Resolution 108. In the guise of "entitling [Indians] to the same privileges and responsibilities as are applicable to other citizens of the United States … and to grant them all of the rights and prerogatives pertaining to American citizenship," the Resolution effectively ended the protected trust status of Indian land and aimed to withdraw federal support of educational, health, and social programs that had been guaranteed by treaties signed by representatives of the federal government and Indian nations in prior centuries. Although federal planners intended that eventually all reservations no longer have trust status, the Resolution stipulated the immediate termination specifically of tribes living in the states of California, Florida, New York, and Texas. It also "free[d]" from "federal supervision and control and from all disabilities and limitations especially applicable to Indians," the Flatheads of Montana, Klamaths of Oregon, Menominees of Wisconsin, Potowatamies of Kansas and Nebraska, and Chippewas of the Turtle Mountain Reservation of North Dakota. The "disabilities and limitations" referred to in the Resolution essentially meant the tax-immune status of Indian land and the monetary support for education and other services provided pursuant to obligations undertaken by the federal government in treaties. One year after the House Resolution, Congress passed the "Menominee Termination Act" (1954) mandating per capita distribution of Menominee tribal funds and ending trust status from the Menominee Reservation. The law did not go into effect until 1961 and thereafter quickly plunged Menominees into poverty as a result of the forced sale of tribal assets to cover newly imposed taxes and the withdrawal of federal support for social programs (Shames 1972). The effects of termination led Menominees and their supporters to appeal to Congress for restoration of their reservation. Finally, in 1973 Congress passed the "Menominee Restoration Act," which returned the Menominees to their previous legal status. And in 1999, the government awarded the Menominees a sum of $32 million for "damages suffered by the tribe as a result of its termination and the mismanagement of tribal property by the BIA prior to termination" (*American Indian Report* 2000a: 18). Still, some 103 reservations were eventually and permanently terminated.

A group of Chiracahua Apaches four months after arriving at Carlisle Indian School.

In the late 1960s and 1970s, Congress passed several important pieces of legislation that affected Indian tribes and marked another shift in federal policies. The Civil Rights Act of 1968, among other provisions, stipulated that in order for states to extend jurisdiction over reservations within their boundaries, the formal approval of a majority of the affected residents was necessary. In 1975, the "Indian Self-Determination and Education Assistance Act" established principles of self-government that have been used to advance Native claims of sovereignty. The legislation was based on Congressional recognition that serious problems on reservations were caused by, among other things, a lack of local control and involvement in administering programs affecting reservation communities and on findings that

> prolonged federal domination of Indian service programs served to retard rather than enhance the progress of Indian people and their communities by depriving Indians of the full opportunity to develop leadership skills crucial to the realization of self-government and has denied to the Indian people an effective voice in the planning and implementation of programs for the benefit of Indians which are responsive to the true needs of Indian communities.

Congressional findings also acknowledged that "Indian people will never surrender their desire to control their relationships, both among themselves and with non-Indian governments, organizations, and persons." The Act empowered tribes to contract directly for the administration of educational, health service, and welfare programs. Significantly, it stated that "nothing in this Act shall be construed as authorizing or requiring the termination of any existing trust responsibility of the United States with respect to the Indian people," putting an end to fears of a return to policies of the 1950s and 1960s.

Indian nations have used the statement of findings as well as provisions of the Self-Determination Act in order to broaden their claims of sovereignty and to extend tribal jurisdiction not only regarding educational, medical, and social services but also regarding claims to control of territory, tax immunity, and economic development. Tribes have also taken advantage of a provision in the Act permitting the acquisition of additional land that could then be protected by federal trust status. Some tribes have implemented this provision in order to acquire and extend jurisdiction over land not adjacent to their reservations. Although this practice is not without controversy, it has been applied to benefit tribal economic development.

Tribal governments throughout the United States are increasingly taking control of local education, incorporating a curriculum that includes tribal history, culture, and language. They are also administering healthcare delivery systems by running clinics and hospitals as well as outreach programs for the prevention and treatment of physical and psychological ailments that particularly affect their community. Tribal agencies have taken charge of constructing and maintaining infrastructure for the delivery of water and energy. And many reservations have established tribal courts based on both traditional and contemporary forms of conflict resolution and adjudication. They are initiating programs for economic development involving local and national businesses. And, finally, tribal governments can now negotiate and conclude leases for their lands without needing to get prior approval from the Secretary of the Interior, although the Secretary does still need to approve the kind of leasing regulation policies that tribes draw up. Furthermore, this new policy does not extend to leases for oil and gas exploration and extraction. Therefore, even though tribal governments have gained greater powers for self-determination, they lack total sovereign authority.

In 1978, the BIA established procedures for federal recognition of Indian groups who were not at that time recognized as legal tribal entities. BIA guidelines set forth seven criteria that groups petitioning for "acknowledgement as an Indian tribe" had to fulfill:

1. evidence that group has been "identified as Indian on a substantially continuous basis"; Claims of identification may be substantiated by relationships with federal authorities, state or local governments, churches or schools based on Indian identity. Other possible supporting evidence might include reports by anthropologists or historians or citations in newspapers and books. Finally, relationships based on Indian identity with recognized tribes or national Indian organizations might also support a claim for acknowledgment.

2. evidence that a "substantial portion of the group" lives in a specific area distinct from other populations;

3. evidence that the group has exerted "tribal political influence over its members throughout history until the present";

4. document describing the group's present governing system;

5. list of known current members and any other former lists;

6. group is "composed principally" of people not belonging to any other tribe;

7. group was not terminated by Congress.

Subsequent to the formulation of the BIA requirements, small Native groups, especially in the Northeast, Southeast, and western states, have sought federal recognition. Although many have been successful, most petitioners have failed to satisfy the BIA's standards of evidence that some critics assert are overly dependent on formal, written sources and ignore personal life histories and oral traditions. In addition, the wording of the necessary criteria is often vague and open to interpretation. The phrases "substantial continuous basis" of identification, "substantial portion of the group," and "composed principally" could be read differently by different evaluators.

Also in 1978, Congress passed the American Indian Religious Freedom Act amid awareness that Indians were often denied "access to sacred sites required in their religion … and at times prohibited in the use and possession of sacred objects necessary to the exercise of religious rites and ceremonies." The Act provided for protection for Indians in their "inherent right of freedom to believe, express and exercise [their] traditional religion, including but not limited to access to sites, use and possession of sacred objects, and the freedom to worship through ceremonials and traditional rites." However, ambiguities in the law continued to make it difficult for some Indians to practice their religions, especially regarding access to peyote, eagle feathers, and some sacred sites. Congress therefore strengthened protection in 1993 by passing the Native American Religious Freedom Restoration Act. The Act was prompted by a Supreme Court decision in 1990 (*Employment Division, Dept. of Human Resources v. Smith*) involving an appeal by two Indians who had been denied state unemployment benefits after they had been fired from their jobs as drug counselors by a private drug rehabilitation service on the grounds that they had used peyote in a ritual of the Native American Church. Their application for unemployment compensation had been turned down on the grounds that they had been discharged from their jobs for "work-related misconduct." Ruling on their appeal, the Supreme Court upheld the state law restricting benefits and upheld the judgment

that the denial was appropriate in the case under consideration. The Supreme Court further ruled that the government need not employ a "compelling interest test" in denying free expression of religious practice. According to the Court, it was possible but not constitutionally necessary to exempt peyote use from the application of federal and state drug laws. The Native American Religious Freedom Restoration Act of 1993 attempted to intervene in the judicial debate by "restoring the compelling interest test" to cases "where free exercise of religion is substantially burdened and to provide a claim or defense to persons whose religious exercise is substantially burdened by government." Additional amendments were passed in 1994 to the American Indian Religious Freedom Act to specifically protect the "use, possession, or transportation of peyote by an Indian for bona fide traditional ceremonial purposes" and exempted such practices from prohibition by the United States or any state government. However, a Supreme Court decision in 1997 declared the 1993 Native American Religious Freedom Restoration Act as unconstitutional. The Court has not yet ruled on the amendments passed in 1994. In 1999, settlement was reached in a class-action suit that now permits Native American prison inmates to possess and employ certain Native religious objects including an unsealed medicine bag, sacred herbs (sweet grass, sage, cedar, sacred tobacco, and calamus root), beaded pendant, smoking pipe, and clan or nature symbols ("Native American Inmates Allowed Religious Items" 1999).

Protection of religious and cultural artifacts was enacted in 1990 in the Native American Graves Protection and Repatriation Act (NAGPRA) that empowered Indians to reclaim the burial remains of their ancestors and objects found in grave sites. In addition to human remains, "cultural items" are also to be returned upon application by a Native group who can demonstrate ownership. Such cultural items include sacred objects as well as objects having "ongoing historical, traditional, or cultural importance central to the Native American group." Items presently in museums, galleries, and other institutions must be returned to Native American groups upon application and demonstration of "rights of possession." Organizers of future excavations must notify Indian groups of their plans and inventory in order to allow them to apply for repatriation of human remains and cultural objects found at the site. In 2010, the Department of the Interior added new provisions to NAGPRA that allow tribes to claim remains and artifacts found in or near their aboriginal territories even if a definite affiliation with that group cannot be scientifically established.

While most federal legislation pertaining to Native Americans deals with legal and social issues, Congress has also passed laws that establish policies regarding economic development. In 1988, legislation was enacted in response to the growing gaming industry that blossomed in the early- and mid-1980s. That growth was initiated by Seminoles in Florida who opened a high-stakes bingo hall and then successfully fought state attempts to restrict their activities. In landmark rulings in 1981 and 1983 (*Seminole Tribe of Florida v. Butterworth*), the US Supreme Court decided that Indian tribes could operate gaming establishments without state regulation provided that similar gaming was not prohibited "as a matter of public policy" in the state (Wilmer 1997: 90). The Court also ruled that states could not unilaterally extend jurisdiction over gaming on reservations. Finally, by the principle of "reserved rights," tribes retained "all powers to regulate activities within their boundaries unless expressly forbidden to do so by Congress" (91). Congress then passed the "Indian Gaming Regulatory Act" in 1988 that distinguished among three types of gaming: Class I (social games for minimal monetary value and traditional forms of gaming associated with ceremonies or celebrations); Class II (bingo, lotto, and similar games); Class III (gaming not included in Class I or II). Class I gaming falls under the exclusive jurisdiction of tribes while Class II gaming is subject to protections and regulations of a newly created National Indian Gaming Commission, which sets standards for gaming on reservations. Finally, the act stipulated that Indian tribes negotiate with the relevant state government for a "compact" to govern Class III gaming on reservations. Regulations of the National Indian Gaming Commission allow for non-Indian participation in funding and operating casinos on reservations but limit the profits of non-Indians to 30 percent. This ensures that proceeds from gaming will primarily benefit Native communities.

Some thirty years after the first tribal bingo hall was opened by Florida Seminoles, there are currently 422 casinos operated by 237 tribal governments in 28 states (some governments operate more than one casino). Native people in Canada operate additional casinos. In 2010, the total US tribal government gross revenue from gaming amounted to $26.5 billion (National Indian Gaming Association 2011). Although casinos run by Native Americans account for a mere 5 percent of gaming revenue in the United States, one of the most lucrative is Foxwoods, owned by the Pequots in eastern Connecticut. With more than 11,000 employees, they are one of the ten largest employers in the state. Their profits, amounting to about $1 billion a year, have been invested in reinvigorating their community and the surrounding area. They have built new housing and roads and provide job training, scholarships, and health services to tribal members. The casino and its accompanying resort generate additional income for nearby hotels, restaurants, and stores. This pattern holds true for casinos throughout the country. In the rest of the United States, approximately 682,000 jobs have been created through Indian gaming both in the casinos and in support services and businesses that provide goods, meals, and other amenities to casino workers and patrons. Nationwide, Native Americans held 25 percent of these jobs whereas people of other races and ethnicities held 75 percent (National Indian Gaming Association 2011). Therefore, non-Native people, both as workers and as owners of businesses catering to casino customers, profit as much or more from Indian gaming as do Native Americans.

In addition, Native American casinos generate $9.4 billion in federal taxes and government revenue savings as well as $2.4 billion in state taxes and revenue sharing profits agreed upon by compacts between tribes and the states in which they are located.

Most of the net profits realized by casino gambling is spent on projects and services in Native communities and also in nearby locations. According to the National Indian Gaming Association report in 2011, revenues were expended in the following categories: 20 percent for education, child care, elder care, cultural endeavors, and charity gifts; 19 percent for economic developments; 17 percent for healthcare; 17 percent for police and fire protection; 16 percent for infrastructure improvements; and 11 percent for housing.

The presence of a casino can boost income for residents of an area, but it can also bring changes to the community that all residents do not desire. The work that casinos create tends to be low-wage jobs with little future. Some people do not approve of gambling on moral grounds or because of its historical connection with organized crime.

And while the public media often focus on casino revenues, in fact, only a small percentage of Indian-run casinos make large profits. For example, in 2010, the majority (55%) of these establishments took in less than $25 million and 62 percent of these earned less than $10 million. Only 21 of the total 422 casinos earn more than $250 million.

Opposition to Indian-run casinos surfaces from time to time in state legislatures and in Congress. Some legislators have proposed that only tribes who had federal recognition in 1988 when the Indian Gaming Regulatory Act was passed should be permitted to operate casinos. Others advocate restrictions on the ability of tribal governments to extend trust status to newly acquired lands and to promote gaming in these areas.

While there is controversy among Indians regarding gaming, arguments in support generally stress the economic benefits, the need to generate money for infrastructural improvements and social programs, especially in a climate of reduced federal funding, and the need to provide jobs for reservation residents. Arguments opposed to gaming emphasize the potential for social problems related to excessive gambling and fears of attracting undesirable individuals or groups to their communities.

CANADIAN GOVERNMENT LEGISLATION

As in the United States, Canadian Indian policy has gone through numerous shifts, reacting to general attitudes in the country as well as to the circumstances, needs, and strength of political activism on the part of members of the First Nations, as Native people of Canada are now called. From the beginning of colonization, French and British explorers proclaimed land that they first encountered to be the property of their respective Crowns. As French settlement in eastern Canada expanded in the seventeenth and first half of the eighteenth centuries, lands were periodically set aside as reserves for Indians. Formal treaties were not signed, but rather lands were conveyed to Indians for their use from a variety of sources such as government grants or donations of private French citizens and church missions. Ironically, the donated land had originally been occupied by a Native nation dispossessed by the Europeans' self-proclaimed "right of discovery."

In 1763, shortly after the "French and Indian War" ended with a British victory and the ouster of the French from eastern North America, King George III issued a Royal Proclamation that significantly affected Native rights at the time. The Proclamation established a boundary separating colonies east of the crest of the Appalachian mountains and Indian territory west of that boundary. In addition, land in the east already granted to Indians under the French system was given official British protection. The Proclamation recognized that some eastern land was still occupied by "several nations or tribes of Indians with whom we are connected, and who live under our protection." These nations "should not be molested or disturbed in the possession of such parts of our dominions and territories as, not having been ceded to or purchased by us." Land lying west of the stated boundary was recognized as the exclusive possession of Native inhabitants except for some territory granted to the Hudson's Bay Company, the principal British traders in Canada. Colonists were forbidden from entering Indian territory except for purposes of trade. Strict regulations were proposed to control and license traders. Individuals were barred from surveying, issuing deeds for, or purchasing land from Indians. Land could only be purchased by the British Crown from Indian governments or recognized leaders "at some public meeting or assembly of the said Indians."

However, as British settlement in Canada expanded in the late eighteenth and early nineteenth centuries, Native rights to territory were jeopardized. In addition to territorial losses, Indians living in central and western Canada who followed a nomadic lifestyle that was considered "uncivilized" by Canadian authorities and missionaries found themselves confronted by policies aimed at encouraging or forcing them to settle on reserved lands and to alter traditional practices. In 1857, an "Act to Encourage the Gradual Civilization of the Indian Tribes" was passed with the goal of leading Indians to eventual assimilation into Canadian society through a process of "enfranchisement." According to the law, an Indian man who was at least twenty-one years old, literate, of good moral character, and free from debt could be declared "enfranchised" on the recommendation of the local superintendent, the local missionary, and a third person appointed by the governor of Canada. Once enfranchised, the person "so declared … shall no longer be deemed an Indian in the meaning thereof." Men who fulfilled all of the necessary requirements except literacy, but who were able to speak English or French and who were deemed "sufficiently intelligent to be capable of managing [their] own affairs," could also apply for enfranchisement. Canadian officials were far more optimistic about the benefits of enfranchisement than were Native people since by 1869 only one man had applied for the privilege. An "Enfranchisement Act" passed in 1869 gave enfranchised men the right to vote and confirmed previous policies regarding the process, but Indians continued to ignore the opportunity offered them. The government then began to more directly interfere in Native communities by imposing a system of elected band councils as the primary governing bodies on reserves. The policy was aimed at accomplishing two goals, that is, accustoming Indians to participate in Canadian-style systems of governance and undermining traditional or hereditary leadership. Superintendents were permitted to impose councils if band members refused to participate. Furthermore, if band members attempted to sidestep the new system by electing traditional or hereditary chiefs, superintendents were given the power to depose councilors who they thought were "incompetent" (i.e., unacceptable).

In 1876, the Canadian parliament passed the first of a series of "Indian Acts" (the last revision was enacted in 1951). The Act defined "Indian" as a legal status, entitling people to be registered as Indians and enabling them to be members of bands and live on reserves. According to Canadian law, "status Indians" were people who were registered on official lists drawn up in 1874, their descendants in the male line, and the wives and children of such persons. Indian women who married non-Indians and the descendants of female Indians but whose fathers were not Indian were not considered "Indian" by legal definition. Such individuals were referred to as "non-status Indians." They and their descendants lost membership in bands and lost the right to live on reserves. It was not until a Canadian Supreme Court ruling in 1985 that Indian women married to non-Indians and the descendants of Indian women were given the power to apply for reinstatement as "status Indians." Indian women who marry non-Indians no longer lose their status and rights.

The Indian Act of 1876 also inaugurated a system of private ownership of property on reserves. Under its provisions, reserves were to be divided and allotted to band members who were deemed capable of management. Such individuals were given a "location ticket" that served as a temporary deed to the allotment. The deed became permanent after a period of three years if the owner had demonstrated his ability to farm and/or raise livestock (note that the masculine pronoun is appropriate here since only men could own land). If band councils resisted the allotment of their reserves by refusing to validate location tickets, superintendents were permitted to approve the tickets and transfer of land. They were also given the power to approve leases and sales without council compliance.

In territory west of Lake Superior, most Indians continued to engage in a nomadic foraging economy and knew little of the English language or of the Christian faith. Therefore, policies of enfranchisement and land allotment that affected Indians in the east were not applied to them because they were deemed not yet fit to assume the responsibilities of civilized life. Instead, between 1871 and 1877 the federal government negotiated seven land cession treaties with nations occupying territory between Lake Superior and the Rocky Mountains. Indians living west of the Rockies did not sign treaties with the federal or provincial governments, but by the late nineteenth century most were living on land reserved for them by agreement or consensus. In an effort to "civilize" western Indians, the Canadian government outlawed some Native ceremonial practices that they considered pagan or dangerous, including the Sun Dance of the Plains and public ceremonial feasts called "potlatches," common in Pacific coast nations.

To further the process of assimilation, the government established boarding schools in the west where boys were taught farming and mechanical skills while girls were taught domestic work. In most of the schools, children lived a highly regimented life and were not permitted to speak their Native languages or follow traditional religious practices. Much recent testimony has been brought forward to document the physical and sexual abuse children often had to endure (see Chapter 3).

Despite the government's stated goals of equality, the majority of Canada's first peoples continued to live in poverty. Their housing and living conditions were much below the standards of Canadian society, and their educational opportunities and health status lagged far behind those of other Canadians, as documented in a report issued in 1967 called "The Survey of the Contemporary Indians of Canada." However, the report's many recommendations to improve living conditions, educational and employment opportunities, and political rights of Native people were ignored by the government. Instead, in 1969 it issued a document called "Statement of the Government of Canada on Indian Policy" that proposed to repeal the various Indian Acts, transfer most responsibility for Indian affairs from the federal to provincial governments, and end the "legislative and constitutional basis of discrimination." With opposition by most Indian leaders, expressed in their own "Red Paper" calling for greater autonomy of First Nations, the government's position paper was withdrawn.

During discussion in the 1970s and early 1980s concerning revision of the Canadian constitution, Native representatives and their supporters advocated for inclusion of guarantees of rights and status of First Nations. They urged explicit recognition of their rights, sparking much debate in the parliament and the country. The Constitution Act of 1982 ultimately included only a short section that affirmed the "existing aboriginal and treaty rights of the aboriginal peoples of Canada," rights that "now exist by way of land claims agreements or may be so acquired." It defined "aboriginal peoples" to include Indians, Inuit, and Métis. It further noted that such rights apply equally to "male and female persons." Finally, it provided that the federal and provincial governments are "committed to the principle" that before any changes in constitutional laws affecting First Nations "the Prime Minister will invite representatives of the aboriginal peoples of Canada to participate in the discussions of that item" (Constitution Act, 1982).

One year after passage of the Constitution Act, the Assembly of First Nations, a national Native organization, issued a draft proposal to amend the constitution. It proposed protections of cultural, economic, and political rights including:

> The right of the First Nations to their own self-identity, including the right to determine their own citizenship and forms of government.
>
> The right to determine their own institutions.
>
> The right of their governments to make laws and to govern their members and the affairs of their people.
>
> Their right to exemption from any direct or indirect taxation levied by other governments.
>
> The right to move freely within their traditional lands regardless of territorial, provincial, or international boundaries. (Assembly of First Nations; quoted in Asch 1984: 29)

In an effort toward reconciliation, the federal government issued a formal apology in 1998 for what it stated were inappropriate and harmful policies of the past 150 years. In particular, the apology noted the hardship faced by Indian children who had been forced to attend residential schools in central and western Canada. The statement acknowledged the psychological, physical, and sexual abuse often meted out to school residents.

While the statement was greeted with approval by some Native leaders, others criticized it as inadequate. They noted that a Royal Commission on Aboriginal Peoples had issued a report in 1996 severely critical not only of past practices but also of current policies and procedures. The Commission had made 440 recommendations, including establishment of a separate aboriginal parliament, recognition of sovereign powers of First Nations, and an increase in the annual federal budget spent on Indian affairs by nearly $1.5 billion by the end of the century, recommendations that were not addressed by the federal government.

NATIVE AMERICAN LANGUAGES

In the past several decades, many members of Native American communities have focused attention on the issue of language, concentrating on developing programs to retain and enhance use of their Native language. Analysis of 2010 US Census data indicates that some 372,095 people speak an indigenous language as their mother tongue. The Census documents speakers of 169 Native American languages, some spoken by only a small number of people, whereas others are well represented.

By far the most frequently spoken language is Navajo in the Southwest with 169,471 people reporting it as their home language. Other languages with more than 10,000 speakers include Yupik in Alaska (18,950), Dakota/Lakota (18,616) in the Plains, Apache (13,063) in the Southwest, Keres (12,945) in New Mexico, Cherokee (11,610) in Oklahoma and North Carolina, and Choctaw (10,343) in Mississippi. Those with between 5,000 and 10,000 speakers are Zuni (9,686) in New Mexico, Ojibwa (8,371) in the upper Midwest, Pima (7,270) in Arizona, Inupik (7,203) in Alaska, Hopi (6,634) in Arizona, Tewa (5,176) in New Mexico, and Muskogee (5,064) in Oklahoma. In addition, some 8,298 respondents reported their home language as "Indian" or "American Indian."

Place of residence is an important factor related to language use. The majority of indigenous language speakers live on reservations or trust territories. That is, of approximately 372,000 speakers of Native languages, about 237,000 live in what are described by federal statistics as "American Indian or Alaska Native" (AIAN) areas. The percentage of indigenous language speakers living in these areas varies by language. For example, 84.5 percent of Yupik speakers live in AIAN areas while 51.5 percent of speakers of Dakota do so. From the perspective of total population, only

5.4 percent of residents of AIAN areas are speakers of their indigenous language. This percentage varies slightly for different age groups: 5.1 percent for children aged 5 to 17 years, 5.6 percent for adults 18 to 64 years, and 5.1 percent for elders 65 years and over. Still, elders are more likely than children to speak their indigenous language. Of the total Native American population, about 20 percent of elders report speaking their Native language while 10 percent of children aged 5 to 17 years are indigenous language speakers. But these figures also vary significantly by language.

Degree of Native ancestry is also a significant factor in the likelihood that people speak an indigenous language. People who identified in the 2010 census as AIAN are more likely to speak their native language than people who reported being "American Indian in combination with another race." For all ages, 14.8 percent of AIAN but only 0.7 percent of AIAN in combination reported speaking an indigenous language at home.

Finally, numbers of Native speakers are concentrated in three states: Alaska, Arizona, and New Mexico. These states account for some 65 percent of all indigenous speakers.

In Canada, data reported from the 2006 Census indicate that overall 22 percent of the Aboriginal population could speak their indigenous language. But rates varied widely among different aboriginal groupings. The Inuit have the highest percentage of people speaking their language, that is, 70 percent, while members of Métis communities have the lowest, or just 4 percent. Among First Nations peoples, residence on- or off-reserve is a significant factor in language knowledge. About 51 percent of First Nations people living on-reserve, but only 12 percent living off-reserve, speak their Native language. Age is another predictor of language ability. Nationwide, about 18 percent of Aboriginal children aged 14 or younger can speak their indigenous language while 37 percent of elders aged 75 or older are Native speakers.

Information collected in the Canadian Census of 2011 revealed that about 213,500 people reported having an Aboriginal mother tongue and nearly 213,400 stated that they spoke an Aboriginal language either most often or regularly at home. In total, more than 60 indigenous languages were recorded in the Census data. Cree, spoken in Saskatchewan, Manitoba, Alberta, and Québec, is the language with the most speakers (83,475), followed by Inuktitut (34,110) of the Canadian north, Ojibway (19.275) in Ontario and Manitoba, Dene (11,860) in Saskatchewan and Alberta, and Innu/Montagnais (10,965) in Québec, Newfoundland, and Labrador. Somewhat fewer speakers reported their mother tongue as Mi'kmaq (8,030) in Nova Scotia and New Brunswick or Atikamekw (5,915) in Québec. Several additional languages have between 1,000 and 3,000 speakers while the majority of Canadian indigenous languages have fewer than 1,000 Native speakers.

The linguistic needs of Native American children in the United States are addressed by several federal laws, including the Bilingual Education Act of 1968, amended specifically for Native Americans in 1972 as the Indian Education Act, funding programs serving Native American communities (Spolsky 1977: 59). Extension of the Bilingual Education Act in 1979–1980 also benefits Native Americans even if they do not speak their tribal language.

Various reservations have developed educational programs designed to meet their specific needs. Some groups accept a transitional model advocated by the federal government. Among the Northern Cheyenne, Choctaw, Ute, and Zuni, bilingual programs teach students English in early grades and switch exclusively to English in third grade. Other Native American peoples employ a maintenance model of bilingual education, stressing acquisition of skills in English while simultaneously developing literacy and fluency in their indigenous language. For example, the Navajo, Yupik, and Cree continue instruction in their Native language in elementary school (65). In addition, Navajo is spoken in community colleges on the reservation.

For groups whose Native language is no longer spoken as a first language, linguistic programs aim at revival, usually in conjunction with instruction in other aspects of traditional culture. Immersion programs are an increasingly popular method to expose children (and sometimes adults) to indigenous language instruction. Language immersion may take place in school settings or in retreats and camp environments where only the Native language is employed for communication. Some school programs have fluent speakers, usually elders, who participate with children, creating master–apprentice relationships. Others employ two or more fluent teachers in each classroom who then model for children the kinds of normal interactions that people have when communicating. In these settings, children are exposed to naturalistic language use as they would in a home or community setting.

In 1990, the US Congress recognized the importance of languages to the continuation of distinctive

Native American cultural identity. The Native American Languages Act (PL 101–477) states:

> The status of the cultures and languages of Native Americans is unique and the United States has the responsibility to act together with Native Americans to ensure the survival of these unique cultures and languages. The traditional languages of Native Americans are an integral part of their cultures and identities and form the basic medium for the transmission, and thus survival, of Native American cultures, literatures, histories, religions, political institutions, and values.

The act specifically endorses use of these codes as "mediums of instruction in order to encourage and support Native American language survival, educational opportunities, increase student success and performance, increase student awareness and knowledge of their culture and history and increase student and community pride."

Programs and policies aimed at maintaining Native languages are supported by the United Nations Declaration on Rights of Indigenous Peoples. Several of the articles specifically mention rights to language, that is, the right to use, develop, revive and teach their indigenous histories, languages, philosophies (Article 14), and the right to an education in their own languages and cultures (Article 15). The intricate relationship between language and other aspects of cultural maintenance have been attended to by members of Native American communities. According to Duane Champagne of the UCLA Native American Studies Center, "languages are holistically interrelated with social, environmental and cultural ways of life. They contain the inherent ways to view or understand the world. When tribal communities renew culture through language, they must also teach about the philosophical processes they convey the ways that indigenous peoples understand being, becoming, ceremony, identity and community" (Champagne 2011:18). And Ojibwa anthropologist and author David Treuer writes, "If the language dies, we will lose something personal, a degree of understanding that resides, for most fluent speakers, on an unconscious level. We will lose our sense of ourselves and our culture" (Treuer 2012). In addition, referring to language and cultural maintenance policies, Treuer states, "This new traditionalism is not a turning back of the clock, but a response to it; modernism (and modern, global capitalism) is

a great obliterator of cultural differences and a great infuser of a new kind of class differences, and language activism is one way Indians are not only protecting themselves and their rights but also creating meaning in their lives."

Efforts to protect and promote the use of Native American languages are especially critical, given the fact that many of these languages have few speakers at this time. The paucity of speakers has resulted from many factors, not the least of which was the federal government's policies, lasting from the nineteenth until the middle of the twentieth century, that banned the use of Native American languages in schools and dormitories for Native American children. In the words of John Atkins, Indian commissioner in 1887, "The instruction of Indians in the vernacular is not only of no use to them, but is detrimental to the cause of their education and civilization, and no school will be permitted on the reservations in which the English language is not exclusively taught" (Commissioner of Indian Affairs 1887: xxii).

Processes of language shift and loss are exemplified in many Native American communities in the United States. Some research raises questions concerning the role of Native ideologies about language itself in the abandonment of indigenous languages and in the subsequent attempts to maintain or restore Native codes. One key issue is the association between language and identity. Language tends to become a marker of identity when the survival of one's language is threatened either from external dominating forces or from the internalization of negative attitudes that results from this domination. In a discussion of Native American language ideologies, Margaret Field and Paul Kroskrity suggest that language becomes a "badge of identity" when the number of remaining speakers dwindles and when community members become alarmed at its approaching loss (2009: 20).

Differences in the speech of younger and older community members may also affect the goals and successes of language maintenance programs. For example, older speakers may promote a kind of "linguistic purism" that denigrates speech that contains borrowings from English or patterns of *code mixing*, the amalgamation of Native and foreign structures and vocabulary.

Finally, concepts related to the issue of "language and thought" underlie the desire to maintain Native languages in some communities. One's indigenous language is felt to express cultural models of the world that differ fundamentally from those expressed by English, and, therefore, the loss of language is seen as a loss of cultural distinctiveness. For instance, analysis of a Hopi tribal court hearing revealed that a Hopi tribal advocate representing a defendant repeatedly insisted on the use of the Hopi language. She stated: "You can't separate Hopi and religion and land, language, court, Constitution. It's all tied up into one. That's why we need special courts, hear us in our language" (Richland 2009: 93). And the Yukon Native Languages Project, sponsored by the Yukon First Nations in Canada, adopted the motto: "We Are Our Language" to stress the interconnections among language, identity, and worldview (Meek 2009:158). Finally, religious rituals and prayers are often thought to lose their power if not spoken in the indigenous monolingual language.

Efforts at revitalizing and maintaining Native American languages have accelerated considerably in the last decade. Innovative learning projects have been initiated in many communities in the United States and Canada. Each project develops in the context of specific language needs based on the number of speakers present in the community and the current vitality of the language as a means of communication. Where languages are still spoken by a sizable percentage of the community, such as among the Inuit in Arctic Canada, Navajo in the southwestern United States, and Cree in central and northern Canada, programs are aimed at language maintenance. The Native language is used in schools as either a primary or secondary code of instruction, books and other teaching materials are printed in the Native languages, and children are encouraged to speak their Native tongue in all appropriate settings. Parents and other relatives, too, need to be involved since the best hope for survival occurs when languages are used in ongoing, spontaneous, and meaningful social interaction. In communities where there are only a small number of Native speakers, other techniques of reintroduction need to be developed. Language immersion programs and the presence of elders as role models help develop the necessary motivation for young children to learn the Native tongue. And of course, there are intermediary cases where people utilize a variety of strategies. For example, in the Mohawk settlement of Kahnawake, located just south of the Canadian city of Montreal, the community operates two elementary schools, one in which English is the language of instruction and the other in which Mohawk immersion predominates. While the majority of Mohawk residents are monolingual English

speakers, a sizable (and now growing) minority are fluent in the Native language. The Mohawk immersion program began in 1984 and was originally used in nursery, kindergarten, and first grade but the program now reaches the sixth grade. A further modification took place in 1994. At that time, full-day language immersion programs were instituted in kindergarten through fourth grade, while in the fifth and sixth grades, language maintenance rather than immersion became the goal (Jacobs 1998:120). About half of the community's children attends the Mohawk immersion school while the other half attends the English language school.

In California, in contrast, most of the remaining Native languages have only a handful of elderly speakers. In the 1990s, a Master-Apprentice Language-Learning Program was initiated. In this program, each "master speaker" was teamed with an apprentice from the same community. Master speakers were first trained in informal interactional teaching techniques (such as managing repetition and rephrasing). Apprentices were also trained in learning strategies, emphasizing the importance of active learning by asking questions and speaking as much as possible. Following their initial work together, the master and apprentice speakers returned to their communities and attempted to involve a wider network of participants. These programs have generated a great deal of interest in Californian Native communities, but they are unlikely to lead to widespread language use. They are, however, important strategies in language survival.

One of the most remarkable instances of language revitalization, or more accurately language reclamation, is the achievement of members of Wampanoag communities in Cape Cod and Martha's Vineyard. Started in 1993 by Jessie Little Doe Baird after recurring dreams in which voices spoke in an unknown language, the Wampanoag language has come from a state of extinction to become a language with a growing number of speakers and at least one child who is a Native speaker. Little Doe Baird began working with Ken Hale of the Department of Linguistics at MIT in Cambridge, Massachusetts, using two major types of sources to reconstruct Wampanoag. First, they used the extensive body of colonial documents written in Wampanoag and English dating from the seventeenth and eighteenth centuries. Indeed, there are more documents written in Wampanoag than in any other indigenous language of North America, including deeds, property transfers, letters to colonial authorities, and agreements between Wampanoag representatives and British and American officials. The documents provide the basis for understanding Wampanoag sentence structure and word formation processes as well as a large body of vocabulary. The second source of information comes from comparative material gleaned from the several dozen languages belonging to the Algonkian linguistic family of which Wampanoag is a member. Study of these languages, some of which are spoken today and others are well-documented by linguists and earlier observers, provides data for the reconstruction of Wampanoag grammar and lexicon as well as clues to pronunciation.

The Wampanoag Language Reclamation Project has involved many community members in organizing immersion camps, master/apprentice teams, and language classes. They have also developed materials for use in these programs such as grammar workbooks, computer files, and board games. The success of this project demonstrates that, provided there are materials available, a community of dedicated people can achieve what might seem impossible. Their work is captured in a documentary entitled *We Still Live Here, As Nutayunean* (Makepeace Productions 2010).

New technologies have been adapted and incorporated into language maintenance programs in many communities. For example, computer programs that teach indigenous languages are increasingly utilized each year. Language apps for young children have been developed for Navajo and Lakota (available at no charge from the iTunes store) with plans to expand into other language communities. The Cherokee syllabary, first developed by Sequoyah in the early nineteenth century, can now be used in social networking media such as Facebook. And speakers can use indigenous languages on Twitter. Indeed, a website called IndigenousTweets.com now collects users of some one hundred indigenous languages worldwide. Interested users can access the website to find other people writing in their own language. Currently included are Navajo, Delaware/Lenape, Lakota, Inuktitut, Mi'kmaq/Micmac, and Secwemctsin. Others can be added by contacting the website. According to its creator, Kevin Scannell, "The important thing is for people to use their language if they want it to survive. The Internet gives people an opportunity to write and chat and be creative while using their language in a natural way" (Meigs 2011:30). While some speakers may have difficulties with advanced technologies, younger people may actually be drawn toward learning and using their language in such contexts. As Peter Austin, director of the University of London's Endangered Languages Project, observes, "Attitudes play a huge role in language maintenance, language shift and language loss. We can't guarantee that someone twittering in the language is going to keep it going, but it does raise the potential for people to say 'Wow, this is something really valuable and a lot of fun'" (31).

In addition, Google launched a project in cooperation with the Alliance for Linguistic Diversity and other universities and linguistic organizations to collect and store data from some 3,054 languages throughout the world, including many Native American languages, that are considered endangered. Maps of the languages' locations and information about populations are collected in the Endangered Languages Project. Many of the languages already have available a full archive of text samples, audio tapes, and video clips. The ongoing goal is to collect such data from as many languages as possible. The Project's website can be seen at www.endangeredlanguages.com and some information about the Project can be obtained at the following web address: http://googleblog.blogspot.com/2012/06/endangered-languages-project-supporting.html

POPULATION DECLINE AND RENEWAL

Just as plants and animals are indigenous to certain parts of the world, organisms that cause disease are also indigenous to specific locales. And when these organisms are transported to new human environments, their effects are often quickly lethal. Such was the case when diseases of European origin came to North America beginning in the late fifteenth century. Among the most devastating were smallpox, measles, and new forms of influenza. The vast majority of excess deaths (numbers of deaths exceeding the normal death rate for a given population) from the sixteenth through nineteenth centuries were caused by disease. Estimates for the aboriginal population of North America vary widely. Any figures given are speculative, particularly because of the unknown rates of death from disease before European or American observers made their earliest calculations. Precontact population densities are difficult to estimate as well. Mooney (1928) suggested an aboriginal North American population of slightly more than

1,150,000, a figure long accepted as a standard but now thought to be much too low. Kroeber's (1939) number of slightly less than 1 million is similarly faulted. Dobyns's (1966) estimates of 9–12 million are considered excessively high. Ubelaker (1976), working with data and estimates provided by scholars preparing the Smithsonian's Handbook of North American Indians, suggests a figure of more than 2,171,000. And Thornton (1987) postulates an aboriginal population for North America at somewhat more than 7 million, including more than 5 million for the area of present-day United States and more than 2 million for Canada. Whatever the figure, rates of decline in the sixteenth through nineteenth centuries were undoubtedly precipitous. By the end of the nineteenth century, only about 250,000 Indians survived in the United States.

The steep population decline had social, economic, and political consequences in addition to the obvious personal suffering and loss. Whole families, sometimes entire lineages or clans, were wiped out in the space of a few years. Not only did the most vulnerable groups, such as young children and elders, die in great numbers, but men and women in their prime also succumbed. Their deaths led to economic as well as social destabilization since they were the principle farmers, gatherers, and hunters upon whom less able family members relied. Political stability was also undermined since established leaders were as likely as others to die from epidemic diseases.

The consequences of disease began soon after the arrival of Europeans in North America. Reports from the sixteenth century and thereafter repeatedly confirm the grim history. For instance, Thomas Hariot, writing in 1590 about people in Virginia, stated "within a few dayes of our departure from everie such towne, the people began to die very fast, and many in short space; in small townes about twentie, in some fourtie, in some sixtie, & in one six score, which in trueth was very manie in respect of their numbers" (1972: 28). Indians interpreted the disasters that were striking them within the framework of their own knowledge about cause and effect. According to Hariot, they "were perswaded that it was the worke of our God through our meanes, and that we by him might kil and slai whome wee would without weapons and not come neere them" (28).

In the next century, French missionaries who lived among Algonkians and Iroquoians for decades witnessed similar devastation and recorded similar interpretations of the suffering that befell them. The number of Hurons, for instance, plummeted from at least 20,000 at the time of French contact in 1610 to no more than 10,000 in less than two decades. Hurons concluded that since the diseases began to flourish only after Jesuits started to live in their communities, the priests had brought the ailments. In accordance with Native beliefs that one possible method of causing disease and death was witchcraft, Hurons accused missionaries of being witches. Since neither Indians nor Europeans of the seventeenth century understood the physical mechanisms of disease transmission, the underlying etiology was misdiagnosed, but the people correctly connected Europeans' arrival with the origin and spread of epidemics. The Jesuits, of course, dismissed the notion that they were witches, but some perceptive priests did admit the justice of the Hurons' accusations against them. Lalemant, writing in 1640, commented,

No doubt, they [Hurons] said, it must needs be that we had a secret understanding with the disease (for they believe that it is a demon), since we alone were all full of life and health, although we constantly breathed nothing but a totally infected air.

Wherein truly it must be acknowledged that these poor people are in some sense excusable. For it has happened very often, that where we were most welcome, where we baptized most people, there it was in fact where they died the most; and, on the contrary, in the cabins to which we were denied entrance, although they were sometimes sick to extremity, at the end of a few days one saw every peron prosperously cured. We shall see in heaven the secret, but ever adorable, judgments of God therein. (*JR* 19: 91–93)

Algonkians living near the Atlantic coast, who were among the first to encounter English settlers in their territories, also remarked on their own destruction. In Virginia, the Powhatan chief, Wahunsonacock, told John Smith "I have seen two generations of my people die. Not a man of the two generations is alive now but myself." And in Massachusetts, Massasoit, a Wampanoag chief, concluded, "Englishmen, take that land, for none is left to occupy it" (Brasser 1978: 66).

In a relatively short time after Europeans' arrival, the numerical balance between Indians and the foreigners shifted due to high rates of death from disease and to endless immigration from Europe. When English settlers first arrived in North America, they needed the help of indigenous people to survive, but as early as 1684, less than eighty years after the first permanent

English settlement in North America, an Iroquois chief remarked to Colonel Thomas Dongan, a British official in Albany: "When the English first came to New York, Virginia and Maryland, they were but a small people and we a large nation, and we finding they were good people gave them land and dealt civilly by them; Now that you are grown numerous and we decreased, you must protect us from the French" (Noon 1949: 15).

When American settlement expanded westward in the nineteenth century, the same process of contact and decline was repeated. As Little Wolf of the Cheyenne noted, "Many have died of diseases we have no name for." And the Lakota chief, Sitting Bull, remarked, "They promised how we are going to live peacefully on the land we still own and how they are going to show us the new ways of living … but all that was realized out of the agreements with the Great Father was, we are dying off" (Thornton 1987: 134).

Indian populations continued to decline until the end of the nineteenth century, some nations reaching their nadir in the last decade or in the first decade of the twentieth century. Thereafter, they began to slowly increase until mid-century, when the rate of growth became more dramatic (159–160). The statistical increase developed because of an actual rise in Native populations due to improved health and lowered death rates along with high fertility. The reported growth is also due to changes in federal census policy of ethnic identification through self-report rather than through census-takers' observation and categorization of respondents. Still, officially counted Native Americans remain a small percentage of the total population of both the United States and Canada. While the actual number of Native people in the United States is higher than in Canada, the percentage of total population is greater in Canada. Bearing in mind the historical and contemporary issues raised by a discussion of Native population figures mentioned in Chapter 1, in 2010, the US Census Bureau reported about 2.9 million Native people (called AIAN in the census terminology) out of a total US population of 308.7 million, constituting approximately 0. 9 percent of the country's inhabitants (US Bureau of the Census 2010). The figure includes residents of some 278 reservations as well as residents of tribal trust lands, designated Native areas of Alaska, and self-identified Native people living in cities and towns throughout the country. Indeed, more than half of Native people live in or near urban areas.

In addition, the Census Bureau reports that another 2.3 million (0.7%) identified as AIAN in combination with one or more other races. Therefore, a total of 5.2 million people (1.7% of the US population) have some American Indian or Alaska Native ancestry. According to some research, an additional 7 or 8 million people who consider themselves "Hispanics" have Indian ancestry as well, raising the total to at least 12 or 13 million (Forbes 1990).

In Canada, the report of Statistics Canada for this census of 2011 noted a total of 1.2 million Aboriginal people including North American Indian, Métis, or Inuit comprising about 4 percent of the Canadian population. Significantly for the future, aboriginal children under the age of 15 comprise 5 percent of their Canadian age group.

Population statistics demonstrate that Native nations have managed to survive despite the policies instituted by European, American, and Canadian authorities that aimed at their physical and/or cultural destruction. Throughout the rest of this text, we will focus on the societies created by Native people in North America, analyzing their aboriginal ways of living as well as the kinds of transformations they experienced as a result of European contact and their situation today in the United States and Canada.

REFERENCES

American Indian Report. February 1999a. "No Dice for Problem Gamblers." pp. 20–21.

American Indian Report. March 1999b. "Reversing the Dawes Act Legacy." pp. 8–10.

American Indian Report. January 2000. "32 Years of Litigation Ends with Justice for Menominee." p. 18.

Asch, Michael. 1984. *Home and Native Land.* Toronto: Metheun.

Bacheller, John. 1997. *A Native American Sourcebook.* New York: McGraw-Hill.

Bonvillain, Nancy. 1986. "The Iroquois and the Jesuits: Strategies of Influence and Resistance." *American Indian Culture & Research Journal* 10: 29–42.

Brasser, T.J. 1978. "Early Indian-European Contacts." *Northeast* (ed. B. Trigger), Vol. 15 of *Handbook of North American Indians.* Washington, DC: Smithsonian Institution, pp. 78–88.

Commissioner of Indian Affairs. 1887. BIA. February 2.

Champagne, Duane. 2011. "Sacred Languages." *Indian Country Today* 1, no. 19 (June 1): 18.

Champlain, Samuel de. 1907. *Voyages of Samuel de Champlain, 1604–1618* (ed. W. L. Grant). New York: Charles Scribners' Sons.

Churchill, Ward. 1999. "The Crucible of American Indian Identity: Native Tradition versus Colonial Imposition in Postconquest North America." *American Indian Culture & Research Journal* 23, no. 1: 39–67.

DeRosier, Arthur. 1975. "Myths and Realities in Indian Westward Removal: The Choctaw Example." *Four Centuries of Southern Indians* (ed. C. Hudson). Athens, GA: University of Georgia Press, pp. 83–100.

Dobyns, Henry. 1966. "Estimating Aboriginal American Population: An Appraisal of Techniques with a New Hemisphere Estimate." *Current Anthropology* 7: 395–416.

Field, Margaret, and Paul Kroskrity. 2009. "Introduction: Revealing Native American Language Ideologies." *Native American Language Ideologies: Beliefs, Practices, and Struggles in Indian Country* (ed. P. Kroskrity and M. Field). Tucson, AZ: University of Arizona Press, pp. 3–28.

Forbes, Jack. 1990. "Undercounting Native Americans: The 1980 Census and the Manipulation of Racial Identity in the United States." *Wicazo Sa Review* 6: 2–26.

Gibson, Arrell. 1988. "Indian Land Transfers." *History of Indian-White Relations* (ed. W. Washburn), Vol. 4 of *Handbook of North American Indians*. Washington, DC: Smithsonian Institution, pp. 211–229.

Hammond, G. P., and A. Rey. 1966. *The Rediscovery of New Mexico: 1580–1594*. Coronado Cuarto Centennial Publications, Vol. III. Albuquerque, NM: University of New Mexico Press.

Hariot, Thomas. [1590]1972. *A Briefe and True Report of the New Found Land of Virginia* (ed. P. Hulton). New York: Dover Books.

Holcombe, Return (ed.). 1894. "A Sioux Story of the War." *Minnesota Historical Collections*, VI: pp. 382–400.

Jesuit Relations and Allied Documents, 1610–1791. 1896–1901. 73 vols. (ed. R. G. Thwaites). Cleveland, OH: Burrows Brothers.

Jackson, Donald (ed.). 1964. *Black Hawk: An Autobiography*. Urbana, IL: University of Illinois Press.

Jacobs, Kaia'Thitahke Annette. 1998. "A Chronology of Mohawk Language Instruction at Kahnawa:ke." *Endangered Languages, Current Issues and Future Prospects* (ed. L. Grenoble and L. Whaley). New York: Cambridge University Press, pp. 117–123.

Kroeber, Alfred. 1939. *Cultural and Natural Areas of Native North America*. Berkeley, CA: University of California Publications in American Archeology and Ethnology, no. 38.

Meek, Barbara. 2009. "Language Ideology and Aboriginal Language Revitalization in the Yukon, Canada." *Native American Language Ideologies: Beliefs, Practices, and Struggles in Indian Country* (ed. P. Kroskrity and M. Field). Tucson, AZ: University of Arizona Press, pp. 151–171.

Meigs, Doug. 2011. "The Tweet Hereafter: Social Media Is Helping Save Native Languages, 140 Characters at a Time." *Indian Country Today* 1, no. 21 (June 15): 30–31.

Meyer, Roy. 1993. *History of the Santee Sioux: United States Indian Policy on Trial* (rev. ed.). Lincoln, NE: University of Nebraska Press.

Mooney, James. 1928. *"The Aboriginal Population of America North of Mexico."* Washington, DC: Smithsonian Miscellaneous Collections 80: pp. 1–40.

Nammack, Georgiana. 1969. *Fraud, Politics, and the Dispossession of the Indians: The Iroquois Land Frontier in the Colonial Period*. Norman, OK: University of Oklahoma Press.

National Indian Gaming Association. 2011. *The Economic Impact of Indian Gaming*. Washington, DC.

"Native American Inmates Allowed Religious Items." 1999. *Indian Time*. October 29.

Noon, John. 1949. *Law and Government of the Grand River Iroquois*. New York: Viking Fund Publications in Anthropology, no. 12.

Quinn, David (ed.). 1955. *The Roankoke Voyages, 1584–1590*. 2 vols. London: Cambridge University Press.

Richland, Justin. 2009. "Language, Court, Constitution. It's All Tied Up into One: The (Meta)pragmatics of Tradition in a Hopi Tribal Court Hearing." *Native American Language Ideologies: Beliefs, Practices, and Struggles in Indian Country* (ed. P. Kroskrity and M. Field). Tucson, AZ: University of Arizona Press, pp. 77–98.

Sauer, Carl. 1971. *Sixteenth Century North America: The Land and the People as Seen by the Europeans*. Berkeley, CA: University of California Press.

Shames, Deborah (ed.). 1972. *Freedom with Reservation: The Menominee Struggle to Save Their Land and People*. Madison, WI: National Committee to Save the Menominee People and Forests.

Simmons, Marc. 1979. "History of Pueblo-Spanish relations to 1821." *Southwest* (ed. A. Ortiz), Vol. 9 of *Handbook of North American Indians*. Washington, DC: Smithsonian Institution, pp. 178–193.

Spolsky, Bernard. 1977. "Asserting Indian Bilingual Education." *International Journal of the Sociology of Language* I, no. 16: 57–72.

Thornton, Russell. 1987. *American Indian Holocaust and Survival: A Population History since 1492*. Norman, OK: University of Oklahoma Press.

Treuer, David. 2012. *Rez Life: An Indian's Journey through Reservation Life*. New York: Atlantic Monthly Press.

Ubelaker, Douglas. 1976. "Prehistoric New World Population Size: Historical Review and Current Appraisal of North American Estimates." *American Journal of Physical Anthropology* 45: 661–666.

US Bureau of the Census. 2010. *American Indian and Alaska Native Areas, 1990*. Washington, DC, 1990 CP-1-1A.

Vecsey, Christopher. 1997. *The Paths of Kateri's Kin*. Notre Dame, IN: University of Notre Dame Press.

Washburn, Willard. 1959. "The Moral and Legal Justifications for Dispossessing the Indians." *Seventeenth Century America* (ed. J. Smith). Chapel Hill, NC: University of North Carolina Press, pp. 15–32.

We Still Live Here, as Nutayunean. 2010. Dir. Ann Makepeace. Makepeace Productions. Documentary.

Wilmer, Franke. 1997. "Indian Gaming: Players and Stakes." *Wicazo Sa Review* 12, no. 1: 89–114.

Native Communities Today

IN THIS CHAPTER, data will document Native population trends in Canada and the United States as well as income, employment, and educational attainment for Native residents. The final section will discuss contemporary political and cultural issues of concern to many indigenous communities.

Native populations in both Canada and the United States have increased dramatically but while their numbers have grown, members of Native communities have not fared well economically. As aggregates, their incomes are below those of other people in their state or province, region, and country. Unemployment rates on Indian reservations and reserves are high as a result both of their rural location and the inadequate education and job training often typical of school systems that serve (or fail to serve) Native children.

CANADIAN DATA

In Canada, statistics on the aboriginal population are derived from two sources that are not exactly comparable, that is, the federal census formulated by Statistics Canada and the Department of Indian Affairs and Northern Development's Registered Indian Population. National and provincial figures from the 2006 census are given in Table 3.1.

As can be seen, Statistics Canada reported that 1,172,785 people listed aboriginal identity, constituting about 4 percent of the total Canadian population of 31,612,897 (Statistics Canada 2006). Of the Aboriginal group, 60 percent (698,025) were North American Indians, 33 percent (389,785) were Métis, and 4 percent (50,480) were Inuit. In addition, 7,740 people reported multiple Aboriginal responses.

Provinces with the highest Aboriginal populations are Ontario, Québec, and British Columbia, followed by Manitoba, Alberta, and Saskatchewan. Ontario and British Columbia have the largest number of North American Indians but Alberta, Manitoba, and Saskatchewan have the highest number of Métis while Québec and Northwest Territories (now Nunavut) have the most Inuit residents.

Differing somewhat from figures released by Statistics Canada, the Department of Indian Affairs and Northern Development (DIAND) publishes a record of people registered under the Indian Act who are members of one of Canada's 608 Indian bands. The total registered Indian population for 2006 was 623,780 (DIAND 2006). DIAND reported an on-reserve population of 360,707 while 275,112 people resided off-reserve. In addition, 24,071 Indians lived on Crown land. The great majority of Indian bands had populations of less than 2,000. Only 10 percent of the bands had more than 2,000 members while 6 percent had fewer than 100. According to DIAND, 44.4 percent of on-reserve Registered Indians lived in "rural zones" (defined as located between 30 and 200 mi. from the nearest service, administrative, or commercial center having year-round road access), 36.4 percent lived in "urban zones" (located within 30 mi. of the nearest service center with year-round road access), 1.7 percent reside in "remote zones" (situated more than 200 mi. from the nearest service center with year-round road access), and a substantial 17.4 percent live in "special access zones," having no year-round access to the nearest service center (DIAND 2000: 84).

Of the major cities in Canada, Winnipeg (capital of Manitoba) has the highest Aboriginal population (68,385), followed closely by Edmonton (capital of

TABLE 3.1	Canadian Aboriginal Population, 2006				
	Total	Total Aboriginal	North American Indian	Métis	Inuit
Canada	31,612,897	1,171,785	698,025	389,785	50,480
Newfoundland	505,469	23,450	7,765	6,470	4,715
Prince Edward Island	135,851	1,730	1,230	385	30
Nova Scotia	913,462	24,175	15,240	7,680	320
New Brunswick	729,997	17,655	12,385	4,270	185
Québec	7,546,131	108,425	65,085	27,985	10,950
Ontario	12,160,282	242,490	158,400	73,610	2,035
Manitoba	1,148,401	175,395	100,645	71,810	560
Saskatchewan	968,157	141,890	91,400	48,120	215
Alberta	3,290,350	188,365	97,275	85,500	1,610
British Columbia	4,113,487	196,070	129,580	59,445	795
Yukon	30,372	7,580	6,280	800	255
Northwest Territories	41,464	20,635	12,640	3,585	4,165

Source: Statistics Canada 2006.

Note: The total "Aboriginal" population is divided into three categories—North American Indians, Métis, and Inuit.

Alberta) and Vancouver (capital of British Columbia). In eastern Canada, only Toronto (capital of Ontario) and Ottawa (the capital of Canada) have more than 10,000 Aboriginal residents. Disaggregating for separate Aboriginal groups, Vancouver and Winnipeg have the most North American Indian residents while Winnipeg has the highest number of Métis (40,980). Ottawa has the largest number of Inuit residents (605), followed closely by Montreal and Toronto. In the west, only Edmonton, Calgary, and Vancouver have more than 200 Inuit residents (Statistics Canada 2006).

Although the Aboriginal population of Canada represents a small minority, they are the fastest growing group as reflected in age distributions. While the total Aboriginal population constitutes about 4 percent of the Canadian population, Native people under 15 years constitute 5 percent of the comparable age group of Canada. The median age of the Aboriginal group was 23.9 years in 2006, that is, 3 years younger than the median Canadian age of 26.5 years. The Aboriginal growth rate is also higher than that of the total Canadian population.

Data concerning languages spoken by people with an Aboriginal identification indicate strong continuation of aboriginal languages, especially as compared to the situation in the United States. However, there are conflicting indications for future trends. According to federal statistics from the census of 2011, most Aboriginal Canadians speak English as their mother tongue (more than 700,000) while only about 36,000 speak French as their mother tongue. The number of people who reported an Aboriginal language as their mother tongue was 144,015, representing about 18.7 percent of the Native population. Some 60 Aboriginal languages are spoken in Canada. Of these, Cree has the largest number of speakers (83,475). Inuktitut (the language of the Inuit) is spoken by 34,110 people, while Ojibway has 19,275 speakers. No other Aboriginal language has more than 10,000 speakers. Table 3.2 lists the largest number of speakers of Canadian Aboriginal languages.

Although about one-fifth of the Aboriginal population reported an Aboriginal language as a mother tongue (the first language they learned at home in childhood), only 11.8 percent of the entire Aboriginal population reported that they actually spoke their Native language at home. However, 21.5 percent reported that they could carry on a conversation in an Aboriginal language. As expected, the ability to speak an Aboriginal language increased with age. People aged 55 years or older were most likely to be fluent speakers and most likely to actually use their Native language in daily conversation. In contrast, children were least likely to speak an Aboriginal language. Also as expected, Aboriginal languages were spoken most frequently on Indian reserves while least used among Native people living in urban areas.

The discrepancy between learning a language in childhood and actually using it at home indicates concern for the future continuation of some Native languages. For every 100 people with an Aboriginal mother tongue, 76 actually spoke their language at home in 1981, but only 65 did so in 1996; 12 did so in 2006. According to Statistics Canada, for every 100 children under the age of 5, 91 spoke their mother tongue at home in 1981, but in 1996 when these children were in their mid- or late teens, only 76 continued to speak their Native language at home. However, DIAND reported that there was an increase in mother tongue knowledge and use by registered Indians residing on reserves.

Statistics from 2006 collected by DIAND concerning income, shown in Table 3.3, indicate a consistent discrepancy among registered Indians, the Aboriginal population, and the general Canadian population. The Canadian population (called "Reference Population" in DIAND tables) has higher household and individual incomes than the total Aboriginal population. Consistently lower than both are the incomes of registered Indians. Finally, in all provinces except Newfoundland, the off-reserve registered Indian population has higher household and individual incomes than on-reserve Indians. These figures indicate that average household income of Canadians was nearly double that of the average on-reserve household income. Table 3.4 reveals that average individual incomes reflect the same discrepancies. Overall, on-reserve Indians earn less than half the money earned by Canadians.

Sources of income for 1991 show trends consistent with the dollar differences in incomes. Table 3.4 presents relevant statistics as percentages. The two sets of figures are correlated. That is, since on-reserve Indians were least likely to receive income from employment, they were most likely to receive income from government transfer payments.

Tables of labor force activity, employment, and unemployment rates for 2006 similarly show consistent patterns favoring the "reference population" while disfavoring the on-reserve registered Indian population. Table 3.5 presents data concerning "participation rate" (the total labor force as a percentage of the total population aged 15 years and older), "employment ratio" (those individuals employed as a percentage of the total population 15 years and older), and "unemployment rate" (those unemployed as a percentage of the total labor force). These figures are internally consistent. That is, while nearly 70 percent of all Canadians over the age of 15 were employed, only about 10 percent of the total labor force was unemployed. In

TABLE 3.2	Aboriginal Languages in Canada
Aboriginal languages	144,015
Cree	83,475
Inukitut	34,110
Ojibway	19,275
Montagnais-Naskapi	10,965
Mi'kmaq	8,030
Dakota/Sioux	1,160
Blackfoot	3,250
Salish languages	2,950
Slavey	1,525
Dogrib	2,080
Carrier	1,525
Wakashan languages	1,075

Source: Statistics Canada 2011.

TABLE 3.3	Individual and Household Income in Canada			
	Reference Population	Aboriginal Population	Off-Reserve Indians	On-Reserve Indians
Individual Average Earning ($)	39,942	32,475	32,177	25,040
Household Income Median ($)	43,261	34,223	15,000	10,500

Source: DIAND 2006: Tables 2, 34.

contrast, while slightly less than half of on-reserve Indians were employed, nearly one-third of those in the labor force were unemployed. Unemployment rates indicate that the percentage of unemployed on-reserve Indians was more than three times as high as the percentage of unemployed Canadians. Although provincial unemployment rates varied, unemployment rates for Indians and Aboriginals were consistently higher than for the reference population.

Statistical tables recording percentage distributions of the experienced labor force by occupation indicate that Indians are the most likely to participate in occupations dependent upon land and resources and least likely to participate in manufacturing jobs. Table 3.6 labels occupations as "primary," "secondary," and "tertiary." Primary occupations include fishing, trapping, forestry, logging, and agriculture; secondary occupations include manufacturing and processing; and tertiary occupations encompass a disparate variety of fields such as managerial, technological, social, religious, teaching, medicine, health, and artistic occupations.

DIAND tables reporting levels of education provide data that are interconnected with occupation and income figures. In 1991, on-reserve Indians were most likely of all the population groups to have less than ninth grade educations and least likely to have graduated from high school. Although Table 3.7 reveals that less than one-third of on-reserve Indians were high school graduates and that less than half of all Aboriginals graduated from high school, the number of Indian graduates has increased in recent years, as has the number of Indians receiving postsecondary educations

Since the 1990s, representatives of numerous First Nations have negotiated self-government agreements with federal and provincial authorities. The agreements vary in scope, ranging from the assumption by bands of responsibility for managing educational and social programs to more extensive local governing arrangements. In all, these agreements affect 506 First Nations and Inuit communities.

Many Canadian First Nations have filed land claim suits with the "Special Claims Branch" empowered to resolve territorial issues. By March 1999, the branch had settled 200 such claims amounting to total monetary awards of $900 million. An additional 139 claims are under negotiation while another 302 are "under assessment" (78).

TABLE 3.4	Sources of Income in Canada			
	Reference Population	Aboriginal Population	Off-Reserve Indians	On-Reserve Indians
Income from Employment (%)	71.5	66.8	59.8	43.2
Income from Transfer Payments (%)	17.0	27.5	35.5	44.7
Source: DIAND 1995: Table 4.				

TABLE 3.5	Employment Data in Canada			
	Reference Population	Aboriginal Population	Off-Reserve Indians	On-Reserve Indians
Participation Rate (%)	63.0	62.7	57.3	46.8
Employment Ratio (%)	53.7	49.7	42.9	32.2
Unemployment Rate (%)	14.8	20.8	25.1	31.0
Source: DIAND 2006: Tables 1, 9.				

TABLE 3.6	Educational Achievement in Canada			
	Reference Population	Aboriginal Population	Off-Reserve Indians	On-Reserve Indians
Primary (%)	6.1	7.3	8.1	11.1
Secondary (%)	14.7	10.8	10.5	5.4
Tertiary (%)	79.2	81.8	81.4	83.5
Source: DIAND 2006: Tables 16, 19.				

TABLE 3.7	High School Educational Achievement in Canada			
	Reference Population	Aboriginal Population	Off-Reserve Indians	On-Reserve Indians
Less than Grade 9 (%)	13.7	18.4	19.4	37.2
High School Graduates (%)	62.1	49.4	44.7	31.1

Source: DIAND 1995: Table 1.

TABLE 3.8	Native Population by State in the United States
States with over 100,000 Native Residents	
Oklahoma	266,801
California	312,215
Arizona	253,542
New Mexico	172,276
Texas	113,755
North Carolina	100,956
States with over 50,000 Native Residents	
Washington	91,299
Michigan	60,842
South Dakota	61,724

Source: US Bureau of the Census 2006: 1.

US DATA

Turning to data from the United States, it is well to recall issues discussed in chapters 1 and 2 concerning the likelihood of undercounting of Native Americans by governmental agencies. With this caution in mind, the US Bureau of the Census of 2010 reports that about 2.9 million people identified as American Indian and Alaska Native belonging to 554 Indian tribes and Alaska Native groups. This figure constitutes 0.9 percent of the US population. In addition, 2.3 million (0.7%) people identified as American Indian and Alaska Native in combination with one or more other races (US Bureau of the Census 2010).

Although Native Americans live in every state of the country, the largest concentrations of Native people are in the west (45.6%), followed by the south (30.2%), the midwest (17.9%), and finally the Northeast (6.3%). Table 3.8 shows that four states had more than 100,000 Native residents and several other states had more than 50,000.

Of the more than 500 Indian tribes in the United States, the Cherokees are the most numerous. According to the 2000 census, they had a population of more than 302,569 (15.9%). The Navajos, with a reported population of 276,775 (14.6%), were the next most numerous. The several "Sioux" tribes accounted for more than 113,713, while the Chippewa tribes accounted for another 110,857. There were an additional 5 tribes or groups of related tribes who had populations of more than 50,000. These include the Choctaws, Puebloans, Apaches, Iroquois, and Lumbees. The Creeks, Blackfoot, and Chickasaws each had more than 20,000 members. Other groups listed in the census with between 10,000 and 20,000 members were the Tohono O'odham, Potawatomi, Seminole, Pima, Tlingit, Cheyenne, Comanche, Osage, and Salish.

Some 169 Native languages are currently spoken in the United States. According to census data for 2010, 372,095 people reported that they speak an Indian language at home. (Note that others may be speakers of Indian languages but do not use the language at home.) Approximately 10,000 people stated that they were monolingual speakers of an Indian language. Most of the languages with the largest percentage of use as home languages are spoken in the Southwest, particularly New Mexico and Arizona. These include Navajo, western Apache, Hopi, and Zuni. Choctaw in Mississippi, Yupik in Alaska, Cherokee in Oklahoma, and Lakhota-Dakota in the northern Plains are also frequently used as home languages (M. Krauss, quoted in "Indians Striving to Save Their Languages" 2006: A22). According to 2000 census data, Table 3.9 lists Native languages that have the most speakers.

Many Indian languages are in grave danger of extinction because they are no longer being learned by children. According to Michael Krauss, of about 200 languages currently spoken by Native people in the United States and Canada, 149 are no longer being learned by children (1992: 5). Krauss distinguishes four categories of languages—Class A: 34 languages still spoken by all generations, including children; Class B: 35 languages spoken only by the parental generation and up; Class C: 84 languages spoken only by the grandparental generation and up; and Class D: 57 languages spoken only by the very elderly, usually less

TABLE 3.9	Native Languages Spoken in the United States

Native Language	Number of Speakers
Navajo	169,471
Yupik	18,950
Dakota/Lakhota	18,616
Apache	13,062
Keres	12,945
Cherokee	11,610
Choctaw (and Chickasaw)	10,343
Zuni	9,686
Ojibwa	8,371
Pima	7,270

Source: US Bureau of the Census 2010: American Community Survey, Native North American Languages, Table 1.

than 10 persons per language (McCarty et al. 1999: 2). Languages in Class D obviously are in serious danger of disappearing, while those in Classes B and C may also face extinction without rapid and well-planned intervention. Many Native nations are responding to the challenge of language survival with innovative programs suited to their particular circumstances such as language-immersion, involvement of elders in the classroom, development of curricula that emphasize conversational uses of language in social contexts, and specialized focus on language use in ritual (McCarty et al. 1999; *Tribal College Journal* 2000). These programs are being implemented in primary and secondary schools operated by tribes. In addition, at least twenty-five of the tribal colleges in the United States offer language courses, some requiring language studies for completion of degrees. To be successful, Native language use must also be encouraged in daily social interactions, not just in school settings. To this end, Clay Slate, director of the Navajo Language Program at the Navajo Community College, suggests that the focus of language planning and use be at the local level of household, clan, and community. He further suggests that in order to protect the Navajo language, English should be restricted from use in some settings. For example, Slate proposes that only Navajo be used in the important interpersonal context of greetings and social introductions where people traditionally locate themselves in "social space" by providing clan identities and other kinship information to establish relationships and exchange social knowledge (1993: 13).

Comparing statistics on incomes for Indians and for the general American population, a consistent disadvantage borne by Indians is revealed. In 1999, the median household income of American Indians was $30,599 while the total US median family income was $41,994. Median family income for Indians was $33,144, compared to a US figure of about $51,046. Per capita income similarly showed disparities that disadvantaged Native Americans. The per capita income for Indians was $12,893, significantly lower than the US per capita of $21,587. Native Americans were consequently more likely to live in poverty than other Americans. In 1999, the percentage of Native families living below the poverty level (defined as a family of four earning less than $12,670) was 21.8 percent while in the general population, 9.2 percent of families lived in poverty. For Native Americans, the individual poverty rate (defined as an individual earning less than $6,300 a year) was 25.7 percent while for the general American population, the rate was 12.4 percent. That is, there were nearly three times as many Indians living in poverty as the general population.

Government statistics on occupation indicate that Indians are more likely than other Americans to be employed in farming, forestry, and fishing; in precision and craft occupations; and to work as machine operators, assemblers, handlers, equipment cleaners, laborers, service providers, and protective service workers. They are less likely than the general US population to be employed in executive, administrative, and managerial jobs; in professional specialty occupations; and in sales and administrative support occupations. The discrepancy between Native and other Americans is most marked in executive, professional, and sales occupations. Occupational differentiation results in differences in income since Indians are more likely to be employed in lower paying jobs and less likely to work in higher paying occupations (US Bureau of the Census 2000: Table 2).

Educational training and achievement statistics reveal another source of disadvantage for Native Americans. Table 3.10 displays percentages of Indians and other Americans with high school and college degrees. In order to improve educational and employment opportunities for Native Americans, 31 tribes now administer their own colleges with total enrollments of over 25,000. The schools provide vocational, technical, and academic training, conferring degrees in two-year, four-year, and graduate programs. Tribal colleges also offer adult education programs, job training,

TABLE 3.10	Educational Achievement of Native Peoples in the United States	
	Native Americans	**All Americans**
Aged 16–19		
High School (%)	83.9	90.2
Aged 25+		
High School (%)	70.9	80.4
College (%)	11.5	24.4

Source: US Bureau of the Census 2000: Table 2.

and continuing education courses and certificates. However, Congressional budgetary appropriations for higher education translates into approximately $3,430 per student enrolled in tribal colleges, a figure much lower than the amount of $4,470 allocated per student attending a state community college (Ambler 1998: 34).

The policy set forth in the federal "Personal Responsibility and Work Opportunity Reconciliation Act" of 1996, commonly referred to as welfare reform, may erode the precarious economic situation of many Indian families. According to the law, tribal governments are permitted to implement their own welfare-to-work programs, but the law does not provide sufficient funding for tribes to realistically be able to do so. Because of the rural location of most reservations, jobs are often difficult to find. For example, The Navajo Nation estimates that it would have to create 2,500 new jobs in order to comply with the work participation requirements of the law (Ambler 1998: 9). However, while many tribes seek to develop high school and college programs for their members in order to improve people's chances of obtaining jobs, federal law stipulates that pursuing college educations and job training for more than one year does not comply with welfare-to-work requirements. Tribal leaders point out that limits on education and lack of adequate funding are inconsistent with the goals of enabling people to qualify and retain skilled jobs that will earn them adequate incomes. For example, while the unemployment rate on the Turtle Mountain Reservation in North Dakota is 50 percent, 87 percent of people who graduate from the Turtle Mountain Community College are employed (9). Similarly, 82 percent of recent graduates of the Navajo Nation's Crown Point Institute of Technology have found employment after graduation, a figure that contrasts sharply with the Navajos' overall unemployment rate of 50 percent (17).

Much has been made in the media of the attempt of Indian tribes to earn income through gaming. Although more than 200 tribes currently operate some form of gaming, the total Native share of gaming revenues amounts to only about 5 percent. According to figures released by the National Indian Gaming Association, Indian gaming has generated over 120,000 direct jobs and 160,000 indirect jobs nationwide. The vast majority of these jobs are held by non-Indians. Native gaming, therefore, benefits not only the tribes that own and operate casinos but also non-Indians who are employed at the casinos as well as people who run hotels, restaurants, and stores frequented by customers drawn into the gaming establishments. Each tribe makes its own decisions about the distribution or investment of profits. In addition to some per capita disbursements, the majority of the funds are used to improve infrastructure on reservations, provide educational, medical, and social services, grant college scholarships, construct and maintain tribal buildings, and subsidize housing for their members. Most gaming profits support Native communities, in the context of declining federal funding for Indian programs, a decline that has accelerated since 1980.

Income and employment data pertaining to Indian and Inuit communities in both the United States and Canada consistently reveal the economic hardships faced by Native people. All measurements indicate that Native people are poorer and more likely to be unemployed than their neighbors in the state or province, region, and country in which they live. Poverty results from the lack of jobs due, among other factors, to the rural location of most reservations and to the low quality of the education and training that many Indians receive. Control over education at all levels is therefore a major goal of tribal governments, although one that many groups are not able to afford to implement.

RESPONSES TO CONTEMPORARY CHALLENGES

Ever since Europeans first arrived in North America, Native people have employed various strategies in reaction to the foreign presence. In some cases, they welcomed the strangers, taking advantage of the opportunity to trade and obtain new products.

At other times, they accommodated European settlers either by sharing their lands and resources or by moving their own settlements to other parts of their accustomed territories. As more Europeans arrived, Native people were often pressured or forced to leave their aboriginal homelands and relocate, sometimes far from their original region. People also resisted the settlers' advance and the consequent loss of land and resources. Modes of resistance depended on the particular economic and political circumstances of the people. Indians sometimes resorted to armed confrontation, defending their own communities and attacking Euro-American settlements. Resistance might also be manifested in spiritual reawakenings or reworkings of traditional beliefs. Frequently, military, social, and spiritual responses were combined.

The following chapters in this text examine the cultures and histories of Native peoples in an attempt to understand the origins and development of the complex Native communities currently living in North America. We focus on aboriginal culture and on indigenous reactions, readjustments, and resistance to European contact. And we explore the ways that Indians and Inuit have shaped their lives today. Here we review some current issues related to sovereignty, self-determination, and protection of political and cultural rights.

Climate Change

We begin with an issue facing everyone on this planet but one that has particular resonance in many Native American communities: that is, climate change. The Arctic, for example, is on the front line of climate change. Rising temperatures due to global warming are resulting in the thinning of ice cover year-round and the erosion and disappearance of glaciers. Temperatures are increasing in the Arctic at faster rates than elsewhere on the planet, as much as 5 degrees centigrade through the twentieth century (Macchi 2008: 32). According to an Inuit observer, "When I was born 60 years ago the ice was 3.5 miles thick, on average. Now, 60 years later, it's 1.5 miles. In just 60 years" (Angaanigaq 2009: 8). Another sign of global warming is the receding of ice caps. In one area, the ice receded 30 mi. in one year. As the ice caps melt, the sea level rises and waves becomes stronger, leading to erosion of coastal land. Weather patterns are becoming unstable, affecting the migratory cycles of both marine and terrestrial animals that Inuit subsistence is still dependent on. With warmer temperatures and melting of the sea ice, hunting becomes dangerous, lessening the food supply. Malnutrition is a serious risk in Arctic communities.

Dramatic effects of climate change can be seen on Baffin Island, the fifth largest island in the world, located in Nunavut in the Canadian Arctic. Inuit Elders there note that the sea ice melts earlier in the year, freezes over later in the summer, the land is warmer, and the land and sea animals are less numerous. And the long Arctic winter darkness is getting lighter. This unusual phenomenon is due to the fact that the warmer air acts as a conduit for light from the south, creating a perceived brightness (Indian Country Today 2011a: 16).

Studies reported in 2011 of more than 62,000 mi. of Arctic coastline indicate that the extent and depth of sea ice are decreasing annually, affecting a rise in ocean levels worldwide. Between 2006 and 2009, 22 cu. mi. of Arctic water were lost yearly, a jump from an annual rate of 7 cu. mi. just two years before. In 2011, sea ice reached its maximum extent early in March, nearly 500,000 sq. mi. less than the average 6.1 million sq. mi. recorded from 1979 through 2000 (Indian Country Today 2011b: 16) The report concluded: "The circumpolar Arctic Coast is arguably one of the most critical zones in terms of the rapidity and the severity of environmental change and the implications for human communities dependent on coastal resources. In the face of unprecedented and jarring changes in the local environment on which traditional livelihoods and cultures depend, Arctic coastal communities are coping with rapid population growth, technological change, economic transformation, and confounding social and health challenges."

For one Inupiat community in Alaska, climate change may mean their imminent forced relocation. Some 427 residents of the village of Kivalina, located on a narrow barrier island 70 mi. north of the Arctic Circle, are faced with a drastic alteration in their local environment. According to their statement, "Due to global warming, the sea ice forms later in the year, attaches to the coast later, breaks up earlier, and is less extensive and thinner. Houses and buildings are in imminent danger of falling into the sea. Critical infrastructure is threatened with permanent destruction" (Indian Country Today 2011c: 18).

In addition to the ecological effects of climate change, Arctic communities are preparing themselves for new struggles over resources and development. As the temperatures warm and the sea ice recedes, land masses and their mineral resources become exposed and available for extraction. In this changing climatic and development context, new opportunities may exist for Arctic peoples to expand and diversify their economic base. They are, however, aware of the dangers of development that is too rapid and does not take into account long-term consequences. Accordingly, leaders of Inuit communities finalized an agreement in 2011 called the Circumpolar Inuit Declaration on Resource Development Principles asserting that resource development must take place "at a rate sufficient to provide durable and diversified economic growth, but constrained enough to forestall environmental degradation and an overwhelming influx of outside labour." Furthermore, "While Inuit look forward to new forms and levels of economic development, the use of resources in the Arctic must be conducted in a sustainable and environmentally responsible way, and must deliver direct and substantial benefits to the Inuit" (Indian Country Today 2011d: 15).

Native peoples in other regions are experiencing alterations in their economies due to climatic changes as well. Northwest coast peoples such as the Quinault Indian Nation in Washington have witnessed sharp declines in salmon catches because of retreating glaciers that no longer sufficiently flow into the rivers that are the salmon's spawning grounds. And in northern Wisconsin, the Ojibwe of the Bad River Reservation have had several years when they have not been able to harvest any wild rice, a traditional staple of their diet and their local economies. The failure of the wild rice crop is due to a combination of warming winters, heavy spring rains that damage young plants, and the spread of plant diseases that proliferate in such a climate.

Several Native nations are constructing new energy projects to replace their reliance on fossil fuels such as coal and oil. The Dine (or Navajos) in Arizona and New Mexico and the Rosebud Lakota in South Dakota are harnessing two sources of energy abundantly available in their territories, that is, wind and sun. The Dine are developing a wind farm near Flagstaff Arizona that is projected to provide power to some 20,000 homes in the area (Navarro 2010). And the Rosebud Lakota began using wind energy at their commercial wind turbine in 2003, generating power for utility companies on and off their reservation.

Treaty Rights

We now look back to the "fish-ins" of the 1950s and 1960s in Washington and Oregon that combined strategies for protecting cultural practices. (See Chapter 20 for details of these events.) Native people of the Northwest were continuing a long tradition of asserting their treaty rights, but rather than employing the methods of pursuing legal suits through the courts or through lobbying public officials and government agencies, they took the action of violating state regulations that restricted their customary fishing activities contrary to treaty guarantees. By fishing "illegally," Native fishermen claimed their rights to fish in "usual and accustomed places as stipulated in treaties." Fish-ins helped unite Indians across North America about the political and legal issues raised by the protestors. Supporters in many communities joined to demonstrate their solidarity with indigenous people of the Northwest. The non-Indian media also played an important part by publicizing the claims of Native fishermen to audiences throughout the United States and Canada. Seeking allies in non-Native communities has been a strategy used for hundreds of years, but the availability of national and international media allowed alliances with other groups to develop much more rapidly.

In 1969, the blockade of an international bridge between the United States and Canada that traverses the Mohawk reserve of Akwesasne between the Canadian city of Cornwall, Ontario, and the New York state mainland was another event that asserted Native claims to free and unhindered crossing of the international border as guaranteed by Jay's Treaty of 1794 (see Chapter 5). The international boundaries that were fixed by foreign powers are culturally meaningless to indigenous people today, but because of the history of state expansion, Native people are restricted by these boundaries. By dramatizing the local problem of a Native nation whose territory was unilaterally divided between two countries, the Mohawks of Akwesasne brought to the fore the issue of unity among all indigenous people in North America.

The occupation of the abandoned federal prison of Alcatraz on an island off the coast of San Francisco in November 1969 was another watershed event. In 1964, one year after the federal penitentiary was closed, five Lakota men living in San Francisco briefly occupied the island, basing their action on their interpretation of the 1868 Fort Laramie treaty signed between Lakotas and the United States that stated that abandoned federal lands could revert to Lakota ownership. The one-day occupation was followed by a suit in federal court claiming title to the island, a suit that was denied. Then, in 1969, after a fire destroyed the San Francisco Indian Center, Native people living in the

Bay area occupied Alcatraz, claiming the island in the name of a newly formed group called "Indians of All Tribes." An initial one-day occupation on November 9 was followed by another on November 20 that eventually lasted for nineteen months, ending in June of 1971 (Johnson and Nagel 1994). The group of about eighty protestors issued a proclamation stating plans to develop Indian institutions on the island, including "a center for Native American studies, an American Indian spiritual center, an Indian center of ecology, an Indian training school, and an American Indian museum" (Fortunate Eagle 1994: 46–47). During the nineteen-month occupation, hundreds of Native and non-Native supporters came to Alcatraz to help strengthen the community and to publicize the grievances of indigenous people against the US government for violations of treaty obligations as well as to provide a forum for educating Americans about the economic and social needs of Indians and Inuit throughout the continent. Although the immediate goals of reclaiming land or establishing Indian institutions on Alcatraz were not successful, "the underlying goals of Indians on Alcatraz were to awaken the American public to the reality of the plight of the first Americans and to assert the need for Indians' self-determination. In this they were indeed successful" (Johnson and Nagel 1994: 20).

In 1972, one year after the end of the Alcatraz occupation, Native people from all across the United States marched from the West Coast to Washington, DC, in the "Trail of Broken Treaties" in order to gain support for their contention that the federal government failed to uphold the treaties it made with Indians in the eighteenth and nineteenth centuries. The "Trail of Broken Treaties" led appropriately to the offices of the BIA in Washington, DC, where marchers delivered a document of "Twenty Points" outlining grievances and proposing new directions in Indian-government relations that stressed the independent and sovereign status of Native nations (Deloria 1974: 48–53). The document included proposals to restore treaty-making authority to Congress, to negotiate new treaties with Native tribes or communities, to review treaty violations committed by the states and federal government, and to acknowledge Native people's right to interpret provisions of treaties signed by their ancestors (52). This point is critical since courts often ignore Native interpretations based on oral tradition and customary knowledge because they lack written documentation. In Canada, the validity of oral tradition and

indigenous testimony was upheld in a 1999 Canadian Supreme Court decision stemming from a land claims case in British Columbia, but similar consideration of Native testimony is lacking as a standard judicial principle in the United States.

In another region, the growing tensions and violence on the Pine Ridge Reservation in South Dakota led to the occupation of the village of Wounded Knee in 1973 and its subsequent encirclement and siege by federal troops (see Chapter 10 for a discussion of these events). In addition to focusing on the failure of federal agencies to guarantee indigenous treaty rights, the seventy-one-day occupation beginning in February 1973 raised issues about the legitimacy (or illegitimacy) of elected tribal leaders and councils. These events brought Native concerns to the attention of many Americans through intense media coverage.

Since then, Native communities in both the United States and Canada have attempted to expand their sovereign powers and to press for governmental action regarding land claims and other treaty rights issues. They have sought to exercise sovereign control in social, economic, political, and judicial domains. Some tribes have begun to levy taxes on corporations doing business within their territories. Some have expanded the jurisdiction of tribal courts or have sought to increase their territorial base through acquiring lands adjacent (and sometimes not adjacent) to their existing reservations. Tribes have lobbied for legislative action to protect their religious, cultural, and economic freedoms. They have so far successfully fought congressional moves to limit tribal sovereignty and to weaken the government's obligations toward tribes. Some Native nations, especially those that have recently prospered through casino gaming, have used their new economic clout in order to wield political influence.

A major step in internationalizing the Native rights movement came with the founding of the International Treaty Council in 1974. The organization, focusing on issues of sovereignty and treaty rights, has reached out to forge alliances with indigenous groups throughout the world. It gained recognition as a nongovernmental organization (NGO) with official observer status in the United Nations (UN). Delegates participate in numerous international conferences in the United States, Canada, and abroad, where they have gained the support of other groups in their struggle for sovereign recognition at home.

In July of 1999, the National Congress of American Indians (of the United States) and the Assembly of

First Nations (of Canada) held its first joint meeting to discuss issues of common concern such as "treaty rights, economic development, education, language and literacy, health, housing, social development, justice, taxation, land claims, and the environment" ("NCAI and Assembly of First Nations Unite" 1999: 5). Leaders of the two groups signed an accord called the "Declaration of Kinship and Cooperation among the Indigenous Peoples and Nations of North America." According to Phil Fontaine, national chief of the Assembly of First Nations, "We have common issues and this accord will allow us to establish a relationship in order to deal with these critical issues and move them forward, both in our mutual political forums and also in international forums such as the United Nations" (quoted in "NCAI and Assembly of First Nations Unite" 1999: 5).

Summarizing issues of concern to "the future of Indian nations," Deloria and Lytle (1984) point to five areas requiring attention: "structural reform of tribal governing institutions, determined and lasting cultural renewal, economic stability, and the stabilization of relations between the tribe and state and federal governments" (245). According to Deloria and Lytle, tribal governments need to become more accountable to their members in ways that are consistent with traditional understandings of the responsibilities of leaders and their requisite sensitivity to community opinion. In some nations, tribal courts have established judicial processes and practices that recognize the "validity of traditional customs in determining cases … [so that] more extensive development of tribal customs as the basis for a tribal court's decision will enable these institutions to draw even closer to the people" (248). Recent developments in the Navajo Nation, for example, demonstrate this connection. By using traditional systems of negotiation by "peacemakers" in domestic conflict cases, Navajo governing institutions have allowed for greater participation of community elders and family and clan members in resolving conflicts and protecting victims (Coker 1999).

Cultural Traditions and Images

Native people have also asserted their rights to maintenance of cultural traditions, attempting to reverse the effects of past policies that undermined indigenous values, practices, and systems of belief. Programs that maintain or revitalize indigenous languages, safeguard religious expression, and teach traditional songs, dances, and arts have become significant vehicles for cultural renewal. Cultural revival might also include the recognition of the centrality of clans or other social and kinship groupings as the basis of family and community life.

Tribal educators stress the importance of language as a basic component in Native heritage, identity, and self-pride. It is a vehicle for the expression of cultural values and philosophies. In an issue of *Tribal College Journal* (Spring 2000) devoted to the subject, Native educators and tribal leaders noted the centrality of language to both their cultural and political goals. As Paul Boyer stated, "Language instruction is not an exercise in sentimentality but part of a strategy of self-determination" (12). And Doris Boissoneau, Anishnabe, commented, "If we are going to call ourselves a Nation with sovereignty rights and inherited rights, we need a language and a culture" (22). Language maintenance is an integral feature of cultural strength because, as Marwin Weatherwax (Blackfoot) observed, the potential "loss of language is more than the loss of words … It would be a loss of the culture as it is. I cannot teach you culture. Culture is something you have to live. Through the language we can give a part of the culture that can be lived" (22). Indeed, "language is a first step in recovering culture. It's authentic culture because the Native perspective is not taken out of it" (Peters, Anishabe, *Tribal College Journal* Spring 2000: 22). Finally, language contains people's values and symbolic meanings; it is the "source of re-discovering our philosophies and knowledge. Our language speaks to us and reveals to us our philosophies. We just have to start listening again" (Mistaken Chief, *Tribal College Journal* Spring 2000: 27).

In addition, Native people and organizations have vocally objected to negative stereotypes and false depictions of Indians prevalent in textbooks for children and in films and other media (see Hirschfelder et al. 1999). Many Native people also object to stereotyped depictions of Indians in advertisements (usually as headdress-wearing chiefs) as well as to the use of words such as "Indians," "Braves," or "Redskins" as the names of sports teams. While some of the most blatant racist cinematic images are not as commonly seen as in the past, Indians are still often portrayed in films as simplistic stock characters rather than as complex human beings (Kilpatrick 1999).

Recent films written and directed by Native Americans, however, convey a more realistic and honest view of Indian life. The films of Chris Eyre (Smoke Signals, 1998; Skins, 2002) and Sherman Alexie (The Business of Fancydancing, 2002) are especially notable. And the work of the Canadian Inuit director Zacharias Kunuk and his associates initiated a new vocabulary in indigenous filmmaking (Atanarjuat: The Fast Runner, 2001; The Journals of Knud Rasmussen, 2006; and Before Tomorrow, 2008). Documentaries have focused on contemporary ecological, cultural, and social issues: In the Light of Reverence (2001) deals with indigenous attempts to protect access to sacred lands; Homeland: Four Portraits of Native Action (2005) depicts efforts to deal with pollution and industrial contamination in Native territories; Coloring the Media (2008) discusses media representation of Native peoples; and The Thick Dark Fog (2012) confronts the history and legacy of Indian boarding schools.

In Canada, the Aboriginal People's Television Network (APTN) began nationwide broadcasting in 1999. The network produces and disseminates programs on Native arts, culture, history, and current issues of concern in indigenous communities. It also plays movies and serials. And it plans programming dealing with indigenous peoples in Central and South America, Australia, New Guinea, and elsewhere. Approximately one-quarter of all programming is broadcast in one of eighteen aboriginal languages ("Old Traditions on New Network: Igloos and Seals" 2000). APTN is carried as a component of basic cable packages throughout Canada.

Protecting and Developing Lands

Building sustainable economic systems depends first on the protection of the Native land base and consolidation of tribally owned land. Reservation land in the United States suffers from the legacy of allotment and fractionated inheritance initiated by the General Allotment Act of 1887 (see Chapter 2 for discussion of this legislation). Although tribal trust land can no longer be allotted, parcels that are already assigned are often further divided whenever a current holder dies. According to standard inheritance codes, if an allottee does not specifically will his/her land to one person, all heirs receive a divided portion. Over the span of only a few generations, hundreds of people may own a fraction of an original parcel. In order to utilize or develop the land, unanimous agreement among all holders must be obtained. Much land therefore remains unused or is leased to non-Indians as an alternative. The income received must then be divided, resulting in meager earnings for each individual. In addition, land can pass out of Native control if an allotment is inherited by a surviving non-Indian spouse, becoming private property and available to be sold.

Land claims cases continue to be of paramount importance in helping to enlarge reservation territory and to establish indigenous rights to self-government. Recent land claims settlements negotiated with federal governments in both Canada and the United States usually stipulate some degree of sovereign Native control over economic, social, and cultural policies in their territory. Hundreds of cases are pending, with outcomes for most likely to be decided in the first several decades of this century. Some analysts expect large amounts of land and monies to be transferred to Native sovereignty, especially in Canada. According to Canadian government estimates, settlements of more than 210 claims may give First Nations control over about 10 percent of the country, an increase from the current Native land base of 0.3 percent ("Indian Affairs Heat Up (Witness the Lobster War)" 1999). In the United States, Native people now control about 2 percent of the country's territory. The increase in their land base is not expected to rise very much since monetary compensation settlements are more the norm in the United States.

Strategies for land development and the use of resources continue to concern tribal governments. Many tribes are attempting to develop their land base through culturally appropriate and economically sound policies. The economic hardships faced by many First Nations have often led tribal governments to allow intensive exploitation of resources through agreements with corporations that do not provide for protection of land for future use, do not give fair monetary compensation, do not help create enduring infrastructure, and do not train the Native labor force.

In their efforts to seek redress and to gain security over their lands and livelihoods, Native peoples in the United States and Canada are using recent actions by the UN to bolster their claims. In 2007, the UN General Assembly voted to affirm the Declaration on the Rights of Indigenous Peoples with overwhelming international support. Only four countries voted against the Declaration: the United States, Canada, Australia, and New Zealand, all the historical descendents of settler colonies, each having a history of violence toward its indigenous peoples and of policies aimed at eradicating these peoples and their cultures. Since the vote, all four governments have reversed their position, beginning with Australia in 2009 and ending with the United States in 2010. The Declaration contains forty-five articles outlining international recognition of indigenous rights. Among these are the right to self-determination, to maintain their cultures, to be protected from genocide, ethnocide, and forced relocation. In addition, the document recognizes indigenous peoples' right to practice, develop, and teach their traditions, histories, languages, and religions. They have the right of access to all forms of media, and they are protected in their right to fully participate in the development of policies and decisions that affect them through their own chosen representatives. And the Declaration acknowledges the equal rights of women to be protected and promoted in all domains.

The Declaration concludes with several articles devoted to implementation of its provisions, including the need for governments to consult with indigenous peoples in the implementation of articles and to provide financial support to help with this process. Finally, the UN makes itself available to ensure that governments comply with all of the provisions. Native nations in both the United States and Canada have already begun using the moral and political force of the Declaration to support their efforts for control in the fields of education, language, healthcare, land rights, and legal practices. These are all issues that relate to claims of sovereignty and self-determination.

As part of the UN initiatives, in 2012, James Anaya, the UN Special Rapporteur on the Rights of Indigenous Peoples, conducted an investigation into discrimination against Native Americans in the United States. Anaya concluded that racial discrimination affects the lives of Native Americans in many domains from their relationships with federal and local governments and their personal experiences in institutional contexts such as education, that is, in the treatment of Native children by teachers and other students, in the educational system itself, and in the way that "native Americans and indigenous peoples are reflected in the school curriculum and teaching" (McGreal 2012). In addition, Anaya found discrimination in "the sense of invisibility of Native Americans in the country overall that is often reflected in the popular media" that presents distorted reporting about the lives of Native peoples today. And referring to both historical and contemporary issues of concern to indigenous peoples, Anaya added, "there have still not been adequate measures of reconciliation to overcome the persistent

legacies of the history of oppression, and there is still much healing that needs to be done."

Among his recommendations, Anaya proposed that the US government should restore to the tribes concerned some lands taken illegally. Anaya commented, "Securing the rights of indigenous peoples to their lands is of central importance to indigenous peoples' socioeconomic development, self-determination, and cultural integrity." In particular, he cited the case of the Black Hills of South Dakota, a territory guaranteed to the Lakota in 1868 by the Treaty of Fort Laramie but then unilaterally expropriated by the US Congress in 1877 after gold was discovered there. The Lakotas' claim to the Black Hills was acknowledged by the US Supreme Court and a financial settlement was awarded, but the Lakota refused the money and instead insisted on their rights to the land. In this context, Anaya advocated the return of the Black Hills to the Lakota, stating, "I'm talking about restoring to indigenous peoples what obviously they're entitled to and they have a legitimate claim to in a way that is not divisive but restorative. That's the idea behind reconciliation."

Another example of building alliances and internationalizing indigenous issues is the current debate about a Canadian omnibus budget bill passed in 2012. The bill, referred to as C-45, includes amendments to the Indian Act that revise procedures for leasing lands in First Nations reserves for economic development projects. Canadian officials assert that these changes will streamline the process of approving leases so that much-needed economic projects can be undertaken in a timely manner. However, opposition on the part of Aboriginal people to the changes began nearly as soon as the legislation was passed. Their opposition, called the Idle No More movement, gained national and indeed worldwide attention early in 2013. Aboriginal leaders are concerned that environmental damage will become widespread if reserve lands can be more easily leased to mineral and timber extraction companies and they fear that environmental protections will be ignored.

Leaders of Idle No More and of some individual First Nations have taken their concerns to the Canadian courts, filing a challenge to the constitutionality of C-45, claiming that the government failed to seek meaningful consultation with First Nations before passing legislation that affects them, a stipulated requirement in the Constitution of 1982. Leaders of the International Indian Treaty Council have also filed a complaint with the United Nations Committee on the Elimination of Racial Discrimination, again asserting that the Canadian government did not adhere to international human rights laws regarding the rights of indigenous peoples to safeguard their environment and their resources.

Participants in Idle No More have taken an active role in the growing environmental movement worldwide. Their concern with their own lands in Canada has expanded to their activism in protecting indigenous lands throughout the globe. And these concerns have led to their participation in an even wider movement that seeks to protect the sustainability of the planet. For example, members of Idle No More had a significant presence and in fact were the lead-off marchers in the People's Climate March in September 2014 that drew more than 400,000 people, timed to coincide with the UN Summit on climate change, voicing their desire to seek international action on this issue facing us all.

Income and Revenues

Tax immunity is a critical issue for Native peoples in both Canada and the United States. The concept refers to the fact that Indian lands are immune, not exempt, from all forms of state, provincial, or federal taxation. This means that Indians living on reservations do not pay property taxes, sales taxes on goods purchased on the reservation, or income tax on wages earned on reservations. The tax-immune status of reservations has become especially contentious in New York State since 1997, when the state government first attempted to collect sales taxes on gasoline and cigarettes sold to non-Native people by Native Americans at reservation stores. Because of objections by the Native governments, the state delayed its move until 2003, two years after the terrorist attacks of September 11, 2001, in New York City caused a sharp decline in state revenues. Then New York governor George Pataki again announced his plan to impose sales taxes on goods purchased by non-Native people from stores on reservations. In 2004, the state legislature authorized collection of those taxes, but in a reversal, Pataki vetoed the bill. Subsequent administrations and legislatures again reinstated the plan to collect taxes but the actual implementation continues to be postponed because of court challenges. According to a new state plan, tribal entities have two options: they may prepay a state tax on all cigarettes coming onto their reservation and

then apply for reimbursement for taxes paid on cigarettes sold to Indians or they may opt for a quota system under which the state will determine how many tax-free cigarettes tribal members can smoke annually. None of the tribal governments in New York have agreed to either plan. For example, the Senecas cited their 1842 Treaty of Buffalo signed with the US government that asserts that the United States "will protect such lands of the Seneca Indians, within the State of New York, as may from time to time remain in their possession from all taxes, and assessments for roads, highways, or any other purpose" (quoted in Toensing 2011: 11). In the context of these controversies, some of the Native nations in the state are moving toward manufacturing their own brands of cigarettes on the reservations, a move that negates any possibility of state taxation.

Elsewhere in the United States, tribal governments continue to struggle against attempts by states to tax property or income generated on reservations. In some cases, the tribal governments win their suits in US courts while in others they are not victorious. For example, in 2012 the Mashantucket Pequots won in federal court against the town of Ledyard, Connecticut, where their Foxwoods Casino is located. Ledyard attempted to tax slot machines used at Foxwoods that are leased from a non-reservation supplier but the court denied their ability to do so, stating, "Indian tribes are distinct sovereign entities that are distinct, independent political communities retaining their original natural rights. States do not have a right to regulate Indian tribes [or infringe] on the right of reservation Indians to make their own laws and be ruled by them" (quoted in Toensing 2012: 12). In another case, however, the US Supreme Court declined to hear an appeal by the Ute Mountain Ute Tribe in New Mexico against lower court decisions that allowed the State of New Mexico to receive tax revenue from oil and gas companies operating on reservation land. The Ute Tribe receives 13.1 percent royalties on these minerals but would receive an additional $1.3 million per year if they were able to collect the taxes currently paid to New Mexico (Berry 2012: 13).

These and other cases reflect the complex struggles between tribal governments and various state and local authorities that attempt to impose taxes on Native lands, businesses, and people. These conflicts undoubtedly continue as tribal governments defend their rights under treaties and their status as tax-immune sovereign entities.

One of the most troubling revelations of recent years has been the discovery of widespread mismanagement of tribal trust fund accounts by the BIA. A class-action suit brought against the BIA by Elouise Cobell (Blackfoot) on behalf of some 300,000 Indians in the United States revealed that the government cannot account for unknown billions of dollars missing from "Individual Indian Money Trusts" that were set up in order to safeguard money earned from government sale of oil, gas, timber, and other resources on Indian land. About 300,000 trust accounts are in the names of individual Native allottees while 1,700 are held by 338 tribes. In response to the lawsuit, called *Cobell v. Babbitt* (for Bruce Babbitt, then secretary of the interior), investigations revealed that the government does not know exactly how much money ought to be in each account nor where the funds currently are located. Most estimates put the missing funds at well over $2 billion, although much more money might be involved. More than $1 billion now flows into the accounts each year. After a Congressional inquiry documented the problem, legislation was enacted in 1994 (the American Indian Trust Fund Management Reform Act) that established the Office of the Special Trustee to clear up the account records. But in 1999, federal judge Royce Lamberth issued contempt-of-court citations against Secretary Babbitt, Secretary Robert Rubin of the Treasury Department, and Assistant Secretary Kevin Gover, head of the BIA, for failure to comply with court orders to present the documentation that it possesses concerning the trust accounts. In his ruling, Lamberth asserted that the named officials and their subordinates had "either ignored or thwarted [court orders] at every turn." He accused them of engaging in "a shocking pattern of deception of the court," adding "I have never seen more egregious misconduct by the federal government. The court cannot tolerate more empty promises to these Indian plaintiffs" ("Babbitt, Rubin Cited for Contempt" 1999: 11). Lead plaintiff Cobell commented, "All this time the government has had this ho-hum attitude—it's just an Indian trust fund case, so what. There was never a sense of urgency about this. Now we are finally on the road to justice" (11).

In December 2010, a major victory for Native American litigants in this case was achieved with a negotiated court settlement, called the Claims Resolution Act of 2010, that awarded a total of $1.5 billion to be divided among the plaintiff class but many probably receive about $2,000 each (Indian Country Today 2010). The settlement also includes a fund of $1.9 billion toward land consolidation that would enable people to buy land parcels that have been fractionated through inheritance in order to consolidate holdings.

Settlement of another long-standing series of claims brought by Native tribes against the federal government was announced in April 2012. The claims of forty-one Nations, some going back 100 years, concerned mismanagement by the Department of the Interior of tribal trust lands and resources including irreparable ecological damage caused by clearcutting timber and extracting coal and oil. The tribal claims also sought compensation for the mismanagement of funds by the Department of the Interior that had been received from resource companies. In its settlement, the government agreed to pay just over $1 billion to be distributed amongst the forty-one Nations according to a formula based on the value of the lands and resources involved. While this settlement concludes a large number of tribal land and resource claims, approximately sixty additional legal actions are still pending, to be worked out between tribal representatives and federal authorities.

The Violence against Women Act

A complex and interrelated set of problems concerns the rates of violence against Native women on reservations and the inability of tribal courts to deal effectively with either the victims or the abusers. The issue of legal authority on Indian reservations is similarly complex and creates confusion about which body (tribal, federal, or state) is responsible for pursuing action in criminal cases. Such confusion leads to extended delays and inaction. While this issue relates to all crimes it affects crimes against women in particular because, according to federal statistics, 88 percent of Native women who are victims of attacks say that their assailant was non-Indian (Walker 2012:10). Data also indicate that the rate of assault against Native women is 2.5 times higher than for other women in the United States. Native women are more than twice as likely as other women to be stalked. Put another way, six out of every ten Native women are likely to be assaulted in their lives and one in three are likely to be raped (10). The US Department of Justice reports that only 13 percent of cases of sexual assaults against Native women end in an arrest (compared to 32% for White women and 35% for African American women) (Williams 2012: A3).

Some relief may be forthcoming with Congressional reauthorization of the Violence against Women Act in 2013. This legislation includes a provision to permit tribal courts to prosecute nonmembers who commit these crimes against Native members on reservations

But even when tribal courts exert authority in criminal prosecutions, they are limited by federal regulations to imposing sentences of no more than one year in most cases. The lack of effective judicial action makes Native women even more hesitant than other women to file formal criminal complaints about sexual assaults that they have been subjected to. Particularly in small communities, women may fear reprisals from their attackers if they try to bring charges against them. Indeed, the rates of sexual and physical assault against Native women in rural and isolated communities in Alaska are especially alarming. Data collected by the Alaska Federation of Natives, for example, indicate that the rate of sexual abuse in rural villages is as much as twelve times the national average (A3).

The arguments about tribal jurisdiction are examples of what James Anaya referred to as the "inherent racism against Native people" in US policies and attitudes. The notion that tribal courts should not have authority over nonmembers is essentially based on principles of race, itself an entirely artificial cultural construct. Territorial jurisdictions routinely have authority over nonmembers of that jurisdiction. For example, state and federal courts prosecute crimes committed within the state or country regardless of the legal residence or citizenship of the accused. Therefore, to exempt tribal courts from the same rights as other sovereign entities contradicts principles of equal justice and is therefore a violation of the UN Declaration on the Rights of Indigenous Peoples.

Residential Schools

The continuing effects of education practices at boarding schools for Native children in both the United States and Canada have been brought to light with testimonies of people subjected to the regimentation, harsh discipline, and abuse common at these schools. One of the most influential of these schools was opened in 1879 in Carlisle, Pennsylvania, under the direction of Richard Pratt, becoming the model for many subsequent schools throughout North America. Pratt coined the motto "Kill the Indian in him and save the man," to emphasize his goal to eradicate Native traditions, languages, philosophies, and attachments

to family and community, that is, a policy that today we would term "ethnocide." By 1900, about 22,000 Native children were enrolled in federal and church-run schools. This number accounts for more than half of all Indian children of school age at that time (Adams 1988).

In the past several decades, revelations have come to light about the systematic abuse of Native children in boarding schools run by both secular and religious organizations from the late nineteenth century lasting in some cases into the 1970s. Children were routinely exposed to harsh physical punishments for minor infractions, even including such "unacceptable" behavior as speaking their Native language or resisting the unending regimentation of their lives. Children might be beaten, whipped, burned, thrown down stairs, and left with no food for long periods of time. Many children suffered sexual abuse such as molestation and rape, often on repeated occasions by the same or multiple perpetrators. The scope of such abuse is astounding. In both the United States and Canada; survivors have come forward to testify about their experiences, leading to lawsuits seeking both punishment for the offenders and compensation for the victims. For example, some 400 survivors of schools in Washington, Oregon, and Alaska won a suit against the Jesuit Order's Province of Oregon totaling $166 million. But legal roadblocks to pursuing these cases exist in some states. The South Dakota legislature, for instance, passed a law in 2010 that denies the ability of a person over forty years old from suing an institution (such as a church organization) from childhood sexual abuse, although individual offenders can be sued. In accordance with this statute, subsequent cases have been denied by state courts but appeals are pending (Woodard 2011: 29).

Although most of the publicized cases of physical and sexual abuse took place at schools for Native children located in the midwest and western states, such practices occurred in the east as well. Indeed, one of the first schools for Indian children was established in 1855 in western New York State by the Quakers. Known as the Thomas Indian School, it took in children from Seneca reservations in the region. In some cases the children were orphans but most were sent there by parents who became convinced that their children would receive a better education than was available on the reservations. The school was run with military-style regimentation, with unvarying schedules for daily activities, classes, and work. Children as young as four years of age were put to work doing heavy physical labor. It addition to physical punishments, children were repeatedly made to feel that their families had abandoned them, that they had no recourse to improve their situation. Some children were able to see their family members on visiting days and during holidays but many others never left the institution from the age of four through sixteen. By the early twentieth century, the Thomas Indian School housed more than 200 Seneca children as well as some from other Iroquoian reservations in the state.

The Thomas Indian School was administered in succession by the Quakers from 1855 to 1875, then by the New York State Board of Charities from 1875 to 1932, and finally by the State Department of Welfare from 1932 until the school was closed in 1957. But regardless of the administrative authorities, the operational policies of regimentation, limited education, and physical and psychological abuse remained the same.

Analysts of the boarding school experience for Native children throughout the United States and Canada point to the long-term effects, not only on children themselves but also on their families and communities. Feelings of isolation, abandonment, low self-esteem, and powerlessness "add up to a powerful formula for self-destructive behavior that would replicate itself generation after generation on reservations across the country" (Burich 2007:93). After years spent in a regimented institution, many people were ill-equipped to create and maintain connections with family and community. Even as adults interacting with their own children, some survivors bear the burdens of psychological isolation and distance.

Recently in Canada, attention has similarly been drawn to the poor quality of education and of living conditions in boarding schools operated from the 1880s until the 1980s under the auspices of the federal government by church groups, especially Anglican, Presbyterian, and Roman Catholic churches. Attendance at the schools was at first voluntary but in 1920, it became mandatory. Tens of thousands of children were removed from their home communities and sent hundreds, sometimes thousands, of miles to be kept in the boarding schools all year long until they reached eighteen years of age. Testimonies from former students of many of these schools document not only the inadequate education that they received, but also the physical and psychological abuses to which they were exposed. As in the US schools, children were punished with beatings for any supposedly bad behavior or even for speaking their own Native languages. And many were subjected to sexual abuses and assaults.

After many years of advocacy by First Nations and their supporters, Canadian Prime Minister Stephen Harper delivered a formal public apology on June 11, 2008, in Canada's House of Parliament. Prior to the event, Harper had appealed through the media to all Canadians to listen to the public broadcast from Parliament. In a lengthy formal statement, Harper asserted, in part:

> I stand before you today to offer an apology to former students of the Indian residential schools. The treatment of children in Indian residential schools is a sad chapter in our history. Today, we recognize that this policy was wrong, has caused great harm, and has no place in our country.
>
> The legacy of the Indian residential schools has contributed to social problems that continue to exist in many communities today. It has taken extraordinary courage for the thousands of survivors that have come forward to speak publicly about the abuse they suffered. The government recognizes that the absence of an apology has been an impediment to healing and reconciliation.
>
> The burden of this experience has been on your shoulders for far too long. The burden is properly ours as a government, and as a country.
>
> The government of Canada sincerely apologizes and asks the forgiveness of the aboriginal peoples of this country for failing them so profoundly. We are sorry. (www.cbc.ca/news/canada/story/2008/06/ll/pm-statement.html)

In addition, the Canadian government agreed to a settlement of reparations for survivors of the boarding schools, currently estimated to number about 80,000 out of the 150,000 children who attended the schools (Indian Country Today 2011e: 17). This settlement includes $1.9 billion Canadian to be awarded to students, $60 million to establish a truth and reconciliation commission to collect testimonies and educate the public about the schools, $20 million for a program of commemoration, and $125 million for an Aboriginal Healing Foundation to provide psychological services for survivors. Each former student is scheduled to receive $10,000 for the first year that they spent in the schools and $3000 for each subsequent year, with average estimated payments of $30,000 (Cherrington 2007:18).

In contrast to the public and detailed statement of apology offered by the Canadian prime minister, US President Barack Obama signed a Native American Apology Resolution in 2009 as an addition to a Department of Defense Appropriations Act. The resolution asks the president to "apologize on behalf of the United States to all Native peoples for the many instances of violence, maltreatment, and neglect of Native Peoples by citizens of the United States." And it "urges the President to acknowledge the wrongs of the United States against Indian tribes in the history of the United States in order to bring healing to this land." Although this resolution is an apology, it lacks the specificity of the Canadian statement without mentioning specific acts of "violence, maltreatment, and neglect." It also focuses on acts committed by "citizens," rather than emphasizing that these acts were committed by or condoned by the US government. And finally, this apology resolution was not delivered by the president in a public national spotlight and even its signing by Obama was an event closed to the press.

Health and Illness Among the serious health concerns facing Native peoples is the continual growth in the rates of diabetes, particularly Type II, adult-onset diabetes. As of 2012, 16.1 percent of Native Americans and Alaskan Natives suffer from Type II diabetes, nearly twice the general US rate of 8.3 percent and Native Americans are three times more likely to die from diabetes than other Americans. Rates for Native Americans vary on different reservations. Some of the highest are reported for the Pima and the Tohono O'odham, both in Arizona, where about 50 percent of adults are diabetic. Reasons for the high incidence of diabetes are complex and not fully understood. Certainly obesity is one of the contributing factors. And while weight gain is a recognized problem throughout the United States, it is even more significant on Indian reservations where adults are 1.6 times more likely to be obese than are Americans on average. The pattern often begins in childhood as it does in other poor communities.

Analysts trace the incidence of both diabetes and obesity to changes in diet. The traditional Native American diet consisted of a healthy mix of foods including (depending on region) corn, beans, low-fat vegetables and fruits, lean meats and fish. According to Karl Reinhard, a professor of forensic science and environmental archaeology who conducted an analysis of Southwestern peoples' coprolites (fossilized fecal remains) from more than 500 years ago, the indigenous diet was high in fiber and low in sugars and carbohydrates, helping people maintain a good balance of energy and nutrition (Richardson 2012). But now many people have adopted the common American pattern of foods containing sugars, sodium, and fats. And, tracing the links even more tightly, this is a diet related to poverty because foods with sugars, salts, and fats are relatively inexpensive compared to whole grains, lean meats, fish, and fresh fruits and vegetables. People living in many reservation communities got their start with this diet from federal programs dispensing surplus commodity foods beginning in the late nineteenth century and continuing in some places even today. The foods distributed include flour, sugar, rice, macaroni, canned meat, canned peas or green beans, canned pineapple, peanut butter, and lard, all foods containing large amounts of sugar, salt, and fat. Following Congressional investigations into food programs in the 1990s, commodity foods now include whole-grain pasta and some fresh fruits and vegetables.

In addition to the general causes affecting all communities, there are some local features that have been identified as possible contributing factors for diabetes. For example, high levels of arsenic in drinking water may lead to higher rates of diabetes. While arsenic occurs naturally in bedrock, its concentration varies throughout the United States, with highest levels in the west and Southwest. Furthermore, arsenic may be released into water tables through mining operations and through agriculture, both common on Indian reservations. And on many reservations, people do not have access to clean, safe drinking water. For example, in the Dine Nation of Arizona and New Mexico, at least 25 percent of homes rely on water from dug wells that are intended for livestock or for household use, but not for drinking. Testing of the samples from these wells indicated high levels of arsenic and in some areas many also tested positively for elevated levels of uranium, a long-term consequence of uranium mining (Hansen 2011:26–27). Scientists link such factors to the high incidence of Type II diabetes as well as to some cancers.

In response to the increasing incidence of diabetes on Indian reservations, in 1979 the Indian Health Service launched its Division of Diabetes to add services and develop programs to combat the disease. Although new clinics have been constructed and new technologies installed, treatment of patients on Indian reservations lags far behind that of other Americans mainly due to the lack of funding. For example, in 2010, the Indian

Health Service spent $2,741 per patient, compared to $4,412 for each federal prisoner, $5,841 for people enrolled in Medicaid, and $7,154 for veterans (Jones 2011: 30). Then in 2010, the Association of American Indian Physicians inaugurated a program among three Native communities to study the interrelated causes of diabetes and to develop prevention and treatment protocols. The selected groups include the Kickapoo Nation in Kansas, the Houma Nation of Louisiana, and the Southeastern Michigan Native community.

Programs to combat diabetes and its underlying causes have been developed on many reservations. These include the basics of nutritional awareness to prevent obesity, an emphasis on regular physical activity, and a reliance on traditional spiritual means to center the body and mind and promote healing. Where possible, a return to traditional foods and methods of cooking is also stressed. An innovative program at the Cherokee Nation in Oklahoma focuses on prevention by identifying people diagnosed as pre-diabetic with higher than normal blood sugar levels and offers them a range of services, including assigning them "life coaches" who encourage them to adhere to weight loss and exercise regimens. Free check-ups and educational classes are also provided. Since the project's inception in 2004, more than 200 people have participated.

DECISIONS OF THE SUPREME COURTS IN THE UNITED STATES AND CANADA

Decisions by the US Supreme Court since 2000 have varied in their implications for Native American sovereignty, particularly the ability of tribal governments to act independently in political and economic matters. In the past, Supreme Court decisions have generally (although not always) given latitude to the interpretation and exercise of Native sovereignty but the Courts led by Chief Justices Rehnquist and Roberts have more frequently reversed this pattern, limiting the ability of tribal governments to act as sovereigns. In 2001, in a case referred to as *Chickasaw Nation v. United States*, the Chickasaws objected to federal attempts to tax some earnings from gaming at their tribally owned casino because the Internal Revenue Service (IRS) exempted states from taxes on similar types of gaming. But the Court ruled against the Chickasaws, declaring that the Indian Regulatory Gaming Act allows the IRS

to require that tribes follow the same reporting and payment obligations as states and it further noted that Indian tribes may be subject to these provisions even in cases where the IRS grants exemptions to states.

In another case involving taxation, *Sherrill N.Y. v. Oneida Indian Nation of New York* (2004), the Court again ruled against the tax-immune status of Indian reservations. The facts of this case originate in the late eighteenth century when the Oneida Indian Nation of New York was established as a reservation by the US Congress. Much of the land was eventually sold by the Oneida Tribe but in the 1990s, tribal members began to buy back acreage as it became available for sale. The Tribe then asserted that these lands are exempt from state and local taxes because they are now part of the Oneida Nation. When the city of Sherrill, New York, attempted to impose taxes, the Oneida Nation sued, claiming their sovereign immunity but the Supreme Court ruled that when the Oneidas sold the acreage in the early ninetteenth century, they relinquished their governmental claims.

Two recent cases indicate differing attitudes of the Supreme Court toward federal responsibility as trustee for Indian tribes. In 2002, the Court ruled against the interests of a Native nation, in this case the Navajos. In 1964 the Navajos, guided by the secretary of the interior, signed a lease with a coal company to extract coal from their lands for a return royalty of 37.5 cents per ton. In the ensuing years, as Peabody Coal Company's profits increased, the Navajos asked the secretary to renegotiate the terms of the lease in accordance with a provision in the original agreement. The secretary decided on a rate of 20 percent of gross proceeds but after private meetings with Peabody and without the Navajos' knowledge, the secretary reduced that rate to 12.5 percent. The Navajo Nation therefore sued the federal government for neglecting its obligations to act for the benefit of Indian tribes and sought $600 million in damages. The Supreme Court, however, ruled that the Navajos had not cited a specific law that requires the federal government to pay monetary damages even if they have been negligent in fulfilling their obligations toward Indian tribes.

In another case that year, the Court did find for the White Mountain Apache Tribe who originally brought suit against the US government for its failure to maintain, repair, and rehabilitate land of the former Fort Apache Military Reservation held in trust by the United States for the White Mountain Apache Tribe. The government claimed that there were no statutes imposing a legal obligation to do so but the Supreme Court favored the Apache's demand that even without a legal obligation, the government does have a duty to protect land held in trust for Native nations.

A decision rendered by the US Supreme Court in 2009 dealt a significant setback to Native American sovereignty by limiting the ability of the secretary of the iInterior to take land into trust status on behalf of federally recognized Indian tribes. The ruling came in a case called *Carcieri v. Salazar* dealing with the Narragansett Indian Tribe of Rhode Island for whom the interior secretary had arranged to put newly acquired land into trust status. However, the Court denied this action on the grounds that the Narragansett were not a federally recognized tribe in 1934 when the US Congress passed the Indian Reorganization Act. The Department of the Interior had argued that nothing in the IRA specifies dates but rather only statuses as "Indian" and the Narragansett are now federally recognized as an Indian tribe. In response, bills have been proposed in Congress to amend the IRA enabling the secretary of the interior to take land into trust status for all current and future Indian tribes but no final action has yet been concluded.

The two most recent Supreme Court rulings, both handed down in 2012, have wider consequences for Indian tribes. In one, *Salazar v. Navajo Ramah Chapter*, the Court agreed with the Navajo plaintiffs, acting as leads in a class action suit, that the federal government was remiss in holding back some funds owed to tribes who subcontracted services from government agencies. Under the Indian Self-Determination Act of 1975, tribes could assume administration of public services such as education, healthcare, police and law enforcement, fire prevention, and infrastructure construction and maintenance. These services are paid for by Congressional appropriations but since 1994 the government unilaterally imposed caps on payment to tribes. The Supreme Court's decision in support of the tribes will result in payments of monies owed as well assurances that new contracts for services administered by tribes will be paid in full.

The second case, *Salazar v. Patchak*, was specifically a dispute about the ability of a band of Pottawatomi Indians in Michigan to operate a casino on land that had been taken into trust for them but its ramifications are potentially much broader than this local issue. The case involves a complaint by David Patchak, a non-Indian living near the casino, who filed a suit claiming that the Department of Interior had wrongly taken the

land into trust for the Pottawatomi Indians because they were not a federally recognized tribe in 1934 when the Indian Reorganization Act was passed by Congress. The issue brought before the Supreme Court was not on the merits of the argument but rather on whether Patchak has standing as a private individual to file suit against the Department of the Interior. By ruling that Patchak does have standing, the Court turned the case back to the US district court for a trial on the specifics of the suit. However, in her lone dissenting opinion, Justice Sonia Sotomayor noted that the Court's majority decision can potentially mean: "After today, any person may sue to divest the Federal Government of title to and possession of land held in trust for Indian tribes so long as the complaint does not assert a personal interest in the land." Native American leaders are urging the US Congress to pass legislation that will amend the language of the 1934 Indian Reorganization Act so that it can refer specifically to all tribes having federal recognition status.

In Canada, recent Supreme Court decisions have dealt with two significant issues: treaty rights and the government's obligations to consult with and accommodate the interests of First Nations. In 1999, the Supreme Court of Canada accepted the argument put forth by a Mi'kmaq man (in *R. v. Marshall*) who claimed aboriginal treaty rights to catch and sell fish after his arrest for fishing in violation of provincial regulations. The Court agreed that catching and trading fish was an aboriginal practice that could evolve into a modern activity for a "moderate livelihood" in accordance with traditional customs.

However, in 2005 the Court dismissed the claims of Mi'kmaq men (in *R. v. Marshall* and *R. v. Bernard*) who had been arrested for logging on Crown land for commercial purposes. The men's argument was based on a treaty of "Peace and Friendship," signed with the British Crown in 1760 that established trading posts for the Mi'kmaqs' dealings with the British but the Court denied this argument, stating that commercial logging was not a modern extension of occasional trade. The Mi'kmaqs' claim that the right to utilize products for trade extended to all natural resources was rejected, and in particular these rights did not extend to commercial logging.

A third related decision was rendered in 2006 when the Court ruled that three men, (two members of the Maliseet Nation and one Mi'kmaq man) who had been arrested for cutting down timber on Crown property in New Brunswick did indeed have a claim based on treaty rights to harvest timber for personal use even on land not currently part of their reserves. The opinion was based on a number of critical concepts. First, the Court considered a determination of aboriginal rights as "integral to a distinctive culture." Second, the Court included a key concept of the "communal aspect of aboriginal rights," allowing activities that help to "preserve the distinctive character of aboriginal communities, not of individuals." The Court also noted that rights spelled out in treaties of prior centuries "must be allowed to evolve" into activities in modern contexts by modern means. And finally, they affirmed that these rights cannot be assumed to have been extinguished unless by specific intent of the Crown. In this case (*R. v. Sappier, R. v. Gray*), the Court found that the Mi'kmaqs and Maliseets had aboriginal practices that included the use of timber for domestic household purposes and affirmed the right to continue these activities in modern contexts since they had not been explicitly extinguished by the Crown.

In several recent cases, the Supreme Courts of Canada and of British Columbia took up the issue of the government's responsibility to engage in prior consultation with First Nations when making decisions that affect their interests. For example, in a case brought by the Gitanyow First Nation against the British Columbia Minister of Forest in 2004, the BC Supreme Court ruled that the government had neglected its obligation to consult with the Gitanyow before they agreed to sell a provinciallyowned timber company that was operating on land claimed by the First Nation. And in the following year, the same Court settled a dispute brought by the Musqueam Indian Band who argued that they had not been consulted prior to the province's agreement to sell land located within a region claimed by the First Nation to the University of British Columbia. In this case as well, the Court sided with the Musqueam in declaring that appropriate consultation and accommodation had not been made prior to the province's decision. The sale was therefore vacated and the parties were required to continue negotiation.

Both of these cases indicate the seriousness with which Canadian courts view the government's responsibilities toward First Nations, in line with the Canadian Constitution of 1982 that sets forth procedures regarding consultation and the rights of indigenous peoples.

URBAN NATIVE AMERICANS

A majority of the Native or Aboriginal population of the United States and Canada currently lives in cities. In the United States, BIA programs of the 1950s and 1960s encouraged Indians to relocate from reservations to cities supposedly in order to relieve reservation poverty but also to disperse the Native population in the context of Congressional "termination" policies (see Chapter 2). In Canada, movement toward urban areas increased somewhat later. By 1998, about half of all Aboriginal people in Canada (including people identified as North American Indians, Métis, and Inuit) lived in urban areas. Table 3.11 presents figures for the ten cities with the largest numbers of Aboriginal residents.

In the United States, by 1980, 54 percent of the 1.5 million people who identified themselves as American Indians lived in metropolitan areas, 10 percent resided on reservations located in or near cities, and about one-third lived in rural areas. Rates of urban residence have steadily increased since then. According

TABLE 3.11	Native Urban Populations in Canada			
	Total Aboriginal Population	**North American Indian**	**Métis**	**Inuit**
Winnipeg	45,750	21,290	24,655	195
Edmonton	32,825	16,405	16,605	275
Vancouver	31,140	22,790	8,580	225
Saskatoon	16,160	9,670	6,565	90
Toronto	16,095	13,155	2,870	300
Calgary	15,195	8,050	7,140	255
Regina	13,605	8,945	4,750	30
Ottawa-Hull	11,605	7,835	3,570	410
Montreal	9,965	6,285	3,485	365
Thunder Bay	7,325	6,070	1,335	20

Source: Statistics Canada 1996: Census.

to the 2010 US census, about 70 percent of American Indians and Alaska Natives live in cities. The following ten cities have the largest number of Native residents (US Bureau of the Census 2010):

1.	New York	111,749
2.	Los Angeles	54,236
3.	Phoenix	54, 724
4.	Oklahoma City	54,572
5.	Anchorage	54,572
6.	Tulsa	54,990
7.	Albuquerque	54,571
8.	Chicago	54,933
9.	Houston	54,521
10.	San Antonio	54,137

During the last half of the twentieth century, hundreds of thousands of Native people permanently moved from their reservations, seeking work in urban areas. Studies published in the 1960s and 1970s document the difficult adjustment of people raised on reservations in their new urban environments (see Ablon 1964 on San Francisco; Price 1968 and 1978 on Los Angeles; Graves 1970 on Denver; Neils 1971 on Chicago). More recent research (Weibel-Orlando 1991 on Los Angeles; Danziger 1991 on Detroit; Bahr 1993 on Los Angeles) has shown that, while adjusting to an urban setting, people have created a new sense of Native identity and community. "Community" is not a geographic concept but one of personal and cultural self-identification on the basis of shared values, expectations, and experiences. Members of the community pursue common interests, meeting frequently or occasionally to exchange information and resources, celebrate rituals, participate in sports, or just socialize. In the words of Susan Lobo, the urban Indian "community" is a "widely scattered and frequently shifting network of relationships with locational nodes found in organizations and activity sites of special significance [that] answers needs for affirming and activating Indian identity" (1998: 91).

Native migrants informally seek out places to socialize where they are likely to find other Indians, but, as the urban Native population grows, more formal organizations are established. In time, such organizations begin to offer social services such as emergency financial relief, educational programs, job-training, job-placement, housing referrals, and some healthcare services. These groups fulfill important roles, particularly since Native people reportedly prefer to rely on other Indians for assistance rather than to seek aid from non-Indians in institutionalized and depersonalized encounters.

Today, urban Native Americans are as diverse as any other ethnic group in North America. Like any other group, their educational, occupational, and income status vary. Some without adequate educations or steady jobs live in poverty; some with skilled trades live comfortably; and those with advanced or specialized educations and professions live in affluence. Indians staff urban organizations and teach Native studies programs in college and university. And they are members of city and state commissions dealing with issues of concern to their communities. The interests of each socioeconomic group are influenced not only by ethnicity but by class as well. People who have greater resources, incomes, and educations obviously are better able to influence local and national policies but organizations, community houses, and service programs geared toward reaching poorer urban Indians are attempting to attend to their educational, employment, and healthcare needs. As the urban Native population continues to grow and to diversify, issues of identity and group interests will become even more complex, calling for innovative solutions to address the disparate concerns of each segment of the population.

Individual and tribal economic issues will undoubtedly continue to be of great concern to Indians and Inuit as they seek to improve employment opportunities and develop their land and resources in ways that suit both their needs and their values. Ensuring the protection of treaty rights as well as strengthening and expanding tribal sovereignty and jurisdiction will also be goals of this century. Today and in the future, members of the First Nations of this continent can assess for themselves to what extent these goals are achieved for their communities. They have already demonstrated their determination to survive and to claim their rights as the original inhabitants of this land.

REFERENCES

Ablon, Joan. 1964. "Relocated American Indians in the San Francisco Bay Area: Social Interaction and Indian Identity." *Human Organization* 23: 296–304.

Adams, 1988.

Ambler, Marjane. 1998. "A Community Responsibility for Welfare Reform." *Tribal College* IX, no. 3: 8–11.

Angaanigaq. 2009. Melting the Ice in the Hearts of Men. Cultural Survival Quaterly.

"Babbitt, Rubin Cited for Contempt." 1999. *American Indian Reports.* March: 11.

Bahr, Diana. 1993. *From Mission to Metropolis: Cupeno Indian Women in Los Angeles.* Norman, OK: University of Oklahoma Press.

Berry, Carol. 2012. "High Court Denies Ute Hearing on Levied Taxes." *Indian Country Today* February 23.

Burich, Keith. 2007. *Cultural Survival Quarterly* 31.3 (Fall).

Cherrington, Mark. 2007. "Oh! Canada." *Cultural Survival Quarterly* 31.3 (Fall).

Coker, Donna. 1999. "Enhancing Autonomy for Battered Women: Lessons from Navajo Peacemaking." *UCLA Law Review* 47, no. 1: 1–111.

Danziger, Edmund. 1991. *Survival and Regeneration: Detroit's American Indian Community.* Detroit, MI: Wayne state University Press.

Deloria, Vine, Jr. 1974. *Behind the Trail of Broken Treaties: An Indian Declaration of Independence.* New York: Dell.

Deloria, Vine, Jr., and Clifford Lytle. 1984. *The Nations Within: The Past and Future of American Indian Sovereignty.* New York: Pantheon.

Department of Indian Affairs & Northern Development (DIAND). 1995. "1991 Census Highlights on Registered Indians, Customized Tables Based on the 1991 Census of Canada." Ottawa.

Department of Indian Affairs & Northern Development (DIAND). 2000. *Basic Departmental Data, 1999.* Ottawa.

Department of Indian Affairs and Northern Development (DIAND). 2006. *Registered Indian Population by Residence.*

Fortunate Eagle, Adam (Nordwall). 1994. "Urban Indians and the Occupation of Alcatraz Island." *American Indian Culture and Research Journal* 18, no. 4: 33–58.

Graves, Theodore. 1970. "The Personal Adjustment of Navajo Indian Migrants to Denver, Colorado." *American Anthropologist* 72, no. 1.

Hansen, Terri. 2011. "Arsenic in Indian Water Table Can Cause Diabetes, Other Diseases." *Indian Country Today* October 25.

Hirschfelder, Arlene, Paulette Molin, and Yvonne Wakin. 1999. *American Indian Stereotypes in the World of Children: A Reader and Bibliography,* 2nd ed. Lanham, MD: Scarecrow Press.

"Indian Affairs Heat Up (Witness the Lobster War)." 1999. *The New York Times.* December 30.

Indian Country Today. 2010. Online newsletter.

Indian Country Today. 2011a. March 9: 16. Online newsletter.

Indian Country Today. 2011b. May 11: 16. Online newsletter.

Indian Country Today. 2011c. December 21 : 18. Online newsletter.

Indian Country Today. 2011d. June 15: 15. Online newsletter.

Indian Country Today. 2011e. 1, no. 5: 17. Online newsletter.

"Indians Striving to Save Their Languages." 2006. *The New York Times.* April 9: A1, A22.

Johnson, Troy, and Joane Nagel. 1994. "Remembering Alcatraz: Twenty-Five Years After." *American Indian Culture and Research Journal* 18, no. 4: 9–24.

Kilpatrick, Jacquelyn. 1999. *Celluloid Indians: Native Americans and Film.* Lincoln, NE: University of Nebraska Press.

Krauss, Michael. 1992. "The World's Languages in Crisis." *Language* 68, no. 1: 4–10.

Lobo, Susan. 1998. "Is Urban a Person or a Place? Characteristics of Urban Indian Country." *American Indian Culture & Research Journal* 22, no. 4: 89–102.

McCarty, Theresa, Lucille Watahomigie, and Akira Yamamoto. 1999. "Introduction: Reversing Language Shift in Indigenous America." *Reversing Language Shift in Indian America. Practicing Anthropology* 21, no. 2: 2–4.

McGreal, Chris. 2012. "US Should Return Stolen Land to Indian Tribes, Says United Nations." *The Guardian* May 4.

Navarro, Mireya. 2010. "Navajos Look to Move Away from Coal in Favor of Sun and Wind." *New York Times.* October 26.

"NCAI and Assembly of First Nations Unite." 1999. *Native Americas* (Fall/Winter): 5.

Neils, Elaine. 1971. *Reservation to City: Indian Migration and Federal Relocation.* Chicago, IL: University of Chicago, Department of Geography, Research Paper no. 131.

"Old Traditions on New Network: Igloos and Seals." 2000. *The New York Times,* February 11.

Price, John. 1968. "The Migration and Adaptation of American Indians to Los Angeles." *Human Organization* 27: 168–175.

Price, John. 1978. *Native Studies: American and Canadian Indians.* Toronto: McGraw-Hill Ryerson.

Slate, Clay. 1993. "Finding a Place for Navajo." *Tribal College: Journal of American Indian higher Education* 4, no. 4: 10–14.

Statistics Canada. 1996. Ottawa.

Toensing, Gale. 2011. "Eeneca President Rebukes New York Post for Editorial." *Indian Country Today* April 9.

Toensing, Gale. 2012. "Mashantucket Court Ruling Re-affirms Non-taxable Status of Residents." *Indian Country Today* March 30.

Tribal College Journal. 2000. 11, no. 3 (Spring).

"The Trust Fund Mess: Historic Trial Begins in U.S. District Court." 1999. *American Indian Reports.* March: 22–23.

US Bureau of the Census. 1996. "Population Projections of the United States by Age, Sex, Race, and Hispanic Origin: 1995 to 2005." Washington, DC.

US Bureau of the Census. 2010.

Walker, Jana. 2012. "Violence Against Native Women Gaining Global Attention." Indian Law Resource Center. Helena, Montana.

Weibel-Orlando, Joan. 1991. *Indian Country, L.A.: Maintaining Ethnic Community in Complex Society.* Urbana, IL: University of Illinois Press.

Williams, Timothy. 2012. "For Native Women, Scourge of Rape, Rare Justice." *New York Times* May 22.

Woodard, Stephanie. 2012. "South Dakota Legislature Quashes New Childhood-Sexual-Abuse Bill." *Indian Country Today* February 9.

THE NORTHEAST

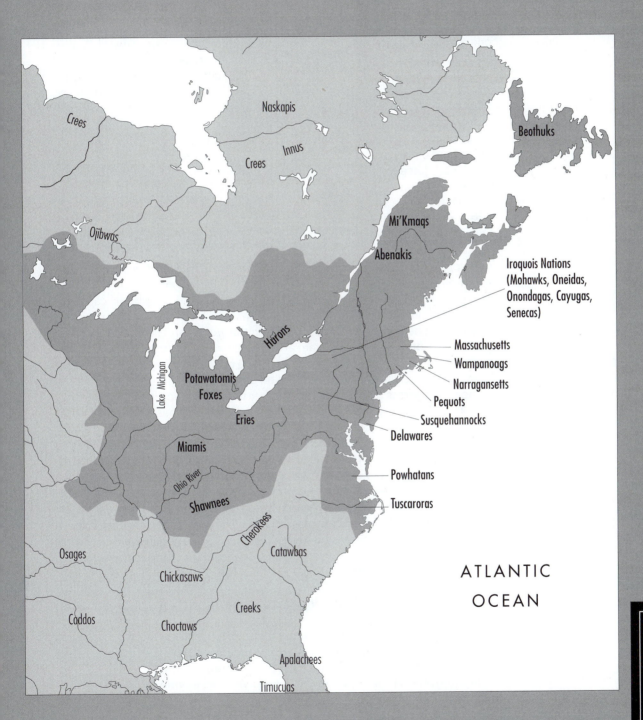

Crees

Naskapis

Crees

Innus

Beothuks

Ojibwas

Mi'Kmaqs

Abenakis

Iroquois Nations
(Mohawks, Oneidas,
Onondagas, Cayugas,
Senecas)

Hurons

Massachusetts

Wampanoags

Potawatomis
Foxes

Narragansetts

Lake Michigan

Pequots

Eries

Susquehannocks

Miamis

Delawares

Ohio River

Powhatans

Shawnees

Tuscaroras

Cherokees

Osages

Catawbas

Chickasaws

ATLANTIC

Creeks

OCEAN

Caddos

Choctaws

Apalachees

Timucuas

PART II

Iroquois Story of the Origin of the False Faces

It was long, long ago, when the earth was new, when the two brothers were contesting as to who would rule the world. Finally, the Good-minded said: "Whoever can make that yonder mountain move, is the one that has the power. We will face away from it and at a command remain so, while the one showing his strength will command the mountain to move forward. At the length of a person's breath, then we shall turn around. So you will now do so." And they both stood facing away from the mountain; then the Evil-minded said: "You, yonder mountain, move towards us." Then they turned and noted that it had moved little. So the Good-minded said it was his turn to show his power. At the command for the mountain to move up to them, the Evil-minded heard some strange noise and turned around quick, forgetting the agreement of the test. As he did so, his face was so close to the cliff he struck it with such force that his face was distorted, his mouth was drawn up one side and his nose was twisted. It was then that the Good-minded spoke: "It was I, who have made everything here about, I am the master of this place. I can create life." Then the Evil-minded said, "It is all as you say, you are the creator here, and it is my own opinion to ask of you to let me be one of your helpers. As the human race will dwell on this earth that you have created, I will be able to help the mankind that will live here in the future. When the people who will dwell on this earth will go about, they shall be troubled with some sort of illness, they shall see me, in vision or in dream. Then the people will cause to be made an image with my likeness; then will I aid the people with my own ceremony of healing; then will people go in the woods and carve a face of my likeness out of the basswood tree, and true enough, my spirit will enter into that mask; then will I help your people by my power to cure illness. I also will have power to control all wind and motion on this earth. Then will mankind say as they will address to me; 'Our grandfather the great medicine man or healer of sickness.' To my grandchildren, I will not only cure sickness, but also will be able to warn them of coming sickness, which they can avoid providing they will fulfill my directions. They can avoid sickness or plague by having their community be visited by the spirits of the Faces to drive away all forms of disease. This will be done by men wearing my likeness, each to be dressed according to my manner of clothes. They shall go to all places of dwelling and go through every part of each home. There also shall be stationed at each spring of water a person wearing the medicine mask, who shall act as one who purifies their drinking water and thus frees them from all things poisoned in their daily use.

The leader of this society as they march from lodge to lodge will carry with him our pole of hickory staff striped with red paint; on it will be hung at the top small specimens of masks. As they go about on this mission, the leader will sing our marching song. As they enter each home, the leader will announce that the Faces are going house to house driving all known and unknown disease; that if there be someone in the place who wish to have the party give her or him any ceremony of curing, they can do so, if their own sacred tobacco is given as token for this ceremony.

In return for all these ceremonies, I will want as payment, a mush made from parched corn sweetened."

Source: Jesse Cornplanter. 1963. *Legends of the Longhouse.* Port Washington, NY: Ira Friedman, pp. 204–210.

Native Nations of the Northeast

THE PEQUOTS' (PEE-KWOT) current prosperity belies a 300-year history of territorial, political, and population decline at the hands of European, colonial, and American authorities since the beginning of the seventeenth century. According to early accounts describing Native territories in the 1630s, Pequots "held dominion over part of Long Island, over the Mohegans, over the sagamores [chiefs] of Quinapeake [New Haven], yea over all the people that dwelt upon the Connecticut River, and over some of the most southerly inhabitants of the Nipmuck country [central Massachusetts]" (Gookin 1972: 7). But Pequots soon fell prey to commercial, political, and military rivalries between the Dutch and English who were expanding their influence in the region. In an effort to establish hegemony in southern New England, the British sought to wrest control from the Pequots and break the commercial alliance between Indians and the Dutch. In 1637, they launched a military campaign against the Pequots, invaded Pequot territory, and destroyed their villages. In an attack against a large village at Mystic, Connecticut, at least 300 men, women, and children were killed. Survivors of the invasion fled to the west, but many were killed or captured, later given to English families as servants or sold into slavery (Bradford 1908: 342–343). Those who remained free eventually obtained small grants of land in Connecticut. Two reservations were established: a 280-acre settlement called Stonington, located at Lantern Hill (1683), and the Mushantuxet reservation (1667), consisting of 2,000 acres originally in Groton, now in the town of Ledyard. Over the next three centuries, both communities lost most of their land, mainly through

A signed petition from the Pequots of Connecticut begging Governor Joseph Talcott for an end to colonial encroachments onto their tribal land.

illegal sales and confiscation by the state. By 1980, the Stonington reservation had been reduced to 224.6 acres while the Mushantuxet (or Mashantucket) settlement held only 175 acres of land.

Until that time, the history of the Pequots was far from unique. Scores of Native societies in the Northeast from the Maritimes in Canada southward in the United States met similar fates. But, due in part to the dynamic leadership of Richard Hayward, elected as tribal president in 1974, the Pequots have changed the course of their history. They first filed a land-claims suit contending that sale of 800 acres of land in the nineteenth century was fraudulent. As a result of the "Mashantucket Pequot Land Claims Settlement Act" passed by Congress in 1983, the Pequots were granted federal recognition as an Indian tribe and were awarded funds for land acquisition. Since then, they have purchased nearly 1,700 acres (Harvey 1996: 181). Pequots also secured federal grants for housing and economic development. And, as the newspaper article that opened this chapter indicates, they have made enormous profits from gaming establishments that they have operated since 1986. In their first year, they netted a profit of $2.6 million (181). In 1992 they built Foxwoods, the largest casino in North America. The complex includes a casino, hotel, conference center, and, in 1998, grew to include a museum, research center, and library that provides visitors with panoramas of aboriginal Pequot culture as well as presenting information on the history and contemporary life of Pequots. The Pequot tribe has used their gaming profits (at one point amounting to about $1 billion per year) to reinvigorate their community. They have built new housing and roads and provide job training, scholarships, and health services to members of the tribe. As living conditions and opportunities at the Mashantucket reservation have improved, many tribal members have returned to establish their homes. From a population of only 13 in 1980, the reservation community grew to 317 in 1995 (152) and numbered almost 1,000 by 2014 (Schlossberg 2014; Sokolove 2012). However, the success enjoyed by the Pequot nation was to be short-lived. The gambling industry was severely impacted by the 2008 recession, and the Foxwoods was over $2.3 billion in debt by 2012. In 2014, the Mashantucket museum was closed for many months due to lack of funding, and stipends to individual tribal members were discontinued. The Pequots' success is not typical of Native nations of the Northeast, most of whom do not make headlines in the national and international press. We turn now to a consideration of the complexity of cultures and histories of these nations.

LANDS AND NATIONS

Northeastern North America was home to speakers of languages belonging to two linguistic families, Algonkian (al-GONG-ki-yan) and Iroquoian (i-ro-KWOY-an). Before proceeding, names used to designate languages and peoples should be clarified. The term "Iroquoian" refers to a linguistic and cultural grouping while the name "Iroquois" refers specifically to members of the "Five Nations Iroquois" consisting of the Mohawks, Oneidas, Onondagas, Cayugas, and Senecas, later joined by a sixth nation, the Tuscaroras. Similarly, "Algonkian" refers to people speaking an Algonkian language while "Algonquin" is the name of one group of Algonkian-speaking people whose aboriginal territory lay in Ontario. Although Algonkians and Iroquoians had different historical roots, as they settled and adapted to ecological conditions in the Northeast, they developed cultures that were alike in significant respects. Most of the cultural differences that did exist were essentially due to constraints or opportunities afforded by diversity in available resources and climatic conditions. Where Algonkians and Iroquoians inhabited similar environments, many aspects of their cultures, especially their economies, settlement patterns, and principles of community organization, tended to develop in similar fashion. Neighboring peoples, whatever their historic roots, tended to be more like each other than did people who inhabited vastly different environments and therefore adapted to vastly different conditions. Since the environments inhabited by Iroquoian-speaking peoples were relatively similar, their cultures tended to share more features than did those of Algonkian-speaking peoples, who lived in a larger and more diverse territory.

Aboriginal Iroquoian culture has been well documented by European traders and missionaries who visited their territories beginning in the early seventeenth century. Although knowledge of Europeans and their trade goods predated the seventeenth century, Iroquoian communities were undisturbed by foreign influences during the earliest period of European documentation. Except for the adoption of manufactured goods and changes in warfare, Five Nations Iroquois retained most of their traditional lifeways until the middle years of the eighteenth century. However, the Hurons, a distinct

Iroquoian-speaking people, were defeated by the Iroquois by 1649, and the few survivors were forced to flee west or merge with neighboring nations.

The record of most aboriginal eastern Algonkian cultures is not as detailed as that of Iroquoians since many Algonkian communities were quickly devastated by European traders, settlers, and soldiers. Within a few years of English settlement, Native lands were appropriated and thousands of people were killed either by military action or, more often, by the spread of deadly epidemic diseases of European origin. Surviving communities were transformed by European hegemony, resulting in economies, political structures, and social systems that, although retaining a Native base, were quite different from aboriginal lifeways.

IROQUOIAN NATIONS

Languages and Territories

The Iroquoian family of languages includes two branches, northern Iroquoian (spoken in the Northeast) and Southern Iroquoian (represented by Cherokee in the Southeast). The two divisions are estimated to have separated approximately 3,500–4,000 years ago. Northern Iroquoian nations include the St. Lawrence Iroquoians, the Huron (a confederation of four closely related nations), Neutral, Petun, Erie, Wenro, Susquehannock, Nottoway, Tuscarora, Mohawk, Oneida, Onondaga, Cayuga, and Seneca. Lounsbury suggests three possible subgroupings of northern Iroquoian languages (1978: 334–336). The oldest division occurred at least 2,000 years ago, separating Nottoway and Tuscarora from the other languages. Huron, Petun, and Neutral form a second subgrouping, while Susquehannock and the languages of the Five Nations Iroquois constitute a third. The Five Nations' languages began to diverge approximately 1,000–1,500 years ago.

Data from comparative studies of northern Iroquoian languages attest to the close linguistic, cultural, and historical relationships of the people. They were concentrated in an area consisting of present-day New York, central and western Pennsylvania, eastern Ohio, and southern Ontario. Northern Iroquoian territory extended into adjacent western New England and southern Québec. The Nottoways and Tuscaroras settled further south in Virginia and North Carolina.

Today, most Iroquoian peoples no longer live in their traditional homelands. Their ancestors fled the region, seeking refuge from the increasing violence and destabilization that characterized the Northeast as a result of European presence and Native involvement in the fur trade. Some Iroquoians sought safety among more westerly peoples, many eventually merging with their hosts and retreating even further west in the eighteenth and nineteenth centuries. The St. Lawrence Iroquoians were the first group to be dispersed from their villages along the St. Lawrence River near the present-day cities of Québec and Montreal. They were, not coincidentally, the first Iroquoians to meet directly with Europeans, specifically with Jacques Cartier in 1534. It is not known exactly what happened to the St. Lawrence Iroquoians, but by the early seventeenth century they were gone from their aboriginal territory. Various theories have been proposed to explain their disappearance. Incursions by Mohawks into the St. Lawrence valley in the late sixteenth century to secure iron tools and weapons from French traders at Tadoussac, located at the mouth of the St. Lawrence River, were likely causes. Desires to control trade routes may have prompted Mohawks to raid the St. Lawrence Iroquoians' villages, leading to the latter's defeat and dispersal. And the influx of European diseases may have weakened the people, contributing to their demise (Trigger 1972: 90–92; Fenton 1940: 175).

Hurons experienced a similar fate at the hands of the Five Nations. Again prompted by the intention to control access to trade and to gain captives and replacements for their declining populations, the Five Nations waged numerous military campaigns against Hurons in the 1640s, causing Hurons to flee to the Petuns and Neutrals who lived west of Huronia. After several intermittent stops, this amalgamated group eventually relocated to the United States. Presently called Wyandots, they obtained a reservation in "Indian Territory" (the state of Oklahoma). When the Huron nations dispersed, a group of Catholic converts established a mission near Québec City under Jesuit guidance. This community, now called "Wendake" (WEN-da-ge; "place of the Wendat," the indigenous name of the Huron) remains the home of Hurons in Canada.

The majority of Nottoways and Tuscaroras who lived in Virginia and North Carolina also fled their homelands. In the early eighteenth century, most Tuscaroras left the south, asking for refuge among the Five Nations Iroquois in New York. They were admitted to the Iroquois Confederacy in 1722 or 1723, becoming the Sixth Iroquois Nation. Additional migrations of Tuscaroras to the north occurred later in the eighteenth century as well as in the early nineteenth. Some Nottoways also traveled north and merged with Seneca villages. Others remained in Virginia, obtaining a small reservation in Southampton County. When the reservation was terminated by the state government in 1824, some residents left to join the Iroquois at the Six Nations Reserve in Ontario. Those who stayed in Virginia eventually blended into surrounding White and Black communities, losing their Native distinctiveness (Boyce 1978: 286–287).

Of all the northern Iroquoians, members of the Five Nations fared best. Although their communities today occupy a fraction of their original territory, most Five Nations Iroquois live on or near their ancestors' homeland. The Six Nations Reserve near Brantford, Ontario, is the largest Iroquois community. As its name suggests, it is home to members of all the Iroquois nations. Mohawks reside on four additional reserves in Canada (Kahnawake and Kanesatake in Québec; Tyendinaga and Gibson in Ontario) and one reserve (Akwesasne) that straddles the international border between Québec/Ontario and New York State. The Onondaga Reservation lies in traditional Onondaga territory south of Syracuse, New York. Oneidas have a small reservation near Rome, New York, similarly located on aboriginal land. Most Oneidas, however, live on lands in Wisconsin. The Tuscarora Reservation is situated in northwestern New York State just inside the US border near Niagara Falls. Senecas reside on three reservations in western New York (Cattaraugus, Tonawanda, and Allegheny). Finally, some Senecas and Cayugas currently live on a reservation in Oklahoma.

Aboriginal Culture

Aboriginal northern Iroquoian cultures had mixed economies, centered on horticulture and foraging. Vegetable products, both cultivated and wild, made up the bulk of their diet, although meat and fish were welcome additions. Women were the farmers, planting fields cleared by men employing slash-and-burn techniques. They grew varieties of corn, beans, squash, and sunflowers using digging sticks to make holes in the earth for the seeds. Most years produced surplus crops that were dried and stored for use throughout the year. Iroquoian women frequently harvested enough crops to sustain their families in the event of poor growing seasons in subsequent years. They also collected a rich assortment of wild plants, including roots, tubers, greens, berries, fruits, nuts, and seeds. Prominent foods were ground nuts, leeks, cabbage, strawberries, huckleberries, hickory nuts, walnuts, and acorns. These foods were eaten fresh or dried, often added to soups and stews. Dried cornmeal and berries were baked into breads. In addition, maple sap was collected in springtime for use as a sweetener.

Men supplied their families with meat from animals, fish, birds, and waterfowl. Among some nations, such as the Hurons, fish provided the bulk of non-vegetable food while among others, including the Five Nations Iroquois, meat was of greater importance (Heidenreich 1971). Hunting gear consisted of bows and arrows, snares, and deadfall traps to catch prey. Deer were especially sought, but other animals were caught, including bear, muskrat, and beaver. Meat and fish were eaten roasted or boiled in soups and stews. Iroquoian men also planted tobacco, which was used primarily in religious contexts.

Northern Iroquoians lived in settlements of varied size, containing from 30 to 150 longhouses surrounded by wooden palisades, presumably built for defensive purposes. Longhouses were rectangular structures, averaging approximately 80 ft. in length and 25 ft. in width. The length could be extended as much as 200 ft., although such large buildings were not common in all northern Iroquoian villages. A residence typically housed 6 or 10 nuclear families consisting of 5 or 6 people each. Villages therefore contained as few as 50 people or as many as 1,000 (Ritchie and Funk 1973: 318–319). Longhouses were constructed of a wooden frame covered with bark, usually cedar or elm. Interior walls were lined with platforms used for sitting and sleeping. They were built about a foot from the ground and were covered with woven reed mats or animals pelts. Higher shelves were used for storing tools, utensils, clothing, and food. A central row of hearths ran down the length of the house, each shared by two nuclear families, one on either side. Family quarters were divided by partitions and bark storage bins that held dried foods.

Residents of longhouses were linked through matrilineal descent and marriage. The core of a household was formed by matrilineages consisting of an elder woman and her daughters. Typical household members were an elder couple, their daughters and daughters' families, and their unmarried sons. Following preferences for matrilocal residence, men moved to their wives' homes after marriage.

Iroquoian society was integrated through matrilineal clans, each bearing the name of an animal or bird. Since clan members thought of themselves and addressed each other as siblings, they were unable to marry one another. In addition to assigning social membership, clans were corporate groups. They owned the longhouses in which their members lived, and they controlled farmland that was worked by women of their group. Clans were united into moieties that functioned mainly as ceremonial groupings. Prominent among their functions was the obligation to prepare and conduct funerals for members of the opposite group. Members of the same moiety were, like

An Iroquois longhouse, Crawford Lake, Milton, Ontario.

clan members, considered to be siblings. Among some people, such as the Five Nations Iroquois, kinship relationships were further symbolized by referring to the two moieties as "Elders" and "Youngers." The literature is unclear as to whether moieties were always, or ever, exogamous (Morgan 1877).

In addition to lineages, clans, and moieties, Iroquoian men and women bound themselves to others through ceremonial friendships. These friendships, invoked and maintained in ritual, involved gift exchanges, mutual aid, and lifelong loyalty. People were prompted to form friendships either as a cure for sickness, a message in a dream, or strong affection (Shimony 1961: 218). The tradition of ceremonial friendships remains an important mechanism of extending reciprocal bonds in contemporary Iroquois communities.

Iroquoian communities were integrated internally and linked externally through political organizations that were based on local social systems. The metaphors of kinship and locality were extended from the family, lineage, clan, and moiety to the village and nation. Among the Hurons and the Five Nations Iroquois, sociopolitical organization was extended further to form confederacies of great strength and vitality. In all of these geopolitical structures, people thought of

themselves, and spoke of themselves, as relatives. Terms having primary reference as siblings, parents/children, and maternal uncle/sister's son were used between members of villages, nations, and confederacies.

Iroquoian men and women generally were held to be autonomous, independent, and equal members of their communities. While their social, economic, political, and religious roles may have differed, the prestige and value accorded to each was equal although not identical. Through the clan and lineage system, women controlled land, houses, and the products from the fields and forests that they grew or collected. They also controlled the distribution of products of the hunt contributed by their husbands and sons. Men were community spokesmen in their roles as clan and confederacy chiefs, but women had a critical role in selecting (and possibly deposing) the candidates. Women's and men's voices were heard directly and indirectly in councils and meetings when issues of war, peace, trade, and other community matters were discussed.

The Iroquois Confederacy

The five nations that came to be known as the Iroquois (Mohawks, Oneidas, Onondagas, Cayugas, and Senecas) bound themselves together in a league or confederacy in order to preserve peace among members and to act as a unified body in dealing, either in peace or war, with other nations. On the whole, these goals were achieved, although internal conflicts were not unknown. Several dates have been suggested for the Confederacy's founding. It certainly predated the arrival of Europeans in North America. While some historians and anthropologists assume a fourteenth- or fifteenth-century origin, Iroquois datekeepers contend that the confederacy began much earlier. Using the arguments of the datekeepers, archeological data, astronomical data of eclipses, and historical sources, Mann and Fields (1997) posit the league's origin in 1142.

Employing the metaphor of family, the Confederacy was symbolized as a great longhouse, stretching from east to west across Iroquois territory. In this longhouse, Mohawks are referred to as "Keepers of the Eastern Door" while Senecas are "Keepers of the Western Door," reflecting their geographic locations as easternmost and westernmost nations.

Local, national, and confederacy leadership was vested in clan chiefs, their advisors, and respected elders. Clan chiefs were men chosen by leading women of their group (often referred to in the literature as "clan matrons"). Chiefs were ceremonially installed in office by having a headdress of deer antlers placed on their heads. They ideally retained their office for life, but if a chief's behavior was deemed inappropriate or contradicted local opinions he could be demoted and replaced by another of his clan. Impeachment was called "dehorning" because the procedure involved removal of the chiefly headdress.

Each chief had assistants or advisors. These people, men and women, advised the chief concerning community opinion on important matters. They could be demoted if their behavior was considered unacceptable. Father Dablon, a Jesuit missionary writing of the Mohawks in 1671, described one such demotion (*Jesuit Relations and Allied Documents, 1610–1791*; hereafter *JR* 54: 281):

> They degraded her from her noble rank, in an assembly of the village notables; and deprived her of the name and title of Oiander—that is, a person of quality. This is a dignity which they highly esteem, which she had inherited from her ancestors, and deserved by her own intelligence, prudence and discreet conduct. At the same time, too, they installed another woman in her place. Women of this rank are much respected; they hold councils,

and the Elders decide no important affair without their advice.

Political integration and expression of public opinion took place in councils that were structured by territory and by social identity. Three types of councils were held in villages: those of elder men (including but not limited to clan chiefs), those of women, and those of young men (often somewhat misleadingly referred to in the literature as "warriors"). Members of each council deliberated together and eventually came to a unanimous opinion concerning the matter at hand. Then each group chose a speaker, who presented its decisions in a unified meeting. Chiefs delegated one of their number to speak for them; women and young men appointed representatives who made their opinions publicly known. These representatives were often chosen among prominent senior men, but in some cases a woman or a warrior was the selected delegate (Lafitau 1974: 298–299). If decisions varied, further discussion was necessary in caucus in order to reach unanimity on the village level. The process of deliberation and consensus was repeated in national and confederacy forums, finally arriving at a universally accepted position. Lafitau described the deliberation process as follows:

> The women are always the first to deliberate…on private or community matters. They hold their councils apart and, as a result of their decisions, advise the chiefs on matters on the mat, so that the latter may deliberate on them in their turn. The chiefs, on this advice, bring together the old people [probably referring to elder men] of their clan and, if the matter which they are treating concerns the common welfare, they all gather together in the general Council of the Nation. The warriors also have their council apart for matters within their competence but all the individual councils are subordinate to that of the Old People which is the superior council, as it were. (1974: 295)

Village councils were concerned with local issues such as planning community events, honoring visitors, and commemorating deaths of respected residents. They also discussed national and international matters such as trade, diplomatic, and military relations with other nations. These concerns took prominence at confederacy councils where decisions had repercussions for all members of society. Local and national councils were held as often as deemed necessary. Confederacy meetings occurred at least once a year but could be called whenever an important issue needed to be discussed. They were, and still are, held in Onondaga, the geographic center of Iroquois territory.

According to Iroquois traditions, the Confederacy was founded by two chiefs, Hiawatha (hi-ya-WA-ta) and Deganawida (de-ga-na-WEE-da), the latter now referred to only as "The Peacemaker." They originated the idea of a united league of Iroquois nations and set out the procedures followed at Confederacy council meetings (Parker 1916). Hiawatha was originally from Onondaga and The Peacemaker was born among the Hurons, but they were both adopted by Mohawks, later becoming Mohawk Confederacy chiefs. There were originally fifty Confederacy chiefs, each having a title that was passed on to another of his clan after his death or demotion. Mohawks and Oneidas each have nine Confederacy titles, Onondagas have fourteen, Cayugas have ten, and Senecas have eight. The titles of the League's founders, The Peacemaker and Hiawatha, are always left unfilled (Morgan 1962).

All decisions of the Confederacy must be unanimous. In reaching consensus, deliberations proceed according to fixed ritual sequences. For procedural and ceremonial purposes, the five Iroquois nations are divided into two groups or moieties, paralleling the kinship division of clans. The Elder moiety consists of Mohawks, Onondagas, and Senecas while Oneidas and Cayugas constitute the opposite, or Younger, moiety. The Elder moiety deliberates first, beginning with Onondaga chiefs, who then "give" the topic to Mohawks for their consideration, followed by the Senecas. When the Elders reach a consensus, the topic is passed "across the fire" to the Youngers. If a decision is unanimous, the matter is settled with a final ceremonial declaration by Thadodaho, the leading Onondaga chief and official spokesperson of the Confederacy. At the conclusion of a session, actions of the Council are "read into" belts of wampum that serve as mnemonic devices for accountings of significant events and agreements. But if consensus is not reached, the problem can be given back to Mohawks for further deliberations, starting the process of negotiation once more. If unanimity is not eventually achieved, the matter is set aside and the council fire is covered up with ashes, ritually indicating the inability of Confederacy chiefs to "roll their words into one bundle." So important is the necessity that all be of "one heart, one mind, one law," that the Confederacy can take no action without unanimous agreement.

The Iroquois Confederacy remains strong as a central symbol of Iroquois cultural and moral continuity. Councils are held at the Onondaga reservation situated near Syracuse, NY. Confederacy chiefs from the Iroquois nations, appointed and installed in office by clan mothers, meet to discuss political, economic, and philosophical issues of importance to the people. Treaty rights, sovereignty, protection of land and resources, and relationships with state, provincial, and federal governments in the United States and Canada are of constant significance. One example of the Confederacy's assertion of sovereignty and autonomy is their issuance of Confederacy passports to members of their nations who travel abroad as representatives

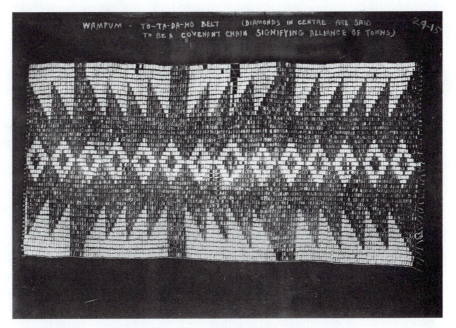

Iroquois Wampum: To-ta-da-ho belt (diamonds in center are said to be a covenant chain signifying the alliance of towns).

of their people. In 1970, Iroquois delegates to an international ecology conference held in Stockholm, Sweden, travelled on such passports as did members of the Iroquois lacrosse team that competed as a national team in a world competition held in New Zealand in 1992. Declarations made by Confederacy chiefs have moral force in Iroquois communities today, as they do for many other Native people who recognize the continuation of the League as a great accomplishment in cultural survival. The Confederacy site at Onondaga is the repository of twelve wampum belts (woven belts of purple and white beads made from clamshells) that commemorate treaties concluded between Confederacy chiefs and Europeans/Americans in the seventeenth and eighteenth centuries. Some of the belts had earlier been sold to collectors and museums, but they were returned in 1989 for safekeeping at Onondaga.

Trade and Conflict

Relations between aboriginal northern Iroquoians and their neighbors combined trade, diplomacy, and warfare. Extensive intertribal trade networks supplied local communities with food, animal skins, and utilitarian and luxury goods. The northern Iroquoian confederacies (i.e., the Huron and Five Nations) excelled in negotiating agreements with their neighbors that solidified trade partnerships and settled disputes. However, members of these confederacies also engaged in warfare against their enemies. Warfare had multiple and complex motivations (Richter 1983, 1992; Jennings 1984). The Iroquois waged war when diplomacy failed to establish peace or secure favorable commercial terms. They fought other Native groups in order to assert their dominance over routes of trade to Dutch, French, and British trading sites. And they engaged in raids against nearby or distant nations in order to take captives to replace family members who had been killed in previous encounters with enemies (Richter 1983; Brandao 2000). These "mourning wars" increased in frequency in the seventeenth and eighteenth centuries as Iroquois deaths rose both from war and disease.

Two forms of warfare were common. Raids by small groups of men were organized by leaders whose reputations were based on prior successes. These forays generally had the goal of exacting revenge for previous losses. Culprits deemed responsible for attacks against one's own community were killed. Such victims might have been the actual perpetrators, or failing that, members of their kin group. The second type of warfare consisted of large war parties, numbering in the hundreds, led by established war chiefs. After the arrival of Europeans in North America and the resulting conflicts motivated by the needs of trade and the need to defend territory from foreign intruders, the goals of Iroquoian warfare sometimes included the destruction of enemy communities. Such confrontations increased in severity as well as frequency in the seventeenth and eighteenth centuries. While some intertribal conflicts grew out of ancient rivalries and animosities, they were worsened by direct and indirect effects of the European presence in the Northeast. As European rivalries intensified over trade and land, Native groups became embroiled as allies and enemies.

As Iroquoian involvement in the European fur trade deepened, cultural influences began to be felt in Native communities. First, of course, Iroquoians incorporated tools, utensils, and cloth of European manufacture into their material culture. They also wanted to obtain guns and ammunition for use in warfare against their enemies. Indeed, the numbers of their enemies grew considerably as commercial rivalry among Native nations intensified and as European powers successfully sought to create and/or exacerbate intertribal tensions.

Emanating directly from participation in the fur trade, the economic pursuits of Iroquoian men shifted focus. Trapping beavers for their fur and then trading the skins for European goods became men's central activities. Such endeavors necessitated men's absence from their communities for longer and longer periods of time as involvement in trade increased. Since Iroquoian lands were relatively poorly supplied with beavers, trappers had to travel further from their villages to secure the animals. In addition, trading posts were located far from the local territory of most trappers, again resulting in extended absences from home. However, despite these economic changes, food production remained stable because of the continuing role of women as farmers, contributing the bulk of the aboriginal diet.

With the exceptions of imported goods and shifts in men's subsistence roles, Iroquoian societies retained their aboriginal patterns in the seventeenth century. Some individuals, though, did come under more intense foreign influence and did alter many of their beliefs and practices. Beginning in the early 1600s, French Jesuit missionaries established missions among Hurons and later in the century among the Five Nations Iroquois as well. From the Jesuits' perspective, the Huron missions were particularly successful, giving the priests a friendly reception no doubt because the Indians were commercial and military allies of France. According to Jesuit records, hundreds of Hurons converted to Catholicism, most often as they lay dying from smallpox and measles. When the Huron confederacy was finally destroyed by the Iroquois in 1648–1649, Jesuits turned their attention to members of the Five Nations. There they found they were less welcome but were still able to make several hundred converts, especially among the Mohawks. By 1667, Jesuits had convinced Iroquois converts to remove themselves from their homeland and resettle in mission communities near Montreal, then a fortified French village. The Iroquois who founded these missions, and others who joined over the next century, adopted many French practices and ideals in addition to the rejection of aboriginal religious beliefs (Bonvillain 1986).

Cultural changes accelerated in the 1700s, especially after mid-century when English, Dutch, and German immigrants occupied large portions of Iroquois territory in eastern and central New York. As their land base shrank and their hunting territories diminished, men were forced to abandon traditional economic pursuits. Dwindling supplies of animals due to overhunting by European settlers also hastened the end of aboriginal subsistence. At the same time, colonial and later state authorities, in conjunction with Christian missionaries, pressured the Iroquois to alter their traditional economic and social roles. Men were encouraged to become farmers while women were to perform domestic work exclusively. Changes in household organization were likewise preached, replacing extended matrilineal households with nuclear units headed by men. Finally, women's roles in political systems and their contributions to council meetings were muted through American/Canadian ideological and material pressure. All of these far-reaching transformations took many years to solidify, but by the middle of the nineteenth century they were fairly complete despite the resistance, continuing into the present day, of some sectors of Iroquois communities.

ALGONKIAN NATIONS

Languages and Territories

The Algonkian family of languages contains an eastern and a central branch. The two subdivisions separated more than 2,000 years ago. At the same time that eastern and central Algonkian languages became differentiated, the eastern branch itself began to diverge into daughter languages (Goddard 1978: 70). Eastern Algonkian languages had a wide aboriginal distribution from the Maritimes southward to North Carolina. They were spoken by people living along the Atlantic coast and in nearby inland regions. The language of the Beothuk, aboriginal inhabitants of Newfoundland, was of uncertain status. Due to the poor quality of the scant word lists collected from Beothuk before its extinction, it is not possible to determine conclusively its relationship to other Native languages. It may have belonged to the Algonkian family or have represented a separate linguistic grouping. If Algonkian, it had split from other members at a very great time depth (77). Central Algonkian languages were spoken in eastern Canada from the coast of Québec west through Québec and Ontario. They were also spoken in the United States by people living near the Great Lakes and Mississippi River valley. Finally, some Algonkian-speaking nations resided far to the west in California and across the Canadian plains.

The cultural diversity of Algonkian societies was primarily caused by differences in climate, geography, and the availability of resources. In most regions of Algonkian territory, horticulture contributed much, if not most, of the people's sustenance. However, even in these areas, farming was never the sole mode of economic production. Hunting, fishing, and gathering wild plants supplemented, and in some cases outranked, the cultivated crops. Availability of resources and the possibility of farming affected community stability, population density, and social organization. Farming communities maintained relatively permanent territories containing villages having several hundred residents who were linked through unilineal clan-based kinship systems. In contrast, foraging people lived in small, temporary camps that fluctuated in membership from season to season. Although residential choices were generally informed by kinship, individual decisions were based on local resource supplies and might change as material conditions changed. Farming people included: the western Abenakis in northern New England; Narragansetts in Rhode Island; Mahicans in eastern New York and western Vermont; Massachusetts, Pequots, and Mohegans in southern New England; Delawares in southern New York, New Jersey, and eastern Pennsylvania; Nanticokes in Maryland; and Powhatans in Virginia. These groups are only the best known of the scores of eastern Algonkian nations. In fact, most of the tribal names listed here actually encompass distinct local identities, often subsumed under the names of the largest and most powerful groups in their vicinity. Many other Northeastern people who lived by farming and foraging have had their cultures and histories obliterated due to early contact with intruding European traders and settlers who waged wars against the people, killing them or forcing them to flee.

In the northern regions of coastal Algonkian territory, subsistence was based primarily on foraging, although in societies such as the Maliseets and Passamaquoddys of New Brunswick and Maine, small-scale gardening was possible. Most Native people whose lands lay to the west, such as the Ottawas, Algonquins, and Southern Ojibwas, also had economies that relied heavily on foraging although in the warmer regions horticulture supplied some portion of the diet. Finally, among people living in the extreme northern regions, including the Mi'kmaqs in New Brunswick and Nova Scotia and Crees in Québec, foraging was the sole mode of subsistence. Modern descendants of eastern Algonkians in the United States constitute but a fraction of the original population. And the land included in their reservations constitutes but a small portion of their former territory. Small reservations controlled by Algonkians exist in most states in the region. Some are located in rural areas while others are situated on the outskirts of major cities. Most have small resident populations. And few have viable economic opportunities that might allow people to remain and build prosperous communities.

In Canada, the Crees especially have benefitted from geographical isolation, at least into the twentieth century. They retain much of their original territory and have rebounded in population from previous declines. Although their lives have changed considerably from those of their ancestors, they do continue some traditional economic, social, and religious practices. However, people whose aboriginal territories were located in areas that have since been populated by Euro-Canadians have lost most if not all of their land and have often been forced to resettle elsewhere—some, like the Ottawas, even as far as "Indian Territory" in Oklahoma.

Algonkians in New England

Aboriginal people of southern New England produced crops in addition to the abundant supplies of natural plant and animal resources available in their territories. Farming was primarily the responsibility of women. They planted corn, beans, squash, and artichokes in fields cleared by groups of women and men. Tobacco was also grown, although, among the Narragansetts and possibly others, men were the producers.

According to Roger Williams's observations of the Narragansetts in the early seventeenth century, women and men cooperated in joint agricultural labor although the bulk of farm work was women's domain:

> The Women set or plant, weede, and hill, and gather and barne all the corne, and Fruites of the field: Yet sometimes the man himselfe (either out of love to his Wife, or care for his Children, or being an old man) will help the Woman.
>
> When a field is to be broken up [readied for planting], they have a very loving sociable speedy way to dispatch it: All the neighbours men and Women forty, fifty, a hundred &c, joyne and come to help freely.
>
> With friendly joyning they break up their fields, build their Forts, hunt the Woods, stop and kill fish in the Rivers, it being true with them: By concord little things grow great, by discord the greatest come to nothing. (Williams 1643: 98–99)

Horticulture produced a substantial harvest, at least where the soil was fertile and weather warm. Among Narragansetts in the seventeenth century, "The woman of the family will commonly raise two or three heaps of twelve, fifteene, or twentie bushells a heap, and if she have helpe of her children or friends, much more" (100).

Algonkian women also gathered a wide variety of wild plants, including many kinds of berries, fruits, and nuts. Among the animals hunted by men, deer were the most important, contributing as much as 90 percent of the meat eaten (Salwen 1970: 6). Deer were caught in traps or stalked by hunters. Communal drives, sometimes involving several hundred people (e.g., among the Narragansetts, Mohegans, and Massachusetts), were organized to hunt deer in the fall. Men also caught freshwater and saltwater fish and hunted many species of waterfowl. In Atlantic coastal regions, women collected shellfish such as clams, oysters, scallops, and lobsters. They were joined in this pursuit by children and sometimes by men too old for the hunt.

Native people of southern New England changed their residences according to seasonal economic pursuits. In the summertime, they dispersed to the seashores in small family groups. They planted fields near the coast, often at distances of a mile or more from each other. In addition to small summer villages consisting of a cluster of houses, people erected temporary shelters when they travelled to fishing stations or to sites for collection of shellfish or wild plants. After harvesting crops in the fall, people moved inland to the forests to hunt deer. There they gathered in larger numbers and cooperated in communal hunts. Some villages were surrounded by stockades in the early seventeenth century, possibly in pre-contact times as well. Among the Pequots in Connecticut, for instance, a stockaded village contained 300 or 400 residents. Although members of such large settlements were usually related, the basis for residential affiliation was flexible. People changed village association depending on resource supplies, available land, and family composition.

The historical literature describing societies of the region is unclear concerning aboriginal social systems. For some people, such as the Narragansetts and Pequots, exogamous matrilineal clans assigned social identity and controlled descent and marriage. For others, such as the Mohegans, descent could be traced through either matrilineal or patrilineal kin.

Village leadership was vested in a chief, or "sachem," whose position tended to be inherited through patrilineal lines, although a son was not necessarily his father's successor. Claims of rights to inherit could also be made by appealing to matrilineal descent. Women, too, could assume sachemships among peoples of Rhode Island, Massachusetts, New York, Maryland, and Virginia (Grumet 1980: 49–52). For instance, in 1673, George Fox, a Quaker minister, reported meeting "the old Empress [of Accomack] [who] sat in council" in her town in Maryland (Fox 1952: 653). And in 1705, Robert Beverley mentioned two women sachems in his description of Indians of Virginia: "Pungoteque, Govern'd by a Queen, but a small nation" and "Nanduye. A seat of the Empress. Not above 20 Families, but she hath all the Nations of this shore under Tribute" (Beverley 1947: 232).

Sachems had influence and authority in their territory, usually confined to a relatively small area where resources were collected and land was farmed by a group of related extended families (Brasser 1971: 65). A sachem's role was one of advisor and leader, but he/she did not have coercive power. Writing of the Narragansetts, Williams observed that sachems did not act or make decisions in ways "to which the people are averse, and by gentle perswasion cannot be brought" (1643: 134). Similarly, of New England nations, Gookin noted that since people could readily leave the village or territory of a particular sachem if they were dissatisfied with local leadership, "sachems have not their

men in such subjection, but that very frequently their men will leave them upon distaste or harsh dealing, and go and live under other sachems that can protect them" (1972: 154). It is possible that some sachems exerted authority in wider regions containing smaller dependent sachemships earlier than the seventeenth century, but complex confederacies and large tribal groupings were political developments that responded to European presence, trade, warfare, depopulation, and community consolidations and dislocations.

In the eighteenth and nineteenth centuries, Native people of southern New England gradually abandoned traditional economic pursuits since their hunting territories were occupied by American settlers and their ability to search out resource sites was curtailed. As the American population of New England increased, towns and cities expanded and engulfed many indigenous communities even though these communities had legal protections as officially recognized state reservations. In fact, reservation lands were diminished, often entirely expropriated. In addition, due to the small Native populations, intermarriage, both with Whites and Blacks, was common. However, although many people left the reservations because of a lack of economic opportunities, those who remained tried to retain their Native identities and distinctiveness.

Today, only a handful of the original Algonkian reservations in southern New England are intact. While several tribes are recognized by individual states, receiving recognition from the federal BIA is an uphill battle, and in recent years many reservations have had their federal "nation" status revoked. These communities are often embroiled in expensive, drawn-out legal suits in attempts to reestablish reservation status, but so far few have been successful. The Nipmuck in Massachusetts, the Narragansetts in Rhode Island, and the eastern Pequot in Connecticut, as well as other tribal groups in New England have had their reservations terminated by the federal government. Only two reservations remain on Long Island (Poospatuck, Shinnecock) as well as in Connecticut (one Pequot, one Mohegan) and in Massachusetts (both Wampanoag).

Algonkians in the Mid-Atlantic Region

Further south in Maryland, Algonkians such as the Nanticokes, Accomacs, and Conoys lived along the coast of Chesapeake Bay, exploiting natural resources and planting fields with corn, beans, and pumpkins.

Women grew the crops while men hunted a variety of animals and birds including deer, bears, squirrels, partridges, and turkeys.

Native people of Maryland lived in villages that were located near rivers and bays. Their houses were rectangular in shape, built of wooden frames covered with bark or woven mats. The length of houses varied but was at least 20 ft long. Their size depended on the number of residents as well as on the wealth and social status of the occupants. Small households consisted of approximately ten people living in a common room but larger ones, especially those of chiefs, were partitioned into separate quarters for each of several families residing within.

Little is known concerning aboriginal social systems and descent rules. Evidence concerning the inheritance of chieftainships hints at the existence of matrilineal descent. Among nations in Maryland, leadership was wielded by chiefs who had authority over several villages. Chiefs were men or women who inherited their position through matrilineal ties. Some chiefs exerted authority over large areas made up of smaller, less powerful chieftainships. Such "paramount" leaders were advised by councils of chiefs and respected elders.

Native people began to leave their ancestral lands in Maryland and Virginia in the late seventeenth and early eighteenth centuries due to the increasing encroachment of British settlers and the turmoil created by warfare in the region. Nanticokes and Conoys abandoned their homes, many seeking refuge among the Iroquois in western Pennsylvania and New York. A subsequent exodus took place after the American Revolution since most Nanticokes and Conoys had aided the British during the war. They resettled on the Six Nations Reserve near Brantford, Ontario, under the sponsorship of Cayugas. Another group of Nanticokes and Conoys migrated westward with Delawares who were also seeking land and security away from their Northeastern homeland. After first establishing villages in southern Michigan and Indiana, they were eventually forced to move even further west by the onslaught of American settlers. Nanticokes and Conoys then moved to Kansas, but when their land there was taken by the state, they finally obtained a reservation in "Indian Territory" in Oklahoma.

The land on which most Indians live today in Virginia does not have reservation status. Only two reservations, that of the Pamunkeys and the Mattaponis, remain intact. Other people have essentially merged with surrounding White and Black communities. Intermarriage among the various populations has led to a decline, but not disappearance, of Native identity.

North-Central Algonkians

To the north and west of the eastern groups lived other Algonkian nations whose economies and sociopolitical systems adapted to different territorial and environmental conditions. The Southern Ojibwas originally occupied land in southern Ontario from the eastern shores of Georgian Bay westward along Lake Huron and Lake Superior. Their economy was described by Jesuit missionaries in 1647: "[They] live solely by hunting and fishing and roam as far as the 'Northern Sea' [to trade for] Furs and Beavers, which are found there in abundance … [They] are nomads, and have no fixed residence, except at certain seasons of the year, when fish are plentiful, and this compels them to remain on the spot" (JR 33: 67, 153). The Ojibwas, like other people in the region, regularly travelled in the summer and early fall to fishing stations along the northern shores of Lakes Superior and Huron where they established camps and caught abundant supplies of sturgeon, trout, and whitefish. They also gathered wild fruits, berries, and roots. The scene was described in 1667 by Claude Allouez:

> The Lake is the resort of twelve or fifteen distinct nations—coming, some from the North, others from the South, and still others from the West; and they all betake themselves to the shore for fishing, or to the Islands, which are scattered in great numbers all over the Lake. These peoples' motives in repairing hither is partly to obtain food by fishing, and partly to transact their trading with one another, when they meet. (JR 51)

Ojibwa settlements contained a localized band consisting of at most several hundred people. They were headed by a chief whose position tended to be inherited from father to son. Chiefs had influence in their communities but their power was probably minimal. It is unclear whether aboriginal kinship systems were based on patrilineal clans but such systems did develop at least by the early eighteenth century.

European contact and involvement in the fur trade had the usual effects on Southern Ojibwas. Depopulation due to disease, relocation from traditional territories, and intensification of warfare all contributed to social destabilization. Writing in 1744 of Native nations of the upper Great Lakes and Ottawa valley including the Ojibwas, Charlevoix noted that "the Amikoues, otherwise called the nation of the Beaver, are reduced almost to nothing; the few remaining of them are found in the island Manitoualin in the northern part of Lake Huron … [and] … the Outaways who were formerly very numerous inhabited the banks of that great river which bears their name. I know not but of three villages of them, very indifferently peopled" (1966, I: 285).

By the early eighteenth century, economic shifts to a focus on trapping and competition for land and resources were the common results of contact between Southern Ojibwas and Europeans. By the middle of the century, reacting to political and military pressure from the British colonial government in Canada and the increased presence of European traders and settlers in their midst, Southern Ojibwas agreed to cede parts of their territory to the intruders. After the first land cession in 1764, Ojibwas were restricted to a relatively small area and therefore were unable to pursue traditional hunting activities. By 1830, they had ceded nearly all of their land in southern Ontario to the British while retaining several small reserves. Ojibwas residing across the border in Michigan signed their first land cession treaty with the United States in 1815. Within less than thirty years, they had been pressured into giving up all of their remaining territory in the state. Thereafter, they lived in small villages scattered among American communities.

After most of their land had been ceded, Ojibwas both in Canada and the United States made their living by fishing in the Great Lakes, selling fish and crafts to Canadians/Americans, and occasionally hiring out as laborers in lumber mills and farms. Ojibwas residing on reserves in southern Ontario gradually adopted farming as a means of subsistence. They grew wheat, oats, corn, potatoes, and a variety of vegetables. Some families added to their income by trapping beavers, muskrats, and bears and selling the pelts at trading posts. Men trapped in hunting territory that was controlled by their families. Such a system of family centered land management was a departure from aboriginal tenure that, in contrast, allocated land and resources to local bands or villages in common.

In the twentieth century, Southern Ojibwas became increasingly incorporated into the rural and urban life of Canada. Many, in fact, left their home communities to seek higher education and employment in cities

such as Thunder Bay, Ottawa, and Toronto, Ontario. Still, the reserves in Ontario are the focus of Ojibwa identity and remain the home of approximately half of the more than 12,000 Southern Ojibwas living in the province. Their number today reflects a dramatic population increase since the low points of the eighteenth century when disease, territorial dislocations, and warfare had taken their greatest cumulative toll.

CONSEQUENCES OF EUROPEAN TRADE AND SETTLEMENT

Commerce between coastal Algonkians and Europeans began almost as soon as European sailors, fishermen, and explorers arrived on the continent. Especially along coastal and nearby interior regions, trade was an early important avenue of contact between Indians and Europeans. However, once English settlements became permanent and expansionist in the early seventeenth century, the quest for land equaled if not exceeded the desire for trade and profit. In Virginia, the colony at Jamestown soon confronted the nearby Powhatans and attempted to bribe or threaten indigenous leaders to relinquish their territory. Although Powhatan leaders at first attempted to be conciliatory, warfare between the two groups erupted several times in the first decades after the colony's founding. Under the leadership of Chief Opechancanough, attacks were made against the English settlement in 1622 and 1644, but Powhatans were unable to oust the unwanted colonists from their midst. The English retaliated by campaigns of genocide against the original inhabitants. The wars ended soon after Opechancanough was captured in 1646. A treaty was signed between the two adversaries that ceded much of Powhatan territory and restricted the Indians' movements. Then, while imprisoned, Opechancanough was murdered, shot in the back by a soldier assigned to guard him.

Several additional colonies were established by English, French, and Dutch settlers in the early seventeenth century. Some were situated near trading posts such as Fort Orange (later Albany, NY), Québec City, Montreal, and New Amsterdam (New York City). Others were founded along the Atlantic coast at sites having good harbors, for example, Plymouth (Massachusetts). In all of these areas, the local indigenous population was quickly decimated by the spread of European diseases. Their demise enabled the settlers to remain and increase their land base. For example, the colony at Plymouth was established in territory previously inhabited by Pawtuxets, a group of people who were completely destroyed by an epidemic in 1619 resulting from visits of English traders, explorers, and slavers. The Pilgrims promptly signed a treaty of peace and friendship with Massasoit, chief of the nearby Wampanoags. Although the two communities did maintain peaceful relations for fifty years, other wars erupted during the period between English settlers and Native nations in New England. The Pequots of Connecticut were attacked by English forces in 1637, followed in 1643 by wars against the Narragansetts of Rhode Island, who had previously been allies of the English.

During this period, some Native groups tried a strategy of accommodation. They sought to protect their remaining territory by making formal alliances with the British government, turning their lands over to the Crown, and becoming royal protectorates. Believing that such an arrangement would compel the English king to safeguard their territory, in 1644 the Narragansetts "freely, voluntarily submit, subject, and give over ourselves, peoples, lands, rights, inheritances, possessions … unto the protection, care and government of Charles, King of Great Britain, … upon condition of His Majesties' royal protection" (quoted in Drake 1995: 118). However, the Indians' strategy failed because colonists ignored boundaries in their quest for additional land. Colonial authorities colluded with settlers' illegal actions, while the government in London did little if anything to protect Native rights as it had pledged to do.

The colonies repeatedly abrogated treaties made with Native nations and invaded lands, often justifying their actions on the basis of rumors that the indigenous people were about to attack them. For example, in 1675, the United Colonies of Massachusetts, Plymouth, Connecticut, and New Haven waged war against the Wampanoags, who were at the time treaty allies of Plymouth colony, after unfounded suspicions circulated about an imminent attack against them. This conflict, known as "King Philip's War" (the English name given to Metacomet, the sachem of the Wampanoags) lasted nearly two years and claimed thousands of Native lives. Philip attempted to enlist the support of other Native nations, recognizing that only a united effort could stem the growing tide of English settlement, but he was unable to muster widespread support among other groups. The war ended with Philip's death and the confiscation of Wampanoag territory.

As a result of depopulation and loss of land, survivors of numerous small nations consolidated into a few villages having larger populations than had been their traditional practice. People thus hoped to regain an adequate subsistence base and retain as much territory as possible. The complex sachemships and confederacies of the seventeenth and early eighteenth centuries that existed in parts of southern New England, Delaware, Maryland, and Virginia probably arose as responses to such changes in circumstance. By consolidating resources and concentrating populations, Native nations tried to fend off colonists' encroachments on their land. Leaders may also have hoped to amass large forces of warriors in defense of their communities. None of these assumptions was borne out as the number of English settlers increased dramatically and as their desire for land came to know no bounds.

An additional strategy for territorial protection was also tried, and also doomed to failure. People who had become converts of the numerous Protestant missionaries who visited the region agreed to separate from their "pagan" compatriots and resettle in protected "Praying Towns" such as those established at Natick in eastern Massachusetts and at Stockbridge in western Massachusetts. Their land, guaranteed by royal and colonial grants, was supposed to be safe from settlers' encroachment. However, even with official land grants, the "Praying Indians" saw their territory diminished and finally expropriated.

While the English were engaged in settling New England and coastal Atlantic regions, the Dutch were encroaching on Native land in eastern New York. Even though Dutch authorities were ousted from New Netherlands by the English in 1664, the villages and farms they established continued to grow, supplemented by immigrants from Germany, Sweden, and England. At the same time, the French established colonies further to the north. Beginning in the early 1600s, French traders and missionaries ventured well inland along the St. Lawrence River and northern shores of the Great Lakes where they met Algonkian and Iroquoian peoples, some of whom, like the Hurons, were settled horticulturalists, while others, like the Crees, were nomadic foragers. Although French colonists did occupy some Native territory, their numbers remained relatively small since few French citizens were willing to settle permanently in North America, probably because there were fewer economic and political incentives for people to leave France than was the case for the English. Still, Indians living in interior regions were affected by the French presence. The Crees and other nomadic groups gravitated to territory near French trading posts and eventually remained there for longer periods of time during the year. They shifted the emphasis of traditional economic activities in favor of trapping beavers to exchange for manufactured goods.

As British and French rivalry increased both in Europe and North America, their Native allies in the Northeast became embroiled in conflicts as well. Warfare in the region intensified in the early eighteenth century and continued nearly unabated until the end of the century. Great Britain enlisted its allies among the Five Nations Iroquois while France depended upon Algonkian nations to support its cause. However, because of the economic power and military prowess of the Iroquois, France, too, often tried to win their allegiance or at least their neutrality. For a time, Iroquois warriors and diplomats were able to hold both the English and French at bay. Pierre Charlevoix, a Recollet priest writing in 1720, observed:

> As the Iroquois were situated between us [French] and the English, they soon found that both would be under the necessity of keeping well with them; and indeed it has been the chief care of both colonies, to gain them over to their own party, or, at least, to persuade them to stand neutral: and as they were persuaded that if either of these nations should entirely get the ascendant over the other, they must soon be subjected themselves; they have found the secret of balancing their success; and if we reflect that their whole force united has never exceeded five or six thousand combatants, and that it is a great while since they have diminished more than one half, we must needs allow, they must have used infinite abilities and address." (1966, II: 28)

Later, during the "French and Indian War" (1756–1763), the British relied heavily on their Iroquois allies to help fight against the French, who, for their part, enlisted the aid of their Algonkian allies. Iroquois' aid was critical to Britain's victory in the war, but the Iroquois did not trust long-term British intentions since the government in London seemed unable, and unwilling, to protect Native lands from encroachment by English settlers. The Proclamation of 1763 issued by the government in London that forbade settlers from advancing beyond a boundary drawn along the crest of the Appalachian mountains did not in fact deter colonial westward expansion. Given the remoteness of the territory from centers of British control, settlers were able to encroach on Indian land without official sanction, but without official interference as well.

In the years leading up to the American Revolution, the British realized that if the Iroquois were not satisfied with their protection, they might turn against the Crown in alliance with colonial rebels. In order to shore up support, Britain signed a treaty at Ft. Stanwix in 1768 establishing definite boundaries between Iroquois and British territory. But, as happened so often, the government failed to protect Native rights to land and resources.

By the 1770s, rebellious colonists also recognized the role that the Iroquois could play in helping or hindering their cause. The Continental Congress sought the Iroquois' promise of neutrality by pledging to honor their territorial boundaries. For their part, the British attempted to use their long-standing alliance to convince the Iroquois to fight against the rebels. However, the Council of Chiefs of the Iroquois Confederacy refused to officially endorse either the British or American side because the member nations were divided in their opinion and therefore unable to speak with unanimity. Without reaching a consensus, the Iroquois Confederacy adopted a position of neutrality, more by default than by conviction. Reacting to insurmountable disagreements among the nations, Iroquois leaders covered up the council fire at the principal Onondaga village in 1777, an act that foreshadowed the end of the Confederacy as a dominant force in international politics. With the waning of the Iroquois' decisive political and military influence in the Northeast came the end of northeastern Native nations as independent, fully sovereign entities. Thereafter, Algonkians and Iroquoians remaining in the region resided on reservations that encompassed only a fraction of their aboriginal territory. However, even though a steady loss of acreage has continually eaten away at their land base, reservations do retain their legal status. Residents of many Indian communities are determined to safeguard their cultural independence, recalling and valuing their heritage and history.

CONTEMPORARY ECONOMIC, POLITICAL, AND CULTURAL ISSUES

Several northeastern nations in the United States have filed land claims suits contending that much of their aboriginal territory was taken from them without their consent and without adequate compensation. Suits were filed in the 1980s and 1990s by Pequots, Mohegans, and Paugussetts in Connecticut; Passamaquoddys, Mi'kmaqs, and Penobscots in Maine; and Oneidas, Cayugas, Senecas, and Mohawks in New York. Recognition for several tribes is perpetually being granted and subsequently rescinded, such as that of the eastern Pequot nation in Connecticut. The eastern Pequot were federally recognized as a tribe in 2002 before their designation was revoked in 2005. They filed for federal status again in 2006, and their application is still under dispute. Some of the cases have been settled, while many are still winding their way through the courts. One of the largest settlements was reached in 1980 between Passamaquoddys and Penobscots and the state of Maine. The Indians received $81.5 million in compensation to settle their claim for 12.5 million acres of land, about two-third of the state. The Aroostock Band of Micmacs (1991) and the Houlton Band of Maliseets (1986), both in Maine, received federal recognition and monetary awards of $900,000 each for land acquisition (Sutton 2000: 131).

Algonkian nations of the Northeast are engaging in cultural programs to strengthen their heritage and identities. Numerous local and regional powwows are held throughout the summer months that bring together Native artisans, dancers, singers, and musicians who display their work. Audiences of Native and non-Native participants help to celebrate Algonkian traditions. Language maintenance programs are also implemented in many communities. For example, the Passamaquoddys in Maine have a "Language Keepers" project to protect and promote use of their Native language. The combined Maliseet-Passamaquoddy language consists of two separate dialectical groups and is currently spoken by about 590 people. The Language Keepers have produced some ninety-five videos of Passamaquoddy people speaking to each other on a wide range of topics including traditional practices, spiritual beliefs, and childhood memories. Recently, they published a near-complete dictionary of the Algonkian language. Online versions contain links from spoken words to dictionary entries as well as links to other videos containing the same words. Plans are also underway to establish an immersion program pairing elder fluent speakers with new learners.

Land claims cases in New York filed by several Iroquois nations have resulted in mixed rulings and some have not yet been finally settled. In 1994, the Cayugas' claim for 64,000 acres in upper New York State was upheld, but decision on a final monetary award is pending. The Cayugas originally filed for return of their land as well as $350 million. They subsequently dropped the demand for the land and have instead pressed for compensation. The Oneidas' claim for territory in central New York was one of the most complex due to the refusal of state authorities to negotiate a settlement even though they were directed to do so by the US Supreme Court in 1985. The claim, concerning about 250,000 acres of Oneidas' aboriginal territory guaranteed to them by the 1794 Treaty of Canandaigua, was filed jointly by the Oneidas of New York, Wisconsin, and Ontario. The latter two groups are descendants of Oneidas who left New York in the middle of the nineteenth century when their homeland was experiencing shrinkage because of settler expansion. The New York Oneidas are currently the smallest group, numbering about 1,300, while there are some 14,000 Oneidas in Wisconsin and 4,700 members of the Thames Band in Ontario. In order to press their claim in the face of state inaction, in 1999 Oneidas filed suit against the state of New York and some 20,000 non-Indians now owning land in the territory the Oneidas assert was illegally taken from them in the first half of the nineteenth century. State authorities, however, have yet to respond to the Oneidas' proposals for negotiation and settlement. In 2006, the US Supreme Court refused to hear the Oneidas' appeal of a lower court judgment against their claim. The lower court based their rejection on the fact that the lands have been out of Oneida control for several centuries and are now owned and occupied by others. A judgment in favor of the Oneidas' claim would have caused hardship to the current owners who are held to be not responsible for the situation.

In 2012, the Onondagas filed a petition in federal court seeking a "declaratory ruling" that would affirm that some lands adjacent to their reservation near Syracuse, NY, were taken illegally by the state of New York in the 1880s, violating the US Indian Trade and Intercourse Act, the US Constitution, and several treaties signed by their ancestors. The Onondagas did not request a return of the lands because they recognize that these lands have been in the control of others for more than two centuries. They instead requested recognition of their rightful claim and their assertion that title to the lands has never been legally extinguished. Their petition was denied in 2013 by the Supreme Court.

Iroquois reservations in New York State have been diminished when dams, reservoirs, and other waterway control projects were constructed. In order to provide inexpensive hydroelectric power to cities in the state, two dam and reservoir systems were built in northwestern New York in the 1960s. One flooded about one-fifth of the Tuscarora Reservation and the second flooded one-third of the Senecas' Allegany Reservation (Hauptman 1986). Both projects were opposed by members of the Indian communities in legal filings. The Federal Power Commission ruled in favor of the Tuscaroras' petition against the New York Power Authority, but the US Supreme Court overturned the ruling and allowed the project to proceed. The Senecas attempted to block construction of the Kinzua Dam at Allegany, but that project too eventually went forward after strong political pressure was exerted by the US Army Corps of Engineers, the agency in charge of developing and constructing the dam.

Senecas of the Cattaraugus Reservation have asserted their rights as owners of valuable land on which the city of Salamanca, NY, is located. When the nearby area in northwestern New York began to be developed as a residential and commercial center, Senecas leased much of their land to non-Indians on terms of ninety years. As the end of the leases drew near in 1991, many town residents refused to sign new leases for forty years as the Senecas had stipulated, but in that year, the US Supreme Court upheld the tribe's right to determine the rental terms (Snow 1994: 201). The Senecas of the Tonawanda Reservation have filed claim for return of Grand Island and other lands near Buffalo, NY. State authorities have tried to block the suit, but federal court rulings affirm the Senecas' right to proceed and have a decision rendered by the courts ("Tonawanda Band of Senecas Win Favorable Ruling from Second Circuit Court of Appeal" 1999: 5).

The Seneca Nation is embroiled in another dispute over claims of sovereignty. In 2012, the tribal government announced that it planned to evict some eighty non-Indian families living in Snyder Beach, along the banks of Lake Erie that is part of Seneca territory. According to the Seneca government, the residents are illegal occupants because they were never approved by the Tribal Council, the only body with authority to grant permits, even though some families have lived in the area for many decades. For their part, the residents say that they were never informed that they were living in the area without proper permission since they had rental agreements with the land's owner. There has been little movement in the case for over three years but the issue will undoubtedly be settled in future court proceedings.

A number of northeastern nations have attempted to improve their economies and develop their communities through profits from casino gaming. The Pequots in Connecticut, despite their recent losses, are the most successful of such groups. The Oneidas of central New York have achieved financial success as well. They have used their profits to acquire more than 7,000 acres of former territory near Syracuse, NY, and to open several small factories and businesses. Their prosperity also benefits non-Indians in the region. The Oneida Nation is now the largest employer in the two counties in which their land is located. They have created about 3,200 jobs, 85 percent of which are held by non-Indians ("Tough Love: Oneidas Push for Land Claim Settlement" 1999: 23). In Ontario, the Chippewas of Rama First Nation, in cooperation with the provincial government, opened a casino in 1996 in a lake resort region about 60 mi. north of Toronto.

The complex relationship among tribal casinos, the state of New York, and local municipalities is dramatized by the refusal of the Seneca Nation of Indians and the St. Regis Mohawk Tribe to make payments from casino earnings to the state. In 2012, the tribal governments asserted that they are withholding payment because the state itself has reneged on its pledge to permit only Indian-run casinos to engage in certain kinds of gaming operations. So far, the Seneca Nation that operates four casinos has refused to pay about $400 million to the state while the Mohawk Tribe has withheld about $35 million. As a consequence, the state has not paid about $100 million to the nearby local communities, a move that has seriously affected the delivery of some services. The Senecas and Mohawks have publicly stated their desire to negotiate but the state has not yet responded.

Some nations without reservations have sought federal recognition as Indian tribes, allowing them to seek redress for loss of lands and to apply for funding under federal programs for housing, education, and economic development. Only the Pequots and Mohegans in Connecticut have been successful in this quest. Others, such as Mashpees of Martha's Vineyard (Massachusetts) and the Paugussetts of Connecticut, have had their petitions for recognition denied.

In New York, controversy arose in 1996 when the state attempted to collect sales taxes on the retail sale of gasoline and cigarettes on Iroquois reservations. Fearing loss of income and threats to their sovereignty, the Indians protested the imposition of taxes, claiming immunity from taxation under treaty provisions.

Demonstrations, blockades, and refusals to pay finally led state officials to rescind the order to collect taxes. The Haudenosaunee (Iroquois Confederacy) reached an agreement with the state of New York that affirmed "the sovereign status of the Haudenosaunee and recognized its exclusive right to regulate economic activities upon its territories" ("Haudenosaunee Nears Trade and Commerce Agreement with NYS" 1997: 1).

The use of Iroquois Confederacy passports became an international issue in 2010 when the Iroquois National Lacrosse Team, made up of players born in the United States and Canada, attempted to travel to the World Lacrosse Championship in Great Britain. The team, ranked fourth in the world, was denied visas for entry to the country by the British government. At first they were also denied permission to travel from the United States without official US passports but after weeks of negotiation, Secretary of State Hillary Clinton granted them a "one-time-only waiver," allowing them to travel and return on Confederacy passports. However, British officials continued to deny them entry visas. For their part, the Iroquois players held fast to their insistence on using their own Confederacy passports as an exercise of their legitimate sovereignty. They then forfeited their games in the championship since they could not travel to Great Britain.

In the following year, a Mohawk woman named Joyce King from the St. Regis Mohawk Tribe at Akwesasne (New York) attempted to use her Confederacy passport when crossing into Canada but was denied entry. Her passport was confiscated by a Canadian border guard who termed it a "fantasy document." King was allowed to enter only after she produced her St. Regis Mohawk identity card as well as her Canadian Indian Status card. In King's words, "This is the real identity theft. They're actually stealing my identity because they only want to acknowledge me as a Status Indian and not as a Haudenosaunee [member of the Iroquois Confederacy]" (Toensing 2011: 21). And Curtiss Nelson, a member of the Mohawk Nation Council of Chiefs, commented, "We're Haudenosaunee Mohawks, those of us who live on both 'sides' [of the US/Canadian border]. We do not see that line called the border as being ours. That belongs to the Canadians and Americans … We have a right under the United Nations Declaration on the Rights of Indigenous Peoples to move freely about in our own homeland" (22–23).

Both of these incidents demonstrate two issues. One is the refusal of national governments to fully acknowledge the rights of Native peoples to express their identities and their sovereignty according to their own practices. And the second is the insistence of Native individuals and communities to assert those rights as they see fit.

Native nations residing in the province of Québec are engaged in a unique controversy over sovereignty. While some political parties (especially the Parti Québecois) have advocated for Québec's independence from Canada, Native nations in the province have asserted their right to remain within Canada. Their position is based on claims of sovereignty and on treaties and other legal agreements made with the federal government (Barsh 1997). The Mohawks and Mi'kmaqs are involved in negotiations on land and fishing rights issues (see chapters 5 and 6). And in 2000, the Huron of Wendake, just north of Québec City, agreed to accept $12 million for a reserve originally established by the Jesuits in 1742 that the Canadian government sold at auction in 1904 ("Two Claims Settled" 2000: 19).

Populations

The number of Native people residing in the Northeast has grown considerably during the twentieth century. Gains in population are due both to natural increase and to the in-migration of people indigenous to other regions who have come to cities of the Northeast seeking employment. Tables 4.1 and 4.2 present data from the US Census Report for 2010 and the Canada registry for 2014.

TABLE 4.1	Native Populations for Selected States	
State	**In-State Native Population**
Maine	8,568
New Hampshire	3,150
Vermont	2,207
Massachusetts	18,850
Rhode Island	6,058
Connecticut	11,256
New York	106,906
New Jersey	29,026
Pennsylvania	26,843

Source: US Bureau of the Census, 2010: Census of Population, American Indian and Alaska Native Areas.

TABLE 4.2	Native Populations for Selected Provinces	
Province	On-Reserve Population	Off-Reserve Population
Atlantic (Novia Scotia, New Brunswick, Prince Edward Island)	23,416	39,008
Québec	53,525	28,376
Ontario	92,346	108,648

Source: Indian and Northern Affairs Canada 2014: Registered Indian Population by Sex and Residence, Ottawa, xv.

Economic Data

US Census data on income for 2009 indicated that Iroquois in New York had an overall per capita income of $18,415 and a median household income of $37,173 (US Census Bureau, 2006–2010 American Community Survey). Both figures are higher than the US American Indian averages of $16,645 and $36,779, respectively. However, Indian incomes were lower than the norm for the general population in New York: $30,948 per capita and $55,603 median household (Statistical Abstracts 2010: 442). Some variation was attested in different Iroquois nations. Per capita income among Mohawks was highest ($11,120) and lowest for the Seneca Nation ($7,443). Median household income was highest for Onondagas ($28,462) and lowest for the Seneca Nation ($15,500). Compared to other American Indian communities, fewer people lived in poverty than elsewhere in Native America. Still, 17.3 percent of Iroquois families and 20.1 percent of individuals lived below the official poverty level. These figures indicate an Indian disadvantage when compared to the general northeastern population where 8.1 percent of families and 10.0 percent of individuals lived in poverty.

Data on Algonkian-speaking nations of the Northeast indicate relatively high incomes as compared to other American Indians, due to their location and accessibility to jobs. Table 4.3 presents data for selected groups. As positive as these figures are when compared to other Native people, only Delaware household income exceeds the northeastern average.

Canadian income statistics provide data of provincial income without specifying band affiliation. Northeastern provinces are listed in Table 4.4.

Per capita and household incomes were uniformly lower for on-reserve Indians as compared to those of off-reserve Indians. And all Indian income statistics were far lower, both provincially and nationally, than figures for all Canadians. As noted in the tables, the average per capita income for registered Indians was $12,800, about half that of all Canadians ($24,100). Average household incomes of all Canadians was 86 percent larger than on-reserve Indians and 45 percent larger than off-reserve Indian households.

Table 4.5 presents figures for unemployment. Except for Prince Edward Island, a larger percentage of on-reserve as compared to off-reserve Indians was unemployed. In all provinces, registered Indians experienced vastly higher rates of unemployment than other Canadians in their province. At the time, the overall Canadian unemployment rate stood at 10 percent.

THE REVELATIONS OF HANDSOME LAKE

In 1795, Handsome Lake, a sixty-year-old Seneca from the Allegany band in western New York, fell gravely ill in his home in northwest New York State. His illness continued for four years, causing periods of delirium and unconsciousness. Then, in 1799, Handsome Lake seemed to die but when mourners gathered to attend

TABLE 4.3	Selected Economic Characteristics for Algonkian Nations			
	Per Capita Income ($)	Median Household Income ($)	Families Below Poverty (%)	Individuals Below Poverty (%)
Abenaki	17,999	35,625	17.3	14.1
Delaware	19,448	40,324	7.4	10.2
Mohegan	17,645	65,398	5.0	9.6
Penobscot	15,980	30,754	20.5	28.2
Pequot	21,673	38,667	11.0	33.7
Shinnecock	12,372	33,081	34.0	33.9

Source: Statistical Abstracts 1999: 442.

TABLE 4.4	Selected Economic Characteristics for Northeastern Provinces			
	Average Household Income ($)		Per Capita Income ($)	
	On-Reserve	Off-Reserve	On-Reserve	Off-Reserve
Prince Edward Island	22,803	24,019	12,500	14,300
Nova Scotia	21,914	33,396	10,300	15,500
New Brunswick	21,293	29,482	10,800	14,200
Québec	30,502	36,639	12,300	17,100
Ontario	27,145	37,698	11,800	17,400

Source: Department of Indian Affairs and Northern Development 1995: Table 34.
Note: Figures are in Canadian dollars.

message that greatly enhanced his popularity and influence not only among the Iroquois but also among non-Indians in western New York State.

Handsome Lake's revelations were welcomed by a people who had been devastated by nearly two centuries of warfare and turmoil. When Europeans came to their territory in the early seventeenth century, the Iroquois were a prosperous and powerful society, but by the late eighteenth century, most of their lands had been confiscated, their population decimated by European diseases, their traditional economies shattered, and their independence abrogated. In the context of personal and communal catastrophes, the Iroquois heard Handsome Lake's message and hoped again for a future of peace and stability.

his funeral, he suddenly recovered and reported that he had had a miraculous experience. He said that he had been visited by four messengers from the Creator who told him to transmit the Creator's words to the Senecas and other Iroquois nations. Handsome Lake's revelations, called the "Good Word" or the "Code of Handsome Lake," consist of a long set of instructions that enumerate the people's wrongdoings and tell them how to correct their errors so that they can live virtuous and peaceful lives. Most of the wrongs pertain to people's behavior in relation to their families and communities. People are told to be kind to their elders, to treat children with patience and love, and to avoid quarrels and malicious gossip. Spouses are urged to be faithful and to respect each other. People should be generous, friendly, hospitable, and compassionate, all interpersonal ethics consistent with traditional Iroquois values (Parker 1913). Handsome Lake's teachings also stressed the importance of sobriety, a

In addition to moral teachings, Handsome Lake's visions supported the traditional Iroquois ceremonies conducted yearly at Midwinter and at times of planting and harvesting crops. Important thanksgiving and funeral rites were also given approval by the Creator's messengers. Handsome Lake's teachings did not create new rituals but rather reinforced those already in existence.

In contrast to the traditional spiritual and ritual messages transmitted by the new religion, Handsome Lake encouraged adoption of Canadian/American gender roles and relationships that differed sharply from the egalitarian gender models of traditional Iroquois society. He argued in favor of household organization based on nuclear families rather than the traditional extended-family residences. He advocated weakening the bonds between mothers and daughters and instead strengthening male authority in marital relationships. And Handsome Lake favored the introduction of Anglo agricultural technology that shifted food production to the domain of men. With Handsome Lake's support, prominent women who

TABLE 4.5	Percent Unemployment for Northeastern Provinces		
	On-Reserve (%)	Off-Reserve (%)	Provincial Average (%)
Prince Edward Island	25.0	36.8	13.4
Nova Scotia	34.5	22.0	12.6
New Brunswick	33.9	27.1	15.3
Québec	33.5	18.1	12.0
Ontario	23.4	17.9	8.5

Source: Department of Indian Affairs and Northern Development 1995: Table 1.

resisted attempts to curtail their economic and political activities were accused of witchcraft. Some were executed as a warning to others who might challenge the new order.

From 1800 until his death in 1815, Handsome Lake travelled to Seneca communities in New York State and Ontario, Canada, to preach his message of religious and social transformation. After his death, disciples carried the teachings of the Handsome Lake Religion to the Six Nations Reserve. By the middle of the nineteenth century, Handsome Lake followers constituted approximately 20–25 percent of the population at Six Nations, a ratio that remains essentially constant today. Since then, the new religion, now usually called the "Longhouse Religion," has spread to all of the Iroquois communities in the United States and Canada. In some places, they constitute a majority; in others only a relatively small minority.

Handsome Lake's teachings had the effect of reconstituting Iroquois religious systems, maintaining traditional elements of ritual but introducing an emphasis on a "Great Creator" that was not ancient in Iroquoian belief and cosmology. Iroquois social order was also reconstituted, shifting the locus of familial allegiance and authority from matrilineal ties, especially between mother and daughter, to spousal bonds, emphasizing male prominence. Handsome Lake's admonitions against the use of traditional abortive and contraceptive practices were further examples of wresting productive and reproductive control from women. While some scholars (particularly Wallace 1969) describe Handsome Lake's achievements as heralding a "rebirth" of the Seneca (and by implication, of the Iroquois generally), as Foster points out, "many Iroquois understood [Handsome Lake's innovations] as the destruction of their culture" (1995: 131). But despite the original thrust of Handsome Lake's teachings, followers of the Longhouse Religion are today among the most active proponents of maintaining aboriginal Iroquoian descent reckoning, clan systems, and the prestige and authority of clan mothers (131). According to Shimony, "the Longhouse helps perpetuate the clan and moiety divisions by giving them roles in the Longhouse ceremonials" (1961: 16). Members of the Longhouse are influential in social and political activities beyond their number. They are strong advocates for treaty rights, land claims, and political sovereignty as well as guardians of traditional values and practices.

REFERENCES

Barsh, Russel. 1997. "Aboriginal Peoples and Quebec: Competing for Legitimacy as Emergent Nations." *American Indian Culture & Research Journal* 21, no. 1: 1–29.

Beverley, Robert. [1705]1947. *The History and Present State of Virginia* (ed. L. Wright). Chapel Hill, NC: University of North Carolina Press.

Bonvillain, Nancy. 1986. "The Iroquois and the Jesuits: Strategies of Influence and Resistance." *American Indian Culture & Research Journal* 10, no. 1: 29–42.

Boyce, Douglas. 1978. "Iroquoian Tribes of the Virginia-North Carolina Coastal Plain." *Northeast* (ed. B. Trigger), Vol. 15 of *Handbook of North American Indians*. Washington, DC: Smithsonian Institution, pp. 282–289.

Bradford, William. 1908. *History of Plymouth Plantation, 1606–1646* (ed. W. Davis). New York: Charles Scribner's Sons.

Brandao, Jose. 2000. *"Your fyre shall burn no more": Iroquois Policy toward New France and its Native Allies to 1701*. Lincoln, NE: University of Nebraska Press.

Brasser, T. J. C. 1971. "The Coastal Algonkians: People of the First Frontiers." *North American Indians in Historical Perspective* (ed. E. Leacock and N. Lurie). New York: Random House, pp. 64–91.

Charlevoix, Pierre de. [1744]1966. *Journal of a Voyage to North America*. 2 vols. New York: Readex Microprint.

Cornplanter, Jesse. 1963. *Legends of the Longhouse*. Port Washington, NY: Ira Friedman, pp. 204–210.

Department of Indian Affairs & Northern Development (DIAND). 1995. *1991 Census Highlights on Registered Indians, customized tables based on the 1991 Census of Canada*. Ottawa.

Department of Indian Affairs & Northern Development (DIAND). 2000. *Registered Indian Population by Sex and Residence 1999*. Ottawa.

Drake, James. 1995. "Symbol of a Failed Strategy: The Sassamon Trial, Political Culture, and the Outbreak of King Philip's War." *American Indian Culture & Research Journal* 19, no. 2: 111–142.

Fenton, William. 1940. "Problems Arising from the Historic Northeastern Position of the Iroquois." *Essays in Historical Anthropology of North America*. Washington, DC: Smithsonian Miscellaneous Collections no. 100, pp. 159–252.

Foster, Martha. 1995. "Lost Women of the Matriarchy: Iroquois Women in the Historical Literature." *American Indian Culture & Research Journal* 19, no. 3: 121–140.

Fox, George. 1952. *Journal of George Fox* (ed. J. Nickalls). London: Cambridge University Press.

Goddard, Ives. 1978. "Eastern Algonquian Languages." *Northeast* (ed. B. Trigger), Vol. 15 of *Handbook of North American Indians*. Washington, DC: Smithsonian Institution, pp. 70–77.

Gookin, Daniel. [1792]1972. *Historical Collections of the Indians in New England* (ed. J. Fiske). [no place] Towtaid.

Grumet, Robert. 1980. "Sunksquaws, Shamans, and Tradeswomen: Middle Atlantic Coastal Algonkian Women during the 17th and 18th Centuries." *Women and Colonization* (ed. M. Etienne and E. Leacock). New York: Praeger, pp. 43–62.

Harvey, Sioux. 1996. "Two Models to Sovereignty: A Comparative History of the Mashantucket Pequot Tribal Nation and the Navajo Nation." *American Indian Culture & Research Journal* 20, no. 1: 147–194.

"Haudenosaunee Nears Trade and Commerce Agreement with NYS." 1997. *Indian Time*. April 4: 1, 4.

Hauptman, Laurence. 1986. *The Iroquois Struggle for Survival: World War II to Red Power*. Syracuse, NY: Syracuse University Press.

Heidenreich, Conrad. 1971. *Huronia: A History and Geography of the Huron Indians, 1600–1650*. Toronto: McClelland and Stewart.

Indian and Northern Affairs Canada. 2014. *Registered Indian Population by Sex and Residence*, Ottawa

Jesuit Relations and Allied Documents, 1610–1791. 1896–1901. 73 vols. (ed. R.G. Thwaites). Cleveland, OH: Burrows Brothers.

Jennings, Francis. 1984. *The Ambiguous Iroquois Empire*. New York: W.W. Norton.

Lafitau, Joseph. 1974 [1724]. *Customs of the American Indians*. Toronto: Champlain Society.

Lounsbury, Floyd. 1978. "Iroquoian Languages." *Northeast* (ed. B. Trigger), Vol. 15 of *Handbook of North American Indians*. Washington, DC: Smithsonian Institution, 334–343.

Mann, Barbara, and Jerry Fields. 1997. "A Sign in the Sky: Dating the League of the Haudenosaunee." *American Indian Culture & Research Journal* 21, no. 2: 105–164.

Morgan, Lewis Henry. [1851]1962. *League of the Ho-de-no-sau-nee, or Iroquois*. New York: Corinth Press.

Morgan, Lewis Henry. 1877. *Ancient Society*. New York: Henry Holt.

Parker, Arthur C. 1913. "The Code of the Indian Handshake." *Albany: New York State Museum Bulletin* No. 163.

Parker, Arthur C. 1916. "The Constitution of the Fine Nations." *Albany: NYS Museum Bulletin* No. 184, pp. 7–154.

Richter, Daniel. 1983. "War and Culture: The Iroquois Experience." *William & Mary Quarterly* 3rd Series, 40: 528–559.

Richter, Daniel. 1992. *The Ordeal of the Longhouse: Peoples of the Iroquois League in the Era of European Colonization*. Chapel Hill, NC: University of North Carolina Press.

Ritchie, William, and Robert Funk. 1973. *Aboriginal Settlement Patterns in the Northeast*. Albany, NY: New York State Museum and Science Service Memoir no. 20.

Salwen, Bert. 1970. "Cultural Inferences from Faunal Remains: Examples from Three Northeast Coastal Sites." *Pennsylvania Archeologist* 40: 1–8.

Schlossberg, T. 2014. *A Connecticut Indian Tribe Faces Its Eroding Fortunes from Foxwoods. The New York Times*. Online.

Shimony, Annemarie. 1961. *Conservatism among the Iroquois at the Six Nations Reserve*. New Haven, CT: Yale University Publications in Anthropology no. 65.

Snow, Dean. 1994. *The Iroquois*. Cambridge: Blackwell.

Sokolove, Michael. 2012. *Foxwoods Is Fighting for Its Life. The New York Times*. Online.

Statistical Abstracts. 2010.

Sutton, Imre. 2000. "Not All Aboriginal Territory Is Truly Irredeemable." *American Indian Culture & Research Journal* 24, no. 1: 129–162.

Toensing, Gale. 2011. "Canadian Border Agent Confiscated Haudenosaunee Passport." *Indian Country Today* August 17.

Trigger, Bruce. 1972. "Hochelaga: History and Ethnohistory." *Cartier's Hochelaga and the Dawson Site* (ed. J. Pendergast and B. Trigger). Montreal: McGill-Queen's University Press, pp. 1–107.

"Tonawanda Band of Senecas Win Favorable Ruling from Second Circuit Court of Appeals." 1999. *Indian Time*. October 22: 5.

"Tough Love: Oneidas Push for Land Claim Settlement." 1999. *American Indian Report*. May: 22–24.

"Two Claims Settled." 2000. *Rencontre*. Quebec: Secrétariat aux affaires autochtones, May: 19.

US Bureau of the Census, 2010. *2010 Census of Population, American Indian and Alaska Native Areas*. Washington, DC.

Wallace, Anthony F. C. 1969. *Death and Rebirth of the Seneca Nation*. New York: Alfred Knopf.

Williams, Roger. 1643. *A Key into the Language of America*. London: Gregory Dexter.

The Mohawks

Many of the contemporary issues that concern Mohawks, such as overlapping and multi-jurisdiction, land shortages and losses, loss of identity, and self-determination can be traced to history and location, all have their roots in historical Canadian colonist practices and the geographic happenstance of each community's location.

Mission statement of the Mohawk/Canada
Roundtable 1995

CONTEMPORARY MOHAWK communities are located in Québec at Kahnawake (gah-na-WA-ge) and Kanesatake (ga-ne-sa-DA-ge), in Ontario at Tyendinaga (tie-yen-di-NE-ga), Wahta (WAH-da), and Six Nations, and at Akwesasne (ah-gwe-SAHS-ne) straddling the borders of Ontario, Québec, and New York State. Together they are home to nearly 50,000 Mohawks. Although the reserves are all situated in territory near to seventeenth-century Mohawk lands, none are in the heart of the aboriginal nation. Complex historical forces led to the creation of each community. Kahnawake and Kanesatake were established as Catholic mission settlements in the late seventeenth century by French Jesuit missionaries. A group of Catholic Mohawks left their homes in New York State in 1667 and established a village on the south side of the St. Lawrence River at La Prairie, a short distance from Montreal. The population there grew throughout the 1670s, attracting Mohawks and Oneidas (a closely related Iroquois nation). The settlement was moved upriver to Sault St. Louis (presently Lachine Rapids) in 1676 because soil at La Prairie was too damp for growing corn. The village was named Kahnawake, meaning "at the rapids," because of its location.

In 1676, the second Mohawk mission, named Kanesatake ("place of reeds" or "at the foot of the hillside"), was established by French Sulpician priests on the island of Montreal. It was soon relocated to the mainland a short distance west of Montreal along the Ottawa River where it has since remained. Converts at Kanesatake were from several Iroquoian and Algonkian groups, but the majority was Mohawks. The settlement at Akwesasne ("where the partridge drums") was founded sometime between 1747 and 1755 by emigrants from Kahnawake who were seeking additional land to grow crops because the soil at Kahnawake was rapidly becoming depleted.

As a result of turmoil created by the American Revolution, the communities of Tyendinaga and Six Nations were established on land given to them by King George III of Great Britain for their loyalty during the war. As the war intensified, Mohawks became both allies and victims of the two parties. Most Mohawks remained neutral, although some sided with the British and some with the Americans. Regardless of their allegiance, Mohawk communities near Albany, NY, were attacked by rebel armies during the war, followed by a final assault ordered by George Washington against all Iroquois villages. Residents were killed and cornfields and houses were burned. In desperation, Mohawks fled from New York, seeking refuge in Ontario. Tyendinaga was founded in 1783 under the leadership of Capt. John Deserontyon, a Mohawk officer who fought for the British during the Revolution. Six Nations was established in 1784 by followers of Joseph Brant, an influential Mohawk leader who was a staunch ally of Great Britain. Toward the end of the nineteenth century, a small number of emigrants left the mission settlement of Kanesatake and founded a new community called Wahta ("maple"), also known as Gibson, along the shores of Parry Sound.

In all six communities, people tried to reestablish their traditional lifeways as much as possible. They were able to do so only with limited success since economic, political, and social forces from Canadian/American society resulted in changes in the conditions to which Mohawks had to react. In order to understand their responses and the new societies they developed, we need to understand their cultural heritage and the history that engulfed all people in the region.

ABORIGINAL CULTURE

Territory

The Mohawks, one of five member nations of the Iroquois Confederacy, settled near rivers and lakes in present-day New York State and western New England. In their own language, the people called themselves "Kanyenkehaka" (ga-nyen-ge-HA-ga) or "people of the place of flint," but to Europeans they were known as Mohawks, from a Narragansett or Massachusetts word meaning "human-eaters." Mohawk territory was described in 1644 by Johannes Megapolensis, a Dutch minister who visited the country:

> The land is good, and fruitful in everything which supplies human needs. The country is very mountainous, partly soil, partly rocks, and with elevations so exceeding high that they appear to almost touch the clouds. Thereon grow the finest fir trees the eye ever saw. There are also in this country oaks, alders, beeches, elms, willows, etc. In the forests, and here and there along the water side, and on the islands, there grows an abundance of chestnuts, plums, hazel nuts, large walnuts of several sorts. The ground on the hills is covered with bushes of blueberries; the ground in the flat land near the rivers is covered with strawberries. Grapevines also grow here naturally in great abundance along the roads, paths and creeks. I have seen whole pieces of land where vine stood by vine and grew very luxuriantly, climbing to the top of the largest and loftiest trees. In the forests is great plenty of deer. There are also many partridges, heath-hens and pigeons that fly together in thousands, and a great number of all kinds of fowl, swans, geese, ducks which sport upon the river in thousands. Beside the deer and elks, there are panthers, bears, wolves, and foxes. In the river is a great plenty of all kinds of fish—pike, eels, perch, lampreys, cat fish, sun fish, shad, bass, and sturgeon. (Jameson 1909: 168–171)

The Mohawks were the easternmost Iroquois nation, located in the Mohawk River valley west of Albany. Their hunting territories extended northward into the Adirondack Mountains and southward along the Susquehanna River to Oneonta. To the west were the four Iroquois nations allied with the Mohawks: Oneidas, Onondagas, Cayugas, and Senecas. They spoke closely related languages belonging to the Iroquoian family and developed very similar cultures. East of the Mohawks were Algonkian nations such as Mahicans, Housatonics, and Wappingers.

At the beginning of the historic period (ca. 1500) Mohawks lived in three large villages, all situated on the south side of the Mohawk River in the heart of the nation's territory (Jameson 1909: 140–155; Grassman 1969: 623). Their territory extended a distance of about 35 mi. from east to west and about 14 mi. from north to south (Starna 1980: 372). Villages were located on hilltops not far from lakes or rivers that were the major routes of travel and sources of drinking water. Villages were surrounded by wooden palisades for protection against enemy attacks. Fields for planting lay outside the boundaries of residential settlements. One village, named Tionontoguen (de-yo-non-DO-gen), meaning "valley" or "between two mountains," was referred to as the center or capital (Lounsbury 1960: 26). The villages, including several smaller ones, were relocated every ten or twenty years when nearby soil became depleted and firewood was scarce.

Figures for aboriginal populations are, of course, estimates, varying widely depending on the source. Based on ethnohistorical and archeological data, estimates of household composition and family size, and calculations of probable mortality rates in seventeenth-century epidemics, Starna suggests a range from a low of 8,258–10,268 (assuming a 50% mortality rate) to a high of 13,763–17,111 (assuming a 70% mortality rate) (Starna 1980: 376).

Economies

Mohawk economy combined horticulture and foraging. Women and men performed different but complementary economic labor. Contributions of both genders were socially recognized and highly valued. Women were responsible for farming. They planted varieties of corn, beans, squash, and sunflowers using wooden hoes to dig holes for seeds that they planted in small mounds of earth. Before planting, seeds were soaked in medicinal solutions for several days in order to keep crows away from the crops. Corn was central to the Mohawk diet. It was eaten in soups and stews, often mixed with berries, meat, or fish. Corn kernels were frequently preserved by being dried in the sun and later baked into breads. In addition to farming, women gathered wild plants, fruits, berries, and nuts, especially potatoes, strawberries, blueberries, hickory nuts, walnuts, acorns, and seeds. In the early spring, women extracted sap from maple trees, which they used to sweeten corn dishes and teas.

Not only were women responsible for food production and gathering wild plants but they also controlled distribution of both the food that they produced and the resources and goods contributed by their husbands and sons. In fact, their control over resources was a crucial factor in women's status in their households and communities (Brown 1975: 236; Bonvillain 1980: 50). In addition to allotting food for daily consumption, women collected and distributed supplies for public feasts and ceremonial occasions (Lafitau 1974: 318). Women dispensed food, typically in the form of dried cornbread, to men setting out on hunting, trading, or warring expeditions. If a woman was opposed to her husband or son joining a group of warriors, she could withhold the expected supplies, thereby symbolically signaling her opposition. Men usually complied with their wives' or mothers' wishes in these matters.

Men's subsistence roles included hunting and fishing to supplement the plant diet. They hunted deer, elk, moose, bear, beaver, partridges, and wild turkeys. Bows and arrows were the basic hunting gear. Hunters also used wooden traps to capture deer and spears and nets to catch birds and fish. Men and women occasionally organized communal deer hunts that resulted in catching as many as 100 animals. They walked through the woods in two lines forming a V, shaking rattles and making noises to frighten the deer, and led them into a narrow space between the two lines. Deer then could not escape and were easily killed. Trading with other Indians for utilitarian and luxury articles was also the work of men.

In addition to economic labor, women cooked meals, took care of children, and made clothing from deer hides. They also made baskets and containers for carrying and storing foods and personal items.

One of men's contributions to Mohawk material culture was the production of wampum belts. Wampum was derived from clam shells obtained through trade with Algonkians on Long Island and coastal New Jersey. Clam shells were cut into pieces and made into small white or purple beads that were strung together or woven into belts. Different patterns of white and purple beads conveyed different messages. An account of a specific event was "talked into the wampum" and thereby preserved forever. Wampum belts had great ritual and moral significance. They were used in community meetings as well as in religious ceremonies including naming and funeral rites. Wampum was also used to commemorate important events such as visits of prominent guests and conclusion of treaties with other nations. Wampum belts retain their political and ceremonial importance for Mohawks today. Belts that commemorate treaties are kept by Iroquois leaders and their provisions are recalled and upheld.

Families and Social Norms

Mohawks lived in "longhouses" built according to Iroquoian design (see Chapter 3 for descriptions of these dwellings). They housed families related in matrilineal clans that formed the basis of Mohawk kinship. The whole society was divided into three clans named after animals: the Bear, Wolf, and Turtle. Since clans were exogamous, kinship groups were linked to others through marriage alliances. In addition to determining descent, clans controlled and distributed farmland to their members.

Clans also owned longhouses in which their members lived. Since matrilocality was the preferred residence pattern, a household typically consisted of an elder woman, her husband, their daughters and daughters' families, and the couple's unmarried sons. Each nuclear group had its own quarters in the house, separated by bark partitions.

Clans currently continue as groupings that assign social identity, but their aboriginal corporate functions have disappeared. Communal ownership of land and housing by clans is not possible in the context of modern nuclear household structure and private, individualized economic pursuits. Clan exogamy has largely disappeared as well. However, if members of the Longhouse Religion wish to marry in a traditional ceremony, they must belong to different clans.

The Mohawk nation was divided into two moieties. The Wolf and Turtle clans formed one moiety while the Bear clan constituted the other. Moieties had mainly ceremonial functions, one of which was to prepare and conduct funerals for members of the opposite group. This custom reflected Mohawks' belief that people from the deceased's clan or moiety were too overcome by grief to be able to conduct a proper rite. Today, the ritual roles of moieties continue to be performed within the context of the Longhouse Religion upon the deaths of members. Moieties similarly conduct funerals for chiefs of the Iroquois Confederacy.

Women traditionally had many critical roles in their households and clans. Senior women of matrilineages composing each clan had responsibility for overseeing domestic tasks performed in their households and for allocating farmland to their kinswomen (Lafitau 1974: 69). Senior women, often referred to as "matrons" or "clan mothers" in the literature, were socially prominent and achieved their status due to combinations of merit, intelligence, and desired social attributes such as cooperativeness, generosity, and good nature.

Although Mohawks were guided by principles of communal responsibility and loyalty, they also believed that all people had rights to independence and autonomy. Rights to individual freedom and autonomy were reflected in gender roles and relations. Men and women had separate but equally regarded and rewarded roles in the society. They were both respected for the labor that they performed in support of their families and for the contributions they made to their society.

Behaviors and attitudes regarding sexuality and marriage were critical reflections of the independence and autonomy of women and men. People freely chose to engage in sexual relationships and to form marriages. No individual had rights to control others in any coercive manner. Marriages were monogamous. In most cases, they were contracted by the couple themselves although parents sometimes took a hand in arranging unions for their sons and daughters. However, arranged marriages did not proceed without consent from the young people involved. Marriages ideally lasted until the death of one spouse, but if the couple became unhappy, they were free to divorce and seek other mates. Although divorce occurred with some frequency, especially in the early years of a marriage, mothers of the two people tried to mediate disputes and reach a reconciliation. As years passed and children were born to a couple, unions were strengthened and less likely to dissolve.

Marriages were marked with a simple ceremony whose primary focus was an exchange of symbolic gifts between a woman and her future mother-in-law, followed by a feast sponsored by the bride's family. A woman gave her mother-in-law a present of corn bread and received in return a gift of deer meat. The two gifts represented the economic roles of wife and husband, together symbolizing the interdependence of women and men.

Mohawk attitudes toward sexuality were permissive. Premarital sexual activity was the norm. Extramarital affairs seem to have been quite common, if one can judge from Jesuit missionaries' complaints about such behavior. Although adultery was met with negative public opinion, no penalties resulted to any party. According to Jospeh Lafitau, an eighteenth-century observer, "the women, being more in the position of mistresses [of the household] fear an outburst less" (1974: 352).

Women were often referred to as "mothers of the nation" in recognition of their role in procreation and the continuity of generations. A symbolic expression of emphasis on women's procreative roles was enacted in practices concerning payment of fines in cases of murder. In order to forestall blood feuds between families that might occur in such circumstances, relatives of a murderer were obliged to give a set number of presents to the victim's family. Number of presents, usually in the form of wampum belts, was based on the gender of murderer and victim. A man's life was valued at ten belts, whereas a woman's was set at twenty. According to a Jesuit missionary, Paul Ragueneau, greater reparation was given for a woman's life because "women cannot so easily defend themselves, and, moreover, as it is they who people the country, their lives should be more valuable to the public" (*Jesuit Relations and Allied Documents 1610–1791* 1896–1901, 33: 243; hereafter *JR*). The system of tribute or fines required that when a man killed another man, his family offered twenty belts, ten for the life of the victim and ten for the murderer's, since by committing murder an individual forfeited his/her own standing in the community and thus rendered their own life without social value. If a man killed a woman, his kin gave thirty belts, ten for his life and twenty for the victim's. If a woman committed murder, her family gave thirty belts to kin of a male victim and forty to a female victim's family.

The respected position of women in Mohawk society was further reflected in the fact that violence against women in the form of wife beating or rape was unheard of. In the words of Gabriel Sagard, a seventeenth-century French missionary, the Indians believed in "leaving all to the wishes of the woman" in sexual matters (Sagard 1939: 125). The Mohawks themselves recognized the difference between their attitudes and those of Europeans. In 1722, Mohawk residents of the Catholic mission of Kahnawake wrote to the French governor of Canada asking for removal of a French garrison posted near the settlement, stating: "Our fields and our cabins, which are left open, and—what is of more importance— our wives and our daughters, are not safe with the French soldiers. Our young men … follow the bad examples before their eyes; and a thousand vices that were formerly unknown amongst us have unfortunately been introduced" (*JR* 67: 73). Even as late as 1779, James Clinton, an American general who led a military campaign to destroy Iroquois villages in New York, wrote in a letter to his confederates: "Bad as these savages are, they never violate the chastity of any woman, their prisoner. It would be well to take measures to prevent a stain upon our army" (quoted in Hewitt 1933: 483).

Political Integration

Mohawk communities were traditionally bound together by strong ties of kinship, friendship, and interdependent responsibilities. These principles were reflected in a political system that integrated village life and united villages within the nation. Village councils were organized into caucuses of elder men, women, and young men to discuss local, national, and international issues and arrive at community consensus through deliberation and negotiation. Clan chiefs, selected and installed by clan mothers, were spokespeople for their kinship groups and communities, but their authority consisted of advice and influence, not of coercive power.

In addition to local and national forums, Mohawks joined with the other four Iroquois nations in forming the Iroquois Confederacy. In the Mohawk language, the Confederacy is called "Ganonsyonni" (ga-non-SHON-ni) "the extended house" or "Rotinonsyonni" (ro-di-non-SHON-ni) "they are of the extended house," reflecting the symbolism of kinship so prevalent in Mohawk (and Iroquoian) polity.

Warfare

Although peace and stability were the goals of Mohawk and Confederacy diplomats, warfare was not infrequent in their history. Indeed, according to stories of the League's origin, the five nations bound themselves together in order to quell retaliatory and revenge attacks among their members. Although the goals of a united league were often fulfilled, conflicts among members of the confederacy did occur. Warfare also erupted between Mohawks and their indigenous neighbors. Raids had complex causes. Animosities, possibly engendered by cycles of killings and revenge killings, seem to have continued for many generations. From archeological and linguistic evidence, Iroquoians were ancient intruders into the Algonkian-dominated Northeast, and therefore animosities might have been created and maintained because of Iroquoian displacement of their neighbors. Mohawks and their confederates often waged war in order to take captives to replace deceased relatives (Richter 1983, 1987). Through these "mourning wars," endless cycles of raid and revenge were perpetuated. Gaining captives replenished a community's and kin group's numbers, but it also served the emotional needs of the bereaved because

> the Iroquois believed that the grief inspired by a relative's death could plunge survivors into depths of despair that robbed them of their reason and disposed them to fits of rage potentially harmful to themselves and the community. Accordingly, Iroquois culture directed mourners' emotions into ritualized channels. (Richter 1983: 531).

Warfare was generally carried out by small groups of men under the leadership of a sponsor or organizer of a particular expedition. Leaders and participants were usually members of a household that had lost a relative in a previous enemy encounter. They were not blood kin because close relatives were thought to be too overcome by grief. Instead, men who had married into the bereaved household were likely participants (532). Participation, however, was voluntary. Men joined only if they thought well of the objectives and plans. Some captives who were taken in raids were adopted by bereaved mothers or sisters but some were tortured to death in ritualized expressions of grief and anger.

Religious Beliefs and Practices

The Mohawks' religion centered around beliefs in the existence of spirit powers in many forms and in the performance of rituals dedicated to spirit beings and to the restoration and maintenance of an orderly universe. Their religious and ethical philosophies were expressed in creation stories. The Mohawks tell that at first there was no earth, only sky above and water below. In the Sky-World lived a woman, Sky-Woman, who, while searching near the roots of a large tree for medicines

Courtesy of the Iroquois Indian Museum

The Iroquois story of creation is depicted in this 1980 painting entitled *Creations Battle* by Mohawk artist John Fadden. The conflict between good and evil in the universe is represented by the struggle between Sky woman's sons, the Good Twin and the Evil Twin. The Good Twin created all the good in the universe, including plants, animals, rivers, and streams. To counteract his brother's work, the Evil Twin produced poisonous plants, thorns, diseases, and monsters. However, the Evil Twin was not ultimately powerful enough to to triumph in the creation battle. As a final stroke, the Good Twin created human beings to enjoy all the good he had made for them.

for her husband, fell through a hole in the sky and descended toward the waters below. Animals in the sea dove beneath the water and took up some mud that they placed on a turtle's back so that Sky-Woman would have a soft place to land. After she landed unharmed on the turtle's back, the mud gradually expanded to become the earth. Sky-Woman soon gave birth to a daughter. The daughter later gave birth to twin sons. One son was born in the normal manner but the second was born through his mother's armpit, killing her in the process. The woman's mother buried her and out of her body grew plants of corn, beans, and squash, plants now called the "Three Sisters" or "Our Life Supporters."

After the deity's death, her twin sons, Sapling and Flint, created many animals and plants. But rather than working in harmony, the twins hated each other and competed in all their endeavors. Sapling created berries and fruits while Flint made briars and poison ivy. Sapling made fish in the rivers and lakes, but Flint put many small bones in their bodies to cause problems for people who eat them. Sapling made rivers and streams flow in two directions so that people could easily travel wherever they wanted to go, but Flint changed the course of water so that rivers flowed only in one direction, making it difficult for people to travel when going "upstream." The Twins continually challenged each other and often came to blows. After many battles, just as Sapling was about to kill his brother, he offered to spare Flint's life if Flint would use his powers to cure the illnesses that he himself had originated. Flint agreed and has since been the spirit source of healing medicines.

Two prominent themes are expressed in the Mohawks' story of creation and transformation. First, the stories emphasize women's fertility, both as creators of new generations and as originators of the plants that are basic to the Mohawk diet. And the crops' origin through the actions of a female deity symbolizes the critical link between women and food production. The second theme that emerges is that of the needed balance between forces of good and evil. Sapling represents the good, beneficial, positive aspects of the world and of society while Flint represents bad, malevolent, and negative aspects of life. Both good and bad exist and must be reckoned with. Sapling's decision not to kill Flint when he had the opportunity to do so is a metaphor for people's inability to totally eliminate evil. But Sapling did not simply let Flint go. He first obtained Flint's promise to use his considerable powers to help people. This bargain expresses people's need to control evil forces both in themselves and in the world around them. However, since humans do not have enough power to control evil on their own, they rely on spiritual aid obtained through prayers and rituals.

Spirit beings and forces affect humans through their use of spirit power, called "orenda" (o-REN-da). Orenda is a spirit force or essence that resides in many forms. Deities and natural phenomena such as the sun, moon, stars, winds, and thunder have orenda. Animals, human beings, and some objects may also have spirit power. Possession of orenda can help people maintain good health and achieve success. Although everyone has the potential for acquiring orenda, not all people are equally successful in obtaining and using it. Those people who have great amounts of orenda are able to foretell the future, find lost objects, interpret messages expressed in dreams, cure illness, and conduct rituals for the benefit of their community.

Mohawk rituals were primarily of three types: calendric ceremonies concerned with foods and crops, curing ceremonies, and death rites. The timing and planning of calendrics were responsibilities of "Keepers of the Faith," men and women who were among the most respected community members. The ceremonies occurred in a seasonal cycle, celebrating maple sap, seed planting, strawberries, beans, green corn, and the fall harvest. Each calendric was composed of a number of separate rites, beginning with a thanksgiving speech offered to supernatural and natural beings and forces, all mentioned and thanked in a ritual sequence reflecting Mohawks' concern with the orderly structure of the universe. Then an invocation was made by sprinkling tobacco on a fire, the smoke attracting spirit beings and carrying people's messages to the spirit realm. Calendrics continued with rites dedicated to seasonal plants and ended with a communal feast, often focused on the particular food associated with the occasion (Shimony 1961: 140–173).

The longest and most complex calendric ceremonial, signaling both the end of one year and the beginning of the next, was a nine-day rite called "Midwinter" (Tooker 1970). It began with selection of a pure white dog that was ritually strangled and burned. As with tobacco smoke, smoke from the burning dog carried people's messages to spirits. Next, messengers called "Our Uncles" went through each house in the village to announce the start of Midwinter and to stir the ashes in every hearth with a large wooden paddle, an act that symbolized community renewal and awakening of life forces for the coming year. Several

days were then devoted to feasting and dream-guessing. People went from house to house, asking others to guess their dreams based on hints or riddles provided by the dreamer. These activities were followed by "Four Sacred Rituals" (Feather Dance, Thanksgiving Dance, Personal Chants, and Bowl Game), ending with dances for "Our Life Supporters" that offered thanks to spirits of corn, beans, and squash on whom Mohawks depended for their survival.

In addition to calendrics, Mohawks performed numerous rituals concerned with curing. A sick person frequently prescribed his/her own treatment through a dream. Indeed, Mohawks believed in the necessity of understanding and fulfilling messages contained in one's dreams. According to their belief, dreams were expressions of a person's innermost thoughts and desires and must be fulfilled in order to maintain health or be cured from illness. If one's dream-wishes were not satisfied, illness or death would ensue. The desires of some dreams were obvious. For example, if a person dreamt of visiting someone or receiving a particular object, that person satisfied the desire by going on the visit or requesting that someone give her/him what was seen in the dream. But messages in some dreams were difficult to interpret, requiring the aid of dream interpreters who understood a dream's hidden or symbolic meanings.

Not all illnesses were related to one's dreams but rather to spirit causes such as failure to honor spirit beings, violation of ritual rules, and the actions of witches. Witches were believed to be jealous or angry men and women who inflicted harm on others by using a variety of methods to cause sickness or death. They might secretly put dangerous concoctions into a victim's food or drink; they might use spells or spirit charms to carry out their intentions. Mohawks believed that witches could change their bodies into ordinary-looking animals so that they could wander near their victims without arousing suspicion. Illnesses caused by witchcraft were difficult to cure, but rituals aimed at breaking harmful spells were performed by specialists who had strong spirit powers.

Curing rituals were frequently conducted by members of various medicine societies, each with its distinctive ceremonial treatments. Choice of society or method of treatment was usually made by a healer based on the patient's symptoms or dreams or on hidden messages that the healer observed in bowls of water or tea. Once a diagnosis was made, members of the prescribed medicine society performed their rituals in the patient's house. Some cures included massaging the patient with ashes from hearths, a recurring metaphor of renewal. In other cures, healers donned masks representing supernatural beings whose restorative powers were applied to a patient. Masks had great spiritual meaning to Mohawks and were thought to be always alive. Masks were either made of wood and associated with spirits of the forest or were made of corn-husks and linked to agricultural spirits. Wooden masks (called "false-faces") were carved into a living tree and only extracted from the tree when completed, thus retaining life-forces and requiring periodic feedings of tobacco to ensure their survival.

A third major ceremonial category consisted of rituals associated with death. Funerals were held within a few days of a person's death. They were marked with speeches of condolence given by members of the opposite moiety from that of the deceased, symbolizing societal interdependence and expressing communal unity and balance. From the time of death until the "Tenth-day Feast" held to release the deceased's soul, food was set out for the deceased's ghost who was believed to remain nearby. At the Tenth-day Feast, personal possessions belonging to the deceased were distributed among guests. The soul then began its journey along the Milky Way to the afterworld. In addition to marking individual deaths, Mohawks conducted a ceremony once or twice a year to commemorate everyone who had died since the last rite, thus reinforcing personal and community bonds.

The religion introduced by the Seneca prophet Handsome Lake at the turn of the nineteenth century came to Mohawk communities in the early twentieth century (see Chapter 4 for discussion of Handsome Lake's revelations and teachings). It was adopted at Kahnawake in the 1920s and at Akwesasne in the 1930s. The lateness of its arrival there is due to the strong influence of the Catholic Church in those communities. Although it has fewer followers than at some of the other Iroquois reservations, believers are influential in their communities because of their social and political activism in upholding Mohawk treaty rights.

THE FUR TRADE AND TRANSFORMATIONS OF MOHAWK SOCIETY

By the beginning of the seventeenth century, Mohawks and their Iroquois allies wielded considerable power, extending their influence far beyond their own territory. Throughout most of the next two centuries, they played a dominant role in the economics and politics of the Northeast. They competed with other Native nations for access to European commerce, seeking by diplomacy or warfare to control trade routes. And they competed for regional hegemony with European powers who were exploiting the resources and the people of the Northeast. Later, as European settlements in the Northeast grew, Mohawks struggled against the foreigners' desires for more land. Finally, the Europeans' presence, their demands for trade and territory, and their economic and political power resulted over the centuries in exacting fundamental transformations in Mohawk society.

By the early 1600s, Mohawks were supplying animal pelts to European merchants in exchange for metal tools, utensils, weapons, and heavy woolen cloth. However, as early as the 1640s, most of the beaver in lands controlled by Mohawks was gone, leading to a desperate situation since without beaver pelts, people could not obtain trade goods. A French traveler, Louis de Lahontan, wrote of their plight, "by these means the [Mohawks], being unprovided with Beaver-skins to be given in exchange for Guns, Powder, Ball and Nets, would be starved to death, or at least obliged to leave their country" (Lahontan 1905: 227). Refusing to withdraw from trade, Mohawks chose instead to acquire pelts from Native groups who still had an abundance of beavers in their territory. Decades of intense intertribal warfare ensued, motivated and often directly encouraged by European powers, to secure beaver pelts and to control routes to trading posts.

In the period following contact with Europeans and the resulting competition over trade and territory, Mohawk warfare altered both its objectives and tactics. Economic goals became entwined with earlier social and personal motivations as Mohawks attempted to control access to trade and establish political hegemony. The so-called mourning wars became a vehicle for pursuit of economic objectives as well (the so-called beaver wars). Large groups, numbering in the hundreds, were organized by war chiefs whose reputations were based on shrewd planning and successful outcomes. Warriors continued to take captives but also plundered enemy settlements, taking furs that they could trade for European weapons that could in turn be used to pursue successful raids (Richter 1987: 20). Richter estimates that "a substantial portion of the pelts that Iroquois traders sold at Fort Orange [now Albany] after 1630 must have been stolen from

Indian enemies" (20). In addition, the desire to obtain captives to replace family members increased as deaths from disease and warfare rose dramatically by the later years of the seventeenth century.

Captives were incorporated into Mohawk communities through adoption, leading to their cultural and linguistic assimilation. For instance, many Mohawk villages had substantial numbers of Hurons who had been taken in war or who had "voluntarily" surrendered (Jennings 1984: 95).

In addition to competition with other Native nations, Mohawks had conflicts with Europeans as well. The first direct confrontation occurred in 1609 near present-day Lake Champlain when a group of some 200 Mohawk warriors was attacked by French soldiers, commanded by Samuel de Champlain, and their Huron and Algonkian allies, numbering approximately 60 in all. Champlain and his men opened fire with muskets, weapons Mohawks had never seen before. The French killed two Mohawk chiefs immediately and critically wounded a third, causing terror among the warriors. Because they fled for their lives, Champlain mistakenly believed that the encounter proved French superiority and thought that French victory over the Mohawks was inevitable (Champlain 1907: 164–169). But although Mohawks were alarmed at the outcome of the confrontation, they were not so easily dislodged from their lands nor dissuaded from trying to tighten their control over trade. Within a mere forty years of the fateful battle of 1609, Mohawks, along with their allies in the Iroquois Confederacy, forced the Hurons to disperse from their homes north of Lake Ontario and subjugated several eastern Algonkian groups, compelling them to trade through Mohawk intermediaries. Exposure to European battle techniques thus had a long-term effect on aboriginal warfare. Native strategists began to seek to destroy their foes, or at least force them to flee the territory, rather than simply inflict a small number of casualties.

When Dutch traders opened the post of Fort Orange (renamed Albany by the British) in 1615, Mohawks saw an opportunity to control regional trade because of the merchants' proximity to their territory. They were soon embroiled in wars against their Mahican neighbors. Both groups wanted to prevent other Indians from trading directly with Dutch merchants, each hoping to force others to trade through them. Mohawks' victories over Mahicans in the 1620s solidified their position as the main suppliers of beaver pelts to Dutch dealers who, in exchange, introduced

Indians to a wide range of foreign products. Metalware such as brass kettles and iron hunting tools were especially desired as were duffel cloth, biscuits, and flour. Mohawks also traded for wampum that the Dutch obtained from Montauks, Shinnecocks, and other Algonkians living on Long Island, then a territory colonized by Dutch settlers. In fact, the Dutch contracted with Long Island Indians to increase production of wampum because it was in such high demand by the Iroquois (Vernon 1978).

Tensions in the area increased not only because of intertribal rivalry over trade but also due to encroachments of Dutch settlers on Native lands around Fort Orange and competition grew for farmland and hunting areas. At the same time, the beaver population in eastern and central New York declined due to heavy kills by hunters trying to keep pace with European demands, thus also increasing intertribal instability. A Mohawk leader expressed his nation's dilemma when he told Dutch officials in 1659: "The Dutch say we are brothers, and joined together with chains, but that lasts only as long as we have beavers; after that no attention is paid to us" (Vernon 1978: 202).

The "attention" that Mohawks wanted was access to European products. They were prepared to secure trade by engaging in warfare against their neighbors. Mohawk raids in the mid-1600s included attacks against Pequots and Narragansetts in New England, Hurons in southern Ontario, Montagnais near Tadoussac in northeastern Québec, Abenakis and Maliseets in the Maritime Provinces, Ottawas and Algonkians in the Ottawa River valley, and Neutrals and Eries in the Great Lakes regions. In all these areas, Mohawks and their Iroquois allies were victorious. One tactic that the Mohawks used was to set ambushes along the Hudson and St. Lawrence rivers, attacking travelers carrying animal skins en route to the trading posts at Fort Orange or Montreal and Québec. Mohawks were so successful that they were able to take as much as one-quarter of the furs transported by other people along the rivers (Vernon 1978). Mohawk prowess was enhanced by the fact that Dutch traders began selling guns to them in the 1640s, an advantage not offered to other Indians at that time.

European settlement increased apace, creating conflict as settlers encroached on Native land. In 1640, only about a thousand Dutch settlers lived in all of the colony of New Netherland, perhaps a hundred in the vicinity of Fort Orange, but by the mid-1640s, settlement grew rapidly (Upton 1980). At the time, the Dutch government followed an official policy of purchasing land fairly from Indians because they wanted to establish good trade relations but despite official intentions, Dutch settlers occupied land without legal purchase. The Dutch then set up local courts and heard complaints brought by Mohawks against illegal expansions of Dutch farms into their territory. Although the courts often ruled in favor of Native claims, little was done to redress the wrongs committed by settlers.

British settlers also made inroads into eastern and central New York from their areas of colonization in New England. British victory over Holland in 1664, both in North America and Europe, resulted in the replacement of Dutch officials by Britons in New York. In the same year, Mohawk and Seneca representatives concluded a commercial agreement with British merchants but antagonisms were soon created as British settlers encroached on Mohawk territory. Since Great Britain allowed settlers to negotiate land deals without official supervision, tensions increased as more settlers arrived and gained control of Mohawk land, ignoring Native claims. As a result of illegal land deals, thousands of acres of Mohawk land were taken by settlers with or without official sanction. Colonial administrators often were guilty of injustices as well. Since many members of local assemblies were themselves wealthy landowners, they used their position to formulate policies from which they benefitted financially at the expense of the Indians (Nammack 1969).

Despite these serious problems, Mohawks remained loyal to their British allies. They continued to trade with Britons and aid them in battles against the enemies of England, most notably France. However, although Mohawks were allied against the French in military matters, they wanted to establish commercial relations with them. In 1653, representatives of the two groups signed a treaty guaranteeing the peaceful flow of valuables. Still, Mohawks preferred trading with the British because British goods were of superior quality and could be obtained at lower cost, often at half the price of French products. In fact, Mohawks signed treaties with the French to put pressure on British merchants to keep their prices low, correctly reasoning that if the two European groups had to compete with each other for Native trade, neither could exert monopoly control.

In the early 1600s, relations with the French expanded as Jesuit missionaries began to contact indigenous people in the Northeast, beginning activity among Algonkian and Huron allies of the French and later visiting the Iroquois as well. The first missionary journey to Mohawk territory was undertaken by Isaac Jogues in 1642. Although Jogues's trip was not successful, he returned in 1646 in a second effort to establish a mission. In the interval between his journeys, smallpox epidemics and crop failures struck Mohawk communities he had visited, disasters that the people attributed to witchcraft based on their discovery of a black box or container that Jogues had left behind in 1642. In the words of Father Lalemant, Mohawks reasoned, "Sickness having fallen upon their bodies after [Jogues's] departure, and worms having perhaps damaged their corn, these poor blind creatures have believed that the Father had left them the Demon among them, and that all our discourses aimed only to exterminate them" (*JR* 30: 229). Although Jogues did not knowingly cause harm to the Mohawks, he may actually have been a carrier of deadly smallpox germs that spread rapidly among the villagers. In any case, when Jogues returned in 1646, he was executed as a witch. Although Jogues's death caused renewed friction between Mohawks and French, Lalemant observed: "It is true that, speaking humanly, these Barbarians have apparent reasons for reproaching us—inasmuch as the scourges which humble the proud precede us or accompany us wherever we go" (*JR* 31: 121–123).

Despite setbacks, Jesuits returned to Mohawk territory in the 1650s. Several leaders welcomed the priests because they hoped to establish trade relations with France and correctly saw the Jesuits as emissaries of French commercial and governmental, as well as religious, interests. One of the now-celebrated converts was a young Mohawk woman named Kateli Tekakwitha who became a fervent believer and agreed to move from her home in central New York State to the Jesuit mission near present-day Montréal. After her death in 1680 at the age of twenty-four, and especially later in the nineteenth and twentieth centuries, several miraculous cures have been attributed to her aid. As a result of the efforts of her champions, Kateli Tekakwitha, now considered the patron of ecology, nature, and the environment, was granted sainthood in 2011 by the Catholic Church. She was ceremonially canonized in October, 2012 at the Vatican in Rome.

On the whole, missionary efforts to convert Mohawks met with little success, but the priests' impact on Native history proved to be considerable. During times of peace, Jesuits were advocates for Mohawk interests, writing favorably about the people and their culture. Father Le Moyne, who visited Mohawk villages in 1656 and 1657, commented:

> No hospitals are needed among them, because there are neither mendicants nor paupers as long as there are any rich people among them. Their kindness, humanity, and courtesy not only make them liberal with what they have, but cause them to possess hardly anything except in common. A whole village must be without corn before any individual can be obliged to endure privation. (*JR* 42: 271)

When the fragile peace turned to war, as often happened, Jesuits' remarks also turned bitter. They counseled French officials to step up attacks against Mohawks, advising that if the Mohawks could be defeated, the other four Iroquois nations would abandon war and agree to treaties with France. The Mohawks, though, remained unbeaten and Jesuits had to write with respect, if not approval, of their military skills. In 1660, Lalemant noted:

> The Agnieronnons (Mohawks) have had to fight with all their neighbors—with the Abnaquois (Abenakis), who are eastward of them; on the south with the Andastogehronnons (Andastes), a people inhabiting the shores of Virginia; with the Hurons on the west; and with all the Algonkin nations scattered throughout the north. But what is more astonishing is, that they actually hold dominion over 500 leagues around, although their numbers are small; for the Agnieronnons do not exceed 500 men able to bear arms, who occupy three or four villages. (*JR* 45: 203–207)

Jesuit activity among the Mohawks led to dissension within the Native communities. When Catholic converts left to found settlements at Kahnawake and Kanesatake in the late 1600s, members of their communities in New York were disturbed by the deep rift in unity, tearing apart the valued principle of "one heart, one mind, one law." And they worried that the converts would come under French political as well as religious influence and would fight with France against the Iroquois. Their foreboding was well founded. Although Kahnawake and Kanesatake residents initially pledged neutrality in Iroquois–French conflicts, they were often drawn in on the side of France.

Although people at both Kahnawake and Kanesatake retained aboriginal economies and clan systems, they abandoned several customs criticized by Jesuit teachings, including easy divorce and indulgent treatment of children. Instead, Jesuits preached that marriages should be indissoluble and that children should be physically punished if they misbehaved. Finally, the priests tried to eradicate Mohawk beliefs about the importance of interpreting and fulfilling one's dreams, practices they thought were signs of devil-worship (Bonvillain 1986). Changes in converts' behavior, of course, made them appear strange to people remaining in New York and gave further evidence of French treachery.

By the late seventeenth century, conflicts between Mohawks and their British allies increased as the settlers' appetite for land was insatiable. Since Mohawks feared that their lands would be taken by colonists, they negotiated peace treaties with the French in the hope of securing protection against Britons' territorial advances but British officials were angered by any sign of Mohawk friendship with France.

Turmoil in the Northeast continued unabated. Mohawks and their Iroquois allies launched attacks against several Native nations, ranging as far west as Lake Superior in raids against Hurons, Neutrals, and Petuns who had relocated there. They made expeditions to the south as well, reaching to Virginia and the Carolinas. Mohawks retained their dominance over other Native groups, defeating enemies and forcing many to abandon their territories and resettle further west or to join the victors and become members of Iroquois settlements. Others remained in the east but pledged not to take up arms against the Iroquois. But despite their successes, the previous hundred years had taken a heavy toll on the Mohawk nation. Thousands of people had been killed, both from deadly European diseases and from the scourge of warfare that continued without respite. Their land was diminished in size as Dutch and British colonies expanded. Because of these difficult conditions, some Mohawks left New York, migrating northward to the mission villages of Kahnawake and Kanesatake near Montreal.

European settlements expanded in the early eighteenth century. Prior to that time, the westernmost colonial communities had been located near Schenectady, but by 1720, settlers moved further west. During the 1720s, German immigrants also invaded the Mohawk and Hudson River valleys. The city of Albany itself laid claim to nearby Mohawk territory. Fearing that all their land would be occupied, Mohawks agreed in 1733 to transfer more than 3,000 acres to the protection of King George III (Nammack 1969). Although Mohawks assumed that their lands were finally safe from settlers' advances, the British government was either unable or unwilling to defend Indians from illegal sales. With their patience at an end, Chief Hendrick told New York Governor Clinton in 1753 that the "covenant chain of friendship" between his nation and Great Britain was broken (Nammack 1969). Alarmed by the possibility of losing Mohawk (and therefore Iroquois) allegiance, the government in London ordered a full accounting of land deals and protection of Native rights. However, as in the past, colonial administrators were ineffectual and typically turned a blind eye to settlers' abuses.

Trading posts expanded their operations, relying on both Native and immigrant commerce. Posts were built along the Mohawk River and even further west as increased British military presence made colonists and merchants feel secure. Although Mohawks prospered from trade, their anger over unscrupulous land transactions made them wary of long-term British intentions.

Despite their misgivings, Mohawks fulfilled pledges of aid for Great Britain during the "French and Indian War" (1756–1763) between Britain and France. When the war ended with British victory and the ouster of France from the Northeast, the two adversaries officially recognized Native land rights. But even though Mohawks had fought as allies of Great Britain, British authorities immediately reduced by half the 40,000 acres originally granted to Mohawks at Kahnawake near Montreal. And the Proclamation of 1763, which forbade settlers from entering land west of a boundary drawn along the crest of the Appalachian mountains, was impossible to enforce. Other provisions of the Proclamation specifying that trade with Indians only be conducted by special license and only at designated posts under government supervision were also largely ignored.

Soon afterward, Mohawks became embroiled in another foreign war. During the American Revolution, most Mohawk leaders and warriors maintained neutrality although some fought with the Americans and others supported the British. The pro-British group was mainly persuaded by warnings that a rebel victory would lead to the end of Native rights to land. Whether the Mohawks would have fared better had the British won is an open question, but the prediction of dispossession was certainly accurate. As an omen of what would happen after an American victory, the New York legislature laid claim during the Revolution to Native lands within its boundaries and offered 600 acres of land to any colonist who enlisted in the rebel army. Increased pressure was applied to Mohawks and other Indians to sell their holdings (Upton 1980).

During the war, Mohawk communities around Albany were targets of retaliation by American settlers regardless of whether the Native residents were neutral or supported the Americans or British. Crops were burned, livestock was stolen, and people were killed. Then, in 1779, Iroquois villages throughout New York were destroyed by General John Sullivan's troops under orders from George Washington, thereafter known to the Iroquois as "destroyer of villages."

The Treaty of Paris in 1783 formally terminated the Revolutionary War and punctuated the end of what little security the Mohawks had in New York. The treaty, transferring British territory as far west as the Mississippi River to the Americans, was silent on the issue of Native rights to land. Only the governor of Canada, Sir Frederick Haldimand, advocated for their claims at the treaty conference, arguing that the Indians did not think Great Britain had the right to cede their lands to the United States and wanted to maintain the boundaries provided in the 1768 Treaty of Fort Stanwix signed between the British and Iroquois (Upton 1980). Haldimand's protests were ignored.

A NATION DIVIDED

By the early 1780s, most Mohawks had left aboriginal lands in New York to seek safety in Canada. Many went to the mission villages of Kahnawake, Kanesatake, and Akwesasne, while others founded new communities at Tyendinaga and Six Nations. The Mohawk settlements grew throughout the nineteenth and twentieth centuries, each confronting and reacting to different local economic and political conditions. As pressure from external governments mounted, Mohawks eventually abandoned most aspects of aboriginal culture. However, sectors of their communities tried to retain traditional values and beliefs and to safeguard their lands and heritage.

Kahnawake

The oldest settlement, Kahnawake (gah-na-WA-ge), relocated several times in the seventeenth and eighteenth centuries because of depletion of soil and its unsuitability for planting corn. Kahnawake came to its present site in 1716 on the southern shore of the St. Lawrence River across from Montreal. The settlement continued to grow, and by 1736 an estimated 300 families resided there.

The fact that Kahnawake was located only a few miles from the growing city of Montreal meant that pressures to adopt Canadian mores were strong. Missionaries instructed married couples to remain together, condemned sexual activity before or outside of marriage, and criticized aboriginal curing practices. And harmful influences from French settlements worried the missionaries. In 1735, Father Nau commented: "The Iroquois are more inclined to the practice of virtue than other nations; they are capable of refined feelings but the bad example and solicitations of the French are a very great obstacle to the sanctification of our Iroquois … taking all into consideration, our Iroquois are much better Christians than the French" (*JR* 68: 267).

The early years were difficult for residents of Kahnawake, especially regarding the breach between themselves and the New York Mohawks. An eighteenth-century French observer, Pierre Charlevoix, commented that in leaving their ancestral territory, the Mohawks had "abandoned everything that was dearest to them," adding: "A sacrifice still more glorious for Indians than for any other nation, because there are none so much attached as they are to their families and their native country" (Charlevoix 1966, 1: 270).

During the eighteenth century, Kahnawake Mohawks pursued a mixed economy of farming, hunting, fishing, raising pigs, poultry, and horses. Large matrilineal families lived together in longhouses built in the Iroquoian style. And the three clans (Bear, Wolf, Turtle) added to their membership by adopting newcomers from other Native nations.

Toward the end of the century, a number of Kahnawake men obtained employment with the North West Company as trappers, loggers, and canoe men, heading west across Canada and establishing a settlement of approximately 250 in Alberta. Many remained in Alberta and married into local communities, especially those of the Cree. The Canadian government gave them 25,600 acres of land in Alberta, later reduced to 15,485 acres. In the 1940s, these lands were taken by the province of Alberta. Although their territory was confiscated, Mohawk descendants still live in Alberta, British Columbia, and Montana (Frisch 1978).

In the nineteenth century, as Kahnawake men abandoned their accustomed hunting expeditions, farming gained in importance, providing food for residents and produce for sale to neighboring communities. In addition, Mohawk women received income from sale of basketry and beadwork embroidery.

In 1830 Kahnawake was legally reconstituted as an Indian reserve. The Canadian government immediately interfered with indigenous custom by allotting individual homesteads to male heads-of-households in an attempt to break up traditional matrilineal households. Years of social and economic pressure resulted in the disappearance of aboriginal household groupings, replaced by nuclear family units headed by men.

Because of Kahnawake's proximity to Montreal, trends toward urbanization grew steadily in the twentieth century. In fact, Kahnawake is now one of the most urbanized reserves in Canada. Although some residents grow a small number of crops in household gardens, farming has been eliminated as a stable source of income. Instead, residents work in Montreal and nearby towns and cities. In 1999, the Kahnawake Economic Development Commission, known as 'Tewatohnhi'saktha,' was established. Many opportunities are available for Kahnawake men and women, from a Young Professionals Program to personal Employment Counselors. The Commission has been quite successful in their mission to provide support for Kahnawake residents. Because of the availability of jobs in a wide range of professional, skilled, and semi-skilled occupations, per capita income at Kahnawake is among the highest for Canadian Native communities. In addition to employment in and around Montreal, residents of Kahnawake work on the reserve in Band offices, schools, health clinics, restaurants, stores, and gas stations.

One of the occupations that has attracted Kahnawake men since the late nineteenth century is that of ironwork in the construction of bridges and buildings. Interest in this industry began in 1886 when the Dominion Bridge Company negotiated with the Kahnawake Council for access to land for a railroad bridge across the St. Lawrence River from Montreal to the Québec mainland. In exchange, the company agreed to hire Kahnawake men. Since then, Mohawks from both Kahnawake and the nearby reserve of Akwesasne have been attracted to ironwork in large numbers, erecting bridges and skyscrapers throughout the Northeast (Mitchell 1960). More than 200 Mohawks were involved in the building of the One World Trade

Center, out of around 2,000 construction employees (Wallace 2012). In fact, most Akwesasne and Kahnawake men are employed in high-steel construction for at least some period of their lives, often commuting to work on a weekly basis to Buffalo, Rochester, Syracuse, New York City, and Boston.

Although ironworkers usually maintain homes at either Kahnawake or Akwesasne, families often establish residences in cities where the men work. A sizeable Mohawk community numbering nearly a thousand developed in New York City's borough of Brooklyn during peak years of construction in the 1960s and 1970s, but with declining construction since the 1980s, most Mohawk families have returned to Kahnawake and Akwesasne.

During the 1950s, the governments of Canada and the United States entered into an agreement to construct locks and other transportation facilities along the St. Lawrence River, affecting the community of Kahnawake located on the shores of the river. The Seaway Authority condemned 1,260 acres at Kahnawake and offered monetary compensation that the Band Council refused to accept. When the land was taken without their consent, Kahnawake Mohawks appealed to the UN, claiming violation of human rights protected by the UN charter. Chief Matthew Lazare petitioned the Secretary General and the Human Rights Commission:

> In violation of treaties between the Six Nations and Britain, and in contradiction to principles of international law, the Canadian authorities have deprived, and continue to deprive, our people of their inherent rights of possession of their land and property by confiscating real and personal property without due process of law and without just, adequate and prompt compensation, in connection with the opening of the St. Lawrence Seaway and other public projects. The method of confiscation is accomplished by brutal force which is unnecessary and unreasonable. (Ghobashy 1961: 57–58)

Lazare pointed out that rates of financial compensation offered to residents of Kahnawake were lower than those offered to non-Indians whose land along the Seaway project was also taken. Lazare and others hoped that the UN would exert pressure on Canada to "reverse its policy of depriving our sacred Reserve which is the only thing of value left to us, and to refrain from further encroachment on our land and infringement of our rights" (60). Although UN delegates sent sympathetic responses to the Kahnawake Council, they took no action to solve the problem.

In an important development in political relations, Québec officials signed a government-to-government agreement with the Kahnawake Band Council in 1984 to construct a hospital on the reserve. This was the first time the Canadian government had, in effect, recognized the equal status and sovereignty of an Indian band. And in 1999, Kahnawake Mohawks signed a series of agreements with Québec that covered a range of economic development, local justice, and cultural matters. One of the agreements broadened Mohawks' rights to tax immunity by not only continuing the tax-immune purchase of goods on the reserve but also enabling Kahnawake Mohawks to buy goods off-reserve without paying taxes "upon presentation of an identification card" (*Rencontre*, June 1999: 5). Further, in 2010, the Canadian government upheld a decision by the Kahnawake Council to evict 35 non-Native residents from the reserve, stating, "these are decisions made by First Nations people on their own land (...) It is not for me to make those decisions, or the Government, and we are not going to be making those decisions" (http://www.caledoniawakeupcall.com/updates/100210np.html).

The people of Kahnawake have taken a significant step in community control by constructing a high school located in their territory. The Kahnawake Survival School, provides residents with the opportunity of completing their secondary education in a high school in their own community rather than having to travel outside the reserve. The school offers a curriculum that includes instruction about Mohawk culture, language, and history, and other topics directly relevant to its students.

Improving living conditions at Kahnawake includes completion of a treatment facility for drinking water and expansion of a water reservoir to meet the community's needs. Since the population at Kahnawake has steadily increased during this century, a larger and more reliable water supply is a prerequisite for the health and safety of the community. The Kahnawake project, completed in 2012, was funded by a portion of the $2.5 billion dedicated by the Canadian government to improving water supplies and delivery systems in First Nation reserves throughout the country.

Despite the problems of land and resources, the population at Kahnawake continues to grow. According to the Kahnawake Council's official website, in 2014 the community had a resident population of around 8,000. Using 1999 percentages as a basis, approximately 1,520 additional Kahnawake currently live off-reserve.,

Kanesatake

The second Mohawk mission village of Kanesatake (ga-ne-sa-DA-ge), established in 1676, found a permanent home in 1721 at Lake-of-Two-Mountains a short distance west of Montreal. At first, residents maintained aboriginal economies and social systems, but as the city of Montreal grew, its influences resulted in an abandonment of traditional lifeways at Kanesatake.

The population at Kanesatake, like nearby Kahnawake, has become increasingly urbanized as the region of metropolitan Montreal has expanded. Because of the small size of the reserve, there is little opportunity for on-reserve work. Therefore, most residents seek jobs in Montreal or other nearby locales. Kanesatake itself has a current population (2013 statistics) of 9,925 residents. An additional 2,280 people are members of the Kanesatake band but reside elsewhere.

In the summer of 1990, the Canadian town of Oka adjacent to Kanesatake announced plans to expand a golf course into wooded land that it said it owned even though Mohawks at Kanesatake claimed that the land belonged to their reserve. In an attempt to stop construction of the golf course, a group from Kanesatake blockaded a road leading to the contested area. Québec provincial police were then called in, leading to an armed standoff between the Indians and the police that lasted about four months. One police officer was killed in crossfire but the origin of the bullet was never determined. In a show of sympathy with the protestors, residents of Kahnawake blockaded the Mercier Bridge linking their reserve to Montreal. Their action was followed by sympathy blockades in several Native communities across Canada. Appeals on behalf of the Mohawks made by the UN Subcommission on Human Rights to the premier of Québec were never answered. After months of negotiations, the Canadian government proposed to pay the town of Oka for the 92 acres of land in dispute and transfer them to Kanesatake, thereby ending the confrontation and blockade.

An additional territorial agreement was reached in 2000 providing for the transfer of about 3,000 acres of land to Kanesatake. The land is currently owned by the Canadian government pending further negotiations aimed at its eventual transfer to full Mohawk jurisdiction ("Kannesatake Mohawks Reach Land Deal with Canada" 2000).

As of 2013, the federal government has made no move to begin the transfer of land to the people of Kanesatake.

Wahta

In the 1880s, a group of people left Kanesatake and established a small reserve called Wahta (WAH-da), meaning "maple," near Parry Sound, southeast of Georgian Bay in Ontario. This settlement, also called "Gibson Reserve," had approximately 250 residents in the nineteenth century. In the twentieth century, the number of members of the Wahta Band increased, although the on-reserve population has actually declined. In 2013, there were a total of 687 band members, but only 166 lived at Wahta. Economic opportunities are extremely limited. Some residents of Wahta own cranberry farms where they produce 10–25 percent of Canada's cranberries, but most people obtain jobs off-reserve on farms or in factories and other businesses.

Akwesasne

Akwesasne (ah-gwe-SAHS-ne), the third settlement of Catholic Mohawks, was founded between 1747 and 1755 by emigrants from Kahnawake at a location along the St. Lawrence River approximately 80 mi. southwest of Montreal. The site was chosen because of its rich soil and easy access to water and timber. French authorities in Montreal encouraged the new settlement because they wanted to have an outpost along the western St. Lawrence.

Soon after its founding, residents of Akwesasne became embroiled in the American Revolution. Although most sided with the British, many fought in support of the rebels. Regardless of their allegiance, the peace agreement between Great Britain and the United States affected the future integrity of Akwesasne since the Treaty of Paris set the boundary between Canada and the United States at 45 degrees north latitude, arbitrarily dividing Akwesasne into Canadian and American sections. Then, in 1791, New York State unilaterally sold a large tract of Akwesasne territory to a New Yorker named Alexander Macomb, leaving Mohawks with an area of only 6 sq. mi. and two islands in the St. Lawrence. In response to Mohawk petitions, an agreement was reached in 1796 granting Akwesasne tracts of 1 sq. mi. along each of two small rivers in addition to the 6-sq. mi. area that they had retained after Macomb's purchase. But additional portions of Mohawk land were sold by New York in the first half of the nineteenth century, leaving Akwesasne with 14,000 acres in the state and 10,000 acres in Canada.

Akwesasne Mohawks were soon affected by another external war. During the War of 1812 between Great Britain and the United States, authorities in New York barred Akwesasne residents from travelling outside the reservation unless they secured official passes, thus severely limiting men's ability to pursue their accustomed hunting. In addition, people were unable to obtain clothing, tools, or other necessary provisions at posts outside the boundaries of the reservation (Hough 1853). Although the US government issued supplies to Mohawks after the people lodged protests, the power of external authorities to interfere with Native life had been amply demonstrated. As in past conflicts between European powers, although both the British and American governments agreed that Akwesasne should remain neutral, Mohawk men became involved on both sides during the war.

Once the war ended, Canada and the United States began to enforce border restrictions against Akwesasne residents who, until that time, had held their land in common, ignoring the international border. The Indians were acting in accord with provisions of Jay's Treaty of 1794 that guaranteed free passage of Mohawks across the border. As a result of border restrictions, the community has been governed locally by two sets of leaders. On the Canadian side, an administrative council consisted of twelve chiefs chosen from kinship groups in accordance with traditional customs. Three chiefs were selected for life terms of service from each of the four clans (Wolf, Turtle, Bear, and Snipe). Today, the twelve members of the Band Council are elected by popular vote. In New York, a council of three trustees, serving three-year terms, carried out government functions. The trustees have been replaced by three Tribal chiefs who are elected by Akwesasne residents. In addition to the elected representatives, the Mohawk Council of Chiefs (now the Mohawk Council of Akwesasne) is composed of hereditary clan chiefs selected by clan mothers in the traditional Iroquoian manner. These chiefs are not recognized by the US or Canadian authorities, but they are respected by the people themselves and have prestige and influence at Akwesasne. Members of the Canadian Band Council, the American Tribal Council, and the traditional Mohawk Council of Akwesasne have formed a "Tri-Council" to discuss and resolve matters of community concern.

In the early twentieth century, Akwesasne Mohawks reasserted claims to some of their aboriginal territory. A state commission of inquiry, headed by Edward Everett,. declared:

> The passing of the title for this ceded territory to the Indians of this state was a legal and proper transaction. And the Indians, as a nation, became possessed of the ceded territory.
>
> The said Indians of the State of New York, as a nation, are still the owners of the fee simple title to the territory ceded to them by the Treaty of 1784, unless divested of the same by an instrument of equal force and effect as the said treaty of 1784. (Quoted in Upton 1980: 103)

In all, Everett concluded that New York Iroquois retained ownership of 6 million acres of land in New York State. State authorities predictably objected to his findings and refused to recognize Native rights

Although Akwesasne territory is predominantly rural, many of its residents participate through their employment in Canadian/American urban life. Akwesasne men often work in the high-steel construction industry along with their brethren from Kahnawake. They too commute long distances to work in cities in the United States and Canada. Residents are also employed in a wide variety of professional, skilled, and semiskilled occupations in nearby cities and towns. And some people work in band or tribal offices, schools, clinics, stores, restaurants, and other businesses located in the community.

Problems of loss of land and treaty rights continue to plague the people of Akwesasne. Construction of the St. Lawrence Seaway project affected Akwesasne since, like Kahnawake, it is located on the shores of the St. Lawrence River. At Akwesasne, the Seaway Authority removed 88 acres at Raquette Point on the American side of the river, promising a payment of $100,000, only $31,000 of which has yet been paid. In addition, the Authority took Barnhardt Island in the St. Lawrence to build a large dam. The three-member Akwesasne Council in New York sued for $34 million in compensation, a claim rejected by state courts and later denied by the US Supreme Court. Despite these decisions, Akwesasne Mohawks have pursued the case and are currently negotiating with the government for a just settlement for Barnhardt Island.

On the Canadian side of Akwesasne, the Seaway Authority expropriated land at Cornwall Island to

A sign posted to a Route 37 marker in June 2009. Route 37 runs through the New York Mohawk Akwesasne Territory; the Canadian government wanted to arm their borders, which was being disputed by Canadian Mohawks.

Policies enforcing customs inspections were not altered until the 1980s. Since then, Akwesasne Mohawks are finally able to exercise rights of free passage guaranteed by George Washington and King George III. Then, in an important treaty-rights ruling in 1998, the Canadian Federal Court of Appeal confirmed the Mohawks' right to "cross the border with goods duty-free for personal and community use and for trade with other First Nations" ("Supreme Court of Canada to Hear Case on Mohawk Border Crossing Rights" 1999: 1).

The issue of border crossings at Akwesasne has been a contentious problem for decades. Many people in the community consider themselves Haudenosaunee citizens and do not identify as citizens of either the United States or Canada. But because the international border runs through their territory, they are frequently faced with the federal authority exerted by these two countries. Various arrangements have been worked out so that members of both the Canadian Akwesasne First Nation and the US St. Regis Mohawk Tribe can cross the border by showing membership cards. The issue of tariffs on goods brought from one side to the other, however, has remained problematic. In 1988, Michael Mitchell, grand chief of the Mohawk Council of Akwesasne, crossed the border into Canada bringing some blankets, bibles, food, clothing, a washing machine, and some motor oil that he had purchased in the United States. He declared these goods but refused to pay duty taxes, stating that he was intending to deliver all of these items (except the motor oil) as gifts to the Mohawk community at Tyendinega. Mitchell claimed exemption from taxes on the basis of aboriginal rights, citing the traditional practices of travel and trade engaged in by his Mohawk ancestors for centuries prior to European settlement.

This case eventually made its way to the Supreme Court of Canada so that the Justices could decide on the issue of aboriginal rights. Their ruling, handed down in 2001, refused to accept Mitchell's claim. Although they recognized the validity of the concept of aboriginal rights and agreed that aboriginal practices are likely to change in modern contexts, they stated that no clear evidence indicated an aboriginal Mohawk pattern of significant trade to the north of traditional Mohawk territory, declaring that the aboriginal pattern of trade was to the east and west.

This debate has not been settled, and in 2009, a protest against alleged Human Rights abuses by Canadian Border Services Officers caused the port of entry to become temporarily vacant. The Cornwall City Police

build an international bridge between Ontario and New York. It condemned additional acreage there for a Canadian customs station and toll booths.

The customs station and toll collection raised serious issues concerning treaty rights. According to Jay's Treaty of 1794 signed between Great Britain and the United States, residents of Akwesasne have rights to freely cross the border, rights the Seaway Authority ignored by compelling the people to undergo customs inspections and pay tolls at the international bridge. After years of attempting mediation, Akwesasne residents blockaded the bridge during the winter of 1969. Canadian authorities then began issuing bridge passes to Mohawks enrolled on the Canadian side of Akwesasne but denied them to those on the American side.

and New York State Police coordinated to block the border and the Akwesasne were denied access to the crossing for over a month after refusing to accept the presence of armed guards on their territory.

The decision in the Mitchell case and the recent decisions by the Canadian government significantly curtail the exercise of indigenous sovereignty in the sense that they disallow the community's ability to make their own regulations that affect their own members. Instead, the sovereign authority of what many Mohawks view as a foreign power takes precedence. In the 1970s, Akwesasne residents, led by hereditary chiefs, began to claim rights to lands that had been taken without treaty or compensation. After occupying two islands in the St. Lawrence River for several months in 1970, Canadian authorities recognized their ownership of the territory. And in New York, the Mohawk Council of Chiefs has filed suit for about 11,600 acres of land and islands that it claims were illegally taken ("Mohawks Statement on Land Claims" 1996: 1). The Mohawks have been negotiating with state officials for many years, but in 1996, Governor George Pataki broke off the talks. The lands and claims remain in dispute.

In a Canadian land claims case filed by the Akwesasne Mohawks, Mohawk and Canadian officials agreed in 2012 to compensation amounting to about $5 million dollars to settle a claim dating back to the 1820s. The suit claimed funds for lands leased between 1820 and 1934 that had not been paid for. The land itself is now part of the Akwesasne Reserve.

Another issue of longstanding concern to Akwesasne residents is the pollution of air, water, and land that emanates from several industrial plants operated by Alcoa, Reynolds Metals, and General Motors nearby in New York State. Chemicals such as PCBs (polychlorinated biphenyls, a likely carcinogen), insecticides, and other toxins have been leaking into the land and water from dumping sites. Autopsies of animals in and near Akwesasne reveal the absorption of more than 500 environmental contaminants (Grinde and Johansen 1995: 175). PCBs, derived from chemicals used at the GM plant, have destroyed many of the fish in Akwesasne's rivers and rendered the remaining fish dangerous for human consumption. In 1981, NY State's Department of Environmental Conservation found harmful levels of PCBs in the reservation's groundwater and concluded that a reversal of the contamination was "not practical" (177). In addition, the Reynolds Metals plant emits flourides that have been found to weaken the bones and teeth of cattle. The loss of fish and cattle has hurt the people's subsistence base since many had relied on these sources of food to supplement their diet. Increased rates of birth defects among Akwesasne children have been another source of worry for the people and their future.

The environmental and health effects of the dumping of PCB's and other contaminants by General Motors and Alcoa continue to be seen at Akwesasne. The General Motors factory, located upriver from the Akwesasne St. Regis Reserve, operated from 1958 until 2009 during which time it dumped contaminated waste in the area. After the area was declared a Superfund site by the US Environmental Protection Agency, General Motors agreed to remove the toxic wastes but some still remain, including a 12-acre landfill topped with a layer of clay and grass. Although the EPA considers this a safe solution, many residents and some scientific studies claim that leakage of PCBs and other toxins continue to affect the land and water, therefore also posing health risks to people and animals. Unusually high levels of PCBs have been found in Mohawk adolescents and in the breast milk of Akwesasne mothers. Additional studies have linked the presence of PCBs to decreases in thyroid hormones and to diabetes in adults, a serious health problem at Akwesasne.

In 2013, the US Environmental Protection Agency announced a settlement that awards the St. Regis Mohawk Tribe at Akwesasne funds of $20.3 million dedicated to resolving problems of pollutants emitted by Alcoa and Reynolds Metals. Most of the money will be used for cleanup of contaminated lands and restoration of bird, fish, and animal habitats. In addition, $8.4 million is earmarked for supporting cultural projects, including programs that support and promote Mohawk language learning, educational programs for young people, and farming practices dedicated to medicine, healing, and nutrition ("Public, Environment to Benefit from $20.3 million from Two Settlements for Natural Resource Damage in St. Lawrence River Area" 2013: 5). The inclusion of cultural projects in the settlement is recognition of the damage done to Mohawk cultural practices because of the loss of lands, resources, and livelihood due to contamination.

To deal with a serious problem of water contamination at Akwesasne, the Nation began operating an advanced water treatment facility in 2006. At that time, an estimated 70 percent of wells serving the community were contaminated, a consequence of industrial runoff and pollution from the nearby Reynolds Aluminum plant. The treatment plant was several years in the planning stage in order to ensure protection of the environment, taking particular care not to disturb animal, fish, and vegetation habitats. Especially important were the groves of butternut and black ash trees, valued for medicinal purposes. The water treatment facility now serves several hundred households. In addition, the community operates a laboratory that analyzes the quality of water delivered through the system as well as specimens of water from existing wells to determine their safety for human consumption. The Akwesasne Mohawks are developing plans to extend the water treatment network to many more homes in the community.

The population at Akwesasne is the largest of all of the Mohawk communities. Since the reservation straddles the border between the United States and Canada, it can be difficult to obtain accurate population data, considering some Akwesasne people are likely counted in both censuses. However, combining figures from the Mohawk Council of Akwesasne and the St. Regis Mohawk Tribe, the total population living at Akwesasne is approximately 23,000. An additional 1,800 people were members of the band or tribe but resided elsewhere. Economic statistical estimates gathered by the US Census in 2014 for the American portion of Akwesasne, based on income earned in 2010, reported a per capita income of $16,829, which is substantially above the overall American Indian per capita income of $16,645. Since 1999, the fortunes of the Akwesasne have turned bleak. In 2014, median household income stood at $33,676, below the average American Indian figure of $36,779, and both individual and household income at Akwesasne were substantially below the norm for their neighbors: $58,687 median household income and $32,829 per capita for New York State. Poverty rates at Akwesasne are more than double those for the region: 25.4 percent of American Akwesasne families and 48.5 percent of individuals are below the official poverty level, compared to Northeastern averages of 12.0 percent for families and 25.3 percent for individuals. (US Bureau of the Census, 2010–2014 American Community Survey 5-Year Estimates). No specific employment data were collected on the reservation. Unemployment rates for the reservation were 9.5 percent as opposed to 5.6 percent for New York residents.

Ganienkeh

In 1974, a group of Mohawks, mostly from Akwesasne and Kahnawake, moved into an unoccupied children's camp at Moss Lake in the Adirondack Mountains of New York that had been purchased by the state shortly before. The land, lying within the Adirondack State Park, was in an area claimed by Mohawks as part of their aboriginal territory never legally sold to New York. Nearby non-Indian residents objected to the move and filed petitions with the state to oust the Mohawks. At first, state authorities refused to intervene, but after a number of violent incidents between Mohawks and town residents, state police set up roadblocks. The police protected the Mohawks by escorting cars along the road, but they were refused entry into the camp. After occupying the camp for three years, the Indians agreed to exchange the site for state land in Clinton County near Altona. Non-Indian residents of Altona then filed suit to have the Mohawks evicted but in 1981 the NY Court of Appeals denied the request, allowing the Indians to remain (Landsman 1988).

The Mohawks named their new community Ganienkeh (ga-NYEN-ge) "at the flint." The people initially hoped to reestablish aspects of traditional Mohawk culture at Ganienkeh but have not been able to produce enough food from the land to make that possible. Most people there are only part-time residents, continuing to work outside the community.

Tyendinaga

During the American Revolution, a group of Mohawks loyal to Great Britain left New York and established a settlement at Lachine, Québec, on the north shore of the Bay of Quinte on the Northeastern waterways of Lake Ontario. The land was purchased in 1783 and settled a year later by Capt. John Deserontyon and his followers. The village was named Tyendinaga ((tie-yen-di-NA-ga)), the Mohawk name of Joseph Brant. It was first administered locally by a council of eleven hereditary chiefs chosen for life from the eleven matrilineal groups that first settled there. It is now governed by an elected band council in accordance with Canadian law regulating representation on Native reserves.

In order to upgrade housing and provide modern services to the community, the Tyendinega Band Council embarked on a program of house construction, emphasizing energy efficiency and conservation. The new houses, completed in 2012, have high-efficiency gas furnaces and ventilation systems for heat recovery. They are available for rental or sale to community members. Residents of the houses report an average 40 percent decrease in their energy bills.

Given its small size and rural location, job opportunities at Tyendinaga are limited. People work on nearby farms or in towns, often in Belleville, located some 8 mi. away. Lack of employment is reflected in the fact that the resident population is approximately half as large as the nonresident band membership. Figures for 2015 indicated that 2,160 Mohawks lived at Tyendinaga while 7,333 additional band members resided away from their home community.

Six Nations

The last community of Mohawks was founded in 1784 in Canada by followers of Joseph Brant. The settlement, called Six Nations because its inhabitants were members of all the nations of the Iroquois Confederacy, was located along the Grand River in southern Ontario, a short distance from the American border city of Buffalo. The land had been purchased for the Iroquois by Sir Frederick Haldimand, governor of Canada, from the Mississaugas. Haldimand was fulfilling a pledge he made during the Revolution to compensate Indians who fought for England for any losses they suffered as a result of their loyalty. The tract encompassed 6 mi. of land along both sides of the Grand River, totaling 675,000 acres. In 1785, Six Nations had 1,600 residents, including 450 Mohawks, 380 Cayugas, 200 Onondagas, 165 Oneidas, 125 Tuscaroras, and 75 Senecas.

Members of each nation set up separate villages along the Grand River. As in other displaced Mohawk communities, people at Six Nations tried to reestablish their aboriginal traditions as much as possible. As a symbol of determination to assert Iroquois identities and traditions, clan chiefs rekindled the Confederacy fire at the Onondaga village at Six Nations. Local government was managed by a council composed of hereditary chiefs from all the nations. Although the six nations were equals, Mohawk prominence was evidenced by the fact that all chiefs spoke the Mohawk language in council deliberations.

Joseph Brant had considerable influence on politics at Six Nations. Although Brant believed that the Iroquois should be politically sovereign in their new home, he also thought that they should adopt Canadian/American economic practices. And he urged leaders to sell a large portion of land to Canadian farmers so that the Iroquois could learn "modern" farming techniques and so that funds from the sale could be used to buy food

and clothing for indigent Iroquois until they could provide for themselves. After years of debate, a large section of land amounting to 350,000 acres was sold to Canadians, many of whom were friends of Brant (Weaver 1972). But despite Brant's plans, most Iroquois retained small farms, planted by women with traditional crops using aboriginal farming methods. Still, a few people amassed larger holdings, adopted plough technology introduced by Canadians, and grew crops such as oats, wheat, and peas. Significantly, these farmers were men, reflecting a shift from the traditional Iroquoian gender roles. Farm production gradually increased in the first half of the nineteenth century until many families at Six Nations were fairly prosperous, producing enough surplus to sell at markets in nearby cities such as Brantford and Hamilton, Ontario.

Influences from Canadian society intensified. Protestant missionaries built churches and schools at Six Nations in the early nineteenth century. In addition to formal education, schools taught domestic skills to girls and farming techniques to boys in an attempt to alter traditional gender roles to conform to Canadian ideals. Fearing that exposure to Canadian education would result in increased assimilation and eventual loss of independence, Mohawks took the lead in establishing their own schools. By 1880, thirteen such schools were operating (Weaver 1972).

Pressures to sell additional acreage continued at Six Nations but the people obtained status as a reserve in order to protect land from sales to non-Indians without public approval through a referendum. At the same time, the Canadian government assumed responsibility for evicting illegal squatters. The Canadian government then initiated a program of dividing lands into individual family allotments. Beginning in 1847, male heads of nuclear households received parcels of 100 acres each. Within one year, 325 families, consisting of 1,271 individuals, had complied with the program. The government's policy had far-reaching cultural consequences. First, it stressed concepts of individual rather than communal ownership of land, thus eroding Iroquois unity. Second, land was allotted to nuclear families, resulting in the breakup of large extended families that had been the basis of economic cooperation and interdependence. And third, the program assigned land to men, undermining the roles and rights of women as producers and controllers of basic subsistence. Not surprisingly, women resisted the changes because they recognized the danger to their own status.

Throughout the second half of the nineteenth century, farming continued to gain importance as a source of subsistence and of income from the sale of products, but by the early years of the twentieth century, the role of agriculture at Six Nations had declined. Small farms were gradually abandoned because they were not financially profitable. However, several large farms were quite prosperous, producing corn, oats, and wheat. People also kept dairy and beef cattle, poultry, hogs, and sheep. They sold surplus produce, milk, and animals in nearby Canadian cities. However, it was not long before these enterprises began to face financial difficulties. The years of the Depression in the 1930s were especially hard. In order to continue successful production and keep pace with technological improvements, Six Nations farmers needed money to invest in new equipment, but Indians living on reserves had difficulty obtaining bank loans because their land was held in trust by the Band and therefore could not be used as collateral for a loan. Since the Depression, farming has continually decreased its contribution to reserve incomes.

During the early years of the twentieth century, conflicts arose at Six Nations regarding the local form of government. Hereditary chiefs who formed the councils tended to be traditionalists; they spoke Native languages and opposed rapid assimilation of Canadian practices. Although the chiefs agreed on many matters, religious differences among them caused animosities that made consensus difficult. As a result, a group of Mohawks petitioned for a change from hereditary chieftainships to a system of elected representatives. Calling themselves the "Dehorners" after the traditional method of "dehorning" or impeaching clan chiefs, they thought that an elected council would be more responsive to the people. However, others at Six Nations preferred to keep the traditional council, arguing that hereditary chiefs symbolized the continuity and sovereignty of the Iroquois Confederacy.

After refusing to mediate the dispute for many years, the Canadian Parliament acted in 1924 to unilaterally dissolve the hereditary system of leadership and promoted an elective system to "modernize" the reserve. Elections were held to select twelve members to serve for two-year terms. At first, only men voted in reserve elections, but suffrage was extended to women in 1951.

Controversy over leadership did not end, however. Hereditary chiefs and 1,300 supporters tried to oust the elected council and reinstate Confederacy chiefs by taking over the Band Council offices in 1959 and proclaiming the end of the elective system. The dissidents occupied the Council house for one week but were evicted by the R.C.M.P. (Royal Canadian Mounted Police) (Weaver 1972). Despite the failure of the traditionalists' actions, dissatisfaction with the elective system continues at Six Nations as well as at other reserves. Hereditary chiefs in all Mohawk communities wield considerable social and political influence even though they do not hold official positions on governing councils. The population at Six Nations includes members of all six Iroquois groups. In 2013, the reserve had a total band membership of 25,660, with 13,389 of that number residing off-reservation. The Six Nations comprises thirteen registry groups, making it the most numerous First Nations band in Canada. Mohawks constitute the largest registry group, but the exact percentage of Mohawks in the Six Nations community is unknown Based on 1999 percentages, in can be estimated that there are 6,136 Mohawks living on-reservation at Six Nations and 6,700 residing in other communities.

Contemporary Populations

Combining the statistics for all Mohawk communities, there are approximately 61,390 Mohawks living in Canada and the United States. Canada estimates that around 45 percent, or 18,900, of Canadian Mohawks live off-reservation, and similar numbers are estimated for the US Mohawk population. This figure represents a considerable increase since the end of the last century when the reservations and reserves had a combined total population of only 6,981. Table 5.1 summarizes the current population numbers by community and by residency.

TABLE 5.1	Mohawk Populations		
	Resident	**Nonresident**	**Total**
Kahnawake	8,000	1,520	9,520
Kanesatake	9,925	2,280	12,205
Tyendinaga	321	1,021	700
Wahta	166	521	687
Six Nations Mohawks	6,136	6,700	12,836
Akwesasne	23,000	1,800	24,800
TOTALS	47,548	13,842	61,390

REFERENCES

Bonvillain, Nancy. 1980. "Iroquoian Women." *Papers on Iroquoian Research* (ed. N. Bonvillain). Occasional Publications in Northeastern Anthropology no. 6, *Man in the Northeast*, pp. 47–58.

Bonvillain, Nancy. 1986. "The Iroquois and the Jesuits: Strategies of Influence and Resistance." *American Indian Culture & Research Journal* 10, no. 1: 29–42.

Brown, Judith. 1975. "Iroquois Women: An Ethnohistoric Note." *Toward an Anthropology of Women* (ed. R. Reiter). New York: Monthly Review Press, 235–251.

Champlain, Samuel de. 1907. *Voyages of Samuel de Champlain 1604–1618* (ed. W. L. Grant). New York: Charles Scribner's Sons.

Charlevoix, Pierre de. [1744]1966. *Journal of a Voyage to North America.* 2 vols. New York: Readex Microprint.

Frisch, Jack. 1978. "Iroquois in the West." *The Northeast* (ed. B. Trigger), vol. 15 of HNAI. Washington, DC: Smithsonian Institution, pp. 544–546.

Ghobashy, Omar. 1961. *The Caughnawaga Indians and the St. Lawrence Seaway.* New York: Devin-Adair.

Grassman, Thomas. 1969. *The Mohawk Indians and Their Valley: Being a Chronological Documentary Record to the End of 1693.* Schenectady, NY: Eric Hugo Co.

Grinde, Donald, and Bruce Johansen. 1995. *Ecocide of Native America: Environmental Destruction of Indian Lands and Peoples.* Santa Fe, NM: Clear Light Publishers.

Hewitt, J. N. B. 1933. "Status of Women in Iroquois Polity before 1784." *Smithsonian Institution Annual Report for 1932.* Washington, DC, pp. 475–488.

Hough, Franklin. 1853. *A History of St. Lawrence and Franklin Counties, New York, from the Earliest Period to the Present Time.* Albany, NY: Little and Company.

Jesuit Relations and Allied Documents 1610–1791 (JR). 1896–1901. 73 vols. (ed. R. G. Thwaites). Cleveland, OH: Burrows Brothers.

Jameson, J. Franklin (ed.). 1909. *Narratives of New Netherland, 1609–1664.* New York: Charles Scribner's Sons.

Jennings, Francis. 1984. *The Ambiguous Iroquois Empire.* New York: W.W. Norton.

"Kannesatake Mohawks Reach Land Deal with Canada." 2000. *Indian Time* May 23.

Lafitau, Joseph. [1724]1974. *Customs of the American Indians Compared with the Customs of Primitive Times.* Toronto: The Champlain Society.

Lahontan, Louis de. [1703]1905. *New Voyages to North America,* 2 vols. (ed. R. Thwaites). Chicago, IL: A.C. McClurg.

Landsman, Gail. 1988. *Sovereignty and Symbol: Indian-White Conflict at Ganienkeh.* Albuquerque, NM: University of New Mexico Press.

Lounsbury, Floyd. 1960. *Iroquois Place-Names in the Champlain Valley.* Albany, NY: State University of NY, State Education Department.

Megapolensis, Johannes. [1644]1909. "A Short History of the Mohawk Indians." *Narratives in New Netherlands* (ed. J. F. Jameson). New York: Charles Scribner's Sons, pp. 163–180.

Mitchell, Joseph. 1960. "The Mohawks in High Steel." *Apologies to the Iroquois* (ed. Edmund Wilson). New York: Farrar, Strauss, & Cudahy, pp. 1–36.

"Mohawks Statement on Land Claims." 1996. *Indian Time* October 11: 1, 4.

Nammack, Georgiana. 1969. *Fraud, Politics, and the Dispossession of the Indians: The Iroquois Land Frontier in the Colonial Period.* Norman, OK: University of Oklahoma Press.

Noon, John. 1949. *Law and Government of the Grand River Iroquois.* New York: Viking Fund Publications in Anthropology, no. 12.

Richter, Daniel. 1983. "War and Culture: The Iroquois Experience." *William & Mary Quarterly* 3rd Series, 40: 528–559.

Richter, Daniel. 1987. "Ordeals of the Longhouse: The Five Nations in Early American History." *Beyond the Covenant Chain: The Iroquois and Their Neighbors in Indian North America, 1600–1800* (ed. D. Richter and J. Merrell). Syracuse, NY: Syracuse University Press.

Rencontre. 1999. June. Québec: Secretariat aux affaires autochtones.

"RJR Nabisco unit admits smuggling." 1998. *The New York Times* December 23: B1, B5.

Sagard-Theodat, Gabriel. [1632]1939. *The Long Journey to the Country of the Hurons* (ed. G. Wrong). Toronto: The Champlain Society.

Shimony, Annemarie. 1961. *Conservatism among the Iroquois at the Six Nations Reserve.* New Haven, CT: Yale University Press.

Starna, William. 1980. "Mohawk Iroquois Populations: A Revision." *Ethnohistory* 27, no. 4: 371–382.

"Supreme Court of Canada to Hear Case on Mohawk Border Crossing Rights."1999. *Indian Time* October 15: 1.

Tooker, Elizabeth. 1970. *The Iroquois Ceremonial of Midwinter.* Syracuse, NY: Syracuse University Press.

Upton, Helen. 1980. *The Everett Report in Historical Perspective: The Indians of New York.* Albany, NY: New York State American Revolution Bicentennial Commission.

US Bureau of the Census. 2010. *2010–2014 American Community Survey 5-Year Estimates.* Washington, DC.

Vernon, Howard. 1978. "The Dutch, the Indians and the Fur Trade in the Hudson Valley, 1609–1664." *Neighbors and Intruders: An Ethnohistorical Exploration of the Indians of Hudson's River* (ed. L. Hauptman and J. Campisi). Ottawa: National Museum of Man Mercury Series no. 39, pp. 197–209.

Wallace, V. 2012. *The Mohawk Ironworkers: Rebuilding the Iconic Skyline of New York. Time Magazine.* Online.

Weaver, Sally. 1972. *Medicine and Politics among the Grand River Iroquois: A Study of the Non-Conservatives.* Ottawa: National Museum of Man Publications in Ethnology no. 4.

The Mi'kmaqs

"Wejgwapniag" (the name of the new village school at a Mi'kmaq reserve in Québec): It's "the time of day just before sunrise." It means a new beginning. At Wejgwapniag, we prepare our children for the outside world, just as the sun prepares itself before rising from behind the mountain.

Rencontre, June 1987: 10

THE MI'KMAQS (MIK-MAK) are an Algonkian-speaking people indigenous to territory in what is now eastern Canada adjacent to the Gulf of St. Lawrence. Prior to European colonization, they inhabited Nova Scotia, Prince Edward Island, the eastern third of New Brunswick, and the southern half of the Gaspé Peninsula in Québec. The Mi'kmaq language is the northernmost member of the eastern Algonkian family. In their own speech, the people call themselves "lnu" or "the people" (currently meaning "Indian"). The name "Mi'kmaq" may derive from "mi:kmaw" (probably meaning "allies") or from "nikmaq" (a greeting that translates as "my kin friends") (Bock 1978: 109, 121; Prins 1996: 2).

ABORIGINAL CULTURE

Territory

Aboriginal Mi'kmaq territory was divided into seven named districts, each inhabited by bands whose membership fluctuated from year to year. A band was more a territorial than a social unit. It was composed at any one time of people who hunted in a given district and who camped together in the spring and summer. Some districts were the habitual territory of only one band while others contained members of several bands. Composition of the bands was unstable as people shifted membership depending upon availability of resources, marriage alliances, and personal choices. A number of the bands were represented by symbols such as a salmon or a cross-like design that were carved into canoes or painted on clothing as a mark of identification.

The "head district" of Mi'kmaq territory was located in "Onamag," known today as Cape Breton Island. Nearby were two districts, Pictou and Esgigeoag, that were politically subordinate to the head district. Another district occupied the central region of Nova Scotia. Further away, on the western end of Nova Scotia and in the Gaspé, New Brunswick, and Prince Edward Island, were three additional districts that were thought of as the "outer ends" (Bock 1978: 110).

Economies

Mi'kmaq economy was based on foraging. Most subsistence tasks were assigned according to gender, although some were performed cooperatively by both men and women. In general, men were responsible for hunting and fishing and thereby supplied the major portion of the diet. Meat came from a great variety of animals including deer, beaver, muskrat, otter, moose, bear, elk, and dog. The latter were also kept as domesticated animals, helping hunters locate large game and beaver lodges.

Hunters used different techniques in pursuit of different game. They were armed with bows and arrows and spears but also used snares and deadfall traps to catch animals. Elaborate hunting methods were employed when pursuing moose. Wearing disguises, hunters attracted the animals by blowing through callers made of birch bark. During the moose's mating season, hunters imitated the call of female moose and "with a dish of bark would take up some water and let it fall into the water from a height. The noise brought the male, who thought it was a female making water" (Wallis and Wallis 1955: 37). Unlike some hunting peoples, Mi'kmaq men usually hunted singly. Cooperative labor was only required for stalking large animals, harpooning seals, and clearing out beaver lodges.

In addition to land species, sea mammals and many kinds of fish were caught in the ocean and in the numerous rivers and lakes in Mi'kmaq territory. Favorite varieties included salmon, sturgeon, cod, trout, smelt, eels, and several kinds of shellfish. Seals were occasionally caught along coastal sites.

Fish were caught with bone fishhooks and nets. On occasion, men fished cooperatively by constructing weirs across rivers. At night, they caught salmon by first attracting them to their canoes using torches and then piercing them with wooden spears. Waterfowl were attracted and killed in similar fashion. Sea mammals were caught with clubs or harpoons.

Women's subsistence tasks included cooking meals and preserving foods for later use. Meat was roasted over fire, sometimes suspended from a twisted cord that rotated as it cooked. An alternative cooking technique was to boil meat in a large wooden trough made from the hollowed-out trunk of a tree and filled with water. Boiling was achieved by placing heated stones in the water. Fish and eels were eaten either freshly roasted on sticks or smoked. Animal grease was separated from broth when cooking or was extracted from fat by heating on hot stones. The grease was stored in birch bark boxes or animal bladders for use both as food and as body ointment to protect skin from the heat of summer, the cold of winter, and the annoyance of mosquitos.

Women gathered wild roots, nuts, and several kinds of berries. Plant resources were eaten fresh, dried, or boiled, sometimes added to meat in stews. Berries were pounded into pulp, dried, and made into small flat cakes. Preserved foods such as smoked meats, dried fruits, and nuts were stored in containers suspended from trees.

Teas were made from boiled winterberries, twigs of yellow birch, roots of sassafras, and leaves of spruce and hemlock. Mi'kmaqs also drank maple sap directly as it came from a tapped maple tree. The sap was sometimes boiled to remove most of the moisture and then hardened into small loaves or cakes. This preparation was considered a delicacy.

The only plant that aboriginal Mi'kmaqs cultivated was tobacco. According to Lescarbot, "our savages plant great store of tobacco. When they have gathered this herb, they dry it in the shade, and have certain little leather bags, hanging about their neck or at their girdles, wherein they always have some" (1928, III: 252). Tobacco was smoked in pipes as an offering during healing rituals and at council meetings. It was also sometimes smoked by men, women, and children to stave off hunger.

Clothing was made of moose hide or skins from the belly of the moose. In summer, people wore light clothing, usually only aprons tied around the

Mi'kmaq people at Tufts Cove, Nova Scotia, Canada, ca. 1871.

waist. In winter, they wore heavy moose-hide clothes consisting of leggings, short capes over their shoulders, and cloaks or robes to cover the entire outfit. Socks made from the skin of muskrat or rabbit were worn in cold weather. Clothes were cleaned with a moose-hide brush. In order to aid the cleaning process, women made a kind of soap by boiling ashes in water and adding animal fat to the mixture.

As summarized by Pierre Biard, a Jesuit missionary who visited Mi'kmaqs in Nova Scotia in the seventeenth century, women's varied work contributed significantly to Native life:

> The [women] besides the onerous role of bearing and rearing the children, also transport the game from the place where it has fallen; they are hewers of wood and drawers of water; they make and repair the household utensils; they prepare food; they skin the game and prepare the hides, sew garments, catch fish and other shellfish; often they even hunt; they make the canoes, set up tents; in short, the men concern themselves with nothing but the more laborious hunting and the waging of war. (*Jesuit Relations and Allied Documents, 1610–1791* 1896–1901, 3: 77; hereafter *JR*)

Biard's summary, however, glosses over an important aspect of economic roles, namely the interdependence of tasks performed by women and men. Much of the necessary work was divided into constituent processes, assigned differently to each gender. For example, in the manufacture of snowshoes or canoes, men made the frames and women completed the item. Likewise, men made bows and arrows while women made the quivers. Hunting and fishing also involved men's and women's work. Large animals were often hunted cooperatively by the whole camp. While men generally killed the animals, women cut the meat and prepared the hides for use. Finally, women caught fish using traps and weirs constructed by men (Gonzalez 1981: 19).

Since Mi'kmaqs were primarily foragers, migration and settlement patterns revolved directly around resource availability. Dependent on natural resources, the people followed an annual cycle of movements to areas where animals and fish were seasonally abundant. Biard described the economic cycle as follows:

> In January they have the seal hunting … in February and until the middle of March, is the great hunt for Beavers, otters, moose, bears, caribou … In the middle of March, fish begin to spawn … often so abundantly that everything swarms with them. After the smelt comes the herring at the end of April; and at the same time geese, sturgeon, salmon, and the great search through the Islets for [waterfowl] eggs. From the month of May up to the middle of September, they are free from all anxiety about their food; for the cod are upon the coast, and all kinds of fish and shellfish. [In September] the eels spawn … In October and November comes the second hunt for elks and beavers; and then in December … comes a fish called by them "ponamo" which spawns under the ice. (*JR* 3: 79–83)

Biard's narration depicts a people whose livelihood was varied and relatively secure. However, there were times of scarcity when resources were limited. According to LeClercq, writing in the late seventeenth century, "when the season was not yet suitable for hunting, nor the rivers in condition for fishing," Mi'kmaqs ate "curdled blood, scrapings of skin, [and] old mocassins" (1968: 111).

Settlements, Families, and Social Norms

The size of settlements was adjusted to best exploit the resources. From the beginning of the fall hunting season until the start of spring fishing, people lived in small camps composed of at most several nuclear families who were generally linked through men, either on the basis of kinship or friendship. In the springtime, large groups, numbering 200 or more, formed in villages along the coast or on the banks of rivers where fish and waterfowl were caught. Each group, sometimes referred to as a "band," had its accustomed site along the coast or river where they camped. Bilateral kinship ties helped solidify such settlements, but they were not the sole basis of residence or cooperation. Bonds created by marriage or by friendship might also organize residential groups. Band composition itself varied from year to year so that membership in any given group was not necessarily consistent over time.

Mi'kmaqs lived in rounded or elliptical homes covered with birch bark, animal skins, or woven mats. The floors were covered with boughs and grass. Bedding was made of animal furs placed on the floor. Dwellings contained a central hearth for cooking and heating. Women constructed the houses when settling in a new camp, completing them within an hour or two after arrival at a chosen site. According to Biard:

> The women go to the woods and bring back some poles which are stuck into the ground in a circle around the fire and at the top are interlaced in the form of a pyramid. Upon the poles they throw some skins, matting, or bark. All the space around the fire is strewn with leaves of the fir tree, so that they will not feel the dampness of the ground; over these leaves are thrown some mats or sealskins soft as velvet; upon this they stretch themselves around the fire; and they are very warm in there around that fire, even in the greatest rigors of the winter. In the summer the shape of their houses changes; for then they cover them with bark or mats of tender reeds, and so skillfully woven, that when they are hung up the water runs along their surface without penetrating them. (*JR* 3: 177)

Dwellings generally housed one family, either a nuclear or extended unit. Some domestic units consisted of polygynous households, while others were enlarged by the addition of a potential son-in-law who was obliged to work for the parents of his future wife for at least two years prior to marriage. In the spring and summer when several groups lived together in a village, houses were somewhat larger than in the winter months, although sources do not specify the family composition of resident households (Bock 1978: 112).

Members of households formed the basic units of economic cooperation, residing and travelling together. Canoes were made of birch bark, shaped into a long, narrow vessel about 8 or 10 ft. in length. They were open in the center but closed over at both ends. According to seventeenth-century descriptions, canoes were "so capacious that a single one of them will hold an entire household of five or six persons, with all their dogs, sacks, skins, kettles, and other heavy baggage" (*JR* 3: 83).

The Mi'kmaq kinship system was bilateral, recognizing as similar the relatives of both mother and father. Corporate kin groups were absent. Postmarital locality patterns were flexible, although there may have been a tendency for patrilateral affiliation following the period of service that a prospective husband performed for his intended wife's family.

Marriages were often arranged by parents, but daughters and sons were never compelled to marry against their wishes. Young girls were sometimes betrothed by the time they reached puberty to men a good deal older,

usually in their twenties. First marriages were marked by a wedding feast with meat supplied by the new husband and attended by members of the community. Parents, elder relatives, and a ritualist made ceremonial speeches to the couple concerning their responsibilities and hopes for long, successful lives. Marital relations were characterized by respect and recognition of each person's independent rights. However, if either husband or wife became dissatisfied with their partner, divorce was their option. Divorces in fact occurred frequently. Subsequent marriages were contracted by the parties concerned and involved neither service to the wife's parents nor ceremony. According to LeClercq:

> They cannot understand how one can submit to the indissolubility of marriage. "Does thou not see" they will say to you "that thou has no sense? My wife does not get on with me, and I do not get on with her. She will agree well with such a one, who does not agree with his own wife. Why dost thou wish that we four be unhappy for the rest of our days?" (1968: 243)

Social interaction was based on the principle that all people were autonomous and deserved to be treated with respect and consideration. It was thought impolite to contradict another person or to try to interfere with their actions. Ethics of sharing and generosity that arose in the familial context were extended to visitors as well. As noted by Lescarbot in the seventeenth century, "If it happens that our savages have venison or other food, all the company have part of it. They have this mutual charity [and] hospitality [receiving] all strangers (except their enemies) whom they accept in their commonality of life" (1928: 227–228).

Leadership and Community Integration

Even though community cohesion was minimal and leadership was diffuse, each band had a leader or "sagamore," a man who had some degree of control over a small territory, although the meaning of their control is not well specified in the literature. Band leadership tended to be inherited from father to son, but inheritance was by no means certain. According to Biard, the sagamore (or "saxamaw" in the Mi'kmaq language) was "the eldest son of some powerful family, and consequently also its chief and leader. All the young people of the family are at his table and in his retinue; it is also his duty to provide dogs for the chase, canoes for transportation, provisions and reserves for bad weather and expeditions" (*JR* 3: 87).

Sagamores evidently amassed extra provisions through the labor of unmarried young men who gave the chiefs all the products of their hunt. Once married, men gave sagamores only a portion of their catch. When new members joined the band, they gave the sagamore some gifts as well.

One of the responsibilities of sagamores was to apportion territories to each band for its use during the current hunting season:

> The occupation of this chief was to assign the places for hunting and to take the furs of the Indians, giving them in return whatever they needed. It is the right of the head of the nation to distribute the places of hunting to each individual. It is not permitted to any Indian to overstep the bounds and limits of the region which shall have been assigned to him in the assemblies of the elders. These are held in autumn and spring expressly to make this assignment. (LeClercq 1968: 235, 237)

Although sagamores seem to have had some measure of authority in their districts, they did not have power in a controlling or coercive sense. As LeClercq remarked, "all his [sagamore] power and authority are based only on the good will of those of his nation just in so far as it pleases them" (234). Lescarbot also noted the circumscribed influence, rather than power, of leaders:

> This Sagamos hath not an absolute authority among them, being not free nor infinite, but they conduct the people rather by example than by commandment … At every proposition [at councils] he demandeth advice and if they give consent they all make an exclamation, saying "haw!"—if not, some Sagamos will begin to speak and say what he thinketh good of it: being both the one and the other well heard. (1928: 308–309)

Sagamores had influence because of their skills, intelligence, and personality, but the degree of their influence depended on their abilities and on the willingness of band members to pay them heed or even to live in their territory. People could, and did, shift location and loyalty when it suited them best to do so.

In the summertime, sagamores from several bands met together to settle disputes and to discuss issues of common interest such as relations with other nations, trade, and war. They concluded treaties with other groups and also settled internal disputes among their members. In addition to summer meetings, councils were held whenever the appropriate situation arose, that is, especially wars and murders. As Biard described, "then messengers fly from all parts to make up the more general assembly [where] they resolve upon peace, truce, war, or nothing at all, as often happens in the councils where there are several chiefs, without order and subordination" (*JR* 3: 89–91). Biard's statement is, in fact, a good description of an egalitarian society with informal rather than formalized, coercive leadership.

Warfare

Although peace between Mi'kmaqs and their neighbors was the norm, warfare did occasionally occur. It was motivated primarily by revenge to punish an enemy for the death or injury of one's relative or friend. In some cases, a deceased relative appeared in a dream, urging their descendants to avenge them. Decisions to go to war might be taken by a council of the whole community or by a few individuals acting on their own. If a person was not able to convince others to join him in an attack against another group, he might decide to go alone, wait in ambush for the enemy, and make off after killing or injuring one or two people.

Warfare tactics centered on the use of surprise and ambush. Men set out on raids after they had been ritually prepared. War dances, feasting on dog meat, and rubbing warriors with powerful medicines protected the men from harm. Women played an important part in the ritual protection of warriors and in the prediction of the outcome of battle:

> The warriors, before setting out, built and entered a stockade, and this was besieged by the women. The men tried to make sallies; the women endeavored to keep them inside. Men who were caught were beaten and stripped. The women's victory was a good sign for the war expedition; if the men escaped, evil would result. (Wallis and Wallis 1955: 212)

Religious Beliefs and Practices

Mi'kmaq religious beliefs centered on a large number of spirit beings and forces that inhabited various regions and affected human activity. Creator or transformer beings were responsible for shaping the world into the one in which we now live. Some creator/transformer spirits were thought to have little direct effect on human life after completing their primordial acts, while others were believed to forever concern themselves with people's activity, bringing success and health or illness and misfortune. One, a "Great Spirit," seems to have been a prime creator deity, also identified as "sun." This being was invoked before setting out on important expeditions, particularly warfare and hunting. Every day at dawn, a member of each household went out of their house, greeted the rising sun, and, bowing, asked for protection for their family. This ritual was repeated at sunset as well, a time considered especially propitious.

The moon was second in importance to the sun, particularly powerful in protecting people at night. The moon also granted human fertility and aided women in childbirth.

The most feared spirit being, called "skadegamutc," was either the ghost of a dead person or the apparition of the living. It could be seen or heard anywhere, especially in the woods at night, appearing as a white light or a vague human figure and uttering the cries of the whooper owl.

Mi'kmaqs believed that human beings were created by a powerful spirit, perhaps the "great spirit," who "planted them in the ground as he did the flowers and trees" (Wallis and Wallis 1955: 144). Consistent with this belief, a Mi'kmaq chief once told a British army officer in 1765: "the land you sleep on is ours. We sprung out of the earth like the trees, the grass, and the flowers" (144).

Stories about the adventures of a spirit giant named "Gluscap" are among the most popular of Mi'kmaq literature. Gluscap is a transformer spirit who assigned living creatures to their proper habitats. Gluscap is intimately linked to the animal world since Bear is his mother and Turtle his father. His kin include Sable, Marten, and Fisher. In addition to Gluscap's role in establishing the order found in the natural world, he taught the early Mi'kmaqs how to make tools and other equipment that would enable them to adapt to their particular environment. Gluscap established social principles for Mi'kmaqs by teaching them to share and cooperate with each other. When a person displeased Gluscap or was haughty or selfish, he transformed the miscreant into an inanimate object. Mi'kmaqs today sometimes point out rock formations in the Maritimes as evidence of Gluscap's work (Guillemin 1975: 106).

Stories of Gluscap's exploits became especially popular in the nineteenth century, a time when Mi'kmaqs' independence was curtailed, their lands reduced by Canadian settlement, and their economic security threatened (Prins 1996: 168, 187).

Another giant, named "Kitpusiagana," appears in some stories as Gluscap's twin. The two are, however, rivals. Unlike Gluscap, Kitpusiagana is vengeful and aggressive. He hurts rather than helps humans and is the cause of disorder rather than harmony and order.

In addition to giants, the spirit world includes a group of dwarflike beings who function as tricksters, performing unusual deeds that are considered both comical and dangerous.

Mi'kmaqs believe that all living creatures, including humans, animals, and plants, as well as many "inanimate" objects are imbued with spirit essence that can be harnessed to enable the holder to be successful and healthy. Everyone has a store of "keskamzit" or "good luck" that in part accounts for their health, well-being, and ability to survive danger and risk. People can, however, attempt to counteract another person's good luck by thinking evil thoughts against them. Such thoughts do not cause death or illness immediately but add to the victim's bad luck or misfortune. Although everyone has good and bad luck and everyone has some spirit resources, some people have more spirit power than others. Their power enables them to foretell the future, know the location of game animals, heal illness, and perform extraordinary deeds of physical strength. A special class of people with unusual powers is that of the "ginap." A ginap is a man or woman who has magical abilities, such as the ability to travel far distances almost in an instant, perform beneficial magic, and defeat enemies simply by wishing it or by raising his/her arm against them. A final group of powerful people, called "buoin" or "puwo:win," use spirit power to harm others through witchcraft. Buoin are feared because they can make people sick or die and may also affect an entire community by causing natural disasters. Buoin cause harm by performing private rituals that include smoking tobacco and wishing evil. Their victim is thought to be struck by the buoin's bad wish and feels either a twitching or quivering sensation in their body. The amazing feats of "ginap" and "buoin" in overcoming seemingly insurmountable obstacles and defeating their enemies reached a height of popularity in the nineteenth century. According to Prins, Mi'kmaqs "created a fabulous repertoire of stories in which the political reality of powerlessness and helplessness was mysteriously turned upside down" (1996: 186).

Aboriginal Mi'kmaqs marked stages in an individual's life with ceremonies at birth, puberty or "coming of age," and death. When women were about to give birth, they left the family lodge and went into the woods or into a special hut that had been prepared for them. Women typically gave birth while kneeling on the ground or squatting and pulling against a pole or stick. They were aided by one or more female relatives who helped the mother by massaging her abdomen and sides in order to facilitate birth. In cases of difficult births or prolonged labor, specialists were called who performed songs and prayers and burned tobacco as an offering to spirits in order to ease the mother's pain and quicken the birth. Newborn babies were immediately washed in the river. They were then given oil from a bear or seal to swallow. Afterwards, they were placed on a board that was covered with soft animal fur. Cradleboards were decorated with beads or porcupine quills both to amuse the child and to indicate the mother's affection for her baby.

Coming of age (in a social, not physical sense) was marked for boys with feasts hosted by their families when they took their first step, cut their first tooth, and killed their first animal. Girls' physical maturity at menarche was noted by separation in a special hut as well as by a variety of ritual avoidances such as prohibitions against stepping over the legs of hunters or hunting equipment. Separation and avoidances were repeated each time a woman menstruated.

The final stage of life was also ritually marked. As soon as a death occurred, several young men were sent to other communities to announce the mournful news. Announcements were made with great solemnity, recounting the deeds of the deceased and inviting friends and relatives to attend the funeral. Relatives of the deceased indicated their loss by blackening their faces, cutting their hair short, and wailing for a period of three days. Preparations for burial included placing the body in a flexed position so that the knees touched the chin and wrapping it in a robe of beaver or elk. On the third day after death, the body was buried in a grave covered with bark and animal skins, surrounded by tools, utensils, and clothing contributed by each person attending the funeral. Among Mi'kmaqs on Cape Breton Island, placing the dead on scaffolds rather than burial in the earth was the general custom. The tools and utensils buried with the dead were meant to aid the deceased in the afterlife. As LeClercq described,

"If it was a man, they add his bow, arrow, spear, club, gun, powder, kettle, snowshoes etc.; if it was a woman, her axe, knife, blanket, necklaces of wampum and of beads, and her tools used for ornamenting and painting clothes, as well as the needle for sewing the canoes and lacing the snowshoes" (1968: 301).

While burial took place in complete silence, as soon as the grave was covered with earth and cedar branches the chief made a long speech reminding the mourners of the qualities and deeds of the deceased. Following the speech, a feast was held to commemorate the occasion. At the end of a one-year period of mourning, widows were permitted to remarry and all mourners were expected to resume their normal lives.

Mi'kmaqs believed that an eternal soul animated a body when a person was alive but that after death the soul left the body and journeyed to the "Land of the Souls" where it lived in settlements similar to those of the living. Souls continue to eat, drink, seek enjoyment, and rest just as they did during life. They are aided in their work by the eternal soul-like aspect of the tools and utensils that were buried with them.

In addition to feasts held at funerals, Mi'kmaqs participated in ritual feasts accompanying lifecycle ceremonies such as marriages and puberty rites. But the most elaborate were "eat-all feasts" given both in anticipation of and thanks for successful hunting expeditions. On these occasions, all of the food prepared for the event had to be eaten so that good fortune would ensue.

Mi'kmaq religion prescribed a number of ritual avoidances or taboos that honored the spirit world. Most important were actions or avoidances related to animal spirits. For example, young hunters were not permitted to eat roasted porcupine meat lest they become slow-moving like porcupines. They were also not allowed to eat certain parts of bear, moose, otter, and beaver lest they have pains in their feet. Animal bones were treated with great respect as well and were never thrown away carelessly. Bones of beaver were never given to dogs for fear that the dogs would lose their sense of smell.

Each animal species was considered different from others, having "a speech of its own which no other animal understands" (Wallis and Wallis 1955: 106). Each species was believed to be under the control or at least guardianship of an animal spirit that would be offended by thoughtless actions on the part of humans. If offended or treated dishonorably, the spirit protector would prevent their animal kind from being caught by hunters. Bear spirits were especially powerful and offenses against them were especially avoided. A further manifestation of the extraordinary power of animal spirits was their ability to change from one form to another. Some animals were believed to be transformed into another species when they reached old age. For example, bear, caribou, and moose were thought to become whales, while beavers turned into black ducks and squirrels turned into snakes.

Aboriginal Mi'kmaqs treated illness with both natural and ritual means. They had a vast knowledge of herbal medicines that they used when people became sick. According to LeClercq, "They are all by nature physicians, apothecaries, and doctors, by virtue of the knowledge and experience they have of certain herbs, which they use successfully to cure ills that seem to us incurable" (1968: 296). Natural remedies included tree barks or seeds used as emetics and animal oils, barks, and plants used to treat wounds, sores, and many internal ailments. Sweat-baths were also considered a helpful treatment for nearly every illness, particularly for chronic inflammations and internal pains. But in cases where illness did not respond to natural treatment, people sought the care of a specialist, that is, a man or woman who had the knowledge and skill to treat people through ritual means. Cures consisted of chants, prayers, and various ritual acts aimed at dislodging the disease-causing spirit that was believed to have entered the body of the sick person. LeClercq described a common healing ritual of the seventeenth century:

> The healer comes near to and draws back from the sick person: he blows several times on the affected part: he plants and drives deep into the ground a stick, to which he attaches a cord and through this he passes his head as if he would strangle himself. Here he makes his invocations until he has worked himself all into a sweat and lather, because of all these violent contortions, the devil has at length come out, and that he even holds him bound in order that he may grant health to the sick person. He shows the Indians the cord which, says he, holds the devil enchained. He cuts from it a piece, and thus lets him escape, promising that the sick man will get well. (218)

Healers possessed "medicine bags" that contained spiritually powerful objects used in curing illness and protecting people from harm:

> [The medicine bag] was made of the skin of an entire head of a moose, with the exception of the ears, which were removed. There was in it a stone the size of a nut wrapped in a box. Then there was a bit of bark on which was a figure made from black and white wampum, representing some monster. There was a little bow a foot in length, together with a cord interlaced with porcupine quills. In addition to these things, this bag contained a fragment of bark on which were represented some little children, birds, bears, beavers, and moose. Finally, I found there a stick, a good foot in length, adorned with white and red porcupine quills; at its end were attached several straps of a half foot in length, and two dozen dew-claws of moose. It is with this stick that the healer makes devilish noise, using these dew-claws as sounders. (221–222)

Although aboriginal ceremonies are no longer performed in Mi'kmaq communities, traditional beliefs about spirit forces, extraordinary powers of ginap and buoin, and stories about spirit beings such as Gluscap remain important features of contemporary Native culture.

CONSEQUENCES OF EUROPEAN TRADE AND SETTLEMENT

Since the Mi'kmaqs were located in territory along the Northeastern Coast of North America, they were among the first Native groups to meet European fishermen, traders, and explorers beginning in the sixteenth century. Although direct documentation for contacts between Mi'kmaqs and Basque, Portuguese, and French fishermen who frequented the coastal waters is lacking, some Europeans did record their knowledge of lands along the bays and inlets of Nova Scotia. Basque fishermen, for example, remarked on land that is probably the Annapolis valley of Nova Scotia: "At the beginning of the coast that turns north is a fine bay, where there is a large [Native] population; and there are in that country things of great price, also nuts, chestnuts, grapes, and other fruits, by which it appears to be a good land" (quoted in Gonzalez 1981: 9). And, when Jacques Cartier explored the region in 1534, he was met by aboriginal inhabitants who clearly had had prior contact with Europeans and were familiar with their trade goods and their interest in exchange. Cartier's first encounter with Mi'kmaqs occurred at Chaleur Bay, New Brunswick on July 7, 1534:

> And when we were half a league from the point, we caught sight of two fleets of Indian canoes that

were crossing from one side of the bay to another, which numbered in all some forty or fifty canoes. Upon one of the fleets reaching this point, there sprang out and landed a large number of Indians who set up a great clamor to make frequent signs to us to come on shore, holding up to us some furs on sticks. But as we were only one boat we did not care to go, so we rowed towards the other fleets which were on the water. And they on shore were seeing that we were rowing away, made ready to move their largest canoes to follow us. These were joined by five more of those that were coming in from the sea, and all came after our long boat, dancing and showing many signs of joy, and of their desire to be friends. (Cartier 1924: 49–50)

The next day, the Indians returned to Cartier's ships and began exchanging furs for iron goods:

The savages showed a marvelously great pleasure in possessing and obtaining these iron ware and other commodities, dancing and going through many ceremonies, and throwing salt water over their heads with their hands. They bartered all they had to such an extent that all went back naked without anything on them; and they made signs to us that they would return on the morrow with more furs. (53)

The Mi'kmaqs returned two days later, presenting the French sailors with a meal of cooked seal. They also traded furs for European hatchets, knives, and other tools and ornaments:

They numbered, both men, women, and children, more than 300 persons. Some of the women, who did not come over, danced and sang, standing in the water up to their knees. The other women, who had come over to the side where we were, advanced freely towards us and rubbed our arms with their hands. Then they joined their hands together and raised them to heaven, exhibiting many signs of joy. And so much at ease did the savages feel in our presence, that at length we bartered with them, hand to hand, for everything they possessed. (55–56)

By the end of the century, trade between Mi'kmaqs and Europeans became more frequent, centered on the exchange of beaver furs brought in by Native hunters. As European interest in Native resources grew, competition intensified between the French and British for hegemony in the region. The French initially took command of the fur trade in the Maritimes, establishing a post at Port Royal (Nova Scotia). Hundreds of European ships arrived each year to trade with indigenous nations. For example, in 1606 more than 6,000 beaver skins were shipped to Europe from Port Royal alone. Mi'kmaqs also supplied Europeans with fur from otter, martin, mink, bear, muskrat, deer, and fox.

In addition, women's handicrafts were also desired by French sailors. The most popular of the handwork was an article called "peschipoty,"

a purse of leather ornamented for holding tobacco; they are the work of the women, rather nicely made. Those Native skins have strings like the purses and all those peschipotys serve to hold tobacco or lead for hunting. The Indian women fixed the price to the fishermen according to the kind of skin and its fantastic ornamentation; it is made from porcupine quills, white, red, violet. With these they obtain many things from the sailors. There is no one of these who is not willing to obtain the peschipoty at the expense of a day's ration of sea biscuits. (Denys 1908: 447–448)

The goods that Mi'kmaqs received were initially perceived as luxuries but soon became desired and even necessary additions to aboriginal material culture. A Jesuit missionary, Gabriel Lalemant, noted the following trade items received by the Indians: "Cloaks, blankets, nightcaps, hats, shirts, sheets, hatchets, iron arrowheads, bodkins, swords, picks (to break the ice in winter), knives, kettles, prunes, Indian corn, peas, crackers or sea biscuits, tobacco" (*JR* 4: 207). Of note in Lalemant's list are items transported from Europe including clothing, tools, and dry foods. And the French were sources of products such as corn and tobacco originally derived from other Indians. That is, the French became a conduit for goods to flow from one aboriginal nation to another. By the end of the seventeenth century, the list of trade items regularly received from European merchants included traps used to snare beaver and other animals, decorative items such as earrings and bracelets, and sea biscuits or crackers that were valued especially in the winter when animal and plant resources were scarce. Mi'kmaqs also obtained small European boats that they preferred to traditional canoes. And they received weapons as trade items, replacing bone and wooden implements with iron-tipped arrows, spears, and harpoons. As Denys observed in 1672: "They practice still all the same methods of hunting with this difference, that in place of arming their arrows and spears with the bones of animals, pointed and sharpened, they arm them today with iron, which is made expressly for sale to them" (Denys 1908: 443). Denys's words indicate that just as Mi'kmaq economy shifted to focus on trade with the Europeans, the French evidently specialized one aspect of their manufacture to suit Native needs.

Although many of the trade items added positively to material culture by freeing labor time required to manufacture traditional tools, utensils, and clothing, people also obtained rum, a product that seriously undermined not only their personal lives but their economic well-being. The consumption of liquor damaged Mi'kmaqs' ability to function as rational traders in addition to its harmful effect on personal and community life:

> The traders make them [the Mi'kmaqs] quite drunk on purpose, in order to deprive these poor barbarians of the use of reason, so that the traders can deceive them more easily; and obtain almost for nothing their furs, which they [the Mi'kmaqs] would not sell except for a just and reasonable price if they were in their right minds. [Traders] thus render themselves the masters not only of the furs of the Indians, but also of their blankets, guns, axes, kettles, etc. which the traders have sold them at a very dear rate. (LeClercq 1968: 254–255)

In other words, Mi'kmaqs traded items that they had originally received from the Europeans back to the same merchants in order to obtain liquor. The Indians, then, were relieved not only of the beaver furs that they had trapped but also of the very goods that they had received for these furs when they were sober.

Involvement in trade led to the development of notions of private property and exchange for profit that gradually transformed social relations and the social fabric of Native communities. This change was well noted by some contemporary observers:

> They are so general and liberal towards one another that they seem not to have any attachment to the little they possess, for they deprive themselves thereof very willingly and in very good spirit the very moment when they know that their friends have need of it. It is true that this generous disposition is undergoing some alteration since the French, through the commerce they have with them, have gradually accustomed them to traffic and not to give anything for nothing; for, prior to the time when trade

came into use among these people, it was as in the Golden Age, and everything was common property among them. (245)

French Jesuit missionaries began their efforts among the Mi'kmaq in the early seventeenth century. Their first convert was Membertou, a "Grand Chief," but the goal of conversion was hampered by aboriginal economic and settlement patterns. Since Mi'kmaqs did not live in stable settlements, they could not be easily contacted. Missionaries therefore attempted to convince the Indians of the virtues of settled residence based on a farming economy. These "virtues," of course, were neither desired nor possible for Mi'kmaqs. Permanent residence requires an economic base that is unlike their traditional subsistence pursuits. As hunters and gatherers, the people followed annual cycles of shifting residence in dispersed and scattered camps. They were not farmers, not only because they had no interest in that mode of production, but also because it was not possible given their technology and environment to reap sufficient harvests to support their population. The missionaries, however, tried to establish colonies of settled Christian converts. Their goal coincided with the goals of traders who also benefitted from semi-permanent settlements of Indians upon whom they could rely as trading partners.

While missionaries' harangues had little effect on Mi'kmaqs of the period, the necessities of trade were more persuasive. During the eighteenth century, Mi'kmaqs adopted two alternative, but compatible, settlement patterns. In order to avail themselves of trade goods, some people established relatively stable camps near French and British trading posts. However, because the Native economy was based on hunting and trapping, men were obliged to leave the camps for extended trips into the interior. And coincidentally, as the beaver supply declined in nearby territory, these men were compelled to range further from their home bases. As a result, hunters' contact with their families became sporadic.

As European colonial penetration expanded in the Maritimes and as Indians became embroiled in conflicts as allies of either the French or British, Mi'kmaqs and some of their neighbors joined together in a "putu'swaqn" ("convention council") that became known as the Wabanaki Confederacy (Prins 1996: 119). The Confederacy, formed in the late seventeenth century, consisted principally of Mi'kmaqs, Maliseets,

Passamaquoddys, and Penobscots. Members aided each other in military conflicts. Their leaders met periodically to discuss matters of common interest and to solidify their alliance with ceremonial exchanges of gifts. The Wabanaki Confederacy generally sided with France against England and its Native allies. After the defeat of France in Canada in the middle of the eighteenth century, the Confederacy's major goal was to stem the tide of English settlement in the Maritimes. Once the border between Canada and the United States divided Wabanaki nations, the Confederacy lost its cohesion. Leaders held a final meeting in 1870 near Montreal and then disbanded until the Confederacy was rekindled in 1978 by Mi'kmaqs in Canada and Penobscots and Passamaquoddys in Maine (212). They continue to meet at alternating tribal headquarters.

In the early eighteenth century the rivalry between France and Great Britain intensified and the goals of both European governments became focused on settlement and territorial control. Reports of the period described the fertility of the land and the possible profits to be made:

> As to the country, I have never seen anything so beautiful, better, or more fertile; and I can say to you, truly and honestly, that if I had three or four laborers with me now, and the means of supporting them for one year, and some wheat to sow in the ground tilled by their labor alone, I should expect to have a yearly trade in beaver and other skins amounting to 7 or 8,000 livres, with the surplus which would remain to me and to their support. I am very sorry that I did not know before my departure what I know now; if I had, I should have left no stone unturned to bring me two or three farmers, and two hogshead of wheat, which is a mere trifle. I assure you it is delightful to engage in trade over here and to make such handsome profits. (*JR* 2)

The European population in Nova Scotia and New Brunswick rose from a mere 300 in 1650 to approximately 6,650 in 1750 (Gonzalez 1981: 25). During the same period, the Mi'kmaq population declined precipitously, an effect of the spread of European diseases such as smallpox and measles. Biard estimated the Mi'kmaqs to number 3,000 in 1616 (*JR* 2: 73) but this reflected losses that had already taken place due to "pleurisy, quinsy and dysentery, which kill them off" (*JR* 1: 177). By the middle of the eighteenth century, their numbers had fallen to only 2,000, less than one-third of the non-Indian population at the time.

Some European settlers occupied Native territory in order to establish farms, but others supplied the Indians with European goods and arranged the transport of furs brought in by Native trappers and hunters. Trading posts established in the Maritimes became centers of commercial activity that attracted increased numbers of colonists as well as Mi'kmaqs, some of whom gradually began to settle in the vicinity.

As European settlement grew, commercial activity in Nova Scotia and coastal New Brunswick expanded to include not only the fur trade but also fishery and lumber industries. Mi'kmaqs became involved in the colonial economy by supplying European merchants with resources. By the middle of the eighteenth century, Mi'kmaqs' reliance on the fur trade actually diminished while participation in fisheries increased. But although Indians benefitted from their work for European markets, they came to play a marginal role in the growing commerce of the region. They were replaced in fish and lumber industries by European colonists, who eventually occupied the most desirable lands along the Nova Scotia and New Brunswick coasts and along their interior river ways. These lands had been the favored territories of aboriginal Mi'kmaqs, who were soon replaced by European settlers.

As the international conflict between England and France intensified both in Europe and North America, Mi'kmaqs became embroiled in hostilities as allies of France. The influence of missionaries was critical in maintaining Mi'kmaq loyalty to France. Although the conflict between the French and British created insecurity in the Mi'kmaqs' lands and lives, once the French were conclusively defeated by the British in 1753, the situation actually deteriorated for the Indians since the expulsion of the French deprived them of a powerful ally. But even after France's defeat, Mi'kmaqs and their Wabanaki confederates were encouraged to raid British settlements (Prins 1996: 147). The British government was hostile toward Native communities that had supported their French rival and instituted policies that marginalized indigenous peoples. When approximately 13,000 French colonists were expelled from Acadia in 1755, they were quickly replaced by settlers from Great Britain and other European countries. More than 4,000 colonists from Scotland and Ireland and nearly 2,000 from Germany emigrated to Nova Scotia. In addition, some 7,000 settlers formerly living in Connecticut, Rhode Island, and Massachusetts took over French homesteads and also ventured further into the interior to develop new farmlands (Guillemin 1975: 54). A final wave of immigrants arrived in the late eighteenth century after the end of the American Revolution when thousands of British loyalists were given grants of land in Nova Scotia by the British government.

In addition to importing settlers who usurped Mi'kmaq territories in the expanding colony, the British deported hundreds of Mi'kmaqs to Newfoundland because they considered them dangerous to British interests. Officials also gave rewards to Nova Scotian colonists for killing Mi'kmaq males. The British government then signed a number of peace treaties with the remaining Mi'kmaq leaders and in exchange Indians received supplies of food, blankets, ammunition, and manufactured goods. The economic and territorial changes that had occurred had been greatly to the Indians' disadvantage, as a Mi'kmaq named Peter Paul recalled,

That time everything plenty; salmon, trout, eels, otter, martin, foxes, wildcat and good many more. My father have a coat—inside beaver, outside otter. That time plenty of fresh fish summer, dry 'em for winter. Not many white men that time; by and by come; cut down woods, kill 'em moose, scare good many away. Spear 'em salmon, most all gone now. Everything eat 'em up, make country cold,— make river small, build sawmills; sawdust and mill dam send all fish away. That time plenty codfish, white men set line scare 'em all. White men burn up all wood for staves, baskets, everything scarce now. That time great many Mi'kmaqs, white people learn 'em to drink and good many bad things, and then get sick and great many die; not many Mi'kmaq now. One time this Mi'kmaq country—my country; now white people say its our country, take 'em from Indian and never pay 'em. (Gonzalez 1981: 55)

ESTABLISHMENT OF RESERVES

The British attempted to deal with the problem of Native poverty by inducing the people to become farmers on settled land. This solution was consistent with goals enunciated as early as the beginning of the seventeenth century by Jesuit missionaries and French traders. In neither case was it actually directed at the Indians' benefit but rather was motivated by a desire to control the indigenous population. By the turn of the nineteenth century, Mi'kmaqs were isolated away from the best land that had already been occupied by European colonists. They were instead given territory in scattered parcels throughout Nova Scotia and New Brunswick. These lands, now called "reserves," were supposed to have been protected from further settler expansion, but in fact they have been periodically diminished. Furthermore, reserves were generally located in regions that were undesirable because of their isolation and/or lack of resources. Writing of the problems faced by the Mi'kmaqs, an Indian commissioner named Joseph Howe noted in 1843:

It is to be regretted that so little judgement has been exercised in the selection of [Native reserve] lands. The same quantity of land if reserved in spots where the soil is good, on navigable streams, or in places where fish was abundant, and game within reach, would now be a valuable resource. All the land reserved [for the Mi'kmaqs] in this county [Halifax] is sterile and comparatively valueless. In Yarmouth, Hants, Colchester, Pictou and Guysborough, there are no reserves, and in Dartmouth and Halifax they have no lands. (57–58)

A few years later, Mi'kmaqs petitioned the governor of Nova Scotia for aid at a time when the Native economy was in sharp decline. Their best lands had been lost and their population had drastically decreased due to poverty and the spread of smallpox and measles. A petition submitted in 1849 by Mi'kmaq "chiefs and captains" stated, in part:

A long time ago our fathers owned and occupied all the land that is now called Nova Scotia, our people lived along the sides of the rivers and were a great many. We were strong but you were stronger, and we were conquered. Tired of a way that destroyed many of our people, almost 90 years ago chief made peace, and buried the hatchet forever. When that peace was made, the English governor promised us protection, as much land as we wanted and a preservation of our fisheries and game. These we now very much want. Before the white people came, we had plenty of wild roots, plenty of fish, and plenty of corn. The skins of the moose and caribou were warm to our bodies. Your people had not enough land, they came and killed many of our tribe and took from us our country. You have taken from us our lands and trees and have destroyed our game. Upon our campgrounds you have built towns, and the graves of our fathers are broken by the plow and hallow. We were never in a worse condition than now. (58)

In addition to attesting to the difficult conditions of their people, the leaders noted that traditional occupations of hunting, fishing, and handicraft no longer provided a secure means of support. And Mi'kmaqs who had attempted to plant crops and become farmers had failed because of natural disasters as well as inadequate technological assistance.

Reserves were set aside for Mi'kmaqs in New Brunswick, Québec, and Nova Scotia, but constituted only a fraction of their original territory. Although the establishment of reserves supposedly protected Mi'kmaqs and allowed them to continue their traditional way of life, in actuality the reserve system did just the opposite. As Pacifique reported in 1926, "the Mi'kmaq were surrounded by more ambitious farmers and merchants who became … by the force of things, dominant, and caused the hunting and fishing in the manner of the savage to disappear, by consequence taking away from them their ancient mode of existence" (Bock 1966: 14). And, once reserves were founded, Catholic missionaries reasserted their position as spiritual leaders for the Native population. As a result of increased missionary activity, combined with social and economic pressures, most Mi'kmaqs were at least nominally Catholic by the middle of the nineteenth century.

The number of reserves in the Maritimes varied throughout the nineteenth century. The size of reserves also varied as their lands were taken by provincial authorities for the use of Canadian settlers. Residents of the reserves attempted to maintain some aspects of their traditional economy but were largely unsuccessful because of limitations of land and resources. For example, the reserve village of Restigouche, Québec, with a population of approximately 300, was described in 1812 by the resident Catholic missionary Father E. L. Painchaud:

> The Indian village of Restigouche is not, according to appearances, as considerable as it had been formerly. One may count here presently about 50 families which come together ordinarily about twice a year in the month of June and towards the beginning of November. This latter season is the time when they are accustomed to come back from their autumn hunts which ordinarily consist principally of beaver skins and otters. (Bock 1966: 15)

Within two decades, Mi'kmaq villages had changed considerably, adopting the outward appearance of their Canadian neighbors. The settlement at Martin's Point, New Brunswick, home to some 200 Mi'kmaqs in 1834, was described as

consisting of a chapel together with a mission house, a burying ground, and 24 dwelling houses. The houses are constructed of logs, covered with shingles or boards; they are all provided with chimneys and stoves; and some of them even have chairs, bedsteads, tables, and similar other conveniences.

> Most of the householders owned livestock consisting of oxen, cows, swine, etc. Some of them have houses; one of them owns a small schooner of 25 tons; and others have small fishing boats.

> The Indians residing here are industrious in their habits. They demean themselves soberly, peaceably, contributing much to their own respectability and comfort, by annually raising small stock of Indian corn, beans, potatoes, etc. (Bock 1966: 16)

As the nineteenth century advanced, much of the resources upon which Mi'kmaqs relied for their subsistence were either confiscated or depleted. Their most fertile lands were incorporated into Canadian farms, while timber resources were depleted by the growing lumber industries. Finally, animals that Mi'kmaqs had formerly hunted either declined in number because of overkill or migrated to more remote regions because encroaching settlement destroyed their natural habitats. Indians were then compelled to rely on farming to support themselves, but the poor quality of their land, lack of training, and the paucity of tools and equipment given by the government undermined their ability to succeed.

In order to supplement their income, many people turned to other occupations. Prominent among these was the manufacture of household utensils and tools made from wood including barrels, hoops, shingles, oars, rafters, and handicrafts of various types. At first, Mi'kmaqs reaped benefits from this work and were encouraged by British officials because they supplied colonists with needed tools and equipment. However, the growing scarcity of lumber in the Maritimes led to a decline in production.

Women continued their traditional handicraft work, transforming a domestic task into an income-producing occupation. They sold baskets, embroidered boxes, and various types of small containers made of wood and hide to residents of nearby towns and occasionally made longer trips to larger communities such as Halifax in order to obtain cash to purchase food, clothing, and household necessities. Women adapted traditional quillwork embroidery to new forms, often using beads in the place of porcupine quills. They expanded their repertory by crafting new items such as eyeglass cases, sewing boxes, and chair seats. In addition to selling handicrafts from door to door, they sold berries and wild fruits that they had gathered in the woodlands. Women's economic contributions to their households were especially critical at times when produce from farming or the catch from the hunt were not sufficient sources of subsistence.

Finally, Mi'kmaqs obtained work as guides for European travelers and sportsmen. Sport hunting and fishing became popular as recreation for European, Canadian, and American city dwellers who wanted to relive a more rural past. Although settlement in the Maritimes had grown considerably, there were enough "wilderness areas" to attract visitors from other regions. Native men were able to apply their intimate knowledge of the territory as guides for sightseers, hunters, and fishermen.

By the middle of the nineteenth century, therefore, Mi'kmaq economy had adjusted to a transformed situation by diversifying. Although a strong preference for the traditional nomadic life based on foraging persisted, people realized that their old way of life was no longer possible. They adapted by attempting to exploit whatever opportunities existed, but since no single occupation could provide sufficient income, people sought work in many domains and pursued several modes of employment or income-producing activities during the year.

Given the realities of their economic situation, Mi'kmaqs could not, even if they had wanted to, remain permanently on the reserve lands that had been set aside for them. To do so would have meant that they were restricted in the kinds of work that would be possible. As a result, the reserves became part-time residences for most people. For example, the reserve at Restigouche, Québec, was described by a writer for *Harper's* magazine in 1868:

Mission Point is the largest settlement of Mi'kmaqs in the Province. They number 200 families and occupy a reservation of 12,000 acres. The majority earn a livelihood by lumbering, hunting, and fishing. They are very expert with the canoe and are always employed by those who have occasion to visit the interior. The women raise a few garden vegetables, and some of the wealthier have a cow. In the winter they manufacture baskets and wooden ware … Their houses are built of boards and logs, furnished like a backwoodsman shanty, and are laid out in streets. For the most part they dress like the whites. Comparatively few of the Indians live habitually on the reserve. (Bock 1966: 19)

Toward the end of the nineteenth and the beginning of the twentieth centuries, Mi'kmaq economy again adapted to new conditions. In addition to subsistence activities, and sale of handicrafts, new occupations became available. In particular, the lumber industry in Nova Scotia grew considerably, providing men with skilled and unskilled jobs cutting lumber and working in subsidiary plants producing pulp and paper. They were also employed in the construction of railroads and in mining and iron and steel works. While the highest wages were earned by skilled workers in lumber mills and coal mines, men and women also performed unskilled work as day laborers, farmhands, and domestic workers.

Mi'kmaqs expanded their repertory of handicrafts to include such items as buckets, axe handles, barrels, hoops, canoes, hockey sticks, snow shoes, and oars. Women produced sewing baskets, chair seats, moccasins, and eyeglass cases. Older men who were no longer able to participate in heavy industry and hard labor also obtained small incomes through handicraft production. However, despite the increasing popularity and market for their work, Native artisans encountered problems because the wood needed for their craft became difficult to obtain due to urbanization of the region and the resulting depletion of wooded areas. As noted in an official Canadian report of 1882:

The timber they require for their handiwork is becoming very scarce. The Indians have to travel some 15 miles to procure more valuable kinds and even the young maple from which the females make the baskets and fancy work are cut and drawn, or in many instances lugged home on their backs a distance from 3 to 5 miles. (Gonzalez 1981: 86)

Finally, Mi'kmaqs were attracted to urban centers of the Maritimes to find either temporary or permanent work. Women found jobs in domestic service while men worked as household laborers and construction workers.

The depression of the 1930s dealt a serious blow to Mi'kmaq economy. Although all Canadian workers were affected by the downturn in industry, agriculture, and commerce, since Mi'kmaqs had been marginal to provincial economies even before the depression, they suffered the most during the period. They were usually laid off permanent jobs earlier than non-Indians. Sources of unskilled and temporary work disappeared as well.

In response to deteriorating economic conditions on the small, isolated reserves in Nova Scotia, the Canadian government began a policy of Indian "resettlement" in the years following World War II. Agents of the Canadian Department of Indian Affairs and Northern Development decided to concentrate Mi'kmaqs on one of two reserves: Shubenacadie located on the mainland of Nova Scotia and Eskasoni on Cape Breton. Once the policy of resettlement was inaugurated, those people who remained on the smaller reserves were no longer entitled to government assistance. By 1945, nearly all Mi'kmaqs in Nova Scotia had relocated in order to avail themselves of new housing, roads, and other public facilities that the government funded at Shubenacadie and Eskasoni. But the economic condition of the people who relocated hardly improved. Farming was difficult on both reserves because the land consisted mainly of marsh and rocky areas. In addition, lumber mills and iron works that were situated near the reserves could not absorb the incoming population seeking employment. As a result, by 1950 many people who had moved to Shubenacadie and Eskasoni had already returned to their former reserves.

CONTEMPORARY MI'KMAQ COMMUNITIES

Most Mi'kmaq families in Québec, New Brunswick, and Nova Scotia continue to rely on a diversified household economy. Earned income is obtained on the reserves through construction and maintenance jobs as well as the staffing of band council offices and community service programs. Government relief provides supplementation to or, in some cases, the major share of money for some residents. Although work in mining, lumbering, and outdoor guiding has declined, handicraft production remains an important source of income for many families. Women and men produce baskets, furniture, beadwork jewelry, and "novelty items" such as birch bark canoes and Indian dolls (Gonzalez 1981: 81). The Nova Scotia Mi'kmaq Arts and Crafts Development Association helps local people train for handicraft work and also markets Native artisans' creations to shops in Canadian cities and to retail outlets and museums in the United States and Europe.

Women's employment on the reserves has increased and in fact expanded into new areas. Young, educated women often work in government positions as band administrators, secretaries, and translators. Others work as nurses, teachers, and social workers. In addition, some individuals and families own businesses such as grocery stores, gasoline stations, shops specializing in cabinetry, handicrafts, and other local services.

Economic data compiled from the 2006 Canadian census reveals that labor force participation rates on Nova Scotia Mi'kmaq reserves (50%) were less than those of other Aboriginal reserves (63%), and participation rates fall far short of the general Canadian figure of 68.1 percent. Mi'kmaq unemployment rates (24.6%) generally exceed those of other Indian reserves (15.5%), which are everywhere far higher than the general Canadian figure of 10 percent.

Incomes are typically higher in Mi'kmaq communities than elsewhere on Canadian reserves ($10,500), but some earn less than the average wage and everywhere Mi'kmaq incomes are far below the general Canadian average of $24,100. The median income for a Mi'kmaq family in 2010 was $16,288 (Prosper and McMillan 2011). Table 6.1 presents specific data from selected reserves.

Table 6.2 presents figures for average individual incomes in 2006 for men and women who received some income from employment.

Data concerning educational achievement reveals an additional source of disadvantage that is intertwined with economic and income factors. The proportion of Mi'kmaq band members who have less than a ninth grade education is consistently higher than for the general population (13.7%). As might be expected, the proportion of Mi'kmaqs graduating from high school is consistently lower. Educational achievement varies considerably, however, among the bands. On some reserves, averages for Mi'kmaqs are close to the Canadian norm while elsewhere the discrepancy is marked. Table 6.3 presents figures for selected bands.

A large number of Mi'kmaqs continue to follow seasonal occupational and residence patterns. Contemporary seasonal cycles revolve around employment as migrant farmworkers in the potato and blueberry fields of Maine as well as work in cities of New England such as Boston, Springfield, and Hartford. Men seek employment in construction industries and women work in factories or in private households as domestics. For some people, out-migration from the reserves is more or less permanent, involving the relocation of whole families, but for most it is a temporary measure.

Even though many Mi'kmaqs no longer reside on their reserves during a substantial portion of their lives, the reserves remain socially and emotionally

TABLE 6.1	Employment Information for Selected Bands		
	Participation Rate (%)	Employment Rate (%)	Unemployment Rate (%)
Nova Scotia	63.0	53.2	15.4
Bear River	73.7	47.4	35.7
Chapel Island	63.5	40.4	36.4
Eskasoni	37.5	28	25.2
Membertoo	64.4	48.9	25.9
Whycocomagh	55.1	38.5	30.2
New Brunswick	62.7	49.7	50.5
Burnt Church	65.8	38.4	42.5
Eel River	56.4	41.0	27.3
Indian Island	80.0	40.0	50.0
Pabineau	75.0	33.0	67.0
Red Bank	70.6	56.9	16.7
Québec	60.8	51.3	15.6
Gesgapegiag	51.0	28.0	44.0
Listuguj	57.2	43.8	24.4
Prince Edward Island	72.0	59.6	17.3
Lennox Island	68.0	40.0	41.0

Source: Statistics Canada 2006: Census, Custom Tabulations.

Note: "Participation rate" refers to percent of population aged fifteen or older in the workforce; "employment to population ratio" refers to percent of the entire population aged fifteen or older that is employed; "unemployment rate" documents the percent of poulation aged fifteen or older that is actively seeking work.

important. People usually return to their Native communities when work is unavailable in the cities of Canada and the United States. And families often leave young children in the care of elderly relatives at home. As Guillemin noted in her study of Mi'kmaqs who had moved from the Maritimes to Boston:

What the reservation actually supports in the way of a stable household is a conglomerate of "home bases," that is, extended families which will host individual adults and children for longer or shorter periods of time, depending on what a visit is prompted by: ill health, good luck and a desire to make a magnificent display, or bad luck and the need to put up somewhere for awhile. (1975: 83)

Such extended family households are typically headed by older women who either have no desire to move to the city or who have reestablished themselves on the reserve when their working days have ended. Among Guillemin's examples of the dynamics of Mi'kmaq households is the story of Peter Dunn, born in Bear River in 1931:

My mother had twelve children in all. Sam, Claude, Ann Mary, and me were the closest. Her brother's two children lived with us for a long while after their mother died. Then there was her own mother who came from Bear River and had a lot of her family there. Well, my father also had a brother who he'd go hunting with and he lived in a little shack right close to our place and he'd eat with us. My cousin Henry lived with us too, he's my age. My mother's younger brother used to come and stay and me and Henry and Sam would have to double up so he could have our bed. That's a lot of people already but we always seemed to have room. Then there was the babies, the little ones who came to us to stay. (86–87)

Families often leave children with relatives on the reserves in part because the adult way of life is unpredictable and entails frequent relocations throughout the year, but children are also left at home because most parents believe that the Native community is the best place for children to grow up, providing a stable, emotionally secure, familiar place with familiar people. Growing up on the reserves also gives children a sense of their identity as Mi'kmaq. They learn to speak the Native language and to socialize with others in ways that are considered appropriate in Native culture. They learn values of family loyalty and cooperation. They learn to respect and appreciate the work of their elders, and they learn that it is necessary to cooperate with others and to share whatever good fortune in the way of money and other material goods comes their way.

TABLE 6.2	Average Earnings for Selected Bands	
	Average Earning ($)	
	Men	Women
Nova Scotia	28,042	19,122
Bear River	11,079	10,635
Chapel Island	13,370	13,579
Eskasoni	16,975	17,010
Membertou	22,764	18,565
Whycocomagh	22,285	16,337
New Brunswick	22,483	17,791
Burnt Church	9,952	9,856
Eel River	15,776	13,632
Indian Island	—	2,826
Pabineau	14,884	7,558
Red Bank	19,258	17,864
Québec	27,858	21,510
Gesgapegiag	12,193	11,874
Listuguj	18,370,	19,558
Prince Edward Is.	23,018	19,529
Lennox Island	11,000	13,318

Source: Statistics Canada 2006: Census, Custom Tabulations.

value in the work setting, so that an Indian usually has to mask his/her real self and hope to escape with their pride intact. The tedium of a job, more than how dirty it gets ones fingernails, is the hardest for the Mi'kmaq to take. Aversion to tedium, the ups and downs of the market, and inexperience basically account for the variety in Indian work histories. (130–131)

Guillemin emphasizes the strength of the Mi'kmaq "urban tribal network" as a reflection and continuation of Native social and cultural norms within a new economic and territorial environment. Again, quoting Guillemin,

the economic strategy of the Mi'kmaq is communal and cannot be understood except as an aspect of their culture. It has sought to maximize the multiple compensation which come out of human interaction. The effect of this has been to keep economics in its proper social context, embedded in rules of human responsibility and cooperation. Kin must be responsible to kin and friend to friend. Out of the social activity of the community comes its solution to economic marginality. (136–137)

As in past centuries, people today make use of their unique cultural resources and strengths in adapting to an economic system over which they have very little control. Given their marginality due to poverty, poor education, and lack of opportunity, they survive by their adaptability and by strengthening communal bonds among family and coworkers. People work together, travel together, share living quarters, and as in the past, share resources so that no one is left without some means of support. When Mi'kmaqs (especially men) come into what is considered a large sum of money through a well-paying job, they often spend that money not only on themselves and their immediate families but also on their friends in the city and at home on the reserves:

Living precariously at the edge of the economy, they celebrate their own existence in the face of brutal poverty, in the face of a society which if it did not succeed in exterminating them, did not fail from trying. There is more optimism than fatalism in spending rather than hoarding money. The goal of Indian behavior is communal, not individualized. When the Mi'kmaq of the seventeenth century

Mi'kmaqs living in urban centers such as Boston generally rely on a variety of jobs that they hold for shorter or longer periods of time depending on fluctuations in demand as well as on the people's own work styles and preferences. Demand in industries rises and falls for market-driven reasons not controlled by the workers. As Guillemin noted, "when strikes or layoffs occur in industry, the first people to lose their wages are those who, like the Mi'kmaq are generally without union protection and work at the level of cheap industrial labor" (1975: 130). However, the jobs that Mi'kmaqs hold tend to conflict with the personality traits of autonomy, initiative, and responsibility that the people value:

the kind of work which the Mi'kmaq ordinarily do requires a real subjugation to industrial goals. There is no intrinsic value to the work being demanded, whether it is washing the cafeteria floor or working on an assembly line. The personal initiative and sociability in which a Mi'kmaq is trained has no

TABLE 6.3	Education Levels for Selected Bands		
	No certificate, diploma, or degree	High school certificate or equivalence	University certificate, diploma, or degree
Chapel Island	50	25	15
Eskasoni	430	200	165
Membertoo	65	50	45
Whycocomagh	80	45	40
Burnt Church	210	65	25
Eel River	15	25	15
Pabineau	10	0	0
Red Bank	30	30	25
Gesgapegiag	0	0	0
Listuguj	165	150	65
Lennox Island	15	15	10

Source: Statistics Canada 2006: Census, Custom Tabulations.

Note: "Post-secondary" refers to attendance in trades, technical, and academic programs.

feasted on their total supply of game, they praised the skill of the hunters who provided for the band and as a community rejoiced in their survival at that point in time. (148–149)

And, as in the past, the person who shares wages and resources with others is sharing "with people who make up the social context of their lives, the people who have the power to give them a good reputation" (149).

Since passage of the federal Canadian Indian Act in 1876, leadership and band council organization has been a matter of national policy. In most Mi'kmaq communities, however, leadership remained a matter of consensus as had been the cultural norm from aboriginal times. While there is little documentation concerning leadership patterns on Mi'kmaq reserves in the nineteenth century, Bock noted that until 1898 chiefs at Restigouche were usually chosen by male consensus "with the consent of the priest" (Bock 1966: 65). Thereafter, a more formal structure was instituted consisting of a chief and four counselors. However, at Restigouche and elsewhere in Canada, the councils were advisory bodies lacking definitive powers and authorities. Control of decision-making on Native reserves continued to be exerted by the federal Department of Indian Affairs and Northern Development.

A greater degree of sovereign control was vested in band councils as a result of revision of the Indian Act in 1951. Band councils increased in membership and gained greater control of policies and programs for their communities, but actual sovereignty is still limited since the Department of Indian Affairs retains veto power over council decisions even though the Canadian government officially follows a policy of "self-rule" on Indian reserves.

Aware of the limitations of their political autonomy and the fragmentation of their people into numerous separately organized bands, in 1969 Mi'kmaqs in Nova Scotia founded the Union of Nova Scotia Indians (UNSI), with a board of governors composed of band chiefs from all reserves in the province. UNSI speaks with a stronger, unified voice to provincial and federal authorities. And in 1978, Mi'kmaqs joined with the Maliseets and Abenakis of Canada and the Penobscots and Passamaquoddies in Maine to reconstitute the Wabanaki Confederacy that had traditionally been a source of political cooperation among the Native nations. The Confederacy had last met in 1870 but was rekindled in order to discuss matters of common concern, particularly land claims and treaty rights advocacy. Members continue to meet regularly at alternating communities (Prins 1996: 214–215).

Emerging from a similar context of the need to organize and speak for larger numbers, Mi'kmaqs in Boston participated in forming the "Boston Indian Council," an organization composed of Indians residing in the city. For Mi'kmaqs, however, participation in the political domain is sometimes difficult because they are unused to and indeed hostile to political organizations that have formal leadership and institutionalized control. Contrary to the bureaucratic style sometimes deemed necessary for practical results, Mi'kmaqs both in Boston and on the reserves are reluctant to "follow the leader" without dissent and resentment. As Guillemin noted about Mi'kmaqs in Boston,

Indians who claim to speak for the group as a whole will quickly be contested by ten or fifteen other Indians voicing dissent, not particularly about the issue in question, but about the right of anyone to speak for the others. Individuals who suggest plans for action are apt to get themselves in trouble if there is any hint of coercion or manipulation in their presentation or if they show themselves impatient with prolonged debate. (Guillemin 1975: 265)

Similar patterns of egalitarian decision-making and hostility toward entrenched leadership were prevalent at Restigouche in the 1960s. Mi'kmaq residents commented: "M was about the best chief we ever had, at least until he started thinking he was high and mighty" and "P started off pretty good as chief, but after awhile he started acting like a dictator, walking around the reserve dressed up in a suit, the people don't like that kind of thing" (Bock 1966: 65).

Differences of opinion are voiced concerning current systems of leadership. In addition to local elected officials who represent their constituents on each of the Mi'kmaq reserves in Canada, a Grand Council centered on Cape Breton is viewed by some as having paramount legitimacy. The Grand Council (or "Sante' Mawio'mi," literally "holy gathering") was originally a body concerned primarily with religious matters within the Catholic church but has now entered the political arena (Prins 1996: 203). The Council is composed of a Grand Chief and a varying number of captains (now more than a dozen) who are appointed for life. In the 1980s, the Grand Council began to assert itself as a custodian of Mi'kmaq sovereignty, sending delegates to international conferences and participating in UN forums. While some Mi'kmaqs view the Council as a principal governing body, most consider its proper role to be a custodian of religious affairs separate from political leadership (215).

Mi'kmaqs have organized and fought for their rights under Canadian law and have been victorious in some instances. In the 1970s and 1980s, they filed more than one hundred suits for land that they claimed had been illegally taken. Basing the suits on the Royal Proclamation of 1763 that stipulated that Indian lands could only be taken by cession or purchase, Mi'kmaqs were able to prove that they had neither ceded nor sold vast tracts of their aboriginal territory. As a result of the cases, Mi'kmaqs either regained control over numerous tracts of land or received monetary compensation (209–210).

More recently in 2005, the Mi'kmaqs, led by Mi'kmaq Nora Bernard, filed a class-action lawsuit against the Canadian government representing around 80,000 Mi'kmaqs that were forced into residential schools. The Canadian government settled the lawsuit for over 5 billion dollars, making the suit the largest in Canadian history. Furthermore, in 2008 then prime minister Stephen Harper publicly apologized to all survivors of the residential school program, and in 2011 the Indian Residential Schools Truth and Reconciliation Commission travelled to Mi'kmaq communities to gather statements from former students (Benjamin 2014).

In addition, Mi'kmaqs have sought recognition of hunting and fishing rights guaranteed by treaties. In 1970s, authorities in Nova Scotia began to enforce fishing regulations that adversely affected Mi'kmaqs, who continued to fish in their customary places regardless of provincial rules. During the decade and into the 1980s, provincial police occasionally raided Mi'kmaq salmon fisheries, confiscating nets and arresting "poachers" (210). But Mi'kmaqs refused to relinquish their rights. In 1990, the Supreme Court of Canada ruled that, under provisions of the new Canadian Constitution of 1982, Native people's fishing rights were protected. And in 1996, the Union of Nova Scotia Indians successfully challenged a dredging project in the Bras d'Or Lakes that would have disrupted Mi'kmaqs' aboriginal rights to fish. A Federal Court Judge suspended the permits that had allowed the dredging of the main channel of the lakes, stating that in the future the environmental impact of such projects should be assessed after consultations with the Mi'kmaqs (*Indian Time* 1996). A case decided by the Supreme Court in 1985 also confirmed the Mi'kmaqs' rights to hunt outside their reserves and their exemption from provincial seasonal hunting regulations. And in 1999, the Supreme Court again reaffirmed aboriginal Mi'kmaq rights based on a treaty signed with Great Britain in 1760. However, although the Court recognized Native rights to hunt and fish year-round, it stated that they can be subject to what it described as "reasonable regulation." While it also recognized the people's rights to mineral and forestry resources, it said that those rights were "not unlimited." Leading to and following these rulings, Mi'kmaq lobster fishermen increased their activity, contributing to significant improvement in their economy. But antagonism has flared between Mi'kmaqs and non-Indian lobstermen who resent the now-recognized rights of all Mi'kmaqs to obtain lobster licenses. As a Native lobsterman in Nova Scotia named Mike Pictou observed, "The resource belongs to us. We shared it for all these years, but somewhere along the line, 'share' became 'take'" ("Indian Affairs Heat Up (Witness the Lobster War)" 1999). Additional fishing rights cases have been decided by the Canadian

Niko Clair places an offering in a tree as part of the Mi'kmaq community's water ceremony on the shores of Pomquet Harbour to support the aboriginal call for a moratorium on oil and gas exploration in the Gulf of St. Lawrence, near Antigonish, NS, in October 2015. The Gulf of St. Lawrence is one of the largest marine breeding regions in Canada, home to endangered whales and hosts some of the largest lobster production in the world.

$25,582, substantially below the incomes of their neighbors in the state and region ($16,248 per capita in Maine, $37,240 median household income in the Northeast) (Statistical Abstracts 1999: 442). About 24.8 percent of families and 26.2 percent of individuals lived below the official poverty level. Employment statistics indicated that 55 percent of the labor force was unemployed while 65 percent of the potential labor force population was not working (US Bureau of the Census 2000, Table 6: 196; US Bureau of Indian Affairs 1995, Table 3). Mi'kmaq unemployment is staggering, particularly in the context of a Maine unemployment rate of 8.1 percent for 2009 (Statistical Abstracts 2009: 405). More recent information is unavailable due to the small population of the Aroostook band.

Supreme Court in 1999, 2005, and 2006. Decisions have been mixed, some favoring Mi'kmaqs' aboriginal rights and others restricting them. (See Chapter 3 for a detailed discussion of these issues.)

In the United States, a group of Mi'kmaqs living in northern Maine joined in 1970 with other Indians in the state to found the Association of Aroostook Indians, dedicated to improving living conditions in their communities. Ten years later, the Mi'kmaqs decided to form their own organization, the Aroostook Mi'kmaq Council, with the goal of seeking state and federal recognition. The Council amassed documentation proving Mi'kmaqs' long and stable occupation of land in Aroostook County. As a result, in 1991, Congress passed the "Aroostook Band of Micmacs Settlement Act" that granted tribal status, entitled members to federal services, and awarded $900,000 for the purchase of 5,000 acres of land (Prins 1996: 213–214).

Members of the Aroostook Band live in rural communities where few jobs are available. According to US census figures for 1999, their per capita income was $9,951 and median household income stood at

In Boston, where Mi'kmaqs constitute the single largest Native group, the Boston Indian Council (BIC; renamed the North American Indian Center of Boston in 1992) sought state recognition to deal with government officials in the hopes of increasing their visibility and influence. In 1976, then-governor Michael Dukakis issued an executive order that recognized the BIC as the "official liaison between state government and Wabanaki Indians" (212). A state commissioner of Indian affairs was appointed with representation by Native members on state commissions. Once recognized by Massachusetts, the BIC became eligible to participate in federal Indian programs.

Since the 1980s, many changes have taken place on reserves in Québec as the province has sought to improve living conditions, economic opportunities, and educational advancement of Native peoples. All three Mi'kmaq communities located on the Gaspé Peninsula have developed programs with cultural and economic goals. Most remarkable are the changes at Restigouche, the largest of the three reserves. Residents have initiated programs in economy, community services, and education to improve their lives and to make Restigouche a place where young people might prefer to remain rather than leave for cities in Canada and the United States.

The band council at Restigouche has signed a joint agreement with the province of Québec to manage salmon resources in the Restigouche River bordering the reserve. Salmon management is aimed at enabling people to use the resource for their own subsistence as well as to engage in commercial fishing, producing a surplus and profit. In addition, the community has launched a tourism development project, awarded a special grand prize by the Québec Ministry of Tourism in 1988, that encompasses several construction and restoration plans. It includes restoration of a church and monastery dating from the seventeenth century and the planting and cultivation of a garden with medicinal plants used by aboriginal Mi'kmaqs. Construction projects include an aboriginal village depicting both summer and winter residences, a museum and cultural center, and an inn and conference facilities.

The reserve of Maria located on the shore of the Baie des Chaleurs at the mouth of Cascapedia River is also developing economic and educational programs aimed at expanding their village. Since the 1980s, residents have built new healthcare facilities, schools, and band council offices. Educational programs foster tribal identity and train students in skills that will enable them to succeed in the Canadian economy. Indeed, the name of the new village school is Wejgwapniag, meaning "the time of day just before sunrise." As a school official explained, "it means a new beginning. For the first time in ages, the people of the village have the power and responsibility of deciding the direction the school will take. At Wejgwapniag, we prepare our children for the outside world, just as the sun prepares itself before rising from behind the mountain" (*Rencontre*, June 1987: 10). Mi'kmaq is the only language spoken in kindergarten whereas French and English are taught beginning in the first grade. The goal of the language program is to encourage children to be trilingual in a province that is officially French and a nation that is officially bilingual in English and French.

People at Maria have formed a panel to manage salmon resources of the Cascapedia River as well as the forests stretching north of the river. They are developing and advertising their region as a tourist spot for fishermen and sightseers.

A concerted effort has been made at the community of Listuguj to emphasize the importance of retaining the Mi'kmaq language as a means of perpetuating Native identity, values, and culture. For example, all documents printed or distributed by the band council are printed in Mi'kmaq and English. In the local school, Mi'kmaq is the language used for instruction in kindergarten and grades 1–4. And, employees of the band council are encouraged to learn Mi'kmaq if they are not already speakers. Although this program is voluntary, most band employees understand the importance participating in the classes. The effort to teach young children to speak Mi'kmaq is coupled with encouraging adults who do speak the language to use it when talking to their children. As educator Eunice Metallic noted, "if you don't teach the language to your children now, who will teach it to your grandchildren?" (*Rencontre*, Summer/Fall 1995: 5).

And in 1999, the Gespeg band of Mi'kmaqs signed a "framework agreement" with the provincial government in Québec to negotiate parameters of self-government encompassing economic, social, and cultural development (*Rencontre*, June 1999: 5). The Gespeg band, located on the Gaspé peninsula of eastern Québec, obtained formal recognition in 1973 but does not have a reserve or any land of its own.

After many years of effort and ten years of formal negotiations with the federal government, the Mi'kmaq living in Newfoundland gained official recognition as the Qalipu Mi'kmaq First Nation Band in 2011. When Newfoundland and Labrador joined the Confederation as provinces of Canada, there was no discussion about the status of indigenous peoples living there until the founding of the Federation of Newfoundland Indians in 1989, representing nearly 8,000 Mi'kmaq who were members of nine local communities. The final agreement establishes the Qalipu Band as status Indians under the Canadian Indian Act, thereby making the people eligible for programs such as college scholarships, healthcare services not covered by federal insurance, and economic development funds. However, the Qalipu Band does not have a reserve and therefore lacks territorial sovereignty.

The small Mi'kmaq community of Miawpukek First Nation, located in Newfoundland, has developed educational programs that focus on their cultural and linguistic heritage. In the past, Miawpukek only had an elementary school to serve their community; students in junior and senior high school had to leave their homes and board at a school away from the reserve. Many students dropped out of school in order to return home. Now that Miawpukek operates its own schools, some of these former dropouts have come back to finish their education. The local schools hire teachers from the community who speak the Native language and understand the cultural orientation of the students. According to Edwina Wetzel, director of education for Miawpukek and herself a Native of the community, children benefit from the local control of schooling and the perspective and understanding that they receive from the teachers. In her words, "children say 'I like our teachers because they understand us better.' It has to do with your language, the way you express yourself, the values you hold. Sometimes when they're writing a test, the way they express their ideas is easier understood by someone who is living in that landscape. Someone from outside can interpret the answer totally differently. Our teachers speak English, but our English comes from a Mi'kmaq perspective" (http://www.aadnc-aadnc.gc.ca/eng/1100100017025).

In addition to classes for children, the school offers adult courses, programs for students with special needs, and cultural and language activities.

Like many other members of First Nations residing in urban centers, the Mi'kmaq living in Halifax, the capital of Nova Scotia, opened a Mi'kmaq Native Friendship Centre to be a focus of community events, provide various kinds of educational and social services, and conduct outreach programs throughout the city. However, due to a federal budget freeze on Cultural Connections for Aboriginal Youth programs, funds allocated to a popular youth initiative called Kitpu were slashed in 2012, threatening the continued existence of the program. In response, the Friendship Centre engaged in emergency fundraising, not only among the Mi'kmaqs but throughout the city and were able to raise enough money to continue operating. They are also undertaking campaigns to pressure the government to unfreeze funding and to gain more permanent access to grants and both public and private sources of support to ensure their long-term survival.

A number of Mi'kmaq First Nations have initiated ecotourism and cultural projects to both generate income and educate visitors about their ways of life and their values and perspectives. For example, Mi'kmaq in Newfoundland, New Brunswick, and Nova Scotia provide visitors with the experience of living in their environment. The Miawpukek First Nation in Newfoundland operates hunting and fishing lodges as well as sightseeing excursions. They also have a park, called Jipujijkuel Kuespern, or "the place that you leave the same as you found it," containing forests, lakes, and streams, replete with campsites, trails for hiking, and cultural exhibits. Pabineau First Nation in New Brunswick sponsors a tour called "Mother Earth's Journey" that exposes visitors both to the people's territory and to their ecological adaptation. They learn to recognize medicinal plants, understand their usages, and share traditional foods. And the Bear River First Nation in Nova Scotia has opened a Heritage and Cultural Centre that houses displays of traditional dwellings and birch bark canoes, photographs and stories about community Elders and leaders, a theater and storytelling corner, and interactive cultural exhibits. The building is also used for community events throughout the year.

Although recent changes on the reserves have opened up new opportunities, people recognize the importance of traditional ethics emphasizing community responsibility, generosity, and other cultural values that maintained Native families and communities for centuries. As Margaret Labillois, a seventy-one-year-old Mi'kmaq from New Brunswick, noted:

> When I was young, we were responsible for bringing food, water and wood to the elders. Nobody asked to be paid, nobody was paid. My mother would say: "the first lobster, the first salmon, the first deer, any food we come by, the first thing to do is share it with those who couldn't get anything. Its our responsibility." In those days we had to get along well with each other. We had to help each other, because we depended on each other to live. (*Rencontre*, Fall 1994: 12)

Examples of current efforts of Mi'kmaqs in the Maritimes demonstrate that the people have set on a path that combines traditional and contemporary ways of life without abandoning the values and underlying social goals of their heritage. Mi'kmaqs in all regions, including those living on reserves in Canada, in small towns in northern Maine, and in the cities of Boston in Massachusetts and in Halifax, Nova Scotia, recognize a common identity based on language, religion, history, and shared experiences. Language maintenance is strong, particularly in Canada. According to data collected in the 2011 Canadian census, 8,030 people reported Mi'kmaq language as their mother tongue, making it the eighth most commonly spoken Indian language in the country (Statistics Canada 2006). On most reserves, about half of the resident population has some knowledge of the Mi'kmaq language although in some communities, especially Eskasoni

Band Name	Total Members	Members On-Reserve	Members Off-Reserve
TABLE 6.4 Population for Selected Mi'kmaq Bands in Canada			
Nova Scotia			
Acadia	1,498	227	1,271
Annapolis Valley	283	119	164
Bear River	330	106	224
Chapel Island	714	581	133
Eskasoni	4,314	3,690	624
Glooscap	359	89	270
Membertoo	1,430	912	518
Millbrook	1,762	882	880
Paqtnkek	565	427	138
Pictou Landing	650	498	152
Shubenacadie	2,554	1,309	1,245
Wagmatcook	810	633	177
Whycocomagh	976	895	81
Woodstock	980	286	694
New Brunswick			
Big Cove	3,245	2,538	707
Buctouche	117	74	43
Burnt Church	1,835	1,324	511
Eel Ground	1,011	566	445
Eel River	708	350	358
Fort Folly	129	36	93
Indian Island	182	104	78
Kingsclear	1,001	704	297
Madawaska	361	156	205
Oromocto	660	315	345
Pabineau	298	101	197
Red Bank	662	452	210
Tobique	2,238	1,485	753
Prince Edward Island			
Abegweit	366	226	140
Lennox Island	927	394	533
Québec			
Gaspeg	727	0	727
Gesgapegiag	1,462	701	761
Listuguj (formerly Restigouche)	3,813	2,074	1,739

Source: DIAND 2015.

Note: Band members who are not counted as living "on-reserve" or "off-reserve" have residence "on crown land."

and Whycocomagh in Nova Scotia, nearly all people speak the language. In contrast, on some of the smaller reserves in New Brunswick and Prince Edward Island, only a fraction of the population has knowledge of their Native language. Furthermore, in most Mi'kmaq communities, only about half of residents who reported knowledge of the language stated that they use it as their "home language." In the United States, however, Mi'kmaq (in combination with non-Spanish, non-Indo-European, and non-Asian or Pacific Island languages) was reportedly spoken at home by only 7 percent of those identified as Mi'kmaq (US Census Bureau 2010), for an estimated total of 115 speakers.

Contemporary Populations

According to 2015 population statistics from the Canadian Department of Indian Affairs and Northern Development, there are slightly fewer than 60,000 registered Mi'kmaqs located in the provinces of Nova Scotia, New Brunswick, Prince Edward Island, and Québec. Of these band members, approximately 56 percent (20,160) reside on their reserves while about 44 percent (15,840) reside off-reserve. These percentages exclude the so-called landless Qalipu, a recognized nation with about 24,000 members but no reservations. Five reserves have populations exceeding 1,000 but most number no more than 400 or 500 and some have fewer than 100 residents. Mi'kmaqs belonging to the Aroostook Band located in northern Maine number about 1,200. Table 6.4 details band membership and residence.

REFERENCES

Benjamin, Chris. 2014. *Indian School Road: Legacies of the Shubenacadie Residential School.* Halifax, Nova Scotia: Nimbus Press.

Bock, Phillip. 1966. *The Micmac Indians of Restigouche: History and Contemporary Description.* Ottawa: National Museum of Canada, Bulletin No. 213, Anthropological Series no. 77.

Bock, Phillip. 1978. "Micmac." *Northeast* (ed. B. Trigger). Vol. 15 of *Handbook of North American Indians.* Washington, DC: Smithsonian Institution, pp. 109–123.

Cartier, Jacques. 1924. *The Voyages of Jacques Cartier* (ed. H. P. Biggar). Ottawa: Publications of the Public Archives of Canada.

Denys, Nicolas. [1672]1908. *The Description and Natural History of the Coasts of North America* (ed. W. Ganong). Toronto: Champlain Society.

Department of Indian Affairs and Northern Development (DIAND). 2015. *Registered Indian Population by Sex and Residence 2014*. Ottawa: Department of Indian Affairs and Northern Development.

Gonzalez, Ellice. 1981. *Changing Economic Roles for Micmac Men and Women: An Ethnohistorical Analysis*. Ottawa: National Museum of Canada, Canadian Ethnology Service, paper no. 72.

Guillemin, Jeanne. 1975. *Urban Renegades: The Cultural Strategy of American Indians*. New York: Columbia University Press.

"Indian Affairs Heat Up (Witness the Lobster War)." 1999. *The New York Times*. December 30.

Indian Time. 1996. November 15. Rooseveltown, NY: Akwesasne Mohawk Nation.

Jesuit Relations and Allied Documents, 1610–1791 (JR). 1896–1901. 73 vols. (ed. R. G. Thwaites). Cleveland, OH: The Burrows Brothers.

LeClercq, Chretien. [1691]1968. *New Relation of Gaspesia*. New York: Greenwood Press.

Lescarbot, Marc. 1928. *The History of New France 1609–1612*. 3 vols. Toronto: Champlain Society.

Lescarbot, Marc. [1618]1968. *History of New France*. 3 vols. New York: Greenwood Press.

Prins, Harald. 1996. *The Mi'kmaq: Resistance, Accommodation, and Cultural Survival*. New York: Harcourt Brace.

Prosper, Kerry, and Jane McMillan. 2011. *Made with Mi'kmaq Hands*. Halifax, Nova Scotia: Mount Saint Vincent University.

Rencontre. June 1987. Québec: Secretariat aux affaires autochtones.

Rencontre. Fall 1994. Québec: Secretariat aux affaires autochtones.

Rencontre. Summer/Fall 1995. Québec: Secretariat aux affaires autochtones.

Rencontre. June 1999. Québec: Secretariat aux affaires autochtones.

Statistical Abstracts. 1999.

Statistical Abstracts. 2009.

Statistics Canada. 2006.

US Bureau of the Census. 2000.

US Bureau of Indian Affairs. 1995. *"Table 3: Indian Service Population and Labor Force Estimates*. Washington, DC.

Wallis, Wilson, and Ruth Wallis. 1955. *The Micmac Indians of Eastern Canada*. Minneapolis, MN: University of Minnesota Press.

THE SOUTHEAST

Eries

Delawares

Miamis

Powhatans

Ohio River

Tuscaroras

Shawnees

Cherokees

Osages

Catawbas

Chickasaws

ATLANTIC

Creeks

OCEAN

Caddos

Choctaws

Apalachees

Timucuas

Calusas

III

PART

Choctaw Story of Creation

At a remote period, the earth was a vast plain, destitute of hills, and a mere quagmire. While the earth was in this situation, a superior being came down from above, and alighting near the center of the Choctaw nation, threw up a large mound, or hill, called "Nunih waiya" ("stooping or sloping hill"). When this was done, he caused the red people to come out of it, and when he supposed that a sufficient number had come out, he stamped on the ground with his foot. When this signal of his power had been given, some were partly formed, others were just raising their heads above the mud, emerging into light, and struggling into life, all of whom perished. The red people being thus formed from the earth, and seated on the area of the hill, their Creator told them that they should live for ever. But not understanding him, they inquired what he said, upon which he took away the grant he had given them of immortality, and told them they would become subject to death.

After the formation of people from the ground, the hills were formed, the earth indurated and fitted to become a habitation. The hills were formed by a great agitation of the waters like that of a boiling liquid, being driven by violent winds, the soft mud was carried in various directions, and being deposited in different places, formed the mountains and hills which now appear on the face of the earth.

Source: John Swanton. 1931. *Source Material for the Social and Ceremonial Life of the Choctaw Indians.* Washington, DC: Bureau of American Ethnology, Bulletin No. 103, p. 201.

Native Nations of the Southeast

Native Americans are still here. We are alive. We are not extinct like the dinosaur. We are proud, strong and beautiful people with many talents and traditions. We have much to offer the world as human beings. We are also God's creatures. We cannot erase the past, but we can change the future, by telling the truth.

Lin Freewolf Sparks, Cherokee [1995]1997

LANDS AND NATIONS

The Southeastern region of North America was the homeland of people whose languages belong to five linguistic families: Muskogean, Caddoan, Iroquoian, Siouan, and Algonkian. The Muskogean family was by far the largest, both in population and in territory. It differs from the other families in that speakers of Muskogean languages were found only in the Southeast whereas speakers of Caddoan, Iroquoian, Siouan, and Algonkian languages lived in contiguous regions as well. Muskogean peoples were among the most numerous and powerful of the Southeastern nations. They included the Choctaws, Chickasaws, Creeks, Seminoles, Natchez, Coosas, Alabamas, Yamasees, and more than fifty additional groups. Southeastern Caddoan nations such as the Cahinnios, Neches, and Washitas were relatively small societies living in parts of Arkansas, northwestern Louisiana, and northeastern Texas. The Iroquoian family was represented by the Cherokees, who resided in the southern Appalachian

mountains of Tennessee, and the Tuscaroras, who lived in North Carolina until the early 1700s, when they went north to New York to join the Iroquois Confederacy as its sixth nation. Siouan speakers included the Ofos, Biloxis, and Quapaws of Mississippi. And Algonkian-speaking nations such as the Chowanocs, Hatteras, and Moratoks inhabited small territories along the Atlantic coast of North Carolina. In addition to these five major families, two other groups of Southeastern peoples spoke languages that are characterized as "isolates," having no known relatives: the Yuchis of eastern Tennessee and the Tunicas of northwestern Mississippi and nearby Arkansas.

Although estimates of aboriginal populations are notoriously inadequate due to the impossibility of ascertaining rates of death from European diseases before a particular group had direct contact with the foreigners, Mooney (1928) suggested the following figures for Southeastern peoples at the time of European invasions, ca. 1500, listed by language family: Muskogean: 83,600; Iroquoian: 30,200; Siouan: 24,000; Algonkian: 16,500; Caddoan: 8,500; Tunica: 6,000; Yuchi: 3,100. Mooney's estimates are based on observations made by European soldiers, missionaries, and traders from the sixteenth through eighteenth centuries, observations that differ widely in their reliability.

Despite the linguistic and ancestral diversity of Southeastern nations, people adjusted to similar environments and through both adaptive processes and diffusion developed cultures that were alike in many respects. Economies throughout the region combined horticulture and foraging; settlements were relatively permanent, although there were some seasonal shifts in the late fall and winter; social systems were based on unilineal descent commonly with clan and/or moiety organizations. The greatest variation in Southeastern cultures was attested in political systems, ranging from informal temporary leadership in egalitarian societies to highly structured hereditary chieftainships in stratified nations.

ABORIGINAL CULTURE

Economies

Aboriginal economies of most Southeastern peoples centered on horticulture, supplemented by hunting, fishing, and gathering wild plants. Several varieties of corn, beans, pumpkins, squashes, and sunflowers were the major crops grown in the region. However, in some areas of south Florida, both coastal and inland, as well as along the Gulf coast of Louisiana, indigenous people did not plant crops but instead focussed their activities on foraging and acquired agricultural products from their farming neighbors. Specific resources varied, of course, depending on particular location. Among the Natchez, a stratified chiefdom located along the Mississippi River in central and southern Louisiana, the yearly cycle of economic activities and food supplies was reflected in names given to the thirteen moons of the calendar:

This nation begins its year in the month of March. The first moon is that of the Deer. The second moon is that of Strawberries. The women and children collect them in great quantities. And the warriors then make their presents [to the paramount chief] of wood ducks, which they have provided by a hunt made expressly for that purpose. The third moon is that of Little Corn. The fourth is that of the Watermelons. This month and the preceding are those in which the sardines run up against the current of the river. The fifth moon is that of the Peaches. In this time, grapes are also brought in. The sixth moon is that of the Mulberries. The seventh moon is that of Maize or Great Corn. The eighth month is that of the Turkeys. The ninth moon is that of the Bison. Then they go to hunt this animal. Everyone sets out, young and old, girls and women, for this hunt being rough there is work for everyone. The tenth moon is that of the Bears. The eleventh moon is that of the Cold Meal [parched corn meal]. At this time, many bustards, geese, and ducks are to be had. The twelfth moon is that of the Chestnuts. Finally, the thirteenth month is that of

the Nuts. It is then that the nuts are broken in order to make bread by mingling them with corn meal. (du Pratz 1758, II: 354, 383)

In the Southeastern region generally, a great variety and abundance of animals, birds, fish, and wild plants were utilized as foods. Men were responsible for procuring animal resources while women gathered vegetables and fruits. Animals such as deer, bison, bears, rabbits, opposums, otters, beavers, and squirrels were the most commonly hunted. Of these, deer were the most significant as a source both of meat and hides. Deer were either stalked singly or were killed in communal drives. When stalking deer, hunters used disguises so that they could approach the animals without alarming them. Techniques employed by Timucuas of Florida were described in 1565:

They manage to put on the skins of the largest [deer] which has been taken, in such a manner, with the heads on their own heads, so that they can see out through the eyes as through a mask. They take advantage of the time when the animals come to drink at the river, and having their bow and arrows all ready, easily shoot them, as they are very plentiful in those regions. (Le Moyne 1875: 10)

Communal deer hunts consisted of driving the animals into a surround or toward a waiting group of hunters either by making loud noises or setting fire to grass. For example, Yuchis of Tennessee drove deer toward rivers or lakes by burning surrounding prairie grass. Hunters who were positioned at the water shot the deer with bows and arrows or killed them with spears.

Bears were caught by inducing them to leave their dens in winter when their reflexes were relatively slow. They were either prodded with poles or called with loud noises. When they emerged from their shelter, they were shot by hunters with sure aim. Buffalo were hunted by some Southeastern people, particularly those groups inhabiting the western sections of the region as well as in Kentucky, Arkansas, and Tennessee (Swanton 1946: 327). Communal hunting of buffalo was the most common technique, often involving hundreds of hunters and their families. Smaller animals were caught using fire-drives. And some were taken in traps and snares. Turkeys were the most important birds in the Southeastern diet. They were frequently hunted by means of fire-drives. In addition, pigeons, partridges, ducks, and geese were caught using bows and arrows or snares. Many kinds of fish were caught, including catfish, barbel, bass, sturgeon, herring, trout, shad, and shellfish such as oysters, mussels, and shrimp. Fishing gear included hooks and lines, nets, weirs, snares, spears, and bows and arrows.

Among the many wild plants gathered were onions, wild sweet potatoes, briars, goldenclub, wild peas, grapes, plums, strawberries, huckleberries, crab apples, walnuts, chestnuts, hickory nuts, and acorns. Finally, salt was collected by people living near natural deposits in Arkansas, Louisiana, and along the Gulf coast. They developed an extensive trade network supplying salt to other groups throughout the region:

> The Indians [of Arkansas] carry salt to other regions to exchange it for skins. They gather it along the river, which leaves it on top of the sand when the water falls. Then they put it into baskets, wide at the top and narrow at the bottom. They hang the baskets to a pole and put water in them, and they place a basin underneath into which the water falls. After being strained and set on fire to boil, as the water becomes less, the salt is left on the bottom of the pot. (Elvas, quoted in Robertson 1933: 192–193)

The proportion of the Southeastern diet that derived from foraging or horticulture differed somewhat, but farm products generally supplied the basis of meals. Farming activities began with the clearing of fields by removing trees and bushes. Typical slash-and-burn techniques were described for the Chickasaws of northeastern Mississippi in 1775:

> In the first clearing, they only bark the large timber, cut down the saplings and underwood, and burn them in heaps; as the suckers shoot up, they chop them off close to the stump, of which they make fires to deaden the roots, till in time they decay. (Adair 1775: 405–406)

Once fields were readied by groups of men, women "plant their corn in straight rows, putting five or six grains into one hole, about two inches distance. They cover them with clay in the form of a small hill. Each row is a yard asunder, and in the vacant ground they plant pumpkins, water-melons, sunflowers, and sundry sorts of beans and peas" (408). Early varieties of corn were ready to be harvested within two months while others took several more months to ripen.

Corn was prepared using a number of different techniques. It was commonly roasted whole, often when it was still somewhat green. Corn was also boiled in soups or stews with meat, fish, and wild plants or berries. A dish of hominy was made by boiling corn kernels that had been pounded with a mortar to remove their skins. A kind of corn mush was prepared by boiling finely pounded corn meal in water. In addition, corn meal was sometimes mixed with chestnuts and then wrapped in husks and boiled. Parched corn was another common dish, made by drying cornmeal over fire and then keeping it for future use. When needed, parched corn was mixed with cold water or boiled briefly in water. It then softened and expanded, supplying a good meal for hunters and travellers away from home. Finally, cornmeal was often baked into cakes and breads. Such recipes included mixtures of meal, sunflowers, berries, and/or nuts.

Pumpkins and squashes were cut into strips and either roasted or dried over fire. Beans were boiled, often mixed with corn or cooked in soups and stews. Wild roots were pounded into flour and made into breads. Some fruits and berries were mixed with meat in stews or with cornmeal in breads while others were dried and eaten whole. Nuts were often pounded into meal and cooked in cakes and breads.

Meat was generally prepared by roasting or boiling. Fish and shellfish were cooked in similar fashion. Bear fat was separated, boiled, and the resulting grease or oil was kept, later mixed with other meats, or used as a sauce. Surplus meat, especially of larger animals such as deer, buffalo, and bear, was preserved by curing slowly over fire. The meat was first removed from the bone, cut into thin strips, and then hung on racks suspended over fire. Fish and shellfish were preserved by smoking as well.

Settlements

Because of a relatively reliable food supply, Southeastern people were sedentary although they did not remain in stable villages during the entire year. Largest settlements existed in spring and summer when people resided in villages amidst their farmlands, often situated along rivers where land was most fertile and drainage provided water for fields. Even in these seasons, though, residence was not completely stable since men frequently left their communities for short hunting or fishing expeditions. After the final harvest of crops in autumn, people prepared to leave their towns and as winter approached, they dispersed in small groups, settling in temporary camps at several locations for hunting and fishing. The annual cycle was renewed in springtime when people returned to their permanent dwellings.

Aboriginal housing consisted of two types of structures, each adapted for and used during different seasons. In spring and summer, large rectangular homes were built. They were constructed of a frame of pine, hickory, or cedar poles over which a covering of either grass or bark was placed both on the sides and on the top. In order to protect the roof from damage by the strong winds and rain common in the Southeast, people tied wooden poles over the grass or bark covering. Houses had shelves along the interior walls or free-standing wooden platforms that were used for sitting, sleeping, and storing possessions. Partitions were built within the dwelling to separate quarters for the several families that shared the space. Most houses had one door although larger structures might have two. The outside and inside walls were plastered with mixtures of clay and grass or moss. Since these dwellings were used during seasons when the weather was typically hot, ovens or small cooking houses were built outside so that the heat from fires would not increase the discomfort of the living quarters.

The second type of dwelling was used in cold winter months. It was usually circular in shape, smaller, and more densely constructed than summer houses. Thatch that covered the wooden frame was woven thick with split saplings. It was then covered with 6 or 7 in. of clay mixed with grass, covered again with grass or bark. Inside the single door a winding passageway six or more feet in length helped protect inhabitants from cold winds. Winter "hot houses" (as they were called by sixteenth- and seventeenth-century European observers) were heated with a central fire. Since these dwellings had no windows and their walls were well sealed, they were quite warm even in the coldest weather.

Houses were furnished with cushions of hide and woven cane or grass mats used as support while sitting or as pillows when sleeping. In winter, people covered themselves with hides of deer, buffalo, or bear that were tanned with the hair retained so that they were soft and comfortable.

Although all houses in a village were constructed using similar designs, they were differentiated by their size. Dwellings of chiefs and their relatives tended to be larger and more elaborately decorated than those of common citizens. Chiefly residences were built on high ground or on sites where earth had been piled so as to raise the structure.

Towns were not dense concentrations of dwellings but rather were small groups of houses scattered throughout an inhabited district that could extend for several miles. Each district usually had a ceremonial and sociopolitical center with distinctive buildings that were venues for rituals, public gatherings, council meetings, and visits of dignitaries. For instance, a town of the Cusabos in South Carolina was described by a British captain in 1666:

> The Towne is scituate on the side or rather in the skirts of a faire forest in which at severall distances are diverse feilds of Maiz with many little houses straglingly amongst them for the habitations of the particular families. On the East side and part of the South It hath a large prospect over meadows very spatious and delightful, before the Doore of their Statehouse is a spatious walke rowed with trees on both sides tall and full branched. (South Carolina Historical Society Collections 1897, 5: 60–62)

The following eighteenth-century Seminole town along the Florida coast was fairly typical of coastal Southeastern settlements:

> There were eight or ten habitations, in a row or street fronting the water [of the bay], and about fifty yards distant from it … There seemed to be several hundred acres of cleared land about the village; a considerable portion of which was planted, chiefly with corn, beans, pumpkins, squashes, melons, tobacco, etc., abundantly sufficient for the inhabitants of the village. (Bartram 1955: 90–91)

Some villages were surrounded by wooden stockades, although it is difficult to be certain that such defenses predated European invasions. As early as the middle of the sixteenth century, people erected temporary palisades to protect against, or at least delay, Spanish soldiers on their destructive marches through the region. Stockaded villages also existed in borderlands between some Southeastern nations. Their antiquity is not firmly known. Some may have been erected as defense against other Native people who entered the region from the north or west earlier than the sixteenth century. Others were constructed after European contact when Indians were forced to move from areas of colonial settlement, infringing on each other's ancestral territories and causing friction and open conflict.

Families and Social Systems

Throughout most of the Southeast, aboriginal kinship systems were based on matrilineal descent. Clans existed in some, but not all, societies. They were usually named after animals, birds, or fish, although in a few nations clans might bear the name of agricultural products or natural phenomena. Clans functioned as corporate groups, followed rules of exogamy, and controlled access to farmland. In many Southeastern nations, exogamous moiety divisions operated as well. They were either named after or associated with colors, most commonly "red" and "white," or termed "peace" and "war." Their primary functions were ceremonial. Moieties prepared and conducted funeral rites for members of the opposite group. And moiety members played against each other in competitive ball games that had a ceremonial as well as athletic character.

Among Southeastern people, consanguineal and affinal kin relationships formed the basis of social obligations. Members of the same clan were obliged to help each other by cooperating in joint labor when required and by giving material support to those less fortunate. Since clans were exogamous, marriages transformed unrelated social groups into families that were bound by reciprocal obligations. Marriages were frequently arranged by clan relatives of the young couple although either of the prospective mates could veto the union. Continuity of family bonds was demonstrated by the possibility of levirate and sororate marriages after the death of husband or wife.

In addition to membership in and responsibilities to households, clans, and moieties, aboriginal social life was structured by sociopolitical systems that both united and differentiated people according to distinctions of merit and birth. Village leadership was vested in clan chiefs and their advisors, usually but not always members of their own clan. The majority of clan chiefs were men, but women chiefs were also common. Inheritance of office passed through women according to principles of matrilineal descent. Daughters, sons, or sisters' children might succeed female chiefs while sisters' children or one's own sibling might succeed a male leader. The authority of chiefs varied due to his/her skills, intelligence, and personality. On the basis of achievement and wisdom, some village chiefs had much greater prestige and influence than others within their nation. Such people were consulted by leaders from neighboring and distant locales. They provided leadership when dealing with representatives of other nations.

While most economic and social practices were fairly similar throughout the region, Southeastern cultures differed markedly in the degree of privilege granted to and assumed by village and national leaders. In most societies, chiefs had influence among their relatives and co-villagers, but their status did not confer power or wealth. Their lives were in most respects no different from those of other people. However, among some groups, chiefs and their close kin had social, economic, and political privileges that set them apart from commoners. As occurred in other parts of Native America, the power and status of chiefs increased after European invasions as a consequence of the amalgamation of smaller communities into larger, more concentrated polities, itself a consequence of depopulation and flight from the path of colonial intrusions. In addition, since Europeans tended to seek out and deal with one or two leaders in any particular nation, those leaders sometimes accrued greater prestige as a result. Still, notwithstanding changes in chiefly status after the sixteenth century, some aboriginal societies invested their leaders with great authority prior to European contact.

One manifestation of rank was the practice of delivering tribute to chiefs. Gifts of farm produce, meat, hides, and wild plants were presented to chiefs at times of harvest or successful hunting expeditions. For instance, the chief of the Chitimachas of Louisiana "is very absolute, as are all those of Florida. He never hunts or shoots but for his diversion, for his subjects are obliged to give him part of their game" (French 1851: 182). Protocol among the Natchez and Taensas of the lower Mississippi region dictated special behavioral and aesthetic marks of chiefly status:

They [chiefs] command and are obeyed. They have their servants who wait upon them at table. They serve them with drink in their cup after having rinsed it, and no one drinks before they do. Their wives and children are treated in the same manner. [When] the chief of the Taensa was coming to see M. de la Salle, a master of ceremonies came two hours before with five or six flunkeys whom he made sweep with their hands the road over which he must pass, prepare a place for him, and spread out a cane mat very delicately and artistically made. Two men preceded him in state, with fans of white feathers. (Margry 1875–1876, 2: 209–210, in Swanton 1946: 649)

Among the Natchez, chiefly prerogatives were the most elaborate of all Southeastern societies. The Natchez national chief, called the Great Sun, was believed to be a matrilineal descendant of a supernatural hero sent by the Great Spirit to rule the people. He had a retinue of slaves and retainers who served him. Whenever a person spoke to the Great Sun, s/he was required to stand at a distance of four paces. After the chief spoke, his hearers bowed and thanked him regardless of what he said. And whenever anyone left his presence, they walked backward. In addition, the Great Sun's bed and eating utensils were never used by anyone else. Natchez families ceremoniously gave as tribute to the chief a portion of any foods that they harvested (Swanton 1911: 100–107).

The Great Sun had the power of life and death over his subjects. If anyone offended him, he could order one of his retainers to "Go and rid me of that dog!" When a chief died, a number of his slaves and retainers were sacrificed in order to provide his soul with services in the afterworld (100–107).

The Natchez chief earned his position and the power associated with it by virtue of his birth as the eldest son of the eldest sister of the previous chief, although presumably an unfit candidate could be bypassed. Chieftainship was interwoven with a complex system of descent and social classes. Natchez society was divided into a noble and a commoner class. The groups are appropriately called classes because they did control differential access to resources, services, and power. The nobility itself consisted of three graded ranks, that is, Suns, Nobles, and Honored Persons. The chief or Great Sun was the highest ranked member of the Sun matrilineage. His eldest sister, called White Woman, was the highest ranking female member and had social and political power nearly equal to that of the chief, including the right to order the death of anyone who offended her. Their younger brother was usually appointed as the Great War Chief.

Although Suns and their close relatives amassed a great deal of power and wealth, they could not develop into an exclusive block because the Natchez social system required that all members of the nobility marry commoners. The Sun matrilineage was perpetuated through children of Sun women who were Suns themselves but children of Sun men, including children of the Great Sun, were not members of that chiefly lineage. Theoretically they should have become commoners but in recognition of their close relationship to Suns, they were termed Nobles. More distant relatives of Suns were called Honored Persons. Although children of male Suns remained in the nobility, children of male Nobles were members of their mother's lineage, that is, commoners. Children of male commoners became nobility if their fathers married noble women. In addition, commoners could raise their status by exemplary services to the nation, usually as warriors. In such cases, their wives' status was raised as well.

A curious note on the relations between Natchez nobility and commoners, and one that might question the complete submissiveness of commoners as reported by eighteenth-century European observers, is that although commoners were usually referred to as "Stinkards" by the nobility, the word was "a name which offends them, and which no one dares to pronounce before them, for it would put them in very bad humor" (du Pratz 1758, 2: 393).

Aboriginal warfare in the Southeast was carried out by small groups of men united under a temporary leader. Only on rare occasions did large forces participate in raids against enemies. Warfare was often motivated by revenge for fatalities suffered by families and/or communities in previous attacks. The goal was injury or death to the person held responsible for one's own losses or to a member of his kin group. Warfare that occurred in borderlands between neighboring nations may have had an underlying ecological purpose, namely to create "disputed regions dangerous to all hunters and allow game populations to recover" from the excesses of overhunting (White 1983: 9). Even in these cases, warfare prior to European invasions was never motivated by desires for territorial expansion. As witnessed by sixteenth-century Spanish observers,

> [Warfare] was not a conflict of force against force with an organized army or pitched battles, or a conflict instigated by the lust and ambition of some lords to seize the estates of others. This struggle was one of ambushes in which they attacked each other on fishing or hunting trips and in their fields and along their roads. As soon as the conquerers had inflicted the desired damage, they regathered in their own lands without attempting to take possession of the land of others. (Garcilaso de la Vega, quoted in Gibson 1974: 130–131)

As we shall see in the next section, aboriginal motivations and military tactics were transformed in the context of European attempts to "seize the estates of others" as societies defended their own lands against intrusions by Europeans and by other Indians seeking refuge from foreign colonizers. In addition, Indians became enmeshed in Spanish, British, and French rivalries and often adopted the Europeans' strategies.

EUROPEAN INVASIONS OF THE SOUTHEAST

The first historically recorded visit by a European to the Southeastern shores was that of Ponce de Leon, who landed along the southwest coast of Florida in 1513. He had brief encounters with aboriginal people, now believed to be from the Calusa nation, and was given an unfriendly reception. Eight years later, Ponce tried to establish a settlement of Spaniards in Calusa territory, but the people repelled the Spaniards' attempt, forcing them to return to Cuba from where they had come. Afterward, several additional groups of Spanish navigators and soldiers explored the coast of Florida, some venturing inland in short expeditions. In 1526, Panfilo de Narvaez received a grant from the Spanish crown giving him "title" to much of south Florida. Two years later, he led a force of more than 300 soldiers on a march into the interior. The Timucuans whose territory the Spaniards first traversed had received advance warning and, as a consequence, had abandoned their villages. After the Spanish raided the Timucuans' stores of corn, they proceeded across the Florida peninsula to the Gulf coast, pursued by Apalachees who successfully defended their homeland.

Expeditions of Ponce de Leon and Panfilo de Narvaez paved the way for the most ambitious and most destructive of the sixteenth-century Spanish invasions, that of Hernando de Soto. After enriching himself from plundering the Incan empire in Peru, de Soto arrived at the Florida Gulf coast north of Tampa Bay in 1539 with a force of 600 soldiers, 100 servants and slaves, 200 horses, and packs of bloodhounds to track Indians. During the next four years, de Soto's group proceeded northward along the coast and then turned inland through Florida, headed north to the coast of South Carolina, turned again across Alabama, Mississippi, and Louisiana, finally following the Mississippi River south to the Gulf coast. They carved a route of murder, rape, looting and disease, disrupting and destroying Native lives and setting in motion chains of events that fundamentally transformed aboriginal societies. The record of their deeds is related by de Soto's chronicler, identified only as a "Gentleman of Elvas," in a *True relation of the hardships suffered by Governor Fernando de Soto and certain Portuguese gentlemen*, a title startling in

Indians burning their village in Arkansas at the approach of Spanish explorer Hernando de Soto. John William Orr engraving 1815–1887

its indifference to the human lives wrecked by de Soto and his gentlemen.

De Soto's expedition embarked on a policy of demanding food, clothing, and carriers from villages that they encountered. They first proceeded through the towns of the Timucuas in northern Florida, plundering stores of food and taking hostages as guides and carriers who they often chained together with iron collars. When people heard of the Spaniards' brutality, they fled their villages in advance of the army. As soldiers marched north into South Carolina, they looted graves for pearls and other luxury goods. They then turned inland, crossing the Appalachian mountains into the country of the Cousas in northern Alabama. Again they looted granaries and captured some people, forcing men to carry their belongings and raping the women. The Spaniards also left one of their number who was sick with smallpox in a Cousa village. His presence proved to be a disaster for indigenous people as they succumbed in great numbers to the ravages of the epidemic unleashed in their midst.

Indians shifted back and forth between two modes of dealing with the invaders. In some cases, they tried to accommodate the Spaniards' demands, hoping to escape death and destruction. In others, they resisted the intruders by either abandoning their villages in advance of the Spanish army or by directly confronting the soldiers with military force. However, although both strategies produced some relief, neither was permanently effective. Accommodation often led to disaster because when provisions and carriers were given to the Spanish, demands for food, servants, and women immediately increased. Hostages were taken, later to be permanently enslaved or murdered. When villages were abandoned, peoples' stores of food and other valuable possessions were stolen by soldiers. And although armed resistance was sometimes initially successful, even those groups who escaped direct destruction were not untouched by the consequences of the invasion.

By the time the Spaniards reached Alabama, enough news of the foreigners had reached the inhabitants that they either fled for their lives or tried to repel the invaders. For instance, the Mobiles of Alabama attacked the Spanish army after their chief, Tascalusa, had been taken as a hostage and forced to guide the foreigners through his territory. Thousands of warriors battled the invading army, killing eighty-two soldiers and wounding nearly all the remainder. But the Spanish army set fire to Mobile houses, killing and burning some 11,000 people.

When the intruders arrived in Mississippi, they were attacked by Chickasaw warriors who killed about a dozen soldiers and sixty of their horses. They also destroyed Spanish equipment, clothing, and provisions but were frightened away from a final assault by stampeding horses and therefore did not venture another attack for several weeks. During the interval, the Spaniards recovered, later admitting that had they been attacked again immediately, they would have all been killed (Swanton 1946: 52). But the Chickasaws' second raid, coming too late, proved ineffective, although it did force the foreigners out of Chickasaw lands.

After de Soto died in 1542, he was succeeded by Luis de Moscoso, who continued his predecessor's destructive policies. As the Spaniards wound their way south along the Mississippi River, Indians offered continual resistance. Pursued and harassed by Natchez warriors, the Spaniards finally left the Gulf coast of Louisiana in 1543, taking with them more than a hundred captives. And, although by that time the Spanish force had lost nearly half of its original number, the toll among indigenous people was far higher.

In 1559, the Spanish attempted to establish a colony of some 1,000 settlers at the head of present-day Mobile Bay, east of the mouth of the Mississippi River. When they arrived, they found that most inhabitants had fled their towns. The Spanish colony too was soon abandoned due to the antagonism of the remaining Indians, who refused to provide food and other assistance. During the same period, the French also planned a number of colonies in the Southeast. The first, in 1562 on the coast of South Carolina, was quickly deserted. The second, made two years later by French Huguenots, was founded in Florida and might have been permanent since settlers were given a friendly reception by local inhabitants, but the colony was destroyed in 1565 by Spanish soldiers on a campaign to rid Florida of French presence. In the same year, the Spanish founded the town of St. Augustine and from there tried to exert control over territory extending from southern Florida north through Georgia into South Carolina. Their authority, at least nominally, remained intact until British settlements spread from Virginia into Georgia in the seventeenth and eighteenth centuries and wrested control from the Spaniards.

Once the British successfully established themselves in coastal Virginia and the Carolinas in the early seventeenth century, they began to spread their trade networks and influence further south and inland. Part of their trade interest was with Indians for deer hides and other goods, but Britons also carried out slave raids against Native communities, capturing men, women, and children for sale to their growing colonies in North America and the Caribbean. Trade both with and for Native people accelerated after 1670 when Charleston, South Carolina, was founded as a colonial capital. Competition between English and Spanish for commercial and military hegemony intensified. At first, the British effectively won support from several Indian nations of Florida and Georgia, such as the numerous Yamasees and Creeks, but the Spanish counteracted by setting their own allies against the English and their supporters. As a result of involvement in foreign trade and wars, conflicts also erupted among indigenous people themselves. And once British and Spanish settlers began to expropriate Native territory for their own use, the original inhabitants were compelled to relocate, often encroaching on territories of others. In addition, masses of people were sometimes forcibly moved by Spanish or British authorities in order to sever ties to rival European merchants and officials. In the process, the Southeastern tribal map was changed considerably by the beginning of the eighteenth century.

Although the early years of European contact in the Southeast were dominated by Spanish and British forces, the French entered (or rather reentered) the region in the late seventeenth century, centering their efforts in the west along the Mississippi River down whose waters they navigated from their burgeoning areas of influence around the Great Lakes. In 1682, La Salle journeyed the length of the Mississippi River to the Gulf of Mexico and promptly declared the entire territory to be a possession of his king. The first permanent French settlement in Louisiana was founded in 1699 at Old Biloxi, and by the early 1700s, several forts and numerous Catholic missions were established in the region. After the French territorial capital of New Orleans was built in 1718, nearby Native people gravitated toward the center for trade and protection from English and Spanish slave raids, among them the Washas, Houmas, Acolapissas, Taensas, Biloxis, Choctaws, Apalachees, Yamasees, and Mobiles. But increasing turmoil and dislocations spread to all areas of the Southeast, resulting in nearly constant wars as aboriginal groups were enlisted as allies of the various European powers and thus pitted against one another in a desperate struggle to survive and retain their own territories. National unity itself was destroyed as some peoples, such as the Choctaws, were divided over their allegiances to the French or British and fought against each other in several disastrous civil wars.

The coerced movement of entire nations was repeated for more than a century, eventually culminating in the infamous "Trail of Tears" of the 1830s. But before that tragedy occurred, dozens of nations were destroyed, forced to flee their lands or be subsumed and merged with other surviving peoples. Some of the victims belonged to small, relatively defenseless groups while others, such as the Natchez, were members of large, powerful societies.

In addition, tens of thousands of people died from the ravages of European diseases. In some cases, entire nations were wiped out. Writing in 1726, the French governor of Louisiana, Jean le Moyne de Bienville, observed the effects of the combination of disease and warfare on indigenous populations:

> It is known that this country is one of the finest climates of America and that it was formerly the most densely populated with Indians but at present of these prodigious quantities of different nations one sees only pitiful remnants that have escaped. Several have been entirely destroyed and about fifty others that are scattered along the Mississippi and [its] tributaries. Only the Choctaws can give us any ideas of what the Indians formerly were. The others are feeble remnants which are diminishing every day because of the different diseases that the Europeans have brought into the country and which were formerly unknown to the Indians. (de Bienville 1726, 3: 526–527)

AMERICAN EXPANSION AND CONTROL

Foreign control of the Southeast was altered again in 1763 when British victory over the French in North America led to the transfer of French territory east of the Mississippi River to Great Britain, while France's territory west of the River passed to Spain. In the next decade, the American Revolution led to another realignment of forces. At the outbreak of the war, many Southeastern nations realized that a rebel victory would threaten their own survival because American colonists were continually encroaching on their territory, attacking border towns, and looting their stores of corn. British officials encouraged Native hostility toward colonists and although British protections were obviously ineffective, most Indians understood the danger posed by an independent country unfettered by British proclamations. Cherokees, Creeks, and Chickasaws were among the most powerful nations to side with Great Britain. At the end of the war, the new American government forced many groups to sign treaties ceding vast expanses of land as punishment for participation as British allies. As historian James O'Donnell has summarized, "If the American Revolution was a time of national beginnings in politics and society, it was equally so in Indian policy, for with the nation's beginnings emerged the ideas of displacement and removal, ideas which came to fruition in the nineteenth century and have not died in the present century" (O'Donnell 1975: 59).

American settlers poured westward after the Revolution, seeking more farmland. In the face of constant encroachment on their land, some Indians renewed their resistance. They were encouraged by Spanish officials who remained in control of Florida and territory west of the Mississippi River that they had obtained from France in 1763. Lands west of the Mississippi were returned to France in 1800 and then sold to the United States in 1803. But even then, Native resistance to American hegemony continued. Among others, the numerous and powerful Creek Confederacy fought the onslaught of settlers into their territory, leading to the so-called Creek War of 1813–1814 that ended with the Creeks' defeat by an American force under Andrew Jackson. Even the Seminoles of Florida were attacked by Jackson's troops although they lived in territory that at that time still belonged to Spain (Florida was not given to the United States until 1819).

Confiscation of Native land and forced relocation of survivors intensified after the War of 1812. Rich, fertile lands east of the Mississippi River were especially valued since they had already been cleared and farmed for generations by Native tribes. Settlers from Virginia, the Carolinas, and Georgia pressured their legislatures as well as the federal government to remove aboriginal inhabitants so that Americans could claim the land. By the 1820s, the Cherokees, Creeks, Choctaws, Chickasaws, and Seminoles (often referred to as the "Five Civilized Tribes" because of their productive agricultural economies and their formal political systems) were besieged by demands for territory. Having signed away a good deal of their homelands, they finally refused to give any more. The election of Andrew Jackson as president in 1829 sealed their fate because he had been one of the strongest advocates of Indian removal. The US Congress added to the pressure by passage of the "Indian Removal Act," which ordered removal of Native people east of the Mississippi River to lands in "Indian Territory," now the state of Oklahoma. Thereafter, officials continued to mount campaigns of unrelenting pressure on Native leaders, often opting to negotiate with those chiefs who they judged to be most easily persuaded, intimidated, and/or bribed to sign treaties relinquishing their people's lands and rights. Disagreement in Native communities about whether to accommodate American demands or resist further losses of territory added to the turmoil, creating dissension and disarray. Whether willing or not, Native negotiators at treaty councils were coerced into signing agreements that set the stage for their nation's removal. The history of these councils is a sordid one indeed. Chiefs were threatened, bribed, and intoxicated until they put their marks on treaty papers.

The first of the documents was signed in 1830 by Choctaws at Dancing Rabbit Creek. They were followed in 1832 by treaties with Chickasaws and Creeks. The Creeks, however, did not leave quickly enough to suit American settlers, who then poured into their lands while the people were still living there. The so-called Creek War ensued in 1836, leading to the Creeks' forced removal. One group of Seminole leaders signed treaties in 1832 and 1833, but the people refused to leave. At the end of the consequent seven-year Seminole War in 1842, many surviving Seminoles were also forcibly ousted. The Cherokees were the last of the "Five Civilized Tribes" to sign treaties of removal. In 1835, one faction agreed to terms in the Treaty of New Echota and emigrated westward, but others refused to comply and were then evicted by the US army in 1837 and 1838. Members of smaller nations were removed as well and assigned lands west of the Mississippi.

Although the majority of Indians were relocated, several thousand managed to elude or escape their army captors and remained in or near their ancestral homelands. Among these were approximately 2,000 or 3,000 Choctaws, 1,500 Cherokees, and 500 Seminoles. In addition, small groups of Seminoles, Koasatis, Alabamas, Biloxis, Pascagoulas, and Choctaws broke away from the march westward and settled in Louisiana and eastern Texas.

CONTEMPORARY NATIVE COMMUNITIES

Today, the majority of descendants of aboriginal Southeastern nations reside in Oklahoma, on lands that once were reservation territory, but have since been removed from that status. Smaller groups continue to live in or near their ancestral homelands in the Southeast. The largest Native nations now in the region are the Cherokees in North Carolina (approximately 15,000 residents) and Seminoles in Florida (a population of about 2,000). In 1970, representatives of four federally recognized tribes (the Seminoles, Miccosukees, Cherokees, and Choctaws) founded an organization called United SouthEastern Tribes, Inc., to coordinate activities related to legal and economic issues and to consult together about their problems and concerns. They later expanded their membership to include several Northeastern nations and in 1979 formed the United Southern and Eastern Tribes.

In addition, an intertribal organization has brought together descendents of the indigenous peoples who were forced out of their territories in the Southeast in the infamous Trail of Tears of 1830. Named the Inter-Tribal Council of the Five Civilized Tribes, the elected leaders of the Chickasaw, Cherokee, Choctaw of Oklahoma, Muscogee (Creek), and Seminole Nations meet periodically to discuss issues of joint concern and to present their positions on these matters. The Council was originally established in 1950 but did not hold meetings for several decades until it was revived in 2012. Of primary importance are discussions of sovereignty, tribal enrollment, repatriation of treasured artifacts and remains, as well as environmental, economic, educational, and cultural programs. The direction and initiatives undertaken by the Council are likely to have regional and even national consequences given that together their tribal population includes some 625,000 members.

The Cherokees

Cherokees who were able to elude the US Army sent to remove them from their homeland to Oklahoma eventually settled in the Great Smokey Mountains of North Carolina. Living on the Eastern Cherokee Reservation (also called Qualla Boundary) that encompasses more than 66,000 acres, the people farmed their land and raised livestock. In the 1950s when the Great Smokey Mountain National Park was established, bordering on the Cherokee reservation, tourists by the thousands came to the region. The parks, motels, restaurants, and other tourist facilities have since provided seasonal employment for many Cherokees. Although most of the businesses are owned by outsiders, Cherokees have established their own enterprises as well. Among the

Dinah George demonstrates basketmaking at the Cherokee village of Oconaluftee in the Great Smoky Mountains, North Carolina.

most successful are the Oconaluftee Indian Village and the Sequoyah Birthplace Museum. Every summer Cherokees host an outdoor drama called "Unto These Hills" that depicts the period of the 1830 Trail of Tears and the forced removal of most Southeastern Indians to Oklahoma. In addition to tourist occupations, Cherokees find employment with the Tennessee Valley Authority, the National Forest Service, and in nearby factories. In 1982, the Cherokee tribe opened a gaming casino that has become profitable, particularly in the summer months when hundreds of thousands of tourists visit the region.

Cherokees who are involved in the tourist industry face an unusual dilemma. While their personal identification is Cherokee, when they work in tourist businesses they often dress up in "stereotypical" Plains Indian war bonnets and regalia. According to Finger, "identification with a non-specific, generic 'Indian' conforming to white stereotypes is common on the reservation, and most Cherokees seem to accept it as a necessary cost of doing business … Yet one should remember that tourism also sustains worthwhile attractions like the Museum of the Cherokee Indian, Oconaluftee Indian Village, and the Qualla Arts and Crafts Cooperative. Thus it entails certain tradeoffs; the tacky merchandise exists in symbiotic embrace with more worthy attractions offering visitors—and the Cherokees themselves—an informed insight into the tribe. More important, tourism puts food on the table. Fortunately most Cherokees seem to understand the difference between the stereotypical image they project and the Cherokee identity they claim" (Finger 1991: 184).

Protection of Cherokee identity and heritage is the goal of several cultural projects. Recognizing the possible loss of Cherokee language ability, programs to enhance the use of the language by speakers of all ages have been inaugurated, including language immersion schools and the use of the Native language in all educational materials. And in 2012, Cherokee became the first Native American language to be fully integrated into Google's Gmail program. In addition, Cherokee was available on Windows 8, although it has not yet been added to Windows 10.

The Cherokee tribal council has expanded its powers and exerted its rights to plan and manage local governmental and economic authority. However, political tensions have arisen, particularly concerning eligibility requirements for tribal enrollment. These tensions are often crystallized in divisions among people on the

basis of blood quantum and ancestry. Such divisions are not new but date to the eighteenth century. After Cherokees established their own constitutional form of government in the 1940s, the elected chief and vice chief of the Cherokee nation had to be at least one-half Cherokee by blood ancestry, but in 1986, the Tribal Council stipulated that any enrolled member could be elected to either of these two offices (Finger 1991: 173). In the same year, the Council enacted new regulations that allowed first generation nonenrolled descendants of enrolled members to inherit possessory rights to land. That is, until that time, people who were ineligible for enrollment on the basis of blood ancestry could not possess rights to land, but they are now permitted to inherit such rights (173). Criteria for enrollment were revised in 1996, stipulating that eligible people must "have direct lineal ancestry" to tribal lists compiled in 1924, "possess 1/16 Eastern Cherokee blood and are currently within three years of the date of birth or within one year following the eighteenth birthday" (Eastern Cherokee Nation 1999).

Under the vigorous leadership of elected officials, eastern Cherokees have expanded their economic investments in enterprises and land. In 1996, the tribe paid $2.1 million for 309 acres that surrounded a sacred ancient site called Kituhwa ("mother town"), the place where Cherokee traditions say that the people originated (Loy 1999: 37). They promoted the writing of a bilingual constitution, in keeping with an emphasis on maintaining traditional culture and language. Today, however, only about an estimated 1,000 eastern Cherokees are fluent speakers of their Native tongue (Finger 1991: 182). While there are no formal ties between eastern and western Cherokees, their representatives meet together at an annual council held alternately in the tribal capitals of the Oklahoma and North Carolina nations.

The US Bureau of the Census has not collected population data for some tribes since the 2010 Census, in which 284,247 respondents identified as "Cherokee alone," while 534,858 more identified as "Cherokee in combination with one or more other race or American Indian tribal grouping." According to this data, the Cherokees are the most numerous Indian nation, accounting for 15.7 percent of all Native Americans (Ogunwole 2002). This figure differs somewhat from official, recent tribal enrollments. In 2011 the Oklahoma Indian Affairs Commission published population data in which 314,162 respondents were enrolled in a Cherokee Tribe. The Commission seperates the

Cherokee into two groups: the Cherokee Nation and the United Keetoowah Band of Cherokee. Approximately 95 percent of Cherokee are affiliated with the Cherokee Nation, while only 5 percent are members of the United Keetoowah Band (Oklahoma Indian Affairs Commission 2011).

However, tribal enrollment has become a contentious issue for the Oklahoma Cherokees. The complicated history of relationships among the Cherokees and descendents of some 1,300 African slaves who made the long journey on the Trail of Tears has contemporary consequences in the Cherokee nation's attempts to define citizenship on the basis of descent from people who were listed as "Cherokee by Blood" on the tribal lists drawn up after passage of the General Allotment Act of 1887. The tribal rolls made a distinction between people who were "Cherokee by Blood" and "Free Colored Persons" living with them. Previously, by a treaty signed between the Cherokees and the United States in 1866, former slaves, then called Freedmen, were entitled to "all the rights of native Cherokees" (Jennings 2012).

Then, in 1970 Congress passed the Principal Chiefs Act that gave the Cherokee the right to vote for their own leaders and in the following year, the BIA mandated that enrolled Freedmen be acknowledged with the same rights as the Cherokees. However, in 1983, members of the tribal leadership began a process of blocking Freedmen from registering and voting in tribal elections. They distributed Certificates of Degree of Indian Blood to the Cherokees, requiring these certificates as identity cards for voting purposes. This process caused growing resentment on the part of Freedmen who felt that they were being unlawfully disenfranchised.

In an effort to counter what she felt was discriminatory, a Freedman citizen named Lucy Allen filed suit in the Cherokee Nation Supreme Court leading to a positive ruling and affirming the rights of descendants of people listed on the tribal rolls to participate with the full rights of citizens. The controversy led to a tribal referendum held in 2007 to amend the Cherokee Constitution that would permanently remove the Freedmen from tribal citizenship. The amendment passed by a margin of 76 percent to 24 percent but without any participation from the Freedmen themselves since they were not permitted to vote. However, the assistant secretary of the Interior for Indian Affairs refused to validate the election. As it currently stands, both sides have filed legal suits in the Cherokee

Nation Supreme Court as well as in federal courts but final determinations have yet to be handed down. In the meantime, the Cherokee Nation has agreed to reinstate the citizenship rights of the Freedmen awaiting definitive court rulings. Additionally, in 2008 the Councils of the Cherokee Nation and the Eastern Band of Cherokee passed a resolution (Resolution #00-08: *A Resolution Opposing Fabricated Cherokee "Tribes" and "Indians"*) asking that no public funding should be granted to non-federally recognized Cherokee tribes, to prevent exploitation of Cherokee culture by non-Cherokees.

This complicated debate can be viewed from several perspectives. A central issue is that of Native American sovereignty. From the beginning of the United States as a distinct country and of US Supreme Court rulings dealing with indigenous peoples, the federal government has taken upon itself the right to define the extent of Native sovereignty, allowing Native tribal entities to act independently in some situations but limiting the full exercise of self-government. The ability to determine the rights of membership is of course one of the powers of sovereign polities. In addition, the use of blood quantum as a principal means of determining the status of "Indian" was introduced by US officials in the nineteenth century so that too can be seen as a colonial imposition on indigenous societies. And finally, in this particular case, the influence of racism toward people of African descent has also been raised by the Freedmen and their supporters as a contributing factor in the attempts to limit their participation.

Federal statistics for 1999 reported the median of the household income is $35,505 for eastern Cherokees and $38,817 for western Cherokees. Median household income for eastern Cherokees was $16,965 and $23,006 for Cherokees in Oklahoma. Figures for eastern Cherokee per capita and household incomes were above the American Indian average but above the median for western Cherokees ($30,693 and $41,994, respectively; US Bureau of the Census 2000, Table 6: 185). Both groups of Cherokees, however, had incomes lower than those of their neighbors in the state. That is, the eastern Cherokee per capita income of $7,374 was less than half the North Carolina average of $15,198 while the western Cherokee income of $9,570 was less than the Oklahoma average of $24,605 (Statistical Abstracts 2000: 442). Median household incomes for Cherokees were similarly below those of the general southern population of $39,184. Consistent with differences in incomes, percentages of families living below the poverty level were higher for eastern Cherokees (18.5%) than for western Cherokees (13.6%) (US Bureau of the Census 2000, Table 6). Again, these numbers compare unfavorably with the general southern figure of 14.7 percent of families living in poverty (Statistical Abstracts 2000: 465). Although average incomes differed for the two groups of Cherokees, employment statistics were roughly the same: 7.3 percent of eastern Cherokee workers were unemployed while 6.4 percent of western Cherokees were unemployed (US Bureau of Indian Affairs 2000, Table 9). These figures reveal a sharply higher rate of unemployment than the norm for their states: 5.3 percent for North Carolina and 5.3 percent for Oklahoma (Statistical Abstracts 2000: 405).

The Seminoles

The second largest Native Southeastern nation is the Seminoles in Florida, a consolidation of at least two and possibly more indigenous groups. These include Yamassees, who left the Carolinas in 1715 because of the increasing strife in their homeland caused by settler encroachment, and the Oconees and the Creeks, who drifted into central Florida following the so-called Creek War (1813–1814). After the Indian Removal Act of 1830, Seminoles resisted removal, and about 500 were able to escape or elude the army by hiding out in the swamps of central and southern Florida. The army, however, pursued them, resulting in the "Seminole War" of 1835–1842. The Native leader Osceola attempted to negotiate a settlement, but when he arrived under a flag of truce, he was taken prisoner and later died in jail. Seminoles continued to reject removal, leading to another war that lasted from 1856 until 1858. At its conclusion, the majority of Seminoles were forced to relocate to "Indian Territory." Thereafter, only about 150 Seminoles survived in Florida (Garbarino 1972: 12).

There are currently five Seminole reservations in Florida with a combined Native population of about

Students help take care of the garden during a sixth grade culture class at the Ahfachkee school at the Big Cypress Seminole Indian Reservation, Florida.

2,000. The largest, called Big Cypress, is located in interior southern Florida about 130 mi. from Miami. Although Seminoles farmed their land and raised cattle in the past, most of the acreage at Big Cypress is now leased to commercial agricultural companies growing vegetables for the northern market. Seminoles work on the farms as seasonal laborers. People also rely on resources such as deer, fish, turtles, birds, and wild plants. Some supplement their incomes by selling crafts, especially skirts and blouses decorated with ribbons and embroidery, a style adopted by Seminoles in the late nineteenth century. Many Big Cypress households are integrated through traditional patterns of social organization that emphasize matrilineal clans and matrifocal households and families. Kin-groups are the primary units of socializing and economic cooperation.

The Seminole community at Big Cypress is linked to the four other reservations in the "Seminole Tribe of Florida" that gained official recognition in 1957. Today, there are six reservations within the state of Florida. Although tribal leaders and council members are elected by the populace, traditional consensus-building is critical to the success of any decision or undertaking. Votes are taken only after prolonged discussion. As a Seminole consultant observed:

> We never vote when anyone is mad. We just talk and talk until everyone understands. If some people are still mad, we don't vote then. We put it off until another meeting. If we have to get something changed which people don't like or don't understand, we may have to talk for a very long time, but it is best for everyone to agree before we vote. (Quoted in Garbarino 1972: 93)

Furthermore, leaders who adopt the Anglo style of decision-making are discredited and quickly replaced: "It isn't good to tell people what to do. Someone gets mad. The people at the agency want us to do some things we never used to do, and the leaders are supposed to tell people to do it. Then no one likes the leader. Most people wouldn't like to be a leader" (94).

The current Seminole economy is based on a combination of farming, cattle raising, tourism, and casino gaming. Because of land reclamation projects and the improvement of herds, Seminoles have become the fifth largest producer of calves in the United States (Gehrke-White 2014). They have also developed a highly specialized farming niche, and currently own over one-sixth of the land used for growing lemons in Florida.

Seminoles began to work in tourism in the early twentieth century. By 1919, men were participating in tourist venues and circuses as "alligator wrestlers." They also worked in "Indian villages" that were opened as tourist attractions near Miami and Fort Lauderdale. Men wrestled alligators and women sold crafts such as dolls, decorated skirts, and belts. Tourism expanded in the 1920s when more land was opened up as a result of the draining of the Everglades and the completion of a highway from Miami to Tampa. In addition, the focus of tourism shifted from the cities to other regions of the state. Seminoles who lived in camps along the new highway began to operate their own tourist attractions, not dependent on non-Indian managers. Throughout the rest of the century, Seminoles kept pace with the demands of the growing tourist industry. However, the ensuing years have brought a change in the type of tourism provided by Seminoles. No longer wrestling alligators, Seminoles now offer glimpses into their traditional lifeways by providing foods, clothing, crafts, and dance demonstrations and allowing visitors to see how people can live in and with their natural environment. This "eco-tourism" is increasingly popular with both American and European tourists (115).

Seminoles have been instrumental in changing the legal and economic landscape throughout Native America. They were the first Indian nation to bring the issue of gaming to the US Supreme Court. When Seminoles opened casinos and bingo parlors in the 1980s, the state of Florida attempted to close them on the grounds that they violated state gaming regulations. The Seminoles responded with a legal challenge that eventually reached the Supreme Court in 1981. In a landmark decision (*Seminole Tribe of Florida v. Butterworth*), the Court ruled that Florida could not regulate gaming on Indian reservations and could not deny an Indian tribe participation in activities that were permitted for non-Indians. The decision led to passage of the federal Indian Gaming Regulatory Act of 1988 that established the rights of Indian tribes to operate gaming establishments on their territory, pursuant to compacts negotiated with the state in which their reservations are located (see Chapter 2 for discussion of the IGRA). Seminoles now operate casinos on four of their five reservations. The money obtained from gaming profits has been used to fund public projects on the reservations, the establishment of museums and visitor centers, and the distribution of per capita payments to enrolled tribal members.

The Seminoles' legal history since federal recognition of the Seminole Tribe of Florida in 1957 and of the Miccosukee Tribe of Florida in 1962 has become increasingly complex because of their new economic and political status. Even before their incorporation as tribal entities, Seminoles filed a suit with the Indian Claim Commission in 1950 covering lands confiscated by the federal government. In 1970, the ICC awarded the Seminoles more than $12 million, with an ensuing final judgment totaling more than $16 million (Seminole Land Rights in Florida 1978: 26). The award was based on the fact that in 1832 the Seminoles had been paid only $152,500 for land that at that time had a "fair market value" of more than $12 million (Kersey 1996: 142). Although many welcomed the award, some Seminoles, particularly those self-identified as traditional "Tamiami Trail Indians" objected to accepting the settlement on the grounds that to do so extinguishes their claim to the land. Instead, they want to retain possessory rights to the land, including rights to traditional subsistence activities such as fishing, hunting, and gathering (142). In 1976, the traditional Seminoles filed a class action suit to block the settlement but were unsuccessful in courts. By 1990, when the award was finally distributed, it had increased with interest to over $50 million (152).

The Seminole Tribe of Florida has recently had a shift in fortune. Due mostly to the gaming empire the tribe has managed to build, tribe-reported per capita distribution of money reached $42,000 in 2003, and $84,000 in 2007 (Tyrer 2010). The year 2007 was the last reported year, as the Tribe has stopped releasing economic data, and the US Bureau of the Census has not released economic data for the Seminoles since 2000. In 1999, the situation was vastly different: 21.4 percent of families were living below the poverty line, almost double the Southeastern US average.

Other Native Nations of the Southeast

In addition to the Cherokees and Seminoles, small groups of Indians continue to live on or near the land of their ancestors in Southeastern states. Some reside on federally recognized reservations, but most live either on lands recognized by the state in which they are located or in communities not recognized by any official entity. In Virginia, the Pamunkeys have a 1,200-acre reservation while the Mettaponis have a reservation of only 125 acres (Rountree 1992: 10). They have recently asserted their rights to fish off-reservation not subject to state regulation. And after years of litigation, the Pamunkeys won an out-of-court land claim settlement for land taken without compensation in 1855 to lay track for a railroad. Land presently unused was returned to them. The agreement also gave Pamunkeys $100,000 in reparations and fair rental value on the land still in use by the railroad. In 2015, the BIA granted federal recognition to the Pamunkeys, after decades of legal battles in which the Pamunkeys were denied recognition in federal bills. The Mettaponis are currently attempting to sidestep the federal bills in the same manner, applying directly to the Bureau (Heim 2015).

Six additional Indian groups are recognized by Virginia as incorporated tribes but lack an official land-base. State recognition, however, enables them to apply for federal grants and funding for education and economic development. A bill introduced in 2011 and still in process would grant these six tribes federal recognition, and is to be introduced favorably to the Senate ("Indian Tribes of Virginia Federal Recognition Act of 2011" 2012).

The only federally recognized Indian nation in North Carolina are the Cherokees. In addition, the Lumbees have been "officially noted by the federal government" but lack full legal recognition or reservation status (Lerch 1992: 45). And there are a number of small groups who have state recognition but no federal standing. Most of these are organized into local Indian associations.

In South Carolina, the Catawbas, who were the only previous federally recognized group in the state, agreed in 1959 to terminate their tribal status. In 1993, after twenty years of discussion, the Catawbas were once again recognized as a tribe and give a $50 million settlement by the federal government. Their land is designated a state reservation. Other Indian communities are dispersed in remote areas of South Carolina. They consist of people who identify as Indian and who form closeknit networks, attend Indian churches, and in the past attended Indian schools. Most of these small groups maintain patterns of endogamy that help ensure their continuity despite their marginalized existence (Taukchiray et al. 1992: 81).

In Alabama, only a group of Creeks, known officially as the Poarch Band of Creeks, have federal recognition. This designation came in 1984 following the tribe's successful petition for acknowledgment. Trust status and protections were then extended to the 230 acres of land that they had purchased in southwestern Alabama. The Poarch Creeks soon opened a bingo hall that has become a profitable enterprise (Paredes 1992: 135). Profits have been used to make further investments in economic development

Four Louisiana tribes have federal recognition: the Chitimachas, Coushattas (Koasatis), Tunica-Biloxis, and the Jena Band of Choctaw Indians (Jena Band of Choctaw Indians 2013). Their reservations are small, totaling about 1,000 acres. Ten additional groups have state, but not federal, recognition. The largest are the Houmas, with an enrollment of about 10,925 (US Census Bureau 2011). The others include three bands of Choctaws, most with two or three hundred members (Gregory 1992: 163). Several Louisiana tribes have filed land claims cases, but only the Chitimachas have so far been successful, winning a settlement of $1.3 million.

When an explosion on BP's Deepwater Horizon oil rig leaked more than 200 million gallons of crude oil into the Gulf of Mexico in 2010, its effects began immediately to destroy the livelihoods of some 20,000 Native people living along the Gulf coast in Louisiana. Their subsistence base, centering around various species of fish, shrimp, oysters, and crabs, was devastated by oil seeping into the bays, inlets, and marshlands where the people live and harvest their foods. And what resources remain continue to be unsafe to eat. The people's health has also been affected by the oil itself and by some 2 million gallons of chemicals pumped into the water in an effort to disperse the spill. Contact with the oil and dispersants through ingestion, inhalation or skin can cause disruption to the central nervous system and respiratory system. Long-term exposure may lead to leukemia and birth defects.

Compounding their problems, members of the six Native groups residing in the region cannot qualify for federal grants available for Indians because they do not have federal recognition. Most are small bands numbering fewer than 1,000 people. These peoples, who have been living in the area since at least the 1600s, are recognized by the State of Louisiana as "tribal entities" but their applications for federal recognition have not been finalized. And although they are eligible for payments from BP's claims fund, the sums amount to at most only $25,000 for businesses and $5,000 for individuals (Hansen 2011: 20).

TABLE 7.1	Population of Native Americans for Selected States
State	**In-State Native Population**
Virginia	24,941
West Virginia	3,139
North Carolina	106,026
South Carolina	14,095
Georgia	23,234
Florida	54,570
Tennessee	15,237
Alabama	25,814
Mississippi	13,610
Arkansas	19,192
Louisiana	27,352

Source: US Bureau of the Census 2011.

These environmental and economic concerns come on the heels of the destruction caused by Hurricane Katrina that barreled through the region in 2005. Katrina caused damage to the Gulf coast from Louisiana to Florida, resulting in erosion and the disappearance of many areas along the coastline where the Houma and other Native peoples sought their livelihoods. In an innovative conservation project, the Houma have contracted with a company to construct floating mats the size of pool tables that are planted with grass. These mats are placed in the water and anchored near marshlands that once were more extensive. The intention is that roots will grow and connect firmly to the underlying ground, eventually extending the shoreline.

Contemporary Populations

Table 7.1 presents data from the 2010 US Census Report, indicating populations of reservations in Southeastern states as well as the number of Native residents living within the state.

REFERENCES

Adair, James. [1775]1930. *The History of the American Indians*. Johnson City, TN: The Watauga Press.

Bartram, William. 1955 [1792]. *Travels through North and South Carolina, Georgia, East and West Florida*, the Cherokee Country, the Extensive Territories of the Muscoguiges or Creek Confederacy, and the Country of the Chactaws. London.

Boykin,. 2002.

de Bienville, Jean Baptiste le Moyne. 1726. "Memoir on the Indians of Louisiana." *Mississippi Provincial Archives: French Dominion* (ed. D. Rowland and A. G. Saunders). Jackson, MS: Mississippi Department of Archives and History, 1927–1932.

du Pratz, Antoine Simon Le Page. [1758]1763. *History of Louisiana.* 3 vols. London: T.E. Becker.

Finger, John. 1991. *Cherokee Americans: The Eastern Band of Cherokees in the Twentieth Century.* Lincoln NE: University of Nebraska Press.

French, B. F. 1846–1853. *Historical Collections of Louisiana.* 5 parts. New York.

Galliland, Hap. 1997. *Voices of Native America.* Dubuque, IA: Kendall/Hunt Publishing.

Garbarino, Merwyn. 1972. *Big Cypress: A Changing Seminole Community.* New York: Holt, Rinehart & Winston.

Gehrke-White, Donna. 2014. "Seminoles Expanding Empire beyond Gambling." *Sun Sentinel.* Online.

Gibson, Jon. 1974. "Aboriginal Warfare in the Proto-historic Southeast: An Alternative Perspective." *American Antiquity* 39.

Gregory, Hiram. 1992. "The Louisiana Tribes: Entering Hard Times." *Indians of the Southeastern United States in the Late Twentieth Century* (ed. J. A. Paredes). Tuscaloosa, AL: University of Alabama Press, pp. 162–181.

Hansen, Terri. 2011. *Indian Country Today.*

Heim, Joe. 2015. "A Renowned Virginia Indian Tribe Finally Wins Federal Recognition." *The Washington Post.* Online.

Jena Band of Choctaw Indians. 2013. *Comments on Procedures for Establishing that an American Indian Group Exists as an Indian Tribe.* http://www.bia.gov/cs/groups/xraca/documents/text/idc1-022887.pdf.

Joint Council of the Cherokee Nation and the Eastern Band of Cherokee Indians. 2008. *Resolution #00-08. A Resolution Opposing Fabricated Cherokee "Tribes" and "Indians."* Catoosa, OK. Online.

Kersey, Harry. 1996. *An Assumption of Sovereignty: Social and Political Transformation among the Florida Seminoles, 1953–1979.* Lincoln, NE: University of Nebraska Press.

Le Moyne, Jacques. 1875. *Narrative of Le Moyne, an Artist Who Accompanied the French Expedition to Florida under Laudonniere, 1564.* Boston, MA.

Lerch, Patricia. 1992. "State-Recognized Indians of North Carolina, Including a History of the Waccamaw Sioux." *Indians of the Southeastern United States in the Late Twentieth Century* (ed. J. A. Paredes).

Tuscaloosa, AL: University of Alabama Press, pp. 44–71.

"Indian Tribes of Virginia Federal Recognition Act of 2011." 2012. *The Library of Congress.* Online.

Lin Freewolf Sparks, Cherokee. 1995. *The Montgomery Journal.* September 15; reprint 1997. *Voices of Native America:* 3

Loy, Wesley. 1999. "Eastern Cherokee: North Carolina's Eastern Band of Cherokees Keep Tradition Alive near the Great Smokey Mountains." *Native Peoples* (Winter): 36–40.

Mooney, James. 1928. *The Aboriginal Population of America North of Mexico.* Washington, DC: Smithsonian Miscellaneous Collections 80, no. 7.

O'Donnell, James. 1975. "The Southern Indians in the War for American Independence, 1775–1783." *Four Centuries of Southern Indians* (ed. C. Hudson). Athens, GA: University of Georgia Press, pp. 46–64.

Ogunwole, Stella. 2002. *The American Indian and Alaska Native Population: 2000.* Census 2002 Brief. Online.

Oklahoma Indian Affairs Commission. 2011. *Oklahoma Indian Nations Pocket Pictorial Dictionary.* Online.

Paredes, J. Anthony. 1992. "Federal Recognition of the Poarch Creek Indians." *Indians of the Southeastern United States in the Late Twentieth Century* (ed. J. A. Paredes). Tuscaloosa, AL: University of Alabama Press, pp. 120–139.

Robertson, James (ed.). 1933. *True Relation of the Hardships Suffered by Governor Fernando de Soto and Certain Portuguese Gentlemen during the Discovering of the Province of Florida.* 2 vols. Florida State Historical Society.

Rountree, Helen. 1992. "Indian Virginians on the Move." *Indians of the Southeastern United States in the Late Twentieth Century* (ed. J. A. Paredes). Tuscaloosa, AL: University of Alabama Press, pp. 9–28.

Seminole Land Rights in Florida. 1978. "Seminole Land Rights in Florida and the Award of the Indian's Claim Commission." *American Indian Journal:* 2–27.

South Carolina Historical Society Collections. 1857–1897. 18 vols. Charleston and Richmond.

Statistical Abstracts. 2000.

Swanton, John. 1911. *"Indian Tribes of the Lower Mississippi Valley and Adjacent Coast of the Gulf of Mexico."* Washington, DC: Bureau of American Ethnology, Bulletin 43.

Swanton, John. 1931. *Source Material for the Social and Ceremonial Life of the Choctaw Indians.* Washington, DC: Bureau of American Ethnology, Bulletin No. 103, p. 201.

Swanton, John. 1946. *The Indians of the Southeastern United States.* Washington, DC: Bureau of American Ethnology, Bulletin No. 137.

Taukchiray, Wesley *et al.* 1992. "Contemporary Native Americans in South Carolina." *Indians of the Southeastern United States in the Late Twentieth Century* (ed. J. A. Paredes). Tuscaloosa, AL: University of Alabama Press, pp. 72–101.

Tyrer, Jill. 2010. "When Fortune Smiles (or not)." Gulfshore Life. Online.

US Bureau of the Census. 2000. *2000 Census of Population: American Indian and Alaska Native Areas.* Washington, DC, 2000 CP–1–1A..

US Bureau of the Census. 2011. *2006–2010 American Community Survey Selected Population Tables.* Washington, DC.

West, Patsy. 1998. *The Enduring Seminoles: From Alligator Wrestling to Eco-tourism.* Gainesville, FL: University Press of Florida.

White, Richard. 1983. *The Roots of Dependency: Subsistence, Environment, and Social Change among the Choctaws, Pawnees, and Navajos.* Lincoln, NE: University of Nebraska Press.

The Choctaws

Choctaw legend says we came from the land, from the great mound, Nanih Waiya. We were told we will always prosper if we remain close to the Mother Mound.

Clay Wesley; quoted in Gildart 1996: 45

THE CHOCTAWS' DESIRE to stay close to their place of origin was thwarted in the early nineteenth century when the US government forced the removal of the majority of the people to lands in "Indian Territory," now the state of Oklahoma. Still, several thousand Choctaws remained on ancestral lands in Mississippi and Louisiana, though their number declined in the early twentieth century due to further removals to the west. Since mid-century, the population has increased to about 8,000, while some 30,000 Choctaws currently reside in Oklahoma, most in the Southeastern region of the state.

ABORIGINAL CULTURE

Territory

Until the nineteenth century, Choctaws lived in what are now the states of Mississippi, western Alabama, and eastern Louisiana. They were the second most populous of the Southeastern nations (only the Cherokee exceeded them in number). The Choctaw language belongs to the Muskogean linguistic family, the largest of the language groupings in the Southeast.

Choctaws settled along rivers, especially the Pearl, Tombigbee, and Pascagaula, and their tributaries. They farmed fertile lands along the rivers and valleys, and they hunted in the forests that stretched beyond. They developed a successful economy, a complex system of social stratification, and a high degree of political integration while they lived in their aboriginal territory. But Choctaw history was abruptly altered in the middle of the sixteenth century when Spanish invaders came to their lands. More than a hundred years later, French and British traders and settlers again disrupted Native lives as they penetrated into the region. Choctaw society was transformed once more in the early nineteenth century when the American government forced most of the people to abandon their homelands and remove to Oklahoma.

Aboriginal Choctaw territory was divided into three or possibly four geopolitical districts: the Okla Falaya or "Long People" located in the Northwestern region; the Okla Tannap (sometimes referred to as the Ahepat Okla) or "People of the Opposite Side" located in the Northeast; and the Okla Hannali or "People of the Six Towns" situated to the south. A fourth and smallest division, called the Okla Chito or "Big People," may have existed in the center of the nation. District differences were not merely geographic; they were also linguistic and to some extent cultural. That is, although all Choctaws spoke a common language, there were some dialectal differences among the regions. Variations in dress and adornment also distinguished members of each division. Finally, because of their diverse locations, external relations between district members and their neighbors differed. The northwestern Okla Falaya were near to and therefore had the strongest ties with neighboring Chickasaws, while the Okla Tannap were closely associated with the Alabamas living to the east, and the Okla Hannali had more frequent interactions with the southern Mobiles. The districts also had different relationships with European colonizers in the seventeenth and eighteenth centuries. People living in the southern region were more closely allied with the French while those in the east were somewhat more likely to be sympathetic toward the British in struggles between the two European powers.

Choctaws developed a complicated relationship with their environment. Through the centuries, they transformed their territory into distinct use areas dedicated to different economic purposes (White 1983). Towns situated in fertile river bottoms contained houses and small garden plots in which women grew crops for their immediate family needs. Outside the concentration of dwellings, people planted fields that were the communal responsibility of larger kinship groups. When nearby fields were depleted of nutrients and lost their productivity, people relocated and once more began transforming wooded areas into tillable land. As towns and fields were abandoned, prairie lands spread and were inundated by small rodents such as rabbits and squirrels that were then caught by Choctaws. Surrounding the inhabited towns and prairie areas, borderlands divided the Choctaw from other indigenous nations. This territory was the habitat of large game animals, especially deer, regularly hunted by Choctaws and neighboring peoples.

Economies

Subsistence was based on a combination of farming and foraging. Farming supplied approximately two-third of the annual diet while hunting and gathering supplied the remaining one-third. Tasks involved in planting and harvesting crops were performed by both women and men although in some cases the work was differentiated. Toward the end of winter, men cleared the fields using slash-and-burn techniques. They stripped off bark near the bottom of trees in order to kill them and then burned all the underbrush and saplings in the new field. In addition to preparing fields for planting, such methods returned valuable nutrients to the soil so that it would remain fertile for a longer period of time.

Small garden plots near each house were planted by women toward the end of April or beginning of May, but larger communal fields were usually planted a month later by the cooperative labor of women and men. Thereafter, women took over most farm work, weeding and tending the plants until autumn when, once again as a cooperative effort, crops were finally harvested. Farm implements included spades and shovels made from cedar and hoes or digging sticks made from wood tipped with flint or animal bones. Aboriginal crops included corn, beans, squash, pumpkins, and sunflowers. Corn seeds were planted in small hills built up from the earth approximately 3 ft. apart. Beans were intermixed with the corn while squash, pumpkins, and sunflowers were planted along the edges of fields and between the hills of corn and beans. Intercropping helped delay soil erosion and depletion of nutrients, but it did not eliminate the problems entirely. People therefore shifted the fields that they brought into production every ten or fifteen years. When land ceased to be productive, they cut and cleared new fields and allowed the old ones to lay fallow. After a while, they relocated village sites in order to be closer to the more fertile land.

Using the best soils in their region and following conservation techniques, Choctaws produced a corn crop that averaged between 40 to 60 bushels an acre, a yield considered extensive even by modern standards. Taking the lower range of the estimate, each family secured approximately 11,200 lb. of corn a year or some 1,600 lb. per person (White 1983: 24). Corn could contribute approximately two-third of the total necessary caloric intake of an adult on a yearly basis.

In addition to food products, Choctaws grew tobacco. The plant was smoked in pipes during rituals and on public occasions such as important meetings and visits by dignitaries. Tobacco was generally mixed with the leaves of other plants, especially dried sumac and sweetgum.

In all, the Choctaw were one of the most successful of the Southeastern farming peoples, as noted by Romans in 1775: "the Chactaws may more properly be called a nation of farmers than any savages i have met with" (1962: 71). They produced a surplus large enough to protect them from a year or two of possible crop failures due to drought and/or insect infestation.

They also traded surpluses to Chickasaws and other neighboring peoples.

Although farming provided the major share of the diet, hunting, fishing, and gathering also contributed valuable food sources. Hunting and fishing were primarily the responsibility of men. Their prey included deer, bear, bison, wild turkeys, ducks, and a number of prairie and forest rodents such as squirrels, beavers, and rabbits. Among the animal foods, deer and squirrel were most commonly eaten. Small animals were typically hunted by men alone, but larger animals, especially deer, were often killed by groups of hunters in communal surrounds or drives, aided by most adult members of the village. The main hunting weapons were bows and arrows, axes, and knives. Boys and girls hunted small animals close to fields near their homes using a kind of blow gun made of reeds 7 ft. long. An arrowhead was inserted into the reed and then ejected by blowing into the pipe.

When stalking deer in lone pursuits, hunters attracted the animals by imitating their call and disguised themselves by use of decoys. Deer decoys were made by scooping out the inside of a deer's head, allowing the skin to dry, and then holding the head upright by inserting sticks into it:

> Thus the hunter with his deer caller and head decoy easily enticed his game within his range; for secreting himself in the woods, he commenced to imitate the bleating of a deer; if within hearing distance, one soon responds. The hunter then inserts his arm in the cavity of the decoy and taking hold of the upright stick within, easily held it up to view, and attracted the attention of the deer by rubbing it against the bushes or a tree. (Cushman 1899: 52)

After a successful expedition hunting deer or bear, the animals' livers were divided among the men in the village.

Women's economic work included farming and gathering wild foods. Nuts such as hickory nuts, walnuts, chestnuts, acorns, and pecans were most valued. Women also gathered blackberries, huckleberries, strawberries, plums, and edible roots such as wild sweet potatoes and jerusalem artichokes.

Meals usually consisted of a corn dish and supplemental foods. Corn was eaten boiled, dried, roasted, or pounded into meal. Cornmeal was then roasted, boiled, or made into breads mixed with sunflower seeds. A popular dish was called "tafala," prepared by first soaking corn to loosen the hulls and then beating off the kernels, which were then broken into several pieces and cooked with beans, wood ashes, and dried hickory nuts. Another corn delicacy was "banaha," prepared by

> first soaking shelled corn in water overnight, separating the hulls from the grain, and then pounding the grain into a meal which is made into dough. The dough is rolled out into cylindrical segments approximately a pound in weight. Each of these is encased in corn shucks and tied around the middle so that the ends bulge somewhat larger than the middle. They are then boiled until done. When ready to serve the shucks are removed. Bread so made was carried in the shuck container by hunters on their long expeditions as it would keep for weeks. After a time it became dried and hard, but the hunter placed it by his campfire to warm and soften it. (Foreman 1933: 308–309)

Animal meat was prepared by either roasting over fire or boiling in water. Corn, acorn flour, and mixtures of dried fruits or roots were added to boiled meats to make stews.

In addition to subsistence tasks, women made clothing. Since Choctaws lived in a mild environment, they generally wore light clothing. Men wore a breechcloth hung in front and back from a belt around the waist. In cold weather, they also wore deerskin leggings. Women's clothing consisted of skirts made either from deerskin or from a fabric woven from buffalo hair or plant fibers treated with yellow or red dyes derived from roots. When it was cold, women and men covered their upper bodies with short capes or shawls made either from deerskin or the feathers of wild turkeys: "They make blankets and other coverings out of the feathers of the breasts of wild turkeys by a process similar to that of our wigmakers, when they knit hair together for the purpose of making wigs" (Romans 1962: 85). Garments were sometimes made by weaving and interlacing the bark of mulberry trees.

Men and women adorned themselves with armbands and necklaces fashioned from stones, seeds, and the pits of nuts. Some people decorated their bodies with tattoos made with black, red, and blue lines. Tattooing was considered a mark of honor as well as a decoration. Warriors, chiefs, and their wives had geometric designs and stylized images of the sun or other natural figures tattooed on their face, arms, shoulders, thighs, and legs. Warriors in particular had tattoos emblazoned on their chests.

Settlements

Choctaws built two types of housing depending on the season. Sturdy winter dwellings in the town of Imoklasha were described in 1770:

> This house is nearly of a circular figure and built of clay mixed with straw or grass. The top is conical and covered with a kind of thatch. The inside roof is divided into four parts and there are cane seats raised about two feet from the ground which go round the inside of the building, broad enough to lie upon, making the walls serve the purpose of a pillow. Underneath these seats or beds they keep their potatoes and pumpkins, covered with earth, but their corn is in a building by itself raised at least eight feet from the ground. The fireplace is in the middle of the floor. The door is opposite one side and is exceedingly small both in height and breath. (Mease, in Swanton 1946: 401)

A summer house was described by the same writer as,

> merely a cabin made of wooden posts of the size of the leg, buried in the earth at one end and fastened together. The rest of the wall is of mud and there are no windows; the door is only from three to four feet in height. The cabins are covered with the barks of cypress and pine. A hole is left at the top to let the smoke out, for they make their fires in the middle of the cabin. The inside is surrounded with cane beds raised from three to four feet above the ground on account of the fleas which live there in quantities because of the dirt. (401)

Villages occupied a relatively large area since houses were commonly scattered along rivers or their tributaries and did not form central clusters. Early eighteenth-century villages were described by du Roullet:

> The village of Boukfouka is one of those of the Choctaw nation the huts of which are the most widely separated from one another; this village is divided into three hamlets, each hamlet a quarter of a league from the others, and all three surrounded by bayous. Lastly this village is at least twenty leagues in circumference.

> The village of Castachas is one of the finest of the Nation; it is situated in a large plain, in the middle of which is a small hill and from its top one can see all the Indian huts placed on the plain and the gardens around the huts of each savage. (Swanton 1946: 637)

In addition to family dwellings, villages contained larger buildings that were used for ceremonials, meetings, and other public community events.

Families and Social Groups

Households consisted of nuclear or extended families who cooperated in economic tasks and formed the basic social and productive units of society. Extended family households were usually composed of people who were related through women since kinship followed rules of matrilineal descent.

Choctaw social organization was based on kinship groupings of matrilineal clans and moieties. Clans, called "iksas," controlled marriage choices through rules of exogamy. They also had some corporate functions, primarily as distributors of farmland to their members, dividing communally held land among the constituent households of the group. People were entitled to use their assigned plots as long as they required, but when a family's need for land declined, their portion was reallocated to another household within the same clan.

Clans were separated into two moieties, the Imoklasha ("their own people" or "friends") and the Kashapa Okla ("divided people"). Although the number of clans in each moiety varied over the years, six or eight clans were usually found in each division. Like clans, moieties were exogamous and had ceremonial functions as well. Of greatest significance, members of each moiety were obliged to prepare and conduct funerals for people in the opposite group. Moiety members also played against each other in ceremonial ball games called "ishtaboli."

Following rules of clan and moiety exogamy, marriages were contracted between people belonging to different kin groups. Either a man or woman might make a proposal of marriage, but it was most common for the man to offer gifts to the parents of the woman he wished to marry after first receiving an indication from her that she was likely to accept. A female relative or an uncle (mother's brother) of the young man might make the formal presentation of gifts. Property received by the bride's family was divided among her female relatives, each of whom was later expected to provide food for a wedding feast. The wedding ceremony itself consisted of exchanges of symbolic gifts between husband and wife, the wife receiving a present of bread and the husband receiving meat. After this exchange, a wedding feast was hosted by the bride's family during which time the village chief delivered a formal ceremonial speech instructing the young couple in their duties and responsibilities.

Most marriages were monogamous but polygyny was possible. Plural marriages usually were unions between a man and women who were sisters. Sororal polygyny was preferred since it did not violate or complicate tendencies for matrilocal residence.

Marriages ideally lasted for a lifetime, but if either spouse became dissatisfied with their mate they were free to divorce. Divorce was more likely in early years of marriage, but once a union was stabilized it was less likely to dissolve. In cases of divorce, children always remained with their mothers, who were considered the primary instructors of children. However, when boys grew older, they came under the guidance of their mother's brother from whom they learned ceremonial and social responsibilities.

Leadership and Community Integration

Choctaw community organization and leadership had both informal and formal aspects. Decisions affecting households were made by members of the household themselves. They organized work, raised children, and settled internal disputes and disagreements. Each clan had a leader, sometimes referred to as a chief, who was selected through informal consensus. They were men of ability, intelligence, good sense, even temper, and generosity. They settled disputes among members of the clan, allocated land to constituent households, organized ceremonial events, and represented their kin group in larger village and district organizations.

Towns had more formal institutionalized leadership. Because of rules of clan exogamy, villages necessarily contained members of several clans, although there was a tendency for different clans to be numerically and therefore politically dominant in particular towns. A village leader or "mingo" usually belonged to the clan that dominated his town. Following matrilineal descent and inheritance patterns, succession to village leadership ideally passed to the eldest son of a deceased chief's eldest sister. However, if the expected inheritor lacked skill, intelligence, or appropriate personality traits, another man would succeed to the position. In addition to kin connections and ability, a prospective chief needed experience as a leader. Prior to becoming chief, therefore, a likely successor functioned as a "tichou-mingo" or "servant chief" who "arranges for all of the ceremonies, the feasts, and the dances. He acts as speaker for the chief, makes the warriors and strangers smoke. These tichou-mingo usually become village chiefs" (Swanton 1918: 54). A tichou-mingo was one of four or five assistants who regularly aided a village chief in his activities and responsibilities.

Civil leadership was one branch of town government, but each village had a war chief and two assistants as well. The position of war chief was open to any town resident who had distinguished himself in combat. When war erupted, these men had considerable authority in their towns, but their influence waned during times of peace.

The final layer of leadership existed at the district level. Each of the three districts had a chief, also called "mingo," who was responsible for dispute settlement, organization of ceremonials, and negotiations with foreigners. Mingos were concerned with matters of trade, peace, and war. In the latter endeavor, they were assisted by district war chiefs who planned and directed military operations. The following description of Choctaw leadership recorded by an anonymous French traveler of the early eighteenth century is, apart from the sarcasm it contains, an apt account: "[the chief's] power is absolute only so far as he knows how to make use of his authority, but as disobedience is not punished among them, and they do not usually do what is recommended to them, except when they want to, it may be said that it is an ill-disciplined government" (Swanton 1918: 54). What is here referred to as an "ill-disciplined government" was in actuality a well-run democratic rather than autocratic polity.

In order to discuss issues of communal importance, mingos convened council meetings consisting of all the village chiefs in their districts. National councils were also held, attended by members of all three district bodies. Ideally, national and district council decisions were made with unanimous consent after an unlimited time for discussion and argument, but if no unified opinion could be reached, the will of the majority was deemed sufficient. Still, no one, including the district mingos, had absolute authority or coercive powers. Even war chiefs led men who were volunteers, free to leave the ranks if they disagreed with the war plans or if they had had a dream foreboding danger and defeat.

Although Choctaw society was based on egalitarian principles concerning equal access to resources through communal control over land, and although there was no system of coercive political power and every person had the same rights to fair treatment and respect in their households and in the community at large, a hierarchy did exist that ranked men in social standing:

> They are divided into four orders, as follows. The first are the grand chiefs, village chiefs, and war chiefs; the second are the Atacoulitoupa or beloved men; the third is composed of those whom they call simply Tasca or warriors; the fourth and last is Atac Emittla. They are those who have not struck blows or who have killed only a woman or child. (Swanton 1918: 54)

These four orders or ranks were based on achievement, not on ascription by birth or accumulation of wealth. The highest rank consisted of men who, because of their experience and accomplishments, had been chosen to be district or village chiefs or who had excelled in warfare and had assumed the title of war chief. The second order was held by men who had extraordinary spirit powers and used them to heal, foretell the future, and in other ways serve the needs and interests of the community. Men who were warriors and had proven their skill and courage in defending their communities occupied the third rank. The fourth and lowest rank consisted of men whose achievements were considered minimal.

Although a male social hierarchy obtained among aboriginal Choctaws, rank did not confer rights different from those of ordinary people. In fact, high status was associated with obligations and responsibilities rather than with privilege. That is, chiefs, warriors, and "holy men" were obliged to be generous to others. It was impossible for a man to succeed to a chieftainship or any other respected position without demonstrating his generosity and public spirit. Indeed, an eighteenth-century French observer noted that a chief's status and prestige depended on "how liberal he was with his possessions" (Bossu 1962: 164).

Chiefs were responsible for redistributing food and other goods that they collected through contributions from the people:

> There is a large crib or granary which is called the king's crib; and to this each family carries and deposits a certain quantity, according to his ability or inclination, or none at all if he so chooses; this in appearance seems a tribute or revenue to the Mingo; but in fact it is designed for another purpose, i.e., that of a public treasury, supplied by a few and voluntary contributions, to which every citizen has the right of free and equal access, when his own private stores are consumed; to serve as a surplus to fly to for succor; to assist neighboring towns, whose crops may have failed; accommodate strangers or travellers, afford provisions or supplies, when they go forth on hostile expeditions; and for all other exigencies of state; and this treasure is at the disposal of the king or Mingo; which is to have an exclusive right and ability in a community to distribute comfort and blessings to the necessitous. (Bartram 1955: 401)

Although Bartram used the terms "king" and "state," the Choctaw nation was not a state and the mingo was not a king in the European senses of the words. Instead, mingos were men who had prestige in their communities but they did not have absolute power or control over members of their district. As Bartram's words do indicate, contributions by the public were voluntary depending on a person's "ability or inclination, or none at all if he so chooses." But whether a person had contributed to the public store or not, persons were entitled to receive help when their own crops had failed or when illness had caused them to be unable to work. Commenting on the egalitarian ethics of Southeastern nations, the English trader James Adair noted:

> Most of them blame us for using a provident care in domestic life, calling it a slavish temper: they say we are covetous, because we do not give our poor relations such a share of our possessions as to keep them from want. There are but few of themselves can blame on account of these crimes, for they are very kind and liberal to everyone of their own tribe, even to the last morsel of food they enjoy. (Adair 1930: 431)

Redistribution was a characteristic element of Choctaw public and private life. At ritual and political feasts, chiefs distributed to all guests portions of food that had been amassed. And when warriors returned from raids with enemy booty, the war chief distributed the goods among his warriors as well as among relatives of men who had been killed in battle. Household hospitality was also the norm: every dwelling contained a pot of "tanfula" (corn soup) given to each visitor as they entered the lodge.

Warfare

Warfare was conducted on a voluntary basis. Men joined a war party if they respected the leader and approved of the goals and plans. According to Romans, "Their leader can not pretend to *command* on an expedition, the most he can do, is to endeavor to *persuade*, or at the extent, he can only pretend to a greater experience in order to enforce his counsel; should he pretend to order, desertion would at least be his punishment, if not death" (1962: 76; italics in original). Once war was declared against an enemy, usually following discussion in council, men who agreed to fight painted themselves with black and red designs and participated in a war dance that lasted for eight days. They fasted and rubbed their bodies with spiritually powerful medicine to promote a successful outcome. Although by far the majority of warriors were men, women sometimes went on raids as well, especially if they were seeking revenge for relatives killed in previous campaigns. Women warriors, however, did not undergo the same ritual preparations and protections as their male comrades (Romans 1962: 75; Swanton 1946: 697).

Warriors carried with them a "war medicine bundle" or an object believed to give spirit protections such as the stuffed skin of an owl. The owl charm was fed meat and guarded against damage. It was "always set with his head towards the place of destination, and if he should prove to be turned directly contrary, they consider this as portending some very bad omen, and an absolute order to return" (Romans 1962: 76). If any warrior had a dream foretelling disaster, he/she was likely to return home. If the war chief had such a dream, the raid would be abandoned.

Raids were considered successful if warriors returned home with captives and booty to be divided among their number. Victorious warriors were greeted with cheers and feted with dances and feasts. Male captives were sometimes burned to death, but women and children were usually adopted into Choctaw families. However, if warriors returned home having suffered many casualties, the raid was considered a failure even if they had been able to harm their enemy. Lack of success often led to the dismissal of the war chief, another taking his place.

Religious Beliefs and Practices

Choctaw religion was based on beliefs in a large number of deities, each of whom had their special province and roles. One of the major deities was a sky god who was associated with but not identical to the sun. After performing primordial acts of a kind only vaguely alluded to in the literature, the sky god seems to have receded into the background. Instead, Sun played a more direct role in everyday life, having the power of life and death:

> He was represented as looking down upon the earth, and as long as he kept his flaming eye fixed on any one, that person was safe, but as soon as he turned away his eye, the individual died. (Swanton 1931: 195)

The powers of Sun were manifest also in fire. Fire had some features of animacy and potency, capable of intelligence. It served as a messenger to Sun, informing him of people's deeds.

Other spirit beings and forces were linked with or took the form of animals or birds. For example, "Ishkitini" was a horned owl who could kill people at night and embodied the evil powers of witchcraft. Thunder and Lightning were conceived as two giant birds. Another deity was half-human, half-deer and frightened hunters in the woods. In addition, a group of spirits called "Oka Nahullo" (or "Okwa Naholo"), meaning "white people of the water," had skin like trout, lived in deep water pools, and sometimes captured people whom they then transformed into beings like themselves (198). Other deities also resided in water bodies such as rivers, lakes, and pools. And there were groups of spirit beings embodied as dwarfs and others as giants.

According to Choctaw belief, the world was flat, covered over with a vault-shaped heaven conceived of as a solid shell. Humans and animals lived on the flat earth, but some beings, including the sky god and other spirits, lived outside on top of the solid shell of heaven. The earth always existed but its form and substance were originally different from that of today. In the beginning, it was completely flat and marshy. Then, a human-like being descended from the heavens and caused a sacred hill to rise out of the ground. The sacred hill, known as Nanih Waiya, is the symbolic and spiritual center of the Choctaw nation. The Choctaws emerged from inside Nanih Waiya, led out by the first being. Later, the ground dried as hills and mountains were formed so that the earth assumed its current appearance.

During the time that the Choctaws resided at Nanih Waiya, deities gave them the gift of corn and also revealed to them the social and political institutions that would form the basis of Native society. In some versions of the origin story, people came to Nanih Waiya not from within but from a westerly direction, reflecting the migration of Choctaws' ancestors from the west.

Choctaws believed that all people had access to spirit powers that could be used for positive or negative purposes. Some men and women, however, had extraordinary powers well beyond those of common people. These individuals, called "alikchi," predicted future events, found lost objects, ensured hunters' success, protected warriors, and influenced the weather. Some were able to make rain with the use of certain herbs, while others produced fair weather. An extraordinary incident of prediction was recounted by a French observer of the early eighteenth century:

> When we were surrounded by the Spaniards in Dauphin island, and were expecting help from France, we wished to know whether it was on the point of arriving … They [Choctaw seers] were then made to conjure, and reported that five vessels would come the next day, three of which were large and two smaller, that one of the little ones would not arrive as soon as the others, but that all would have arrived the next day toward evening. This actually took place, for the next day at eight in the morning the first vessel was discovered, and about three or four in the afternoon four anchored at Dauphin island, but the fifth did not come in until the next day. (Swanton 1918: 63)

A special class of alikchi consisted of healers. They employed herbs, roots, tree barks, and animal oils to treat internal ailments, external inflammations, and wounds. They acquired their knowledge as apprentices to established healers. As noted by a Choctaw named Folsom living in the nineteenth century,

> The doctors made use of herbs and roots in various forms, applied and given in different modes—emetics, cathartics, sweat, wounds, and sores; they also made use of cold baths, scarification, cupping, and practice suction to draw out pain; at a high price and much expense the doctors of both sexes learned the mode and manner of the use of herbs and roots. (Cushman 1899: 367–368)

In addition to natural healing techniques, doctors treated patients by means of ritual cures consisting of prayers, songs, and drumming.

According to Choctaw belief, sickness might result from witchcraft or the harmful powers of some spirits. It might also come from food that a person ate. Specific locations evidently might adversely affect some individuals, since a person who had lived for a long time in one place and had often been ill might be advised by a doctor to move elsewhere.

The most important ceremony was a rite of renewal and thanksgiving called "Green Corn Dance," performed in late July or early August when corn was first ripe to eat. The Corn Dance, lasting five days, included feasting, dancing, and giving thanks to the spirit world for the gift of corn. During the period of the festival, community regulations were drawn up for the new year. On the final day, a large communal feast was held, overseen by the village chief, who delivered long orations concerning people's responsibilities to one another. The chief ate last and then was addressed by members of the community with words of praise. The Green Corn Dance thus was not only a religious rite but also a public communal gathering that celebrated the well-being, health, and fertility of the nation as well as of the natural environment upon which people depended for survival.

There were numerous other occasions for public feasting and dancing. Although the contemporary literature describes them as having a social rather than ritual character, the fact that they were named after animals (e.g., Turkey, Bison, Bear, and Alligator) suggests a spiritual component. Additional evidence is found in the fact that for the Bear and Alligator Dances, one or two participants donned masks resembling the animal to whom the dance was dedicated and chased five or six impersonators of animals that the named species regularly ate for food. These activities suggest a religious component in the symbolic representation of animals and the metamorphosis of human and animal forms.

Ceremonial and social dances and feasts were sometimes accompanied by a ball game called "ishtaboli," similar to one known today as lacrosse. Teams were composed of about a hundred men, pitting members of the two moieties against each other. Played in a large field with goals at each end, the object of the game was to hit a ball into the opposite team's goal. Although players used racquets to hit the ball, there was a great deal of body contact, requiring strength and skill in order to evade one's opponents. After many hours of play and the conclusion of the men's game, teams of women took their turn at the sport.

A number of additional ceremonies marked stages in an individual's life, such as birth, naming, and death. When a woman was about to give birth, she retired to a small hut or cabin separate from the household lodgings, assisted by elder female relatives. While she was in labor, her husband fasted and, if labor lasted more than a day, he ate only after sunset. If the baby were a girl, the father repeated his daily fast for eight days, eating only after sundown. As soon as the baby was born, it was washed and placed in a cradle. If it were a boy, a process of applying pressure gently to the baby's head was begun in order to produce a flattened skull. Bartram described this process:

> The Choctaws are called by the traders "Flatheads," all the males having the fore and hind part of their skulls artificially flattened or compressed; which is effected after the following manner. As soon as the child is born, and put in its cradle a bag of sand being laid on his forehead, which by continual gentle compression, gives the head somewhat the form of a brick from the temples upwards; and by these means they have lofty foreheads, sloping off backwards. (Bartram 1955: 515)

Children were named in response to a portentous incident or event that happened at the moment of

Men of the Choctaw tribe playing the traditional ball game ishtaboli with rackets and tall goalposts. Hundreds of players can take part in one game, and other members of the tribe lay extravagant bets on the outcome. *Ball-Play* by George Catlin.

their birth. Later in life, people received additional names in recognition of their achievements. Men usually received names connected with their war exploits. Nicknames and other terms of address were most commonly used in Choctaw conversation since people were reluctant to tell or mention their own name. Partly for this reason, men who were fathers became known by the name of their child. Mentioning the name of the dead was also considered dangerous.

Burial customs and funerals were the most elaborate of Native ceremonials. When a person died, his/her house and its contents were burned. The deceased's head was painted red and the body was covered with bear or buffalo skins. It was placed on a scaffold approximately 5 or 6 ft. from the ground, along with some of the deceased's property meant to accompany the soul to the afterworld. If the deceased were a person of renown, the scaffold and the poles holding it were painted red. A small fire was lit under the scaffold and continued to burn for four days. During this period, mourners were hired by the deceased's relatives to cry and wail loudly three times every day, at sunrise, noon, and sunset. However, if the deceased had been a murderer or had committed suicide, the body was quickly buried in the ground without ceremony or commemoration.

Choctaws believed that people had two souls. One, called "shilombish" or "outside shadow," had the same shape as a human form. It became a ghost after a person's death and sometimes uttered the cries of a fox or owl. The shilombish or ghost remained near the deceased's body and might harm living people. If anyone dreamed of a ghost, sickness or death was thought likely to follow. Nightmares were brought on by a ghost's attempts to wrest the dreamer from among the living. The second soul, called "shilup" or "inside shadow," travelled after death in a westerly direction to the Land of the Souls. If a person had died in war or had been a victim of witchcraft or murder, the shilup did not begin its journey until its death had been avenged. There were two forms of the afterworld: one was a pleasant, fertile land to which most souls travelled, but souls of people who had committed murder went instead to a place that was always cloudy and rainy and had very few animal or plant resources.

Funerary practices continued after the deceased had been placed on the scaffold. When the body became decayed, a ritual specialist called a "bone picker" or "buzzard man/woman" removed the flesh from the bones with long fingernails that they never cut. The bones were placed in a box and given to the deceased's

family to be taken to a village mortuary house. Bones of chiefs were placed in a separate bone house. In late fall every year, a feast was given for all the dead whose bones were at the village bone house. At these events, the moiety system became ritually and socially significant. Each of the two moieties alternated in crying and dancing for the deceased belonging to the opposite group. People demonstrated their respect not only for their own relatives but for relatives of the opposite social grouping, thus both mourning the dead and in effect celebrating the unity of the nation.

Finally, after a period of time, bone boxes were removed in a ritual conducted by bone pickers of a number of neighboring towns. The bone pickers carried the boxes to a designated place in a solemn procession, arranged them in a pile, and covered them with earth. These piles, known as "burial mounds," were the eternal resting place of Choctaw ancestors.

CONSEQUENCES OF EUROPEAN EXPANSION IN THE SOUTHEAST

The Choctaws escaped most of the direct brutality of the Spanish expedition led by Hernando DeSoto that began in Florida in 1539 and ended in Louisiana four years later, leaving in its wake the rape and murder of tens of thousands of Southeastern people and the looting and destruction of their fields and villages. DeSoto and his soldiers arrived in Choctaw territory in the middle of November 1540 following their nearly total annihilation of the Mobile nation and immediately asked chiefs for provisions, carriers, and guides. The Choctaws denied the Spaniards' request, quickly removing most of their stores of food to the opposite side of the Tombigbee river where the foreigners had met them. By the time the Spanish had succeeded in crossing the river, the Choctaws had retreated further into the forests and the intruders were reduced to merely stealing their corn. Then, proceeding north along the river, the Spanish came to an inhabited town and, as was their practice, took the chief captive as their "guide" and forced him to lead them through his territory. Most of the towns through which DeSoto passed had been abandoned by their inhabitants since news of the foreigners and their deeds had already reached the populace. The Spanish took whatever provisions remained in the towns and continued through Choctaw territory into the lands of the neighboring Chickasaws.

Although Choctaws were spared direct military confrontation with the Spanish, they did not escape the epidemic diseases that European presence had either directly or indirectly caused. Some estimates put the death toll of Southeastern people at approximately 80 percent during the sixteenth and seventeenth centuries. No nation, however isolated, escaped the devastating population destruction that was the universal Native American experience.

Following their encounters with Spanish soldiers in the middle of the sixteenth century and the ravages of disease that followed in their wake, Choctaws remained relatively isolated from European contact until the very end of the next century. By that time, British colonists who had settled in what had been Indian territory along the Atlantic coast and French traders who had established themselves along the southern reaches of the Mississippi River began to make inroads into Choctaw territory. British policies were most harmful in the early period, bringing new diseases and a different kind of terror into Native lands. The British and their Creek allies raided Choctaw villages to obtain slaves who were sold to Europeans in eastern North America and the West Indies. In addition to depopulation and hardship, fear of slavers compelled many people to abandon towns situated near rivers such as the Big Black, Pearl, and Tombigbee that were used as entry by the intruders, retreating for safety into the hill country of east and central Mississippi.

Slave raids carried out either by English colonists from South Carolina or by their allies among the Creek, Chickasaw, and Yamasee nations continued into the early decades of the eighteenth century. They not only captured men, women, and children but also burned towns and crops, thereby inflicting damage even to survivors. Villages in the eastern and northern districts suffered the most destruction and depopulation, possibly losing as many as 4,000 people in a 30-year period from 1690 to 1720.

While the British were invading from the east, French traders and explorers landed along the Gulf coast of Louisiana and Mississippi. Since they were primarily interested in trade with Native peoples, they needed to have friendly relations with the inhabitants. Peace rather than war was a necessary condition for profitable commerce. French traders and diplomats recognized that their best chance of forging alliances with Indians was to follow aboriginal customs regarding gift exchange. That is, according to Native practice, allies demonstrated their friendship by exchanging gifts in a quasi-ceremonial context. As described in the early eighteenth century,

> When a Frenchman wishes to go trade among them, he usually chooses the time when they return with their presents. When one has reached the village he is conducted to the house of the chief, where, having entered without uttering a word, he is seated on a cane bed. Then they throw you a pipe called calumet with a pouch full of tobacco which you smoke. It is to be noticed that all this is done without speaking, after which the chief says to you, "You are come then?" Having answered that he had, one tells him the object of his journey and the kind of merchandise which he has brought to sell to his warriors. The next day the chief informs all his people of the arrival of the Frenchman at his house, what he has brought, and what he asks for it. Each one comes to his ship, and takes away his goods, and when the trader desires to return he informs the chief, who has the payments which he has agreed upon with his warriors brought to him. (White 1983: 43)

This description of an exchange encounter not only indicates the ceremonial and economic nature of the proceedings, but also highlights the critical role played by chiefs in negotiating with foreigners and acting as brokers between foreign sources and Native people. Chiefs continued their traditional role as mediators and redistributors by first settling upon the value of imported merchandise and then distributing the goods to their warriors. Through this process, chiefs gained influence because they became conduits for the flow of European goods to their communities.

In addition to metal tools, utensils, and cloth, Choctaws received guns in trade, enabling them to more efficiently hunt the deer whose hides were desired by the merchants. As chief Chahta Imnataha recalled,

> In the course of two or three winters, all the hunters had guns, and it changed the nature of the hunt entirely. In place of the large companies and laborious running, surrounding, and driving, men would sneak out alone and could accomplish more than twenty men could with the bow and arrow, and never go out of a walk. Besides it did not frighten off the game the old way of yelling and driving. (44)

Chiefs enhanced their roles as brokers by giving guns to hunters, collecting the meat and hides brought in by the hunters, exchanging the animal products to

French merchants for European manufactures, and then finally distributing the goods to members of their communities. They became the sources both of the means of production and of the goods obtained from production.

Gradually, differences in accumulation of property began to emerge in Native communities as chiefs, their relatives, and closest supporters benefitted more than others from the expanding trade networks. Although no one was permitted to go hungry or to lack the basic necessities of life, those most directly involved in trade began to form a social and economic group apart from the majority of people.

The French monopoly on Choctaw trade was broken in the middle of the eighteenth century when British traders were invited into the nation by Northeastern District Chief Conchak Emiko. But although British traders offered goods of better quality at lower prices, most people preferred dealing with the French because of their well-remembered encounters with British slave raiders.

As British and French competition for trade and settlement intensified, the European powers drew their Indian allies into an increasingly tumultuous era as indigenous nations fought each other to protect their dwindling lands and resources. De Bienville, a French governor in Louisiana, noted in 1723 that "putting these barbarians into play against each other is the sole and only way to establish any security in the colony because they will destroy themselves by their own efforts eventually" (Rowland and Sanders 1927, 3: 343). Choctaws were at war with the neighboring Chickasaws for more than two decades, both groups acting as surrogates for European powers, Choctaws as allies of the French and Chickasaws as British allies. Choctaws also aided the French in wars against the Natchez from 1729 to 1731, resulting in the near-annihilation of the Natchez nation.

Intertribal wars were not the only threat to Choctaw security and stability. By the late 1740s, tensions within the nation and the growing disparities in power and influence that separated chiefs and their families from other people began to take a violent turn. Dissension and internal struggles for power led to civil war between the Northeastern district, situated closest to British settlements, and other regions more closely allied with the French. During 1748–1750, hundreds of Choctaws were killed by members of their own nation. And, at the same time, the people suffered and died from smallpox and other European diseases. The dual burden of war and disease severely weakened the nation. Finally, in 1750, the two factions agreed to a peace settlement that contained provisions imposed by the French governor of Louisiana in an attempt to control Native life. For instance, the Treaty of Grandpré stated that any Choctaw who either killed a French citizen or who invited an English settler or trader to visit their village would be executed. Within a few years, however, the French were forced to relinquish their "possessions" in North America east of the Mississippi River to the British after their defeat in the French and Indian War of 1756–1763. The Choctaws' homeland then became part of the British colony of West Florida. After removal of French influence, the British government and their traders became dominant in Choctaw territory but Indians continued to resent British behavior. Unlike the French, British traders refused to enter into the indigenous system of economic and ceremonial exchange but insisted on understanding trade as a purely commercial transaction. And they showed little respect for Choctaw women, as recalled by Chief Albinmanon Mingo:

> They [traders] lived under no government and paid no respect to either wisdom or station. And often when the traders sent for a basket of bread the generous Indian sent his own wife to supply their wants instead of taking the bread out of the basket they put their hand upon the breast of the wives which was not to be admitted, for the maxim in our language is that death is preferable to disgrace. (Rowland 1911: 241)

By the middle of the eighteenth century, Choctaws had come to rely on manufactured goods. As Chief Ouma told a British delegation in 1772, the people were "ignorant and helpless as the beasts in the woods incapable of making necessaries for ourselves our sole dependence in upon you" (White 1983: 79). During the period of British commercial hegemony, the power of chiefs began to decline since they were no longer courted by traders as they had been under French monopoly. In contrast to the French policy of supporting and encouraging the power of civil chiefs, the English supported and promoted war chiefs who they believed could aid them against indigenous nations outside the British sphere of influence. For instance, the British fomented conflicts between Choctaws and the neighboring Creeks that continued for more than a decade. By the 1770s, the Choctaw Nation had been racked with intertribal wars, civil warfare, disease, and yet another factor that undermined its stability, namely the increasing desire of hunters to obtain liquor from English merchants. The growing trade in liquor no doubt reflected the personal demoralization that followed decades of turmoil for the nation as a whole. As one English trader noted in 1776, "in this destructive commerce, for one skin taken in exchange for British manufacture, there are five gotten in exchange for liquor; the effect of which is that the Indians are poor, wretched, naked, and discontented" (84–85). Comments like these clearly depict people in despair.

AMERICAN CONTROL OF THE SOUTHEAST

As conflict between the British government and its American colonists moved toward war, the situation in the Southeast was once again destabilized. Although most Choctaws had never been sympathetic toward the British, they distrusted American intentions since they had seen colonists continually encroaching on their land despite British treaties and proclamations to the contrary. Given their apprehensions about both parties, Choctaws did not aid either the British or the Americans. When the war ended, the American government sent agents to establish formal relations with Choctaws and other indigenous groups in the region. Although treaties were signed declaring friendship, American officials intended to eventually force Indians to relinquish much if not all of their aboriginal territory so that it could be available for American settlement. Such a policy was alluded to in a letter written by Thomas Jefferson in 1803: "When we shall be full on this side [of the Mississippi River], we may lay off a range of States on the western bank [of the river] from the head to the mouth, and so, range by range, advancing compactly as we multiply" (DeRosier 1975: 88). Since Choctaws would not willingly give up their land, the government employed two techniques to coerce them to accede to their demands. One technique, used with some frequency in dealings with Native nations, was to intoxicate leaders attending treaty meetings and then induce them to sign agreements that they probably would not have signed if sober. The second technique, popularized by Thomas Jefferson during his presidency, was to establish government-run "factories" or trading posts that granted credit and then force leaders to sign documents ceding land in return for the forgiveness of enormous debts that their people had incurred to the traders. In Jefferson's words,

> We shall push our trading houses, and be glad to see the good and influential individuals among them run in debt, because we observe that when these debts get beyond what the individual can pay they become willing to lop them off by a cession of lands. (DeRosier 1975: 86)

Both of the strategies worked to produce a series of treaties between the United States and the Choctaw Nation, the first in 1786 and the last in 1830. The initial agreement, called the Treaty of Hopewell, confirmed existing Choctaw boundaries, encompassing about two-third of the present state of Mississippi and parts of Alabama. The second (Treaty of Fort Adams, 1801) ceded 2.6 million acres of land in the Southwestern district and allowed the United States to construct roads through their territory (DeRosier 1970: 29–30; Champagne 1992: 108). The Choctaws received $2,000 in compensation for their land and in the following year, they ceded an additional 500 acres of land north of Mobile, receiving one dollar in compensation.

American settlers then streamed into the Mississippi River valley north of Natchez and Mobile. Not satisfied, however, in 1803 the government coerced Choctaw leaders to sign the Treaty of Hoe Buckintoopa, relinquishing more than 850,000 acres of land north of Mobile in return for the government's payment of Indian debts to the British merchants Panton, Leslie and Company (DeRosier 1970: 30–31). Two years later, Choctaws gave up an additional 4.1 million acres in their southern district, again in exchange for payments of debts to Panton, Leslie, and Company (32). The treaty also stipulated that the Choctaw Nation would receive a cash payment of $50,000 and an annuity of $3,000 to be used at the discretion of district chiefs who were given direct cash payments of $500 and yearly salaries of $150 as well. These payments (one could call them bribes) were a new feature of American treaties with Indians, a feature used with some regularity in the early decades of the nineteenth century. Then, in 1816, Choctaw representatives once again put their signatures on a treaty giving up more land in their eastern district and receiving $10,000 in goods and a $6,000 annuity to be paid for twenty years (37).

REMOVAL AND ITS AFTERMATH

Pressures on Choctaws to relinquish even more land mounted after 1817 when the US Congress established the state of Mississippi and proclaimed the state of Alabama two years later. As statehood expanded into Choctaw territory, more settlers came to the region. Assuming that they had unlimited rights to Native territory, they urged the government to force Indians to remove completely from their homelands. As a result of nearly constant harassment, Choctaws agreed in the Treaty of Doak's Stand (1820) to cede more than 5 million acres of land in exchange for 13 million acres to be granted them between the Red River and the Arkansas and Canadian Rivers in "Indian Territory," now the state of Oklahoma (65). This land had previously been acquired by the United States from the Quapaws. When Choctaw leaders at first balked at signing the treaty, US officials threatened to take control of the land even without an agreement, leaving the Indians without any compensation (Champagne 1992: 147). Although some Choctaws began to relocate to their newly designated land, the great majority did not. In addition to personal preferences for their own homeland, the boundaries of the reservation in Oklahoma were not clearly described and, moreover, settlers were already living on the land supposedly given to the Choctaws. In order to clarify the treaty's provisions, a Choctaw delegation travelled to Washington, DC, in 1824 to renegotiate the terms. American officials lavished dinners and drinks on their guests, spending more than $2,000 on liquor and an additional $2,000 on food and lodgings. An eventual agreement (Treaty of Washington City, 1825) resulted, redefining the boundaries of Choctaw land in Oklahoma with a loss of approximately 2 million acres in exchange for a perpetual annuity of $6,000 plus an additional $6,000 per year for sixteen years (82). However, before the treaty was signed, Pushmataha, the leading Choctaw chief, became ill and died in Washington. Andrew Jackson called Pushmataha "the greatest and bravest Indian I ever knew. He was wise in counsel, eloquent in an extraordinary degree, and on all occasions and under all circumstances the white man's friend" (83). Five years later, as president, Jackson was to repay Pushmataha's friendship with the Indian Removal Act that would force the majority of Choctaws out of their homeland.

In a vain attempt to stave off further American expansion by consolidating Choctaw authority and establishing a formal legal polity, Native leaders adopted a constitution in 1826 (Champagne 1992: 151–152). Like the traditional method of governance, the new system was based on a division into three districts with local and national councils and district chiefs. A national legislative committee, composed of members from each district, was formed to enact laws and negotiate treaties. The national committee steadfastly opposed removal and instead planned to strengthen civil order and advance education. But in 1829, the state legislature unilaterally dissolved the tribal government and extended its laws over the Choctaws.

By the late 1820s, Native culture had been radically transformed. Although conditions had changed for all Choctaws, new ways of living were most pronounced among descendants of Native women and White traders and settlers. They advocated changes in traditional culture that accommodated to American society and promoted the establishment of schools run by Protestant missionaries who had begun proselytizing among Choctaws in the early nineteenth century. The same group was responsible for economic changes as well, that is, cotton was grown as a cash crop with the labor of Black slaves and livestock such as horses, cows, pigs, and chickens were kept for household and commercial use.

In addition to economic changes, social transformations affected traditional family, clan, and moiety systems. Clans relinquished one of their most fundamental functions when they lost corporate control over land. Aboriginal matrilineal rules governing clan membership and descent were replaced by patrilineal descent and inheritance in keeping with dominant Euro-American patriarchal principles. Rules of clan exogamy were weakened and largely disregarded. And ceremonial duties of clans and moieties in conducting funerals and mourning for the dead disappeared.

All the transformations of Choctaw culture had a similar direction, namely the weakening of communal cooperation and responsibility and the development of individual ownership of property and tendencies toward confining one's obligations only to members of nuclear families. Of course, none of these changes came about without opposition and resistance, especially from people who retained traditional ideals and customs and primarily lived outside the concentration of new towns. But as these changes intensified, the nation became increasingly divided once again. Some people were oriented toward traditional values and practices and others toward assimilation to American culture.

Although the former group was composed mainly of "full-bloods" and the latter of "mixed-bloods," the groups did not divide solely along lines of parentage. Wealth played an important part in people's orientation. Many privileged Choctaws favored accommodation to American society since much of their income came from selling agricultural surpluses to American settlers. Although it is true that the majority of wealthier Choctaws were of mixed-blood parentage, some mixed-bloods allied themselves firmly with Native society and in fact owed their prestige in the communities to their adherence to traditional life.

Attitudes toward removal divided the more privileged segments of Choctaw society as well. Some favored removal because they thought that they would be able to secure land in Oklahoma and reestablish profitable farms as well as retain their influence in a Native community away from the increasing encroachment of White Americans. Others wanted to remain in Mississippi because they had large plantations, principally growing cotton for export, and did not want to risk the loss of their wealth by removing to a land whose future was uncertain. Division among poorer Choctaws also was manifested since some preferred removal in order, they hoped, to reestablish traditional modes of living while others wanted to remain in their homelands in isolated areas away from White settlement.

Although in principle, diversity within a society is neither positive nor negative, for the Choctaw in the early nineteenth century, cultural dissension within led to weakness in dealing with external powers. Therefore, when the US government convened a treaty meeting at Dancing Rabbit Creek in 1830 in order to force the people's removal, Native leaders did not speak with a unified voice. More than 6,000 Choctaws attended the conference. American negotiators set the stage by allowing saloons and gambling tables to operate on the treaty grounds but banned missionaries from the American Board who were opposed to removal (DeRosier 1970: 120–121; White 1983: 142). In the face of Native resistance to removal, Secretary of State John Eaton threatened that without an agreement, the US government would declare war on the Choctaw Nation and force the people out of Mississippi. When the majority of Native leaders left in anger and disgust, officials continued to deal with those who remained, most of whom were amenable to signing a treaty of removal. Many of these leaders were of mixed-blood descent and had achieved ascendancy in Choctaw politics because of their wealth and expertise in dealing

with American authorities. As an American delegate to land cession meetings in 1826 observed, "the government seems to be in the hands principally of half-breeds and white men, who dictate to some of them without regard to the interest of the poor Indians" (Wells 1986: 51). This comment points out the significance of economic as well as ancestral differences developing in the Choctaw community. In the end, succumbing to threats and bribes, 172 Choctaw leaders signed the Treaty of Dancing Rabbit Creek on September 27, 1830 (DeRosier 1970: 122–123). According to its provisions, the Nation relinquished their remaining land in Mississippi and agreed to remove to "Indian Territory" in return for promises of protection and an annuity of $20,000 for twenty years, with additional funds for the construction of schools and churches

Despite the objections of most Choctaws, the vast majority of people were forcibly removed from their lands beginning in the late fall of 1831, embarking on a 550-mi. walk that has become known as the "Trail of Tears." The removal of the Choctaws was mismanaged by the US government and its military. Due to the lack of suitable means of transportation and inadequate supplies of food and clothing, nearly one-fourth of the 14,000 people who left Mississippi died from starvation, disease, and exposure to winter blizzards. Another 4,500 were forced west in removals during the years 1854–1857. It was not until 1859 that Choctaws finally received some financial compensation for land cessions that they had made. According to the Treaty of Dancing Rabbit Creek, they were entitled to money from the sale of their Mississippi homelands, minus the cost of removal. Even ignoring the moral flaw in this arrangement, Choctaws had not received the nearly $3 million owed to them after their former territory was sold for $8 million while the cost of removal was estimated at $5 million. And most of the $2,981,247.30 allotted to the Choctaws never reached them because they had to pay legal fees out of the sum (DeRosier 1970: 163).

Even the majority of the 6,000 Choctaws who remained in Mississippi never received the land to which they were entitled. Some were refused outright, others' applications were lost or misplaced, and the names of some were simply removed from registration lists. Landlessness rapidly transformed Mississippi Choctaws from a thriving nation into an impoverished sector of the growing regional population. Most became squatters, sharecroppers, or hired farmworkers.

In addition to the Choctaws who lived in Mississippi, a smaller number retained some of their traditional lands in southeastern Louisiana. They lived in scattered, isolated settlements, farming or working as day laborers for White farmers and townspeople. Some earned money from producing file from sassafras leaves or handcrafting baskets, both for sale to White communities. Winter trapping, carpentry, and work in logging industries also provided wages for some men (Peterson 1975: 106–107).

For the Choctaws who had removed to Oklahoma, a radical readjustment of lives and culture began. The new Choctaw Nation was divided into three territorial and administrative districts, each named after chiefs who had signed the Treaty of Doak Stand, that is, Pushmataha, Apukshunnubbee, and Moshulatubbee. Settlements were concentrated near the Arkansas, Red, and Kiamichi Rivers where people established farms, growing traditional corn, beans, and pumpkins, European peas, oats, rye and wheat, and raising cattle, sheep, and horses. By 1833, they were producing a surplus of 40,000 bushels of corn for sale to the US government. Some Choctaws consolidated their wealth by growing cotton on large plantations, often with the work of Black slaves they had brought from Mississippi.

In 1834, the people adopted a new constitution, written in both Choctaw and English, that provided for a tribal council composed of one chief and nine representatives from each of the three territorial districts. They later revised the governing structure following the US federal model with a senate, house of representatives, and supreme court. Schools were founded to instruct children in both English and Choctaw and to teach them academic and vocational subjects. Tribal meetings and other public gatherings were held in a large building named Nanih Waiya to commemorate their place of origin in Mississippi.

The population of the Nation increased during the 1840s and 1850s with the arrival of nearly 6,000 Mississippi Choctaws as well as settlements of Chickasaws who, like the Choctaw, had ceded their homelands in Mississippi and Alabama to the United States. But by mid-century, Choctaws lost control of part of their tribal estate, receiving $530,000 from the Chickasaws for the right to settle and establish a fourth district for themselves west of the major Choctaw towns. And in 1855, Choctaws leased land in the westernmost section of their nation to the United States for a sum of $800,000 in order to provide land for Wichitas and several other groups who had formerly lived in the plains.

When the US Civil War began in 1861, the Choctaw government declared neutrality, but within a few months, they decided to sign a pact of alliance with the Confederacy because they had been greatly disillusioned with the federal government regarding its failure to uphold treaties and its continuing pressure to secure more Native land. Although very few Choctaws actually fought in the Confederate Army, when the war ended they were compelled to surrender to the United States and to relinquish the lands that they had been leasing to the US government in their western section. Choctaws also agreed to allow the construction of railroads across their territory, a provision that had far-reaching consequences since the railroads brought thousands of trappers and settlers into the region. In addition, mining companies developed coal mines in Native territory, bringing European and American workers to the area. As a result, by 1890 the resident population of the Choctaw Nation consisted of some 10,000 Indians, nearly 30,000 Whites and 4,500 Blacks.

In the same period, as the non-Indian population increased and as Choctaw lands became more valuable to outside interests, government officials pressured the people to divide their land into small allotments assigned to families and individuals. Although a majority of Choctaws were firmly against this plan, a small group of tribal councilors agreed to institute the policy and urged people to register for allotments. Choctaws who had remained in Mississippi were also permitted to claim land if they removed to Oklahoma. In 1903, nearly 1,800 people from Mississippi and Louisiana joined their compatriots in Oklahoma and received shares of the tribal estate. Following the end of the allotment process in 1906, the Choctaw Nation was unilaterally dissolved by the US government and its citizens became residents of the state of Oklahoma.

CONTEMPORARY CHOCTAW COMMUNITIES

Choctaws in Oklahoma

As elsewhere throughout the Native west, much of the land allotted to individuals in Oklahoma was sold soon after they gained title because of the poverty of the owners and their need to have money to support themselves. Choctaws then went to work on farms owned by non-Indians on land that they had previously controlled. Some also found employment in the growing timber and mining industries that exploited the resources of their former territory. The multinational timber company Weyerhaeuser Corporation, in particular, has had a critical impact on Choctaw communities (Faiman-Silva 1997). Weyerhaeuser was attracted to the region in 1969 not only because of its timber resources but also because of the possibility of paying low wages to non-unionized and poorly educated workers. Men and women are employed planting trees and logging, organized into teams hired by independent contractors. Since their employment is seasonal and temporary and they are considered independent workers rather than direct employees of Weyerhaeuser, they do not receive health benefits, vacation time, or sick days. In addition to the timber industry, there are jobs available in chicken-processing plants located in nearby towns in Arkansas and Oklahoma. However, like Weyerhaeuser, these companies also pay low wages. Finally, some Choctaws earn income by producing traditional arts and crafts such as basketry, beadwork, clothing, and quilts. Despite the availability of some jobs, however, unemployment is high, even by rural state standards. For example, in 1970 rates of unemployment for Choctaws were twice the state average: while the state of Oklahoma had an unemployment rate of 4.8 percent, the Native rate was approximately 10 percent. By 2000, the unemployment rate fell to 5.0 percent (US Census Bureau 2000), about twice the Oklahoma state unemployment rate of 3.3. Poverty rates among the Choctaws similarly are far higher than state averages. A survey conducted in 1980 of two of the ten counties inhabited by Choctaws found that nearly half of the people lived below the poverty level, compared to an overall state average of 18.8 percent (112). A more recent study by the Choctaw nation suggest that 32.3 percent of children in the tribal service area live in poverty, as opposed to the overall rate in Oklahoma of 23.9 percent (Smallwood n.d.).

Of the original 6.8-million-acre Choctaw reservation in Oklahoma granted by treaty in 1825,very little is still owned by Choctaws, and a great deal of reservation land is occupied by non-Choctaws. Even reservation land is not unified but instead is scattered in parcels averaging fewer than 200 acres each. The size of individually owned parcels dwindles each generation because of patterns of inheritance and competing claims and interests of heirs. As is true on many reservations that were allotted, all children inherit a share of their parents' estate, resulting over time in the decreasing size and therefore productive usefulness of land parcels. Furthermore, in order to put the land to use, all heirs must be contacted and agree on a course of action. When people cannot be contacted or do not agree to a plan for land utilization, the parcel is often sold or leased to non-Indians instead (131). Through such means, much of former Choctaw territory is currently in the hands of large agribusinesses or owned by timber companies such as the Weyerhaeuser Corporation. Weyerhaeuser has gained additional acreage by paying delinquent taxes on Choctaw land and then purchasing the land at reduced prices (132). Choctaw owners are often not aware of the taxes owed or of the procedures through which they lost control.

As land is alienated, Choctaws have become an increasingly small proportion of the regional population. As early as a census report taken in 1907, Choctaws constituted only 9.1 percent of the region's population while 79 percent of the residents were White (Faiman-Silva 1993: 46). The trend continued well into the 1960s as Native communities experienced sharp population declines, a result of lack of opportunities at home as well as federal US relocation programs developed in the 1950s, to train Indians for jobs in urban centers of the west and Midwest. In the late twentieth century, however, Choctaws returned to their communities because of improved conditions, particularly in housing, education, and health services. According to the 2010 census, there are 195,764 Choctaws in the United States, up from 158,774 in 2000.

In order to cope with conditions of poverty and job insecurity, people depend on networks of extended families and close friends to share household resources, living quarters, childcare, and other domestic responsibilities. Many people also rely on federal and local public assistance programs to help make ends meet (136–139). Since 1969, more than 2,500 homes have been built with funds provided by HUD (Housing and Urban Development) grants (122), and in 2013, the HUD awarded about $375,000 to continue the grant program (US Department of Housing and Urban Development 2013). To be eligible for the program, applicants must own at least 1 acre of land and contribute some labor in the construction of the house. The Choctaw Nation of Oklahoma independently offers housing service for the elderly and for families, as well as other assistance.

Choctaws are attempting to improve their situation by sponsoring development programs in economy, education, and social services. Although their land is no longer a reservation, a form of local self-government was reinstituted in 1971 with power to make and enforce laws, manage tribal assets, and administer community programs. The governing structure consists of an elected chief, assistant chief, and a tribal council drawn from the twelve Choctaw districts. An independent judiciary functions as a court. In addition to its central offices in Durant, regional offices and community centers serve people in each district. The Oklahoma Choctaw Nation currently employs over 6,000 people in administration, casino management, construction, maintenance, and delivery of social assistance, health, and education programs. The Nation is now the biggest employer in Durant, OK.

The Choctaw government implements long-range goals for economic development emphasizing the need to create jobs in tribally owned and managed enterprises. Their goal is for full employment for Choctaws in their local communities. The tribe operates a cattle-raising project, a clothing factory, a tourist lodge and convention center, and a gaming hall in Durant. Profits from these enterprises are used to provide specialized medical services no longer funded by the federal government, since spending for social programs has been severely reduced. The tribe has also taken over the operation of many BIA programs and services under provisions of the 1975 American Indian Self-Determination Act. They operate the Choctaw Nation Indian Hospital in Talihina, three local health clinics, several community centers, and head-start programs.

In addition, the tribe has attempted to attract national and multinational businesses to their area to provide employment. In 1989, Texas Instruments set up a chemical finishing plant where Choctaws now work. However, indicative of the predicament that rural Native American communities find themselves in, Texas Instruments chose rural Oklahoma for its plant when it closed its factory in El Salvador due to the continuing civil war there (214–215). Although Choctaws find work at Texas Instruments, most of the jobs are relatively unskilled, hazardous, and low-paid. Since 1988, the tribe gains income from a sales tax that it collects from businesses operating on their lands.

Despite economic and political uncertainties, Choctaws maintain their Native identity and distinctiveness. According to Faiman-Silva, Choctaws perpetuate their identity and "a sense of transgenerational boundedness … [because of] kin-based residential communities, exchange networks, nonmarket subsistence strategies, and tribal political and cultural traditions" (199). Many Choctaws also maintain traditional expertise in the arts, including material production such as basketry and beadwork and the skills of Native dancing and athletics. These skills are displayed every year during an annual tribal festival held on Labor Day at the nation's capital of Tuskahoma, OK. Projected attendance at these events is around 100,000.

Choctaws in Mississippi

Choctaws who remain in Mississippi form a very small minority in their state and live in isolation from other communities in scattered settlements, most with populations of no more than 500 or 600. However, they have received some aid from the federal government since a congressional investigation in the early twentieth century revealed high rates of poverty, ill health, and substandard living conditions. The BIA established a Choctaw Indian Agency at Philadelphia, MS, in 1918 and provided funds for economic development, education, and health improvements. From that year until 1931, Congress authorized twelve bills of appropriation for the Choctaws (Lujan and Hill 1980: 39). In 1921, a program designed to purchase land for the Mississippi Choctaws began and eventually resulted in the establishment of a reservation in 1944 that encompassed about 17,000 acres. The following year, the people set up a governing tribal council and constitution.

However, conditions improved only slightly during most of the century. Even in the 1960s, tribal chairman Phillip Martin reported:

> More than half, possibly two thirds, of the total Choctaw population live away from the seven reservations. Inadequate acreage of tillable and productive lands accounts for the majority of them engaging in share cropping. Only a few Choctaws are skilled workers. Most are farm laborers. Farming, stock raising, poultry, pulpwood and lumber industries are the only source of income. (McKee and Murray 1986: 126)

A report submitted to hearings prior to passage of the Economic Opportunity Act of 1964 noted that "at least 90 percent of the Mississippi Choctaw Indians live in poverty with inadequate housing, insufficient land base and annual incomes of less than $1,000 per person" (126).

But 1964 was a turning point in the economic history of Mississippi Choctaws. First receiving a federal planning grant of $15,000, within twenty years, the Choctaw Tribe was managing grants and contracts worth over $10 million (Peterson 1992: 143–144). The Tribe set itself a major objective: the development of a "restructured and more assertive tribal government operating all programs in terms of the long-range goals of self-government and self-development" (144). Choctaw leaders believed that economic development could only be achieved by first establishing a strong, independent, stable government with consistent mechanisms for planning and implementing long-range projects and policies. At the same time, they began to assert their sovereign rights in relation to the BIA and other federal and state agencies. The tribal council eventually negotiated contracts with the BIA and other agencies to manage their own health, education, and social service programs.

An early major effort at self-development was the formation of a Choctaw construction company to build homes for the people. Their success led to complaints by local non-Indian construction firms, prompting the Mississippi State Tax Commission to apply state sales tax rates for materials purchased by the Choctaw company. The Choctaws, however, asserted their rights to immunity from state taxes on the grounds that their land was a federally recognized reservation. When the issue of the Choctaw lands' status reached the courts, both the state courts and the US Court of Appeals ruled against the Indians, but in 1977, the US Supreme Court handed down a decision that confirmed the legal status and rights of the Choctaw Tribe and their lands (Lujan and Hill 1980: 41–46; Peterson 1992: 149).

In the past several decades, Choctaws have vigorously sought to attract industries to their communities in order to provide jobs for residents. They built an industrial park and attracted Packard Electric, a subsidiary of General Motors, to manufacture wire harnesses under the aegis of a newly formed tribal entity called Chahta Enterprises. Chahta currently produces wire harnesses for Ford and Navistar and also makes telephones for AT&T, audio speakers for several companies, and greeting cards for the American Greetings Corporation, and operates a printing plant for direct-mail services. Chahta Enterprises now consists of three main parts: a commercial laundry service, a wire harness operation, and a metal fabrication operation. These companies helped to reduce the Choctaws' 80 percent unemployment rate of the 1980s to a low 4 percent by the mid-1990s (Gildart 1996: 45,49; Bordewich 1996: 71). Choctaw employment in 1998 was around 85 percent, a figure much higher than the national average of 65 percent (Ferrara 1998: 82). In addition to Chahta Enterprises, the Tribe also established Applied Geo Technologies, Inc., Choctaw TechParc, and Choctaw-Ikhana Laboratory Services. There are over 350 Choctaw employed in high-tech jobs such as robotics and

Terry Ladnier, council leader of the Vancleave Live Oak Choctaw tribe, raises his ceremonial staff for his grandson and great-grandson, Jon and Ryder Ladnier, during the 2014 naming ceremony for tribal members at Saint's Retreat in Ocean Springs, MS.

meteorology. Chahta Enterprises has expanded and opened factories in many locations around Mississippi as well as one in Mexico (Mississippi Band of Choctaw Indians 2016). While the people realistically have few present alternatives, the Tribal Council is dedicated to advancing the incomes and opportunities of their people through education and training. A recently developed Scholarship Fund, along with other incentives, is supporting this model. These are important efforts that look to the future for enhancing people's skills for available jobs, management positions, and technical and professional careers.

In addition to owning or controlling most of the local plants making products for national or multinational corporations, the Tribal Council sponsors construction companies to build new housing, schools, and community centers on their reservations. They also operate the Choctaw Health Center, described as "among the best clinics in Mississippi" (Bordewich 1996: 71). Indeed, improvements in health have been marked, a result both of better care and economic advance. Life expectancy has risen from about 45–50 years in the 1950s to about 65–70 currently, while infant mortality has dropped to below national and state averages (Ferrara 1998: 83).

In order to improve healthcare services to Choctaws in Mississippi, the Tribal Council signed an agreement with the Indian Health Service to build a new hospital that will more than double the size of the existing facility. When it opened in spring 2015, people became able to access expanded services including acute care, advanced technology diagnostic devices, ambulatory procedures, dental care, behavioral and community health services. In addition to this central facility, seven regional clinics are already providing healthcare services to people in their local communities.

In addition, in 2012 the Mississippi Choctaw Tribe received a grant of $1 million from the United States Department of Agriculture to upgrade its sewer services and water treatment plants. These funds are used not only to maintain existing pipelines but also to extend sewer and water delivery services to rural settlements.

The Choctaw Tribe also owns a local television station that broadcasts programs in both English and Choctaw and provides production services to Indians and non-Indians. Finally, since 1994 the tribe has operated a successful casino, although not without controversy and dissension among some Choctaws who fear its potentially disruptive effects on family and community life.

Choctaw businesses not only provide jobs for Choctaws but for non-Indians as well. By the early 1990s, they ranked together as the fifteenth largest industrial enterprise in the state of Mississippi, benefitting the economic expansion of the entire region (Peterson 1992: 157). By 2009, the Choctaw Tribe was creating over 23,000 jobs per year and was the third largest employer in Mississippi (Boykin 2002). As Ferrara observed, "The descendants of the Mississippi Choctaws that the locals were so desperate to ship to Oklahoma 170 years ago are now local heroes" (1998: 85).

As a result of growth in economic resources and improvement in standard of living and opportunity, the population of Mississippi reservations has increased in the latter half of the twentieth century, more than quadrupling to some 8,300 residents in seven communities: Pearl River, Bogue Chitto, Conehatta, Red Water, Tucker, Standing Pine, and Bogue Homa. The strength of their communities is reflected not only in population increases but in the maintenance of the Choctaw language, spoken in nearly all households and used, along with English, as a medium of instruction in bilingual, bicultural educational programs in reservation schools.

Improvement in educational programs and job opportunities has led to a growth in levels of education, but a high-school drop-out rate of 50 percent persists. Still, many Choctaws have graduated from college, assisted by funding from the tribal government. The availability of employment has also resulted in a dramatic rise in income levels to approximately $36,670 per year for a family of four, an increase of over 800 percent since 1980 (US Census Bureau 2010). However, because education and job training remain essential requirements for success, some Choctaws continue to be left out of the prosperity that surrounds them. The improved educational programs becoming available on the reservation will make it possible for future generations to take advantage of economic opportunities.

Choctaws in Alabama

In addition to the Choctaw communities in Mississippi and Oklahoma, there are now and have been for centuries villages of Choctaws living in southwestern Alabama. This community, named the MOWA Tribe, lived in remote villages without making their presence known in the nearby vicinity until the 1940s when they began to send their children to Indian schools in other states. At that time, the Choctaws started the process of applying for state recognition as an Indian tribe and were awarded that status in 1979 by the State of Alabama, with the official name of the MOWA Band of Choctaw Indians. They also instituted claims for federal recognition. In 1991, the Senate Select Committee on Indian Affairs did grant them recognition but their petition to the BIA was rejected in 1997. The BIA asserted that the MOWA Choctaws failed to prove Native American ancestry.

This case highlights a fundamental problem for Native Americans attempting to achieve federal recognition, that is, the BIA relies solely on documentary evidence in the Western academic tradition and does not value the legitimacy of oral testimony and oral histories of the people concerned. The historical issues in this case are also complicated. The Alabama Choctaws remained isolated because they did not want to be sent to Oklahoma as were many other Native peoples in the Southeast. They therefore did not appear on official documents in Alabama government agencies. And although the names of some Alabama Choctaws are found on letters to officials asking for help, this evidence is inconclusive according to the BIA because of the inconsistency in spelling and the use of an X to mark a signature. Despite this setback, the MOWA Choctaws continue to seek additional avenues toward federal recognition. The irony of their predicament was noted by Loretta Cormier, an anthropologist from the University of Alabama who is working with the tribe, "throughout their history, they have been discriminated against and taken advantage of because they were Indian. And now that it could be a benefit to them to be Indian, to be federally recognized and get some approved education and job opportunities, then they're not Indian anymore" (Burgess 2009).

Contemporary Populations

There are currently about 195,764 Choctaws in the United States (US Census Bureau 2010). In Oklahoma, only about 780 people speak the Choctaw language fluently, but in Mississippi the number of speakers is much higher. A survey conducted in the 1970s indicated that 80 percent of Mississippi Choctaws reported speaking primarily Choctaw at home while only 7 percent said they spoke primarily English at home (Lujan and Hill 1980: 40). In 1997, about 87 percent

TABLE 8.1	Population for Selected Choctaw Reservations, 2000
Name of Reservation	**Population**
Mississippi Choctaw Reservation	7,892
Jones County	136
Kemper County	38
Leake County	569
Neshoba County	2,363
Newton County	549
Mississippi Choctaw Trust Lands	277
Jones County	7
Leake County	24
Neshoba County	89
Newton County	112
Winston County	45
Oklahoma Choctaw Tribal Jurisdictional Area	12,524
Atoka County	1,587
Bryan County	3,513
Choctaw County	2,319
Coal County	955
Haskell County	1,592
Hughes County	212
Latimer County	1,574
LeFlore County	5,112
McCurtin County	4,873
Pittsburg County	5,005
Pushmataha County	1,669
Louisiana Choctaw Designated Area	1,057
Apache Choctaw	639
Clifton Choctaw	153
Jena Band of Choctaw	265

Source: US Bureau of the Census 2010: American Indian and Alaska Native Areas, 2000, CP-1-1A, pp. 38, 48–50.

of Mississippi Choctaws over the age of five reported that they understand their Native language very well, while 63 percent said they speak it very well (33–34). Table 7–1 presents population figures for officially designated Choctaw communities in Oklahoma, Mississippi, and Louisiana as reported by the US Census Bureau in 2000. According to the US Census Bureau (2011), there are 9,635 speakers of Choctaw as of 2015.

An estimated 90 percent of Mississippi Choctaws are speakers, while about 30 percent of Oklahoma Choctaws are speakers (Heritage Voices Collection 2013).

REFERENCES

Adair, John. [1775]1930. *The History of the American Indians*. Johnson City, TN: The Watauga Press.

Bartram, William. [1792]1955. *Travels through North and Travels through North and South Carolina, Georgia, East and West Florida, The Cherokee Country, The Extensive Territories of the Creek Confederacy, and Country of the Chactaws*. London.

Bordewich, Fergus. 1996. "How to Succeed in Business: Follow the Choctaws' lead." *Smithsonian* (March): 71–81.

Bossu, Jean-Bernard. [1751–1762]1962. *Travels in the Interior of North America*. Norman, OK: University of Oklahoma Press.

Burgess, Claire. 2009. "Alabama's Lost Tribe." *UAB Magazine*. http://www.uab.edu/uabmagazine/2009/july/losttribe.

Champagne, Duane. 1992. *Social Order and Political Change: Constitutional Governments among the Cherokee, the Choctaw, the Chickasaw and the Creek*. Stanford: Stanford University Press.

Cushman, H. B. 1899. *History of the Choctaw, Chickasaw, and Natchez Indians*. Greenville, TX.

DeRosier, Arthur. 1970. *The Removal of the Choctaw Indians*. Knoxville, TN: University of Tennessee Press.

DeRosier, Arthur. 1975. "Myths and Realities in Indian Westward Removal: The Choctaw Example." *Four Centuries of Southern Indians* (ed. C. Hudson). Athens, GA: University of Georgia Press, pp. 83–100.

Faiman-Silva, Sandra. 1993. "Decolonizing the Choctaw Nation: Choctaw Political Economy in the Twentieth Century." *American Indian Culture and Research Journal* 17, no. 2: 43–73.

Faiman-Silva, Sandra. 1997. *Choctaws at the Crossroads: The Political Economy of Class and Culture in the Oklahoma Timber Region*. Lincoln, NE: University of Nebraska Press.

Ferrara, Peter. 1998. *The Choctaw Revolution: Lessons for Federal Indian Policy*. Washington, DC: Americans for Tax Reform Foundation.

Foreman, Grant. 1933. *Advancing the Frontier, 1830–1860*. Norman, OK: University of Oklahoma Press.

Gildart, Bert. 1996. "The Mississippi Band of Choctaws: In the Shadow of Nanih Waiya." *Native Peoples* (Summer): 44–50.

Heritage Voices Collection. 2013.

Lujan, Philip, and L. B. Hill. 1980. "The Mississippi Choctaw: A Case Study of Tribal Identity Problems." *American Indian Culture & Research Journal* 4: 37–53.

McKee, Jesse, and Steve Murray. 1986. "Economic Progress and Development of the Choctaw since 1945." *After Removal: The Choctaw in Mississippi* (ed. S. Wells and R. Tubby). Jackson, MS: University Press of Mississippi, pp. 122–137.

Mississippi Band of Choctaw Indians. 2016. Governments. www.choctow.org.

Peterson, John. 1975. "Louisiana Choctaw Life at the End of the Nineteenth Century." *Four Centuries of Southern Indians* (ed. C. Hudson). Athens, GA: University of Georgia Press, pp. 101–112.

Peterson, John. 1992. "Choctaw Self-Determination in the 1980s." *Indians of the Southeastern United States in the Late Twentieth Century* (ed. J. A. Paredes). Tuscaloosa, AL: University of Alabama Press, pp. 140–161.

Romans, Bernard. [1775]1962. *A Concise Natural History of East and West Florida*. Gainesville, FL: University of Florida Press.

Rowland, Dunbar (ed.). 1911. *Mississippi Provencial Archives: English Dominion, 1763–1766*. Nashville, TN: Press of Brandon Printing Company.

Rowland, Dunbar, and A. G. Sanders (eds.). 1927–1932. *Mississippi Provencial Archives: French Dominion*. 3 vols. Jackson, MS: Mississippi Department of Archives and History.

Smallwood, Sarah-Jane. n.d. *Choctaw Nation Promise Zone Fact Sheet*. The Chocktaw Nation of Oklahoma. Durant, OK. Online.

Swanton, John. 1918. "An Early Account of the Choctaws Indians." *Memoirs of the American Anthropological Association* 5: 53–71.

Swanton, John. 1931. *Source Material for the Social and Ceremonial Life of the Choctaw Indians*. Washington, DC: Bureau of American Ethnology, Bulletin No. 103.

Swanton, John. 1946. *The Indians of the Southeastern United States*. Washington, DC: Bureau of American Ethnology, Bulletin No. 137.

US Census Bureau. 2000.

US Bureau of the Census. 2010. *2010 Census CPH-T-6. American Indian and Alaska Native Tribes in the United States and Puerto Rico: 201*. Washington, DC.

US Department of Housing and Urban Development. 2013. *HUD Announces $374,476 to Support Affordable Housing for Mowa Band of Choctaw Housing Authority in Alabama*. Washington, DC. Online.

Wells, Samuel. 1986. "The Role of Mixed-Bloods in Mississippi Choctaw History." *After Removal: The Choctaw in Mississippi* (ed. S. Wells and R. Tubby). Jackson, MS: University Press of Mississippi, pp. 42–55.

White, Richard. 1983. *The Roots of Dependency: Subsistence, Environment, and Social Change among the Choctaws, Pawnees, and Navajos*. Lincoln, NE: University of Nebraska Press.

THE PLAINS

Carriers

Saroees

Crees

Crees

Ojibwas

Shuswaps

Thompsons

Blackfeet

Sanpoils

Gros
Ventres

Assiniboins

Yakimas

Hidatsas
Mandans

Nez
Perce

Crows

Arikaras

Flatheads

Cheyennes

Lakotas

Lake Michigan

Potawatomis
Foxes

Pawnees

Shoshones

Washos

Arapahos

Miamis

Utes

Ohio River

Paiutes

Shawnees

Kiowas

Walapais

Hopis

Diné

Osages

Mohaves

Pueblos

Chickasaws

Tohono
O'odham

Zunis

Comanches

Caddos

Choctaws

Cochimis

Apaches

Pimas

Rio Grande

White Buffalo Calf Woman Brings the Sacred Pipe to the Lakotas

A very long time ago, they say, two scouts were out looking for bison; and when they came to the top of a high hill and looked north, they saw something coming a long way off, and when it came closer they cried out, "It is a woman!" and it was. Then one of the scouts, being foolish, had bad thoughts and spoke them; but the other said: "That is a sacred woman; throw all bad thoughts away." When she came still closer, they saw that she wore a fine white buckskin dress, that her hair was very long and that she was young and very beautiful. And she knew their thoughts and said in a voice that was like singing, "You do not know me, but if you want to do as you think, you may come." And the foolish one went; but just as he stood before her, there was a white cloud that came and covered them, and the beautiful young woman came out of the cloud, and when it blew away the foolish man was a skeleton covered with worms.

Then the woman spoke to the one who was not foolish: "You shall go home and tell your people that I am coming and that a big tipi shall be built for me in the center of the nation." And the man, who was very much afraid, went quickly and told the people, who did at once as they were told. And after a while she came, very beautiful and singing, and as she went into the tipi this is what she sang:

"With visible breath I am walking. A voice I am sending as I walk. In a sacred manner I am walking. With visible tracks I am walking. In a sacred manner I walk."

Then she gave something to the chief, and it was a pipe with a bison calf carved on one side to mean the earth that bears and feeds us, and with twelve eagle feathers hanging from the stem to mean the sky and the twelve moons, and these were tied with a grass that never breaks. "Behold" she said. "With this you shall multiply and be a good nation, nothing but good shall come from it. Only the hands of the good take care of it and the bad shall not even see it." Then she sang again and went out of the tipi; and as the people watched her going, suddenly it was a white bison galloping away and snorting, and soon it was gone.

Source: John. G. Neihardt, *Black Elk Speaks*, reprint by permission of the University of Nebraska Press. Copyright 1932, 1959, 1972, by the John G. Neihardt Trust. Copyright © 1961 by the John G. Neihardt Trust.

Native Nations of the Plains

THE GREAT PLAINS ENCOMPASSES a large territory in central and western North America, extending from the foothills of the Rocky Mountains on the west and eastward to the Missouri River and its tributaries. Its southern limits are in Texas while its northern boundaries lie in southern Canada. Elevations rise to about 7,000 ft. above sea level in the western Plains and then drop about 10 ft. per mile toward the east (Gilbert 1980: 8). Except for the Missouri River, most of the region's rivers flow from west to east. The Plains contains grasslands, canyons, gullies, mesas, rolling hills, and buttes. Plains climate is characterized by high temperatures in the summer and low readings in winter. Rapid changes frequently occur over short periods of time. Most precipitation falls as rain from May to July, averaging about 40 in. annually in the southeastern Plains to only 14 in. in the northwest. Because of relatively low precipitation in most of the region combined with high summer temperatures and rapid rates of evaporation due to constant winds, moisture in the ground is scant and therefore farming is difficult. However, the Missouri River drainage system provides rich, well-watered bottomlands suited to farming.

LANDS AND NATIONS

The Plains was the homeland of numerous nations, some of long occupation while others were relatively recent arrivals. Situated along the eastern banks of the Missouri River were village communities whose economies were focused on horticulture. Farming nations included the Arikaras (a-RIK-a-ra), Mandans and Hidatsas (hi-DAT-sa) living in the Dakotas, and the Omahas, Iowas, Missouris, and Osages located in Nebraska and Kansas. Throughout most of the rest of the region, nomadic foraging societies exploited bison and other large animals that inhabited the grasslands. These included the Comanches, Wichitas and Kiowas in Oklahoma, Colorado, and Texas, and the Arapahos (a-RAP-a-ho), Pawnees, and a number of Dakota bands living in the central Plains. Other Dakota bands, as well as the Cheyennes, Crows, and Gros Ventres, lived in the north. Finally, western Canada was home to the Blackfeet, Assiniboins (a-SIN-a-boin), Plains Crees, and Plains Ojibwas (o-JIB-wa).

The Plains is an area of great linguistic diversity. Languages belonging to six different linguistic families were spoken in the region: that i, Algonkian, Athabaskan, Caddoan, Siouan, Kiowa-Tanoan, and Uto-Aztecan. Algonkian languages include Arapaho, Blackfoot, Cheyenne, Plains Cree, and Plains Ojibwa. Athabaskan languages spoken in the Plains are Apache (in Texas and Oklahoma) and Sarsi (in Alberta). Caddoan-speaking nations include the Arikaras, Caddos, Pawnees, and Wichitas. Languages belonging to the large Siouan family include Assiniboin, Crow, Hidatsa, Iowa, Kansa, Mandan, Omaha, Osage, Oto, Ponca, and Dakota (or Lakota). Two smaller linguistic families are represented by single Plains languages: Kiowa (a Kiowa-Tanoan language) and Comanche (a Uto-Aztecan language). Finally, Tonkawa is classed as a linguistic isolate with no demonstrable links to other languages.

Most indigenous Plains languages are still spoken today on reservations and reserves in the United States and Canada (Hollow and Parks 1980: 75). The strength of language maintenance varies considerably and is related to community size. According to data reported in the 2011 Canadian Census, there are 83,475 speakers of Cree, including Plains Cree, Swampy Cree, Woods Cree, and other unspecified dialects. Similarly, there are 19,274 speakers of Ojibwa. The Canadian Census does not specify dialects, so it is difficult to determine the number of speakers of Plains Cree or Plains Ojibwa alone, but it is safe to assume that the numbers are much lower (Statistics Canada 2011a). Additional speakers of both languages reside in the United States but have not been recently surveyed. A number of Siouan languages also have sizable Native-speaking populations: that is, Teton Lakota (6,000), Santee Dakota (2,000), and Crow (4,500). Blackfoot, Cheyenne, Comanche, Hidatsa, and Assiniboin each have between 1,000 and 2,000 speakers. Other Plains languages have far fewer speakers, most numbering between 100 and 300.However, these statistics were last collected in 2000, so the current fate of many Native Languages is unknown.

Many members of Plains nations were bilingual or multilingual, able to communicate with each other when they met for trade, travel, or attendance at each other's ceremonial events. In addition, a sign language developed among aboriginal nations, possibly originating in the southern Plains (Wurtzburg and Campbell 1995: 164–165). It may have begun in order to fulfill the needs of deaf people, or it may have arisen for use in contexts such as war or hunting where silence was mandatory. Whatever its origin, the expanding interactions that occurred among people of different nations as a result of trade and migration encouraged its diffusion throughout the region. By the middle of the eighteenth century, sign language was in common use. It continued to be employed by members of many contemporary nations, especially Crows, Cheyennes, Blackfeet, Assiniboins, northern Arapahos, and Crees into the 1980s, most commonly at intertribal social and ceremonial gatherings (Farnell 1995: 11–12). Signs are formed with hand position and movements. For example, the sign for "bad" (meaning: thrown away) is made by holding the right fist near the chest, throwing it out and down to the right and while doing so opening the hand; "eat" is made by first holding the right hand compressed and then passing the tips of the fingers in a curved downward motion in front of the mouth two or three times by action of the wrist; and the word "dog" is formed by extending and spreading

the middle and index finger toward the left, and then drawing the hand across in front of the body from left to right (West 1960, 1: 70, 112). The number of signs in a lexicon varies from individual to individual. A late-nineteenth-century vocabulary contained some 3,000 entries (Mallery 1880). A vocabulary collected in 1960 from an Arapaho signer consisted of about 3,500 items, while several other twentieth-century lexicons contained some 1,000 signs (West 1960, 1: 2).

Many indigenous nations have lived in the Plains for countless centuries, but others arrived a few hundred years ago, coming from adjacent areas in the east and west. Some people were drawn to the region in order to exploit new environments; others were pushed out of their previous homelands by European expansionism along the Mississippi and Missouri Rivers and the Great Lakes system in the eighteenth and nineteenth centuries. Among the earliest to relocate from the Northeast were Cree and Ojibwa bands who left the Canadian woodlands and moved westward into Manitoba and Saskatchewan. By 1730, Cree settlements were established near Lake Winnipeg and within fifty years the people had altered their woodland economies, finally becoming culturally differentiated from eastern Crees. Ojibwas experienced similar processes of migration and economic change, resulting in a distinctive Plains Ojibwa culture.

In a short time, Crees and Ojibwas who had obtained guns from European traders were able to force a number of eastern farming people such as the Cheyennes, Crows, and Lakotas out of their sedentary villages onto the Plains. Cheyennes originally inhabited western Wisconsin and Minnesota but by at least the late eighteenth century were living in South Dakota. And Lakotas who had earlier lived in the upper Mississippi region gradually migrated onto the Plains in the early eighteenth century. Teton Lakotas eventually occupied territory extending as far west as the Black Hills, Wyoming, and eastern Montana while Santee Dakotas remained in Minnesota, retaining much of their aboriginal horticultural economy. In addition, Assiniboins were first located in the eastern woodlands of southern Ontario, but by the early nineteenth century had found their way to western North Dakota and southern Saskatchewan. Similar processes affected some groups in the south. For example, Apaches were pushed south into Texas and New Mexico by well-armed and mounted Comanche raiders coming out of the eastern Basin into Oklahoma and northern Texas. Finally, Caddoan-speaking nations such as the Pawnees, Arikaras, and Wichitas, who originally inhabited the Southeast, gradually moved northwest onto the Plains. Pawnees settled in Nebraska while Arikaras migrated further north, eventually establishing themselves along the Upper Missouri River in southern North Dakota.

EARLY ECONOMIES

Prior to transformations of indigenous economies, horticulture was the "dominant culture of the area" (Ewers 1955: 331). Farming was practiced by the Mandans, Arikaras, and Hidatsas along the Upper Missouri River and by the Pawnees, Wichitas, Osages, Omahas, and others in the central and southern Plains. The people lived in permanent villages located in rich bottomlands along the rivers. Some settlements were fortified, presumably as protection from invaders (Holder 1970: 27). Although village sites were permanent in construction, people left in the summer for buffalo-hunting expeditions while in winter they set up temporary camps in places sheltered from the winds and snowstorms characteristic of the region. Together, the farming nations had aboriginal populations estimated at totalling some 45,000–50,000 (Kroeber 1939).

Horticulturists produced great quantities of corn, beans, squash, and sunflowers. Nearly all of the farmwork, that is, planting, weeding, and harvesting, was done by women although men contributed by clearing new fields when necessary. Fields were generally small, averaging from 1–3 acres per household (Lowie 1954: 20). Women supplemented farm produce by gathering wild berries, fruits, turnips, and various roots and greens. In addition to food crops, tobacco was grown, usually by men. Of the nomadic nations, only the Blackfeet, Sarsis, and Crows planted tobacco; the others obtained their tobacco through trade (26).

Living to the west of the village people were nomadic nations who depended on buffalo herds and other animals for their food. Prior to the eighteenth century, they travelled on foot, carrying preserved foods and possessions or transporting them with the aid of domesticated dogs pulling wooden travois loaded with goods. Their mobility was restricted because of difficulties of transport, and their economic security was limited due to uncertainties in locating and processing resources.

Nomadic economies centered on hunting, especially buffalo, deer, antelope, elk, rabbits, and other rodents. Men hunted individually or in small groups, sometimes wearing animal disguises. Periodically, though, communal buffalo hunts were organized. Aboriginal methods included encircling a herd by setting fire to grass, keeping the animals within the circle, and driving them to a fire-free opening where hunters awaited. Buffalo and other game were sometimes driven over cliffs where they were either killed by the fall or shot by hunters. Finally, corrals were constructed with an opening leading to two converging lines made of fences, rock piles, or bundles of brush. Men and women positioned themselves beyond the fences for a distance of perhaps several miles, shouting and waving robes to keep the animals within the lines leading to the corral. When the animals were finally enclosed, they were killed by hunters with bow and arrows. Grinnell quoted Weasel Tail, a member of the Blood Nation, on methods used in the eighteenth century:

> After swift-running men located a herd of buffalo, the chief told all the women to get their dog travois. Men and women went out together, approaching the herd from downwind so the animals would not get their scent and run off. The women were told to place their travois upright in the earth … spaced so that they could be tied together, forming a semi-circular fence. Women and dogs hid behind them while two fast-running men circled the buffalo herd and drove them to the travois fence. Other men took their positions along the sides of the route and closed in as the buffalo neared the enclosure. Barking dogs and shouting women kept the buffalo back. The men rushed in and killed the buffalo with arrows and lances.
>
> After the buffalo were killed the chief went into the center of the enclosure, counted the dead animals, and divided the meat equally among the participating families. He also distributed the hides to the families for making large covers. The women hauled the meat to camp on their dog travois. This was called surround of the buffalo. (Grinell 1923: 234)

Significant in this description is the cooperative labor of women and men and the equal community sharing of meat and hides from the kill.

A portion of plants (both wild and farmed) was eaten fresh after being boiled or roasted, but much of it was dried and stored in rawhide bags for later use. When needed, dried corn was pounded into meal and some was made into breads or cakes. Settled villagers boiled vegetables in earthenware pots while nomadic people cooked by "stone boiling," that is, dropping heated stones into pits lined with rawhide and filled with water. Some plants were baked in hot ashes or earthen ovens. Meat and fish were roasted on spits or boiled in water. Women also prepared pemmican consisting of dried and pounded buffalo or deer meat mixed with melted fat, marrow, and dried berries or crushed chokecherries. Pemmican was a preserved food that lasted for many months and could be eaten at home or taken when travelling or on hunting and warfare expeditions.

Aboriginal dwellings consisted of permanent structures in the sedentary villages and portable tipis among the nomadic nations. Most village people built circular, dome-shaped lodges based on a frame of heavy poles connected with beams and covered with earth. The lodges were entered through an earth-covered passageway. Wichita and Caddo dwellings were of similar design but were covered with grass thatch instead of earth. Pawnee and Omaha lodges were built over an excavation of ground dug to a depth of a few feet. Earth lodges were large enough to house an average

of forty residents. Benches used for sitting and storing possessions were built inside the lodges. A fireplace was made in the middle of the house, while an opening was left in the roof to permit the emission of smoke from a central fire. Firewood was stored inside for heating and cooking. Horses were sometimes kept in a section of the lodge as well. Pits were dug in the flooring to store dried foods.

Nomadic people erected temporary dwellings called "tipis" that were made of buffalo hides sewn together and draped over a frame of poles set in the ground in a circular formation. The poles were pulled together and fastened at the top, forming a conical shape. Tipis were constructed and maintained by women and were usually considered the property of the woman who made them. A smoke hole was created by an opening in the top of the tipi, covered over with flaps attached to poles that could be left open for the emission of smoke from a central fire or ventilation in warm weather or closed to keep out the cold or rain. An opening in the side of the tipi cover was also made as an entrance or doorway, covered over with one or two buffalo skins. In warm weather, the bottom of the tipi could be rolled up to allow increased ventilation. Possessions such as

A Pawnee family poses outside their earth lodge at Loup, Nebraska. Pawnees are Plains Indians, most of whom were nomadic and lived in tipis.

clothing, tools, household utensils, and weapons were stored on poles in the tipi. The size of tipis varied depending upon the wealth of the household and the number of occupants intended. After acquiring horses, tipis increased in size considerably since horses were able to carry or drag larger structures than could dogs.

ACQUISITION OF HORSES

The acquisition of horses, originally obtained from Spanish settlements in the Southwest, revolutionized aboriginal economies and led to social and political transformations. Although some southern nations such as the Kiowas and Apaches may have acquired horses by the middle of the seventeenth century, diffusion of these animals into the central and northern Plains did not occur until the early eighteenth century. The use of horses increased the mobility of nomadic people and was a stimulus for the nomadism of previously settled farming groups such as the Cheyennes, Crows, and Dakotas. The ability of mounted hunters to locate and pursue buffalo herds was a boon to the expanding economies of the region. Two areas of aboriginal intertribal trade became central in the spread of horses. One was located in Shoshone territory in western Wyoming and the second at the Mandan and Hidatsa villages on the Upper Missouri River. Several nations established themselves as intermediaries, obtaining horses at the centers and then trading them to more distant groups. By the early eighteenth century, Comanches were middlemen in the southern Plains, Cheyennes and Arapahos functioned as brokers from the Missouri villages, while Crows were intermediaries between the Shoshonean center and northern nations (Ewers 1955: 333).

The commerce in horses and other products of European origin that developed in the eighteenth and nineteenth centuries was built upon established and extensive aboriginal trade networks linking not only the nations of the Plains with one another but with adjacent and even distant regions. For example, one prehistoric site in South Dakota contained beads from the Tennessee River in the Southeast, beads and pendants from the Gulf coast, pendants from Florida and the Atlantic coast, and shells from the Pacific coast (Wood 1980: 99). The Hidatsa, Mandan, and Arikara trading centers were supplied through networks radiating around two temporary trading "rendezvous," one in South Dakota and the other in southwestern Wyoming. The Wyoming rendezvous was itself supplied by the Dalles rendezvous of northern Oregon and southern Washington, thus linking nations of the Northwest Coast, Columbia Plateau, and Basin regions with the Plains (100). Plains nations were supplied with products from the Southwest as well, trading through Shoshones and Utes in Utah (Ewers 1954: 430–431). Aboriginal commerce was facilitated by social and ceremonial ties established between trading partners who regularly exchanged goods. When European traders entered the area, they were incorporated into similar fictive relationships (Bruner 1961: 201).

Among the many cultural transformations resulting from the introduction of horses was a change in methods of transportation. Prior to that time, dogs were used for transporting goods but the amount of possessions that could be carried was limited. Ewers (1955) estimated that a strong dog could carry a load of about 50 lb. or drag 75 lb. on a travois, while horses could carry some 200 lb. on their backs or haul 300 lb. on travois. When heavily loaded, dogs could not travel more than 5 or 6 mi. a day while horses could cover distances of at least twice as far. In addition, horses relieved people of the burden of carrying possessions when they moved and instead allowed them to ride horseback. Finally, people who were ill or disabled could be transported by lying on a travois pulled by a horse.

Acquisition of horses had social consequences as well. Horses came to be regarded as measurements of wealth and social status. The horses that a family owned were differentiated according to their use and consequently had distinct economic and social value. Some served as pack animals, others for riding when moving camp, while the swiftest and most valuable were reserved for hunting and warfare. Typically about one-fourth of a family's herd consisted of the latter type. The number of animals owned, particularly those used for hunting and war, contributed significantly to a family's social standing. Since horses embodied wealth, they were used as payment for services rendered as well as in ceremonial exchanges at marriage and public giveaways, further adding to a family's prestige. In addition, horses became endowed with spiritual value and were incorporated into rituals. For example, the Blackfoot believed that horses were originally a gift from Sky or Water Spirit and possessed spirit powers of their own (Ewers 1955). Horses might transmit power to their owners in dreams. They were ritually protected to prevent their illness or death and to ensure their success on hunting or raiding expeditions. And they were sacrificed at the death of their owner, thus reflecting the deceased's wealth and status. If the deceased's family could not spare a horse, the animal's mane or tail might be cut off and buried with the dead as a substitute.

Wealth in horses differed considerably among indigenous nations. Inhabitants of the western Plains held the most horses. By the beginning of the nineteenth century, the Crows were probably the richest of the northern nations, owning some 10,000 horses among 400 households (Maximilian 1906, I: 174). On the southwestern Plains, the Comanches, with a population of less than 2,000 reportedly owned about 15,000 horses in 1867 (10–11). In contrast, settled villagers held far fewer horses than did the nomadic people. Since villagers used horses mainly as pack animals and on summer buffalo hunts, their requirements paled beside those of their nomadic neighbors. For example, two Mandan villages with populations of approximately 1,000 each owned only about 300 horses. All of the cited figures are composite numbers for communities as a whole, but the animals were not evenly distributed among the population. The number of horses owned by families differed greatly, resulting in and reflecting differences in wealth and consequent social status. For instance, the Kiowa, with a population of about 1,500 probably owned some 6,000 horses, but many families owned no horses, average people owned between 6 and 10 animals, well-to-do families held 20 to 50 horses and the richest had herds numbering in the hundreds (Mishkin 1940: 19). Wealthy Lakota men owned between 30 and 40 horses each. And according to Maximilian writing in the early nineteenth century, a Blackfoot chief named Sackomaph held between 4,000 and 5,000 horses. One hundred and fifty animals were sacrificed when he died (Maximilian 1906, I: 259).

Although horses were initially acquired through trade, raiding became a common means of obtaining the animals, intensifying intertribal hostilities. Horses contributed to the growth of warfare both by providing a motive for raids and by enabling warriors to launch sudden and successful attacks followed by speedy retreats. For example, although Lakotas had first been pushed from the eastern woodlands by Ojibwas, who were armed with guns obtained in European trade, once Lakotas reached the Plains and acquired horses, they were able to "halt the western movement of their pedestrian enemies" (Lowie 1954: 34). In the words of an Ojibwa leader recorded by British trader David Thompson in 1798:

> While they (Sioux) keep to the Plains with their horses we are no match for them; for we being footmen, they could get to windward of us, and set fire to the grass; when we marched for the woods, they would be there before us, dismount, and under cover fire on us. Until we have horses like them, we must keep to the woods, and leave the Plains to them. (Thompson 1962: 264)

Once mounted on horses, Plains warfare changed in strategies and techniques employed. Aboriginal warfare had consisted either of small raiding parties seeking revenge for previous deaths or pitched battles between opposing groups who lined up in formation and attempted to injure or kill their enemies with bow and arrows. After acquiring horses, warriors were more likely to execute quick raids against villages or ambushes of enemies, often charging into close contact and engaging in deadly combat that resulted in higher numbers of casualties. In addition, earlier raids and revenge warfare were organized by temporary leaders but formal or permanent military leadership was lacking. However, at later times, the need to organize hundreds of warriors for large-scale expeditions required more centralized and organized leadership. Finally, while in earlier times civil or peace leaders clearly were the principal authorities in a camp, later the functions of war and peace chiefs came to be equal. And some war leaders eventually challenged the authority of the elder peace chiefs, seeing them as impediments to warfare. For their part, civil leaders considered the younger war chiefs to be upstarts who were reckless and difficult to control.

Throughout the Plains, war exploits were accorded differing amounts of prestige depending upon the action involved. Although each nation followed its own rules, "counting coup" (touching an enemy with one's hand or a special coup stick) was generally the most prestigious achievement. Counting coup garnered more renown than killing an enemy. Among the Kiowa, for instance, highest ranked exploits included counting coup, rescuing a comrade, and helping to cover a retreat by charging the enemy. Next in importance was killing an enemy or receiving a wound in hand-to-hand combat. Fighting on foot and stealing horses brought distinction as well (Mishkin 1940: 39). Men made their accomplishments known by publicly reciting their actions and wearing distinctive types of ornamentation. Assiniboin warriors who killed enemies wore an eagle feather for each slain foe. Lakota warriors also wore feathers to advertise their achievements while Blackfoot men sported white weasel skins and the Crows wore wolf tails attached to the heels of their moccasins (Lowie 1954: 109).

EUROPEAN TRADE AND ITS CONSEQUENCES

The introduction of horses was not an isolated event in Plains history but rather coincided with the expansion of European trade along and across the Mississippi and Missouri Rivers. Commercial and exploratory expeditions began in the southern Plains in the late seventeenth century. French troops under LaSalle entered the southern Plains from the Southeast, visiting the horticulturists of the southern Missouri, while Spanish explorers came from their bases in the Southwest. These forays into the region were relatively short-lived and involved few individuals but in the early years of the eighteenth century, the penetration of French traders advanced further into the Plains. By the middle of the century, they had reached as far north as the Arikara and Mandan villages on the Upper Missouri River and had also proceeded along the Platte and Arkansas Rivers. After 1763, when France ceded all of its territory east of the Mississippi to England and west of the Mississippi to Spain, British and Spanish traders were more frequent intruders into the Plains. The Spanish established a fort at present-day St. Louis and from there strengthened their position as traders to southern and central Plains nations while British merchants visited the farming villages of the Upper Missouri River in increasing numbers. British interest continued in the early nineteenth century, but it was soon rivaled by traders from the United States, who followed quickly on the heels of the exploratory expeditions of Lewis and Clark after the American purchase of Louisiana Territory from France in 1803.

Involvement of indigenous nations in European trade was not everywhere swift or all-inclusive. Traders' goods were not immediately appealing to Native people but in time their desire and need for the goods became entrenched. According to Tabeau, writing in the early 1800s, "It is evident that with the bow and arrow that the savages of the Upper Missouri can easily do without our trade, which becomes necessary to them only after it has created the need … The idea of luxury will give birth among the savages to new needs; and the necessity of enjoying will produce the activity required to produce the means for them" (Abel 1939: 72, 166). Traders were eventually able to create "new needs" and Native hunters were willing to "produce the activity required to procure them," that is, hunt buffalo and prepare the hides for market. Hunting became more effective on horseback and communal surrounds characteristic of earlier periods that required the participation of women and men were replaced by predominantly male hunting activities. Such a shift also ensured that women's productive time could be spent preparing hides for market rather than joining in the hunt itself. But their elimination from participating in the procurement of animals did not lessen their work. Rather, as Jablow noted, "As far as the women were concerned, what the horse gave, the fur trade took away, for the latter only added to her burden of labor" (1950: 21). In addition, the animals killed belonged to the men who had shot them, so identified by distinctive markings or decorations on their arrows. Methods of distributing meat therefore changed from one that benefitted all members of the community equally to one that benefitted some individuals more than others.

At first, villages were sites of exchange, allowing nations such as the Mandans, Hidatsas, and Arikaras to become significant intermediaries between European traders to the east and nomadic nations of the west. Village people acquired hides from nomadic nations in exchange for manufactured goods obtained from the Europeans. They then traded the hides to the foreign merchants, receiving iron tools, utensils, and weapons. They also traded surpluses of food, increasing their productivity to supply merchants with corn, beans, dried meat, and pemmican. In the middle of the nineteenth century, F. V. Hayden noted that Arikaras,

> By tilling the soil … have two markets for their surplus produce. The first is the fort of the American Fur Company, located near their village, at which they trade from five hundred to eight hundred bushels in a season. This trade is carried on by the women, who bring the corn by panfuls or the squashes in strings, and receive in exchange knives, hoes, combs, beads, paints, etc.; also ammunition, tobacco, and other useful articles for their husbands. The second market for their grain is with the several bands of the Dakotas. These Indians make

their annual visits to the Arikaras, bringing buffalo robes, skins, meat, etc., which they exchange for corn; and the robes and skins thus obtained enable the Arikaras to buy at the trading post the various cloth and cooking utensils needed by the women, and the guns, horses, etc. required by the men. (Hayden 1863: 353–354)

Similarly, Mandans raised great surpluses of corn, beans, squash, and pumpkins for sale to both European traders and nomadic peoples, while Pawnees grew as much as twice the amount of produce necessary for their own use in order to have ample supplies for trade (Jablow 1950: 30).

Due to the substantial profits that flowed from trade, village nations attempted to prevent direct commerce between Europeans and nomadic groups, desiring instead to function as intermediaries. As Ewers noted, "It was common practice for the Indians to exact a markup of 100 percent on the goods they offered. Thus the Crow sold horses to the Mandan at double the price they paid for them in their distant commerce with the Shoshoni, and the Mandan again doubled the price of these horses in trading them to the Assiniboine or Cree" (1997: 40). But the villagers' role as brokers was soon eclipsed as European traders penetrated further west and dealt with suppliers of hides directly. As economic competition deepened, horticultural nations became increasingly vulnerable to mounted raiders because they lacked the rapid mobility to escape attacks. At the same time as the economic role of village nations declined, their very survival was threatened by the spread of epidemic diseases. Since they were the first of the Plains nations to have intensive contact with Europeans, they were the first to fall victim to measles, smallpox, and other foreign diseases. And their sedentary settlement patterns made them more vulnerable to the spread of epidemics. Although all indigenous nations suffered from the spread of European diseases, the toll among settled villagers exceeded that of their nomadic neighbors. As Boller noted in the mid-nineteenth century,

Smallpox was an enemy that neither stockades nor bravery could keep away. The Mandans, from a large nation, have become reduced to a mere handful. All the tribes have suffered, but the Sioux have escaped with the least loss as they, immediately upon the appearance of the disease, scattered in small camps throughout their country and thus confined it to a single locality. (1959: 246)

As village nations lost population because of disease and warfare, survivors tended to concentrate in fewer settlements in order to sustain their cultures and protect themselves from attacks. Therefore, during the same period that the nomadic nations were expanding both economically and geographically, the settled farmers experienced territorial contraction, economic decline, and social instability. These changes in fortune were due to the new focus of regional economies, namely the intensification of trade and the shift from subsistence to exchange that brought wealth to nomadic hunters and traders. But the nomadic way of life was also inherently unstable. As Holder noted, "In sober fact the life of the nomads has little of stability about it. Having once committed themselves to the horse and bison, they were increasingly drawn into a new and dynamically imbalanced situation. Many factors were at work. The most basic was the appearance of Europeans as harbingers of a new economy which would ultimately disrupt and reorient all native modes of life" (1970: 110–111).

In a relatively short period of time, Plains economies were transformed into systems of commodity production and exchange that had consequences for the immediate as well as long-term functioning of indigenous social systems, political independence, and military security. Quoting Klein (1980: 136):

Articulation with the fur trade only lent the appearance of autonomous external exchange, for in reality the division of labor, structural economic priorities, and methods and goals of the equestrian system had decidedly eroded its economic autonomy. [The fusion of hunters and traders was] a complex, complementary yet skewed set of interdependencies that collapsed when faced with the elimination of the resource on which they depended.

Although participation in trade led to economic and military advantages for equestrian people, the egalitarian nature of aboriginal societies was dramatically altered as social hierarchies based on wealth, age, and gender were created or enhanced. While some segments of Native nations benefitted, others were increasingly marginalized as their access to production declined in favor of those more able to exploit available resources and engage in trade. The division of labor between the genders became more marked and rigid. And status differences based on wealth and military success were emphasized.

Changes in Women's Status

Women's autonomy in many (but not all) nomadic nations was undermined as the desire for European goods expanded, forcing hunters to kill more buffalo and accumulate the hides for trade. But in order to ready the hides for market, men needed to control the labor of women. While the labor of both men and women was crucial to expansion of trade, they served in different capacities. Men were directly involved in commercial networks. They travelled to trading posts and received guns, ammunition, iron knives, and other metal tools and weapons. Women's labor was also essential to Plains trade. They helped butcher animals, transport meat and hides to camp, and, most significant, they tanned the hides and prepared them for market. Although women's and men's work was complementary, a critical difference lay in the kind of control exerted over one's activities. Men were generally independent producers, organizing and controlling their own hunting and trading expeditions. Furthermore, they directly benefitted from their labor in two ways. First, they exchanged the hides for manufactured articles that in turn helped them achieve subsequent success. Second, through trade, men were able to amass the wealth that came to be the measurement of social prestige. In contrast to men's autonomy in directing their own labor, women's work was organized and controlled largely by others. First as daughters and then as wives, women worked tanning hides obtained by their fathers and husbands. Women became engaged as necessary but adjunct workers in a trade economy.

Allocation of tasks based on gender and the differential control over one's work led to critical changes in familial and social relations, all of which subverted women's equal participation in society. In order to fulfill needs stemming from the new economic mode, the frequency of polygyny increased. Although an individual man could kill buffalo by the score, the hides were worthless unless rendered marketable. Since one woman could not prepare such a large number of hides in a timely manner, men sought several or even many wives in order to gain additional workers. A man's wives also provided him with children whose labor he managed. Sons helped

in hunting and raiding while daughters aided their mothers in tanning hides. Polygyny was therefore not so much a feature of social structure as it was of the mode of economic production. Wealthy men especially used their wealth to obtain more wives. According to Lewis's study of the Blackfoot, by the mid-nineteenth century, some men were married to as many as twenty women. Significantly, the sharpest growth in polygyny occurred after 1833, "a period which coincides with the increase in the buffalo hide trade both in Canada and the United States" (Lewis 1942: 39). As reported by the Earl of Southesk, a Blackfoot chief responding to missionary preachings against polygyny stated that he could not afford to be deprived of any of his eight wives because they "could dress a hundred and fifty skins in a year whereas a single wife could only dress ten, supposing that she was always well, and that such a loss was not to be thought of" (39). The growth of polygyny was intertwined with the growth of herds of horses since men had to give horses in marriage exchanges to their prospective wife's father. Men with large herds and many wives were able to continually increase their wealth, using horses to acquire wives and usingtheir wives' labor to accumulate wealth. As a result, social and economic differences among the population continued to widen. As Lewis noted, "this expansion [of polygyny] perpetuated and intensified social gradations that already existed, for men with large herds were the ones who could purchase many wives, and in the exchange thereby transform idle capital (surplus horses) into productive capital (women)" (40). But although polygyny was essentially an economic necessity for men desiring to expand their wealth and raise their social standing, given the intensification of warfare in the late eighteenth and throughout the nineteenth centuries, polygyny was also a societal strategy that enabled all women to be married in the context of disproportionate war casualties resulting in a sex imbalance favoring women.

Concomitant with the development of polygyny, the age at which women and men married became markedly distinguished. Prior to the period of expanding involvement in trade, women married in their late teens to men in their early twenties. But afterward, girls were married when they were as young as thirteen while men usually did not marry until they reached their thirties. Girls were productive workers at a very early age, but it took many years for a man to prove himself an able hunter and amass the horses needed for bridewealth. The substantial age difference between a husband and wife was especially significant in the Plains where seniority was an important component in status and authority. Therefore, age and gender combined to enhance rights of husbands.

Men's dominance in their households was solidified by increased emphasis on patrilocal residence. Preferences for affiliation with a husband's family combined with strengthening bonds between fathers and sons and among brothers and male cousins. Patrilocal residence deprived women of the support of their own kin groups for daily companionship and for aid in the event of conflict with their husbands.

Plains cultures contained a double standard concerning sexual behavior reflective of male dominance. Men's sexual exploits were condoned, but unmarried girls were expected to be chaste and married women to be faithful to their husbands. Girls who violated the norms were ostracized and unlikely to find suitable husbands. The transgressions of errant wives were severely punished by beatings, facial disfigurement, or, in a few communities, group rape.

Despite the substantial changes in women's position in nomadic Plains societies with the development of male dominance as a consequence of the expansion of trade and warfare, women's roles and prestige were not totally subverted. And, of course, the processes that undermined women's equality were not everywhere as powerful. Among the sedentary village nations of the Missouri River valley, women retained their autonomy and equality even as the people became involved in expanding trade networks and even as they became embroiled in the intensifying warfare and instability that characterized the region. Even for some nomadic groups such as the Crows, women did not lose their equal voice in household and community life (Foster 1993). Perhaps Crow women's status was protected by a matrilineal descent system, preferences for matrilocal residence, and an enduring symbolic tradition of women's equality. Throughout the Plains, women's achievements in female tasks such as robe making and quillwork embroidery were highly respected, qualifying a woman for membership in prestigious voluntary associations. Women healers and midwives also were recognized and respected for their skills. In addition, some women chose to participate in and excel at occupations usually performed by men such as hunting and warfare. Such women were not viewed as deviant but rather as fulfilling "normative statuses which permitted individuals to strive for self-actualization, excellence, and social recognition in areas outside the customary sex role assignments" (Medicine 1983: 269). Women participated along with men in forming group consensus in their households, kin groups, and communities. Finally, women played important roles in family and communal ceremonials.

Development of Social Hierarchies

By the nineteenth century, systematic social hierarchies founded on wealth and military success developed in nomadic nations. Men's status was based primarily on their own wealth and achievement while women's status was usually derived first from that of their father and later from that of their husband. Kiowa society, for example, was divided into four categories of rank. The highest consisted of people ("fine, distinguished, perfect, fast") who were valiant in war, generous, good looking, and "aristocratic in bearing and courteous" (Mishkin 1940: 36). Most chiefs belonged to this highest grade. The second rank ("second best") consisted of people with wealth who were generous and courteous but who lacked exemplary military records. Ritualists, skilled hunters, and artisans usually belonged to the second rank. The third grade ("poor, property-less") had no particular achievements to their credit. They were neither valiant warriors nor people of wealth. Although such people might try to improve their ranking, they were usually unsuccessful. Instead "most of the time they were forced to remain attached to their more fortunate relatives from whom they borrowed horses to hunt and for transportation and in exchange performed certain duties in the household of their benefactors" (36). The lowest Kiowa rank ("useless, helpless, criminal") were virtually outcasts, often being denied help by their own relatives. Success in war, with its consequent economic and social benefits, underlay the distinction between the first and second classes and also was relevant to the third since failure to achieve in war meant failure to obtain horses and therefore led to relative poverty.

Members of village nations were also differentiated by status and wealth although the strength of stratification varied. It was probably most intense among the Caddoan people of the southeastern Plains and weakest among the Siouans of the Upper Missouri region.

CHAPTER 9 • Native Nations of the Plains / 185

LEADERSHIP AND POLITICAL INTEGRATION

Patterns of political integration differed widely in Plains nations. Leadership was most formalized among the village-dwelling, horticultural nations of the eastern Plains and prairies, while it was weakest and most diffuse among the nomadic nations, although political centralization probably increased among the latter in the nineteenth century as the need for defense, coordination of military and economic endeavors, and negotiation with other nations (including the United States) increased. Among the most formalized political systems was that of the Osage, a central Siouan nation living along the Missouri and Osage Rivers (Bailey 1980). Village leadership derived from a system of patrilineal clans, twenty-four in number, that were grouped into Sky and Earth moieties. The people lived in five permanent villages, each with populations of 1,000–2,000. Each clan had a number of leaders, called "little-old-men," who had both civil and religious functions. The little-old-men residing in a village constituted a village council that governed activities within the community and with other Osage villages and neighboring nations as well. Councils might also declare war and bestow spirit protection on military expeditions. On occasion, the "little-old-men" of all villages met together as a tribal council. In addition to councils, every village had two chiefs, one selected from each of the two moieties. Village chiefs helped settle disputes among members of their communities. Their decisions were enforced by appointed "police" societies. In rare cases, wrongdoers were executed. The two village chiefs organized communal buffalo hunts that took place in summer and fall, alternating their days of leadership. They were assisted by five soldiers who helped coordinate communal hunts and carried out the decisions of the chiefs in civil matters.

In contrast to the formalism of the Osage, political systems among nomadic nations were generally diffuse. Tribal polities probably developed as an outgrowth of collective hunting efforts. As formerly disparate bands united to more efficiently exploit available resources, political leadership emerged to plan and direct economic activities. Chiefs and councils of elders assumed prominent positions. Such men achieved their status by successes in hunting, trading, and warfare. Their authority was based on personal influence. They gave advice and led by the good example of their generosity, sound judgment, and even temper.

Among the nomadic nations, the Cheyennes had the most highly formalized central governing body consisting of a "Council of Forty-Four" made up of men chosen from each of the ten constituent bands (Hoebel 1978). Members served for a term of ten years. They met together only during the summer when the nation as a whole gathered for communal buffalo hunts. Council members (often referred to as "peace chiefs") were responsible for settling internal disputes, organizing and overseeing communal hunting, and appointing members of military societies to function as camp police. Separate from the civil leaders were war chiefs who organized and led military expeditions. Although civil chiefs initially had greater influence and authority than war chiefs, later in the nineteenth century, war chiefs attempted to gain ascendancy and control in their communities, leading to friction between the two sets of leaders.

Although most nomadic nations did not have formally constituted governing bodies comparable to the Cheyenne's Council of Forty-Four, they did have leaders or "chiefs" who were looked to for advice, counsel in disputes, and general management of camp order and movements. These men were usually informally chosen by community consensus. Councils of elders advised the chiefs and made decisions affecting the group as a whole. The leaders were aided by military societies whose members functioned as police when large groups of people congregated for buffalo hunting. During those periods, they acted as agents of social control, ensuring that no man go out hunting on his own. The stricture against individual hunting was most critical since such activities might frighten away an entire herd and thereby ruin the success of a cooperative endeavor. These and any other infractions against public order were dealt with harshly. Wrongdoers were subjected to a range of punishments including destruction of their tipis, confiscation of property, beatings, and even execution for the most serious offenses. However, punishments meted out to wrongdoers were not merely reprisals or retribution but were aimed at correcting antisocial behavior. Proof of this is found in the fact that although policing societies might well destroy or confiscate a person's property, when the wrongdoer showed remorse and corrected his/her behavior, the very people who had carried out the punishment later donated goods, clothing, and equipment to replace what they had destroyed.

Although leadership positions were generally held by men throughout the Plains, women played a more direct and active role in decision-making and public participation in ceremonials in the farming societies than they did in nomadic foraging nations. Everywhere, intelligence, personality, and achievements were the essential requisites for leadership and prestige.

PLAINS SOCIAL SYSTEMS

Social systems attested in Plains nations differed considerably. The Hidatsas and Mandans had matrilineal clans grouped into moieties while the Omahas, Osages, Poncas, Kansas, and Iowas were organized into patrilineal clans. Ponca clans were divided into moieties while in the other patrilineal nations, clans were linked into a number of phratries. In contrast to the unilineal clan systems of the farming people, most nomadic nations had bilateral kinship and descent systems. Such systems were ancient among some groups whereas for others, changes in economies and settlement patterns led to transformations of previous unilineal systems to ones of bilateral descent (Eggan 1966). For example, the Cheyennes and possibly the Lakotas had previously been organized into matrilineal clans but had reoriented their kinship systems as a result of adaptations to their new way of life. Once having migrated from the eastern woodlands onto the Plains, bilateral affiliation became adaptive in the context of increased mobility. The need to maximize alliances, to widen one's network of kin, and to be able to shift membership in local and territorial units led to the disappearance of matrilineal clans and the emergence of bilateral descent. Only the Crows continued to have matrilineal clan membership and descent.

Where they existed, clans were exogamous while moieties were commonly, but not universally, exogamous as well. Where clans were lacking, looser restrictions on marriage choices prevailed, but people could not marry close relatives. The sororate and levirate were common forms of marriage in most Plains societies.

Postmarital residence rules varied. Wherever kinship was based on unilineal descent, postmarital residence generally was consistent with the descent system. That is, matrilineal clan organization, such as found among the Mandans, Hidatsas, and Crows, was associated with preferences for matrilocal residence while among the patrilineal Omahas, Osages, and Kansas, patrilocal residence was common. The nomadic Cheyennes, Lakotas, and Arapahos preferred matrilocal residence while Blackfoot couples usually lived with the husband's kin.

In most Plains nations, marriages were usually monogamous, but polygyny was possible and in fact became dramatically more frequent in the late eighteenth and nineteenth centuries as a response to new economic conditions, the developing hierarchy of status and wealth, and the growing numbers of male casualties from war. Sororal polygyny was generally preferred in order to better guarantee cooperative bonds between cowives. Women taken as captives in raids might also become wives of their captors.

Although kinship informed people's most frequent and continual interactions and provided networks of economic, social, and political support, cross-cutting associations linked individuals to others outside their sphere of kin. Some associations or societies were ranked by age while others were based solely on interest and talent. Most nations had societies for men and women, but men's groups were more numerous. Some men's societies had military or police functions while others were oriented around ritual. Hidatsa, Mandan, Blackfoot, Arapaho, and Gros Ventre young men began their careers in the first age-graded society and then gradually moved into successive groups by collectively purchasing the rights to dances, songs, regalia, and other privileges. The sellers subsequently moved on to the next grade. Men eventually sold their privileges in the eldest group and retired in old age. The formation of and procedures entailed by age-graded societies helped men form and solidify social and ceremonial bonds. In other Plains nations, membership in associations was voluntary. Since the most prestigious groups were the military societies, men hoped to qualify by success and bravery in warfare. Most Plains nations had women's associations as well. Mandan and Hidatsa societies were age-graded, requiring the collective buying and selling of membership. Their functions typically involved the performance of planting and hunting ceremonials. Elsewhere, women's societies were voluntary. The most prestigious recruited women who achieved the highest perfection in arts such as robe making and porcupine-quill embroidery.

PLAINS POLITICAL HISTORY IN THE NINETEENTH CENTURY

Beginning in the early nineteenth century, the American government sought to extend its control over lands west of the Mississippi River. The purchase of Louisiana territory from France in 1803, the defeat of the

British at the end of the War of 1812, and the defeat of Mexico after the Mexican-American War in 1848 left the United States the sole foreign power over the vast lands between Mexico and Canada. The government had first become aware of the number and strength of Plains nations after the exploratory expeditions of Lewis and Clark in 1804–1805. It then commenced in earnest its attempts to hold and exploit these territories. A number of treaties of "peace and friendship" were signed with indigenous leaders in order to protect traders and settlers who began to enter the region in the 1830s. In addition to the influx of settlers, Indians whose aboriginal homelands lay east of the Mississippi came to the Plains after they were compelled to relocate in the west when their own lands were inundated by settlers and taken by the government. Reservations were established for eastern people in what is now Kansas, Nebraska, and Oklahoma, thus putting pressure on the land base of Plains nations. After the discovery of gold in California in 1849, followed soon thereafter by gold and silver finds in Nevada and Montana, thousands of prospectors and settlers streamed across the Plains on their way west. Although most intended to travel through the region, some stayed or returned once their hopes for quick fortunes had faded. But even the transient population damaged local resources. When Indians were faced with loss of resources and pressure on their lands, they sometimes responded with armed resistance and attacks against the intruders. At the same time, intertribal hostilities intensified due to conflicts over resources, the confiscation of territory to make room for displaced eastern nations, and competition over access to trade and horses. The government responded to the growing destabilization on the Plains, brought about by its own policies, by attempting to "pacify" the region in order to make it safe for settlers and traders and to acquire more land to satisfy American expansionism.

Two approaches were used to secure land and establish peace in the Plains. Native leaders were coerced or bribed into signing treaties that essentially restricted their rights. The first such agreements were the Treaties of Fort Laramie (1851) and Fort Atkinson (1853). In the Fort Laramie Treaty, the Arapaho, Assiniboin, Blackfoot, Cheyenne, Crow, and Gros Ventre agreed to relinquish some of their hunting ranges and to allow passage of settlers through their territory and the construction of transcontinental railroads, trading posts, and military forts. Boundaries were drawn among the nations with the aim of ensuring that people remain in their assigned territories, a provision that was impossible to enforce. The Fort Atkinson Treaty, negotiated with Comanches, Kiowas, and Apaches, made nearly identical demands on the Native signatories. Similar agreements were signed with a number of Dakota bands.

Additional treaties were negotiated in the late 1860s, providing for formal boundaries delineating Native territories, establishment of reservations, and the cession of millions of acres of land. Not all Indians, however, were willing to comply with government demands without resistance. Many refused to accept reservation boundaries and preferred to continue their traditional economic pursuits in their accustomed territories. The second strategy of the US government therefore gained prominence. Although the use of the military to advance its goals was nothing new, the government became increasingly determined in its desire to break Native resistance and take the land. The military mobilization that occurred during the Civil War provided troops that could be used to threaten and attack nations in the Plains. In addition, settler communities in the west organized volunteer militias composed of men whose hatred of Indians led to frequent attacks, murders of defenseless noncombatants, mutilation of their victims, and the display of body parts as trophies. The massacre of several hundred Cheyennes at their village at Sand Creek, Colorado, in 1864 was but one of the many ignominious events of the period. Another common American tactic was the use of "Indian scouts" and warriors from one nation against members of other nations. In the words of General George Crook, "To polish a diamond there is nothing like its own dust. It is the same with these fellows. Nothing breaks them up like turning their own people against them … It is not merely a question of catching them better with Indians, but of a broader and more enduring aim—their disintegration" (Smits 1998: 77). And, once the Civil War ended, units of emancipated Black soldiers were enlisted to fight Indians in the west.

During the 1860s and 1870s, the government continued to strengthen military posts throughout the region and to search for and attack Indian settlements. As a result of relentless campaigns, much of the resistance was quashed despite a number of Native military successes, most dramatically the Lakota/Cheyenne victory over General George Custer in 1876. The surrenders of prominent leaders such as Crazy Horse, Sitting Bull, Chief Joseph, and others in the 1870s and the 1880s signaled the effective end of Native independence and their forced acquiescence to the US government's demand for land.

Governmental policies in Canada were similarly aimed at acquiring Native territory, although less military force was generally employed than in the United States. Canadian officials negotiated seven land cession treaties with indigenous nations between 1871 and 1877, resulting in the transfer of most of the region between Lake Superior on the east and the Rocky Mountains on the west. The affected area encompassed the homelands of Crees, Ojibwas, Assiniboins, Dakotas, Bloods, Piegans, and Blackfeet. Reserves were established in a small fraction of aboriginal territories. Native people, though, did not give up their land and independence without struggle. The last demonstration of military resistance to Canadian control was the unsuccessful Métis rebellion of 1887 led by Louis Riel and joined by Crees.

Traditional ways of life for Native people in the United States and Canada were all but impossible by the late nineteenth century. In addition to the loss of territory, buffalo were virtually extinct by 1880, a result both of decades of intensive hunting that had begun to reduce their numbers and especially the deliberate slaughter of the animals advocated by American officials in order to reduce Indians to a state of starvation that would force them to comply with government demands. As efforts to kill the buffalo gained popularity among sportsmen in the 1860s and 1870s, products made from the animals glutted military and civilian markets in the United States and Europe. Makers of bone china sought enormous numbers of buffalo skeletons to make into powder used in the production of dishes. One of the many companies involved in the trade estimated that in the seven years between 1884 and 1891, they obtained bones from 5,950,000 buffalo skeletons (Sandoz 1954). The demand for buffalo products on the part of commercial interests coalesced with the government's policy of eliminating buffalo as a source of food for Indians, resulting in the slaughter of millions of buffalo and the destruction of the aboriginal way of life. In the words of Col. R. I. Dodge speaking to a visiting British sportsman in 1867, "Kill every buffalo you can. Every buffalo dead is an Indian gone" (Weltfish 1971: 218). Similar sentiments were expressed by General Phil Sheridan in 1870, suggesting that the state legislature of Texas issue bronze medals of honor to buffalo hunters engraved with drawings: "A dead buffalo on one side and a discouraged Indian on the other" (218).

During the same period, Native communities were devastated by epidemic diseases such as smallpox and measles. In some cases, the outbreaks were deliberately spread by disease-laden blankets that were distributed by the government as rations to the people.

Once most of Native territory in the west was acquired, federal and local authorities began pressure on surviving indigenous culture. Missionaries arrived in reservation communities, attempting to convert the residents to Christianity and inculcate American values in schools operated by church organizations. It was hoped that Indians would live in nuclear family households, adopt farming, acquire the love of private property, and strive for personal wealth. Government programs tried to undermine aboriginal norms of communal ownership of land and resources and reliance on strong extended networks of kin. In furthering the goals of federal policies and satisfying the demands of land-hungry settlers, Congress passed numerous laws affecting Native communities. Among the most devastating was the General Allotment Act of 1887 that provided for the division of reservation land into allotments of 160 acres each assigned to heads of households and 80 acres for individuals. In addition, land that remained after all allotments had been assigned was considered "surplus" and opened to homesteading by settlers. The law, in the guise of helping Indians assimilate to American society, accomplished long-held goals of acquiring territory guaranteed by treaty to indigenous nations. Although many people objected to the allotment procedures and refused to accept individual parcels, eventually most of the land was allotted. As a result, nearly 60 million acres of "surplus" land was sold (Gibson 1988: 227). Further government provisions enacted in the late nineteenth and early twentieth centuries effectively deprived Native people of more land by allowing the sale and leasing of allotments to American farmers and ranchers. By 1934, therefore, an additional 27 million acres of land (two-third of the allotted acreage) had been taken from Native control (227).

The history of the Cheyenne-Arapaho Reservation in Oklahoma is an instructive case. After allotment of 500,000 of its 4 million acres, the remaining 3.5 million "surplus" acres were signed over to the federal government in exchange for $1.5 million (Berthrong 1985: 34). By 1900, about one-third of the allotted parcels had been leased to outsiders. Then, responding to ranchers' demands for permanent control of Indian land, Congress passed modifications of the General Allotment Act that freed certain allotments from trust status and allowed their sale. Officials of the BIA also advocated the sale of reservation land because they felt that simply leasing land gave Native owners an income that enabled them to get by without working. Indian Affairs Commissioner William Jones commented in 1900: "The Indian is allotted and then allowed to turn over his land to whites and go on his aimless way" (35). Instead, Albert Smiley, a member of the Board of Indian Commissioners, urged that Native people be forced to "Earn their bread by labor … Work is the saving thing for the Indians. We have coddled them too much … Put them on their metal; make them struggle, then we will have some good Indians" (37). Both men thought that Native people should sell their land and then either invest the proceeds in farm equipment or, once their income was exhausted, be employed for meager wages in the growing towns and ranches established on their former territory. Despite protests by Cheyenne and Arapaho leaders, many restrictions on sales of land were modified or eliminated. As a result, the remaining tribal land base continued to shrink. By the 1920s, 56.3 percent of all allotted land had been sold (48).

Although the laws affecting Native people in Canada differ from those in the United States, essentially similar processes were at work that deprived Indians of land, independence, and cultural traditions. Native leaders in the Canadian Plains eventually signed treaties with the federal government in which they agreed to cede most of their territory and live within boundaries of reserves set aside for their use. The Canadian government attempted to instill the virtues of private property and agricultural labor in indigenous nations that were traditionally based on principles of communal ownership and use of land and resources. However, in contrast to conditions in the United States, because of the relatively small Euro-Canadian population resident in the west, Native nations have been able, even now, to retain much of the land that they originally reserved by treaty. But Indians of the Canadian Plains were compelled to reorient their economies because the buffalo on which they had depended were nearly extinct by the late nineteenth century. The government then introduced farming on western reserves but with little success. For example, people living on the Blood Reserve in Alberta attempted to grow oats, barley, and potatoes even though the short

growing season and the frequent infestations of grasshoppers made their efforts futile. They also attempted to raise cattle, again with little initial success. Then in the early twentieth century, the Canadian government invested additional sums to acquire cattle and horses that could be bred for sale. The investment proved beneficial. Within a few decades, the Bloods had accumulated more than 7,500 cattle and netted a cash income of $40,000 annually (Goldfrank 1945: 25–26). However, the increase in income was not spread evenly throughout the community. Rather, individuals and families who had been able to retain their prereserve wealth benefitted disproportionately from the new economic system by continually reinvesting their profits in more animals. Therefore, "the bulk of the wealth still rested in the hands of the horse owners who in the first seventeen years of the reserve succeeded in freezing the only valuable form of property that remained to the Blood after the Treaty of 1877" (30).

After 1910, wheat crops that suited the climate and soil of southern Alberta were introduced, resulting in a general improvement in incomes for a majority of reserve residents. But by the middle of the century, the older pattern of wealth distribution reemerged. Successful farmers and herders were able to concentrate their holdings in land and animals and reinvest in business expansion, consequently reaping greater financial benefit from the new economy. The gap between rich and poor continued to widen.

REVITALIZATION MOVEMENTS IN THE PLAINS

Because of the irretrievable loss of land, eradication of resources, military campaigns against their people, and government programs aimed at destroying their culture, most Indians lived in poverty and despair. In such a context, a number of revitalization movements spread quickly across the Plains. The Peyote religion, based on aboriginal practices in Mexico, gained adherents in many Native communities in the 1870s. It was probably first learned by Lipan Apaches in the late eighteenth or early nineteenth century from Native people in Mexico (Stewart 1980: 189). Lipans taught the ceremonial use of peyote to Comanches and Kiowas in Oklahoma sometime in the middle and late nineteenth century. From there it was carried throughout the Plains.

Peyote is thought by believers to be a spirit being as well as a means of obtaining visionary messages and absorbing spirit power. It grants people direct contact with the spirit world, allowing them to receive knowledge, power, and physical and emotional health. Participation in peyote rituals is a learning experience that expands one's understanding of the spirit world. In the words of a Comanche practitioner, "You can use Peyote all your life, but you'll never get to the end of what there is to be known from Peyote. Peyote is always teaching you something new. The only way to find out about Peyote is to take it and learn from Peyote yourself" (Slotkin 1975: 100).

Peyote rituals or "meetings" follow a standard pattern although certain elements may be adapted to suit the traditions of different groups or the individual visions of participants. Ceremonies take place in a tipi erected so that the doorway faces east, the direction bestowing the sacred power of the rising sun. Inside is an altar that holds ritual paraphernalia combining aboriginal artifacts such as eagle feathers, gourd rattles, drums, bowls of water, and plates containing peyote buttons, as well as Christian crosses and bibles. Meetings begin at sunset and end at sunrise of the following morning. They are sponsored by a ritualist, called a "road chief," who organizes the proceedings and supplies the peyote. During the meeting, members eat peyote buttons from a common plate and in turn each participant sings his/her peyote songs. The songs may consist of standardized verses or spontaneous lyrics revealed in visions. The ceremony ends at dawn when members share a communal breakfast prepared by a "morning water woman," usually the wife of the road chief.

Participants in peyote rituals form a community of believers who rely on each other for support in all contexts of their lives. They aid each other when in financial, social, or emotional crises. Members follow traditional ethical values of generosity, helpfulness, and cooperation toward others.

The Peyote religion quickly grew in strength during the late nineteenth and early twentieth centuries. As it gained thousands of followers, it also attracted criticism. Since peyote is officially listed as a controlled substance, participants in peyote meetings were sometimes arrested and charged with possession of dangerous drugs. In response to mounting harassment, peyotists incorporated as the Native American Church in 1918, hoping to thereby be protected in the free practice of their faith. However, harassment and arrests of participants continued. The issue of peyote use in ritual was reviewed by the US Supreme Court in 1990 in the context of a case stemming from the application for unemployment insurance by two Indian peyotists in Oregon following their dismissal by their employer, a private drug rehabilitation program (*Employment Division, Dept. of Human Resources v. Smith*). The Court confirmed the right of the state to deny unemployment benefits, ruling that the government may restrict the free practice of religion without needing to show "compelling interest" if such practices violate federal or state laws (see Chapter 3 for more detailed discussion of the case). In response to criticism of the ruling voiced by Native American groups, Christian and Jewish leaders, and civil

Arapaho Ghost Dance, painting by Mary Irvin Wright, ca. 1900.

liberties organizations, Congress passed the "Native American Religious Freedom Restoration Act" in 1993. Among other provisions, the law counteracted the Supreme Court ruling by requiring that the government show a "compelling interest" when restricting Native peoples' exercise of religion. However, in 1997, the Supreme Court declared the law to be unconstitutional. Amendments passed by Congress in 1994 specifically protecting the use of peyote in religious contexts are still in effect.

A second revitalization movement, the Ghost Dance religion, originated among the northern Paiutes (Paviotsos) in 1889 and rapidly gained great popularity (see Chapter 12 for a discussion of the origins of the Ghost Dance). Its founder, Wovoka, initially advocated reconciliation to the social and political conditions prevailing at that time, saying "You must not fight. Do no harm to anyone. Do always right." But Wovoka also prophesied a return to an earlier, peaceful life. He said that the earth would soon begin to tremble and come to an end and non-Indians would disappear while Indians who had died would return to their families. As the religion spread into the troubled Plains, the message of renewal was greeted with celebration. Not surprisingly, the hope of a return to an earlier way of life had great appeal to people devastated by warfare, poverty, starvation, and disease. They responded to the words of hope and participated in dances and songs dedicated to achieving the dream of a returned peace and a renewed prosperity. But also not surprisingly, settlers were alarmed by a prophecy predicting their disappearance, even though Ghost Dance celebrants never resorted to direct means to hasten the transformation. Despite the peacefulness of the dances, settlers' fears were used to enflame hostility against Indians. Government repression of Ghost Dance ceremonies and reprisals against participants intensified, culminating in the murder of the Hunkpapa Lakota leader Sitting Bull on December 15, 1890, and the massacre of more than 300 Oglalas at Wounded Knee Creek, South Dakota, on December 29 (see Chapter 10 for a more detailed discussion of these events).

The violence and tragedy of Wounded Knee aroused enough outrage on the part of some influential Americans to call for an official investigation of the massacre. Public hearings were held in 1891 to gather testimony from government officials, missionaries, and army officers concerning conditions on Lakota reservations. For example, General Miles quoted from a report written by the commander of Fort Yates in North Dakota listing factors contributing to poverty and demoralization:

> Failure of the government to provide the full allowance of seeds and agricultural implements to Indians engaged in farming.
>
> Failure of the government to issue such Indians the full number of cows and oxen.
>
> Failure of the government to issue the Indians the full amount of annuity supplies to which they are entitled.
>
> Failure of the government to have the clothing and other annuity supplies ready for issue.
>
> Failure of the government to appropriate money for the payment of the Indians for the ponies taken from them. (Mooney 1965: 79–80)

Similar conditions of poverty, frustration, and despair engendered by government actions and inactions prevailed on other reservations throughout the region.

CONTEMPORARY ISSUES

An important continuing issue for many Plains peoples concerns control of natural resources. The use of water, in particular, has been a critical problem. As settlement of the region expanded and settlers' needs for water for their farms and herds soured, projects were undertaken to divert water from rivers that fed Native land so that it could be used by non-Indian communities. Plains nations in the United States were adversely affected by the Pick-Sloan plan initiated in 1944 that diverted water from the Missouri River and constructed dams that flooded Native land. According to Lawson, "The Pick-Sloan plan … caused more damage to Indian land than any other public works project in America" (1985: 171). Six dams were eventually built on the Missouri, collectively destroying over 500 sq. mi. of Native land and causing the displacement of more than 900 families. Five Lakota/Dakota reservations (Standing Rock, Cheyenne River, Yankton, Crow Creek, and Lower Brule) and the Fort Berthold Reservation (home to the Three Affiliated Tribes of Mandans, Arikaras, and Hidatsas) were affected. When families were forced out of their homes to make way for the construction of dams, they lost valuable acreage containing woods, water, and pasturage for their livestock and were instead removed to less fertile areas. The Pick-Sloan dams and related projects led to the loss of 90 percent of the timberland and 75 percent of the wild game and plant supplies of the affected reservations (72). Livestock holdings were seriously curtailed as a result of the loss of river bottomlands and grazing areas. And people were forced to abandon or disturb the graves of their ancestors, a burden that was emotionally and spiritually wrenching.

In addition to the economic and spiritual consequences for Native people, implementation of the Pick-Sloan plan violated treaties that had been signed with the federal government in the nineteenth century. According to those agreements, reservation land was not to be confiscated without the people's consent. Ignoring this restriction, the government did not consult with tribal governing bodies before devising the program and continued with the project despite the people's objections. The governments' actions also violated a Supreme Court decision rendered in 1908 (*Winters v. United States*) that has come to be known as the Winters Doctrine. The ruling stipulated that when treaties reserved land for Native people, they also implicitly reserved rights to waters that flow through the reservations for both present and future needs. However, instead of supplying either the domestic or commercial needs of people on the affected reservations, water provided by the Pick-Sloan projects has benefitted non-Indian communities and non-Indian industrial and agricultural development.

Valuable oil and mineral resources located on many reservations have not always benefitted local communities either. In the past, tribal governments often signed long-term mineral extraction leases with national corporations that severely limited indigenous rights and incomes. Because of inadequate legal advice provided by the Bureau of Indian Affairs, most leases did not give tribes fair market rates for their minerals. In the 1980s, tribes received average royalties of only $2 a barrel for oil at the same time that OPEC nations were receiving $40 a barrel (Fixico 1985: 230). In addition, tribal land has been seriously damaged by industrial processes, especially strip mining. Once recognizing the environmental degradation caused, some nations have attempted to stop strip-mining operations in their territory. For example, in 1974, the Northern Cheyenne Tribal Council unilaterally terminated a mining project. A subsequent suit filed by the coal companies was rejected by a federal appeals court in Montana. The decision recognizing Native rights paved the way for other tribal governments to assert control over industrial projects in their territory and to renegotiate long-term leases containing royalty payments that are much lower than prevailing market rates. Following a favorable ruling handed down by the US Supreme Court in 1982, some tribal governments are imposing severance taxes on oil and gas extracted from their land.

During the 1940s, the federal government instituted a Job Relocation Program that was supposedly aimed at alleviating the poverty of reservation communities by providing job training for people who agreed to relocate to cities in the Midwest and west. Participants received one-way bus fares to their destinations and promises of training and aid in seeking jobs. In all, thousands of people accepted the offers, but most found that their hopes of economic improvement were not fulfilled. Job training was inadequate and most people either became part of the urban poor or returned home, where they at least had the social and spiritual support of their families. Migration away from the reservations, though, has had a negative effect on local communities both by draining off college-educated, potential contributors to the community and by weakening the social base and potential political strength of the reservations. But, despite these trends, reservations do represent and actualize social and economic support for their members. Many of the larger Plains reservations have accredited junior or senior colleges that teach vocational and academic subjects with an emphasis on Native history, culture, and language. And many of the traditional social gatherings, highlighted by generous giveaways, are used to mark important events in the lives of individuals and the community as a whole. Finally, the Sun Dance, the major communal ceremonial of eighteenth- and nineteenth-century Plains nations, has reemerged as a central social and spiritual festivity. Some nations such as the Cheyennes, Arapahos, and Assiniboins have maintained their Sun Dances from earlier times, but others such as the Oglalas and Crows have revived a ceremony that they had abandoned by 1900 (Liberty 1980: 168). People not only participate in Sun Dances in their own communities but travel to nearby and even distant reservations to attend ceremonials and visit with friends and relatives (see Chapter 10 for a description of the Lakota Sun Dance).

A young fancy dancer performs during an annual dance competition.

TABLE 9.1	Native Populations for Selected States, 2010

State	Native Population
North Dakota	34,798
South Dakota	68,215
Nebraska	15,651
Kansas	24,442
Oklahoma	259,809
Texas	119,680
Montana	60,135
Wyoming	12,786

Source: US Bureau of the Census 2011b.

TABLE 9.2	Selected Economic Characteristics

	Per Capita Income ($)	Median Household Income ($)	Families Below Poverty (%)	Individuals Below Poverty (%)
Kansas	16,907	38,517	18.2	23.8
Montana	12,230	28,561	31.6	36.7
Nebraska	11,259	26,932	37.7	38.5
North Dakota	11,967	25,255	37.4	39.8
South Dakota	9,191	23,565	42.4	47.3
Wyoming	17,185	40,696	23.1	24.0

Source: US Bureau of the Census 2011a.

TABLE 9.3	Populations for Selected Canadian Provinces

	Population	
	On-Reserve	Off-Reserve
Alberta	45,753	50,976
Manitoba	61,267	44,548
Saskatchewan	53,954	40,206

Source: Statistics Canada 2011b.

Contemporary Populations and Economic Data

The US Census Bureau reported figures for the 2010 Native population in Plains states and on reservations given in Table 9.1 (differences between state and reservation numbers indicate the off-reservation Native population; also note that the large gap between reservation and state figures in Oklahoma and Texas is due, in part, to the loss of reservation status for land originally set aside by treaties).

Economic statistics for Plains nations reveal generally low incomes and consequent high rates of poverty. Most fall below the averages for American Indians as a whole although some earn higher incomes, but as elsewhere in the United States, all Plains average incomes are substantially lower than those of most residents of their states. Table 9.2 presents data for American Indian Populations in Plains states. For comparative purposes, 2010 per capita incomes (general population) for Plains states are: North Dakota ($25,803), South Dakota ($24,110), Nebraska ($25,229), Kansas ($25,907), Montana ($23,836), Wyoming ($27,860) (US Bureau of Census 2010).

The Canadian provinces of Manitoba, Saskatchewan, and Alberta are also home to Plains nations. Table 9.3 is a listing of the registered Indian populations of these provinces (note, however, that the figures are aggregates of all First Nations people within the province, not including Inuit or Metis populations).

Income statistics compiled by DIAND based on the 2010 US and 2011 Canadian census reveal a consistent pattern of disadvantage for First Nations. For measures of both per capita and average household income, on-reserve Indians' incomes were about half that of the overall provincial averages while off-reserve Indians fared only slightly better than their on-reserve counterparts. Relevant figures for the three Plains provinces are given in Table 9.4. Provincial averages were as follows. Alberta: per capita $24,600, household $47,789; Manitoba: per capita $21,600, household $41,090;

Saskatchewan: per capita $21,100, household: $39,597. Unemployment rates (see Table 9.5) for the three populations consistently indicated disadvantage for First Nations.

REFERENCES

Abel, Annie. 1939. *Tabeau's Narrative of Loisel's Expedition to the Upper Missouri*. Norman, OK: University of Oklahoma Press.

Bailey, Garrick. 1980. "Social Control on the Plains." *Anthropology on the Great Plains* (ed. W. R. Wood and M. Liberty). Lincoln, NE: University of Nebraska Press, pp. 152–163.

Berthrong, Donald. 1985. "Legacies of the Dawes Act: Bureaucrats and Land Thieves at the Cheyenne-Arapaho Agencies of Oklahoma." *The Plains Indians of the Twentieth Century* (ed. P. Iverson). Norman, OK: University of Oklahoma Press, pp. 31–54.

Boller, Henry. 1959. *Among the Indians: Eight Years in the Far West, 1858–1866*. Chicago, IL: The Lakeside Press, R.R. Donneley & Sons.

Bruner, Edward. 1961. "The Mandan." *Perspectives in American Indian Culture Change* (ed. E. Spicer). Chicago, IL: University of Chicago Press, pp. 187–277.

Department of Indian Affairs and Northern Development (DIAND). 2000. *Registered Indian Population by Sex and Residence 1999*. Ottawa.

Eggan, Fred. 1966. *The American Indian: Perspectives for the Study of Social Change*. Chicago, IL: Aldine Press.

Ewers, John. 1954. "The Indian Trade of the Upper Missouri before Lewis and Clark: An Interpretation." *Missouri Historical Society Bulletin* 10, no. 4: 429–446.

Ewers, John. 1955. *The Horse in Blackfoot Indian Culture*. Washington, DC: Bureau of American Ethnology, Bulletin No. 159.

Ewers, John. 1997. *Plains Indian History and Culture: Essays on Continuity and Change*. Norman, OK: University of Oklahoma Press.

Farnell, Brenda. 1995. *Do You See What I Mean?: Plains Indian Sign Talk and the Embodiment of Action*. Austin, TX: University of Texas Press.

Fixico, Donald. 1985. "Tribal Leaders and the Demand for Natural Energy Resources on Reservation Lands." *The Plains Indians of the Twentieth Century* (ed. P. Iverson). Norman, OK: University of Oklahoma Press, pp. 219–236.

Foster, Martha. 1993. "Of Baggage and Bondage: Gender and Status among Hidatsa and Crow Women." *American Indian Culture & Research Journal* 17 no. 2: 121–152.

Gibson, Arrell. 1988. "Indian Land Transfers." *History of Indian-White Relations* (ed. W. Washburn), Vol. 4 of *Handbook of North American Indians*. Washington, DC: Smithsonian Institution, pp. 211–229.

TABLE 9.4	Per Capita Income for Selected Canadian Provinces	
	Per Capita Income ($)	
	On-Reserve	**Off-Reserve**
Alberta	15,451	30,936
Manitoba	13,098	23,285
Saskatchewan	12,517	22,997

Source: Statistics Canada 2006. Special Interest Profiles: Aboriginal Ancestry (14), Area of Residence (6), Age Groups (8), Sex (3), and Selected Demographic, Cultural, Labour Force, Educational and Income Characteristics (227A) for the total population of Canada, provinces and territories.

TABLE 9.5	Unemployment Rates for Selected Canadian Provinces		
	On-Reserve (%)	**Off-Reserve (%)**	**Provincial Average (%)**
Alberta	25.9	11.7	6.9
Manitoba	28.5	32.0	7.9
Saskatchewan	28.9	23.3	6.6

Source: Statistics Canada 2006. Labour force characteristics of population aged 15–24 by aboriginal identity and province or region, 2007

Gilbert, B. Miles. 1980. "The Plains Setting." *Anthropology on the Great Plains* (ed. W. R. Wood and M. Liberty). Lincoln, NE: University of Nebraska Press, pp. 8–15.

Goldfrank, Esther. 1945. *Changing Configuration in the Social Organization of a Blackfoot Tribe During the Reserve Period (The Blood of Alberta, Canada)*. Seattle, WA: University of Washington Press, Monographs of the American Ethnological Society No. 8.

Grinnell, G. B. 1923. *The Cheyenne Indians*. New Haven, CT: Yale University Press.

Hayden, F. V. 1863. "On the Ethnography and Philology of the Indian Tribes of the Missouri Valley." *Transactions of the American Philosophical Society* 12: 231–461.

Hoebel, E. Adamson. 1978. *The Cheyennes: Indians of the Great Plains* (2nd ed.). New York: Harcourt Brace.

Holder, Preston. 1970. *The Hoe and the Horse on the Plains*. Lincoln, NE: University of Nebraska Press.

Hollow, Robert, and Douglas Parks. 1980. "Studies in Plains Linguistics: A Review." *Anthropology on the Great Plains* (ed. W. R. Wood and M. Liberty). Lincoln, NE: University of Nebraska Press, pp. 68–97.

Jablow, Joseph. 1950. *The Cheyenne in Plains Indian Trade Relations 1795–1840*. Seattle, WA: University of Washington Press, Monographs of the American Ethnological Society No. 19.

Klein, Alan. 1980. "Plains Economic Analysis: The Marxist Complement." *Anthropology on the Great Plains* (ed. W. R. Wood and M. Liberty). Lincoln, NE: University of Nebraska Press, pp. 129–140.

Kroeber, Alfred. 1939. *Cultural and Natural Areas of Native North America*. Berkeley, CA: University of California Publications in American Archeology and Ethnology, Vol. 38.

Lawson, Michael. 1985. "Federal Water Projects and Indian Lands: The Pick-Sloan Plan, a Case Study." *The Plains Indians of the Twentieth Century* (ed. P. Iverson). Norman, OK: University of Oklahoma Press, pp. 169–186.

Lewis, Oscar. 1942. *The Effects of White Contact Upon Blackfoot Culture with Special Reference to the Role of the Fur Trade*. Seattle, WA: University of Washington Press, Monographs of the American Ethnological Society No. 6.

Liberty, Margot. 1980. "The Sun Dance." In *Anthropology on the Great Plains* (ed. W. R. Wood and M. Liberty). Lincoln, NE: University of Nebraska Press, pp. 164–178.

Lowie, Robert. 1954. *The Indians of the Plains*. Garden City, NY: Natural History Press.

Mallery, Garrick. 1880. *A Collection of Gesture-Signs and Signals of the North American Indians*. Washington, DC: Government Printing Office.

Maximilian, Prince of Wied. 1906. *Travels in the Interior of North America* (ed. R. G. Thwaites). 3 vols. (Vols. 22, 23, 24 of *Early Western Travels*). Cleveland, OH: Arthur H. Clark.

Medicine, Bea. 1983. "'Warrior Women': Sex Role Alternatives for Plains Indian Women." *The Hidden Half: Studies of Plains Indian Women* (ed. P. Albers and B. Medicine). Lanham, MD: University Press of America, pp. 267–279.

Mishkin, Bernard. 1940. *Rank and Warfare among the Plains Indians*. Seattle, WA: University of Washington Press, Monographs of the American Ethnological Society No. 3.

Mooney, James. 1965. *The Ghost Dance Religion and the Sioux Outbreak of 1890*. Chicago, IL: University of Chicago Press.

Sandoz, Mari. 1954. *The Buffalo Hunters*. New York: Hastings House.

Slotkin, J. S. 1975. "The Peyote Way." *Teachings from the American Earth: Indian Religion and Philosophy* (ed. D. Tedlock and B. Tedlock). New York: Liveright, pp. 96–104.

Smits, David. 1998. "'Fighting Fire with Fire': The Frontier Army's Use of Indian Scouts and Allies in the Trans-Mississippi Campaigns, 1860–1890." *American Indian Culture & Research Journal* 22, no. 1: 73–116.

Statistics Canada. 2006. "Special Interest Profiles." *2006 Census*. Ottawa.

Statistics Canada. 2011a. "Language Highlight Tables." *2011 Census*. Ottawa.

Statistics Canada. 2011b. "Distribution of First Nations people, First Nations people with and without registered Indian status, and First Nations people with registered Indian status living on or off reserve, Canada, provinces and territories." *2011 Census*. Ottawa.

Stewart, Omer. 1980. "The Native American Church." *Anthropology on the Great Plains* (ed. R. W. Wood and M. Liberty). Lincoln, NE: University of Nebraska Press, pp. 188–196.

Thompson, David. 1962. *David Thompson's Narrative of His Explorations in Western America, 1784–1812* (ed. J. B. Tyrell). Toronto: The Champlain Society, Publications of the Champlain Society, Vol. 12.

US Bureau of Census. 2010.

US Bureau of the Census. 2011a. "2006–2010 American Community Survey Selected Economic Characteristics." *2011 Census*. Washington, DC.

US Bureau of the Census. 2011b. "2006–2010 American Community Survey Selected Population Tables." *2011 Census*. Washington, DC.

Weltfish, Gene. 1971. "The Plains Indians: Their Continuity in History and Their Indian Identity." *North American Indians in Historical Perspective* (ed. E. Leacock and N. Lurie). New York: Random House, pp. 200–227.

West, LaMont, Jr. 1960. *The Sign Language*. 2 vols. PhD dissertation. Ann Arbor: University Microfilms.

Wood, W. Raymond. 1980. "Plains Trade in Prehistoric and Protohistoric Intertribal Relations." *Anthropology on the Great Plains* (ed. W. R. Wood and M. Liberty). Norman, OK: University of Oklahoma Press, pp. 98–109.

Wurtzburg, Susan, and Lyle Campbell. 1995. "North American Indian Sign Language: Evidence of Its Existence before European Contact." *International Journal of American Linguistics* 61, no. 2: 153–167.

The Teton Lakotas

Our sense of history works this way: everything is connected. In order to understand where you're going and how to get there, you must know where you are now; in order to understand that, you must know where it is that you've been.

Matthew King, Oglala; quoted in
Churchill 1997: 120

THE TETON ARE the most populous of seven bands known collectively as the Lakota, a name meaning "allies" or "friends." In some dialects, the word is pronounced with a "d" as Dakota, from which the states of North and South Dakota get their name. The name "Teton" comes from the Native word "tetonwan" or "dwellers of the prairie" and aptly describes their original homeland in what is now central Minnesota. Later, from the mid-eighteenth century nearly to the end of the nineteenth, they inhabited a vast territory in the northern prairies and plains of the present-day states of Minnesota, North and South Dakota, Nebraska, and Wyoming. Today, most Lakota live in or near reservation communities within a small portion of their traditional region.

The Teton are a sociopolitical unity of seven distinct bands. The largest constituent group is the Oglala ("they scatter their own"). The other six bands are the Sicangu or "burnt thighs" (sometimes referred to as the Brule, from the French word meaning "burnt"), the Hunk-papa ("those who camp at the entrance"), Sihasapa ("blackfeet"), Itazipco ("without bows"), Oohenonpa ("two kettles"), and the Miniconjou ("those who plant by the stream").

ABORIGINAL CULTURE

Territories

In addition to the Teton or western division of Lakota, there are northern and eastern groupings, each containing a number of separate bands. The northern group consists of the Yankton, from the Native word "ihanktunwan" or "dwellers of the end," and the Yanktonai ("little Yankton"). The eastern peoples are called the Santee, a term derived from the word "isanti" or "knife" that refers to their location near "Knife Lake" in present-day Minnesota. The four Santee bands are the Wahpeton ("dwellers among the leaves"), Mdewakantan ("people of Spirit Lake"), Wahpekute ("shooters among the leaves"), and the Sisseton ("camping among the swamps").

The Lakota divisions refer to themselves collectively as members of the "Seven Council Fires." Although they are distinct social and political entities, they recognize a common culture and heritage, sharing most characteristics of history, economy, social systems, and religious beliefs. And while they were never integrated into a fixed political structure or confederacy, they generally were at peace and cooperated in matters of common interest. The people speak separate dialects of the Lakota language, a member of a large linguistic family called Siouan whose languages are found throughout the plains and prairies and in the Southeastern regions of North America.

Before migrating to the plains, the Teton inhabited prairie lands in central Minnesota, building their villages along the eastern banks of the Missouri River and the upper valleys of the Minnesota. Their economy combined farming and foraging. Women planted gardens of corn, beans, and squash in fertile fields near the rivers and gathered wild rice, roots, tubers, fruits, and berries. Men hunted animals on the prairies and in the forests, especially buffalo, deer, and elk. In addition to procuring resources by farming and foraging, the Teton had extensive trade networks with nearby Arikaras, Mandans, and Hidatsas, whose large and productive fields secured surpluses that they exchanged for meat and animal hides.

Although the Teton were well adapted to their prairie environment and had developed a successful economy and generally peaceful relations with their neighbors, their stay in that region was gradually made difficult because of changing conditions set in motion by the arrival of Europeans in North America. As a consequence of the expropriation of Northeastern Native territory by European settlers and the penetration of European traders beyond the Great Lakes, aboriginal societies of the prairies were destabilized by the mid-seventeenth century. When Indians were forced out of their ancestral Northeastern homelands, they fled toward the west and inevitably entered territories inhabited by other Native nations. A steady process of western movement and relocation continued for centuries, disrupting and transforming all aboriginal societies. Competition for the remaining land and resources accelerated. Sometime in the early years of the eighteenth century, Lakotas left their villages in the prairies, reacting to the presence of Native people entering the region and of French and British traders and soldiers who were making their way into the area. Lakota were at a disadvantage because they were not well-armed but instead became the targets of others, particularly Crees who received weapons from the French. In 1680, a French missionary, Louis Hennepin, noted that the "Sioux" were west of the Mississippi River in the vicinity of the Sauk Rapids. Twenty years later, Lakotas were met by a French fur trader in south central Minnesota and evidently claimed territory between the upper Mississippi and Missouri Rivers. Twenty-two years afterward, Lakotas were located near the headwaters of the Minnesota River (Hassrick 1964: 63). By that time, they were described as having abandoned their settled farming economy and instead had adjusted to life as nomadic

foragers. In 1743, Lakotas were situated some 50 mi. north of present-day Pierre, South Dakota, reaching the western shores of the Missouri River, where they were safe from attacks by their more easterly enemies. Finally, by 1775, Lakotas had migrated as far west as the Black Hills.

Adaptation to the Plains

In order to secure their new territory, Lakotas carried out raids against people such as the Omahas, Arikaras, Kiowas, and Cheyennes. Then, after defeating the Crows in the early nineteenth century, they were able to expand even further west into eastern Wyoming. By that time, they were in possession of firearms, although they do not seem to have been well-supplied (69).

Although population figures for the Teton during the seventeenth, eighteenth, and early nineteenth centuries are uncertain, they were consistently described as the largest of the Lakota divisions. Originally one group, as they expanded both in number and territory several subdivisions began to develop. In 1838, Nicollet described the Teton as consisting of three "grand tribes," each further divided into constituent bands (Nicollet 1978: 259). The largest of the three divisions, called the Saonis ("the whitish people, whose robes are always whitened with white earth"), was made up of five bands: the Minikanoju, who resided in 180 lodges; the Wanonwakteninan, 80 lodges; the Itazichonan, 110 lodges; the Sia-sappa, 100 lodges; and the Onkpapa, who had at least 100 lodges. The second subdivision, the Oglalas, were divided into three bands: the Onkp'hatinas, 100 lodges; the Ku-inyan, 100 lodges; and the Oyurpe, 100 lodges. The final Teton subdivision, the Brules, contained four bands: the Chokatowanyans, 90 lodges; the Wazazi, 70 lodges; the Minishanan, 60 lodges; and the Kiuksa, 80 lodges (260–261).

Economies

After arriving in the Plains, the Teton abandoned their former farming economy, becoming nomadic hunters and gatherers living in temporary camps and small villages. During the course of the next one hundred years, they developed a distinct and thriving culture adapted to their new social and ecological environment. Some features of Teton culture relied on previous knowledge and skills, but other aspects were more closely adapted to their new surroundings. The most important innovation in eighteenth-century Native culture was the incorporation of horses into their economy. When the people crossed the Missouri River around 1750, horses were just beginning to make their appearance in the northern plains. The Teton obtained horses primarily from Cheyennes who themselves secured the animals from Comanches and Kiowas. The Teton, like other aboriginal people of the plains, immediately realized the enormous potential for travel and transport afforded by use of these animals. As an indication of the importance ascribed to horses, they were called "sunka wakan" or "sacred dog," modifying the name for the animals that were previously used to carry or haul loads.

Teton men hunted a great variety of game including buffalo, deer, elk, antelope, coyote, fox, porcupine, beaver, muskrat, prairie dog, and rabbit. Many species of water and land birds were caught as well. Hunters used various techniques depending on the animals that they sought and the specific conditions of the hunt. Most hunting was done by men living within a small settlement or camp although larger, more complex groups were formed for communal buffalo or deer drives. In addition to organized hunting, men went out on daily hunts when their family's store of food had declined. They used deerskin disguises when hunting deer because these animals were sensitive to sound and odor and therefore difficult to catch. Bears were killed after being lured with bait tied to a log or stick. Foxes and small animals such as raccoons and badgers were often trapped in narrow stockades. Beaver were enticed from their holes and then clubbed to death. Rabbits and squirrels were caught by young boys hunting in groups who killed the animals by throwing "rabbit sticks" or heavy clubs at them. Birds such as prairie chickens, ducks, cranes, pigeons, meadow larks, and owls were either shot, clubbed, or snared. Their eggs were also valued as food. Fish were caught as well, most often with bone hooks attached to pieces of sinew fastened to the ends of willow poles. A kind of fishing net, made by piercing holes in a piece of buffalo hide, was held by two men walking upstream on opposite sides of a brook or river, catching fish swimming downstream. Finally, turtles were caught by hand in the early morning.

Although hunters required training and knowledge of the habits of animals to be successful, they understood their accomplishments as gifts from the spirit world. Animals were protected by spirit guardians who allowed their kind to be caught only if hunters showed them proper respect. Before departing on hunting expeditions, men smoked tobacco as a prayer to the spirit world and after animals had been killed, they made offerings to the spirit guardians. Finally, when eating meat, small pieces were given to the spirits: "when eating, one should put a piece of meat aside for the spirit, holding it up and throwing it away saying, 'recognize this, ghost, so that I may become the owner of something good'" (Hassrick 1964: 194). When planning a particularly important hunt, men sought spirit aid in visions or might enlist the help of a shaman. Since hunting eagles was considered a particularly spirit-laden endeavor because of the birds' sacredness, a shaman's prayers were deemed necessary to protect the hunter.

Communal buffalo hunts were held at least once every summer or early fall but may have occurred more often depending upon availability of game, need for food, and the advice of a shaman. The most common technique was the "two group surround," in which hunters divided into two sections and, at a signal, charged toward the herd, attacking the animals with wooden lances or bows and arrows tipped with stone arrowheads. Each hunter had arrows painted with designs particular to him so that after the hunt the animals that he had killed could be identified. Communal drives or surrounds were sometimes accomplished by setting a circle of small fires on the plains grass and killing the animals within the circle. Another method was to drive buffalo over the edge of a cliff, lured by a "buffalo caller" who, disguised as a buffalo and mimicking its call and movements, enticed the herd toward the cliff. Meanwhile, all able-bodied men, women, and children formed a V heading toward the cliff, shouting and stamping their feet to frighten the buffalo and keep them within the enclosure. The animals blindly plunged over the edge where they either died in the fall or were killed by hunters waiting below.

During communal buffalo hunts, individuals' activities were strictly monitored. Hunt organizers established rules of behavior that all people were to follow so that no man went out on his own, potentially risking the danger of frightening the herd to the detriment of the entire community. In order to ensure compliance with regulations, civil chiefs appointed members of a warrior society to act as marshals or "akicitas." If anyone violated the rules of the hunt, akicitas had the right to destroy all of the man's belongings and to beat him if the offense was considered serious enough. Then, if the offender showed remorse for his actions, his property was usually replaced either by the akicitas from their own possessions or from donations made by other members of the community.

Women's primary subsistence activities included gathering wild foods and preparing meals. They collected varieties of berries, wild plums and other fruits, edible roots, wild potatoes, turnips, onions, cactus fruits, and prairie grasses. Foraging tasks were often performed by girls and women working in teams. Some wore specially designed aprons to collect the produce while others carried hide containers or skin bags. Dogs were also employed to pull travois carrying the produce.

Prior to the Teton's migration into the plains, women had made earthen pottery for use as cooking vessels, but when the people became nomadic foragers, they gave up the art because pottery was too easily broken in transport. Thereafter, food was cooked in pits dug into the ground, lined with animal skins, and filled with water. Stones that had been heated on fire were placed in the pit to cause the water to boil. Fruits and berries were usually eaten fresh although some were dried in the sun and preserved for use in stews and in mixtures with meats. When making soups, peppermint leaves were sometimes added as a seasoning. Acorns and other nuts were usually roasted and then boiled or dried and crushed to make a kind of mush, often with the addition of box-elder sap collected in the early spring. Meat was generally roasted or boiled in soups, although liver and kidneys were considered delicacies when eaten raw. Turtles were boiled in soups as another delicacy.

Women accompanied hunters, sometimes participating in the hunt itself but more often waiting to prepare the meat for transport to camp. Buffalo meat was cut into thin strips, hung on wooden racks to dry, and then packed into tight bundles for storage. When needed for food, the meat was unpacked and boiled together with wild berries or plants. Some of the dried meat was made into pemmican by pounding it into a powder and mixing it with dried berries. The various methods of preserving meat ensured that supplies obtained in one hunting expedition could sustain people for a long period of time.

Animals were not only used as a food resource, however. Many articles of material culture including tools, utensils, and clothing were made from hides of buffalo, deer, and elk. In order for the hides to be converted into useful objects, they first had to be softened or tanned. Women began the process by scraping all animal flesh and fat from the hide with an elk antler blade. They removed the animal's hair if the skins were to be made into clothing or dwellings, but hair was left on the hides if they were destined for bedding and covers. Once the hides were cleaned, they were soaked in water until pliable and then rubbed with oils and fats to maintain their softness.

Buffalo hides were used to construct tipis, the most common form of dwelling. Tipis and their domestic contents were the property of the woman who made them. Most tipis measured from 12 to 16 ft. in diameter at the base, large enough to house a nuclear or small extended family. The first step in their construction was the preparation and sewing of eight to ten buffalo hides. Women, usually working in small groups, used sinew to form the required shape and then stretched the material over a frame made of wooden poles spaced to form a circular base and laced together at the top. Two additional buffalo skins were loosely hung at the top to provide an exit for smoke from a central hearth. The flaps could be opened to emit smoke and/or closed to keep out rain, snow, or cold air. The bottom of the tipi was held in place on the ground by pegs or stones spaced around the edge, but in hot weather the skins were rolled up so that fresh air could enter. A doorway was covered with an extra hide and held with pins made of wood or bone. The exterior skins of tipis were sometimes decorated by men with paintings made from natural dyes. Pictographs recorded successful hunting expeditions or bravery in warfare. Interior furnishings used for seating, bedding, and coverings were made of tanned buffalo hides. Despite their large size, tipis were light in weight and could be dismantled in a matter of minutes when people relocated their camps. The skins were rolled up and placed on a travois pulled by horses.

Clothing was made from animal hides, usually from the soft, tanned skins of deer and elk. Women's clothing consisted of knee-length dresses and leggings reaching to the knee. Men wore sleeveless or long-sleeved shirts, breechcloths, and leggings that covered their thighs and were fastened to a belt worn around the waist. In cold or rainy weather, people covered themselves with buffalo robes. Daily clothing was usually undecorated, but both men and women also had clothing for ritual or social occasions that was painted and decorated profusely. Moccasins, robes, dresses, and shirts were embroidered with beads or porcupine quills colored with red, yellow, black, green, and blue dyes derived from boiling roots or berries. Women often received ideas for designs from spiritually powerful dreams or visions.

Men and women ornamented their bodies with necklaces and arm bands of bones or beads. Some people painted or tattooed designs on their face and/or body. All children of about five or six years old had their ears pierced by an elder man or woman using a bone needle. Strings of colored beads were thereafter worn as an ear ornament.

Most women and men wore their hair in two braids, often intertwined with colored cloth or beads. Older women, however, wore their hair loose on their backs. Some young men preferred a hairstyle called a "roach," made by shaving the sides of the head and allowing the hair in the center to grow. Young men successful in war ornamented their hair with eagle feathers, while older war leaders wore feather bonnets on ceremonial occasions.

Families and Social Systems

Camps consisted of groups of related families who cooperated in economic and social tasks. Households were composed of nuclear families although extended-family units were also attested. Since the Lakota kinship system was based on bilateral descent, either matrilocal or patrilocal postmarital residence was possible, but camps were more likely composed of people on the basis of patrilateral affiliation. Groups of fathers and sons or of brothers usually formed the core of settlements whereas women left their parent's households after marriage to take up residence near their husband's family. Patrilateral affiliation was preferred because men more than women depended on each other in cooperative tasks such as communal hunting and raiding or warfare, but decisions about location and residence were made on the basis of group composition, economic resources, and personal preferences. An additional factor in settlement decisions was the renown of the camp leader.

Families were relatively small; five or six children were considered a large group (Mirsky 1937: 393). Upon marriage, the couple often initially resided near the wife's family but gradually shifted their residence to near the husband's kin. Given rules of strict social distance between a mother-in-law/son-in-law and between a father-in-law/daughter-in-law, it was not deemed respectable for a couple to reside in the household of either set of parents but instead erected a new tipi for themselves near their kin.

The actual physical arrangement of settlements was symbolically significant. Winter camps were the largest and most stable and therefore conformed to the ideal plan more than did the small temporary summer camps that were established in places where game was seasonally available. In winter camps, tipis were placed in circular formation with a small space left unoccupied on the side of the circle facing the rising sun. This space was the entrance to the encampment, and a person who entered from any other direction was considered hostile. The place opposite the entrance, known as the "chief's place," was the residence of the most highly respected man and his family. It was also the place where a public lodge was erected to be used for council meetings and other communal gatherings. All lodges within the camp had their doors placed so that they faced the center except for two tipis situated at either side of the entrance that faced east (Walker 1992: 23).

Most marriages were arranged by parents for their daughters and sons although ideally the wishes of the young couple were taken into consideration. Formal proposals of marriage were made by male relatives of the prospective husband, accompanied by gifts of horses and other valuables presented to the young woman's family. If the woman's parents thought the young man acceptable, usually on the basis of his skill as a hunter and success as a warrior, they accepted the presents offered. Marriage ceremonies consisted of further exchanges of clothing and ornaments between the families of bride and groom. Some marriages, however, were not preceded by formal proposals to relatives but instead began with the couple's elopement if they could not obtain their families' approval.

Although monogamy was the most frequent form of marriage, polygyny was also possible. Sororal polygyny was the most common form of plural marriage. Men in such unions were typically wealthy and influential members of their communities, able to give adequate gifts to their wives' families and able to support large households. Polyandry was also possible, although it required the consent of the first husband and was evidently a rare occurrence. According to Walker, a woman might take a second husband if her marriage was childless. Children born after her second union were considered offspring of her first spouse (Walker 1992: 55).

Marriage ideally lasted for a lifetime, but divorce often occurred, particularly early in a couple's life together. Either jointly or separately, a husband or wife might choose to end their marriage. A husband could announce his wish to divorce by beating a drum at a warrior society dance and proclaiming that he wished to "throw away [his] wife," thus not only ending the marriage but publicly humiliating his wife as well. No such strategy was available to women. Men also had means of shaming wives who committed adultery by punishing them with disfigurement, cutting off the tips of their noses as a form of humiliation and as a way to render them unattractive to other men. Although a husband's adultery was criticized, men who committed these offenses were not treated as harshly.

Differences in attitudes toward women's and men's sexuality were also manifested in expectations concerning premarital behavior. Girls and unmarried women were expected to be chaste. The emphasis on female chastity was enacted in feasts of "Virgin Fires" that were held by young unmarried women to publicly proclaim their virginity (Mirsky 1937: 410). Although social pressure was subtly and overtly applied for young women to participate, if any woman made a false claim to living a chaste life, she ran the risk of being denounced by the man with whom she had had sexual relations. Such women thereafter suffered the social consequence of losing value as potential wives. In contrast, unmarried men might boast of their sexual exploits regardless of the obvious fact that their relationships were, by necessity, with women who were either unmarried (thereby violating the norm of premarital chastity) or married (thereby committing adultery). Such double standards in attitudes toward sexuality were indications of the male dominance that existed in Teton culture, at least in the nineteenth century.

Kinship ties were the basis of social and economic cooperation, group solidarity, and personal loyalty. As Mirsky observed, "to lack relatives was the great dread of Dakota, for on kin everything depended. A man was safe as long as he had a group of relatives with whom he could cooperate and who would help him" (1937: 392). And a modern consultant of DeMallie noted:

Relatives are anyone who depends upon us for anything, and so we respect them. Like if someone comes here and eats with us, maybe stays here out of the cold, he depended on us, and so we are related. We respect one another, have established relationship. We become relatives like that. (DeMallie 1994: 132)

Furthermore, as Deloria described, the system of social integration became widespread, inclusive, and dense:

It was true that everyone was related to all the people within his own circle of acquaintances. But all those people had other circles of acquaintances within the large tribe. All such circles overlapped and interlocked. Any Dakota could legitimately find his way to any other, if he wished or needed to do so. And thus, with relatives scattered over the many camp circles and communities, anyone could go visiting anywhere, and be at home. (Deloria 1944: 37–38)

Relatives were classified into two general categories: close kin or members of one's extended family and more distant consanguineous as well as affinal kin (DeMallie 1994: 136–137). In contrast to relatives, strangers were thought of as potentially dangerous since they were unknown. In order to establish trust, strangers were transformed into relatives by address with kin terms. According to Deloria, when a new arrival entered a community, s/he would soon be addressed as son, grandson, daughter, or granddaughter, a terminological practice usually initiated by an old woman in the settlement (Deloria 1944: 29). New arrivals immediately became enmeshed in wide networks of relationships based on ties to the woman who had begun to call them by kin terms.

The importance of relatives was not only demonstrated in social life but was legitimated in Native religion as well. The smoking of a sacred pipe, a gift from a deity called White Buffalo Calf Woman, established kinship bonds between people. In primordial times, when the Woman gave the pipe to the people, she addressed them as "brothers and sisters," saying, "I am proud to become a member of your family—a sister to you all … I represent the Buffalo tribe. When you are in need of buffalo meat, smoke this pipe and ask for what you need and it shall be granted" (DeMallie 1994: 128). The sacred pipe itself signifies the kin-like reciprocity between the spirit of Buffalo and humanity. The Woman told people how they should treat their relatives and emphasized the importance of sharing and reciprocity. Kinship is not only conceived of as a relationship among people but also unites people, animals, spirit beings and forces and is understood to be "a contract with Wakan Tanka [great sacred], which thereby unites all forms of being into an unbroken network of relationship" (142).

Behavior within the family and the settlement group was attuned to complex rules of public etiquette.

Differences in age, gender, and kinship influenced the way in which people interacted. Some relatives were treated with formality and social distance while others interacted casually and jokingly. The most formal relationship obtained between parents-in-law and children-in-law of the opposite gender (i.e., father-in-law/daughter-in-law and mother-in-law/son-in-law). These sets of relatives were expected never to look directly at or even to speak to one another. If they had to convey messages to each other, intermediaries were employed. Behavior between children and their parents was also rather formal even though they did not entail the social distance required of in-laws. Children spoke respectfully to their parents and generally followed their advice. Interactions between siblings were characterized by a lack of formality, but the degree to which they were truly casual depended upon age and gender. If the age difference between the two siblings was great, the younger spoke respectfully to the elder, but if they were close in age and of the same gender, they interacted with easy rapport and affection. Sisters-in-law and brothers-in-law behaved in a casual, joking style consistent with marital practices of the levirate and sororate. That is, a man was expected to marry the widow of his deceased brother while a woman might marry a deceased sister's spouse.

The close affectional and social loyalties of siblings was replicated in the institutionalization of formal friendships that might be established between men or women, often beginning as childhood friends and formalized upon reaching adulthood. Friends, called "kola," had reciprocal responsibilities, shared resources, and gave emergency support to each other, following the typical behaviors expected of relatives.

Kinship as well as residence underlay the formation of bands. The primary kinship grouping was the "tiyospaye," an extended bilateral family usually consisting of from ten to twenty nuclear families. Members did not all reside in one encampment, but commonly each encampment was dominated by one such family group. Each tiyospaye was headed by a chief or headman, usually but not always the eldest man. His advice was sought by family members concerning individual and communal decisions but his actual influence depended upon the regard with which he was held.

Community Leadership

Bands also had chiefs, selected by common consent, who typically came from respected families and could rely on the support of large networks of kin. However, according to Walker:

> A chief's authority depended on his personality and his ability to compel others to do his will, and if he were successful in his undertaking, followers were apt to flock to him and his authority be correspondingly great. If he were weak or cowardly, or unsuccessful, his people deserted him, and he became a person of little consequence. (Walker 1992: 24)

Succession to chieftainships ideally passed from a man to his oldest son, but if the son was deemed unworthy, another descendent or even an unrelated man might succeed.

In small camps, chiefs acted on their own but in larger settlements a council of elders was formed, composed of headmen of resident families, ritualists, and successful warriors and hunters. The council was not formally selected; its members were acclaimed by agreement among the respected men of the community. Women's contributions to the selection process were stated in contradictory terms by one of Walker's consultants,

> Women never took part in these meetings, nor had anything to say in the matter, except on rare occasions when an old woman would make a speech, which was always listened to with respect. But the women would talk to the men in their families about it and give their opinions as to the candidates. (Walker 1992: 29–30)

Councils discussed matters of public interest, enacted regulations that governed people's behavior, made decisions concerning movement and location of camps, negotiated and concluded treaties with foreign groups, and declared war on their enemies. Decisions were made after unlimited debate and discussion but could not be taken unless unanimity was achieved. In addition, if conflicts arose between settlement members, people could seek advice from the council, who heard arguments presented by the parties concerned and sought additional information when needed. Their decisions had influence but they did not have absolute authority and instead relied on public opinion to support them. Chiefs and councils appointed "akicitas," translated as "marshals," to carry out and enforce their decisions. Any member of the camp could be chosen as a marshal, an honor that it was not possible to refuse. Women were appointed only on rare occasions (30). One of the marshals was named as a public herald to make announcements telling of decisions reached by the council concerning movements of camps, organization of hunting expeditions, and other public business.

In some bands, the council of elders appointed a smaller group from among themselves to function as a kind of executive committee. This committee, usually consisting of ten members, implemented the broad policy initiatives of the larger council. An even smaller group of officers, called "shirt-wearers," was appointed by the executive committee to be spokesmen to the public for the committees' decisions and policies (Hassrick 1964: 25–27). Their name derived from the fact that, as an emblem of their responsibilities, they were given shirts painted with designs symbolizing spirit beings who controlled and protected the world and humanity. Although men of high-status families usually achieved these posts, young men of extraordinary wisdom, ability, and spirit powers might be named as shirt-wearers.

Indian chiefs who counciled with Gen. Miles to settle the Indian War: (1) Standing Bull, (2) Bear Who Looks Back Running (Stands and Looks Back), (3) Has the Big White Horse, (4) White Tail, (5) Liver (Living) Bear, (6) Little Thunder, (7) Bull Dog, (8) High Hawk, (9) Lame, (10) Eagle Pipe.

Warfare

Military expeditions were organized by war leaders whose status depended on their continued success. Men were willing to follow the advice of a warrior who had proven his valor and strategic skills in previous campaigns, but they were never compelled to join a raid or to remain in the ranks if they became dissatisfied with the plans. Aboriginal warfare was generally motivated by revenge for injury or death suffered in prior raids, but by the late eighteenth century, raids were also motivated by a desire to obtain enemies' horses. And as competition for land and resources increased in the middle of the nineteenth century, warfare was often necessary as a means of defense against intruders.

Warfare had several ritualistic traits. Men who wanted to participate in war had to abstain from sexual activity for four days prior to leaving their settlements. They were ritually purified in sweat to cleanse their bodies and spirits and to give them strength and courage to face the dangers encountered in conflict. In addition, actions in raids or war were judged according to complex rules of bravery known as "counting coup" that ranked exploits on the basis of their danger. The most prestigious act was to touch or strike an enemy at close range. Wounding or killing an enemy by clubbing him brought more honor than shooting from a distance because it meant that the warrior exposed himself to direct danger of retaliation. Success in face-to-face combat was considered honorable. Other daring actions included wresting a weapon from an enemy's hand or stealing a horse from inside an enemy village.

Wealth and Status

As Teton culture developed in the late eighteenth and early nineteenth centuries, it became focused on the acquisition of wealth, especially symbolized by horses but also displayed in personal property such as ceremonial clothing, ornamentation, and finely decorated household items. However, the accumulation of goods was not motivated by desire for private consumption but rather was meant to be given away and, through generosity, to enhance the reputation of the donor. That is, "the ownership of things was important only as a means to giving. Property was for use, not for accumulation, and its chief use was bestowing it on others … Wealth, therefore, was counted in terms of a man's ability to accumulate for disposal" (Hassrick 1964: 36, 296). Native ethics and attitudes thoroughly condemned the acquisition of personal property as a goal in and of itself. Indeed, the desire for possessions was considered suspect and dishonorable. Furthermore, "the Dakota feel that property is of no importance when compared with human relations. Property achieves importance only when it is used to bring out and emphasize one's relationship to another human being" (Mirsky 1937: 385). Property was given away on informal occasions, as gift exchanges, and as charity to those who were elderly, sick, or needy. Through various means within the household, extended family, and community, people who were able to accumulate more possessions because of their skills and good fortune were obliged by principles of generosity to distribute their wealth to others. "If a person is rich all his life, the tribe is suspicious of him. As they say, death visits all families; then why all these riches?" (387). Greedy persons were without honor and had no prestige.

The Teton recognized three kinds of gifts: "a solicited gift that required repayment by an article of greater value; a voluntary gift acknowledged by repayment of something not of the same value, but highly personal and 'from the heart,' and a charity gift that was given in such a way that no return was implied in the giving" (388–389). Gifts were given and status enhanced on many public and private occasions. Families sponsored public giveaways during rituals such as a daughter's first menstruation, a son's first successful war expedition, and funerals for family members. In addition to these public occasions, people shared informally with those less fortunate than themselves. Young men and women brought food to the dwellings of elderly people who could not provide for themselves, women gave gifts of clothing and food to orphans and elders, and all people helped others who had lost possessions or whose fortunes had declined. All of these circumstances provided opportunities to both ensure the adequate survival of all and to promote the status and prestige of those who through good fortune, skill, and intelligence had been able to accumulate more than others. Although striving for wealth was a legitimate goal in Native culture, it did not result in distinct classes of people because those who possessed wealth were obliged to share with those who were needy. The obligation to be generous was not only inculcated in people as a moral duty but also was a means to another end, namely the attainment of high status in society. That is, positions of leadership as civil authorities, akicitas, and war chiefs were based on a man's generosity and concern for the welfare of others.

Competition existed among individuals for public acknowledgment of skills and abilities. For men, personal achievement was especially demonstrated in war. Men kept records of their military valor, noting successes in "counting coup" on their clothing, tipis, and ornamentation. Everyone in the community was aware of the accomplishments of individual men, not the least because the men's families were proud to publicly proclaim their son's or spouse's success. For women, similar records were kept of achievement in domestic skills such as abilities to make tipis, buffalo robes, and ornamented clothing. Quilling was considered an especially honored occupation, enabling a woman who had produced many elaborate quilled robes to join the "robe quilling society," a group that had comparable status to the young men's akicita and warrior societies. Although the paths to status and renown differed for men and women, both were publicly acknowledged and earned community respect for their abilities and accomplishments.

Religious Beliefs and Practices

Lakota religion is concerned with understanding and respecting "wakan tanka," a spirit essence or force that pervades all beings and all nature. It can be embodied in human, animal, or object form or have no physical shape whatsoever. It can be seen as a visible entity or unseen as an abstract essence. Anything and everything that has power partakes of wakan tanka. It is demonstrated in the power of deities, in the power of human healers and visionaries, in the power of animals, and in the power of objects to cure, bring good fortune, and protect people from harm.

The spirit realm is inhabited by many kinds of beings and forces. The most important are Sun ("Wi"), Sky ("Scan"), Earth ("Maka"), and Rock ("Inyan"). Sun, Sky, and Rock are endowed with male characteristics whereas Earth is thought of as female. The four major deities each have their particular roles. Sun is the protector of the four Lakota moral principles, that is, bravery, integrity, fortitude, and generosity. It is visible not only as the celestial body but also as fire. Sky, however, is not visible but is thought of as the source of power and motion. Earth, addressed as "all mother," is a visible deity embodied in the earth itself. It is considered the "ancestor of all material things, except the Rock" (Walker 1917: 82). Earth is the protector of everything that grows from the ground and also of food and drink, and of the home. It is a symbol of generation, birth, and growth. Finally, Rock is a visible god, addressed as "all father," who resides in the mountains and is the protector or "patron of authority and vengeance, of construction and destruction, and of implements and utensils" (82).

Next in importance are spirits of winds, the four cardinal directions, whirlwind, the Thunderers, and spirits of Buffalo and Bear. There is also a deity, called Iya, who embodies evil forces and powers, frequently personified as a cyclone. Harmful or treacherous forces are represented as monsters, evil spirits that dwell in the forests or in waters, and deities who control the powers of witchcraft.

A special role in Native religion is given to a deity named White Buffalo Calf Woman. Her origin is said to have been in the ancient past when there was warfare between human beings and buffalo (Erdoes and Ortiz 1985: 48–52). After many conflicts, the spirit of Buffalo sent White Buffalo Calf Woman to the people to bring peace and knowledge. She gave humans a sacred pipe to smoke and send messages to the spirit world, thus creating bonds between inhabitants of earthly and spirit realms of existence. White Buffalo Calf Woman also gave seven rituals that formed the basis of Lakota religious practice. Of these, the four most important are the sweatbath performed to purify people's bodies and minds; the vision quest through which people seek visions and guidance from spirit beings; the girl's puberty ceremony; and the Sun Dance, performed every summer in thanksgiving for life, health, and good fortune.

Lakota religion is imbued with symbolism of number, color, and shape. The number four is sacred, reflected in the division of deities into groups of four and in the fact that ceremonial actions are repeated four times or multiples of four. The sacredness of the number four originates from the fact that there are four directions, four divisions of time (day, night, moon, and year), four segments of things that grow from the ground (roots, stem, leaves, and fruit), and four kinds of creatures that breathe (those that crawl, those that fly, those that walk on four legs, and those that walk on two legs) (Walker 1917: 159–160).

Color symbolism is reflected in the association of each of the four major deities with a color: red is the color of Sun, blue the color of Sky, green is the color of Earth, and yellow is Rock's color. Red is also employed in ceremonial designs and ornamentation as a general representation of sacredness. Finally, the color black signifies "intensity of emotion or firmness of purpose" (82).

The most important symbolic shape is that of the circle, a reflection of the circularity or roundness of everything in nature. The circle is the symbol of the roundness of the world, the roundness of celestial bodies, the roundness of animate bodies, and the roundness or circularity of the passage of time. Consistent with the shape of the sacred circle, Lakota tipis are round, camps are set up in a circular formation, and people sit in circles during ceremonials. Also, when offering tobacco smoke to deities, the pipe is passed in a circular direction to reflect circularity of time and energy. When a ritualist begins a ceremonial, he lights a pipe, offers it to the deities, to the four winds and four directions, and makes the following invocation:

> I pass the pipe to you first. Circling I pass to you who dwell with the father [Sun]. Circling pass to beginning day. Circling pass to the beautiful one [White Buffalo Calf Woman]. Circling I complete the four quarters and the time. I pass the pipe to the father with the sky. I smoke with the great spirit. (Walker 1917: 157)

Lakotas believed that all people had access to spirit power and could accumulate spirit protections, but those men and women with extraordinary powers were among the most respected members of their communities. They were consulted before setting out on important expeditions or before making crucial personal or family decisions. They could foretell the future, find lost objects, communicate with the spirit realm, and treat illness. Healers were aided by spirit guardians to diagnose the cause of patients' ailments. Ritual cures included songs, prayers, and dances aimed at securing the powers of spirit forces to cure disease and restore the body's physical and psychological harmony. But although practitioners were well-trained in practical and ritual techniques, spirit forces and beings were the ultimate source of healing power. As the Oglala healer, Black Elk, remarked, "If I thought that I was doing it [curing] myself, the hole would close up and no power could come through" (Niehardt 1961: 209).

Some men and women were chosen by spirits to become "heyokas," named for the deity, Heyoka, whose "functions are to cleanse the world from filth and to fight the Monsters who defile the waters and to cause all increase by growth from the ground" (Walker 1917: 83; Mirsky 1937: 416). After receiving a dream or vision from Thunderer beings of the west, they were initiated through a complex ritual reenacting their vision. Heyokas demonstrated their unusual powers by reversing the normal pattern of life: they walked backward, sat backward while riding horses, and reversed their clothing. Their actions were both serious and comical to onlookers, a dual role explained by Black Elk:

> The people shall be made to feel jolly and happy, so that it may be easier for the power to come to them. The truth comes into this world two faces. One is sad and suffering and the other laughs; but it is the same face, laughing or weeping. When people are already in despair, maybe the laughing face is better for them; and when they feel too good and too sure of being safe, maybe the weeping face is better for them to see. (Niehardt 1961: 192–193)

A person's passage through life was marked with rituals at critical stages such as birth, naming, puberty, and death. During pregnancy, a mother-to-be or one of her female relatives made a small pouch that would later contain the child's umbilical cord. When the baby was born, it was cleaned with sweet grass soaked in warm water and then wiped with buffalo grease and wrapped in blankets. Its umbilical cord was placed in the pouch and initially kept by the mother, but when the child was able to walk the pouch was attached to its clothing. Later, the pouch was taken from the child and safeguarded by the mother. The umbilical cord was believed to contain the individual's substance or essence and was preserved as a symbolic representation of the protection given to the child. When twins were born, people believed that one or both were likely to die but if they both survived, they were thought to be spiritually powerful or "wakan."

Four days after the birth of a child, a feast was held that honored the mother and was the occasion for bestowal of the baby's name. The father and maternal grandmother gave presents to everyone in attendance, particularly to people of importance and to those who were poor. Children were usually named for their oldest living grandparent, but a child might be named for a deceased relative who was especially respected. If, however, a grandparental name had already been given to an older child, the new baby was named in accordance with a dream or an important event that had happened to its parents. After the name was publicly announced, the father donated a horse in honor of his child to a poor member of the community.

Coming of age rituals were held for girls and boys. When a girl reached puberty, she retired for four days to a separate tipi or hut within hearing distance of her family's dwelling. The girl was accompanied by older female relatives who instructed her in the work and responsibilities of adult women. She spent her time in handicrafts such as sewing and embroidery. Following are the recollections of Nellie Star Boy Menard whose puberty rite was held in 1925 when she was fifteen years old.

> Grandma took a little ax cut into the ground made a little dug out about 4 inches deep, she put loose dirt in then got some sage and made a bed. All I had to wear was dress and underskirt. I sat on these sage when too uncomfortable she will take the soiled sage and the dirt where blood soaked through, then put fresh in. If I itched anywhere I can't scratch. I had to use a special little forked stick....During the day all I did was sit and do either beadwork first....Next I have started a pair of moccasins and within 4 days or as long as I can see without lamp I had to finish at least one side of moccasins … Of course I was clean up every so often. Wash and eat. I cannot look outside or go near any men or boys.
>
> End of my time 4 days evening Grandma boiled sage and bath me with the sage water then she wipe me off with sage—no towel. I put on all new clothes. (Bol and Menard 2000: 26)

The period of seclusion was followed by a Buffalo Ceremony that announced the girl's new status to the community:

> A man gave a talk first then he told me I was a woman now and said always to do right. (26)

Afterward, a ceremony called "Throwing the Ball" took place. The pubescent girl threw a specially prepared hide-covered ball to another girl selected for the honor. If the receiver dropped the ball, bad luck ensued. According to nineteenth-century accounts, the pubescent girl threw the ball four times, once in each direction. The last stage of the ritual process was a feast hosted by the young girl's father to mark the conclusion of his daughter's passage to womanhood.

A boy's passage to manhood was marked when he achieved success in activities typical of men. When a boy killed his first animal or when he joined a raiding or war group, his family hosted a public feast in his honor.

Young adults engaged in rituals called vision quests, seeking visions of spirit beings who would afterward become their guardians. Although vision quests were especially important for men, women sought spirit guardians as well. Before setting out on the quest, the seeker prepared him/herself by fasting for four days and by ritual purification in a sweat bath. The act of sweating was understood to be a sacred shedding of physical and psychological impurities, cleansing people to face the world of spirit beings.

The seeker left camp alone and proceeded to a lonely place for four days to pray and sing for aid. S/he did not eat or sleep during the quest, thinking only of encountering a spirit being. If the quest were successful, a spirit came to the seeker and gave songs or instructions to follow when in danger or need. Afterwards, whenever the seeker was in peril or suffered misfortune, s/he could use these songs and prayers to call on spirit help. During vision quests, people often found distinctive objects such as eagle feathers, oddly shaped stones, or animal bones that embodied the power received from the spirit world. The charms were placed in deerskin pouches and kept at home or carried whenever the seeker travelled from camp.

Additional visionary experiences could occur anytime thereafter. People might actively seek contact with the spirit world through prayer and fasting but visions might also appear spontaneously. Unsought visions were especially powerful since they were the will of the spirits.

Death was marked with burial rituals and the rigors of mourning. When a person died, the body was dressed in fine clothing and a pair of "spirit moccasins," wrapped in buffalo robes and tied securely with sinew. While the body was being prepared, female relatives wailed loudly and sadly. When preparations were completed, relatives of the deceased participated in a "worship ceremony" to indicate their loss and to sacrifice themselves in grief (Hassrick 1964: 335).

Men inserted small wooden pegs into their arms and legs while women slashed their limbs with knives and might cut off their little fingers at the first joint. Both men and women cut their hair short and continued to weep and wail in sorrow. The period of intense mourning lasted for four days. Then, women of the deceased's family carried the body out of the tipi in which it was resting and placed it on a scaffold that had previously been erected. Men were accompanied in death by hunting equipment and war weapons; sewing utensils and household goods were placed with a woman's body. A favorite horse might be sacrificed at the scaffold and its tail tied to one of the supporting poles.

After death, the spirit that animated a living person left the body of the deceased to travel westward on the "spirit trail" (identified as the Milky Way) to the afterworld where souls were reunited with friends and relatives in the midst of fertile land and abundant resources. Souls of the dead continued activities similar to those of the living but without fear of starvation, misfortune, warfare, or unhappiness.

If a person died in childhood or as a young adult, his/her parents might hold a ritual called a "spirit-keeping rite" (302). Although all parents might wish to conduct such a ceremony for a deceased child, since the rites were accompanied by giveaways of large amounts of food, clothing, horses, and other possessions, it was in practice limited to those who could afford it. The ritual brought honor both to the spirit of the deceased and to the family who was able to carry it out. Parents announced their intention of performing the rite approximately one year in advance so that they could amass many possessions and quantities of food. During this period, they continued to paint their faces red as a sign of mourning. On the appointed day, guests came to witness the release of the deceased's soul contained in a lock of hair that had previously been cut from the person's head and hung in a quilled bag kept in a "ghost lodge" erected in front of the parents' tipi. The spirit of the dead was released by a ritualist who carefully unwrapped the bundle containing the lock of hair. At the moment of final unwrapping, the practitioner walked out of the tipi to release the spirit on its journey to the afterworld. The parents then hosted a feast and distributed all the clothing, food, and other possessions that they had collected, even dismantling and giving away the lodge in which they lived, leaving nothing but the opened spirit bundle that had held the soul of their dead child. Their act of generosity and self-sacrifice was honored by members of the community who donated enough belongings so that the couple could begin life again.

In addition to ceremonies marking events in the life of individuals, several communal rituals were performed that blessed the entire band or nation. The most dramatic of these was the Sun Dance, held in conjunction with summer buffalo hunts. Preparations began months before when a man or woman made a vow to sponsor the rite in thanks for recovery from illness or alleviation of misfortune. When the appointed time arrived and many Lakota bands had gathered together in an encampment possibly numbering in the thousands, four days of preparatory activities began, including the selection of a cottonwood tree and its installation as the central pole of the Sun Dance lodge. The chosen tree, thereafter considered sacred, was approached by men on horseback who set upon it in mock attack as though it were a prize buffalo. Next, another group of men and women walked in procession to the sacred tree, and when they arrived, the women felled the tree with axes. The tree was then carried to the Sun Dance lodge and decorated with feathers and an effigy of the spirit of Buffalo. An altar erected in the lodge was also dedicated to Buffalo.

The most dramatic episode of a Sun Dance occurred on the last day, centered on activities of male dancers who had pledged sacrifice. Candidates were expected to embody the four moral values of Native society. As a mark of their special status, they were given hide shirts painted red (the sacred color of Sun) and sets of armbands and anklets. The men prepared themselves for their ordeal by praying, fasting, sweating, and concentrating their minds on achieving strength, courage, and good fortune. When the final day approached, dancers rose early to view the rising sun and walked in slow procession to the Sun Dance lodge. Flesh on their backs and chests was pierced with small skewers attached to sinew cords tied to the Sun Dance pole. After many hours of singing, praying, and dancing in circular movement inside the lodge, dancers broke free of the cords tying them to the central pole, in the process wrenching pieces of skin from their bodies. Men who performed acts of such physical and spiritual daring gained prestige and honor because their self-sacrifice was dedicated to the good of all members of their communities.

TRADE AND CULTURAL TRANSFORMATION

During the hundred years after 1750, Lakotas thrived in their northern plains territories, developing a robust economy and broadening their political and social interactions with neighboring peoples such as the Cheyennes, Arapahos, and Crows. Relations among Native groups were sometimes friendly, leading to trade and intermarriage, but they might also be hostile, especially as conflicts erupted because of economic and political changes brought about by contact with European and American traders. Involvement in trade first increased the people's fortunes but then proved to be a cause of conflict.

Trade between Lakotas and Europeans began in the late seventeenth century when the people still inhabited lands in Minnesota. At that time, they received goods from French merchants who were expanding their commercial networks westward from their bases in eastern Canada. After the people left the upper Midwest and migrated into the plains, they obtained European goods through intermediary nations such as the Mandans, Hidatsas, and Arikaras living along the Missouri River. Then, in the early nineteenth century, American traders from St. Louis contacted Lakotas and exchanged American products for animal hides and meat. Although buffalo hides were the Indians' major marketable item, they also traded beaver and muskrat skins. Lakotas soon established themselves as middlemen between American traders and other Native people living in the plains, thereby asserting economic dominance in the region. Indeed, in 1805, the American explorers Meriwether Louis and William Clark described the Lakotas as the dominant economic and political power along the Missouri River. Trade expanded as a number of large posts were opened in Lakota territory by the American Fur Company and the Rocky Mountain Fur Company. One of the largest was a post, later known as Fort Laramie, situated on the North Platte River in Wyoming that became a major commercial center for the region, attracting people from many nations including Lakotas, Cheyennes, and Arapahos (Josephy 1958: 264).

As involvement in trade deepened, aboriginal economies and societies were radically transformed. An immediate economic change was a shift in the amount of time and energy that both men and women spent procuring and preparing animal products for market. Hunters focused their attention on killing numbers of animals far above their subsistence and household requirements. Women spent more time processing buffalo meat into dried pemmican and tanning hides for trade. As a result, animal resources declined, creating conflict among indigenous nations over the remaining supply.

Shifts in fundamental social principles were also stimulated by economic changes that were taking place. In contrast to aboriginal ethics of equality and the redistribution of goods through sharing and generosity, differences in wealth and rank emerged and were outwardly manifested in the number of horses that an individual or family owned. People accumulated horses either through purchase or, more commonly, through raiding neighboring groups. Wealthy individuals were able to translate their economic and military success into social prestige in two ways. First, the number of horses a person owned was a demonstrable symbol of their fortune as the accumulation of personal property became an acceptable goal. Second, wealthy individuals and families enhanced their social prestige by manipulating traditional values of generosity, rising in honor and influence by their ability to be generous to others. However, unlike past practices when successful people gave away all, or nearly all, of their surplus abundance, wealthy individuals later retained a portion of their personal goods, leading to differences in standards of living among families.

Expansion of trade also had an effect on gender relations within households. A complex relationship developed between gender and wealth. In order to accumulate property and increase status, a man needed the services of women to transform a raw product into a marketable item. Women's work was indeed essential but, given the time-consuming nature of tanning, one woman could not keep pace with the supply of animals that a man could procure by hunting. Estimates vary but, depending on the amount of time spent in other domestic tasks, three to ten days of work were probably required to tan one buffalo hide, yielding a seasonal rate of 20–30 hides (Klein 1983: 155). Because ambitious men needed to secure the labor of more than one woman, polygynous marriages increased in frequency. But in order to marry, men first had to accumulate wealth in horses because the animals were necessary gifts to a woman's parents upon proposal of a union. Age of marriage for men therefore rose as they required more experience to prove their worthiness as hunters and warriors and to accumulate wealth through trade and raiding. At the same time, age of marriage for women declined since fathers were willing to agree to unions of young daughters in exchange for the horses that they would receive as gifts, horses that could then improve the fathers' own wealth and status. The widening gap in age between spouses also solidified the marital control exerted by husbands since seniority itself conferred prestige in Lakota society. All of these interrelated changes resulted from the transformation of a subsistence economy to one that emphasized trade. And, as Klein noted, "The overall prosperity concealed an erosion of women's position through her being increasingly circumscribed to a few tasks related to processing and domestic production. On the other hand, men were increasingly free to pursue wealth" (156).

Interaction with American traders had a destabilizing effect on power relations within the Lakota nation. Traders and the government officials who soon followed endeavored to establish ties with Native men who they thought could control hunters and warriors, helping to shift the economic balance in favor of hunting and trapping for the market. Although the "chiefs" that Americans contacted did not traditionally have rights to dominate members of their communities, "the more the agents treated them as powerful, the more powerful they became" (Schusky 1994: 263–264). And as Native leaders became the conduit for wealth to their nation, they were able to manipulate their position to their material and social advantage.

As trade expanded in the early and middle nineteenth century, intrusions by American travelers and settlers increased as well. When farmers and ranchers encroached on Lakota territory, the people responded by defending their aboriginal rights, but the steady stream of intruders created a crisis in Native societies. At first, leaders attempted to negotiate with American officials in order to guarantee their borders, but within a very short period of time such negotiations proved to be fruitless because settlers ignored any official (albeit weak) attempts to curtail their greed for land. After the discovery of gold in California in 1849, the number of Americans crossing through the Plains accelerated sharply. Although most of these seekers of instant wealth were only temporary nuisances, some decided to stay and establish farms in the region, resulting in intensification of hostility between Indians and settlers. Military conflicts also erupted between indigenous people and the United States Army, which systematically sided with the intruders against the original inhabitants.

As conflict and warfare increased, the aboriginal balance of power between civil and war chiefs was altered. Although war chiefs planned and carried out raids against enemies, they were traditionally under the authority of elder civil leaders, but as warfare intensified and shifted in focus from personal revenge to raiding for horses and defense of communities, young warriors grew increasingly independent of the reasoning abilities and negotiating skills of civil chiefs. They began to exert more authority within their communities, often acting without the approval of civil leaders.

In addition to traders and settlers, missionaries were another source of foreign intrusion. Missionary activity among the Lakota had begun in the late seventeenth and early eighteenth centuries with visits by French Jesuits to Native communities then located in central Minnesota. Their attempts to convert Lakotas were unsuccessful, but later British and American Protestant and Catholic missionaries were able to convert a small number of people in the early nineteenth century. Although the number of converts was at first minimal, their influence in transforming ideological and behavioral features of Native culture increased throughout the century.

AMERICAN EXPANSION AND ITS CONSEQUENCES

Conditions changed once again in the plains after the US government and its military ousted foreign competitors from the region with the purchase of Louisiana from the French in 1803 and the defeat of the British in the War of 1812. The government then intensified its efforts to obtain Native land west of the Mississippi in order to expand its own borders. Officials began the process of acquiring land for settlement by negotiating treaties with aboriginal nations in the region. The first treaty that Lakotas signed was a "treaty of friendship" in 1816, pledging "Every injury or act of hostility, committed by one or either of the contracting parties against the other, shall be mutually forgiven and forgot … There shall be perpetual peace and friendship between all the citizens of the United States, and all the individuals composing the aforesaid tribe." Soon afterward, the government attempted the formal acquisition of territory that had been the Lakotas' prior homeland. In 1837, Native leaders agreed to cede all their land east of the Mississippi River to the United States in

exchange for a cash payment of $300,000 and annuities in the form of tools, livestock, and provisions for a period of twenty years. Although the treaty did not actually harm the Lakotas' land base since they no longer used the territory that they sold, it set a precedent that was dangerous to their long-term security. The first major land cession treaty was signed in 1851, essentially marking the end of the period of economic and political growth for the Lakotas. In the document, known as the Treaty of Fort Laramie, Lakotas gave up a portion of their lands in present-day South Dakota but retained the territory bounded by the rivers Heart, Missouri, White, and North Platte and reinforced their title to the Black Hills in western South Dakota. In exchange for their land and for granting safe passage to Americans through their territory, Lakotas received annuities for a period of fifty-five years (Josephy 1958: 268). Although the Treaty's terms were unfavorable, Native leaders signed the document because of the increased pressure of American settlements in their region and their hope that by relinquishing some land, they would secure peace and safety in their remaining communities.

But despite land cessions and treaty guarantees, warfare in the plains intensified in the 1850s and 1860s as more settlers entered the region. Reacting to nearly constant turmoil and raids by soldiers and settlers, Lakotas agreed to terms of another treaty signed at Fort Laramie in 1868 abandoning much of their remaining land in South Dakota although they still retained approximately half of the present-day state from the Missouri River in the east, westward to the state's current border. These lands were thereafter transformed officially into the "Great Sioux Reservation," an area supposedly protected from further settler encroachment. The US government also promised to supply the people with some 25,000 cows, 1,000 bulls, unspecified numbers of oxen, farming tools, and seeds for planting (Utley 1963: 60), demonstrating its commitment to encouraging the Lakota to take up a settled farming life.

Once more, despite treaty guarantees, the government denied Lakotas the rights to their own land after gold was discovered in the Black Hills in 1874. Officials hoped to settle the issue of the Black Hills by offering $6 million for the sacred territory, an offer that was immediately refused. But discovery of gold lured prospectors, traders, and settlers into Native land in violation of the Fort Laramie treaty of 1868 and the government continued to pressure the people to sell the Black Hills, in the words of Edward Smith, Commissioner of Indian Affairs, "For the sake of promoting the mining and agricultural interest of white men" (Hagan 1988: 56).

In March of 1876, the government responded to the growing crisis created by settlers' intrusions by ordering the cavalry to round up all Lakotas and force them to remain on reservations. The army and volunteer militia attacked Native villages, killing the inhabitants and plundering their property. In some cases, the people were able to retaliate, as recounted in the words of Black Elk describing a raid against an Oglala village headed by Crazy Horse:

> Crazy Horse stayed with about a hundred tepees on the Powder River. It was just daybreak. There was a blizzard and it was very cold. The people were sleeping. Suddenly there were many shots and horses galloping through the village. It was the cavalry of the Wasichus [Americans], and they were yelling and shooting and riding their horses against the tepees. All the people rushed out and ran, because they were not awake yet and they were frightened.

> The soldiers killed as many women and children and men as they could while the people were running toward a bluff. Then they set fire to some of the tepees and knocked the others down. But when the people were on the side of the bluff, Crazy Horse said something, and all the warriors began singing the death song and charged back upon the soldiers; and the soldiers ran, driving many of the people's ponies in front of them. Crazy Horse followed them all that day with a band of warriors, and that night he took all the stolen ponies away from them, and brought them back to the village. (Niehardt 1961: 90–91)

Still, federal officials were determined to exert control over Native territory. In June of 1876, the Seventh Cavalry led by General George Custer was sent to locate and destroy Indian villages. On 26 June, they came upon a Teton camp near the Little Bighorn River in South Dakota and began firing on the inhabitants. But Lakota warriors, with the aid of Cheyenne allies, defeated Custer, killing the general and all of his soldiers. However, even the Indian victory did

The Battle of the Little Bighorn, showing Native Americans on horseback in foreground, painting by C. M. Russell, 1903.

not deter the American government from its goal of obtaining Native land. After suffering numerous attacks and losses of life, Lakota chiefs decided to surrender to the US government, hoping that their people would be protected from further raids. In 1877, Crazy Horse agreed to negotiate with officials at Fort Robinson, Nebraska, in order to establish peace, but upon his arrival he was arrested and imprisoned. Events immediately following Crazy Horse's arrest, as recounted by Black Elk, became an indelible part of Lakota history:

> They told Crazy Horse they would not harm him if he would go and have a talk with a Wasichu Chief there. But they lied. They did not take him to the chief for a talk. They took him to the little prison with iron bars on the windows, for they had planned to get rid of him. And when he saw what they were doing, he turned around and took a knife out of his robe and started out against all those soldiers. A soldier ran a bayonet into Crazy Horse on one side and he fell down and began to die. Crazy Horse was dead. He was brave and good and wise. He never wanted anything but to save his people, and he fought the Wasichus only when they came to kill us in our own country. He was only 30 years old. They could not kill him in battle. They had to lie to him and kill him that way. (Niehardt 1961: 146–147)

Sitting Bull (1834–1890), the famed chief and spiritual leader of the Hunkpapa, led his followers into Canada, hoping that as conditions improved in the plains they would be able to return to their homes in peace. But no peace was ever established, and in 1881 Sitting Bull returned to South Dakota and surrendered at Fort Buford, Montana.

Pressure on Lakotas increased to cede more territory and abandon their traditional lifestyle. After passage of the General Allotment Act in 1887 and the granting of statehood to South Dakota in 1889, the government hoped to "pacify" the remaining Indians and force them to accept allotments and open surplus land for sale to settlers. The Great Sioux Reservation was divided into the four separate reservations of Pine Ridge, Rosebud, Standing Rock, and Cheyenne River, each to be the home of one or more of the seven bands. The Oglalas were to reside on the Pine Ridge reservation; the Brules at Rosebud; the Hunkpapas at Standing Rock; both the Miniconjous and Itazipcos

at Cheyenne River; the Sihasapas at either Cheyenne River or Standing Rock; and the Oohenonpas at Cheyenne River and Rosebud.

Land on reservations was allotted to nuclear families and single individuals, but by terms of the Sioux Act of 1889, the usual allotment of 160 acres per family was doubled so that heads of households were assigned a total of 320 acres and single individuals were given 80 acres of land. In clear violation of the Fort Laramie treaty of 1868, the remaining territory was open to claims from "homesteaders." By 1890, the reservations carved out of the Great Sioux Reservation together comprised only half of their original territory. In order to compel reluctant Lakotas to accept allotments, the amount of rations was reduced by half, another violation of treaty guarantees. Many people lived on the brink of starvation and many died from general debilitation and malnutrition. Adding to their difficulties, a severe drought occurred during the same period, resulting in the loss of crops grown by some Native families. By 1890 government actions and policies had had a devastating effect on the people. Their territory was greatly reduced in size, their economies were subverted by the slaughter of buffalo, and the people were confined within reservation boundaries. Indigenous customs and religious practices were constantly criticized by American religious and secular authorities.

The year 1890 was critical in Lakota history. The year before, a delegation of Native leaders had travelled to Nevada to hear the message of the Ghost Dance from the northern Paiute (Paviotso) prophet Wovoka (see Chapter 12 for a discussion of the origin of the Ghost Dance). They returned to South Dakota in April of 1890 and began spreading the doctrine and practices of the new religion (Mooney 1965). In the context of their desperate situation, people welcomed a message that gave them hope of a renewed life of harmony and well-being. But settlers and government officials greeted the people's enthusiasm for the Ghost Dance with alarm. Rumors spread that Indians were planning raids against settlers in order to rid their territory of the intruders, hastening the apocalyptic vision prophesied by Wovoka. In truth, Ghost Dance participants never organized raids against settlers, believing instead that a miraculous transformation would save them and return to aboriginal conditions. But government authorities advocated military actions against Ghost Dance followers. For instance, D. F. Royer, head of the BIA at Pine Ridge (and known to the Lakotas as "young man afraid of Indians"), wrote to his superiors in Washington, DC, on October 30, 1890:

> Your department has been informed of the damage resulting from these dances and of the danger attending them of the crazy Indian doing serious damage to others. I have carefully studied the matter and have brought all the persuasion to bear on the leaders that was possible but without effect and the only remedy is the use of military and until this is done you need not expect any progress from these people. (Utley 1963: 105)

In November, agents at Standing Rock decided to withhold food rations from people on the reservation. Participation in Ghost Dances was outlawed and soldiers were sent to break up ceremonies and arrest those considered responsible for leading them. In response to President Harrison's order to "suppress any threatened outbreak" of the Ghost Dance, more than 1,000 US troops were sent to Pine Ridge and Rosebud. Tensions in the communities mounted as federal agents intensified their intimidation of the people. James Mclaughlin, agent at Standing Rock, ordered the arrest of Sitting Bull on December 15 and sent a police force composed of both American and Lakota officers to his cabin in the early morning hours. While his supporters tried to prevent his arrest, the great spiritual and moral leader was killed by one of the Lakota policemen. A melee then broke out that resulted in casualties among both the policemen and Sitting Bull's supporters.

As fears among settlers mounted, General Nelson Miles ordered additional troops into Lakota territory to arrest Big Foot, chief of the Miniconjou. While Big Foot and his followers were on their way to Pine Ridge to negotiate a peaceful resolution of the conflict, their encampment at Wounded Knee Creek was surrounded and attacked by soldiers on December 28, 1890. When the people refused to surrender to the army, shots rang out from the soldiers and the Lakotas. The army responded by massacring the people, killing more than 300 unarmed men, women, and children, later to be buried in a mass grave. One eyewitness to the tragedy, a man named Turning Hawk, described the scene:

> All the men who were in a bunch were killed right there, and those who escaped that first fire got into the ravine, and as they went along up the ravine they were pursued on both sides by the soldiers and shot down. The women were standing off at a different place, and when the firing began, those of the men who escaped the first onslaught went in one direction up the ravine, and then the women, who were bunched together at another place, went entirely through a different direction through an open field, and the women fared the same fate as the men who went up the deep ravine. (Mooney 1965: 139)

Another witness, American Horse, added more details:

> The women as they were fleeing with their babies were killed together, shot right through, and the women who were very heavy with child were also killed. All the Indians fled, and after most of them had been killed a cry was made that those who were not killed or wounded should come forth and they would be safe. Little boys who were not wounded came out of their places of refuge, and as soon as they came in sight a number of soldiers surrounded them and butchered them there. (139–140)

When people residing at Pine Ridge heard news of the massacre, they fled for fear that they too would be killed. Soon thereafter, most people returned and their leaders surrendered to government authorities. The last chief to surrender was Kicking Bear, giving himself over to the power of the United States on January 15, 1891.

In the early decades of the twentieth century, government pressure on Lakotas did not abate. The BIA coerced people to divide the reservations into individual allotments following procedures outlined by the General Allotment Act of 1887. As a result, Native lands were reduced by millions of acres because "surplus" land remaining after assignment was sold either to the US government or to American farmers and ranchers. Additional land was lost when Native owners were permitted to sell their allotments at the end of a period of twenty-five years. Some sold out of ignorance or from trickery and some because of dire poverty and their need to have money to support themselves. All reservations experienced large losses of land. For example, by 1934 the Rosebud Reservation had lost 2,195,095 acres of its original territory while Pine Ridge lost 182,653 acres (Grobsmith 1981: 15). Since the 1920s, more than half of reservation land in individual allotments has gone out of Native control.

Some has been sold and the rest leased to American farmers and ranchers.

CONTEMPORARY LAKOTA COMMUNITIES

Reservation communities are differentiated by many factors, including location, economic pursuits, language, religion, and cultural values and orientation. Although they are not simple polar opposites, people are often characterized (and characterize themselves and others) as "traditionalists" or "progressives." People who live in reservation towns tend to have lifestyles that more closely resemble American norms, while people living in rural areas are more apt to conform to a Lakota identity. Housing in towns is of better quality than in rural communities, some of it built and subsidized by federal programs administered by HUD. Homes in towns have electricity, sewage systems, and telephone service, while those in remote areas often do not. Even with the popularization of cell phones, Lakotas on reservations rarely have the means or methods through which to purchase them, and cell service is spotty at best. Access to education and employment is also more likely for town dwellers. Differentiation of communities has led to distinctions in economic class that have an obvious consequent effect on political interests and sociocultural values.

For most members of reservations, levels of unemployment and underemployment have been extremely high throughout the century, with correspondingly high rates of poverty. Available jobs are more likely to be found in towns than in rural areas. However, much, if not most, employment is connected directly or indirectly to the local tribal government and its maintenance and social service programs. Given the relationship between government and jobs, town dwellers are often dependent on tribal council members for their economic security. They therefore are apt to support the council in its policies since they benefit directly from them. And employees' dependency further enhances the power of tribal councilors. In contrast, the economic and political interests of rural residents are not tied to local government and, in fact, are often overlooked by tribal officials. This process exacerbates divisions between rural and town segments of reservation populations, a division also reflected in cultural orientation. Rural residents tend to retain use of the Lakota language and are more likely to follow traditional religious and social practices than townspeople, who instead tend to be monolingual speakers of English and are oriented toward adoption of American culture.

In 1968, some Lakotas then living in Minneapolis helped found the American Indian Movement (AIM). Among the leaders were two Oglala men, Russell Means and Dennis Banks, and two Chippewas, Vernon and Clyde Bellecourt. In the 1970s, several events galvanized local and national action and involved AIM in Lakota politics. The first was the murder in 1972 of Raymond Yellowthunder, an Oglala man from Pine Ridge, who was set upon by two men in Gordon, Nebraska, stripped naked, and forced to enter an American Legion Hall where a dance was in progress. He was later beaten to death, but his attackers were charged only with second degree manslaughter rather than murder and served a one-year jail sentence for their crimes. Outrage among people at Pine Ridge and other South Dakota reservations led to demonstrations in Nebraska protesting the lenient treatment of Yellowthunder's killers.

In the same year, the Oglala Sioux Civil Rights Organization was established at Pine Ridge after a bitter election for president of the Tribal Council that highlighted the split between the segment of the population who maintained traditional beliefs and values and those who were more oriented toward American lifestyles. Richard Wilson, the candidate supported by the "progressive" faction, won the post over the "traditional" candidate, Gerald Onefeather. After the election, Wilson and his supporters attempted to block organizing activities of their opponents, intensifying divisions among the people at Pine Ridge. After a group of tribal councilors called for Wilson's impeachment, Wilson declared a state of emergency and called in US marshals to keep the peace. In response to an invitation made by some traditional leaders, members of AIM came to Pine Ridge and staged a protest at the village of Wounded Knee. In the words of Leonard Crowdog, one of the AIM leaders, "Here we come going the other way. Its just like those Indian soldiers in Big Foot's band who were going to Pine Ridge, and now they're coming back. We're those soldiers, we're those Indian people, we're them, we're back, and we can't go any further" (Zimmerman 1976: 127). And as Dennis Banks of AIM recalled, "Everything pointed to one course of action—retake Wounded Knee. The medicine men brought wisdom to us. They gave us the spiritual direction we needed. There was no writing letters to the government and sending them demands anymore. That's exactly what the medicine men said to us—"when you put your words on paper, then they step on them" (127–128).

Within a few weeks, 300 people were barricaded in the village. They called on the government to investigate activities and policies of the BIA and to adhere to promises made in treaties. The protestors were surrounded by a force of more than 300 federal marshals, FBI agents, and police officers. By the end of the seventy-one-day occupation at Wounded Knee, two Indian men had been killed and two more wounded; one federal marshall was also wounded. Russell Means, Dennis Banks, and more than thirty other demonstrators were charged with a variety of felonies in connection with the occupation, but were all acquitted because of governmental use of illegal wire taps, paid witnesses, altered evidence, and the perjuring of prosecution witnesses.

After the end of the Wounded Knee occupation, further controversies continued to embroil Lakotas regarding land and legal rights. For more than a century, they had struggled to regain possession of the sacred Black Hills, unilaterally appropriated by an act of Congress in 1877. After congressional hearings in 1974, the Lakotas were awarded a sum of $17.5 million as compensation for the Black Hills and an additional sum of $85 million in interest payments. The Court of Indian Claims confirmed the Lakotas' claim in 1980, awarding the nation a total of $105 million, a ruling later upheld by the US Supreme Court. Despite a favorable monetary judgment, the people refused to accept payment in exchange for title to the land, instead continuing to claim the right of return of the Black Hills based both on the Treaty of 1868 and on the American Indian Freedom of Religion Act passed by Congress in 1978. The matter is still pending in courts, and the money awarded remains in trust in a BIA account. In 2012, one parcel of privately owned prairie land totaling 1,942 acres located in the Black Hills was put up for sale for $9 million. The Rosebud Sioux Tribe, with financial support from a coalition of Plains tribes, paid the purchase price for the acreage, called Pe' Sla, so that they could regain at least a part of their traditional sacred territory.

Another lingering legal controversy concerns the case of Leonard Peltier, an Oglala from Pine Ridge, who was involved in a shooting incident on the reservation in 1975. Details remain uncertain, but an exchange of gunfire took place between several Oglala men and four FBI agents, resulting in the deaths of one Oglala and two of the agents. Peltier and three Oglalas were arrested and charged with murder. Two of the men were put on trial and both were acquitted, but Peltier sought refuge in Canada instead of standing trial. After his extradition from Canada, protested by members of the Canadian Parliament, Peltier was tried, convicted, and sentenced to two life terms. Peltier and his lawyers appealed the verdict and requested a new trial based on uncovered information indicating the government's illegal investigation and prosecution of the case, including tampering of evidence, suppression of ballistics' reports, and coercion of prosecution witnesses. Requests for new trials have been repeatedly denied by the courts although they are supported by members of Congress, religious leaders throughout the world, and Amnesty International, declaring Peltier to be a political prisoner of conscience. Requests for presidential executive clemency have also been denied even though they too are supported by some members of Congress and other public figures including Judge Gerald Heaney, who had previously denied Peltier a new trial.

The legacy of conflicts on the Pine Ridge Reservation, dating especially from the 1970s when political turmoil erupted into violence, continues to raise troubling questions about justice for the memories of people killed during those years. In 2012, the Tribal Council asked the US Department of Justice to reopen investigations into the cases of some twenty-eight people whose deaths, they say, have not been adequately explained. However, officials in the Justice Department claim that most of the deaths were not murders but were either suicides or accidents.

In an act of commemoration and unity, some 400 Lakotas participated in a prayer ritual to mark a century since the massacre at Wounded Knee. The ceremony, held on December 29, 1990, memorialized the victims of Wounded Knee at the site of their mass grave. More than 200 participants rode on horseback to retrace the path that Big Foot and his band had taken, a journey of 220 miles. Commenting on the events, spiritual leader Arvol Looking Horse said, "The ride was for unity and peace … an effort to mend the sacred hoop and bring our people back together" (*The New York Times*, December 30, 1990: 12).

Although issues such as the Black Hills land claim and the Peltier case have gained national and international attention, Lakotas are also faced with serious problems at home. High rates of unemployment and

Chief Arvol Looking Horse, Lakota Keeper of Sacred White Buffalo Pipe, leads group of Lakota Sioux on the Big Foot Memorial Ride.

underemployment, lack of capital to invest in economic enterprises, and poor healthcare services continue to plague the communities.

In the mid-1980s, for example, unemployment at Pine Ridge reached as high as 82 percent and average family income was the lowest of all American households (Kehoe 1999: 87). Data obtained for 2010 reveal low per capita and median household incomes for all Lakotas. Table 10.1 shows the disparity between incomes of Lakotas and other chosen groups. Although average Lakota per capita income are higher than the American Indian averages, Lakota median household incomes fall far below the Midwestern averages. What this data does not show, however, is the shocking poverty that plagues individual reserves. Although the US government has not surveyed individual reserves since 2000, the American Indian Humanitarian Foundation has created economic characteristic estimates for one Lakota reserve, Pine Ridge. Their data states

that 97 percent of the reserve lives below the federal poverty line, while the unemployment rate oscillates from 85 to 95 percent (American Indian Humanitarian Foundation 2016). Table 10.2 shows the most recent individual reserve data, taken from the 2000 US Census.

TABLE 10.1	Comparative Incomes for Selected Population Groupings	
	Income ($)	
	Per Capita	Household
Lakota	18,433	40,829
American Indian	16,645	36,779
South Dakota	24,110	46,369
Midwestern	26,205	50,276

Source: US Bureau of the Census 2011, Table 6: 204–206.

TABLE 10.2	Poverty Rates for Selected Lakota Reservations	
	In Poverty (%)	
	Families	**Individuals**
Cheyenne River	40.2	41.2
Lower Brule	45.6	46.3
Pine Ridge	29.9	41.2
Rosebud	42.8	47.1
Standing Rock	40.3	43.6

Source: US Bureau of the Census 2000, Table 6.

Lakota communities are facing difficulties due to revisions of federal welfare requirements enacted by Congress in 1996. While the number of families on welfare statewide in South Dakota declined between 1995 and 1998, few Lakota families were able to leave the welfare rolls. In 1995, Lakota families constituted about half of the state's welfare families, but by 1999, their percentage had risen to 66 percent ("Welfare Reform Comes Slowly to Reservations" 1999). The Personal Responsibility and Work Opportunity Reconciliation Act (PRWORA) of 1996 allowed tribes to create and implement Temporary Assistance for Needy Families (TANF) policies. However, the effectiveness of their programs varied broadly by reservation. For example, the Pine Ridge Reservation, due to tensions over sovereignty and refusal to cooperate from both the tribal leaders and the state, was unable to enact positive change in the community. The Rosebud Reservation, on the other hand, had good relationships with the state and nonprofit groups. Since 1996, they have constructed two childcare centers and created a Tribal Employment Services center, which has catered to over 500 people. It is obviously unrealistic to assume that overarching assistance programs will have the same effect wherever they are implemented; Pine Ridge is a much larger reservation with a better established social economy and history of conflict with the state and federal government ("Perspectives on Poverty, Policy, & Place" 2004). In order to help local residents, several Lakota colleges have expanded high-school equivalency services as well as job-training programs. However, they too face difficulties because federal laws limit the amount of time a welfare recipient may be enrolled in college to one year, even though most academic and job-training programs last a minimum of two years.

In both 1980 and 1990, Shannon County on the Pine Ridge Reservation was ranked the poorest county in the United States. Because of the dismal economic situation at Pine Ridge, in 1999 President Clinton visited the reservation as part of his tour of economically depressed communities and announced its designation as an "Empowerment Zone," thus making it eligible to receive $20 million over ten years to improve infrastructure and hopefully to attract business and employment ("Challenging the Traditional View of Tribal Economics" 1999: 17). However, the Bush administration reduced the funding, cutting the grant to $1.5 million in 2004 and stopped the grant in 2005, just as the program was starting to take off (Nieves 2004).

In 2014, Buffalo County, the home of the Crow Creek Indian Reservation, was the poorest county in the United States by median household income, which sat at $21,658, less than half of South Dakota's average of $50,979 (US Census Bureau 2014).

Despite often severe economic problems, many people attempt to maintain aspects of traditional culture and beliefs. In some reservation communities, traditional social and ceremonial life continues to bind the people together. Followers of Native religion mark some of the ancient sacred rites and seek support and instruction from the spirit world through vision quests. Maintenance of the Lakota language is also critical to a continuation of Native culture. According to US census figures for 2010 and Canadian census figures for 2011, a total of 20,110 people reported speaking Lakota/Dakota (note that the census did not disaggregate according to reservation or dialect). People living in rural areas and those involved in traditional lifeways are more likely to speak Lakota fluently, using it especially in religious and social contexts. The language is now taught in schools on the reservation at all levels including elementary and high school, as well as in two local community colleges at Pine Ridge and Rosebud.

To promote the use of the Lakota language, members of the Standing Rock Tribe and the Lakota Language Consortium have developed innovative programming to appeal to young children, encouraging them to learn and use their indigenous language. One of these initiatives is the translation of the popular Berenstain Bears animation series into Lakota. It can be accessed online at the website lakotabears.com. And both the Standing Rock and Pine Ridge communities have set up "immersion nests" for infants and toddlers where speakers of the Lakota language will act as caregivers, exposing very young learners to their Native language. It is hoped that children who have this early exposure to Lakota will develop fluency and be encouraged to use their language as they grow up. At Pine Ridge, an immersion school opened in 2012, and is currently poised to open a primary school section in the fall of 2016. Recently, they have been recognized by President Obama and given a TEDx talk on their work. Currently, only about 6000 (or 14%) of Lakota people are speakers of their indigenous language, with an average age of about sixty-five years. Without younger speakers, the language's survival is in danger.

And although traditional patterns of kinship and communal solidarity have often been criticized by American authorities as impediments to "modernization" and "assimilation," it is in fact this very structure that has enabled the Lakotas to survive. Throughout their history, the Lakotas' ethics emphasizing "sharing, voluntary cooperation, equality, and solidarity have sustained these communities under conditions which would otherwise have destroyed their membership" (Wax 1971: 76).

To help maintain Lakota communities, the South Dakota Department of Education is working with the Lakota reservations to develop programs that will encourage Lakota high school and college students to remain in school. The programs involve students and their families to help students continue their educations and meet graduation requirements. Outreach to all of the Lakota communities is planned to stress the importance of education as preparation for rewarding careers.

And in order to enable people to connect to others and to their jobs on the 2,000,000-acre Pine Ridge Reservation, since 2009 the Oglala Sioux Transit has been providing bus services throughout the territory. The system is used by people who want to save money otherwise spent on gasoline or by people who have no reliable transportation of their own. People can more easily travel to stores on the reservation, helping to support those local businesses as well. Resource conservation and energy efficiency are additional benefits to a public transportation system.

All of the Lakota reservations are vulnerable to periods of drought, due in part to their natural environment, the negative effects of climate change, and the poor condition of infrastructure in their communities. Water supplies for most people come either from surface water (streams and rivers) or groundwater accessed by wells. The surface water is plentiful during some seasons but unreliable year round. Its quality and purity is not controlled. In some places, it may be of high quality but in others it may be contaminated or polluted. Well water is also not treated and therefore often not safe for human consumption. And in periods of drought, the wells often go dry.

Constructing and maintaining safe and adequate supplies of water are therefore primary concerns of the reservation communities. In addition to the effects on human consumption, the primary livelihoods of cattle-raising and farming are seriously jeopardized by a lack of consistent water. Unfortunately, funding for pipelines and water supply systems is seriously lacking in most communities.

In 2012, the Oglala Lakota of Pine Ridge signed an agreement with the National Park Service to become the managers of the first tribal national park located in the South Unit of the Badlands National Park in South Dakota. For the past forty years, the Oglala have worked with the National Park Service in overseeing operations in the South Unit but the agreement allowed the national park to come under the jurisdiction of the Oglala alone. The Oglala Lakota planned to operate educational and recreational activities, open to the public, and construct a Lakota Heritage and Education Center. However, conflicts between the Park Service and the Oglala Lakotas have escalated, with the Lakotas accusing the Park Service of not honoring an agreement from 1976 that turns money from North Gate receipts over to the Tribe, and the Park Service attests that the Lakotas have not submitted required budget reports, along with other paperwork. They are currently in a stand-off, with the Lakota requesting complete turnover of the land and the Park Service refusing to do so (Tupper 2015).

Despite a high rate of out-migration to urban centers seeking employment, populations on the reservations continue to grow. According to estimates from the US Department of Housing and Urban Development, the Pine Ridge Reservation is the largest, having 28,787 residents. Rosebud is next, with 10,869 members. Somewhat smaller is the Standing Rock Reservation with a population of 8,217. Next is the Cheyenne River Reservation with 8,090 residents. And the smallest of the Lakota Reservations is Lower Brule, numbering 1,505, and the Mdewakanton Sioux, numbering 658 (the smallest is Mdewakanton Sioux: 403) (US Census Bureau 2010a & b).

REFERENCES

American Indian Humanitarian Foundation. n.d. *Pine Ridge Statistics*. Brigham City, UT. Online.

Bol, Marsha C., and Nellie Z. Star Boy Menard. 2000. "'I Saw All That': A Lakota Girl's Puberty Ceremony." *American Indian Culture and Research Journal* 24, no. 1: 25–42.

"Challenging the Traditional View of Tribal Economics." 1999. *American Indian Reports*. pp. 16–17.

Churchill, Ward. 1997. *A Little Matter of Genocide: Holocaust and Denial in the Americas 1492 to the Present*. San Francisco, CA: City Lights Books.

Deloria, Ella. 1944. *Speaking of Indians*. New York: Friendship Press.

DeMallie, Raymond. 1994. "Kinship and Biology in Sioux Culture." *North American Indian Anthropology: Essays on Society and Culture* (ed. R. DeMallie and A. Ortiz). Norman, OK: University of Oklahoma Press, pp. 125–146.

Erdoes, Richard, and Alfonso Ortiz. 1985. *American Indian Myths and Legends*. New York: Pantheon Press.

Grobsmith, Elizabeth. 1981. *Lakota of the Rosebud: A Contemporary Ethnography*. New York: Holt, Reinhart and Winston.

Hagan, William. 1988. "United States Indian Policies, 1860–1900." *History of Indian-White Relations* (ed. W. Washburn), Vol. 4 of *Handbook of North American Indians*. Washington, DC: Smithsonian Institution, pp. 51–66.

Hassrick, Royal. 1964. *The Sioux: Life and Customs of a Warrior Society*. Norman, OK: University of Oklahoma Press.

Josephy, Alvin Jr. 1958. *The Patriot Chiefs: A Chronicle of American Indian Resistance*. New York: The Viking Press.

Kehoe, Alice. 1989. *The Ghost Dance: Ethnohistory and Revitalization*. New York: Holt, Reinhart and Winston.

Klein, Alan. 1983. "The Political-Economy of Gender: A Nineteenth Century Plains Indian Case Study." *The Hidden Half: Studies of Plains Indian Women* (ed. P. Alvers and B. Medicine). Lanham, MD: University Press of America, pp. 143–173.

Mirsky, Jeannette. 1937. "The Dakota." *Cooperation and Competition among Primitive Peoples* (ed. M. Mead). Boston, MA: Beacon Press, pp. 382–427.

Mooney, James. 1965. *The Ghost Dance Religion and the Sioux Outbreak of 1890*. Chicago. IL: University of Chicago Press.

The New York Times. 1990. 30 December: 12.

Nicollet, Joseph. 1978. *Joseph N. Nicollet on the Plains and Prairies: The Expeditions of 1838–39 with Journals, Letters, and Notes on the Dakota Indians* (ed. E. Bray and M. Bray). St. Paul, MN: Minnesota Historical Society Press.

Niehardt, John (ed.). 1961. *Black Elk Speaks: Being the Life Story of a Holy Man of the Oglala Sioux*. Lincoln, NE: University of Nebraska Press.

Nieves, Evelyn. 2004. "On Pine Ridge, a String of Broken Promises." *The Washington Post*. Online.

"Perspectives on Poverty, Policy, & Place." 2004. *Rural Policy Research Institute Newsletter* 1, no. 4. Online.

Schusky, Ernest. 1994. "The Roots of Factionalism among the Lower Brule Sioux." *North American Indian Anthropology: Essays on Society and Culture* (ed. R. DeMallie and A. Ortiz). Norman, OK: University of Oklahoma Press, pp. 258–277.

US Bureau of the Census. 1990a. "American Indian and Alaska Native Areas." *1990 Census of Population*. Washington, DC, 1990 CP–1–1A.

US Bureau of the Census. 1990b. "Table 6: Income and Poverty Status in 1989 of American Indian Tribes." *1990 Census of Population*. Washington, DC.

US Census Bureau. 2000.

US Bureau of the Census. 2010a. "Small Area Income and Poverty Estimates." *Census 2010*. Washington DC.

US Bureau of the Census. 2010b. "2010 Demographic Profile Data: Census Counts by Age and Sex for the Populations Living on Minnesota's American Indian Reservations and Trust Lands." *Census 2010*. Washington DC.

US Bureau of the Census. 2011. "Selected Economic Characteristics." *2006–2010 American Community Survey*. Washington, DC.

US Census Bureau. 2014.

US Department of Housing and Urban Development. n.d. *Indian Housing Block Grant Formula*. Washington, DC. Online.

Utley, Robert. 1963. *The Last Days of the Sioux Nation*. New Haven, CT: Yale University Press.

Walker, J. R. 1917. *The Sun Dance and Other Ceremonies of the Oglala Division of the Teton-Dakota*. Anthropological Papers of the American Museum of Natural History, Vol. 16, Part 2. New York: American Museum of Natural History.

Walker, J. R. 1992. *Lakota Society* (ed. R. DeMallie). Lincoln, NE: University of Nebraska Press.

Wax, Murray. 1971. *Indian Americans: Unity and Diversity*. Englewood Cliffs, NJ: Prentice-Hall.

"Welfare Reform Comes Slowly to Reservations." 1999. *Pequot Times*. April.

Zimmerman, Bill. 1976. *Airlift to Wounded Knee*. Chicago, IL: Swallow Press.

The Hidatsas

THE HIDATSAS (HI-DAT-SA) are an indigenous nation of the eastern Plains who inhabited villages and hunting territories in present-day central North Dakota. Today their descendants live on the Fort Berthold Reservation, constituting one of the "Three Affiliated Tribes" along with their Mandan and Arikara neighbors.

ABORIGINAL CULTURE

Settlements

By sometime in the eighteenth century, Hidatsas lived in three villages along the Knife River near its juncture with the Missouri.

Each village was occupied by an autonomous group of people with their own name and origin. Although they later amalgamated and became known as Hidatsa, they were independent groups who shared similarities of language and culture albeit with some local variations. The three groups are called the Hidatsa ("people of the willows"; sometimes referred to in the literature as "Hidatsa-proper"), Awatixa ("people of rock village"), and Awaxawi ("people of mountain village"). The Hidatsa-proper resided on the north bank of the Knife River about 3 mi. from its juncture with the Missouri; the Awatixa occupied a village on the south bank of the Knife about a half mile from the Missouri; and the Awaxawi village was located on the south bank of the Knife at the mouth of the Missouri. According to David Thompson, a British trader who visited the region in 1797, the Hidatsa-proper dwelt in eighty-two earth lodges while the Awatixa lived in thirty-one lodges and the Awaxawi village contained only fifteen lodges (Thompson 1916: 235–236). Thompson estimated their total population at 1,330. These are, of course, only conjectural estimates, and other European and American observers in the next several decades offered varying figures ranging from 1,500 to 2,500 (Meyer 1977).

The environment of the Hidatsa nation was formed by the Missouri River Valley and therefore differed from the topography and climate of the central and western Plains. The region consisted of river valleys, rich floodplains, and upland hills and plains rising 200–400 ft. above the valley. The floodplain contained dense woodlands of cottonwood, willow, elm, ash, and oak. Water from the river was used to irrigate the fields in which women grew corn, squash, beans, and sunflowers. Although the soil was well suited to farming, the area was not ideal for year-round habitation because every spring the Missouri River overflowed its banks, causing widespread flooding. While the floodwaters enriched the soil and helped create conditions conducive to farming, people could not live nearby because their houses too would have been flooded. Instead, villages were located on high ground above the rivers, in some places as much as 100 or 200 ft. above the bottomlands. Village sites lacked the densely wooded areas of the valley, but some edible grasses and wild fruits grew nearby. They were gathered to supplement the farm diet. To the west of the villages stretched open prairies and plains more typical of the region as a whole. These lands were the habitat of buffalo, deer, elk, antelope, and other animals that were important to the aboriginal diet. Although village sites were habitable during the summer, in winter their exposure to cold winds and snowstorms made their occupation difficult. Therefore, once winter came, most people moved to wooded areas in the valley where they could find wood for fuel and be sheltered from the wind-swept plains.

The Missouri Valley climate was one of low rainfall, averaging about 15 in. annually in the area of Hidatsa settlement. Drought was relatively common and therefore impeded the development of intensive farming. Temperatures varied widely throughout the year, from scorching heat in summer to bitter cold in winter. Strong winds made the winter cold more intense.

The Hidatsa language belongs to the large Siouan linguistic family whose component languages span a good deal of territory in the eastern and central Plains. Most closely related to Hidatsa is the language of the Crows. Indeed, the modern Hidatsa and Crow nations are descendants of a common cultural and linguistic group whose history and adaptation followed two different paths. Crows developed a nomadic, buffalo-hunting economy, while Hidatsas settled along the Upper Missouri, focusing their subsistence on horticulture, supplemented by hunting and gathering.

The Awatixa were the first to settle along the Missouri River and adopt a farming economy, while the Hidatsa-proper and the Awaxawi were more recent arrivals in the region. According to histories told by Maxi-diwiac (Buffalobird-woman), a Hidatsa woman born in 1839, the Hidatsas learned to farm from the Mandans, another Siouan-speaking people living along the Upper Missouri south of its juncture with the Knife:

One day a war party that had wandered west to the Missouri River saw on the other side a village of earth lodges like their own. It was the village of the Mandans. Neither they nor the Hidatsas would cross over, each party fearing the other might be enemies.

It was in the fall of the year, and the Missouri was running low, so that an arrow could be shot from shore to shore. The Mandans parched some ears of ripe corn with the grain on the cob, these ears they broke in pieces, stuck the pieces on the points of arrows and shot them across the river. "Eat!" They called.

The Hidatsas ate of the parched corn. They returned to their village and said, "We have found a people on a great river, to the west. They have a strange kind of grain. We ate of it and found it good."

After this, a party of Hidatsas went to visit the Mandan. The Mandan chief took an ear of corn, broke it in two and gave half to the Hidatsas for seed. This half the Hidatsas took home and soon every family in the village was planting corn. (Wilson 1972: 38–39)

Hidatsa villages were relatively compact, but the houses did not form any particular pattern or street plan. The villages were fortified by stockades made of upright logs and/or by ditches dug around the enclosure of houses. Dwellings were large circular earth lodges that housed extended families, usually of matrilineally related kin. Lodges were built on a wooden frame erected over an excavation of about one foot in depth. They measured from 30–40 ft. in diameter, with a domed roof that was 10–15 ft. high in the center and sloped to 5–7 ft. at the sides. Lodges typically housed 40–50 people (Matthews 1877: 4–5). The frame was made of two rows of supporting posts, the outer consisted of 10 or 15 posts while the inner row was made of 4 posts. Heavy beams were laid across the posts to support the domed roof. When the support frame was finished, willow branches were laid on top and the whole structure was covered with layers of sod blocks, grass matting, and earth. Finally, loose earth was placed on the roof and packed solid.

In the center of the lodge, a circular depression about 1ft. deep and 3 or 4 ft. wide was made in the ground for a fireplace that was lined with an edging of flat rocks. A smoke hole was made in the roof above the hearth in order to emit smoke and to let in light. Houses had a doorway made of rawhide stretched on a wooden frame. A passageway measuring about 6–10 ft. in length led to the door. A partition of poles was erected between the fireplace and the door in order to block the winds and cold air. Clothing, utensils, tools, and weapons were hung from pegs inserted in the supporting posts and in horizontal logs linking the posts. Most lodges also contained an area near the door for stabling the family's most valuable horses during the night. Beyond the fireplace, a partition was made of cottonwood planks covered with buffalo robes to shield the bed of the leader of the household. The bed was used for sleeping at night and for sitting and entertaining guests during the day. The beds of other members of the household were arranged against the back walls of the lodge. Headrests and bedding were made of buffalo skins. According to Maxi-diwiac, "We thought an earth lodge was alive and had a spirit like a human body, and that its front was like a face, with a door for a mouth" (Wilson 1972: 45). Houses therefore were blessed with prayers when they were built and medicines were hung within the lodge to protect the dwelling and its inhabitants.

Lodges constructed in winter camps were of similar design but generally smaller than the permanent lodges of summer villages. Families sometimes constructed a second or "twin lodge" that had a connecting covered passageway to the main dwelling. "The twin lodges were very small, covered with bark and thick layers of earth. They provided more warmth than the ordinary houses and were used by elderly or sick members of the household who needed extra warmth in the coldest days of winter" (17). Hidatsa families owned tipis made of buffalo hides that they used when travelling and when camped for summer buffalo hunts.

In addition to household dwellings, larger ceremonial earthen structures were built. They were used for rituals and dances attended by several hundred people.

Economies

Hidatsa economy combined horticulture and foraging. In the bottomlands along the Knife and Missouri Rivers, women planted corn, beans, squash, and sunflowers. New fields were cleared with the assistance of older men. Digging sticks used for planting were made of ash, "slightly bent and trimmed at the root end to a three cornered point. To harden the point it is oiled with marrow fat, and a bunch of dried grass is tied around it and fired. The charring makes the point almost as hard as iron" (19–20). Some hoes were made from the shoulder bone of buffalo bound with rawhide thongs to a wooden handle. Fields were claimed by whoever cleared them and who thereafter retained rights to the area by use and occupation. People identified their fields by placing small piles of earth or stones around them. In the absence of such markers, fields were distinguished by wild weeds and grasses that were allowed to grow between the gardens. When the land was no longer used by a particular household, it was available for claim by anyone who needed it. In Maxi-diwiac's words, "We Indians thought our fields sacred, and we did not like to quarrel about them. A family's right to a field once having been set up, no one thought of disputing it. If anyone tried to seize land belonging to another, we thought some evil would come upon him; as that one of his family would die or have some bad sickness" (41).

Corn seeds were planted in small hills of earth. Beans were planted around each of the corn hills and squash was planted between every ten rows of corn. Sunflowers were planted as a border around the garden. Once plants were in full growth, women put up small platforms or stages in their gardens, typically tended by young girls, in order to chase away birds. When corn was ready, young men were invited to come and husk the corn. After the husking was completed, the men were thanked with a feast. As was Hidatsa custom, guests brought containers to carry home food that was not consumed at the meal since it was considered impolite to leave over any food offered at a feast (113).

The farming accomplishments of Hidatsa women were all the more remarkable because of the relatively short growing season and poor climatic conditions of the region. According to Waldo Wedel, Hidatsa, Mandan, and Arikara women transformed corn "from a lush warm weather plant requiring high day and night temperatures during a growing season of 150 days or more into a tough, compact plant three or four feet high, maturing in 60 or 70 days, and possessing marked resistance to drought, wind, cold, and frost. [Their work] ranks high as an achievement in plant breeding" (Wedel 1961: 161).

Some surpluses of corn, beans, and squash were dried and stored in pits or caches dug inside the lodges. Caches were deep holes shaped like bottles, that is, wide at the bottom tapering to a small opening at the ground. Some were so deep that a ladder was needed in order to retrieve supplies stored at the bottom. The top of the cache was covered over with earth and patted smooth so its location was undetectable to all but members of the household. Women protected their fields and encouraged the growth of crops by singing sacred songs to the spirits who helped ensure a good harvest. They also cleansed their bodies and clothing when returning from farm work by rubbing themselves with sage. Meat and pieces of hide were offered to water birds on their northward and southward migrations in the spring and fall because these birds were the harbingers of the changes in seasons that coincided with planting and harvesting. In addition, every spring, women who belonged to the Goose Society, an age-graded ceremonial organization, performed protective and thanksgiving rituals dedicated to the growth of crops.

In addition to farm work, women gathered wild potatoes, turnips, grasses, fruits, and berries. Plant foods (both wild and farmed) were prepared by boiling in earthen pots or roasting over fire. Some corn was picked and roasted while still green, but most was first ripened. Corn kernels were pounded into meal and either boiled into a kind of pudding or cooked in cakes. Some corn was parched, then pounded into powder and eaten without further preparation. Corn to be stored was first boiled, then dried and shelled. When it was needed, it was boiled again. Beans were boiled or dried and later mixed with corn. Squash was cut into thin slices and dried on racks. When needed, it was cooked by boiling. Sunflower seeds were dried in the sun, slightly scorched in pans over fire, and then pounded into meal that could be boiled or made into cakes mixed with grease or oil. As Matthews observed, "Sunflower cakes are often taken on war parties, and are said, when eaten even sparingly, to sustain the consumer against fatigue more than any other food" (1877: 26).

Buffalo were the most important animals in the aboriginal economy. During the late spring and summer, communal drives were organized west of the villages on the prairies and plains. Corrals were constructed with brush and rocks, and then lines of women, children, and older men formed a V leading toward the corral. The animals were driven between the lines to the enclosure where waiting hunters shot them with bow and arrows. After horses were acquired in the middle of the eighteenth century, men on horseback surrounded buffalo herds and chased the animals into corrals or over cliffs, or simply outran them and shot them at close range. Once trade became critical to Hidatsa economy, hunters marked their arrows with designs to identify themselves so that they could claim the animals that they had shot (Peters 1995: 27). Such practice was a departure from previous custom in which the entire community shared equally in the products of a successful hunt. It marked a transformation from a society that stressed sharing of resources to one that noted individual ownership of subsistence products because of their utilization in trade and the accumulation of wealth.

After men had completed the hunt, women went to the site to prepare the meat and hides. Meat was cut into strips and dried on wooden frames. Then the hides and dried meat were packed into bundles and transported back to camp overland on travois pulled by dogs or on boats along the rivers.

Meat from buffalo, deer, elk, and other animals was roasted over fire, broiled on coals, or boiled in pots. Meat was sometimes chopped into small pieces and put inside a section of animal bowel to make a kind of sausage that was then boiled. Some meat was cut into thin sheets or long strips and dried in the sun or in the smoke of a fire. Dried meat was eaten raw, boiled, or broiled. Pemmican was prepared using dried buffalo or deer meat that was broiled, pounded into powder, and mixed with animal fat and berries.

Fish were caught in the Knife and Missouri Rivers using spears or wooden traps. Turtles and water birds were taken in snares or shot with bow and arrows. Eagle hunting required special training and ritual observances. Traps were dug into the ground in high places on nearby hills and covered over with sticks. A dead rabbit or other small animal was tied on the top as bait. The hunter hid himself in the excavation below. When an eagle flew down to pull up the bait, the hunter put his hand up through the opening, caught the bird by both legs, drew it into the hole and tied it. When several eagles were caught, they were brought back to camp. Their tail feathers were plucked and then the bird was set free (Matthews 1877: 58). The men fasted the day before they began the four-day expedition and did not eat until they returned from their work each evening. Hunters who were unable to catch any eagles did not sleep during the night but instead prayed for spirit assistance.

When travelling on summer buffalo hunts or when changing village locations, people used wooden travois to transport their possessions. Before the eighteenth century, small travois were pulled by dogs, but after Hidatsas acquired horses they made larger travois that could be pulled by horses for hauling greater quantities of clothing, utensils, and foods.

People used boats, called "bull-boats," to transport themselves and their possessions on the Missouri and Knife Rivers. The boats, shaped like tubs with flat bottoms and rounded sides, were made of a frame of willows over which buffalo skin was stretched. They were ferried by wooden oars. Heavy articles such as tipi poles, hide robes, and bedding were tied in bundles and attached to the boat so that they could be pulled behind while people and lighter goods were carried inside (Wilson 1914: 13).

Hidatsa clothing varied with the occasion. For daily wear, men wore buffalo robes as their main covering, often with no other garment. They sometimes wore breechcloths made of tanned deerskins or buffalo hide and a sleeveless shirt of deerskin. Women wore a sleeved deerskin dress of two pieces sewn together at the sides and belted at the waist. In cold weather, leggings, moccasins, and gloves with the fur side turned inward were worn by all. On ceremonial occasions, people wore garments made of finer skins ornamented with pieces of animal hooves or fur, porcupine quills, and dentalia shells (Catlin 1973).

Women wore their hair in two braids, sometimes painting the part with red pigment. Men had a number of hairstyles. They often parted their hair across the head from side to side and combed the hair both forward and back. The sides were cut shoulder-length while the hair in front and back was sometimes braided.

Certain households owned special rights to craft production such as pottery making and basketry. These skills were taught from mother to daughter through purchase and apprenticeship. Secrecy and ritual observances were associated with these occupations. When other members of the community needed pots or baskets, they paid for the production of the item.

Trade with other nations was an integral part of the Native economy. Hidatsa villages, along with those of their Mandan and Arikara neighbors, were aboriginal commercial centers frequented by Lakotas, Assiniboins, Crows, Crees, and Cheyennes. Hidatsas exchanged farm produce, tobacco, and eagle feathers for buffalo hides, robes, and meat. Such exchanges were critical to the economies of both village and nomadic nations. When crops failed due to drought or insect infestation, Hidatsas relied on meat obtained in trade to supplement their own supplies, while the nomads depended heavily on farm produce both for variety in their diet and as a mainstay when hunting was poor. Cheyennes and Crows were especially avid consumers of corn, probably reflecting their previous experience as horticulturists before their migration into the Plains in the seventeenth and eighteenth centuries (Ewers 1954: 433–434). Both men and women carried on trade, but men's commercial activity was often formalized by establishing ceremonial father/son bonds between trading partners through adoption rites. These bonds not only facilitated trade but also ensured peaceful relations. They were especially necessary because nomadic raiders frequently attacked Hidatsa villages in order to plunder the crops. Therefore, because of the uneasy relations between the two groups, whenever nomadic people came to Hidatsa villages to trade, their plans were announced in advance and a mutual truce was acknowledged.

Families and Social Systems

Hidatsa social organization was based on a system of matrilineal clans and moieties. The Awatixa have a tradition of thirteen clans that originated in mythical times when a spirit being named Charred Body descended from the sky and created thirteen household groups. Eight of these clans continued into historical times while five either died out or merged with other groups. The Hidatsa-proper and Awaxawi have seven matrilineal clans separated into two moieties, called the "Four-Clan Moiety" and the "Three-Clan Moiety" (Lowie 1917: 19). Members of a clan addressed each other with kinship terms of "sister" and "brother" and extended the reciprocal cooperative bonds typical between siblings to members of their own clan. Members of one's father's clan were called "father" or "father's sister," extending kinship obligations to these relatives as well.

Clan members were responsible for training and supervising younger clan relatives. The primary disciplinarians for boys were "older brothers," including actual older brothers, mother's brothers, and mother's sister's older sons. "Older sisters," that is, actual older sisters, mother's sisters, and mother's sister's older daughters, were the disciplinarians for girls. Most discipline was relatively mild, consisting of verbal reminders and corrections, but when restraint of belligerent or aggressive behavior was needed, older clan relatives might resort to corporal punishment, typically ducking the offender in the river. In extreme cases beatings might be administered.

Clan relatives played an important part on many ceremonial occasions. When a young boy reached the age of about twelve or fourteen, older clansmen began to encourage him to fast in order to receive a spirit protector. An elder clansman accompanied the boy to a secluded spot, possibly a bank overlooking a river or a pile of rocks, and left him there to fast, standing all day and most of the night crying for a vision. A successful faster was encouraged to make more frequent fasts and to participate in ceremonials that were related to success in war. Clansmen helped a young man accumulate gifts to give to sponsors and "ceremonial fathers" who aided him in acquiring spirit powers.

Members of a clan also participated in avenging assaults and murders of their relatives. They avenged their kin by either killing the offender or exacting reparations from the wrongdoer and his/her clan people. Finally, members of one's own and one's father's clan carried out major duties at the time of one's death. People in the deceased's father's clan prepared the body for burial and organized the funeral. Members of the deceased's own clan acknowledged these services by providing a feast and payment in goods. The greater the quantity of goods offered, the more honored was the deceased and the greater was the clan's reputation for generosity.

Hidatsa moieties may have at one time been exogamous but by the eighteenth century moiety exogamy was not in practice. Moieties did, however, have some ceremonial functions and, according to Lowie, "Though it is not easy fully to comprehend the nature of the Hidatsa moieties, it is clear that their functions were in part political. Whenever matters of tribal moment were to be debated, the grouping of men was based on the dual division" (1917: 21). Because of their lack of clear-cut social or economic functions and their lack of distinctive names, Lowie concluded that moieties were much more recent in Hidatsa cultural history than clans and "had developed historically as combinations of several clans" (22).

Membership in households revolved around a stable core of lineally related women. As Bowers noted, "The household group was a stable unit of generations as long as there were daughters to inherit the lodge complex. With strong loyalties to the mother's household group, any study of a Hidatsa male or female must take these ties into account. The Hidatsa say that a person without relatives is nothing" (1992: 163).

Kinship informed most daily interactions. The bond between mother and daughter was the most intense since, given matrilineal descent and matrilocal residence, mothers and daughters usually lived in the same household and cooperated together in their work. Mother/son relationships were also close, but given preferences for matrilocal residence, most men did not live in their mother's household. However, men usually married within their natal village in order to remain near the household of their mother or close female kin. Married sons continued to help their mothers and contributed to their sustenance. Men often ate meals in their mother's lodge if their own wife was away because it was not proper for a man to be alone with his parents-in-law. Relationships between fathers and their children differed from that of mothers and children because of their divergent clan membership. However, fathers took great interest in their son's economic, military, and ceremonial training. Men's relationships with their daughters were more attenuated than with their sons because a man and his daughter shared neither economic nor ceremonial roles. Behavior between father and daughter became increasingly formal once the girl reached her teenage years.

Relationships between siblings of the same gender were close, cooperative, and supportive. Sisters often lived together in the same household and helped each other with domestic duties. Brothers hunted together and joined in war expeditions. And a brother was obligated to avenge his sibling's death. Brothers and sisters tended to avoid each other in public after the age of about six or seven as a marker of social restraint and deference, but as adults they provided mutual economic and ceremonial support. Brothers often brought meat to their sister's families and sisters helped accumulate goods for their brother's ceremonial participation.

Deferential behavior occurred between parents-in-law and their children's spouses. They avoided speaking directly to one another or being alone together. These taboos were strongest on the part of a son-in-law and his mother-in-law. However, if the two lived in the same household, the son-in-law could break the restriction by giving his mother-in-law a scalp that he had obtained in warfare (Bowers 1992: 121).

Informal and joking behavior was appropriate between certain classes of kin who were considered "joking relatives." Principal among these were people belonging to the same clan, people whose fathers were members of the same clan, sisters-in-law and brothers-in-law, people whose fathers were of the same moiety, and grandparents and grandchildren. Joking relatives addressed each other as brother and sister. People joked their relatives by teasing, ridiculing, or criticizing their errors or violations of customary behavior. According to Maxi-diwiac, the function of joking relationships was to instill the virtue of modesty and to correct errant behavior: "It is never good for a man not to know his faults, and so we let one's clan cousins tease him for any fault he had. Especially was this teasing common between young men and young women" (Wilson 1972: 67–68). Joking behavior, however, was less likely to occur in public if there were a great age difference between the two people. Members of the same household were similarly unlikely to joke each other because to do so might cause a strain in the ethic of harmonious household interaction (Bowers 1992: 125).

Marriage united families and created economic and social relationships. Parents might arrange marriages for their children, but more often a young man and woman who were attracted to each other made their decision to wed. Although the couple acted on their own initiative, they preferred to have their families' approval. Marriage ceremonies involved an exchange of gifts between the households of the couple. On the appointed day, relatives of the groom brought gifts to the bride's family. By the nineteenth century, such gifts typically were in the form of horses and guns. The bride's relatives gave gifts in return to the groom's household. According to Maxi-diwiac, "It was a point of honor for the bride's father to make a more valuable return gift than that brought him by the bridegroom and his friends" (Wilson 1972: 124–125). The exchange of gifts was followed by a feast hosted by the bride's kin. Postmarital residence was typically matrilocal, although exceptions were easily made depending upon the composition of already existing households as well as personal preferences. By the rule of clan exogamy, people did not marry members of their own clan. They were reluctant as well to marry into their father's clan.

Bonds between wives and husbands were initially rather weak, but after several years had elapsed, especially with the birth of children, marriages tended to become more stable. Polygyny was a possible marriage form. Sororal polygyny was preferred because it was thought that cowives were more likely to get along if they were sisters. By the early nineteenth century, women outnumbered men by a ratio of about 3:1 as a result of male casualties in warfare, making polygyny a socially beneficial practice. In the event of the death of a spouse, the sororate and levirate were considered appropriate.

Divorce might occur on the initiative of either wife or husband, most commonly because of adultery or mistreatment. When conflicts or difficulties arose, the couple's families tried to achieve a reconciliation but if none were possible, divorce was a socially acceptable option. The couple's children usually remained with their mother.

Age-Grade Societies

Most adults belonged to age-graded societies that had social, economic, and ceremonial functions. Both men and women began their participation in the age-grade system when they were in their early teens and then proceeded from one to the next until they retired in old age. The entire system was a means of uniting individuals that cross-cut families, clans, and moieties. Each

group had officers who were chosen by the membership because of their outstanding achievements. Male leaders were usually acknowledged for their military success, while female leaders were chosen because of their artistic skills or ritual effectiveness. Each society also had a crier, invariably a man, who made public announcements concerning the group's activities. Members of a society aided each other when communal work or support in emergencies was needed. And society members presented food and gifts to relatives of a deceased colleague. Certain women's and men's societies were linked as "friends"; their members gave reciprocal aid to each other, assisting in rituals and feasts. Rights to a society were purchased collectively by people advancing to the appropriate group because of their age and achievements. The relationship between the buyers and sellers was phrased as a relationship of parent and child (i.e., mother/daughter, father/son). Purchase of membership included transfer of spirit powers and sacred bundles associated with the group. Women obtained spirit power directly from the previous holders, but men needed the assistance of their wives in order to finalize the transfer. As part of the ritual of purchase, wives of the buyers invited the sellers to have sexual intercourse with them in the belief that the spirit power of the elder man was passed to the woman in the sex act and that she later transferred it to her husband when they had intercourse.

Twelve age-grade societies existed for men while four were open to women. Most of the male societies were connected in some way to military participation. One of the major male associations was the Black Mouths. They were

> an intermediate and transitional position between the lower societies (whose members had recently begun their first fast, ceremonial adventures, ritualistic feasting, and participation in the war expeditions as beginners and immature men) and those older males who had obtained the principle objectives prescribed by the culture. (Bowers 1992: 184)

Black Mouths served as police, enforcing decisions of a village council of elders and informing the people of significant community activities. They also enforced regulations that applied during communal buffalo hunts that forbade men from hunting on their own prior to the collective effort. And they organized group movements from summer to winter camps. Finally, Black Mouths attempted to arbitrate disputes and to dissuade victims of assaults or the kin of a murdered relative from exacting blood revenge for the crime. "If a Hidatsa killed another, the relatives of the slain man might plot revenge; but the Black Mouths would gather together property and offer it to the aggrieved people, fill a pipe for them to smoke, and by gentle words would conciliate and cause them to give up projects of revenge" (Lowie 1917: 19). Because of the Black Mouths' community control functions, Hidatsas considered it crucial that men not be advanced to the society until they were mature and showed sound judgment. Consequently, most Black Mouths were between thirty and forty-five years of age (Bowers 1992: 194). Members of the most senior male age-grade society, called the Bull Society, formed a council of elders who made decisions concerning community matters and chose village leaders. They also had the important task of performing "buffalo-calling" rituals of renewal and thanksgiving for the buffalos.

The most prominent of the women's associations were the Goose Society and the White Buffalo Cow Society. The Goose Society was composed of mature women, usually between the ages of thirty and forty. Members performed planting rites in the spring when the first water birds appeared in the region, celebrating the renewal of the earth and the fertility of crops. They also performed dances during the summer whenever villagers so requested. Their aid was sought during droughts to bring rain and protect crops. And the Goose Society performed rituals at the time of the fall migration of water birds in thanks for a successful harvest. Some members were thought to have corn spirits in their body and were especially powerful and effective ritualists for corn fertility. Maximilian described one such ceremony in 1832:

> The medicine woman danced alone near the fire to which she sometimes put her hands, and then laid them upon her face. She began to totter, to move her arms backwards and forwards, and to use convulsive motions, which became more and more violent. Now, as she threw her head backwards, we saw the top of a white head of maize fill her mouth, and gradually came more forward, while her contortions greatly increased. When the head of maize was half out of her mouth, she fell into convulsions, and the music became overpowering violent. Other women brushed the arm and breast of the performers with bunches of wormwood, and the head of maize gradually disappeared; on which

> the jugleress rose, danced twice round the hut, and was succeeded by another female. (1906, III: 33–34)

The eldest women's association was the White Buffalo Cow Society. When the people moved to their winter settlements, members performed rituals to attract buffalo near the camps so that they could be caught easily during that difficult season.

Community Leadership

Leadership was vested in different individuals depending upon the unit of consideration. The most senior and prominent man in a household was acknowledged as its leader. His place within the lodge was positioned directly behind the central fireplace so that he had a favored spot to entertain guests. The household head was looked to for advice and leadership. People followed his counsel because of his proven good judgment and ability.

Each village had a council composed of mature men who were beyond the age of membership in the Black Mouth Society. Anyone could speak at council meetings, but the influence of the participant varied with his/her age and achievements. Representatives of all households in the village were asked to express their opinions about important community matters before decisions were made. Approval by all households was critical if a decision were to have any weight. Accordingly, "at best, the council is only as strong as the bond which held households together" (Bowers 1992: 34).

After the disastrous population decline following smallpox epidemics in the late eighteenth century, the three autonomous Hidatsa villages established a joint tribal council whose membership consisted of successful war leaders from each settlement. The council was responsible for planning raids and defending all of the villages. Unanimity in tribal meetings was paramount. If a unanimous decision could not be reached, action was postponed in order to attempt to sway the minority. If eventual agreement were not possible, the matter was dropped.

Summer hunting expeditions were carried out under the stewardship of elder, able hunters who selected a hunt leader having both practical skills and spirit powers. Such men usually were the owners of sacred bundles that assured successful hunting expeditions. They planned and directed rituals dedicated to attracting large herds. During the hunt, members of the Black Mouth Society acted as police to ensure that everyone obey camp regulations, particularly the restriction against hunting alone before the communal endeavor was completed.

In the late fall, the village council selected a man to serve as community leader during the winter. The winter leader chose the site for the winter encampment, set the date for the move, and planned ceremonials that were aimed at attracting buffalo near the camp.

Fortunate occurrences during any leader's term of office, such as successful summer buffalo hunts, victorious raids, the appearance of buffalo near the camp in winter, and the general health and good fortune of the community, were all attributed to the practical and spiritual abilities of the leader. Similarly, any failures were attributed to his lack of power:

> He [the chief] was responsible for the safety and welfare of the people. He was entitled to credit if the buffalo were abundant and if many enemies were killed during his incumbency. However, sometimes there was no chief because the man chosen was unwilling to risk the responsibilities of the position. The ideal chief seems to have been a man of general benevolence who offered smoke to the old people and feasted the poor. (Lowie 1917: 18)

Personality traits of generosity, intelligence, even temper, and compassion were critical requisites for being chosen for leadership. A chief's generosity was particularly essential, as attested by Boller's description of a mid-nineteenth-century man of wealth and accomplishment who nonetheless was not an acknowledged leader:

> The old man was not a chief, although his many dashing exploits when he trod the warpath richly entitled him to that distinction. He preferred to keep a large band of fine horses, make plenty of robes, and provide well for his family, instead of giving away nearly everything he possesses, although he would thereby gain much coveted distinction of being a big man, which distinction is too often acquired at the sacrifice of wealth and comfort. (1959: 55–56)

Finally, spirit power was a necessary adjunct to civil and military success. However, as one assumed greater responsibilities, spirit powers eventually waned. In fact, the more responsibilities one had, the greater was the loss of spirit power. Hidatsas therefore thought that, "an individual should not remain in authority too long and no man aspired to continue his leadership" (Bowers 1992: 63–64). As a result, "we find constant changing of top leadership as the situations of life change" (64).

Warfare

Although Hidatsas regularly carried on trade and intermarried with many neighboring nations, intertribal relations were not always friendly. Particularly by the nineteenth century, Hidatsas and other farming people became increasingly vulnerable to attacks by mounted nomadic nations of the central and western Plains. Warfare was organized by proven successful warriors. Most raids were motivated by the desire to avenge previous losses although economic goals grew important in the nineteenth century. Young men who desired to participate in raids and eventually become leaders periodically fasted to obtain spirit power. A potential leader invited other men to accompany him. The goal of warfare was not the annihilation of the enemy but rather the killing of one person. Even if "the enemy was greatly outnumbered and there was a fine opportunity to kill a great many of them, the battle was stopped and both groups retired" when one killing had taken place (232). And even though previous encounters had resulted in multiple losses in one's own group, the death of only one enemy was considered sufficient revenge.

In addition to their role in raids, war chiefs were responsible for the defense of their village, entrusting most of the actual defensive activities to members of the Black Mouth Society. If, as evidently occurred frequently, members of a foreign group were visiting a Hidatsa village when it was attacked, the visitor was obliged to assist the Hidatsas even against their own nation.

In common with other Plains nations, military exploits were ranked in terms of the honor they received. The most prestigious act was to go out alone, kill an enemy, and return safely. Other important honors were obtained by men who struck enemies and were able to retreat without harm to themselves. Such actions entitled men to decorate their clothing or their bodies with ritual insignia.

Women and Men

Hidatsa men and women had different economic, social, and ceremonial roles that complemented each other and brought value and prestige to both. Women grew the crops that had great economic and ritual value. Corn was the staple of the village diet and also provided an abundant surplus that was used in the critical networks of intertribal trade, allowing villagers to obtain meat, hides, and other products from nomadic nations to supplement their household economy. Later, after the influx of European and American traders, surplus corn was exchanged for manufactured goods, tools, and weapons. Men's labor supplied their families with meat and hides, while women's labor was necessary to prepare the meat for meals and to process the hides into useful objects such as containers, bedding, and clothing. Later, hides were exchanged with foreign traders for tools and weapons. The Hidatsa social system provided women with lifelong emotional and economic support by patterns of preferential matrilocal residence. The participation of both men and women in age-grade societies provided all people with networks of support and methods of social recognition and advancement. Both women and men were keepers of sacred bundles that validated rituals and endowed people with spirit protection and guidance. Although many rituals were performed either predominantly by men or women, both men and women participated in auxiliary functions when the other gender's rituals were held. For example, when women of the Goose Society conducted their dances in the spring and fall, the music was provided by male drummers. And whenever men's societies put on dances and feasts, the food was prepared by the mothers, sisters, and wives of the male participants. Resource renewal rites highlighted the necessary economic contributions of women and men. Ceremonies in the spring and fall dedicated to crops and vegetation focused on women's roles as farmers while winter and summer rituals centering on buffalo emphasized men's work as hunters. Men's contributions as warriors and seekers of power through fasting and self-torture were socially recognized and aided by women's preparation of feasts and participation in dances celebrating the return of successful war expeditions and the courageous completion of fasting and self-torture on the part of their sons, brothers, and husbands. Men served their communities as chiefs and leaders, but group approval and consensus of all respected members of the community, both women and men, were necessary before any communal actions were undertaken.

Religious Beliefs and Practices

In primordial times, say the Hidatsas, the land was covered with water. Spirit beings named First Creator and Lone Man decided that they would make the land habitable and called on some birds to dive below the water and bring up mud. Lone Man took the earth, divided it, and gave half to First Creator. First Creator made lands west of the Missouri River while Lone Man made the lands on the east side. Ancestors of the Awatixa, Awaxawi, and Hidatsa-proper eventually populated the region, but their stories of origin differ, presumably reflecting a difference in historical roots. According to the Awatixa, a spirit being named Charred Body who was living in a village in the sky heard buffalo in a land below. When he looked through a hole in the sky and saw the land underneath, he changed himself into an arrow and descended to the earth. He formed thirteen earth lodges and then made thirteen couples to occupy the dwellings. These were the ancestors of the thirteen Awatixa clans. Descendants of each pair eventually inhabited thirteen separate villages (Peters 1995: 27). Stories of the Hidatsa-proper and Awaxawi tell that the people originally lived in an underworld beneath Devil's Lake but one day they climbed a vine to reach the surface. The vine was broken when a pregnant woman attempted to ascend, leaving behind those people who had not yet emerged. The people on the earth surface moved from place to place in order to find a suitable home. They travelled northward but later separated when a fire came from the sky. The Awaxawi eventually settled south of Devil's Lake while the Hidatsa-proper remained farther north. Myths relate different time sequences for the arrival of the three groups near the Missouri River. The Awatixa were the first to settle near the River, followed later by the Awaxawi, while the Hidatsa-proper were the last to arrive (Bowers 1992: 298–302).

Hidatsas believed in a spirit essence or "mystery" that pervades the universe and endows all living creatures, celestial bodies, forces of nature, and many aspects of the natural world with spirit power. As Edward Goodbird explained, "All things in this world have souls, or spirits. The sky has a spirit; the clouds have spirits; the sun and moon have spirits; so have animals, trees, grass, water, stones, everything. These spirits are our gods; and we pray to them and give them offerings, that they may help us in our need" (Wilson 1914: 27). People prayed to spirits and received answers in dreams or visions. Men sometimes engaged in acts of self-torture to receive visions and power. Self-torture principally involved dragging buffalo skulls on the ground by attaching them to thongs that were tied to skewers inserted in the man's back or chest:

> Sometimes a man fasted and tortured himself until he fell into a kind of dream yet while awake; we call this a vision. A man who the gods helped and visited in dreams, was said to have mystery power; and one who had much mystery power, we called a Mystery Man, or Medicine Man. Almost everyone received dreams from the spirits at some time; but a Medicine Man received them more often than others. (28)

For men, obtaining spirit protection was a critical antecedent to engaging in warfare. Therefore, when a boy reached his middle teens, his parents or older brothers encouraged him to seek a spirit guardian:

> Finding one's god was not an easy task. The lad painted his body with white clay, as if in mourning, and went out among the hills, upon some bluff, where he could be seen by the gods; and for days, with neither food nor drink, and often torturing himself, he cried to the gods to pity him and come to him. His suffering at last brought a vision. Whatever he saw in this vision was his god, come to pledge him protection. Usually this god was a bird or beast; or it might be the spirit of someone dead; the bird or beast was not a flesh and blood animal, but a spirit.
>
> The lad then returned home. As soon as he was recovered from his fast, he set out to kill an animal like that seen in his vision, and its dried skin, or a part of it, he kept as a sacred object or medicine, for in this sacred object was his god. (29)

Spirit protection and aid was important to women as well, although their means of acquiring it differed. Women sometimes fasted for spirit power but never tortured themselves in order to achieve visions. They more often received spirit guidance and protection in dreams. Men and women gradually built up personal sacred bundles containing objects that were their protectors and helpers. These objects were prayed to and given offerings of food and cedar incense. They helped ensure health, good fortune, protection of crops, and success in hunting and warfare. The validity of one's

power was demonstrated in one's success. That is, good crops, success in war, good health, and long life were demonstrations of the spirit power that one had obtained while misfortune, illness, or failure were the outcomes of the lack or loss of spirit protection. In times of sickness, misfortune, or bad luck, "a man would throw away his moccasins, cut his hair as for mourning, paint his face with white clay, and again cry to the gods for a vision" (33).

Spirit power could be accumulated and augmented but it could also be diminished. It could be augmented through additional visions, spontaneous unsought dreams, prayers, and offerings made to sacred objects, while it could be diminished by the failure to abide by ritual regulations. Spirit power could also be diminished by its too frequent exercise. Successful men were sometimes reluctant to take on positions of leadership and authority too often because it was believed that they thereby overused their spirit powers.

In addition to personal bundles that were privately accumulated and usually buried with the owner at his/her death, Hidatsas had a number of tribal bundles that were handed down from generation to generation. The contents of these bundles were validated by myths explaining the original collection of the objects, their purpose, and their association with specific ceremonies. Edward Goodbird recalled that there were about sixty such bundles in the late nineteenth century (Wilson 1914: 36). Owners of sacred bundles were asked to officiate at ceremonies and were feasted and paid with gifts for their assistance. They could sell rights to their bundles and usually did so when they got older. The purchase of a bundle enabled the buyer to make use of the ceremonies and songs associated with it. Bundles were usually sold from father to son or mother to daughter, whether actual blood relatives or people standing in parent-child social relations. Ownership of sacred bundles contributed greatly to a person's social prestige.

Hidatsas celebrated a number of community rituals dedicated to renewal of plant and animal resources. One of the central summer rituals was the Naxpike (meaning "hide beating"). The Naxpike reenacted the torture and suffering of Spring Boy in mythic times. The ceremony was sponsored by a man who had rights to the appropriate sacred bundles. The ceremonial grounds were prepared and blessed by eight elder women belonging to the Holy Women's Society. After a central post of cottonwood tree was selected and placed in the ground, several young men charged the post as though it were an enemy. The lodge was then constructed around the post under the direction of the Holy Women. The ceremony itself consisted of four days of singing and dancing. Dancers were men who volunteered to endure self-torture to achieve visions and renew the earth. Flesh on the men's arms, chest, or back was pierced with thongs attached to a rawhide strip tied to the central post. By dancing around the post, the men gradually pulled away bits of flesh. Their sacrifice for the good of the community brought them great public acclaim. The Hidatsa Naxpike rituals may have been borrowed from the similar but more complex Okipa ceremony of the Mandan. The Sun Dance of the nomadic Plains nations was probably a borrowing from these village rituals.

Another central ceremonial complex was associated with Old-Woman-Who-Never-Dies. These rites were dedicated to the growth and fertility of cultivated crops and indeed of all vegetation. Members of the Goose Society who owned the relevant sacred bundles conducted formal ceremonies in the spring and summer that dramatized episodes in myths dealing with farm crops and water birds that were messengers of Old-Woman-Who-Never-Dies. If pleased by the rites, the deity sent buffalos near the villages in winter so that the people could survive until new vegetation grew in the spring. Associated with this ceremonial complex were the "buffalo-calling rituals" of the winter. In these rites, six elderly men were chosen to represent buffalo bulls. The rituals began with several hours of singing, feasting, and prayers of thanksgiving. Then each woman who had pledged to "walk with the buffalo" approached one of the men representing the bulls, "passed her hand over his arm, from the shoulder downwards, and withdrew slowly from the lodge. The person so summoned follows her to a solitary place in the forest" (Maximilian 1906, III: 30). Most of the

Scalp Dance of the Minatarres (members of the Hidatsa Tribe were referred to as the Minnetaree by their allies, the Mandan).

women who participated were wives of young men who aspired to military or civil leadership. A woman obtained spirit power from the "bull" through the sex act and then subsequently transferred it to her husband when the couple had intercourse. Women who "walked with the buffalo" were thought to have intercourse with the spirit Buffalo. In addition to receiving power through the sex act, the woman took the elder man's sacred bundle, held it to her breast and thereby transferred to her body the spirit powers contained in the bundle (Peters 1995: 41). Older men sometimes refused the women's invitation lest their own spirit powers begin to wane.

In addition to community ceremonies, Hidatsas marked the beginning and end of life with ritual observances. They believed that in order for conception to occur, spirits must enter the mother's body and cause the baby to develop. Spirits that produce babies inhabited a number of nearby hills or caves where childless women and men prayed and gave offerings. A woman who desired a child went to the cave at sunset, placed a small ball and a bow and arrow at the cave's mouth and waited until dawn. If the ball were missing in the morning, she would have a daughter, while if the bow and arrow were gone, she would have a son (Matthews 1877: 51).

Women preferred to give birth at their mother's lodge. If they were not already living there, they returned when the baby was due. In cases of difficult delivery, specialists who owned sacred rites dealing with childbirth were called for assistance. They eased labor by stroking the woman with a fox or wolf cap, turtle shell, or feather, accompanied by singing and rattling (Maximilian 1906, II: 382). Hidatsas believed that a baby was an incarnation of a previous being, either a person, bird, animal, or plant. Adults sometimes remembered the bird or animal that they had been in a prior life (Wilson 1914: 40).

Children were given names when they were ten days old. Their parents asked a relative or other respected elder to select a name for the child and thanked the elder for the service with a feast and gifts. The name chosen had some sacred meaning or association with a propitious occurrence. The name giver blessed the child and asked for good health, courage, industriousness, and long life. Children and adults frequently received additional names at critical points in their lives.

The end of life was marked with ceremonial preparation, burial, and mourning. Young children who "died before they teethed or were old enough to laugh" (Goodbird in Wilson 1914: 41) were not given formal funerals but were wrapped in animal skins and placed in trees. Hidatsas "thought if such a baby died, that its spirit went back to live its former life again, as a bird, or plant, or as a babe in one of the babe's lodges" (41). When an older child or adult died, the funeral was directed by an individual often chosen before death by the person about to die. It was customary to paint a person near death in the designs that they preferred and to dress them in their burial garments. Burial optimally took place on the day of death, but if the person died at night, a pair of old moccasins containing hot coals was placed in the entranceway of the lodge to keep away evil spirits until burial the next day. The body was then removed from the lodge and carried in a procession to its place of rest, either on a scaffold or in the ground. The scaffolding or grave was prepared by men and women of the deceased's father's clan. Some of the deceased's property was buried as well, especially personal sacred bundles, but most of their possessions had already been willed to specific individuals before the death or was divided among siblings or close members of the deceased's clan. The mother and sister of the deceased cut their hair short and jagged and tore the sleeves from old dresses that they would wear in mourning. Some women also cut off a section of their finger. After the body was deposited in its final resting place, a member of the deceased's father's clan spoke: "My son/daughter, do not look backwards but go to the Ghost Land. You will meet many of your beloved ones there. You must not expect us, your family are remaining here. Go alone. We are poor" (quoted in Lowie 1917: 52). When the rites were completed, anyone who had touched the corpse rubbed themselves with a ball of sage to be protected from illness.

Hidatsas believed that life in the afterworld was much like on earth. Murderers, however, were not permitted to enter the villages of the dead but instead were "aimless wanderers." Some Hidatsas believed that the land of the dead was located under the earth and that after death the souls of the dead were reunited with primordial people who had not emerged onto the surface. Others believed that the village of the dead was located on earth, either at the mouth of the Knife River or at Devil's Lake (Bowers 1992: 174). Since souls could carry messages from the living to those who had died before, when it seemed that a person was near death, relatives or members of the community might visit them and request that they give messages to their loved ones.

TRADE AND ITS CONSEQUENCES

Hidatsa villages, along with those of the Mandans and Arikaras, became focal points in the developing European trade in the late eighteenth and early nineteenth centuries, incorporating new products and new personnel into an already existing economic, social, and ceremonial system. When European traders entered the region, they were often adopted into fictive father/son relationships in order to establish bonds of trust that would facilitate trade. Also in accordance with aboriginal custom relating to power held by men and its transmission through women, Hidatsa men extended invitations to European traders to have sexual intercourse with their wives in the hopeful expectation that the wealthy foreigners' spirit power would be transmitted through the sex act to the women and consequently to their husbands (Peters 1995: 153–154). Not surprisingly, Europeans took full advantage of the Native practice although its underlying meaning was not of concern to them. As British trader David Thompson remarked in 1797, "The white men who have hitherto visited these villages, have not been examples of chastity" (Coues 1897: 233).

Guns and horses quickly became the most important of the European trade items. Hidatsas received guns from French and British traders coming up the Missouri River or overland from eastern Canada and then traded the weapons to nomadic hunters for the horses that the nomads obtained through intertribal trade networks in the central and southern Plains. According to the early-nineteenth-century British trader Charles Mackenzie, Hidatsas carried on a large volume of trade with nomadic nations: "The Hidatsas gave the Crows two hundred guns, a hundred rounds of ammunition each, a hundred bushels of corn, and other articles, in return for which they received two hundred fifty horses and immense numbers of buffalo robes, leather leggings, leather shirts, and the like" (Meyer 1977: 42). Nomadic hunters were valued as suppliers of meat, hides, horses, and finished products such as leather clothing and equipment, and as recipients of trade goods such as guns, surplus corn, and other farm produce.

Because of the profits obtained and the important political and economic position that resulted from monopolizing intertribal trade, Hidatsas were reluctant to permit European merchants to proceed west and deal directly with nomadic nations. Instead, they wanted to function as intermediaries in order to gain wealth and influence. But as commercial activity expanded, the hunting nations had more incentives to trade directly with Europeans and to plunder the villagers' provisions. Thus began a cycle of conflicts among indigenous nations. Hidatsas' sedentary settlement patterns made them vulnerable to attack by equestrian raiders armed with guns. The growing frequency of warfare was reflected in a sex imbalance due to male casualties. According to George Catlin's estimates in 1834, "The proportion of women to the number of men is two or three to one" (1973, I: 187). And by the early nineteenth century, Hidatsas were weakened by epidemics of smallpox that rendered the survivors even more likely targets of raiders.

Trade continued in spite of the sharp population declines of the period. Commercial involvement led to cultural and political changes as more foreign traders entered the region following the expedition led by Lewis and Clark, which passed through the Missouri villages in 1804. Of all the village nations, Hidatsas evidenced the greatest skepticism concerning the purposes and motives of the interlopers. For instance, although Lewis and Clark claimed that they were merely exploring the region and desired friendship with indigenous inhabitants, Charles Mackenzie reported that Hidatsas "concluded that the Americans had a wicked design on their country" (Meyer 1977: 42). American and British trade grew rapidly thereafter. And in 1837 Native villages were devastated by smallpox that originated with passengers on an American Fur Company steamboat travelling up the Missouri River from St. Louis. Although all villages suffered, the Awaxawi and Awatixa experienced the greatest number of deaths. Due to both population loss and warfare, particularly with Lakotas, the three Hidatsa villages relocated to sites near the mouth of the Knife River. They established a tribal council consisting of twelve members to coordinate ceremonial and military activities among the villages. Then in 1845 people from all settlements built a new village called Like-A-Fishhook at a bend in the Missouri River just upstream from the mouth of the Knife. They were joined there by survivors from nearby Mandan settlements. The period leading up to the formation of Like-A-Fishhook was one of social, economic, and political instability. The extent of the consequent despair was reflected in a high number of suicides, particularly among women. Bowers' consultants in the early twentieth century stated: "In those days the Hidatsa did not believe that any people would survive. Therefore, these women claimed, people committed suicide during the periods of epidemics simply to catch up with and join their recently deceased relatives at a time when the household was largely destroyed by these newly introduced diseases" (1992: 173).

By 1850, two competing American trading companies had established posts near Like-A-Fishhook. One, called Fort Berthold, was run by the American Fur Company, and the other, Fort Atkinson, by the Opposition Company. Fort Berthold became the largest and most active post in the region, although the presence of rival establishments benefitted Indian traders because competition kept prices for American goods lower and induced foreign merchants to pay more for Native products in order to secure their business (Boller 1959: 60).

As settlers and traders penetrated further into the Plains in the mid-nineteenth century, the government negotiated treaties with Indians in order to "pacify" the region and guarantee rights for Americans to travel through their territory, establish trading posts and military forts, and allow for the construction of transcontinental railroads. In 1851, the Fort Laramie Treaty established boundaries among Native nations of the northern Plains, including Hidatsas, Mandans, and Arikaras as well as the nomadic Arapahos, Assiniboins, Blackfeet, Cheyennes, and Crows. However, the boundaries drawn were inadequate and in any case meaningless because neither the Indians nor the federal government paid any attention to them. Indeed, intertribal warfare intensified because of economic and territorial instability in the Plains, the encroachment of American settlers on Native lands, the disruption of traditional economies and the increasing pressure felt by all groups as their involvement in trade expanded. The list of Hidatsa enemies during the period included the Lakotas, Assiniboins, Blackfeet, Cheyennes, and Arapahos, while their main allies were the Mandans, Arikaras, and Crows (Maximilian 1906, II: 383–384). Adding to the distress within their community, epidemics of smallpox and cholera swept through Like-A-Fishhook in the 1840s and 1850s.

From time to time, the federal government sent surveyors and "Indian agents" to Like-A-Fishhook. Henry Boller, an employee of the Opposition Trading Company in the mid-nineteenth century, gave an apt although sarcastic description of a typical encounter:

The Agent held the usual council, gave the usual stereotyped advice to love their Great Father and their enemies, to which they responded with the usual grunt, and the council broke up, without

the Indians having a very exalted opinion of the Agent, or his ability. The annuities were landed and, compared with the preceding year, the pile was beautifully less, so insignificant that the Indians considered it rather an insult than otherwise. The government appropriations are supposed to be liberal, but it so happens by the time they reach their destination they have, and not mysteriously either, dwindled down into a paltry present. (1959: 343)

Agency corruption at Fort Berthold was further reflected in Joseph Taylor's observations of 1869:

They had made a treaty with the government—had ceded large tracts of land for promises unfulfilled. A pair of pants to a chief, a calico dress or a shawl for some female favorite was about all that reached them after passing through the gauntlet where the agent, the inspector and the issuing clerk took turns in their stands along the line. (Taylor 1930: 222)

Government surveillance and intervention in the region increased in the 1860s when additional forts were established and those existing were strengthened. As Matthews described the period,

About this time (1863), the immigration to the Montana gold mines by way of the Missouri River began; and, instead of one steamer a year ascending the river as in the old days, they came up by dozens, some making two and three trips during the season of navigation. The Indians were thus brought into more intimate contact with the Americans, the seclusion of their country was ended, and a change more general and rapid in their affairs initiated. Since then, their game has been killed off, they have grown weaker, poorer, and more dependent, and, in many other respects, they have altered for the worse … The Mandans and Minnetarees [Hidatsas] claim never to have shed a white man's blood, although some of their number have been killed by whites. For their fidelity they have been repaid in starvation and neglect. (1877: 31–32)

THE FORT BERTHOLD RESERVATION

Once the Civil War ended, the government turned its attention to exerting control in the Plains, endeavoring to reduce the size of aboriginal land holdings. In 1866, officials pressured Hidatsa, Mandan, and Arikara representatives to cede 4 million of the 12 million acres of hunting territory guaranteed them in the 1851 Treaty of Fort Laramie. The remaining 8 million acres were to become a reservation for the three nations. Since Congress never ratified the agreement, an executive order issued by President Ulysses S. Grant in 1870 established the Fort Berthold Reservation. Ten years later, a second executive order reduced the size of the reservation to less than 3 million acres at the insistence of the Northern Pacific Railroad Company in order to appropriate land for rail lines. Shortly thereafter, Hidatsas began leaving Like-A-Fishhook, settling in several smaller communities throughout the reservation to have access to more farmland and wood needed for fuel. The move was not without its hardships. Hidatsas had for centuries lived in compact villages where they could rely on relatives and community members for economic assistance, social and ceremonial cooperation, and emotional support. Once they dispersed into smaller settlements and homesteads, they lost the social network that underlay their community integration. But government officials were pleased with the move since they had encouraged Hidatsas to dismantle large extended family residences and reliance on kin in favor of American-style housing, nuclear family household composition, and individual ownership of land. By the 1870s, only about thirty-five of the Hidatsa houses were of the earth-lodge type while sixty-nine families lived in log cabins (Matthews 1877: 4). Seasonal movements from summer to winter communities were no longer undertaken. With the encouragement or insistence of government officials, Native men took up farming in accordance with the gender division of labor prevailing in Euro-American society:

> Within the last few years, [1877] there has been an improvement in their farming. The bottom to the west of the village is still divided up and cultivated in the old way [i.e., women working in small gardens using aboriginal technology]; but the bottom to the east and a part of the Upland have been broken up by the Indian Agency, fenced, and converted into a large field. A portion of this field is cultivated (chiefly by hired Indians) for the benefit of the Agency, and the rest has been divided into small tracks, each to be cultivated by a separate family for its own benefit. Potatoes, turnips, and other vegetables have been introduced. The men apply themselves willingly to the labors of the field; and the number of working men is constantly increasing. (11–12)

What Matthews described as "an improvement" reflected a transformation of aboriginal subsistence and gender roles. Hidatsa women did not adopt the new system without resistance or resentment. Maxi-diwiac's life history is replete with examples of elderly women who insisted on tilling their fields as their ancestors had done for generations. She ends by remarking,

> Sometimes at evening I sit, looking out on the big Missouri. In the shadows I seem again to see our Indian village, with smoke curling upward from the earth lodges; and in the river's roar I hear the yells of the warriors, the laughter of little children as of old. It is but an old woman's dream. Our Indian life, I know, is gone forever. (Wilson 1972: 176)

In order to effect wide-sweeping cultural changes, schools and missions were opened on the reservation. Indicative of officials' attitudes, in 1879 William Courtnay, agent at Fort Berthold, urged the government to dissolve the Indians' "tribal organization, dances, ceremonies and tomfoolery … and compel them to labor and accept the alternative of starvation" (Meyer 1968: 226). The American Board of Commissioners for Foreign Missions began work at Fort Berthold in 1876 but met with resistance and outright hostility, particularly by the Hidatsa chief Crows Breast. Eventually, however, a number of converts were made. Still, many aboriginal beliefs and practices continued among the majority of the population. As Edward Goodbird, the first Hidatsa missionary, remarked,

> Worshipping as we did many gods, we Indians did not think it strange that white men prayed to another god; and when missionaries came, we did not think it wrong that they taught us to pray to their god, but they said we should not pray to our god. "Why," we ask, "do the missionaries hate our gods? We do not deny the white man's great spirit; why, then should they deny our gods?" (Wilson 1914: 33)

In the climate of federal policy that culminated in passage of the General Allotment Act in 1887, officials convinced representatives of the Hidatsas, Mandans, and Arikaras to sell nearly two-third of their reservation, at that time consisting of some 2.9 million acres, for an annuity of $80,000 for ten years to be spent on education, missions, and new housing. The remaining reservation was divided into allotments of 160 acres for a family or 80 acres for individuals. Unlike the General Allotment Act, however, the Fort Berthold agreement stated that surplus lands remain as communal tribal property held in trust by the US government, but in 1910, Congress voted unilaterally to allow the sale of the communal surplus acreage to non-Indians.

In the closing decades of the nineteenth century, farming and raising livestock grew in economic importance. Farm work was done by men although a few, mostly elderly, women continued to plant small plots for subsistence needs. The communal land base continued to shrink as additional allotments were made from tribal land. By 1928, only 1,652 acres remained unallotted (Meyer 1977: 167). And as increasing numbers of allotments were fractionated through inheritance, many were leased or sold to outsiders.

In response to the growing complexity of laws affecting them, in 1910 Hidatsas, Mandans, and Arikaras formed a business committee consisting of ten members whose responsibilities included overseeing reservation land and resources. At first, committee members were chosen by respected elders through consensus but later, as members withdrew or died, their successors were chosen by the committee itself.

In the 1920s, the Fort Berthold Reservation filed a claim with the US Court of Indian Claims requesting compensation for lands illegally taken since the signing of the Fort Laramie Treaty in 1851. The Court's ruling in 1930 allowed a settlement for some 10 million acres, fixing a rate of $0.50 per acre, which was the prevailing price at the time of the expropriation of land. The sum finally awarded amounted to $4,923,093 but $2,753,00 was deducted as "offsets," that is, money given by Congress for the "support and civilization" of the Fort Berthold Indians. Thus the three tribes received $2,169,000 or about $1,091 per capita (Meyer 1977: 188).

After passage of the Indian Reorganization Act in 1934, members of the Fort Berthold Reservation adopted a constitution that provided for their incorporation as the "Three Affiliated Tribes" and set up a tribal council with representatives elected for terms of two years. The constitution also set an eligibility requirement for tribal membership, that is, at least one-fourth Hidatsa, Mandan, or Arikara ancestry.

CONTEMPORARY HIDATSA COMMUNITIES

Just as members of the Three Tribes were recovering from the economic downturns of the depression years and began to establish a unified community and government, federal agencies instituted a plan that, although aimed at controlling flooding along the Missouri River, had devastating effects on the Indians. Despite the fact that floodwaters actually helped the Three Tribes by replenishing the nutrient content of their fields and providing rich grazing lands for their cattle, Congress acted to control the river because of pressure from residents of cities downstream. Ignoring strong Native objections, the Pick-Sloan project was approved in 1944. A total of twenty-three tribes were affected by the plan, but people at Fort Berthold were the most seriously harmed. Five dams were built along the Upper Missouri with loss of more than 550 sq. mi. of reservation land. The government's actions violated provisions of the 1851 Fort Laramie Treaty guaranteeing that no Native land be taken without the people's explicit approval. In addition, the Pick-Sloan plan violated the Winter's Doctrine enunciated by the US Supreme Court in 1908 in a case concerning the Blackfoot of Montana. According to the ruling, when treaties with Indians reserved rights to land, they also reserved rights to water for present and future needs. Contrary to such guarantees, the waters provided by the Pick-Sloan projects destroyed much of the Tribes' territory. Even after the plan was finalized by Congress, delegates from the Three Tribes continued to protest the taking of their land. Testifying at congressional hearings in 1947, one woman stated:

> I object to leaving my land and home where my children have walked and played ... Where can the Army [Army Corps of Engineers] find a place as good as our land? If there are such lands the whites would not give them up. Our cemeteries will be molested—here where we have placed flowers on the graves of those who have gone on ahead of us. (Meyer 1977: 215)

And Carl Whitman, Jr., president of the Three Tribes Tribal Council, remarked:

> We kept our promise and have worked to build up a strong cattle industry and steadily expanding agricultural programs. Just as we were in sight of

economic independence you began to build a reservoir and take away the heart of our reservation and divided it into five isolated segments. The homes which we built, the bottomlands on which 85 percent of our people live and on which our cattle industry depended, our churches, our schools, our government, and our social life will be disrupted. (Meyer 1968: 257)

But the federal plan moved ahead. Representatives of the Three Tribes, some with tears in their eyes, signed the final agreement allowing construction of the dams. In compensation, the Tribes received a settlement eventually totaling some $12.5 million.

The Garrison Dam was completed in 1956, flooding more than 150,000 acres of Native farmland to create a reservoir called Lake Sakakawea. The name chosen is an ironic reminder of the Shoshone woman who guided Lewis and Clark on their journey through the Plains and Northwest in 1804. Perhaps, though, it is a historically fitting appellation, recalling British trader Charles Mackenzie's comment that when the expedition passed through Hidatsa territory, the people "concluded that the Americans had a wicked design on their country" (Meyer 1977: 42).

The relocation of about 90 percent of Three Tribes families began in 1951, and the once-unified Fort Berthold Reservation was divided into five noncontiguous segments. The sense of community was completely shattered. Extended families were dispersed, undermining a system of relationship that relied on mutual economic assistance and emotional support. The lands that were flooded had contained woodlands, rich farmlands, surface coal deposits that were used for fuel, springs of fresh water, and wild fruits and animals that were gathered and hunted to supplement household economies. Instead, people were relocated to more remote, less fertile and productive areas of the reservation. As an indicator of the economic deterioration that ensued, the percentage of people requiring welfare assistance rose dramatically. Before relocation, only about 1 percent of the population received welfare but by 1960 the figure had climbed to 9 percent (Meyer 1968: 27).

Some improvements in income were made in the late 1950s as reservation coal and oil resources were exploited. However, only those people whose land held the deposits received payments. Studies in the 1970s showed an improving economic situation. On average, more families were deriving income from land, either from their own production of crops or livestock or from leases of land to non-Indian farmers and ranchers. In fact, lease income rose more rapidly than production (Meyer 1977: 253–254).

In 1970, three law suits that had been filed by the Three Tribes in the Court of Claims were settled, awarding the people a total of $1,850,000 for land ceded in the late nineteenth century. Per capita distributions were made of 80 percent of the funds while the remaining 20 percent was earmarked for land purchases and other tribal expenses. Subsequent land claims suits were settled in 1974 for an award of $9.7 million (254–255).

In the late 1970s and 1980s, the government of the Three Tribes began to regulate the activities of non-Indian individuals and companies on their lands. Their ability to do so was supported by a US Supreme Court ruling in 1987 giving the tribal council the right to sue a contractor in state court for faulty workmanship.

In 1984, the Three Affiliated Tribes sued the federal government for actions undertaken by the Pick-Sloan plan, claiming that "the building of the Garrison Dam amounted to an unconstitutional taking of the real property owned by a sovergn nation" (VanDevelder 1998: 48). A congressional inquiry acknowledged the legitimacy of the claim, awarding a settlement of $149.5 million (48).

Fort Berthold residents have slowly rebuilt their sense of community, maintaining a core of Native values, especially the ethic of generosity and sharing with others. In the Native view, success and good luck are the outcomes of having fulfilled one's obligations to family and community. Traditional giveaways are held in conjunction with tribal and intertribal powwows, community celebrations, and holidays. Giveaways are also held to mark individual and family events such as graduation from school, marriages, or retirement. Although the occasions differ from those of aboriginal times, traditional feasts and displays of generosity are important signs of the strength of Native values.

While traditional social ethics are favored by a significant segment of the community, economic changes have led to the differentiation of people at Fort Berthold based on access to land and capital (McLaughlin 1998). In particular, cattle ranching grew in importance after allotment of reservation land in the early twentieth century and people who had greater financial resources and greater wealth in land and livestock, "particularly those who were relatively educated and of mixed heritage, began to engage in commodity livestock production and to adopt the ethics and management practices requisite to capital accumulation" (107). Changes in economic relations led to alterations in social outlook because "under pressure to assimilate and increasingly invested in market exchange, agrarian entrepreneurs [began] to disengage partially from social and moral networks and associated responsibilities" (108). The Fort Berthold community, then, became divided by differences in economic and social orientation. Financial policies of the federal and reservation governments resulted in widening the rift between richer and poorer residents. Through loans and other supports, people with large amounts of land and numbers of animals were able to increase their advantage. After relocation and shrinkage of the land base, fewer people were able to remain in the cattle business, but those who did were able to increase their herds. By 1990, only about 10 percent of Fort Berthold residents were full-time farmer/ranchers (120–121).

Economic development on the Ft. Berthold Reservation has focused recently on exploring for and extracting oil and natural gas. Reservation land is located atop the Bakken Formation of North Dakota, representing one of the largest energy sites in the United States. By 2012, there were some 300 producing wells, and another 1,000 planned for the next ten years. Since production began in 2008, royalty revenues have steadily increased, and in 2015, new laws simplified the process of leasing tribal land and increased prices for doing so, boosting royalties to over $20.6 million per year (US Department of the Interior 2012). The oil slump of 2015 has not seemed to affect the Ft. Berthold production numbers, where the average oil production is over 100,000 barrels per day (Andrist 2015). The revenues are paid to the tribal government as a collective, although some monies are owed to individual Native owners of mineral leases.

In 2012, Tex Hall, chairman of the Three Affiliated Tribes testified at a US Senate hearing concerning regulations of the Bureau of Land Management (BLM). Hall voiced opposition to attempts by the BLM to treat Indian reservations as "public lands," ignoring their special status as trust lands held by United States. He reminded the Senate that Congress had specifically exempted Indian trust lands from BLM control when it established that agency in 1976. Hall concluded, "If we do not have the right to determine ourselves if a public land regulation is in our best interest or not, then it will result in our treaty rights and our sovereignty being made subordinate to public lands policies,

in violation of the federal government's trust responsibility and our treaty rights."

According to figures from 1980, about 1,000 Hidatsas were speakers of their Native language (Hollow and Parks 1980: 75) but the US Census for 2000 recorded that 571 Hidatsas reported themselves as speakers of Hidatsa. Six people said they were monolingual Hidatsa-speakers (Broadwell 1995: 146). In 2015, the MHA (Mandan, Hidatsa, and Arikara) Language Project estimated that there are only one hundred fluent speakers of Hidatsa. Community schools now emphasize the teaching of the Hidatsa language, culture, and history. And a tribally run community college continues the local education. Programs to maintain the use of the Hidatsa language are oriented toward creating fluent speakers by stressing the importance of identity as reflected in and transmitted through one's Native language. Efforts centering on language also incorporate cultural traditions and values in an integrated approach to learning.

Foreshadowing recent efforts on the part of Native Americans to protect their cultural and spiritual heritage, members of the Hidatsa Waterbuster clan regained possession of the Waterbuster sacred bundle from the Museum of the American Indian in New York City. The bundle had been sold in 1902 by its keeper after he converted to Christianity but was returned to the clan in 1938 (Meyer 1968: 236).

Despite many advances, economic problems remain. Because of its rural location, there are few jobs available on the reservation other than those sponsored by tribal or federal governments. Most people, therefore, either work in the public sector or have incomes derived from agriculture, cattle raising, or leasing of land to non-Indian ranchers and farmers. As of 2010, the US government does not collect Hidatsa economic data separately from Ft. Berthold data. However, data from different counties and census-designated places (CDPs) within the reservation is highly variable. For example, per capita income for the Mandaree CDP is $8,035 while per capita income for Mercer County is $37,570. Because of oil royalties, it can be very hard to determine actual incomes, as median household income for Mercer county is $9,688, with a variance of $205,807. Poverty rates throughout the reservation are quite high, though, ranging from a 28.1 percent individual poverty rate in McKenzie county to a 51.6 percent family poverty rate in the White Shield CDP. As a result of income, although a high percentage of Hidatsas were living above the poverty level, others at

TABLE 11.1	Poverty Rates for Selected Locations within Hidatsa Reservations	
	Living below Poverty Level (%)	
	Families	**Individuals**
Ft. Berthold McKenzie County	32.1	28.1
Ft. Berthold McLean County	42.4	40.9
Ft. Berthold Mercer County	—	40.0
White Shield CDP	51.6	44.0
Four Bears Village CDP	45.7	28.9
Mandaree CDP	35.8	34.1

Source: US Bureau of the Census 2011.

Reservation (total reservation population of 1,262) (132). The number of Hidatsas continued to decline, reaching its nadir in 1906 when there were only 136 Hidatsa residents at Fort Berthold (total reservation population of 1,118)(136). Since then, the Hidatsa population, as well as that of the Mandans and Arikaras, has rebounded. Hidatsas experienced the sharpest increase, eventually becoming the most numerous of the three nations. By 1946, just before the flooding of most reservation land to build the Garrison Dam and the increased out-migration because of deteriorating economic conditions, Hidatsas numbered 897 (total Fort Berthold population of 2,034) (201). Figures from the 2010 census distinguish among the three tribes: there are 6,609 members of the Three Affiliated Tribes, of which 3,379 were residents at Fort Berthold. There are 1,201 registered Hidatsa, 1,171 Mandan, and 1,356 Arikara. The BIA has slightly different numbers, with an estimated tribal enrollment of 10,249 members and 4,053 living on-reservation (US Department of the Interior 2016).

Ft. Berthold were even more likely to be poor. Relevant data are presented in table 11.1. These composite figures gloss over marked income disparities. According to data for 2010, 5.8 percent of reservation households had annual incomes of over $100.000, while 21.2 percent had incomes of less than $10,000.

BIA statistics on employment report reservation trends, but they do not disaggregate by tribe. In 2010 the unemployment rate stood at 14.0 percent while the North Dakota unemployment rate was 3.6 percent (Statistical Abstracts 2009: 405).

Figures for aboriginal Hidatsa population are, of course, lacking. The first European estimate, made by David Thompson in 1797, reported 1,330, but on the basis of his description of the number of lodges in Hidatsa villages, Stewart revised the number to more than 2,000 (Meyer 1977: 34). In any case, this is not an aboriginal number because by the time of Thompson's visit, Hidatsas had experienced at least one major smallpox epidemic. Maximilian gave a figure of 2,100 during his visit in 1832 that agrees well with government figures of between 2,000 and 2,500 in 1837, before the devastating smallpox epidemic that occurred later that year (97). There are no figures for the number of Hidatsas who died during that epidemic or in warfare during the next forty years, but in 1876 there were 403 Hidatsa residents of the Fort Berthold

REFERENCES

Andrist, Steve. 2015. "Bakken Briefs for Wednesday, Nov. 25." *The Bismarck Tribune*. Online.

Boller, Henry. 1959. *Among the Indians: Eight Years in the Far West, 1858 to 1866*. Chicago, IL: Lakeside Press, R. R. Donnelley & Sons.

Bowers, Alfred. 1992. *Hidatsa Social and Ceremonial Organization*. Lincoln, NE: University of Nebraska Press.

Broadwell, George. 1995. "1990 Census Figures for Speakers of American Indian Languages." *International Journal of American Linguistics* 61, no. 1: 145–149.

Catlin, George. 1973. *Letters and Notes on the Manners, Customs and Conditions of North American Indians*. 2 vols. New York: Dover Press.

Coues, Elliott (ed.). [1897]1965. *New Light on the Early History of the Greater Northwest: The Manuscript Journals of Alexander Henry and David Thompson, 1799–1814*. 2 vols. Minneapolis, MN: Ross & Haines.

Ewers, John. 1954. "The Indian Trade of the Upper Missouri before Lewis and Clark: An Interpretation." *Missouri Historical Society Bulletin* 10, no. 4: 429–446.

Hollow, Robert, and Douglas Parks. 1980. "Studies in Plains Linguistics: A Review." *Anthropology on the Great Plains* (ed. W. R. Wood and M. Liberty). Lincoln, NE: University of Nebraska Press, pp. 68–97.

Lowie, Robert. 1917. *Notes on the Social Organization and Customs of the Mandan, Hidatsa and Crow Indians.* New York: American Museum of Natural History, Anthropological Papers, Vol. 21, pp. 1–99.

Matthews, Washington. 1877. *Ethnography and Philology of the Hidatsa Indians.* Washington, DC: US Geological and Geographical Survey, Miscellaneous Publications No.7.

Maximilian, Prince of Wied. 1906. "Travels in the Interior of North America" (ed. R. G. Thwaites). *Western Travel*, Vols. 22, 23, 24. Cleveland, OH: Arthur H. Clark.

McLaughlin, Castle. 1998. "Nation, Tribe, and Class: The Dynamics of Agrarian Transformation on the Ft. Berthold Reservation." *American Indian Culture and Research Journal* 22, no. 3: 101–138.

Meyer, Roy. 1968. *Fort Berthold and the Garrison Dam. North Dakota History: Journal of the Northern Plains* 35, no. 3–4: 217–355.

Meyer, Roy. 1977. *The Village Indians of the Upper Missouri: The Mandans, Hidatsas, and Arikaras.* Lincoln, NE: University of Nebraska Press.

Peters, Virginia. 1995. *Women of the Earth Lodges: Tribal Life on the Plains.* North Haven, CT: Archon Books.

Statistical Abstracts. 2009.

Taylor, Joseph. 1930. "Fort Berthold Agency in 1869." *North Dakota Historical Quarterly* 4, no. 4: 220–226.

Thompson, David. 1916. *David Thompson's Narration of His Explorations in Western America 1784–1812.* Edited by J.B. Tyrell. Vol. 12. Toronto: Champlain Society.

US Bureau of the Census. 2011. "2006–2010 American Community Survey Selected Economic Characteristics." Washington, D.C.

US Bureau of Indian Affairs. 1995. "Table 3: Indian Service Population and Labor Force Estimates." Washington, DC.

US Department of the Interior. 2012. *Energy Production on Ft. Berthold Reservation in North Dakota Provides Substantial Economic Benefits to American Indian Communities.* US Department of the Interior Press Releases, Washington, D.C.

US Department of the Interior. 2016. *Indian Affairs Agencies: Fort Berthold Agency.* Online.

VanDevelder, Paul. 1998. "A Coyote for all Seasons." *Native Peoples* 11, no. 4(Summer): 42–48.

Wedel, Waldo. 1961. *Prehistoric Man on the Great Plains.* Norman, OK: University of Oklahoma Press.

Wilson, Gilbert. 1914. *Goodbird the Indian, His Story.* New York: Fleming H. Revell.

Wilson, Gilbert. 1972. *Waheenee: An Indian Girl's Story Told by Herself.* Lincoln, NE: University of Nebraska Press.

THE GREAT BASIN

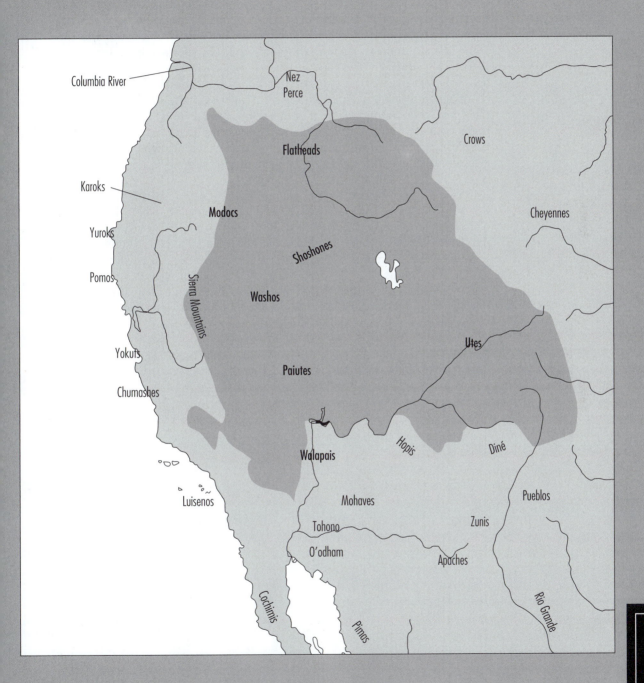

Columbia River

Nez Perce

Flatheads

Crows

Karoks

Modocs

Cheyennes

Yuroks

Shoshones

Pomos

Sierra Mountains

Washos

Utes

Yokuts

Paiutes

Chumashes

Walapais

Hopis

Diné

Luisenos

Mohaves

Pueblos

Tohono

Zunis

O'odham

Apaches

Cochimis

Pimas

Rio Grande

Shoshone Story of the Theft of Fire

A long time ago, the animals were people. They had no fire in any part of this country.

Lizard was lying in the sunshine. He saw a tule ash, blown by the south wind from a long way off, fall to the ground near him. The people sent Hummingbird up into the sky to find out where it had come from. Coyote was watching him. He saw that Hummingbird looked to the south and saw something. Hummingbird told the people that there was a fire in the south.

They all started for the south. On the way, Coyote stationed the different animals at intervals. They went on until they could see the fire. The people there were having a big celebration and dance. Coyote made himself false hair of milkweed string. He joined the people and danced with them. As he danced he moved close to the fire and leaned his head over so that his hair caught on fire. Then he ran away. The fire in the camp went out, and the people began to pursue Coyote to recover their fire.

Coyote ran to the first man he had posted and passed the fire to him. This man ran with it to the next man, and in this way they passed it along. Every time the pursuers caught one of Coyote's people, they killed him. There were fewer and fewer of them left, but they kept the fire. At last only Rabbit remained. As he ran with the fire, he caused hail to fall to stop the pursuers. Rat, who was living alone on the top of a big smooth rock, went down to meet him. Rat took the fire from Rabbit and ran with it to his house. The pursuers gathered around his house, but could not get into it. They all died right there. They can be seen now piled on a mountain nearby.

Rat scattered the fire all over the country.

Source: Julian Steward. 1943. *Some Western Shoshone Myths.* Washington, DC: Bureau of American Ethnology Bulletin No. 136, pp. 254–255.

Native Nations of the Great Basin

We should adhere to the law the Creator gave the Indians: "Live with the land." In living with this law, we should also adhere to the law our ancestors laid down for us: "This is our land, for us and our children, their children's children, and the children to come after them forever, in like manner."

We should educate the white people to this end. We need their technology, we should not accept their way of life entirely. They are beginning to think our way. They are opposing development and tearing up the land. They are concerned with environment.

Walter Voorhees, Walker River Paiute; Inter-Tribal Council of Nevada 1974: 14–15

LANDS AND NATIONS

The Great Basin encompasses a large region of western North America in the present-day states of Nevada, Utah, western Colorado, southern Oregon, Idaho, Wyoming, eastern California, and northern Arizona and New Mexico. Its distinctive natural feature, giving it the name "Great Basin," is the fact that its rivers and streams have only interior drainage into lakes; none of its waterways empty into the sea. The region is one of high mountains, intervening valleys, and deserts. To the west are the Sierra Nevada Mountains of California and to the east are the Rocky Mountains of Colorado and Wyoming. The climate is generally arid or semi-arid with relatively meager precipitation, although at higher elevations rates of rain and snow increase. Most

of the moisture coming from the Pacific Ocean far to the west is blocked by the high Sierra Nevadas, leaving much of the region dry. In some parts of the Great Basin, large lakes such as Pyramid Lake, Walker Lake, and Lake Tahoe have formed, but most of the area is watered only by small rivers, streams, springs, and seeps. Temperatures vary widely, with lowest readings in the high mountains and warmest temperatures in the valleys and desert flatlands. Due to vast differences in elevation, topography, and climate, the flora and fauna of the region vary widely as well.

From archeological evidence of human habitation before the European and American invasions of the eighteenth and nineteenth centuries, 82 percent of the most populated sites were situated from 5,000 to 7,000 ft. above sea level. This figure suggests a concentration of population because that area contains only about one-quarter of the total Great Basin territory (Harper 1986: 58). People evidently avoided the highest mountain ranges and the low flatlands and deserts because of climatic conditions and the consequent scarcity of resources. Of the Great Basin land mass as a whole, approximately one-fifth consists of desert characterized by shrubs; flatlands and grasslands typified by sagebrush and grasses constitute about 40 percent while an additional 40 percent consists of mountains and forests of juniper, piñon, oak, pine, aspen, and fir. In addition, there are marshes in basins and near lakes that, although small in area, provided people with rich nutrients (Madsen 1982; Harper 1986: 52–55).

Indigenous to the Great Basin were eight cultural groupings who, although differentiated, shared many practices and beliefs. Aboriginal nations included the Utes, Washoes, southern Paiutes (PA-yute), Owens

Valley Paiutes, and northern Paiutes (or Paviotsos). The eastern Shoshones (sho-SHO-nee), northern Shoshones, and western Shoshones were also indigenous to the Great Basin.

Given the environment, climate, and scarcity of resources, population densities were quite low, averaging about one person per 15 sq. mi. (Price 1980: 46). Among the highest were the Utes, possibly reaching as much as one person per square mile (Jorgensen 1980: 447), and the Washoes, who may have averaged about one person per 2.7 sq. mi. (Price 1980: 46).

With the exception of Washoe, all of the languages spoken by aboriginal people of the Great Basin belong to a linguistic family called Uto-Aztecan and constitute its northernmost branch, called Numic (Miller 1984). Numic languages include Mono, northern Paiute, Panimint, Shoshone, Comanche, Kawaiisu, and Ute. These language names do not coincide exactly with the names of cultural groupings. For instance, Mono is spoken by Owens Valley Paiutes, northern Paiute is spoken by northern Paiutes and Bannocks, while southern Paiutes speak a dialect of the Ute language. Most Shoshone groups speak the Shoshone language but others speak Panimint. In contrast to the other languages, Washoe is a member of a large linguistic family called Hokan, which contains thirteen branches located primarily in California.

There are today few monolingual speakers of Great Basin languages, but many people are bilingual in English and their mother tongue. The percentage of speakers of Native languages varies in different communities and for different age groups. People living on reservations are more likely to speak their Native language, while those living in small colonies near towns and cities are less likely to do so. According to Victor Golla's 2007 "Encyclopedia of the World's Endangered Languages," there are approximately 2,760 fluent speakers of Numic languages, with another 1,500 or so "passive speakers," that is, those who could understand the Numic languages but had difficulty communicating when speaking them (Moseley 2007). This number has decreased rapidly from the 6,769 who reported in the US Census of 2000 that one of the Numic languages was their "home language" (US Bureau of the Census 2000). Only several dozen fluent speakers of Washo exist, although the Washoe tribe has been successful at creating a K-8 immersion school (Moseley 2007). Most speakers of both Washo and the Numic languages are over fifty-five, indicating danger of language loss in a few generations. Given the linguistic

situation, numerous other projects are underway in many reservation communities to encourage and deepen young people's knowledge of their ancestral language.

Bearing in mind the unreliability of population estimates for aboriginal people in North America, Leland suggests a probable figure of approximately 40,000 for the Great Basin, an estimate based on a depopulation ratio of about 3.4:1 (depopulation refers to excess deaths occurring after contact with European and American traders and settlers due to the spread of foreign diseases, starvation resulting from depletion of natural resources, and deaths from warfare) (1986: 609). The first official population census of Great Basin people, made in 1873 after a sharp decline had occurred, listed a total of 21,544. The indigenous community continued to decrease until 1930 when they numbered approximately 12,000. Since then, their populations have slowly risen, but as of 1980 their number, estimated at about 29,000, had not yet achieved the pre-contact level. There are now forty-five officially recognized reservations and colonies in the Great Basin region. Some of these communities are inhabited by members of the same nation while others are made up of allied or confederated tribes. In addition, there are a number of unrecognized groups whose petitions for official status are pending before Congress. The largest proportion of Great Basin Indians live in Nevada (32%), followed by Idaho (17%), California (12%), Wyoming (12%), Colorado (11%), Utah (11%), and Oregon and Arizona (2.5% each) (Leland 1986: 613). According to the 2010 US Census, there are 55,473 people who identify as Great Basin people in these states. These statistics include those who identify as Ute, Washoe, Paiute, Shoshone, or Kawaiisu, Mono or Comanche (except for the Oklahoma Comanche).

ABORIGINAL CULTURE

Economies

Great Basin economies were based on foraging. Given the variability of environment and climate, plant and animal resources differed considerably from place to place, from season to season, and from year to year. Since adjacent territories might contain vastly different plants and animals, people needed extensive knowledge of the resources available in what Steward called "microenvironments" (Steward 1938). By necessity, people were nomadic, ready to shift their settlements in adjustment to resource availability. The contribution of various types of foods to the diet depended on ecological factors. People living near the few large lakes and rivers had diets that consisted mainly of fish and wild plants, supplemented by some animal meat. However, in other areas, particularly where animals were scarce and fish were entirely absent, plant resources accounted for the majority of the diet (Driver and Massey 1957; Morris et al. 1981).

Many kinds of plants were gathered and usually contributed the major share of the Native diet. In many areas, piñon nuts were a staple food. Harvesting of pine cones usually began in late summer and lasted into the fall. Acorns were also important although they were not as abundant and therefore not as critical to the food supply. Several varieties of beans made significant contributions, especially mesquite, screwbean, and agave. Seeds from cattail, rice-grass, and bullrush were gathered as well. Camas, other roots, and many kinds of greens such as amaranth leaves, thistles, and wild grasses were collected. Berries and fruits were also important to the aboriginal diet. Where possible, surplus foods were dried and cached in pits for future use. When necessary, people returned to their caches and retrieved the stored foods, but even these supplies were usually exhausted by the end of winter. Early spring before new plants had grown was often a difficult time of want (Kelly 1976: 22).

Plant cultivation was practiced only by a few societies in the southern Great Basin such as some southern Paiutes, Utes, and Shoshones. Sometime in the early or mid-nineteenth century, some southern Paiutes adopted farming techniques from their Native neighbors in the Southwest. They planted corn, squash, beans, sunflowers, and several varieties of melons. Fields were cleared and planted near rivers or lakes if possible, but elsewhere water was brought to the field from a spring through ditches. Small plots of an acre or so were farmed by one man; larger fields were tended by brothers or other relatives. Farming was commonly the responsibility of men but women assisted in most of the work as well. Aboriginal Paiute practices were observed by federal agents in southern Utah and Nevada in the mid-nineteenth century:

One of the chiefs, Que-o-gan, took me to his farm and showed me the main irrigating ditch which was to convey the water from the river to his land, which I found to be a half a mile long, four feet

wide, four feet deep, and had been dug principally through a gravel bed with wooden spades, and the dirt thrown out with their hands—the last being performed by the women and children while the men were employed in digging. He also showed me a dam, constructed of logs and brushwood, which he had made to turn a portion of the water from the river and convey it through the ditch. (Malouf 1966: 24)

Most other Basin peoples engaged in practices that manipulated their environment and exerted some control and direction to the natural resources. They encouraged the growth of wild plants through the broadcast sowing of wild seeds, irrigation, pruning of wild plants, and burning brush to stimulate productivity (Downs 1966b: 46–47).

Different species of animals were available in different regions. Among the larger were deer, bighorn sheep, elk, and antelope. More common were small animals such as rabbits, wood rats, badgers, gophers, squirrels, and mice. Buffalo were hunted only by the eastern Utes and Shoshones who lived on the fringes of the western Plains. The most frequently sought bird species were grouse, larks, and waterfowl such as ducks, geese, and swans. In the lakes and rivers that formed in some areas, people fished for sturgeon, chub, salmon, trout, carp, and whitefish. Lizards, snakes, and insects were also common foods. Most hunting was done individually, but where deer were available, communal hunts were organized in the fall. Rabbits were often taken in drives in the winter with the assistance of women and children. Among southern Paiutes, boys participated in hunting as soon as they were able, but they could not eat the meat of animals they had caught lest they become lazy. Instead, they donated their catch to elderly men and women in their camps (Kelly 1976: 47). The Washoe caught many hundreds of rabbits in fall communal drives organized by a "rabbit leader" who had spirit powers. The animals were driven into nets sometimes measuring 300 ft. in length (Downs 1966a: 27). The general scarcity of animals was reflected not only in the diet but also in the paucity of clothing that people wore since they had only meager supplies of animal hides. Adults wore little clothing and children usually wore none at all. Women's clothing consisted of skirts made of bark or woven fibers reaching from the waist to the knee. Men wore breechcloths made of animal hides. Moccasins were worn only in very cold weather or when travelling on unusually rough terrain. Instead, people sometimes coated the soles of their feet with pine pitch in order to protect their skin (Malouf 1966: 3). The most common type of overgarment was a cape or robe made of rabbit skins since these were the most plentiful animals in the region. The skins were hung loose or woven to make the garment. Rabbit skin robes were also used as bedding and as insulation to cover water bottles when the weather was hot (3). Since rabbit skins were often infested with lice, some people cleaned them by placing them over anthills so that insects would eat the lice.

Economic tasks were ideally assigned according to gender. Women were responsible for collecting plants, seeds, and nuts while men contributed by hunting and fishing. However, in most societies actual work roles were not rigidly differentiated. Instead, people cooperated in the performance of many tasks, especially communal hunting drives and harvesting of piñon nuts when they became abundant.

Among their crafts, people of the Great Basin are best known for their basketry. Women produced baskets using several techniques such as twining, coiling, and plaiting. They most commonly employed bark and fibers of willow, juniper, yucca, and sumac. Their products included open burden baskets, conical-shaped gathering baskets, trays for winnowing and parching seeds and nuts, baskets for catching fish, roasting trays, gathering scoops, and seed beaters. Baskets for carrying water and boiling foods were made watertight by coating them with pine pitch and/or clay. Articles of clothing such as woven capes, aprons, hats, and sandals were made from fibers as well.

Settlements

People lived in small, temporary encampments in most areas, although near lakes and rivers larger, more stable villages were possible. While the lack of reliable food sources required a nomadic existence, people's mobility was somewhat restricted due to the need to be near sources of water. Camps were ideally located near springs, but when people travelled from one resource site to another, they carried water in large baskets (or "ollas") that held no more than 2 gallons of water. According to Steward, "A two-day trip would require one and a half ollas of water. The burden would include 27 pounds of water, all essential equipment, varying amounts of food, and perhaps an infant or small child. In view of the loads and the slow pace, 15 or 20 miles is probably the maximum daily travel, which would limit a two-day travel between water holes to 30 or 40 miles" (Steward 1970: 120–121).

Members of the southern branch of the Paiute tribe, camped near Mendocino. They live in wickiups—huts of stick and brush fastened to poles made from willow trees.

Several kinds of dwellings were constructed depending on the permanence of residence and the climate. Southern Paiutes built conical houses made of a frame of juniper poles set in the ground in a circular formation and covered with layers of juniper bark. The floor was covered with bark to increase comfort and provide insulation. House size varied depending on the number of expected occupants. Caves or rock shelters were also utilized in the winter. In the summer, sunshades and light circular enclosures made of poles with a covering of willow branches or other materials were erected. The sides of such shelters were either covered with willow matting or left open, depending upon the weather. Washoe houses were of two types. "Winter houses," built in locations of permanent settlements, were round structures about 10–20 ft. in diameter supported by long poles set in a circle and tied together at the top. The poles were covered with bark slabs tied with willow thongs or with bundles of grass or willow. Such houses usually were the domicile of as many as ten people. In the summertime, small domed dwellings made of brush woven together were erected in temporary camps. People also found shelter in windbreaks and sunscreens made of willow and brush leaned against a wooden frame. Ute habitation also consisted of several kinds of dwellings, some more permanent than others. Domed-shaped houses made of willow, approximately 8 ft. high and 15 ft. in diameter were common. They were covered with willow branches, brush or bark. Utes also constructed tipis made of buffalo or elk hides for temporary use in summer and winter.

Territory was not owned by individuals or groups, but there was a sense that certain resource areas were controlled by the people who habitually used them. Control of springs and seeps was particularly important. For example, although southern Paiutes considered most of their resources and territory to be available for use by all members of the community, springs were recognized as the property of kin groups who regularly resided nearby. Other valuable resources were sometimes claimed by individuals or groups. Ownership of piñon trees was claimed by the women who harvested them. Eagle nests were also privately owned, usually by members of a nearby community. Eagles were not eaten, but their feathers were used for arrows and also had ceremonial value. Ownership of aeries was inherited from father to son (Kelly 1976: 92–93). For all Basin nations, however, resources, whether water or plants, were never withheld from people from other areas who were in the vicinity. Usually as a courtesy, the visiting group asked permission of the resident community, but their request was never denied.

Families and Social Systems

Settlements were composed of a small number of related nuclear families forming a "cluster" of people who cooperated and shared resources and support (Steward 1970: 131). Kinship was organized by principles of bilateral descent. In addition to the region-wide formation of bilateral kindreds, the Washoe probably had patrilineal, nonexogamous moieties (Lowie 1939). The functions of moieties are uncertain although they seem to have had a role in organizing and identifying families who congregated together for fall pine nut harvesting. At that time, people evidently camped in specific sections of a settlement according to moiety membership and may have decorated themselves with white or red paint to identify their group (Freed 1960). Since comparable systems are lacking in other Great Basin societies, it is possible that the moiety system was borrowed from Miwoks or other Native nations of California with whom Washoes had close social and economic relations.

Residence after marriage was flexible, the new couple living in the camp of either the wife or husband. An initial period of uxorilocal residence was common but not mandatory. Independent nuclear families allied themselves with others to whom they were related, forming a group of cooperating members. The composition of these "family clusters" was not stable since people could and did change their association from one cluster to others depending upon changes in resource availability, group composition, or personal preferences. Flexibility and adaptability were critical to the continuation and survival of aboriginal societies since the resources upon which people relied were not always available, changing from year to year depending upon cycles of natural growth as well as variations in climatic conditions. According to Downs, "the freedom of the small social unit to make its own decisions within limitations of Basin environment, and the freedom of individuals to shift from group to group and choose their own alternatives without reference to even the smallest of units is one of the most significant social facts of Basin life" (Downs 1966b: 42).

The size of communities varied from area to area depending upon the abundance or scarcity of resources but an aggregate of five families was probably the norm

(Steward 1970). These small residential and cooperating groups were not isolated, however, since bonds of blood and marriage linked one encampment to others nearby and even to groups in more distant territories. In some areas, larger concentrations of people were possible either annually or seasonally because of more abundant resources.

In addition to local units, some groups, such as the Washoes and Utes, formed regional communities or bands. Washoes recognized regional communities that tended to exploit particular resource areas and live in identified places. Members of such communities were likely to be linked either through descent or marriage. They might on occasion cooperate together in economic pursuits and attend communal feasts and festivals. Intermarriage and exchange of resources added to the cohesiveness of regional communities, but they lacked permanent unity and structured leadership. Rather, leadership was vested in the head of a family or cluster of families. These men or women were consulted and gave advice to members of their families. They were older people with proven skills and success and embodied valued personality traits of generosity, peacefulness, and modesty. The heads of large families or clusters sometimes were recognized as leaders or spokespeople of their local communities. These people, usually men, represented their communities in interactions with other such groups (Downs 1966a: 45). Utes were organized into a number of bands that were named for geographic features in their area or for food resources that were particularly abundant. These bands, possibly numbering a dozen or so, were territorial groups whose actual composition might vary from year to year as people and families shifted their membership from one to another. Bands had leaders who were respected and recognized for their abilities. They were men of skill, intelligence, and valued personality traits who organized communal activities and helped settle disputes but who lacked coercive or regulatory powers.

Consistent with the small community size characteristic of the region and the necessary flexibility of settlements and economic pursuits, leadership was informal and flexible. Local groups often had a leader who was the head of a family cluster and was respected because of his abilities, knowledge of the territory, sound judgment, and oratorical skills. Leaders did not have coercive powers but rather were heeded because of the respect that they engendered. If their abilities or judgment diminished, they were ignored in favor of others who showed themselves worthy. Leaders gave advice and organized the few communal economic activities that occurred from time to time such as hunting drives and piñon harvesting. Among the southern Paiutes, camp leaders occasionally addressed their communities in the early morning from the doorway of their house or from a nearby hilltop, giving advice and instruction about hunting and the movement of camps. They admonished people to "be good, not to fight, not to steal" (Kelly 1976: 27). Leaders also hosted visitors to their communities. They had little or no role in settling disputes. Instead, disputes were solved by the independent actions of the people directly concerned.

Family clusters often came together in larger concentrations, even including members of other nations, for festivals and feasting that took place at the time of the fall piñon harvest or animal hunting drives. These communal activities might last several days or more than a week. At that time people cooperated in economic activities, shared resources, and socialized. These were times of dancing and gaming, as well as occasions for intergroup and interregional trade. A great variety of goods was exchanged, including animal skins, rabbit skin robes, moccasins, and resources that were available in particular areas such as dried fish, ornamental shells, obsidian, tobacco, feathers, and ceremonial paints.

EUROPEAN INVASIONS OF THE GREAT BASIN

Because of the scarce resources and inhospitable climate and topography of the Great Basin, indigenous nations were spared the early invasions of their territory by Spanish military, missionaries, and traders that occurred in the surrounding regions of the Southwest and California beginning in the middle of the sixteenth century. Although direct foreign incursions did not occur until the late eighteenth century, Native people were influenced by European contact through neighboring groups. They received goods through aboriginal trading networks from the Southwest and California and some acquired horses from Plains nations. Horses became central to the economy and group composition of some eastern and northern Utes and Shoshones, who were thus able to exploit animal resources, particularly buffalo, on the western plains adjacent to the Great Basin.

Direct contact with the Spanish occurred in the late eighteenth century when expeditions attempted to find a route connecting the provincial capital at Sante Fe, New Mexico, to California. The Utes had the dubious honor of being the first among Great Basin nations to meet Spanish explorers. In 1776, an expedition led by two Franciscan priests, Francisco Dominguez and Silvestre Velez de Escalante, made a brief and uneventful incursion into Ute territory near present-day Utah Lake. They were followed by others during the next several decades. Then in 1805, the American explorers Meriwether Lewis and William Clark travelled through Shoshone territory in Idaho. Soon afterward, American and Canadian trappers entered the region from the north and east, while more Spanish traders came from the Southeast and Southwest in violation of Spanish colonial regulations forbidding individual commerce with Indians. Spanish influence was also reflected by the growth of the slave trade. Native people, especially women and children, were frequently captured and taken as slaves to New Mexico to work on farms and in households as domestics.

Ute communities in southern Utah and Colorado had early contact with Spaniards based in the Southwest. Beginning in the late seventeenth century, Utes raided Spanish settlements in New Mexico, especially taking horses. Once on horseback, they attacked Puebloan communities in New Mexico and northeastern Arizona. Utes also ranged further west in the Great Basin, raiding Shoshone and southern Paiute communities. For several decades, they were unchallenged among Great Basin nations because of their ability to make sudden and rapid incursions on horseback and to retreat as quickly as they had come. They also ranged to the south, entering Navajo territory in northern New Mexico and Arizona by the middle of the eighteenth century and pushing the Navajo out of their traditional homeland. With the expansion of the Spanish slave trade, Utes captured members of other Native nations to sell to the Spaniards as domestic workers or ranch hands and shepherds. With the use of horses, Utes were able to effectively utilize resources on the Plains. And, during the summer, they congregated in groups of at least 200 lodges, many more than had been possible in pre-contact times (Jorgensen 1972: 29). But the Utes faced enemies to the east when Plains nations such as the Arapahos, Lakotas, Cheyennes, and Comanches entered their hunting territories.

When Spanish rule ended in 1821, official authority passed to the Mexican government, but the Mexicans never exerted control over the Great Basin although their traders and slave raiders frequently entered the region, particularly on its southern periphery. American and Canadian traders and trappers stepped up their activities in the region as well. Hudson's Bay Company merchants came from the north into Idaho and Oregon, while traders from the Rocky Mountain Fur Company, based in St. Louis, entered both from the north and the east. Native people subsequently acquired weapons, tools, and some items of clothing.

AMERICAN CONTROL IN THE GREAT BASIN

By the middle of the nineteenth century, European and American traders, explorers, and settlers created conditions that led to devastating changes in Native nations. As elsewhere in North America, diseases of European origin spread quickly and took a great toll in health and lives. Slave raiding became even more acute after the 1830s when new routes and trails were opened through Paiute territory. In 1839, for example, a trader named Thomas Farnham commented that Paiutes were "Hunted in the spring of the year, when weak and helpless, by a certain class of men, and when taken, are fattened, carried to Sante Fe and sold as slaves during their minority. A likely girl in her teens brings often times sixty or eighty pounds. The males are valued less" (1843: 11). As a result of the intensity of the slave trade and the spread of European diseases, Native populations declined rapidly. According to Garland Hurt, an Indian agent to the southern Paiutes, "Scarcely one half of the Py-eed children are permitted to grow up in a band; and a large majority of these being males, this and other causes are tending to depopulate their bands very rapidly" (Hurt 1876: 462).

In addition to population losses, the fragile balance that aboriginal people had maintained with their environment and its resources was destroyed. Trails and trade routes cut through areas of most abundant resources and water, destroying habitats of many of the plants and animals that people had depended upon for centuries. Land near rivers and lakes was particularly devastated. Indians were pushed out of the most plentiful areas, resulting in pressure on remaining resources that the environment could not bear. As natural resources were depleted, people either resisted or withdrew into even more remote regions. Water sources were especially the targets of expropriation, depriving the indigenous population of their most essential life-sustaining resource. As early as 1843, less than fifty years after initial European penetration in the region, Charles Preuss, accompanying the explorer John Fremont, noted: "The white people have ruined the country of the Snake Indians [northern Paiutes]. Almost all the Natives are now obliged to live on roots, game can scarcely be seen any more" (Gudde and Gudde 1958: 86). His comments apply equally well to members of other Native nations.

Permanent White settlements were established in midcentury, especially by Mormons (members of the Church of Jesus Christ of Latter Day Saints). They came to Utah in 1847 even though at that time the region was nominally Mexican territory, first settling in the Salt Lake Valley between the territories of Utes and Shoshones. Although Mormons ostensibly hoped to avoid conflict with the indigenous population, their very presence created environmental, economic, and cultural pressures on Native communities. Despite official policies of noninterference, Native territory was occupied and Indian communities and cultures were disturbed and transformed, especially through missionary activity, which was motivated in part by the belief that aboriginal people of the Americas were descendants of one of the ten lost tribes of Israel (Malouf 1966:20). As the Mormon population increased, Ute and Shoshone land was occupied and water from their rivers was diverted for Mormon use. Missionary activity had a serious impact on Native families as well because Mormons attempted to "adopt" Indian children into their own households and educate them in Christian beliefs and behaviors.

After the discovery of gold in California in the mid-nineteenth century, more travelers trespassed on Native territory. Those who journeyed through the region disturbed the floral and faunal resources, and settlers who remained consumed grasses, seeds, and roots without regard to conservation or natural balance that had been fundamental principles underlying aboriginal resource adaptation. Animals were either hunted or driven from their former habitats both by the expanding settlements and the loss of vegetation upon which they fed. As a result of combined environmental changes and diminution of available resources, Indians were unable to maintain an adequate level of subsistence. Many succumbed to European diseases and to widespread malnutrition.

In response to American expansion and in their desperate economic situation, some Indians raided livestock held by settlers. As F. Dodge, an Indian agent of the period, observed: "The encroachments of the Emigrant have driven away the game upon which they [Native people] depend for subsistence. They must therefore steal or starve" (Knack and Stewart 1984: 65). Armed conflict grew more serious as the US Army tried to exert control. When federal agents were to the region, Indians often complained about the encroachment of settlers on their territory, the disruption of the natural habitat and the diverting of their water supplies. For example, in 1855, one of the federal agents, Armstrong, reported:

> The chief complained to me that they could not catch their usual supply of fish, in consequence of some of the citizens using seines and nets to their disadvantage…The Indians then attempted to take fish in their usual way, that of trapping, shooting with bow and arrow, etc. But in consequence of the high stage of water in the river, they were unable to catch but a few … The chiefs frequently complained that they now had no place of safety where their animals could feed as in former years, in consequence of so much land having been improved and fenced by the settlers. (Malouf 1966: 21–22)

The discovery of gold and silver in Nevada brought even more prospectors and settlers, touching off a renewed cycle of resource depletion, Native resistance or impoverishment, and armed conflict. In 1860, northern Paiutes living near Pyramid Lake and the Humboldt Sink resisted settler expansion in the so-called Pyramid Lake War, followed a few years later by Goshiutes and eastern Shoshones, who defended their territory after the confiscation of more than two dozen waterholes by overland stage routes. The "Owens Valley War" erupted in 1862 and 1864 when Owens Valley Paiutes acted for similar reasons. In all cases, the American army overcame Native resistance and "pacified" the region. Afterward, more than a dozen treaties were signed in which the original inhabitants agreed to cede much of their territory to the United States and were assigned to reservations, usually away from areas of settlements, in return for guarantees on the land that they retained. However, many of the treaties were never ratified by Congress and the government's promises of protection were never fulfilled. Instead, the Native land base was further eroded by agreements signed in the late nineteenth and early twentieth centuries with consequent deterioration of economic conditions. Captain Sam, a Shoshone leader, told federal agent Levi Gheen in 1876:

> The game was all gone; trees that bore pine nuts cut down and burned in the quartz mills and other places; the grass seeds, heretofore used by them for food, was no more; the grassland all claimed by and cultivated by the white people; and that his Indians would soon be compelled to work for the ranchers for two bits (25 cents) a day or starve. (Malouf 1966: 30–31)

Even though reservations were established for all indigenous nations of the region, less than 60 percent of the Native population actually lived on them because of the poor conditions of the land, particularly its unsuitability for farming and scarcity of water.

Consistent with the federal government's attempts to alter the values and behavior of Native people, education was advocated as a means of indoctrinating children. C. S. Young, a superintendent of public instruction in Nevada, commented in 1887:

> Our Nevada Indians should be educated. They are now an important factor in our western civilization. They should be taught how to work, how to make a living; should be taught the principles underlying our government, and the duties of citizenship. They should be taught not only to read and write, but the various trades, domestic work, ranching, all kinds of handiwork. Then they might be substituted for Chinese servants, or other people foreign to our institutions and obnoxious to our American civilization. (Stewart 1978: 105–106)

After passage of the General Allotment Act of 1887, much of reservation land was allotted even though most Indians either did not understand the procedures or opposed them. For instance, when allotments were to be made on Ute reservations, the people objected, preferring to hold their land in common as they had always done. Their resistance was unheeded even though federal agents were well aware of their opposition. One agent, H. P. Myton, wrote:

> If the consent of the Indians is necessary to be obtained in order to open the Uintah reservation, it will be useless for Congress to pass any more laws or spend any more money for that purpose, for I do not believe there is an Indian on the reservation who is willing or favors selling any part of their land. (Jorgensen 1972: 53)

But Congress did pass laws and did spend money for allotting Native land. As a consequence of congressional provisions that allowed "homesteading" on "surplus land" and permitted allottees to sell their parcels, the land base controlled by Native people dwindled once again.

THE GHOST DANCE

In the context of monumental environmental, economic, and political changes that had wrought devastation in Native communities, a new religion was born to bring hope to the people. Sometime in the mid-1860s, a northern Paiute (Paviotso) man named Wodziwob had visions of a ritual and dance that Indians should perform in order to revitalize their communities, restore the environment and its resources, and bring the dead back to life. In order to hasten and celebrate this occurrence, Wodziwob taught that people should perform a round dance with men and women alternating in a circle and interlocking their fingers. The dances, accompanied by special songs, were to be performed for at least five nights in succession. During the dancing, some participants received visions, acquiring new songs and communicating their wishes to the spirit world. The "Ghost Dance," as it came to be known, thus reinforced elements of traditional Great Basin beliefs and practices, including the importance of personal visionary experience and contact with the spirit world as well as a ceremonial emphasis on mourning rituals that honored the dead. Jorgensen, (following Aberle 1966), refers to the first Ghost Dance as "a transformative movement" (1972: 6–9). It focused on a rejection of the conditions of life that existed for Native people at that time and a spiritual transformation in which the world would be magically rid of White trespassers, aboriginal resources would be restored, and the dead would return.

The Ghost Dance spread rapidly throughout the Great Basin and further into California and Oregon. It was inaugurated and accepted at a time of devastating changes in indigenous communities. The people's land had been taken, their resources depleted, and their independence and autonomy abrogated. They were assigned limited territory on reservations that lacked the resources to sustain them. In a state of economic loss, population decline due to disease and warfare, and oppressive military and governmental actions, the people hoped for a new beginning. From its origin in Nevada, the Ghost Dance was taught to Paiutes, Utes, and Shoshones in Nevada, Utah, Colorado, Wyoming, and Idaho, where it was frequently performed in the 1870s and early 1880s. By the middle of the 1880s, however, Ghost Dance practices had dissipated among Great Basin people. But then, on January 1, 1889, during an eclipse of the sun, another northern Paiute man named Wovoka (also known by his English name, Jack Wilson) experienced a series of visionary revelations. He was taken by spirit beings into heaven to meet with God: "When the sun died, I went up to heaven and saw God and all the people who had died a long time ago. God told me to come back and tell my people they must be good and love one another, and not fight, or steal or lie. He gave me this dance to give to my people" (Mooney 1965: 2). Wovoka's message emphasized the transformation that should be sought within the individual and in Native communities. People were admonished to live according to aboriginal ethical principles, to be good and help one another, to cooperate and treat each other kindly. During a visionary experience, God showed Wovoka the land of the dead and told him that the living would be reunited with their deceased loved ones if they followed the ways that he set out for them. God told Wovoka, "You must not fight. Do no harm to anyone. Do always right. If people faithfully obey the instruction, there will be no more death or sickness or old age" (171–172). Wovoka taught moral lessons to Native communities and foretold God's plan that the world as it was would soon come to an end. According to this prophesy, the earth would tremble mightily at that time and the dead would be brought back to earth, led by a spirit figure in the shape of a misty cloud. Wovoka told the believers, "When the earth shakes do not be afraid, it will not hurt you." In Jorgensen's terms, this new movement was "redemptive," focusing not on a transformation of external conditions but rather on changes within individuals and communities that would enable people to cope with the external situations understood as unalterable. Moral admonitions to be peaceful, industrious, truthful, cooperative, and generous were at the center of Wovoka's teachings. Wovoka's original message was one of peace, cooperation, and harmony but as it spread to communities throughout the Great Basin and into the Plains, the message was reinterpreted and adapted to local beliefs and to local economic and social circumstances. In the Plains particularly, it took on a more urgent, apocalyptic message seeking the immediate reversal of external conditions, the disappearance of Whites, and the return of the dead.

By the end of the nineteenth century, Ghost Dance practices had waned in the Great Basin. And with the massacre of more than 300 Lakotas at Wounded Knee, South Dakota, in December 1890, the Ghost Dance religion was crushed in the Plains. But it survives today in some Native communities in the western United States and Canada, although in somewhat different form (Kehoe 1989).

CONTEMPORARY BASIN COMMUNITIES

By the middle of the twentieth century, Native communities were beginning to regain a small percentage of the territory they had lost. When allotments of land and their sale ended in the 1930s under the administration of BIA director John Collier, the Native land base was made more secure. Additional acreage was added to reservations with funds provided by Congress. But even before these policies were initiated, some Native groups in the Great Basin filed suit against the US government in order to regain territory or at least be compensated for land that had been illegally taken. The first case was settled in 1910, awarding the Utes $3.5 million. After establishment of the Indian Claims Commission in 1946, additional suits were brought by Native claimants. The total funds awarded in compensation amounted to more than $130 million for all of the Great Basin petitioners (US Indian Claims Commission 1980).

In the early years of the claim period, most of the money received was divided among tribal members, but since the actual amounts distributed per capita were relatively small, they provided only a temporary boost to household income. Since the 1960s, in contrast, most Native nations utilized the majority of funds for tribal purposes and investments in the future. They established tribal enterprises, sought to improve living conditions, and build or upgrade reservation infrastructure (Bennett 1972).

In a major land claims settlement of 1999, the Utes signed an agreement with the federal government that returns some 84,000 acres to the Uintah and Ouray

Reservation in northern Utah. The land was originally part of the reservation but was appropriated by the United States in 1916 because it wanted access to shale oil deposits in the region. The land has since become seriously contaminated with more than 10 tons of low-level radioactive waste because of industrial milling on the site. In the document of land transfer, the Utes have agreed to contribute toward the projected $300 million cost of clean-up by donating 8.5 percent of their future mineral royalties from oil sales elsewhere on their 4.5-million-acre reservation (U.S. Is Returning 84,000 Acres to Indians 2000.). Another incident, still pending, occurred in 2014 when the Confederated Tribes of the Goshute Reservation (a Utah tribe of western Shoshone) along with the Great Basin Water Network sued the Bureau of Land Management and Department of Interior for their decision to construct a water pipeline starting in the ancestral lands of the Goshute (Confederated Tribes of the Goshute Reservation 2014). The pipeline would pump large amounts of water away from the reservation, causing cultural and environmental repercussions for the Goshute.

Economic conditions in Native communities vary considerably although certain common traits are attested. Reservations that have received large land claims awards have invested in tribal enterprises, provided welfare and social services, increased tribal employment, and set aside scholarships for young people. The economies of some groups are enhanced by income from royalties and leases to national corporations for resource extraction. However, while some reservations such as Wind River (Shoshone), southern Ute, Walker River, and Ute Mountain have benefitted from relatively large revenues, others receive only small amounts of money while still others lack resources for exploration and extraction. The success of tribally owned enterprises is also uneven. Some tribes operate campgrounds, small retail stores, construction companies, and fish hatcheries that employ the local population and earn income for the tribe, but other communities have not been able to generate enough capital or income for investment. In addition, the ancient art of basketry provides some Basin women with income. Employing aboriginal techniques and materials while incorporating both traditional and modern designs, they have found a profitable market, selling their baskets to shops throughout the United States.

The economic situation for Native residents does not measure well when compared to that of their non-Indian neighbors. On larger reservations, most employment is associated with tribal administration, the delivery of services in healthcare, education, and welfare, and in construction and maintenance of roads and housing. However, on small reservations and "colonies" where the majority of Great Basin Indians reside, rates of unemployment are higher due to the lack of tribal enterprises or government agencies that can provide jobs.

Data obtained by the US Bureau of the Census reporting for 2010 indicate low per capita incomes in most Indian communities. Table 12.1 presents figures for income and for percentages of families and individuals living in poverty. Note that these figures are averages combining all reservations for each nation. In some cases, significant disparities are attested in different communities. For example, while the per capita income for reservation Utes is $16,474, local averages range from a low of $12,005 at Ute Mountain to a high of $20,834 at the Ignacio CCD (census county division), in the Southern Ute Indian Reservation. For comparison, note that per capita income in Nevada was $25,284 while it was $22,059 in Utah. Unemployment rates also vary in the Great Basin, from a low of 16.2 percent at Pyramid Lake to a high of 35.4 percent at Walker River These numbers compare unfavorably with Great Basin states. The unemployment rate in Nevada in 2010 was 9.0 percent and in Utah, only 5.9 percent (US Census Bureau 2010).

TABLE 12.1	Selected Economic Characteristics for Great Basin Tribes

	Income ($)	
	Per Capita	**Household**
Paiutes	21,262	32,152
Utes	16,472	38,373
Washoes	21,283	47,763

	Below Poverty (%)	
	Families	**Individuals**
Paiutes	22.4	24.6
Utes	17.5	20.8
Washoes	23.0	27.7

Source: US Bureau of the Census 2011.

In recent years, the issue of Native hunting rights has become a significant test of treaty guarantees. In 1978, the US District Court of Colorado confirmed the rights of people at Ute Mountain to hunt off-reservation for subsistence needs and for religious or ceremonial purposes. While Utes must adhere to tribal hunting regulations, they need not obtain state licenses and may hunt at times when non-Indian hunting is prohibited.

Acknowledging that Native people rely on scarce water resources both for household use and economic development, tribal governments have sought to protect their rights to water. In 1908, the US Supreme Court handed down a ruling in *Winter's v. United States* (now known as the "Winter's Doctrine") affirming that when reservations were established in the nineteenth century, the people's right to water for present and future needs was also confirmed. But since then, states and local business interests have repeatedly abridged Native access to water by diverting water to industrial or utility uses. In some cases, Indian communities have taken their claims for water to federal courts but have had a mixed record of success in gaining recognition of their aboriginal rights. For example, after years of litigation, the Pyramid Lake Paiutes lost an appeal to the Supreme Court in 1983 stemming from their attempts to preserve the water supply of

Pyramid Lake that would have sustained Native fisheries. Instead, the courts have permitted the century-old practice of non-Indian diversion of indigenous water sources, in this case by allowing water to be taken from the Truckee River that feeds Pyramid Lake (Knack and Stewart 1984). However, an agreement signed between the Pyramid Lake Paiute Tribe and the US government in 1999 reversed the usual trend by granting Paiutes control of management of the Truckee River. The agreement is especially significant because although Pyramid Lake is located on the Paiute Reservation, the Truckee River is not. The Paiutes planned to use their control of the river to replenish the supply of water in Pyramid Lake and to thus aid the recovery of cutthroat trout and other species of endangered fish indigenous to the lake. In 2008 the agreement was finalized and the Tribe has already published Water Quality Ordinances and reviews the Water Control Quality Plan every three years (Wright 2015). The Tribe monitors three tribal fish hatcheries, collects fees from recreational fishing, camping and boating, and manages monthly water sampling and the regulation of water rights. The 2015 review outlines several future projects, including pollution management, low water flow studies, and several scientific research initiatives.

In order to develop energy efficiency and conservation, the Moapa Band of Paiute Indians in Nevada is embarking on the construction of a solar energy project that will deliver efficient electricity without the use of water, a scarce resource in their arid territory. The Paiutes are particularly dedicated to developing clean energy because of their current location within sight of a coal-powered plant, the Reid Gardner Generating Station. The people assert that illnesses and deaths have been caused by pollution emanating from the plant even though federal authorities say that population numbers of the Moapa Band are too small to allow statistical verification.

Calvin Meyers (far right) of the Moapa Paiute Tribes makes a statement during a 2003 US Nuclear Regulatory Commission hearing in southern Nevada about plans for full-scale safety tests on nuclear waste shipping casks.

The Moapa Paiutes are one of many Native American tribes who are concerned about balancing the issue of the energy development and protections of human health and the environment. Reservations whose lands are located near coal-burning plants to produce energy are particularly in danger since coal burning releases carbon monoxide, sulfur dioxide, and other pollutants into the air. Respiratory ailments and heart disease can result from continual exposure. Children are especially at risk for developing health problems that may last a lifetime and many elderly people already have compromised health, making them vulnerable as well.

The Paiutes are not alone in this predicament. The Ute Indian Tribe in Utah is concerned about pollution coming from a Deseret Power plant where emissions result in ozone readings that are about twice the limit that the Environmental Protection Agency considers safe. Nationwide, about 10 percent of all power plants are located on or near Indian lands, affecting 48 tribes living on 50 reservations even though Native Americans account for less than 2 percent of the US population. Despite the health risks and environmental concerns, many tribal governments allow energy companies to operate in their territories because of the need to provide jobs for their residents. Given the high rates of unemployment on most rural reservations, the benefit of jobs is hard to resist. Still, many groups are attempting to impose limits on energy production and safeguards to protect their citizens.

The Ute Mountain Ute Tribe in Colorado is participating in a Food Systems Capacity Building Project under the guidance of the First Nations Development Institute. The Ute project focuses on developing a community garden accompanied by outreach and educational activities centered on conservation and sustainable farming practices.

Since the 1970s, many tribes have sponsored local historical projects to gather data regarding their communities. A number of "people's histories" have been published, some detailing tribal histories and others presenting the reflections and reminiscences of tribal members (Jefferson et al. 1972; Johnson 1975; Fallon Paiute-Shoshone Tribe 1977; Inter-Tribal Council of Nevada 1976a,b). Some of these projects are sponsored by local funds while others have been supported by the Inter-Tribal Council of Nevada, an organization formed in 1963 that is dedicated to the protection and promotion of Native interests. As a unified group representing the disparate Indian communities in the state, the Council is better able to advocate for Native rights and coordinate activities for the common interest.

Traditional ways of interacting and organizing households and communities persist in some Basin communities. Clusters of households related to one another through bilateral kinship form the core of group social and economic activities among southern Paiutes and others (Bunte and Franklin 1987: 244). These family clusters control land and make decisions concerning its use. After marriage, a couple typically resides with the family of either spouse but, as in prior times, couples may change their residence from one family cluster to another to which they are related, depending upon availability of land and resources as well as personal preferences. Marriage to a member of the community is preferred although not always possible.

Modern communities have both formal and informal leadership. Members of elected tribal councils are responsible for managing tribal funds and programs, but communities also have informal leadership very much in the traditional style. These leaders, both men and women, are elders who have valued skills and knowledge that they impart through advice and example to community members. In addition, they often have spirit powers received in visions and dreams (275).

REFERENCES

Bennett, Robert. 1972. "Building Indian Economies with Land Settlement Funds." *The Emergent Native American* (ed. D. Walker). Boston, MA: Little, Brown & Company, pp. 693–702.

Bunte, Pamela, and Robert Franklin. 1987. *From the Sands to the Mountain: Change and Persistence in a Southern Paiute Community*. Lincoln, NE: University of Nebraska Press.

Confederated Tribes of the Goshute Reservation. 2014. *Confederated Tribes of the Goshute Reservation Join Water Coalition*. Ibapah, UT: Confederated Tribes of the Goshute Reservation Press Release. Online.

Downs, James. 1966a. *The Two Worlds of the Washo*. New York: Holt, Rinehart, & Winston.

Downs, James. 1966b. "The Significance of Environmental Manipulation in Great Basin Cultural Development." *The Current Status of Anthropological Research in the Great Basin, 1964* (ed. W. D'Azevedo et al.). Reno, NV: Desert Research Institute, pp. 39–56.

Driver, Harold, and William Massey. 1957. "Comparative Studies of North American Indians." *Transactions of the American Philosophical Society*, no. 47 (2): 165–456.

Fallon Paiute-Shoshone Tribe. 1977. *After the Drying Up of the Water*. Fallon, NV: Fallon Paiute-Shoshone Tribe.

Farnham, Thomas. 1843. *Travels in the Great Western Prairies*. New York: Greeley & McElrath.

"The Flow of Power: Paiute's Control of the Truckee River Bodes Well for Fish and Waterways." 2000. *American Indian Report*. February, p. 24.

Freed, Stanley. 1960. "Changing Washoe Kinship." *University of California Anthropological Records* 14, no. 6: 349–418.

Gudde, Erwin, and Elizabeth Gudde (eds.). 1958. *Exploring with Fremont: The Private Diaries of Charles Preuss*. Norman, OK: University of Oklahoma Press.

Harper, Kimball. 1986. "Historical Environments." *Great Basin* (ed. W. D'Azevedo), Vol. 11 of *Handbook of North American Indians*. Washington, DC: Smithsonian Institution, pp. 51–63.

Hurt, Garland. 1876. "Indians of Utah." *Report of Explorations across the Great Basin* (ed. J. Simpson). Washington, DC: US Government Printing Office, pp. 459–464.

Inter-Tribal Council of Nevada. 1976a. *Numa: A Northern Paiute history*. Reno, NV: Inter-Tribal Council of Nevada.

Inter-Tribal Council of Nevada. 1976b. *Nuwuvi: A Southern Paiute history*. Reno, NV: Inter-Tribal Council of Nevada.

Jefferson, James *et al.* 1972. *The Southern Utes: A Tribal History*. Ignacio, CO: The Southern Ute Tribe.

Johnson, Edward. 1975. *Walker River Paiutes: A Tribal History*. Schurz, NV: Walker River Paiute Tribe.

Jorgensen, Joseph. 1972. *The Sun Dance Religion: Power for the Powerless*. Chicago, IL: University of Chicago Press.

Jorgensen, Joseph. 1980. *Western Indians: Comparative Environments, Languages and Cultures of 172 Western American Indian Tribes*. San Francisco, CA: W.H. Freeman.

Kehoe, Alice. 1989. *The Ghost Dance: Ethnohistory and Revitalization*. New York: Holt, Rinehart, Winston.

Kelly, Isabel. 1976. *Southern Paiute Ethnography*. New York: Garland Publishers.

Knack, Martha, and Omer Stewart. 1984. *As Long as the River Shall Run: An Ethnohistory of Pyramid Lake Indian Reservation*. Berkeley, CA: University of California Press.

Leland, Joy. 1986. "Population." *Great Basin* (ed. W. D'Azevedo), Vol. 11 of *Handbook of North American Indians*. Washington, DC: Smithsonian Institution, pp. 608–619.

Lowie, Robert. 1939. "Ethnographic Notes on the Washo." *Publications in American Archeology and Anthropology* 36, no. 5: 301–352.

Madsen, David. 1982. "Get It Where the Gettin's Good: A Variable Model of Great Basin Subsistence and Settlement Based on Data from the Eastern Great Basin." *Man and Environment in the Great Basin* (ed. D. Madsen, and J. O'Connor). Washington, DC: Society for American Archeology Papers no. 2.

Malouf, Carling. 1966. "Ethno-History of the Great Basin." *The Current Status of Anthropological Research in the Great Basin, 1964* (ed. W. D'Azevedo et al.). Reno, NV: Desert Research Institute, pp. 1–38.

Miller, Wick. 1984. "The Classification of Uto-Aztecan-Languages Based on Lexical Evidence." *International Journal of American Linguistics* 50, no. 1: 1–24.

Mooney, James. 1965. *The Ghost Dance Religion and the Sioux Outbreak of 1890*. Chicago, IL: University of Chicago Press.

Morris, Elizabeth *et al.* 1981. "Nutritional Content of Selected Aboriginal Foods in Northeastern Colorado." *Journal of Ethnobiology* 1, no. 2: 213–220.

Moseley, Christopher. 2007. *Encyclopedia of the World's Endangered Languages*. New York: Routledge.

Price, John. 1980. *The Washoe Indians*. Reno, NV: Nevada State Museum Occasional Papers no. 4.

Steward, Julian. 1938. *Basin-Plateau Aboriginal Socio Political Groups*. Washington, DC: Bureau of American Ethnology Bulletin No. 120.

Steward, Julian. 1943. *Some Western Shoshone Myths*. Washington, DC: Bureau of American Ethnology Bulletin No. 136, pp. 254–255.

Steward, Julian. 1970. "The Foundations of Basin-Plateau Shoshonean Society." *Languages and Cultures of Western North America* (ed. E. Swanson, Jr.). Pocatello, ID: Idaho University Press, pp. 113–151.

Stewart, Omer. 1978. "The Western Shoshone of Nevada and the U.S. Government, 1863–1950." *Selected Papers from the 14th Great Basin Anthropological Conference* (ed. D. Tuohy). Socorro, NM: Ballena Press, pp. 77–114.

US Bureau of the Census. 2010. "American Indian and Alaska Native Tribes in the United States and Puerto Rico: 201." *2010 Census*. Washington, DC, CPH-T-6.

US Bureau of the Census. 2011. "2006-2010 American Community Survey Selected Economic Characteristics." Washington, DC.

US Bureau of Indian Affairs. 1995. "Table 3: Indian Service Population and Labor Force Estimates." Washington, DC.

US Indian Claims Commission. 1980. *Final Report 1979*. Washington, DC: House Document no. 96–383.

"U.S. Is Returning 84,000 Acres to Indians." 2000. *The New York Times*. January 14.

Wright, Mervin, Jr. 2015. *Tribal Response to Truckee River Water Quality & Water Quality Impacts*. Sutcliffe, NV: Region Tribal Operations Committee Pyramid Lake Paiute Tribe. Online.

The Shoshones

*Our legends tell us how we were brought to this land
by the Coyote. We know that we are the first people
upon this continent and the true owners. We will
continue to hold our treaty and our lands and no
part of our heritage, our birth right to this mother
earth, is for sale.*

Chief Frank Temoke, Western Shoshone,
quoted in Clemmer 1974: 38

THE SHOSHONES (SHO-SHO-NEE) are aboriginal inhabitants of the Great Basin whose territorial
expanse comprised about one-third of that region.
They were not a unified nation but rather adapted to
somewhat different environments and therefore developed economic, social, and political practices that differentiated local groups from one another. Western
Shoshones inhabited territory from Death Valley in
the west through the mountains, highlands, and deserts of central Nevada into northwestern Utah. Northern Shoshones lived in Idaho in the northern regions
of the Columbia Plateau and the Snake and Salmon
River drainage systems, while eastern Shoshones held
land in western Wyoming centered on the Green,
Sweetwater, and Big Horn Rivers in the central Rocky
Mountains. The territory inhabited by western Shoshones was probably the ancient center of Shoshone
cultural development, whereas the groups living in
Idaho and Wyoming were descendants of people who
had migrated from their original base. Although there

are cultural distinctions among the three groups, they
are united by some shared similarities. Most Shoshones spoke a language called Shoshone that is a member of the Central Numic branch of the Uto-Aztecan
linguistic family. The Panamint western Shoshone,
however, were speakers of a language called Panamint that is closely related to Shoshone. The name
"Shoshone" was first recorded by Meriwether Lewis in
1805, but like most names of Native nations, it is not
a self-designation. In their own language, the people
call themselves "niwi" or "newe," meaning "people."
Shoshones referred to various internal groupings not
by distinct terms for the groups themselves but rather
for the locations in which they commonly lived. These
terms generally referred either to a distinctive feature
in the geographic region or to a food that the people
typically ate, for example, "buffalo-eaters," "mountain
sheep-eaters," "seed-eaters," and so forth.

WESTERN SHOSHONES

Western Shoshone economy centered on the collection
of plants, particularly piñon nuts, seeds, and roots.
Piñon nuts, which were the single most important
resource, were gathered in the fall by groups of cooperating households. The nuts were shaken from trees
using a long, hooked pole. According to Steward's estimates, western Shoshone families collected approximately 1,200 pounds of pine nuts during the fall
harvest, supplying enough food for about four months
(1938: 27). Some of the nuts were transported from
the piñon groves back to villages in twined carrying
baskets, but most were cached nearby. People often set

up winter camps not far from the piñon groves so that they could have easier access to their cache of stored supplies when other foods became scarce. Piñon nuts were roasted in coals and some were then ground into flour for storage. Later the flour was mixed with water to make gravy. In addition to piñon, women collected a variety of seeds using woven seed beaters. The seeds were threshed with woven paddles and then roasted on trays with added charcoal and ashes. Seeds were also boiled in cooking baskets made watertight with coatings of pine pitch. And they were sometimes pounded into meal and made into cakes. Roots such as camas, sego, morning glory, and cattail were dug from the ground with long digging sticks and then boiled in soups or dried for winter storage. Currants, berries, and chokecherries were gathered, eaten raw or dried in the sun. Chokecherries were ground into pulp and made into cakes. Currants and buckberries were ground and made into pudding (Inter-Tribal Council of Nevada 1976: 6–8).

Although the bulk of the western Shoshone diet was derived from plant foods, animals were hunted as well, particularly bighorn sheep, antelope, rabbits, ground-hogs, other rodents, and reptiles. Most hunting was an individual or small-group effort but occasionally larger groups hunted communally. Bighorn sheep were caught by hunters from behind rock walls or hunting blinds. Antelope were most commonly hunted in drives under the direction of "antelope dreamers" who attracted the animals by spirit means. Then all able-bodied men and women in the camp formed a V-shaped line leading into a corral constructed of brush, stone, and poles. As the animals entered the corral, they were enclosed in the structure and shot with bows and arrows. Cooperative rabbit hunts, directed by "rabbit chiefs," were undertaken in the fall when large numbers of the animals could be caught in long nets made of twisted grass that were held by men and women. Rabbits were a significant source of both food and fur for most western Shoshones. Rabbit hunts often coincided with piñon harvests and were celebrated by feasting and festivals having economic, social, and religious purposes.

Birds such as sage hens, quails, doves, and water-fowl were also taken where available. Fish were a slight contribution to the Native diet given the scarcity of rivers and lakes in the region, but they were significant for people living near the Reese River, Humboldt River, and Ruby Valley (Steward 1938). And everywhere insects such as grasshoppers and crickets were collected and eaten.

While the western Shoshone environment provided a variety of resources, none was totally predictable. The amount of food available varied seasonally as well as from year to year. Adapting to resource uncertainty, people developed a flexible subsistence strategy based on intimate knowledge of resources and climate. Of necessity, they lived a nomadic existence, travelling and cooperating in small family clusters. Periods of greatest mobility obtained from the spring through the fall, whereas in the winter, people remained in larger, more stable encampments. Winter settlements, typically composed of several bilaterally related families, were located in valleys that were generally warmer than the mountain ranges. Although family clusters had preferred locations, they did not automatically follow the same routes every year due to the need to adapt to existing conditions. People's knowledge of vast territories was necessary so that in times of scarcity in one locale, they could find food in other familiar places.

Due to their mobility, western Shoshones erected temporary shelters. During the winter, they lived in conical huts made of a light wooden frame covered with pieces of bark. Such a dwelling typically housed a family of six that, according to Steward, was the average household size (1938: 240). In the summer, fully constructed houses were not needed because of the hot weather. Instead, people provided shelter in semicircular dwellings or sunshades made of brush. Communities often had a sweathouse that was either conical or domed in shape. Separate small menstrual huts were set up for the use of women during their menstrual periods and when giving birth.

Western Shoshones generally wore little clothing even in cold weather. However, in the coldest of winter people covered themselves with robes, most often made of woven or sewed rabbit skins but sometimes of antelope or deer hides. Women wore skirts made of bark or grass while men wore breechcloths of tanned hides or twined bark. Hats made of twined bark or hide were occasionally worn. People usually went barefoot except in cold weather or when walking on rough ground. Then they wore moccasins made of fur or twined sage bark stuffed with bark, grass, or fur (Steward 1940: 486). Both men and women wore earrings and necklaces made of shell and bone tubing. Some people applied mineral pigments as paint on their faces and bodies.

In adapting to their environment and the resources it provided, western Shoshone settlements were small, comprising no more than a few bilaterally related families, although larger groups formed for brief periods during the fall piñon harvests. Each "family cluster" tended to center its activities in certain territories. The group itself derived its name from a local distinctive geographic feature or from a food resource that was abundant in the area. These named groups had flexible membership since individuals and families could and did alter their alliance depending on the availability of resources and group composition. Kinship bonds were strongest within nuclear or small extended families. Ties between siblings were particularly supportive and enduring. Additional kin bonds were created by marriage. The sororate and levirate exemplified and underscored the bonds created between families at marriage and also exemplified the linkage of siblings. Although most marriages were monogamous, polygamy was possible. Sororal polygyny and fraternal polyandry were favored although the latter was probably less common than the former (Steward 1938: 240–241). Postmarital residence was flexible. Newly married couples typically lived with the wife's family for at least an initial period after marriage, but afterward they might change residence whenever practical.

Shoshone gender relations were generally egalitarian (Steward 1938; Eggan 1980). Men and women contributed their labor in both individual and joint efforts. While much of work was assigned according to gender, many activities consisted of component elements that united men and women in collective goals. Women's work as skilled basket makers was highly regarded, providing many of the utilitarian products needed for subsistence. Marriage practices also reflected gender equality with neither husband nor wife having authority over the other. Preferences for initial uxorilocal residence after marriage provided continuity and security to women. The possibilities of both polygyny and polyandry further reflected a balanced view of male and female. And women and men could equally achieve community prestige as curers.

Households were the basic units of economic cooperation. Surpluses were unusual given the paucity of resources, but when additional food was collected, women shared with their neighbors and relatives. However, in areas of great scarcity such as western Nevada and eastern California, sharing was restricted due to the need to conserve available food for one's own family (Eggan 1980: 177). Households or family clusters travelled over a large area, commonly ranging at least 20 miles or more from their winter villages (Steward 1938: 232). The largest of winter villages consisted of no more than fifteen or twenty families. Population density was relatively light, but differences depended upon resources. Where resources were scarcest, population density was probably no more than 1 person per 20 square miles, but where more abundance was found, population density rose to about 1 per 3 square miles (Steward 1943a). The Goshute in western Nevada had population densities that were the lowest of all Shoshone groups, while people living in the Ruby Valley or near the Humboldt River had among the highest densities (Steward 1938: 134, 153).

Given the small concentrations of populations and the high degree of mobility, community leadership was diffuse and informal. Each family cluster had an acknowledged leader, a man of intelligence, hunting ability, good character, and oratorical skills. Leaders gave advice, organized communal economic and religious activities, and exhorted followers to behave properly. They did not interfere in disputes. Instead, disputes between members of a community were settled by relatives of the people concerned. Small villages had no recognized leaders, but large villages sometimes had a single "headman." In Shoshone, his title was "degwani" meaning "talker," a term that aptly sums up "his most important function. As a 'talker,' he gave long orations, telling of his information [about the availability of plants] and giving directions to families who cared to cooperate. Any family was at liberty to pursue an independent course at any time" (Steward 1938: 247). When large gatherings came together for fall harvests or at festivals, village headmen gave public "harangues, exhorting the people to behave, have a good time, prepare food for feasts, etc." (247). In addition, "dance specialists" organized and directed the group's activities.

NORTHERN SHOSHONES

The northern Shoshones, living in the upper Columbia Plateau south of the Salmon River in Idaho, shared a core of cultural features with Shoshones further south but also had distinct practices due primarily to their adaptation to a different ecological zone. Their environment was richer in resources and provided a more stable subsistence base than that of the western people. They principally lived near rivers such as the

Snake, Salmon, and Boise, and in the intervening valleys. They also occupied territory in the Sawtooth and Bitterroot Mountains, whose peaks rose as much as 12,000 ft. above sea level. Climate varied depending upon location but it was generally dry, averaging only about 15 in. of rain per year. In the mountains, though, heavy snows fell in the winter, sometimes blocking mountain passes and thus limiting mobility and resulting in the isolation of communities from one another.

Northern Shoshone economy combined hunting, fishing, and plant-gathering. Variations were attested among different groups due to differences in ecology and cultural influences. Shoshones in eastern Idaho acquired horses by the end of the seventeenth century from Plains nations and thereafter hunted buffalo in the Snake River valleys and plains until about 1840, when the animals became extinct in the region. Shoshones in western Idaho, in contrast, did not incorporate horses into their subsistence strategies but rather maintained economies that centered on fishing and gathering plants.

Where they were found, large animals such as buffalo, antelope, elk, mountain sheep, and deer were hunted, using various techniques depending on the species sought. Antelope, elk, deer, and mountain sheep were taken by individuals or in group hunts. Antelope were sometimes stalked by lone hunters wearing disguises made of antelope skins. In communal hunts, animals were driven by men on horseback in relays until the quarry tired. Then they were surrounded and either shot or clubbed to death by men, women, and children (Lowie 1909: 185). Buffalo were usually sought in expeditions by men on horseback who rode their horses on the flanks of the herd and shot the animals with bows and arrows. Various species of rodents such as groundhogs and rabbits were hunted by boys. Sage hens were snared or driven into enclosures.

Fish were a significant contribution to the northern Shoshone diet, especially in western Idaho where salmon, in particular, were a mainstay. Salmon were taken during their spring spawning runs by several methods. They might be caught with harpoons by fishermen standing on wooden platforms or wading in the water. Weirs made of stone and brush or woven willow were built across small streams while handheld nets and basketry traps were used as well. Trout, perch, and sturgeon were also speared, netted, or trapped in weirs. Shoshones also caught fish by erecting barriers of woven brush and forcing the fish toward them, where they became entangled and could be easily speared. Insects, snakes, and lizards were collected and roasted in large trays.

Due to the availability of animals and fish, plants made a smaller contribution to the diet than among western Shoshones. Women collected camas bulb, yampa, and bitterroot with sharpened digging sticks. These and other roots were boiled in watertight baskets or steamed in pits dug in the ground into which heated rocks were placed. The pits were then covered with earth, allowing the plants to cook. Camas roots were kept in the pit for several days until they turned brown and sweetened (Lowie 1915: 188). A variety of berries and seeds was also gathered. Berries were eaten fresh or dried for later use. Seeds were collected with seed beaters and were roasted on woven trays. Sunflower seeds were mixed with berries and then pounded into flour to be made into bread. The bread mixture was sometimes roasted in long trays made of willow. Chokecherries were pounded, dried in the sun, and made into cakes. In a few areas, pine nuts were collected.

A variety of resources was seasonally available, but since none was entirely predictable, northern Shoshones lived in temporary encampments and followed annual cycles of movement from one resource area to another. Settlement size varied considerably, depending on the seasonal subsistence needs that were the focus of activity. During much of the year, small groups of related families travelled and camped together, while at other times larger groups accumulated. In reverse of the western Shoshone pattern, northern Shoshones tended to form larger villages in the summer and disperse into small groups in winter (Eggan 1980: 187). Lewis and Clark reported a summer village in 1805 that consisted of about 25 lodges and a population of perhaps 100 men and 300 women and children (Lewis and Clark 1905, II: 379). They noted frequent changes of location as people pursued their subsistence rounds. According to Nathaniel Wyeth, who was at Fort Hall, Idaho, in the 1830s, commenting on the Shoshone:

> None of the roving tribes claimed the ownership of its soil; they visited only to hunt game … They exist in small detached bodies and single families, and change their location so widely they seem to have no particular claim to any portion … No considerable body of these Indians can be found whose lines of wandering have not continually interlocked with those of similar bands." (Wyeth in Schoolcraft 1851, Part I: 244)

Although settlements tended to focus around rivers, particularly the Snake, Boise, and Weiser, fixed villages did not develop. And while settlement size was greater among northern Shoshones in the east than in the west, nowhere were villages permanent or composed of the same families year after year (Murphy and Murphy 1960: 332). During the fall, large groups gathered, many moving into western Montana and Wyoming for communal buffalo hunts and then fissioning into smaller groups and migrating to river encampments for the winter. However, forays into the western Plains became less frequent by the middle of the nineteenth century because of the increasing enmity between Shoshones and Blackfeet, who were better armed with guns acquired from European and American traders. During the spring, people gathered for salmon and trout spawning runs. John Fremont, writing in 1844, noted that northern Shoshones "grow fat and become poor with the salmon, which at least never fail them—the dried being used in the absence of the fresh" (Nevins 1956: 269). Later in the spring and summer, subsistence activities focused on collecting roots, berries, and grasses and hunting deer, elk, and mountain sheep.

Relations between northern Shoshones and most of their neighbors were friendly. In fact, members of the Bannock nation, a northern Paiute-speaking people, migrated from their original homeland in Oregon and lived peacefully among northern Shoshones and were integrated into their communities. Intermarriage between the two groups was common. Shoshones maintained friendly social and economic ties with the nearby Nez Perce and Flatheads, sometimes joining them in buffalo hunts. A nineteenth-century trapper, Osborne Russell, remarked that Shoshones often camped together with members of these two nations (1955: 41). They also participated in annual intertribal trading fairs along the Weiser River. Shoshones were the conduit for the horse trade in the region, supplying other indigenous nations with the animals.

Social and economic life centered on family clusters consisting of bilaterally related households. Local clusters were linked loosely to others through intermarriage, temporary coresidence and cooperation, and communal activities such as hunting and feasting. Residence rules were flexible, enabling couples to align themselves with any set of relatives depending on available resources and personal preferences. Exogamous marriages were effective means of linking groups and strengthening ties of cooperation and support. Most marriages were monogamous, but polygyny and polyandry were both possible. Preferences

for the levirate and sororate were further means of continuing alliances formed by marriage. Like most other Great Basin people, gender relations in northern Shoshone communities were generally equal. Both men and women contributed significantly to their household economies and received respect for their accomplishments.

Leadership in most northern Shoshone communities was diffuse and informal. Senior men were recognized for their skills, intelligence, and achievements and were thus accorded prestige and solicited for advice. However, in some groups, more formalized chieftainships developed in response to greater concentrations of people and the need to organize and coordinate buffalo hunting expeditions and community defense, especially in the nineteenth century (Steward 1938). The influence of Plains culture was undoubtedly a factor in the growth of chieftainships as well. Even in such communities, however, chiefs had only advisory rather than coercive powers. As Meriwether Lewis noted in 1805, "the authority of the chief being nothing more than mere admonition supported by the influence which the propriety of his own exemplary conduct may have acquired him in the minds of the individuals who compose the band" (1905, II: 370). The position of chief was a temporary one. Individuals' prominence and prestige waxed and waned depending on their skills and the regard with which people held them. As Russell noted in 1844: "The Government is a Democracy … deeds of valor promotes the Chief to the highest points attainable from which he is at any time liable to fall for misdemeanor in office" (1955: 144). Also borrowed from the Plains, Shoshone chiefs had assistants and "police" societies that kept order during communal hunting expeditions, dances, and ceremonies. In addition, settlements had councils of elders who made decisions and gave advice to the chiefs. And they had "criers" who made announcements and notified people of the council's decisions and directives.

Northern Shoshone clothing varied in its materials and styles, influenced in the east by Plains culture while in the west, the characteristic Great Basin garments were common. In eastern Idaho, men and women wore breechcloths made of tanned elk skins year-round and in the winter covered themselves with buffalo robes held close to the body with belts. Men and women wore leggings of antelope skin with fringed flaps on the side. Men's shirts, extending to mid-thigh, were also fringed on the sides and sleeves.

Women wore longer shirts or chemises, decorated with porcupine quills (Lowie 1909: 180–181). In western Idaho, people wore similar styles but utilized rabbit skins instead (Murphy and Murphy 1960: 295). People went barefoot much of the time but they sometimes wore moccasins made of deer, elk, or buffalo hide. For summer moccasins, the hair was taken off the hide, but in the winter it was kept on and worn toward the inside. In very cold weather, moccasins were stuffed with sagebrush bark for extra insulation.

Housing also varied depending upon the location of the group and the degree of Plains influence. In the east, people erected buffalo-skin tipis while in much of Idaho they constructed Basin-style conical lodges made of sagebrush, grass, or woven willow branches. They also built small huts for use as sweatlodges and menstrual huts.

Northern Shoshone basketry styles were consistent with the people's Great Basin origins. Women made coiled, twined, and woven gathering baskets, roasting trays, cooking vessels, and hats. Cooking baskets were made watertight by lining them with pine pitch.

EASTERN SHOSHONES

Eastern Shoshones differed from their western and northern relatives in several significant respects. Eastern Shoshones migrated into western Wyoming at least by 1500, possibly earlier. They later advanced into the northern plains, especially after acquiring horses in the late seventeenth or early eighteenth century, but then retreated, pushed south by Blackfeet, Arapahos, and Lakotas. Eastern Shoshones were nomadic, following annual and seasonal movements throughout a wide territory. According to Osborne Russell, "They seldom stop more than eight or ten days in one place" (Russell 1955: 145). For much of the year, people travelled in small groups of related families, but communal hunting, particularly of buffalo, brought together larger aggregates of people. Winter camps, formed after the fall buffalo hunts, were the most stable settlements. They were preferably located in valleys protected from snowstorms and the high winds of the Plains (Murphy and Murphy 1960: 307). Unlike other Shoshones, Eastern Shoshone economy centered on hunting although gathering of berries, roots, and seeds was also significant. Eastern Shoshones hunted large animals such as buffalo, elk, deer, and antelope and also caught beaver, rabbits, and sage hens. Minks, otters, and lynx were taken for their fur but were not eaten. Fish, especially trout and whitefish, were also caught. The most common plant foods were currants, gooseberries, wild roots, camas, wild onions, sunflower seeds, thistles, and various kinds of greens. Meat was either roasted or boiled while plants and berries were boiled or dried for later use. Pemmican was prepared by pounding buffalo or elk meat and mixing it with fat and dried berries. Fish were eaten roasted fresh, dried in the sun, or smoked.

After horses were acquired, the eastern Shoshone economy began to focus on buffalo, providing food and raw materials for the manufacture of clothing, tipis, and containers of many types. Communal buffalo hunts in the spring and fall involving hundreds of hunters were organized by chiefs and policed by members of a military society called the "Yellow Brows," whose name derived from their distinctive cockscomb hairdo painted yellow. Once "buffalo scouts" had located a herd, they signaled the camp and the hunters then approached the herd on horseback, shooting the animals with bows and arrows or piercing them with lances. But after about 1840, the number of buffalo in Shoshone territory declined and the danger of pursuing them further east increased due to enmity between Shoshones and Blackfeet, Lakotas, and Arapahos. Intertribal antagonism grew more intense as Plains nations were pushed westward by the continual pressure of American expansion from the eastern states during the nineteenth century. In mid-century, Charles Preuss, a cartographer for John Fremont, reported attacks on Shoshones by several Plains nations including the Gros Ventres, Arapahos, Lakotas, and Cheyennes (Gudde and Gudde 1958: 26, 30, 84). Eastern Shoshone households, as elsewhere in the Great Basin, were composed of bilaterally related kin. There were no absolute rules of residence although it was likely that newly married couples lived with the wife's family for at least an initial period. During that time, the husband was expected to work for his wife's parents and contribute to their household economy. Parents arranged marriages for their daughters, endeavoring to find husbands who were accomplished hunters. Young women, often just passed menarche, were thus frequently married to men much older than themselves. Most marriages were monogamous but polygyny was possible. In contrast to other Basin societies, polyandry was not reported for eastern Shoshones.

Alta Washakie, Shoshone girl.

or another depending upon economic and personal factors. Bands may have developed in response to the need for group cohesion in the face of increasing pressures due to threats from neighboring nations as well as the need to coordinate activities for resource exploitation after acquiring horses. These conditions were lacking in western Shoshone communities and corresponded with a lack of band organization.

The eastern Shoshone shift to an economy based on hunting led to a number of transformations from the basic Shoshonean model of political and social organization. The role of community leader became more prominent and permanent. Chiefs were respected men who had demonstrated skills in hunting and warfare and possessed spirit powers as well. They directed movements of their group from one location to another, organized collective hunting expeditions, and gave advice about communal activities. They also greeted and provided hospitality to visitors. However, they lacked coercive powers and did not solve or mediate internal disputes (Hoebel 1940). A chief's special status was signified by the painting of a broad yellow band on the outside of his tipi. In addition, chiefs wore special feathered headdresses and carried eagle staffs when in battle (Bourke 1891: 337).

Unlike most Great Basin people, eastern Shoshones developed military societies consistent with a more specialized emphasis on warfare than existed elsewhere (Lowie 1915). No doubt both the organization of military societies and of warfare itself was a diffusion from Plains nations as well as a response to growing competition over resources and the real possibility of conflict with neighbors. Military societies were under the direction of chiefs. The "Yellow Brows" were young men who constituted the advance guard in military campaigns. They engaged in daring maneuvers and sometimes pledged to hold their ground even if doing so led to their deaths. Similar to the "contraries" of the Plains, Yellow Brows used ritual "backwards speech" in which "no" meant "yes" (Shimkin 1986: 311). The second military society, called the "Logs," was composed of middle-aged but able warriors who acted as the rear guard in battles. Members of military societies held high prestige in their communities, but all skilled participants in warfare earned respect as well. Military success was rewarded with the privilege of painting black finger marks, with red fingermarks beneath, on both sides of the tipi door.

Once eastern Shoshones obtained horses, military techniques changed considerably. Prior to the eighteenth

By the turn of the nineteenth century, eastern Shoshones were organized into bands that were associated with particular territories. Bands were unnamed groups whose membership was flexible. Individuals or families might shift their alliance with one group century, warfare was infrequent, but when it occurred, men fought on foot, grouped into lines for both offensive and defensive purposes. Later, warfare was transformed into ambushes on horseback and quick raids into and retreats from enemy villages. Warriors protected themselves and their horses with antelope-hide armor. A man's favorite horses were painted on the face and their tails and manes were decorated with feathers.

In addition to their role in hunting and warfare, horses were used to transport goods when moving camp. Their association with their owner was evidenced in the practice of killing a man's favorite horse at his death and burying it in the grave to accompany him in the afterworld. Horses were thought to have spirit powers as well. They could foretell their owner's death by making three rapid pawings with their front hoof that left a column of half-moon marks on the ground (Shimkin 1986: 319).

After acquiring horses and developing a robust economy, eastern Shoshones began to measure wealth in possessions, particularly in numbers of horses. The animals were used as tokens of wealth in gifts from a man's family to that of his prospective bride. And they might be won (and lost) in gambling. Wealth was also received as payment for curing and midwife services. However, although obtaining wealth was considered a proper goal, societal and ethical values mitigated against the accumulation of great amounts of property and the surfacing of economic disparities. Wealthy people were obligated to be generous to their relatives and needy community members. Material goods were routinely distributed in giveaways that accompanied feasts and life-cycle rituals.

In concert with economic and political transformations in eastern Shoshone society, status between men and women became unequal in contrast to the basic egalitarian gender relations of Shoshonean and Great Basin peoples generally. Eastern Shoshone men were able to exert dominance once they held important community roles as chiefs, hunters, ritualists, and members of military societies. The increased frequency of polygyny and the absence of polyandry also reflected some degree of female subordination. The possible great age difference between an older husband and a young wife also enhanced men's dominance since seniority itself conferred prestige. But the exertion of male authority in marital relationships was at least initially tempered by preferences for a period of uxorilocal residence after marriage, providing a new wife with the security and familiarity of her own family. And although men

occupied the dominant roles in eastern Shoshone society, individual women could and did achieve personal prestige, particularly after reaching middle age when they functioned as midwives and curers and earned respect as craftswomen.

SHOSHONE RELIGIOUS BELIEFS AND PRACTICES

Although there were significant regional differences in religious beliefs and practices, Shoshones shared a basic constellation of beliefs. Spirit power, called "puha" or "poha," was conceived of as a vague spirit essence that was inherent or resided in spirit beings, forces of nature, sacred places, and powerful objects. According to Shoshone belief, the world was formed, or more accurately transformed, by the actions and exploits of two figures, Wolf and Coyote. Wolf was generally thought of as benevolent and helpful to humans whereas Coyote often played the part of trickster. The exploits of Coyote are responsible for the origin of people. There are numerous variants in details but in all of the stories, Coyote somehow has possession of a water jug in which, unknown to him, are human beings. Coyote is told, sometimes by Wolf and sometimes by an old woman, not to open the jug. However, consistent with his trickster traits, Coyote opens the jug before he is instructed to do so. When he removes the stopper, the men and women inside the jug jump out and run away to found new communities. They are sometimes identified with particular locales and with particular Native nations (Steward 1943b: 261–268).

The universe is somewhat vaguely described in Shoshone cosmology. The sky is thought of as a dome of ice atop the earth. A huge serpent forms the rainbow, lying against the domed sky. Snow is caused by the friction of the serpent against the ice, but in summer it melts and turns to rain (Lowie 1909: 230–231). Some stories recount that the sun was originally very close to earth and scorched the people. After sending Hare to kill the sun, a new sun was formed from the fragments of the first and was put into the sky high above the earth.

In primordial times, all beings had the shape of animals although their speech and behavior was humanlike. During the transformation of the primordial era into the world we now know, these beings took on the shapes that are familiar to us today, separating animals and humans.

In addition to Wolf and Coyote, other animal spirits had subsidiary roles in the transformation of the world and as helpers of humans. They might appear to people in visions and dreams and thus become guardian spirits and impart one of their attributes to the recipient. For example, Antelope spirits impart speed, Bear spirits give strength, and so forth. Shoshones also believed in a vaguely described deity, sometimes referred to as "our father," who seems to have been a figure of benevolence and protection. However, this spirit did not play a direct or active role in people's daily lives.

The world of nature was thought to be imbued with spirit powers. Among the most significant were Thunder, Lightning, Winds, and "Our Mother Earth." Whirlwinds were thought to be dangerous spirits, sometimes associated with death and the dead. People who encountered whirlwinds might become sick or suffer some other misfortune. Certain places were also associated with spirits whose contact might be dangerous. Lakes, streams, caves, and the sites of rock drawings were particularly powerful.

Shoshones believed that people could acquire spirit power or "puha" and benefit from its protective and curative qualities. Most people held some power, usually received spontaneously in dreams or waking visions. Among eastern Shoshones, it was also obtained through vision quests, most commonly by men but by woman as well. The notion of acquiring power through vision quests probably entered eastern Shoshone culture from contact with Native nations of the Plains among whom the practice was widespread. Eastern Shoshones who desired to obtain power went alone to sacred places and cleansed themselves in a nearby stream or lake. Clad only in a blanket, the supplicant waited and prayed for a spirit visit. The seeker was not to eat or sleep until a vision appeared, typically in the form of a person or animal. During the encounter, the vision often changed shape, consistent with Shoshone beliefs about the changeability or metamorphosis of spirit forms. Alternatively, as a contemporary eastern Shoshone healer recalled, "the Puha approaches you like a strong light" and may fade away as it leaves (Hultkrantz 1987: 54).

Among all Shoshones, spirits that appear in visions or dreams give specific instructions consisting of songs, prayers, or procedures that the recipient is obliged to follow in order to be protected. If any of the taboos imposed upon them are broken, the power departs and may actually become dangerous to the person who has transgressed.

Although every person is able to acquire some spirit power, and most people do, some individuals are able to accumulate more spirit protectors and more intense powers than others. These people are recognized as healers and can use their abilities to cure illness, to predict future events, and to perform extraordinary acts. Healers cured illness by a variety of techniques depending upon the cause of the ailment. Soul loss and object intrusion were the most frequent causes of illness according to Shoshone disease concepts. Typical complaints usually attributed to soul loss were high fever, debilitation, and overall weakening or lack of energy. Healers treated the ailment by sending their spirit helpers in search of the patient's missing soul. When retrieved, the healer replaced the soul in the patient's body through the top of the latter's head since this was thought to be the passage through which souls depart and return (77). Ailments caused by object intrusion were diagnosed by healers who were able to see into the patient's body and find where the object was lodged. The healer then extracted the object by brushing the patient with an eagle feather or by blowing or sucking on the spot where the object was lodged. Once the object was removed, it was blown away or spat out and thrown into a fire. Healers did not volunteer their services but rather waited to be asked. Once asked, however, they could not deny treatment. Payment for services usually consisted of specific ritually prescribed items and were limited in the amount considered appropriate.

Shoshones accompanied life-cycle changes with ritual observances at birth, puberty, and death. Observances during pregnancy and at birth were for the protection of the child, ensuring its health and long life. Pregnant women, and usually their husbands as well, avoided eating meat or heavy foods to ensure that the child would be healthy and energetic. When the expectant mother was about to give birth, she went to a separate hut, accompanied by a midwife or female relatives. Once the woman entered the hut, her husband abstained from eating meat and instead drank great quantities of water to facilitate the birth. Birth itself was usually not accompanied by ritual, but in cases of difficult labor, the midwife or a healer might sing powerful songs to aid the delivery. When the child was born, it was bathed in warm water. At the same time, the father bathed himself in a cold creek or lake. Mother and child remained in the delivery hut for a month during which time the mother refrained from eating meat and could not scratch herself with her fingers but instead used a scratching stick. During the same span of time, the father rose early in the morning and tried to remain as active as possible to ensure that the child would be industrious. At the end of the period of separation, the mother, her husband, and the baby were bathed in a creek or lake to purify themselves.

Puberty for girls was marked by ritual isolation and adherence to taboos. Upon menarche, the young girl entered a "menstrual hut" not far from her family's dwelling where she remained for at least four days, abstaining from eating meat lest the flow of blood continue indefinitely. During this time, she was visited only by female relatives and was instructed in the skills and responsibilities of adult women.

At the end of life, rituals of burial and mourning took place. When a person died, their body was cleansed and dressed in fine clothing. A period of intense mourning lasted for four days during which time relatives of the deceased mourned loudly in expression of their grief. Both men and women mourners cut their hair short and wore it loose. Among eastern Shoshones, women also slashed wounds in their legs and arms. Relatives and friends donated gifts to the deceased. A woman knelt by the body and shouted into its ears the names of donors and told what had been given (Lowie 1909: 214–215). The body remained in the camp for four days and then was taken to its burial site. Methods of disposing of the dead varied. The body might be buried in the ground, placed in a rock shelter or cave, or cremated. Personal possessions of the deceased were sometimes buried with the body or destroyed. Some property might be distributed to relatives of the deceased. After the burial, close relatives of the deceased continued mourning by remaining quiet, wearing old clothes, and not attending to their appearance. After a year had passed, the mourners cleansed themselves in a bath and put on fresh clothing. Surviving spouses were then able to remarry if they wished. Shoshones believed that the soul, located in the head during life, leaves at death and travels to the afterworld where it is washed by Wolf. Ghosts remaining on earth can cause harm to the living and were thus greatly feared. Dreaming of the dead was considered a bad omen, foretelling the dreamer's death or misfortune.

In addition to individual ceremonies, Shoshones celebrated a number of collective rites. Some rituals were associated with food resources. Rituals of thanksgiving and celebration were performed by western Shoshones at times of piñon harvests and rabbit drives in the fall.

Some groups, such as the Goshute, conducted resource renewal festivals in the spring in order to make the seeds grow (Steward 1938: 139). Western Shoshone festivals brought together large groups of people from neighboring and even distant areas. Villages alternated as hosts of the rituals from year to year, thus establishing and perpetuating wide networks of ceremonial, economic, and social reciprocity. Northern Shoshones performed collective rites in the spring to celebrate the return of salmon at the start of the spawning season.

All communal rites included prayers, songs, and dances. The most common dance, performed on nearly all ritual occasions, was the "round dance" in which men and women participated, alternating in a circle. Round dances were performed at night for a number of nights in succession. In addition to their religious functions, they were occasions for feasting, socializing with relatives who lived in distant settlements, and gaming and gambling. Northern and eastern Shoshones also performed the "father dance," which differed from the round dance mainly in its intention of protecting the community from illness and misfortune. Eastern Shoshones performed the "shuffling dance" at the time of the full moon during the three winter months. Shuffling dances lasted for three or four nights in succession. All participants danced and shook out their blankets in a symbolic gesture that metaphorically shook disease away from the community.

Shoshone collective rituals had similar purposes in uniting a community of people who were separated into relatively small groups during most of the year but who came together for cooperative economic activities. The rites also celebrated the renewal of resources and life forces. Finally, they protected members of the community from harm.

EURO-AMERICAN INCURSIONS AND THEIR CONSEQUENCES

The earliest effects of the European presence on Shoshone society were indirect, beginning with the acquisition of horses in the late seventeenth or early eighteenth centuries. Horses were obtained through trading networks with other Native people, particularly Comanches, who got them from Spanish settlements in the southwest. After acquiring horses, Shoshones spread northward into Montana and Canada but by the nineteenth century they were pushed out of the western and northern plains by Blackfeet who had obtained guns from European traders. Conflicts with Arapahos and Lakotas underscored the dangers for Shoshones on the western Plains.

In the early nineteenth century, Shoshone communities were disrupted by the presence of Euro-American trappers and traders who operated in their region. When Lewis and Clark made their expedition along the Missouri River and through the Northwest in 1805, they encountered eastern Shoshones living on both sides of the Rocky Mountains. Trading posts were established in and near territories of eastern and northern Shoshones of Wyoming and Idaho in the first few decades of the century by employees of the Hudson's Bay Company, NorthWest Company, and Rocky Mountain Fur Company. One of the early consequences of this activity was the depletion of beaver and buffalo by the 1840s. During the same period, American explorers such as Jedediah Smith, Peter Skene Odgen, and John Fremont journeyed through western Shoshone lands in Nevada and California, contributing to the depletion of resources. Indeed, Odgen remarked, "The banks of the river are now lined with Indians. It appears on our arrival they apprehended we were a war party, but they are now convinced we are come merely to wage war on the beaver, and this I trust we shall do most effectually" (Inter-Tribal Council of Nevada 1976: 15).

American settlement in western Shoshone territory began in earnest in 1847 with the arrival of Mormons in Utah and Nevada. They were soon followed by other settlers and prospectors when gold was discovered at Gold Canyon on the Carson River in 1849 and at the Comstock Lode in 1857. Encroachment on eastern and northern Shoshone territory accelerated during the same period by Americans on their way to mining camps in California and Oregon and others settling in the region. Passage along the "Oregon Trail" following the Snake and Boise Rivers intensified in the second half of the century. The most notable effect of these incursions was the disturbance of the environment and the plant and animal resources upon which Shoshones depended. Indigenous economies were precariously balanced on scarce resources that were carefully managed and conserved, but the large-scale movement of people and livestock eradicated the best grazing lands, resource sites, and water sources, leaving Shoshones without adequate resources. Charles Preuss noted in 1843: "The white people have ruined the country of the Snake (Shoshone) Indians and should therefore treat them well. Almost all the Natives are now obliged

to live on roots; game can scarcely be seen any more" (Gudde and Gudde 1958: 86). In response to depletion of their resources and pressure on their lands, eastern and northern Shoshones congregated in larger bands under stronger and more centralized leadership. In 1861, Benjamin Davies, the Utah superintendent of Indian affairs, noted:

> At some springs were immense quantities of … chub which the Indians used to eat in winter, but the overland California mail company has built stations for convenience, and located men and quartered stock about these spots, and the Indians no longer visit them. No sign of antelope, deer, mountain sheep, elk, not so much as a prairie dog, weasel, bear, buffalo. (Inter-Tribal Council of Nevada 1976: 47)

In the 1850s and 1860s, the American government began to sign treaties with some Shoshone bands in order to settle Indians on reservations, obtain land cessions, and clear the way for increased settlement. The first agreement, the Treaty of Ruby Valley signed in 1863 by twelve "captains" representing "western bands of Shoshone," was a pact of "peace and friendship" not a treaty of land cession. The Shoshones' control and ownership of the territory was acknowledged by the US Secretary of Interior in 1862, stating that the land was "owned by the Indians" (Clemmer 1974: 27), and was reaffirmed by US Senator James Nesmith who commented, "The object of the amendment is not for the purpose of making a treaty that contemplates the purchase of any land" (27). However, the Treaty of Ruby Valley did put certain restrictions on Shoshone actions. Shoshones agreed to allow railroads, mail lines, and citizens to traverse their territory and permitted construction of mines, settlements, and timber mills. And they agreed that at some future time, "whenever the President of the United States deemed it expedient," they would "abandon the roaming life" and "become herdsmen or agriculturalists" and "remove their camps to such reservations as he [the president] would indicate, and to reside and remain therein" (28). But Shoshones never agreed to cede their lands or extinguish title to their territory. In return for allowing American settlements on Native land, the government promised annual payments of $5,000 for ten years to be delivered in clothing and livestock. Although Shoshones never relinquished title to their land, they agreed to move to reservations if they were established within their original borders. As Shoshone leader Obiaga stated, "We don't feel like going away too far. This is our country and we would like to remain here" (Inter-Tribal Council of Nevada 1974a: 60). However, much of their land was overrun by farmers and in some cases, Shoshones had to pay rent to settlers for the opportunity to farm on land that was rightfully their own (65). Finally, in 1877, they were assured reservations at Carlin Farms and Elko and began to farm the land, trying to reorient their economies given the loss of their aboriginal resource base. Within a few years, however, they were ordered out of their reservations because these had become valuable to American farmers and ranchers. The people were told to join the northern Shoshones on the Duck Valley Reservation, which had been established at the Idaho border in 1877 following signing of treaties between northern Shoshones and US officials. The directive was carried out against the unanimous opposition of all sixteen Shoshone leaders, including Temoak and Tutuwa, who had been given the authority to speak for their communities. Later they were ordered to leave Duck Valley and relocate to the northern Shoshone reservation at Fort Hall, Idaho, once more against the people's wishes. One leader, Captain Buck, spoke of his frustration at the frequent moves they were forced to make:

> After one year government give us some cattle in Ruby Valley. Next spring I find little piece [of land] and sow wheat, potatoes, turnips. Next time I go to Carlin farm. Next time Duck Valley. That is way I move all time. Just now I'm tired. That is why I no go Fort Hall. (76)

In the same year as the signing of the Treaty of Ruby Valley, the Gosiute band of western Shoshones signed the Treaty of Tooele Valley, which provided some safeguards to a portion of their traditional homeland. Gosiutes were largely ignored because of the remoteness of their territory and the scarcity of its resources. By the end of the nineteenth century, many western Shoshones had actually left their reservations because of the lack of economic opportunities. Instead, they lived near mining camps and towns, attempting to find employment in the mines or on farms and ranches owned by American settlers.

The first treaties between northern Shoshones and the United States, signed in 1863 and 1864, ceded land to the government and established the Fort Hall Reservation. The reservation originally consisted of 1.8 million acres but was soon reduced by more than two-third. Some land was taken in order to provide track and rights of way to the Union Pacific Railroad, while additional acreage was confiscated to accommodate the growing town of Pocatello and neighboring communities. Settlers pressured their legislators to reduce Shoshone land in order to increase American holdings. For example, an Idaho newspaper editorial of 1880 implied that Shoshones did not require as much land as they had: "Here in southeastern Idaho we have an Indian reservation containing more than two millions of acres of land, the finest in the territory. On this reservation there is less than 1,500 Indians to occupy this large body of land" (Jorgensen 1972: 82). Soon thereafter, about 1 million acres were taken. A reservation for the Lemhi band of northern Shoshones was set aside in 1875, but when it was dissolved in 1907, the people were ordered to go to Fort Hall, thus exacerbating the pressure on land and resources there.

Economic hardships for northern Shoshones increased in the last decades of the nineteenth century as their land and resource base was eroded. In the words of a US census officer, writing in 1890: "The material conditions of the Shoshones is easily summed up: they are as poor as they can be and live" (US Census Office 1894: 631; Shimkin 1986: 523).

Although the government officially encouraged Shoshones to become settled farmers, actual policies interfered with the success of agriculture. In addition to the unsuitability of most reservation land for farming and the inadequacy of funding and technical support, water sources were often diverted away from Native territory. For example, the Fort Hall Irrigation Project of 1912 diverted water from the Fort Hall Reservation to neighboring non-Indian farmers. And the American Falls Reservoir flooded the Snake River bottomlands on the northern Shoshone reservation. Additional acreage was ceded to companies extracting timber and asphalt.

In the middle and late-nineteenth century, eastern Shoshones, under the leadership of Washakie, attempted to accommodate the American government in the hope of retaining their lands and resources. He urged his followers to accede to American requests for rights of passage through their territory and for land to construct forts and rail lines By the late 1860s, Washakie and other leaders signed several treaties, notably the Treaty of Fort Bridger in 1868 that ceded territory to the United States and established the Wind River Reservation in Wyoming. In return, Shoshones

Last photograph of Chief Washakie (1804?–1900, at far left, pointing) at Fort Washakie, Wyoming, surrounded by Shoshone Indians, 1892.

received twenty payments and annuities of $10,000 each. The money and goods were given directly to Washakie for distribution, thus augmenting the chief's power and prestige (Shimkin 1942: 452).

But regardless of all the concessions made by Washakie and other Shoshones, the reservation that initially contained 2.8 million acres was reduced in 1872 in exchange for a payment of $25,000. Then in 1878, the US government unilaterally assigned the eastern half of the remaining land to Arapahos without consulting the resident Shoshones and despite the enmity between the two nations. Problems of political coordination ensued and lasted well into the twentieth century.

In the context of their poverty, loss of land and independence, and population declines due to disease and warfare, Shoshones participated in two waves of Ghost Dance activity that spread through the Great Basin toward the end of the nineteenth century. They were especially enthusiastic supporters of the second Ghost Dance movement, espousing a militant interpretation of prophesy that predicted a cataclysmic end to the world and a return to economic and social conditions prior to the intrusions of Euro-Americans in the region.

Shoshone Ghost Dance rituals were built upon traditional religious and ceremonial practice and incorporated the ancient round dance form to a new setting. The ceremony included round dances performed for four or five successive nights, accompanied by songs that were contributed by individuals who had acquired them in dreams and visions.

Ghost Dance activity began to wane in the late nineteenth century following the US Army's massacre of more than 300 Lakotas at Wounded Knee Creek, South Dakota, in December 1890. However, Ghost Dances continued to be performed in some communities, again with a change of meaning and focus. Among eastern and northern Shoshones, Ghost Dances are performed today with an emphasis on community and individual health. The rites now combine the traditional round dance with elements of the father dance. As in the father dance, people cover themselves with blankets and then shake the blankets out in a symbolic gesture ridding people of disease and harmful ghosts and attracting good health.

By the twentieth century, all Shoshone groups had been assigned reservations that encompassed only a fraction of their aboriginal territory, and even these lands, guaranteed by treaty, were continually reduced in size. Enforcement of provisions of the General Allotment Act of 1887 resulted in division of communally owned territory into individual parcels and the eventual leasing or sale of reservation land to non-Indian ranchers and farmers. Even with such losses, pressure from settlers intensified to force Shoshones out of the farms and productive lands that they still retained. When the government failed to act immediately, intimidation and violence were some of the methods employed. According to recollections of a western Shoshone, for example:

> There used to be an Indian lady lived on that little farm near Palisade. One day she disappeared and nobody ever found out what happened to her. That was about 1922 … An old Indian man named Cortez used to live in this little valley near Immigrant Pass. He had an apple orchard up here. He told me this story: One day three ranchers rode up there and told Cortez to get out, cause they wanted the spring for their cattle. They told him if he didn't get out they would throw him and his family in the spring. So he had to get out. (Clemmer 1974: 32)

Because of the isolation of reservations and their scarce resources, many Shoshones resided instead in small "colonies" on the outskirts of American towns. Eventually, a number of these settlements were given official recognition as Indian lands, especially those in Nevada that were set aside for western Shoshones, such as Skull Valley, Bishop, Fallon, Reno-Sparks, Battle Mountain, Goshute, Elko, Yomba, Odgens Ranch, South Fork, Ruby Valley, Duckwater, and Wells.

CONTEMPORARY SHOSHONE COMMUNITIES

After passage of the Indian Reorganization Act of 1934, several Shoshone communities filed suits against the federal government seeking the return of or compensation for land illegally taken in the nineteenth century. Suits by eastern Shoshones led to congressional action in 1939 that almost tripled the acreage of the Wind River Reservation, increasing from some 800,000 acres to more than 2.2 million, returning the reservation to nearly its original size. The Act also provided $3.5 million for economic development (Shimkin 1986). In addition, suits filed in 1957 and 1965 with the Indian Claims Commission awarded Eastern Shoshones of Wind River the sum of $433,000 for land and $120,000 for gold illegally taken from them. And in a joint case settled in 1968, Eastern and Northern Shoshones received $15.7 million as compensation for their land (US Indian Claims Commission 1980).

Western Shoshones also filed suits concerning land that had never been relinquished by treaty or agreement. In 1962, the Indian Claims Commission ruled that although the Shoshones had never ceded their territory, the land had been lost through "gradual encroachment" of settlers (Crum 1993: 176). When the Court ordered compensation based on 1872 land values, some Shoshones objected, insisting instead on a return of their territory, while others were willing to accept a monetary award. Among the opponents of the settlement was Edward McDade from South Fork who stated: "You will find out that you are actually selling your Indian rights. The land will always take care of you…For myself, no one will ever buy my Indian rights. They are sacred" (ibid: 177). While the land claims case was being contested, "traditional" Shoshones organized the United Western Shoshone Legal Defense and Education Association (later re-named the Sacred Lands Association) to press for return of the land rather than acceptance of a monetary settlement. However, in 1979, the Indian Claims Commission rejected their suit on the grounds that the land had been relinquished and awarded the Shoshones the sum of $26 million. On appeal in the following year, a federal court gave some ground to the Native petitioners, ruling that although Western Shoshone title had indeed not been extinguished in 1863, title was extinguished in 1979 as a result of the Indian Claims Commission's decision. The Western Shoshone Legal Defense Association next appealed to the Supreme Court, which ruled in 1985 that the $26 million awarded to the Shoshones in 1979 had effectively extinguished their title to the 24 million acres under contention. Still, Western Shoshones refused to accept the monetary payment and continue to press their claim for title to their land.

A related case surfaced in 1974 when two Shoshone sisters, Carrie and Mary Dann, were fined by the Bureau of Land Management for failure to pay permit fees for grazing cattle on what the BLM called public domain land. In their defense, the Danns claimed that the land belonged to Western Shoshones and that they were within their treaty rights to graze their stock on the land. A federal judge in Nevada ruled in 1980 that the Danns did not have to pay permit fees dating before 1979 because at that time title to the land was still held by Western Shoshones, but after the Indian Claims Court transferred title to the United States, the Danns were liable for the fees. An appeal to the federal circuit court ended in a decision favorable to the Danns, invalidating the 1980 ruling and stating that title to Shoshone land had not been extinguished. However, a subsequent appeal to the Supreme Court in 1985 reversed this decision, upholding previous rulings by the Indian Claims Commission. Still, the Court allowed some leeway for Shoshones by permitting them to sue for "individual aboriginal rights" in the lower courts (Crum 1994: 182). Based on this opinion, in 1986, the federal district court recognized the Danns' rights to use (but not own) aboriginal Shoshone lands.

Differing strategies of land use have emerged in Shoshone communities. Western Shoshones have opposed expansion of nuclear testing facilities in Nevada, construction of MX missile sites, and the dumping of nuclear waste near their territory (Crum 1993: 174). In contrast, in 1999, Skull Valley Goshute Shoshones granted a 50-year lease to eight electrical companies for storage of nuclear waste by-products on their 18,000-acre reservation. Tribal leaders entered into the agreement because they hope to create fifty permanent jobs for their members. There are currently some 120 members of the band, but only about 30 live on the reservation because of the scarcity of employment. The agreement has sparked controversy among Skull Valley Shoshones since some support and others oppose it. It has also generated debate among Utah state officials. The governor opposes the plan but cannot block it because the Goshutes have sovereign powers over their lands ("Tribe in Utah Fights for Nuclear Waste Dump" 1999: A16).

Another group, the Timbesha Shoshones, whose aboriginal homeland is located in what is now the Death Valley National Park, reached an agreement with the federal government in 1999 to manage the park and to reacquire about 300 acres of land in the park and an additional 5,000 acres nearby that are administered by the Bureau of Land Management. The tribe planned to build about fifty homes, a tribal complex, a cultural center, and an inn on the land in the park, known as Furnace Creek ("Tribe Strikes Deal with Feds to Manage National Park" 1999). In 2014

the tribe held a contest where students were given 48 hours to create a unique design for the new cultural center, and construction was set to begin in May 2016 ("WSU Design Students Collaborate on Death Valley Cultural Center" 2014).

Residents of the Wind River Shoshone Reservation are currently in the midst of an environmental and health investigation, carried out jointly by tribal agencies, the Rocky Mountain Tribal Epidemiological Center, the US Environmental Protection Agency, and the Department of Energy. The investigation focuses on several interrelated concerns. First are the high rates of cancer on the Reservation and an unusual incidence of birth defects. Second are findings of contaminated water supplies throughout the territory. Third are the waste products, especially uranium tailings, that were emitted and then left behind by production at the Susquehanna-Western uranium mill that operated on the Reservation from 1958 until 1963. Once the mill was closed, the owners left piles of uranium tailings without properly capping or containing them. By the time they were removed in the late 1980s, the groundwater was already contaminated. Additional sources of contamination were the natural processes of rainfall and melting snow that seeped through the tailings and then into the ground. According to officials from the Department of Energy, once the tailings are removed, they expect that the sites and the water table will clear up naturally, perhaps in about a hundred years (Ahtone 2012: 27). However, when the area experienced frequent flooding in 2011, the levels of groundwater contamination increased, indicating that any estimate of a timeframe for a natural cleanup is impossible.

The fact that the US government permitted operation of a uranium mill on Shoshone territory was a violation of Native sovereignty. Additional examples of these violations were the test explosion of a nuclear weapon on western Shoshone land in Nevada in 2006 and the current plans to cut down groves of piñon trees in order to develop a biomass industry that officials from the Bureau of Land Management claim will create jobs and generate income. However, members of the western Shoshone community are opposed to these endeavors. The nuclear weapons case in 2006 led to a complaint filed by the western Shoshone National Council to the UN Committee for the Elimination of Racial Discrimination after they failed to get a hearing in US federal courts. The UN Committee ruled that the US government had indeed violated western Shoshone sovereignty by using the people's lands without their consent. They ordered the United States to "desist and stop" their actions and instead to acknowledge the Shoshones' rights to "own, develop, control and use their land and resources." The US government did not heed this warning but instead went forward with their tests, and plans are proceeding to develop biomass production on territory claimed by the western Shoshone. The specific acreage under question was unilaterally taken by the US government and turned into public lands in violation of the Treaty of Ruby Valley of 1863. The western Shoshone have been trying to regain control of these lands for decades.

The Duckwater Shoshone tribe acquired their land in 1940 under provisions of the 1934 Indian Reorganization Act, which provided that Indians without a territorial base could begin to purchase land that would then be incorporated into a reservation. The Duckwater Shoshone Reservation now includes 3,272 acres, home to about 130 members. In recent years, the tribe has expanded services including an elementary school, community park, health department and clinic, and a senior center. They are also working with the US Fish & Wildlife Service to restore the habitat of a threatened fish species, the Railroad Valley Spring Fish. In prior days, this species of fish was a traditional food for the Shoshones.

A more recent civil lawsuit was filed in 2015 by members of the Fort Hall Shoshone-Bannock tribe. The suit alleges that the BIA is admitting those without Shoshone-Bannock ancestry to the tribe. The filer of the suit, William Beasley, claims that the BIA is doing so with criminal intent, and that the new "members" are paying for membership. Beasley and other members of the tribe have requested that federal payments to the Fort Hall BIA are halted and that a federal investigation is opened before any more money is released to the tribe (Jones 2015).

It is about 150 years since the massacre at Bear River in Idaho when some 300 northwestern Shoshone men, women, and children were killed by a detachment of volunteers, led by US Col. Patrick Connor. Remains of some of the victims have been held by the Smithsonian Institution in Washington, DC. But in 2013, skeletal remains of two of the victims, a teenage boy and a young woman in her twenties, were repatriated to their northwestern Shoshone homeland.

Economic conditions on Shoshone reservations vary widely depending on location, quality of land, awards from land claims cases, mineral extraction leases and royalties, as well as possibilities for local employment. Larger reservations such as Fort Hall, Idaho, and Wind River, Wyoming, tend to have more diversified sources of income and provide greater job opportunities, while small reservations and colonies tend to depend on off-reservation employment for their residents. Given the paucity of such jobs combined with the lack of adequate education and training of many Shoshones and the prejudice and discrimination they face, rates of unemployment and underemployment are extremely high.

Even at larger reservations, rates of unemployment are high and consequent incomes low. Economic disparities within reservation populations are also attested. Reservation communities continue to be disproportionately poor, whether judged by national or local standards. In 2010, the average per capita income of all Shoshones was $17,340 while the median household income was $38,116. At that time, about one-fourth of Shoshone families (24.3%) and nearly one-third (26.8%) of individuals were living below the poverty level. Per capita incomes were much lower than the Shoshone average at Fort Hall ($10,304) while they were somewhat higher at Fort Hall ($13,085). The Shoshone figure for median household income ($38,116) is higher than the overall American Indian median household income of $36,525. But average household incomes at all Shoshone reservations lagged far behind those of other Americans in their states, for instance in Nevada ($55,726), Utah ($56,330), and Idaho ($46,423). Employment and unemployment rates in different Shoshone communities generally hovered between 15 and 25 percent. Comparison with their neighbors reveals another source of disadvantage since the average unemployment rates for Nevada was 9.0 percent, for Utah 5.9 percent, and for Idaho 7.0 percent (US Census Bureau 2010).

Shoshone reservations are currently administered by elected tribal councils or business councils whose members are responsible for planning and implementing local projects for economic development, education, and social service programs. Funding for some services and projects come from federal grants while on a few reservations, lease rents and royalties from mineral extraction companies provide additional money. However, only at Wind River is the amount from oil and gas resources substantial. In 2014, the government settled a lawsuit from 1970 where they failed to pay royalties for oil and gas development. A sum of $157 million was given to Shoshone and

Arapahoe tribal members in reperation. None of the reservations or colonies have been able to set up highly profitable tribal enterprises, due mostly to the difficulty of raising capital for investment. Tribal government and its functions account for a sizeable percentage of jobs available on the reservations but cannot provide full employment for residents.

In the 1960s and 1970s, western Shoshones obtained funding from federal antipoverty programs that helped improve living conditions and provided some employment for residents (Crum 1994). The first such program, and the one with perhaps the most significant permanent effect, was housing initiatives for constructing new dwellings, renovating existing houses, and providing electricity and running water. However, while the new housing was beneficial, there were some drawbacks to the building programs, especially the construction of housing clusters that violated Shoshones' preferences for "space and openness" (150).

During the same period, the federal government provided funds for job training through the Economic Development Administration and the Office of Economic Opportunity. Under these programs, western Shoshones were trained and employed to construct community centers, build and upgrade irrigation works and corrals, and maintain roads and tribal infrastructure (154–157).

Recognizing that education is a key to economic success in the future, some communities have established their own local or alternative schools that stress the importance of acquiring job skills and training as well as fostering knowledge of Shoshone history, culture, and language. Several books detailing Native history and reminiscences of tribal members have been published by the Inter-Tribal Council of Nevada to provide educational and historical records from the people's perspective (Inter-Tribal Council of Nevada 1974a,b; 1976). The Shoshone language is spoken by most residents of the larger reservations (Wind River and Fort Hall) and by members of smaller colonies. Economic, social, and religious activities that focus on kin groups and communities are important means through which people maintain their ties to each other. According to Liljeblad, commenting on the northern Shoshone at Fort Hall,

> The most deep-rooted indigenous elements of culture which have resisted re-orientation are social, religious and folkloristic in nature …
>
> The durability of the [traditional social structure], favoring a strong family solidarity and reciprocal obligation between kinsmen, meets the need for social security in a rapidly changing world. (1972: 82)

For western Shoshones, Clemmer noted: "Although Western Shoshones are now incorporated into Euro-American economic pursuits, most still participate in traditional food gathering behavior to some extent, primarily to enforce their cultural and psychological ties to the land which formerly provided the sole support for human life in the Great Basin" (Clemmer 1978: 70). And Stewart concurs,

> Although the physical and material conditions of Western Shoshone life were nearly completely and permanently changed by occupation of their territory as ranches and mines reached to the limits of their territory and particularly the better valleys, some ancient Shoshone emotional, social and psychological values and behavior patterns appear to have persisted in spite of material cultural changes … [among these] is the strong

A Shoshone Indian boy, age ten, Fort Washakie, Wyoming, learns traditional dance from a video.

attachment they have to their home territory very narrowly defined. (Stewart 1978: 80–81)

Members of Shoshone communities have retained their traditional philosophical orientation to the world, one that respects the natural world and understands people's relationship to other creatures and to their environment as one of balance and harmony. Festivals and rituals have been revived and maintained. Many today, especially at the eastern and northern Shoshone reservations, participate in Sun Dances both as an expression of fundamental religious and philosophical beliefs and as a means of creating and reinforcing their unity. Eastern Shoshones first began performing Sun Dances around 1880 as a result of diffusion from Comanche teachers, especially the Comanche visionary Yellow Hand, who learned the dance from Kiowas. Once absorbed into eastern Shoshone communities, the Sun Dance later spread to northern Shoshones and Utes in the Great Basin. While the Sun Dance of the Plains focused on earth renewal and successful hunting, Shoshone Sun Dances were reinterpreted with a shift to community renewal, protection, and individual and group health (Jorgensen 1972). The Shoshone Sun Dance is therefore a "redemptive" movement, enabling people through inner spiritual means to cope with external conditions beyond their control.

The modern Shoshone Sun Dance is a ritual of thanks and renewal, continuing themes of aboriginal religious practice. Its focus on health and curing perpetuates concerns that were part of Great Basin rites. The Sun Dance is also consistent with traditional beliefs about acquiring power through visions. Furthermore, traditional curing rites aimed at extracting harmful objects lodged in patient's bodies are performed on the last day of the Sun Dance (Hultkrantz 1987: 74). And in the final evening, continuation of ancient Shoshone religious practice is reflected in feasting, performance of round dances, and giveaways of gifts donated by participants and spectators.

Changes have taken place, however, from Sun Dances of past decades and indeed past centuries. Symbolic features of the rites are now identified with both aboriginal and Christian meanings (Hultkrantz 1987; Liljeblad 1972). For example, while the central pole in the Sun Dance corral is decorated with the head of a buffalo, which is said to represent spirits and forces of nature and is a traditional means of transmitting spirit power, it is also equated with Jesus and the Crucifix. In addition, the twelve outer poles used to construct the corral represent the twelve apostles of Jesus. One of the early-twentieth-century innovators of the Wind River Sun Dance, Pablo Juan Truhuja, explicitly compared Sun Dance practices and artifacts with Christianity. According to Truhuja, the three black bands that are painted on the central pole "meant the Lord laid in the tomb three days and the third day they opened up his tomb—the resurrection" (Voget 1984: 175). Truhuja also compared the cane traditionally used by the drum chief when accompanying songs to the "shepherd's hook" carried by Christ, and the rattles used in Native rituals were likened to church bells. Finally, people today often have visions of Jesus while participating in Sun Dances.

A further modern innovation in some communities is the participation of women as dancers. In the past, women could only act as singers and spectators, but now at Fort Hall they participate as dancers and Sun Dance chiefs (Liljeblad 1972: 98). Sun Dances are performed at the Fort Hall northern Shoshone reservation in Idaho and Wind River eastern Shoshone reservation, Wyoming (Liljeblad 1972). These celebrations are attended by members of western Shoshone and Ute communities as well (Jorgensen 1972). As Jorgensen demonstrates, traditional Shoshone beliefs and practices have been integrated into the modern Sun Dance as an expression of power and identity in the context of a national economic and political system that abrogates Native rights and undermines individual autonomy and esteem. In the Sun Dance, people achieve personal spirit power that is validated by their community:

> Although power is achieved by individuals, it can be achieved only within the group context. Indeed, the power that is earned is sanctioned by the group, and it is expected that individual power will be used for broad ends—family, the wider network of kin, friends and community. The communitarian ideology of the dance compliments the collective Indian ethic. Both preach that Indians must work together in order to achieve. (235)

In the process of participation and achievement, individuals are transformed and redeemed:

> Redemption is critical to Shoshone life now, as it has been in the reservation past, because the redeemed are instructed to reject hedonism and other forms of narrow individualism. The redeemed are

expected to keep "good heart," to "help out" family, kin, friends, and the Indian community, and to be exemplars of how Indian life ought to be lived all of the time. These are instructions for lifelong commitment. (235)

Contemporary Populations

The earliest reports of Shoshone populations suggest a figure of approximately 3,000 each for the northern and eastern groups in the early or mid-nineteenth century and perhaps somewhat more for the western Shoshone. Numbers for all groups declined during the nineteenth century due to disease, starvation, and warfare. By 1890 an official census put the Shoshone population at 3,480. Of these, 639 were western Shoshones, 916 were eastern Shoshones, and 1,925 were northern Shoshones and Bannocks (Leland 1986: 610–611). Shoshone populations continued to decline into the twentieth century. The western and eastern groups reached their lowest point in 1910 while the northern Shoshone nadir was reached in 1930. Since then, all groups began to rebound and have continued to increase steadily.

In the combined 2000/2010 data, there are an estimated 4,442 western Shoshones, 2,278 eastern Shoshones, and 3,196 northern Shoshones. In 1980, census data reported 3,648 western Shoshones, 3,559 eastern Shoshones, and 4,768 northern Shoshones. Compared to other Great Basin nations, the Shoshone have experienced the most dramatic population increase. In 1873, they comprised 25 percent of the Native people in the region, but in 1980 their percentage had risen to 41 percent (610). Among the Shoshone groups in 1873, the western people constituted the largest proportion, but in 1980 the northern Shoshone population was the largest. In 2010, the US Census reported the figures shown in table 12.1 for residents on Shoshone reservations and officially recognized colonies.

TABLE 13.1	Population for Selected Shoshone Reservations	
Eastern Shoshone		
Wind River	2,278	
Northern Shoshone and Bannock		
Fort Hall	3,196	
Western Shoshone		
Duck Valley	1,014	
Duckwater	115*	
Ely Colony	52*	
Fallon	517*	
Fallon Colony	150*	
Goshute	238*	
Reno-Sparks Colony	262*	
Skull Valley	32*	
Te-Moak	1,974*	
Yomba	88*	

Source: US Bureau of the Census 2000: 32–34, 41, 44–46.

*Populations are from 2000 census, more recent data unavailable.

REFERENCES

Ahtone, Tristan. 2012. "A Cancer Runs through It: The Wind River Reservation, Where Cancer Is Epidemic, Is Fighting the EPA over Water Supplies Contaminated with Uranium." *Indian Country Today* 2, no. 1 (January 18): 26–29.

Bourke, John. 1891. *On the Border With Crook.* New York: Scribner's Sons.

Clemmer, Richard. 1974. "Land Use Patterns and Aboriginal Rights: Northern and Eastern Nevada, 1858–1971." *The Indian Historian* 7, no. 1: 24–49.

Clemmer, Richard. 1978. "Pine Nuts, Cattle and the Ely Chain: Rip-off Resource Replacement vs. Homeostatic Equilibrium." *Selected Papers From the 14th Great Basin Anthropology Conference* (ed. D. Tuohy). Socorro, NM: Ballena Press, pp. 61–76.

Crum, Steven. 1994. *The Road on Which We Came: A History of the Western Shoshone.* Salt Lake City, UT: University of Utah Press.

Eggan, Fred. 1980. "Shoshone Kinship Structures and Their Significance for Anthropological Theory." *Journal of the Steward Anthropological Society* 11, no. 2: 165–193.

Gudde, Erwin, and Elizabeth Gudde (eds.). 1958. *Exploring with Fremont: The Private Diaries of Charles Preuss.* Norman, OK: University of Oklahoma Press.

Hoebel, E. Adamson. 1940. *The Political Organization and Law-ways of the Comanche Indians.* Menasha, WI: Memoirs of the American Anthropological Association No. 54.

Hultkrantz, Ake. 1987. *Native Religions of North America.* New York: Harper & Row.

Inter-Tribal Council of Nevada. 1974a. *Life Stories of Our Native People: Shoshone, Paiute, Washo.* Reno, NV: Inter-Tribal Council of Nevada.

Inter-Tribal Council of Nevada. 1974b. *Personal Reflections of the Shoshone, Paiute, Washo.* Reno, NV: Inter-Tribal Council of Nevada.

Inter-Tribal Council of Nevada. 1976. *Newe: A Western Shoshone History*. Reno, NV: Inter-Tribal Council of Nevada.

Jones, Luke. 2015. *Federal Lawsuit Claims BIA Defrauding Shoshone-Bannock Tribe Members*. NPG of Idaho. Online.

Jorgensen, Joseph. 1972. *The Sun Dance Religion: Power for the Powerless*. Chicago, IL: University of Chicago Press.

Leland, Joy. 1986. "Population." *Great Basin* (ed. W. D'Azevedo), Vol. 11 of *Handbook of North American Indians*. Washington, DC: Smithsonian Institution, pp. 606–619.

Lewis, Meriwether, and William Clark. 1905. *Original Journals of the Lewis and Clark Expedition* (ed. R. G. Thwaites). New York.

Liljeblad, Sven. 1972. *The Idaho Indians in Transition, 1805–1960*. Pocatello, ID: Idaho State University Museum.

Lowie, Robert. 1909. *The Northern Shoshone*. New York: Anthropological Papers of the American Museum of Natural History, Vol. II, Part 2, pp. 165–306.

Lowie, Robert. 1915. *Dances and Societies of the Plains Shoshone*. New York: Anthropological Papers of the American Museum of Natural History No. 11, pp. 803–835.

Murphy, Robert, and Yolanda Murphy. 1960. *Shoshone-Bannock Subsistence and Society*. Berkeley, CA: University of California Anthropological Records, Vol. 16, No. 7, pp. 293–338.

Nevins, Alan (ed.). 1956. *Narratives of Exploration and Adventure by John Charles Fremont*. New York: Longmans Green & Company.

Russell, Osborne. 1955. *Journal of a Trapper, or Nine Years in the Rocky Mountains, 1834–1843*. Lincoln, NE: University of Nebraska Press.

Schoolcraft, Henry. 1851. *Historical and Statistical Information Respecting the History, Condition and Prospects of the Indian Tribes of the United States*. Washington, DC: US Office of Indian Affairs.

Shimkin, Demitri. 1942. "Dynamics of Recent Wind River Shoshone History." *American Anthropologist* 44: 451–462.

Shimkin, Demitri. 1986. "Eastern Shoshone." *Great Basin* (ed. W. D'Azevedo). Vol. 11 of *Handbook of North American Indians*. Washington, DC: Smithsonian Institution, pp. 308–335.

Steward, Julian. 1938. *Basin-Plateau Aboriginal Socio-Political Groups*. Washington, DC: Bureau of American Ethnology Bulletin no. 120.

Steward, Julian. 1940. "Native Cultures of the Intermontane (Great Basin Area)." *Essays in Historical Anthropology of North America*. Washington, DC: Smithsonian Miscellaneous Collections no. 100, pp. 445–502.

Steward, Julian. 1943a. "Culture Element Distributions, XXIII: Northern and Gosiute Shoshoni." Berkeley, CA: University of California Anthropological Records no. 8, pp. 263–392.

Steward, Julian. 1943b. "Some Western Shoshone Myths." Bureau of American Ethnology Bulletin no. 136, Anthropological Papers no. 31: 249–299.

"Tribe Strikes Deal with Feds to Manage National Park." 1999. *Pequot Times*. April.

"Tribe in Utah Fights for Nuclear Waste Dump." 1999. *The New York Times*. April 18: A16.

US Census Bureau. 2000.

US Census Bureau. 2010.

US Census Office. 1894. *11th Census, 1890*. Washington, DC: US Government Printing Office.

US Indian Claims Commission. 1980. *Final Report, 1979*. Washington, DC: US Government Printing Office, House Document no. 96–383 (serial no. 13354).

Voget, Fred. 1984. *The Shoshoni-Crow Sun Dance*. Norman, OK: University of Oklahoma Press.

"WSU Design Students Collaborate on Death Valley Cultural Center." 2014. *Standard Examiner*. Online.

Wyeth, Nathaniel. 1851. "Indian Tribes of the South Pass of the Rocky Mountains." *Historical and Statistical Information Respecting the History, Condition and Prospects of the Indian Tribes of the United States* (ed. Henry Schoolcraft). Washington, DC: US Office of Indian Affairs, Part I: 204–228.

THE SOUTHWEST

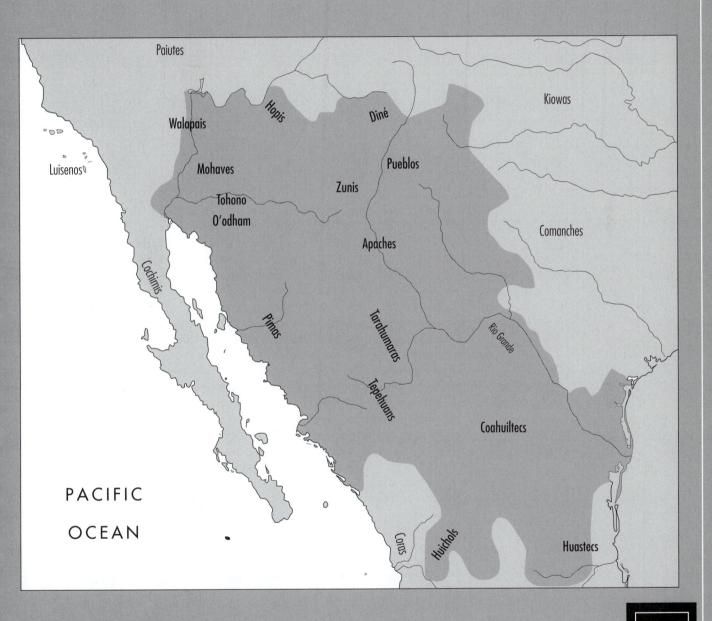

Paiutes

Kiowas

Hopis

Diné

Walapais

Luisenos

Mohaves

Pueblos

Zunis

Tohono
O'odham

Comanches

Cochimís

Apaches

Pimas

Tarahumaras

Rio Grande

Tepehuans

Coahuiltecs

PACIFIC

OCEAN

Coras

Huichols

Huastecs

Diné Creation Story

The surface of the fourth world was unlike the surface of any of the lower worlds. For it was a mixture of black and white. The sky above was alternately white, blue, yellow, and black, just as it had been in the worlds below. But here the colors were of a different duration. As yet there was no sun and no moon; as yet there were no stars.

When they arrived on the surface of the fourth world, the exiles from the lower worlds saw no living thing. But they did observe four great snow-covered peaks along the horizon around them. One peak lay to the east. One peak lay to the south. One peak lay likewise to the west. And to the north there was one peak.

It was now evident to the newcomers that the fourth world was larger than any of the worlds below.

Twenty-three days came and went, and twenty-three nights passed and all was well. And on the twenty-fourth night the exiles held a council meeting. They talked quietly among themselves, and they resolved to mend their ways and to do nothing unintelligent that would create disorder. This was a good world, and the wandering people meant to stay here, it is said.

[Eventually the people were visited by the Holy People who gave them instructions about how to prepare themselves to live in the fourth world. The Holy People promised to give them advice and to teach them to live properly.]

Proceeding silently the gods laid one buckskin on the ground, careful that its head faced west. Upon its skin they placed two ears of corn, being just as careful that the tips of each pointed east. Over the corn they spread the other buckskin making sure that its head faced east.

Under the white ear they put the feather of a white eagle. And under the yellow ear they put the feather of a yellow eagle. Then they told the on-looking people to stand at a distance.

So that the wind could enter.

Then from the east the white wind blue between the buckskins. And while the wind thus blew, each of the Holy People came and walked four times around the objects they had placed so carefully on the ground. As they walked, the eagle feathers moved slightly. Just slightly. So that only those who watched carefully were able to notice. And when the Holy People had finished walking, they lifted the topmost buckskin. And lo! The ears of corn disappeared.

In their place there lay a man and there lay a woman.

The white ear of corn had been transformed into our most ancient male ancestor [First Man] and the yellow ear of corn had been transformed into our most ancient female ancestor [First Woman].

It was the wind that had given them life: the very wind that gives us our breath as we go about our daily affairs here in the world we ourselves live in. When this wind ceases to blow inside of us, we become speechless. And we die.

In the skin at the tips of our fingers we can see the trail of that life-giving wind. Look carefully at your own fingertips. There you will see where the wind blew when it created your most ancient ancestors out of two ears of corn, it is said.

Source: Paul Zolbrod. 1984. *Diné Bahane: The Navaho Creation Story*. Abuquerque, NM: University of New Mexico Press, pp. 45–51.

Native Nations of the Southwest

We have lived upon this land from days beyond history's records, far past any living memory, deep into the time of legend. The story of my people and the story of this place are one single story. No man can think of us without thinking of this place. We are always joined together.

Taos Pueblo, quoted in Henry et al. 1970: 35.

LANDS AND NATIONS

The southwestern region of North America, centered in the present-day states of New Mexico and Arizona and including adjacent territory in Utah, Colorado, California, and the Mexican state of Sonora, is an area of great environmental, cultural, and linguistic diversity. Most of the land is high above sea level, with altitudes from 3,000 to as much as 10,000 ft. Precipitation rates are generally low although amounts of rainfall vary from one year to the next and from one region to others. Higher elevations tend to receive more rain and/or snow, while lower altitudes may be nearly devoid of precipitation. Given differences in climate and topography, local districts also vary in their natural resources, particularly water, wild plants, and animals.

The Southwest was the aboriginal home of people of many distinct nations whose cultures and histories shared similarities as well as unique differences. Four major groups are distinguished by linguistic affiliation and cultural emphases: the Puebloans, Apacheans, Pimans, and Yumans. Most Puebloans lived in small compact villages along the Rio Grande River in New Mexico, while others, often referred to as western Puebloans, resided further west in New Mexico and Arizona. Apacheans (the several Apache nations and the Diné or Navajos) occupied territory on the Colorado Plateau in New Mexico, Utah, Colorado, and Arizona. Piman nations include the Pimas and Tohono O'odham, whose lands are located in southwestern Arizona and nearby northern Mexico. Finally, the Yumans held territory in western Arizona and adjacent areas of eastern California. Nearly all of the Native nations that inhabited the Southwest at the time of the first European invasions in the sixteenth century were descendants of people who had lived there for many millennia. Only the Apacheans were relatively recent immigrants into the area, arriving from the Northwest by the fourteenth century.

The languages spoken by aboriginal southwestern people belong to six linguistic families, most with ties to languages spoken outside the region as well. The Puebloans called the Tiwas, Tewas, and Towas speak languages that belong to the Tanoan branch of the Kiowa-Tanoan linguistic family. Other eastern Puebloans and some western Puebloans (the Acomas and Lagunas) speak languages of the Keresan family. The Uto-Aztecan family is represented in the Southwest by the Hopis and the Piman nations (the Pimas and Tohono O'odham). Another Puebloan nation, the Zunis of western New Mexico, speak a language that is classed as an isolate having no known relatives within the Southwest, although it may be related to Penutian languages of California. The genetic link between Zuni and Penutian, however, has not yet been fully demonstrated. If they are related, their separation goes back at least 7,000 years (Newman 1964). Additionally, some southwestern peoples speak Yuman languages, that is, the Havasupais, Walapais, Yavapais, Mohaves, Maricopas, and Quechans. Finally, the languages of Apaches and Diné (Navajos) comprise the southern branch of a large family called Athabaskan, whose northern relatives live in western Canada and northern California.

The effects of climate change are predicted to be particularly serious for Native nations in the Southwestern region. A report issued in 2012 by the Southwest Climate Science Center of the University of Arizona stated in part, "Native American lands, people and culture are likely to be disproportionately affected by climate change. Effects are likely to be greater than elsewhere because of endangered cultural practices, limited water rights and social, economic, and political marginalization ... The marginal landscape of reservations in the United States, particularly in the Southwest with some of the driest resource-poor areas [was] established by policy, not by coincidence" (quoted in Allen 2012). Southwestern nations are already suffering from increased drought and water shortages that are negatively affecting farming and animal husbandry, and this problem has been accentuated by the recent California drought. Many people rely on their crops for household subsistence and on raising cattle and sheep both for domestic use and for sale. At times, drought alternates with heavy storms and flooding, causing soil erosion and further destroying the ability of the land to support farming and herding. Excessive heat and dry conditions also lead to dangers from wildfires. Reacting to the Climate Center's report, Francie Spencer, an economic development specialist with the San Carlos Apache tribe in Arizona, commented: "Our existence is still based on practices rooted in the land. There's a water shortage across the reservation and because cattle are still one of our top economic drivers, without water, our stock numbers have been reduced." And Lawrence Snow, a land resources manager for the Shivwits Band of Paiutes in Utah stated: "Our 30,000 acre reservation is dry because of drought. Wildfires in the last decade have burned half our acreage and changed the landscape. Once the fires happened and took out the ground cover, major storms brought big flooding. Seasons have changed."

There are many grant and funding initiatives to support economic development, Native language acquisition, Native culture preservation, and other important projects among Southwestern tribes. The First Nations Development Institute, for example, has provided over $3.3 million in grants to Native youth programs throughout the United States. In 2012, they awarded grants to the Mescalero Apache Tribe, the Navajo Technical College in Crownpoint, the Notah Begay III Foundation, the Zuni Youth Enrichment Program, the Sante Fe Indian School, and the Pueblo of Pojoaque. Programs aimed at youth will encourage young people to develop skills that they can use to benefit their communities. Results from the program are yet to be published (Whiting 2012).

Shasta Dazen, 21 (center), and Deandra Antonio, 17 (right), of the White Mountain Apache Nation and who serve on the White Mountain Apache youth council, vie for a glimpse of first lady Michelle Obama, after she spoke at the first White House Tribal Youth Gathering in July 2015.

PUEBLOAN CULTURE

Puebloans inhabit two distinct ecological zones: relatively fertile lands near the Rio Grande River in New Mexico and the warmer and drier mesas and steppe regions of northern Arizona. The word Puebloan is derived from the Spanish word "pueblo" (town) with which these diverse peoples were named by Spanish invaders of the sixteenth century because of their compact village settlements. Despite differences in climate and topography that necessitate a different use of land and water, Puebloan cultures share a distinctive orientation and value system. Although Puebloans are of different linguistic and presumably historical roots, they share cultural traits and orientations that are usefully distinguished from other aboriginal residents of the region. According to Ortiz,

> The peoples called Pueblos, despite their linguistic diversity and wide geographical range, have, at various times reaching far into dim pre-history, shared a sense of cultural similarity, just as they have shared a common homeland. This sense of cultural similarity has probably never settled on any single thing held or believed in common among all Pueblos in their long existence…With the Pueblos we must assume a long term interactionist perspective, one which does not assume that there is a shared property common to all of them, but rather that there have always been shifting clusters of experiences and meanings that have overlapped several groups at the same time, and different groups at other times. (Ortiz 1994: 296–297)

Puebloans are united by their worldview, their assumptions about and orientation to the universe and their strong sense of land and place, no doubt deepened by their long residence in the region. But despite ideological similarities among Puebloans, differences in subsistence techniques, social organization, and political integration and leadership are attested. Some of the boundaries demarcating cultural differences are those of geography. That is, eastern Puebloans utilize different economic strategies and different principles of social organization than those of western Puebloans. Linguistic affiliation frequently overlaps with geographic divisions. While the easternmost Puebloans (i.e., the Tanoan-speaking Tewas, Tiwas, and Towas) are most differentiated from the western Hopis and Zunis, the centrally located Keresan-speaking people demonstrate internal variations, some traits more closely resembling the Tanoans and others more closely resembling the western nations. However, even these distinctions are not sharp or discrete but rather are differences of emphasis and gradation.

Aboriginal economies of all Puebloans were centered on farming and included the same basic inventory of crops: corn, beans, squash, and cotton. The people obtained most of their foods from farming, supplemented by gathering wild plants and hunting and fishing where possible. At the time of the earliest Spanish invasions, Puebloans lived in approximately ninety compact permanent villages. Population estimates are unreliable, but in the early seventeenth century they probably numbered some 30,000–40,000, undoubtedly a decline from the population of a century earlier before European diseases and warfare greatly reduced their size. Village populations generally averaged about 400 although they varied from a high of 2,000 to possibly as few as 50 (Dozier 1961: 99). Village plans differed somewhat, but houses were everywhere made of adobe and some utilized sandstone slabs as well. Tanoan village plans featured houses oriented around one or two central open plazas that were used for public gatherings and ceremonies whereas Keresans and western Puebloans constructed parallel rows of houses. All Puebloan villages had one or more kivas, that is, underground structures used for the performance of rituals and storage of ceremonial objects.

Major economic distinctions between eastern and western Puebloans were the methods of obtaining and utilizing water for their fields. People living near the Rio Grande irrigated their fields with runoffs from the river's floodwaters and by building dams and irrigation ditches to bring water to their fields. Irrigation works were constructed, maintained, and cleaned by the communal labor of men and women. In contrast, western Puebloans lacked year-round sources of water but instead relied on rainfall to water their crops. Such reliance was risky because rainfall was relatively meager, averaging only about 10 in. per year. In addition, the rain tended to be concentrated in severe thunderstorms in the summertime. The timing of precipitation was crucial to the success of farming because if rain fell too early it could damage or destroy young plants and if it came too late the crops would have by then withered and died. Both in the east and west, farmland was not individually owned but rather was controlled communally, usually by kin groups. Farm production was organized by groups of male relatives who worked on land where they had use-rights, that is, by birth in patrilocal households and by marriage in matrilocal communities. Men cleared fields, planted seeds, and harvested the crops. They also hunted and fished where possible, secured firewood, produced the tools used in their work, and made baskets, blankets, and sashes. Women's work included gathering wild foods, preparing meals, taking care of children, and making pottery (Dozier 1961: 102). Houses were built by men, but women were responsible for plastering the walls and maintaining the dwellings. Puebloans kept turkeys, principally using their feathers for ceremonial paraphernalia and decoration. Domesticated dogs were kept as pets.

The social organization of Puebloan communities varied in different regional and cultural groupings. Western Puebloans were organized into matrilineal exogamous clans and lived in matrilocal extended family households. Eastern Keresans also had matrilineal exogamous clans but these clans were not corporate groups and held no land in common. Keresan residence after marriage was bilocal, enabling couples to make choices based on availability of land, household composition, and personal considerations. Eastern Keresan clans were grouped into two moieties, Turquoise and Squash, that were each associated with one of the two ceremonial kivas in their villages. Although kiva recruitment was initially through patrilineal affiliation, people could switch membership for a variety of reasons. Among the Tanoans of the Rio Grande region, several different social principles organized village and kinship life. The Towas were most similar to the nearby eastern Keresans, having both matrilineal exogamous clans and a dual organization based on two kivas, the Turquoise and Squash. Tiwa kinship was thoroughly bilateral, lacking clans or any rules of exogamy. Villages were, however, divided into two groups associated with kivas. The Tewas also had a bilateral kinship system and a dual organization, called Summer and Winter, linked to kivas. Membership in the Summer or Winter moiety followed patrilineal lines, but one's membership was not automatic and in fact could change during a lifetime. Women commonly joined the kiva of their husband if they were not already members. Tanoan residence was bilocal. Land, owned by villages, was assigned to families who had use-rights that could be inherited by either sons or daughters (Dozier 1961).

Navajo Hogan.

In most Puebloan communities, sociopolitical integration and leadership were associated with ritual roles. As in other cultural domains, variations were influenced by both location and cultural ancestry. Particular practices and patterns seem to have been strongest in some nations while more weakly manifested in others. Among western Puebloans, especially the Hopis and Zunis, political organization was most closely associated with ritual functions. For Zunis in particular, secular leaders were appointed and managed by members of priesthoods. In the eastern Pueblos, in contrast, political organization was more centralized and less tightly linked to ritual roles. In Tanoan villages, governmental and religious functions were associated with the two moieties (Summer and Winter among the Tewas; Turquoise and Squash among the others). Much of public life was organized and directed by the leaders and members of social, political, and ritual societies. Various societies had responsibilities to announce dates for public rituals, organize communal dances and celebrations, direct the cleaning of villages and irrigation ditches, plan communal hunting and warfare expeditions, and set dates for planting and harvesting (Dozier 1961: 112–113).

Today there are a total of twenty-one federally recognized Pueblos in New Mexico, Texas, and Arizona (Department of the Interior 2002). The western Keresans of Acoma and Laguna each occupy one principal town. The eastern Keresans live in five pueblos near the Rio Grande: Cochiti, San Felipe, Santa Ana, Kewa (formerly Santo Domingo), and Zia. Each of the three Tanoan societies occupy several villages. The Tiwa villages are called Isleta, Picuris, Sandia, Taos, and Tigua. Towas reside in the pueblos of Jemez and Pecos. Finally, Tewas occupy six villages, including Ohkay Owingeh (formerly San Juan), the largest, Santa Clara, San Ildefonso, Nambe, Pojoaque, and Tesuque. In addition to these twenty-one Pueblos, the Hopis reside in thirteen villages atop mesas and in the foothills of the western Colorado Plateau and Arizona. The Zunis have one principal village, called Zuni, and several small satellite settlements nearby.

Tewa Worldview

The Tewas are one of the Tanoan-speaking nations residing in the northernmost reaches of the Rio Grande. They currently inhabit six villages that are considered politically independent although they recognize a common language and shared culture. Tewa kinship is based on bilateral principles of organization and affiliation. In addition, Tewas are organized into two moieties, Summer and Winter, that have social, political, and ceremonial functions. People are initiated into the moiety of their father although such membership must be achieved and may change during one's lifetime. That is, belonging to a moiety and being a Tewa are not automatic facts but rather deliberate acts. In Ortiz's words, "The two most meaningful things one can say about the Tewa life cycle are first, that one is not born a Tewa but rather one is made a Tewa and second, once made, one has to work hard continuously throughout one's life to remain a Tewa" (Ortiz 1979: 287).

Basic to Tewa worldview is the distinction of matter between "unripe" and "dry or hardened food" (Ortiz 1969: 16). The term for the latter, "seh t'a," refers not only to food but to all matter and includes as well children after the age of six or seven. Before that age is reached, children are considered unable to reason and therefore not "dry." Although children are incorporated into their appropriate moiety through a "water-giving" rite during their first year and receive a moiety-specific name, they are not considered to be a Tewa adult (or "Dry Food Person") until they have undergone a "water-pouring rite" performed by each moiety for children between the ages of six and ten. These rites are held every four years in the kiva and appropriate season for each moiety (i.e., in the summer for the Summer

moiety and in winter for the Winter people). The successful conclusion of the ritual makes the child a Dry Food Person. During the water-pouring rite when children are brought into the ceremonial kiva of their moiety, masked gods appear to them, exposing them for the first time to the physical presence of deities. The moiety initiation process concludes with a "finishing" rite when children are at least ten years old. At this rite, held when a group of fifteen or twenty children of the appropriate age are available, the masked gods appear again and then take off their masks to reveal that they are in fact relatives of the initiates. The "finishing" rite makes a person an adult member of the Tewa community and is a prerequisite for marriage.

While the dual organization separates Tewas into Summer and Winter moieties, the groups are linked through their parallel structure and through the transference of secular and ceremonial authority over time. The Summer moiety and its associated officials lead the village during the summer half of the year and are replaced by officials from the Winter moiety during the winter. The system thus both divides the community into social and ceremonial groups and integrates them through cycles of replacement and symmetry.

Tewas conceive of human and spirit beings in three linked pairs (Ortiz 1969: 17). The first pair are the "Dry Food People" and the "Dry Food Who Are No Longer," the latter being the souls of Dry Food People who have died. The second category is made up of two groups of "Towa e," one human and one spirit. The human Towa e include three types of secular and ceremonial officials. The civil officials, including a governor, two lieutenants, and a sheriff, are responsible for dealing with the outside world. Another group of Towa e consists of six people, three selected from each moiety, who have ritual functions. They protect and clean the kivas, coordinate rituals conducted in the village, and set the ceremonial calendar. A final category of human Towa e are the four "fiscales" who maintain the town's Catholic church and assist the resident priest. All Towa e are chosen from among Dry Food People for terms of one year.

Linked conceptually to the human Towa e are spirit beings, also called Towa e, who are the six primordial pairs of brothers whose origin is in the beginning of creation. When the Tewas' ancestors first emerged from inside the earth, they were led out by the spirit Towa e who then retired to the sacred mountains surrounding the Tewa homeland and now watch over and protect the people.

The third paired category in the Tewa universe are the "Made People" and the "Dry Food Who Never Did Become." Made People are humans who have a variety of political and ceremonial roles. They are the chiefs of the Summer and Winter moieties as well as the members of a number of specialized societies such as the Bear Medicine Society, the Kossa (clowns), the Hunt Society, the Scalp Society, and the Women's Society. Tewas become members of these societies in several ways. Some receive a calling in a dream, others may be cured by the society or may find a sacred object associated with the group. In addition, a parent may dedicate a child to membership in a particular society. Once selected, people undergo a series of rites of incorporation, culminating in a "finishing" rite that formally installs them as members of the group.

Paired conceptually with the Made People are the Dry Food Who Never Did Become. These are the deities responsible for creation of the Tewa and their culture. They live in sacred lakes that are associated with each of the four sacred mountains delineating the Tewa world.

Just as Tewa concepts of "persons" organize their sense of being, Native concepts of space similarly situate the people in their physical and spiritual universe. The outer limits of the Tewa world are marked by the four sacred mountains that are the abodes of the spirit Towa e, the six pairs of brothers who helped the Tewa at the time of emergence. Inside the boundaries of the space set off by the mountains and next closer to the Tewa villages are four sacred mesas that were created by the Towa e and are the locales for spirit beings called "Tsave Yoh" who appear or are impersonated in initiation rituals. The next closer set of boundary markers are shrines to the four cardinal directions. Finally, the link to sacred space is maintained in Tewa villages by the open dance plazas in their center, connecting all of the directions, hills, and mountains that have sacred meaning (Ortiz 1969: 18–20). Like the spatial perspectives of other Puebloans, Tewas emphasize the importance of the center or "middle place," a place not only of emergence from the earth in primordial times but also a spiritual place of timelessness connecting all of the beings and energy of the universe.

Spanish Invasion of Puebloan Lands

In 1539, Fray Marcos de Niza travelled north from the Spanish bases in Mexico and reported seeing the "Seven Cities of Cibola," an imaginary kingdom that Spaniards believed possessed untold treasures. In reality, de Niza viewed some of the Zuni villages in western New Mexico. Even though he never approached the settlements but only surveyed them from a distant hilltop, he claimed possession of the region for the king of Spain and then returned to Mexico. On the basis of de Niza's false reports, in 1540 Francisco Vasquez de Coronado was sent to conquer the Puebloan villages. Some 300 soldiers accompanied by Mexican Indian slaves and six Franciscan missionaries entered Puebloan territory but instead of finding the fabled cities of gold, they found small villages settled along the Rio Grande and the mesas of the west. Coronado stayed in the area for less than two years, but in that short time he and his soldiers succeeded in terrorizing the indigenous inhabitants in whose midst they established camps and missions. The Spaniards demanded food, clothing, and housing from the people, who initially complied out of friendship and later out of fear. Spanish soldiers raped Native women and punished whoever attempted to stop them. As the soldiers' demands intensified, some Puebloans balked and finally staged local, and unsuccessful, rebellions. Coronado then returned to Mexico and it was not until the 1580s that Spanish authorities again sought to conquer Puebloan territory. The first major expedition was led by Antonia de Espejo in 1582. Like Coronado, he was accompanied by soldiers, Mexican Indian slaves, servants, and Franciscan priests. Espejo's troops travelled through the Rio Grande villages and westward as far as the Zunis and Hopis in Arizona. As others before him and others to follow, Espejo's campaign left a trail of rape, death, and theft of property. Continually demanding provisions and servants, Espejo also occasionally incited Native resistance and, as others had done, dealt brutally with any rebellion. The following account of an assault on a Tiwa village was recorded by one of Espejo's chroniclers:

> The people were all in the Sierra except for some thirty Indians on the flat roofs of their houses. When we asked them for food, as they were our friends, they mocked us like the others. In view of this, the corners of the Pueblo were taken by four men, and four others with two servants began to seize those Natives who showed themselves. And as the Pueblo was large and the majority had hidden themselves there, we set fire to the big Pueblo, where we thought some were burned to death because of the cries they uttered. We at once took

out the prisoners, two at a time, and lined them up close to the cottonwoods against the Pueblo, where they were garroted and shot many times until they were dead. Sixteen were executed, not counting those who were burned to death. (Hammond and Rey 1966: 204)

In 1598, Juan de Oñate crossed into Tewa lands and set up headquarters in one of their villages. There the provincial capital remained until 1610 when it was moved to Sante Fe. Oñate, like his predecessors, established rule through terror. Soldiers occupied Native towns, demanded food, provisions, and slaves and punished with beatings and death anyone who disobeyed. According to one of his captains, Oñate's policy was to

send people out every month in various directions to bring maize from the Pueblos. The feelings of the Natives against supplying it can not be exaggerated … for they weep and cry out as if they and all their descendants were being killed. The Spaniards seized their blankets by force, leaving the poor Indian women stark naked, holding their babies to their breasts. (Hammond and Rey 1953, 2: 608–610)

When Oñate encountered resistance in the village of Acoma, he ordered the burning of the town, the killing of a large number of residents, and the enslavement of men, women, and children. As a further punishment, men over the age of twenty-five who survived the assault had one of their feet amputated (Dozier 1970: 47). In this incident alone, at least 500 people were enslaved (Simmons 1979: 181).

Accompanying and assisting the soldiers, Franciscan priests began their missionary activities in earnest. By 1630, one priest reported that they had converted some 60,000 Puebloans and had forced them to build ninety chapels in Native villages (Dozier 1970: 47). Most of the "conversions" were manifested by mandatory attendance at Catholic masses. Absences were brutally punished. In addition to compelling Puebloans to attend church services, missionaries tried to eradicate performances of indigenous ceremonies, but the people continued to conduct their own rituals and dances underground in the kivas or in other places far from view. Whenever the priests learned of the celebration of Native rituals, they ordered soldiers to punish the participants, whipping religious leaders and executing those held most responsible.

The brutality with which the Spanish forced Puebloans to comply with their demands prompted the people to forge a united resistance. In 1680, a Tewa religious leader named Pope, who himself had been the victim of a public beating, emerged as an organizer of a rebellion. With coordination among all Pueblos including those in the west, the revolt was set for August 11, 1680, but because news of the uprising had been leaked to Spanish authorities, the leaders decided to stage the revolt on August 10. The people destroyed the churches, killed the resident priests, and forced Spanish settlers out of their territory. They were even successful in attacking the provincial capital at Sante Fe and routing the inhabitants. A total of twenty-one missionaries were killed along with some 400 settlers (out of a population of 2,500). Puebloans, though, also suffered many casualties, especially in the Tewa and Tiwa nations, who were the most active in the rebellion (Dozier 1970: 59).

Following the revolt, twelve years of peace returned to Puebloan territory but the people fell prey to raiding by other Indians living on their periphery, especially Apaches, Diné, and Utes who stole sheep that Puebloans had begun to raise after their introduction by the Spanish. Then, in 1692, the government in Mexico reconquered Puebloan territory, successful in part by internal dissension within Native communities as well as the people's fear of incursions by Apacheans and Utes. Although Spanish civil and religious functionaries in the eighteenth century pledged to respect Native people and customs, in fact, Puebloans were often forced to work in shops producing blankets and clothing or in mines and on farms. In addition, the Spanish continued to abuse the Indians, especially committing sexual assaults on women.

After the reconquest, the Pueblos were declared "republicas" with some degree of self-government but the Spaniards imposed a new set of officers to deal with external authorities. The civil leadership included a governor, a lieutenant governor, war captains, a sheriff responsible for internal law and order, a mayor domo who supervised the cleaning and maintenance of irrigation ditches, and sacristans to assist the missionaries. These officials were elected by the male populace for one-year terms. However, the traditional ritual and secular leadership continued as the actual authorities in most villages, directing the activities of the men selected as civil officers. And traditional religious beliefs and rituals continued, usually far from foreign eyes so as not to provoke repression. Compliance with church rules was generally superficial, as one of the priests, Fray Dominguez, noted on a visit to several villages in 1776:

> Even at the end of so many years since their reconquest, the specious title of neophytes is still applied to them. This is the reason their condition now is almost the same as it was in the beginning. Their repugnance and resistance to most Christian acts is evident, for they perform the duties pertaining to the church under compulsion, and there are usually many omissions. (Dozier 1961: 143)

By the end of the eighteenth century, life in Puebloan villages had returned to some degree of calm although people were forced to conform outwardly to foreign regulations. However, disease and military attacks had resulted in thousands of deaths. From an estimated population of 14,000 in 1700, Puebloans numbered some 9,732 in 1799 (149). Diseases such as smallpox, measles, typhus, and influenza caused the vast majority of deaths. In only a two-year period, 1780–1781, more than 5,000 Puebloans died during a devastating smallpox epidemic.

The Imposition of American Control

When Mexico won its independence from Spain in 1821, a new foreign authority took nominal control of Puebloan territory, but because of internal problems in Mexico and the vast distance between the center of government and Puebloan lands, the Indians were little affected by the administrative change except for a revision in their legal status. Under Spanish rule, indigenous inhabitants had been considered wards of the crown, but under Mexican jurisdiction, they became citizens of Mexico with full rights to land and protection. Puebloan status was to change yet again in 1846 when the US government took control of the region after the Mexican-American War. Under federal law, most Native people were considered wards of the government and faced restrictions on their legal autonomy and rights. It was not long before American officials began to exert an actual physical presence in the territory. They were motivated both by the discovery of gold in California and the desire to extend control from coast to coast in fact as well as in law. Once perceiving the change in government, Puebloan communities sent numerous delegations to federal authorities to seek redress for two problems that they

faced, namely encroachment of Hispanic settlers on their territory and incursions by Apache, Diné, and Ute raiders seeking sheep and other livestock. The US government attended to both problems, although not with the same degree of zeal. Using Puebloan requests as a pretext, American authorities ordered attacks against the Indian raiders to "pacify" the region, not only restoring peace to Puebloan communities but making the territory safe for Anglo settlement. The culmination of this policy was the campaign launched in 1864 against the Diné that resulted in the killing of hundreds of people and the incarceration of the majority of survivors at Fort Sumner, New Mexico, for four years. In instructions reminiscent of Spanish policies of the sixteenth and seventeenth centuries, General James Carleton, commander of the troops, summed up the approach to be taken to the Diné:

> [T]he Indian men are to be killed whenever and wherever you can find them: the women and children will not be harmed but you will take them prisoners. If the Indians send in a flag and desire to treat for peace, say to the bearer; they have broken their treaty of peace and that now we are going to punish them for their crimes, and that you are there to kill them wherever they can be found. I trust that this severity in the long run will be the most humane course that could be pursued toward these Indians. (Beck 1962: 189)

Disputes over claims to land were dealt with in due course. By the time the United States took jurisdiction over the Southwest, much of Puebloan territory supposedly protected under Spanish and Mexican land grants had been invaded by Hispanic and Anglo settlers. Some of the land had been sold with the acquiescence of the Indians who probably did not fully understand the finality of the transfers. When the Indians pressed for return of their land, settlers argued that since Puebloans had been citizens under Mexican rule, they had full rights to sell land if they chose to do so. While this argument supported Indians' rights to some of the advantages of citizenship, in fact it was promoted in order to undercut Puebloan communal rights to land and thereby benefit non-Indian residents. Territorial courts in New Mexico supported the settlers' arguments, but in 1913 the US Supreme Court reversed lower court rulings, declaring that Puebloans had the same ward-like status as other Indians and therefore could not sell their land. Moreover, they were entitled to reclaim lands that had already been sold. The Supreme Court's decision had the practical effect of promoting the communal integrity of Puebloan villages even though its wording revealed their own ethnocentrism:

> The people of the Pueblos, although sedentary rather than nomadic in their inclinations and disposed to peace and industry are nevertheless Indians in race, customs, and domestic government, always living in separate and isolated communities, adhering to primitive modes of life, largely influenced by superstition and fetishism, and chiefly governed according to the crude customs inherited from their ancestors. They are essentially a simple, uninformed, and inferior people. (Dozier 1961: 157)

Following the Court's decision, in 1924 Congress passed the Pueblo Lands Act that established a Pueblo Lands Board to review claims concerning Native land grants. Some of the land previously sold was returned to Native villages and funds were provided for the compensation of non-Indian owners. Once these immediate problems had been settled, Congress provided money for the acquisition of additional acreage since they recognized that serious problems of soil erosion and increases in both the human and animal populations required additional farming and grazing territory. By the middle of the twentieth century, more than 600,000 acres were added to the Puebloan land base, a 50 percent increase over the territory that they held in the 1930s (Aberle 1948: 16). Later, in the 1960s, the people of Taos petitioned for the return of some 48,000 acres contained in the Carson National Forest (New Mexico), including Blue Lake, sacred to the Taos people. Their suit was affirmed in 1965 by the US Indian Claims Commission and officially ratified in 1970 by an act of Congress.

Contemporary Population, Economic, and Cultural Data

Today, Puebloan villages are integrated into local and national economies. Their cumulative population is estimated at nearly 78,386 in 2014 (US Census Bureau 2014). Most people are engaged in wage work either in their villages or more commonly in nearby towns and cities. People also earn a substantial portion of their income from craft production as the market for Puebloan jewelry has expanded both nationally and internationally. However, rates of unemployment and underemployment are high. The 2010 per capita income for Pueblos ranges from $9,687 in Kewa Pueblo to $28,148 in Sandia Pueblo. However, a far greater number of people have per capita incomes on the lower side: seventeen of the Pueblos have a per capita income under the average of New Mexico ($22,966), and all but one have a per capita income under the average of Arizona ($25,537). Similarly, the Picuris Pueblo has the lowest household median income ($11,500) while the Tesuque had the highest ($68,750). Poverty rates vary, but are generally between 15 and 30 percent, with a few outlier on each side.

Some Pueblos have recently begun to take advantage of their proximity to Albuquerque and Santa Fe by opening casinos that attract people from the nearby cities, even though gaming is controversial at many Pueblos and many segments of the communities vigorously oppose it, often on the grounds that it undermines traditional religious and cultural beliefs. Advocates of casinos, however, stress that the well-needed jobs and tribal income that they provide will strengthen Puebloan communities and culture. In the words of Roy Montoya, chief administrator of Santa Ana,

> Our culture and religion was very strong when we got our subsistence from farming right here on the reservation. Then when the economy started changing and Dad had to go off the reservation to work, things got weak. But with jobs on the reservation now you have more time to spend with your family and in 15 or 20 years, the religion and culture will become stronger again. (Brett 1999: A24)

As elsewhere throughout Native America, these issues will be debated for many years to come.

Additional cultural concerns continue to reverberate in Puebloan communities. For example, Puebloan nations have sought application of the federal Native American Graves Repatriation Act to recover sacred masks and ceremonial objects from public museums. However, when these objects are owned by private collectors or foreign entities, the US law does not apply. In a recent case of this sort, in 2013 some seventy Hopi masks and ceremonial headdresses were auctioned in Paris by a collector who said that he had acquired them legally over a period of thirty years while living in the United States. Still, the Hopi Tribe appealed to a French court to have the auction canceled on the grounds that these were items of great religious significance but the judge ruled that the sale did not violate laws. Despite protests by the Hopis and by the US ambassador to France, the masks were auctioned although two foundations and private collectors purchased several of the masks to return to the Hopi tribe.

Given their location in the arid Southwest, access to clean water supplies is a central environmental and economic issue to Puebloan peoples. In 2013, a water rights settlement conferred access to sufficient water supplies from rivers in the Rio Pojoaque Basin located north of Santa Fe, New Mexico, to the nearby Pueblos of Tesuque, Nambe, Pojoaque, and San Ildefonso. The agreement was reached between the four Native groups and the US Department of the Interior and the state of New Mexico after forty-six years of litigation and negotiation ("Four New Mexico Pueblos and Secretary Salazar Finalize Historic *Aamodt* Water Rights Settlement" 2013: 6). Projects supported by the agreement include construction of water delivery systems, irrigation canals, and surface water diversion systems from the Rio Grande.

APACHEAN CULTURES

Apacheans are presumed to have entered the Southwest around 1300, migrating south from their prior homeland in the Mackenzie River Basin of western Canada. Linguistic and cultural evidence points to their origin in the region of Athabaskan concentration in Saskatchewan, Alberta, and eastern British Columbia. Although it is impossible to know why the Proto-Apacheans left their ancestral territories, their migration southward might have been caused by deteriorating resource supplies (Helm 1965). Furthermore, the route or routes by which the Proto-Apacheans migrated southward are not established. An intermontane route through Utah or Colorado and the Great Basin is perhaps the most likely, although a second possible route may have been through the western and central plains close to the eastern edge of the mountains. Neither possibility can be definitely confirmed by archeological, ethnographic, or historic data although an intermontane route seems to be most favored. It is, of course, possible that some groups of Apacheans took a more westerly route while others migrated closer to the plains. Only the Kiowa-Apaches exhibit significant Plains features in their culture. From linguistic evidence, they are thought to have diverged the earliest from the Apachean family, probably some 650 years ago. In other words, at least until 1300, the Apacheans were a relatively unified and closely related group of hunting and gathering people. They are believed to have made their entrance into the Southwest or at least have been on its northern boundaries by that time. Since then, distinct cultural and linguistic groups have emerged, each responding to different ecological and historic conditions and each receiving cultural influences from neighboring indigenous people among whom they settled.

Historical linguistic calculations suggest that the Proto-Apacheans separated from their northern relatives in approximately 950–1000 (Hoijer 1956). They were probably then a relatively homogeneous group although there may have been some slight differences in culture and dialect. The divergence of Apachean peoples themselves probably began about 1300, as evidenced by glottochronological data pointing to the separation of the easternmost (Kiowa-Apache) and western Apache languages. Apachean languages, comprising the southern branch of the Athabaskan language family, include Diné, western Apache, Chiricahua, Mescalero, Jicarilla, Lipan, and Kiowa-Apache. The western Apache and Diné languages are closest to each other and more distinct from the eastern Apache languages, suggesting that these two peoples have been closely united until fairly recently. Their cultures also share the most similarities in economic and social organization and again are distinct from eastern Apache nations. The Diné and western Apaches inhabit territory that is ecologically similar, consisting of desert, steppe, and mountain zones with relatively light precipitation although more rain (and snow) falls in mountainous regions. The eastern Apache nation of the Chiricahua occupied territory in southwestern New Mexico while the other eastern Apaches (i.e., the Jicarillas, Mescaleros, Lipans, and Kiowa-Apaches) lived further east in eastern New Mexico, Colorado, Texas, and Oklahoma.

The economies of Apacheans varied according to region occupied and cultural emphasis. The Diné, western Apaches, and Jicarillas combined farming with foraging activities while the Mescaleros, Chiricahuas, Lipans, and Kiowa-Apaches were primarily or exclusively foragers. However, the reliance on farming differed somewhat even among Apachean farmers. For instance, western Apaches derived no more than 25 percent of their annual diet from farming whereas among the Diné, farming supplied at least half of food resources (Griffin et al. 1971). To water their fields, Apachean farmers relied principally on rainfall and runoff from streams and flashfloods in summer rainstorms. Farming was accomplished with the cooperative labor of small groups formed with no gender preferences or restrictions. Although men were responsible for the initial clearing of land, both women and men might plant, weed, and harvest crops. The lack of rigidity in economic roles also extended to other activities, especially ceremonial roles. Both men and women might function as curers, diagnosticians, and ritualists of other types.

The social systems of Apacheans were not identical although there was a similar tendency to emphasize matrilineal kin and a preference for matrilocal residence. Matrilineal extended families lived in scattered communities, each nuclear family occupying a separate dwelling. Local groups consisted of a number of related extended families who formed the basic units of economic and ceremonial cooperation. Among the eastern Apaches, territorial groupings were linked into named bands having some form of established leadership. Diné and western Apache kinship groups were more complex than in eastern nations. They had named exogamous matrilineal clans and phratries that exercised some corporate and ceremonial functions. Western Apache local clan groups controlled farmland, assigned use-rights to their members, and claimed gathering and hunting areas as well. Among the Diné, land was controlled by local clan groups too, but they made no claims to foraging resource areas.

Mescalero Apache Culture

The Mescalero Apaches occupied territory in southeastern New Mexico, western Texas, and adjacent areas of Mexico. Their settlements were concentrated between the Pecos River on the east and the Rio Grande on the west, although they made use of extensive lands both east and west for buffalo and antelope hunting expeditions. They held a vast territory but their population was never highly concentrated. Farming was not possible either in the high mountains because of a short growing season or in the flat bottomlands and valleys, which were hot and dry and lacked sources of year-round water. Mescaleros therefore relied on foraging for their subsistence and traded with settled farming people for vegetable products. While most hunting

was carried out by men working singly or in small groups, occasionally larger expeditions were formed for buffalo hunting. In addition, all able-bodied members of a settlement might cooperate in rabbit hunting. Women frequently accompanied men on buffalo hunts to help butcher the meat and carry it back to camp where it was prepared for storage or cooking. Most of women's subsistence activities centered on gathering a wide variety of plants including mescal, edible grasses, cactus, wild peas and beans, fruits, berries, and nuts such as piñon, acorns, and walnuts. They also prepared the inner bark of box elder, pine, and aspen for use as sweeteners. Other tasks were divided between men and women. Women tanned animal skins, which they used for making clothing, containers, and tipis. They wove baskets and gathered firewood and water. In addition to hunting, men cared for the herds of horses that they owned and protected the community from enemies (Opler 1969: 20–21).

Mescalero settlements consisted of a number of extended family units. Within an extended family cluster, each nuclear group of parents and children resided in a separate dwelling. After marriage, people followed rules of matrilocal residence. The Mescalero kinship system was bilateral and lacked clans or other large organized kin groups. Extended families composing a settlement cooperated in economic, military, and ceremonial activities. Men worked with their brothers-in-law and fathers-in-law to supply food and give protection to the community. A man who married into the group was at first only loosely integrated into the unit, but with time and with the growth of his family, particularly if he had a number of daughters, he eventually became the head or leader of a large extended family cluster.

Each local group, possibly consisting of as many as thirty families but often far fewer, had a central place of residence, usually that of its leader. Most of the families within the local group were related to the leader through blood or marriage. Although the leader had influence and prestige in his community, he was more of an advisor or director than an enforcer of decisions and policies (11). His title, literally "he who speaks," aptly denotes his principal roles and means of influencing his followers. Leaders also were expected to be brave warriors, successful hunters, and eloquent speakers. They cemented the allegiance of their followers through their generosity and oratorical ability.

The Consequences of Foreign Intervention

At the time of Spanish invasions of the Southwest in the sixteenth century, Apache bands occupied a large territory in Texas, Oklahoma, New Mexico, Arizona, and the northern Mexican province of Sonora. They may have begun to develop a raiding complex before the appearance of the Spanish, taking farm produce from Puebloan settlements, but Spanish farms and ranches later became even more attractive targets. And when Puebloans adopted domesticated animals such as sheep and horses, they too were vulnerable to Apache raids. By the middle of the eighteenth century, Apache raids became even more frequent and posed a danger to many Puebloan communities along the Rio Grande as well as to the growing Spanish population. At the same time, processes unfolding in the Plains had an effect on Apache raiding in the Southwest as well as on Apaches' determination to survive. Because of population dislocations that became endemic in the Plains due to the westward movement of eastern people attempting to find safety away from the advancing Euro-American settlements, the Comanches in particular began to move southward, pushing Apaches further to the south and west into the territory of Puebloans, Pimans, and Yumans. Apaches ranged far into the Sonora River Valley of northern Mexico, raiding Native communities and those of Spanish settlers. The raids became so frequent that by the end of the eighteenth century Sonora was practically depopulated as people relocated further south into Mexico (Spicer 1962: 239). Apaches found some degree of safety in their mobility and were able to evade or defeat Spanish soldiers sent to control them. Spanish authorities therefore decided to make peace with separate Apache bands, encouraging them to settle more permanently in exchange for rations. Although the policy was effective with some groups, it was not always successful, and by the early nineteenth century, raiding and warfare increased. Mexicans then embarked on a policy of exterminating Apache communities. In response, Apache raids increased in frequency and destructiveness. Mexican officials offered bounties on Apache scalps brought in by vigilantes and regular soldiers, thus increasing the brutality of Mexican retaliation against Native communities.

Although the southwest was still nominally part of Mexico in the early nineteenth century, American trappers and traders filtered into the area in growing numbers. After the US government took possession of the region in 1846, they turned their attention to "pacifying" the Apaches, partly by making treaties with them and partly by making threats followed up by attacks against resistant communities. When gold was discovered near Prescott, Arizona, in 1863, the government stepped up pressure on Native communities. Soldiers and vigilantes increased their attacks, killing Apaches wherever they found them. In at least one incident, Anglo settlers arranged for a peace council with nearby Apaches only to feed them poisoned food (247). By the 1870s, some Apache bands decided that peace with Anglos was the only option available, while others believed that armed resistance was the best course since they distrusted official promises of protection and aid. In 1871, the US government began to establish reservations for Apaches in New Mexico and Arizona. Although some people agreed to remain within the borders of the reservations, many refused to stay, prompting the military to seek out resistors. By 1873, most Apaches had either been confined to reservations or had been killed. But even on the reservations, Apaches were not safe from Anglo harassment. The discovery of large deposits of copper, silver, and gold enticed prospectors and settlers, leading to the confiscation of large portions of Apache reservations. Although Native leaders protested, the federal government did nothing to stop the erosion of their land base. Agents in charge of the reservations were no help in protecting Apache interests and in some cases even invested their money in new mines and ranches. In addition, water from the San Carlos River was diverted by Anglo farmers to flow into their own fields, leaving Apache lands without water.

By the end of the nineteenth century, Apaches were settled on five reservations and were compelled by conditions to reorient their economy to farming rather than hunting and gathering. However, farming was difficult given the poor quality of most of their land. Cattle raising was then introduced as a source both of food and income. Apaches also began to work as hired hands on Anglo cattle ranches and in mines near their territory.

Contemporary Issues and Data

Efforts to develop sustainable farming practices are the concerns of a group formed by the White Mountain Apache Tribe called "Ndee Bikiyaa" or "People's

Farm." Supported by the First Nations Development Institute, this group is developing organic farming methods in ways that involve community members of all ages. Their goal is to provide nutritious foods that are locally grown and culturally significant.

Today most Apache families are integrated into the surrounding local and national economies. Wages from employment is the predominant form of income although cattle ranching continues to engage members of some households. Apache reservations have some of the lowest incomes and highest poverty rates in the United States. Averages for per capita income varied, from a low of $9,771 for Mescaleros to a high of only $15,614 for the Jicarillas. Both numbers are far below the New Mexico average of $22,966 and do not even reach the American Indian average of $16,446. Median household income ranged from the Jicarilla high of $44,301 to the Tonto low of $16,667. Unemployment rates for Apaches in New Mexico were about 20 percent while nearly a quarter of Arizona Apaches were unemployed. As a method of comparison, the Arizona state average unemployment rate was 9.9 percent and the New Mexico state average was 7.2 percent (US Census Bureau 2010). Several Apache tribes have opened casinos and resorts to generate jobs and profits. The White Mountain Apaches, for example, have taken advantage of their scenic mountain location to provide hotels, restaurants, and tourist services. According to US Census data for 2010, there are 147,413 registered Apaches in the United States.

PIMAN CULTURE

Pimans occupied territory in southwestern and south-central Arizona as well as in the northern Sonoran desert of Mexico. Environmental variations were principally due to differences in precipitation rates. Least amounts of rain fall in the west, sometimes no more than 5 in. per year and in some years none at all. Moving toward the east, more rainfall is likely, but even in the best areas it averages only between 10 and 15 in. annually. Some Piman groups had the advantage of living near year-round water supplies from the Gila, Salt, and Colorado Rivers. In these places, river flooding provided rich silt deposits that made the land productive for farming. Given the warmth of the region, the combination of fertile land and climatic conditions resulted in long growing seasons, enabling people to harvest two or three crops per year.

In aboriginal times, three different types of settlement patterns were attested, each with economic and social correlates. The first type was a nomadic pattern of small encampments exemplified by one group of Tohono O'odham formerly called Sand Papago, who lived in the lower Colorado Valley where the climate was extremely hot and dry. Their economy was based on foraging. Water was their scarcest resource, forcing people to rely on springs and ponds formed by rainfall. Men hunted a variety of animals including bighorn sheep, deer, coyote, birds, and several species of rodents, snakes, and lizards, while women gathered wild roots, beans, cactus, prickly pears, and saguro fruit. Although they had a variety of foods, none occurred in abundance. Consequently, the people lived in small bands composed of extended family groups, with populations of no more than eighty or ninety per band. There was a tendency toward patrilocal residence, but given the climate and scarcity of resources, residence was in fact flexible (Fontana 1968–1974, 2).

The second cultural type was exemplified by the Tohono O'odham (formerly called Papagos) who commonly shifted residence between two seasonal settlements (Underhill 1939). Tohono O'odham territory received an average of 5–10 in. of rain per year, and since they had no permanent streams, they were dependent upon rainfall and small springs and seasonal water sources. Their economy included farming but the actual percentage that crops contributed to their diet varied annually due to rainfall. In some years no food at all was harvested, while in the best years farming might supply about half of the diet.

A third cultural type were the Pimas, who resided in stable villages on the borders of Piman territory near the Gila River. Rainfall in their region averaged about 10–17 in. per year. Rainfall combined with water from the Gila River gave Pimas the most reliable water supplies of all of the Piman people. Their economy combined farming and foraging. Their fields were supplied with rainwater and floodwater from the river channeled through irrigation canals. However, due to seasonal and annual variations in precipitation rates, farming was not always productive. At best, farm products contributed approximately 60 percent of the Pimas' diet (Castetter and Bell 1942: 57). In good years, Pimas were able to obtain two corn crops. Surplus foods were kept for times of scarcity when harvests were poor. Pimas also traded surpluses to neighboring people for wild plants and meat.

Among both the Pimas and Tohono O'odham, farmland was owned or controlled by the village as a communal entity. Settlements consisted of residential compounds surrounded by farmland. Nuclear families lived in separate dwellings whose construction was relatively simple. The houses had brush walls and dry earthen roofs supported by mesquite posts and rafters. Village compounds contained shared open roofless cooking enclosures, roofed sunshades, and food storage receptacles. Villages also had open ceremonial grounds that were used for rituals performed in conjunction with corn harvests and hunting expeditions. Residence in household compounds and in villages ideally followed patrilocal principles but was flexible in practice. Piman social organization was based on membership in patrilineal clans that were not exogamous and had no corporate functions. The clans were organized into two moieties, called Buzzard and Coyote.

Every village kept a sacred basket containing relics or medicines that gave it power and protection. These baskets were hidden in the desert surrounding the village and were taken out and displayed on ceremonial occasions. The baskets were under the guardianship of village headmen whose other responsibilities included organizing public meetings and mediating disputes. Headmen had influence but lacked power to enforce their decisions. Instead, they were sensitive to public opinion and were effective only insofar as members of their communities chose to listen to their advice. In order to obtain and retain leadership positions, headmen were generous to their followers, giving gifts and sharing resources in times of need. They were aided by a number of assistants who advised them and helped in carrying out their duties. The wife of the headman also had community responsibilities in organizing women's work and ritual activities. Local groups were loosely recognized as belonging to regional bands that corresponded to dialectal groups. Each band was named for a distinctive geographical feature in its area. Regional bands were in actual practice little more than nominal associations since they lacked cohesion or leadership.

Tohono O'odham Culture

The Tohono O'odham inhabit the driest and hottest regions of North America, living in southwestern Arizona in flat valleys and low mountain ridges. Their territory receives an average of only 5 in. of rain per year, concentrated in the months of July and August. When heavy rains come in the summertime, it provides enough moisture in the hot ground for the sprouting of seeds of cactus, small trees, prickly pear, and other desert plants. The relatively abundant growth continues for two months, and during that time women gathered wild foods, dried them in the hot sun, and stored them for later use. After the rains ceased and the land dried, the people moved to the foothills where there were springs from which they obtained drinking water. Due to the environment and scarcity of resources, the Tohono O'odham did not have permanent settlements but rather shifted their camps between the "fields" and "wells" (Underhill 1939). In years when rainfall provided enough water, men cleared their land and planted crops, principally corn, beans, and pumpkins. Farm plots were small, no more than 2 or 3 acres. Land was controlled by a local group of kin, usually formed by patrilineal affiliation. Each family within the local group was allotted land that was planted by a man and his sons. In addition, the community cooperated in a number of projects that made farming possible such as clearing the land and digging irrigation ditches and reservoirs. The irrigation ditches brought water from flooded areas and the reservoirs were made in order to catch rainwater for drinking purposes (95). Both the ditches and the reservoirs were constructed and cleaned periodically at the direction of the leader of the local community. Most of Tohono O'odham economy, however, was focused on foraging. Some tasks were carried out individually while others were communally organized. Men cooperated in deer hunting whereas women participated in gathering expeditions. Economic cooperation within local groups was underscored by patterns of food distribution. Hunters distributed meat from deer that they killed to each household in their community. Women also brought cooked food to each other's homes. Most of these exchanges occurred between relatives since communities were formed on the basis of kinship ties, but all members of a community were aided on a regular basis and certainly in times of need. Economic cooperation was the glue that held Native communities together. As Underhill noted, "food was the currency of the Papago economic system. Small gifts of it were continually passing within the intimate family group, and penetrating now and then to further connections" (100).

The composition of local communities depended on the season and resource availability. A village was ideally composed of families related through patrilineal descent following patrilocal residence patterns. Each village was an independent, autonomous economic, ceremonial, and political unit. It had a leader, usually the eldest male head of one of the founding families. Leaders gave advice and organized communal activities but had no coercive power. They could, on occasion, help settle disputes among community members. They also had ceremonial functions since it was they who kept sacred paraphernalia associated with the settlement (73). Village leaders were often succeeded by one of their brothers rather than a son since seniority was an important requisite of leadership. In addition, each settlement had an informal council consisting of the elder men resident in the camp. According to Underhill, it was the council that was the "real governing power of the community. It decided on communal activity, agricultural work, hunts, war, the dates of ceremonies, and games with other villages. It approved the installation of a chief or new residence in the village." Furthermore, according to one of Underhill's consultants, "if there was nothing to discuss, they would come together and talk" (78).

Villages were ceremonial as well as territorial units. Each settlement kept a collection of sacred objects in a special basket that was hidden in the hills away from houses because "sacred things are considered too powerful to keep near human dwellings" (71). Sacred objects included carvings of spirit animals, slate pendants, arrowpoints, dried animal hearts, eagle feathers, and carved and painted prayer sticks. The basket and its contents were considered the communal property of village members but were kept in their name by the ceremonial/secular leader of the village.

Men and women had control over and rights to dispose of their own personal property as well as the distributions of foods that they procured. Men managed the distribution of meat and agricultural products; women supervised the use of household utensils, cooked food, and wild plants that they gathered (92). Personal property consisted of clothing, tools, utensils, and articles of adornment. Sacred songs and rituals were also considered personal property. Such songs came to people in dreams and could help in economic pursuits. A person's property could be inherited by their sons or daughters, but much of it was instead either buried or destroyed when they died. Houses, too, were sometimes burned if a death occurred inside.

Tohono O'odham society was based on a system of patrilineal clans grouped together into two moieties named Coyote and Buzzard. Although clans and moieties were means of social and kinship identification, they had no corporate functions. There may have

been some totemic beliefs regarding moieties since, for example, a Coyote man should never kill a coyote. Even if a man found a coyote eating crops in his garden, he would never harm it because "We can't chase away our partner" (32).

Among kin, the closest, most enduring relationships were those between a parent and their same-sex child and between same-sex siblings. Bonds between fathers and sons were underscored by economic interdependence, while the mother-daughter bond was less complex because at marriage a daughter usually moved to her husband's camp. Relationships between brothers also involved economic as well as social cooperation. Sisters, too, had close and affectionate ties but they, like mothers and daughters, resided in different households and often in different camps after marriage. In contrast to relationships between same-sex siblings, interactions between opposite-sex siblings and parent/child dyads were marked by respectful behavior. Although men were recognized as the heads of households, husbands and wives were treated equally. Both men and women were considered knowledgeable in their spheres of activities and neither one interfered with the other.

European and American Control

The Spanish invasions of the Southwest had a direct impact on Piman communities. Since they were settled farming people, their villages were relatively easy targets for Spanish slave-raiders. Their sedentary lifestyle attracted missionary attention as well. Some Indians accepted missionaries in their communities, but from time to time resistance to foreign authority arose and was met with brutal reprisals reminiscent of Spanish actions against Puebloans. Spanish officials and missionaries forced the Indians to work on their farms, in their churches, and in mines and workshops, but the people did not submit easily. According to Spanish records, the Indians "objected to working for themselves as much as for the church and were so lazy and wasteful that they had to be whipped to make them do anything" (Underhill 1939: 25).

In the seventeenth century, Piman farmers added European crops and domesticated animals to their economies, but the livestock quickly became targets of Apache raiders. In response to raiding, Pimans concentrated their population in a few villages for defense purposes, with a consequent decline in the number of villages and a contraction of the inhabited range of territory.

By the late eighteenth century, Pimas were trading surpluses of wheat to the nearby Tohono O'odham as well as to Mexican Indians and Hispanic settlers. Once they had external markets for their crops, Piman farmers expanded production by making improvements in irrigation ditches and canals for transporting water to the fields. The need to organize communal labor and plan village projects thus developed and led to greater authority for village chiefs.

As Pimans became vulnerable to Apache raids in the early nineteenth century, some groups decided that an alliance with the Spanish and/or Mexicans would be beneficial if it offered protection. However, these alliances also brought more Hispanic settlers into their region seeking farmland, leading to conflicts over land and water.

The United States took possession of most of Piman territory in 1853, but conditions hardly changed for the Indians. They remained vulnerable to Apache attacks as well as to the confiscation of their water supplies by Anglo farmers and ranchers. Hoping to survive, some Piman communities forged alliances with the American government and aided the military in attacks against Apache raiders. When the Overland Mail Company contracted with Pimas to supply wheat to California mining camps, farm production and profits grew (Fontana 1976). At about the same time, the Tohono O'odham expanded their economy by developing cattle ranching. In the late nineteenth century, gold, silver, and copper mines were operating in and near their territory. Settlement patterns began to change in response to both historic and environmental conditions. After 1870, when Apache and Navajo raiders had been suppressed by American armies, there was a tendency for the concentrated Pima and Tohono O'odham villages to disperse into smaller scattered settlements typical of aboriginal times. During the same period the climate became drier, also forcing the dispersal of populations.

As a consequence of economic changes and national policies, reservations were established for the Pimas and Tohono O'odham in the late nineteenth century. In 1874, a presidential executive order set up the first Tohono O'odham reservation at San Xavier, followed by others in the 1880s. As elsewhere in the Southwest, the establishment of reservations was prompted by the discovery of precious metals in Native territory. By the end of the century there were dozens of silver mines that attracted thousands of Anglo prospectors and ranchers. The largest of the reservations, consisting of two million acres in southwestern Arizona, was set aside in 1918. Significantly, the founding agreement contained a clause that denied Tohono O'odham rights to minerals that might be found on their land (Spicer 1962: 140).

For the Pimas of Gila River, the late nineteenth century was a time of increased farm production to supply Anglo travelers and settlers. After gold was discovered in California in 1849, as many as 60,000 prospectors and settlers passed through Native villages and were supplied with wheat, corn, and other produce in exchange for metal implements (147). After 1858, when the stagecoach trails from Texas to California passed through Pima villages, production again increased in order to supply the growing traffic. As elsewhere, the desirability of Pima land and resources led the federal government to establish a reservation for the Indians but, as elsewhere, even after reservations were set aside, Anglo demand for land and particularly for water harmed the Native economy. For example, in 1887, an irrigation canal diverted all of the water from the Gila River to Anglo settlements so that no water reached any of the Pima fields downstream (149). It was not until 1924 that the government began construction of a dam on the San Carlos River that would bring water to their lands.

Contemporary Issues and Data

The Pimas (or, in their language, Akimel O'odham, "the river people") living in the Gila River Indian Nation in Arizona have the unfortunate distinction of having the highest incidence of diabetes in the world. In the late twentieth century, more than 50 percent of adults over the age of thirty-five years suffered from Type II diabetes. This figure is about five times the rate for the general US population, at 11 percent. The Pima population has been the focus of a long-term study conducted by the Centers for Disease Control since 1965 when the high rates of diabetes were first systematically reported. Since then, the incidence of diabetes has stayed relatively stable in the Pima, with about 38 percent of adults suffering from the condition, although a significant rise was noted in youth (Pavkov et al. 2007; Schulz et al. 2006). The study centers on investigating the possible causes, including genetic predisposition, diets, and lifestyle activities.

An important component to the research is a comparison of the incidence of diabetes among Pimas living in Arizona and their relatives located in the Sierra

Madre mountains of northern Mexico. It is estimated that the Gila River Pimas migrated north from Mexico approximately 2,000 years ago but the two populations are genetically similar. Until the late nineteenth century, the Gila River Pimas sustained their traditional economy of farming, hunting, and gathering. These are economic patterns still followed by the Pimas in Mexico. Comparison of the two groups reveals that the incidence of diabetes among the Mexican Pimas is much lower than for their American counterparts. According to a 2006 article, about 7 percent of Mexican Pima men have diabetes while the rate is 34 percent for Gila River men. Similarly, about 20 percent of Pima women in Mexico suffer from the disease while the rate for Gila River women is 41 percent (Schulz et al. 2006).

The striking contrast in the diabetes rates can be correlated with a significant difference in lifestyle and cultural practices. Whereas the Pimas in Mexico have a diet that centers on the traditional crops of beans, corn, okra, and a small amount of lean meat, the Gila River Pimas have adopted a diet high in fats, sugars, and white flour. The change in the Pimas' diet is itself related to another significant transformation in their lives. In the late nineteenth century, the Gila River was diverted by American settlers in order to supply their own farmlands with water, leaving the Pimas without clean drinking water and that necessary to nurture their irrigated fields. As a result, the Pimas became largely dependent on government rations, that is, foods distributed to Native peoples that emphasized white flour, sugar, and lard. Consumption of these foods has led to obesity, one of the precursors to developing diabetes. Therefore, some of the underlying causes of the high rates of diabetes among the Pimas are traceable to government policies that go back more than a century.

To redress one part of this historical legacy, in 2004 the Pimas won an agreement with the US government and the State of Arizona to return water from the Gila River to the reservation. The Gila River Indian Community Water Rights Settlement, Title II of the Arizona Water Settlements Act, reverts water from the Gila River to be used for agricultural use and household consumption. The Act also provides funds to enable the construction of water delivery and irrigation systems. In response, the Gila River Pimas are developing community gardens and individual farmlands once again. Community leaders hope that these efforts will have a lasting and positive effect not only on reviving cultural traditions and lifestyles but also on lowering the incidence of diabetes.

In the twentieth century, there has been a trend among both Pimas and Tohono O'odham toward the division of communally held lands into individual farms tended by nuclear families. Farming has declined, however, both because of the increasing aridity of the climate and intensification of soil erosion processes and because of competition with non-Indian farmers who have more capital to invest in advanced technology. Many people are therefore engaged in wage work, ironically, often as farm workers on land owned by non-Indians while much of Piman land is leased to outside companies that operate corporate farms (Schulz et al. 2006: 176). Per capita income for the Pimas and Tohono O'odham ranges by reservation from $9,438 in Papago to $15,791 in Salt River. Similarly low median household incomes were attested: $21,827 for Papago and $32,022 for Salt River. All income statistics were substantially lower than the American Indian averages. Per capita incomes were also startlingly lower than the $25,537 figure for Arizona. Consequently, more than a third of Pima and Tohono O'odham families (35.1%) and individuals (40.3%) was living below the poverty level. Income and poverty statistics obviously reflect high unemployment rates. Approximately 21.5 percent of Pimmas and Tohono O'odhams were unemployed in 2010, more than double the Arizona state average of 9.9. Currently, Pimas reside on three reservations in Arizona: Gila River, Salt River, and Ak Chin. Some of the Tohono O'odham also live at Ak Chin and in addition reside on three reservations of their own, called Papago, San Xavier, and Gila Bend. In all, the Pima and Tohono O'odham reservations have a population of approximately 28,926

YUMAN CULTURES

Yumans occupied two somewhat different ecological zones in central and western Arizona. The Upland Yumans lived in the deserts of northern Arizona while the River Yumans occupied the flood plains of the Lower Colorado and Gila Rivers in southwestern and central Arizona and the extreme southeast of California. The most numerous of the River Yuman nations were the Mohaves, Maricopas, and Quechans. Even though their territory only received about 4 in. of rain per year, due to the warmth of the climate the growing season lasted some 300 days (Jorgensen 1983: 689). River Yumans lived in small, scattered farming settlements rather than compact villages. They supplemented farm produce with a variety of wild beans, roots, and edible plants and also hunted small game, especially rabbits. Fish were caught in the rivers where available. Farmland was owned by the individual men who cleared it, but both men and women worked cooperatively to plant and harvest the crops. Principal foraging sites were also owned by men even though gathering activities were the responsibility of women. Yuman social organization was based on patrilineal exogamous clans. Postmarital residence rules were flexible although there was a preference for patrilocal affiliation.

The Upland Yumans, principally the Havasupai, Walapai, and Yavapai, occupied the deserts of central Arizona. Due to lack of rainfall or year-round water sources, the region was sparsely populated. Upland Yuman economies emphasized foraging although Havasupais were able to do some farming along a creek in the Grand Canyon where they resided in the spring and summer. In early fall, Havasupais dispersed into small foraging groups and sought wild resources on the Colorado Plateau above the canyon. They hunted bighorn sheep, rabbits, deer, and antelope and gathered wild plants such as yucca, grasses, mesquite, mescal, juniper berries, and piñon nuts. Walapais and Yavapais inhabited territories at the bases of cliffs and along washes and valleys of the central desert, relying solely on foraging for their subsistence. Upland Yuman social organization was based on principles of bilateral kinship. Postmarital residence was flexible but there was a tendency to prefer patrilocally formed households.

Mohave Culture

The Mohaves occupied territory in the Mohave Valley of extreme western Arizona and southeastern Nevada and California. Their settlements were concentrated near the Colorado River, whose floodwaters were used to irrigate fields of corn, beans, and pumpkins. Farming through irrigation enabled Mohaves to secure a relatively stable subsistence in the midst of an otherwise dry and hot region. Men were responsible for clearing the land and planting the crops while women assisted in harvesting. Fields were relatively small, consisting of at most a few acres (Stewart 1966). Unused land was open to all, but once a man cleared a field and began cultivating it, the land thereafter was his own property. Mohaves usually obtained sufficient food from farm production, but in years of drought,

people relied more heavily on wild plants, fishing, and hunting. Hunting was the least productive of their economic strategies since few animals were available in the immediate vicinity and people rarely went on distant hunting expeditions.

Mohaves had patrilineal, exogamous clans whose sole purpose seems to have been the organization of kinship groups since they lacked corporate functions and had no leaders or ceremonial roles. Clan names were derived from plants, animals, or natural phenomena. Consistent with a fairly flexible social pattern, residence after marriage followed no preferential rule. Decisions about location were made on the basis of the composition of already existing groups and personal inclinations. Communities extended for a mile or two along the river and were separated from each other by 4 or 5 miles. People lived during most of the year in open-sided shelters with flat roofs and only used sturdier houses covered with sand in colder weather (Kroeber 1925).

Although Mohaves did not live in concentrated settlements, they thought of themselves as a nation with a distinct territory. The nation as a whole was organized into at least three bands, a northern, central, and southern division. Each division, and possibly the nation as a whole, had a leader whose actual role was one of advisor and spokesperson rather than commander. Local settlements also had group leaders whose influence depended on their ability to gain people's respect. Their prestige was enhanced by their generosity and oratorical skills.

Walapai Culture

The Walapais inhabited land in northwestern Arizona, bounded by the canyons of the Colorado River on the north, the Black Mountains on the west, and the Santa Maria River on the south. On the east, Walapai lands abutted those of the Havasupais. Although Walapai territory was extensive, the population was always sparse because of the difficulty of obtaining subsistence in the region. Aboriginal economy, based on hunting and gathering, required a high degree of mobility and the shifting of small camps to resource areas. In the spring, the people gathered mescal in the northern canyons and foothills. In the summertime, they collected fruits of several cactus species as well as other wild fruits and seeds. Then in the late summer and fall, Walapais gathered nuts, piñon cones, and juniper berries. In winter, resources were scarcer than during the rest of the year, leading to the development of larger and more stable camps subsisting on hunting and surplus foods stored from previous foraging expeditions. Few large animals were available in significant numbers in the region so that hunters focused on catching rabbits and other rodents. Bighorn sheep and antelope were occasionally hunted, either by a cooperative drive or individually (Kroeber 1935).

In the context of their environment and the necessary mobility consistent with their economy, social organization was relatively flexible. Walapai camps usually were composed of some twenty-five members (Martin 1973). Residence was in practice bilocal, although an idealized pattern included an initial period of uxorilocal residence followed by a shift to the husband's camp. In the summer, people lived in small dwellings that were made of branches and leaves supported by tree limbs. In the winter, they constructed sturdier dwellings with domed roofs covered with thatch or juniper bark.

Each small camp had a recognized leader whose main role was to give advice and coordinate community activities. A number of neighboring camps were considered to form local bands, each named for a geographical feature in their territory. The Walapai nation as a whole was organized into three subgroups that were regionally distinct, although boundaries between them were not strongly delineated and people might shift their membership among the groups (Dobyns and Euler 1970).

European and American Control

Yuman communities were very little affected by the Spanish or Mexicans because of their remote location and relatively unproductive territory. Significant numbers of Spanish intruders did not enter their lands until the late eighteenth century. Later, Anglos began moving into the region after the discovery of gold in California, leading to the first serious disruption of Yuman culture. Greater pressure was exerted against the River Yuman Mohaves and Maricopas, whose territory was more fertile and suitable for farming and settlement while the Upland Yumans remained in isolated areas. But in the 1860s, Upland Walapais were affected when gold and lead mines were opened and attracted prospectors. Cattlemen came to the region as well, eventually taking over Walapai land and waterholes. As elsewhere, Native resistance prompted US military reprisals. In the late nineteenth century, several small reservations were established for the separate Yuman nations. There the people lived by farming and wage work in mines and on Anglo ranches. In 1935, the Hoover Dam was constructed on the Colorado River, ostensibly to aid the irrigation of Native farms, but as the land was improved it attracted more Anglo settlement, presenting a further obstacle to the Yumans' ability to maintain their land base. In addition, during World War II, 25,000 Japanese Americans were incarcerated on a portion of the Colorado River Mohave reservation, depriving the people from using some of their own land (Spicer 1962: 274).

Contemporary Population and Economic Data

Currently, most Yumans have abandoned an agrarian economy and instead seek wage work to support their families. However, employment opportunities are limited in most communities. Statistics for 2010 indicate unemployment rates mostly between 12 and 16 percent. Several Yuman reservations report comparatively low numbers (5.1% on the Colorado River Reservation) while others report even higher levels of unemployment (24.8% for Gila River) All figures indicate unemployment much above the Arizona norm of 9.9 percent Average incomes on all Yuman reservations were low. The overall per capita income was $13,651 in 2010, ranging from $9,691 for Gila River to $18,599 for Cocopah. Median household income has increased since 2000, ranging from a low of $27,600 for Yavapai to $43,300 for Cocopah. Consequent rates of poverty were high. While 28.5 percent of all Yuman families and 33.5 percent of individuals lived in poverty, rates varied as well. Lowest percentages of poverty were attested for Cocopah (15.7% for families) and Salt River (12.5% for individuals), and highest for Hualapai (50.4% for families) and Gila River (47.8% for individuals). The comparatively low averages despite high unemployment at some reserves may be because some individuals earn money from tourism. Havasupais, for example, whose reservation includes land at the floor of the Grand Canyon earn about half their total income from work as guides and outfitters for sightseers. Some Yuman communities also obtain income from leasing their land to corporate farming and mining interests, and others, such as the Cocopah, have opened casinos and other gaming facilities to generate income. According to 2010 Census data, there are approximately 14,204 people who identify as Yuman (US Census Bureau 2010).

REFERENCES

Aberle, Sophie. 1948. *The Pueblo Indians of New Mexico: Their Land, Economy and Civil Organization.* Menasha, WI: American Anthropological Association Memoir No. 70.

Allen, Lee. 2012. "Southwest Tribes Struggle with Climate Change Fallout." *Indian Country Today.* June 14. http://indiancountrytodaymedianetwork. com/2012/06/14/southwest-tri.

Beck, Warren. 1962. *New Mexico, A History of Four Centuries.* Norman, OK: University of Oklahoma Press.

Castetter, Edward, and Willis Bell. 1942. *Pima and Papago Indian Agriculture.* Albuquerque, NM: University of New Mexico Press.

Dobyns, Henry, and Robert Euler. 1970. *Wauba Yuma's People: The Comparative Sociopolitical Structure of the Pai Indians of Arizona.* Prescott, AZ: Prescott College Studies in Anthropology No. 3.

Dozier, Edward. 1961. "Rio Grande Pueblos." *Perspectives in American Indian Culture Change* (ed. E. Spicer). Chicago, IL: University of Chicago Press, pp. 94–186.

Dozier, Edward. 1970. *The Pueblo Indians of North America.* New York: Holt, Rinehart and Winston.

Fontana, Bernard. 1968–1974. *Man in Arid Lands: The Piman Indians of the Sonoran Desert.* Vol. 2 of *Desert Biology* (ed. G. W. Brown). New York: Academic Press.

Fontana, Bernard. 1976. "The Faces and Forces of Pimeria Alta." *Voices from the Southwest* (ed. D. Dickinson *et al.*). Flagstaff, AZ: Northland Press, pp. 45–54.

"Four New Mexico Pueblos and Secretary Salazar Finalize Historic Aamodt Water Rights Settlement." 2013. *Indian Country Today* 3, no. 14 (April 17): 6.

Griffin, P. Bion *et al.* 1971. "Western Apache Ecology: From Horticulture to Agriculture." *Apachean Culture History and Ethnology* (ed. K. Basso and M. Opler). Tucson, AZ: Anthropological Papers of the University of Arizona No. 21, pp. 69–76.

Hammond, G. P., and A. Rey. 1953. *Don Juan Oñate, Colonizer of New Mexico, 1598–1628.* Sante Fe, NM: University of New Mexico Press.

Hammond, G. P., and A. Rey. 1966. *The Rediscovery of New Mexico: 1580–1594.* Vol. III. Albuquerque, NM: University of New Mexico Press.

Helm, June. 1965. "Bilaterality in the Socio-Territorial Organization of the Arctic Drainage Dene." *Ethnology* 4, no. 4: 361–385.

Henry, Jeannette *et al.* 1970. *Indian Voices: The First Convocation of American Indian Scholars.* San Francisco, CA: The Indian Historian Press.

Hoijer, Harry. 1956. "The Chronology of the Athabaskan Languages." *International Journal of American Linguistic* 22: 219–232.

Jorgensen, Joseph. 1983. "Comparative Traditional Economics and Ecological Adaptations." Southwest (ed. A. Ortiz). Vol. 10 of *Handbook of North American Indians.* Washington, DC: Smithsonian.

Kroeber, Alfred. 1925. "The Mohave." *Handbook of the Indians of California.* Washington, DC: Bureau of American Ethnology, Bulletin No. 78, pp. 726–780.

Kroeber, Alfred. 1935. *Walapai Ethnography.* Menasha, WI: American Anthropological Association Memoir No. 42.

Martin, John. 1973. "On the Estimation of the Sizes of Local Groups in a Hunting-Gathering Environment." *American Anthropologist* 75, no. 5: 1448–1468.

Newman, Stanley. 1964. "A Comparison of Zuni and California Penutian." *International Journal of American Linguistics* 30, no. 1: 1–13.

Opler, Morris. 1969. *Apache Odyssey: A Journey between Two Worlds.* New York: Holt, Rinehart and Winston.

Ortiz, Alfonso. 1969. *The Tewa World: Space, Time, Being and Becoming in a Pueblo Society.* Chicago, IL: University of Chicago Press.

Ortiz, Alfonso. 1979. "San Juan Pueblo." *Southwest* (ed. A. Ortiz). Vol. 9 of *Handbook of North American Indians.* Washington, DC: Smithsonian Institution, pp. 278–295.

Ortiz, Alfonso. 1994. "The Dynamics of Pueblo Cultural Survival." *North American Indian Anthropology: Essays on Society and Culture* (ed. R. DeMallie and A. Ortiz). Norman, OK: University of Oklahoma Press, pp 296–306.

Pavkov, M. E. et al. 2007. "Changing Patterns of Type 2 Diabetes Incidence among Pima Indians." *Diabetes Care* 30, no. 7: 1758–1763.

Schulz, L. O. et al. 2006. "Effects of Traditional and Western Environments on Prevalence of Type 2 Diabetes in Pima Indians in Mexico and the US." *Diabetes Care* 29, no. 8: 1866–1871.

Simmons, Marc. 1979. "History of Pueblo-Spanish Relations to 1821." In Southwest (ed. A. Ortiz). *Handbook of North American Indians* vol. 9. Washington, DC: Smithsonian, pp. 178–193.

Spicer, Edward. 1962. *Cycles of Conquest: The Impact of Spain, Mexico, and the United States on the Indians in the Southwest, 1533 – 1960.* Tucson, AZ: University of Arizona Press.

Stewart, Kenneth. 1966. "Mohave Indian Agriculture." *Masterkey* 40, no. 1: 4–15.

Underhill, Ruth. 1939. *Social Organization of the Papago Indians.* Contributions to Anthropology No. 30. New York: Columbia University.

US Bureau of the Census. 2010.

US Bureau of the Census. 2014.

US Bureau of Indian Affairs, Interior. 2002. *Federal Register, Vol. 67, No. 134/Friday, July 12, 2002/Notices. Indian Entities Recognized and Eligible to Receive Services From the United States Bureau of Indian Affairs.* Washington, DC.

Whiting, Marsha. 2012. "First Nations Development Institute Grants $400,000 to 22 Native American Organizations." Office of Juvenile Justice and Delinquency Prevention Press Release. Longmont, Colorado. Online.

Zolbrod, Paul. 1984. *Diné Bahane: The Navaho Creation Story.* Abuquerque, NM: University of New Mexico Press, pp. 45–51.

The Zunis

Today as we live in the present ways of our people, we live also within the realm of our ancestors, for we are sustained through the rituals and beliefs of long ago. We live in accordance to the ways of our people, which bring life, blessings, and happiness.

Quam, *The Zunis: Self-Portrayals* 1972: 180

THE ZUNIS (or 'A:shiwi in their own language) are aboriginal and ancient inhabitants of western New Mexico, residing along the banks of the Zuni River. They are one of several nations of people referred to as western Puebloans, a group that also includes the Hopi, Acoma, and Laguna. Although western Puebloans share many cultural features of economy, sociopolitical structure, and religious organization, the Zuni language is different from that of all other inhabitants in the region. Its genetic status is currently uncertain. It may be a language isolate with no known linguistic connections, or it may belong to a language family called Penutian, most of whose members are located in California.

ZUNI SOCIETY

Territory and Settlements

The Zuni homeland is of a diversity of terrain and resources, including flat plains, plateaus, deserts, woodlands, foothills, and mountains. On the plains and desert grasslands grow shrubs, roots, herbs, cactus, rabbit brush, and yucca. White oak, spruce, juniper, and piñon trees are found in woodlands and mountainous regions. The mountains and foothills are the habitats of many species of animals including elk, deer, antelope, mountain sheep, bears, and foxes. Reptiles and rodents such as rabbits, mice, and squirrels abound in all areas of the region.

Today, Zunis reside in one large town (presently called Zuni but formerly known as Halona) and several small settlements located along nearby rivers and streams. Before the arrival of Europeans in the early sixteenth century, they lived in six villages situated within an area of 25 mi., all with access to good farmland. The six villages, named Halona ("red ant place"), Hawikkuh, Kiakima ("house of eagles"), Matsaki, Kwakina ("town of the entrance place"), and Kechipauan ("gympsum place"), were located in western Zuni territory and were the results of population concentrations that took shape as eastern villages were abandoned by the late fourteenth century (Hodge 1907, I). Most of the six villages were deserted in the seventeenth century when the people merged their settlements as a defensive strategy against Spanish invaders. Zuni land traditionally extended 35 mi. to the east and north of the settled villages toward the Zuni Mountains rising to altitudes of 9,000 ft. above sea level. Native territory also stretched 50 mi. to the west and south where altitudes are somewhat lower and the climate is drier and hotter.

The Zunis' central town has been inhabited from ancient times. Called 'itiwa'a ("middle place"), it was founded, say the Zuni, at the time of emergence after people left the darkness of the earth where they had been created. When people emerged from inside the earth, they were instructed by deities to go forth and find the "middle place" where they should build their villages. During their journey of many years, they stopped several times but continued on, realizing that they had not yet found the middle place of the world. At last, during a heavy rainstorm, a water strider came by, spread out its six legs, and told the people that the "middle place" was directly under its heart. Zunis' ancestors then built their village at that spot and founded six others at locations marked off by the six legs of the water strider. In their central village, the people erected an altar and placed on it a stone that contains the eternal beating heart of the "middle place" of the world. The Zunis' understanding of their origin and emergence firmly establishes them in a place that has sacred meaning and provides them with knowledge of their past as well as with the spiritual and practical resources to survive.

In accordance with their story of origin, Zunis conceive of their world divided into six, or more precisely seven, regions: north, east, south, west, zenith or above, nadir or below, and the all-important middle or navel, which is thought of as the place of synthesis of all regions or directions. The importance of the number six is reinforced by the six-fold division of sacred colors associated with each direction: north is associated with yellow, west with blue, south as red, east as white, the zenith or upper region is multicolored or speckled, and the nadir or lower region is black. Finally, the center or navel is an accumulation or concentration of all colors as it is also the synthesis of all directions, all matter, and all energy.

From the seventeenth century, after the period of most intense Spanish invasions, the central town remained the only inhabited village until the nineteenth century. Although the present town of Zuni remains the largest Native settlement and the focus of social and ceremonial life, four outlying farming villages have been founded: Nutria (in Zuni, To'ya), Ojo Caliente (K'apkwayiana or "water comes up from the depth"), Pescado (Hesota c'ina or "marked house"), and Tekapo ("full of hills, hilly") (Hodge 1907, II).

The architectural plan of Zuni as seen in the late nineteenth century by Frank Cushing was representative of aboriginal settlement patterns:

Imagine numberless long, box-shaped adobe ranches, connected with one another in extended rows and squares, with others, less and less numerous, piled up on them lengthwise and crosswise, in two, three, even six stories, each receding from the one below it like the steps of a broken stair flight—as it were, a gigantic pyramidal mud honeycomb with far outstretching base—and you can gain a fair conception of the architecture of Zuni.

Everywhere this structure bristled with ladder poles, chimneys, and rafters. The ladders were heavy and long, with carved slab crosspieces at the tops, and leaned at all angles against the roofs. Wonderfully like the holes in an anthill seemed the little windows and doorways which everywhere pierce the walls of this gigantic habitation; and like anthills themselves seemed the curious little round-topped ovens which stood here and there along these walls or on the terrace edges.

All round the town could be seen the regular, large and small adobe or dried mud fences, enclosing gardens in which melon, pumpkin and squash vines, pepper plants and onions were most conspicuous.

The view extended grandly from the outlying, flat lower terraces, miles away to the encircling mesa boundaries north, east, and south, while westward a long, slanting notch in the low hills was invaded to the horizon by the sand plain through which, like molten silver, the little river ran.

All over the terraces were women, some busy in the alleys or at the corners below, husking great heaps of many-colored corn, while children romped in, out, over and under the flaky piles. Many, in little groups, were cutting up peaches and placing them on squares of white cloth, or slicing pumpkins into long spiral ropes to be suspended to dry in the protruding rafters. In one place, with feet overhanging the roof, a woman was gracefully decorating newly made jars, while, over in a convenient shadow, sat an old blind man, busy spinning on his knee with a quaint bobbin shaped spindle-whorl. (Cushing 1979: 48–49, 56–58)

And in the interior of houses:

The room was forty feet in length by twelve in width. The white-washed walls and smooth, well swept floor of plastered mud, paved near the center and at the entrance with flags of sandstone, gave it a neat appearance. Huge round rafters supported the high ceiling, pierced near one end with a square hole for entrance and exit, and along the center with lesser apertures for the admission of light. Two or three portholes in the walls served

A corner of Zuni, ca. 1903.

as additional windows, and as many square openings led into other rooms. A carved pine slab, hung on heavy wooden hinges and secured by a knotted string, served as the door of one, while a suspended blanket closed another. A low adobe bench around the room appeared to be the family sitting place. It was interrupted near one end by a fireplace.

Between the fireplace and the end of the room, eight or ten metlatls were slantingly set side by side in a trough of stone—the mills, course and fine, of the household. Along the opposite side of the room, suspended from the rafters a smooth pole, upon which hung blankets, articles of clothing, and various other family belongings. More of the like, including quivers and bows, war clubs, and boomerangs or "rabbit sticks," disks of shell and other ornaments, depended from pegs, and deer and antelope horns on the walls. Some large, finely decorated water jars, and a black earthen cooking pot by the fireplace, two or three four pronged stools of wood, sundry blanket rugs and robes, made up the furniture of the apartment. (62)

Houses were constructed from sandstone blocks and slabs. Men built the outside structure with stone quarried from nearby deposits; women plastered the interior walls and later applied fresh coats of plaster when walls deteriorated over time. Houses were (and are) inhabited by families, occupying a series of adjacent rooms, who are usually related to each other through women. Consistent with rules of matrilineal kinship and descent, a household typically includes an extended family of an elder couple, their daughters, daughters' husbands and children, and the couple's unmarried sons. In accordance with preferences for matrilocal residence, daughters remain in the household into which they are born but sons usually leave at marriage to move into their wife's home. Contrary to the typical pattern, however, women sometimes move to their husband's home, especially if the man has no sisters (Kroeber 1917: 105).

Economies

In addition to their social functions, households are the basic economic units of society. The woman who is head of household is responsible for organizing and assigning work to unit members. Men's work traditionally centered on the production of food, preparing the land, planting seeds, and harvesting crops. Some work was carried out individually while other tasks were done collectively, usually by a group of relatives consisting of fathers, their unmarried sons, and their resident sons-in-law. Before marriage, men worked the land controlled by their mothers while after marriage they worked on land under the direction of their wife's mother. Farming required meticulous planning and care, in part due to the difficulties caused by the Southwestern climate and weather conditions. The summertime climate is generally dry, with annual rates of rainfall averaging only 10–15 in. per year. Timing of precipitation is of critical importance since if rain comes in sudden and severe storms too early in the growing season, young plants may drown or wash away, while if rain is too late, plants wither and die from lack of water. Changes in temperature also affect the survival of crops since although daytime temperatures are quite warm, nights can be cold in late spring and early fall. Given the conditions of weather and terrain, Zuni farmers planted crops in several locations, some closer to sources of water while others were situated in drier spots.

Due to the difficulty of farming in an arid environment, the people developed a system of floodwater irrigation that made best use of available water from rainfall and from the small Zuni River and a few nearby springs that are the only natural sources. When a man cleared new land for planting, he built small dams and canals with mud walls to direct water from rainfall and overflowing streams. The walls were constructed by packing mud over a row of stakes made of branches, rocks, sticks, and earth. The farmer also selected a ball of clay that had been previously deposited by a stream of water in a river or arroyo and redeposited it in the irrigation channel that he built. Since the clay had once been pushed along by water, it was believed that it would attract water (Cushing 1979: 252). When the new field was prepared, the farmer blessed it by planting a prayer stick cut from red willow and decorated with plumes of various birds. Even though the field was then fully prepared, it was left unplanted until the following year so that water from rainfall and streams could properly nourish it.

Although a variety of crops were planted, corn (in Zuni, *ta'a* or *a'ta'a* meaning "the seed of seeds") was given the most attention both in terms of human activity and ceremonial care. The seeds that were used for planting were obtained from a store of dried corn selected from the most perfect ears taken in the previous harvest. Seeds of all six colored varieties of corn (white, yellow, blue, red, black, and speckled) were kept in a family "corn room" or "granary." They were prayed over when put away for storage and again when taken out for planting. The farmer next chose six kernels of corn, one of each of the different colors, proclaiming to the women there, "We go!" And, as he steps out of the doorway, "the corn matron hustles after him with a bowl of fresh, cold water, with which she lavishly sprinkles him, laughingly telling "them" to go. Thoroughly drenched, he shuffles down the hill, across the river, and out to his field" (Cushing 1979: 261). The act of water-sprinkling symbolized the hoped-for rain needed to nourish the seeds. Once in the fields, the farmer planted the first seeds into small holes in the ground, covered the grains and returned home, remaining away from the fields for four days, during which time he fasted and prayed at sunrise. When he finally returned to the fields, he buried the seeds into small holes dug from 4 to 7 in. into the earth, putting some 15–20 kernels in each in order to assure that at least some would yield plants.

Corn was harvested by cooperative work teams of related men. Some of the ears were husked in the fields so that the husks could decay and fertilize the earth, but most were taken back to the village for husking and drying by groups of women. A large supply was kept in sealed storage rooms as a surplus to be used in years of poor harvests.

Corn was made into a great variety of recipes, most using ground cornmeal. Indeed, grinding corn was one of the most time-consuming tasks of Zuni women, requiring many hours of work to produce the large quantity of meal needed for breads and cakes. Grinding stones have different types of edges, yielding meal of varying consistencies. Traditional corn dishes, many still prepared today, are either cooked in large pots of boiling water, on flat stones in open fireplaces within homes, or inside the dome-shaped ovens built outdoors on terraces. Boiled breads or dumplings are made from small balls of fine and coarse cornmeal and salt. After boiling in water, they harden and become somewhat pasty. A kind of pudding is made with yellow cornmeal, sweetened with dried flowers. The batter is then wrapped in green corn leaves and boiled or baked. Some types of corn bread are prepared with the addition of ashes or lime yeast used as a leavening. After the flour is prepared, it is molded into thick cakes and cooked on hot coals or baked under hot ashes (Cushing 1979: 285–287). The most prized corn bread is a delicacy called *hewe*, a paper-thin bread prepared on large baking stones. Fine flour is made from all six varieties of corn and mixed with hot water to form a thin paste, which is then poured onto heated cooking stones. As soon as the batter is lightly toasted, it is peeled away from the stone. *Hewe* is eaten on ceremonial as well as domestic occasions and is given as gifts in ritual exchanges.

Zunis also grew varieties of beans and squash. Beans were prepared for eating by soaking and boiling. They were sometimes preserved by drying and later boiled in water or soups. Squash was eaten boiled or roasted while its seeds were preserved by drying. In addition to the crops planted by men, women grew some produce in "waffle gardens" along the banks of the Zuni River. Waffle gardens were divided into small square or rectangular cells surrounded by low mud walls that helped conserve water and protect the plants from wind. They were watered by hand, using ladles to distribute water brought from the river or from nearby wells in water jars that women balanced on their heads.

In the past, wild plants also contributed to the diet. Women gathered walnuts, acorns, piñon nuts, watercress, yucca, juniper berries, sunflowers, wild rice, peas, potatoes, parsnips, and milkweed. The nuts in particular provided rich sources of protein at times when crops failed due to drought or flooding.

Animal protein was a supplemental part of the aboriginal diet, adding variety to the basic plant fare. Rabbits, mice, and other desert rodents were found in abundance nearby while in the woodlands and mountains at some distance from villages, deer, antelope, elk, mountain sheep, and bears were hunted. Men hunted individually or in groups as large as 100 or 200. They fanned out on open land and caught rabbits with sticks thrown like boomerangs. Deer were hunted collectively by driving them either into fenced enclosures or into pits dug in the ground. Eagles, ducks, wild turkeys, hawks, owls, crows, and blue jays were caught using traps of wood and twine designed specifically for each species. Birds were prized both as food and as a source of feathers used in clothing, decoration, and ceremonial equipment. Flocks of turkeys, tended by all household members, were eaten when other foods were scarce, but they were kept primarily for their feathers, which were woven into clothing or used for decoration. Meat from animals and birds was generally cooked in boiling water or roasted over coals.

Zunis offered food to visitors as part of their gestures of hospitality. Generosity and hospitality were due to anyone, whether relative, friend, stranger, or even enemy, who entered one's home. As Cushing observed,

> The instant greeting to a Zuni house is "Enter, sit, and eat!" Enter any house at whatever time day or night and the invariable tray of "hewe" will be brought forth, also parched corn, or in their seasons peaches, melons or pinon nuts, nor once having taken to the sitting block or bench, may you state your errand without first making a fair show of eating. Toward one another, the Zunis exercised these rights of hospitality. A Zuni may not be on speaking terms with another, but if by chance the other should happen inside his door he will certainly have a bread tray placed before him and be bidden to eat. (Cushing 1979: 297, 301)

In addition to subsistence work, women and men produced tools, equipment, and household utensils. Women made pottery from red, blue, yellow, and white clay. They carefully dug out clay deposits from the ground and then returned the earth to its original condition. They made jars, bowls, plates, and many kinds of containers, some used for cooking, others for storing dried or fresh foods. Pottery was painted with contrasting colors in geometric designs. When a pot was nearly complete, the potter paused in her work, offered a short prayer, and then threw a few crumbs or bits of dried bread into the vessel. This ritual act was called a "feeding period." While women were decorating their pottery, they were careful not to laugh, whistle, or make any unnecessary noises because "it was feared that the 'voice' would enter into the vessels, and that when the latter were fired, would escape with a loud noise and such violence as to shiver the ware into chards. That this should not in any event happen, the voice spirit in the vessels, especially those designed for water and food, was fed during the burning" (Cushing 1979: 248).

Men produced tools and equipment used for farming and hunting such as digging sticks, shovels, axes, and bows and arrows. Some tools, utensils, and weapons were made or decorated with silver, copper, obsidian, and turquoise obtained from nearby mines and quarries. Underground mines had tunnels as deep as 200 ft. with pits 300 ft. in width. Men made baskets from twine and coiled yucca and rabbit brush of natural color or of contrasting colors woven in geometric designs. In addition, they wove cotton cloth that was then fashioned into blankets, clothing, and sashes. Cloth might be dyed with brightly colored mineral and vegetable pigments. Women's clothing consisted of cotton blouses, skirts, and sashes while men wore cotton shirts, sashes, and aprons over deerskin leggings. Men and women wore moccasins and boots made of deer and antelope hides. Clothing was often embroidered with bright colors in geometric designs. Finally, men used turquoise, shell, and coral to craft jewelry that was worn by all.

Many of the products produced by Zunis were traded with neighboring villages as well as with people living in far distant regions. Indeed, local and regional trade was a significant feature of aboriginal life. As early as 600 to 900, Zunis' ancestors had trade relations with people in Mexico, California, and the Great Plains. By 1250, Zuni villages were centers for intertribal trade. The village of Hawikkuh in particular became an active commercial hub, visited by people from throughout the Southwest and adjacent regions. Numerous trails linked Zunis to near and distant lands. One trail led to the Pueblos situated near the Rio Grande River, another further east toward the Plains, and others travelled north to the Hopis, northwest to the Grand Canyon, and south into the Sonora region of northern Mexico (Ferguson and Hart 1985: 55). Zunis traded corn, salt taken from the Zuni Salt Lake located some 60 mi. from their villages, turquoise from local mines, and buffalo hides obtained by hunters in expeditions into the Plains. They also traded cotton cloth, jewelry, baskets, pottery, moccasins, and a distinctive blue paint. Zunis received pottery, copper, and parrot feathers from Mexico, buffalo hides from the western Plains, and seashells and coral from people in California (53). As noted by a Spanish traveler in 1605, "In the winter they [Zunis] wear skins or hides of the buffalo which are tanned and very well dressed and which are brought to these provinces to trade for corn, flour and cotton blankets by the Indians who live among the buffalo" (Forbes 1960: 107).

Families and Social Systems

Zuni social organization and descent centers on membership in matrilineages. Matrilineages are the core of Zuni households, functioning as they do as social, economic, and ceremonial units. The matrilineage is headed by the senior resident woman, who plays an active role in the lives of members of her group, giving advice, helping settle disputes, and organizing economic, social, and ceremonial activities. In addition, she is the guardian of lineage property, especially sacred objects that are used in kin-group ceremonies. These objects, kept in a medicine bundle, are placed on an altar erected in a special room of her house. Medicine bundles contain an ear of corn wrapped in feathers and may also include seeds, stone images representing animal spirits, and ceremonial masks. The eldest brother of the head woman is also an important figure in a lineage. He, too, is consulted when decisions must be reached or conflicts need to be settled. And he plays an important part in supervising and preparing lineage rituals.

Matrilineages are combined into more than one dozen matrilineal clans, most bearing the name of an animal or bird such as bear, coyote, deer, badger, frog, turkey, eagle, and crane. Other names are derived from trees, plants, and natural forms including dogwood, tobacco, corn, and sun. Although one's first loyalty is to one's own clan, people also have close ties to their father's group and speak of themselves as "child of my father's clan." Clans are exogamous, and even though one's father is not a member of one's own group, marriages between an individual and someone in her/his father's clan are strongly condemned. At least into the twentieth century, clans were organized into six phratries, each associated with the six sacred directions. Although the linkage of specific clans into phratries seems to have varied from time to time, Eggan listed the following groupings: North (crane, gross, yellowwood, evergreen oak), West (bear, coyote, spring herb), South (tobacco, corn, badger), East (deer, antelope, turkey), Above (sun, sky, eagle), Below (frog, water, rattlesnake), and Middle (macaw) (Eggan 1950: 198). The Macaw clan was, according to Cushing, considered "the all-containing or mother clan of the entire tribe" (Cushing 1979: 186).

In addition to their role in kinship, clans own land in common, each with control over certain areas of farmland allocated by elder women to the lineages and households in their group. Farmland is said to be "owned" by women of the household but it is not "private property" belonging to individuals. Rather, land is a resource controlled in common by the clan as a whole, its members having rights to use according to their needs.

Bonds between relatives are deep, strong, and enduring. Relatives live and work together, share food and other resources, and are generous, cooperative, and supportive. Bonds between mothers and daughters and between sisters are deepened by lifelong residence in the same household. Although men leave their natal households after marriage, bonds between parents and sons and between sisters and brothers remain strong. Men return to their first home to help celebrate family occasions, participate in kin-group rituals, and give aid and advice to their relatives.

The importance of kinship in Zuni life is further demonstrated by the way that people talk to each other. Kinship terms are extended to clan-mates: elder women are called "mother" while elder men are called by the term meaning "mother's brother." Older men in one's father's clan are called "father" while elder women are called "father's sister." And older people call their younger clan-mates by words meaning "daughter" or "son." When addressing or referring to people who are not relatives, the practice of teknonymy prevails. That is, instead of employing someone's personal name, Zunis use an expression meaning "Father (or Mother) of X" (Kroeber 1917: 72). Kinship terms are also employed for people with whom men and women form "ceremonial friendships." These bonds are established between children who are especially close, and then throughout their lives they call each other "brother" or "sister," extending words for "mother" and "father" to each other's parents. Finally, certain natural forms are spoken of with words usually labeling relatives. The earth is called "mother" and the sun "father." Words for grandparents are used for some aspects of nature: rain clouds and fire are called "grandmother"; water is called "grandfather"; and corn may be called "sister" or "brother" (Eggan 1950: 188).

Networks of relatives are widened through affinal bonds. Marriages are based on the affections and wishes of the couple. After a man and woman decide that they want to marry, the woman consults with her mother to make sure the union will meet with family approval. Then the man comes to the woman's home at night, stays with her "in secret," and leaves before dawn (Ladd 1979b: 486). The period of "trial marriage" lasts for several weeks during which time the man or woman may change his/her mind. If the woman decides against marriage, the matter is ended immediately, but if the man changes his mind, he must give the woman a gift before the bond is broken. In most cases, the couple decides to continue their relationship. As part of a ceremonial exchange of gifts, the woman grinds a large supply of corn to present to her mother-in-law, who reciprocates with a set of ceremonial clothing consisting of a black dress, moccasins, shawl, and strings of beads. The next morning, the husband leaves after sunrise and returns in the early evening to share the day's meal with his new family, thus publicly acknowledging his marriage (485–486).

If a man wishes to propose marriage without prior discussion, he may bring gifts to the woman's house. When he states his desire for marriage, the woman's father responds by saying "it is up to my daughter." At that point, the woman can accept or reject the man's proposal.

Wives and husbands form a cooperative team as equal partners having equal rights in their households. If a couple does not get along, either party is free to divorce. If the man chooses to divorce, he simply leaves his wife's household, returning to his mother's home. If the woman wants to end the marriage, she puts her husband's personal belongings outside the house. All property acquired during marriage belongs to women, inherited from mothers to daughters.

The birth of children of either gender is welcomed although girls are preferred. All children are treated

A Zuni girl, ca. 1903.

kindly by relatives and by the community as a whole, but grandparents are especially affectionate and indulgent of their grandchildren. Children are taught by example and encouragement, not by punishment. However, if a child misbehaves often, adults may tell him/her frightening stories about owls, witches, and other creatures who could come and harm the child. Girls and boys acquire the values of their society by observing the kind of behavior that is socially approved. People who are generous, helpful, considerate, and moderate are respected while those who are boastful, argumentative, uncooperative, or stingy are strongly condemned. According to Ruth Bunzel,

> In all social relations whether within the family group or outside, the most honored personality traits are a pleasing address, a yielding disposition, and a generous heart. The person who thirsts for power, who wishes to be, as they scornfully phrase it, "a leader of the people" receives nothing but criticism. (Bunzel 1938: 480)

Zuni communities are held together by strong bonds of cooperation and loyalty. Disputes among kin are settled by respected members of households and clans. If conflicts continue or people behave in ways considered unacceptable, public teasing, ridicule, and gossip usually convince wrongdoers to mend their ways.

Community Leadership

Formal village leadership is based on both civil and religious authorities. In the past, civil leadership was intertwined with religious organization. Ultimate authority and responsibility rested with a council of priests who planned the yearly calendar of ceremonies, appointed village officials, and organized public events. The council consisted of members of a number of religious societies including the Rain Priests, Sun Priest, and heads of kiva groups and medicine societies. The council of priests set moral examples rather than involve themselves directly in village disputes. They encouraged others to act properly by their own behavior and by exhortations that they made to village members. As a Spanish soldier named Castaneda remarked in 1540:

> They have priests who preach; these are aged men who ascend to the highest terrace of the village and deliver sermon at sunrise. The people sit around and listen in profound silence. These old men give

them advice in regard to their manner of living, which they think it their duty to observe; for there is no drunkenness among them, no unnatural vice; there are no thieves; on the contrary, they are very laborious. (Tyler 1964: 11)

Although the council of priests is the underlying authority in the village, the members themselves do not exert overt civil control since, as people who are "pure of heart," they are expected not to engage in argument or conflict. Therefore, members of another priesthood, called the "Bow Priesthood," serve as representatives and implementers of council decisions (Ladd 1979b: 488). Bow Priests were traditionally a warrior society that protected villages from external enemies and internal problems. They obtain their power from the twin war gods who led the Zunis out of the earth in primordial times. As civil functionaries, they act on behalf of the religious leaders who make up the council of priests. Bow Priests notify people of the council's decisions, oversee public functions, and ensure that people behave properly during public rituals or gatherings. In the past, they also conducted trials of people accused of witchcraft. In times of war, Bow Priests organized and led armed forces in defense of their villages. They also guarded the many trails that were used to conduct local, regional, and long distance trade.

Each village had a "house chief" who was named to the position by the council of priests. The chief, called "Pekwin," was always a member of the Dogwood clan. He was installed in office in a ceremony conducted by the head Rain Priest of the village, who placed a staff made of feathers in the chief's hands, recited a prayer, and then blew on the staff four times. The house chief had two assistants who were members of the Bow Priesthood and who acted directly to settle disputes within the village and to protect the community from outside enemies. The chief could be removed from office by the council of priests that appointed him if the people disapproved of his behavior.

Religious Beliefs and Practices

The Zuni universe consists of nine realms or layers of existence. We now live in the middle realm while beneath the earth are four layers of underworlds, and above, over an inverted stone bowl that is the sky, are four upper worlds. Each of the underworlds is home to different species of trees while the upperworlds are inhabited by birds. Around the earth toward the north, west, south, and east lie the oceans, all interconnected by underground links that provide water for the springs, ponds, and caves of the earth. In the oceans are four mountains whose mountaintops are the "sacred old places" or shrines of the world (Stevenson 1904; Bunzel 1932c).

There are two types of persons who inhabit the realms of existence: "Raw People" and "Cooked or Daylight People." Raw People are spirit beings who eat both raw foods and the cooked foods given to them as offerings by humans, the Cooked or Daylight People. In exchange for offerings and prayers, Raw People protect humans and give them long life, health, and good fortune. Among the most powerful Raw People are Earth Mother, Sun Father, and Moonlight-giving Mother. Earth Mother, the place of life's origin, wears a robe of yellow flowers in the summertime while in the winter she is clad in a robe of white snowflakes. Sun Father and Moonlight-giving Mother are husband and wife, givers of light and life. Sun Father, the source of daylight, is offered daily gifts of cornmeal at sunrise, the most sacred time of day, to rejoice in the beginning of new life. Indeed, in the Zuni language, the word "tekohananee" means both "life" and "daylight" (Bunzel 1932a: 481).

In the ocean surrounding the earth live four giant feathered serpents of the colors yellow, blue, red, and white. Along the shores live "Rain Priests" of the six directions who become clouds, rain storms, fog, and dew when they leave their usual habitats. They are assisted by six "Bow Priests" who are the makers of thunder and lightening (498).

The world is oriented by division into six directions, associated with colors, animals, birds, and trees. This system of linkages underscores a basic principle of Zuni philosophy, namely the spiritual order, unity, and interconnection of all life in the universe. Associations among various lifeforms, colors, and directions are described in Table 15.1.

Within every household is kept a sacred bundle that contains spiritually powerful objects and substances representing the eternal forces and bounty of the universe. These bundles include water, seeds, stone images of animals, and ceremonial masks. They are reminders of the sacred relationship between Zunis and the Raw People who guard and protect them. People show their respect and thanks to spirits by making offerings of tobacco smoke, small portions of cooked food and cornmeal that may be mixed with crushed turquoise, shells, and coral. They also sacrifice wooden prayer sticks carved with faces, painted, and decorated with feathers. Since the sticks represent or stand in for the person making the sacrifice, the supplicant is essentially sacrificing a surrogate of him/herself. Women offer sacrifices to Moonlight-giving Mother while men give to Sun Father and all people sacrifice to the ancestors, a generalized class of spirits. Offerings are always made at the summer and winter solstices although they may be made at many other times throughout the year as well.

Zunis conceive of life as a path or road that is given to each person by Sun Father at his/her birth. The length of the road corresponds to the years that a person will live. Therefore, a fundamental hope is to be able to live out one's apportioned path, not to die before one's time through accident or witchcraft. Families mark stages in the road of a person's life with rituals at birth, puberty, and death. During pregnancy, a woman and her husband can go to nearby shrines to make offerings depending on whether they desire to have a daughter or son (Stevenson 1904: 296). Then, when a baby is about to be born, the maternal grandmother aids in the delivery. Since a newborn child is considered unripe or soft "as are germinating seeds or

Direction	Color	Prey Animal	Game Animal	Bird	Tree
North	Yellow	Mountain Lion	Mule Deer	Oriole	Pine
West	Blue	Bear	Mountain Sheep	Bluejay	Douglas Fir
South	Red	Badger	Antelope	Parrot	Aspen
East	White	Wolf	Whitetail Deer	Magpie	Cottonwood
Zenith	All Colors	Eagle	Jackrabbit	Purple Martin	
Nadir	Black	Mole	Cottontail Rabbit	Swallow	

TABLE 15.1 Associations

Source: Dozier 1970: 205–206.

unfinished clay vessels" (Cushing 1979: 205), it is kept inside the house away from sunlight for eight days so that it will gradually become hardened and safe for exposure to "the world of daylight." At the end of the period of seclusion, the baby's umbilical cord is buried in the soil nearby, that site becoming the "midmost shrine" of the child, connecting it to Earth Mother and the underworld from which the ancestors emerged in primordial times. At sunrise on the eighth day after birth, the baby's paternal grandmother washes the baby's head, puts it in its cradle, places cornmeal in its hands, and takes it out into the dawn air, facing east toward the rising sun. While other female relatives of both parents sprinkle offerings of cornmeal to Sun in the east, the paternal grandmother recites a blessing prayer (Bunzel 1932b: 635). A baby is not given its name immediately after birth but instead awaits a time when the parents are confident that it is healthy, likely to survive, and therefore hardened and safe. Then the baby's paternal grandmother bestows a name on the child, usually the name of a relative on either side of the family who has lived a long life.

When a young girl reaches puberty, she goes to her paternal grandmother's house and spends the day grinding corn. Zunis believe that it is important for the girl to "work hard at the dawn of her womanhood" so that she will not suffer pain during menstruation (Stevenson 1904: 303). It is believed that if she is idle on the first day of her new life as a woman, she will always suffer from cramps and pain.

The final stage of life is marked with rituals of burial and mourning. Zunis believe that death may result from spirit causes such as witchcraft, the revenge of ceremonial masks against a person who does not truly believe, or jealousy of the dead who may appear to people in dreams in order to take the living with them (Bunzel 1932d: 634). All deaths are preceded by omens that typically manifest in people's dreams. When death occurs, the deceased father's sister or another female relative bathes the body with suds made from yucca, rubs it with cornmeal and dresses it in new clothing, making a gash in each garment so that the clothes' spirits can accompany the deceased's soul on its journey to the afterworld. On the day after death, the deceased's brother digs a grave and carries the body out for burial, placing it so that its head faces east. Some of the deceased's possessions are placed in the grave for the soul's use in the afterlife, but the majority of personal belongings are either given to descendants or are burned or buried in a separate place (D. Tedlock 1975: 260–261).

A period of intense mourning lasts four days. A surviving spouse is washed with yucca suds and cold water. S/he must stay away from fire, bathe only in cold water, and refrain from eating meat or salt. S/he sleeps with a kernel of black corn and a piece of charcoal under the head in order to avoid dreaming of the deceased (Stevenson 1904: 306–307). And s/he should remain quiet, keeping away from others as much as possible. A widower never remains in his wife's family's household but instead returns to his mother's or sister's home. As Zunis say, "death takes two, not one" (Eggan 1950: 195).

The deceased's soul remains in the village during the four days of mourning and may make itself known by scratching on surfaces, opening and closing doors, or appearing in dreams. Doors to the house of the deceased are left ajar so that the soul can enter and exit at will. Souls can be dangerous to the living because they may want to take a companion along on their journey to the afterworld. At the end of the mourning period, the soul travels west to Koluhwala:wa, the village where souls reside, located at the bottom of a sacred lake a journey of two days from the town of Zuni. However, if death was premature, the soul cannot reach its final destination immediately but must wait at "Spirit Place" just 1 mi. west of Zuni where it remains until its preordained road reaches an end when it can finally join the ancestors in their village. Existence in the afterworld is similar to that of the living. Souls plant, feast, dance, and even die. When they have died four deaths, they return to the place of emergence from inside Earth Mother (D. Tedlock 1975: 262–268).

The dead are never spoken about by personal name but instead are addressed as members of a general class of ancestors. To Zunis, the living and dead are eternally linked. The living honor their ancestors with prayers, food, and rituals while the dead reciprocate by protecting people from harm and, when transformed into clouds, bring rain, the life-giving water that nurtures crops upon which people depend for survival.

In addition to participation in life-cycle ceremonies, people may belong to a number of religious societies that periodically perform private and/or public rituals. Many rites are organized by members of the six "kiva societies," each associated with one of the six ceremonial kivas linked with one of the six sacred directions believed to have their origin in the beginnings of time when the Zunis founded their village in the "middle place." Each kiva is governed by a ceremonial society that plans its rituals and initiates new members. Boys are initiated into a kiva society when they reach the age of five or six to "save them" or "make them valuable" (Bunzel 1932b: 975). Girls needs not undergo initiation because they are thought to be already "valuable" by their nature. A boy is initiated into the kiva of his ceremonial father, a man selected at the child's birth from among the men in his father's sister's household. The ritual process begins when the ceremonial father carries the boy to his kiva where initiation takes place. When all eligible boys have been assembled, they are whipped by men dressed in costumes and masks that impersonate "kachinas" (or more accurately are transformed into kachinas), who are spirit beings associated with ancestors and with rain. The second stage of initiation occurs when boys are between ten and twelve years old. The second rite follows the same pattern as the first, but after the boys are whipped by the kachinas, the adults remove their masks, revealing that they are human beings representing gods. Participants then reverse roles as the boys whip the men. Initiates are told never to reveal the secret of the transformation of deities. Each boy acquires a mask that he may wear during the public performance of kachina dances held four times every year: just before the winter solstice, later in winter, in summer, and at harvest time. Dancers don their masks and costumes, enter the village at dawn, and proceed to dance in the town's open plazas. Dances may continue for many hours, with audience requests for encores of particularly beautiful dances (Bunzel 1932c).

Two other groups of masked impersonators are organized into religious societies as well. One group consists of six beings called "Shalakos," deities who are bringers of rain, fertility, good fortune, and abundant crops. Shalakos are impersonated by dancers wearing costumes and masks that are as much as 10 ft. tall. Their dances are performed every year in the late fall. A final group of masked dancers are called "mudheads" or ritual clowns. Their costumes include mud-colored masks with distorted, quizzical, or foolish-looking faces. They participate in many public dances, engaging in comical and outrageous behavior. As comics, they make fun of spectators, kachina dancers, and priests and may present parodies of current events. In addition, clowns behave in ways that violate standards of normal behavior, shouting obscenities and making lewd gestures (B. Tedlock 1975: 108, 114). They drink what is undrinkable, including urine, and eat what is inedible, including ashes, pebbles, woodchips, and feces. Zunis say that clowns are able to perform unusual and inappropriate acts because they have medicines that take away their sense of shame. Despite their comic appearance and antics, clowns' behavior teaches a serious lesson, namely that human societies can exist only if people follow common rules of decency and normalcy. By their own outrageous actions, clowns dramatize the danger of violating normal standards, thus in effect emphasizing the limits of social order.

In addition to the groups of masked gods, there are more than a dozen medicine societies, each performing dances and rituals intended to cure illness. Any man or woman may volunteer to join a medicine society or may be compelled to join after receiving successful medical treatment from the group. Members learn both natural and ritual methods of curing. Each society receives its knowledge and powers from particular patron spirits, called "Beast Priests," that represent prey animals such as Bear, Wolf, and Eagle. The most prestigious healers are those who have received their knowledge from the spirit of Bear, considered the most powerful of animal patrons. Such healers are able to see into a patient's body, locate a hidden object believed to have caused the illness, and draw it to the surface either with an eagle feather or by sucking on the body. Members of some medicine societies engage in especially dramatic displays of their skills. For example, healers of the "Snake Medicine Society" and the "Little Fire Society" bathe in fire, swallow fire, and dance on hot coals without getting burned while members of the "Sword People" bathe in icy water in winter and swallow swords and sticks without getting cut (Stevenson 1904). Medicine societies treat patients whenever their services are needed. They also perform public rituals that bring good health to the community in general. At the time of ceremonies marking winter solstice, each society holds an open meeting and performs cures for anyone who asks.

A final group of religious societies consists of priesthoods, the most important of which are the Rain Priesthood and the Bow Priesthood. The prestige of the Rain Priesthoods is indicative of the significance of rain for the Zunis' survival. Rain Priests, who pray for rain and for the well-being of the people, derive their knowledge and powers from the "Rain-bringing Spirits." Rain Priests are men of high moral character, "pure of heart," generous, and kind. They function both as ritualists and as civil authorities in their role of appointing village leaders who represent them and implement their wishes. Bow Priesthoods are assistants to or spokesmen for Rain Priests. They announce ritual calendars, carry out the decisions of Rain Priests, and serve as assistants to civil leaders.

The annual cycle of agricultural activities is intertwined with rituals that legitimate and sustain the practical work that people do. Most of the rituals performed during the summer months are concerned with rain and crops while most winter ceremonials are concerned with medicine, war, human fertility, and earth renewal (Eggan 1950: 209). Zunis participate either as active members or as audiences for public rituals that reinforce their unity as a people as well as their unity with all life forces of the universe. Indeed, the perseverance of Zuni culture today is fundamentally related to the strength of Native beliefs. Religious beliefs, spiritual ties to place and to the powerful forces that created and sustained them have given the people the strength to withstand hundreds of years of Spanish, Mexican, and American invasions and the direct and indirect pressures exerted upon them to abandon their traditions. As Cushing remarked, "The Zuni faith is as a drop of oil in water, surrounded and touched at every point [by more than 350 years of Spanish intercourse] yet no place penetrated or changed inwardly by the flood of alien belief that descended upon it" (Cushing 1979: 181).

SPANISH INVASIONS AND THEIR CONSEQUENCES

The Spanish invasion of the Southwest began in the early years of the sixteenth century when officials based in Mexico began to extend their control over Native people further north. Hoping to find cities filled with gold and other treasures, explorers and missionaries eventually mounted expeditions into Zuni territory. One, named Marcos De Niza, advanced toward Zuni lands in 1539, sending a small group in advance of the main contingent under the leadership of an African slave named Esteban. Upon reaching Native villages, Esteban tried to assault several women and was killed by the men (Forbes 1960: 7). When Niza learned of Esteban's fate, he turned back toward Mexico, but before retreating caught sight of the village of Hawikkuh. Although

Niza viewed Hawikkuh from a far distance, he reported that he had found a wealthy kingdom, richer even than that of the Aztecs. Calling the kingdom "the Seven Cities of Cibola," Niza told of houses decorated with turquoise and other jewels. A large force was immediately sent to the region to conquer the inhabitants and plunder their reputed treasures. The expedition, led by Francisco Vasquez De Coronado, consisted of 230 soldiers on horseback, 70 foot soldiers, several Franciscan priests, and hundreds of Mexican Indians. When the Spaniards reached Hawikkuh, they "found all the Indians of Cibola and the people of other places who had gathered to meet us with force" (10). In the resulting battle, 600 Zuni warriors delayed the Spaniards' assault but then abandoned the town. Since the Spanish failed to find the treasures they sought, they turned eastward, leaving several priests and soldiers at Hawikkuh in order to assert Spanish authority in the region. When these men finally left in 1542, a Spanish officer recounted that "for two or three days, the Zuni never ceased to follow the rear guard of the army to pick up any baggage or Indian servants. They rejoiced at keeping some of our people" (23).

For nearly forty years, Zunis were spared further invasions by the Spanish, who by that time were concentrating their control among Puebloan villages along the Rio Grande. The Zunis' lives continued as before, as described in 1540 by Coronado:

> They have very good homes and good rooms with corridors and some quite good rooms underground and paved, built for the winter. The town of Granada [Coronado's name for Hawikkuh] has 200 houses, all surrounded by a wall. There is another town nearby, but somewhat larger than this, and another of the same size as this; the other four are somewhat smaller.
>
> The food which they eat consists of maize, of which they have great abundance, beans, and game. They make the best tortillas that I have ever seen anywhere. They have the very best arrangement and method for grinding that was ever seen. They have very good salt and crystals, which they bring from a lake a day's journey distance here. (*Zuni History* 1991, I: 18)

The Zunis' prosperous and tranquil life was again disrupted in 1598 when the Spanish government established colonies in the Southwest. It was during that period that the people, who called themselves 'a:shiwi, were first mentioned in Spanish reports as the "Zuni," a name adapted from the Acomas' appellation for the people (Miller 1965). Juan de Õnate, the first governor of the Spanish colony, declared that all Puebloans were subjects of the king of Spain and ordered Native leaders to declare their obedience to the monarch. In response to the foreign presence in the early seventeenth century, Zunis abandoned several of their towns and sought safety in nearby communities, thus concentrating populations in fewer large settlements rather than maintaining small scattered villages that could not be adequately defended. In 1604, a Spanish official noted that six Zuni villages were "almost completely in ruins" (Forbes 1960: 104).

Since Zuni territory was hundreds of miles from the center of foreign settlement near the Rio Grande, the people escaped the most intense forms of control. When Spanish soldiers re-entered the region in 1529, demanding that the people submit to their authority, the council of priests refused to comply. Zunis killed two priests residing in their village and then abandoned their towns, settling together in a large community atop a nearby mesa that afforded protection from assaults. Unable to penetrate the Zunis' defenses, the Spanish left the area and the people returned to their former homes.

Throughout the middle years of the seventeenth century, Zunis defied demands imposed upon them by Spanish civil and religious authorities. Catholic priests, however, arrested a number of religious leaders, punishing them with public beatings, confiscating ritual objects, and burning ceremonial kivas. When the "Pueblo Revolt" against Spanish authority erupted in 1680, Zunis participated by killing their resident priests, burning churches, and expelling colonists who had intruded on their land. Although the Spanish reconquered the region in 1692, they found it difficult to control the Zunis and other western Puebloans. By that time, Zunis had abandoned their smaller villages and settled together in the town of Halona.

In the eighteenth century, relationships between Zunis and nearby Indians deteriorated as Navajo and Apache raiders stole their crops and livestock and carried out several attacks against Halona. In order to protect themselves, Zunis sometimes joined Spanish soldiers in expeditions against the raiders but never formed stable alliances with Spain or any other foreign power.

Although Zunis remained independent throughout the period of Spanish rule, contact with the foreigners affected their economy, settlement patterns, and systems of governance. They adopted numerous articles of European manufacture, especially metal knives, axes, saws, scissors, nails, pots, and kettles. Native economy expanded with the incorporation of new crops including wheat, oats, peaches, apples, melons, tomatoes, and chili. The latter two foods actually originated among the Aztecs in Mexico but were adopted by Spaniards and taken with them into the Southwest. Sheep were also a significant addition to indigenous economy, valued both for their meat and for the wool that women wove into blankets and clothing both for personal use and for sale to Spanish and Mexican traders. In order to tend large herds, Zunis turned some of their land into pasture. Acquisition of sheep altered traditional ownership and inheritance patterns as well. Unlike land and houses, which were controlled and inherited through women, sheep were individually owned by men and inherited patrilineally (Bunzel 1938: 354).

An indirect result of the Spanish invasion was a change in Native settlement patterns. By the end of the sixteenth century, Zunis had abandoned all but one of their six villages, consolidating their population in Halona. Furthermore, the architectural plan of the village was adapted for defensive purposes as the multistoried houses were built to face inward around central plazas with only a few narrow passages leading into open areas. Rooms on the ground floor had few doors or windows so that in order to enter a house people had to climb up ladders onto rooftops and then descend through entrances in the roofs. If intruders approached the village, the ladders to rooftops could be pulled up quickly, barring any access to the rooms below.

In the early nineteenth century, several small farming communities and herding camps were founded as an adaptation to the changing economy. At first, these settlements were inhabited only during the summer, but later in the century three of the communities (Nutria, Ojo Caliente, and Pescado) became permanent residences. During the period of Spanish influence, indigenous governing systems were altered by the introduction of civil authorities including a governor, lieutenant governor, and village council. The Spanish appointed the head of the Bow Priesthood as governor, but by the middle of the nineteenth century when Mexico became the nominal authority in the region, the governor and all other civil officials were chosen by Native religious leaders as had been traditional custom.

Finally, several devastating epidemics of smallpox and measles struck Zuni villages in the sixteenth and seventeenth centuries. Although population figures for early years of the foreign invasion are not reliable, the

Zuni probably numbered 10,000 in the middle of the sixteenth century, but by the time of the Pueblo Revolt of 1680, their population had fallen to 2,500. Further declines continued so that by the end of the eighteenth century, the Zuni numbered only 1,600. Their population did not begin to recover until late in the nineteenth century.

THE PERIOD OF AMERICAN CONTROL

After the Spanish rule in the Southwest ended in 1821 and the Mexican government assumed territorial jurisdiction, Zunis continued to live in relative isolation, benefiting from their great distance from governmental centers. Then during the Mexican-American War, Zunis supported the American military effort by supplying soldiers with food and fighting alongside the troops. In 1845, two American officers visited Halona, exchanging official pledges of peace and friendship with the governor, Lai-iu-ah-tsai-ah:

> As soon as our horses were unsaddled, they [the Zuni] furnished us with a house, and took us all off to different houses to eat. I went to one house where they set out a soup made with mutton and various kinds of vegetables, and a kind of bread as thin as paper. They have the reputation of being the most hospitable people in the world, which I believe they merit in every respect.
>
> We were out of provision and proposed to buy from them but they said they did not sell their provision and more particularly to Americans. So they brought in sufficient bread and meal to last our party into camp, which is three days from here. Our saddles, bridles, and all equipment was left exposed to them, but in the morning, not a single article was gone. Where can such a mass of honest people be found? (*Zuni History* 1991, I: 21)

At the conclusion of war in 1846, the Treaty of Guadalupe-Hidalgo granted the United States possession of the present-day states of New Mexico and Arizona. Although Zuni officials had signed agreements with the United States guaranteeing that the "Zuni shall be protected in its full management of all its rights of private property and religion," the United States began to assert its authority over its newly acquired land and the indigenous inhabitants (21). In addition, the influx of American settlers accelerated dramatically.

After discovery of gold in California in 1849 brought a stream of travelers across the Southwest, the people sought protection of their land. In response, President Hayes, by executive order in 1877, created the Zuni Reservation but it encompassed only one-tenth the territory that the people had occupied. Despite their losses of land, however, Zunis maintained a prosperous economy, as observers of the period noted:

> They breed sheep, keep horses and asses, and practice agriculture on an extensive scale. In all directions, fields of wheat and maze, as well as gourds and melons hold testimony to their industry. In gardens, they raise beans and onions. And the women are skillful in the art of weaving, and manufacture durable blankets. (22)

The late nineteenth century was another period of accelerated settlement of Anglos and Hispanics near Zuni lands and deepening influences of American society in Native life. After trading posts were established and the Atlantic and Pacific Railroad extended to the Anglo town of Gallup, New Mexico, located 40 mi. northeast of Halona, Zuni economy shifted to herding sheep and cattle for sale to livestock markets in eastern and western states. The new economic pattern affected values concerning wealth and property. Since sheep and cattle were individually owned, notions of private property began to develop that were consistent with a market-oriented economy (Bunzel 1938: 356). However, traditional ethics regarding reciprocal kin obligations and communal generosity moderated the development of private ownership and mitigated against a system of personal acquisition of wealth that might have resulted in marked differences in standards of living. As Goldman noted,

> [R]arely can wealth remain for long in the same family or in the same hands. If a man has poor relatives he will feel obligated to support them with gifts of food. Out of motives of friendship he may give expensive gifts to his "kihe" [ceremonial friends]. He will be called upon to entertain the masked god impersonators at the Shalako ... Most of his fortune will be dissipated among the community. (Goldman 1937: 330)

While Zunis were increasing their livestock holdings, Anglo and Hispanic sheepherders and cattle ranchers also entered the Southwest looking for grazing pasture, leading to competition over land between the original inhabitants and the newcomers. Indeed, some army personnel also appropriated Zuni land for grazing their own herds. Settlers encroached on eastern and southern portions of the Reservation while Mormons expanded their holdings in the west. As the population of immigrant communities grew, Zunis lost access to most of their former territory. In addition, American companies began to exploit timber resources in the region. Beginning in the 1890s, more than 2 billion ft. of timber were cut in the Zuni Mountains. Once the trees were taken, Anglo herders grazed their animals on the deforested land.

Zunis also lost part of their original territory to other Native people through treaties that the Indians signed with the US government. In 1868, they lost a northern section of their reservation to Navajos who had that year been released from confinement at Bosque Redondo in New Mexico and needed land on which to reestablish their communities. Then, three years later, creation of the Apache White Mountain Reservation took in a southwestern portion of Zuni lands. Compounding the problem of decreases in land base, the Zuni population began to slowly increase in the early twentieth century, exacerbating population pressure. In response to numerous appeals by Native leaders, several parcels of land were added to the Zuni Reservation, bringing the total area to about 340,000 acres by 1935 (Spicer 1962: 199).

By the early decades of the twentieth century, the developing Zuni economy led to economic growth and security. People produced a variety of crops for their own use and for sale to outsiders, increased the size of their herds, and earned money from jobs working for railroads, government agencies, and businesses located in nearby Anglo towns. But in the 1930s, the BIA unilaterally instituted a program of stock reduction aimed at limiting the number of animals grazed, supposedly for the purpose of arresting soil erosion that had become a serious problem due, however, not to traditional methods of farming, but rather to adoption of "'modern' water management techniques [that caused] extensive erosion and gullying" (Sadler 1992: 6). The Zuni Reservation was divided into eighteen grazing units, each assigned a quota of livestock based on what federal authorities believed the unit could sustain without further depleting the soil. If herders in the unit had holdings that exceeded their limit, they were forced to sell surplus animals to the government at fixed prices. Despite Zunis' vigorous protests against imposition of quotas and forced reductions of livestock, many families had to relinquish much of their herds, thereby losing a stable source of income. Although the government paid herders for their sheep, prices given were low. Furthermore, a single payment for herds did not reflect the sheep's true value since people relied on income from sale of wool from the same animals year after year.

CONTEMPORARY ZUNI COMMUNITIES

Zuni communities have adopted external features of modern technology and developed an increasingly diversified economy, but the people have retained much of their traditional culture and orientation.

Students from A:shiwi Elementary School in Zuni, NM, take part in a writing, art, and dance workshop at the Aztec Ruins National Monument.

Most people are bilingual, speaking the Zuni language in homes and at secular and religious community events. In 2010, 9,686 Zunis of a population that numbered 11,828 were speakers of their Native language (US Bureau of the Census 2010). Zunis have shown a remarkable stability in the face of hundreds of years of physical and ideological assaults from agents of foreign military, religious, governmental, and educational control.

The Zuni Reservation has grown in size as additional acreage has been obtained. It now encompasses nearly 420,000 acres or 654 sq. mi. adjacent to the western border of the state of New Mexico (*Pueblo of Zuni* 2016). The population has also grown in the latter half of the twentieth century, revealing a particularly dramatic recovery from a low of 1,514 recorded in 1905 to a total of 9,946 people according to the 2010 US census count (US Bureau of the Census 2010).

There have been many infrastructural improvements on the reservation in the past thirty years. New housing and modernization of older units have upgraded living conditions both inside the village of Zuni as well as in nearby "suburban" areas. Improvements have also been made in public services, including installation of electricity, construction of piped water systems, paving of roads, and completion of a sewer system and indoor plumbing. Government buildings containing the headquarters of the tribal council, five schools, and a public health service hospital have all been constructed to serve the community.

The Zuni economy has grown and diversified while maintaining some of its traditional resources. People now support themselves through farming, herding, wage work, and craft production (Ladd 1979a: 494–497). In order to increase farm production and livestock holdings, water supplies have been expanded and upgraded. Approximately 95 percent of the reservation's land is currently used for grazing, divided into ninety-five grazing units for sheepherding and four pastures for cattle. All grazing land is regulated by a Zuni Range Code, adopted in 1976, that sets limits for the number of animals allowed in each grazing unit or cattle range.

Farming continues to be an important endeavor although few families rely on agriculture as their main economic activity. Only about 1,000 acres of land are currently under cultivation, a sharp decrease from the 10–12 thousand acres farmed a century ago. As in past centuries, most farming is done by men, although a number of older women plant small traditional waffle gardens near their homes.

In 2012, the Zuni Pueblo was designated a Main Street Project by the National Trust for Historic Preservation. The designation provides the Zunis with funds for economic development, particularly aimed at revitalizing commercial neighborhoods.

Most families support themselves through wage work either as their sole income-producing activity or as a supplement to farming and/or herding. Craft occupations provide income for many people who specialize in such arts as silverwork, pottery, painting, and sculpture. Native work is promoted and marketed by the Zuni Craftsman Cooperative Association, selling to local and national outlets. Employment is obtained in the public sector with tribal and federal agencies while jobs in local businesses, industries, and tribal enterprises are also available. However, despite the range of potential jobs, rates of unemployment and underemployment are high because the actual number of jobs does not meet all the needs. In 2010, 8.6 percent of the labor force was unemployed, as opposed to 7.2 percent in New Mexico. Zunis' 2010 per capita income was a low $11,404, a figure about two-third that for the total American Indian population and about half the New Mexican average of $22,966. Zuni median household income stood at $35,724. Given the low incomes and high unemployment rates, it is not surprising that many Zunis are poor. In 2010, more than a quarter (28.5%) of families and over a third (35.9%) of individuals were living below the poverty level (US Bureau of the Census 2010).

Civil governance at Zuni is now regulated by a constitution, ratified in 1970, that established leadership by a governor, lieutenant-governor, and tribal council, all elected to terms of four years. Civil officials are installed in office in accordance with traditional custom by the Head Rain Priest who "charges [them] with the responsibility of taking care of the people, whether rich or poor, clean or dirty" (Ladd 1979b: 489). As a symbol of office the governor is given a cane that was presented to Zuni leaders by Abraham Lincoln in 1863. It is a symbol parallel to the ceremonial feathered staff that is the property of the village House Chief appointed by the traditional council of priests.

Since the 1970s, Zunis have won significant land claims cases that have addressed the issue of rights to land and compensation for territory illegally confiscated during past centuries. As a result, Zunis have regained access to some portions of the vast territory that they had lost. After many years of litigation, pursuing their claim to the BIA and the US Court of Claims, and after exerting political pressure locally and in Washington, DC, Zunis and their supporters persuaded the US Congress to pass legislation in 1978 enabling the people to regain possession of Zuni Salt Lake, located 62 mi. south of Zuni village. In traditional times, the lake not only provided salt for the people but also was (and is) an important religious site. By the act of Congress, Zunis were able to acquire the Lake and surrounding lands from the state of New Mexico, title to the lands to be held in trust "in the name of the United States for the benefit of Zuni Indian tribe of New Mexico" (Hart 1995a: 82). The law also enabled the people to sue for compensation for additional lands taken by the US government without payment. The Zuni tribe immediately filed suit in the Court of Claims seeking compensation for land confiscated between 1846 and 1946. The Court issued a ruling in 1987 recognizing that Zunis had held "aboriginal title" to a large portion of the states of Arizona and New Mexico and had been wrongfully deprived of 14,835,892 acres of land during the period from 1876 to 1939. The tribe was awarded $25 million (approximately $1.69 per acre) in compensation, a sum that the tribal council placed in a trust account for investment and purchases for "the benefit of the tribe as a whole" (Hart 1995b: 87). Funds were subsequently allocated for construction of a new elementary school and for purchase of additional acreage, which increased the total acreage of the reserve from around 410,000 to around 420,000. The Zuni Elementary Magnet School for Communication and Technology was built in 2015, using approximately $24.1 million of the awarded money, and opened later that year (HB Construction 2015).

A dispute over another sacred area has also ended in victory for Zuni claims. The people had filed suit for return of a site called Kolhuwala:wa, located at the juncture of the Zuni and Little Colorado Rivers. Kolhuwala:wa is the place where Zuni souls travel after death and is therefore a central sacred site in the Native universe and the focus of pilgrimages by Rain Priests. Although Zunis won the return of Kolhuwala:wa in 1984, they were sometimes denied access to the site by Anglo ranchers who own surrounding land. Finally, in 1990, a federal judge granted the Zunis easement rights to Kolhuwala:wa for the pilgrimages that occur every four years at the time of the summer solstice (Hart 1995c: 206).

In 1990, after additional legal battles, Zunis reached an agreement with the United States acknowledging that the government had illegally sold Native land in the nineteenth century to railroad companies that were extending track throughout the Southwest, as well as to army officers stationed at Fort Wingate for incorporation into private ranches. The government also admitted that they had permitted Anglo ranchers to encroach on and overgraze Zuni land and had allowed timber companies to overcut Native forests. The suit against the government ended in an agreement ratified by Congress as the Zuni Land Conservation Act of 1990, establishing a permanent Zuni Indian Resource Development Trust Fund of $17 million (Enote 1992: 5; Sadler 1992: 6). Interest from the account is used to implement the Zuni Sustainable Resource Development Plan aimed at developing renewable resources, rehabilitating the watershed and water resources, and acquiring land for future use. A Zuni Conservation Project aims to replant vegetation, control soil erosion, improve soil quality, and reduce the loss of water (Enote 1992: 5). The project also collects data on fish and wildlife resources, water sources, and forestry needs. In addition, a Zuni Sustainable Agricultural Project is dedicated to developing local agriculture using the knowledge and skills of traditional farming techniques (*Zuni Farming for Today and Tomorrow* 1993: 8). Zunis understand economic recovery in the context of their principles of social, cultural, and spiritual integrity: "For the Zunis, sustainable development includes more educational opportunities for young people, provision of Medicare for the sick elderly and the acquisition of sacred sites that are outside reservation boundaries" (Sadler 1992: 7).

Additional tribal projects serve the interests of preserving Native cultural heritage and advancing opportunities for the future. These include establishment of the A:shiwi A:wan Museum and Heritage Center (A:shiwi A:wan means "belonging to the Zuni people") as a center for maintaining, displaying, and enhancing knowledge of Zuni history and culture. In the words of the museum's statement of purpose, it is not a "temple" of the past but a "community learning center that links the past with the present as a strategy to deal with the future" (*Zuni Museum Matters* 1993).

And the Zunis operate the first Native American eagle sanctuary, caring for injured eagles that could not survive in the wild. The sanctuary receives eagles from communities throughout the United States, many from as far away as Alaska. Through the sanctuary, Zunis are able to acquire eagle feathers for use in their ceremonies, a vital part of their religious practice. Prior to establishing the sanctuary in 1999, Zunis could only obtain eagle feathers by applying to the US Fish and Wildlife Service, National Eagle Repository located in Colorado. Because of the high demand from Native American communities, delays in obtaining the feathers often meant that ceremonies had to be postponed or canceled. In addition to the practical benefits of having their own supply, the Zunis are keeping many injured birds alive. In 2012, they cared for twenty-six eagles that otherwise would have died. And they are asserting their sovereignty by working out agreements that recognize their rights to maintain their ceremonial practices.

The integrity and continuity of Zuni communities are in large part attributable to the strength of traditional social systems based on cooperative households and clans and to the people's commitment to their spiritual heritage, perpetuated in homes, kivas, and public spaces. It is in their hearts and minds that their social and religious beliefs are kept strong, as they say in prayer, "I hope you will let me live. May I have a good heart. May I raise much corn and many sheep. Let me be happy; let all people have much and be happy" (quoted in Stevenson 1904: 145).

REFERENCES

Bunzel, Ruth. 1932a. *Introduction to Zuni Ceremonialism*. Bureau of American Ethnology, Washington, DC. Annual Report No. 47. pp. 467–544.

Bunzel, Ruth. 1932b. *Zuni Katcinas*. Bureau of American Ethnology, Washington, DC. Annual Report No. 47. pp. 837–1086.

Bunzel, Ruth. 1932c. *Zuni Origin Myths*. Bureau of American Ethnology, Washington, DC. Annual Report No. 47. pp. 545–609.

Bunzel, Ruth. 1932d. *Zuni Ritual Poetry*. Bureau of American Ethnology, Washington, DC. Annual Report No. 47. pp. 611–835.

Bunzel, Ruth. 1938. "The Economic Organization of Primitive People." *General Anthropology* (ed. F. Boas). Boston, MA: D.C. Heath.

Cushing, Frank. 1979. *Zuni: Selected Writings*. Lincoln, NE: University of Nebraska Press.

Dozier, Edward. 1970. *The Pueblo Indians of North America*. New York: Holt, Rinehart, and Winston.

Eggan, Fred. 1950. *Social Organization of the Western Pueblos*. Chicago, IL: University of Chicago Press.

Enote, James. 1992. "Saving the Land and Preserving Culture: Environmentalism at the Pueblo of Zuni." *Global Pages* (August): 4–8.

Ferguson, T. J., and E. R. Hart. 1985. *A Zuni Atlas*. Norman, OK: University of Oklahoma Press.

Forbes, Jack. 1960. *Apache, Navajo, and Spaniard*. Norman, OK: University of Oklahoma Press.

Goldman, Irving. 1937. "The Zuni of New Mexico." *Cooperation and Competition among Primitive Peoples* (ed. M. Mead). Boston, MA: Beacon Press, pp. 313–353.

Hart, E. Richard. 1995a. "Zuni Relations with the United States and the Zuni Land Claim." *Zuni and the Courts: A Struggle for Sovereign Land Rights*. Lawrence, KS: University Press of Kansas, pp. 72–85.

Hart, E. Richard. 1995b. "The Zuni Land Claim Victory." *Zuni and the Courts: A Struggle for Sovereign Land Rights*. Lawrence, KS: University Press of Kansas, pp. 86–87.

Hart, E. Richard. 1995c. "Protection of Kolhuwala:wa: Litigation and Legislation." *Zuni and the Courts: A Struggle for Sovereign Land Rights*. Lawrence, KS: University Press of Kansas, pp. 199–207.

HB Construction. 2015. *HB Construction Begins Work on $24.1 Million Zuni Elementary School*. HB Construction Company News. Online.

Hodge, Frederick. 1907. *Handbook of American Indians North of Mexico*. 2 vols. Washington, DC: Bureau of American Ethnology Bulletin No. 30.

Kroeber, Alfred. 1917. *Zuni Kin and Clan*. New York: Anthropological Papers of the American Museum of Natural History, pp. 39–205.

Ladd, Edmond. 1979a. "Zuni Economy." *Southwest* (ed. A. Ortiz), Vol. 9 of *Handbook of North American Indians*. Washington, DC: Smithsonian Institution, pp. 492–498.

Ladd, Edmond. 1979b. "Zuni Social and Political Organization." *Southwest* (ed. A. Ortiz), Vol. 9 of *Handbook of North American Indians*. Washington, DC: Smithsonian Institution, pp. 482–491.

Miller, Wick. 1965. *Acoma Grammar and Texts*. Berkeley, CA: University of California Publications in Linguistics No. 40.

Pueblo of Zuni. 2016. www.ashwini.org/.

Quam, Alvina. 1972. *The Zunis: Self-Portrayals by the Zuni People*. Albuquerque, NM: University of New Mexico Press.

Sadler, Barry. 1992. "Zunis Search for a Sustainable Future." *Alternatives* 18, no. 3: 6–7.

Spicer, Edward. 1962. *Cycles of Conquest: The Impact of Spain, Mexico and the United States on the Indians in the Southwest, 1533–1960*. Tucson, AZ: University of Arizona Press.

Stevenson, Matilda. 1904. *The Zuni Indians*. Twenty-Third Annual Report of the Bureau of American Ethnology, Washington, DC.

Tedlock, Barbara. 1975. "The Clown's Way." *Teachings from the American Earth: Indian Religion and Philosophy* (ed. D. Tedlock and B. Tedlock). New York: Liveright Publishing, pp. 105–118.

Tedlock, Dennis. 1975. "An American Indian View of Death." *Teachings from the American Earth: Indian Religion and Philosophy* (ed. D. Tedlock and B. Tedlock). New York: Liveright Publishing, pp. 248–271.

Tyler, Hamilton. 1964. *Pueblo Gods and Myths.* Norman, OK: University of Oklahoma Press.

US Bureau of the Census. 2010. "American Indian and Alaska Native Tribes in the United States and Puerto Rico: 201." *2010 Census.* Washington, DC, CPH-T-6.

Zuni Farming for Today and Tomorrow. 1993. Nos. 1, 2.

Zuni History. 1991. Sections I, II.

Zuni Museum Matters. 1993. 1, no. 1.

The Diné (or Navajos)

I will never leave the land, this sacred place. The land is part of me, and I will one day be part of the land. I could never leave. My people are here, and have been here forever. My sheep are here. All that has meaning is here. I live here and I will die here. That is the way it is, and the way it must be. Otherwise, the people must die, the sheep will die, the land will die. There would be no meaning to life, if this happened.

Katherine Smith, Big Mountain, Testimony to US Senate Investigators; quoted in Churchill 1993: 163–164

THE ORIGINS AND FORMATION of the Native nation now known as the Diné (dee-NEY) or Navajo are historically and culturally complex. The earliest identifiable Diné territory in the Southwest was located in northwestern New Mexico and northeastern Arizona. This region, called Dinetah ("among, in the area of the people"), is thought by contemporary Diné to be their ancestral homeland. It is bounded by four sacred mountains: Hesperus Peak and Blanca Peak (Colorado), Mount Taylor (New Mexico), and the San Francisco Peaks (Arizona). Near the center of Dinetah are two additional sacred mountains: Gobernador Knob and Huerfano Mesa. Dinetah is probably where the formation of what is currently referred to as traditional culture took place. Some subsequent cultural developments were shaped by internal innovations and diffusion from nearby Puebloans, while others resulted from European and American pressures. Puebloan influence on Diné culture increased during the late seventeenth and early eighteenth centuries when members of Puebloan villages fled Spanish invaders and joined Diné settlements. Puebloan influence is evidenced in the diffusion of ceramic traditions and motifs in Diné religious practice and in the adoption and/or strengthening of principles of matrilineal descent and clan organization. Indeed, some contemporary Diné clans date their origin to immigrants from Jemez, Zia, and Zuni (Vogt 1961: 301; Reiter 1938: 38).

In their own language, the people call themselves "Diné" or "the people." The name "Navajo" is an English form of the Spanish "Apaches de Nabaju," first recorded in 1626 by Salmeron (Milich 1966: 94). The Spanish "Nabaju" is itself derived from the Tewa word "navahu:," a compound of "nava" (field) and "hu: " (wide arroyo, valley) that was used to designate a large arroyo with cultivated fields (Hewett 1906).

The Diné language is a member of the Apachean or southern branch of the Athabaskan language family. Northern Athabaskan languages are spoken mostly in western Canada and parts of California and Oregon. Other southern Athabaskan languages include those spoken by the six Apache groups.

The Diné nation began to take its modern shape during the middle of the eighteenth century as internal and external events forced the people to abandon Dinetah and move in a southerly and southwesterly direction. Droughts in the region caused economic hardship while attacks from Utes descending from the north compelled people to seek safer lands. The People then inhabited northeastern Arizona as far as the Colorado and Little Colorado Rivers. The expanse of land under their control continued to grow until the pivotal year of 1863, when a military campaign carried out by the US Army succeeded in rounding up the majority of people and forced them to march more than 300 mi. to an army base in New Mexico, where they were detained until 1868. After that time, a reservation was established through treaty that initially encompassed only one-tenth of their prior territory. However, in the late nineteenth and early twentieth centuries, the Diné gradually increased their acreage both through presidential executive orders and through the unofficial recognition of land holdings outside the original borders. Today, the Diné or Navajo Nation is the largest Native territory in the United States, encompassing more than 17 million acres (27,000 sq. mi.) in the states of New Mexico, Arizona, Colorado, and Utah. It is also first in full-blooded population, with some 286,000 full-blooded members, 379,540 total members, and 44,398 living off-reservation (US Bureau of the Census 2010).

TRADITIONAL CULTURE

Diné territory is located on the Colorado Plateau, which ranges in elevation from 3,500 to more than 10,000 ft. above sea level. Approximately half of the present 17-million-acre nation is characterized by warm, dry desert conditions, while another two-fifths consists of steppe regions, with a vegetative cover of piñon, juniper, and sagebrush. Precipitation is light, averaging about 12 in. annually. The remainder of the land is located in high mountainous elevations with ranges of pine, oak, aspen, and fir. This region is colder than elsewhere and receives higher precipitation rates although even there rainfall averages only about 22 in. per year (Vogt 1961: 278–279). Most precipitation comes in the form of summer rainstorms although winter snowstorms occur in the mountains. Due to differences in altitude, topography, and precipitation, growing seasons vary significantly. There are only a few rivers traversing the territory, especially the Colorado River to the west and the San Juan River to the north. However, since most of the people are not concentrated in these river zones, they rely upon small streams and springs for their water.

Economies

Diné subsistence was based on a mixed economy, combining foraging, farming, and herding. Foraging had its roots in Athabaskan culture and presumably was the main productive method utilized by Apacheans as they migrated southward. Principal animals hunted included deer, antelope, big-horn sheep, and such abundant small animals as rabbits and prairie dogs. It is not known exactly when farming was incorporated into Diné economy, but by the sixteenth century the People were noted by Spanish chroniclers to be successful farmers, probably having learned the techniques from their Puebloan neighbors. Like Puebloans and other Native people of North America, corn was the People's basic crop. They may have grown small amounts of beans and fruits but these were of minor significance. The third element in Diné economy, that is, herding, was adopted from Puebloan people from original Spanish sources. The People primarily herded sheep and kept a smaller number of goats and cattle as well.

Each of the productive modes that the Diné pursued required different kinds of residence and land-utilization practices. Flexibility and adaptability were necessary features of their economies, settlement patterns, and community organization. A seventeenth-century Spanish observer noted that the Diné "move from mountain range to mountain range looking for game on which they live, although each camp group has a recognized area of land on which they plant corn and other seeds [i.e., beans, squash, gourds, and melons]" (Reno 1981: 13). Farming required fixed residence during the late spring and summer growing seasons. In contrast, sheepherding entailed not only daily movement of herds but periodic shifting to new grazing areas. Given these requirements, families generally established two different residences, one in summer and one in winter. An entire family might relocate from one place to another, but sometimes only some members would make the move. Herders utilized two different sets of pastureland, usually moving from lower flatlands to higher elevations in the summertime. Since farmland tended to be located away from the best pastures, daily trips to the crops during the growing season were necessary (Aberle 1961: 145).

Land was under the control but not ownership of the family or individual who used it. The lack of definite ownership reflects both cultural values and objective factors of land quality that made flexible utilization practices advantageous. Some sites might be abandoned due to water scarcity, and although sites near streams and springs might be highly desirable, soil erosion resulting from heavy summer thunderstorms might make them worthless in a relatively short period of time. Lack of competition over land resulted from the necessary flexibility of landholding patterns and the availability of sufficient land for farming, at least until the early twentieth century. Although persons who first worked a new field had a claim on the land that could be transmitted to their heirs, if they stopped using the land, others could begin to farm there. Pastureland was also controlled but not owned by individuals and groups. Since grazing areas, like farmland, vary in their yearly supply of water, rigid control of land would be a barrier to each group's productivity. People generally had rights to pastureland near where they resided. Herders in the same community might make and assert overlapping claims to the same territory, but people were expected to keep herds away from cultivated fields and crops (Haile 1954: 18).

In addition to domestic production, people participated in intertribal trade networks that involved all Native nations of the Southwest, supplying foods, hides, and household and ceremonial goods (Hill 1948; Kluckhohn and Leighton 1946). From Hopis, the Diné received cotton, woven clothing, and peaches; they received gourd rattles and salt from Zunis, while from the Tohono O'odham they obtained salt and saltwater shells for use as ornaments and in ceremonial paraphernalia. The Diné traded piñon nuts, firewood, deer meat, and antelope and deer hides to the Hopis and other Puebloans, while they supplied jet, coiled baskets, woven blankets, silver, sheep, and mutton throughout the Southwest.

Productive activities were performed singly and cooperatively by members of residence units generally consisting of two or more families related through women in accordance with rules of matrilineal descent and clan organization. Settlements consisted of clusters of houses or "hogans" (eight-sided domed earth dwellings) that were inhabited by separate nuclear families. Although some work was ideally assigned to

Navajo weavers.

one gender or the other, most productive tasks could be and were performed by either or both women and men. Hunting of large animals was predominantly a male endeavor; cooking and the care of young children were mainly women's work. Women did, however, hunt small animals such as rabbits and sometimes participated in communal deer hunts, while men cared for their children and performed other household tasks when necessary. Weaving and making pottery and baskets were women's work; men hauled water and wood, did the heavy work of house building, and tended horses and cattle (Aberle 1961: 142). Following the Puebloan pattern, farming was most often the work of men, sometimes aided by their wives and children. Sheepherding was a task that could be performed by any and all able-bodied members of the residence group, including young children, but women generally were the principal herders and owners of the stock (Haile 1954: 19). Sheep and goats were owned by individuals, but all animals were combined into one herd that was tended as a single unit.

Families and Social Systems

The Diné descent system continues today as the foundation of social life. It is based on matrilineal clans that are often named for their reputed places of origin. Clans are grouped into phratries, approximately twenty in number, that are unnamed associations whose main functions are to guarantee mutual aid and support for their members. Although people's primary allegiance and closest bonds are to their mother and her clan, they recognize strong ties to their father's clan as well. People say that they are "born of" or "born in" their mother's clan and "born for" their father's clan. Rules of clan exogamy forbid marriage within the clan and proscriptions forbid marriage between a person and members of his/her father's clan as well. Furthermore, people should not marry anyone whose father is of the same clan as oneself since people who are "born for" the same clan consider themselves siblings.

Residence rights stem from two relationships. One, a relationship that endures throughout one's life, is that established by the mother/child bond. Second, people can claim rights to residence on the basis of marital ties. That is, they may reside wherever their spouse has the right to live (Witherspoon 1975). In most cases, married couples live with the wife's family, but a couple may choose to reside with the husband's kin instead or they may change residence from one group to another over time. The eldest woman in the residence group is usually recognized as the "head mother" of the unit. She organizes the economic activities of her daughters and may make requests, through her daughters, for aid from her sons-in-law. When men move into their wife's residence unit, they usually do not become fully integrated for several, possibly many, years depending upon the strength of their loyalty to and affection for their wife. Much later, as couples age and the stability of their marriages is secured, men assume more responsibilities and leadership roles within their residence unit. Eventually, the husband of the head mother takes on the duties of representing his group to outsiders. Both the head mother and her husband are looked to for advice and support by members of their family.

The death of a spouse has varying consequences on residence depending upon the age of the survivor and the availability of other mates within the household in which they are living. In accordance with levirate and sororate preferences, a surviving spouse is encouraged to remarry within his/her deceased mate's family. After the death of the head mother, residence groups may fission as each surviving daughter establishes herself as the head of a growing settlement composed of her own daughters and their husbands and children. Residence groups therefore pass through developmental cycles, with membership that first grows and expands and then changes through births, marriages, and deaths.

Relationships within the nuclear family are affected by rules of etiquette and propriety. The strongest kinship bond is that between mother and child. Mothers are primary cultural symbols of love and benevolence and in practice they are central to people's social, economic, and philosophical worlds (Witherspoon 1975). Children, in return, owe their mother loyalty, kindness, and support. A child's bond to the father is much less intense, in part due to their membership in different clans. Relationships between siblings are generally strong and supportive, but age and gender affect actual behavior. An elder sibling is given more respect than is a younger sibling, especially if many years separate the two. Same-sex siblings have particularly close and supportive relationships, frequently characterized by public joking. Joking may also occur between a brother and sister but they must be careful to avoid sexual overtones.

Marriage creates additional bonds upon which people can depend for cooperation and aid. Formerly, marriages were arranged by parents for their children although the wishes of sons and daughters were ideally taken into consideration. Marriages were typically proposed by maternal relatives of the man to the mother and/or matrilineal relatives of the woman. The concerned families negotiated an appropriate gift to be given by the husband's kin to those of the wife. People understood such gifts as contributions of the husband's family to at least symbolically balance the much greater contributions that the wife's family made by providing most of the livestock, food, and equipment that the new couple used (Leighton and Kluckhohn 1947: 79). It was considered appropriate but not necessary for the woman's family to give presents to the husband's family, although these gifts were generally of lesser value than those given by the husband (Dyk 1947). Traditional weddings typically take place in the evening in the woman's matrilineal settlement. After a brief ceremony during which the bride and groom eat white and yellow cornmeal (symbolizing maleness and femaleness, respectively) the fathers of the couple instruct them in the duties of husband and wife (Leighton and Kluckhohn 1947: 81). Finally, the ritual ends at dawn with songs from a ceremonial corpus known as "Blessingway."

Relationships between men and their in-laws are characterized by "bashfulness," demonstrated by respect and social distance (Aberle 1961). Bashfulness is strongest in the relationship between a man and his mother-in-law. The two should avoid speaking to or looking at one another or being alone together unless circumstances make direct interaction necessary. Women are also expected to show respect and restraint when interacting with their fathers-in-law, but since the two usually do not live in the same settlement, their daily lives are little affected by these patterns of behavior. A man's responsibility to his wife and her family results in orderings of priorities for requests and offers. That is, people generally are reluctant to ask a married man directly for assistance or for resources but instead approach his wife first to get her approval. And if a man does not want to accede to a request, even from relatives, he can postpone or deny compliance by stating that he has prior commitments to his wife and her family (Lamphere 1977). Even though a man may move to his wife's homestead, he continues to have strong personal and social responsibilities toward his relatives, especially his mother, siblings, and sister's children, who are all members of his own clan.

Although people owe their greatest loyalty to their household and extended family residence group, they are also aware of strong bonds of cooperation and responsibility to members of what Aberle calls the "local clan element," described as "consisting of the members of a given clan residing in a given area, plus some of the close relatives of these members living in nearby areas. It is loosely organized and constitutes the unilineal unit of collective responsibility and joint action" (Aberle 1961: 108). As Aberle notes, clans themselves are dispersed and not centrally organized. They have "no head, are not organized, do not congregate, and do not hold property" (109). Given the large number of people possible within a clan (some with 3,000 or 4,000 members), it is the smaller, localized "clan element" that has salience for individuals.

Community Leadership

Traditionally, a local clan group had a leader, usually a man who was an older brother or other close relative of the eldest woman who functioned as the head mother. The local clan leader represented his group in dealings with members of similarly organized units, mobilized his kinspeople to participate in communal activities, and helped settle disputes with other such groups. However, a leader's authority was based solely on his prestige and ability to gain the support of members of his group. He did not have formal authority, but rather his influence rested on his personality, intelligence, generosity, and ability to persuade others through oratorical skills.

In addition to leadership exercised by heads of residence groups and clan elements, leaders of territorial areas were chosen by all the men and women in the community. Although most such leaders (called "natani") were men, women were occasionally selected. Because of people's knowledge of the reputations of others, selections were usually unanimous, but if two candidates appeared as competitors, they might be asked to give speeches so that the people could judge their opinions as well as their oratorical ability (Hill 1940: 25–26). Natani often had two or three advisors appointed by them to assist in carrying out the requisite duties. Leaders were installed in office through ceremony, probably a Blessingway rite, in order that they "make powerful speeches" (Wyman and Kluckhohn 1938: 19). The position of territorial leader was generally held for life, but an inadequate incumbent could be informed that the community no longer wanted their services. Territorial leaders acted as spokespeople for their group but had no authoritarian or coercive powers. According to Hill,

> He was expected to address his own and other communities at public and ceremonial gatherings. While these talks might refer to specific problems, they were usually ethical and moral in their scope, admonishing the people to live in peace, righteousness, and to be diligent and hardworking. As most headmen were accomplished raconteurs, various traditional and mythological tales were used to emphasize the points. (Hill 1940: 27)

Natani planned and supervised communal work such as cooperative planting and harvesting. They also attempted to settle disputes and act as mediators when problems arose between individuals or families in their community. And they were representatives of their community in consultations and negotiations with other similarly organized communities or other nations.

When community decisions needed to be made, matters of public concern were talked over with all interested men and women. Discussion ideally led to unanimity, but in any case people could comply or not with decisions as they chose. As described by an American army sergeant in 1855:

> They have no hereditary chief—none by election. Even those who by superior cunning have obtained some influence are extremely careful lest their conduct should not prove acceptable to their criticizing inferiors. The council's decisions are of little moment unless they meet the approbation of the mass of the people; and for this reason these councils are exceedingly careful not to run counter to the wishes of the more numerous class, being well aware of the difficulty, if not the impossibility, of enforcing any act that would not command their approval. (Shepardson 1963: 52)

Participation in raiding and warfare was voluntary. Men looked to recognized war leaders for planning and conducting expeditions. The success of campaigns was deemed to result from the leader's military prowess and strategy as well as from his ritual knowledge and the proper performance of War Way songs and rites (Hill 1940: 24).

Religious Beliefs and Practices

The Diné universe consists of a number of worlds thought of as platters or hemispheres stacked one on top of another. The number varies according to different traditions, but at least five or possibly as many as a dozen worlds are envisioned. The hemispheres or platters of each world are supported by pillars made of precious stone: four of white shell at the east, four of turquoise at the south, four of abalone at the west, and four of redstone at the north (Reichard 1950: 14). The space in between each world is filled with stars. Primordial people, animals, and plants existed in prior worlds and had humanlike shapes and the powers of thought and speech. Primordial people lived in conditions that should have made them happy, but because of their own failings they were not content. Instead, they quarreled among themselves, were jealous and envious of each other, and failed to control their sexual urges, leading to disorder and chaos. As conditions worsened, spirit beings warned people to mend their ways, but even though they tried, they were unable to live properly. Spirit powers therefore decided to destroy the worlds and force the people out, sometimes by flood, fire, or drought. When threatened with destruction, people sought entrance into the next world by proceeding upward, led by a helper being who showed them the way out. They found themselves again in pleasant surroundings, but each time life began anew, primordial people were unable to curb their desires, quarrels, and discord.

Stories of emergence reveal a world of initial harmony that descended into chaos and disorder because of people's uncontrollable urges that destroyed their own good fortune. In those earlier times, people lacked not only the ability to regulate their behavior but also the ritual knowledge that might help them control the evil forces unleashed both within themselves and their environment. As a result, evils such as adultery, incest, and witchcraft originated, ever threatening the People's existence.

Finally, the deities First Man and First Woman created yet another world for people to inhabit. The place of emergence into this, the fifth world, was at first covered with water, but eventually the winds of the four directions dried the earth and revealed a landscape that would later be transformed into the Diné world. First Man and First Woman began the process of creation by thinking and talking about how the new world was to be formed. They built a ceremonial hogan in which, at nightfall, they took objects from a medicine bundle and transformed them into holy figures. Then First Man shaped the figures into humanlike forms that are the "inner life forms" of all living things and dressed these representations in the outer shapes that they would take (i.e., plants, animals, celestial bodies, mountains, and other aspects of the landscape). The ceremonial unfolding of representations of the world continued throughout the night until, at dawn, the objects were transformed into the present world after being smoked over and transported to their proper places. Finally, when creation was completed, the deities of Dawn and Evening Twilight toured the earth and saw that it was full of beauty, order, and harmony (Zolbrod 1984).

Once the world was created, some of the most important Diné deities were born, among them Changing Woman, whose name refers to the fact that she never dies but instead upon reaching old age is transformed again into a young woman, eternally proceeding through cycles of birth, childhood, adulthood, and old age. After performing the first "kinaalda" (girl's puberty rite), she mated with Sun and bore twin boys, Monster Slayer and Born-for-Water, who set out to rid the world of monsters. Afterwards, Changing Woman created the Diné by rubbing skin from her body and mixing it with cornmeal, forming four pairs of men and women who were the ancestors of the four original clans.

The Diné world is watched over by numerous Holy People who exist as forces in the universe and are prayed to for aid and support (Reichard 1950: 63–66). Among the most dependable helpers are Changing Woman, Sun, First Man, First Woman, and a number of animal spirits including Beaver, Otter, Spider, and various birds. Wind is also considered a helper of human beings and carries messages from the Holy People to humans (McNeley 1981). A final group of potentially helpful powers are Sky, Dawn, Evening Light, the stars, and precious stones such as whiteshell, turquoise, rock crystal, and jet. In contrast to beings upon whom the Diné can rely for aid, there are some who harm humans. In this group are monsters having various names and symbolizations, often appearing as colors under rocks and at the base of cliffs. Many monsters were defeated or at least held in check by Changing Woman's twin sons, but some who bring troubles, sadness, and discomfort to humans—such as Old Age, Cold, Poverty, Hunger, Sleep, Desire, and Want—have survived. The story of their survival gives insight into the Native view of the balance between positive and negative aspects of life. When Monster Slayer came upon these creatures in their dwellings,

> He found them a disgusting lot. They had sore eyes, sticky eyebrows, and mucus running from their noses, but each gave a good reason why it should not be destroyed and he was powerless before their words and gentle ways. His mother [Changing Woman] explained when he got home: "These you should not kill because they meet somewhere in-between good and bad. Poverty and hunger are somewhere between that which gives pleasure and that which gives pain. That is why they should not be destroyed. That is why we have these things today." (Reichard 1950: 72)

Diné religious and social systems are based on the concept of "beauty" (hozho). In the Native language, "hozho" refers to harmony, order, peacefulness, and appropriateness (Reichard 1944, 1950; Wyman 1950, 1957). Beauty resides in the proper functioning of a

person's body, mind, and spirit, in their proper relationship with the holy beings and forces that inhabit the universe, in proper relations with other people, and in the harmony of their environment. However, the attainment and maintenance of beauty is not always achieved because of a person's weakness, because of harmful spirit forces, or because of malevolent people who interfere with one's good fortune. In order to achieve beauty and goodness, one must control one's thoughts and actions, to be ritually purified if necessary, and generally to counteract forces that are out of control. As Reichard noted, "what is wholly good is merely an abstraction, a goal that people as individuals never attain. Similarly very few things are wholly bad; nearly everything can be brought under control and when it is, the evil effect is eliminated (1950: 5). Furthermore, "one who knows how to keep things in order has the key to life's problems" (14). In contrast, improper behavior is an indication of the need for control. Even excesses of normal activities (including such benign or pleasurable activities as weaving, silversmithing, sexual relations, or undue concentration of the mind) are suspect and are thought of as "symptoms of disease amenable to ritual cure" (Wyman 1983: 537). Like all Diné religious philosophy and practice, ritual is concerned with the notion of beauty and restoration of harmony and balance. It is the "correct performance of traditional orderly procedures" (537), allowing people to bring the "out of control" under control and restore harmony in the individual and in the group. Disturbance of beauty may result in illness and therefore require a cure. Among the possible reasons for disturbance are violations of spiritual taboos or regulations, bad dreams, and excess of any activity. In addition, illness may result from contact with the dead or with any of a large number of potentially harmful animals, plants, or natural forces including coyote, ants, cactus, moths, bears, rattlesnakes, lightning, and whirlwinds. Direct contact with any of these agents may bring illness but indirect contact may be just as harmful. Leaning against a tree that has been struck by lightning, stepping on rocks that have been crossed by rattlesnakes, or dreaming of coyotes may result in illness just as readily as direct contact. Contact with any spiritually powerful person or ritual may also lead to illness because an ordinary person may be too weak to withstand the power of a ritual, a song, or an especially effective healer. Illness may also result from witchcraft. In addition to the common techniques of contagious magic, witches may invert sacred substances and procedures in order to cause illness and death. They may grind up the bones of a dead person so that it resembles corn pollen (the most sacred, beneficial substance known to the Diné) and sprinkle it on the victim's clothing or on their body while they sleep or they may recite curing prayers backward, thereby subverting and manipulating the most sacred of Diné practices. However, witchcraft may also be dangerous to the witch him/herself, since if a person is cured of a witchcraft-induced ailment, the spell may revert to the witch.

When people become ill and are unable to treat themselves through rest, common herbal remedies, or purification by sweating and fasting, they seek the care of specialists whose aim is to discover and eliminate underlying causes of illness. Patients first consult diagnosticians, most of whom employ a technique called hand-trembling in which they enter a trance state that results in shaking and trembling of their hands and arms and may encompass the entire body. In the state of trance and trembling, the diagnostician is able to see a symbol of the ritual needed to cure the patient and then recommends a healer (or "singer") who specializes in the appropriate ceremonial. Healers treat by administering medicinal substances and performing curing rites that are learned after a long apprenticeship to an already established practitioner. Healers acquire songs and medicine bundles for which they must pay a fee at the end of their training. The payment may be very small and is considered mainly a token but "the sing [ceremonial] is not valid without payment" (Aberle 1961: 139).

Curing rituals are long and complex procedures. Although there are dozens of separate ceremonials, most are performed according to procedures of a class called "Holyway," conducted over a period of five or nine nights (the Diné count time from sundown to sundown). According to Wyman (1983: 556), a Holyway ceremonial contains at least eleven component rituals, beginning with blessing of the hogan in which the cure is held, various purification rites to cleanse the patient and healer, and presentation of offerings to attract the Holy People and obtain their aid. Then, the singer and his/her helpers make a sandpainting (or dry painting) on the floor of the hogan by trickling ground bits of red, yellow, and white sandstone and charcoal through their fingers to make stylized representations of Holy People and mythic episodes. The patient sits on one of the figures depicted, the singer moistens his/her palms with herbal medicines, takes up sand

from the painting and applies it to the corresponding parts of the patient's body, thus identifying the patient with the Holy People and allowing him/her to absorb their protective powers and exchange evil for good. The penultimate rite is an all-night sing that ends with dawn songs after which the patient leaves the hogan, faces east, and "breathes in the dawn" four times. The ceremonial is terminated with a final prayer and song from a corpus known as "Blessingway" that correct any errors or omissions as well as bless and protect the participants.

The lengthy and complex procedures performed during curing and blessing rites necessitate vast ritual knowledge, requiring singers to have learned several hundred songs and prayers for each ceremonial. Since there are an enormous number of ceremonials, singers typically specialize in only a few. Perhaps the knowledge of six or eight ceremonials is the most an individual can attain although they may know smaller sections of several others.

In addition to curing rituals, people participate in a number of lifecycle ceremonies. According to Diné traditions, menstrual blood is the principle material substance that forms the fetus, although it must be united with male semen (Leighton and Kluckhohn 1947: 14). In addition, the fetus has within it two winds, one from each parent, that grow as the baby grows (McNeley 1981: 49). Then as the baby emerges from its mother, a third wind comes into it, thus giving it life. When a child is about to be born, a Blessingway song is sung over the mother in order to protect the child and to help with an easy delivery, but if the birth is difficult, a midwife or healer will aid by kneading the mother's abdomen and motioning the baby out with an eagle feather brush. After the baby is bathed, white and yellow corn pollen is sprinkled on its head and it is then shaped by gently pressing its body to ensure a healthy life. When the baby's umbilical cord dries, it is buried outside in an appropriate place. A girl's umbilical cord is often buried under a weaving loom while boys' cords may be buried under a horse corral (Leighton and Kluckhohn 1947: 17). Babies are not named immediately but must await the passage of at least four days or as much as a month to receive their names. The honor of bestowing a name is usually given to a relative of one of the parents, who typically chooses a name held by a well-liked or capable kinsperson.

The "kinaalda" or girl's puberty rite is a central ceremony, celebrating the onset of fertility and the assumption of adult roles. The kinaalda is a four-day ritual that has a number of recurring activities (Frisbie 1967). At dawn and noon each day, the pubescent girl, accompanied by a few friends or relatives, races to the east in order to build up her strength and endurance. Lying on a blanket in front of her hogan, the girl's body is repeatedly kneaded or "molded" by an older woman who has led an exemplary life. During the first three days of kinaalda, the girl and some female relatives grind great quantities of corn that on the evening of the fourth day will be mixed into a batter and placed in a pit oven lined with corn husks to be baked into a cake during the night. The last night of the ceremony culminates in singing that begins shortly before midnight and ends at dawn. After the girl's hair is washed and her cheeks painted with white lines, she distributes the baked corncake to all the guests. Once a girl has had her kinaalda, she is ready for marriage.

In contrast to the joyous celebration that accompanies passage to adulthood, the end of life is treated with intense fear. Death and the dead are the most contaminating and potentially dangerous entities in the Diné universe. At death, the life- activating wind that entered the body at birth leaves through the fingers. The whirls of the fingertips are thought to be traces of the trail of the first death (Leighton and Kluckhohn 1947: 91).

When death occurs, the deceased's kin hire four mourners to prepare and bury the body. They bathe the body and dress it in fine garments, taking care to put the left moccasin on the right foot and the right moccasin on the left foot. If a death occurs inside a hogan, the body is carried out through a hole made in the north side of the dwelling so as not to contaminate the normal path of the living. The hogan is then abandoned or burned down. During the transport of the deceased to the burial site, the mourners must remain completely silent. The body is placed in a rock niche sealed shut or buried in the ground in an isolated spot. In the winter, when the ground is frozen, the body may be left inside a hogan and the structure torn down to cover it. Some personal property belonging to the deceased may be buried with the body but the deceased's parents, siblings, and maternal aunts and uncles have first claim to the remainder. If the deceased is a woman, her children also have primary claims. The rest of the property is distributed among the deceased's friends, spouse, and children if the deceased is a man. Distribution of goods to relatives not in the deceased's clan (i.e., spouse and a man's children) is viewed as a courtesy, not as a formal obligation (Dyk 1947: 185).

Following the burial, the mourners return taking a different path back to the settlement, hopping and skipping rather than walking in the normal fashion. They then purify themselves in smoke from a sage fire and observe four days of isolation. Members of the deceased's family also observe four days of mourning, remaining indoors and weeping. However, if a person is killed by lightning, no funeral or burial is observed because the deceased is believed to be especially dangerous.

CONSEQUENCES OF THE SPANISH PRESENCE IN THE SOUTHWEST

When the Spanish arrived in the Southwest in the middle of the sixteenth century, the Diné were already settling the region known as Dinetah. They were first mentioned in 1582 by Antonio de Espejo, who noted the presence of "peaceful Indian mountaineers" near Laguna, New Mexico (Reno 1981: 15). Their economy combined foraging and farming but they continued their older semi-sedentary settlement patterns. Because the Diné lived in scattered clusters rather than the compact villages of the Puebloans, the Spanish were unable to exert control over them. Contact between the two nations was intermittent, varying from friendly encounters to armed conflict. One reason for the deterioration of relations was the prevalence of Spanish slave raiders who captured men to work in mines and seized women and children to serve as household domestics. For their part, the Diné raided foreign settlements along the Rio Grande for sheep and horses. As the Spaniards increased their slave raids, the Diné also stepped up retaliation against the intruders so that as the seventeenth century wore on, the uneasy relations between Indians and Spaniards deepened. However, due to the size of the Native population, their scattered settlements and the renown of their warriors, the Spanish never attempted a full-scale conquest of the Diné nation, an effort that surely would have failed. When Puebloans rebelled against Spanish authority late in the century, the People came to their aid by warning them of impending assaults and attacking soldiers on the march. And when the Spanish later began their reconquest of the Southwest, the Diné harbored thousands of refugees.

Diné and Spanish hostilities continued throughout most of the eighteenth century, interrupted at brief periods when several truces were negotiated but these were short-lived.

During the early and mid-eighteenth century, the Diné had to contend with harassment by other Indians, especially Utes, who stepped up raiding campaigns from their lands in Utah and Colorado. As a result of Ute incursions, by 1754 the Diné had effectively abandoned most of Dinetah, moving south and west into unoccupied territory as well as land settled or used as hunting grounds by other Southwestern people, principally Havasupais.

After Mexico gained its independence from Spain in 1821, Hispanic settlers in New Mexico increased slave-raiding and attacks against the Diné. Although Native warriors were able to defend their territory on the eastern borderlands, they lost many people to the slave trade. Underhill estimates that by the end of the Spanish and Mexican periods in 1846, as many as 4,500 of the Diné were enslaved as domestics and ranch workers in Hispanic settlements (1956: 80).

By the middle of the nineteenth century, Diné territory had expanded south and west of their original lands, holding the area from the Rio Grande River in the east to the Colorado River in the west and stretching south to the Zuni River and north into southern Utah and Colorado. Native economy was centered on herding sheep, goats, and horses, supplemented by farming and foraging. Economic differentiation was based on the ownership of sheep, but egalitarian ethics prevailed in expected generosity and sharing of resources, especially among kin. A division of labor based on gender developed in animal husbandry, that is, men owned and herded horses while women owned and herded most of the sheep. In addition, women butchered and sheared sheep and wove wool into blankets and clothing. Clothing styles had changed from an aboriginal use of animal skins to garments made of woven wool. Women wore black woolen dresses made like a double blanket fastened at the shoulders while men wore deerskin breechcloths, shirts, and leggings although some wore Spanish-style trousers made either of cloth or deerskin.

THE DEVELOPMENT OF AMERICAN CONTROL IN THE NINETEENTH CENTURY

Soon after the United States took possession of the Southwest in 1846, the government attempted to exert authority over Native people in the region. Several meetings were held between American and Diné negotiators but none led to a lasting peace. The results of some meetings only further convinced the people of the danger posed by an American presence. On August 31, 1849, a council between a group of Diné under the leadership of Narbona, one of their most respected headmen, and Col. John Washington ended with the murder of Narbona and six of his associates following a dispute about the ownership of a horse. The Native men were shot in the back as they were departing and then were scalped (McNitt 1972).

During the next few years Diné leaders signed several treaties with the US government but it all proved ineffective, in part because the Native signatories had no legitimacy in their own communities to conclude binding agreements with other nations. In fact, men who signed such agreements lost status at home because they were acting in ways that violated traditional norms. The treaties were also ineffective because the US government did not uphold its promises to protect Indians from incursions by slave-raiders. Recognizing that they would not be protected, the People continued to retaliate against nearby settlements in an attempt to repulse the raids.

The American government then built Fort Defiance in the middle of Diné territory and threatened full-scale warfare if the people did not stop raiding New Mexican settlements, despite the fact that these raids were often in defense of Native land, resources, and residents. Then, in 1858, the Diné and Americans signed a treaty of peace and friendship (the Bonneville Treaty), stipulating that the Indians cede some of their best grazing land in exchange for government protections. But conditions worsened as the People continued to lose valuable land. Indeed, an agent named Samuel Yost recognized the People's precarious economic situation, one that might have dire consequences:

> Depriving the best of the Indians of the grounds they cultivate graze—whereon they raise corn and wheat enough to support the whole nation … thus forcing them either to violate the agreement forced upon them, or to abandon cultivating the soil and stock raising or become pensioners on the government, or plunderers. (Bailey 1964: 102)

Soon after the Bonneville Treaty was signed, Henry Connelly (governor of New Mexico) prepared a military campaign against the Diné, motivated by the desire to acquire Native land, and reports of deposits of gold, silver, and other minerals (Keleher 1952). General James Carleton planned to remove the People from their territory and hold them at Fort Sumner in southeastern New Mexico, supposedly in order to aid their progress toward civilization:

> To collect them together, little by little on a reservation, away from the haunts and the hills and the hiding places of their country; there teach their children how to read and write, teach them the truths of Christianity. Soon they will acquire new habits, new ideas, new modes of life; and the old Indians will die off. The young ones will take their place, and thus, little by little, they will become a happy and contented people. (Secretary of the Interior 1863; quoted in Vogt 1961: 313)

Col. Christopher (Kit) Carson was charged with carrying out the removal following an ultimatum issued by Carleton: "Say to them, 'Go to Fort Sumner or we will pursue and destroy you. We will not make peace with you on any other terms. This war will be pursued against you if it takes years until you cease to exist or move'" (Kelly 1970: 52).

In the late summer and fall of 1863, Carson's troops rounded up the Diné, shot resistors, destroyed corn fields and peach orchards, burned hogans, contaminated waterholes, and confiscated thousands of sheep and horses. By destroying Native resources, Carson hoped to starve the People into submission. In the winter of 1864, about 4,000 people left their homeland for Fort Sumner. It is unknown how many died during the military campaign, but hundreds more died en route during the "Long Walk" to Fort Sumner in the midst of winter. They died of starvation, exposure to the cold, and continued depredations by New Mexicans who captured stragglers on the forced march. According to family histories told by survivors, the journey cost many lives and even the survivors were harassed: "There were few wagons to haul some personal belongings but the trip was made on foot [over a distance of 300 mi.]. People were shot down on the spot if they complained about being tired or sick, or if they stopped to help someone. If a woman became in labor with a baby, she was killed. There was absolutely no mercy" (Roessel 1973: 103–104).

During the remainder of 1864 and into 1865, more people surrendered, driven by starvation because their resources had been destroyed. A census taken in March 1865 at Fort Sumner counted 9,022 people (Bailey 1964: 214). Until their release in 1868, thousands died, most from starvation and exposure to bad weather.

Living conditions at the fort were never good and rapidly deteriorated. Shelter was inadequate, many people living in holes dug in the ground and covered with tree branches. Food rations were insufficient to supply the large number of people there and, changes in diet led to diarrhea and other intestinal disorders, causing more deaths. Criticism of the inhumane conditions came not only from the Diné but from influential American authorities, among them Judge Joseph Knapp, a member of the New Mexico territorial Supreme Court, who accused Carleton of calculated policies directed at "alienating and souring the minds of those peace Indians" in order to have an excuse to launch a campaign against them. Furthermore, Knapp asserted that "old men and women too decrepit to walk, little ones equally, yet more helpless, women and children, non-combatants, and those not able to take care of themselves much less to fight, are all held as prisoners of war—persons who have voluntarily come in for their protection and food" (Keleher 1952: 449–451). Finally, at a meeting in 1868 held to negotiate a settlement, the Diné headman Barboncito, who was a principal orator, declared "I hope to God you will not ask me to go to any other country except my own. We do not want to go to the right or left, but straight back to our own country" (Roessel 1971: 32). After signing a treaty of peace, the Indians left Fort Sumner and reached their reservation of some 3.5 million acres, an area encompassing less than 10 percent of their prior territory. Difficulties arose almost immediately because of the scarcity of land and encroachment by non-Indian ranchers and sheepherders. An executive order issued in 1878 added nearly a million acres to the west of the first reservation. During the next several decades, more lands were added, most through executive orders. In total, four geographically separate reservations were eventually established. The largest is the original territory with several major additions, amounting to some 17 million acres. Three nonadjacent parcels were created as well: the Cañoncito reservation in New Mexico consisting of nearly 58,000 acres, the Alamo reservation of 62,000 acres, and the Ramah reservation containing 91,000 acres (Correll and Dehiya 1972).

Federal actions that expanded Diné territory were taken in recognition of the increasing Native population, the size of their herds, and the poor quality of their land. Indeed, in 1883, an Indian agent described the reservation as more than "10,000 square miles of the most worthless land that ever laid outdoors …

three quarters of it is about as valuable for stock grazing as that many acres of clear sky" (White 1983: 216). A further difficulty was that a good portion of reservation land had been granted as a right of way to the Atlantic & Pacific Railroad Company in 1866. In addition, non-Indian cattle ranchers and sheepherders continued to move into Native territory, taking some of the better grazing lands in the eastern portion of the reservation. Therefore, although the boundaries of the reservation were expanding, the actual land available per capita for grazing was shrinking (White 1983). Despite these problems, people were building up their herds and strengthening their economy by involvement in local and national trade, selling woven woolen blankets and silver jewelry. Commercial expansion was also facilitated by the establishment of trading posts on the reservation in the late nineteenth century. Traders operated as middlemen in the Diné market, buying rugs woven by women as independent producers and then selling them to the American domestic market. Trading posts eventually came to exert an enormous influence in Native communities, often through unethical and even illegal practices that began in the nineteenth century and continued until recently. For example, after extensive investigative research conducted in the 1970s, the Federal Trade Commission found that traders charged excessively high prices, demanded illegal interest rates on pawn, frequently "lost" pawn when people tried to redeem their articles, and practiced "credit saturation." Credit saturation was achieved by a complicated process of keeping people's paychecks and/or social security and welfare benefits, allowing a purchaser's credit to reach a predetermined limit, withholding the check until the person's credit equaled the amount of the check, and then requiring the purchaser to sign over the check directly to the trader (Federal Trade Commission 1973: 16–26; Southwestern Indian Development 1974: 10–19). People therefore rarely had cash available for disposal but rather were bound to the trader in a system of debt-peonage. Although traders provided some useful services such as disseminating information about jobs, extending credit in difficult times, and in the past providing the service of burying the dead (a task that to traditional Diné is considered dangerous), they tended to exert influence that were detrimental to the economic independence of their clientele.

As stock raising and the sale of wool and rugs grew in importance, farming for subsistence gradually declined. But the economic shift away from farming was uneven. Subsistence farming remained important for families who did not own large herds. According to Bailey and Bailey, even if high estimates of Diné sheep are accepted, the numbers suggest a human-to-sheep ratio of approximately 1:30. Since Bailey and Bailey estimate that a human-to-sheep ratio of 1:40 or 1:50 is required for adequate subsistence, Diné herds of the mid-nineteenth century were below the requisite level (1986: 49). These facts indicate that although herding was an important element in the economy, it had to be supplemented by farming and foraging. In years of crop failure, evidently a fairly frequent occurrence, people also gathered roots, piñon nuts, acorns, seeds, sunflowers, grasses, and fruits.

During the last years of the nineteenth century, the People were encouraged both for internal and external economic reasons to increase production for market. They supplied a growing quantity of wool for sale outside the reservation and also produced more blankets and silver jewelry. As the tourist trade grew, national companies became involved in the commercialization of handicrafts. Several companies sent raw materials (silver, turquoise, and other jewels) to traders on the reservation who "farmed out" the supplies and gave orders for particular designs. Diné jewelers were paid by the ounce for their finished product (Weiss 1984: 48). Beginning in the late 1880s, commercial dyes and yarns were supplied to Native weavers, replacing the time-consuming process of carding the wool and dyeing it with natural plants as women had done previously. The replacement of natural products with commercial dyes and yarns both increased output and cheapened the product. Soon, wholesale houses sprang up and became the primary sources of Diné blankets to American cities. These large commercial enterprises were able to accumulate more rugs, again cheapening the product and increasing their own profits (52). Although many Diné benefitted from access to markets for wool and other products, prosperity was uneven. Some families, for reasons of location, household composition, or bad fortune, were never able to accumulate large enough herds to be self-sustaining. And farming was difficult for people who lived on inadequate land and suffered through seasons of drought, insect infestation, and other difficulties. Added to these problems, distribution of rations promised in the Treaty of 1868 ended in 1879, but even these rations had not reached the population uniformly because many residents of remote communities had no means of transportation to agency offices where the goods were stored. By 1882, a federal agent on the reservation noted the existence of a "pauper class" consisting of "about one third of the adult population who own no property, and have no means of earning a livelihood, who are compelled to live off the bounty of their more prosperous friends, it being a custom among them to share the necessaries of life with each other, even to the last meal in the house" (Weiss 1984: 68).

Among the poorer segments of society, wage work necessarily increased. Men obtained work on the railroads and through the federal government in construction and transportation, usually at about half the wages as off-reservation workers (69). In addition, some men worked as agency police.

At the same time, the market for Diné commodities diversified. Weavers produced blankets, saddle blankets, sash belts, garters, saddle cinches, women's dresses, and knitted socks and leggings. Silverwork included buttons, bracelets, bridle ornaments, concha belts, tobacco cases, and jewelry with turquoise stones (Bailey and Bailey 1986: 51–54). Silversmithing grew in importance when trading posts on the reservation initiated the practice of accepting silver ornaments as pawn in exchange for goods. In time, people began to think of their jewelry as a form of "savings" to be converted into utilitarian goods. Meanwhile, other crafts such as pottery and basketry declined because these products had little or no commercial value and could be replaced by store-bought items. Diné baskets continued in importance only for ceremonial use.

Government intervention in Native life intensified with attempts to "civilize" the people and convert them to American values and Christianity. Teachers and missionaries tried to convince people to live in permanent settlements in nuclear family households, speak English, wear American-style clothing, and attend church. The first school on the reservation was a boarding school operated at Fort Defiance, but most parents did not want to send their children away from home. Many of the children who were enrolled ran away. According to the reminiscences of Frank Mitchell,

> One of the main objections to enrolling the children was that white people were not Navajos. They are foreign people, people of another race. The People were suspicious; they thought that if they put their children in school, the white people would take the children away from them and either kill them or do something so they would never be seen again. Even

if they remained alive, the children would just go further and further from their homes and before the People knew it, they would never come back. (Frisbie and McAllester 1977: 55–56)

Such fears were not unfounded given the history of relations with foreigners. Since children had often been kidnapped for the New Mexican slave trade, it is understandable that Diné parents distrusted the underlying intentions of the boarding-school system.

People had ambivalent attitudes toward American-style clothing as well. Although some did adopt certain American garments, reluctance to wear American clothing was expressed by others:

> The People were suspicious of those things at first; there were times when they would find clothing, like pants, shirts, coats and even hats, and they were scared to wear those things. The old people said you were not supposed to wear anything made by a white man or belonging to a white man … we were told not to wear white men's clothes because those people were our enemies and we would get sick from the effects of using their clothing. If the People were given some clothes, they would just throw them out. (Frisbie and McAllester 1977: 35–36)

Such attitudes reflect traditional views of possible causes of illness, especially contamination from one's enemy or from dangerous substances.

The Diné continued to have difficulties protecting their borders from settlers. During the 1870s, Mormons entered the Little Colorado River Valley from the north and west, Anglo ranchers encroached in the San Juan Valley, and Hispanic settlers crossed into Diné territory along its southern and eastern borders. All of these foreign groups also competed with the Diné for public domain lands that lay outside the reservation. Construction of railroads brought more settlers into the Southwest, and the growth of the cattle industry also had a deleterious effect on Native grazing land.

In addition, the national economic collapse of 1893 led to a dramatic fall in prices for wool and livestock. While people had prospered initially from their integration into the national economy by having outlets for the sale of their products, this same integration proved disastrous because the people were vulnerable to fluctuations in prices for their goods. Moreover, since they could not diversify their economy, they were caught in a classic bind of underdevelopment.

A further obstacle to prosperity was that as the market for Diné handiwork expanded, competing non-Indian establishments were opened off the reservation that produced imitation rugs and jewelry. In response to these pressures, some companies established workshops on the reservation where they oversaw the production process (Weiss 1984). Although this practice aided sales, it undermined the creative and autonomous role of the artisans, essentially turning them into wageworkers.

POLITICAL AND ECONOMIC CHANGES IN THE EARLY TWENTIETH CENTURY

The 1920s and 1930s were decades that had far-reaching effects on Diné economy and polity. When oil was discovered on the reservation near Shiprock, New Mexico, in 1921 and oil companies applied for leases to begin drilling operations, the BIA organized a Navajo Council that would have nominal authority to approve leases. The Council consisted of twelve delegates and twelve alternates appointed by the Secretary of Interior. Although it was designated as an official governing body, it lacked true administrative or executive powers, intended as it was to be nothing more than a consultative group. As such, the council granted authority to the superintendent in charge of the Navajo agency to sign oil and mineral leases on behalf of the tribe.

Throughout the next several decades, the Navajo Tribal Council underwent changes in composition and powers. In 1928, women were given the right to vote, returning to traditional practices in which group decisions were made on the basis of discussion and consensus by all community members. The reservation was organized into local chapters, each with representatives who called periodic meetings. Eventually, these representatives were included in an expanded tribal council, currently having eighty-eight members. A tribal chairman and vice-chairman were also elected, first by members of the council and then by general election. Since 1992, the position of council chairman has been renamed and now a president and vice-president are elected.

The second critical event of the 1930s was the federal imposition of reductions in the number of sheep grazed on the land. The BIA, led by John Collier, was advised of the seriousness of soil erosion on the reservation, but the problem was blamed exclusively on Diné herds even though, coincident with the increase of stock, the region periodically experienced climatic changes that led to cycles of erosion with accompanying gullying of land (White 1983: 226). Sometime in the middle of the nineteenth century, soil erosion began to intensify, with a consequent lowering of the water table. Both problems accelerated in the early twentieth century and were exacerbated, but not caused, by overgrazing. Compounding the problem, people concentrated their herds near the few available sources of water, thus placing even greater pressure on natural resources and leading to new cycles of overgrazing and erosion.

In addition to the local problem that drew the attention of Collier and his advisors within the BIA, pressure to reduce Diné sheepherding came from western cities whose growing populations and economic importance dominated Southwestern Indian policy. In the late 1920s, the Boulder Dam (renamed the Hoover Dam) was built on the Colorado River to supply water to California. Although the Colorado River and Hoover Dam were west of Diné territory, silt from the reservation's rivers was blamed for contributing to the silt of the Colorado itself. As one official remarked, "the fact is the Navajo Reservation is practically public enemy number one causing the Colorado silt problem" (White 1983: 251). The Soil Conservation Service reported in 1936:

> The physical and geological processes which have occurred within the reservation, if unchecked must ultimately have an important effect on areas outside the reservation principally through the vastly increased deposit of silt in the Boulder Reservoir. If erosion continues unchecked, ultimately the entire alluvial fill of most of the valleys of the Navajo Reservation will be deposited behind the dam, threatening the enormous federal, state, municipal, and private investments involved in, or directly or indirectly dependent on, the maintenance of the storage capacity of the reservoir. (251)

And therefore, according to White,

> the dam was the catalyst that prompted drastic stock reduction. The government saw itself not only as saving the Navajos from themselves but also saving much of California, and indeed the entire

southwest from Navajo herds. Unfortunately while others reaped benefits the Navajos were called on to make the sacrifices. (252)

Collier initiated a program of stock reduction in 1933, the first phase of which was to be voluntary but soon a 10 percent reduction was ordered. Although the percentage figure was uniform, herders were unevenly affected. Reducing herds by 10 percent did not seriously affect large stockholders since they were able to cull less desirable animals from their herds, but it was disastrous for small holders since they were forced to eliminate stock required for subsistence.

The program of stock reduction had more than an economic effect, however. The Diné traditionally viewed their livestock as wealth and security. Older people and especially women had become increasingly dependent upon their herds, while younger men had some opportunities for wage work. The stock reduction program therefore undermined the economic security of many of the more traditional people and especially of women, the matrilocal residence unit, and the traditional homestead. The loss of sheep put particular strains on women's autonomy and economic independence because supplies of wool, the source of raw materials for weaving, were depleted as well. As White noted, stock reduction policies "threatened to destroy the entire fabric of Navajo social and economic life in the name of preserving it" (289). And in Aberle's words, "livestock reduction was the most disturbing event in Navajo life since the Fort Sumner captivity" (1983b: 643).

In order to manage stock reductions, the reservation was divided into grazing districts, each assigned a livestock carrying capacity. The number of animals owned by each individual was matched against a maximum permit set for his/her grazing district. People who owned more than the permissible limit were forced to sell animals to bring them to the requisite number. According to Aberle, between 1933 and the early 1950s per capita holdings of animals dropped dramatically, some 65 to 80 percent (643). An additional difficulty was that permits specified not only how many animals a person might own, but where they might be grazed, severely limiting the movement of herds from one area to another and making it difficult not only to move a herd between grazing areas, but within them as well. Furthermore, it undermined traditional land-use practices that emphasized flexibility.

During World War II, some of the pressure on Native resources was ameliorated by opportunities for work in the war industry. However, after the war, when soldiers returned home and industrial workers were laid off, pressures on resources accelerated once again, leaving families who had no steady incomes and did not own large herds to suffer disproportionately. Wage work that was offered by the federal government was in fields such as construction and mining that were open only to men, creating for the first time in their history the economic dependence of some women on their husbands or other kin (Hamamsy 1979).

CONTEMPORARY DINÉ COMMUNITIES

The Diné or Navajo Nation is one of great diversity, not only in its natural resources but also in the quality of life of its residents. Distinctions stem from uneven distribution of resources, access to technological improvements, job opportunities, and participation in societal decision-making. For many years, the traditional agrarian sectors of farming and herding were marginalized both in real monetary terms as well as in efforts to maintain them, but since the 1960s, the tribal government has encouraged herders and farmers by reseeding some pastureland and digging wells to increase productivity. And as a measure that both raises income and helps conserve resources, herders are permitted to graze additional stock provided that pastureland improvements are maintained (Aberle 1983b: 645). The tribal government also established a Navajo Wool Program to collect, purchase, and market wool and livestock directly to buyers, eliminating outside intermediaries and therefore increasing herders' incomes. Still, tribal planners in the 1970s believed that even with improvements no more than 5,000 people could be supported by herding at an adequate income level (Navajo Nation 1972).

Subsistence farming has also declined as a reliable mode of production for most people. Most reservation land is not suitable for production for profit without substantial capital investment in technology for irrigation and machinery far beyond the ability of individuals. The tribally owned Navajo Agricultural Products, Inc. (NAPI) manages a project now encompassing about 60,000 acres, with plans to nearly double that amount. Because of the arid environment, the farming enterprise requires a large input of water diverted from three reservation rivers. NAPI currently grows corn, alfalfa, wheat, potatoes, and fruit. It markets produce to off-reservation wholesalers and to national companies such as Campbell Soup and Frito-Lay ("Indian Agriculture Restores Traditions and Economy" 1999: 17). NAPI also operates a cattle feedlot that consumes much of the corn grown locally. They constructed a potato-processing plant in the late twentieth century that planned to employ about 450 people and increase the profits obtained from agriculture and food production. However, the plant has been steadily losing money for over two decades and is not the economic opportunity that was expected (*Livestock Weekly* in Levek 1997).

Another profitable enterprise is a tribally owned timber industry. In 1959 the Tribal Council established the Navajo Forest Products Industry (NFPI) to oversee lumber production and milling. Juniper, piñon, pine, fir, and spruce are used locally in heating, cooking, and construction. The NFPI also exports lumber and other wood products, generating income through sales and wages paid to Diné workers (Reno 1981: 86–87). In addition to direct economic advantages, the NFPI paid for the construction of more than 2,000 mi. of roads through Diné forests and has established water conservation programs that benefit not only the forest areas but nearby grazing and pasture land as well.

While there has been some growth in Native ownership of retail facilities, particularly small shopping centers in several locations, expansion of such establishments is sorely needed. Even most of the trading posts of the past have fallen into decline, especially those located near border areas, because off-reservation stores offer a greater variety of merchandise, sell goods at lower prices, and are generally more attractive for consumers. Only 15 of the 65 posts operating in 1990 were owned by the Diné (Volk 2000: 78) and the Navajo Tourism Department now only lists eight. Because of the scarcity of stores on the reservation, Diné wages and incomes are siphoned off to border towns rather than remaining on the reservation to generate new sources of income.

Despite some growth in their economy, the Diné remain one of the poorest ethnic groups in the United States due primarily to lack of employment. Most existing jobs are supported by some government agency whether it be the tribe or the federal system. The tribal government supports an array of programs in construction of schools, roads, and health facilities, in administering and providing healthcare, education,

and social support programs and in reservation policing and a tribal judicial system, but the number of these jobs also falls far short of what is necessary for full employment. The gap between the Diné and the general US population is substantial. By 2010, Diné per capita income of $12,245 was less than one-half the US average of $27,334. Their income was about two-third that of the American Indian average of $16,446 and about half of the average for New Mexico ($22,966) and Arizona ($25,537). Median household income for the Diné stood at $31,613, a bit more than two-third that of the American Indian average of $36,525. Not surprisingly, therefore, more than a quarter of all Diné families (28.4%) and a third of individuals (33.0%) were living below the poverty level.

Employment statistics indicate serious individual and community economic problems. In the year 2010, 14.0 percent of workers were unemployed (US Bureau of Indian Affairs 2010: Table 3). Citing comparable figures for their states, New Mexico had an unemployment rate of 7.2 percent while 9.9 percent of Arizona residents were unemployed (US Bureau of Census 2010). Given these realities, Diné households rely on multiple sources of income and subsistence, combining wages, social service benefits, and some participation in the agrarian sectors of farming and herding in order to have a buffer against poverty. According to tribal figures, 66 percent of full-time employed residents work in public services, principally for the tribe as well as for the BIA, public schools, and the public health service.

The Nation has reserves of oil, natural gas, coal, and uranium, but the profits generated by exploitation of these resources have overwhelmingly benefitted national and multinational corporations rather than the Diné. The Nation has been selling water rights to power plants, fracking, and mining for over forty years, and in April 2015, a group of Navajo sued the Nation for doing so, citing impoverishment of the people as a result of the Nation's water policies (Paskus 2015). In prior decades, companies negotiated agreements with the Tribal Council that granted leases and tax exemptions in exchange for relatively low royalties and rental fees. Much of the income received by the tribe from resource extraction is used to fund social service programs, building infrastructure, and supplying emergency benefits because adequate funds are not available from any other public or private source. As Aberle noted, "Navajos have no control over their non-renewable energy resources; profits from extracting and processing flow elsewhere; and tribal income goes to operate government and to supply welfare but not to develop the Navajo economy," exemplifying another feature of underdevelopment (1983b: 651). Mining of coal and uranium presents serious problems, especially those of air and water pollution, land desecration, and health hazards to workers and nearby residents. For example, coal on Black Mesa, mined by the Peabody Coal Company, is extracted by stripmining that both pollutes the air and destroys the earth. According to Ted Yazzie, a resident of Black Mesa:

The Kerr McGee uranium mine at Cove on the Navajo Reservation is manned by Navajo workers.

> It's terrible when they work. Since they started, people began to change. The air began to change. It is something we have not known before. The plants seem to have no life. When the wind blows our way, coal dust covers the whole ground, the food, the animals, the hogans, the water. The dust is dirty, it is black. The sun rises, it is grey. The sun sets, yet it is still grey, I imagine the night is grey. (Gordon 1973: 47)

Ironically, the Diné often do not even benefit from energy produced by their resources. For example, some of the coal mined by Peabody is used to operate plants in the Four Corners region of the reservation to produce energy destined for southern California, Arizona, and New Mexico (30–31).

In addition, operation of coal mines and power plants requires water—the scarcest resource in the Southwest. Based on advice given to the tribe by the BIA in the 1960s, the Council agreed to limit Diné rights to water from the Colorado River in exchange for monetary compensation. The agreement was harmful because the loss of water undermined efforts at agrarian development, but the Council agreed to the arrangement on the advice of BIA employees who were evidently pressured by the Secretary of Interior to present the tribe with an either/or option: "either the tribe accept limitations on its water rights or it would not receive any economic benefits from the Black Mesa coal mines" (Levy 1980: 5).

Uranium mining entails some of the same and some additional problems. Compounding the familiar disadvantages of unfair lease and royalty arrangements and of environmental degradation, uranium is a radioactive substance that presents health dangers to workers and nearby residents. Miners have been exposed to levels of radon gas (a byproduct of the decay of uranium into radium) that are between one hundred and one thousand times the safe dosage. Radioactive substances also are inhaled in tiny filings of uranium ore. And some miners' families have been found to live in houses constructed of radioactive materials. According to Johansen, "by 1990 the lung cancer death toll among former Diné miners stood at 450. Relatives of the dead recalled how the miners had eaten their lunches in the mines, washing them down with radioactive water, never having been told it was dangerous" (1997: 12). According to a 2000 study, these miners contracted lung disease at a rate of twenty-nine times the general population. In 2014, a $1 billion settlement with one of the many mining companies will provide for cleanup of only a few of the 521 ghost mines, which are still haunting the tribe. Beyond the miners' fiasco, a whole new generation of Navajo are growing up drinking from contaminated wells (Loomis 2014).

Arrangements concluded between the Diné Nation and resource extraction industries point out several interconnected problems. First, because of their under-developed economy, and lack of capital, they were dependent on outside corporations to extract and process their resource wealth. Second, the lease agreements, negotiated through BIA advisors, resulted in generally unfavorable terms. And third, the BIA does not even enforce contracts that it helped negotiate. For example, while all contracts with national corporations contain a "local preference" clause, indicating the intention of hiring within the community, the BIA has been negligent in protecting Native workers according to testimony at hearings held by the US Commission of Civil Rights at Windowrock in 1973:

> The BIA makes no valid effort to monitor or enforce the employment provisions [of contracts]. The chief BIA contracting officer for the Navajo area was not sure how Indian employment data reached his office, or whether the office even had such a reporting system. The contracting office has never required breakdowns on Indian employment and has never cancelled or threatened to cancel a contract for noncompliance with the EEO clause. Overall, the Commission found the BIA's response to the Navajo unemployment problem has ranged from obstructionist to, at best, insufficient to change the status quo. The BIA, in short, has created and maintains an elaborate machinery that intrudes on every aspect of Navajo life but is incompetent—or unwilling—to enforce Navajo rights." (US Commission of Civil Rights 1975: 124–126)

In an attempt to redress at least part of the problem, the Navajo Nation filed a lawsuit in 1999 against the Peabody Coal Company for allegedly attempting to pressure the Department of Interior to block a 1985 departmental recommendation that the Diné be awarded an increase in royalties from 12.5 percent to 20 percent. The suit also charges Interior with bowing to Peabody's pressure by withdrawing the recommendation for higher royalties. According to the suit, the Diné lost an estimated $600 million by accepting the lower royalty payments ("Navajo Lawsuits Contend US Government Failed the Tribe in Mining Royalty Deals" 1999: A19). In 2000, the US Court of Federal Claims ruled in favor of the Diné's suit contending that the Department of the Interior violated its trust obligations when Interior Secretary Donald Hodell consulted with lobbyists for Peabody while negotiations for royalties to the Navajo Nation were in progress. However, the judge denied the claim for monetary

compensation, citing technicalities of law and jurisdiction. The Navajo Nation has appealed the denial of compensation (*American Indian Report*, April 2000). In 2011, the issue was settled quietly between the two parties with a $50 million cash payment to the Nation and $1.5 million divided among certain affected areas within the reservation (Shebala 2011).

The Native government has expanded its powers and authority considerably since the tribal council was established in 1923, assuming financial, taxation, judicial, and social responsibilities. The executive branch of government is represented by a president and vice-president, both elected for four-year terms; the legislative branch consists of an 84-member Tribal Council; and judicial functions are served by a court system. In order to exert local control over education, the Tribal Council created the Navajo Division of Education to coordinate planning and implementing curriculum in the four reservation school systems, that is, BIA schools, public schools operated by the states of New Mexico and Arizona, mission schools run by Protestant and Catholic organizations, and community-controlled "contract schools." The school systems now all stress bilingual, bicultural approaches that include instruction in Native history, language, and culture. In addition, two tribal colleges are located in the Nation, one at Tsaile and the other in Shiprock.

The Navajo Health Authority works to improve sanitation and living conditions, upgrade health facilities, operate programs of visiting nurses and healthcare paraprofessionals, and generally provide better healthcare to remote areas. However, although clinics and hospitals have been constructed, they are understaffed and underequipped. Furthermore, people who live in remote areas still suffer from a severe shortage of healthcare professionals as well as difficulties in access to the facilities that exist. As healthcare improves and becomes more available, utilization rates have increased (Kunitz 1983: 164–165). However, there are still many issues that impede Diné from accessing heathcare, including lack of transportation, language barriers, and economic hardship. There are also high rates of alcoholism and drug abuse, which may inhibit patients from seeking help.

Many people have come to rely on both standard and traditional healthcare systems. They recognize that standard medicine helps relieve symptoms of disease but seek Native curing rituals for counteracting and eliminating what they perceive as underlying causes of illness. Programs developed by the Navajo Nation and the Indian Public Health Service are geared to sensitizing professional healthcare workers about the value of Native healing practices and to encourage traditional healers to recommend that their patients seek standard care for conditions that are well treated by that system.

Since the 1950s, the Diné have been embroiled in disputes over access to land jointly occupied by themselves and the Hopis. Both nations have claims to land in part because of the language of an 1882 presidential executive order that established the Hopi Reservation, stating that the land was to be reserved for "the use and occupancy of the Moquis [Hopis] and such other Indians as the Secretary of the Interior may see fit to settle thereon." In the context of this wording, some Diné moved onto parts of the Hopi reservation when their own population grew rapidly in the twentieth century, but as both nations increased, competition arose over grazing and settlement rights. Even though the conflict was often phrased as a dispute between the two Native nations, it occurs in a context of attempts by coal companies to obtain leases on Native lands, attempts that are hindered by the lack of clear, undisputed claims to the land under consideration (Churchill 1993). In 1962, the US District Court of Arizona determined that the Hopi tribe had exclusive rights to a portion of the land but that Hopis and Diné "have joint, undivided and equal rights and interests both as to the surface and subsurface, including all resources" on the remainder, referred to as the Joint Use Area. The Court's decision itself was indeterminate since the mechanisms implementing a "joint" arrangement were not specified. The area concerned was settled mostly by Diné, who maintained a traditional way of life dependent on grazing pastures for their herds of sheep. Rather than allowing the people themselves to resolve the problem, Congress passed the "Navajo-Hopi Indian Settlement Act" in 1974 that provided for separation of the Joint Use Area into Navajo and Hopi regions. People who lived on land assigned to the other nation were advised that they would have to relocate. Both Diné and Hopi objected to the partition but a greater number of Diné were affected by the relocation order.

Some 100 Hopi families and 4,000 Diné families (about 11,000 people) agreed to relocate, but 1,200 of the Diné refused, especially members of traditional households who relied on the land and their animals. Some felt emotionally and spiritually as well as economically bereft. As one elderly woman remarked, "the Wind won't know me there. The Holy People won't know me and I won't know the Holy People.

And there's no one left who can tell me" (Benedek 1992: 272). Most of the Diné who moved faced difficult obstacles. Some, unable to find new homes, had to join relatives who themselves did not have adequate space and land. Some extended family households were unable to relocate together, resulting in the breakup of the traditional kinship network central to Diné social and ceremonial life. Leaders of the Hopi and Diné nations agreed to allow the Diné families to lease land from the Hopis for a period of seventy-five years provided that they adhere to Hopi laws (*American Indian Report*, March 2000: 26–27).

The Diné and Hopis have formed an alliance aimed at protecting territory that both peoples consider sacred, especially a group of mountains called the San Francisco Peaks that are said to be part of the sacred boundaries of the original Hopi and Diné homelands. These mountains contain sacred sites where spirit beings long ago emerged from inside the earth. Although the mountains are controlled by the US Forest Service, a ski resort called Snowbowl is operating on the peaks. The Diné and Hopis filed suit against the Forest Service, asking that the expansion of Snowball be halted and that future development to be blocked. The case was dismissed but the Diné and Hopis have continued to object, and in 2002 brought a case against the city of Flagstaff for allowing the ski resorts to make snow out of wastewater.

The operators of Snowbowl utilize wastewater to make artificial snow so that the skiing period can be extended into the spring season. The Diné and Hopis object to the use of wastewater because of their fears that existing groundwater resources, already scarce in the region, will be contaminated and polluted. They depend upon this water both for drinking and for irrigating their arid fields in the growing season. Native leaders object to the use of wastewater in part because they see it as disrespect for the sacred mountain and for the spirits living there. In the words of Hopi Raleigh Puhuyaoma, the use of wastewater on the mountain is like "pumping dirty water on somebody's face. The Katsinas [Hopi spirit beings] and other people are living over there." And Raymond Maxx, a member of the Navajo Nation Council, referred to important shrines on the San Francisco Peaks, "Just the other day my father was out their gathering herbs. Wastewater is sewer water. That's what it is to us. If you allow this to happen, our people will have heavy hearts." Finally, Lisa Talayumptewa remarked: "Our elders tell us that everything has life. We all need private time. The beings on the mountain need private time, not noise all day and all night. [The Forest Service says they] and can accommodate our views. We don't need accommodation" (Wilson 2002).

The tribal suits, later joined by an environmental group called Save the Peaks Coalition, were dismissed in federal Appeals Court in 2012, allowing construction of an expanded ski resort and the use of wastewater for snowmaking. However, ironically it may be an endangered plant, rather than the wishes of human beings, that halts the project. Scientists have determined that high winds may blow artificial snow onto the habitat of an endangered species called ragwort or groundsel, resulting in long-term damage, in violation of the Endangered Species Act. The tribes have requested review by the US Forest Service and the US Fish and Wildlife Service in the hopes of ending the snowmaking development. The case was greenlighted by the Arizona Supreme Court in 2014 and is still pending (Macmillan 2014).

It is understandable that for a nation with a large population, a large territory, and complex historical forces affecting them, diversity in attitude and orientation would emerge. Although the people have different economic and social goals, most agree on the need for improvements in living conditions, educational opportunities, healthcare services, and political sovereignty. But beyond this constellation of basic concepts, diversity in lifestyle, economic pursuits, and attitudes toward the family and community are attested. Recently, the growth of towns and large settlements has been stimulated by the search for jobs and steady income. In these towns, concentrated in the eastern sections of the nation, most people live in nuclear family households in American-style housing, whereas people who reside in more remote areas tend to maintain traditional matrilineal extended families. Notions of private property, home ownership, and accumulation of personal wealth are more pronounced in towns, while in rural areas, communal ownership and control of resources are prevalent. Traditional notions of sharing among kin, cooperation with one's community, and responsibility for a wide network of relatives are maintained in traditional families, while in towns, focus has shifted to responsibilities to the nuclear family resulting in a tendency for extended kin bonds to dissipate. The nuclear family model that some people have adopted tends also to lead to changes in authority within the household. As in the American system, wage work and the money earned tend to be reflected in influence and

authority in the home. In most cases, such families rely more on the wages of men than of women, leading to a shift in authority that favors men and a concomitant erosion of authority, influence, and status of women in their households (Hamamsy 1979).

Changes in settlement patterns and subsistence activities have also affected clans. Although clans continue to be important in a person's identity and to function in regulating marriage choices, the responsibilities that people traditionally felt to clan members have weakened for town dwellers, who no longer live and work amidst their clan relatives and have shifted their social and economic focus toward individual rather than communal goals. Furthermore, people who have achieved some prosperity may feel burdened by clan responsibilities and the need to share resources with relatives. Land use practices and control of property have changed dramatically as populations of people and animals have increased and as a shift away from traditional values has occurred. Speaking in 1971, then tribal chairman Peter MacDonald remarked, "now there is not a foot of Navajo land someone does not claim" (in Reno 1981: 21).

Despite economic, social and political transformations of Diné society, most people support the value of maintaining the Native language and certain aspects of traditional beliefs and practices. Although there has been a shift toward more frequent use of English among younger people, the majority of the Diné speak their Native tongue. According to US census data collected in 2010, 169,471 people reported speaking Navajo. School curriculum aimed at maintaining the use of the Diné language is encouraged by the tribal council and its Division of Education in all of the schools on the reservation.

In addition, despite changes in Diné society, people's loyalty to their families and communities remains strong. Cooperation, helpfulness, and consideration for others are valued personality traits. And traditional understandings of the equality of men and women continue to influence behavior and expectations. These principles permeate Diné religious and ethical thought, reflected in the complementarity of genders and "teachings [that] stress male and female as a basic form of symbolism; the notion is that only by pairing can any entity be complete" (Reichard 1950: 29).

As in other societal domains, religious participation is diverse. There are three religious movements now coexisting among the People. First are the traditional beliefs and ritual practices that are strongly maintained, especially in rural areas. Second, various Christian sects attracted Native converts and have expanded their influence by operating schools and health clinics. And third, a growing number of people are members of the Native American Church, the official name of the Peyote religion. Although the Peyote religion began to spread in North America in the late nineteenth century, it had very few Diné adherents until the 1940s. The emergence and growth of the Peyote religion in the Navajo Nation was initially a response to the increasingly overt domination exerted by the American government in the stock reduction program of the 1930s (Aberle 1966). As Aberle discovered, communities that had experienced more precipitous declines in livestock holdings tended to have higher concentrations of Peyote believers. Since that time, the number of members of the Native American Church has risen steadily. Although exact figures are lacking, possibly half of all of the Diné are now followers of the Peyote religion (Aberle 1983a: 558).

Access to safe drinking water is a pressing concern throughout the Navajo Nation. Some residents get their water from rainfall, reservoirs, and rivers but an estimated 40 percent of Diné carry barrels of water obtained from wells that are never checked for contaminants or impurities. The Navajo Nation long planned to construct a system of pipelines to deliver clean drinking water but those plans were complicated by the fact that their territory is located in three different states, receiving water from several basin systems including the Upper Colorado River, Lower Colorado River, and the Rio Grande. After many years of negotiation, in 2009 the Navajo Nation signed an agreement with the State of New Mexico and the US government that allows construction of a 280-mi. pipeline to be completed by 2024. It will eventually serve some 250,000 people on the reservation as well as delivering water to sections of the Jicarilla Apache Nation and the city of Gallup, New Mexico. An additional immediate benefit to the project is the creation of some 450 construction jobs, slated to increase to 650 in a few years (Donovan 2012). More funds were appropriated for this purpose in December 2015, and the pipeline should soon begin delivering water to the Eastern Navajo Agency, home to about 6,000 people in one of the more populated areas in the Nation (Office of Senator Tom Udall in KRWG 2015).

Additional jobs are being generated by funds distributed by the Environmental Protection Agency and other federal organizations to train and employ Navajos in numerous projects designed to clean up toxic sites on the reservation. There are approximately 520 such sites containing hazardous waste byproducts, including tailings and radioactive materials, from mining that has contaminated land, water sources, and homes (Minard 2013:32). The projects will replace contaminated homes, construct wells and water delivery systems, and remove toxic wastes.

The Diné have received grants enabling them to set up photovoltaic solar energy systems in remote parts of the reservation that are far from established electricity power grids and therefore lack energy sources for their homes. The first area of the reservation to receive the service is Cameron Chapter, the majority of whose residents currently lack power. A Navajo-owned energy company, Shonto (Shaa'tohi) Energy Solutions, is set to construct and maintain the installations.

In response to a growing awareness of conservation and environmental concerns, especially among young Diné, the Tribal Council established a Green Economy Commission that will seek funding for economic and ecological projects emphasizing conservation and sustainability. Some potential projects include energy efficient housing, a textile mill for processing wool, and farmers' markets. Council members hope that these projects will not only improve the environment but will encourage young people to return or remain on the reservation and contribute to their communities.

A similar concern is the focus of an organization called "Dine be lina" (The Dine Lifeway) whose members are developing projects related to the herding of sheep and the production of wool. Their goal is to support economic self-sufficiency in ways that maintain traditional cultural practices of herding and farming.

Hi-tech jobs are also being promoted through college scholarships for youth who want to major in business, communication, computer science, engineering, and information technology. The scholarships are funded by a tribally owned IT company hoping to expand services and recruit local employees. More jobs will become available as high-speed internet services expand throughout the Navajo Nation although many sections, particularly in remote areas, are not yet served.

Seeking to launch new development projects and to attract tourists to their territory, the Diné have proposed construction of a resort on the East Rim of the Grand Canyon on land within the Grand Canyon National Park. Plans include a hotel, restaurant, tramway, and an RV park. The site itself sits near the confluence of where the Little Colorado River flows into the Colorado River. While the resort may generate between $50 and $95 million annually and create about 2,000 jobs, it is not without controversy (Yurth and Beyal 2012). Most of the opposition comes from the Hopis for whom this location is sacred because it borders their Salt Trail and Sipapuni, their place of emergence. In response to these objections, Diné President Ben Shelly has promised that there will be restrictions on travel to the Hopi sacred sites. As of 2016, the Navajo Nation has yet to approve the resort development plan (The Wave 2016).

This controversy highlights the difficulties of planning for economic development, an obvious benefit, in the context of conflicting interests and strategies. In this case, the interests of two different Native nations are in competition. In any case, before the project can go forward, it requires approval by the full Tribal Council, an action that has yet to happen.

In an affirmation of sovereignty, the tribal council began issuing Navajo Nation Identity Cards in 2012 that can be used not only as proof of membership in the Navajo Nation but also, according to federal standards, as valid identity cards for use both domestically and to cross the borders into Canada and Mexico. Membership in the Navajo Nation is currently based on a blood quantum requirement of at least one-quarter Navajo ancestry.

The Navajo Nation faces many social, economic, and political dilemmas that its leadership and its people must address. How these questions, particularly of sovereignty, economic development, and social change amidst traditional values and cultural continuity will be answered will determine the future of the nation.

REFERENCES

Aberle, David. 1961. "Navaho." *Matrilineal Kinship* (ed. D. Schneider and K. Gaugh). Berkeley, CA: University of California Press, pp. 96–201.

Aberle, David. 1966. *The Peyote Religion among the Navaho.* New York: Viking Fund Publications in Anthropology No. 42.

Aberle, David. 1983a. "Peyote Religion among the Navaho." *Southwest* (ed. A. Ortiz), Vol. 10 of *Handbook of North American Indians.* Washington, DC: Smithsonian Institution, 558–569.

Aberle, David. 1983b. "Navajo Economic Development." *Southwest* (ed. A. Ortiz), Vol. 10 of *Handbook*

of North American Indians. Washington, DC: Smithsonian Institution, pp. 641–658.

American Indian Report. April 2000.

American Indian Report. March 2000.

Bailey, Garrick, and Roberta Bailey. 1986. *A History of the Navajos: The Reservation Years.* Santa Fe, NM: School of American Research Press.

Bailey, Lynn. 1964. *The Long Walk: A History of the Navajo Wars, 1846–68.* Los Angeles, CA: Westernlore Press.

Benedek, Emily. 1992. *The Wind Won't Know Me: A History of the Navajo-Hopi Land Dispute.* New York: Knopf.

Churchill, Ward. 1993. *Struggle for the Land: Indigenous Resistance to Genocide, Ecocide and Expropriation in Contemporary North America.* Monroe, ME: Common Courage Press.

Correll, J. L., and Alfred Dehiya. 1972. *Anatomy of the Navajo Indian Reservation: How It Grew.* Window Rock, AZ: The Navajo Nation.

Donovan, Bill. 2012. "Navajo-Gallup Pipeline Groundbreaking Set." *Navajo Times,* May 31. http://navajotimes.com/politics/2012/0512/053112pip.php.

Dyk, Walter (ed.). 1967. *Son of Old Man Hat: A Navajo Autobiography.* Lincoln, NE: University of Nebraska Press.

Federal Trade Commission. 1973. *The Trading Post System on the Navajo Reservation: Staff Report to the Federal Trade Commission.* Washington, DC.

Frisbie, Charlotte, and David McAllester. 1977. *Navajo Blessingway Singer: Frank Mitchell.* Tucson, AZ: University of Arizona Press.

Gordon, Suzanne. 1973. *Black Mesa: The Angel of Death.* New York: John Day.

Haile, Berard. 1954. *Property Concepts of the Navajo Indians.* Anthropological Series No. 17. Catholic University of America. Washington, DC.

Hamamsy, Laila. 1979. "The Role of Women in a Changing Navajo Society." *American Anthropologist: 101–111.* Reprinted in *Women and Society* (ed. Tiffany). Boston, MA: Eden Press Women's Publications, pp. 75–91.

Hewett, Edgar. 1906. "Origin of the Name Navaho." *American Anthropologist* 8: 193.

Hill, W. W. 1940. "Some Aspects of Navajo Political Structure." *Plateau:* 23–28.

Hill, W. W. 1948. "Navajo Trading and Trading Ritual: A Study of Cultural Dynamics." *Southwestern Journal of Anthropology* 4, no. 4: 371–396.

"Indian Agriculture Restores Traditions and Economy." 1999. American Indian Report. August. pp. 16–18.

Johansen, Bruce. 1997. "The High Cost of Uranium in Navajo Land." 1997. *Akwesasne Notes* 2, no. 2 (Spring): 10–12.

Keleher, William. 1952. *Turmoil in New Mexico, 1846–1868.* Sante Fe, NM: Rydal Press.

Kelly, Lawrence. 1970. *Navajo Roundup: Selected Correspondence of Kit Carson's Expedition against the Navajo, 1863–1865*. Boulder, CO: Pruett Press.

Kluckhohn, Clyde, and Dorothea Leighton. 1946. *The Navaho*. Cambridge, MA: Harvard University Press.

Kunitz, Stephen. 1983. *Disease, Change and the Role of Medicine: The Navajo Experience*. Berkeley, CA: University of California Press.

Lamphere, Louise. 1977. *To Run after Them: Cultural and Social Basis of Cooperation in a Navajo Community*. Tucson, AZ: University of Arizona Press.

Leighton, Dorothea, and Clyde Kluckhohn. 1947. *Children of the People: The Navaho Individual and His Development*. Cambridge: Harvard University Press.

Levek, A. 1997. "Huge Navajo Farm Project Still Losing Money after Two Decades." *Livestock Weekly*. Online.

Levy, Jerrold. 1980. "Who Benefits from Energy Resource Development: The Special Case of the Navajo Indian." *The Social Science Journal* 17: 1–19.

Loomis, Brandon. 2016. "Abandoned Uranium Mines Continue to Haunt Navajos on Reservation." *The Republic*. Online.

Macmillan, Leslie. 2014. "Hopi Lawsuit against Wastewater Snowmaking Gets Green Light in Arizona." *High County News*. Online.

McNeley, James. 1981. *Holy Wind in Navajo Philosophy*. Tucson, AZ: University of Arizona Press.

McNitt, Frank. 1972. *Navajo Wars, Military Campaign, Slave Raids and Reprisals*. Albuquerque, NM: University of New Mexico Press.

Milich, Alicia (trans.). 1966. *Relaciones by Zarate Salmeron*. Albuquerque, NM: Horn and Wallace.

Minard, Anne. 2013. "Waste Makes Jobs." *Indian Country Today* 3, no. 13 (April 10): 32–33.

Navajo Nation. 1972. *The Navajo Ten Year Plan*. Windowrock, AZ: The Navajo Tribe.

"Navajo Lawsuits Contend US Government Failed the Tribe in Mining Royalty Deals." 1999. *The New York Times*. July 18: Sec. A, p. 19.

Office of Senator Tom Udall. 2015. "In Depth: New Mecixo Prioritizes in Spending Bill Lauded by Udall, Heinrich." New Mexico State KRWG TV. Online.

Paskus, Laura. 2015. "Why Is the Navajo Nation Giving Water to Fracking While Its People Are Parched?" *Indian County Today* Media Network. Online.

Reichard, Gladys. 1928. *Social Life of the Navajo Indians*. New York: Columbia University Contributions to Anthropology No. 7.

Reichard, Gladys. 1944. *Prayer: The Compulsive Word*. American Ethnological Society Monograph No. 7. New York: J. J. Augustin.

Reichard, Gladys. 1950. *Navaho Religion: A Study of Symbolism*. New York: Bollingen Foundation.

Reiter, Paul. 1938. *The Jemez Pueblo of Unshagi*. Santa Fe, NM: Monographs of the School of American Research Nos. 5–6.

Reno, Phillip. 1981. *Mother Earth, Father Sky, and Economic Development: Navajo Resources and Their Use*. Albuquerque, NM: University of New Mexico Press.

Roessel, Ruth (ed.). 1971. *Navajo Studies of Navajo Community College*. Many Farms, AZ: Navajo Community College.

Roessel, Ruth (ed.). 1973. *Navajo Stories of the Long Walk*. Tsaile, AZ: Navajo Community College Press.

Shebala, Marley. 2011. "Peabody, Tribe Mum on Lawsuit Settlement." *Navajo Times*. Online.

Shepardson, Mary. 1963. *Navajo Ways in Government: A Study in Political Process*. Washington, DC: American Anthropological Association, Memoir 96, vol. 65, no. 3, pt. 2.

Southwestern Indian Development. 1974. *Traders on the Navajo Reservation: A Report on the Economic Bondage of the Navajo People*. Windowrock, AZ.

Underhill, Ruth. 1956. *The Navajos*. Norman, OK: University of Oklahoma Press.

US Bureau of the Census. 2010. "American Indian and Alaska Native Tribes in the United States and Puerto Rico: 201." *2010 Census*. Washington, DC, CPH-T-6.

US Bureau of Indian Affairs. 2010. "Table 3: Indian Service Population and Labor Force Estimates." Washington, DC.

Vogt, Evan. 1961. "Navaho." *Perspectives in American Indian Culture Change* (ed. E. Spicer). Chicago, IL: University of Chicago Press, pp. 278–336.

Weiss, Lawrence. 1984. *The Development of Capitalism in the Navajo Nation: A Political-Economic History*. Studies in Marxism, Vol. 15. Minneapolis, MN: MEP Publications.

White, Richard. 1983. *The Roots of Dependency: Subsistence, Environment, and Social Change among the Choctaw, Pawnees, and Navajos*. Lincoln, NE: University of Nebraska Press.

Witherspoon, Gary. 1975. *Navajo Kinship and Marriage*. Chicago, IL: University of Chicago Press.

Wyman, Leland. 1950. "The Religion of the Navajo Indians." *Forgotten Religions* (ed. V. Ferm). New York: Philosophical Library.

Wyman, Leland. 1957. *Beautyway: A Navajo Ceremonial* (trans. B. Haile). New York: Pantheon Books.

Wyman, Leland. 1983. "Navajo Ceremonial System." *Southwest* (ed. A. Ortiz), Vol. 10 of *Handbook of North American Indians*. Washington, DC: Smithsonian Institution, pp. 536–557.

Wyman, Leland, and Clyde Kluckhohn. 1938. *Navaho Classification of Their Song Ceremonials*. Memoirs of the American Anthropological Association, No. 50. Menasha, WI.

Yurth, Cindy, and Duane Beyal. 2012. "Targeting the Confluence." *Navajo Times* June 4.

Zolbrod, Paul. 1984. *Diné Bahane: The Navajo Creation Story*. Albuquerque, NM: University of New Mexico Press.

CALIFORNIA

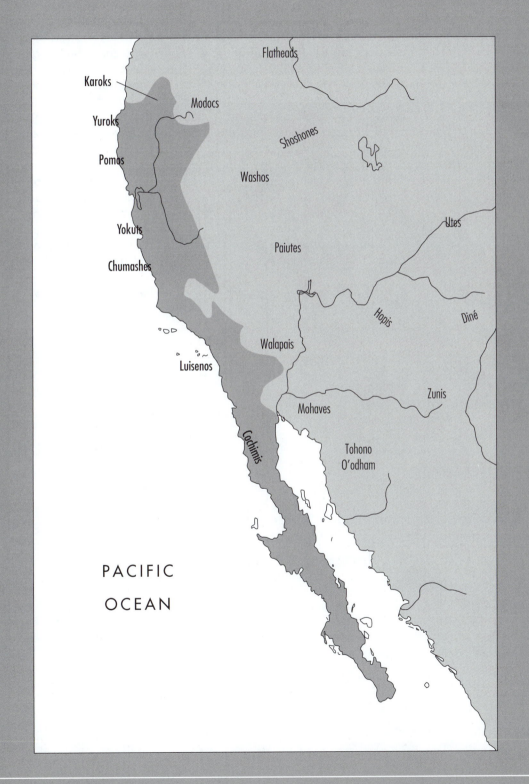

Flatheads

Karoks

Modocs

Yuroks

Shoshones

Pomos

Washos

Yokuts

Paiutes

Chumashes

Utes

Hopis

Diné

Walapais

Luisenos

Zunis

Mohaves

Cochimis

Tohono O'odham

PACIFIC

OCEAN

Origin of the Pomo Ghost Ceremony

Hawk, the captain of a village, was killed by Vulture. After being absent from the village for some time, Hawk suddenly returned, came into the dance house, and sat down in front of the center pole, at its foot. A ceremony was about to begin, and the people noticed nothing out of the ordinary about Hawk and were perfectly willing to allow him to participate in the dancing. Meadowlark, however, noticed an odor about Hawk which showed that he had just returned from the realm of the dead. With his characteristic garrulity, he commenced to chatter about the improprieties of mortals dancing with dead people. Hawk was a chief and one of an important family and felt especially offended by these reflections upon him and left at once, never again returning to the village. Meadowlark had, in those days, a long tail like most other birds. His action upon this occasion, however, so enraged the other members of the village that someone struck at him with a fire poker which happened to be near at hand. Meadowlark was able to dodge the blow, but the poker clipped off a large part of his tail. He has had only a stub of a tail since that day. The people then fell to discussing what could be done to atone in some way for the insult to Hawk. A number of men immediately went out into the woods and dressed themselves as the ghost dancers now do, returning to the village to impersonate the spirits of the departed. From this mythical source has descended the present-day Ghost ceremony.

Source: S. A. Barrett. 1917. *Ceremonies of the Pomo Indians*. Berkeley, CA: University of California Publications in American Archeology and Ethnology 12.10, p. 406.

Native Nations of California

We built our culture center for our people to learn and enjoy the richness of the past as part of the present … Our land keeps us alive; our cultural ways make us proud to be Indian…Our spirit must not die … In this material world, the material things which represent our heritage, the baskets, the songs, the dances, the language, can house the spirit of our culture.

Inscription on the Cupa Cultural Center, Pala, California; quoted in Bahr 1993: 142

LANDS AND NATIONS

The culture area called "California" is not coterminous with the present-day state but is somewhat narrower, particularly in its south-central and southern regions. Although it encompasses a smaller territory than other culture areas of North America, California was the homeland of a large number of autonomous and independent aboriginal groups who spoke at least sixty-four and perhaps as many as eighty separate languages belonging to five different linguistic stocks. Nations indigenous to California shared a core of similar practices and beliefs, but their differences also were marked. The area as a whole can be divided into regions based on ecological and cultural distinctions. Central California is the area of greatest homogeneity, while cultures that developed in the northwest and

south were most distinct. Northwestern Californian nations shared similarities with neighboring groups in southern Oregon and Washington, while those of southern California were influenced by southwestern Puebloans.

California is divided by the long, narrow Great Central Valley that extends from north to south. The valley is surrounded on the east by the high Cascade Range and Sierra Nevadas and on the west by the somewhat lower mountains of the Coast Range. North of the Great Central Valley are the Klamath Mountains; to the south are the Transverse Ranges and to the southwest lies the Mojave Desert. The climate in most of California is relatively mild with moderate precipitation although in the highest mountain elevations, cold temperatures and heavy snows prevail in the winter. In the Mojave Desert, in contrast, temperatures are high year-round and precipitation is exceedingly light.

Aboriginal languages of California, numbering in the sixties or seventies, are grouped into five language stocks or families: Hokan, Penutian, Uto-Aztecan, Algonkian, and Athabaskan (Bright 1964; Shipley 1973). Hokan is probably the oldest linguistic stock of California. Hokan languages were once spoken in most of the region but were pushed into peripheral areas by the intrusion of Penutian-speaking people who spread through the Great Central Valley. Later, speakers of Uto-Aztecan languages entered from the Southwest and Mexico. At the same time or possibly earlier, speakers of Algonkian languages entered California from the east and/or north. Finally, Athabaskan speakers arrived from the north or northeast. Major languages comprising the Hokan stock include Karok,

Shasta, Yana, and the Pomoan languages, all spoken in the northern third of California. In addition, Chumash and Yuman were spoken in southwestern and southern California. The Penutian stock, including Wintu, Maidu, and Yokuts, is distributed in central and northcentral California. Algonkian languages, that is, Wiyot and Yurok, were spoken along the Northwestern Coast. Speakers of Athabaskan languages such as Hupa and Tolowa also lived in northwestern California. And, finally, Uto-Aztecan languages, including the Takic and Numic families, were spoken in southern and southcentral regions.

All of the linguistic stocks of California are related to languages spoken outside the territory. Hokan and Penutian have only minor ties to languages of other regions, but Uto-Aztecan, Athabaskan, and Algonkian languages are mainly spoken outside the area. Uto-Aztecan languages are attested in the Southwest and Mexico; Athabaskan languages predominate in the Northwest, western Canada, and interior Alaska; while Algonkian languages are found throughout central and eastern North America. The linguistic connections between aboriginal nations of California and other regions are reflections of migration patterns of Native people and their successive arrivals in the area. Although ancestors of Californian nations came from very different historical origins and undoubtedly brought traits indigenous to other regions, once in California, their various original cultures merged and borrowed from one another until they developed ways of living that were similar in many respects. Shared traits are results of adaptations to similar environments and diffusional processes from one group to another.

Population

As elsewhere in North America, population figures are uncertain but Sherburne Cook, the preeminent authority on Californian demography, estimates an aboriginal figure of some 310,000, plus or minus 30,000 (1978: 91). Populations were most concentrated in central and northwestern California while they were less dense in the northeast and south. Where resources were scarce, densities were probably as low as 0.5 person per square mile, whereas in areas of most abundant resources, population densities rose to as high as 10 or more persons per square mile (Bean 1976: 101).

From the late eighteenth century when Spanish invasions commenced until the late nineteenth when the destructive forces of European and American settlement had taken their full toll, the Native population declined to approximately 20,000, a rate of loss of over 90 percent (Cook 1978: 91). The onslaught began first along the coast from San Diego to San Francisco as Spanish priests established missions and forced Indians to congregate there in order to be converted to Christianity and to work for the resident priests. By 1830, there were at least 18,000 neophytes at the missions. According to Cook, disease was the major killer of Native people during that period. Changes in diet also contributed to malnutrition and early deaths. Disease and death quickly spread to other regions of California as many inmates of missions escaped into remote regions. After 1800, Spanish authorities sent soldiers into the interior to capture more potential converts, introducing disease and fear throughout the region. By 1830, the total Californian population had declined to about 245,000. During the next destructive era, ending with the Mexican-American War in 1845, disease spread to the Central Valley while at the same time European settlement expanded. Epidemics of malaria, smallpox, and syphilis took their toll on the Native population, probably killing at least 60,000 in the 1830s alone. An additional 40,000 people died as a result of warfare and the destruction of the food supply. By 1845, then, there were probably no more than 125,000 to 150,000 aboriginal inhabitants, a loss of more than 50 percent. After the discovery of gold in 1848, an enormous number of American settlers and prospectors poured into the region, exacting a heavy toll on the Native population. As Cook summarized the situation:

The Indian territory that until this point had escaped direct contact with European influence now succumbed, for it was exactly the remote valleys of the Sierra Nevadas, Cascades, and Siskiwous that attracted miners, while commerce and agriculture took possession of the Central Valley and coast ranges. The overwhelming assault upon the subsistence, life, and culture of all Californian Natives during the short period from 1848 to 1865 has seldom been duplicated in modern times by an invading race … It is evident that by 1850 the Indian population of the entire state had been reduced to about 100,000. The decline during the worst decade, 1845 to 1855, was incredible—from approximately 150,000 to 50,000. This desolation was accomplished by a ruthless flood of miners and farmers who annihilated the Natives without mercy or compensation. The direct causes of death were disease, the bullet, exposure, and acute starvation. The more remote causes were insane passion for gold, abiding hatred for the Red Man, and complete lack of any legal control. (1978: 93)

The Native population continued to decline until at least 1880 or 1900, falling to less than 20,000, and then began to rebound slowly. By 1910, it probably reached about 25,000. By 1960, the official California census listed somewhat more than 39,000 Indians living in the state, and only ten years later, the census reported 91,000 Native residents. And in 2014, there were about 286,631 Indians in California. These figures, however, do not represent only people indigenous to California since the state has been the recipient of the largest influx of Indians in modern times from throughout the United States. They are currently concentrated in the San Francisco Bay region and Los Angeles county, accounting for 25 percent of the total (US Bureau of the Census 2010).

ABORIGINAL CULTURES

Economies

Although nearly all aboriginal societies had economies based on foraging, subsistence activities varied depending on environment, location, and available resources. The Yuroks, Wiyots, Pomos, Miwoks, Yukis, and Tolowas who lived along the Pacific coast in central and northern California focused their economies on marine life. They gathered shellfish such as clams, oysters, mussels, and abalone, caught fish near the shore, and supplemented a marine diet with acorns and land animals including deer, elk, and antelope. Oak trees that provided such an important staple in much of California were relatively scarce along the coast, but coastal people were able to obtain acorns and animal hides and meat from inland groups through extensive trade networks. In turn, coastal people provided inland groups with sea shells utilized in the manufacture of small disks that served as money throughout California. The Chumash and Gabrielinos who lived along the southern coast and on the Channel Islands had economies centered on sea-fishing, hunting sea mammals such as sea otters and seals, and gathering shellfish. Their marine diet was supplemented by acorns, seeds, fruits, and land animals including deer, raccoons, badgers, and squirrels. They constructed

sturdy wooden plank canoes to enable them to fish in the deep ocean, whereas the people on the northern coast made small boats, called balsas, constructed of tules and other fibers or small dugout canoes that were not seaworthy but better used for bays and inland rivers. The Hupas, Tolowas, Karoks, Shastas, Pomos, Yanas, Yokuts, Wintus, and Maidus who lived near the Klamath and Sacramento Rivers and other waterways had economies focused on fishing for salmon and trout, catching waterfowl, and gathering acorns and marsh plants. Hunting was the least important of their subsistence strategies. Economies of inhabitants of the Central Valley and nearby plains such as the Wintus, Patwins, Maidus, and Yokuts centered primarily on gathering plants, especially acorns, chia or sage seeds, and yampa. Acorns, collected from at least ten varieties of oak, were their single most important food. Some Miwok, Yokuts, Mono, Yana, Maidu, Wintu, Patwin, Cahuilla, Chumash, and Luiseno communities living in foothill or mountain regions also had plant-collecting economies. Their territories provided abundant and variable resources, permitting the development of the most densely populated communities of California (Beals 1951: 80–81). People such as the Serranos and Cahuillas who lived in the Colorado and Mohave Deserts collected piñon nuts, mesquite, and other desert roots and plants. And finally, the Yumas, Mohaves, and Diegueños living along the Colorado River farmed small plots of land, planting corn, beans, and pumpkins (82).

Of all the plant foods available in California, acorns were the most important staple. Once gathered and shelled, they were prepared first by grinding them into meal and then leaching them with hot water to remove the bitter tannic acid. Acorn meal was usually mixed with water and boiled until it had the consistency of mush or soup. The meal was cooked in watertight baskets filled with water and hot stones. It was then eaten cold (Reid 1968: 23). Buckeyes were also collected, leached, and cooked. Women gathered berries, chokecherries, wild plums, and other fruits. In southern California, mesquite beans were dried, ground, and baked into cakes. Mescale or agave roots were also collected and eaten. Seeds were shaken loose with woven seed beaters and collected in flat baskets. They were usually parched and then ground into flour and roasted or boiled. Seeds such as chia or sage and amaranths were the most commonly abundant varieties. Many kinds of greens were collected and eaten raw or boiled in cooking baskets (Kroeber 1962: 53–54).

Although most Native Californians were not farming people, many engaged in a number of practices that contributed to the conservation of resources and encouraged prolific growth of natural plants both for human and animal consumption. Burning of grasslands, particularly in the Central Valley, was done both at the beginning of the spring growing season and after plant and seed harvesting in the fall. Clearings in forests were sometimes burned in order to prevent overgrowth (Bean and Lawton 1976: 29–32). Such practices were noted by Spaniards in the eighteenth century:

Yurok Nation basketmaker teaches basketry to girls at a cultural camp in Klamath, California.

> In all of new California, the gentiles have the custom of burning the brush, for two purposes; one, for hunting rabbits and hares (because they burn the brush for hunting); second, so that with the first light rain or dew the shoots will come up upon which they feed when the weather does not permit them to seek other food. (Longinos Martinez 1792, quoted in Simpson 1939: 51)

In addition, some people engaged in "semicultivation" (Bean and Lawton 1976: 37). They planted wild seeds in order to produce a better crop or transplanted wild plants close to their villages so that they would be easier to tend and gather. True farming, probably diffused from the Southwest, was practiced on a small scale in the Colorado Desert of southeastern California west of the Colorado River. Farming was adaptive in the Colorado Desert because of the relatively scarce natural resources there but further north, in contrast, abundant food supplies made farming unnecessary.

Among the most important aboriginal crafts were basketry and the production of shell money. Baskets were made by women utilizing methods of twining and/or coiling. Many types of baskets were produced, including conical-shaped carrying or seed-gathering baskets fitted with carrying straps, woven trays or flat baskets used for shaking and separating acorn meal or sifting acorn flour, seed beaters, storage baskets of many shapes, sizes, and uses, and closely woven watertight baskets for boiling and cooking. In addition to household basketry, women produced twined fish traps, bird traps, hats, mats, and cradles. They also made water bottles sealed with pitch or asphaltum. Special baskets were made for ceremonial purposes or as gifts to important visitors, sometimes decorated with feathers and shell beads. Designs were made by using contrasting colors and materials.

Native Californian money was produced by men from dentalium shells or clamshell beads. The former were common in southern California, but throughout the rest of the region clamshell money predominated. Clam shells were broken into pieces, shaped, bored with holes, strung on cordage, and then rounded and polished on a slab of sandstone (Kroeber 1971: 20–21). Each disk was somewhat less than an inch in diameter and from a quarter to a third of an inch thick. Differences in value derived from the size, thickness, polish, and age of the disks. Value was also measured by the length of strings of clamshell beads.

Aboriginal clothing was relatively simple. Women wore short skirts consisting of two pieces worn in front and back. The skirts were made either of plant fibers such as inner barks of trees, grass, and tule or of buckskin. Men rarely wore clothing except in cold or damp weather. In such conditions, men and women covered themselves with blankets or capes made of animal skins that they wrapped around their bodies or fastened over their shoulders. Sea otter, land otter, deer, and rabbit furs were used in their manufacture. Moccasins were made from animal skins, sometimes lined with grass in cold weather. In southern California, sandals were often worn instead. In particularly cold climates and especially when heavy snows had fallen, leggings made of animal skins were worn. Headgear for women consisted of basketry caps that protected their heads from chafing from the straps of carrying baskets that they used when collecting plants.

Native Californians supplemented the resources in their own region with goods obtained through intertribal trading networks. Exchange of products occurred whenever visitors came to a community or participated in ceremonies and festivals. In addition, trade was frequent between neighboring groups, particularly when each had access to different ecological zones and resources.

Surpluses were traded in order to obtain resources that were lacking in one's own area. Friendly relations between neighboring groups were therefore essential to economic integration and supply and highlighted the importance of social and ceremonial cooperation. Intertribal trade generally consisted of bartering one product for another, but goods were occasionally purchased with standardized money, that is, dentalium or clamshell beads and disks.

Many kinds of foods, raw materials, and finished products were exchanged. Shell beads were the most commonly traded items (Swanton 1907). In fact, archeological evidence indicates trade in shell beads derived from the central California coast dating back to at least 6600 BC. Additional frequently traded items included baskets, salt, animal hides, and foods such as acorns and fish. A vast series of trails linked villages to one another, extending north and south from the Mexican border to Oregon, mainly along the valleys of the Coast Ranges and the Great Central Valley. Trails also ran east to west from the Pacific shore across the Coast Ranges, the Central Valley, and again across the Sierra Nevadas into the Great Basin (Heizer 1941, 1946; Bennyhoff and Heizer 1958).

In southern California, the Chumash developed extensive intervillage trade among island, coastal, and inland communities, exchanging regionally specific resources (King 1976: 292–293). Shell beads and fish were traded from the islands to the mainland while acorns, seeds, animal skins, and baskets were traded from mainland to island settlements. Coastal villages functioned as trade centers to which people from island and inland communities congregated to exchange their products.

Women's and Men's Roles

In general, egalitarian economic and social relations prevailed between men and women in most Californian societies, but prestigious political and religious roles were usually held by men. Rigid sexual division of labor was absent in most groups, especially within the household (Willoughby 1963). Cooperative labor was the norm although phases of a given task might be separately allocated. Hunting was probably the most regularly segregated task, being almost always the occupation solely of men. However, in some groups women aided men in hunting and might separately hunt small animals. Fishing was also predominantly done by men but women aided in these endeavors. Women typically caught small fish in baskets whereas men used spears or nets. Gathering plants was usually a female occupation, but men aided and sometimes gathered nuts and seeds independently. Differentiation in technique applied to gathering acorns and pine nuts: women used poles to shake the nuts loose whereas men often climbed trees to shake down the nuts. Household tasks such as food preparation and childcare were usually assigned to women but in most groups men helped. Men were responsible for butchering meat, while cooking, preserving, and storing foods were women's tasks. The production of crafts also generally followed gender lines but again with flexibility. Women were the primary basketmakers and producers of matting, cradles, and clothing whereas men made fishing nets and the tools and weaponry used for hunting. Houses were constructed mainly by men but often with the aid of women.

The roles of chief and shaman were gender-linked in most cases. Chiefs were almost always men although occasionally a woman might serve. In some societies men predominated as shamans, while in other groups women were the more likely practitioners and in some women or men were equally represented. The only medical specialty that was universally associated with a particular gender was midwifery, always the work of women (59–60).

Men's social and political advantages mainly derived from their prominence as chiefs and counselors. The social system itself, particularly the tendency for patrilineal descent and patrilocal residence, also favored men in household and community life. And, although divorce could be initiated by either partner, men were more likely to divorce their wives than the reverse. Symbolic separation of the sexes was reflected in the institution of the sweathouse that functioned not so much as a ceremonial structure but as an exclusive clubhouse and sleeping quarters for men.

Cahuilla house in the desert, California.

Settlements

House styles varied depending on materials available, intended permanence of the structures, and other cultural influences. In the Northwest nations of the Hupa and Yurok, houses were generally made of large planks in a rectangular formation. Following is a description of Yurok houses of the mid-nineteenth century:

> The huts are constructed of planks made of split fir [redwood] trees. The floor dimensions are approximately sixteen by twenty feet, the height of the walls is four to six feet, and the height of the gable ten to fifteen. In one corner is the door, a two foot wide oval hole through which the inhabitants crawl in and out … In the middle of the floor, which is dug out several feet is the fireplace, over which in the roof is a hole which can be closed by means of a cover, which serves the double purpose of flue and a window. The fire is never permitted to go out. The Allequas [Yurok] sit and sleep around the fire, always with the seniors nearest to the fire, while the younger members range themselves around them according to their ages … If the settlement constitutes a village, the huts stand in straight lines next to each other two to four feet apart, surrounded by a mound of earth. (Meyer 1851; in Heizer and Whipple 1971: 265)

In northcentral and central California, houses were constructed of poles covered with bark. Some were of rectangular shape but more often they were conical, covered with earth or brush rather than bark. Earth-covered houses were more common among the Modoks, Yukis, and Miwoks of central California as well as most peoples of the south. A nineteenth-century description of Chumash houses follows:

> Their houses, shaped like half globes, are neatly built; each one is capable of sheltering four or five families which, being kin, are accustomed to living together. The houses have one door on the east, and one door on the west, with a skylight in the roof, halfway between … The men do not often sleep in their houses at night; but are accustomed to congregate in numbers in great subterranean caves. (Pedro Fages; quoted in Heizer and Whipple 1971: 255)

In some nations, different kinds of houses were constructed in different regions. For example, among the Miwoks of central interior California, dwellings built in mountainous regions were conical in shape and covered with three or four thicknesses of bark slabs, while houses in communities situated at lower elevations had brush, grass, or tule thatch over a framework of poles. In winter, some people constructed semi-subterranean dwellings covered with earth (Kroeber 1925: 447). The floors of houses were layered with pine needles, mats, or deerskins used as bedding.

In many communities throughout California, large assembly or council houses were built to serve for communal gatherings—meetings and festivals. Assembly houses were constructed according to the same design used for domestic dwellings but were generally much larger. Most groups erected sweathouses that were used for ritual purposes and as clubhouses and sleeping quarters for men. Sweathouses were constructed of logs and poles covered with earth. They were smaller than family dwellings and were heated by fire, not steam, as elsewhere in North America. Women usually did not enter sweathouses except on ceremonial occasions (Kroeber 1971: 8).

Local Communities

Aboriginal people of California were organized into what Kroeber (1962) termed "tribelets." The choice of this nomenclature reflects the small size of indigenous cultural groups and indicates that each territorial unit considered itself autonomous even though it recognized kinship, cultural, and linguistic links to nearby groups. Territories occupied by tribelets varied from a low of 50 sq. mi. to a high of about 6,000 sq. mi. (29). Populations of each tribelet also varied from only a few hundred to a thousand or more. In California as a whole, therefore, there were several hundreds of such groups. Tribelets held territory in common, their ownership legitimated by both occupancy and use. Tribelets, and sometimes villages, owned or controlled resource sites such as oak groves, salmon streams, and coastal beaches for the gathering of shellfish and seaweed. The boundaries of each tribelet's territory were definite and recognized both by members of the group and by members of neighboring groups as well. According to Powers,

> The boundaries of all tribes are marked with the greatest precision, being defined by certain creeks, canyons, boulders, conspicuous trees, springs, etc. each of which object has its own individual name. Accordingly, [women] teach these things to their children in a kind of sing-song ... over and over, time and again, they rehearse all these boulders etc., describe each minutely and by name, with its surroundings. (Powers 1877: 109–110)

Tribelets contained at least one but usually several villages. In some cases, one of the constituent villages was numerically and politically dominant while the others were "suburban" satellites (Kroeber 1962: 33). In other tribelets, all of the villages were more or less the same size and were independent. In all tribelets, one village was recognized as a center where communal festivals and councils were held. Village and tribelet cohesion was common throughout most of California except the Northwest. In Northwestern nations, in contrast, village atomization or what Kroeber referred to as "fractionation" occurred (43). Each village was autonomous, and even within villages separate lineage groups were recognized as socially and politically distinct. In contrast to tribelet communal ownership of resources in the rest of California, resource sites in the Northwest were owned by lineages.

Land was important for the resources it contained, providing people with food and raw materials for the manufacture of clothing, shelters, household utensils, tools, and weapons. But land had intangible values as well. As Kroeber noted,

> Each territory contained spots which had religious, magical, or other affective associations to its inhabitants. Some landmarks were sacred. Others were dangerous. Some brought blessings if prayed to ... The Indians were also sensible of pleasant landscapes and views. They picked their settlement sites, of course, primarily for utilitarian and practical reasons, but at the same time so many of these sites command an agreeable or beautiful prospect that this factor, too, must have entered into their attitudes ... Allied to this, in turn, is the tremendously strong attachment which all California Indians had for the place for which they were reared and had lived most of their lives. They wanted to go on living where they had always lived. Again and again old people speak of having been born here and of dying in the same spot; the cycle has come around ... With these sentimental attachments, it is evident that dispossession from it or even disturbance from its utilization was bound to be extremely upsetting to Native customs and to Native morals. Enforced transfer to a new habitat, even if only a few miles away, deprivation of familiar areas for food gathering, and the necessity of learning a wholly new mode of life, all came as a very real and genuine shock. (57–58)

Although most tribelets were fully autonomous and independent, political confederations may have existed in some groups such as the Chumash, Pomo, Miwok, Patwin, Shasta, Gabrielino, and Tipai-Ipai (Holt 1946; Heizer 1968). Since these groups were distributed throughout California, such organization does not seem to have had an areal bias.

Families and Social Systems

The social units that constituted tribelets included households of either nuclear or extended family composition. Parents and children formed the core of household units, but other blood or affinal relatives and sometimes even nonrelatives added to household size. According to Kroeber, families usually contained seven or eight members, with a range of perhaps five to ten (1962: 30). Lineage organization was also critical to the formation of households and tribelets. In nations of southcentral and central California, patrilineages were common. Such lineages typically had a depth of from three to five generations (32). Among the Pomos of northcentral California, however, lineages were based on matrilineal descent. Elsewhere, lineages were either patrilineally or ambilineally organized. Residence after marriage generally followed descent principles. That is, where patrilineal kinship groups dominated, couples followed rules of patrilocal residence, while among the Pomo postmarital residence was generally matrilocal and elsewhere ambilocal residence prevailed (Bean and Theodoratus 1978: 298–305; Kunkel 1974).

Many, but not all, nations of southcentral and southern California had exogamous totemic moieties that were linked through ritual exchange of services (Gifford 1926). They were named after animals thought to be guardians of the members. In some groups, people belonging to a particular moiety were responsible for ensuring the survival of their animal guardian, thus helping to maintain and conserve the animal populations upon which people depended.

Families were allied to one another through marriages that were usually contracted for girls shortly after puberty and for boys in their late teens. Polygyny was possible although only likely for men of highest status and wealth, particularly chiefs and shamans. Where it occurred, sororal polygyny was preferred. Polyandry, though rare, was also acceptable in some nations. And the sororate and levirate perpetuated affinal bonds between families. Where lineages or moieties existed, people could not marry within such kinship units but everywhere generational rules prevailed so that close relatives within three to five generations could not marry. Since marriage restrictions made it difficult for people to find mates within their own local group, tribelets tended to be exogamous. As a consequence of exogamy, affinal bonds created between separate communities led to economic, political, and ceremonial exchanges between tribelets.

In the event of unhappy or ill-suited marriages, divorce was a possibility, but families put pressure on their sons and daughters to remain in unions that had been contracted in order to maintain already-established economic, political, and ceremonial alliances. Given the predominant rules of patrilocal residence, women sometimes had difficulty integrating themselves into their husband's family. And while both men and women could opt for divorce, it was generally easier for a man to divorce his wife than for a wife to divorce her husband.

Social Hierarchies

Social distinctions among members of Californian nations gave certain privileges to those of higher class while social stigma was attached to people of the lowest groups (Bean and King 1974; Gayton 1945; Kroeber 1925). In most nations, the populace was differentiated into three groups: elites, commoners, and poor people. A fourth class consisting of vagabonds or slaves also existed in some groups. Although social mobility was possible in theory, high-class people tended to marry members of their own group and thus maintain patterns of inheritance both of rank and wealth. Highest status accrued to chiefs, men of wealth and prestige, who belonged to elite or chiefly lineages. Chieftanships were usually hereditary, passing from a man to a brother or eldest son. If no such person were available, a near kin was chosen as successor (Reid 1968:15). Although chiefs ideally held their positions for life, they could be replaced if their behavior was deemed unacceptable. In addition to membership in a chiefly lineage, qualifications included wealth, hunting skills, intelligence, and personality traits valued by their communities such as honesty, moderation, generosity, self-restraint, industriousness, and self-respect (Bean 1975: 28). Access to and control of spirit power that was either inherited or acquired were also valuable and necessary assets (30).

Once in office, chiefs generally did not perform economic tasks but rather were supported by the work of others. Chiefs often had more than one wife, usually selected from neighboring tribelets so as to extend networks of alliances with high-status families elsewhere. Chiefs had certain material benefits as well. Their houses were larger, their adornment finer, and their possession of ceremonial and material wealth exceeded that of others (32). Furthermore, they assumed a dignified demeanor and speech patterns that distinguished them from common people. However, in spite of marked differences from others, chiefs lacked coercive powers but rather were advisors and managers of community affairs. They collected and redistributed food, money, and other symbolic and real community wealth. From the stores of food that they collected, they provided for the needs of the poor and welcomed and hosted visitors with displays of hospitality and generosity (Blackburn 1974: 233; Kroeber 1962: 46). They were prominent figures at community ceremonies and public meetings, giving advice, making public speeches, admonishing people to behave properly, and contributing substantially to the costs incurred. Chiefs also exerted social control because their advice and approval were sought when public opinion clamored for the execution of wrongdoers, especially people accused of causing the death of others through direct assault or spiritual manipulation (Blackburn 1976: 233–234; Gayton 1930). But chiefs rarely became involved in personal disputes except in cases of "protracted inter-family feuds" (Gayton 1930: 375). In sum, as Blackburn noted for most of California, "The position of chief could be characterized as one of considerable moral authority combined with little apparent power" (1976: 234).

Chiefs were aided by an array of advisors and administrators who were usually sons, brothers, or other close relatives of the incumbent. Assistant chiefs functioned as auxiliaries and substituted in the chief's absence, thereby gaining experience in the event that they would be chosen as successor. In addition, chiefs were assisted by messengers who made public announcements and travelled to other settlements to give or receive news. Messengers were appointed because of their oratorical skills and their "powers of observation," often serving as "Native gossip columnists" (Beals 1933). Chiefs and/or their assistants planned and coordinated ceremonial activities. Their ritual duties were augmented by designated dancers and singers.

In addition to individual aides, councils of elders gave advice to chiefs and ratified the decisions that were made. Councils were formed at several levels of sociopolitical integration. Lineage councils were composed of the lineage chief and his assistants and advisors. Councils of tribelets consisted of leaders of lineages, heads of large extended families, and other officials and administrators. Finally, chiefs of several neighboring or related tribelets formed intertribelet councils as well.

Second only to chiefs in social status were shamans. Shamans figured centrally in rituals and were the principal medical practitioners. They had access to spirit knowledge that enabled them to cure, foretell the future, control the weather, and perform magical acts such as transcending the bounds of space or transforming themselves into birds or animals. Shamans were respected members of their communities, but they were feared because they were thought to be able to use their spirit powers both for good and evil. They could cure illness and save a person from misfortune but they could also cause illness and death.

Gayton's (1930) study of Yokuts chiefs provides a blueprint for their behavior in many Californian nations. Yokuts chiefs were wealthy and respected members of their communities. Chiefly position was inherited, first by a younger brother and then by the former chief's eldest son (365). People were chosen on the basis of wealth, ability, and personality, but a person so selected could decline if they did not want to take on the responsibilities of office. Chiefs lived in a style somewhat better than others, but in practice there was not much difference because although accumulation of wealth was highly regarded, the actual range was slight. In fact, there were many mechanisms for circulating wealth, especially in giveaways that were held at mourning rituals (364). Chiefs accumulated food and other resources through gifts or tribute from young unmarried hunters. These supplies were given to visitors and messengers from other villages and were also distributed to elderly or poor members of the community. Chiefs also accumulated wealth through their roles as the center point of intertribal trade. When traders came to the village, chiefs might select the choicest products, which they could buy and resell at a profit. They shared in payments received by shamans who officiated at mourning rituals. And they obtained a percentage of all money, food, and other resources donated by spectators and participants in public rites and festivals. In addition, Yokuts chiefs had complex alliances with shamans. The two provided one another with reciprocal economic and political support. For example, chiefs could deflect accusations against a shaman suspected of causing illness or death through spirit means. And they could use their alliance with a shaman either to protect someone or to cause harm to a rival or enemy. In the words of a Yokuts consultant:

The chief always had money. People always made him presents when he was going to give a ceremony. If he got short of money he would have his doctor kill somebody who was rich. The victim chosen belonged to another tribe. He would send a gift of money to the chief of that tribe asking that he have his doctor kill the man. If the chief accepted the money he had his doctor proceed with the process of sickening and killing the man. The money received was divided between the chief and the doctor. Doctors who killed this way made sure that the patient would finally send for him by making him more sick for every other doctor the sick man sent for.

Usually we had good chiefs with good doctors, but sometimes even a good chief would bribe a doctor to kill some man he thought ought to be killed. (Quoted in Gayton 1930: 408)

Chiefs might order the killing of doctors and/or the chiefs with whom they were allied: "Sometimes a doctor would be killed who lost a patient. A doctor and his chief would meet the bereaved family and their chief for the supposed purpose of making an adjustment. A discussion was held and often the family killed the doctor and his chief right on the spot" (408).

In addition to chiefs and shamans, a number of other categories of people were differentiated from the common folk in aboriginal societies, principally specialists in various occupations. The number and distinctiveness of specialties differed in different nations. Occupational specialization was more likely in communities with high population densities and abundant resources. Specialists included traders, basketmakers, manufacturers of money, arrow-makers, potters, canoe-makers, and so forth. Most craft or occupational specializations were linked to gender. Women specialized in basketry and certain kinds of medical arts such as midwifery and herbal treatments while men made tools and equipment used in fishing and hunting. Together the elites constituted approximately 25 percent of the population. The majority of the population was commoners, people without rank or distinction in terms of wealth or ability (Bean 1976: 110).

In most indigenous nations, there also existed lower classes who were socially stigmatized in a variety of ways. They might be poor, physically handicapped, or orphaned and without the ability to support themselves. Others might be criticized as inept or lazy and therefore also incapable of full self-support. An additional group was even more strongly stigmatized as unacceptable, especially people who were vagabonds, morally loose, irresponsible, or criminals.

Finally, in some nations there was a small slave class, typically derived from people who were taken in raids from other groups. The children of slaves were not themselves in the slave class but they tended to

have lower social status than other people. Slaves usually remained with their "owners" for a relatively short time, however, being freed as part of negotiated settlements or by their own escape. Among some groups of northwestern California, people became slaves as the result of debts incurred by their actions. For example, a Yurok man who assaulted another or destroyed property became the slave of the person he had wronged and thereafter worked for his owner (Kroeber 1925: 32).

Although Californian nations recognized differences in status accruing from birth and inheritance, upward mobility from the lower groups was theoretically possible but limited in practice. According to Bean,

The elites, with their inherited power that brought wealth and privileges were in continual conflict with individuals from beneath their ranks who sought to acquire power, since power was potentially available to anyone. The elites, however, possessed control mechanisms for the sanctioning of power such as secret societies, initiation, and inheritance of rank, knowledge and control of ceremonial equipment. These mechanisms provided a means by which persons of lower rank, possessing skill and ambition might enter the system. Through such a licensing of power, bright young people of lower ranks were able to move upward, yet the power structure was always kept safe from serious disruption by malcontents with talent. (Bean 1975: 31)

Warfare

Despite generally friendly and cooperative relationships between neighboring groups, warfare occasionally occurred. Motives for conflicts varied but appear to have been of two general types: conflict over resource areas and revenge killings (McCorkle 1978). Disputes sometimes arose when trespassers entered a region without making proper requests and giving compensation for hunting, fishing, or gathering acorns in another's territory. Revenge killings might occur when the death of one's relative was thought to have been caused by witchcraft or the malevolent ministrations of a doctor. Military strategies included surprise attacks on villages or formal battles involving opposing lines of warriors who met at agreed-upon times and places. Relatively few casualties resulted from armed conflict although surprise attacks on villages probably resulted in more deaths than formal battles. Women and children were sometimes taken as prisoners whereas men were more likely to be killed. Most Californian nations had formal procedures for settling armed conflict. Among the Yuroks and other people of northwestern California, formal negotiations were carried out by go-betweens, who arranged for the amount of property to be paid as compensation for injuries incurred in raids and battles (Kroeber 1925: 20). Accordingly, victorious groups paid more compensation than did losers (Wallace 1949: 11). Elsewhere in California, chiefs acted as peacemakers, arranging for gifts to be exchanged in an attempt to settle disputes and end conflicts.

Aboriginal Ceremonial Systems

Californian nations were integrated through ceremonial networks that brought together hundreds of communities and thousands of people (Bean and Vane 1978: 662). The three major aboriginal religious systems were the World Renewal, Kuksu, and Toloache cults (Bean 1975, 1976; Kroeber 1925; Loeb 1932, 1933). Although they were primarily religious and ceremonial in nature, they included economic redistributions in the form of donations from participants and presentations of gifts made by hosts and visitors. One village in each tribelet usually functioned as a ceremonial center, attracting people from neighboring and even distant tribelets as well (Bean and King 1974; Blackburn 1974; Kroeber 1925).

The World Renewal religion was indigenous to Northwestern nations such as the Karok, Hupa, Yurok, and Tolowa. The constituent rituals performed annually focused on maintaining the world in its harmonious order, ensuring the replenishment of plant and animal life, protecting and augmenting human health, and securing the assistance of spirit powers. World Renewal rituals were planned and supervised by male shamans although female practitioners participated in subsidiary activities as curers. The annual ceremonials included the recitation of sacred stories describing the origin of the rites and their necessary reenactment in order to preserve the world and its creatures. Death and rebirth were symbolized by the rebuilding of sweathouses and ceremonial structures (Kroeber and Gifford 1949).

The religious system known as Kuksu was practiced in central and northcentral California by the Pomo, Miwok, Patwin, Maidu, and Yuki (Loeb 1932, 1933). The component rituals of the Kuksu religion focused on initiation of members (usually men) into secret ceremonial societies, temporary transformation of society members into spirit beings, and restoration of the sacred order that existed at the time of creation. Kuksu ceremonials also included public curing rites performed by shamans who extracted disease-causing objects that had invaded patients.

The third aboriginal religious system, called Toloache, involved the ceremonial use of Datura, a plant with narcotic properties that can produce altered states of consciousness. The Toloache cult, common in much of southcentral and southern California, was practiced by the Ipais, Luisenos, Serranos, Gabrielinos, and Cupeños (Blackburn 1974; Kroeber 1925). Datura was mixed into a drink and imbided by shamans, granting them access to spirit power that could be used for healing, performing magical acts, and causing harm. The drug was also taken in initiation rituals, especially by boys. Although men predominated in Toloache rites, women might participate in some groups.

THE SPANISH INVASION OF NATIVE CALIFORNIA

In 1542, an expedition led by Juan Cabrillo sailed up the coast of California to the Bay of San Diego and the Channel Islands in a vain quest for the mythical Strait of Anian or Northwest passage. Several subsequent explorations in the late sixteenth and early seventeenth centuries established ports along the coast, but none of these ventures was long-lasting. It was not until 1769 that the Spanish sent another expedition of soldiers and missionaries north from Mexico to California. Spanish forces eventually established twenty-one missions along the coast from San Diego to Sonoma by the early years of the nineteenth century. The missions and military forts (or "presidios") together achieved the virtual enslavement of tens of thousands of Native people who were forcibly removed from their homes and compelled to convert to Catholicism and labor for the financial benefit of the priests and soldiers.

Soon after their establishment, Spanish missions developed economies based on farming, ranching, and textile production. Native laborers grew corn, beans, wheat, barley, and various fruits and vegetables and tended cattle, horses, and sheep. In the early years of the nineteenth century, as agricultural and livestock production grew, farm produce, livestock, and textiles were sold to settlers and to the Spanish military (Jackson and Castillo 1995: 15–17).

In addition to compelling Native people to work at the missions, Spanish authorities attempted to alter aboriginal customs and beliefs. They forced people to convert to Catholicism, but they were not always successful in eradicating indigenous practices, especially at the larger missions where the inmates' numerical strength helped them withstand pressures to change by providing group support. Furthermore, new arrivals continued to reinvigorate indigenous culture and beliefs. The Spanish tried to undermine the role of traditional chiefs by appointing new leaders (called "alcaldes") but they rarely attained prestige among their fellow inmates. As noted by missionaries at the San Fernando Mission, "The Indians respect only those who were the chiefs of their rancherias in paganism" (quoted in Jackson and Castillo 1995: 38).

Inmates of the missions lived in virtual slavery. The slightest infractions were punished by beatings, solitary confinement, mutilation, branding, and execution (Castillo 1978: 101). Men were beaten in public view of others in order to serve as examples but, according to a French naval officer visiting the mission at San Carlos in 1786, "Women are never whipped in public, but in an enclosed and somewhat distant place that their cries may not excite a too lively compassion, which might cause the men to revolt" (Jackson and Castillo 1995: 83). And as one man recalled in the nineteenth century, "When I was a boy the treatment of the Indian was not any good—they did not pay us anything—they only gave us food, a loin cloth and a blanket every year, and many beatings for any mistake even if it was slight, it was more or less at the mercy of the administrator who ordered the beatings whenever and how many he felt like" (Castillo 1978: 102). In contrast to the testimony of captives, a Spanish priest named Francisco de Lasuen remarked: "It is evident that a nation which is barbarous, ferocious and ignorant requires more frequent punishment than a nation which is cultured, educated and of gentle and moderate customs" (Cook 1976a: 124). Not all priests, however, shared de Lasuen's attitudes. One, Antonio Horra, wrote in 1799 to the viceroy in Mexico, "The treatment shown to the Indians is the most cruel I have ever read in history. For the slightest things they receive heavy floggings, are shackled, and put in the stocks, and treated with so much cruelty that they are kept whole days without a drink of water" (Bancroft 1886–1890, 1: 593).

Unmarried men and women were housed in separate locked dormitories, described by the Russian explorer Otto von Kotzebue on a visit to Santa Clara Mission in 1824,

These dungeons [large dormitories without windows] are opened two or three times a day, but only to allow the prisoners to pass to and from church. I have occasionally seen the poor girls rushing out eagerly to breathe the fresh air, and driven immediately into the church like a flock of sheep. After mass, they are in the same manner, hurried back to their prison. (Jackson and Castillo 1995: 81)

From the first founding of missions in 1769 until they were secularized by the Mexican government in 1832, the decline in the Native population was catastrophic. The most significant cause of death, accounting for about one-half of the reduction, was disease (Cook 1976a: 13). While pneumonia, diphtheria, measles, dysentery, and influenza took many lives, the most devastating disease was syphilis. Spaniards began to infect Indian women with syphilis almost from the moment of their arrival in the territory. Cook cites numerous excerpts from Spanish journals commenting on the frequent rape of Native women by soldiers and settlers. One, for example, written in 1785, concerned soldiers near San Juan Capistrano: "The officers and men of these presidios are behaving themselves in the missions with a vicious license which is very prejudicial on account of the scandalous disorders which they commit with the gentile and Christian women" (Cook 1976a: 25). Cook estimates that by the nineteenth century, syphilis had become nearly universal in the indigenous population. The disease had a disastrous effect not only by causing deaths but by leaving survivors with chronic disabilities that made them more likely to contract and die from other illnesses. Syphilis may also have had a role in lowering birth rates and thereby reducing the population over time.

The crowded and unsanitary conditions of the missions also contributed to the spread of disease and the incidence of early deaths. As one nineteenth-century observer remarked,

The Indians in their wandering life as savages enjoyed good health … Afterward very harmful to them was enclosure within infected walls, according to the system adopted by the missionaries … The walls usually were a yard thick and lacked necessary ventilation: imagine the odor which would emanate from those never-washed bodies, without being able to change the air. (Cook 1976a: 32)

Once housed at the missions, Indians were restricted in their diet, mainly consisting of grains and beef. In fact, missionaries barred neophytes from utilizing the wild foods in adjacent land that might have afforded them a balanced nutritional supply because they wanted to prevent the people from engaging in any activities that were derived from their aboriginal life.

In addition to missions, the Spanish established numerous forts, the largest at San Diego, Santa Barbara, Monterey, and San Francisco. Indigenous inhabitants of the area nearby were captured and forced to work in the forts and in the homes of soldiers and settlers. And Native women were often kept to serve the soldiers sexually.

Resistance to foreign control began shortly after the Spanish invasions of 1769. Uprisings occurred sporadically but the numbers of people involved were usually too small to effect a lasting victory over the intruders. Never previously having had a need for unified political or military action, Indians were not in the habit of large-scale coordinated military campaigns, but resistance intensified in the nineteenth century nonetheless. Missions were destroyed, soldiers were attacked, and occasionally the priests were killed. Most resistance was small scale and uncoordinated but more organized revolts also took place. The largest was that of the 1824 Chumash rebellion that involved residents of three missions. The revolt lasted about one month but ended unsuccessfully.

More common than military action, however, was a kind of passive resistance that took several forms. The most frequent was escape from the missions. In most instances, people fled individually or in small groups, but in a few cases, hundreds managed mass escapes. Although successful escapes benefitted the individuals involved, they began a process of introducing diseases that had been contracted in the missions into interior territory that had been untouched by direct Spanish conquest.

Another form of passive resistance was the resort to abortion and infanticide. Although such practices occurred in aboriginal times either to limit family size to adapt to available resources or to eliminate deformed infants, both abortion and infanticide increased in the missions as a conscious or unconscious attempt to defy the oppressors and as an "escape for the child from the environment of the progenitor, resistance to the

system which seeks to augment the number of [captives]" (Cook 1976a: 112).

The psychological toll that mission life exacted on Native people must have been enormous. The confinement, change of diet, restrictions on behavior, forced labor, punishments, segregation of men and women, and total loss of independence and respect were all devastating personal traumas.

Although initially not as severely traumatized, Indians who escaped from the missions or who continued to live in the interior also suffered a number of ancillary effects. Soldiers who were sent on raids to recapture escapees attacked their settlements, capturing or killing the inhabitants, destroying their property and stores of food. As a result, many villages were deserted and aboriginal subsistence patterns undermined. Furthermore, diseases spread from mission residents to those of the interior when the former escaped. Syphilis, dysentery, tuberculosis, and influenza spread throughout Native California in the first few decades of the nineteenth century. One of the worst episodes was the pandemic of 1833 which, although uncertain in its specific etiology, was possibly cholera or typhus. Citing just a few examples of the devastation, contemporary authorities estimated mortality in the San Joaquin Valley at 12,000 and another 8,000 in the Sacramento Valley (Cook 1976a: 211). According to observers describing the results of the epidemic, "whole tribes [were] exterminated," "the stench of dead bodies was almost intolerable," and "heaps of bones were a common sight" (211). Only four years later, an epidemic of smallpox spread through much of northern California with similar results.

After Mexico won its independence from Spain in 1821, the colonial administration of California passed to the Mexican government. Little changed initially for indigenous people but previous trends continued. As settlement of interior California expanded, enslavement and exploitation by Hispanic settlers increased. In response, Indians turned to armed resistance that, while successful in certain encounters, was not sufficient to counter the Mexican military. And more people died as diseases continued to spread inland.

In 1832, the Mexican government began the process of secularizing the missions, relieving the Franciscan priests of control. However, rather than freeing Indians from their plight, secular authorities established a system of peonage that replaced religious personnel with civilians. Ranches that had been established by Spanish soldiers and settlers with coerced labor continued to expand and become more numerous under

Chumash musicians at Mission San Buenaventura, 1873.

as they reached our shore the troops, the civilians and the auxiliaries surrounded them and tied them up … We separated a hundred Christians. At every half mile we put six of them on their knees to say their prayers, making them understand that they were about to die. Each one was shot with four arrows. Those who refused to die immediately were killed with spears … On the road we killed in this manner one hundred Christians [Then the non-Christians] should be told they were going to die and they should be asked if they wanted to be made Christians. We baptized all the Indians and afterwards they were shot in the back. At the first volley seventy fell dead. I doubled the charge for the thirty who remained and they all fell. (Cook 1962: 197–198)

Mexican jurisdiction (Forbes 1969: 31). And once the missions were converted into towns (or "pueblos"), their resources, tools, and food supplies were often taken by settlers, leaving the Indians destitute. Still, many remained in the pueblos or sought work at ranches because their options were limited by the loss of their land and resources. As a prior resident of Mission Delores observed: "I am very old … my people were once around me like the sands of the shore … many … many. They have all passed away. They have died like the grass. I had a son. I loved him. When the palefaces came he went away. I do not know where he is. I am a Christian Indian, I am all that is left of my people. I am alone" (Castillo 1978: 105).

Although the Mexican government officially recognized Indians as citizens having rights to their land by reason of occupancy, Hispanic settlers continued to invade Native territory, taking land for their farms and towns. Warfare increased throughout California as settlers penetrated further into the interior, disrupting Native life, destroying resources, capturing children for the slave trade, and murdering the adults. It was not unusual for Mexican militias and vigilantes to massacre whole villages of people. In the words of a Mexican chronicler writing in 1837:

Amador [leader of an expedition] invited the wild Indians and their Christian companions to come and have a feast of pinole and dried meat. As soon

Faced with imminent starvation, Indians sometimes raided Hispanic settlements, stealing livestock in order to eat. These "depredations" were answered with repeated invasions into Native territory, resulting in retaliatory executions of many innocent people. Still, the Native response intensified and, realizing that they had few options but to fight, attacks against Hispanic settlements increased, leading to more retaliation and violence.

US CONTROL OF CALIFORNIA

The end of Mexican hegemony in California with the signing of the Treaty of Guadalupe-Hidalgo did not end the conditions that indigenous inhabitants faced. After the discovery of gold in California lured thousands of American prospectors and settlers to the region, Indians experienced even more brutality and devastation than they had known under Spanish and Mexican rule. Americans viewed the aboriginal inhabitants as impediments to their access to and control over the region. Accordingly, Indians were hunted down and murdered in order to open more land for settlement. Raids against Native communities carried out by private militias and vigilantes were paid for by the federal government, which reimbursed expenses for guns, ammunition, horses, and supplies (Castillo 1978: 108).

Laws were passed in California that harassed those Native Californians who survived. For example, in 1850, the state legislature enacted a law entitled "Act for the Government and Protection of Indians," providing that "Any Indian able to work who shall be found loitering and strolling about … shall be liable to be arrested on the complaint of any resident citizen … and brought before any Justice of the Peace … who shall [authorize] him to hire out such vagrant to the best bidder … for four months" (Heizer and Almquist 1971: 215). After passage of the law, nearby Indians were forced into indenture through procedures having the stamp of law. Excursions into the interior to kidnap children became common. According to the Humboldt Times in 1855: "A large number of children have been brought down and sold in the agricultural counties. They bring from $50 to $250 each" (41). And in 1862, an army officer named Colonel Frances Lippitt reported: "Individuals and parties are constantly engaged in kidnapping Indian children, frequently attacking the rancherias, and killing the parents for no other purpose. This is said to be a very lucrative business, the kidnapped children bringing good prices, in some instances hundreds of dollars apiece" (43). Raids on Native communities to steal children increased at least until 1867 when the fourteenth amendment of the constitution forced the California legislature to repeal their laws. But by then more than 4,000 Indian children had been taken (Castillo 1978: 109).

Unlike Hispanic settlers who were concentrated along the coasts, Americans ventured into the interior, taking land and resources and wreaking havoc on indigenous communities. Diseases, too, continued to take their deadly toll. In addition to the widespread incidence of syphilis, diseases such as dysentery, tuberculosis, cholera, typhoid, malaria, smallpox, measles, influenza, and diphtheria were common (Cook 1976a: 274).

Hunger and starvation were also endemic in many communities due to the loss of resources, the fencing of land by American settlers, destruction of grasses and seeds by cattle and hogs, and dispersal of Indians from their traditional villages. People were often forced to flee their homes, not only abandoning their familiar communities but leaving behind their stored provisions. In desperation, raids on American livestock increased, only to be met by wholescale retaliation. Many men, unable to provide from their environment, sought work farming the fields and tending the livestock of settlers while women worked as domestics and prostitutes, but the conditions under which Indians labored were often no better than what they had experienced in the missions. For example, in the words of James Clyman, a visitor to Sutter's Fort in 1846:

> The captain [Sutter] keeps 600 or 800 Indians in a complete state of Slavery and I had the mortification of seeing them dine I may give a short description 10 or 15 Troughs 3 or 4 feet long were brought out of the cook room and seated in the Broiling sun all the laborers grate and small ran to the troughs like so many pigs and feed themselves with their hands as long as the troughs contain even a moisture. (Heizer and Almquist 1971: 19)

Responding to accounts of the deplorable conditions of Native Californians, the federal government began to negotiate treaties and establish reservations in the 1850s, which would offer protection from invasions and confiscation of land and persons. The government initially distributed rations, tools, and clothing but these were in short supply and of inferior quality. After conducting an investigation of federal aid policies, J. Ross Browne observed sarcastically:

> The blankets, to be sure, were very thin, and cost a great deal of money in proportion to their value; but then, peculiar advantages were to be derived from the transparency of the fabric. By holding his blanket to the light, an Indian could enjoy the contemplation of both sides of it at the same time; and it would only require a little instruction in architecture to enable him to use it occasionally as a window to his wigwam. (Browne 1944: 28–29)

In any event, most of the money provided for food and equipment was embezzled by agents in charge. As Browne concluded, "The results of the policy pursued were precisely such as might have been expected. A very large amount of money annually expended in feeding white men and starving Indians … What neglect, starvation, and disease has not done, has been achieved by the cooperation of the white settlers in the great work of extermination" (50–54).

Farms that Native people had begun to work on their reservations were often destroyed by livestock and occupied by Anglo and Hispanic squatters. As Browne remarked in congressional hearings:

> In the history of Indian races I have seen nothing so cruel and relentless as the treatment of these unhappy people by the authorities constituted by law for their protection. Instead of receiving aid and succor, they have been starved and driven away from the reservation, and then followed into their remote hiding places, where they sought to die in peace, and cruelly slaughtered, till but few are left, and that few without hope. (Castillo 1978: 111)

In response to growing pressure exerted by settlers, the California state government began to withdraw support from reservations, forcing many residents to leave and eke out a bare survival wherever they could. Not surprisingly, the Native population continued to decline from disease, poor living conditions, and armed attacks against their surviving communities.

In the 1870s, the federal government again established reservations for Indians in southern California. Some funds were provided to aid people in farming. Schools were established in an attempt to teach children American values and practices but many parents did not want their children to go to schools, preferring that they grow up in Native traditions. Within a few decades, most Native territory in southern California was once again confiscated. For example, in 1903, Cupeños were evicted from their homes at Warner's Ranch, forced to gather their belongings and move to Pala, California. One evictee later recalled:

> First they said, "Go see your relatives for the last time." They went to the cemetery, there they wept. Then it was time to move out. Still they did not move … they still stayed there by the gate. And my greatgrandmother went running to the mountain. And she said, "Here I will stay, even if I die, even if the coyotes eat me." The people moved out from the cemetery. They were weeping. And then from there they moved us. And they said to them, "Now, look behind you, see your homes for the last time." But no one turned around … they did not look back again. They were very angry. And they said, "Tomorrow up there sometime that water will dry up, then you'll learn your lesson." (Quoted in Bahr 1993: 46–47)

Land continued to be taken from Native control through procedures established earlier by the General Allotment Act of 1887, providing for the breakup of reservations into individually owned parcels of 160 acres each and the eventual sale of much of the property to outsiders. "Surplus" land remaining after allotment was opened for American settlement. Additionally, land was taken out of Native use by the frequent leasing of reservation acreage to ranchers and farmers.

Given the dismal economic conditions of Native communities in the late nineteenth century, the population decline that left nearly 300,000 dead and the survivors physically and psychologically debilitated, the continual pressure on what little land they still controlled, the abridgement of their civil and human rights, and the bleak outlook for the future, a number of new or syncretic religious movements arose or were integrated into existing beliefs. When the Ghost Dance originating among the Nevada Northern Paiutes in 1870 spread to California, it was received with enthusiasm, particularly among Native communities in the north (DuBois 1939). Prophecies of a new beginning, the return of better conditions, and the renewal of the earth gave hope to a people on the brink of despair. The teachings of the Ghost Dance also provided people with a feeling of unity and connectedness in a social and psychological environment that was otherwise fraught with division. The Ghost Dance often became amalgamated with aboriginal beliefs and practices. For example, beliefs in individual access to spirit powers, long a part of traditional shamanistic and healing practices, became a focus of the Ghost Dance. And the ritual structures that had been used for the ancient Kuksu rites were transformed into Ghost Dance lodges.

Among the Pomos, Patwins, and Maidus, a new religion developed called the Dreamer or Bole-Maru religion (DuBois 1939). Bole-Maru dreamers had access to spirit power that they used for curing. They preached the importance of cooperative social relations and forbade disruptive behavior such as drinking, stealing, and quarreling. In addition, the Shaker Church, founded in the 1870s by the Coast Salish in the state of Washington also spread to northwestern California in the 1920s. It was most accepted by Hupas, Yuroks, Tolowas, and Wiyots. Shakers stressed the importance of people's personal access to the spirit world and the unity of believers dedicated to following principles of moralistic and cooperative behavior. Both the Bole-Maru and Shaker religions are practiced today in several northern California Indian communities.

In the early twentieth century, some lands were again set aside for indigenous residents of California so that by 1930, thirty-six reservations had been established, most in the north. Although people attempted to farm their land, they faced difficulties primarily because of the lack of water sources, which had been diverted to surrounding communities. By that year, approximately 19,000 Native people resided in the state of California, approximately one-half living on reservations (Castillo 1978: 121).

CONTEMPORARY NATIVE COMMUNITIES

Recognizing that they lived in small communities scattered throughout the state, Native Californians formed a number of regional and statewide organizations in order to have a more unified voice when dealing with state and federal authorities. In 1919, the Society of Northern Californian Indians was established to advocate legal representation and land rights for its members. The Federation of Mission Indians was also founded, similarly to improve conditions for the descendants of the southern California mission Indians.

A principal priority of both organizations was securing compensation for lands ceded in 1851 and 1852 when reservations were first established. After years of litigation, the US Congress voted in 1928 to permit the state of California to submit claims on behalf of Native residents to the US Court of Claims. However, the bill was actually detrimental to Native interests for several reasons. First, the money to be awarded as compensation was not to exceed $1.25 per acre. Second, all funds that had been dispersed by the federal government from 1851 until passage of the act were to be deducted from the award (Forbes 1969: 104). During the ensuing decades, numerous attempts at reaching settlements were negotiated and renegotiated. Finally, in 1944, a compromise was achieved in which $17,530,941 was granted in compensation, subject to a deduction of over $12 million for federal expenses, leaving Californian Indians with just over $5 million as compensation for 75 million acres of land covered by 18 treaties that their ancestors had signed.

A second series of land claims cases were settled in the 1950s and 1960s, involving some 91 million acres not included in the first case since the acreage concerned had not been covered by the treaties of 1851 and 1852. In 1964, a compromise settlement of $29.1 million was agreed upon as compensation. By 1971, the amount plus interest had increased to more than $37 million, available for per capita distribution to approximately 65,000 Native residents of California who were judged to be eligible descendants of nineteenth-century inhabitants (Stewart 1978: 708, 13 Ind. Cl. Comm. 369).

Shortly after World War II, the federal government adopted a new policy toward reservations, intending to "terminate" the special trust status of Native land and end funding of services to their communities. Congress acted to terminate reservation status in California despite the opposition of the majority of the people affected. Succumbing to pressure from the BIA in support of termination, thirty-six rancherias in California voted to end their trust status, resulting in the loss of some 5,000 acres of land and the end of federal support (Castillo 1978: 123).

Since the 1960s, organizations have been formed to address health, educational, and social needs of California Indians. The American Indian Historical Society has advocated the protection of aboriginal burial grounds. The California Indian Education Association has attempted to address educational needs of Native students. In southern California, regional organizations have been formed to address health, educational, and community needs, including the All-Mission Indian Housing Authority, Inter-Tribal Council of California, and California Rural Indian Health Program. Finally, the founding of several Native American studies departments in major universities in the state has energized historical and anthropological research of Native California and also supports modern literatures and cultural developments.

Despite the dislocations, migrations, and transformations experienced during the past two centuries, many aboriginal ethical principles continue to integrate Native families and communities in California. The importance of extended kinship ties, providing reciprocal aid and emotional and financial support, remain important features of family life. Feelings of responsibility to members of one's family and community are strong, reflected in generous aid and willingness to share whatever resources one has with others in need. And although most Native Californians are Christians, there is evidence of the continuity of aboriginal beliefs as well. For example, Bahr's study of Cupeño women in Los Angeles indicates beliefs in individual healing powers and access to spirit power through visionary experience, the importance of dreams as vehicles for receiving messages from the spirit world and from deceased relatives, the revelatory aspect of dreams in foretelling the future, and beliefs that omens or premonitions may also foretell future events (119–135).

Discussion of indigenous communities in California is complicated because of the migration of tens of thousands of Indians from elsewhere in the United States to the state, particularly since the 1940s and 1950s when the federal government instituted its Job Relocation Program. The program was supposedly an attempt to better economic conditions of people living on reservations who lacked employment opportunities by providing job training and transportation to major cities in the Midwest and west. In fact, the program was a failure, in part because training was either not provided or was inadequate to meet the demands of the existing job market in the cities to which people were drawn. Many participants either ended up returning to their own reservation communities or living in poor ghettos in cities like San Francisco and Los Angeles. There has also been a high rate of in-state migration from rural areas in California to the cities by people seeking work. The increase in the Native urban population during the twentieth century has far outpaced the rural communities. While the rural population in 1970 (16,476) was just slightly more than it had been in 1890, the number of Native residents of California cities in 1970 (69,802) was a dramatic increase over the figure of 281 reported for 1890 (Cook 1976b: 178). The 1980 US census reported some 200,000 Indians in California, about half of whom live in and around San Francisco, Los Angeles, and Long Beach (Bahr 1993: 54). By 2010, the Native population of Los Angeles alone was estimated at about 54,000.

Indigenous communities suffer from economic, educational, and health deficits. A study conducted in 1999 of Indians in Los Angeles indicated 15.6 percent were living below the poverty line (58). Rates of unemployment and underemployment are obviously extremely high. Economic statistics compiled for 2010 indicate that incomes of most recognized California Indian tribes are about the average for American Indians, although some deviate from the norm by a considerable amount. Table 17.1 presents data for selected groups. Only a few groups have per capita income that comes close to the California average of $27,353.

And only the Cahuilla and Elk Valley poverty rates are near the norm for California, that is, 11.8 percent

TABLE 17.1	Selected Economic Characteristics for California Tribes			
	Income ($)		Below Poverty (%)	
	Per Capita	Household	Families	Individuals
Cahuilla	25,054	39,375	5.8	14.8
Pala	19,549	48,542	28.8	32.4
Morongo*	53,397	84,167	35.6	30.6
Hoopa Valley	13,017	31,654	23.1	27.8
Karok	8,057	17,500	54.2	64.3
Trinidad	16,520	39,375	20.0	20.5
Quartz Valley	16,789	25,625	32.3	31.5
Grindstone	8,273	19,500	50.0	60.8
Tule River	15,018	37,604	17.3	17.7
Santa Rosa	10,347	48,750	17.5	17.5
Elk Valley	31,497	69,750	0.0	0.0
Smith River	25,326	28,125	24.0	29.6
Yurok	13,729	26,953	34.6	32.6

Source: Selected Economic Characteristics, 2006–2010: American Community Survey 5-Year Estimates.

*Data is from 2009 community survey. Some tribes/rancherias/reservations were not included because the data sample was unavailable or too small to be statistically significant.

for families, 15.8 percent for individuals, while most California Indians have poverty rates that are twice or three times the California average (465).

In order to improve economic conditions, numerous tribes have opened casinos in the very profitable California market. Estimates suggest that statewide economic benefits are provided by Indian casinos, such as over $7 billion in taxes and the creation of over 56,000 jobs. Native casinos as a whole earned $26.5 billion in 2011, which explains the high income and low poverty rates for some nations in table 17.1 (500 Nations; Wood 2012; Beacon Economics 2014). Native representatives of fifty-eight tribes negotiated a pact with state authorities that allows and expands some forms of gaming, sets the number of permissible slot machines, and provides for a revenue-sharing arrangement so that tribes without gaming can obtain a portion of the profits from the casinos. The state will receive a percentage of the profits as well. The new-found wealth of a small number of California tribes has increased their political clout in the state. They are in a position to influence state and congressional representatives through political contributions, a position quite different from the past when Native interests were generally ignored.

Indigenous California was and continues to be an area of cultural and linguistic diversity. But from an estimated eighty to one hundred languages spoken prior to European colonization, about thirty still have speakers. However, in many cases, these languages are now spoken by one or only a few elderly people. An organization called Advocates for Indigenous California Language Survival was formed in 1992 to address the issue of language loss. According to their data, people in about thirty of the communities where the languages are no longer spoken have begun efforts to regain their linguistic heritage. Because of the work of linguists and anthropologists from the University of California at Berkeley and other universities in the state, many of these languages are well documented but the path from written resources to spoken language is not always an easy one. The use of immersion retreats and master-apprentice pairings, matching fluent elders with younger learners can be quite helpful. And the use of computer and video technologies can also encourage young people to participate. Much of this work is supported by money donated by various tribes from earnings produced by casino revenues. For example, the Chukchansi Indians living in the Sierra Nevada foothills donated $1 million to the linguistics

department at California State University at Fresno to develop resources to help restore and preserve their language.

Contemporary Populations

According to federal census figures for 2010, there were 281,908 Indians living in California but only around 11,000–12,000 were resident on reservations and trust lands (US Bureau of the Census 2010). Of 103 reservations and trust areas in the state, 67 contain less than 1,000 acres of land, 15 contain between 1,000 and 10,000 acres, while only a few contain more than 10,000 (Bureau of Indian Affairs 1985). The largest is the Hoopa Reservation, consisting of some 93,000 acres, located in northwestern California. Several Cahuilla and Ipai-Tipai reservations in southern California contain approximately 30,000 acres of land. Most reservations have small populations, numbering in the hundreds. Even the relatively large Hoopa Reservation has only 3,115 Native residents. Reservation populations, however, do not account for the majority of Indians because of the history of land tenure and displacement in California. Since most of the treaties signed by Native representatives in the nineteenth century were never ratified by Congress, indigenous communities have not always been officially recognized as such. Numerous additional reservations and rancherias were "terminated" in the 1950s and 1960s. Even though California has the largest number of recognized tribes compared to other states, it also has the largest number of "unacknowledged Indian people and more groups seeking to apply for federal acknowledgement" (Goldberg 1997: 185).

REFERENCES

Bahr, Diana. 1993. *From Mission to Metropolis: Cupeño Indian Women in Los Angeles*. Norman, OK: University of Oklahoma Press.

Bancroft, Hubert. 1886–1890. *The History of California*, 7 vols. San Francisco, CA: The History Company.

Barrett, S. A. 1917. *Ceremonies of the Pomo Indians*. Berkeley, CA: University of California Publications in American Archeology and Ethnology, 12.10, p. 406.

Beacon Economics, LLC. 2014. *2014 California Tribal Gaming Impact Study*. The California Nations Indian Gaming Association. Online.

Beals, Ralph. 1933. *Ethnology of the Nisenan.* Berkeley, CA: University of California Publications in American Archeology and Ethnology No. 31, pp. 335–414.

Bean, Lowell. 1975. "Power and Its Application in Native California." *Journal of California Anthropology* 2: 25–33.

Bean, Lowell. 1976. "Social Organization in Native California." *Native Californians: A Theoretical Retrospective* (ed. L. Bean and T. Blackburn). Ramona, CA: Ballena Press, pp. 99–124.

Bean, Lowell, and Thomas King (eds.). 1974. *Antap: California Indian Political and Economic Organization.* Ramona, CA: Ballena Press Anthropological Papers No. 2.

Bean, Lowell, and Harry Lawton. 1976. "Some Explanations for the Rise of Cultural Complexity in Native California with Comments on Proto-Agriculture and Agriculture." *Native Californians: A Theoretical Retrospective* (ed. L. Bean and T. Blackburn). Ramona, CA: Ballena Press, pp. 19–48.

Bean, Lowell, and Dorothea Theodoratus. 1978. "Western Pomo and Northeastern Pomo." California (ed. R. Heizer), Vol. 8 of *Handbook of North American Indians.* Washington, DC: Smithsonian Institution, pp. 298–305.

Bean, Lowell, and Sylvia Vane. 1978. "Cults and Their Transformations." California (ed. R. Heizer), Vol. 8 of *Handbook of North American Indians.* Washington, DC: Smithsonian Institution, pp. 662–672.

Bennyhoff, James, and Robert Heizer. 1958. "Cross-Dating Great Basin Sites by Californian Shell Beads." Berkeley, CA: University of California Archeological Survey Reports No. 42, pp. 60–92.

Blackburn, Thomas. 1974. "Ceremonial Integration and Social Interaction in Aboriginal California." *Native Californians: A Theoretical Retrospective* (ed. L. Bean and T. Blackburn). Ramona, CA: Ballena Press, pp. 225–244.

Bright, William. 1964. *Studies in Californian Linguistics.* Berkeley, CA: University of California Publications in Linguistics No. 34.

Browne, J. Ross. 1944. *The Indians of California.* San Francisco, CA: Colt Press.

Bureau of Indian Affairs. 1985. *Annual Report of Indian Lands.* Washington, DC.

"California Elections Confirm Tribal Gaming Is the Force to Be Reckoned with." 1999. *American Indian Report.* pp. 8–9.

"California Tribes Reach a Compromise with the State." 1999. *American Indian Report.* October. pp. 20–21

Castillo, Edward. 1978. "The Impact of Euro-American Exploration and Settlement." *California* (ed. R. Heizer), Vol. 8 of *Handbook of North American Indians.* Washington, DC: Smithsonian Institution, pp. 99–127.

Cook, Sherburne. 1962. "Expeditions to the Interior of California: Central Valley, 1820–1840." Berkeley, CA: University of California Anthropological Records No. 20, pp. 151–214.

Cook, Sherburne. 1976a. *The Conflict between the California Indian and White Civilization.* Berkeley, CA: University of California Press.

Cook, Sherburne. 1976b. *The Population of the California Indians: 1769–1970.* Berkeley, CA: University of California Press.

Cook, Sherburne. 1978. "Historical Demography." *California* (ed. R. Heizer), Vol. 8 of *Handbook of North American Indians.* Washington, DC: Smithsonian Institution, pp. 91–98.

DuBois, Cora. 1939. *The 1870 Ghost Dance.* Berkeley, CA: University of California Anthropological Records 3.1, pp. 1–151.

Forbes, Jack. 1969. *Native Americans of California and Nevada.* Healdsburg, CA: Naturegraph Publishers.

Gayton, Anna. 1930. *Yokuts-Mono Chiefs and Shamans.* Berkeley, CA: University of California Publications in American Archeology and Ethnology, No. 24, pp. 361–420.

Gayton, Anna. 1945. "Yokuts and Western Mono Social Organization." *American Anthropologist* 47: 409–426.

Gifford, Edward. 1926. "Miwok Lineages and the Political Unit in Aboriginal California." *American Anthropologist* 28: 389–401.

Goldberg, Carole. 1997. "Acknowledging the Repatriation Claims of Unacknowledged California Tribes." *American Indian Culture & Research Journal* 21, no. 3: 183–190.

Heizer, Robert. 1941. "Aboriginal Trade between the Southwest and California." *Masterkey* 15, no. 5: 185–188.

Heizer, Robert. 1946. "The Occurrence and Significance of Southwestern Grooved Axes in California." *American Antiquity* 11, no. 3: 187–193.

Heizer, Robert. 1968. *The Indians of Los Angeles County: Hugo Reid's Letters of 1852.* Los Angeles, CA: Southwest Museum Papers No. 21.

Heizer, Robert, and Alan Almquist. 1971. *The Other Californians: Prejudice and Discrimination under Spain, Mexico and the United States to 1920.* Berkeley, CA: University of California Press.

Heizer, R., and M. Whipple (eds.). 1971. *The California Indians: A Source Book.* Berkeley, CA: University of California Press.

Holt, Catharine. 1946. *Shasta Ethnography.* Berkeley, CA: University of California Anthropological Records No. 3, pp. 299–349.

Jackson, Robert, and Edward Castillo. 1995. *Indians, Franciscans, and Spanish Colonization: The Impact of the Mission System on California Indians.* Albuquerque, NM: University of Mexico Press.

King, Chester. 1976. "Chumash Inter-Village Economic Exchange." *Native Californians: A Theoretical Retrospective* (ed. L. Bean and T. Blackburn). Ramona, CA: Ballena Press, pp. 289–318.

Kroeber, Alfred. 1925. *Handbook of the Indians of California*. Washington, DC: Bureau of American Ethnology, Bulletin No. 78.

Kroeber, Alfred. 1962. "The Nature of Land-Holding Groups in Aboriginal California." Berkeley, CA: Report of the University of California Archeological Survey No. 56, pp. 19–58.

Kroeber, Alfred. 1971. "Elements of Culture in Native California." *The California Indians: A Source Book* (ed. R. Heizer and M. Whipple). Berkeley, CA: University of California Press, pp. 3–65.

Kroeber, Alfred, and Edward Gifford. 1949. *Renewal: A Cult System of Native Northwest California*. Berkeley, CA: University of California Anthropological Records, No. 13, pp. 1–156.

Kunkel, Peter. 1974. "The Pomo Kin-Group and the Political Unit in Aboriginal California." *Journal of California Anthropology* 1: 7–18.

Loeb, Edwin. 1932. *The Western Kuksu Cult*. Berkeley, CA: University of California Publications in American Archeology and Ethnology No. 33, pp. 1–137.

Loeb, Edwin. 1933. *The Eastern Kuksu Cult*. Berkeley, CA: University of California Publications in American Archeology and Ethnology No. 33, pp. 139–232.

McCorkle, Thomas. 1978. "Intergroup Conflict." California (ed. R. Heizer), Vol. 8 of *Handbook of North American Indians*. Washington, DC: Smithsonian Institution, pp. 694–700.

Powers, Stephen. 1877. *Tribes of California*. Washington, DC: US Geographical and Geological Survey of the Rocky Mountain Region, Contributions to North American Ethnology No. 3.

Reid, Hugo. 1968. *The Indians of Los Angeles County: Hugo Reid's Letters of 1852* (ed. R. Heizer). Los Angeles, CA: Southwest Museum Papers No. 21.

Shipley, William. 1973. "California." *Current Trends in Linguistics* (ed. T. Sebeok), Vol. 10. The Hague: Mouton, pp. 1046–1078.

Simpson, Lesley. 1939. *California in 1792: The Expedition of Longinos Martinez*. San Marino, CA: Huntington Library.

Stewart, Omer. 1978. "Litigation and Its Effects." *California* (ed. R. Heizer), Vol. 8 of *Handbook of North American Indians*. Washington, DC: Smithsonian Institution. pp. 705–712.

Swanton, John. 1907. "Media of Exchange." *Handbook of North American Indians North of Mexico* (ed. F. Hodge), vol. 1. Washington, DC: Bureau of American Ethnology Bulletin No. 30, pp. 446–448.

US Bureau of the Census. 2010.

Wallace, William. 1949. *Hupa Warfare*. Los Angeles, CA: Southwest Museum Leaflets No. 23.

Willoughby, Nona. 1963. *Division of Labor among the Indians of California*. Berkeley, CA: University of California Archeological Survey Reports, No. 60, pp. 7–79.

Wood, Robert. 2012. "Native American Casino and Tax Rules That May Surprise You." *Forbes*. Online.

The Pomos

It's time for us to stand up, speak out … It's who we are in the history of things.

Violet Chappell; quoted in Sarris 1992: 79

THE POMOS are aboriginal inhabitants of coastal and interior California north of San Francisco. They were not a unified nation but rather were members of seven distinct linguistic groups whose separate languages, although related to each other, are mutually unintelligible. The seven Pomoan groups are known as the Kashaya, southern Pomo, central Pomo, northern Pomo, eastern Pomo, northeastern Pomo, and southeastern Pomo.

These names have been used in the anthropological literature since the late nineteenth century, but they are territorial designations, obviously not translations of the people's names for themselves. In the past, two forms of the general word naming the people were used, that is, "Pomo" and "Poma," but the former has eclipsed the latter. In the northern Pomoan language, "pomo" means "at red earth hole" while "poma" is added to placenames with the meaning "people who reside at X" (McLendon and Oswalt 1978: 277).

With the exception of the northeastern Pomo, Pomoan territories were contiguous. Together, the lands of the Kashayas, central, and northern Pomos extended about 70 mi. along the Pacific coast north of Bodega Bay and inland about 50 mi. at its widest point. The southern, eastern, and southeastern Pomos held inland regions. Kashaya and southern Pomo territory encompassed the Russian River valley while that of eastern and southeastern Pomos included Clear Lake and two smaller connected lakes called East Lake and Lower Lake. The land of northeastern Pomos was separated from that of other Pomoan groups, lying to their northeast along Stony Creek on the northeastern side of the Coast Range (277–287).

Of the Pomoan languages, those of the Kashaya, southern Pomo, and central Pomo are most closely related while the language of southeastern Pomos is the most distinct (Oswalt 1964). Pomoan languages constitute one of the linguistic families belonging to the Hokan stock, probably the oldest linguistic grouping of aboriginal California. Speakers of other Hokan languages are found elsewhere in the southern, southwestern, and northern regions of California.

ABORIGINAL CULTURE

Settlements

Pomoan nations differed from one another in cultural practices but recognized a common heritage and both cultural and linguistic similarities. According to Gifford and Kroeber, "What we call Pomo refers to … a sort of nationality varying around a basic type … There was a series of highly similar but never quite identical Pomo cultures, each carried by one of the independent communities or tribelets" (1939: 119). Each Pomoan group consisted of several dozen villages and smaller settlements. Most villages contained several hundred inhabitants, although some were smaller and a few were much larger, possibly numbering more than 1,000. Kroeber estimated their total aboriginal population at about 8,000, living in some seventy-five stable villages (1925: 237–238). There were probably about 500 settlements in all, many of them seasonal encampments (229). According to Stewart (1943), the Pomo constituted 34 tribelets occupying some 3,370 sq. mi. of territory. Based on estimates of about 8,000 indigenous Pomoans, Cook concluded that population density averaged 2.3 persons per square mile, a relatively high figure for people with a foraging economy and one of the highest in aboriginal California (Cook 1976: 173).

The whole of Pomoan territory occupied three distinct ecological zones: the Pacific coast on the west, the Russian River valley in the south and central regions, and the lake district in the east. People inhabiting each of these zones developed somewhat different economies regardless of their linguistic affiliation. Differences in material culture, social organization, leadership, and religious beliefs also somewhat distinguished residents of the three zones. The coastal region included the Pacific shore, the mouths of rivers and creeks that emptied into the ocean, and a densely forested area of giant redwood that extended inland from 5 to 20 mi. The majority of the coastal people lived between the shore and the redwood forests but even there, population density was lighter than in other Pomoan regions. Most coastal settlements were located near the banks of rivers and streams away from the immediate shoreline because the coast itself was relatively inhospitable due to its rugged cliffs and foggy, wind-swept climate (Kroeber 1925: 225). The redwood forest also did not offer appealing settlement sites although a number of permanent villages were found there, mainly in isolated prairies or valleys. In contrast, more numerous communities were established in the Russian River valley that ran through the territory of the Kashayas and southern Pomos. The river and smaller waterways provided abundant fish, while the valleys provided numerous varieties of nuts, seeds, roots, grasses, and animals. Accordingly, more than one-third of Pomoan settlements were found in this region (226). Finally, the lake district was probably the most densely populated of the Pomoan zones. It was the territory of eastern and southeastern Pomos who built villages along streams near the lakes, on small islands, and in nearby open clearings. Kroeber noted that most of the principal Pomoan villages were established on the northern or eastern sides of streams because "the vegetation is invariably thickest on the northern and eastern slopes of hills, where ground and foliage hold moisture better through the long rainless summer" (235).

Economies

Pomoan economies were everywhere centered on gathering, fishing, and hunting. Except along the Pacific coast where oak trees were scarce, acorn meal was the staple of the Pomo diet. Acorns were gathered, shelled, and then pounded into meal. The meal was sifted, spread over a bed of sand and leached with hot water to remove the bitter tannic acid. It was then made into bread or mush mixed with water. Buckeyes were also collected in the fall, shelled and leached in order to remove their poisonous substances. They were cooked on a bed of hot rocks for about two and a half hours, placed in baskets, squeezed into a mush-like substance, allowed to dry, and then soaked in cold water, again spread on a bed of sand and leached with hot water. Hazelnuts and pine nuts were eaten raw. Blackberries, thimbleberries, huckleberries, strawberries, and raspberries were eaten raw, dried and mixed with

A Pomo woman uses a seed beater to gather seeds into a burden basket.

other foods, or squeezed into juices. Various seeds, grasses, and roots were also collected. These included clover, mushrooms, wild onions, wild potatoes, anise roots, several kinds of fungus, and tule found near lakes. Roots, grasses, and other plants were eaten raw or baked in hot ashes. Foods were seasoned with salt or pepper. Pepper balls, collected in the fall from bay trees, were roasted, ground up, and formed into small cakes. People bit into the pepper cakes when they wanted seasoning for their foods. Salt was obtained from a deposit located in northeastern Pomo territory or from the Pacific coast rocks where it was left by the ocean water. Salt was usually made into cakes that were baked in hot ashes. People living near the coast also obtained salt by drying kelp and then chewing the dried kelp and extracting its salt.

Coastal people made use of the ocean resources for fish, shellfish, sea lions, seaweed, and salt. However, their exploitation of the ocean was limited by the fact that they did not have seaworthy boats but rather used simple rafts made of logs and were thus not able to venture far out into the ocean. Ocean fish such as sea trout, bullhead, and codfish were caught by men standing along the rocky shoreline, using a line made of kelp attached to a wooden hook. Smelts and other small fish were taken with dipnets. Crabs and lobsters were caught with bait tied to strings or were taken in nets at low tide. Seals and sea lions were caught at low tide in the summertime, but since Pomos lacked seaworthy craft, hunters had to swim a mile or more to the sea rocks where the animals congregated. Even though seal hunters were of necessity good swimmers, because of the danger of their work they followed ritual restrictions before undertaking the risk. These included abstaining from eating meat and engaging in sexual activity for a day before the hunt. The hunters prayed to sharks before they left shore in order that they not be attacked. The seals were clubbed while they slept and then were dragged back to shore by ropes. Seal meat was first cut into strips and then roasted. The skins were used for clothing. Women collected shellfish such as mussels, barnacles, snails, sea urchins, and abalone. They also gathered seaweed and kelp from which they scraped the salt that adhered to the surfaces. Fish were roasted fresh on hot coals. Some were dried on wooden racks, a process that took about a week. Afterward, the dried fish was rubbed with salt and stored in large baskets kept inside houses. Shellfish, crabs, lobsters, and turtles were cooked in hot ashes.

Inland rivers and lakes were also exploited for their fish. Salmon, suckers, and trout were abundant in the Russian River, coming to spawn every year. Lake fishing equipment included poles made of willow and lines of milkweed fiber attached to hooks made from the leg of a deer. Worms were used as bait. Fish were also taken with nets that were about 10-ft. wide attached to poles of pine or fir. Salmon were caught in dipnets as they came up the rivers to spawn in the fall. The nets were held by fishermen wading into the river. A more elaborate technique consisted of building a dam across a river, making a hole in the dam and positioning a man behind it, the man holding a dipnet with which he scooped up salmon as they swam upstream. Large baskets about 12 ft. in length were sometimes set out at night over breaks in the dam, and the fish were retrieved in the morning. Salmon were also caught with harpoons. Similar methods were used to catch trout in the summertime.

Fishing was accompanied by a number of ritual observances and restrictions. Men whose wives had recently given birth or were menstruating did not go fishing lest they get sick. When the first fish of a species was taken for the year, the fisherman made a wish, translated as "lots will come" (Loeb 1926: 169). Eastern Pomos who fished in Clear Lake purified their poles and nets before use by rinsing them with boiled water mixed with herbs. If fishing were unsuccessful, the cleansing rites were repeated.

Meat obtained by hunting provided Pomos with nutritional variety but did not constitute a major share of the diet in most regions. Animals hunted included deer, bear, elk, wildcat, raccoon, otter, beaver, rabbit, and other woodland and prairie rodents. Animals were commonly hunted with bow and arrow, but squirrels were often clubbed by fast runners who outran them, and rabbits and raccoons were usually caught in traps. Deer hunting was a specialized occupation requiring training and the acquisition of songs and charms. Before departing on a hunt, men rubbed themselves with herbs and leaves so that they would be protected from spirits in the forests. They purified their hunting equipment in the smoke of a fire made from herbs, leaves, and seeds. The singing of deer songs accompanied all of their activities. Hunting deer was sometimes done singly by a man keeping watch over a deer trail or using a disguise consisting of a deer's head. More commonly, however, groups of men cooperated in drives. After surrounding the animals, men chased them to waiting hunters who wore deer-head disguises and sang deer songs. Another technique consisted of first placing fences and nets over deer trails, driving the animals using sticks, and then shooting them with arrows. Deer caught in communal hunts were butchered and divided among the hunters. Upon returning to their villages, hunters gave a generous supply of meat to their mothers-in-law. If a man was recently married, he brought an entire deer to his wife's mother (171). Meat from animals was usually eaten fresh after being roasted in ashes or on hot coals, but some deer meat was dried and stored for later use.

Hunting of any kind was accompanied by prayers, not addressed to the specific animal sought but rather to spirits that were thought to influence or control the outcome. The spirit of Panther and Wildcat were guardians of big game, while Eagle and Falcon controlled bird hunting and Otter was the spirit overseeing fish (171).

A great variety of birds were caught, supplying food and feathers used in decorating clothing, ritual paraphernalia, and baskets. Among the many species sought were quail, woodpecker, lark, robin, sparrow, bluejay, pigeon, crane, buzzard, and grouse. Some birds were shot with bows and arrows, some were surrounded on the ground and driven into baskets, while others were caught in traps. Ducks were shot with bows and arrows from boats or were trapped with nets. Bird's eggs were eaten, especially those from quail and ducks. They were first wrapped in grass and then baked in hot ashes.

Subsistence tasks were typically allocated according to gender although some were accomplished with joint labor by men and women. Hunting, particularly of large animals, was the work of men, but women sometimes cooperated in hunting small animals. Fishing was men's work but women collected shellfish and seaweed. Gathering plants, seeds, and roots was usually women's work although men helped collect acorns and insects. Men also collected salt and wood for household use (Willoughby 1963: 17, 22, 28). Tasks associated with preparing meals and preserving and storing foods were nearly always performed by women.

Craft occupations were also allocated according to gender. Men built houses and rafts and manufactured the tools and equipment needed for hunting and fishing. Women produced baskets and other items made from fibers except fish traps and fish baskets, since these were used in men's work. Both women and men made basketry cradles. Although men butchered

animals, women prepared, cooked, and preserved the meat. Men made clothing, rabbitskin blankets, and ceremonial costumes. Some crafts and subsistence tasks were performed by specialists whose skills were learned and handed down within families.

Although all women learned to make baskets, some were especially gifted and provided other women with finished products in exchange for other goods. Pomos were (and are) renowned for their basketry. Women produced baskets using both coiling and twining techniques. They employed several kinds of fibers including conifer and hazel roots, tule, bullrush, willow, grapevine, and fern. Among the numerous types of baskets made were boiling baskets, hot serving baskets, circular storage baskets, carrying baskets, seed-gathering baskets, flat or shallow woven trays, hoppers, seed beaters, scoops or dippers, work baskets, winnowing baskets, and woven baby cradles. Pomoan artistry was demonstrated in ornamentation and decoration. Some baskets were colored with dyes made from alder and poison oak. Designs were woven into the baskets with added fern and tule. Clamshell beadwork was used to decorate baskets as well (Barrett 1908; Gifford and Kroeber 1939). A unique feature of Pomo baskets was the use of feathers of different colors taken from various species of birds to decorate the ware. Feathers were woven into the baskets or hung as ornamentation. The entire surface of some baskets was covered with feathers, producing a patterned effect from the coloration of the feathers. Decorative designs on baskets were named with terms referring to animals, birds, and plants. However, the designs were not realistic depictions of the named source but rather, were "primarily decorative and seemed to have been named from some real or fancied likeness to the object bearing the same name" (Barrett 1905: 31).

All men knew how to make the clamshell beads that were used as money, but specialists were paid to perform some of the necessary work. Indeed, Pomos supplied money to most other groups in central California, obtaining clamshells on the shores of Bodega Bay. In order to manufacture money, clamshells were first broken into small pieces and their edges were chipped off with flint so that they had a circular shape about half an inch in diameter (Loeb 1926: 177). Next, the shell disks were drilled by specialists whose knowledge was passed from a man to his son or sister's son. The specialist drilled a hole in the center of each disk, strung the disks together on wire grass, rounded and smoothed their edges by rubbing them over a flat stone, and finally polished the disks with deerskin. Strings customarily held about 200 beads. Clamshells were also used to made cylindrical-shaped beads that had about the same diameter as ordinary beads but were much longer. They were worth from 20 to 40 common beads (177). The value of beads depended upon their size, thickness, degree of polish, and age (Kroeber 1925: 249). According to Kroeber, "The handling of a lifetime imparted a gloss unattainable in any other way" (249). Cylindrical beads 1–3 in. long were also made from magnesite found in southeastern Pomo territory. After being ground and perforated, they were baked in a pit filled with hot ashes. After about four hours, they were removed and dropped into a basket filled with boiling water. The combination of heat and water caused the stone to break into pieces, while the heating process transformed the color of the beads from white or gray to a shiny tan, salmon, or red, with additional banding or shading of coloration. Each piece was then shaped and chipped in order to make it smooth and even (Hudson 1897: 15–16). Because of their beauty, magnesite cylinders were more valuable than clamshell disks. They were not strung but rather sold individually or hung as pendants on strings of clamshell beads.

Certain resource sites were communally owned by residents of villages or members of kinship groups. Villages owned hunting territory in surrounding areas and marked off their borders by twisting the branches of oak trees. Among some eastern Pomos, juniper, acorn, and pepperwood trees located on land owned by a village were said to belong to particular families. Such trees were marked by scraping off a piece of bark in an identifiable design that was recognized by everyone in the village. Although the trees were said to belong to the eldest member of the family, in fact they were communal property. Among eastern Pomos living near Clear Lake, landings from which people fished were the property of individual families. In order to identify their ownership, people marked nearby trees or stuck posts in the ground. Since fishing was a specialized occupation, the fish landings were considered the property of the fishermen and were passed from a man to his sister's son or his own son (Loeb 1926: 197–198). Coastal Pomo fishermen owned sections along the streams that flowed to the sea, but no area of ocean shoreline was considered private property. And among eastern Pomos, whenever a new field of plants, seeds, or roots was discovered, a family could mark its claim to the area by setting a long pole in the center. The claim was publicized throughout the community and was maintained as long as the family used it. However, if a family's resource areas were unproductive in any given year, they might ask permission to gather plants and seeds or hunt and fish in land claimed by a relative or neighbor. Such requests were customarily granted.

Although most Pomo regions were supplied with a variety and abundance of resources, people sometimes wanted to obtain products that they lacked and therefore developed a complex system of intercommunity trade. Exchange of products from coastal to inland villages occurred systematically in order to supply coastal people with acorns and animal meat and to supply inlanders with fish, shellfish, and seaweed. Trading expeditions were organized as feasts (Vayda 1967: 495). For example, when people near Clear Lake accumulated a larger supply of fish than they required for their own needs, they invited other communities to visit them and attend a feast (Loeb 1926: 192–193). The invitation was made by a messenger sent to the guest village with woven "invitation" sticks representing the number of days until the feast was scheduled. After accepting the invitation, the guest villagers amassed strings of clamshell beads to be presented later to their hosts. When they arrived at the host settlement, their chiefs deposited the beads in a pile. After several days of feasting, socializing, and gambling, the actual transaction of fish for beads took place. Men in the host village piled up their fish and each took the amount of shell beads that he was owed for his share. After all donors had given their fish and obtained their beads, the guest chiefs divided up the fish to each family in equal portions and they departed. The guests thereby received food while the hosts obtained beads. Similar trade feasts were held for acorns, seeds, and seaweed. Such exchanges allowed people to secure resources that were scarce in their own region and allowed those with abundant resources to obtain shell beads that counted as money and could be used to purchase food, equipment, and services. The importance of trade feasts as mechanisms to equalize resources was demonstrated by the fact that the amount of shell beads a host obtained depended upon the amount of fish (or acorns, seeds, and so forth) that s/he had given, but when the foods were distributed among the guests, they each received an equal portion regardless of how many strings of beads they had contributed.

Dwellings

Pomo dwellings varied depending upon environmental zone. In the region located between the coast and the redwood forests, conical houses were made by leaning slabs of redwood bark and split wood against a center pole. When arranging the wood against the pole, an opening was left to allow the smoke from an interior fire to exit. A space was left in one side of the house to function as a doorway that could be closed by placing slabs of bark over it (Barrett 1916: 37). Such dwellings were generally 8–12 ft. in diameter and 6 or 8 ft. high. They typically housed one family although additional people might reside there as well.

Houses built by Pomos living in the valleys of the Russian River were usually circular or rectangular in shape, while some were formed like an L. The houses were constructed around a framework of vertical poles either brought together at the top or connected with a horizontal ridge pole. Once the framework was erected, layers of thatched grass were placed as a covering, providing a watertight surface. A portion of the top was left open in order to allow smoke from interior fires to exit. These thatched grass houses were commonly used in the winter but had to be repaired or rebuilt each year. They housed several related families. According to Barrett, "each two families ordinarily had an independent door and fire, while a single baking pit sufficed for all" (38). Barrett described a typical example that measured about 20 ft. wide and 40 ft. long, having five fires and five doors (38). Inside such houses, people stored dried foods, personal possessions, and tools and utensils. They slept near the fires in small indentations hollowed in the ground that were lined with soft tule covered with a woven sleeping mat. When the weather required, people covered themselves with rabbitskin blankets.

Pomos living in the lake region built circular or elliptical houses with domed roofs, covered with tule or brush. The framework was similar to the wooden frame employed in the valleys but tule was used instead of grass thatching. The tule was first made into small bundles and then attached to the frame. Such houses usually had one doorway measuring only a few feet in height so that people had to stoop or even crawl in order to enter (41). The doorway was closed with a tule mat when necessary. The inner walls were lined with mats to keep out drafts. The earthen floor was also covered with loose tule or tule mats. Dwellings built by Clear Lake Pomos were large enough to house at least two but more often several related families (Gifford 1926: 291). Each family had their own entrance and interior fire.

Pomos in all regions erected small brush shelters when they set up temporary camps near hunting or gathering sites. They also made shades or shelters consisting of posts covered on the top with brush but having no sides. These shelters were used in the daytime during the summer to protect people from the hot sun.

In addition to household dwellings, Pomo communities had semisubterranean structures covered with earth that were used both as sweathouses and clubhouses for men. Men and boys congregated in the buildings during the daytime and often slept there at night, especially in the winter, because such houses were made warmer than regular dwellings by their earth coverings. Men generally sweated everyday, heated by a fire built in the sweathouse. Sweats were thought to be beneficial for health and were part of men's daily regimen. Women, however, rarely participated in sweat baths except as a cure for illness (Barrett 1916: 44–45).

Finally, most Pomo villages contained a large, semisubterranean building that was used for community meetings, ceremonials, and dances. It was usually located in the center of the village. The foundation was dug about 3–6 ft. deep and 40–60 ft. in diameter. Then a circular framework of poles was erected and covered over with tule matting, a layer of dried grass, a layer of mud, and a final covering of loose earth (48). Ceremonial houses were entered through tunnels 10 or 20 ft. long and 3–6 ft. wide. The floor was covered with a layer of black earth and a topping of coarse sand.

Clothing and Adornment

Pomo clothing was relatively simple. Men usually wore no clothing at all except when weather necessitated some garments. In cold and damp weather, they covered themselves with rabbitskin blankets or cloaks and capes made of shredded tule that were held over the shoulder or tied around the neck. Coastal Pomos sometimes made robes from sea otter skins instead. Women wore a double or overlapping buckskin skirt tied around the waist. In the wintertime, extra warmth was provided by an outer skirt made of shredded tule in the lake region, shredded inner redwood bark along the coast, and willow bark in the Russian River valley (Loeb 1926: 154). Like the men, women covered themselves with rabbitskin robes in cold and damp weather. Pomos generally did not wear shoes, but in cold weather or on rough terrain, buckskin moccasins were worn. Sandals and leggings made of tule were occasionally worn as well. Women decorated their skirts with clamshell beads, bird's feathers, and dangles of abalone shells. Both men and women wore clamshell bead necklaces and beaded or feathered belts. Girls and boys had their ears pierced when they were about six or seven years old and thereafter wore bone or shell ear ornaments. Men occasionally wore nasal ornaments that were inserted in holes pierced in the septum of their noses.

Women and men wore their hair long, sometimes tied in the back with milkweed strings. They adorned their hair with pins made from the leg bone of a deer. The hairpins were often decorated with feathers. Both men and women also wore hairnets made from milkweed cord. They wore beaded and feathered headdresses on ceremonial occasions. Finally, both women and men tattooed designs on their legs, arms, and faces.

Residential Groups

Pomo social and political organization was based on local residential groups, commonly called "tribelets" in the anthropological literature concerning aboriginal California. (See Chapter 17 for a discussion of Californian tribelets.) Each village community was functionally autonomous and independent. Its boundaries were recognized by members of the group as well as by members of nearby groups. Outsiders were careful not to trespass on resource sites that were communally owned by other tribelets. In several instances, Pomo villages located along the Russian River formed confederations that probably came into existence in order to maximize military defense (Kunkel 1974: 288). Tribelets were regularly linked through intermarriage, trade, feasts or festivals, and participation in each other's ceremonials.

Tribelets consisted of groups of kin related to each other through bilateral ties. A preference for matrilateral affiliation and descent seems to have been prevalent but, as Kunkel remarked, "matrilaterality was a statistical trend, not an inflexible rule" (1974: 12). Decisions regarding residence after marriage were made by the couple concerned based on resource availability, household composition, and personal preferences. It was common for couples to live with the wife's family initially after marriage and then at

some point, possibly within a few months or at most a year, shift to the husband's kin, then back and forth between the two families until they settled with one or the other. Future moves were never ruled out. When a first child was expected, the couple typically went to live with the wife's family until sometime after the birth. They might choose to remain there or remove to the husband's family if they wished.

Community Leadership

Residential kin groups constituted the basic economic and political units of Pomo society. They pooled resources and cooperated in subsistence tasks, trade exchanges, and ceremonial events. Each residential group had at least one leader or chief, a position that was usually hereditary although the line of descent was not always rigid. Among some groups, chieftainships passed from a man to his sister's son while in others the position passed from father to son or from a man to his brother. Among the Central Pomo, chiefs were elected by a council composed of the heads of related families. Some tribelets also had women chiefs, usually a sister or daughter of a male chief. Women chiefs had somewhat different roles in different Pomoan communities. Among the central Pomo, women chiefs performed similar functions as those of their male counterparts except that "a chieftainess … did not address the people in person, but conveyed her messages through a male chief, who did the talking to the people" (Gifford 1928: 676). Coastal Pomo women chiefs prepared food for communal ceremonials and may have had other responsibilities as well (Loeb 1926: 236). Large villages having 1,000 or possibly 2,000 residents usually had several chiefs. One might be considered the head chief, while in some communities they were all recognized as equals (Gifford 1928: 677).

In addition to their necessary kinship support, men who were chosen as chiefs had to be "good hearted," generous, intelligent, and skilled in oratory (Gifford 1926: 333). They were usually wealthier than others, but differences in wealth and standard of living were actually slight. Once selected from among possible contenders, the chief was relieved of subsistence duties and was instead supported by donations from his relatives of food, animal hides, and other goods. The wealth he accumulated was not kept privately but rather was expended when communal ceremonies were held or when dance houses were built (Loeb 1926: 237).

Chiefs provided moral leadership in their communities. They made public speeches admonishing people to behave properly. According to Gifford describing the Clear Lake Pomo, "Each morning and evening the chief harangued the people as to righteous and proper conduct. 'Work, do not steal, do not fight, do not become angry'" (1926: 342). However, as important as what they said to their followers, chiefs led by the example of their own behavior. They helped settle disputes within their communities and served as peacemakers to other groups when raids or war had erupted. Chiefs or their messengers made public announcements, informing people of communal activities and plans. And they either initiated or participated in organizing ceremonies and feasts.

Chiefs had assistants, sometimes called "captains" or "boy chiefs" (a title that does not connote their age but rather their subsidiary position) who helped prepare ceremonies and participated in discussions at village councils. Boy chiefs also aided in welcoming and hosting visitors to the community. Their duties prepared them for possible succession to chieftainships. A chief sometimes vacated his position before his death and might name a successor, formally presenting a gift of clamshell beads to the one so chosen (239). Just before his death, a chief notified the community that any planned ceremonies or social events should take place as scheduled so that no period of public mourning followed his death.

Village councils were composed of chiefs, boy chiefs, and other respected elders. They planned and approved communal activities and organized trade feasts and ceremonials. No action of any kind was possible without unanimous agreement. Furthermore, no action was undertaken without the approval of public opinion as well. Differences in status and wealth in Pomoan communities stemmed from kinship ties, inheritance, and ability. Chiefs and their close relatives held highest status and were the beneficiaries of labor and donations given by members of their community. Religious practitioners such as shamans and healers also had high status. Members of specialized professions such as money makers, skilled basketmakers, and other craftspeople also were highly respected.

Families and Social Systems

Families were linked through marriages that established social, economic, and ceremonial ties. Parents sometimes arranged marriages for their children but never without the children's consent. Men and women who were attracted to each other might decide to marry but always sought their families' approval. The sororate and levirate were possible, although not common, marriage choices (Gifford 1926: 319). Polygyny was also possible in some Pomo communities but was of rare occurrence. Among the lake Pomo, marriages were always monogamous (324). Marriages began with an exchange of gifts between the families of husband and wife. The husband's family initiated the exchange by bringing gifts to the wife's household. Acceptance of these presents signaled approval of the marriage. The husband then moved in with his wife, contributing his labor to the family's subsistence. The presents brought by the husband's family were later reciprocated by gifts of roughly equal value offered by the woman's family to that of the husband. Among the eastern Pomo, and possibly others as well, the gifts exchanged had symbolic significance. First, both sides exchanged foods, that is, items produced by women; then they both exchanged a valuable made by men, that is, clamshell beads. Finally, the husband's family gave another men's product (rabbitskin blankets) and in return received a woman's item (baskets) (Loeb 1926: 278, 284). Marriages were publicly acknowledged by the chief, who made a speech announcing the union and advised the couple to "care for one another in health or in sickness, and to defend one another, and to be good to their parents-in-law" (278). Certain deferential behaviors were expected between people and their spouse's parents. Men and women were bashful in the presence of their parents-in-law, particularly those of the opposite sex. Men avoided looking at or speaking directly to their mothers-in-law. Although women displayed similar patterns of deference toward their fathers-in-law, the restrictions on speaking were less fully imposed. In addition, whenever parents-in-law and children-in-law spoke to each other, they used a plural form of address (Gifford 1926: 327).

Divorce was possible but did not occur often. Customs differed somewhat regarding the breakup of families. In some Pomoan groups, children remained in the household in which they were living at the time of the divorce, while the parent who did not belong there returned to his/her own family. In other groups, children always remained with their mother. And, in some cases, boys stayed with their fathers and girls with their mothers although if there were only one child, s/he always stayed with the mother (Loeb 1926: 281).

Social control was usually the responsibility of kin-groups, but when conflicts arose between different kin-groups or villages, chiefs of the relevant units attempted to settle the disputes. If a murder were committed against someone in another village, the chief of the murderer's village presented the victim's family with reparation in the form of clamshell beads collected from the culprit's kin.

Warfare

Although peaceful relations perpetuated by intermarriage, trade, and ceremonial participation were the norm among Pomoan communities, disputes that led to war sometimes arose. Conflicts might erupt when trespassers gathered acorns or hunted in another group's recognized territory, but more often they were motivated by the desire to seek revenge for an alleged poisoning death of a member of one's community. Warfare was not considered a noble alternative but was nonetheless resorted to on some occasions. There were no established war leaders, but any man might organize a group of followers. War leaders were temporary figures who were looked to because of their military skills but were not universally admired. In the words of one of Loeb's consultants, a war leader was "a good bad man" (1926: 200). Battles usually entailed confrontations between the two sides organized into lines, perhaps consisting of about 100 men each, standing about 30 yards apart. They shot arrows, threw stones, and hurled insults at one another but never engaged in direct contact. In some Pomoan groups, women and boys accompanied warriors and assisted on the sidelines by picking up arrows and stones, that had been thrown, resupplying their own warriors. The battle might end as soon as anyone was seriously wounded or it might continue, but fighting always ceased at night. In addition, raids were sometimes carried out against an enemy village, generally resulting in higher casualties than the formal line battles.

After armed conflict ended, chiefs of the victorious party acted as peacemakers, bringing a peace offering of clamshell beads collected from their villagers to the community of their defeated foe. Negotiations were prefaced by sending a messenger to the enemy village, often a person related to them through marriage. When the chief arrived, he made a formal speech apologizing for the suffering that had been caused. The chief of the defeated village accepted the reparations and made a speech voicing hope that peace would

be restored. The beads received from the victors were divided among the mourning families who had lost men in battle.

Religious Beliefs and Practices

Pomos conceived of the earth as a flat surface floating in water with the sky arching above. They believed that spirit protectors were associated with six cardinal directions, that is, south, east, north, west, sky (above), and earth (below). There were a number of variants of creation stories. According to an eastern Pomo myth, the earth was created from a ball of gum taken from the armpits of the first man, Kuksu, and a creator called Marumda. Coast and northern Pomos believed that Coyote rather than Marumda was the creator and protector of people (Loeb 1926: 300).

Pomoans believed in a world of nature imbued with a spirit essence or power. According to an eastern Pomo consultant, "the people believe that the whole of nature contains spirits … All animals were once people, but at the destruction of the world were turned into animals. Unusual rocks and natural objects were thought to be alive … Plants are thought to be alive, the juice is their blood, and they grow. The same is true of trees. All things die, therefore all things have life" (Loeb 1926: 302).

Spirit force or essence was concentrated in powerful beings of nature, certain objects, and humans who obtained power either through inheritance or the acquisition of charms. Forces of nature such as thunder, lightning, and wind were personified, having humanlike shapes and language. Certain places, particularly unusually shaped rock formations and bodies of water, were the abodes of powerful and potentially dangerous spirits who had to be placated with prayers and offerings lest they harm people. Good fortune was the result of spirit protections, whereas bad luck and illness came from failure to show proper respect to powerful beings or to abide by ritual restrictions and taboos. People could acquire power and good fortune by rubbing their arms or hands against a powerful object or person. And they might acquire power contained in charms that they found. When someone saw objects such as unusually shaped rocks or bird feathers, s/he collected them and performed prayers and rites that released their inherent power so that it could be used for the person's benefit. Such objects might help gain success in fishing, hunting, and gambling as well as protect their owner from illness or other misfortune. Charms were sometimes acquired through inheritance, usually from maternal kin. People could also acquire power through dreams. According to Pomoan belief, dreams were initiated by Coyote in primordial times. They might bring either good or bad luck. For example, dreaming about a charm or powerful object gave even more good fortune than actually seeing the object while awake, and dreaming about the dead would likely cause illness.

While everyone was able to acquire spirit powers and protections, some people had access to more power than others. Chiefs and other people of high status were thought to have more spirit power than ordinary people. Curers and other ritual practitioners also had extraordinary powers and abilities. Their skills were sought by members of their communities both for individual and communal needs. They officiated at public ceremonials and could influence the weather by making it rain or, even more commonly, making the rain cease. And curers or doctors treated illnesses and prevented death.

According to Pomoan medical theories, illness and other misfortunes resulted from contact with harmful agents, failure to adhere to ritual taboos, or the evil ministrations of doctors or poisoners. Pomo curers had a vast knowledge of plant and animal remedies for ordinary illnesses, but if an ailment failed to respond to natural therapy or when its etiology was unknown, poisoning was considered the likely cause. Sudden deaths, that is, those occurring within a month or two after the onset of an ailment, were routinely suspected of resulting from poisoning. An enemy of the victim, a stranger, or even a doctor was thought to be the evildoer. Assignment of likely guilt was made after careful consideration of the patient's activities before the illness or death occurred. Contacts were reviewed and the person's whereabouts were discussed in order to ascertain the guilty party. Once blame was laid, the family of the victim sought revenge by an outright murder of the accused or a close relative, or by a counterpoisoning. If no one in the victim's family knew the art of poisoning, they hired someone who did. Poisoners generally learned their techniques through training and inheritance from a relative: fathers taught their sons; mothers taught their daughters. Because of the fear of poisoning, people were wary of contact with strangers but were also careful not to slight them lest they retaliate by poisoning. Old people were often thought to have knowledge of poisoning techniques and consequently were treated with deference.

Poisoning was accomplished by a number of techniques. First, poisons were collected from spiders, snake venom, and bee stings. Then the poisoner, often aided by assistants, made a doll out of sticks to represent the victim and rubbed it with poison and with the victim's urine or feces, collected surreptitiously. While applying the concoctions, the poisoner called out the real name of the victim and thereby transmitted the harmful spell. When the doll became sick and died, it was burned and buried in imitation of rituals performed at human funerals. Poisoning could also be accomplished by placing the victim's urine or feces on a grave and leaving it there for four days. Sticks from a poison oak tree could be stuffed with poison mixed with the victim's excrement or hair and placed under the victim's house. Lizards were sometimes fed a poison mixture and then tied under the victim's house, preferably under the doorway or bed. As the lizard sickened, the victim similarly took ill and died.

If someone suspected that they had been poisoned, they or their relatives could try to search out the hidden substance or object used and purify it, thus breaking the spell and making it revert to the original poisoner. Failing this, however, people sought the aid of either of two types of doctors: "sucking doctors" and "outfit doctors" (Gifford 1926: 330). "Outfit doctors" learned their craft through training, usually from a close relative who passed on their knowledge, and their "outfits" or "medicine bundles" containing spiritually powerful objects that had been collected and/or inherited by their owners. Such objects included unusually shaped rocks, bird's feathers, animal bones, and the like. Outfit doctors performed ritual cures that included singing over the patient, dancing, and sometimes impersonating a spirit being who had frightened the patient into illness. Outfit doctors cured either singly or in collaborating teams. In contrast to the training needed by outfit doctors, "sucking doctors" derived their powers from visions and dreams. They cured by removing a harmful spell or disease-causing object or "pain" by sucking the part of the victim's body where the object was lodged. When extracted, the pain often took the form of a blood clot or some other amorphous substance. Both women and men might doctor, although men were more likely to be outfit doctors while women were more often sucking doctors. All doctors were paid for their services but did not have set fees. Instead, patients and their families gave as many strings of clamshell beads as they could afford.

It was understood, though, that the more one gave, the more likely was a cure (Loeb 1926: 325).

Illness and death might also be caused by a special class of evildoer called a "bear doctor." "Bear doctors," most often women, dressed in bearskin costumes, hid in the woods, and attacked hunters or travellers, thereby causing them severe fright that led to illness and potentially to death (Barrett 1917b). A bear doctor's power was contained in the bearskin suit and could be augmented by ritual procedures. Before dressing in the suit, the doctor covered her/his body with an "armor" consisting of belts of shell beads, presumably to protect themselves from the power of the suit.

Finally, spirits might cause illness if ritual restrictions or taboos had been violated or if their abodes had been trespassed upon. They usually made a person sick by appearing to them and causing fright, manifested by fainting or losing consciousness (Aginsky 1976: 320–322). Such cases were often handled by outfit doctors who impersonated the spirit and repeated the episode of fright and thus broke its spell. The relationship between breaking taboos and the onset of illness was illustrated by a Pomo woman's recollections in the 1940's. According to Sophie Matinez,

> My uncle didn't know that his wife had the month-sick. After he went to Green Lake, she got it. Green Lake is no good, they claim. He shouldn't have gone there. That's why he got sick. For about two months, he suffered. He told everything. He said he saw a fish there; "A big fish," he said. "I feared it," he said. I was there when he came home. He told us what happened. He had gone down to the water, he said, and a big fish made him sick. Then somebody was doctoring him there. It was a singing doctor that heard him that time. The doctor made a fish and water, and he showed it to my uncle. My uncle just stood there. Everybody hold him, and he just stood there. He never moved, never breathed, just stood there. And the doctor was singing—making him breathe. That's the way Indians doctor. We call it sopka, "scare something." The doctoring made him well, and after he was well he became a maru. (Colson 1974: 52)

The uncle evidently had broken a taboo requiring men to avoid fishing and hunting while their wives were menstruating. Ignorance of his wife's menstruation was irrelevant. In order to effect a cure, the doctor replicated the conditions that had caused the man's fright and subsequent sickness, thus removing the spell and making the patient well. After he recovered, the man too became a dreamer or maru.

Ritual observances marked the passage of people from birth to death. Pomoans believed that sexual intercourse was not sufficient for a woman to become pregnant. She also needed to pray and employ a number of ritualistic techniques. Among eastern and northern Pomos, a woman wanting a child asked a man to make a doll of white clay and wood that she put inside a baby basket or cradle and treated as though it were a child. The dolls were stylized representations of people. They were flat, relatively shapeless figures, but breasts were formed if the woman desired a daughter. In addition, women who wanted children went alone to particular rock formations after having fasted for four days and performed a number of rites, circling the rock first counterclockwise four times and then clockwise four times. The woman then took a flint knife, cut into the rock to extract small pieces of dust that she marked on her own body, and asked the rock for a child (Loeb 1926: 246–247).

When a woman realized that she was pregnant, she and her husband began to observe taboos that were aimed at protecting the coming child. The husband was not permitted to hunt, fish, gamble, or drill clam-shell beads while his wife was pregnant or for a month or two afterward. Pregnant women and their husbands refrained from eating meat and other hot foods.

Childbirth itself was not accompanied by ritual except in cases of difficult labor, when specialists were called to perform songs and prayers that would hasten the birth. After the birth, the placenta and umbilical cord were buried in a secret place to keep them safe from an enemy who might use them to poison the child. A few days after the birth, the mother was given a clamshell-beaded belt and a basket made by a woman who had never been sick. The paternal grandmother came to the house every morning and evening to wash the child. The basket used to wash the child was later given to the child when grown up.

Both parents observed restrictions for a period of time after the birth. Eastern Pomo fathers remained at home for eight days and then bathed in warm water and prayed for their wife's and baby's health. For a month afterward, they continued to observe the same restrictions on food and activity as before the baby's birth. During this time, the mother could not wash, scratch herself with her hands, or look directly at the sun.

Gifts were given to the baby in order to protect it and ensure its health. Girls were given small baskets so that they would grow up to be skilled basketmakers, while boys were given a quail or dove head "in order to make the boy mild-tempered and beautiful" (256).

About a month after birth, children were named, usually after a respected living or deceased relative, in a brief ritual that essentially blessed the child and wished it health and success. It was hoped that the child would grow up to be like the person s/he was named for. Names were considered private property and were not used except by parents. People were therefore usually called by kinship terms or nicknames.

Coming of age was not marked with ceremony for boys, but when they were about ten years old, a feast was given in their honor by both maternal and paternal families. They were presented with hairnets and cottontail robes. Girls' puberty, in contrast, was marked with elaborate ritual. Upon reaching menarche, the girl went to reside in a small menstrual hut erected near her family's house, often connected to it with a doorway. A space on the floor was dug out to about 4 or 5 in. in depth and a layer of heated coals was placed inside, covered over with tule stalks. The girl lay on the bed and refrained from eating meat or fish. In addition, she could not drink cold water, wash herself with cold water, or scratch herself except with a special scratching stick. On the fourth night or early on the fifth morning, she was given a hot bath and dressed in a robe made of panther, a new buckskin skirt, a hairnet, and a necklace of clamshell beads. She then ground up a large supply of acorns, in real and symbolic representation of her future responsibilities. She prepared acorn mush and served it to her family and friends at a public feast.

During subsequent menstrual periods, a woman followed many of the same observances as at her menarche except that she remained in her family's house in a private corner. Married men also observed restrictions during their wife's menstruation, refraining from hunting, dancing, fishing, or gambling. When his wife's period ended, the husband cleansed himself in a bath.

Death was accompanied by ritual observances and mourning. When a death was imminent, men and women mourners began to cry and wail. They continued to cry after their relative died, praising the deceased's good qualities. Women also scratched their faces with their fingernails as a sign of mourning. Once the death was known in the community, people placed gifts of clamshell bead strings on the deceased's body. The number of strings given was noted so that the deceased's relatives could return an almost equal value to the donors. After two or three days, the body, wrapped in a robe, was removed from the house on a stretcher, covered with skin robes and decorated with beads. Four men who were not relatives of the deceased carried the stretcher to a place not far from the village that functioned as a cremation ground. The body was placed in a shallow pit with its face downward and its head toward the south. The kin-group chief made a speech extolling the virtues of the deceased but avoiding the use of her/his personal name. A fire brought from the deceased's house was used to light the body. While it burned, mourners wailed and cried, acting "as though they were in the utmost frenzy of mind" (Loeb 1926: 287). Some Pomoans burned the gifts donated by relatives and friends for fear that the deceased's ghost would like the presents and want to remain close to them. The day after the cremation, the father or another close relative returned to the site, gathered together any pieces of bone that had not been fully burned and placed them in a basket or wrapped them in a robe, later to be buried nearby.

During a mourning period lasting as much as one year, close relatives of the deceased kept their hair cut short and even singed the ends. Women continued to "feed the spirits of the dead" during the year's mourning, singing mourning songs and sprinkling acorn meal over the places where the deceased was wont to walk.

Pomos believed that when a person died, their soul departed from the body and might remain nearby for four days. It often continued to visit places where the deceased had been accustomed to go. And it might appear to people in dreams. Souls were thought to eventually find their way to a "ghost place," located somewhere in a southerly direction. Souls continued to live at the "ghost place" as they had during their lifetime, but they were always at peace and did not suffer illness (290).

In addition to individual rites of passage and curing rituals, there were two communal ceremonials of great importance: the Ghost Ceremony and the Kuksu. Both contained a core of shared beliefs and practices in all Pomoan groups, but there were distinctive variations in each as well. Among the coast Pomo, who Loeb thought practiced the "most original form" (1926: 338), the Ghost Ceremony was performed and witnessed by men who had been initiated into the "Ghost house." Women and children did not attend these performances. The Ghost Ceremony was an annual rite conducted in the spring but not held every year in the same village. Rather, villages took turns sponsoring the rite, attracting participants and spectators from neighboring settlements. The ritual took place in a semisubterranean ceremonial house. The principal performers were initiated men who wore costumes and masks and painted their bodies with black, white, and red designs. They prepared themselves in the woods and then appeared in the village and proceeded to the Ghost house, some entering through the doorway and others through the smoke hole in the roof. As they entered, they imitated the sounds of birds. The performers were impersonators of the dead and as they entered the Ghost house, their leader called out the name of a deceased person. They then danced and sang, making both frightening and comical movements. They also used a special way of talking, reversing the meanings of their words, and made jokes in an attempt to make spectators laugh. However, if anyone did laugh, they were fined. Some dancers handled live coals and tried to put fire in each other's mouths. When their dance ended, they stripped themselves in the house and ran to the river to wash off their paint (339). Women who stood by outside during the performance acted as though they were in mourning. At the end of the ritual, the village chief announced that the dead had returned and people should stop mourning. The women then brought food to the Ghost house and later returned home. Ghost rites were repeated twice daily for four days, followed each day by dances and feasts that were attended by everyone in the village. The purpose of such dances and festivities was, according to Gifford's Clear Lake consultant, "to make people feel good and to keep them from feeling 'huffy'" (quoted in Gifford 1926: 350).

Boys could be initiated into the Ghost house when they reached adulthood. Candidates were sponsored by a maternal or paternal relative who was already a member. The initiation rite, occurring as part of the Ghost Ceremony, replicated death and rebirth. When the initiates entered the Ghost house, they lay down in a line, were covered with straw and remained as though dead. After the performance was over and the feasting had ended, the initiates were brought to life and given a ritual bath.

Although the Ghost Ceremony differed somewhat among northern, central, and eastern Pomos, the purposes of the rites were similar (Barrett 1917a). In all cases, male members of the Ghost house impersonated the dead, returned to the village, danced and sang, and were feasted by the community.

Kuksu ceremonies also took somewhat different forms among the Pomoan nations, but everywhere Kuksu participants (both men and women) were members of secret societies. In the rites, they impersonated the spirit being Kuksu, the first man according to Pomoan creation stories. People became members of the Kuksu society through an initiation rite that symbolized death and rebirth. Among the coast Pomo, initiates were taken into the woods, made to stand in a row facing east, and subjected to a mock assault by Kuksu impersonators who charged at them with spears. After four repetitions of the charge, the initiates fell down as dead. When the Kuksu impersonators departed, the remaining members picked up each initiate, carried them back to the dance house, and laid them down in the rear of the building. The mothers of the initiates raised up their children, removed their clothing, bathed them, and dressed them in new clothing. Their rebirth was celebrated with dances and feasting. Afterwards, the initiates returned to the hills for four days during which time they were taught the songs and dances of the Kuksu society. When they finally returned home, they were washed and given clamshell-beaded necklaces and belts. A feast was held in their honor a few days later.

CONSEQUENCES OF FOREIGN CONTROL

Pomos may have first seen Europeans in 1579 when Francis Drake travelled up the California coast and visited Coast Miwok villages just south of Pomoan territory, but certainly by the late 1700s, European products reached Pomos from their point of importation in the Spanish missions and forts near San Francisco, not far to the south. Then in the early decades of the nineteenth century, Russian traders began to visit Pomo territory and in 1812 established their first Californian settlement at Fort Ross in Kashaya land. Ninety-five Russians were accompanied by eighty Aleuts and Inuit from the Russian colony in Alaska. They were primarily interested in obtaining foods to supply their Alaskan colonies (Essig 1933: 191). They set up small farms on a tract of land about 2 mi. in length and 1 mi. in width that the Pomos had allowed them to use. The Russians hired some 100 Pomoans as laborers on their farms and in their homes (192). Since few Russians came to settle in the region and the Russian stay ended in 1841, Pomoan society was little affected by their presence, although missionaries managed to convert about forty Pomos to the Russian Orthodox Church at Fort Ross (Veniaminov 1972).

The Spanish, however, continued to expand their control in California, establishing additional missions in the north. After a mission was opened at San Rafael in 1817 and at San Francisco de Solano in 1823, Pomos were subjected to raids by Spaniards seeking to capture potential converts and workers for their missions. During the first few years after the missions were founded, Spanish records indicate 600 Pomo conversions, but Cook estimates that at least 1,200 Southern Pomoans alone were held at the missions (1976: 173–174).

When California became a province of the independent country of Mexico in 1822, Hispanic settlers penetrated further north, making incursions into Pomoan land and raiding for slaves and workers. Settlers were awarded land grants by the Mexican government, giving them a legal claim to indigenous territory. By 1840, all of Pomoan territory was settled or claimed by Mexicans. These years witnessed not only appropriation of land but increasing violence by slave raiders and Mexican militia and vigilantes. In 1833 and 1834, Pomos were attacked by soldiers commanded by Gen. M. V. Vallejo, resulting in at least 200 dead and 300 captured (205). Vallejo again attacked Pomos at Clear Lake in 1841 and killed at least 150. Another 170 were killed by his troops in 1843 (205). Vallejo had personal economic motives driving his military campaigns since he obtained land near Pomo territory and required a source of cheap labor. They captured and coerced Native workers into peonage and virtual slavery (Forbes 1969: 41).

During the same period, thousands of Pomos died from European diseases that swept through their communities. A cholera epidemic in 1833 was followed four years later by a smallpox epidemic originating at Fort Ross that spread throughout the Russian River and Clear Lake districts. Eyewitness accounts reported that "in the region, the Indians were almost exterminated" (Cook 1976: 213). Additional epidemics in the 1840s severely crippled the Pomoan population. According to George Gibbs who visited Clear Lake in 1851, "There is but little doubt of the principle cause of diminution in the ravages of smallpox, at no very remote period. Some old Indians who carry with them the marks of the disease state it positively" (214–215).

By the end of the period of Mexican control in California, Pomo communities were devastated by decades of war, slavery, disease, and capture for missions. Many people had fled the missions after they were first forced there in the 1820s and many others died as a result of the conditions and hard work that they were forced to do. The effects of raids and capture have been amply documented by eyewitnesses. As Cook concluded, "From these and other instances the impression is gained that capturing, or perhaps better kidnapping, had grown to the dimensions of a major industry by 1848" (224).

Soon after the United States assumed jurisdiction over California, two American adventurers, Charles Stone and Andrew Kelsey, established a ranch in the Clear Lake region using indigenous labor. In a few short years, they had earned a notorious reputation because of the ill-treatment given their Native laborers including beatings, rapes, and murders. Finally, in 1849, Pomos retaliated and killed Stone and Kelsey. But the killing of Americans was answered with a military campaign against the Pomos. In 1850, troops attacked Pomos at a fishing camp on an island in Clear Lake, killing 135. According to an eyewitness of the event known as the Bloody Island Massacre,

The white warriors went across in their long dugouts. The Indians said that they would meet them in peace so when the whites landed the Indians went to welcome them but the white man was determined to kill them. Ge-wi-liw said he threw up his hands but the white man fired and shot him in the arm … Many women and children were killed on around the island. One old lady said she saw two white men flinging their guns up in the air and on their guns being a little girl. They brought it to the creek and threw it in the water. And a little while later, two more men came. This time they had a little boy on the end of their gun and also threw it in the water. She said when they gathered the dead, they found all the little ones were killed by being stabbed, and many of the women were also killed by stabbing. (Forbes 1969: 55)

American settlement in the Pomoan region increased in the 1850s with raiding, confiscation of land and disruption of indigenous communities. Even lands that had been isolated from Spanish and Mexican contact were inundated by American settlers, prospectors, and adventurers of all sorts. In 1851, the federal government began to contact Native groups in California in an attempt to negotiate treaties and establish reservations that would essentially clear the way for American settlement while "pacifying" the Indians. A treaty signed between Pomoans in 1851 was, however, never ratified by Congress. Five years later, the Mendocino Indian Reserve and the Round Valley Reservation were established for Pomos. Some people were coerced into resettling at these sites, but within a few years the land was occupied by American settlers and the Indians were forced out. Pomos were then obliged by necessity to work as ranch hands, farm laborers, and domestics. By the end of the nineteenth century, many were working as migrant laborers, picking fruit, hops, and beans and harvesting grain.

In 1872, Pomos began to participate in the Ghost Dance religion originating among northern Paiutes in Nevada. The Pomos learned the dance from the neighboring Patwins. The Ghost Dance (not to be confused with the aboriginal Pomoan Ghost Ceremony) shared some features of belief and practice with traditional Pomo ceremonies but diverged in important ways as well. Both the aboriginal Ghost Ceremony and the nineteenth-century Ghost Dance focussed on the dead, but whereas the traditional rite was a memorial to the deceased, the Ghost Dance was intended as a ritual that would bring the dead back to life. In addition, the leaders of the new religion, unlike those of traditional ceremonials, did not belong to specialized societies and did not require initiation. Instead, the form that the Ghost Dance took among the Pomo centered on practitioners called "Maru" (from the eastern Pomoan word meaning "myth" or "Marumda") who obtained their power through dreams. The dreamer was instructed by a recently deceased person appearing as a messenger from the deity Marumda with instructions about new songs and dances that should be incorporated in the ceremonies. Upon awakening, the dreamer taught people the new rites that s/he had been given. Maru dances were held in newly built ceremonial houses constructed on the model of the traditional brush dance house. Maru dreamers often cured illness, employing songs and prayers that they were taught in dreams. The Pomo Maru religion (or Bole Maru, as it is often called from words derived from the Patwin and Pomo languages, respectively), also preached against behavior that was considered socially disruptive such as drinking, gambling, and sexual promiscuity (Sarris 1992: 74).

The enthusiasm with which the Ghost Dance was greeted stemmed from the disastrous economic and social conditions existing at that time. Having lost nearly all of their aboriginal territory, having endured deaths from disease or raids that decimated their population, and being deprived of their independence and autonomy, Pomos sought relief and reassurance in a religion that promised a new beginning. Although the specific philosophy of the Ghost Dance of the 1870s concerning the imminent return of the dead, cataclysmic end of the world, and return to precontact conditions lost its appeal among Pomos by the end of the nineteenth century, Maru performances continued (and continue) to evolve and in fact became central to Pomoan belief and practice. Dreamers, most often women, were respected members of their communities and, in accordance with instructions from their dreams, assumed some of the social and political functions previously served by chiefs (Sarris 1992: 74).

In the late nineteenth and early twentieth centuries, a number of Pomoan communities took the novel approach of purchasing land for themselves with money that they had saved. For example, in 1878 and 1879, members of four villages bought 90 acres north of Upper Lake, constructed houses and barns, farmed their land, and raised livestock. In 1881, another group purchased 120 acres with money that they had earned farming and selling baskets (Kasch 1947: 212). They incorporated as an independent rancheria known as Yokayo. The land was deeded to their four chiefs "and their tribe," always to be held communally (212). The people attempted to reestablish traditional social and political patterns despite economic changes that were irreversible. Residents of these and similar rancherias hoped that their land holdings would provide economic security and social support. As economic conditions improved at communally owned rancherias, they attracted Pomos from other areas (Colson 1974: 24).

In the early years of the twentieth century, a number of Christian missionary organizations came to Pomo communities, seeking converts and influence. Catholics and Methodists soon established missions and schools in the region (25). They were followed by Baptists, Presbyterians, and Episcopalians, who visited Pomo communities and attracted small numbers of converts.

During the economic depression of the 1930s, Pomoan economy suffered due to declines in local farm production and in employment opportunities.

However, Pomos were able to participate in the federal Work Projects Administration and the Civilian Conservation Corps to help build and improve infrastructure on rancherias and obtain jobs for local residents. By the 1940s, most Pomos were either living on trust land rancherias or near towns and cities in California. Many obtained work on ranches and farms as either seasonal or year-round laborers. The people hunted and gathered acorns and other plants to supplement their incomes. And Pomo women made baskets both for household use and for sale to outside markets (27). Jane Adams, a Pomo of Oak Valley, described life during that period:

> I hard working lady—work even summer. Pick hops, train hops, pick grapes. Work every day. Winter time come—make baskets. Busy with the basket. People come around, buy basket. That help too. And I catch fish with net in Oak River. Swim all way under bank, catch about ten, fifteen at a time. Kill rabbit. Then we go to coast, every summer. Dry sea weed, dry mussels for winter time for eats. Sometime we want real meat, and we goes out and shoot wild rabbit. We gather basket root when we out of job. We gather this fall, and use them next winter. (206)

After World War II, as the economy of California expanded both in agricultural production and industrial development, Pomos secured jobs in greater numbers. Nonetheless, they still faced discrimination and suffered from poorer living conditions than many nearby communities.

CONTEMPORARY POMOAN COMMUNITIES

Pomos have been actively involved in regional and statewide organizations dedicated to securing Native rights and improving living conditions, expanding political involvement, and securing justice for their people. They helped found the Society of Northern California Indians and the Inter-Tribal Council of California and participate with service organizations such as Northern California Indian Education, California Indian Legal Services, and California Indian Rural Health Service that provide funding for local programs. In an attempt to strengthen their political voice, Pomos founded the Sonoma County Coalition for Indian Opportunity and the Mendo-Lake Pomo Council in order to unite people from various communities and address common issues. And as Forbes observed, since aboriginal independent tribelets and villages have lost their land base and autonomy, Pomos no longer identify themselves as members of distinct and separate groups but instead have adopted the ethnic label of "Pomo." Although such designation was originally incorrect, it has advantages today "since a unified Pomo people, several thousand strong, possess stronger political power than a number of small groups of a few hundred individuals each" (1969: 143).

While most Pomo lands lost their trust status since the 1950s and 1960s, not all rancherias have been terminated. Those that remain as officially recognized Native communities are governed by elected councils and officials who are responsible for representing their people and coordinating local programs. In contrast, rancherias that were terminated have gradually gone out of Pomo control because many people sold their land to pay taxes that were required once they lost trust status. Some people have remained near their old communities and others have moved to Californian cities, especially San Francisco.

There are today twenty separate Pomo communities living in California that have official federal recognition. These are located in three counties: Sonoma, Lake, and Mendocino. Several of them operate casinos in the lucrative and populous California market. In 2012, two Pomo groups, the Federated Indians of Graton Rancheria and the Dry Creek Rancheria Band of Pomo Indians, purchased land outside their original reservation with plans to construct new casinos there. The Graton Rancheria Pomo's compact with the state has been approved but the Dry Creek Pomo signed an agreement in 2015 to not begin construction on another casino until 2025, in exchange for a deal to reduce their taxes to the state (Mason 2015). In another casino negotiation, the Coyote Valley Band of Pomo Indians has agreed to provide up to 15 percent of its net earnings to local communities in exchange for permission to expand gaming operations.

In support of other types of economic development, the Hopland Band of Pomo Indians has received a grant of $122,000 from the US Department of Agriculture to expand farming practices. The Pomos have initiated a program stressing the interconnections between agriculture and traditional environmental knowledge.

The Hopland Band of Pomos is dealing with another environmental challenge. Their water supply, originating from a tribal well, is contaminated with dangerous materials deriving from the ground, especially arsenic. The Pomos do not have a safe, affordable source of drinking water. They have therefore been awarded a grant from the Environmental Protection Agency, amounting to $228,000, to clean up a water supply on a 6.5 acre section of land that they will then be able to use in their community. In addition, funds are also being used for ongoing monitoring of soil and water conditions, a new Recycling Center, and other environmental protection projects (Tobin and Carre 2007).

Traditional cultural knowledge is emphasized among children and teenagers through participation in school programs and summer camps. In these programs, children and teens learn about the ancestral uses of environmental resources and traditional food collection and preparation. Efforts at language maintenance are stressed as well. These are supported by a $20,000 grant from the Native Youth and Culture Fund of the First Nations Development Institute to help create southern Pomo language apps for iPhones and Android phones. Internet links to photos, language audio recordings, and videos are additional features of language maintenance projects.

Economic conditions vary considerably at the numerous Pomoan rancherias and communities. According to federal statistics based on 2009 earnings,

Pomos' average per capita income was $12,572, a figure somewhat below the American Indian average of $16,446 Compared to other Native Americans, their poverty rate is moderate but still extensive. In 2010, 39.7 percent of Pomoan families and 42.0 percent of individuals were living below the poverty level (Tobin and Carre 2007). Pomoan income and poverty figures are startlingly lower than those for other residents of California. In the same year that Pomos' per capita income was $12,572, the overall Californian figure was $27,353. Pomos were about three times as likely to be living in poverty than other Californians.

Employment and unemployment statistics for Pomos are also varied. Of the seventeen federally recognized Pomo rancherias and bands reported by the Native American Liaison Branch, Coyote Valley had the highest percentage of potential workers not employed (44.7%) while several, Stewart's Point, Redwood Valley, Sulphur Bank, and Guidiville had the lowest (0%). However, several of the above communities had very small sample sizes, so these numbers are likely unrepresentative. Average unemployment for all Pomos was 18.2 percent, compared to a California rate of 12.8 percent.

Despite all of the changes that have taken place in Pomo economy and political organization, traditional extended families continue to provide financial and emotional support to their members. Interest in use of the Pomoan languages has developed, but the outlook for linguistic maintenance is not good. Data collected from the 2000 census reveal that 216 people reported use of the Native language as their "home language" but only four people between the ages of 5 and 23 were speakers (Broadwell 1995: 147; US Bureau of the Census 2000, Table 18: 874).

Traditional beliefs about contact with the spirit realm through dreaming remain strong for some Pomos. Bole Maru dreamers and traditional curers treat ailments by aboriginal means such as dreaming, singing, and sucking out pains. Indeed, according to Sarris, survival of the Bole Maru

Kashia Pomo woman weaving a "gambling tray"; weaving remains an important art in California.

religion is the "foundation for a fierce Indian resistance that exists in many places to this day ... Bole Maru leaders inculcated an impassioned Indian nationalism in the homes and ceremonial roundhouses" (1992: 75). It is also a religion that is adaptive and creative, constantly reinvigorated by the addition of new rites given by Dreamers and the abandonment of old songs and dances when their originator dies unless she explicitly permits their continuation (78). Among the most prominent Pomo Dreamers in the second half of the twentieth century were Essie Parrish (Kashaya) and Mabel McKay (Lolsel Cache Creek). Both women received their doctoring spirits in dreams and practiced according to instructions given by their spirit helpers. As McKay recalled, she heard the voice of her spirit speaking to her and felt her tongue move: "The spirit said, 'it's me. And what is happening is that you have an extra tongue. Your throat has been fixed for singing and sucking out the diseases. It's talking. It's me in you'" (quoted in Sarris 1994: 38). McKay later became a colleague of the well-known Essie Parrish, already an established doctor with a dedicated following. After Parrish's death, McKay obeyed her colleague's wishes, locked the Roundhouse where Parrish had practiced, and threw away the key (124). These procedures were consistent with Pomo traditions that emphasize the personal association between Dreamers and their ritual practice, allowing for a continual process of innovation and creativity based on individual spiritual inspiration.

Contemporary Populations

From a probable aboriginal Pomoan population of 8,000, Cook estimates a decline to about 5,000 in 1851, 1,450 in 1880, and a recorded 747 in 1908 (1976: 239). Pomoan populations have increased slowly since then. In 2010, the US Census counted 4,688 residents of Pomoan rancherias in California. See table 18.1 for a breakdown of population in several areas.

TABLE 18.1	Acreage and Population of Pomoan Rancherias	
Rancheria	**Area (in acres)**	**Population**
Big Valley	171	274
Coyote Valley	70	182
Dry Creek	75	530
Hopland Ranch	400	357
Manchester-Point Arena	350	404
Middletown	109	58
Pinoleville	99	131
Redwood Valley	177	91
Robinson	113	225
Stewarts Point	100	477
Sulphur Bank	50	123
Upper Lake	119	96

Source: http://www2.bren.ucsb.edu/mlpa3/tribes.html; http://www.census.gov/population/www/cen2010/cph-t/t-6tables/TABLE%20(1).pdf; http://library.sdsu.edu/guides/sub2.php?id=195&pg=195; http://www.courts.ca.gov/.

REFERENCES

Aginsky, B. W. 1976. "The Socio-Psychological Significance of Death among the Pomo Indians." *Native Californians: A Theoretical Retrospective* (ed. L. Bean and T. Blackburn). Ramona, CA: Ballena Press, pp. 319–329.

Barrett, S. A. 1905. "Basket Designs of the Pomo Indians." *American Anthropologist* 7: 648–653.

Barrett, S. A. 1908. *Pomo Indian Basketry*. Berkeley, CA: University of California Press.

Barrett, S. A. 1916. "Pomo Buildings." Washington, DC: Holmes Anniversary Volume, pp. 1–17.

Barrett, S. A. 1917a. *Ceremonies of the Pomo Indians*. Berkeley, CA: University of California Publications in American Archeology and Ethnology 12.3, pp. 397–441.

Barrett, S. A. 1917b. *Pomo Bear Doctors*. Berkeley, CA: University of California Publications in American Archeology and Ethnology 12.11, pp. 443–465.

Broadwell, George. 1995. "1990 Census Figures for Speakers of American Indian Languages." *International Journal of American Linguistics* 61, no. 1: 145–149.

Colson, Elizabeth. 1974. *Autobiographies of Three Pomo Women*. Berkeley, CA: University of California Archeological Research Facility.

Cook, Sherburne. 1976. *The Conflict between the California Indian and White Civilization*. Berkeley, CA: University of California Press.

Essig, E. O. 1933. "The Russian Settlement at Ross." *Quarterly of the California Historical Society* 12, no. 3: 191–216.

Forbes, Jack. 1969. *Native Americans of California and Nevada*. Healdsburg, CA: Naturegraph Publishers.

Gifford, Edward. 1926. *Clear Lake Pomo Society*. Berkeley, CA: University of California Publications in American Archeology and Ethnology 18.2, pp. 287–390.

Gifford, Edward. 1928. "Notes of Central Pomo and Northern Yana Society." *American Anthropologist* 30: 675–684.

Gifford, Edward. 1967. *Ethnographic Notes of the Southwestern Pomo*. Berkeley, CA: University of California Anthropological Records 25, pp. 1–47.

Gifford, Edward, and Alfred Kroeber. 1939. *Culture Element Distributions, IV: Pomo*. Berkeley, CA: University of California Publications in American Archeology and Ethnology 37.4, pp. 117–254.

Hudson, John. 1897. "Pomo Wampum Makers: An Aboriginal Double Standard." *Overland Monthly* 30: 101–108.

Kasch, Charles. 1947. "The Yokayo Rancheria." *California Historical Society Quarterly* 26: 209–216.

Kroeber, Alfred. 1925. *Handbook of the Indians of California*. Washington, DC: Bureau of American Ethnology, Bulletin No. 78.

Kunkel, Peter. 1974. "The Pomo Kin-Group and the Political Unit in Aboriginal California." *Journal of California Anthropology* 1: 7–18.

Loeb, Edwin. 1926. *Pomo Folkways*. Berkeley, CA: University of California Publications in American Archeology and Ethnology 19.2, pp. 149–405.

Mason, Clark. 2015. *No Petaluma Casino Until 2025 under Deal with the Dry Creek Rancheria Band of Pomo Indians*. The Press Democrat. Online.

McLendon, Sally, and Robert Oswalt. 1978. "Pomo: An Introduction." *California* (ed. R. Heizer), Vol. 8 of *Handbook of North American Indians*. Washington, DC: Smithsonian Institution, pp. 274–288.

Native American Liaison Branch, Caltrans. 2016. *California Federally Recognized Native American Tribes*. California Department of Transportation. Online.

Oswalt, Robert. 1964. *Kashaya Texts*. Berkeley, CA: University of California Publications in Linguistics No. 36.

Sarris, Greg. 1992. "Telling Dreams and Keeping Secrets: The Bole Maru as American Indian Religious Resistance." *American Indian Culture & Research Journal* 16, no. 1: 71–86.

Sarris, Greg. 1994. *Mabel McKay: Weaving the Dream*. Berkeley, CA: University of California Press.

Tobin, Phyllis, and Kris Carre. 2007. *Household Hazardous Waste Management Plan for the Hopland Band of Pomo Indians*. US Environmental Protection Agency. Online.

US Bureau of the Census. 2000. "Table 18: American Indian Language Spoken at Home by American Indian Persons in Households, by Sex and Age." Washington, DC.

Vayda, Andrew. 1967. "Pomo Trade Feasts." *Tribal and Peasant Economies* (ed. G. Dalton). Garden City, NY: Natural History Press, pp. 494–500.

Veniaminov, Ivan. 1972. "The Conditions of the Orthodox Church in Russian America." *Pacific Northwest Quarterly* 63, no. 2: 41–54.

Willoughby, Nona. 1963. *Division of Labor among the Indians of California*. Berkeley, CA: University of California Archeological Survey Reports 60, pp. 7–79.

THE PLATEAU

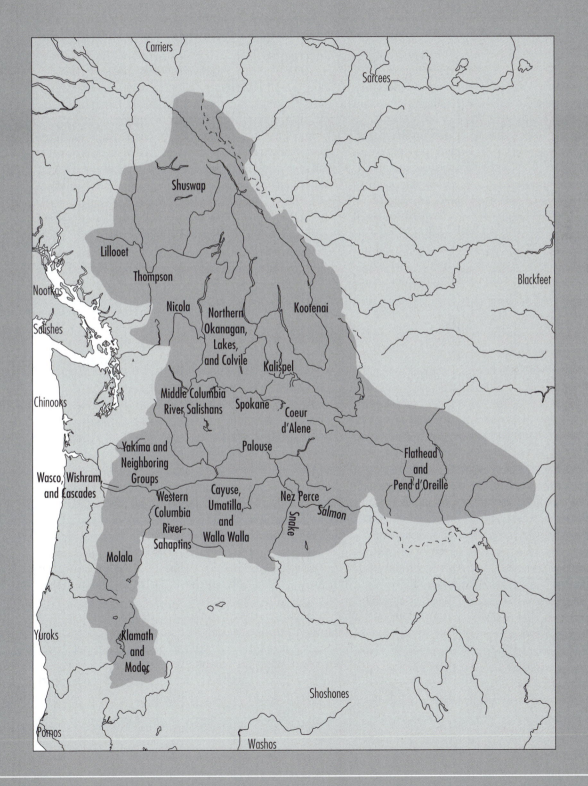

How Coyote Saved the People Swallowed by the Monster

A Nez Perce Narrative of Transformation

Coyote was just wandering downriver, and it was quiet around for a long time. And he learned that a Monster had swallowed everyone. Then one who was left, whoever he was, said, "Monster swallowed them all now. And you too are to go there also." Now Coyote made plans. He went up this way here, high up, and he came to place called Passasonam. Then Coyote made seven rawhide ropes there, and he tied himself to the Seven Devils mountains. Then he shouted to the Monster, "Let us inhale each other." Now the Monster heard him. Then it heard again, "Let's inhale each other."

Now the Monster got ready, and breathed in. The wind moved Coyote, but he was held because he had himself tied down. Then Monster tried again, breathing more strongly; it was anxious to swallow Coyote. Now one rope broke. Then again Monster tried, and another rope broke, then all seven broke. Now Coyote was pulled and Monster took him in; Coyote was quickly pulled to Monster's mouth. "Now I swallowed you." He went on inside and first saw a rattlesnake acting vicious. Coyote said, "Why, what for are you being so vicious?" And he stepped on, kicked, and flattened its head. For this, rattlesnakes have flat heads. Then he walked into a grizzly bear and it acted vicious toward Coyote. He said to the grizzly bear, "Why, what for are you being so vicious?" And he grabbed the grizzly bear's nose and flattened it with his hand. For this reason, grizzly bears have concave noses.

Then he saw so many people already starving to death. "Why are you making yourselves hungry, while this much meat is here?" Then people said, "No, you are not going to do that. Monster will soon kill us all." Now he pulled out five agate knives. One he took out and he started cutting its heart. Then the knife broke. Then again he took out another and kept cutting like this, and all he pulled out. He broke the last knife as he was cutting. Now by a little bit the heart was attached, and Coyote pulled its heart loose. Then Monster dropped dead. Then Coyote cut Monster's meat for each, and he threw it to them saying, "Eat this!" Then the poor ones ate. Then Coyote told them, "Now we are going out." Then everyone came out of the Monster. Monster now lay dead.

Then Coyote cut it into pieces and threw them as he proceeded. He threw its leg to the eastern country of the Sioux, saying, "There they will be tall people." He threw each of its short arms to the south, and there they became short people. In this way, Coyote cut and distributed meat from various parts to each of the different people. But he forgot the Nez Perce people. Then he said, "I surely forgot these people who are living right here. I have not given them anything." Then he washed his hands, which were all bloody, and moistened the earth with the bloody water. And he told them, "Right here people will be brilliant and they will feel brave. They will be brilliant in everything."

The head of that Monster was up the river at Kooskia. And his body came down the river over the bluffs and all the way to Kamiah. Monster had such a body and down the river to the Udder Place. Its tail was down the river on the other side at the Lolo Creek. This was the size of that huge Monster. And Coyote killed it in that way. Then people were happy and became settled.

Source: Haruo Aoki. 1994. "Nez Perce Texts." *Nez Perce Dictionary*. University of California Publications in Linguistics 90. Berkeley, CA: University of California Press, pp. 27–28.

Native Nations of the Plateau

LANDS AND NATIONS

The region called the "Plateau" is an area comprising parts of what are now the states of Idaho, Oregon, and Washington and adjacent sections of the Canadian province of British Columbia. The principle ecological features that helped shape Plateau cultures are the major regional waterways including the Columbia River, Fraser River, Clearwater River, and the Snake River. These waters provided the focus of Plateau economies and settlement patterns. Most peoples established their villages near the rivers in order to most efficiently avail themselves of the many resources both in the waters and in the nearby foothills, plains, prairies, and forests. The Plateau is also characterized by its boundaries of mountain ranges, that is, the Cascade Range on the west, the Blue Mountains on the south, and the Rocky Mountains on the east and north.

In addition to the major rivers, many smaller streams and lakes provided resources that Plateau peoples utilized. The region includes forested areas and extensive grasslands, contributing to an abundant resource base for indigenous peoples. Climatic conditions affected the seasonal distribution of resources and therefore the adaptive strategies developed by local populations. The Plateau is characterized by dramatic variations in temperature and precipitation at different times of the year and in different localities. Moist air coming from the Pacific Ocean results in summer thunderstorms and heavy snow falls in the winter but in some places these conditions are tempered by the high mountains of the Cascade Range to the west. The greatest amount of precipitation occurs at higher elevations while foothills and plains receive relatively less rain and snowfall. Temperatures vary in a similar pattern, with colder readings further north and at higher elevations and warming to the south and at lower levels. The warmest regions are in the Columbia River basin.

Although the cultures of the Plateau nations shared many similar practices, there were also significant local differences. The Plateau region, therefore, encompassed northern, southern, and eastern variants, each one influenced by the environments and the peoples living in areas adjacent to them from whom they borrowed some practices. The diversity of cultural origins is demonstrated by the distinctions of Plateau languages into three separate language families: Athabascan, Salishan, and Sahaptian. Athabascan speakers include the Kootenai and Nicola while Interior Salish is represented by the Lillooet, Thompson, Okanagan, Spokane, Shuswap, Coeur d'Alene. and Flathead. Sahaptian languages are spoken by the Sahaptin, Nez Perce, Cayuse, Wasco, Wishram, Klamath, and Modoc peoples.

Archeological evidence suggests that aboriginal peoples inhabited the Plateau region for at least 11,000 years and have left a continuous record of cultural development culminating in the practices attested from historical data. Earliest peoples were gatherers and hunters, dependent on the foods found naturally in their environment. Resources included many species of fish, animals, and wild plants and fruits. At the earliest time of human settlement, the region was relatively dry in the winter and hot in the summer. Therefore, forests and their resources were less abundant than during later periods. Because of the variability in available resources, people were nomadic, moving frequently depending on food supplies. Their settlements were small and their dwellings were quickly built and easily dismantled (Chatters and Pokotylo 1998; Stryd and Rousseau 1996).

About 5,000 years ago, increased rates of rainfall encouraged the growth of forests and many types of plants, supporting animal, fish, and plant resources and therefore increases in the size of human populations. The expanded resource base included deer, elk, rabbits, birds, many varieties of fish, especially salmon, sturgeon, and minnows, and fruits and root crops.

Another significant finding from this period is evidence of trade among peoples. Implements and ornaments made from obsidian derived from other regions and from dentalium and other shells from the Pacific Ocean have been found in inland Plateau sites, firmly connecting the Plateau region to other peoples living to the south in the Great Basin and to peoples living along the Pacific coast in western Oregon and Washington. In the Plateau, trading was made easier by travel along the Columbia and Fraser Rivers and their tributaries. Trade networks later expanded north into British Columbia.

As local resources became more dependable, settlements became more stable. Houses were larger and were dug deeper into the earth. In addition to settled communities, people resided in small, temporary camps when fishing, hunting, or collecting roots and plants, all major sources of food. These camps were located in the river valleys for best access to resources. Techniques for storing food also developed and became more frequently utilized. Houses contained pits for storage and sometimes ovens for processing food (Stryd and Rousseau 1996).

The next series of climatic changes began about 2,000 years ago, resulting in warming and drying trends. New flood plains were formed along the Columbia and Snake Rivers, especially in summer when heavy rain storms flared up, helping to support increased vegetation. With expanding plant growth, people traveled further to procure new food sources, including into the higher elevations spreading out from river basins. Root crops were especially exploited and processing technologies were refined. There is evidence that people may have used fire in order to control and direct plant growth in regions upland from the rivers. In the southeastern regions of the Plateau, bison migrated onto the lands from the adjacent western Plains.

Growth in food supplies led to changes in settlement patterns. Rather than living in many small settlements dispersed along the rivers, people sometimes gathered together in large villages, some containing more than a hundred dwellings. And, significantly, the size of houses within a village often varied, some measuring more than 12 meters (36 ft.), suggesting differences in relative wealth and social status (Chatters 1989, 1995; Ames 1991).

Finally, goods obtained from peoples in other regions increased in number and variety. These included dentalium shells, beads made of shell, pipes for smoking, and many types of ornaments made of stone, whalebone, and animal antlers. There is evidence of differences among households in both the number and quality of trade goods, further supporting assumptions that some people were wealthier and had higher status than others. The importance of trade is reflected in the development of communities that were strategically located on trade routes, some later expanding into large centralized trading centers that became critical in the eighteenth and nineteenth centuries to the fortunes not only of indigenous peoples but of European and American merchants as well.

The final set of changes in Plateau cultures were in place by about 1,000 or 1,500 years ago. Variations in community size and settlement patterns are indicated by the growth of some villages while at the same time population densities in other communities declined as the number of people in some concentrated settlements dispersed into many smaller communities living along the primary rivers of their territory, especially the Columbia, Frazer, Snake, Clearwater, and Salmon Rivers. Within villages, social inequalities that were earlier indicated by differences in household size and in the number of possessions largely disappeared, presumably reflecting egalitarian social ethics.

ABORIGINAL CULTURE

Economies

Environmental conditions in the Plateau created a rich resource base utilized seasonally by indigenous peoples. The principal food sources included root crops and other plants as well as numerous species of fish. Some 135 varieties of plants were collected as were more than 35 species of freshwater fish. Food collecting work was generally allocated according to gender. Women were responsible for gathering the majority of wild plants while men caught fish and hunted animals. Although the percentages varied in different locations, women's work contributed more to their household's nutrition (possibly 50–70%) than did the productive work of men (Hunn 1981).

The most important root crops were camas and other varieties in the lily family, bitterroot, wild carrots, wild onions, and parsnips. These foods were prepared by cooking in pits heated with hot stones and then dried on woven mats or hung on strings. In this form, they could be stored in baskets for later use at which time they would be soaked in water or combined in soups. In addition to root crops, Plateau peoples gathered shoots, leaves, fruits, berries, and mushrooms. These foods were either eaten fresh or dried for winter storage. Pine seeds, acorns, and hazelnuts were also collected. The inner tissues of the bark of pine and cottonwood trees were scraped off and eaten fresh. Finally, tree lichen from fir or pine branches was collected, cleansed with water, pounded, and cooked in pits, sometimes mixed with wild onions or berry juice.

Fish provided the most significant source of protein in the Plateau diet. The amount of fish consumed varied for different locations but estimates suggest a range of about 400–600 lb. per capita annually (Hewes 1973). Many varieties of fish were sought but by far the most important was several species of salmon. The major waterways of the region, especially the Columbia and Fraser Rivers and their tributaries, were spawning grounds of five species of salmon. These fishes were taken at many sites with the use of varied technologies including spears, dip nets, rectangular nets, and traps. The most abundant catches were taken at waterfalls and rapids where migrating fish could be easily caught as their journey to their spawning grounds was made difficult by blockages and turbulent waters. These sites included the Cascades and Kettle Falls in present-day Washington as well as the Dalles and Celilo Falls in Oregon. Additional fishes taken included species of lampreys, sturgeon, and suckers.

Fish were generally either boiled in heated pits or roasted over fires. Fish not eaten immediately were then dried in the air and stored for winter use in baskets or bags. Indeed, the majority of these foods provided nutrition during the winter when fresh plants and fish were scarce.

Finally, men hunted animals to supplement their families' diets. In most areas of the Plateau, animal meat was a less significant source of food than fish but in some localities, especially in the northern Plateau,

hunting provided a more substantial resource because of the lack of plant crops. The most important animals taken included deer, elk, bighorn sheep, and caribou. In the eastern Plateau, bison could be hunted as well. Smaller animals such as rabbits, squirrels, and marmots were also hunted. Many species of birds were caught and their eggs collected for food.

In addition to the consumption of foods within households and communities, many resources were exchanged among Plateau peoples in local and regional networks. Indeed, these exchanges were a distinguishing feature of Plateau economies, connecting nearby and distant peoples. Trade routes extended from the Pacific Ocean coast, inland along the Columbia River and its numerous tributaries, and through the prairies and plains of the upper Northwest. The trading season lasted from late spring until late in the summer. There were several key centers of intertribal trade to which the Plateau peoples had regular access. The most important was the Dalles, located on the Columbia River just east of the Cascade Mountain range in what is now northern Oregon. A second significant trading site was located nearby at Celilo Falls and a third was at the Cascades, about 50 mi. distant. These centers were positioned in the territory of the Sahaptin, Wasco, and Wishram who came to dominate the trade but Plateau peoples from all over the region exchanged their goods. Men and women traders from coastal areas in western Oregon, Washington, and British Columbia brought marine shells, whale oil, and blubber; peoples from the western regions of the Plateau brought animal skins, woven mats, and breads made from roots; and from the southern Plateau, people brought horses, camas roots, animal hides, and buffalo robes. Buffalo robes were obtained both from forays into the plains of Montana and from trade with western Plains groups, especially the Flatheads. Salmon pemmican was an especially favored item, produced by people living in villages near the Dalles along the Columbia River basin. Salmon pemmican was made of dried salmon pounded into a paste and then kept in baskets lined with salmon skins. This food could then be stored and eaten in later seasons. Estimates suggest that about 1,000,000 lb. of salmon pemmican was produced and traded each year (Griswold 1970: 21).

In addition to the major centers at the Dalles, Celilo Falls, and the Cascades, Plateau traders participated in other commercial centers located in eastern Oregon at the Grande Ronde, in eastern Washington at Kettle Falls, and at other sites in the area. And southern Plateau peoples exchanged goods at the annual Shoshone rendezvous in northern Wyoming. People from all over came to exchange goods that they themselves procured and surplus products that they had obtained through trade with others. In this way, the continual flow of goods in and out of the Plateau was sustained.

For the indigenous peoples of the region, commerce was not merely an economic exchange but was embedded in social networks and social relationships. People established stable partnerships with particular individuals at the same trading centers. Trade itself was viewed as an exchange of gifts of equal value, not as a context for making a profit. If people did not know each other well, then some bargaining might take place but eventually people who traded regularly with one another established social relations as well. For example, the following is a description of an encounter between Nez Perce and Spokane traders in Washington:

> The Nez Perce lined up on one side, each man holding the lead rope of his "trading" horse. Each Spokane came forward and placed his pile of trade goods in front of the horse he liked. If the Nez Perce was satisfied, he handed over the lead rope and took the goods. If not, he might try for an extra article, or he might lead his horse to some other pile which interested him. It might take all of a pleasant summer day to trade 40 horses, but this seemed to worry nobody. (Haines 1964:80)

Settlements

Plateau settlements were of two distinct types. The most stable were winter villages located in basins created by the regional waterways. These villages typically consisted of rectangular longhouses positioned linearly near the rivers. The houses were constructed of a wooden frame covered by woven mats and straw. They varied in size and could therefore accommodate different numbers of families. The smallest might be the home of only two or three related families while

Two Skokomish women by mat shelter and rowboat, ca. 1913.

the largest might extend about 100 or 150 ft., able to house several families. Villages themselves also varied in size, some containing only a few longhouses while the largest might contain about a hundred separate dwellings. The population of villages therefore differed, ranging from 50 to as many as 1,000, although the latter size was less common.

Riverine villages were inhabited during the winter so that residents could take advantage of the somewhat milder climate characteristic of river basins. But resources even in these areas were relatively scarce in winter so that people relied on their stores of dried foods that had been prepared during the spring and summer.

In the summer, Plateau peoples generally moved to temporary camps at higher elevations. Summer dwellings were sometimes constructed on the same model as the winter longhouses but were generally smaller and accommodated fewer families. Another type of summer lodge consisted of a conical wooden frame covered with animal hides or woven mats.

Families and Social Systems

Plateau social systems were based on ethical principles of equality and personal autonomy. All people were understood to have the same rights to resources and social respect, and could aspire to fulfill prestigious roles in their households and communities. One's intelligence, skills, and personal charisma were the deciding factors in determining how one was viewed by other community members.

The thoroughgoing equality characteristic of Plateau societies extended to both women and men. Although men and women had different productive roles, their contributions to their households were equally valued. Women and men owned property individually and made decisions about the distribution and consumption of resources and property without interference from others. Spouses cooperated jointly in providing for their families but did not have rights to control each other's activities or decisions. Both men and women could participate in household or community discussions leading to decisions that affected the group. Age, and the life experience it implied, rather than gender was a factor in the influence one had. Although chiefs were usually men, the abilities, intelligence, and personality of a man's wife was a significant factor in his being chosen to lead because a chief's wife was one of his major advisers. And in some

nations, she could function as chief in her husband's absence. Finally, women and men could equally participate in the important sphere of religious activity. Both girls and boys sought personal spirit guardians and as adults could become shaman or specialists performing rituals to cure illness or foretell the future.

Kinship systems in Plateau nations followed principles of bilateral descent. Household organization was structured around an extended family, generally consisting of an elder couple, their sons and/or daughters and these people's spouses and children. Siblings might also form the center of an extended family household that included their own spouses and children. Therefore these households might be based on multigenerational or collateral bonds. Since the kinship system reckoned relationships bilaterally, extended households could be linked through descent from a founding mother or father. People chose their affiliation to the core group either in the male or female line depending on their personal ties, the composition of already existing households, and the availability of resources. In addition, one's affiliation with an extended household could change during one's lifetime. This was especially true for young couples and individuals who were relatively mobile although older people tended to have more stable residence patterns, in part because they themselves might be the focal members of such households.

Extended family households had a spatial focus since they occupied a communal longhouse in a winter village. The number of related nuclear families forming an extended household varied and therefore the size of the composite group varied as well. Since extended families were the core of economic, social, and political cooperation, larger units could provide more resources and in turn attract new members. That is, given the choices that a bilateral kinship system allowed, people favored affiliating themselves with stable and successful households, thus reinforcing the appeal that such households had.

There was little variation in household and kinship systems throughout the Plateau. However, some groups in the western Plateau borrowed elements of social organization from neighboring peoples further to the west in coastal Washington and British Columbia. For example, the Lillooet had a system of clan organization that was based on bilateral descent allowing people to affiliate with either or both their mother's or their father's group. These clans were said to have originated in mythic times, founded by an animal or spirit being (Teit 1906:252). Although Lillooet clans organized people into recognized groups, they did not have any particular corporate functions and did not restrict marriage choices as clans often do elsewhere.

In Plateau nations, marriage was forbidden between known relatives but otherwise there were no restrictions or preferences. Parents and/or other older relatives arranged marriages for young men and women. A couple was considered married at the end of exchanges of goods between their respective families, beginning with gifts going from the family of the future husband to the wife's kin, followed by reciprocal exchanges offered by the wife's relatives. Although arranged marriages were the ideal, either the man or woman could elope with another partner if they objected to their parents' choice. First marriages might end in divorce, possibly initiated by either spouse. There was no social stigma associated with divorce and remarriage therefore was common. Marriages beyond the first were not arranged by parents but instead were the result of personal choices. Although people were free to marry because of their own inclinations, families expressed some preference for the levirate or sororate after the death of husband or wife. These patterns allowed for the continuity of an alliance between families that had been established by the original marriage.

Most couples lived in monogamous marriages but polygyny was possible. Although a man could marry unrelated women, sororal polygyny was the most common type since the likelihood of friction between cowives was minimized by the fact that the two women were sisters and already had strong emotional and social bonds. Men who were chiefs, shaman, or successful fishermen and hunters were more likely than other men to contract marriages with more than one woman due to their ability to provide for larger households and to their social prestige.

EUROPEAN TRADE AND ITS CONSEQUENCES

Influences from European sources reached Plateau nations long before people of European descent actually entered the region. Trade items of foreign origin made their way through indigenous intertribal networks from Pacific coastal peoples who traded directly with British, Russian, and Spanish merchants beginning in the early eighteenth century. These items, including beads, coins, and copper kettles and other metal utensils, and later guns and ammunition, were traded and retraded along the Native commercial networks.

One of the most significant effects of European trade was the acquisition of horses. These animals made their appearance among southern Plateau nations in the early eighteenth century through long-established trade networks linking this region to the Great Basin and the Southwest. Horses originated from Spanish settlements in present-day New Mexico and were traded by indigenous groups such as the Apache, Navajo, Ute, and Comanche to more northerly nations. Peoples in the southern Plateau initially received horses from the Shoshones in the northern Great Basin region. Some of these Plateau peoples, especially the Nez Perce, soon became the conduits for horses into the western Plains. Later, horses were obtained through trade and through raiding other peoples. As elsewhere in North America, horses led to greater mobility and were thus useful in procuring resources and in transporting both goods and people. Horses also led to increased hostilities between groups, enabling warriors to range further from their home villages and to return safely. The goal of acquiring additional horses became a motive for raids. In the border regions of the Plateau eastward toward the Plains and south toward the Great Basin, raiding grew to be especially frequent, with increasing numbers of fatalities. Finally, ownership of horses resulted in systems of social differentiation based on this new form of measurable wealth. Families who owned more horses were better positioned to acquire resources and to excel in warfare, both sources of social prestige and political influence. Some families might own more than 1,000 horses (Osborne 1955).

A deadly consequence stemming from European contact was the devastating effect of introduced diseases, especially smallpox and measles, to which indigenous populations had no natural resistance. Although population estimates before European contact and recordkeeping are always questionable, the Plateau region as a whole was probably inhabited by at least 87,000 people in aboriginal times (Boyd 1998: 472). Even this estimate is likely to be an underrepresentation of the actual population because it is based on figures collected by missionaries, travelers, and government agents well after the first waves of disease spread through the region.

The earliest documented smallpox epidemic in the Plateau occurred sometime in the 1770s (Boyd 1994). It originated in communities along the Pacific coast where Europeans first arrived in 1774. Contemporary observers noted that this epidemic was "a dreadful visitation" with the "most virulent form of the smallpox" (Drury 1958: 137). It is probable that these early epidemics led to the deaths of about half of Plateau populations (Boyd and Richerson1985). A second deadly wave of smallpox hit the Plateau in 1801 and 1802. This episode may have originated in the Plains, brought to the Plateau by Nez Perce and other hunters seeking the buffalo that inhabited that region. Although many people died during this period, the disease seems to have been in a milder form, causing fewer casualties. Smallpox entered the region again twice in epidemic form, in 1853 and in 1862, causing additional deaths.

After trading posts were opened in the Plateau by British and American merchants in the 1820s and 1830s, new infectious diseases, especially influenza and whooping cough, spread through the Native villages that congregated around the posts, especially in winter when their own food supplies had dwindled. Another source of disease came from American children who entered the Plateau in the 1830s and 1840s, offspring of missionaries and settlers. They brought with them typical childhood diseases such as chickenpox, whooping cough, and measles.

Exploration and Trade in the Nineteenth Century

By the early nineteenth century, the US government began to take a more active interest in exploration of the west, especially following the purchase of Louisiana Territory from France in 1803. An exploratory expedition, led by Meriwether Lewis and William Clark, departed from St. Louis, Missouri and, with the guidance of a northern Shoshone woman named Sacagawea, reached the Plateau in the fall of 1805. Their first encounter with Plateau peoples was a meeting with the Nez Perce near present day Wieppe, Idaho. After a stay of several weeks in the area, Lewis and Clark continued westward along the Clearwater, Snake, and Columbia Rivers, heading west toward the Pacific coast. These travels took them through territory held by the Nez Perce, Walla Walla, Cayuse, Wasco, Umatilla, and Yakima. By that time, these peoples were thoroughly familiar with articles of European origin that they obtained through indigenous intertribal trade networks. They were already in possession of copper and iron utensils including knives, hatchets, and files in addition to blankets and wool and cotton cloth (Moulton 1983).

Shortly thereafter, following in the footsteps of Lewis and Clark, American and European traders established direct commercial relations with Plateau peoples. Their initial interest was in acquiring animal furs, especially beaver, extending the reach of the fur trade that had begun in the east of North America in the sixteenth century and somewhat later on the Pacific coast. The first foreign trader to enter the Plateau was David Thompson, employed by the British North West Company, who established several posts beginning in 1807. Others soon followed, leading to competition between several companies but after 1821 British trade was monopolized by the Hudson's Bay Company after its merger with North West. The British fur companies initially established trading posts near the centers of indigenous trade along the Columbia River and its tributaries but later attempted to widen their territorial scope. Additional competition soon came with the presence of American fur traders, especially the Rocky Mountain Fur Company, who entered the region in 1829.

At first, Native peoples insisted on embedding commercial transactions within the kind of social relationships that characterized their own trading networks. The British complied with this etiquette, holding feasts and ceremonial gift exchanges with the Natives. American merchants were less likely to adhere to these norms but instead focused solely on trade as an economic matter divorced from social relations. For their part, indigenous peoples tried to get the better bargain by encouraging competition between British and American traders, attempting to lower prices for the goods they wanted to receive. American traders were willing to lower the prices for their goods in order to attract indigenous trade away from the British. Both the indigenous and American strategies were successful for several decades but by the middle of the nineteenth century, most of the companies had departed the region because of the depletion of beaver in the area.

By the early nineteenth century, some groups were receiving guns and ammunition from European and American sources. Some guns were obtained directly from the foreign traders while others were obtained from Native people through a series of exchanges. Members of villages situated along the Columbia River closest to the commercial centers tried to monopolize the trade in weapons in order to prevent peoples living upriver from obtaining them. But the people whose ability to acquire guns was blocked sought to open up the trade. Increased access to weapons in the context of depleting resources and the imminent departure of American and European traders led to intertribal conflicts as well as hostilities toward the foreign merchants.

Within Plateau communities, conflicts also arose when some people tried to monopolize trade in their villages, seeking to become intermediaries and raise their status as sources of European goods.

Missionaries soon followed traders into the Plateau, beginning their attempts to convert Native peoples to Christianity in the 1830s when Roman Catholic, Anglican, and Presbyterian missionaries visited villages and established missions among them. The Roman Catholics proved to be the most successful throughout the Plateau except among the Nez Perce where the Presbyterians were able to gain adherents. However, there were few early converts, some of whom were village and band headmen who hoped to benefit from their association with the missionaries to gain greater access to trade goods and influence. They further hoped to become middlemen in trade between the outsiders and their own village members, supplying people with desired articles and therefore gaining supporters and allies.

An important reason for the lack of enthusiasm for conversion on the part of most Plateau peoples was that, according to their own traditions, ritual practice was understood to lead to the maintenance of good health, prosperity, and power. But since people who converted to Christianity did not seem to be more likely than others to have these advantages, there was no perceived benefit to following the Christian path. In addition, the rivalries and struggles for power that ensued among headmen who had converted were sometimes disruptive to village and community stability. Finally, Plateau aboriginal religious practices remained strong, continuing to furnish the people with a coherent understanding of the world in which they lived.

US SETTLERS AND GOVERNMENT POLICY

In addition to traders and missionaries, American settlers began arriving along the Oregon Trail, first in 1845 with the passage of about 3,000 settlers. Between that year and 1850, some 11,500 American settlers passed through Plateau territory (Unruh 1979). Policies of the US government supported the intrusion of

settlers and the extension of American power tipped the balance in their favor. The influx of settlers also prompted negotiations between the United States and Great Britain over the boundary separating the United States and Canada, resulting in the Oregon Treaty of 1846 establishing the current borders. The Treaty was, however, silent on the status of Native peoples and their claims to ancestral territory. Government officials then extended their reach into the Northwest in order to obtain Native lands for settlement and to "pacify" the indigenous tribes inhabiting the region so that settlers could enter the territory without fear of attack. They also sought to establish reservations for the Natives and to convince them to remain there and to alter many of their cultural traditions.

The first step in this process was the creation of Oregon Territory in 1848 by an act of the US Congress. The Act protected the "rights of person or property" of Native inhabitants "so long as such rights shall remain unextinguished by treaty." And it allocated $10,000 for presents to Native tribes for the purpose of securing "peace and the quietude of the country" (Oregon Territorial Legislature 1854: 28–37). Following on the wording of this Act, the government set out to negotiate treaties with the indigenous peoples in order to obtain their land and impose cultural changes. Military posts were opened throughout the Plateau in the 1850s, enabling the government to keep close supervision of the region. And the government sought to prevent Plateau peoples from crossing into Canada to trade with the British Hudson's Bay Company. In addition, the federal BIA sent superintendents to oversee local operations. Washington Territory was then created by Congress in 1853 under the governorship of Isaac Stevens, who began negotiating treaties in 1854 and 1855 with indigenous nations in Washington and Oregon.

The Walla Walla Treaty Council in 1855 was the first to be held with Plateau peoples. In all, eleven treaties were negotiated with several nations acting together, under the guidance of Stevens and the Indian superintendent of Oregon, Joel Palmer. A number of additional treaties were concluded by the US officials with single nations. Nearly all of the treaties followed a standard pattern pursuant to the government's interests in obtaining large tracts of indigenous territory, establishing reservations, promoting economic and social changes in indigenous cultures, and protecting Native people's fishing rights while at the same time guaranteeing Euro-American fishing rights as well.

Governor Stevens's words at the Walla Walla Treaty Council outlining the government's wishes summarizes not only the government's intentions but also their attitudes about promoting agricultural work and transforming gender roles:

> My children, we want you to agree to live on tracts of land, which shall be your own and your children's; we want you to sell the land you do not need to your Great Father; we want you to agree with us upon the payments for these lands; we want you to have schools and mills and shops and farms; we want your people to learn to read and write; your men and boys to be farmers or millwrights or mechanics, or to be of some profession as a lawyer or doctor. We want your wives and daughters to learn to spin and to weave and to make clothes and all the labor of the house. (Quoted in Slickpoo and Walker 1973: 93)

The Treaty of 1855 guaranteed Native rights to continue gathering plants, fishing, and hunting on lands ceded to the government as long as the land remained unoccupied by settlers. And it guaranteed that the government would continue to support schools and agricultural services in perpetuity unless limited by further treaties. However, conditions for Plateau peoples deteriorated by the increasing numbers of settlers encroaching on their lands, new and virulent outbreaks of smallpox and measles, and the discovery of gold deposits that attracted even more miners and settlers. These conditions led to armed conflicts and retaliations but rather than protecting the rights and lives of indigenous peoples, the army arrested and imprisoned Native people accused of attacking or killing settlers. Some of these prisoners were hanged without trial, thus prompting more anger and leading to intensified warfare between the US Army, local militiamen, and indigenous peoples. The wars ended in 1858 but not before the Army burned Native farm fields, destroyed stored foods, and killed hundreds of horses, all in an attempt to force the people to submit to government demands.

Another wave of miners and settlers entered the Plateau in the late 1850s and 1860s after the discovery of gold in the Thompson and Fraser River watersheds in British Columbia and in the United States in Oregon and Idaho. The influx of settlers, numbering as many as 35,000, led Congress to create Idaho Territory in 1863 (Bancroft 1890). New roads, railroads lines, and towns sprang up throughout the region, many intruding on protected Indian lands. Congress also approved the rights of non-Indian settlers to drive their cattle and sheep herds through reservations and to take reservation acreage for the expansion of American towns. In both the United States and Canada, the growth of the fishing industry further compromised the ability of Native peoples to secure resources for their survival. Commercial fisheries interfered with salmon runs that had for millennia given the people their major protein source.

These conditions led in the 1870s to renewed resistance on the part of indigenous peoples to the presence of settlers, the loss of their ancestral territory and even those lands guaranteed by treaty, and government pressures for cultural change. In northern California, in 1872, Captain Jack of the Modocs led a small group of dissidents from their location as part of the Klamath Reservation with the goal of returning to their prior lands. When the US Army was sent to capture them, warfare ensued, ending in the Native defeat the following year. Four Modoc leaders were hanged and about 150 were sent in exile to the Quapaw Reservation in Oklahoma (Murray 1959: 304–306). A few years later, in 1877, Chief Joseph of the Nez Perce led another valiant effort to resist being moved from their ancestral lands in Oregon and for a time they were successful in evading and defeating army units sent to capture them. But they were finally stopped 40 mi. from the Canadian border, ending armed resistance in the Plateau.

In addition to reservations established by treaties, US presidential executive orders created some reserved lands for indigenous peoples in the Plateau. However, the orders did not provide for protections of fishing or hunting rights and could be, and often were, either revoked or unilaterally amended by the president or the US Congress without consultation with the people concerned. Some of these orders created composite reservations intended for several tribal groups. For example, the Colville Reservation was set aside in 1872 for members of the Okanagan, Sanpoil, Nespelem, Lakes, Colville, Methow, Kalispel, Spokane, and Coeur d'Alene nations with no regard to allocating specific territory to each group. Conflicts inevitably arose among the various peoples over the boundaries of the lands that they controlled. Furthermore, subsequent executive orders and congressional mandates arbitrarily reduced the acreage contained in the reservation. In similar fashion, executive orders created the Coeur d'Alene Reservation in Montana, the Spokane Reservation and the Kalispel Reservation in Washington, and the Grand Ronde Reservation in Oregon (Lahren 1998: 492–493). The land base contained within all of these reservations was reduced by subsequent executive orders.

The territorial situation in British Columbia was equally, if not more, complex for Plateau First Nations. Shifts in government policies throughout the late nineteenth and early twentieth centuries left the indigenous people vulnerable to reductions in their land base. Reserved lands were first established in the 1850s under the governorship of James Douglas whose efforts were based on recognition of aboriginal title to lands customarily inhabited and utilized by indigenous peoples. Under his guidance, Native groups were directed to select the lands that they wanted based on their traditional patterns of use. This procedure created relatively small reserves inhabited by separate bands generally consisting of no more than several hundred members. Shortly thereafter, however, the following governor reversed the policy and unilaterally reduced the size of reserves. The next process was set in motion after 1871 when British Columbia joined the Canadian Confederation as a province. Although the federal government asserted its primacy in dealing with First Nations, conflicts arose between federal policies that recognized aboriginal title and British Columbia provincial interests that sought to limit indigenous landholdings.

As administrative personnel came and went, policies also vacillated between these two goals. The one consistent practice is that numerous reserves have been established for separate bands in recognition of their autonomous indigenous territories. That is, most people secured reserves within the boundaries of their aboriginal lands, although much reduced in size. As a result, there are now more than 400 small reserves in the province together encompassing about 500,000 acres.

The Prophet Dance and the Seven Drum Religion

Resistance to forced changes may take many forms. People may resist external control by strengthening and reinforcing their own system of beliefs, sometimes manifested as religious movements that promote indigenous culture and seek solutions to current problems through spiritual means. Revitalization movements arise in situations of rapid cultural change that undermines traditional beliefs, erodes economic stability, and curtails and limits political independence.

Several new indigenous religious movements found adherents in Plateau communities in the late nineteenth century, a time of military conflict and cultural upheavals. Although these movements were to some degree innovative, they also emphasized continuation of aboriginal beliefs and practices. One of the earliest was the Prophet Dance, a circular dance with men and women stepping in a rhythmic pattern while singing and praying. Each dance was organized by a leader who had received inspiration in visionary contacts with spirit beings. These visionary experiences usually occurred when a person was thought to have been nearly dead or was thought to have actually died. The vision came in a kind of reawakening or rebirth. The leader or prophet then announced his or her message of hope and renewal for the whole community. The dance was a means of honoring the vision and of hastening the time of world renewal. During the dance, some of the participants also received visions. Dances might be led by different prophets, some of whom might attract large followings if their prophecies and visions were especially compelling.

Another religious movement that developed was called "Washat" or the "Seven Drum" religion. In this tradition, ceremonies were also inspired by a leader who received spiritual messages in visions and dreams. He or she imparted prophecies and sometimes performed miraculous cures, often while in a trance state. The ceremony itself centered on drumming and singing. Seven drummers positioned themselves in a row at the western end of a rectangular longhouse, accompanied by bell-ringing in keeping with the drumming. Each drummer, beginning with the youngest, sang songs in succession. At the same time, the men and women in attendance danced and sang, holding fans made of eagle feathers in their right hands. At intervals of rest between the songs and dances, elders from the community might speak to those present, encouraging them to maintain their cultural traditions and beliefs.

As the nineteenth century wore on, ceremonies for the Prophet Dance and the Seven Drum Religion drew increasing numbers of participants. These rituals appealed to people because they conveyed messages that validated Native customs and offered hope to a people overwhelmed by changes that they could not control.

Promoting Cultural Changes

In order to further the goal of promoting changes in indigenous behavior and attitudes, government officials established schools for Native children. Some of the schools were day schools while others were boarding schools that housed children for the entire school year. Boarding schools were deemed the most effective because they separated children from their homes and families for long periods of time. Most of the teachers were either missionaries themselves or were assigned by missionary boards that oversaw Native education. Eventually, children were made to feel ashamed of their parents, of their traditional customs and beliefs, and of their own Native language.

Educational policies were spelled out by Edward Geary, Superintendent of Indian Affairs for the Pacific Northwest region. Writing in 1859, Geary stated:

> The children educated at these institutions should be taken entirely from the control of their parents, and boarded under the care of a judicious matron, where habits of cleanliness, punctuality, and order should be carefully cultivated. The education of the schools should not only embrace letters, but the boys should be instructed in agriculture and trades; the girls in the use of the needle and the various branches of domestic economy. These schools should be governed and taught by persons of not only capacity, firmness, and ability, but by those of decidedly religious character. (ARCIA 1860: 755).

And the basic philosophy of educators was summed up later in 1878 by James Wilbur, agent to the Yakima Reservation:

> The Bible and the plow (which must never be divorced) have brought them up from the horrible pit, and put a new song into their mouths, and new hopes into their hearts. They are washed and clothed in their right minds. There can be no lasting good accomplished with the children in school, without taking them to a boarding school, where they are taught to talk, read, and write the English language. (ARCIA 1878: 141)

However, during most of the late nineteenth century, very few children actually attended the schools. Those who did later became proponents of accommodation to government policies that promoted cultural changes, not just in education, but in work roles, housing styles, and basic family organization. Along with the shift toward farming, the agents favored breaking up large, extended family residential patterns and replacing them with nuclear family dwellings. It was an attempt to separate generations that, along with schooling, removed children from the direct influence of their families, particularly of their grandparents who were likely to retain traditional cultural practices and ideals.

In 1880, a further step in separating children from their families was begun with the founding of the Indian Training School, located in Forest Grove, Oregon, later moved to Chemawa, near Salem, Oregon. The Indian Training School drew students from many reservations in the Northwest. It was a boarding school that included a summer work program so that children would not return to their home communities until they had completed their many years of training. The school operated under an "outing system," first developed for Indian institutions at the Carlisle Indian School in Pennsylvania. In this system, students worked, without pay, during the summer on the farms and in the homes of American citizens. Boys worked as farm hands and ranch hands while girls did domestic labor in the households. The founder of the Indian Training School, M. C. Wilkinson, a lieutenant in the US Army, commented on his intentions: "The first rule here after cleanliness and obedience is 'No Indian Talk.' Children are to be divided up until all tribal association is broken up and lost. Their entire removal from family and reservation influences are the points of highest hope (ARCIA 1881:199). All of the schools, whether day or boarding, whether on or off the Reservation, followed military style discipline. Corporal punishment was meted out to children who did not follow the many regulations governing their behavior and their speech.

Finally, both day and boarding schools stressed the development of patriotism toward the United States. Celebrations for the Fourth of July lasted four full days and included foot races, horse races, feasting, and parades. Soon, celebrations for other national holidays, including George Washington's birthday, Memorial Day, Thanksgiving, and Christmas were added to the list. Observance of these holidays promoted allegiance to the United States and to Christian beliefs and principles.

As elsewhere in the western United States, the General Allotment Act of 1887 led to the breakup of communal landholdings on Plateau reservations as families and individuals were assigned specific parcels for their use. Land on some reservations was actually allotted earlier according to provisions of the treaties negotiated by Isaac Stevens and others in the 1850s and 1860s. Although the allotment policy was implemented in somewhat different ways and at different times on the various reservations, by early in the twentieth century, all of the Plateau peoples saw their control over land holdings diminished as their family acreage was reduced. In addition, "surplus" land that had not been allotted was opened up for homesteading by American settlers, resulting in a further decline in the indigenous territorial base.

Similar procedures were adopted by the provincial government in British Columbia for the allotment of lands despite protests by the indigenous residents of assigned reserves. In an effort to secure their rights, a number of Native groups formed the Allied Tribes of British Columbia, one of the first intertribal organizations whose goal was protection of their land base and their hunting and fishing rights. Although they were not immediately successful, the Allied Tribes established a model that was repeated by other Native intertribal organizations in the Plateau and Northwest.

A decision rendered by the US Supreme Court in 1908 gave significant protections for Native water rights in the region. In *Winters v. United States*, the justices ruled that Indians have priority water rights from rivers and streams within the boundaries of existing reservations as well as in lands that had originally been part of reservations as negotiated by treaty but subsequently lost to Native control. However, many groups had a difficult time asserting these rights because of competing interests by non-Indian users and the lack of funds to construct dams, canals, and other irrigation projects that would give the people access to the waters. The issue of water rights was contentious throughout the twentieth century and remains so today.

Passage of the Indian Reorganization Act by Congress in 1934 was met with only minor approval by Plateau nations. Only three groups approved its provisions but it nonetheless marked a change in federal policy, especially in ending allotment procedures and in providing funds for the purchase of additional acreage for Indian reservations. Shortly after the Indian Claims Commission was established in 1946, most of the Plateau nations filed suits claiming illegal seizures of their territory. Although many of these claims were eventually successful, they took decades to be resolved.

However, any security that Native peoples might have felt at the time was short-lived since a new government policy was introduced in the 1950s, aimed at terminating the trust status of Indian reservations. Bills enacted by Congress in 1954 provided for the termination of the Colville Confederated Tribes and the Klamath Reservation. Both of these reservations had rich timber resources that were coveted by lumber companies then able to negotiate favorable contracts to extract forest products. The Klamath Reservation was particularly hard-hit by the termination policy. The loss of federal funding meant the end of support for educational and healthcare facilities. Then subject to state and federal taxation, many residents were forced to sell their allotments but had nowhere else to go. Efforts by Klamath people to reestablish trust status finally led in 1986 to congressional approval for the renewal of reservation status.

CONTEMPORARY COMMUNITIES

Regional Resource Issues

Rights to fishing, as guaranteed by treaties signed in the nineteenth century, continues to be one of the most contentious issues for Plateau nations. All of the treaties agreed to by Plateau peoples and the US government contain language that guarantees rights to fish "at usual and accustomed places" but this phrase has been variously interpreted by different courts at different times. Several cases in the late nineteenth century resulted in rulings that acknowledged the rights of indigenous fishermen to have access to traditional fishing stations even if they had to cross through land owned by non-Indians. An additional Supreme Court ruling in a case in 1919 interpreted the treaty phrase "at usual and accustomed grounds and stations" to include fishing sites located on lands originally encompassed by early treaties but subsequently lost through cession or sale.

A new set of problems arose beginning in the 1930s when Congress authorized the construction of dams on the Columbia River. These dams, especially the Grand Coulee and Bonneville dams, caused serious disruption to salmon runs and thus interfered with the subsistence and livelihood of Plateau peoples. Indeed, construction of the Grand Coulee dam resulted in flooding of large sections of the Colville Reservation, rendering people homeless until funds were later allocated for the purchase of new acreage. In the 1950s, representatives of Plateau nations including the Nez Perce, Yakama, Umatilla, and Warm Springs nations, participated in negotiations with the US Army Corps of Engineers in a dispute over compensation for the loss of fishing sites at Celilo Falls in Oregon. These sites were principal fishing locations for Native peoples for hundreds of years but were flooded by construction of the Dalles Dam, completed in 1957. Finally, after years of negotiations, the several Indian tribes were awarded a total of about $27 million. The money received was a direct compensation for loss of fishing sites.

Then, in 1977, Plateau nations took part in founding the Columbia River Inter-Tribal Fish Commission, a network of Native peoples in the Northwest whose goal is protection and rehabilitation of the rivers and streams that are critical to the preservation of salmon and steelhead trout runs. These runs are, in turn, critical to the livelihood, sense of identity, and cultural integrity of Plateau peoples. (For more detailed discussions of Northwest fishing rights, see Chapter 21.)

Native peoples in British Columbia have also initiated legal suits regarding fishing rights and land claims. A major ruling was handed down by the Supreme Court of Canada in 1973 in a case brought by the Nisgha who claimed that their aboriginal rights to territory in the Nass Valley had never been extinguished. The Court ruled in their favor and indeed set a precedent for aboriginal status in Canada by affirming that aboriginal title to territory derived from their "long-time occupation, possession, and use" regardless of whether this concept was recognized by European governments at the time of initial settlement (Ministry of Aboriginal Affairs 1995).

Another significant ruling was handed down in 1990 by the Canadian Supreme Court in a case involving a fisherman from the Musqueam Indian Band in British Columbia who sought to overturn a conviction for using a net longer than that allowed under the federal Fisheries Act. The Court vacated the conviction, citing the 1982 Constitution Act granting protection of aboriginal rights. Furthermore, the Court enumerated principles for understanding aboriginal rights, beginning with the notion that aboriginal rights may evolve over time and must be interpreted generously. Second, provincial and federal governments can only regulate aboriginal rights given compelling reasons to do so, including conservation and resource management. And, finally, aboriginal peoples have priority in the allocation of fish for subsistence over other groups (Ministry of Aboriginal Affairs 1991).

In the same year, the British Columbia Claims Task Force began to discuss formulating treaties with First Nations aimed at specifying and securing treaty rights and resolving land claims through negotiation. Since then, most territorial

Staff from Yakama Nation Fisheries load mature sockeye salmon into a waiting semi-truck in 2012, for reintroduction to Cle Elum Lake as part of the Cle Elum fish passage project, led by the Yakima Nation fisheries department.

claims brought by Native peoples in British Columbia have led to the acquisition and protection of additional acreage. This result is consistent with the negotiation process that assumes that First Nations should have control of territory "proportional to their population."

Native peoples in both the United States and Canada have recently focused on environmental concerns regarding pollutants in the waters and on the land that interfere with their economic pursuits and with their goals of sustainable resource management. For example, six tribes in Oregon are working together to pressure the federal Environmental Protection Agency to develop strategies to clean up a Superfund site that is the source of contamination of salmon and other fish that eventually reach the Columbia River and its tributaries. The nations of the Umatilla, Nez Perce, Yakama, Grand Ronde, Warm Springs, and Siletz are negotiating with the federal Fish and Wildlife Service and the Oregon Department of Fish and Wildlife to remove toxins including arsenic, cyanide, heavy metals, PCBs, and various pesticides from the Portland Harbor whose waters flow into the Willamette River and from there into the Columbia River. Native access to several species of salmon that become contaminated from these toxins is guaranteed by treaty as well as by negotiated agreements between the tribes and state and federal agencies.

In 2012, the Colville Confederated Tribes won an important victory in a US court against an industrial polluter located in Canada. A smelting company called Teck Metals Ltd. (formerly Teck Cominco) admitted in court to having knowingly emptied millions of tons of toxins into the upper Columbia River during the period from 1896 until 1995 (McNeel 2013). These toxic byproducts of the smelting process, including zinc, lead, mercury, and arsenic, polluted the river and the many lakes into which it flows and therefore contaminated fish and other resources crucial to the Native economies and to their environmental foundation. When the Colville Tribes first filed charges against Teck, the company claimed that they were immune from prosecution for polluting US waters since they were located in Canada but the US District Court in Washington ruled against the company and further stated that Teck is responsible for funding cleanup as well as for other damages.

The issue of water rights in the Northwest continues to be a source of conflict among tribal and nontribal interests in the region. In the state of Oregon, a successful agreement was reached that will affect local farmers and fisheries. The agreement guarantees water supplies for fisheries along the Columbia River that flows through tribal lands and for farm irrigation throughout the rural eastern parts of the state (Lies 2013). In Montana, however, an agreement between the Confederated Salish and Kootenai Tribes, the Montana Reserved Water Rights Compact Commission, and the federal government has been stalled because of opposition from the Western Montana Water Users Association, an organization of non-Indian, off-reservation farmers and ranchers who claimed that granting water rights to the Confederated Tribes and to the Flathead Indian Reservation might decrease their own supply (Hanners 2013). The negotiated settlement has, however, been submitted to the Montana state legislature for their approval, pending the outcome of litigation.

Issues of Taxation

The ability of state and federal agencies to impose taxes on businesses located on Indian reservations proves to be another source of conflict in the Northwest as elsewhere in the United States and Canada. For example, the federal Alcohol, Tobacco and Trade Bureau has assessed excise taxes on cigarettes manufactured by a member of the Yakama Nation. The manufacturer, King Mountain Tobacco, instituted a suit to block taxation, claiming that tax immunity extends to businesses operating on Indian lands as provided by the Yakama Treaty of 1855. However, a US District Court judge ruled against this claim in 2013, stating that since tobacco originating on the reservation is blended with tobacco grown elsewhere in the production of cigarettes, the business is not wholly derived from on-reservation sources. The state of New York is also seeking to tax cigarettes made by King Mountain Tobacco that were shipped to stores on the Poospatuck Indian Reservation on Long Island, New York (Ferolito 2013a)

In another tax case concerning the Yakama Nation, the US District Court again ruled against the Yakamas, this time regarding Washington state's withdrawal from an agreement that would have imposed state taxes on only 25 percent of bulk fuel purchased by Native owners of reservation gasoline stations (Ferolito 2013b). The state claimed that the Yakama Nation had not complied with the requirement to submit records of sales and is therefore attempting to impose full taxation. The controversy arises, in part, from the fact that given the history of allotments of reservation lands and the subsequent sale of parcels to non-Indians, the Yakama Nation is a patchwork of acreage owned by Indians and non-Indians. Therefore, many non-Indians living on the reservation purchase their gasoline from nearby stations that are on Native-owned land. The state claims that the station owners are liable for taxes on gasoline sold to non-Natives.

Contemporary Populations

Economic problems within the Plateau region are not as severe as in other Native regions, but unemployment continues to be a large problem, and all income rates lag far behind state averages. Poverty rates in many reservations and for many tribes are double or triple that of the general region. Unemployment is worst for the Bridge River Indian Band in British Columbia, with 43.5 percent of the 457 members unemployed, more than five and a half times the British Columbia rate

of 7.8 percent. Poverty levels for Plateau nations are generally between 15 and 30 percent, with the Umatilla and the Modoc on the low side, and the Warm Springs reservation on the high side at 46.5 percent. For tribes in British Columbia for which data was available, the 2011 census estimated the average earnings at $23,384, as compared to the British Columbia average of $40,005. See tables 19.1 for an overview of rates for given Plateau tribes in the United States, and 19.2 for an overview of rates for given Plateau tribes in British Columbia.

Programs to support Native language maintenance and development as well as other cultural projects have been instituted on reservations in the Plateau region. Participation in language immersion schools is growing in recognition of the fact that few tribal members are fluent speakers of their indigenous tongue. The Montana legislature approved funding in 2013 for language preservation projects on the state's

---

TABLE 19.1 | **Selected Economic Characteristics for Plateau tribes**

Tribe/Reservation	Per Capita Income ($)	Unemployment (%)	Poverty Rate (overall) (%)
Nez Perce	18,428	17.0	21.7
Flathead	15,357	19.0	34.7
Colville	15,487	14.9	29.3
Spokane	14,287	28.2	27.4
Coeur d'Alene	13,486	17.6	24.6
Sahaptin	14,918	13.4	30.3
Klamath	14,145	20.6	24.8
Modoc	18,133	26.5	15.4
Warm Springs	10,043	24.6	46.5

Source: Selected economic characteristics, 2006–2010: American Community Survey, American Indian and Alaska Native tables.

TABLE 19.2 | **Selected Economic Characteristics for Plateau Tribes (Canada)**

Tribe/Reservation	Average Earned Income ($)	Unemployment (%)	Median Household Income ($)
Lower Nicola	23,681	24.0	28,375
Xaxli'p	20,564	26.9	31,347
Tit'q'et	19,007	29.6	27,999
Tasl'alh	23,047	23.8	31,128
Shuswap	27,292	9.1	47,902
Okanangan	22,677	13.5	41,567
British Columbia (all)	40,005	7.8	60,333

Source: http://fnp-ppn.aadnc-aandc.gc.ca/.

Indian reservations (Dennison 2013). This funding is consistent with the goals of the Indian Education for All program that mandates teaching Native American culture in classes throughout the public school system in Montana and thereby exposes all students, Indian and non-Indian, to the indigenous heritage of the state.

REFERENCES

ARCIA. 1860. *Annual Reports of the Commissioner of Indian Affairs to the Secretary of the Interior*. Washington: Government Printing Office. New York: AMS Press.

ARCIA. 1878. *Annual Reports of the Commissioner of Indian Affairs to the Secretary of the Interior*. Washington: Government Printing Office. New York: AMS Press.

ARCIA. 1881. *Annual Reports of the Commissioner of Indian Affairs to the Secretary of the Interior*. Washington: Government Printing Office. New York: AMS Press.

Ames, Kenneth. 1991. "Sedentism: A Temporal Shift or a Transitional Change in Hunter-Gatherer Mobility Patterns." Between Bands and States (ed. Susan Gregg). Carbondale, IL: Southern Illinois University, Center for Archaeological Investigations. Occasional Paper 9, pages 108–134.

Aoki, Haruo. 1994. "Nez Perce Texts." *Nez Perce Dictionary*. University of California Publications in Linguistics 90. Berkeley, CA: University of California Press, 27–28.

Bancroft, Hubert. 1890. *History of Washington, Idaho, and Montana, 1845-1889*. San Francisco, CA: The History Company.

Boyd, Robert. 1994. "Smallpox in the Pacific Northwest: The First Epidemics." *BC Studies* 101: 5–40.

Boyd, Robert. 1998. "Demographic History until 1990." *Plateau. Handbook of North American Indians*, Vol. 12 (ed. Deward Walker). Washington, DC: Smithsonian Institution, pp. 467–483.

Boyd, Robert and Peter J. Richerson. 1985. *Culture and the Evolutionary Process*. Chicago: University of Chicago Press.

Chatters, James. 1989. "Resource Intensification and Sedentism on the Southern Plateau." *Archaeology in Washington*, 1: 3–19.

Chatters, James. 1995. "Population Growth, Climatic Cooling, and the Development of Collector Strategies on the Southern Plateau." *Journal of World Prehistory* 9, no. 3: 341–400.

Chatters, James, and David Pokotylo. 1998. "Prehistory: Introduction." *Plateau. Handbook of North American Indians*, Vol. 12 (ed. Deward Walker). Washington, DC: Smithsonian Institution, pp. 73–80.

Dennison, Mike. 2013. "Montana Senate OKs bill for Indian language preservation pilot program." Missoulian. February 27. http://missoulian.com/news/state-and-regional/montana-legislature/.

Drury, Clifford. 1958. *The Diaries and Letters of Henry H. Spalding and Asa Bowan Smith Relating to the Nez Perce Mission, 1838–1842*. Glendale, CA: Arthur H. Clark.

Ferolito, Phil. 2013a. "Yakama Tribal Cigarette Maker Could Face $30 Million Tax Bill." *Yakima Herald Republic*. February 20.

Ferolito, Phil. 2013b. "Judge Rules against Yakamas Again in State Fuel Tax Fight." *Yakima Herald Republic*. February 21.

Griswold, Gillett. 1970. "Aboriginal Patterns of Trade between the Columbia Basin and the Northern Plains." *Archaeology in Montana* 11, nos. 2–3: 1–96.

Haines, Francis. 1964. "How the Indians Got the Horse." *American Heritage* 15, no. 2: 16–22, 78–81.

Hanners, Richard. 2013. "Judge Rules for Irrigators in Water Compact." *Hungry Horse News*. February 27. http://www.flatheadnewsgroup.com/hungryhorse-news/news/article

Hewes, Gordon. 1973. "Indian Fisheries Productivity in Pre-Contact Times in the Pacific Salmon Area." *Northwest Anthropological Research Notes* 7, no. 2: 133–155.

Hunn, Eugene S. 1981. "On the Relative Contribution of Men and Women to Subsistence Among Hunter Gatherers of the Columbia Plateau: A Comparison with Ethnographic Atlas Summaries." *Journal of Ethnobiology* 1:124–134.

Lahren, Sylvester. 1998. "Reservations and Reserves." Plateau (ed. Deward Walker). Vol. 12 of *Handbook of North American Indians*. Washington, DC: Smithsonian, pp. 484–498.

Lies, Mitch. 2013. "Environmentalists, Tribes and Farmers Agree on Water Strategy." February 19. http://www.dailyastorian.com/news/local/environmentalists-tribes-and-farmers.

McNeel, Jack. 2013. "Watershed Heroes: Colville Confederated Tribes Win Sierra Club Award." *Indian Country Today* 3, no. 12 (April 3): 18.

Ministry of Aboriginal Affairs. 1991. *The Report of the British Columbia Claims Task Force*. June 28. Victoria, BC: Ministry of Aboriginal Affairs.

Ministry of Aboriginal Affairs. 1995. *Information about Landmark Court Cases*. Victoria, BC: Ministry of Aboriginal Affairs.

Moulton, Gary (ed.). 1983. *The Journals of the Lewis and Clarke Expedition*. Lincoln, NE: University of Nebraska Press.

Murray, Keith. 1959. *The Modocs and Their War*. Norman, OK: University of Oklahoma Press.

Oregon Territorial Legislature. 1854. *The Statutes of Oregon, 1853*. Salem, OR: Asahel Bush.

Slickpoo, Allen, and Deward Walker. 1973. *Noon-Nee-me-poo (We, the Nez Perces): Culture and History of the Nez Perces*. Lapwai, ID: Nez Perce Tribe of Idaho.

Stryd, Arnoud, and Michael Rousseau. 1996. "The Early Prehistory of the Mid-Fraser- Thompson River Area." *Early Human Occupation in British Columbia* (ed. Roy Carlson and Luke Dalla Bona). Vancouver: University of British Columbia Press, pp. 177–204.

Teit, James. [1906]1975. *The Lillooet Indians. Memoirs of the American Museum of Natural History* (ed. Franz Boas). New York: AMS Press.

Unruh, John. 1979. *The Plains Across: The Overland Emigrants and the Trans- Mississippi West, 1840- 1860*. Urbana, IL: University of Illinois Press.

The Nez Perce

The earth is the mother of all people, and all people should have the equal rights upon it. You might as well expect the rivers to run backward as that any man who was born a free man should be contented penned up and denied liberty to go where he pleases. I have asked some of the great white chiefs where they get their authority to say to the Indian that he shall stay in one place, while he sees white men going where they please. They cannot tell me.

Whenever the white man treats the Indian as they treat each other, then we shall have no more wars. Then the Great Spirit Chief who rules above will smile on this land, and send rain to wash out the bloody spots made by brothers' hands upon the face of the earth. For this time the Indian race are waiting and praying.

North American Review April 1879: 431–432; in
Beal 1963: 288

THE NEZ PERCE LIVE IN LANDS in the southeastern region of the Plateau, concentrated in present-day western Idaho and nearby territory in eastern Oregon and Washington. The Nez Perce and their direct ancestors have lived in this region for at least 2,500 years.

The name Nez Perce is derived from a French term meaning "pierced nose," based on the people's custom of piercing their noses in order to wear ornaments made of dentalium shells. The people themselves have other names for their own group. The most common is "Ne-mee-poo," sometimes also written as "Nimipuu" or "Nimipoo" by members of the contemporary tribe. In their own language, this name means the "real people" or "we, the people." Although the custom of nose piercing ended in the early nineteenth century, the term "Nez Perce" is still in general use today.

TRADITIONAL CULTURE

Territories and Settlements

The current size of the reservation now inhabited by the Nez Perce is a small fraction of their aboriginal territory of approximately 13,000,000 acres or 27,000 sq. mi. Although the reservation today comprises about 750,000 acres, the Nez Perce themselves do not own even this amount but instead only control about 13 percent, or 97,500 acres. In former times, the people occupied land centering around three rivers in Idaho, Oregon, and Washington: the Snake, Clearwater and Salmon Rivers, and in addition encompassed tributaries, small streams, deep canyons, hillsides, and high plateaus. Temperatures and rates of precipitation varied, depending on elevation, that is, valleys and lands near rivers were warmer while upland hills and high plateaus were colder. Rates of precipitation in the form of summer rains and winter snows were greater at higher elevations. Because of these differences, people adjusted their living sites to changes in the seasonal availability of plant, fish, and animal resources, providing the Nez Perce with a balanced and nutritious diet. This lifestyle was an ancient one, dating back many centuries and indeed many millennia.

The country of the Nez Perce was described by Meriwether Lewis when he and William Clark visited in 1805 and 1806 during their exploratory expedition:

> To its present inhabitants nature seems to have dealt with a liberal hand for she has distributed a great variety of esculent [succulent] plants over the face of the country which furnish them a plentiful store of provision; these are acquired with but little toil, when prepared after the method of the Natives afford not only a nutritious but an agreeable food. Among the other roots those called by them "quawmash" [camas, a member of the lily family] and cows [cous] are esteemed the most agreeable and valuable as they are also the most abundant. (Moulton 1983, 5: 11–12).

The Nez Perce lived in distinct types of settlements during different seasons. During the winter, they resided in villages situated along the banks of rivers and streams. Some villages contained only a few dwellings but others might contain more than one hundred. In the summer, they lived in smaller, temporary camps located in the upland regions where they moved to exploit seasonally available resources. In 1800, there were seventy permanent villages, populated by between 30 and 200 people depending on the season. At that time, there were a total of 300 living sites, including the villages and smaller camps (Walker 1998:420).

The structures erected in the villages and summer camps differed. The largest houses, used during the winter, were longhouses, rectangular in shape, made of a wooden frame covered with woven mats and straw. Some of these houses measured 100–150 ft. in length, but others were smaller. Lewis described one of these large dwellings:

> It is 156 feet long and about 15 wide, built of mats and straw. In the form of the roof of the house having a number of small doors on each side, it is closed at the ends and without divisions in the intermediate space, this lodge contained at least 30 families. Their fires are kindled in a row in the center of the house and about 10 feet apart. All the lodges of these people are formed in this manner. (Moulton 1983, 4: 358–359)

Summer lodges erected in temporary fishing and hunting camps were sometimes built on the same design but were smaller, accommodating fewer families. Others were conical in shape, framed by wooden poles covered with hides or mats.

In addition to household dwellings, settlements contained sweat lodges, built partially underground, that were used for ceremonial purification and for cleansing and health purposes. Participants entered the lodge through a small hole on the top. Finally, menstrual lodges were used by girls and women during their menstrual periods. Located near main dwellings, they were built with the same materials as longhouses but were much smaller.

Economies

The Nez Perce were foragers, dependent upon the natural cycles of the earth, and like all foragers, they had a great deal of knowledge about the seasonal growth of plants, the migration patterns of animals and birds, and the spawning cycles of fish. This knowledge was learned and refined many centuries ago and then passed down from generation to generation. Their connection to the specific lands that they occupy is intimate and sacred.

Economic tasks were generally allocated by gender although some were performed cooperatively by men and women. Women's work centered on gathering the many wild plants, roots, and fruits available in their territories. In total, about 135 species of edible plants were eaten. These resources accounted for about 50–70percent of the annual diet (Hunn et al. 1998:526). The most important of these were the root crops, especially camas, a member of the lily family. Other significant root plants included couse, bitterroot, and wild carrots and onions. Women used wooden digging sticks to clear the ground and extract the roots. Root crops, the people's principal food, were prepared in a variety of methods:

> The principal roots [camas] which they made use of for food are plenty. These prairies are covered with them. They are much like potatoes when cooked, and they have a curious way of cooking them. They have places made in the form of a small coal pit and they heat stones in the pit. Then they put straw over the stones, then the water to raise steam. Then they put on large loaves of the pounded potatoes and 8 or 10 bushels of potatoes on at once. Then cover them with wet straw and earth. In that way they sweat them until they are cooked, and when they take them out, they pound some of them up fine and make them in loaves and cakes. They dry the

cakes and string them on strings, in such a way that they would keep the year and handy to carry, any journey. (Moulton 1983, 7:161)

In addition to roots, women collected many kinds of greens, shoots, mushrooms, pine nuts, sunflower seeds, fruits and berries, especially gooseberries, huckleberries, currants, and chokecherries. If food supplies stored from the summer and fall dwindled by late in the winter, women gathered lichen and black moss until spring plants became available. Moss, seeds and nuts were generally roasted or boiled. They might be eaten plain or cooked in cakes or stews. Finally, people sometimes peeled the bark of pine trees and ate the inner layers, providing a sweet and nutritious food.

Nez Perce men were the primary fishers and hunters although women participated in communal hunting and fishing endeavors. Men's work accounted for about 30–50 percent of the annual diet. Most animal protein came from fish. Indeed, it is estimated that each person consumed an average of about 500 lb. of fish per year. Altogether, there were about thirty species of fish caught, principal among them were salmon, sturgeon, and lake trout although other fish such as whitefish, minnows, suckers, and lampreys were also taken. The people had a complex and diverse technology for catching fish, using spears, harpoons, and hooks to catch fish individually and dip nets, traps, and weirs to catch large numbers of fish. Some of the nets measured about 330 ft. in length. People from several villages often cooperated in the construction of large traps and weirs, usually built on smaller streams that were tributaries of the major regional rivers. This work was overseen by fishing specialists who were also in charge of distributing the catch among all residents of the villages.

Of all the fish sought by the Nez Perce, the prize catch were salmon. Five varieties were taken, depending on the season and the sequence of spawning runs. When the rivers were thick with salmon, people paddled in canoes and caught the fish with spears or nets. They sometimes erected platforms on the rivers from which they could suspend their nets, enabling them to catch a large number of fish simultaneously.

Fish were prepared by drying them in the sun or smoking them over a slow fire. Dried salmon was sometimes broiled or roasted. A majority of the catch was stored in large pits and storage baskets for use during the winter when the fresh supply of fish was exhausted.

Hunting supplied significant sources of protein although meat was not as important as fish in the diet. The major large animals sought included deer, elk, moose, mountain sheep, black and grizzly bear. Smaller animals, especially rabbits, squirrels, and birds were also taken. Bows and arrows were the most common weapons used in hunting. Hunters occasionally covered the tips of their arrows with rattlesnake poison to increase the likelihood of a kill. All able-bodied men and women participated in communal hunting of deer and elk. The animals were sometimes lured into traps in open areas where hunters awaited and could then easily kill their prey or the people might attract the animals by erecting scarecrows or using decoys made of deer heads. For example,

These decoys are formed of the skin of the head and upper portion of the neck of that animal extended in the natural shape by means of a few little sticks placed within. The hunter when he sees a deer conceals himself and with his hand gives to the decoy the action of the deer at feed, and this induces the deer within arrowshot. In this mode the Indians near the woody country hunt on foot in such places where they cannot pursue the deer with horses which is their favorite method when the grounds will permit. (Moulton 1983, 4: 371)

Small animals and birds were most commonly taken with snares. When rabbits were plentiful, all men, women, and children in a village participated in catching them by walking through the fields holding long nets to capture the animals. The most common birds taken were Canada geese, ducks, swans, and grouse.

Animal meat was prepared employing similar methods to those used for fish. In order to boil meat, women put heated stones in large cooking baskets filled with water. They roasted the meat in earthen ovens situated either inside or outside their dwellings. Finally, women might broil meat by attaching it to sticks suspended over an open fire.

Subsistence activities followed a yearly cycle beginning with the gathering of plants in the early spring when the first root crops ripened in the lower river valleys. Communal hunts in search of deer and elk also took place in early spring, using snowshoes when snow was still deep upon the ground. Soon thereafter, fishermen sought the first salmon as the fish began their spawning runs on the Snake and Columbia Rivers. Crucial components of the spring cycle were the rituals performed to welcome the arrival of the first roots and the first salmon in the local environment. The ceremonies were led by specialists reciting prayers to please the spirits who were the guardians of plants and fish. If the rituals were not performed properly, spirit guardians would withhold their bounty and the people would suffer.

Later, as summer arrived, plants, fish, and animals became more abundant and were gathered or caught in all regions of the territory. People then often moved to campsites in the higher elevations in order to procure these resources. As fall and winter approached, the majority of foods taken were prepared for winter storage. At that time, people moved back to their winter villages near the rivers where temperatures were milder than at higher elevations.

In addition to consuming resources, the Nez Perce utilized plant and animal products in their tools, utensils, and clothing. In particular, most clothing was made from deer or elk hides. Men wore long shirts, leggings, breechcloths, and short moccasins. Women's clothing consisted of deer or elk skin dresses and knee-length moccasins. They also wore caps made of woven fibers. In cold weather, people wore buckskin gloves. Men and women decorated their faces with painted designs made with dyes obtained from plants and berries. People's clothing was also decorated with paints as well as with porcupine quills and shell or bone beads. Women's dresses, in addition, were decorated with elk teeth and shells originating in the Pacific Ocean that were obtained through trade networks.

Families, Households, and Social Systems

Nez Perce households were composed of people who were related through ties of bilateral descent. Kinship organization was based on the formation of informal groupings of relatives called "kindreds," consisting of all people related to one another through their mothers and fathers. People belonging to a kindred showed hospitality and generosity to one another, assisted each other in times of economic need, supported each other in conflicts with others, and were allies in political or military endeavors.

Kinship and descent were the basis of the most important social bonds among people. Marriage also formed critical social bonds between families that ideally endured after the death of one spouse through the practice of both the levirate and sororate but marriage was prohibited between any known relatives, whether close or distant.

Households usually consisted of extended families formed through multiple generations or through combinations of two or more nuclear families. An extended household might consist of an elderly couple, their unmarried children and their married children and these children's families or several siblings or cousins and their families could combine to form an extended household. Although the rules for residence after marriage were flexible, the ideal pattern was for a newly married couple to live in the husband's household since men's work required cooperation in fishing and hunting. However, actual residence patterns showed a great deal of variation. Indeed, many couples moved back and forth at various times to the relatives of each spouse, choosing residence on the basis of available resources, the composition of already existing households, and personal preferences. Younger couples and individuals, in particular, tended to be quite mobile but as people grew older, they had more stable living arrangements. Elderly couples were especially likely to live permanently in one place, attracting younger relatives on the basis of their knowledge, experience, and good reputation. Indeed, grandparents played a central role in the care and socialization of their grandchildren. The bond between these generations was perhaps the most affectionate of all kin relationships.

Family and community relationships were based on ethics of sharing and reciprocity. In the words of a contemporary Nez Perce woman,

> Indians were a really close-knit family. Everybody helped each other then. I can remember when living by the river, we never went anyplace or traveled that much, but we were in the area where people would come by our place, and our place was a convenient stopping place, so that older people were coming through, sometimes they would stop overnight, or sometimes they would stop and visit for a while, and Mom would say, "Go out there and pick some cherries for them. Get some cantaloupes, tomatoes, whatever we had, and we would give it to them. Giving was a strong part of our culture." (Quoted in James 1996: 88–89)

Community Leadership

Nez Perce society was based on egalitarian ethics. All people were understood to have equal rights to resources, to opportunities for prestige and respect, and to being valued for their contributions to their households. Seniority did confer some degree of influence and respect because a person's life experiences gave them knowledge and insight. And although men and women might have had somewhat different roles in their families and communities, they had equal status and their opinions were equally valued. But of course in practice some people were more respected by community members than others because of their good judgment, wisdom, success, and favored personalities.

Each winter village had a leader or headman, selected by members of the village council who were themselves the heads of the extended families that resided there. The council usually chose the eldest family leader resident in that settlement but the eldest might be overlooked in favor of another candidate deemed more fitting. The intelligence, experience, and personality of a candidate's wife were also taken into account because a leader's wife was often one of his trusted advisers. In addition, leaders were usually assisted by younger men. The headman acted as a spokesman for his village, settled disputes among members of his village, and promoted the well-being and security of the community. Headmen led by influence and example but could not force their will on others.

Although each village was autonomous and independent, villages that were located along the same stream or tributary formed bands that had councils made up of their constituent village leaders. Bands were named entities, usually adopting the name of the largest village within its territory (Walker 1973:104–105). Like villages, band councils selected a leader, usually himself the leader of the largest village in that grouping. Bands cooperated in some economic pursuits and they participated collectively in the defense of their member villages. Several bands might similarly be joined into a larger grouping, referred to as a "composite band," each again having a council composed of the leaders of the various bands. Prominent community leaders and warriors were also members of these councils.

Disputes that occurred in Nez Perce communities were settled in various ways depending on the units where the conflicts arose. Conflicts among members of a family grouping were negotiated by the leader in consultation with elder men and women who were respected for their sound judgment and personal charisma. If disputes arose between members of different families within a village, the village leader and council helped solve the problem but their influence was personal rather than structural. That is, they could not impose a solution but rather could only offer advice and hope that their reputations would add weight to their opinions. Only on rare occasions did village councils intervene and then only in situations where specific individuals were thought by the community to be unredeemable troublemakers. In those cases, the offenders might be exiled from the community.

Village and band councils held periodic meetings to discuss issues relevant to their groups. At these meetings, headmen and leaders solicited the opinions of members of their communities before taking any actions. All men and women in the community could participate and voice their opinions. Leaders could not act alone but only after achieving support from their constituents.

In addition to village and band leaders, known as peace chiefs, warriors who excelled in the defense of their communities were recognized for their courage and bravery. These men sometimes served as assistants to the peace leaders but their roles were separate. War chiefs could organize expeditions against their enemies and were in charge of home defense. The men who accompanied them did so voluntarily because they approved of the plans that the war chief formulated. Although prestige came to men who took part in war, no one was compelled to participate.

Religious Beliefs and Practices

The Nez Perce world is inhabited by many kinds of "persons" including human beings, plants, animals, and spirits. In their system of belief, people need to establish relationships with all of these "persons," cooperating with other humans, showing respect to the plants and animals that they depend upon for survival, and honoring the spirits who protect them, give them knowledge, and help them survive and succeed.

To the Nez Perce, the world is imbued with a spiritual essence or power that pervades all living creatures, including people, animals, plants, and the earth itself. Celestial bodies, mountains and rivers, winds, and thunder also contain spirit essence. Consistent with their egalitarian ethics, everyone can have access to spirit powers and can make direct contact with the spirit world through prayer, song, dance, dreams, and visions. Participation in rituals is a way of both obtaining and enacting spiritual knowledge and power.

Although in principle everyone has access to spirit power, in practice some people gain more knowledge and power than others. Success in any endeavor is a demonstration of power while failure and misfortune are indications that a person lacks these powers. A man or woman who has a great deal of spirit power may become a shaman. Such people have extraordinary abilities and insights, are able to foretell the future, locate game and other food sources, and intervene in conflicts. They can interpret spiritual omens seen by people in dreams or visions. Shaman may be called on to cure disease because of their medicinal knowledge and expertise in the rituals that treat illness. Indeed, this is one of their most important functions.

People began their search for spirit powers in the form of "tutelary spirits" or helpers sometime during adolescence. At that time, boys and girls prepared themselves through cleansing and purification in sweat lodges and then went into the woods or to a mountain-top and dedicated themselves by fasting, not sleeping, taking cold baths if possible, and concentrating their minds on spiritual matters. If successful, a spirit might appear to the seeker and give them a song that they could sing when summoning aid. Spirits appeared in human form although they might have qualities of animals as well. The seeker might also find an unusually shaped stone, bird feather, or animal tooth that gave them spiritual protection. Some people sought visions several times, acquiring additional powers. People who failed to receive visionary help in their first attempt usually went out again in order to achieve the desired result.

A major winter ceremonial involved practices that demonstrated people's tutelary spirits. These ceremonies have recently been revived by some members of the Nez Perce community. During the Spirit Dance, lasting from five to ten days, young people who had that year received their tutelary spirits sang the songs given to them. Then anyone in the community who wished to do so could also sing their own spirit songs. Finally, shaman demonstrated their powers, singing, performing dances given by their tutelary spirits, and demonstrating their extraordinary powers to locate lost objects, foretell the future, and control the weather by causing thunderstorms.

Winter dances were also occasions for the transfer of power from people with stronger powers to those with weaker ones. The stronger person carried the weaker one around the dance area, eventually leading the weaker person to enter a trance state and receive powers from the stronger person. As a result of exposure to strong power, the recipient often became ill and was subsequently cured by a shaman (Walker 1968:24).

In addition to the function of winter dances to validate personal spirit powers, they also helped strengthen allegiances between nearby villages. Each year, the winter dance was sponsored by the headman of a band of neighboring villages who provided the accompanying feasts and giveaways. The host amassed the necessary gifts through his own labor and that of his relatives whose generosity enhanced their collective prestige.

The ceremony itself was directed by one or more shaman who were allies of the sponsoring headman.

In addition to spirit dances, the Nez Perce commemorated major stages in a person's life. When a baby was due, the mother retired to a small lodge, accompanied by a midwife, her mother and other female relatives. A small hole was dug into the ground so that during the birth, "all of the blood and the afterbirth and everything was buried in this hole after the child was born" (James 1996:36). In cases of a difficult delivery, a specialist assisted the birth by using medicinal herbs, massage, and songs received from spirit helpers. As soon as a baby was born, its umbilical cord was cut and placed in an animal hide container attached to the baby's cradleboard so that it would remain with the baby as it grew because the umbilical cord was considered a vital part of one's being. Feasts were then held to honor the mother and baby.

Names for the baby were selected from those of successful, prominent, and respected ancestors because it was thought that the same qualities associated with these names would then develop in the child. In addition, people could take new names at any point in their lives, reflecting significant events, accomplishments, and personality traits.

The next transition marked by ritual occurred when a young girl or boy made their first major contribution to their family's subsistence, usually when they were about six years old. When a girl first independently dug up root crops or a boy made his first catch of a fish or animal, a feast was held in their honor, accompanied by speeches praising the child. A child's future was deemed especially favored if a renowned hunter or a skilled gatherer ate the child's first food offering (Walker 1973:109).

As they grew older, young girls participated in rituals at the time of their first menstruation. When menarche occurred, the girl went to a menstrual lodge constructed near her family's dwelling, joined there by her mother and several older female relatives. She stayed in the lodge all day but could go out in the evenings for short periods of time. She ate food cooked on a separate fire and used a carved scratching stick so that she did not touch her body. This was deemed a powerful time in a girl's life, exhibiting a power that could affect others, particularly men. For this reason, her menstrual blood was buried in a hole in the lodge. The girl's separation, lasting about one week, was followed by a public ceremony welcoming her into her community as an adult woman, ready for marriage.

Marriages were celebrated primarily through feasting and exchanges of gifts between the families of the bride and groom. First marriages were generally arranged by the heads of the respective families, initiated by an elder female relative of the prospective groom. If the woman's family agreed, the couple began to visit and the families met periodically for feasting and the exchange of gifts, begun first by the groom's family and then reciprocated by the bride's kin. As recalled by a contemporary Nez Perce woman, "Fish, meat, and related foods are usually served at the first trade, the men's sphere. Roots, berries, and such are represented at the second, the women's trade. Before each occasion, ten women are chosen by and from each side to conduct the trade. They kneel in two facing lines, with their goods on the floor in front of them. A leader of the host's line commences, handing a first gift to the opposite guests. The guest reciprocates, and so on" (James 1996:86). The symbolism of men's and women's roles was also enacted by the foods served when each group hosted the feasts, that is, women's families served varieties of roots while men's relatives served meat. At the end of the second exchange, the couple was deemed married. And although most marriages were stable, in the event of an unhappy relationship, either spouse could initiate divorce by taking their belongings and leaving the household.

At the final stage of life, news of a person's death was announced by a chosen crier, followed by wailing of the deceased's female relatives. The deceased was given a ritual bath and a new set of clothing and his or her face was decorated with red paint. On the next day, the deceased was taken to burial on a slope overlooking the village, the place marked by a wooden stake. People thereafter avoided the spot.

Some possessions were buried with the deceased to accompany them in the afterlife, symbolic of the roles and interests of the deceased. Men might be buried with their fishing or hunting gear or with war weapons while women were buried with cooking baskets, utensils, and beaded bags. In the historic period,

horses owned by the deceased might be sacrificed at the site of the grave. The tutelary spirits that a person had acquired during their lifetime departed at death. However, sometimes the spirit might appear to one of the deceased's relatives in a dream, thus indicating that it wanted to remain nearby. However, funerals conducted in the proper manner freed the deceased's soul for its journey to the afterworld. To the Nez Perce, the afterworld was very like the present world. People continued the same types of activities in the afterlife as they had done while living. The name of the deceased was never spoken. In some cases, his or her household furnishings and the house itself might be abandoned or destroyed. At the end of a year of mourning, a surviving spouse was given a new set of clothing and could then remarry.

Illness and Healing

Nez Perce concepts of illness and healing center on notions of harmony and balance, that is, health is a state of balance between people and their social and spiritual environments. In order to remain healthy, people should establish good relationships with others, obtain tutelary spirits, honor the spirit beings, and avoid behavior that offends them.

Health can also be maintained by the use of medicinal plants and by acts of cleansing and purification. Sweatbaths were taken prior to participating in rituals and as an occasional practice to cleanse their bodies and minds. And as part of a daily regimen for health, people took cold baths in the waters of nearby rivers in every season of the year. They also drank herbal teas that worked as emetics and laxatives. And tobacco was burned and smoked as a cleanser and as a mode of communication with the spirit world.

When people fell ill, they might seek the help of medicinal specialists who had vast knowledge of the healing qualities of plants and animals in their environment. Indeed, there were over 120 species of plants used to treat colds, coughs, indigestion, headaches, nausea, swellings, and various internal pains (Hunn et al. 1998:534). Medicinal practices also had a spiritual component because whenever specialists collected plant specimens they had to recite prayers honoring the spirit sources of these medicines.

If medicinal treatment alone did not succeed in curing the patient, people had recourse to shaman who performed rituals treatments to counteract spiritual causes, especially a curse sent to the patient either by a spirit as a punishment for some ritual transgression or by a human being acting out of ill will. The curse manifested itself as an object or substance that came suddenly within a person's body. The shaman sang their power songs, then located and extracted the curse by using a sucking horn although some shaman could extract an ailment by touching the spot with their index finger. Especially powerful shaman were able to extract the curse simply by concentrating their minds on the endeavor.

The Nez Perce believed that nearly anyone could cause illness and misfortune to others by purposely thinking evil thoughts or simply by a passing wish triggered by some intentional or unintentional offense or slight on the part of the victim. However, some people engaged in more elaborate practices to harm others. Shaman themselves might be suspected of causing harm since they controlled powerful spiritual sources. Care, therefore, needed to be taken to avoid offending other people.

Nez Perce man on horseback, ca. 1910.

TRADE AND CULTURAL TRANSFORMATION

The Consequences of Trade

Europeans did not enter Nez Perce territory until the exploratory expedition of Meriwether Lewis and William Clark in 1805, but their effects were felt by the people in the early eighteenth century. At first, the Nez Perce prospered from contact with Europeans, obtaining goods that benefited them and enriching themselves through widening networks of trade.

In the early eighteenth century, probably by around 1730, the Nez Perce began to acquire horses through trade with other indigenous peoples who themselves had obtained the animals from Spanish traders and settlers in what later became known as the American Southwest (Lavender 1992:21). Horses revolutionized Nez Perce economies and ways of living as they did for other Native peoples. People on horseback were able to expand their resource base by traveling further from settlements. Horses also enabled warriors to move with greater speed to confront their enemies. Finally, the number of horses that an individual or family owned became a significant measure of wealth and status. Lewis and Clark report family herds of 50–100 horses (Moulton 1983, 7: 252–254). By mid-century, some bands owned thousands of horses and individuals might own several hundred (Josephy 1965:38). As a group, the Nez Perce owned more horses than any other peoples in the Plateau region (Sappington 1989:29). They were known as skilled horsemen and horsewomen. And, unusual in Native America, they concentrated on breeding their horses for qualities of speed, strength, and endurance (Beal 1963:10). Their horses were among the finest on the continent.

The Nez Perce actively participated in intertribal trade that had been well-established hundreds of years earlier (see Chapter 19). The trading season lasted from late spring until late in the summer. The most important intertribal trading center frequented by the Nez Perce was the Dalles, located on the Columbia River just east of the Cascade Mountain range in what is now northern Oregon. There, men and women traders from coastal regions in Oregon, Washington, and British Columbia brought marine shells, whale oil, and blubber; peoples from the western regions of the Plateau brought animal skins, woven mats, and breads made from roots; and from the southern Plateau, the Nez Perce and their neighbors brought horses, camas roots, animal hides, and the buffalo robes that they obtained both from their own forays into the plains of Montana and from their trade with other indigenous groups, especially the Flatheads. The Nez Perce sought many types of goods in these exchanges, especially marine shell beads and salmon pemmican that was produced by people living in villages near the Dalles along the Columbia River basin (Lavender 1992:13).

Nez Perce traders also participated in commercial centers at the Grande Ronde and at Celilo Falls, both in eastern Oregon and at Kettle Falls in eastern Washington as well as at other sites in the area. Although many languages were spoken at these trading centers, the Nez Perce language began to be used by other peoples in trading interactions, reflecting the dominance that the Nez Perce exerted in their region.

In the fall of 1805, the Lewis and Clark expedition arrived in Nez Perce territory, remaining there for about one month. They then continued westward but on their return trip, they again crossed Nez Perce territory for about four months in the following spring. Surveys taken by the explorers estimated the Nez Perce population to be about 6,000 (Sappington 1989:3). They were said to be the largest of all of the indigenous groups in the Plateau. Clark described their first meeting with members of a Nez Perce village:

> Soon after a man came out to meet me, and with great caution, and conducted me to a large, spacious lodge, which he told me by signs was the lodge of his great chief who had set out three days previous with all the warriors of the nation to war in the southwest direction, and would return in 15 or 18 days. The few men who were left in the village and great numbers of women, gathered around me with much apparent signs of fear, and appeared pleased. They gave us a small piece of buffalo meat, some dried salmon, berries and roots in different states. Of this they make bread and soup. They also gave us the bread made of this root, all of which we ate heartily. I gave them a few small articles as presents, and proceeded on with the chief to his village

> 2 miles in the same plain, where we were treated kindly in their way, and continued with them all night. (Slickpoo and Walker 1973:68)

Despite the friendliness of these first encounters, the Lewis and Clark expedition opened the door to disruptions in the lives and security of the Nez Perce and other peoples in the region.

British and American traders entered the region in the early nineteenth century. In 1812, the British North West Company opened a trading post in Nez Perce territory at the joining of the Snake and Clearwater Rivers. The people traded horses and beaver furs in exchange for metal tools and utensils, blankets, shell and glass beads, and ornaments. However, from the point of view of the Company, the amount of trade brought in by the Nez Perce was disappointing. According to one of the Company's agents, writing in 1829:

> The Post has never been very productive, as the country in its neighborhood is not rich [in beaver], and the Natives who are a bold warlike race do little else than rove about in search of scalps, plunder and amusement. It is necessary, however, on many accounts, to keep on good terms with them, and to maintain the post for their accommodation whether it pays or not. (Slickpoo and Walker 1973:71)

These words exaggerate the "warlike" nature of the Nez Perce but do acknowledge their regional prominence. And as noted, the supply of beaver in the area was quickly depleted because of overkill. The people then maneuvered to set themselves up as middlemen in trade between the Hudson's Bay Company (which had bought out the North West Company) and Native groups living far from the posts. This strategy proved successful for several decades but eventually the Company sent its men into the interior to trade directly with indigenous peoples. American companies, heading northwest from St. Louis, competed with the British Hudson's Bay Company, establishing posts and sending trappers into the Plateau region. The first among the Nez Perce was opened in 1829 by traders from the Rocky Mountain Fur Company but by the 1840s, trapping and trading directly with interior peoples essentially eliminated the middleman role that the Nez Perce had adopted.

Deepening involvement in trade led to several changes in indigenous cultural practices. People began to spend more time obtaining the products that the foreign merchants wanted, principally horses and buffalo hides and meat. Horses were obtained both through trade with and raiding against other Native peoples. And in order to acquire the buffalo hides, men had to make more frequent and prolonged journeys eastward into the plains of Montana where the buffalo were numerous. In doing so, they risked confrontations with indigenous peoples in that region, particularly the Flatheads. Raiding and intertribal warfare then increased, resulting in casualties on all sides.

Second, the requirements of trade encouraged Nez Perce men to take more than one wife. In traditional society, polygyny was possible but the practice was not common. The increase in polygyny was associated with commercial demands for buffalo hides because in order for the hides to be marketable, they had to be softened by tanning, a process that took many days to accomplish. And since women prepared the hides, a man with only one wife could supply few hides for trade whereas a man with several wives could increase his participation in trade and his wealth and social status.

Trade also led to the acquisition of guns, in turn exacerbating intertribal hostilities. The Nez Perce attacked several of the Columbia River villages in 1811 and 1814 in order to obtain goods and attempt to exert control. Raids and retaliations continued to occur through the first half of the nineteenthcentury as different groups vied with each other for access to trade and for dominance in the region. The Nez Perce were generally successful in this competition because of their supply of guns and horses.

Beginning in the late eighteenth century, the Nez Perce experienced dramatic declines in their population from epidemic diseases, especially smallpox and measles. One of the earliest smallpox epidemics, spreading to the Nez Perce from its origin along the Pacific coast in the 1770s, took a heavy toll. According to one observer, "the people almost to an individual dead... Very few surviving the attack of the disease" (quoted in Boyd 1998:472). Later, in the early nineteenth century, the Nez Perce were especially affected by whooping cough and influenza.

While the aboriginal population figures are not known, the Lewis and Clark expedition estimated some 6,000 Nez Perce in 1805 (Sappington 1989:3). By 1865, a government census reported 2,830 tribal members. Their numbers declined to 2,085 in 1890. And a further decline to 1,387 was reported by government figures collected in 1927. After that, the Nez Perce population began a slow recovery (Boyd 1998).

The Consequences of Cultural Changes

Missionaries, teachers, and government agents were the major proponents of change in indigenous culture. The missionaries who had begun work in Nez Perce villages in the 1830s with few adherents gradually gained an influential following. The most successful of the Christian missions was established at Lapwai Creek in 1836, later renamed for its founder, Henry Spalding, a Presbyterian minister. Some people gravitated toward the missionaries in order to seek alliances with these powerful representatives of American society and appreciated the technological innovations that the missionaries introduced (Walker 1968:40, 43). However, tensions eventually surfaced between the missionaries and those people who resisted conversion. Tensions also arose between followers of Christianity and those who adhered to Native beliefs.

The missionaries' attitude toward traditional customs was ambivalent. They admired certain aspects of indigenous society, particularly the people's generosity and hospitality but they objected to customs that violated Christian principles or were incompatible with an American way of life such as rituals involving drumming, dancing, singing, and vision quests seeking tutelary spirits. They also opposed the freedom with which Native men and women engaged in sexual activity prior to marriage and the ease with which they might seek to end an unhappy marriage. Instead, the missionaries advocated monogamous and stable marriages without divorce, keeping of the Sabbath, and attendance at Christian rituals.

Missionaries also promoted changes in economic and social life. They urged people to abandon their foraging strategies and instead become farmers, encouraging men to farm and women to do household tasks. This new pattern of work fundamentally affected the productive roles of men and women. In the past, women's work contributed more than half of their household nutrition but with changes sought by the missionaries, men were to do the major work of providing for their families whereas women's occupations became secondary and supportive.

A further change promoted by the missionaries altered the household arrangements of Nez Perce society, emphasizing a shift from extended family households to nuclear family arrangements with the husband (and father) as the head. Just as the change in economic roles reduced the importance of women, the change in household arrangements also favored men's position and made women secondary members. Contemporary Nez Perce women recall the words of their mothers and grandmothers commenting on these changes:

> Women were involved side-by-side with men in all walks of their lives. In the Nez Perce culture, indirect involvement of women or their presence with men was sufficient to influence political discussions… Women did have leadership and power and they were kind of looked to as counselors. These women were from chieftain families as well as from the common families. It was quite an accomplishment; they could be someone. (James 1996:119–120)

In addition to missionaries, settlers soon entered Native lands, protected by the American military. Government agents also followed, establishing posts from which they sought to control the indigenous peoples. These developments were summed up by a Nez Perce observer:

> The introduction of missionaries … played an important role in breaking down our way of life, demoralizing and weakening our cultural values, and ending our power and freedom so that we would be dependent on the whites.
>
> To do this the missionaries came and taught new ways which were alien to us. The military followed to enforce these teachings and clear the way to the vast numbers of encroaching settlers, miners and traders. We asked for the Bible, and that's all we have left. (Quoted in Slickpoo and Walker 1973:72)

In the 1870s, the Nez Perce educational system was given over to the control of the Presbyterian mission. Henry Spalding, the Presbyterian minister who had worked among the people from 1836 to 1847, returned as the superintendent in charge of the agency. Religious instruction was merged with training in farming and various trades such as blacksmithing and mechanics for boys and domestic work for girls.

The transfer of schools to religious rather than secular authorities heightened conflicts between different constituencies. Divisions between Christian and non-Christian believers became more intense as parents who followed traditional beliefs and practices feared the influence of Christian teachers. Assignment of the schools to the Presbyterians also created conflict between the majority of Christians who were Presbyterians and the minority who had converted to Catholicism (Walker 1968:54). Gradually, each of these three groupings (Presbyterians, Catholics, and traditionalists) gravitated toward spatial separation in different areas. The Presbyterians resided in the towns of Lapwai and Kamiah, the sites of government posts, agencies, and churches. These towns grew to be the politically dominant areas on the Nez Perce lands.

In addition to local schools, an intertribal boarding school, called the Indian Training School, was founded in Forest Grove Oregon. Children from the Nez Perce communities began attending the Indian Training School in 1884, sending an initial contingent of thirty-four.

Treaties and Reservations

In 1855, Governor Isaac Stevens of the newly declared Oregon Territory began a process of negotiating treaties with Native peoples in the region. In that same year, Stevens concluded the Walla Walla Treaty with the Nez Perce and other indigenous nations of the southern Plateau. This treaty established three reservations, including one for the Nez Perce that consisted of approximately 7,787,000 acres, located in an area situated in western Idaho, eastern Oregon, and a small amount of acreage in southeastern Washington (Lahren 1998). This represented a reduction of their aboriginal territory comprising some 13,000,000 acres, a loss of nearly 50 percent of their land. In return for the land loss, the government agreed to make financial outlays of $100,000 during the first two years and an additional $200,000 over the next twenty years to be spent on maintaining schools, health services, and agricultural services.

Although some opposition to the treaty provisions was voiced by Nez Perce delegates to the Council, eventually their leaders were persuaded to sign it. Stevens stressed the fact that many White settlers were already encroaching on Native territory, taking their resources and occasionally attacking individuals. Stevens said that the government would only protect the people from further harm if they agreed to the treaty.

In 1863, only eight years after Nez Perce ownership of their reservation was guaranteed by the government, a second treaty was negotiated. It was prompted, in part, by the discovery of gold on and near the Nez Perce Reservation in 1860. Following reports of this discovery, more than 10,000 miners flocked onto reservation lands in the 1860s and extracted gold worth an estimated $50 million (Beal 1963:19). The major provision of the new treaty made a further reduction in Native territory, taking away the lands that contained the gold reserves and additional acreage. Of the original 7,787,000-acre Reservation, only 757,000 acres remained, a loss of more than 7,000,000 acres or about 90percent of their land. This treaty was, and still is, controversial because the Nez Perce negotiators who were invited to the treaty meetings were members of the so-called Upper Nez Perce and did not actually represent the entire nation. In fact, the chiefs who signed were heads of bands that lived on lands included in the reduced reservation while leaders of bands whose lands were signed away were not present at the treaty council. The majority of the Upper Nez Perce was Christians and more receptive to policies that encouraged cultural change than were the so-called Lower Nez Perce, the majority of whom followed the traditional religion and was more resistant to government policies. The Lower Nez Perce, or the Non-Treaty Nez Perce, objected to the new treaty and especially to giving away more of their lands (Slickpoo and Walker 1973:147).

Antagonisms between the two groups grew into open conflicts. At the same time, a new wave of Presbyterian missionary activity commenced. Members of the Upper Nez Perce converted in large numbers while very few members of the Lower Nez Perce did so, heightening the growing rift between the two communities.

A final treaty was signed in 1868 that clarified some of the provisions of the Treaty of 1863. In particular, it guaranteed the people's rights to the resources on their lands, especially to the timber reserves that American companies were trying to gain access to.

The provisions of these treaties, with the loss of land and livelihood, led quickly to dissension among the people. The division between the Upper Nez Perce, living near the administrative center at Lapwai, and the Lower Nez Perce, living in an area about 100 mi. south, created conflicts over land and over cultural changes that have continued into the twenty-firstcentury.

By the 1870s, most of the Nez Perce were living on the reservation assigned to them in the treaties of 1855 and 1863. Because they had lost the vast majority of their ancestral lands, many adapted themselves to farming wheat, various vegetables, and fruit crops although women and men supplemented these crops with resources obtained by their traditional foraging activities. There were, however, some people who refused to adopt the lifestyle imposed on them by the US government. Prominent among these were the people who lived in a band in the Wallowa Valley of northeastern Oregon, headed by a man whose Native name was Hin-mah-too-yah-lat-kekht, meaning "thunder rolling in the mountains." He came to be known in English as Chief Joseph. When the Treaty of 1855 was agreed, lands of the Wallowa valley were included as part of the Nez Perce Reservation but when the Treaty of 1863 was drawn up, these lands were ceded to the United States. Joseph and his followers were not signatories to that Treaty and therefore refused to accept their loss of land. In 1873, in response to their objections, US President Ulysses S. Grant created a separate Wallowa Reservation for Joseph's band. Conflict over this land continued, however, because American settlers pressured the government to reverse its decision so that they could have access to the excellent grazing and farming lands contained within. Armed clashes between Nez Perce and intruding settlers occurred,

Chief Joseph, Nez Percé chief, head-and-shoulders portrait, painting by E.A. Burbank, Nespelem, WA.

eventually persuading Grant to reverse Wallowa reservation status in 1875 and instead allow American settlement (Beal 1963:35).

General Oliver Howard was assigned the task of either convincing or forcing Joseph and his followers, numbering between 700 and 750, to leave Wallowa and take up residence on the Nez Perce Reservation in Idaho (Lavender 1992:323). In meetings in 1877 between Native leaders and the army the difference in attitudes can be summed up by two statements, one from Chief Tulhuulhulsuit and one from General Howard:

> Chief Tulhuulhulsuit: You white people measure the Earth and divide it. The Earth is part of my body, and I never gave up the Earth. I belong to the land out of which I came. The Earth is my mother.
>
> General Howard: We do not wish to interfere with your religion, but you must talk about practical things. Twenty times over you have repeated the Earth is your mother, and that chieftainship is from the Earth. Let us hear it no more, but come to business at once. (Quoted in Josephy 1965: 502–503)

The Nez Perce finally agreed to relocate to the Reservation and were given thirty days to make the move but conflicts between the Native people and settlers continued, prompting Howard to send an army unit against the Nez Perce, leading to a battle that ended in a Native victory even though they were outnumbered and poorly armed. Several important battles ensued as the soldiers followed Chief Joseph and his band, all with Nez Perce victories, escaping capture throughout a period of three months by moving east toward the plains, through Yellowstone National Park, and then turning north through Montana, hoping to find refuge in Canada. However, they were finally stopped at Bear Paws in Montana, just 40 mi. from the Canadian border. Approximately 200 people were able to escape prior to the final confrontation. After a long battle, Chief Joseph surrendered, handing his rifle to General Howard and stating:

> I am tired of fighting. Our chiefs are killed. It is cold and we have no blankets. The little children are freezing to death. My people, some of them, have run away to the hills and have no blankets, no food; no one knows where they are, perhaps freezing to death. Hear me, my chiefs, I am tired; my heart is sick and sad. From where the sun now stands, I will fight no more, forever. (Quoted in Slickpoo and Walker 1973:193)

Although the earlier goal of the government had been to force Joseph and his followers to move to the Nez Perce Reservation in Idaho, after the surrender, they refused to let him join his people. Instead, he and his band, then numbering 431, were ordered to go to Oklahoma to lands originally part of the Ponca Reserve. Within a few months, forty-seven of the exiles had died from exposure to the heat, lack of clean drinking water, and poor sanitation conditions (Slickpoo and Walker 1973:195). Then in 1885 the Nez Perce were allowed to go north but not as a united group. The people who were followers of the Presbyterian Church were permitted to repatriate to the Lapwai community on the Nez Perce Reservation but the non-Christians, including Joseph, were sent instead to join other Native peoples living on the Colville Reservation in northern Washington where they established a community called Nespelem.

GOVERNMENT POLICIES OF THE LATE NINETEENTH AND EARLY TWENTIETH CENTURIES

Allotment of lands, in accordance with the General Allotment Act of 1887, commenced on the Nez Perce Reservation in 1890. In the first year, 1,000 allotments were assigned, with an additional 905 allotments made by 1893 (Lahren 1998:489). Some of the best parcels were immediately taken by White men who had married Native women. Then, after continuing pressure by the US government, in 1893, Nez Perce leaders agreed to sell some additional 542,000 acres of "surplus" lands in exchange for about $1,626,000 (Slickpoo and Walker 1973:224). Of this money, $1 million was placed in a trust fund for collective use while the remainder was distributed per capita to registered tribal members. Allotments amounted to 182,938 acres, leaving only 32,020 acres in tribal trust. The total land base, then, was 214,958 acres by the turn of the twentieth century. Soon, however, an additional 130,000 acres were sold or otherwise lost by individuals or families. In all, the aboriginal homeland of 13,000,000 acres was reduced to fewer than 80,000 acres by the year 1975 (Lahren 1998:437). It has since increased to about 770,000acres through the success of tribal policies of acquiring land that had previously been sold or lost (Peterson 2009). But the legacy of past actions is reflected in the fact that more than 85percent of the land within the Nez Perce Reservation is owned by people who are not

Indians. And the land still owned by Native people is a patchwork of allotments scattered throughout the territory.

Surveys conducted on the Reservation in conjunction with congressional investigations begun in 1926 indicated a great deal of variation in living standards. While many people lived in good homes, had productive gardens, and kept some domesticated chickens, horses, and cattle, others were poor and lived in substandard housing. The surveys documented the increasing reliance of tribal members on rental income obtained from leasing their lands to White farmers and ranchers. Indeed, investigators counted about 1,300 Nez Perce and about 20,000 White people living on the Reservation (Slickpoo and Walker 1973:242).

A tribal organization called the Nez Perce Indian Home and Farm Association was formed, consisting of a general council that included all adult members of the tribe. A Business Committee was charged with implementing economic development plans for the Reservation. Its "Declaration of Purpose" summarized the forces at work that led to the situation in which the people found themselves at that time:

> We see many of our people—particularly our young people—without permanent homes of their own, and in many cases, leasing to white men the land which they themselves should farm. We see neglected homes, and children growing up without proper parental guidance and control; we see the majority of our people depending on the income from their leased lands for their support; we see our allotted land and the homes of our fathers gradually passing into the hands of the white man—title to more than 900, or almost one half of the original allotments having thus passed, leaving many of our people without land. (Quoted in Slickpoo and Walker 1973:243)

The Association developed plans to improve homes and living conditions and encourage people to farm their own lands rather than leasing them to outsiders. In addition, fifteen local chapters were established so that people could directly participate in tribal affairs. A constitution was drawn up in 1927, creating a nine-person governing body known as the Advisory Council and Business Committee, elected by the adult members of the tribe. The group's functions included approving land leases, loan applications, timber sales permits, and grazing permits. In addition, the Committee pursued land claims suits against the federal government.

Following passage of the Indian Reorganization Act in 1934, an election was held on the Nez Perce Reservation to decide whether to accept or reject its provisions. Those in favor believed that the IRA would strengthen the tribe's ability to oversee its own affairs but people opposed fearing that their lands would eventually be vulnerable to federal taxation. And many of the Christians opposed the support given by the IRA to the maintenance of traditional religious ceremonies. In this atmosphere of controversy, by a vote of 252 to 214 (142 members not voting), the Nez Perce chose to exclude themselves from the provisions of the Indian Reorganization Act (Slickpoo and Walker 1973:270). Indeed although most reservation communities in the United States voted to accept the IRA, a majority of groups in the Plateau and Northwest rejected it.

A new constitution was then drafted in 1948, establishing a general council again consisting of all adult members of the tribe, led by the Nez Perce Tribal Executive Committee (NPTEC). The Committee administers a wide range of projects including the protection and expansion of fish and water resources; social service and welfare programs in education, health, and housing; law enforcement; and legal affairs and land claims.

When the constituency of the general council was originally envisioned, only people who lived within the borders of the Reservation described in the Treaty of 1863 were given membership and allowed to vote but in 1961, people who lived in the wider area encompassed by the original Reservation as established by the Treaty of 1855 were included. This change has created some conflicts because of the contrasting interests of people living on the current Reservation and those who are living officially off the Reservation. Some of the issues that divide these two groups concern plans for economic development, the amount of power vested in the NPTEC, and funding for cultural and language heritage programs.

Beginning in the 1950s and congressional passage of the Relocation Act, many people left the Reservation to settle in urban centers located in the Midwest and west. However, this process also undermined the stability of Native reservations by leading to a loss of income and talent from their home communities. In the words of one Nez Perce woman:

> The relocation programs of the 1950s and 1960s did have tremendous impact on Indian people nationally and on the Nez Perce Tribe... They created large urban populations without any sort of support

system for that population…[And] there is a draw of skilled Indian people away from the Reservation, away from the tribal communities through education, jobs…Nez Perce people have now a base, a family system out there in Seattle or Portland or Los Angeles or San Francisco and other places. The Nez Perce Tribe has a lot of really talented people within the tribe, but there are a lot of talented people who are members of the tribe who are living outside. (James 1996:210)

The western regions of the Reservation, closest to Oregon and Washington, have become socially and politically dominant, especially around the town of Lapwai, located 10 mi. from the urban centers of Lewiston-Clarkson in Idaho, that has drawn people both from nearby western areas and from the east, including the town of Kamiah. Residents of Lapwai are more likely to speak English rather than the Native language and to marry people who are not Nez Perce (Walker 1968:80). Marriages with Anglo Americans accelerated beginning after 1895 when Whites were permitted to live on the Reservation. This pattern continued throughout the twentieth century but the frequency of such unions varies with location, that is, those people living in the west around Lapwai are more likely than people living in the eastern Kamiah region to marry members of other groups. These differences in rates of intermarriage are associated with other constellations of attitudes and behaviors. For example, Nez Perce married to other Nez Perce are more likely to retain traditional social values, especially related to family and household obligations. In contrast, people who have married members of other groups are more likely to accept changes in their ways of living, influenced as they are by their spouses and children.

Finally, in the twentieth century, Nez Perce religious affiliations have become quite complex. A significant number of people became disillusioned with the Presbyterian and Catholic churches because of these groups' support for land allotment policies that resulted in huge land losses for the Reservation and fractioning of individual allotments (Walker 1968:87). Some people turned to Pentecostal Protestant sects that offered cathartic emotional experiences, similar to those of the spirit quests and visions of traditional belief. Like aboriginal practice, Pentecostal believers strive to make direct contact with the spirit world through prayer, song, and movement. In addition, many people are returning to traditional religious practices, especially seeking personal tutelary spirits through vision quests and participation in the Winter Spirit Dances and the Seven Drum Religion.

Revitalization of indigenous religions is also associated with emphasis on other aspects of Native traditions. Many people have become interested in learning the Nez Perce language. And many participate in festivals and "powwows" that celebrate their musical, visual, and dance arts, strengthening people's community ties.

The continuing legacy of government policies, especially of allotments and of the resulting loss of land through surplus homesteading and sales to non-Indians has led to a contemporary problem of patchwork ownership of acreage by the Nez Perce themselves even within the borders of their own reservation. A study of relationships between Nez Perce and "settlers" in a town of about 2,000 residents located on the reservation but inhabited by a majority of settlers reveals underlying tensions and conflicts in attitudes (James 1999). Although on the surface both Nez Perce and

Nez Perce women performing their "Welcome Dance."

settlers describe attempts to reconcile differences and support each other, segregation is reflected in lack of participation in events sponsored by the other group, whether that be Native or settler. And although children from both communities attend the same schools, indigenous representation on school boards or other official town bodies is negligible. In addition, settlers expressed some hostility toward what they viewed as benefits given to tribal members but not to themselves, such as monetary support for education and healthcare services as well as preferential hiring policies mandated by the Nez Perce Tribal Executive Committee guidelines (James 1999:157–158). But most settlers did not acknowledge that these "benefits" were in fulfillment of treaty responsibilities agreed to by the US government in exchange for millions of acres of land that the Nez Perce had ceded in the nineteenth century.

As many members of the Native community have pursued their rights to their land and sovereignty, limited though it is by federal policies and regulations, conflicts in attitudes have grown between the assertions of the Nez Perce to their aboriginal claim and those of the settlers to a subsequent claim. In the words of a Nez Perce woman in the town:

> It's scary right now for the white people in this community because they have always known the Indians to be doormats and lie down and take whatever comes to them. But now we've got very well educated people that are not going to be like that. They're not going to be the passive Indians anymore; they're going to speak out… Whereas our Indians in the past were, you know, too friendly! (James 1999:161)

CONTEMPORARY COMMUNITIES

Economic and Social Issues

According to tribal data, the Nez Perce Reservation currently contains some 770,000 acres of land but only 154,478 acres of this territory are owned by Native people. The majority of land is therefore owned by others, mostly White people. The reservation spans three states: the largest section in Idaho contains some 137,500 acres while 15,200 acres are located in Oregon and the remaining 1,300 acres in Washington (Peterson 2009). The Tribe continues policies to buy back some of the 7,500,000 acres of land that was originally guaranteed to them in the Treaty of 1855.

Regulations established by the NPTEC mandate that in order for a person to be a tribal member, he or she must have at least one-quarter Nez Perce ancestry. There are currently 3,513 members of the Nez Perce Tribe. This number varies somewhat with statistics reported by the US Bureau of the Census in the year 2000 that counted 3,499 Nez Perce residents of the Reservation. The Census Bureau also reports that Nez Perce Indians account for only 11.7 percent of the Reservation population while White people (numbering 15,186) constitute 84.6 percent, a vast majority. People of other races make up the remainder.

Age distribution statistics reveal that in 2010, 8.9 percent of the Nez Perce living on the Reservation are children under the age of five years while at the other end of the lifespan, only 0.3 percent are 85 years of age or older. These figures contrast with comparable data for the United States as a whole but are similar to figures for Indian reservations in the country. That is, 6.8 percent of all US residents are under the age of five years while 1.5 percent are age 85 or older. The Nez Perce population is therefore a relatively youthful one.

Economic and employment data collected by the Bureau of the Census for the year 2014 indicate higher rates of unemployment for the Nez Perce than in the United States as a whole and correspondingly lower levels of income. In that year, of the Nez Perce living on the Reservation who were 16 years and over, 64.5 percent were in the labor force; 55.4 percent were employed while 8.4 percent were unemployed. The remaining 35.5 percent were not in the labor force either because they did not want to work or because they were discouraged workers no longer looking for jobs. The most striking contrast between the Nez Perce and all Americans is the percentage of unemployed people. Although nearly the same percentage of Nez Perce and all Americans were in the labor force (63.4% for the Nez Perce and 63.9 % for all Americans), the Nez Perce unemployment rate was double that of the United States (8.4% for the Nez Perce and 9.2% for the United States as a whole) (US Census Bureau 2014).

Statistics reporting income indicate that Nez Perce workers and families have relatively low earnings as compared to the general US population. Table 20.1 presents comparative data for the year 2010.

In addition, 7.7 percent of Nez Perce households had annual incomes of less than $10,000 while a smaller percentage (7.2%) of all Americans had similarly low incomes.

TABLE 20.1	Nez Perce and U.S. Individual and Family Income	
	Nez Perce ($)	**Total US ($)**
Median Family Income	45,367	53,482
Per Capita Income	19,841	28,555

Given the low incomes of Nez Perce families, the poverty rate for the year 2010 was high, that is, 16.9percent of Native families were living below the poverty level. Figures were even higher for families with children and the highest rates of poverty were experienced by families headed by single women with young children.

Statistics on educational attainment reveal that the Nez Perce are somewhat better educated than the American averages at the high school and community college levels but are less well-educated at the level of four-year college and graduate degrees. These data might predict successful employment but underemployment for reservation residents is caused, not by a lack of training, but by a paucity of job opportunities.

The governing council, or NPTEC, has spearheaded the expansion of economic, social, and legal services to their communities, generating income by leasing land and purchasing additional acreage adjacent to the reservation. A Natural Resources Subcommittee declares its goal to "expand and protect our precious natural resources, which are fundamental to who we are as a people" and specifically to guarantee rights of access to natural resources both on and off the Reservation as agreed by the Treaties of 1855, 1863, and 1868. Programs include protection of fisheries, forestry, water resources, and wildlife and developing sustainable resource utilization.. In addition, the Tribe works to enhance control over cultural and historical resources. These include efforts, in accordance with provisions of the Native American Grave and Repatriation Act of 1990, to regain ownership of cultural artifacts that were taken illegally or sold to private collectors or museums in the past. In 2009, the federal government agreed to repatriate several objects of human remains and funerary artifacts to the Nez Perce that were held by the US Department of Defense, Army Corps of Engineers and housed in museums at the University of Washington and the University of California at Berkeley.

The Human Resources Subcommittee implements programs to improve enrollment in schools, acquires additional funds for education, and awards scholarships to Nez Perce students who want to attend college and graduate degree programs. The Subcommittee also oversees the Nimiipuu Health Board that administers programs dealing with health and wellness, including a new health facility, staffed by additional doctors and expanded services to the community.

In order to both generate income and expand people's knowledge of Native history, the Tribe opened a Nez Perce National Historical Park with sites both on the Reservation and outside its current boundaries. There are thirty-eight sites that commemorate the location of battlefields, trading posts, missions, and forts, including the trails and campsites used by Chief Joseph and his followers in their attempt to escape from US Army control. The site of ancient petroglyphs are marked, as well as places described in sacred narratives such as the "Heart of the Monster" where Coyote killed the Monster and released the Nez Perce people into this world (see the narrative that opens Chapter 19).

Some Nez Perce leaders participated in 2004 in national events marking the 200th anniversary of the Lewis and Clark Expeditions. The numerous trails that the expedition followed across Native territory are part of the Nez Perce National Historical Trail Park, a major tourist attraction in the region. But Allen Pinkham, a Nez Perce member of the National Lewis and Clark Bicentennial Council, raised concerns about the programs: "The general population wants to see heroes, and to them Lewis and Clark are heroes. To us, they mean something completely different." And Clara HighEagle, a member of the NPTEC, noted that the Bicentennial should be "commemorated, not celebrated" (Sequoyah Research Center).

Land and Resource Claims Cases

The Nez Perce Tribe is an active participant in several regional coalitions concerned with protecting Native people's fishing and resource rights as guaranteed in numerous treaties signed in the nineteenth century. One of their first actions was a suit brought by the Nez Perce, Yakima, Umatilla, and Warm Springs nations against the US government for the loss of fishing sites at Celilo Falls in Oregon, an area flooded by construction of the Dalles Dam, completed in 1957. A negotiated settlement awarded a total of $27 million in direct compensation for the loss of fishing sites. Of this sum, the Nez Perce received $2,800,000.

The Nez Perce have also sought protection of their water rights based on their treaties. Negotiations that began in the 1990s finally ended in 2007 with an agreement between the Tribe and the US Department of the Interior and the State of Idaho over claims to use the Snake River waters. The claim stems from the Treaties of 1855 and 1863 that guaranteed the people enough water for uses on the Reservation. The Treaty of 1855 also guaranteed fishing rights in "all usual and accustomed places" not only on the Reservation but also on the lands that were ceded to the US government. Finally, the Treaty of 1863 grants the Nez Perce the right to use any springs or fountains that are located in the area first guaranteed as their Reservation in the 1855 Treaty but subsequently ceded to the government.

The water rights agreement, called the Snake River Basin Adjudication, grants the Tribe consumptive water rights from the Clearwater River and some tributary sources. They were also granted claims to springs and fountains on federal lands within the area ceded in the Treaty of 1863 but were denied their claims to springs on lands within that area if controlled by the State of Idaho or private owners. In addition, certain lands under the control of the federal Bureau of Land Management, valued at $7 million, were given to the Tribe. The Tribe was established as comanager, along with federal agencies, of national fish hatcheries. Finally, the Tribe received $73 million for acquisition and restoration of lands for fish habitats, fish production, agricultural development, water resource development, sewer and water system projects, and cultural preservation projects.

In conjunction with their desire to manage fish production and habitats, the Nez Perce have embarked on a program aimed at increasing the population of steelhead trout in the Columbia River basin. These fish are listed as a threatened species in northern Washington and Idaho. The project involves a method of artificial spawning in which fish eggs are extracted from the female trout without harm to the fish and then the eggs are combined with sperm and cared for in a fish hatchery. The rate of survival of fish eggs in this artificial environment is higher than that in natural conditions. Once the eggs are extracted, the adult fish are returned to the river to make their journey toward the Pacific Ocean (Oregon Public Broadcasting 2013). Although it is unlikely that the population of steelhead trout will ever rebound to the numbers prior to river contamination, dam construction, and commercial overfishing, it is hoped that a significant increase will result from the project.

REFERENCES

Beal, Merrill. 1963. *"I Will Fight No More Forever": Chief Joseph and the Nez Perce War*. Seattle, WA: University of Washington Press.

Boyd, Robert. 1998. "Demographic History until 1990." *Plateau. Handbook of North American Indians* (ed. Deward Walker) Vol. 12. Washington, DC: Smithsonian Institution, pp. 467–483.

Hunn, Eugene, Nancy Turner, and David French. 1998. "Ethnobiology and Subsistence." *Plateau. Handbook of North American Indians* (ed. Deward Walker) Vol. 12. Washington, DC: Smithsonian Institution, pp. 525–545.

James, Caroline. 1996. *Nez Perce Women in Transition, 1877–1990*. Moscow, ID: University of Idaho Press.

James, Darcy. 1999. "The Continuing Impact of Manifest Destiny in a Small Town." *Wacazo Sa Review* 14, no. 1: 147–163.

Josephy, Alvin. 1965. *The Nez Perce Indians and the Opening of the Northwest*. New Haven, CT: Yale University Press.

Lahren, Sylvester. 1998. "Reservations and Service." *Plateau. Handbook of North American Indians* (ed. Deward Walker) Vol. 12. Washington, DC: Smithsonian Institution, pp. 484–498.

Lavender, David. 1992. *Let Me Be Free: The Nez Perce Tragedy*. New York: HarperCollins.

Moulton, Gary (ed.). 1983. *The Journals of the Lewis and Clark Expedition, July 28–November 1, 1805*. Lincoln, NE: University of Nebraska Press.

Oregon Public Broadcasting. 2013. "Tribes Work to Maximize Columbia River Basin Steelhead." March 28. http://earthfix.opb.org/water/article/maximizing-columbia-river-basin-steelhead.

Peterson, Steven. 2009. "The Updated 2009 Economic Impact Analysis of the Nez Perce Tribe." http://www.nezperce.org/official/PDF/Updated 2009Economic Impact.

Slickpoo, Allen, and Deward Walker. 1973. *Noon Nee-me-poo (We, The Nez Perces). Culture and History of the Nez Perces* Vol.1. Lapwai, ID: Nez Perce Tribe.

Sappington, Robert. 1989. "The Lewis and Clark Expedition among the Nez Perce Indians: The First Ethnographic Study in the Columbia Plateau." *Northwest Anthropological Research Notes* 23, no. 1: 1–33.

Sequoyah Research Center. "Along the Lewis and Clark Trail." American Native Press Archives.www.anpa.ualr,edu.

US Census Bureau. 2014.

Walker, Deward. 1968. *Conflict and Schism in Nez Perce Acculturation: AStudy of Religion and Politics*. Portland, WA: Washington State University Press.

Walker, Deward. 1973. *American Indians of Idaho*. Anthropology Monographs of the University of Idaho, No. 2. Moscow, ID: University Press of Idaho.

Walker, Deward. 1998. "Nez Perce." *Plateau. Handbook of North American Indians* (ed. Deward Walker) Vol. 12. Washington, DC: Smithsonian Institution, pp. 420–438.

THE NORTHWEST COAST

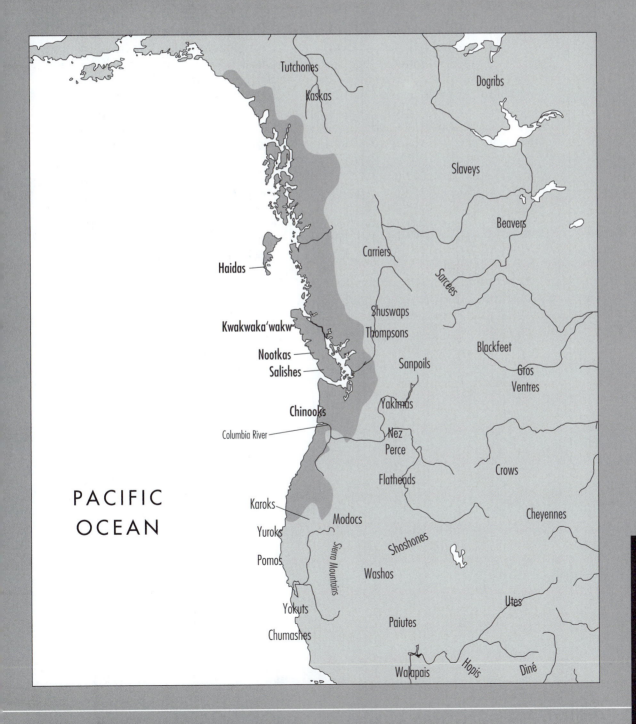

Tutchones

Kaskas

Dogribs

Slaveys

Beavers

Haidas

Carriers

Sarcees

Shuswaps

Thompsons

Kwakwaka'wakw

Blackfeet

Nootkas

Sanpoils

Gros
Ventres

Salishes

Yakimas

Chinooks

Columbia River

Nez
Perce

Flatheads

Crows

PACIFIC
OCEAN

Karoks

Modocs

Cheyennes

Yuroks

Pomos

Shoshones

Sierra Mountains

Washos

Yokuts

Paiutes

Utes

Chumashes

Walapais

Hopis

Diné

Tsimshian Story of the Theft of Light

Giant (the Raven) flew toward the east for a long time. When he was tired, he rested on a rock in the sea, refreshed humself, and took off the raven skin. At that time there was always darkness, no daylight. Again Giant put on the raven skin and flew toward the east, finally reaching the mainland at the mouth of Skeena River. There he scattered salmon roe and trout roe, saying "Let every river and creek have all kinds of fish!" He scattered fruits all over the land, saying "Let every mountain, hill, valley, plain, the whole land, be full of fruits!"

The whole world was still covered with darkness. When the sky was clear, people would have a little light from the stars; and when clouds were in the sky, it was very dark all over the land. The people were distressed by this. Then Giant thought that it would be hard for him to obtain food if it were always dark. Then he made up his mind to bring down the light from heaven to our world. He put on his raven skin and flew upward through a hole in the sky. He took off the raven skin and came to a spring near the house of the chief of heaven. There he waited. The chief's daughter came out to fetch some water. Giant transformed himself into a cedar leaf and floated on the water. The chief's daughter dipped it up in her bucket and drank it. After a short time, she was with child, and gave birth to a boy. The boy grew quickly and continually cried for a box hanging in the chief's house. The box contained daylight. The chief took the box down and let the boy play with it. The boy kept it near him for four days. Then, when no one was watching, he put it on his shoulder and ran out with it. When Giant got to the hole in the sky, he put on the raven skin and flew down to our world. Later, Giant broke open the box and it was daylight.

Source: Boas, Frank. 1899–1900.*Report of the Bureau of American Ethnology*. Washington, DC: Smithsonian Institution, Vol. 21, p. 60.

Native Nations of the Northwest Coast

We, as Indian leaders, have responsibility to preserve our right [to fish], just as our elders fought to preserve it. We must preserve that right, for more than the value it carries today, for more even than the value of saving the past. Our obligation is to preserve the right to fish for our future, for the many Indian children who will wake to the far-off sound of the first splash of the first salmon of the season.

Andy Fernando, former chairman, Upper Skagit Tribal Community, Washington, May 1984; quoted in Cohen 1986: xxvi

LANDS AND NATIONS

The Northwest Coast is a geographically small but culturally complex region extending along the north Pacific coast from southern Alaska through British Columbia and Washington, and reaching to the southern coast of Oregon, a distance of more than 1,500 mi. On the west it is bounded by the Pacific Ocean, on the east by the Chugach and St. Elias Mountains in southern Alaska, the Coast Mountains of British Columbia, and the Cascade Range in Washington and Oregon. Some of these peaks are more than 10,000 or 15,000 ft.above sea level. Mountains also rise along the Pacific coast, especially on some of the islands offshore. The region is widest in central British Columbia where it extends about 200 mi.inland, but it is

narrower in the north and south. The Northwest Coast is not only exposed to the ocean on the west but also has many inland bays, lakes, rivers, and streams. In the central sections of British Columbia the area contains numerous large and small islands. Islands dot the coast in other regions as well. Because of numerous indentations in the coastline, the actual shoreline in British Columbia measures some 10,000 mi.(Kroeber 1939: 170).

The climate is influenced by both the Pacific Ocean to the west and the mountain ranges to the east that make for differences in average temperatures and rates of precipitation. In general, the Pacific Ocean cools the air in summer and warms it in the winter, but variations in temperature are attested, with milder readings to the south and colder readings in the north. Furthermore, temperatures are mildest along the coast and coldest near the mountains that define the region's eastern boundaries. Precipitation rates also vary, influenced by ocean air coming from the west. Heaviest rainfall is found along the western slopes of the outer ranges of mountains, that is, on the Queen Charlotte Islands, Vancouver Island, the Olympic Mountains of Washington, and Oregon's Coast Range. Precipitation is also heavy along the western slopes of the Coast Mountains and the Cascade Range. In contrast, the eastern slopes of the outer peaks experience least precipitation. Variations can be extraordinary. For example, in the eastern slopes of the Olympic Mountains less than 30 in.of rain may fall, while on the western side rainfall averages 83 in.per year (Phillips 1960). Some regions of southeastern Alaska receive more than 300 in.of rain or snow each year, while others receive less than 40 in,. Throughout most of the Northwest Coast,

424 PART IX • The Northwest Coast

precipitation falls as rain, but in some areas, particularly in the north, heavy snows also occur.

Aboriginal nations of the Northwest Coast shared many cultural traits, no doubt as a result of extensive contact through trade, travel, and intermarriage. However, although there were similarities, specific practices and beliefs were not everywhere identical but rather were more or less elaborated in different societies. The northernmost groups were the Tlingits of southern Alaska and northern British Columbia, the Haidas of the Queen Charlotte Islands, and the Niskas, Gitksans, and Tsimshians of northern and central British Columbia. South of these nations lived the Bella Coolas, the Kwakwaka'wakw or Kwakiutls, and the Nootkas of Vancouver Island, the Coast Salish, and Quileutes of southern British Columbia and northern Washington. Finally, the Salish, Chinooks, Tillamooks, and Coos, among others, inhabited southern Washington and north and central Oregon. While population estimates are unreliable, it is probable that the region was home to at least 200,000 people, making it one of the most densely populated areas of the world inhabited by foraging people (Boyd 1990: 135).

An unusual feature of the Northwest Coast is the diversity of languages spoken there. At least forty-five different languages were indigenous to the region, comprising nine different language families and three language isolates. Some of the language families represented are related to others outside the region but most are confined to this particular territory. The Northwest Coast therefore is a dense and complex linguistic area. Languages belonging to the Eyak-Athabaskan group are spoken in southern Alaska. In the same vicinity, Tlingits speak a language that is classified as an isolate with no demonstrable relatives. Another language isolate is Haida, spoken by indigenous inhabitants of the Queen Charlotte Islands. Next further south are speakers of Tsimshian languages, that is, Tsimshian and Gitksan. The Wakashan languages, that is, Kwakwala and Nootkan, are spoken in central and southern British Columbia. The Chimaquan language family has speakers known as Chemakums and Quileutes who live in southern British Columbia. Overlapping southern British Columbia and northern Washington are speakers of Salishan languages, that is, Bella Coola, Salish, Squamish, Chehalis, Nooksack, and Quinault. Four additional language families are represented in Washington and Oregon: the Chinookan, Takelman, Alsean, and Coos, and one language isolate, Siuslaw.

Chinookan language, called Chinook, was the major contributor to a trade jargon that developed in the nineteenth century and was used by European and American traders, missionaries, and settlers.

One of the most unusual features of Northwest Coast linguistic history is that although its numerous languages belong to nearly a dozen separate families, there are many area-wide linguistic features shared in the region that are distinct from languages elsewhere in Native North America. Among the most striking are aspects of the sound systems, particularly their rich inventory of consonants. In fact, Northwest Coast languages tend to have far greater numbers of consonants than most other languages of the world.

Most of the languages indigenous to the Northwest Coast are no longer spoken today or have only a small number of speakers. In general, the further south their territory, the less likely there are to be current Native speakers. According to statistics collected by the US Census Bureau in 2000, only the Tlingit language had a large number of speakers. But although there were 1,088 people reporting Tlingit as their "home language," only eighty-one children between the ages of 5 and 17 spoke their Native tongue (US Bureau of the Census 2000, Table 18: 875). Wakashan and Salishan languages had a total of 1,105 speakers but most of the member languages had fewer than a hundred speakers. Salish was spoken by the most people: 540 speakers, 181 of whom were children (Table 18: 875). In Canada, according to the census of 1996, 2,520 people spoke Salishan languages while 1,360 spoke languages belonging to the Wakashan family. In some regions, particularly on the reserves in British Columbia, language programs have been instituted since the 1980s that aim to either maintain or introduce the languages to young speakers.

ABORIGINAL CULTURES

Economies

Because of its relatively mild temperatures and abundant rainfall, the Northwest Coast is rich in flora and fauna both in the sea and on land. Indigenous people had an intimate knowledge of the sea, the cycles of daily, monthly, and yearly tidal changes, and the possibilities of obtaining food from the sea at different times of the day or year. On land, differences in temperature and altitude result in differences in the types of trees and plant life that also contributed to aboriginal economies. In Alaska and northern British Columbia, the trees are predominantly spruce and hemlock, while further south, hemlock and fir trees abound. Cedar, pine, maple, birch, and redwood grow in different areas. All of these varieties were utilized, where they were found, for the extensive woodworking technology of aboriginal people. Wood was used in the manufacture of tools, weapons, and household goods such as boxes, trunks, dishes, and spoons. Most importantly, wood was used in the construction of houses and canoes. People also made extensive use of plants as foods, medicines, and raw materials in the manufacture of other products. Among the most abundant plants prepared for foods were numerous varieties of wild grasses, ferns, lilies, onions, the roots of clover, lupine, parsley, cattail, and skunk cabbage. Of the more than forty varieties of fruits and berries found in the region, the most important to the Native diet were gooseberries, currants, raspberries, blackberries, strawberries, cranberries, wild plums, and crab apples. Marine vegetation such as seaweed and kelp were also collected and prepared for food. In some regions, acorns and hazelnuts were gathered as well. Some plants were used in the manufacture of clothing and household utensils. Cedar bark was made into baskets, matting, and bedding and was shredded and woven into clothing. Cordage was prepared from kelp, hemp, and the roots of cedar, spruce, and willow. Tobacco was grown in western Oregon where it was smoked or chewed. In other regions, wild plants were sometimes tended in order to conserve and ensure their survival.

Among the faunal resources available, fish and marine animals were the most important to the aboriginal diet. Five species of Pacific salmon formed the basis of aboriginal economies. Each of the species (Chinook, Sockeye, Coho, Pink, and Chum) lived their adult life in the sea and returned to rivers and streams where they had been born and where they would spawn and die. The migratory patterns of the various species differed somewhat in their timing and thus provided great abundance and nearly year-round availability. In addition to salmon, men caught trout, eulachon, sturgeon, and lamprey in rivers and lakes, while in the ocean they caught halibut, herring, smelt, and cod. Women collected mussels, scallops, oysters, barnacles, and sea urchins exposed at low tide. They also dug for clams along the beaches. Crabs and octopus were taken by wading in the water or spearing from a canoe.

The sea provided seals, sea lions, porpoises, and whales. Land animals including deer, elk, mountain goat, and black bear were hunted both for their meat and their hides. Smaller furbearing animals such as otters, beavers, hares, squirrels and mice were taken as well. Hunters also caught a large number of birds, particularly waterfowl such as ducks, swans, geese, loons, and heron. Birds were also important as sources of eggs.

Economic activities followed an annual cycle as fish, plants, and animals became seasonally available. For Tlingits along the northern coasts, for example, the year began in March when ocean fishing commenced (Oberg 1973: 73–74). In April, women collected seaweed and shellfish. Huge numbers of eulachon were also taken, primarily for their oil. As spring plants began to bloom, they were collected and stored for winter use. Throughout the late spring and early summer, people continued to focus on fishing in the sea, hunting land animals, and collecting berries and roots. In late July and August, men caught salmon that entered the streams of Tlingit territory to spawn. As more salmon arrived in September, the focus on their catch intensified. Some fish were eaten fresh, but most were dried for winter use when they became the main staple of the Native diet. Sometime in October, people returned to their villages after having spent the summer and fall fishing, hunting, and plant-collecting, amassing enough food from their varied resources to be dried and preserved for use throughout the winter. People then turned their attention to producing and repairing tools and utensils. Men made wooden boxes, dishes, tools, and equipment while women made clothing from fur and animal hides and utilized cedar bark, roots, and mountain goat wool in the manufacture of baskets, mats, and blankets.

All of the indigenous nations of the Northwest Coast had foraging economies that were primarily centered on aquatic resources such as fish, shellfish, and sea mammals found in great abundance in the Pacific Ocean and in tributaries and lakes. Subsistence activities tended to be at least ideally divided between men and women. Men's primary responsibilities were fishing and hunting whereas women collected shellfish and gathered wild plants. Technological skills also tended to be aligned with gender. Northwest Coast technology, in fact, was highly developed and specialized, utilizing many tools and procedures that aided in transforming raw materials into useful objects and structures. Women made clothing, bedding, containers,

Two Tlingit women with children near the Kotsina River, Alaska, in 1902.

found their way up and down the coast and into the interior. In addition to local trade, the Northwest Coast was part of a larger commercial system that linked it to other regions. Indians exchanged marine and forest products for raw materials and finished goods made by inland people in the western subarctic and northern plateau.

Settlements

Aboriginal settlements, often containing more than 500 residents, were constructed along the shore. People occupied the villages during the winter when their economic activities were generally suspended. The "winter villages" contained large wooden houses facing the ocean, often built on pilings or platforms so that unusually high tides would not damage or destroy them. During other times of the year, people established smaller temporary seasonal camps near fishing sites, berry patches, hunting grounds, or other resource areas that were exploited in accordance with seasonal cycles. Among the Tlingits, for example, permanent winter villages were built along the ocean or riverbanks. Houses were built in a row with their doorways facing the water. Racks for drying fish were erected in front of the houses. Canoes were pulled up on the beaches or riverbanks and covered over with mats or bushes to protect them from the sun. Behind the rows of houses were the graveyards, each belonging to clans resident in the village. In aboriginal times, when the bodies of the dead were cremated, each clan also had a funeral pyre. Ashes of the dead were placed inside totem poles that were carved with clan crests and erected in front of houses (Oberg 1973: 10–11).

and many household tools and utensils from fibers, while men produced wooden tools, weapons, storage containers, and dishes and constructed houses and canoes. Although labor was generally associated with gender, in most societies of the region much work was done cooperatively by men and women. Tasks that were primarily assigned to one gender might be performed by the other if people were so inclined or if the need arose. Even cooking and childcare, which were usually the domain of women, could be performed by men as the occasion necessitated. And women frequently joined their husbands on hunting and trading expeditions. In fact, among the Tlingit, it was common for at least one woman to accompany male traders because the people believed that "women were better bargainers" (86). European traders noted the prominence of Tlingit women on trading expeditions, usually complaining both because of the shrewdness of the Indians and the fact that they were women: "The women are far keener at 'dicker' than the men, and much more difficult to cheat" (Knapp and Childe 1896: 61–62).

Northwest Coast people developed extensive trading networks so that utilitarian and luxury goods

Tlingit houses were made of spruce or cedar planks (Oberg 1973: 10; Swanton 1908; Shotridge and Shotridge 1913: 86–89). They were usually about 30 to

50 sq.ft., 6 ft.high at the eaves and 14 ft.high at the center ridge. Such houses accommodated several families, perhaps as many as six, with an average resident population of forty or fifty people. The floor inside was dug to a depth of one or 2 ft.below the door in order to minimize drafts. A fire was built in the center of the house for communal cooking and heating. Platforms, placed along the interior walls several feet above the floor and covered with mats of woven cedar bark, were used for sleeping and seating. A higher row of platforms was built along the walls for storage of food and personal belongings. Houses had one central door covered over with a heavy cedar bark mat. The door was usually a couple of steps above the ground so that when it snowed, the snow would not pile higher than the entranceway. In addition, since the door was not quite high enough for an adult to enter without bending, its placement was a defensive strategy because an enemy could only enter awkwardly. A central smoke hole was opened in the roof over the fire to give light and ventilation. A few feet in front of the back wall of the house, Tlingits erected a large screen with a hole in the center that was painted with crest animals or spirits representing the kinship group of the inhabitants. People stored ceremonial gear such as masks and totemic figures behind the screen. Clan crests were also carved and painted on the four main posts supporting the frame of the house as well as on its exterior facade.

Each family residing in the house had their own quarters, usually partitioned off with wooden screens or cedar bark mats. The area in front of the back screen was considered "the head of the house" and was reserved for the owner of the house and his family to sit and rest. When guests came to visit, they were entertained in this place.

Like those of the Tlingits, Coast Salish villages in southern British Columbia were constructed along the water, preferably near sandy beaches, with their front doors facing the water (Barnett 1938, 1955). The composition of villages varied, some consisting of a single dwelling, others of one or two rows of houses. Houses generally measured some 20 to 60 ft.wide and 40–100 ft.long. Some were even larger, as much as 640 ft.in length and 60 ft.wide. Large houses were partitioned into separate areas for the resident families. House posts were decorated with carvings or paintings representing ancestral spirits. Some Coast Salish people built semi-subterranean houses for use during cold weather, and some erected fortified shelter for safety during raids. Houses in a village were sometimes said to belong to one named local group descending from an important ancestor, but a village might contain two or more local groups, each with its own kinship history.

Further south, Coosans inhabited at least seventy villages, constructed along the banks of rivers or bays. Their largest houses measured about 80 ft.in length and 40 ft.in width (Zucker et al. 1983: 35). Houses were dug into the ground to a depth of 1–5 ft. They were partitioned by wood planks or tule mats into separate areas for each resident nuclear family. The inside walls were lined with tule mats, and the dirt floor was also covered with mats or hides as were platforms used for sleeping and sitting. A series of hearths was placed in the center, each with drying racks and cooking utensils. Members of households were usually related by birth or marriage. They functioned as an economic unit, sharing resources and domestic tasks. Each house had an acknowledged leader who gave advice and served as a spokesman for his group. The size of houses varied and was indicative of the social status of its residents. Houses belonging to people of highest status were sometimes named (35). When at temporary camps, people lived in small sheds made of thatched grass.

Families and Systems of Social Stratification

In all regions of the Northwest Coast, kinship groups were the defining and coordinating units of economic, social, and ceremonial activities. Among northern people such as Tlingits, Haidas, and Tsimshians, social organization and descent were based on membership in exogamous matrilineal clans. Tlingit clans were grouped into exogamous moieties called Raven and Wolf while Haida moieties were named Raven and Eagle (DeLaguna 1952: 2). The major function of moieties was ceremonial. Funerals were performed by members of the opposite moiety from that of the deceased. Other ritual services, such as ear piercing for babies and the washing of newborns, were provided by a person not in the child's own moiety, usually by a father's brother or sister. Tlingit clans were corporate groups holding certain kinds of property in common, including salmon streams, berry patches, and other resource sites. Clan-owned resource areas were available to any member of the group. Clans also owned house sites in winter villages and owned or controlled trade routes. In addition, they owned ceremonial privileges and paraphernalia, especially names and crests that were carved on houses, utilitarian goods, and ritual gear. The Tsimshian organized their clans into four phratries: Raven, Eagle, Wolf, and Grizzly Bear (Sapir 1966: 40–43). In central regions, membership in lineage groups was also of paramount social, economic, and ceremonial importance, but the descent system was based on bilateral flexibility. A child might become a member of either the mother's or father's lineage through a formal naming process. The choice of group was based on strategic decisions aimed at maximizing one's status and wealth. In the south, social organization was thoroughly bilateral and lacked the lineage group identifications of central and northern people.

In contrast to foraging societies elsewhere in the world, Northwest Coast societies developed complex systems of social rank and status differentiation. The specific workings of the system of rank differed in different societies. In general, people were divided into three groupings: nobles, commoners, and slaves. In northern nations, the distinction between nobles and commoners was of great cultural significance and the drive to acquire and enhance one's social rank was a strongly motivating force, particularly for people who had a potential to reach high status in the society. Elsewhere, although social status was important, it was less a central cultural focus.

The relationship between noble and common status was quite complex. These were not discrete groups but rather were places on a continuum of rank. Nobles were people who held high-ranking names or titles such as chiefs and their close relatives, whereas commoners were people who lacked social significance of this sort, although mobility between the groups was possible. Commoners were sometimes related to nobles, often their youngest siblings and more distant kin. They could aspire to and perhaps achieve noble status by inheritance of prestigious names and titles. Slaves were a distinct category composed of people who had been captured in war or were the children of slaves. They were not mistreated but lived in the houses of their owners and performed menial subsistence and household tasks. However, they carried a significant social burden by their exclusion from the system of status that was important in most societies. In addition, in some groups, a slave might be sacrificed at the funeral of his/her owner, particularly if the latter were a high-ranking chief.

Tlingits were keenly aware of their own and others' social status but not in terms of clearly delineated classes. However, "there was a kind of aristocracy, composed of chiefs and their immediate families, in contrast to ordinary people" (DeLaguna 1972, I: 462). A chief or rich man was referred to as a "man of the town" while poor people and those of very low status were called "those who live at the front of the house." The most derogatory term was "child of the empty beach," a term used for lazy people, paupers, freed slaves, or anyone with slave ancestry (462). There evidently were no specific labels for the majority of Tlingits, that is, common or ordinary people.

The highest ranked people were the chiefs of clans and their immediate family. These men and women were called "one who is heavier than others" or "crystal person" (463). The latter term implies their lack of any social or spiritual stain upon themselves or their ancestors. People of high status strove to increase their wealth and social standing through their industry, generosity, kindness, and unblemished moral character. They were taught the histories of their group as well as its songs and rituals. They were also expected to be gifted speakers in ceremonial and social contexts, using complex metaphorical language that ordinary people could not understand. Desired personality traits for anyone of high status included self-restraint, mildness of temper, sympathy for the unfortunate, courtesy and polite manners, and modesty about one's own achievements or abilities. As one of DeLaguna's consultants remarked, "They used to say, 'Don't brag about yourself! Be kind to everybody and not hurt somebody's feelings. Don't brag. Let somebody find out how good you are!'" (467).

Status and rank were interconnected with marriage patterns. Parents attempted to arrange marriages for their children with people of at least equal but preferably higher status. Polygamy was possible among elites, both for men and women, although it occurred only occasionally. Among the Tlingits, cross-cousin marriage was common for high-status people because it solidified wealth and rank. Since a person's status was derived from that of their mother and father, a mother's brother's children and a father's sister's children were of the same rank as oneself. Cross-cousin marriage not only solidified lineage wealth and prerogatives but also served to unite the principles of matrilateral and patrilateral descent (DeLaguna 1952: 6; Oberg 1973: 37). Furthermore, since the young people concerned belonged to different lineages, repeated cross-cousin marriage patterns resulted over generations in the transfer of property back and forth between two kinship groups, creating a stable exchange of inheritance and wealth.

Central Coast Salish society was divided into three groups: first, high-class people (now referred to by Coast Salish as "ladies" and "gentlemen"); second, a class referred to as "poor people," "nothing people," or "low-class people"; and third, slaves (Suttles 1958: 499). By far the majority of people belonged to the upper or "respectable" class (500). Relative mobility within the upper class was frequent as people rose into positions of leadership, gained wealth, acquired ceremonial privileges, and achieved prestige through their own accomplishments. The lower class was composed of people with no material, spiritual, or social advantages. They comprised a relatively small group "upon which the upper class imposed its will and which it treated with contempt" (500). Mobility from the lower to upper class was difficult. Slaves were people who had been captured in war or purchased from others. Their lowest social status was hereditary. They were the least numerous group in Coast Salish communities. High status and prestige accrued to people of good birth and wealth. Wealth was derived from the possession of material goods, rights to productive resource sites, and spirit power. High-status people also had "private or guarded knowledge" or "advice" consisting of family genealogies and stories that attested to unblemished family histories, access to spirit knowledge and protections, and "a good deal of solid moral training" (501). Lower-class people, in contrast, were those who had "lost their history" or "had no advice." According to Suttles, the existence of a small lower class who had "lost their links with the past and their knowledge of good conduct" served to remind people (especially those in the upper class) of the importance of moral knowledge and behavior (501).

Among the Skagit, a southern Coast Salish nation, although wealth was a necessary component of high status, it was not sufficient (Collins 1974: 124–125). Rather, Skagit etiquette required that a person of high class demonstrate through their demeanor and behavior that they were deserving of the respect they received. High-status people were quiet and carried themselves with dignity in public. They did not argue or act violently but rather were peaceful and accommodating. They were expected always to tell the truth. The Skagit believed that people learned how to act properly by belonging to families that encouraged and demanded moral and ethical behavior. It was therefore difficult to rise from lower status to higher status categories since

a lower-status person, almost by definition, was born into and trained in habits that diverged from those of the upper class.

Although Skagit society was concerned with principles of status, many aspects of behavior and beliefs also indicate an egalitarian social ethic. Resources and property were frequently distributed throughout the community. For example, goods were circulated among relatives and villagers in a system of gift exchange. Whenever someone visited a relative in another settlement, they brought gifts, especially specialties of their region that were scarce or lacking in the village of their host: "People from up-river villages brought prepared skins, dried venison, mountain goat wool blankets, and coiled baskets as gifts. In return those on salt water might give smoke clams, oysters, saltwater fish, and matting" (77–78). Gifts were regularly exchanged between affinal relatives, even after their connecting link was deceased. In addition, gifts were distributed at feasts or "potlatches" (from the Chinook jargon word meaning "to give"). Such gifts included ceremonial articles and raw materials and foods that equalized levels of consumption in different households and villages. Property was also given away when a person died, most passing to relatives of the deceased. Furthermore, most household items belonging to anyone in the household of the deceased were taken away by other relatives or visiting mourners, a practice that could have left the deceased's relatives with few possessions, but in fact replacements were usually given so that the family would not be impoverished. In sum, Skagit mechanisms of exchange resulted in a general recirculation of property and resources within a village or kinship group. An interesting consequence of the recirculation of goods was that although the acquisition of possessions was a proper value, people did not develop claims on particular items since all of their property would some day be distributed to others and replaced with goods that had previously belonged to other people.

The Coosans of Washington and Oregon divided the populace into four groups. The highest were people of wealth and status including leaders or "chiefs" and their close kin. Leaders were selected because of their wealth and accomplishments. Chiefly families were a relatively closed group who tended to marry within their class and held the few positions of limited authority that existed in their communities. Second were common but respectable people. Next were people who were poor and of low status, a combination that was intrinsically linked. Finally, there was a small class of slaves derived from people captured in raids or more likely obtained through trade. In contrast to more northerly nations, the social status and lifestyle of slaves approximated that of poor commoners (Zucker et al. 1983: 56). Poor people may not have owned as much property as the majority of the population but they did not live beneath an adequate level of subsistence. Redistribution of goods took several forms. Poor people received support through gift exchange from their more affluent relatives. And whenever communal fishing or hunting expeditions returned to the community, the catch was distributed to everyone in the village. In addition, people in need could visit more affluent families at mealtime and receive food.

Throughout the Northwest Coast, ceremonial property such as names, dances, ritual paraphernalia, crests that portrayed animal ancestors, and myths of lineage origin were of both religious and social value. Rights to acquire and display ceremonial property were obtained primarily through inheritance and secondarily through marriage. Ceremonial wealth was owned by individuals as representatives of their lineage group or clan. Crests in particular were powerful ritual and social symbols that depicted animals who figured in lineage or clan origin myths. These animals were believed to have long ago removed their animal masks and outer forms to reveal their inner human shape and become the ancestors of people living today. Crests depicting animal ancestors were displayed on many structures and objects. They were carved or painted on totem poles that were erected in front of people's houses, the facades and/or posts of the houses themselves, ritual gear, and utilitarian objects such as dishes, boxes, spoon handles, and pipes.

In most Northwest Coast societies, an exchange of property took place at marriages. The husband's family gave material wealth to the wife's family and in return received ceremonial property that was initially held by the husband but later passed on to the couple's children. In the northern societies that followed rules of matrilineal descent, children inherited from their mother's brother while elsewhere they primarily inherited from their fathers and mothers. Whatever the line of transmission, the acquisition or inheritance of ceremonial property was confirmed at public feasts or potlatches. Potlatches differed widely from north to south, displaying their most elaborate form in the northern and central groups such as the Tlingits, Tsimshians, and Kwakiutls. In all cases, however, they involved sponsoring a feast for guests who came to witness and thereby validate the transfer of social rights to names and rank and to ceremonial property such as dances and membership in ritual organizations. Potlatches were also held to mark lifecycle events including naming, girl's puberty, marriage, and death. They also celebrated the building of a new house and the erection of a lineage or clan totem pole. In some central and northern groups, they were occasions for the public display of rivalry between high-ranking chiefs or those who aspired to enhance the prestige of the titles or names that they held. This competitive element was lacking in potlatches in most of the central and especially southern groups, where potlatches were more simply occasions for the display of ceremonial property and the marking of ritual occasions. Even in the north, there is evidence that the competitive aspect of potlatching was a post-contact phenomenon.

Community Leadership

Northwest Coast societies were not unified nations, but rather each village was politically autonomous. High-ranking chiefs had social influence but nowhere did they have coercive powers either over their relatives or others living in their villages. Instead, group decisions were reached through open discussion and consensus among the respected men and women in the community. People (except perhaps slaves) were never compelled to follow the advice or will of others except through the usual means of social pressure.

Among the Tlingits, leadership in house groups was usually vested in the most senior man belonging to the resident lineage. He was designated the "yitsati" or "house keeper" (Oberg 1973: 42). Within every village, the head of the highest ranking and most respected house group was called an "ankaua" (rich man). The heads of each house and of the leading clan house group in the village had symbolic functions but lacked coercive powers. In general, succession to leadership followed rules of primogeniture, first among brothers and then from uncle to sister's sons (DeLaguna 1952: 6; Oberg 1973: 42). When a leader died, his next eldest brother was the likely successor. Once succession through all siblings had been exhausted, inheritance passed to the eldest son of the eldest sister.

Skagit households were headed by the oldest male and oldest female in the senior generation. They had authority and influence over their juniors. They did not exercise power but rather were heeded because of their greater experience and better judgment. Within villages, the eldest member of the most important household was deemed a village leader. This leader often called community-wide meetings that were attended by all members of the village. Anyone present could contribute to the discussion and speak as long as they wished. No decisions could be made without reaching unanimous agreement. Whenever group activities were necessary, such as the construction of wooden fish weirs or communal hunting or warfare expeditions, the person who was the most knowledgeable in the specific domain took charge of organizing the activity. Even though people were never compelled to contribute labor or property to any group effort, they usually did so because they understood that it was in their own interest and that they would benefit from the communal activity. According to Collins: "Lazy persons were allowed to benefit by the industry of others. Those who do not help, say in food-getting activities, were fed by others. People sneered at them and insulted them. The indigent might be given spoiled salmon or a piece which the cook had dropped in the dirt" (1974: 113). While direct compulsion was not exerted on people to comply with group norms, clearly some social pressure led to generally cooperative behavior.

Further south among the Coosans, formal political unity was lacking, but each large village had a chief and an assistant whose decisions and actions were taken after consultation with respected men and women in the community. Chieftainships were usually inherited by sons or other close male relatives. Although primogeniture was preferred, if an eldest son was deemed unfit, he was passed over in favor of another son or other relative. In cases where no male heir was thought adequate, a woman could succeed to the position of chief. Chiefs helped settle disputes within their villages and organized communal activities. They also aided community members who were less fortunate than the majority and needed food or other supplies.

Among most Northwest Coast societies, the techniques of and motivations for intergroup raiding and warfare were fairly similar. Although relationships among neighboring nations were generally friendly, hostilities were also possible. They were usually motivated by revenge for a death in one's own group. People sought to punish either the person responsible for the death or a member of the person's kin group or nation. Victims of raids, especially if they were men, were frequently beheaded and their heads brought back to the home village and kept as trophies. Women

and children were more typically taken as slaves and adopted into their owner's household.

RELATIONS WITH EUROPEANS

Beginning in the late eighteenth century but accelerating in the nineteenth, Native people of the Northwest Coast became involved in the fur trade with Russian, Spanish, British, French, and American merchants. Permanent establishments began in 1799 when Russians opened a fort at Sitka (Alaska) that was soon to become the center of the RussianAmerican Company as well as the administrative base of Russian control in Alaska. In 1827, the Hudson's Bay Company established Fort Langley on the Fraser River (British Columbia), followed by other forts in the next several decades.

Native involvement in trade did not cause a radical shift from aboriginal patterns because local and long-distance trade had been indigenous to the region. The Europeans simply brought new items of value, particularly iron and copper goods, cloth, blankets, firearms, clothing, and ornaments that were obtained in exchange for otter and beaver furs. In addition, food was traded between both groups. Native people supplied traders with meat and fish, both fresh and prepared, and received rice, bread, and molasses (Gibson 1978). They also obtained alcoholic beverages, particularly rum. Europeans actually depended upon Native supplies more than the Indians depended upon European trade goods. For instance, Russians in Alaska were nearly totally dependent on Tlingits to supply them with the basic necessities of life, as one Russian official reported in 1860:

> [T]he Kolosh [Tlingit] cannot in any respect be regarded as dependent on the Company rather it may be said that the Company's colonies on the American coast depend on them; for the Kolosh have only to begin to make a little noise to deprive the port and its entire population of all fresh food and even of the opportunity to show their faces a few yards outside the fortification. (Okun 1951: 207)

Native people of the Northwest Coast were evidently eager to trade with Europeans. According to George Vancouver's recollections of a meeting with the Coast Salish:

> In the morning, soon after they [men from Vancouver's ship] had landed to breakfast, they were

visited from a large canoe full of Indians, who were immediately followed by a hundred more of the Natives, bringing with them the mats for covering their temporary houses, and, seemingly every other valuable article belonging to them. (Vancouver 1801: 162)

Indians greeted Europeans with traditional marks of friendship and hospitality: "a middle aged man, in all appearance the chief or principal person of the party, was foremost in showing marks of the greatest hospitality, and perceiving our party at breakfast, presented them with water, roasted roots, dried roots, fish, and other articles of food. This person, in return, received some presents, and others were distributed amongst the ladies and some of the party" (162).

Spanish explorers of the same period had similar encounters with Coast Salish people:

Several Indians ran down to the beach got into a canoe and steered for the schooner, pursuing them with as much skill as the most experienced sailor could do. In it an old man and four young ones came boldly alongside and gave us brambleberries. We gave each a metal button and they repeated their gifts in small portions to obtain something else in exchange, seeing that we gave them a string of beads or a piece of ship's biscuit for each present. They also gave us dried shellfish, threaded on a cord of bark, and others of different kinds on slender skewers. We accepted a sufficient quantity of them and also obtained from them a blanket of dog's hair, quilted with feathers and a tanned deerskin. (Wagner 1933: 246)

European observers were quick to note, and complain about, the shrewd bargaining of Northwest Coast people and their refusal to trade when they believed that the terms were unfavorable. For example, journals of a British trader in 1795 noted that the Indians "began to set their own price on the skins which was not moderate, we were plagued the whole day to break trade on their own terms" (Elliott 1927: 263). People who lived closest to the coastal harbors were quick not only to trade for their own uses but to establish themselves as intermediaries between Europeans and upriver or interior nations. Tlingits and Tsimshians played these roles among northern groups, while the Kwakwaka'wakw acted as middlemen in the central Northwest Coast, and Chinooks were the primary brokers to the southern region. Indeed, an English trader at the post of Fort Astoria on Puget Sound noted in 1849 that "the crafty Chinookes fomented and nourished the misunderstanding of us and the distant tribes, monopolizing all the trade themselves" (Ross 1849: 77).

Furthermore, Vancouver observed that the people who were the direct recipients of trade sometimes settled near areas where the Europeans had landed"until an opportunity was afforded them to barter their commodities for valuable productions of Europe, which are afterwards disposed of the inhabitants of the interior country at a very exorbitant price" (Vancouver 1801: 164).

European merchants benefited from traditional fishing and hunting activities to supply their food but the aboriginal economic focus shifted from subsistence to trade. Changes in social life gradually occurred, particularly in the area of leadership. None of the aboriginal Northwest Coast groups had formal, centralized leadership, but since Europeans preferred to deal with representatives of communities both for trade and political purposes, they helped solidify and augment the authority of kinship-based chiefs. Chiefs who became wealthy from the trade enhanced their status in their communities and were often instrumental in furthering commercial ties with Europeans since they benefitted both materially and socially.

Changes also took place in women's status and roles in Native society (Klein 1980). Although women's productive contributions in preparing fur pelts for market were highly valued, women were eclipsed in some of their important traditional activities by preferences that Europeans showed toward dealing with men. Female traders were ignored and belittled by European merchants and women chiefs, although not common in aboriginal times, were likewise ignored by foreign authorities. Missionaries who came to the region in the early nineteenth century also helped undermine women's status by attempting to impose a European model of gender in which men were the heads of households and women were relegated to subordinate domestic work.

CONSEQUENCES OF EURO-CANADIAN/AMERICAN SETTLEMENT

By the middle of the nineteenth century, European and American traders penetrated further into the US and Canadian interior. Treaties were eventually signed that called for the cession of most aboriginal land and the assignment of indigenous groups to reservations and reserves. The Treaty of Washington signed in 1846 by the United States and Great Britain divided aboriginal Northwest Coast territory between the United States and Canada, separating some Native nations between the two jurisdictions. Government policy differed regarding the composition and status of Indian communities. In general, the Canadian government recognized each large Native village as a separate autonomous band with jurisdiction over one or more reserves, whereas according to US policy, neighboring villages were combined into tribes, some obtaining reservations but others being deprived of land.

The second half of the nineteenth century was a period of restrictions on Native access to land and the people's gradual incorporation as a political and numerical minority in the states and provinces in which they lived. One of the most difficult problems that Indians faced at that time, and continue to face today, is the lack of certainty about their lands. In Canada, British Columbia was not incorporated into the Canadian confederation until 1871 and therefore developed its own policies regarding Native rights. As towns grew, they began to absorb Indian land, but during the governorship of James Douglas, Indian communities could choose or "pre-empt" land that they wanted to reserve for residential use. Some Native groups received monetary compensation for relinquishing most of their territory, retaining village sites and some fishing stations. Indians also retained aboriginal rights to hunt and fish on lands that were at that time unoccupied. However, although land was taken and reserves were established, many of the agreements between Indians and colonial authorities were never ratified. Beginning only one year after Douglas' retirement (i.e., in 1865), land was taken from reserves in southern British Columbia. After British Columbia joined the Canadian system in 1871, federal jurisdiction extended to Indians in the province. In the agreement of union, the federal government pledged to continue "a policy as liberal as that hitherto pursued by the British Columbia Government" (Fisher 1977: 176). Indians continued to be vulnerable to changing attitudes of federal and provincial commissioners. In 1875 commissioner Joseph Trutch stated: "The Indians have really no rights to the lands they claim, nor are they of any actual value or utility to them; and I cannot see why they should either retain these lands to the prejudice of the general interest of the colony, or be allowed to make a market of them either to government or to individuals" (164).

Accordingly, Trutch implemented a policy of "adjustment" of acreage to suit what he thought were the Indians' needs. He instituted reductions that allocated only 10 acres per family. Although the exact amount of land lost to Indians in the process is unknown, one surveyor's report of the period noted that with new boundaries, some 40,000 acres were opened for settlement (164).

Although the government wanted to negotiate treaties with Native groups to extinguish their aboriginal title to land, none of the coastal nations agreed to do so. The lack of treaties has been the foundation of land claims suits throughout the twentieth century. As Tennant observed: "The British Columbia Indians, as an integral aspect of their political development, came to demand that provincial and federal governments acknowledge that the absence of treaties was not to be taken as an absence of agreement on the land question, but rather as proof that Indian title remains in effect" (1982: 14).

British Columbian Nations

By the late nineteenth century, the earlier numerical strength of the Native population in British Columbia had declined. According to a census taken in 1881, Indians numbered 25,661, representing just over one-half of the province's population of 49,459. Ten years later, Native figures remained about constant but the non-Indian population doubled to 98,173, and in 1901 it reached 178,657, relegating the Indians (at 25,488) to a small minority (Fisher 1977: 202). The population disadvantage was most marked in and near cities and towns, while in rural areas Indians tended to be the majority.

In response to their marginal situation, Indians began to organize for their economic and political rights. In 1913, the newly formed Nishga Land Committee filed a petition in Ottawa for recognition of their territorial rights (27). Three years later, a province-wide group, the Allied Indian Tribes of British Columbia, was formed, followed in 1931 by the Native Brotherhood of British Columbia, now the longest-lived Canadian Indian organization (28). Beginning among coastal people, it gradually widened its membership to include all Northwest Coast nations. And in 1969 Indians whose lands were not protected by the treaty and reserve system organized the British Columbia Association of Non-Status Indians in an attempt to obtain official recognition of their needs. Although the large, province-wide groups continue to function, many smaller, local organizations have formed that are based on independent linguistic and cultural identities. Some of these organizations began as district councils that unite separate bands or reserves whose members belong to the same nation (Tennant 1983: 119–121).

As a result of litigation in British Columbia brought by the Gitksan, the Supreme Court of Canada ruled in December 1997 that aboriginal rights to land and resources must be taken into consideration when mining, logging, and other resource exploration projects are undertaken in indigenous territory, including in lands where Indians have outstanding claims. Additionally, the ruling recognized the validity of oral traditions in supporting claims to land. As Chief Justice Antonio Lamer stated: "In practical terms, this requires the courts to come to terms with the oral histories of aboriginal societies, which, for many aboriginal nations, are the only record of their past" ("Canadian Court Ruling Broadens Indian Land Claims" 1997). While the court's ruling was specifically directed at affairs in British Columbia, it has application elsewhere in Canada, as was noted by Paul Fontaine, chief of the Assembly of First Nations, "What it does is send a clear message to all of Canada. Neither the government of Canada nor any province can unilaterally engage in development without taking into account the first nations because these activities affect the fundamental rights of our people" ("Canadian Court Ruling Broadens Indian Land Claims" 1997).

The first treaty subsequent to the Supreme Court's ruling was signed in 1998 by the Nisga'a and the governments of British Columbia and Canada. In the agreement all parties acknowledged the Nisga'a's sovereign jurisdiction over their land in northwest British Columbia just south of Alaska, allowing the Nisga'a to own their homeland rather than have it held as Crown property and to exert rights of local government. In addition, they received a payment of $380 million. The Nisga'a band numbers about 5,000 but only some 2,000 members are living on reserves. The Nisga'a treaty is widely viewed as an important step in the process of achieving sovereignty for First Nations in Canada. In 1999, the Haidas filed suit for their aboriginal homeland, encompassing 10,000 acres of Queen Charlotte Island. The federal and provincial governments are in the process of negotiating land claims with forty-three additional nations representing 70 percent of the indigenous population of the province. The claims cover nearly all of the province, including the capital city of Vancouver.

In a fishing rights case in British Columbia, the Canadian Supreme Court ruled in 2011 that the Lax Kw'alaams First Nation retains their right to harvest fish and crabs for household use and for ceremonial purposes but does not have the right to sell those products commercially. Lawyers for the Lax Kw'alaams had argued that for generations prior to the arrival of Europeans the people had engaged in extensive local and regional trading networks and therefore their commercial sale of seafood is a contemporary expression of these practices. However, the Supreme Court justices stated that earlier trade involved only one product, that is eulachon (or smelt). Trade in other types of seafood was judged to be "sporadic" and therefore not central to the people's economy. The ruling curtails the ability of the people to develop a profitable fishing industry that would utilize one of their major resources.

A province-wide tourism organization was founded in British Columbia in 1996. Called the Aboriginal Tourism Association of British Columbia, it promotes and coordinates tourism activities at eight regional cultural centers throughout the province. In addition, the Association sponsors art galleries and museums that showcase the artistic achievements of Northwest Coast sculptors, painters, and artisans. Individual First Nations members sponsor their own ecotourism expeditions and educational displays. These include guided canoe trips on area rivers and lakes and hikes along forest trails that bring visitors into contact with traditional plants whose nutritional and medicinal uses are explained.

Development projects managed by British Columbia's First Nations include a hydroelectric plant on the China Creek operated by the Upnit Power Corporation (a partnership of the Hupacasath and Ucluelet First Nations) that produces electricity for some 6,000 homes and a railway project in association with regional governments on Vancouver Island. Although economic development is an obvious positive goal, some First Nations insist on the importance of protecting their lands and environments. For example, the Nuu-chah-nulth nations have instituted regulations that ban clearing and cutting logging and industrial mining, instead focusing on ecotourism, the restoration of plant and animal habitats and safe energy generation.

And several First Nations in British Columbia have united in opposition to construction of a natural gas pipeline intended to run some 288 mi.through indigenous territories. The Pacific Trails Pipeline would bring natural gas obtained through hydraulic fracturing (or fracking) that is a procedure stirring controversy in many parts of North America because of the dangers of chemical pollution and increased risk of earthquakes. For example, in 2012, the Wet'suwet'en Nation in British Columbia began to evict surveyors working for the project. The Wet'suwet'en are also forming alliances with other groups throughout North America to support their opposition to fracking and the construction of the pipeline.

Alaskan Nations

Trends in Alaska during the nineteenth and twentieth centuries were similar to those in Canada. After the United States purchased the territory in 1867, the government sent troops to exert control over the region. Although the Organic Act that established territorial government in Alaska recognized the rights of Native people to the possession and use of their traditional territory, as non-Indian settlements increased, particularly after the 1880 gold strike in Juneau, settler encroachment on Native land widened. Reacting to infringements on their land and independence, Alaskan Natives organized the Alaskan Native Brotherhood in 1912 to protect their social, economic, and territorial rights. The Alaskan Native Sisterhood was founded in the next year. In addition, Tlingits and Haidas filed suit against the US government to retain land or receive compensation for land taken in the creation of the Tongass National Forest. Although the US Court of Claims ruled against the petition, the effort was an important unifying issue for all Native people in Alaska.

After the discovery of oil in the North Slope of Alaska in the 1960s, the federal government moved to settle Native claims to land in order to extinguish aboriginal title and clear the way for oil exploration. Negotiations between Native people and US officials culminated in the Alaskan Native Claims Settlement Act of 1971. The Act extinguished aboriginal title to land held previously in common by Native people and granted 44 million acres to indigenous communities that were subsequently required to organize regional and local corporations to manage the land and the compensation payments totaling nearly $1 billion. The corporations were required to invest at least part of their settlement monies in profit-making businesses. Income generated was either reinvested or divided among the residents of the communities, thereafter referred to as shareholders in the local corporations. Alaskan Natives of the Northwest Coast region formed the Sealaska Regional Corporation, obtaining title to 280,000 acres of land and $200 million (Worl 1990: 156).

Native Nations in Washington and Oregon

In Washington and Oregon, American settlement accelerated in the middle of the nineteenth century, prompting government officials to negotiate treaties with Native nations in the region. In 1854 and 1855, representatives of many indigenous groups in the two states attended councils that ended with the signing of treaties at Medicine Creek, Point Elliott, and Point-No-Point, all ceding much of aboriginal territory and retaining some land that was converted into reservations. Until that time, Native nations had no formal political structure or permanent leadership outside kinship groups, but since American officials insisted that each band be represented by a chief, the people had to reorient their leadership and decision-making systems. For example, according to a contemporary Skagit, "The old people got together and decided he was capable for that position. After he was chosen, then his son was chief. They pick out the oldest son to be chief. When the old man gets too old, then the young man acts as chief." And, "there was one kind of people. There was one kind of people, no chief, no headman, no bishop. This white man came and called a man 'chief.' When this head man died, his son was the head man" (Collins 1973: 37).

Several additional treaties were signed by other Native nations but most were never ratified. In their precarious legal situation, some groups in Oregon and Washington appealed to local and federal courts to guarantee their rights. Some of these claims ended with small monetary compensation ranging from $1,000 to $15,000. During the 1950s and 1960s, a number of reservations in Oregon and Washington were affected by federal policies aimed at "terminating" their legal status as reservations and ending federal support, tax-immunity, and other guarantees protecting Indian lands. Among the largest of the affected groups on the coast were the Grand Ronde and the Siletz Reservations in Oregon. After years of pressing their case through the courts and Congress, members of the Confederated Tribes of Siletz achieved restoration of the land's reservation status in 1977 (Zucker et al. 1983: 113–115). For many others, it was not until 1978 and the formation of the Federal Acknowledgement Program in the BIA that most Washington and Oregon nations had their requests for federal recognition reviewed. As a result, some groups received recognition and rights to participate in programs and obtain funds from the BIA but many others did not (113–115).

The Puyallup claims case in Washington was one of the most successful. Until the claim was settled in 1989, the Puyallup tribe controlled 130 acres of land near Tacoma, 99 percent of which was owned by non-Indians. The Puyallup's suit claimed some 20,000 acres, but they agreed to settle for 900 acres and a multimillion dollar trust fund. The land is suitable for fisheries, marine terminals, and recreation facilities (Sutton 2000: 133).

In addition to land claims, another fundamental issue of great importance to Indians in the northwest is that of fishing rights guaranteed by treaty. In 1854 and 1855, six treaties were signed between Native nations of Washington and the US government in which the indigenous people agreed to cede most of their land but secured their right to fish. Even though these rights were reaffirmed by the US Supreme Court, state and local authorities repeatedly attempted to erode Native claims to fish off-reservation. Particularly in the 1950s and 1960s, Indian fishermen were harassed by state and local authorities. After first trying to evade authorities, the people began a policy of publicly exercising their fishing rights, even though they risked confiscation of their boats, nets, and fish and also risked imprisonment. In order to dramatize their claims, they staged "fish-ins," fishing at times and places considered illegal under state regulations but within their rights as stipulated by treaty (see Chapter 3 for further discussion).

Finally, after years of litigation, a landmark decision was made in 1973 by Judge George Boldt of the Federal District Court in Tacoma, Washington. Boldt ruled that Native people retained rights to fish both on and off reservations, basing his decision on passages in all the relevant treaties. For example, the Point-No-Point Treaty states: "The right of taking fish, at all usual and accustomed grounds and stations, is further secured to said Indians, in common with all citizens of the United States" (quoted in Cohen 1986: 5). The Boldt decision held that Native rights to fish for salmon, steelhead trout, and other species had to be considered separately from the rights of non-Indian fishermen

and commercial operations. Furthermore, Boldt interpreted the treaty guarantee of "taking fish in common" to mean "sharing equally." That is, Native people have rights to 50 percent of the "harvestable fish that were destined to pass through their usual and accustomed fishing grounds and stations. As most of these traditional places were situated along the rivers—the end point of the salmon's migratory journey—the decision meant that the authorities would have to limit those fishing farther out, either on Puget Sound or the ocean, so as to permit enough fish to reach the Indian fishermen" (11). Boldt defined "harvestable fish" to exclude fish that Indians catch on reservations as well as fish caught for ceremonial and subsistence needs. According to Boldt, after these fish are subtracted from the total run, the remainder can be divided equally. Finally, in 1979, the US Supreme Court upheld Judge Boldt's original interpretation of the treaties and the decision that he issued but ruled that fish caught for ceremonial and subsistence uses were to be included in the 50 percent share that Native people could retain (114). However, in the years since the Boldt decision, the Native fish harvest has declined because of the disappearance of salmon from the Columbia River. The fish harvest has dropped about 80 to 90 percent in the past twenty years alone ("One Fish, Two Fish: Northwest Tribes Fight against Formidable Odds to Save Endangered Salmon"2000:22–23). The decline is due largely to construction of dams on the Columbia and Snake Rivers that impede salmon migrations. Although Native nations have developed several fish restoration projects, their efforts may be futile without removal of the dams, an unlikely prospect given strong opposition by state authorities and commercial interests. The number of Native people earning a living from fishing has decreased correspondingly. A decline in salmon fishing has had an impact on Native health as well because salmon had previously formed a large part of the people's diet, providing a rich source of protein and other nutrients.

In 1999, in an assertion of treaty rights, members of the Makah nation of coastal Washington revived their traditional whale hunts after a lapse of some seventy-five years. Hunting gray whales had been illegal since 1937 when the animals were declared an endangered species, but when restrictions were lifted in 1994, Makahs applied to the international whaling commission for permission to resume their hunts. Based on guarantees included in a treaty signed by Makah leaders in 1855, the commission

The king of the seas in the hands of the Makahs, in Washington, ca. 1910.

granted the Makahs the right to take twenty gray whales during the next five years. The Makahs stated that they intend to hunt only for subsistence and ceremonial purposes, not for profit from sale of whale meat. Makahs support the revival of whale-hunting because of both its economic and spiritual significance to their culture. In the words of Arnie Hunter, vice president of the tribal whaling commission, it "restores a missing link in our heritage" ("Reviving Tradition, Tribe Kills a Whale"1999: A18). Whalehunting is not without controversy, however, especially among members of environmental and animal rights groups.

Contemporary Economic Data

Economic conditions vary widely in contemporary Northwest Coast communities. In the United States, income statistics indicate that some groups exceed the national norm for American Indians while others fall below the average. Table 21.1 presents economic data for selected nations. Even the nations whose

income is higher than American Indian averages fall short of other residents of their states. For example, although Tlingit and Tsimshian per capita incomes exceed the American Indian norm of $17,134 by about $3,000, they are less than half the average for Alaska of $33,129 (US Bureau of the Census 2010: Table 6: Selected Economic Characteristics, 442). Indian residents of Washington and Oregon have incomes much below others in their states (i.e., $18,878 for Washington, $17,134 for Oregon).

Labor force participation data as seen in Table 21.2 reveal high levels of unemployment in most Northwest Coast communities. Indian unemployment figures are many times higher than comparable rates for the states in which they reside: Alaska (8.4%), Oregon (10.5%), Washington (8.8%) (US Bureau of the Census 2010: Table 6: Selected Economic Characteristics).

TABLE 21.1	Income Data for Selected Northwest Nations			
	Per Capita Income ($)	Median Household Income ($)	Families Below Poverty (%)	Individuals Below Poverty (%)
Chehalis	23,108	31,625	17.1	16.0
Chinook	24,856	44,104	6.7	7.2
Coos	9,654	23,015	12.7	23.5
Lummi	14,588	37,273	20.1	21.2
Makah	27,334	53,098	25.1	39.8
Tlingit	22,672	50,046	11.3	10.5
Tsimshian	20,070	40,938	20.8	16.4
Upper Skagit	7,591	46,290	32.0	34.2

Source: US Bureau of the Census 2000; 2010: Table 6.

TABLE 21.2	Employment Data for Selected Northwest Nations	
	Labor Force Employed (%)	Civilian Labor Force Unemployed (%)
Chehalis	55.9	10.8
Coos	57.0	7.1
Lummi	48.6	11.5
Makah	44.7	15.1
Quileute	60.8	7.4
Tlingit/Haida	57.0	6.9
Upper Skagit	27.0	33.1

Source: US Bureau of Indian Affairs 2000: Table 3; US Bureau of the Census 2010: Table 6.

THE SHAKER CHURCH

In the late nineteenth century, a new religious movement originated among the southern Coast Salish in Washington through the revelations and practices of John and Mary Slocum, members of the Squaxin band. It began in 1882 when John Slocum became deathly ill and, according to tradition, died. While his relatives were preparing for his funeral, Slocum revived and reported revelations that had come to him while he had been dead. He said that God took him to heaven, showed him happiness there, and said that Indians would be saved if they gave up immoral or harmful behaviors such as drinking, smoking, and gambling. He also warned against using ritual and medical treatments ministered by shamans. Slocum's relatives organized a church on Shaker Point in Washington for him to preach his message. In the following year, Slocum again became gravely ill. Fearing that he would die, his relatives summoned a shaman to heal him, but Slocum's wife, Mary, angered over the contradiction to her husband's teachings, left the house, weeping and praying. As she prayed, she began to tremble and shake. She then returned to the house and prayed over her husband, restoring him to health. News of Mary Slocum's "shake" and its curative powers spread throughout western Washington Native communities. Later that year, at a meeting at Slocum's church, many participants experienced the same "shake" as Mary had done. When word spread, new converts were attracted to subsequent meetings.

As the movement gained adherents, the Shakers, as they came to be known, were criticized by federal and local authorities as well as by missionaries. In an attempt to protect their rights to freedom of religion, the Shakers formally constituted themselves as a church in 1892 (Barnett 1957: 111–112). They established a governing body that included a bishop and a board of elders who served through election every four years. The Shaker Church grew during the first half of the twentieth century, reaching throughout Washington, Oregon, and northern California.

The Shaker Church is an amalgamation of Christian and aboriginal beliefs and practices. From the Christians, Shakers employ the sign of the cross, repeated three times, at the beginnings and endings of prayers. Shakers believe in an omnipotent God, in his son Jesus, and in the "Spirit of God" that is manifested in believers as they begin to shake. The shaking power enables people to heal, foretell the future, and fight evil. After death, the "Shaker Spirit" leads the deceased to heaven. Consistent with aboriginal beliefs in guardian spirits, the Shaker Spirit is received when a person is in trance. And similar to aboriginal concepts, occurrences of visions and prophecies are individual experiences not rigidly controlled by dogmatic teachings but rather are personalized contacts with the spirit world. As Barnett noted, "The Shaker ideal encourages individual deviation" (9). Although Shakers ostensibly reject shamanistic treatments, traditional beliefs in disease causation, such as soul loss or attacks by ghosts or witches, continue in the Shaker Church. And even though afflicted people seek treatment within the Shaker community, many Shaker healing methods are reminiscent of shamanistic practices. For example, Shaker healers remove disease-causing objects or essences by brushing patients with their hands or passing a lighted candle over the patient's body, just as aboriginal curers relieved patients suffering from object intrusion.

Shakers follow ethical principles common to those of most Native revitalization movements. They refrain from using alcohol, smoking, gambling, and socially disruptive behavior. They stress the importance of sharing and cooperating with members of their community. Because of their ethical practices, Shakers are often influential members of their communities even though they probably number no more than one thousand (Amoss 1990: 639).

REFERENCES

Amoss, Pamela. 1990. "The Indian Shaker Church." *Northwest Coast* (ed. W. Suttles), Vol. 7 of *Handbook of North American Indians*. Washington, DC: Smithsonian Institution, pp. 633–639.

Barnett, Homer. 1938. "The Coast Salish of Canada." *American Anthropologist* 40: 118–141.

Barnett, Homer. 1955. *The Coast Salish of British Columbia*. Eugene, OR: University of Oregon Monographs. Studies in Anthropology No. 4.

Barnett, Homer. 1957. *Indian Shakers: A Messianic Cult of the Pacific Northwest*. Carbondale, IL: Southern Illinois University Press.

Boas, Frank. 1899–1900. *Report of the Bureau of American Ethnology*. Washington, DC: Smithsonian Institution, Vol. 21, p. 60.

Boyd, Robert. 1990. "Demographic History, 1774–1874." *Northwest Coast* (ed. W. Suttles), Vol. 7 of *Handbook of North American Indians*. Washington, DC: Smithsonian Institution, pp. 135–148.

"Canadian Court Ruling Broadens Indian Land Claims." 1997. *The New York Times*. December: 12.

Cohen, Fay 1986. *Treaties on Trial: The Continuing Controversy over Northwest Indian Fishing Rights*. Seattle, WA: University of Washington Press.

Collins, June. 1974. *Valley of the Spirits: The Upper Skagit Indians of Western Washington*. Seattle, WA: University of Washington Press.

DeLaguna, Frederica. 1952. "Some Dynamic Forces in Tlingit Society." *Southwestern Journal of Anthropology* 8: 1–12.

DeLaguna, Frederica. 1972. *Under Mt. Saint Elias: The History and Culture of the Yakutat Tlingit. 3 parts*. Washington, DC: Smithsonian Contributions to Anthropology No. 7.

Drucker, Philip. 1958. *The Native Brotherhoods: Modern Intertribal Organizations on the Northwest Coast*. Washington, DC: Bureau of American Ethnology, Bulletin No. 168.

Elliott, T. C. 1927. "The Journal of the Ship Ruby." *Oregon Historical Quarterly* 28, no. 3: 258–280.

Fisher, Robin. 1977. *Contact and Conflict: Indian-European Relations in British Columbia, 1774–1890*. Vancouver: University of British Columbia Press.

Gibson, James. 1978. "European Dependence upon American Natives: The Case of Russian America." *Ethnohistory* 25, no. 4: 359–385.

Klein, Laura. 1980. "Contending with Colonization: Tlingit Men and Women in Change." *Women and Colonization: Anthropological Perspectives* (ed. M. Etienne and E. Leacock). New York: Praeger, pp. 88–108.

Knapp, Frances, and Rheta Childe. 1896. *The Thlinkets of Southeastern Alaska*. Chicago, IL: Stone and Kimball.

Kroeber, A. L. 1939. "Cultural and Natural Areas of Native North America." Berkeley, CA: University of California Press.

"One Fish, Two Fish: Northwest Tribes Fight against Formidable Odds to Save Endangered Salmon." 2000. *The Nation*. January 24: 22–24.

Oberg, Kalervo. 1973. *The Social Economy of the Tlingit Indians*. Seattle, WA: University of Washington Press.

Okun, S. V. 1951. *The Russian-American Company*. Cambridge, MA: Harvard University Press.

Phillips, Earl. 1960. *Climates of the States: Climatography of the United States*. Washington, DC: US Department of Commerce.

"Reviving Tradition, Tribe Kills a Whale." 1999. *The New York Times*. May 18: A18.

Ross, Alexander. 1849. *Adventures of the First Settlers on the Oregon or Columbia River*. London: Smith, Elder (repr. New York: Citadel Press, 1969).

"The Salmon People: Tribes in Crisis." July 2000. *American Indian Report*. pp. 12–16.

Shotridge, Louis, and Florence Shotridge. *1913*. "Indians of the Northwest." *University of Pennsylvania Museum Journal* 4, no. 3: 71–100.

Suttles, Wayne. 1958. "Private Knowledge, Morality, and Social Classes among the Coast Salish." *American Anthropologist* 60: 497–507.

Sutton, Imre. 2000. "Not all Aboriginal territory IsTruly Irredeemable." *American Indian Culture & Research Journal* 24, no. 1: 129–162.

Swanton, John. 1908. *Social Conditions, Beliefs, and Linguistic Relationships of the Tlingit Indians*. Washington, DC: Bureau of American Ethnology, 26th Annual Report, pp. 391–485.

Tennant, Paul. 1982. "Native Indian Political Organization in British Columbia, 1900–1969: A Response to Internal Colonialism." *BC Studies* no. 55 (Autumn): 3–49.

Tennant, Paul. 1983. "Native Indian Political Activity in British Columbia, 1969–1983." *BC Studies* no. 57 (Spring): 112–136.

US Bureau of the Census. 2000.

US Bureau of the Census. 2010. Washington, DC.

US Bureau of Indian Affairs. 2000.

Vancouver, George. 1801. *A Voyage of Discovery to the North Pacific Ocean, and Round the World*. 2 vols. London: John Stockdale.

Wagner, Henry. 1933. *Spanish Explorations in the Strait of Juan de Fuca*. Santa Ana: Fine Arts Press.

Worl, Rosita. 1990. "History of Southeast Alaska since 1867." Northwest Coast (ed. W. Suttles), Vol. 7 of *Handbook of North American Indians*. Washington, DC: Smithsonian Institution, pp. 156.

Zucker, Jeff et al. 1983. *Oregon Indians: Culture, History, and Current Affairs*. Press of the Oregon Historical Society.

The Kwakwaka'wakw (or Kwakiutls)

THE KWAKWAKA'WAKW (Kwakwala-speaking people) inhabit territory on the central coast of British Columbia along the Queen Charlotth Sound to Cape Cook. In aboriginal times, they lived on the northern end of Vancouver Island, on the opposite mainland along the inlets leading to Queen Charlotte Strait and eastward into the interior. The land is most suitable for settlement closest to the shoreline where the terrain is level. In contrast, immediately to the east, rugged mountains rise from 4,000 to 12,000 ft. above sea level. The name "Kwakiutl" is the original designation of only one of approximately thirty independent and autonomous groups usually referred to as "tribes." In the anthropological literature, the tribal name of Kwakiutl has been generalized to refer to the entire collection of separate groups. This is a misnomer in a further sense because the autonomous "tribes" did not form a political unity and did not recognize themselves as a cohesive nation. They did, however, recognize a shared language, albeit with dialectal differences, and a similar culture with regional variations. The people themselves currently employ a different designation, that is, the "Kwakwaka'wakw" meaning "Kwakwala-speaking people." Their language, called "Kwakwala," is one of two languages making up the Wakashan linguistic family. The other member is Nootka, spoken by indigenous inhabitants of Vancouver Island.

Each of the autonomous Kwakwaka'wakw tribes occupied a distinct territory that contained at least one large sedentary village and several smaller temporary communities. The large settlements or "winter villages" were inhabited during the winter, when economic activities were generally suspended. During the rest of the year, people dispersed to camps near where they exploited seasonally available animal, fish, and plant resources.

The climate of the region is primarily influenced by the Pacific Ocean to the west, whose waters contribute to cooling the air in the summer and warming it in the winter. As a result, temperatures in the summertime are relatively cool while in the winter they are mild. The ocean's moisture helps produce an average annual rainfall of 100 in. The territory is consequently rich in both floral and faunal resources, enabling the people to obtain their food from foraging and yet live in sedentary and densely populated villages.

KWAKWAKA'WAKW SOCIETY

Economies

Aboriginal economy focused on fishing, supplemented by gathering plants and hunting land animals. Among the most significant species of fish in the diet were salmon, halibut, eulachon, cod, and herring. Women contributed to the marine economy by gathering sea urchins, clams, and mussels. The people had a specialized technology for fishing and hunting. They used barbed harpoons attached to lines made of cedar bark to catch sea lions and seals. Codfish and halibut were caught with fish lines made of kelp to which hooks and sinkers were attached. When salmon ascended the rivers, they were caught in wooden weirs and fish traps or by the use of nets dragged between two canoes. Fish found in deeper water were sometimes harpooned. Small fish such as herring and eulachon were taken with long rakes by men in canoes. A variety of cooking and food preservation techniques were employed for different products. Seals and sea lions were roasted and eaten fresh. Salmon, cod, and halibut were roasted over fire or boiled in watertight wooden boxes that had been heated by red-hot stones. Fish intended for use later in the year were cut into strips and dried over fire or in the sun. Herring and eulachon were cooked in heated water. The oil produced by the cooking process was separated and kept in containers made of dried kelp. In the wintertime, dried halibut and salmon were eaten dipped in eulachon oil. Clams and mussels were eaten either fresh or dried by being strung on sticks or strips of cedar bark. Fish roe, especially that of herring, was considered a delicacy. It was prepared dried and eaten with fish oil (Boas 1966: 9–10).

Although marine products provided the bulk of the diet, men also hunted land animals such as deer, elks, and bears. They usually hunted deer and elk with bows and arrows, but the animals were sometimes driven into large nets made of cedar bark. Deer and bears were also caught in traps. Birds were hunted with bows and arrows. Women gathered a variety of sea grasses, roots, clover, berries, and wild fruits. Sea grass was cut and formed into square cakes that were dried and stored for later use. Berries were eaten either fresh or dried and then moistened in water and mixed with fish oil. Crab apples were preserved by boiling, kept in their juice, and later eaten with fish oil (10). A kind of chewing gum was made by refining hemlock pitch over fire and straining it through a basket (Ford 1941: 9).

Native women prepared three daily meals. The main meal of fish or meat and berries or roots was eaten at night, while lighter meals were taken in the morning and late afternoon. People used shredded cedar bark as towels to wipe fish oil from their hands.

Although economic tasks were associated with gender, the actual production or collection of food resources was a cooperative effort because many tasks required the contributions of both male and female labor. Husbands and wives often formed economic teams:

> Most often the man made the tools, digging sticks, drying stages, and containers necessary for the collecting work of the women, but in some cases the women made or collected objects necessary for the man's work, such as fishlines, bait, cedar bark pack straps, and mats. Men and women were equally occupied and important in the production of food. (Codere 1950: 16)

Resource areas such as salmon streams, shellfish sites, or berry patches were considered the property of specific Kwakwaka'wakw tribes and/or constituent lineages. Other sites, however, were considered common property, exploitable by any of the tribes. People whose territory lacked a particular resource could trade for it with those more strategically located.

Resources were utilized not only for food but also for raw materials needed for a sophisticated technology. Animal intestines were used for fishing lines, bow strings, and bags while bladders were used as containers. Blankets were made from either tanned deer hides or the woven wool of mountain goats and birds' feathers. Wood was employed by men in the manufacture of a large number of products including tools, boxes, dishes, spoons, canoes, and houses. Bark from cedar and other trees was cut or woven by women into clothing, mats, baskets, bedding, and many kinds of containers.

Clothing was relatively light. In warm weather, men usually wore no clothing at all while women wore aprons made of strands of cedar bark. In cooler weather, both women and men wore blankets made either of woven yellow cedar bark, mountain goat wool, birds' feathers, or mixtures of wool and feathers. Cedar bark blankets were often trimmed with fur. Rain capes and conical-shaped hats made of tightly woven or matted cedar bark were worn when necessary. People usually wore no shoes or leggings. Women wore their hair long and braided, while men's long hair was worn loose or knotted in the back and kept from their faces with a piece of fur tied around their heads. Both men and women adorned themselves with nose and ear pendants made of abalone shell or bone. Some women in northern tribes wore labrets as well. Women also wore necklaces, bracelets, and anklets made of dentalia shell. People often painted their faces and bodies for protection against sunburn (Boas 1966: 10–11; Drucker 1950). Parents reshaped the heads of infants in order to suit their standards of beauty by applying wads of bark to the head while the baby lay in the cradle. In most regions, both boys and girls had their heads somewhat flattened and broadened, while in some tribes girls of high-ranking families had their heads elongated (Boas 1909).

Large wooden canoes made by men from the hollowed-out trunks of red cedar trees served as the primary means of transportation. The manufacture of canoes was both a practical endeavor and one surrounded with ritual precautions. When the tree selected for the canoe was felled and the branches removed, the canoe builder remained continent lest he find rotten places in the wood. He did not comb his hair in order to avoid splitting the wood. His wife did not boil water for fear that the rising steam would dampen the wood and cause it to split (Boas 1966: 31–32). Once the tree was felled, the canoe was shaped inside the tree and the interior was then cut into blocks and broken out while the outer side was smoothed. Next, the canoe was filled with a mixture of water and urine, heated with hot stones to bring the mixture to a boil while the underside was heated by a small fire. This process rendered the wood watertight. Any holes or cracks found in the wood were sealed by caulking with rotten pitchwood. If large cracks appeared, they were filled with a mixture of shredded yellow cedar bark and pitchwood.

Settlements

Technological skills of Native woodworkers were also demonstrated in the construction of large, permanent houses. In the late eighteenth century, houses had flat roofs, but by the middle of the nineteenth they were made with pitched roofs and heavy wooden planked walls. By late in the century, houses were even larger and had painted facades and carvings on their exterior. In order to construct houses, cooperative labor was required principally in order to raise the heavy side planks, roof beams, and roofing:

> The framework of the house rests on heavy posts and beams. The front side of the hole in which the post is to stand is protected by heavy planks driven into the ground. The post is shoved into the hole and gradually shored up. The machinery used for raising the heavy roof beam … consists of a lever and guides. The wall beams of the house are generally shored up and guided by men standing on top of the posts, who hold the beams with ropes. The cross piece on the two door posts is raised on boxes. These are covered with planks and more boxes are put on until a sufficient height has been reached. (Boas 1966: 33–34)

Late nineteenth century houses measured about 40–60 sq. ft. They were built along the shoreline, with a central door facing the water. Some houses were built on pilings and others had front platforms. Inside the house, a platform measuring 4 or 5 ft. wide was built along the interior walls about 2 ft. from the floor. It was used for sleeping, sitting, and storing food, possessions, and firewood. Houses were usually divided into four sections, each containing a fireplace. Racks of poles were hung above the fireplace to dry fish, meat, and berries. Each section was occupied by a separate family generally related to one another. According to Boas, "the place of honor is the middle rear of the house, then the right side, next the left, and finally the door side" (Boas 1909: 416). Families also kept small buckets that were used as chamber pots, later emptied into large boxes outside near the door to the house (Ford 1941: 11–12).

Settlement sizes varied seasonally. Larger settlements, numbering some 500 residents, were those occupied during the winter. In the summer, villages were abandoned in favor of smaller seasonal camps located near customary fishing, hunting, and plant-collecting sites. People living within the village were usually related by descent or marriage. In the late eighteenth century, George Vancouver recorded his observations of a Nimkish village on what has become known as Vancouver Island:

> The Ty-eie, or chief of the village, paid us an early visit, and received from me some presents which highly delighted him. I understood his name to be Cheslakees … Accompanied by some of the officers, and our new guest, I repaired to the village, and found it pleasantly situated on a sloping hill, above the banks of a fine freshwater rivulet discharging itself into a small creek or cove. It was exposed to a southern aspect, whilst higher hills behind, covered with lofty pines, sheltered it completely from the northern winds. The houses, in number thirty-four, were arranged in regular streets; the larger ones were the habitations of the principal people, who had them decorated with paintings and other ornaments, forming various figures … The house of our leader Cheslakees was distinguished by three rafters of stout timber raised above the roof; … the whole, from the opposite side of the creek, presented a very picturesque appearance.
>
> On our landing, three or four of the inhabitants, came down to receive us at the beach; the rest quietly remained near their houses. These, Cheslakees informed me, were his near relations, and consequently received, in the shape of presents, compliments from me, with which they seemed greatly pleased.
>
> Several families lived under the same roof; but their sleeping apartments were separated. The women, who in proportion appeared numerous, were variously employed; some in their different household affairs, others in the manufacture of their

garments from bark and other materials … The fabrication of mats for a variety of purposes, and a kind of basket, brought so curiously close, as to contain water like an earthen vessel without the least leakage or drip, comprehended the general employment of the women, who were not less industrious than ingenious. (Vancouver 1984, II: 625–626)

Families and Social Systems

Kwakwaka'wakw social organization was based on a unit called a "numaym," meaning "of one kind." A numaym consisted of people related through lineal descent, but an individual could affiliate with either the mother's or father's group. Each village contained members of more than one numaym, although one of them might be numerically and socially dominant. Numayms collectively owned the houses in which their members lived and owned access to fishing sites, berry patches, and other resource areas. Ritual property such as songs, dances, and ceremonial paraphernalia were also owned by numayms. A tribe or village usually contained at least three or as many as seven numayms.

Boas thought that numayms had originally been village communities whose descendants had since dispersed into several local areas (Boas 1966: 42). Each numaym had a myth relating its origin from a supernatural ancestor. The tales usually told of a mythic guardian figure who was part-animal, part-human in form and who, in a series of episodes, finally took off an animal mask, became human, and was the originator of the numaym. These ancestors were called "'fathers' or 'grandfathers,' or 'chief root,' and the myth is called 'home myth,' indicating that the numaymn is essentially a family or house community" (Boas 1966: 42). Among the many numaym origin tales, the following relates the story of the Koesotenok, current members of the Gilford Island band:

> The first Koeksotenok man came from a cedar tree. His name was "one who comes from the cedar." Later in life he changed his name to Tseikami, "Supreme." He survived the flood or deluge. Transformer arrived where Tseikami was residing…Transformer put Tseikami through many trials. He put a rock around the neck of the latter and attempted to drown him …When he turned around he was amazed to see that Tseikami was alive and singing. Later Transformer put Tseikami in the fire and when he reached the same distance as before, he again heard singing. When he turned around, he saw Tseikami was alive and singing. After many such trials Tseikami and Transformer became friends as equals. Transformer could not vanquish Tseikami.
>
> Tseikami had several daughters. Qolus, "Thunderbird," was up on the mountain and looking down, saw Tseikami's fair daughters. He liked their looks and descended from the mountain. After making his face human by removing the Thunderbird headpiece he sang a song before Tseikami. He asked Tseikami's permission to

Two totem poles in front of a wood frame house in the Nimkish village Yilis, on Cormorant Island, ca. 1914. The totem poles depict an eagle representing the owner's paternal crest and a grizzly bear symbolizing the maternal one.

marry one of his daughters and was granted permission. Qolus then removed the Thunderbird cloak from himself and commanded it back to the mountain. He then became fully human. It is from the union of Qolus and one of Tseikami's daughters that the Koeksotenok descended. (Rohner 1967: 26–27)

Numayms intersect with the system of social rank and inheritance fundamental to Kwakwaka'wakw society. Although membership in a numaym followed lineage principles, individuals could choose to affiliate with the group of their mother, father, or one of their grandparents. Choices were made as they might best advance a person's social position:

> The child does not belong by birth to the gens [numaym] of his father or mother, but may be made a member of any gens to which his grandparents belonged. The child becomes a member of a gens by being given a name belonging to that gens. By taking a name belonging to another gens to which one of his ancestors belonged, a man may become at the same time a member of that gens. Thus chiefs are sometimes members of many gentes, and even of several tribes. (Boas 1891: 609)

Most marriages took place between people of different numayms, with expectations of postmarital residence with the husband's family. Intertribal marriages were common as well. There were in fact very few restrictions on marriageable choices other than constraints against unions between parents and children, full siblings, or first cousins. Although it was not common, marriages might occur between people who had the same father but never the same mother. A marriage might also take place between a man and his younger brother's daughter. Marriages between close relatives such as these occurred in an effort to consolidate wealth and social status within a numaym. The higher one's social position, the more necessary it was to marry one's social equal or, even better, to marry someone of higher rank. However, since high-status people did not want to marry beneath them, it was unlikely that a person of low rank could achieve social advancement by marrying far up the social scale. In effect, then, most marriages took place between people of more or less similar social standing.

Negotiations for marriages were a complex process that often began years before the actual wedding took place. The higher the social standing of the families involved, the lengthier and more serious the negotiations concerned with the amount of material and ritual property to be transferred between the families. By the nineteenth century, material wealth principally was given in blankets although other household gifts might be included. Ritual wealth consisted of titles, songs, and ceremonial masks. The amount of wealth given was an indication both of the social standing of the husband's family and the perceived prestige of the wife's family. It was an insult both to the potential recipient and the donor to offer less than the appropriate number of blankets, for example. Once the fathers of the boy and girl agreed upon an appropriate number of blankets to be given, preparations for the transference of property at a subsequent potlatch began. When the day came, the husband's kin proceeded to the wife's house and presented the blankets to her father, reciprocated by the bride's father in an amount "often almost, if not quite, equal" to the amount received (Boas 1966: 54). The husband and wife were then instructed by their parents in the proper behavior of married couples. They were told of their duties as economic contributors to their household and admonished to be loyal and treat each other with respect.

Several years after the wedding, often after the birth of a child, the wife's father "repaid the marriage debt" by giving wealth to the husband, principally in the form of ritual or social property such as songs, ceremonial dances, and titles that would later be inherited by the couple's children. Although the wealth was presented to the husband, it was not his to retain but rather was a gift of inheritance to the couple's children. In Native custom, repayment of the marriage debt officially ended the marriage, leaving the wife free, if she wanted, to return to her parents. If she chose to stay, evidently the more likely occurrence, a new marriage contract was made between the parties similar to the first but generally exchanging less property. A marriage was considered solid when four cycles of payment and repayment had been concluded.

Although couples were under some pressure to remain together because of the economic and social alliances created by marriage, divorce was possible in cases of incompatibility or mistreatment. Couples of common or low status probably felt much less constrained in decisions to divorce than did people of high status. And while adultery was frowned upon, it was not considered a serious breach and rarely led to divorce unless the guilty spouse behaved in excess or let their extramarital affairs become public knowledge.

Even if a wife became pregnant from an adulterous affair, the matter might not cause serious disruption in the marriage (Ford 1941: 38–39). In fact, women whose husbands were sterile might deliberately have an affair in order to become pregnant. The child would be considered a child of the woman and her husband.

Because of the complexities of inheritance and marriage payments, a man holding wealth and social standing wished to have both sons and daughters although strong preferences were expressed for sons. Because marriage repayments for daughters were usually of higher value than payments received at a son's wedding, a man with many daughters and no sons bore an economic deficit. However, it was also necessary to have daughters because social rank and ceremonial property were passed on to a daughter's children. In order to accommodate these necessities, several types of fictive marriages could be arranged by men who had no sons or no daughters:

> Difficulties arise when no daughters are available through whose marriage a name may be transmitted to offspring. It cannot be done directly through the marriage of a son. Then the chief "… turned the left side of his son's body" into a woman and gave him the name belonging to the oldest daughter of his line. Soon another chief, who wished to get the names belonging to the father of the man whose one side had been turned into a woman, wooed her, and the whole marriage ceremony was performed. The young man stayed in his father's house, but when the time for the transfer of names occurred, the appropriate ceremony was performed as though a real marriage had been performed. If there is no son, the father may call his foot or one side of his body, his daughter. The marriage ceremony is performed as though these were the women married, and the names are transferred in the usual manner. (George Hunt, quoted in Boas 1966: 55)

If a man had no children at all, a marriage ceremony could be performed with one of his feet or another part of his body. This was called "taking hold of the foot" (Boas 1897: 359).

High-ranking people chose spouses for their children with great care in order to maximize economic and social advantages. Restrictions on marriage choices were exemplified by Charles Nowell's recollections in the early twentieth century: "When I was old enough to get a wife—I was about twenty-five—my brother looked for a girl in the same position that I and my brothers had. Without my consent, they picked a wife for me. The one I want was in a lower position than me, so they wouldn't let me marry her. I argued about it and was very angry with my brother, but I couldn't do anything" (Ford 1941: 149). In contrast, marriages between commoners or people holding only low rank were less complicated. In fact, low-ranking people or commoners actually had more choices and were less constrained by formal rules of marriage and postmarital residence because for them the consequences were less momentous.

Social Rank and Potlatching

In order to understand the ways in which individuals made marriage choices and maximized their potential options for social advancement through affiliation with numayms, it is necessary to consider the system of social rank that developed in Native society. All Kwakwaka'wakw tribes and all of their constituent numayms were ranked in relation to all others. In addition, each numaym possessed a number of names (or ranks, seats, positions) that were also serially ranked. Each name was held by a particular individual, although people could hold more than one at a time. Names were inherited from parents or grandparents and could be acquired through marriage as well. Numayms therefore were groups "consisting of a series of ranked social positions plus children and adults who do not have one of the ranked positions but who may receive one as a relative of one who has one to pass on or who may have held one and retired from it" (Boas 1966: 154). According to Codere, there were a total of 794 ranks within all of the numayms combined. People strove to become holders of prestigious names (or occupiers of prestigious seats) and to manipulate their position within the system to enhance the status of the names that they held. Status was manipulated through potlatches (from the Chinook jargon meaning "to give"), that is, public feasts with economic, social, and ritual functions. Codere gives perhaps one of the best definitions of the potlatch:

> The Kwakiutl potlatch is the ostentatious and dramatic distribution of property by the holder of a "fixed rank" and named social position, to other position holders. The purpose is to validate the hereditary claim to the position and to live up to it by maintaining its relative glory and rank against the rivalrous claims of the others. There did not

need to be any special occasion to giving a potlatch, or the occasion could be merely nominal. Potlatches were always given however, on the occasion of the numerous changes of name from birth to child's name to young man's name to potlatch name, on marriages, and the birth of children to the married couple, and on initiation to the secret societies of the winter dance ceremonial. "Potlatching" is, however, more than any single potlatch. The public distribution of property by an individual is a recurrent climax in an endless series of cycles of accumulating property—distributing it in a potlatch—being given property—again accumulating and preparing. The whole potlatch system is a composition of these numerous individual potlatch cycles and is supported and maximized in Kwakiutl by certain social and economic features, the details of which clarify the general definition. (Codere 1950: 63)

Hosts of potlatches gave away wealth (by the late nineteenth century it was principally, but not exclusively, in the form of blankets) and made claim to names or titles. Such claims were validated and publicly acknowledged by the presence of invited guests who in effect were witnesses to the social displays that were central to the potlatching system. Recognition of high status, particularly of a chief, benefitted both the individual and the numaym to which s/he belonged. Potlatch ranks were referred to as "seats" because social rank was symbolically and materially displayed at potlatch feasts by the seating of invited guests and by the relative order in which they were served and received property distributions. Highest-ranking guests were seated and served first, they received property first and the property that they received was of greater value than that given to lower-ranking guests.

Inheritance of ranked positions followed rules of primogeniture to the first-born child, whether boy or girl. According to George Hunt,

> when the head chief of a numaym has no son, and his child is a girl, she takes the place of her father as head chief; and when the head chief has no child, and the younger brother of the head chief has a child, even if she is a girl, then the head chief among the brothers takes the eldest one of the children of his younger brother, and places him or her in his seat as head chief to the numaym. (Quoted in Boas 1921: 824)

Although the rule of primogeniture was absolute, rivalries between siblings sometimes surfaced but

when "the younger brother of the eldest sister tries to take away from his sister the office of giving away property, the chiefs do not agree because it never goes to the next one to the eldest" (George Hunt, quoted in Boas 1925: 91). However, when a woman was the chosen inheritor, she generally received a man's name and transmitted her social position to her own eldest son as soon as he was grown. Siblings could manipulate the system by succession to seats or ranks in different numayms to which they were eligible. And if siblings belonged to the same numaym, Hunt observed that the younger brother might resort to witchcraft against the elder brother, particularly if the latter did not yet have children, so that the first successor would die and allow the younger to inherit (Boas 1921: 1358).

It was common for holders of rank to choose their successor and pass on their name before their death, often beginning the process of transfer when the child was young. The assumption of seats or ranks was part of the naming process. When a child was born, it was given a name derived from its place of birth. After about a year, a second name was bestowed in conjunction with the distribution by its parents of a small gift such as a paddle (for boys) or a mat (for girls) to each member of the numaym. Then, when the child was ten or twelve years old, s/he received a third and more important name that marked their entry as a participant in the potlatching system. At this feast, the child gave small gifts to members of their numaym, aided by his/her relatives. And the child received a "potlatch name" from the person, usually their father, from whom they inherited status and who thus relinquished his own seat.

The Kwakwaka'wakw social system has often been described as differentiating among three groups: nobles (*noxsola* "chiefly class"), commoners (*bagil* "man of the house"), and slaves (*baganamqala* "only a man, entirely human") (Berman 1991: 71). The first two groups were, however, not discrete classes but rather gradations of relative rank. Slaves, in contrast, were socially distinct. Most slaves were acquired in warfare or were the descendants of slaves. They generally performed menial subsistence and productive tasks, but their major deficit was that they could enter into the system of social rank and prestige that was fundamental to Native society. Although there was no absolute bar to marriage between slaves and commoners, marriages with slaves were disadvantageous to commoners' social standing, it was unlikely that commoners would contract such unions. The contrast between nobles and commoners was much more complex. They were not fixed categories but rather were places on a continuum from lowest to highest social standing:

> "Commoner" in Kwakiutl refers to a person who at the moment of speaking is either without a potlatch position, chief's position, or standing place—all these being interchangeable "noble" terms—or applies to one who has low rank which is nevertheless a "standing place" or position. The man referred to at that moment might have passed on his position just the moment before, or he might just the next moment be a successor to a position. "Commoners" in Kwakiutl society cannot be considered a class, for they have no continuous or special function; they have no identity, continuity, or homogeneity as a group. Individuals can at will become commoners by retirement from potlatch positions, and they customarily did so; individuals are raised from a common to a noble position at the will of others; individuals chose to consider "common" the lower positions of noble social rank; brothers and sisters of the same parents were given positions greatly varying in social rank and the younger ones might receive a position so lowly to be "common." (Boas 1966: 150)

People of highest status (sometimes referred to as "chiefs") constituted the informal leadership of kin-groups and villages. Chiefs were recipients of portions of animal, fish, and plant products secured by members of their group. They were usually exempt from most subsistence tasks such as fishing, hunting, and collecting wood or drinking water. Chiefs were responsible for organizing cooperative productive activities, but these were relatively infrequent since hunting and fishing were usually individual endeavors. House-building, though, did require cooperative labor of many men and was organized by the chief (Boas 1921: 1333). Chiefs acted as representatives of their numayms in potlatching both as hosts and as guests.

While acquiring, validating, and enhancing one's status were central social goals, at least for the elite, the system of rank was complicated by the fact that the exact ranking of a title, a numaym or a tribe was not absolutely fixed but could be manipulated in the competitive displays and distributions of wealth made by potlatch hosts. Within each tribe and numaym, named seats were divided into three somewhat flexible categories. For example, according to George Hunt's manuscripts, one of the numayms of the Gwetela, the highest-ranking Kwakiutl tribe, contained

> fifty-three individually named seats, of which the first eighteen apparently represent one category; seats nineteen to thirty-six are described as being held by old men who have given up their seats to their sons; and seats thirty-seven to fifty-three are listed as "common man." The distinction between the first two categories relates to the difference between those who have high rank now and those who have held it in the past. (Rosman and Rubel 1971: 136–137)

In other words, as Codere suggested, differences between noble and common status were flexible, enabling people to move from one category to another, rising higher in the social system and then returning to their former status when their seat was transferred to a successor.

Non-chiefly people could aspire to chiefly status through manipulation of kinship ties, accumulation of wealth by hard work, and currying favor with established chiefs (Drucker and Heizer, 1967). Chiefs sometimes aided candidates by creating new positions, but they could harm an aspirant's chances by spreading gossip about the person's kin and questionable lineage history. Chiefs also used their ties to a shaman in order to bolster the reputation of their own spirit power or to harm competitors through witchcraft.

The potlatch system was further complicated by the continual increases in the amount of wealth needed to validate one's claim to social standing and to surpass that of one's rivals. In order to enhance one's social position, it was necessary to give a potlatch that distributed more wealth than the previous holder of one's named position had been able to do. However, although people conceived of potlatching as a system of rivalrous competition, there were a number of ways in which solidarity was also manifested. For instance, to be invited as a guest to a potlatch given by a high-ranking person was a public acknowledgment of one's own high status since for a host to enhance his/her own claims, s/he had to distribute wealth to high-ranking guests. To fail to do so would not only not raise the host's social standing but would actually diminish it by the public shame that would ensue. In addition, as Rosman and Rubel point out, although "rivals are in opposition, it is apparent that they need each other—this is the essence of the potlatch … Opposites need each other, and serve the important function of witnessing the ascension to office of one another. A great chief needs great rivals. It is an honor, therefore, to be selected as a rival by one acknowledged as a great chief" (1971: 151, 168).

Three types of goods were distributed or displayed at potlatches. By the late nineteenth century, the most common were blankets. Indeed, blankets became easily standardized tokens by which wealth was measured. At the time of Boas's fieldwork, the basic article was "a cheap white woolen blanket, which is valued at fifty cents … These blankets form the means of exchange for the Indian, and everything is paid for in blankets or in objects the value of which is measured by blankets" (Boas 1895: 341). Second, "coppers" or parts of them were presented to rivals at potlatches. Coppers were plates or shields originally made of metal traded from people in Alaska, but by the late nineteenth century they were made of European or American copper. The coppers had a rectangular lower section and a flared upper section etched or carved with a design representing an animal ancestor of the first owner. The value of a copper was expressed in terms of the number of blankets that were paid for it at the time of its last transfer. The more often a copper was sold, the higher was its value, since every new owner had to pay more than it fetched at its previous sale. Because of their expense, only wealthy chiefs could purchase coppers, but even for them the cost usually exceeded their means and therefore they had to borrow blankets (i.e., wealth) from others within their numaym. The process of borrowing wealth helped solidify the economic and symbolic unity of numayms. Since chiefs represented their numayms and tribes, it benefitted all members of the group to participate in the purchase of coppers, and it was to their detriment if the attempt to buy the copper failed. Once purchased, coppers were next offered for sale to a rival of equal or presumed higher status. To be offered a copper was therefore an acknowledgment of one's social standing and of the high esteem of the current owner. But it was also a challenge, because to fail to make the purchase if offered was in effect a public admission of one's lack of wealth and consequent social status.

A third, but rare, type of potlatch was "grease feasts" at which property was doused with oil and set afire in a destructive display of wealth and status. These potlatches took place only between the highest-ranking rivals. They probably did not develop until the late nineteenth century.

In addition to their social and symbolic value, potlatches served economic functions. Along with the distribution of blankets or surplus wealth, food was consumed in the feasting that took place. Foods eaten or distributed included dry salmon, fish oil, crabapples, and cinquefoil roots. The highest chiefs in attendance were also given seal meat, halibut skins, and currants (Walens 1981: 94). Other goods including clothing, ornaments, and utilitarian items such as boxes and dishes were also given away. People of high status could circulate these goods in turn when they hosted potlatches, but lower-ranking people made direct use of them in their domestic consumption.

Finally, potlatches had ceremonial functions when they marked lifecycle changes such as birth, naming, girl's first menstruation, boy's assumption of adult roles, marriage, and death. They also celebrated initiations into winter dance societies and the inheritance of songs, dances, and ceremonial regalia that were part of marriage repayment debts.

Significant changes took place in economic and social aspects of potlatches from the late eighteenth century when European contact began until the late nineteenth when Boas visited the Kwakiutl. One of the major changes was the enormous increase in the amount of property distributed. According to Codere, before the pivotal year of 1849 when the Hudson's Bay Company established Fort Rupert in Kwakiutl territory, the largest potlatch distribution consisted of 320 blankets but by 1869, a mere twenty years later, a potlatch reportedly included the distribution of 9,000 blankets. Significant increases continued to occur. In 1895 a potlatch of over 13,000 blankets was held and, finally, the greatest recorded Kwakiutl potlatch took place in 1921 with the distribution of some 30,000 blankets (Codere 1950: 89–97). This staggering rise in the amount of goods distributed was stimulated by growth in wealth as well as a severe population decline. In the second half of the nineteenth century, increased wealth was available through trade with the Hudson's Bay Company and employment in the fishing industry, canneries, and sawmills. A substantial portion of the income received was converted into blankets to be used in potlatching. During the same period, populations sharply declined due to epidemic diseases. The steep drop in the Native population had an impact on the potlatching system because the number of ranked positions remained constant while the number of people plummeted, enabling a much larger proportion of the community to compete in potlatching and thus deepening a cultural focus on social rank and competition.

Another feature that grew in importance was the rise in interest payments for loans of wealth:

> When a Native has to pay debts and has not a sufficient number of blankets, he borrows them from his friends and has to pay the following rates of interest: For a period of a few months, for five borrowed blankets six must be returned; for a period of six months, for five borrowed blankets seven must be returned; for a period of twelve months or longer, for five borrowed blankets ten must be returned." (Boas 1966: 78)

People evidently could amass wealth not only by borrowing from others but also by lending to others and receiving a handsome return. This wealth could then be socially reinvested by sponsoring potlatches that enhanced one's own status.

The eradication of regional intertribal warfare in the mid-1800s also affected potlatching by replacing armed conflict with symbolic rivalry. This process was noted by many of the people themselves. For example:

> We are the Koskimo [a Kwakiutl tribe], who have never been vanquished by any tribe neither in wars of blood nor in wars of property. Of olden times the Kwakiutl [tribe] ill-treated my forefathers and fought them so that the blood ran over the ground. Now we fight with button blankets and other kinds of property, smiling at each other.
>
> We used to fight with bows and arrows, with spears and guns. We robbed each others' blood. But now we fight with this (pointing at the copper which he was holding in his hand), and if we have no coppers, we fight with canoes or blankets. (Quoted in Codere 1950: 118)

Furthermore, speeches given by leaders of numayms and tribes to encourage support from members of their groups often employed military metaphors. Following are the words of a Kwakiutl chief rallying his supporters:

> Friends, I ask you to keep yourself in readiness, for the Koskimo are like to a vast mountain of wealth, from which rocks are rolling down all the time. If we do not defend ourself, we shall be buried by their property. Remember this is our village battlefield. If we do not open our eyes and awake we shall lose

our high rank. Remember, Kwakiutl, we have never been vanquished by another tribe. (119)

Aboriginal Warfare

Before the end of warfare, the people had engaged in raids against other groups, especially the Bella Collas and Nootkas. Conflicts among Kwakwaka'wakw tribes occurred as well. Warfare was usually motivated by the death of a member of one's numaym or tribe. If a member of one's own group had been killed, it was considered honorable to take a victim from another group, but the people attacked might or might not have been the ones responsible for the first death. According to Boas, "the loss of a relative was felt as an insult to one's dignity and as a cause of shame and sorrow. The reaction to this feeling was the wish to make someone else, no matter who, feel sorrow and shame at least equal to one's own" (Boas 1921: 1364). By taking another life, the original victim was honored and the new victim became the "pillow" of the first. When a murder occurred between members of different numayms in the same tribe, relatives of the deceased generally attempted to take the life of someone in the offender's numaym at least equal in rank to that of the victim. Acceptance of a payment of wealth as restitution instead was theoretically possible but was unlikely because it was considered shameful.

Men participating in raids were essentially volunteers, following the leadership of a man of proven skill. War leaders were often the younger brothers of chiefs. Although successful warriors were respected for their achievement, they were disliked and feared because they were quick to anger and behaved in ways that disregarded normal social rules. Boys who were chosen by their fathers to become warriors were trained from their youth in physical skills such as running and using weapons. Warriors might take booty when they attacked a village but they were not permitted to keep it. Instead, they gave it to their chief to be redistributed. Many warriors never married, partly because they could not accumulate wealth necessary for potlatching and partly because of their aggressive and ill-humored demeanor (Boas 1966: 106).

Many ritual precautions were necessary for men about to engage in a raid. Prior to their departure, warriors had to undergo four days of purification by bathing in cold water, rubbing their bodies with hemlock branches, and eating sparingly. Canoes used in travelling on a war expedition also had to be protected. They were kept on the beach turned upside down and could not be touched by anyone. If chiefs accompanied the warriors, they did not actually fight but remained with the canoes. Raids generally occurred early in the morning in a surprise attack against the targeted village. Adult male victims were usually beheaded and their heads taken home, covered with birds' down, and kept as trophies. They were often displayed in the home village on poles put in the ground along the beach near the village. Women and children might also be killed but they were just as likely to be taken as slaves.

Religious Beliefs and Practices

According to Native belief, the world is imbued with a vague but essential spirit power called "nawalakw." Beings and forces having extraordinary powers or abilities are also called "nawalakw." The term is for any supernatural being that appears to a person in visions or dreams. All aspects of nature including the sun, moon, stars, rocks, islands, waterfalls, and animals and plants have spirit power that can be used to help or harm human beings. People prayed to these entities in order to obtain their aid. In addition, many daily or routine activities were prefaced or followed with prayers thanking the spirits who were in charge of or in some way affected their outcome. When fishermen dipped their nets into the water, they prayed to the fish and the water; hunters prayed to game animals that they were seeking, and after making a kill, they greeted the animal and thanked it for its powers. For example, after killing a beaver, a hunter prayed: "Welcome, friend, for you have agreed to come to me. I wanted to catch you because I wished you to give me your ability to work that I may be like you; for there is no work that you cannot do; and also that no evil befall me in what I am doing, friend" (quoted in Boas 1930: 196). When migratory or seasonally available birds appeared in the territory, they too were welcomed with prayers and thanked for their return. Wild plants such as roots, ferns, and berries were also thanked for their help in human survival (207).

According to Native conceptions, primordial beings were not distinguished into animal and human form. All beings had an inner form or substance that was humanlike and an outer form that was animal-like. At some time in the ancient past, some beings took off their animal "masks," consisting of coverings over their entire bodies, to become human while others remained animal in outward appearance. Modern humans and animals therefore are linked through sacred bonds of ancestry and interdependence.

The people believed that most living things (people, fish, animals, birds, trees, and bushes) had souls, described as having "no bone and no blood, for it is like smoke or like a shadow" (Boas 1966: 169). People's souls were in some way identified with owls. Each person had its own owl and when the owl was killed, the person's soul died as well. When a person was asleep, their soul might leave the body, resulting in feelings of weakness. Furthermore, if the soul remained outside the body for an extended time, the person might become sick and die. In fact, according to Native theories of disease, soul loss was the most frequent cause of illness and death. A second frequent cause was the intrusion of a foreign object into a person's body as a consequence of spirit action or witchcraft. Contact with or the effects of spirit powers might also lead to illness. Most types of spirit-caused illnesses were treated by ritual healers or shaman. Souls that either got lost or were abducted by a spirit or witch had to be located, retrieved, and reincorporated into the victim's body. Objects that had been thrown into a person had to be removed, usually by sucking and secondarily by rubbing the patient. When the object was removed, it was frequently found to have the form of a small splint of bone or piece of slate.

People who became healers were often first afflicted with illness as a sign or calling from the spirit world. Such episodes were manifested by sudden fainting or disorientation. The patient appeared to be near death or was thought to have died before their cure. As part of their therapy, patients were required to be initiated as shaman. The following account was reported by a shaman about her initiation:

For almost three months I lay sick in my bedroom. No longer strong enough to sit up. One morning I thought I had died. Now I saw a large shining house and was invited to enter. The chief spoke to me, "On account of the sorrow of your husband and your relatives I shall send you back." He called his shaman of his house who sang his sacred song and rubbed with both hands down along the sides of my body. Then the chief sent me home, gave me the name of his shaman and told me to sing the sacred songs I had heard. He ordered me to put the sun in front of my head ring of red cedar bark and to wear a twisted neck ring. Then I went back into my body. Mourners went out of the house and listened to my sacred songs. For four days I was left alone in the house. During this time, the people purified themselves and on the fourth day they came in and sang my songs. Then I was a shaman. (Quoted in Boas 1930: 54)

This account includes the common elements of direct contact with a spirit being or force, the teaching of sacred personal songs, the return of the patient to health, and her final presentation to the public. Although the spirits who helped the novice were not identified here, certain beings such as Wolf, Whale, and Toad frequently had this role. The beings who trained the shaman remain as personal guardians and helpers, giving songs and dances to use in healing other patients.

When treating illness, shaman used rattles and purification rings made of hemlock branches or cedar bark that were large enough to pass over and around patients' bodies. Some ritual cures required that the shaman enter a mild trance state in which s/he manifested a violent trembling of the body. According to Boas, shaman report that "all the strength gathers in the stomach. He has the feeling as though knives were cutting his insides" (quoted in Boas 1966: 136).

Difficult cases of illness were often attributed to witchcraft. Witchcraft techniques could be used by anyone who had learned the proper procedures. Most witches utilized their intended victim's body waste such as nail clippings, strands of hair, sweat, urine, or feces. These substances or objects were wrapped in a rag and then stuffed into a skull or long bone or placed into the mouth or head of a lizard, snake, or toad. The entire package was then covered up with tree gum and tied to the top of a hemlock tree or buried in the ground. Witches operated secretly at night or early in the morning. If their actions were discovered or if they smiled or laughed, the spell was broken and caused no harm. If someone believed that they were the victim of witchcraft, they attempted to find the "witchcraft box" and clean its contents. Failing this, the victim could go into the woods and pray to the plants for recovery. They might also purify their body by rubbing it with shredded cedar bark. Another possible cure was to have a menstruating woman step four times over the small of the victim's back as he/she lay on the ground, face downward (Boas 1966: 152).

The most spectacular of the rituals were the "cedar bark dances," usually referred to in the literature as "winter ceremonials" because of their occurrence during the winter season. The songs, dances, and sacred paraphernalia involved in the cedar bark dances were the property of individuals who inherited them from their maternal grandfathers. When a successor, usually the grandson or granddaughter of the current owner, came of age, they were initiated into the ceremonial society that they inherited. Each society had particular rituals but shared a fairly similar outline. The initiate was first abducted by the spirit guardians who originated the dance. During their absence from the community, they came under the control of their spirit abductors, took on personality or behavioral characteristics of their spirit guardians, and were taught the songs and dances relevant to their ritual. The third phase of the ceremonial involved the initiate's sudden return to the community, their capture by other members of the dance society, and their gradual taming from the wild forces that affected them. The fourth and final phase was their reemergence as full members of the group. One of the most dramatic and lengthy of the cedar bark dances was the "Hamatsa" or "Cannibal Dance." In these rituals, the initiate was believed to be abducted by the Cannibal Spirit and accordingly also became a cannibal, desiring to eat human flesh. James Sewid, a high-ranking Kwakiutl man born in 1913, recalled his initiation into the Hamatsa society when he was sixteen years old:

I was supposed to disappear into the woods and go and seek the supernatural power of the Cannibal Spirit. I lived up in the woods for about ten days. In the early days, they used to stay up in the woods for three or four months. I left all my clothes in the village and just dressed in some hemlock branches that were put around me. Every morning I took a cold bath and rubbed myself down with branches. It was winter time but that was supposed to make me tough and feel light so that I would feel ready when the day came to come back to the village and dance. Sometimes during the day I would come into the village and show myself to the public for a minute or two and rush back to the woods. All I had around me was the hemlock branches and when I did this all the different kinds of whistles would be blowing. They all had different tones which imitated the raven and geese and all the birds.

Every night the people were all called into the big house where different dances were performed. They did these dances in order to bring back Hamatsas from the woods. While we were in the woods we were supposed to become wild men and they were trying to bring us back to civilization. It was at this time that all the retired Hamatsas would teach me how to dance and the new songs. My grandfather hired singers and composers for the songs that were sung each night. All these new songs were telling the history of my father's side of the family and my mother's side. Finally the night came when I was going to return and all the people from all over the Kwakiutl nation were giving their dances. Nobody could ever do a dance that did not belong to them or one of their relatives.

I was waiting up [on the roof of the house] for my time to come. [Another dancer] shouted, calling for me to come. On his third time, [a helper] began to blow this whistle. As soon as the people heard this whistle they knew I was coming. [The helper] held my legs and I lowered myself halfway into the house and showed half my body to the crowd. I was making the Hamatsa noise and I could see all the people standing up swaying their hands, which is the way they would greet one another. Some of them were chanting and beating sticks and there was a terrific noise. I had a strange feeling when they received me that night as I was hanging down through the roof. They were all chanting the songs and swaying their hands. It was out of this world what they were doing, and I can't express how I felt. It made me feel out of this world. Then we moved to another place [on the roof] and that is where I slid in. And all the Hamatsas of the different villages were there with a big strong blanket to receive me. I jumped onto this blanket and I'll never forget that when I came through my mother cried. She just cried and cried because I guess she thought that I had come back to civilization again after I had been away so long. (Spradley 1972: 83–87)

Another dramatic cedar bark dance was the Towidi in which the main dancer, usually a woman, entered the ceremonial house and stood at the front facing a fire. She then asked for implements that could aid her in some act of self-destruction, such as a knife to cut her head or a hammer to crush her skull. When no one offered the requested tools, she proceeded to sing personal sacred songs and perform acts of supernatural power such as giving birth to giant animals, producing serpents out of the air, making birds fly around the house, or altering the cycles of the moon (Ford 1941: 118–119).

Rituals marking significant stages in the lifecycle were observed including pregnancy, birth, naming, girl's puberty, and death. There were numerous regulations that pregnant women followed to ensure that their babies would be healthy. Expectant mothers and their husbands avoided seeing anything that was frightening, especially a dead person or animal, lest the child be stillborn. They also tried to avoid seeing any deformed or unusual people lest the baby resemble the infirmities. However, if any of these experiences accidentally occurred, parents could attempt an antidote by waving a piece of cedar bark four times over the object or person who had frightened them and then passing the bark down the back of the mother four times. Pregnant women avoided certain foods that might make birth difficult, especially salmon eggs or tree gum, because it was believed that the stickiness of the substances would make the fetus adhere to the woman's womb. Most women gave birth in a hut separate from their main house, assisted by three or four midwives. The husband might enter the delivery hut before the birth but no one else was permitted inside. The mother and her baby remained in the hut for four days after the birth. Twins were believed to have great spirit powers and could influence the weather and cure diseases (Ford 1941: 30–31).

After the birth of a child, both parents abided by special precautions. According to Charles Nowell: "At the birth of my child, I and my wife go to the tub where it is to be washed and wash my eyes and her eyes and our ears and our noses, too, four times in that water. After we got back, the baby is washed in that, and we do that for four days after. They say that is why our children never had any sickness" (Ford 1941: 158).

The people believed in a connection between babies and ancestors through reincarnation. They thought that the spirit of a dead ancestor would eventually be reborn into one of his/her descendants. Accordingly, people whose relatives had died would be comforted with the saying, "After all, the departed one will come again, born to his niece or his granddaughter" (Ford 1941: 29). If a baby resembled a deceased relative, had some distinguishing physical or behavioral trait or a special skill or talent similar to that of an ancestor, s/he was assumed to be a reincarnation of that person.

When a girl reached puberty, she remained indoors or in a special hut for four days and could only eat or drink sparingly. At the end of this period, her hair and fingernails were cut and she received a new set of clothing. Her father then sponsored a potlatch in her honor and gave her a name belonging to her mother's family. Girls were often betrothed and married within a few years of their menarche.

Boys were honored with coming-of-age potlatches when their voices changed, an event that was referred to as "the boy's first monthly" (Ford 1941: 35). At this feast, the boy's father announced the potlatch position that his son would eventually inherit. Although boys were then eligible for marriage, they rarely did so until their late teens.

When a person died, their soul left the body and travelled to an afterworld much like this one. In preparation for the journey, the body was washed and dressed and then taken out of the house through an opening in the wall rather than through the door that was the normal way of humans. The body was arranged in a flexed position and placed in a canoe, dry cave, or burial hut, or on scaffolding in a spruce tree. Its head always faced west. For four days after burial, a general period of mourning barred the performance of potlatches or other public events. Relatives of the deceased sang mourning songs during the day but never at night. At the end of the four days, the relatives washed themselves and put on clean clothing. All residents of the village emptied whatever containers of water they had in their houses and filled them with fresh supplies (64). Afterward, a ritual of departure was enacted. The deceased's spirit was called to return to the community and enter the house to be greeted by all the people in the village. A man then put on a mask representing lineage ancestors of the deceased, entered the house, danced in silence, and left again. This ritual symbolized the departure of the deceased. Then the person who succeeded the deceased in his/her social rank gave a potlatch in honor of the deceased and in validation of his/her inheritance (39–40). The surviving spouse endured a longer period of mourning, as much as one year, followed by a memorial potlatch.

CONSEQUENCES OF EUROPEAN TRADE AND SETTLEMENT

Europeans, principally from Great Britain and Spain, entered the northern Pacific Ocean waters in the 1770s and began exploratory and commercial expeditions along the coast. The first direct contact between the Kwakwaka'wakw and the foreigners took place in 1792 when George Vancouver observed a Lekwiltok village as he circumnavigated Vancouver Island. There were brief encounters between the two groups in which Indians exchanged fish and wild berries for European goods. Vancouver then sailed to the village of the Nimkish on the shores of Alert Bay. He noted that the Nimkish had already obtained a "great variety of European commodities," which he was told they had received in trade from Nootka intermediaries. The following is Vancouver's description of one encounter:

> The next morning showed the village in our neighborhood to be large; and from the number of our visitors it appeared to be very populous. These brought us the skins of the sea-otter, of an excellent quality in great abundance which were bartered for sheet copper and blue cloth; those articles being in the highest estimation amongst them. (Vancouver 1984, II: 625)
>
> [Our goods] were solicited by [women] in every house we entered; and so abundant were their demands, that although I considered myself amply provided for the occasion with beads, hawks' bells, and other trinkets, my box, as well as my pockets, and those of the gentlemen who were of the party, were soon nearly emptied. At the conclusion of this visit we were entertained at the house of an elderly chief, to whom Cheslakees [the chief], and every other person paid much respect, with a song by no means unmelodious. The song being finished, we were each presented with a strip of sea-otter skin; the distribution of which occupied time.
>
> Their total number we estimated at about five hundred. They were well versed in the principles of trade, and carried it on in a very fair and honorable manner. Sea-otter skins were the chief objects of our people's traffic, who purchased nearly two hundred in the course of a day. When we refused them firearms and ammunition, nothing but large sheets of copper, and blue woolen cloth engaged their attention in a commercial way; beads and other trinkets they accepted as presents, but they returned nothing in exchange. (Vancouver 1984, II: 626–627)

Vancouver's associate, Archibald Menzies, described the shrewdness of Native traders, noting that "Upwards of 200 sea otter were procured from them during our short stay at more than double the value I ever saw given for them on any other part of the coast, consequently many of our articles of commerce begin now to lose their intrinsic value amongst them" (Newcombe 1923: 88).

Contact and trade between several Kwakwaka'wakw tribes and European and later American merchants continued intermittently during the first half of the nineteenth century. In addition to acquiring some tools, utensils, clothing, and blankets, the major effect of the European presence was the spread of new diseases. The first recorded comments concerning disease were made in 1837, a year that was "marked by the frightful progress of the smallpox among the Native tribes" (Codere 1950: 51). Subsequent smallpox epidemics occurred in 1862 and 1876. Measles, influenza, and tuberculosis were also widespread and accounted for many deaths. In 1841, the Kwakwaka'wakw were reported to number 23,586 while only twelve years later their population was put at about 7,000 (52). Beginning in 1872, the Canadian Department of Indian Affairs began to take more regular census and reported 3,500 people. Figures for the remainder of the century and through the first quarter of the next reflected a continual but more gradual decline. The lowest census report showed the Kwakwaka'wakw to number only 1,039 in 1924. A reversal then took place and the population began to slowly rebound.

A significant change in relations began in 1849 when the Hudson's Bay Company established Fort Rupert in Kwakiutl territory. Immediately, four Kwakiutl numayms that lived nearby moved directly to Fort Rupert and became intermediaries between Company traders and other Kwakiutls as well as members of other Native nations. In addition, the growing city of Victoria attracted Indians for trade and jobs. By the 1860s, some people had temporary employment as day laborers or domestics. Native women also earned money as prostitutes and often thus became transmitters of venereal disease and other ailments to the indigenous population. A further effect of the colonization of the region was occasional armed conflict with the British, leading to the destruction of the village of Nahwitti in 1850 and of the Native village at Fort Rupert in 1865. Conflicts with other aboriginal people, particularly the Bella Coolas, also resulted in the destruction of at least one Kwakiutl village in the 1850s.

In 1876 the Canadian government began to establish reserves for Indians in British Columbia with an administrative center called Kwakkewlth Agency at Alert Bay. Agency commissioners were "officially enjoined as little as possible to interfere with any existing tribal arrangements; and they were to be careful not to disturb the Indians in the possession of any villages, fishing stations, fur trading posts, settlements, clearing which they might occupy, and to which they might be specially attached" (quoted in Codere 1950: 25). But in fact the government did interfere in Native life. Most important, the founding of reserves effectively decreased aboriginal territory, turning it over to the province. In addition, the Indian Act of 1876 outlawed potlatching and the winter ceremonials. Finally, in keeping with a single-minded federal directive to encourage all aboriginal people in Canada to become farmers, officials attempted to turn the Indians from successful fishermen into people who would "take to the plow and rely less upon the chase and the results of fishing sports" (25).

By 1887, fifty-four Kwakwaka'wakw reserves had been established, including thirty-two fishing stations. By 1890, the people controlled an additional forty-two reserves. Most of these areas were relatively small, with a median of 38.5 acres, while the largest at Knight Inlet contained 350 acres (26).

Missionary activity began in the 1870s when Anglican ministers commenced their work at Fort Rupert and soon afterward at Alert Bay. Missionaries inaugurated education programs in 1881 and controlled Native schooling for a number of years. In 1894 provincial law mandated compulsory education for Indian children. By the early twentieth century, most people were at least nominally Anglican but they incorporated the Kwakwala language in hymns and prayers, a practice that continues today.

Native contributions to the Canadian fishing industry expanded considerably after the 1870s when canneries opened in the region, employing many Native men, women, and children. A total of seventeen canneries were functioning in Kwakwaka'wakw territory between 1881 and 1929 (Galois 1994). The people were thus able to continue their traditional settlement arrangements with seasonal occupations at the canneries and employment on fishing boats. Throughout most of the late nineteenth century, the Kwakwaka'wakw and other Northwest Coast Indians monopolized jobs in the fishing and canning industries, but by the end of the century they were faced with competition from White, Chinese, and Japanese workers. At first, competition did not adversely affect Native incomes, but by the 1930s the rapid growth of the non-Indian population had a serious impact on the people. By 1921 when there were just over 1,000 Kwakwaka'wakw, there were nearly 40,000 Chinese, 9,000 Japanese, and a total of 500,000 British Colombians (Codere 1961: 457). In order to protect their jobs, the Indians began participating in work-related organization and strikes. Job actions started in 1900 among Native and non-Native fishermen demanding higher prices for their fish and in 1907 among Native women cannery workers seeking higher wages for their work.

In the 1920s, the Kwakwaka'wakw were affected not only by the worldwide economic depression but by changes in the fishing industry itself. The introduction of gas boats hurt Indians because they were unable to get credit to purchase the new equipment due to government regulations that made it difficult for Native people to obtain independent financing. In addition, the number of canneries operating in the territory declined, eliminating many employment opportunities for women. In 1936, the Kwakwaka'wakw helped organize the Pacific Coast Native Fishermen's Organization in order to protect their jobs and wages. Then, to further their economic and political goals, they joined with the Native Brotherhood of British Columbia to negotiate contracts with fishing companies. Participation thus brought Kwakiutls into close working relationships with other Indians in the province.

CONTEMPORARY KWAKWAKA'WAKW COMMUNITIES

Kwakwaka'wakw fishermen and cannery workers are no longer independent because of changes in fishing industries and the consequent necessity of large amounts of capital investment in technology. Instead, they are employees who depend upon and are affected by industry and market decisions in which they do not participate. The economic difficulties faced by women are especially serious because the canneries that once operated in their territory have closed, while large modern commercial canneries operate far to the south, making it difficult for local women to travel or relocate there. In addition, domestic production of food, food preservation, and crafts, which used to be an important component of women's work, are largely replaced by cash purchases. Despite changes in local economies, most residents of reserves work in some capacity for commercial fishing companies although they are often seasonal employees. Men also find employment in logging, mining, and construction, while both men and women may work for local band administrations in clerical, construction, teaching, and social service capacities.

According to Wolcott's study of a small Kwakiutl village in the 1960s, many families relied on traditional subsistence activities to supplement their incomes and diets. They collected plants, shellfish, and seaweed and caught halibut, salmon, and eulachon. Hunting for deer, black bears, and birds also added to the diet. Wild berries were gathered and canned for year-round use. Still, the Native diet relied heavily on store-bought foods as well (Wolcott 1967: 15–16). As in the past, the economic year followed seasonal cycles although the focus had changed. From June through October, fishing dominated the local economy. Clam-digging took over as an important domestic and commercial task from the late fall until March. During the spring, fishing for subsistence concentrated on cod, halibut, and eulachon (32).

A study of the village of Gilford during the same period documented essentially similar trends. About 75 percent of the men identified their primary occupation as fishing, followed in importance by clam-digging and logging. Because of provincial regulations, the fishing season was limited to the period from May to October and on a weekly basis from Sunday evenings to Tuesday evenings (Rohner 1967: 45). Fishing activities were thus seasonal and restricted by law, resulting in people's need to obtain income from other sources. Households relied on domestic production including berry-gathering, fishing, clam-digging, and hunting.

Most households were based on nuclear family composition but other kin often resided in the home, at least on a temporary basis (21). People maintained ties through kinship or friendship with members of other bands and frequently were away from their own homes visiting or living elsewhere.

Many people, particularly elders, were aware of distinctions of social rank and knew their own and others' positions, but friendships and marriages were no longer influenced by one's status as they were in the past (72–73). Consensus was lacking regarding the specific ranking of lineage groups (numayms), but there was agreement and stability concerning the social ranking of the Kwakwaka'wakw tribes in relation to each other.

There are currently fifteen recognized Kwakwaka'wakw bands, each with an elected governing council consisting of one counselor for each one hundred band members. There are, in addition, two intertribal councils, the first established in 1974 called the Kwakiutl District Council and the second, the Musga'makw Tribal Council, founded eight years later. Both groups were formed in order to

TABLE 22.1	Employment Rates for Selected Canadian Kwakwaka'wakw Bands		
Band Name	**Participation Rate (%)**	**Employment Rate (%)**	**Unemployment Rate (%)**
British Columbia (overall)	64.6	59.5	7.8
Campbell River	59.4	48.4	21.1
Cape Mudge	64.6	52.3	19.0
Dzawada'Enuxw	46.2	46.2	0
Gwa'Sala-Nakwaxda'xw	48.3	32.8	32.1
Khikwasat'inuxw	55.6	33.3	40.0
Haxwa'mis			
Kwakiutl	51.3	43.6	15.0
Kwiakah	ua	ua	ua
K'omoks	52.6	36.8	30.0
Mamalilikulla	ua	ua	ua
Namgis	47.6	37.8	20.5
Quatsino	56.7	43.3	23.5
Tlatlasikwala	ua	ua	ua
Tlowitsis	ua	ua	ua

Source: National Household Survey, Statistics Canada 2011b: data tables.

Notes: ua, data unavailable. Tabulation: highest certificate, diploma, or degree (7); age groups (8B); major field of study—Classification of Instructional Programs (CIP) 2011 (14); labor force status (8); attendance at school (3); and sex (3) for the population aged 15 years and over, in private households of Canada, provinces, territories, census divisions, and census subdivisions.

have a more united and therefore influential voice in dealings with the Canadian Department of Indian Affairs. Each of the local band councils administers programs concerned with housing, sanitation, healthcare, social services, and education. Some bands operate economic enterprises such as marinas, shipyards, salmon or oyster hatcheries, and retail businesses (Webster 1990: 387).

Current economic data compiled from the 2006 Canadian census document labor-force participation rates generally higher than for most Indian reserves (45.5%), but lower than the general Canadian average (67.2%). The participation rate is 65.2 percent for people who are twenty-five years and older, and the employment rate is 54.1 percent. The unemployment rate is 16.8 percent. For most Kwakwaka'wakw reserves, unemployment rates are somewhat higher

than the on-reserve Indian average of 33.6 percent and much exceed the Canadian norm of 10 percent. Table 22.1 presents relevant data from representative bands.

Table 22.2 presents averages for men's and women's earnings for individuals who received income from employment in 2006. While incomes for members of Kwakwaka'wakw bands usually exceed the average for on-reserve populations of s, they fall short of the general Canadian average of $24,100.

Most children attend nearby provincial schools, but a number of bands administer their own schools that emphasize Native culture, language, and history. The Kwakwala language is used as a first language by a minority of contemporary people. According to 2011 census data, about 500 people have knowledge of Kwakwala, but only about 80 of these use it as their "home language" In an effort to increase children's knowledge of their heritage, local primary schools are offering instruction in Kwakwala. However, the effectiveness of these programs seems to be limited, as only about half as many people spoke Kwakwala in 2011 as did in 1996 (US Bureau of the Census 2011).

Despite some advances, educational achievement for members of Kwakwaka'wakw bands lags behind that of the general Canadian population. For some bands, the proportion of people with less than a ninth-grade education is just slightly above the Canadian norm of 16.7 percent but for others, more than one-fifth of reserve residents have not attended high school. Table 22.3 presents data from selected bands.

Traditional ceremonial activity continues in the form of initiations for members of dance societies. Ritual dances have undergone changes from the past, particularly a shortening of the period of abduction by guardian spirits, requirements for fasting and purification, and a general decrease in the number of days committed to the dance sequence. Of all the dances, the Cannibal Dance has continued with fewest alterations (Holm 1990: 381).

TABLE 22.2	Average Income by Sex for Selected Canadian Kwakwaka'wakw Bands	

Band Name	Average Income ($)	
	Men	Women
British Columbia (overall)	47,480	31,683
Campbell River	39,231	24,448
Cape Mudge	39,957	22,423
Dzawada'Enuxw	ua	ua
Gwa'Sala-Nakwaxda'xw	20,672	17,390
K'omoks*	21,939	18,852
Kwakiutl (overall)	21,901	20,567
Kwiakah	ua	ua
Khikwasat'inuxw Haxwa'mis	ua	ua
Mamalilikulla	ua	ua
Namgis	21,319	19,427
Quatsino	ua	ua
Tlatlasikwala	ua	ua
Tlowitsis	ua	ua

Source: Statistics Canada 2011a: NHS profile of First Nations.

* 2006 numbers; ua, data unavailable.

Since the 1950s, potlatching has been legally permitted and has resurfaced in some Native communities. However, potlatches no longer stress status differences within villages, as noted by Charles Nowell:

> If I am giving a feast to the Kwekas nowadays, I call everybody—men, women, and children. When I was a boy this wasn't so. When I was a boy, my brother would only call those that has positions and are old enough to have positions and go to feasts. (Ford 1941: 193)

Although contemporary potlatches do not equal the splendor and competitive rivalry of the past, they are still held to commemorate lifecycle changes at naming, girl's puberty, marriage, and funeral memorials, the latter occurring one year after a death. Potlatches also are sponsored to mark a person's acquisition of ceremonial names, dances, crests, and other sacred paraphernalia. A modern adaptation includes giving potlatches to celebrate openings of community

TABLE 22.3	Education Levels for Selected Canadian Kwakwaka'wakw Bands		

Band Name	No Certificate, Diploma, or Degree	High School Certificate or Equivalent	University Certificate, Diploma, or Degree
British Columbia (overall)	607,660	1,009,395	1,014,210
Campbell River	110	80	25
Cape Mudge	110	85	30
Dzawada'Enuxw			
Gwa'Sala-Nakwaxda'xw	195	60	0
K'omoks	65	45	0
Kwakiutl	110	30	25
Kwiakah	ua	ua	ua
Khikwasat'inuxw Haxwa'mis	20	10	0
Mamalilikulla	ua	ua	ua
Namgis	195	65	30
Quatsino	95	30	0
Tlatlasikwala	ua	ua	ua
Tlowitsis	ua	ua	ua

Source: Statistics Canada 2011a: NHS profile of First Nations.

Note: ua, data unavailable.

Gary Humchitt (right) of the Kwakiutl First Nation in Fort Rupert, BC, and Shawn Edenshaw (left) of the Haida First Nation wear traditional carvings on their heads while waiting to take part in the 2013 Walk for Reconciliation in Vancouver, British Columbia, which wrapped up a week of Truth and Reconciliation Commission of Canada events in the city. From the nineteenth century until the 1970s, more than 150,000 aboriginal children were required to attend state-funded Christian schools in an attempt to assimilate them into Canadian society. They were prohibited from speaking their languages or participating in cultural practices. The commission was created as part of a $5 billion class action settlement in 2006 between the government, churches, and 90,000 surviving students.

buildings, receptions of dignitaries, and fund-raising dance performances (Webster 1990: 389).

Two Kwakwaka'wakw communities have built museums to preserve ceremonial masks, coppers, and ritual objects that were returned to the people by the Canadian government in 1978. These objects had been handed over to the government in 1922 in exchange for reduced sentences for forty-five people who had been arrested for holding a potlatch in violation of Canadian law. The sacred objects are now kept at the Kwagiulth Museum in Cape Mudge and the U'Mista Cultural Center at Alert Bay. Both centers have broadened their scope and currently sponsor projects to record oral histories, to generate curriculum dealing with language and Native culture, and to help organize

classes in the teaching of traditional songs, dances, and Native arts. The art of carving, in fact, has continued as an important domestic and income-producing skill in most communities. In addition, new crafts such as jewelry-making and print-production have developed as well.

The U'Mista Cultural Society has the goal of protecting and enhancing Kwakwaka'wakw heritage and identity through programs concerning language, cultural traditions, and Native history. They have collected and exhibited photographs, artwork, and artifacts that document the lives of Kwakwaka'wakw First Nations peoples in the past and present. They have also transcribed numerous texts of sacred narratives that embody the spiritual knowledge and worldview of the people. And

TABLE 22.4	Populations for Selected Canadian Kwakwaka'wakw Bands		
Band Name	**Total Membership**	**On-Reserve**	**Off-Reserve**
Campbell River	808	395	413
Cape Mudge	1,113	391	722
Dzawada 'Enuxw	225	55	170
Gwa'Sala-Nakwaxda'xw	981	599	382
Kwakiutl	774	343	431
Kwiakah	22	7	15
Kwikwasat'inuxw Haxwg'mis	304	79	225
Mamalilikulla	417	64	353
Namgis	1,837	979	858
Quatsino	543	244	299
Tlatlasikwala	65	44	21
Tlowitsis	415	74	341

Source: Statistics Canada 2011a: NHS profile of First Nations.

another of its major accomplishments is the establishment of the Kwakwaka'wakw First Nations Centre for Language Culture that will collect copies of original documents in the Native language, along with commentary by contemporary Elders who are fluent speakers. Plans are also under way to digitize an estimated 30,000 of such documents so that they can be available to students and researchers. Planning for the Centre began in 2005 but is not yet complete. According to anthropologist Guy Buchholtzer of Simon Fraser University, "the anthropological discourse had too often become a long monologue, in which the Kwakwaka'wakw had nothing to say. The Kwakwaka'wakw will re-appropriate the material on their own terms."

There are currently an estimated 500 speakers of Kwak'wala, accounting for a mere 4 percent of the tribal population. Nearly all of these speakers are bilingual in English and Kwak'wala although there are a very small number of monolingual indigenous speakers, all quite elderly. The Native language is used mostly on ceremonial occasions of public speaking in meetings, feasts, and church services. Language maintenance measures include classes in schools, immersion "nests," and the use of technologies such as creating Kwak'wala computer fonts, CD ROMs, and video "talking dictionaries." However, the success of these efforts depend, as elsewhere, on stressing the importance of intergenerational and community-based speaking in the Native tongue.

Contemporary Populations

Populations of Kwakwaka'wakw bands steadily increased in the latter half of the twentieth century. According to statistics from the Canadian government for 2011, there were 7,504 members of Kwakwaka'wakw bands, somewhat less than half, living on reserves. Table 22.4 reports specific figures for bands.

REFERENCES

Berman, Judith. 1991. *The Seal's Sleeping Cave: The Interpretation of Boas' Kwakwala Texts*. PhD dissertation. University of Pennsylvania.

Boas, Franz. 1891. *Second Generation Report on the Indians of British Columbia*. London: Sixtieth Report of the British Association for the Advancement of Science for 1890, pp. 562–715.

Boas, Franz. 1895. *Fifth Report on the Indians of British Columbia*. London: Sixty-Fifth Report of the British Association for the Advancement of Science for 1895, pp. 522–592.

Boas, Franz. 1897. *The Social Organization and the Secret Societies of the Kwakiutl Indians*. Washington, DC: Report of the US National Museum of 1895, pp. 311–738.

Boas, Franz. 1909. *The Kwakiutl of Vancouver Island*. New York: Memoirs of the American Museum of National History No. 8(2).

Boas, Franz. 1921. *Ethnology of the Kwakiutl (Based on Data Collected by George Hunt)*. 2 parts. Washington, DC: Thirty-Fifth Annual Report of the Bureau of American Ethnology, pp. 43–1481.

Boas, Franz. 1925. *Contributions to the Ethnology of the Kwakiutl*. New York: Columbia University Contributions to Anthropology No. 3.

Boas, Franz. 1930. *The Religion of the Kwakiutl Indians*. 2 parts. New York: Columbia University Contributions to Anthropology No. 10.

Boas, Franz. 1966. *Kwakiutl Ethnography* (ed. H. Codere). Chicago, IL: University of Chicago Press.

Codere, Helen. 1950. *Fighting with Property: A Study of Kwakiutl Potlatching and Warfare, 1972–1930*. New York: Monographs of the American Ethnological Society No. 18.

Codere, Helen. 1961. "Kwakiutl." *Perspectives in American Indian Culture Change* (ed. E. Spicer). Chicago, IL: University of Chicago Press, pp. 431–516.

Drucker, Philip. 1950. *Culture Element Distributions XXVI: Northwest Coast.* Berkeley, CA: University of California Anthropological Records 9.3, pp. 157–294.

Drucker, Philip, and Robert Heizer. 1967. *To Make My Name Great: A Re-examination of the Southern Kwakiutl Potlatch.* Berkeley, CA: University of California Press.

Ford, Clellan. 1941. *Smoke from Their Fires: The Life of a Kwakiutl Chief.* New Haven, CT: Yale University Press.

Galois, Robert. 1994. *Kwakwaka'wakw Settlements, 1775–1920: A Geographical Analysis and Gazeteer.* Vancouver: University of British Columbia Press.

Holm, Bill. 1990. "Kwakiutl: Winter Ceremonies." *Northwest Coast* (ed. W. Suttles), Vol. 9 of *Handbook of North American Indians.* Washington, DC: Smithsonian Institution, pp. 378–386.

Newcombe, C. F. (ed.). 1923. *Menzies' Journal of Vancouver's Voyage.* Archives of British Columbia, Memoir No. 5.

Rohner, Ronald. 1967. *The People of Gilford: A Contemporary Kwakiutl Village.* Ottawa: National Museum of Canada, Bulletin No. 225, Anthropological Series No. 83.

Rosman, Abraham, and Paula Rubel. 1971. *Feasting with Mine Enemy: Rank and Exchange Among Northwest Coast Societies.* Prospect Heights, IL: Waveland Press.

Spradley, James. 1972. *Guests Never Leave Hungry: The Autobiography of James Sewid, A Kwakiutl Indian.* Montreal: McGill-Queen's University Press.

Statistics Canada. 2011a. *Language Highlight Tables, 2011 Census.* Ottawa, CA.

Statistics Canada. 2011b. *2011 National Household Survey Data Tables.* Ottawa, CA.

Vancouver, George. [1798]1984. *The Voyages of George Vancouver* (ed. W. K. Lamb). 4 vols. The Hakluyt Society.

Walens, Stanley. 1981. *Feasting with Cannibals: An Essay on Kwakiutl Cosmology.* Princeton, NJ: Princeton University Press.

Webster, Gloria. 1990. "Kwakiutl since 1980." *Northwest Coast* (ed. W. Suttles), Vol. 9 of *Handbook of North American Indians.* Washington, DC: Smithsonian Institution, pp. 387–390.

Wolcott, Harry. 1967. *A Kwakiutl Village and School.* New York: Holt, Rinehart and Winston.

THE SUBARCTIC AND ARCTIC

Bering Strait

Kutchins

Tananas

Hans

Ingaliks

Inuit

Hares

Tutchones

Kaskas

Dogribs

Inuit

Chipewyans

Slaveys

Inuit

Beavers

Carriers

Crees

Haidas

Sarcees

Crees

Naskapis

Shuswaps

Thompsons

Innus

Kwakwaka'wakw

Nootkas

Salishes

Sanpoils

Blackfeet

Gros
Ventres

Crees

Ojibwas

PACIFIC

OCEAN

Yakimas

Nez
Perce

Assiniboins

Chinooks

Columbia River

Hidatsas
Mandans

Hurons

Karoks

Flatheads

Crows

Arikaras

Sauks

Yuroks

Modocs

Cheyennes

Lakotas

Potawatomis

Foxes

Eries

Pomos

Shoshones

Washos

Pawnees

Miamis

Illinois

Yokuts

Paiutes

Utes

Arapahos

Ohio River

Chumashes

Shawnees

Cherokees

Walapais

Hopis

Diné

Kiowas

Osages

Chickasaws

Catawbas

Lake Michigan

Inuit Bear Story

Many moons ago, a woman obtained a polar bear cub but two or three days old. She gave it her closest attention, as though it were a son, nursing it, making for it a soft warm bed alongside her own, and talking to it as a mother does to her child. She had no living relative, and she and the bear occupied the house alone. The bear, as he grew up, proved that the woman had not taught him in vain, for he early began to hunt seals and salmon, bringing them to his mother before eating any himself, and receiving his share from her hands. Learning to excel the Inuit in hunting, he excited their envy, and after long years of faithful service, his death was resolved upon. On hearing this, the old woman, overwhelmed with grief, offered to give up her own life if they would but spare him who had so long supported her. Her offer was sternly refused. Upon this, when all his enemies had retired to their houses, the woman had a long talk with her son, telling him that wicked men were about to kill him, and that the only way to save his life and hers was for him to go off and not return. At the same time she begged him not to go so far that she could not wander off and meet him, and get from him a seal or something else which she might need. "Good mother, I will always be on the lookout for you and serve you as best I can."

Not long after this, being in need of food, she walked out on the ice to see if she could not meet her son, and soon recognized him as one of two bears who were lying down together. When she told him her wants, he ran away, and in a few moments the woman looked upon a terrible fight going on between him and his late companion, which, to her great relief, was soon ended by her son's dragging a lifeless body to her feet. She continued to ask for his help for a long time, the faithful bear always serving her and receiving the same unbroken love of his youth.

Source: Franz Boas. 1888. *The Central Eskimo*. 6th Annual Report of the Bureau of American Ethnology for 1884–1885.

Native Nations of the Subarctic and Arctic

We are open to changes from the past practice of governance to improve our lives. The culture that we have, in addition to being open, is very adaptive to change.

> Paul Okalik, the first premier of the new
> Canadian territory called Nunavut or "our land"
> that came into existence on April 1, 1999; quoted in
> American Indian Report July 1999: 14

Inuit power! We've been waiting for this for a long time.

> Darcy Kablalik, attending the ceremony marking
> the birth of the territory of Nunavut; quoted in
> "Canada's Eskimos Get a Land of Their Own"
> April 2, 1999

LANDS AND NATIONS

The Arctic and Subarctic together encompass by far the largest region in North America, bounded on the east by the Atlantic Ocean, on the west by the Pacific, and extending through the Canadian provinces of Labrador, northern Québec, Ontario, Manitoba, Saskatchewan, Alberta, the Yukon, Nunavut ("Our Land," the new Inuit territory), Northwest territories, and interior British Columbia, as well as the US state of Alaska. Although there are local variations in topography, climate, and resources, the region presents basically similar environmental and ecological challenges to human residents, resulting in a relatively low population density throughout the entire area. While population estimates for aboriginal inhabitants are unreliable and variable, the region as a whole sustained no more than 1 or 1.5 individuals per 100 sq. mi. Population densities of less than 1 person per 100 sq. mi. were probably the norm in many locales (Kroeber 1939: 141–142; McKennan 1969: 105–106). The north continues to be a region of relatively few residents. In 2010, the Juneau office of the BIA reported a total of 98,210 Indians and Inuit in Alaska (US Bureau of the Census 2010). The Canadian census of 2011 recorded figures for Indians and Inuit in Subarctic and Arctic provinces and territories as shown in Table 23.1. Figures for Native people in the provinces of Québec and Ontario indicate substantial numbers of Inuit in the north (12,575 and 3,360, respectively). Numbers of Indians in the two provinces are much higher (108,425 and 242,495, respectively), but the data given include all Native residents, not exclusively those living in the north. Table 23.2 lists residency data for Indians compiled by Canada's Department of Indian Affairs and Northern Development.

TABLE 23.1	Populations of Indians and Inuits for Selected Provinces	
	Indian	**Inuit**
Newfoundland and Labrador	23,455	6,265
Yukon	7,580	175
Northwest Territories	20,635	4,335
Source: Statistics Canada 2009.		

Languages spoken by people in the arctic belong to three linguistic families. The largest, called Inuit-Inupiaq, consists of closely related languages spoken from coastal Alaska in the west, through interior arctic Canada, and east along the coasts of Québec, Labrador, and Greenland. A second family, Yupik, contains five languages indigenous to coastal Alaska and Siberia. The third, and smallest, family is that of the single language Aleut, spoken by Aleuts living in the Aleutian Islands extending in a chain in the Pacific Ocean southwest from the Alaskan peninsula. Subarctic languages belong to two linguistic families: Algonquian and Athabaskan. Algonquian languages of the Subarctic include Cree and Ojibwa. Cree contains three geographically distinct dialects (Cree, Innu or Montagnais, and Naskapi) spoken from Labrador through central and northern Québec, Ontario, Manitoba, Saskatchewan, and Alberta. Ojibwa has four regional dialects (Chippewa, Saulteaux, Ottawa, and Algonquin) whose speakers are concentrated in western Québec, central and southern Ontario, Manitoba, and eastern Saskatchewan (Rhodes and Todd 1981: 52). Cree and Ojibwa are widely spoken today, but the extent of language maintenance in Native communities is correlated with their territorial isolation. Cree has more speakers than any other Native language in Canada, due in part to the remoteness of most Cree communities as well as to the fact that the Crees are the largest of the Canadian First Nations. According to statistics gathered in the 2011 census, 83,475 reported Cree as their "mother tongue," making it the most commonly spoken aboriginal language in Canada Ojibwa has a reported 19,275 Native speakers, the third most numerous in Canada (52). In the United States, the 2010 census indicated that 8,371 reported speaking Ojibwa at home. The second language family represented by speakers in the Subarctic is the northern branch of Athabaskan. It contains twenty-three languages indigenous to northwestern Canada and the interior of Alaska (Krauss and Golla 1981: 67). Northern Athabaskan languages currently having more than 7,4751,000 speakers include Chipewyan, Slavey, Dogrib, Carrier, Babine, Chilcotin, and Kutchin (77).

TABLE 23.2	Distribution of Native Populations for Selected Provinces	
	On-Reserve	**Off-Reserve**
Newfoundland	6,780	12,535
Yukon	ua	ua
Northwest Territories	280	13,070
Québec	59,346	23,079
Ontario	74,407	126,693

	On-Reserve	**On Crown Land**	**Off-Reserve**
Newfoundland	675		1,560
Yukon	696	3,103	3,634
Northwest Territories	219	10,422	4,009

Source: DIAND 1999.

The Subarctic territory is varied, containing mountains, flat tundra, forests, swamps, meadows, lakes, and rivers. Indigenous people occasionally exploited resources in the tundra or barren grounds at the northern limits of their territory, but the area served mostly as a buffer between Subarctic and Arctic nations (Helm and Leacock 1971: 345). Forests of spruce, fir, tamarack, pine, birch, willow, and poplar grow throughout the Subarctic although different types of trees are prevalent in different sections depending on climate, altitude, and topography. The ground within forested areas is covered in the south with moss and in the north with lichen. The Arctic environment is a landscape devoid of trees, consisting of mountains, plains, coastal seas, and inland rivers and lakes.

Climate is an important factor that affects people in the Subarctic and Arctic since it constrains and influences the development of many aspects of culture including subsistence, settlement patterns, housing, clothing, and technology. The Subarctic is characterized by long cold winters and short warm summers, often with great differences between daytime and nighttime temperatures. Warmest temperatures prevail nearest to the Pacific coast and rapidly fall further inland. In most of the Subarctic, there is frost nearly all year although in Alaskan river valleys there may be as much as 120 days without frost. Precipitation is relatively light in most areas although local variations are attested, increasing inland and decreasing near the western coasts. However, while snowfall is not heavy everywhere, snow cover is continual and deep throughout the long winter since there is little evaporation of moisture. Average temperatures in the Arctic are colder than in the Subarctic. Coldest readings are found in central Canada, while warmer weather prevails in western Alaska. Precipitation, which mostly falls as snow, is highest in eastern Canada and lowest in the west. Even though the snow melts in the brief summer, the ground remains frozen all year because of the long, cold winter.

Economies

Local ecological and resource variations differentiate specific areas within the Arctic and Subarctic. Coastal waters in the Atlantic, Pacific, and Arctic seas provide mammals such as seals, walrus, and whales as well as numerous species of fish. The lakes and rivers of the Subarctic are the habitats of fish and waterbirds, while land animals range throughout the interior. Arctic people concentrated on hunting sea mammals and some land animals such as polar bears and wolves and also exploited the southern perimeter of their region to hunt caribou and other species that migrated north in the summertime. In the Subarctic, caribou were hunted as well, but other large animals such as moose and bears were also caught. In the east, deer were found in significant numbers while in the west, people hunted musk ox, woods bison, mountain goats, and Dall sheep (Helm and Leacock 1971). Smaller animals such as beaver, fox, hare, marten, porcupine, muskrat, lynx, and wolf were also taken. In most sections, birds were not central to the diet, but in some places, such as in the vicinity of Hudson Bay, waterfowl migrated in great numbers and were taken for food. In the west, ptarmigan and grouse supplemented the Native fare. The availability of fish also obviously depended upon location. Salmon, lake trout, sturgeon, whitefish, and eels were taken where they were found. Aboriginal people of the western Subarctic were more dependent on fish as a food source than were most of the people in the east, having access to rich supplies of salmon, whitefish, char, and several species of freshwater fish. Given the environment, plant products contributed only a small proportion of the Subarctic and an even smaller proportion of the Arctic diet. Blueberries, cranberries, currants, and some edible shoots and bulbs were abundant only in the late summer in most areas, although in some sections of the southern Subarctic, wild rice and maple sap were gathered when in season.

Indigenous economies depended chiefly on hunting and secondarily on fishing. In winter, each adult required approximately 4,500 to 5,000 calories per day while in summer they needed somewhat less (Burton and Edholm 1955; Feit 1973). In order to obtain the requisite calories, people ate an average of at least 4 lb. of flesh food every day, including a substantial percentage of animal fat (Rogers 1963). Hunting large animals was therefore the most efficient method of securing the calories and nutrients needed.

Since aboriginal people depended almost entirely on resources obtained through hunting and fishing, men's labor contributed most of the direct subsistence. Hunting activities were generally performed in small groups, although men sometimes hunted singly when families were dispersed during seasons of scarcity. On other occasions, an entire community consisting of men, women, and children participated in cooperative caribou drives, especially in the late fall when the animals congregated in large numbers and their bodies were plump with fat and their coats thick. For example, Chipewyans of central Canada erected a circular enclosure consisting of trees and brush. Within this area, which might be as much as 1 mi. in circumference, people set up a maze of brush hedges and tied snares to poles or tree stumps within it. The animals were maneuvered into the entrance of the enclosure and driven through the maze where they were caught by the snares and then killed by hunters with spears or bows and arrows (Hearne 1958: 49–50). In Alaska, caribou were hunted in communal drives when the animals were in large migratory concentrations during the fall and spring. They were driven into an enclosed surround or corral through a series of two converging lines of fences. This method enabled twenty or thirty hunters to entrap and kill several hundred caribou, a supply that provided enough meat and hides for their seasonal needs. Caribou were also tracked and speared as they crossed rivers or lakes or in winter when they became trapped by deep snow.

Moose usually roamed singly or in small groups and they too were trapped in deep snow or killed as they foraged near rivers or lakes. Beaver were not abundant in all areas of the north but where they appeared they were hunted, usually during the winter when their lodges could be located and the animals were trapped inside. Escape routes were blocked, the lodges were dismantled, and the animals taken. Other small animals were caught with snares, deadfall traps, or bows and arrows.

The hunting of sea mammals in the Arctic was accomplished by specialized techniques. Hunters located the breathing holes of seals in the ice covering the seas, waited for the animals to surface for air, and shot them with harpoons. Since it was impossible to predict where a seal would surface, several men cooperated by positioning themselves at nearby breathing holes in a given area. Whaling was done cooperatively by teams of men under the leadership of "umialiks," who were the owners of boats and whaling equipment.

Fishing provided an important supplementary food source for all people in the region, principally exploited when large game animals were scarce. Fish were speared or caught with hooks and lines. In the Subarctic, fishing was sometimes a cooperative effort with construction of wooden weirs or netting woven from rawhide or the inner bark of willow. Wires and nets set across streams enabled the catch of large numbers of fish. In the winter, holes were made through the ice covering rivers and lakes, and nets were suspended through the holes to catch fish. In Alaska, fish supplied a more significant portion of the diet than elsewhere. They were caught either with nets, lines, and hooks, or weirs consisting of wooden fences erected across streams or at the mouths of lakes. Baskets were attached at openings in the fences to collect the fish. But even though fishing was successful, it rarely was central to Native economy, not because of a dislike of the flesh but rather because fish do not supply the necessary calories and fat that were required in the Subarctic and Arctic environment for human survival.

Women's labor was not often directly involved in procuring food although women did participate in cooperative caribou drives and also caught fish, birds, and small animals such as hares. Their work, however, consisted mainly of preparing and preserving food, making clothing, bedding, and domestic utensils, and taking care of children. Some foods were eaten freshly cooked while others were preserved for later use. Fresh meat and fish were either roasted or cooked in water brought to a boil by dropping heated stones into bark or hide containers. Preservation of meat was achieved by cutting it into strips and drying it on racks over slow-burning fires. The strips were packed into bundles and stored. Some dried meat was made into pemmican by pounding it into a powder and mixing it with fat and occasionally with dried berries. Fish were preserved either by "freeze-drying" them whole in the cold air or cutting them into strips and drying them on racks. In the Arctic, meat, fish, and berries were preserved by burying them in "ice-cellars" dug into the ground.

Much of women's time was devoted to the manufacture and repair of clothing made from animal hides, most commonly of moose and caribou in the Subarctic and of sealskin in the Arctic. Continual supplies of hides were required since a set of garments usually lasted only one or two seasons (Hosley 1981: 539). Hides were first de-haired and then softened or tanned by scraping, soaking, and rubbing with animal brains or grease. The softened hides were cut and sewn together with sinew. In the Subarctic, clothing consisted of shirts, dresses, and coats or parkas, some with and some without hoods. Men wore breechcloths and leggings as well. Moccasins and mittens were also made of animal hides. In some areas, strips of hare skins with the fur left on were woven into tunics and capes. In the eastern Subarctic, clothing was often decorated with painted designs. Throughout the western Subarctic, people wore shirts and leggings, some with moccasins attached. Some of the clothing was elaborately decorated with fringes, seeds, porcupine quills, bird claws, and red ochre paint. In Alaska, clothing was made from caribou, moose, or sheep skins that had first been rubbed with a paste of moose or caribou brains to soften the material. Garments, essentially similar for women and men, included shirts, often belted and fringed at the bottom and across the chest, leggings with moccasins attached, and hooded parkas or coats and caps. People wore the same styles of clothing throughout the year, although in the summer the hides were de-haired while in winter the hair was left on. Arctic clothing consisted of a set of softened sealskin or caribou undershirts and pants and outer garments of shirts, pants, hooded parkas, knee-high boots, and mittens. Undergarments were worn with the animal hair turned inward while outer garments had the hair turned out.

Natural resources were used in the production of a great variety of utensils and tools. In general (but with exceptions), women made clothing, netting, and containers while men produced tools, hunting equipment, and weapons. Both women and men cooperated in the construction of shelters, toboggans, canoes, and snowshoes. Bone and antler were used to make awls, needles, arrow points, fishhooks, and the frames of arctic boats and sleds. Wooden arrows, spear shafts, shovels, and the frames of Subarctic snowshoes and toboggans were constructed. Bark, woven spruce root, animal hides, and internal organs such as stomachs, bladders, and intestines were useful in the manufacture of many kinds of coverings and containers.

Aboriginal life was attuned to the climatic changes that occurred yearly. The nomadic lifestyle of indigenous people was made possible by the development of a technology that enabled people to travel during most of the year. In order to traverse the Subarctic territory in wintertime when rivers and lakes were completely frozen and snow covered the ground, people wore snowshoes made of a frame of birch laced with thongs of rawhide. Toboggans made of two sideboards of birch bound together with crossbars were used to travel and transport goods. During the summer, people traveled on the waterways in canoes made of cedar, fir, or spruce frames covered with birch bark. Seams in the coverings were closed with gum from black spruce to make the craft watertight. Canoes were relatively small and light, weighing only 40 lb. or 50 lb., and could easily be carried overland from stream to stream. Logs were sometimes tied together to make rafts for use in crossing streams. In the Arctic, people travelled and transported their possessions over frozen land or sea ice in sleds pulled by teams of dogs. The sleds were constructed of a frame of driftwood or whalebone laced together with sinew. For hunting or travelling on the seas, boats or "kayaks" of whalebone covered with sealskins were used.

Mobility in the Subarctic was restricted during two periods of the year, that is, the spring "breakup" of ice and the autumn "freeze-up." Exactly when these changes occurred depended upon location, but for all people throughout the region they were times when travel was hampered. When snow began to melt and ice to thaw in early spring, snowshoes and toboggans were useless, but it was not yet possible to travel by canoe since the water was not ice-free. Similar conditions obtained in the fall as a thin layer of ice began to form, too restrictive for canoes but not solid enough to walk upon. During spring breakup and autumn freeze-up, people were forced to remain close to available food resources, particularly those of small animals and fish.

In the western Subarctic, seasonal rounds of settlement and economic activity included two periods of relatively stationary residence. In summer, people accumulated at rich fishing sites where they caught large numbers of fish and dried them for winter use, cutting them into strips and air-drying the strips on racks. After fish were dried and stored, people moved into the mountains for hunting. Animals were generally snared or shot with arrows. A majority of the meat, whether from caribou, moose, or smaller animals, was dried and stored for winter when it became the primary items of sustenance, supplemented by hunting when possible. Toward late in the winter, just before the spring ice break-up, hunger and even starvation were not uncommon.

Dwellings

Seasonal variation affected the dwellings constructed by indigenous people. In wintertime, a secure shelter was required in order to avoid the bitter cold, but dwellings needed to be constructed quickly since the

Inuit hut and family, 1899. Note the seals hanging from poles in front of the hut.

people were nomadic and changed location frequently. Subarctic people lived in lodges that were conical in shape, made of a frame of light poles covered with hides, brush, or pieces of bark sewn together. In some areas, particularly among Algonquians, the typical dwelling was dome-shaped rather than conical but the construction materials were essentially the same. Fires were lit in a hearth in the center of dwellings to serve for cooking and heating. A third type of housing design was the ridge-pole lodge. In these rectangular dwellings, a series of light poles was erected and supported by a ridgepole suspended on frames at both ends. Small lodges had one central hearth, but larger ones had a row of fireplaces extending under the ridgepole. One door sufficed as entrance in small houses while larger dwellings had a door at either end. In warm weather, lighter lodges were built and in some areas tents were used instead.

In the Alaskan Subarctic, people lived in different kinds of shelters in the summer and winter. In summertime, they constructed rectangular lodges made of sheets of bark that were placed between poles stuck in the ground. In the winter, they lived in circular, dome-roofed houses made of poles covered with animal skins. Sturdier winter dwellings were made of a framework of poles covered with moss or dirt and dug 1–2 ft. into the ground, sometimes with a protective passageway to lessen the flow of wind and cold air into the house. In all areas, bedding and coverings for the ground inside dwellings were made from caribou, moose, or seal skins with the animal fur left intact.

Arctic houses were also seasonal. Two types of dwellings were constructed for winter: one, oval in shape, was made of sod and had a long entrance passageway lined with stone, driftwood, and whalebone; the other (commonly called an igloo) was made of blocks of snow carved to fit together. Igloos belonging to separate families in a camp were sometimes joined together with passageways so that people could visit without having to go out into the cold air. In the summer, people lived in conical or rounded tents made either of sealskin or caribou hides.

Families and Social Systems

Subarctic households consisted of two or more nuclear families who lived together in a dwelling. Affiliation tended to be through men, particularly fathers and sons, brothers, or brothers-in-law. However, any combination of related groups was possible, and if a couple had no sons, it was likely that their daughter and her family would live with them and form a domestic unit. In fact, such units were common, at least temporarily, since there was a preference for residence with the wife's family for a year or two after marriage. During that time, the new son-in-law worked with and aided his wife's parents. When a child was born to the couple, they usually remained with the wife's family for a time and later might decide to move to the husband's kin. Such decisions were based on combinations of resource availability, household composition, and personal preferences.

In the Arctic, domestic units generally consisted of a nuclear family, possibly with the addition of one or two relatives. Camps were composed of autonomous households related to each other through kinship or marriage. As elsewhere in the north, there was a tendency for patrilateral affiliation although a period of uxorilocal residence followed marriage.

Kinship systems differed in different regions of the Arctic and Subarctic. In the Arctic and in eastern, central, and most of the western Subarctic, kinship was reckoned bilaterally. Although kin relationships were critical means of affiliation and social organization, there were no formally recognized groupings such as clans. However, in the Alaskan Subarctic, most people reckoned kinship according to matrilineal descent and had named exogamous matrilineal clans. The clans were not territorial but rather were widely dispersed throughout a region, enabling people to expand their cooperative and supportive networks. After marriage, men usually moved to their wife's band and contributed to the aid of her parents. Men thus became familiar with hunting territories of at least their own and their wife's group, an adaptive advantage in an environment of scarcity. After a year or two, the couple might remain with the wife's group or move to the husband's kin. In addition to kin relations, men established wider social and economic networks by forming partnerships. Partners were people who maintained close, lifelong alliances and shared hospitality and support. They usually belonged to different clans, thereby extending linkages with other social groups, another obvious adaptive advantage.

Some groups in the western Subarctic, particularly those toward the Pacific coast, had matrilineal clans that were organized into moieties. The development of clans and moieties was no doubt a diffusional influence from Northwest Coast nations such as the Tlingits, Tsimshians, and Bellacoolas, all of whom lived in coastal British Columbia. In addition to organizing kinship groupings, the most important function of western Subarctic moieties was to conduct funeral feasts or for members of the opposite group.

Community Relations

Household productive units in the Subarctic were linked with others in what can be termed local bands. These groups were composed of separate and autonomous households who cooperated with each other, travelling and settling together for at least part of the year, but the actual composition of such bands was fluid and people shifted their association depending on availability of resources, the composition of the bands themselves, and personal preferences. Larger local groups or "regional bands" were loose associations, generally not exceeding 400 or 500 people and frequently consisting of far fewer. They occupied a familiar territory but did not have exclusive rights to resources. That is, resources were available and exploited by any person or group who had need of them. Although regional bands might come together for communal hunting and fishing in the summer and fall, they dispersed into smaller units of households or associated households during most of the year. A number of regional groups occupying adjacent hunting territories might form a loosely defined unit that had a common identity and was interconnected by kinship and marriage. Sizes of such groups varied from perhaps a few hundred to several thousand. They did not, however, assemble in a common location or cooperate in economic or political endeavors.

In Alaska, some households (with an aggregate population of between 15 to 75 individuals) formed a camp or small village under the informal leadership of the most dominant extended family. Such residential groups tended to live together throughout the year, but their actual composition was fluid and changeable. Local groups or bands were generally separated from one another by at least 50 mi. with a territory consisting of as much as 5,000 sq. mi. (Hosley 1981: 540). Local bands were usually exogamous. They were associated with similar groups with whom they intermarried and shared a vaguely defined territory. Such associated groups or "regional bands" were typically endogamous.

Arctic settlements varied in size and composition in different seasons. Winter camps were the largest, numbering some 50 or 100 residents. The camps or villages, situated on the frozen sea ice, were inhabited from October through May. In the summer, people dispersed into smaller units of at most several related families and moved inland for hunting caribou and other land animals and birds and for river and lake fishing.

Aboriginal people in the western Subarctic carried on regular and widespread trade between inland and coastal groups. Coastal people, both in the Subarctic and Northwest Coast, traded abalone and dentalium shells, dried seaweed, clams, baskets, and wooden boxes for the tanned hides of moose, elk and caribou, squirrel skins, sinew, quillwork, and raw copper supplied by inland groups (McClellan 1964). Alaskan people had particularly extensive trading networks that reached north, west, and south. They traded throughout the interior of Alaska and with coastal Inuit, exchanging animal hides, ivory, shells, and other goods. Commercial networks also obtained between Athabaskans in Alaska and aboriginal people of Siberia. Alaskans received iron tools, tobacco, and reindeer skins for furs, wooden utensils, and red ochre (Hosley 1981: 546). "Trade fairs" were held in summer, particularly in Kotzebue Sound, Norton Sound, and the Yukon Delta, which were attended by large numbers of Athabaskans and Inuit (545).

Sociopolitical organization among Subarctic and Arctic people was diffuse, lacking systems of formal leadership. Occasionally, individuals in local or regional bands who were skilled hunters or shamans might assume prestige but such prestige or influence lasted only as long as the person's skill and knowledge aided the community. Respected individuals were sought for advice in the areas of their expertise, but group decisions were made through consensus by all concerned. In order to be recognized as an able and respected person, one needed more than just technical and subsistence skills. The individual needed to embody the personality traits valued by aboriginal people including generosity, good judgment, even temper, and cooperativeness; and in addition, respected people generally had acquired and could demonstrate spirit powers.

EUROPEAN TRADE AND ITS CONSEQUENCES

Interactions between Native people in the Subarctic and Europeans began as early as 1500 when Innu (or Montagnais) located along the north shore of the Gulf of St. Lawrence traded with fishermen from France, Portugal, and Spain. Soon afterward, explorers and traders ventured along the St. Lawrence drainage system, contacting members of the Algonquin, Ottawa, and Ojibwa nations. Toward the end of the century, explorers expanded their voyages north to the seas and waterways of the eastern Arctic, meeting Inuit with whom they had sometimes friendly and sometimes hostile interactions. Traders often joined exploratory expeditions along the Subarctic and Arctic coastlines and into the interior, hoping to establish trade relations with indigenous people in order to obtain furs of beaver, fox, mink, and other valued animals. As elsewhere in North America, commercial ties between indigenous nations and Europeans began as peripheral activities, particularly for the Natives, but eventually came to have a central role in local economies, accompanied by social, political, and ideological transformations of aboriginal culture.

In 1667, a major step was taken in the developing North American fur trade when the Hudson Bay Company was founded. First known as the "Company of Merchant Adventurers to Hudson Bay," it was established by two French merchants, Pierre Radisson and Medart Chouart des Groseilliers, who obtained financial backing from commercial interests in London. The company began as a small enterprise with a handful of trading posts in northern Canada but later played a critical role in relations between Native nations and Europeans, having far-reaching effects on the livelihood and lifeways of aboriginal people.

After 1670, exploration and trading expeditions penetrated further inland, contacting the Crees, Ojibwas, and Chipewyans who inhabited the Hudson Bay drainage region. Later in the seventeenth century and throughout the eighteenth, trade with Subarctic and Arctic peoples intensified as did competition between Great Britain and its commercial, political, and military rivals. In competition with the British, the French government sent explorers and traders into the northern waters of the Atlantic. Expeditions by Radisson, des Groseilliers, and Louis Jolliet travelled north along the coast of Labrador where they traded with Innu, Naskapis, and Inuit, from whom they bought caribou hides, seal skins, and whale oil. Indigenous people had already acquired a variety of goods such as wooden boats and barrels, iron screws, nails, knives, and woven cloth from traders, sailors, and fishermen by the late seventeenth century.

During the same period that the British and French were exploring the eastern Atlantic and nearby interior, Russians were navigating the western coasts of Alaska. The first Russian voyage across the Bering Strait, led by Semen Dezhnev in 1648, was followed by Russian merchants principally interested in obtaining sea otter furs from Aleuts living on the Aleutian Islands and western coast of Alaska for trade to Europe and the Orient.

Both in the eastern and western north, expeditions were undertaken in the eighteenth century to seek out indigenous groups to expand trade networks and to solidify imperial claims to territory. France and Great Britain established trading posts and forts in the east while Russians did the same in the west. In 1717, British traders of the Hudson Bay Company founded a major center, named Fort Churchill (now Churchill) on the western coast of Hudson Bay, later to become a major trading center and government outpost. During the same period, the French developed seal-hunting stations and cod fisheries off the coast of southeast Labrador, hunting seals year-round and fishing for cod in the summer. Nearby Native people traded with the French fishermen, an exchange network that became regularized after 1743 when a trading post was opened on the Labrador coast.

After 1763 when France was defeated by Great Britain in the French and Indian War, British merchants built additional trading posts in the territory. In 1770, a British sailor, Samuel Hearne, aided by Chipewyan guides, made the first European overland journey from Fort Churchill to the northern Arctic, proceeding north along Coppermine River and arriving at the shores of the Arctic Sea. British exploration of the western Arctic coasts was initiated by James Cook in 1776 and followed by George Vancouver in 1790 and 1795. Expeditions by Britons into the western Subarctic interior reached throughout the Mackenzie River drainage system, contacting indigenous people belonging to the Beaver, Slavey, Dogrib, Hare, and Kutchin nations. At the same time, Russians were making further voyages along the Alaskan coast, meeting Aleuts living on Kayak and Kodiak Islands. In 1781, the Russian Grigorii Shelikov established a post on Kodiak Island, inaugurating a growing enterprise called the "Shelikov Company." In 1792, the company was renamed "The Russian-American Company" and granted a monopoly charter by the Russian government.

During the nineteenth century, Russians continued to stake their claim to Alaska while Great Britain deepened its hegemony in the Canadian Arctic and Subarctic. Competition between the two powers for economic and political influence consequently intensified. After 1821, the Hudson Bay Company solidified its control over British trade when it bought out a rival trading firm, the NorthWest Company of Montreal, and monopolized trading activities in the north. Thus began a long period of Hudson Bay Company dominance and the stabilization of trade relations in the Canadian north.

Once trade in sea otters became less profitable because the animals had become nearly extinct due to more than a century of overhunting Russian traders turned to obtaining the furs of land animals such as beaver, marten, fox, and lynx, but greater expense was required in order to maintain interior trading posts and less profit was returned. As Russian interest in Alaska waned in the middle of the nineteenth century, American interest there increased, leading to the sale of the territory of Alaska from Russia to the United States in 1867. An American company, Alaska Commercial Company, replaced the older Russian-American Company as the principal traders in the region. Trade was expanded, new posts were established in the interior, and Native hunters and trappers were supplied with improved weapons and dog-pulled sleds to transport the furs that they procured.

In the same year that Alaska was sold to the United States, Canada achieved confederation, uniting the provinces and territories that comprised the country. Beginning in 1871 and continuing until 1921, the Canadian government signed eleven land cession treaties with Native nations in the provinces of Ontario, Manitoba, Saskatchewan, British Columbia, and the Northwest territories. Official treaties were not signed in Québec, but indigenous people obtained title to reserves in the province nonetheless.

Until fairly recently, most of the Subarctic and Arctic was inhabited primarily by indigenous people. Few non-Natives entered the region for more than temporary stays. Most came as traders, government officials, military personnel, and missionaries. Their number increased only gradually in the late nineteenth and early twentieth centuries except for two periods of more intense intrusion. The first, in 1855, was stimulated by the discovery of gold along the Thompson and Fraser Rivers in the west. The second occurred in 1898 after the discovery of gold in the Klondike region of Alaska, bringing more than 40,000 prospectors and adventurers. Although the Klondike gold rush brought an influx of non-Natives into the area, when it ended most of the intruders returned to the south of Canada or the United States. Interactions in the twentieth century between indigenous Subarctic and Arctic people with Canadians and Americans continued to be relatively restricted. Indians and Inuit met and dealt with personnel at trading posts but had little direct or prolonged contact with any other agents of Canadian and American society.

Aboriginal culture was not undermined because traditional economic pursuits of hunting and trapping were in the interests of traders to supply their commercial needs. Still, as people shifted their economies to emphasize trapping for markets to obtain manufactured goods, several important changes were exacted. Competition arose between different groups for access to European commerce. Various nations attempted to assert themselves as intermediaries between the traders and more remote communities. Those people who inhabited territory closest to the trading posts were able to take earliest and best advantage of their territorial position. First the Innu in northeastern Québec, then Crees in central Canada, Chipewyans in northcentral Canada, and finally Kutchins in the western Subarctic were the most successful at fulfilling roles as brokers for European traders. Such roles were not benign but rather stimulated conflicts with other indigenous people who objected to dealing through intermediaries.

In response to demands on labor and the desire to participate in trade, people gradually abandoned fully nomadic lifestyles and eventually resettled near trading posts, leading to development of "trading post bands" whose members became increasingly reliant on metal tools, weapons, clothing, and food supplied by traders. In general, families settled near trading posts during at least part of the year, particularly after procurement of animal skins in the fall. Eventually, trappers' wives and children were likely to remain at the settlements during most if not all of the year while men hunted in more remote areas, usually in pairs or small groups of kin.

In addition, settlements and villages grew more populous as people came to reside near trading posts. Although Native villages remained much smaller than their Canadian and American counterparts, many more people aggregated there than had been the aboriginal norm. And in response to needs to coordinate larger groups of residents, leaders emerged to represent their constituents in trade relations with

Canadians and Americans and eventually also in dealings with government officials.

As a further consequence of trade, family or individually allocated "trapping territories" developed as Native economies shifted more toward market exchange and extended cooperative networks began to lose their importance. Traditional ethics of sharing and generosity sometimes became perceived as impediments to one's own accumulation of goods. However, control over territories was limited to trap lines and furbearing animals and did not involve control over subsistence resources found in the area, which were still exploited according to aboriginal egalitarian principles.

Finally, in conjunction with European trade, a novel ethnic group emerged in central and western Canada. Known as "Métis," they were descendants of Cree or Ojibwa women and French, French Canadian, or British traders, trappers, and woodsmen. The Native wives of foreign traders acted directly and indirectly as models and vectors of acculturative influences. Both the wives and their Métis offspring introduced a wide variety of European goods in addition to the standard metal tools and utensils, such as new styles of clothing, decorative artwork, and foods (Slobodin 1964, 1966). But Métis' experiences and identifications with their society were somewhat different for sons or daughters. Sons were likely to work for trading companies as canoemen, trappers, packers, and employees of trading posts. They therefore tended to have less prolonged or intimate contact with indigenous groups than did their sisters. In contrast, given the strong ties between daughters and mothers prevalent in Native society, women were more likely to remain closer, both physically and emotionally, to indigenous communities (Brown 1994: 211). Since Métis offspring were usually bilingual in their Native mother tongue and French and/or English, they were often employed as interpreters and negotiators. These positions were more likely held by sons, although daughters might function as interpreters. By the late eighteenth and early nineteenth centuries, Métis became critical intermediaries between aboriginal nations and the developing Canadian society. And while they primarily served direct economic interests, they came also to represent and broker Canadian culture to aboriginal people.

Christian missionaries were an additional source of acculturative change. In Canada, French Jesuits began proselytizing among indigenous people of the eastern Subarctic in the seventeenth century. Their early endeavors met with little success and most of the first missions among nomadic people were attenuated and abandoned. Later, in the eighteenth and nineteenth centuries, Catholics, Anglicans, Presbyterians, Moravians, and others followed the path of the expanding network of trails and roadways into aboriginal communities, while in the western Subarctic, Russian Orthodox clergy attempted conversions of indigenous people. By the late nineteenth century, in all areas of the Subarctic and in some communities in the Arctic, missionaries of various denominations established churches, schools, and small health clinics for the Native population. As a result of missionary activity in various societal domains, most of the people in the Subarctic were nominally Christian by the early twentieth century, although in the Arctic such religious conversions did not occur until much later. While missionaries provided important educational and health services, they also attempted to eradicate aboriginal customs that they found contrary to their own beliefs. Among these were the celebration of girls' puberty, the amassing and distribution of goods at funeral feasts in the western Subarctic, shamanistic performances such as the "shaking tent" rite of the eastern Subarctic, and the shaman's trances and journeys to the spirit world that were central to beliefs and practices in the western Subarctic and Arctic.

Still, despite the many influences toward culture transformation, much of the region remained unchanged well into the twentieth century. Until the middle of the century, most of the non-Natives were government personnel, teachers, health workers, traders, and missionaries. Few permanent settlers resided in the area. After World War II, however, the pace of cultural change accelerated considerably. During and after the war, American and Canadian presence was much more visible as the two governments cooperated in the construction of the Distant Early Warning system in the Arctic, an installation of radar stations spread throughout the north. Government control both in Canada and Alaska increased with a new impetus for education, health services, subsidized housing, police presence, and social welfare aid. Improved transportation and communication facilities brought more non-Natives into the region, particularly in Alaska and especially after statehood was granted to the territory in 1958. Compulsory education and the construction of schools stabilized family settlements since schooling required children and therefore their families to remain in one place during most of the year.

Access to healthcare also was a stimulus for permanent or near-permanent settlement, particularly after the 1950s when health services in the north were expanded and upgraded.

CONTEMPORARY NATIVE SUBARCTIC AND ARCTIC COMMUNITIES

Throughout the Subarctic and Arctic, Native people have become incorporated as wageworkers for mining companies, oil and gas companies, lumber industries, and commercial fisheries. Most Indians and Inuit, however, are relegated to unskilled and low-paying positions within these industries, due partly to discrimination and partly to the lack of educational opportunities and training required for skilled, professional, or managerial posts.

Although the non-Native population in the Subarctic and Arctic has steadily increased, Native people remain the majority in the Northwest territories, the Yukon territory, Nunavut, and Nunavik (Arctic Québec) as well as elsewhere in northern Ontario, Saskatchewan, Manitoba, Alberta, and Alaska. Most Native people live in communities that are predominantly indigenous, isolated from non-Native settlements and in many cases isolated from access to modern technology and advanced infrastructure.

While indigenous people no longer live independently of the Canadian or American countries in which they live, local economic and ideological autonomy persists. People's lives today are a mixture of modern technological conveniences and traditional forms of economy, social integration, and values even though these aspects of culture have also undergone change in the past century. Most Native people live in permanent settlements, many originating as trading posts and/or administrative governmental centers. As populations of towns have increased, indigenous ties to the "bush" have declined for a myriad reasons. On the one hand, there are attractions to permanent residence; on the other, there are difficulties engendered by life in the bush that have gradually dissuaded people from those pursuits. Town living has become attractive because of subsidized housing, year-round schooling, healthcare facilities, stores for the purchase of food, equipment, household goods, and luxury items, opportunities for fulltime or parttime employment, and the possibility of socializing with a variety of people. In contrast, life in the bush is often arduous, unpredictable, and lonely (Fried 1972: 707–708; Van Stone 1972: 309, 313). Still, there is evidence that at least in some northern communities, people continue to rely on traditional subsistence resources. For example, for the Slavey in the Northwest territories, Asch cited Canadian government figures indicating that people secured a yearly supply of more than 180 lb. of edible meat per capita, enabling them "to sustain their meat needs at a level equal to that of the average Canadian without one purchase from the store" (Asch 1984: 17). Similarly, research conducted among people at Fort Franklin, Northwest territory, demonstrated that the community procured over 400 lb. of meat per capita annually, equivalent to one-third

Cree family in their "bush camp" cabin at night, lit by oil lamps. Québec, Canada.

of their total food requirements. According to Rushforth, the amount of food obtained through local production saved the community approximately $200,000 annually (Rushforth 1977: 40). Corroborating studies indicate that as a whole, northwestern ubarctic people obtained approximately 34 percent of their domestic consumption of food and furs through the exploitation of local resources (Asch 1984: 18).

In addition to supplying food and other household needs, hunting and trapping continues to be important for social and ideological reasons. As Asch noted for the Slavey, meat from large animals is shared not just within the hunter's family but also within a network of cooperating and related households in keeping with aboriginal ethics of reciprocity and community responsibility (20). Similarly, Dunning noted that in an Ojibwa community in northern Ontario great prestige accrued to hunters, particularly those who return with a large supply of meat that can be shared within their communities (Dunning 1959: 30). Problems, however, have been generated for local hunters by several new factors. First, the number of animals locally available has declined because of greater pressure on resources resulting from the growth of human populations. The concentration of people in fixed settlements has created an imbalance in the relationship between humans and the resources on which they depend. There are simply not enough animals in the vicinity to support the local population (Dunning 1959: 34–35; Fried 1972: 708). Another factor contributing to the ecological imbalance is that, at least in some areas, the size of trapping regions has declined as hunters prefer not to leave their families for extended periods of time, thus restricting the area in which they trap (Van Stone 1972: 312).

Consistent with shifts favoring permanent residence in towns, changes have occurred in families and social groups. In some areas, traditional local bands have lost their importance as territorial and social units. However, extended family households or groups of associated households remain as the primary economic and social units in many indigenous communities (Asch 1984: 19; Dunning 1959: 64). For both the Slavey and Ojibwa, these are the functioning units of production, consumption, cooperation, and reciprocity. Dunning noted additional social changes among northern Ojibwas including an emphasis on patrilateral kin and the solidarity of siblings, especially brothers (Dunning 1959: 108). The patrikin group is the basis of

economic cooperation, social solidarity, and control over territorial rights. It is this group, not individuals, that allocates trap lines and makes decisions concerning their inheritance (107). In addition, Dunning noted that as populations become concentrated at settlements, people have more face-to-face contact with local band members and less with members of other groups. This shift in social interaction led to an increase in the dichotomy between community members and strangers as well as to an increase in band endogamy (70–71, 164).

Northern communities differ in their degree of "urbanization," and residents within such communities also differ in their commitment to town life or their involvement with indigenous economic pursuits and principles of social integration. The location of the settlements themselves is an important factor: those communities more advantageously located in resource-rich environments are more likely to continue pursuing traditional activities, while those communities established in poorer resource bases are obviously less likely to be involved in hunting and trapping. As Fried observed, many northern settlements were founded in order to suit Canadian government, military, and economic needs rather than those of the Native population (1972: 706). Residents of such towns are more apt to experience ecological imbalance, loss of autonomy, and "de-involvement" with traditional activities as they become dominated by "alien white members of the larger society to the south" (711).

Subarctic and Arctic peoples belonging to many different nations have developed united political efforts in order to assert their rights to land and indigenous culture. In Alaska, the discovery of oil in Prudoe Bay in 1968 led to far-reaching changes in Native people's relationship to their land and resources. As soon as oil was discovered, petroleum companies requested permits to drill for oil, but the US government did not immediately grant leases because the land rights of indigenous people had not been resolved. The Alaska Statehood Act of 1958 did not specifically award land to either Natives or non-Natives, but while it asserted that the state had no claim to Native land, it granted the state the right to select 140 million acres from the public domain that were "vacant, unappropriated, or unreserved," an amount that was approximately one-third of the total land in the public domain at that time (Arnold 1976). Disputes immediately arose between indigenous people and the state because some of the land chosen by the state was claimed by Indians and Inuit. An organization called the Alaska Federation of Natives (AFN) met with state and federal officials to negotiate a settlement to land claims. In 1971, an agreement was reached between the concerned parties and accepted by the US Congress as the Alaskan Natives Claims Settlement Act (ANCSA), providing that Indians and Inuit could select 44 million acres of land and then relinquish legal claim to the remainder of the state. In exchange, Native people received $962.5 million to be distributed over a period of 11 years (Arnold 1976). The Act further ordered the creation of thirteen regional corporations and over 200 village corporations in Native territory, granting shares to residents. Regional corporations receive cash payments awarded under the Settlement Act and can either invest the money or distribute it to shareholders. In addition, each regional corporation must operate one or more businesses for a profit that is then either reinvested or distributed. Village corporations receive cash payments through their regional corporation and also operate businesses, but these may be for profit or nonprofit. Additional regulations allow corporations to restrict the sale of shares to non-Natives.

Protections of indigenous resource rights were not included in the original legislation but were enacted ten years later in the Alaska National Interest Land Conservation Act. However, the bill was not as all-encompassing as Indians and Inuit intended. Rather than guaranteeing subsistence rights to all Alaskan Natives, it allowed "rural people" to hunt and fish in times of shortage. According to Robert Lancaster, a president of Sealaska Corporation, the largest of the regional corporations set up under ANCSA with 16,000 shareholders, "We reserved unto ourselves our subsistence rights—our human rights—to take fish and game and gather from the land ... We believe our Native rights should prevail as enacted under the US Constitution" ("Subsistence Is a Human Right" 1999: 26).

Following the discovery of oil in Alaska and plans to construct a pipeline through the Northwest territories for delivery of oil to southern Canada and the United States, the Dene (Athapaskan-speaking nations of western Canada) began to press for recognition of their aboriginal rights to land and resources. They also called for recognition of their sovereignty as an independent nation within Canada. In 1975, two regional organizations (the Indian Brotherhood of the Northwest territories and the Metis Association of the NWT) issued a declaration of rights that stated:

> We the Dene of the Northwest Territories insist on the right to be regarded by ourselves and the world as a nation ... The Dene find themselves as part of a country. That country is Canada. But the Government of Canada is not the government of the Dene. The Government was not the choice of the Dene, [it] was imposed upon the Dene ... We insist on the right to self-determination as a distinct people and the recognition of the dene Nation ... What we seek then is independence and self-determination within the country of Canada. (Watkins 1977: 3–4)

In 1988 the Dene Nation signed an agreement with Canada giving the Dene clear title and subsurface rights to about 6,000 sq. mi. of land as well as surface rights and royalties to 100,000 sq. mi. The Dene also secured rights to traditional use of more than 600,000 sq. mi. And they received a monetary award of $500 million.

In another Canadian land rights case, in 2013, the Supreme Court of Canada rendered a decision in a case dating back 143 years to a claim by Métis people in Manitoba seeking rights to 1.4 million acres. The claim resulted from the failure of the government of Canada to abide by its agreement that ended the Metis uprising in 1870 led by Louis Riel. In its ruling, the Supreme Court acknowledged the government's responsibility to uphold its promises.

The industrial use of natural resources in northern Québec led to controversy over land rights and self-determination. In the early 1970s, the provincial government proposed a plan to build hydroelectric projects surrounding James Bay, including construction of dams on rivers that would result in flooding millions of acres and disrupting the migration patterns of animals, birds, and fish, consequently harming Native subsistence activities. The energy generated by the projects would not benefit indigenous communities but rather would be delivered to utility companies in New York and New England. At hearings called to investigate the long-term ecological impact of the project, Native people and many non-Native scientists testified to the negative results that would ensue from diverting rivers and flooding the land. Crees and Inuit concluded the James Bay and Northern Québec Agreement in 1975, which relinquished indigenous rights to ownership of land in the area covered by the James Bay hydroelectric projects in exchange for $60 million in immediate payment and an additional $30 million as an "indemnity on future development." The agreement also recognized Native people's rights to control their own political and economic systems. The James Bay Agreement divided the region into three sections. Land Category One consists of land where no mineral extraction is permitted without formal permission of community councils representing every Native village. Land Category Two contains land where Crees and Inuit keep exclusive rights to hunt, fish, and trap. Land Category Three consists of land where Native people have no special rights and thus the government can proceed with resource development projects as it chooses (Niezen 1998). When the Québec administration proposed a second project, called James Bay II, in 1983, Crees and Inuit had already witnessed the ecological damage of the first project and mounted stiffer opposition to the new plan. They noted the virtual extermination of beaver, muskrat, hare, mink, and otter in the affected region and the rotting wood and silt in the rivers that caused the disappearance of many species of fish and waterbirds. Crees and Inuit convinced the major proposed recipients of James Bay energy production (i.e., utility companies in New York, Vermont, New Hampshire, and Maine) to cancel their contracts with HyrdoQuebec, thus defeating the project.

In the Northwest territories, Inuit residents claim that Canadian and multinational companies mining the rich supplies of zinc, nickel, and uranium disturb the herds of caribou that the people rely on for their subsistence. In 1979, Inuit filed a legal suit to prevent further mining, but the court ruled against the people, stating that they had no legal rights to property in the Arctic because property rights had been given in 1670 to the Hudson Bay Company by the British monarch, King Charles II. The ruling affirmed that Inuit were entitled to land-use rights but not to land-ownership rights. In response, Native representatives founded the Committee for Original People's Entitlement with the goal of protecting and advancing indigenous rights in the western Canadian Arctic. A nationwide group, called the Inuit Tapirisat of Canada (ITC), was also formed, uniting all Inuit in the country and working to better their economic, political, and social welfare. In the 1980s, the ITC proposed that the Northwest territories be divided into two areas: one, to be called Nunavut (our land), under the control of the Inuit and the other to remain under provincial and federal control. Their proposal led to an historic accord, the "Nunavut Final Land Claim Agreement," that establishes the new region:

> The formal signing of the land claim agreement represent[s] a landmark accomplishment in nation building, according to Minister of Indian Affairs, Tom Siddon, "… It finalizes the settlement of the largest land claim agreement in Canada and confirms the commitment to create the Nunavut territory by 1999. It signifies a bold new partnership between Canada and the Inuit of the northwest territory."
>
> The agreement gives title to 350,000 square kilometers (136,000 square miles) of land to the Inuit and will provide financial compensation of 1.14 billion dollars, to be paid over 14 years. (Communique issued by the Government of Canada, May 25, 1993)

As provided by the agreement, the territory of Nunavut came into being on April 1, 1999, with ceremonies at its capital of Iqaluit. The territorial parliament has 19 legislators, 15 of whom are Inuit. Nunavut comprises about one-fifth the land mass of Canada and has some 27,000 residents, about 85 percent of whom are Inuit. According to its first premier, Paul Okalik, education is the government's first priority in a territory where nearly half of residents do not graduate from high school. Economic concerns are also prominent. The cost of living is extremely high, with groceries in particular costing hundreds of dollars a week for a family of three. Average annual household income, on the other hand, ranges from $4,000 to $45,000 less than in other parts of Canada ($63,300 in Nunavut compared to $76,550 in Canada) (http://www.statcan.gc.ca/tables-tableaux/sum-som/l01/cst01/famil108a-eng.htm).

In Arctic Québec, the Inuit territory now known as Nunavik established regional autonomy and self-rule, but remains within the province and recognizes the ultimate authority of Québec laws. Nunavik, encompassing some 300,000 sq. mi., is home to about 9,000 Inuit who comprise 88 percent of the total population of the region ("Québec Forms the Nunavik Commission" 2000: 6). A referendum held in 1987 set up a Constitutional Committee that led in 1999 to a formal "Political Agreement" establishing a Nunavik Commission charged with developing plans to organize and implement self-government. Although there are similarities between the procedures and aims of the formation of Nunavik in Québec and Nunavut in Northwest territories, a significant political difference lies in the degree of autonomy and sovereignty enjoyed by each. While Nunavut is now a territory independent of any other entity except the Canadian federal government and has legal standing equal to that of other territories and provinces, Nunavik remains within the borders of Québec.

Industrial pollution and contamination of waterways are threats both to the environment and to the human and animal inhabitants. Recent studies have discovered dangerous levels of contamination from mercury and PCBs in the waters of the Arctic Ocean and of inland lakes and rivers in the Subarctic and Arctic. Contaminants have also been found in high concentrations in fish, marine mammals, and land animals that Native people rely on for subsistence (Price 1979; "PCB Pollution in Québec's Far North" 1989). These conditions pose both short- and long-term dangers to people's health, to their food supplies, and to their way of life. For example, when methyl mercury was discovered in northern Ontario's English-Wabigoon River in 1970, it set off a downward spiral for members of the Grassy Narrows Ojibwa community whose economy, land-use patterns, social systems, and spiritual moorings had been formed by their ecological adaptation. In a study of the community, Shkilnyk (1985) documents how the pollution of the river was the final blow in a series of changes that disrupted the people's activities and beliefs. Problems began when the Canadian government organized a relocation of the Grassy Narrows Reserve from the river to a site 5 mi. away near Kenora, Ontario, in order to "modernize" the community, allowing greater access to healthcare, schooling, and employment. In fact, though, few jobs were available, often because of local discrimination against Indians. After 1963, when the move took place, family bonds based on sharing work and resources began to disintegrate, resulting in loss of the traditional sense of "togetherness" of kin networks and larger collective units. Changes in economic pursuits led to the disappearance of women's and men's cooperative productive roles in household subsistence, undermining conjugal and family cohesion. In addition, previously unknown economic and social hierarchies developed based on access to jobs and to administration of benefits derived from government sources. The decline in societal stability was reflected in

the rapid replacement or resignation of elected chiefs. Whereas in the eighty-nine years between 1873 and 1962, the reserve had only nine different leaders, in the fourteen years following relocation, eleven chiefs "attempted to govern" (103). Some community members tried to maintain a semblance of older ways by continuing to trap beaver and mink, but the price for furs fell by the late 1960s, leading to a loss of income and an abandonment of the activity. Fishing that had sustained the people both for subsistence and for commercial endeavors also became impossible because of the discovery of methyl mercury in the river, a result of industrial pollution from a chemicals plant and a pulp and paper mill in Dryden, Ontario. As Shkilnyk observed, "To accept the fact that their 'River of Life' had turned into a river of poison meant to lose forever their faith in nature and in the source of life itself" (179). Blood samples from the community were tested to evaluate levels of mercury and ascertain health risks, but the government was unable to state categorically whether the levels that they found were dangerous. The resulting uncertainty was disastrous: "To have a gnawing fear that there is a poison in one's body, not to know the difference between being at risk and being poisoned, is to live in a state of constant apprehension" (198). Finally, after years of litigation, the governments of Canada and Ontario and the companies responsible for the pollution agreed to pay $8.7 million to compensate members of the Grassy Narrows band, with an additional $8 million to be paid to members of another affected group, the Islington Whitedog band.

Dealing with another environmental issue, in 2002 the people of Grassy Narrows began a blockade of logging operations that were being carried out in their traditional territories. The Grassy Narrows Trappers Center built a log cabin at the site in order to house people participating in daily 24-hour blockades until

TABLE 23.3	Unemployment Percentages for Selected Native Populations			
	On-Reserve (%)	Off-Reserve (%)	Aboriginal (%)	Provincial (%)
Newfoundland	42.5	57.1	18.6	27.8
Yukon	34.0	26.5	9.4	9.3
Northwest Territories	32.9	20.6	10.4	11.0
Source: DIAND 2006: Table 1.				

2008 when the company, named Resolute Forest Products, terminated their logging activities in the area. Then, in 2012, an Ontario provincial court ruling ordered that the province could not grant forestry licenses in violation of indigenous treaty rights and recommended the establishment of an advisory committee that would negotiate agreements with First Nations consent.

As a result of recent agreements with Canadian and US administrations, Subarctic and Arctic people have achieved recognition of their sovereignty, legal rights to land and resources, and support of their cultural integrity. However, problems remain for the vast majority of indigenous residents. Rates of unemployment and underemployment are staggering in the context of few job opportunities, lack of educational and training facilities, and remoteness of most Native communities from areas of stable and expanding employment. Table 20.3 presents unemployment rates for registered Indians and non-status aboriginals in the Yukon, Northwest territories, and Newfoundland as reported by the Canadian Department of Indian Affairs and Northern Development based on 2006 census data. Note, however, that Arctic and Subarctic nations in northeastern and northcentral Canada are not included in the data since the provincial figures for Québec, Ontario, Manitoba, Saskatchewan, Alberta, and British Columbia are not disaggregated by region. Given high rates of unemployment, per capita and household incomes were correspondingly low, in fact, much lower than those of all Canadians in the provinces. Tables 23.4 and 23.5 present relevant data.

According to statistics compiled by the US Bureau of the Census for 2010, some Alaskan Native households and individuals had incomes substantially above those of most American Indians while others fell below the norm. Table 20.5 presents data for the two categories of Alaska's indigenous population as delineated by the census tables. These data indicate that the aggregate Native and Athabaskan-speaking groups per capita and median household incomes are higher than the American Indian norm of $16,446. Where incomes were higher, poverty rates were correspondingly lower. However, even Indians and Inuit whose

TABLE 23.4	Per Capita Income for Native Populations in Selected Provinces		
	On-Reserve ($)	Off-Reserve ($)	Total Aboriginal ($)
Newfoundland	14,400	12,500	25,255
Yukon	13,400	17,300	23,560
Northwest Territories	10,600	18,500	21,216

Source: DIAND 2006: Table 34.

TABLE 23.5	Selected Economic Characteristics for Native Alaskan Populations			
	Per Capita Income ($)	Median Household Income ($)	Families Below Poverty (%)	Individuals Below Poverty (%)
Alaska Native	16,968	41,963	18.7	21.8
Alaskan Athabaskan	18,409	36,958	17.9	21.2

per capita incomes were relatively high fall far below the overall Alaskan average of $30,598

Although Native Alaskans' incomes are in some cases higher than American Indian norms, unemployment rates in Native communities are extremely high, much higher even than those of other American Indian reservations. According to statistics from the Juneau office of the BIA, the average unemployment rate for all of Alaskan Natives in 2010 was 20.8 percent. In 2000, of about 230 communities reporting, only 5 had unemployment rates below 50 percent and these were in the 40–49 percent range, while 81 communities reported rates higher than 80 percent. These figures contrast sharply with the unemployment rate of 9.6 percent for the state of Alaska.

Given the seriousness of obstacles to healthcare, educational and job advancement, and the desire for an improved standard of living, many indigenous people are forced to choose between remaining in relatively isolated communities or leaving their homes for towns and cities to the south in Canada. These are difficult choices, neither of which guarantees protection for the people or for their land, resources, and cultural heritage.

REFERENCES

Arnold, Robert. 1976. *Alaska Native Land Claims.* Anchorage, AK: Alaska Native Foundation.

Asch, Michael. 1984. *Home and Native Land: Aboriginal Rights and the Canadian Constitution.* Toronto: Metheun Publications.

Boas, Frank. 1888. *The Central Eskimo.* 6th Annual Report of the Bureau of American Ethnology for 1884–1885.

Brown, Jennifer. 1994. "Fur Trade as Centrifuge: Familial Dispersal and Offspring Identity in Two Company Contexts." *North American Indian Anthropology* (ed. R. DeMallie and A. Ortiz). Norman, OK: University of Oklahoma Press, pp. 197–219.

Burton, Alan, and Otto Edholm. 1955. *Man in a Cold Environment: Physiological and Pathological Effects of Exposure to Low Temperatures.* London: Arnold.

Department of Indian Affairs and Northern Development (DIAND). 1999. *Registered Indian Population by Sex and Residence, 1998.* Ottawa.

Department of Indian Affairs and Northern Development (DIAND). 2006. Ottawa.

Dunning, R. W. 1959. *Social and Economic Change among the Northern Ojibwa.* Toronto: University of Toronto Press.

Feit, Harvey. 1973. "The Ethno-Ecology of the Waswanipi Cree: Or, How Hunters Can Manage Their Resources." *Cultural Ecology: Readings on the Canadian Indians and Eskimos* (ed. B. Cox). Toronto: McClelland and Stewart.

Fried, Jacob. 1972. "Urbanization and Ecology in the Canadian Northwest Territories." *The Emergent Native Americans: A Reader in Culture Contact* (ed. D. Walker, Jr.). Boston, MA: Little, Brown and Company, pp. 704–711.

Government of Canada. 1993. *Communique. Formal Signing of Tungavik Federation of Nunavut Final Agreement.* Ottawa: Indian and Northern Affairs Canada.

Hearne, Samuel. 1958. *A Journey from Prince of Wales Fort in Hudson's Bay to the Northern Ocean in the Years 1769, 1770, 1771, and 1772.* Toronto: McMillan.

Helm, June, and Eleanor Leacock. 1971. "The Hunting Tribes of Subarctic Canada." *North American Indians in Historical Perspective* (ed. E. Leacock and N. Lurie). New York: Random House, pp. 343–374.

Hosley, Edward. 1981. "Environment and Culture in the Alaska Plateau." *Subarctic* (ed. J. Helm), Vol. 6 of *Handbook of North American Indians.* Washington, DC: Smithsonian Institution Press, pp. 533–545.

Krauss, Michael, and Victor Golla. 1981. "Northern Athapaskan Languages." *Subarctic* (ed. J. Helm), Vol. 6 of *Handbook of North American Indians.* Washington, DC: Smithsonian Institution Press, pp. 67–85.

Kroeber, Alfred. 1939. *Cultural an Natural Areas of Native North America.* Berkeley, CA: University of California Publications in American Archeology and Ethnology No. 38.

McClellan, Catharine. 1964. "Culture Contacts in the Early Historic Period in Northwestern North America." *Arctic Anthropology* 2, no. 2: 3–15.

Niezen, Ronald. 1998. *Defending the Land: Sovereignty and Forest Life in James Bay Cree Society.* Boston, MA: Allyn and Bacon.

"On Top of the World: Inuit's Aspirations Realized in a New Canadian Territory Called Nunavut." 1999. *American Indian Report* July. pp. 12–15.

"PCB Pollution in Québec's Far North." 1989. *Rencontre* June.

Price, John. 1979. *Indians of Canada: Cultural Dynamics.* Salem, WI: Sheffield Publishing Co.

"Québec Forms the Nunavik Commission." 2000. *Rencontre* May: 6–7.

Rhodes, Richard, and Evelyn Todd. 1981. "Subarctic Algonquian languages." *Subarctic* (ed. J. Helm), Vol. 6 of *Handbook of North American Indians.* Washington, DC: Smithsonian Institution Press, pp. 52–66.

Rogers, Edward. 1963. *The Hunting Group-Hunting Territory Complex among the Mistassini Indians.* Ottawa: National Museum of Canada Bulletin No. 195, Anthropological Series No. 63.

Rushforth, Scott. 1977.

Shkilnyk, Anastasia. 1985. *A Poison Stronger than Love: The Destruction of an Ojibwa Community.* New Haven, CT: Yale University Press.

Slobodin, Richard. 1964. "The Subarctic Métis as Products and Agents of Culture Contact." *Arctic Anthropology* 2, no. 2: 50–55.

Slobodin, Richard. 1966. *Métis of the Mackenzie District.* Ottawa: Saint Paul University Canadian Research Centre for Anthropology.

Statistics Canada. 2009. "Aboriginal Identity Population, by Province and Territory." *2006 Census.* Ottawa, Canada.

"Subsistence Is a Human Right." 1999. *American Indian Report.* June. p. 26.

US Bureau of the Census. 2010. "2006–2010 American Community Survey Selected Population Tables." Washington, DC.

Van Stone, James. 1972. "Changing Patterns of Indian Trapping in the Canadian Subarctic." *The Emergent Native American: A Reader in Culture Contact* (ed. D. Walker, Jr.). Boston, MA: Little, Brown, pp. 308–321.

Watkins, Mel. 1977. *Dene Nations: The Colony Within.* Toronto: University of Toronto Press.

The Innu (or Montagnais)

Our parents did not wait for the caribou to come to them, they went looking for it. Young Montagnais have to do the same.

Quoted in *Rencontre* June 1989: 7

WITH THESE WORDS, Armand McKenzie, director general of the Innu (EE-nu) or Montagnais (man-tan-YEA) band of Matimekosh in interior northeastern Québec, spoke of an innovative program funded by the Band Council to help young unemployed residents create their own jobs through education and training under a project called the "Young Volunteers." Within a year of its inauguration, twenty-three people from Matimekosh had submitted proposals and were on their way to learning new skills and, in some cases, establishing small businesses. The Young Volunteers program is an important initiative directed at achieving goals that are widely shared by people who want to remain in their own communities, benefitting from the experience and knowledge of their elders while making an income that enables them to prosper in a difficult economic situation.

Although all of the nine Innu reserves in Québec are in need of economic development, job creation, and community infrastructure, Matimekosh was acutely affected by the closing of the Iron Ore Company in the town of Schefferville (adjacent to Matimekosh) in 1982, eliminating employment and support for nearly two dozen Native families. In fact, Schefferville has been virtually abandoned. Stores and homes are boarded up, only the most visible signs of the loss of jobs and incomes. But the people of Matimekosh, one of the smaller and more remote communities, have responded by mobilizing their skills to find independent alternatives. In addition to supporting training for new jobs, the Matimekosh Band Council encourages young people to learn traditional hunting and survival skills. Although approximately 10–20 percent of the nearly 600 residents of the reserve continue to trap, hunt, and fish in nearby territories, most young people no longer are trained in the required skills. However, some recognize that such activities not only can provide subsistence for their families but can lead to income-producing work as outfitters and guides for Canadian and American visitors. A group of Young Volunteers chose to go "into the bush" to acquire techniques involved in hunting, trapping, preserving meat, and making clothing from animal skins. According to one of the participants, they learned to understand the natural world as their ancestors had. Said Elisabeth McKenzie: "We learned more than just the techniques. We also learned the words, the language of the places and acts we must perform and which we had lost. These words, this way of perceiving nature is essential to find your way in the forest" (quoted in *Rencontre*, June 1989: 6).

INNU SOCIETY

The present situation of the Innu is the legacy of a combination of indigenous and historical processes. Traditional culture survives, with adaptations to changing economic, social, and political conditions brought about by the presence of Europeans in Native territory beginning in the late fifteenth and early sixteenth centuries. At that time, the aboriginal people, who called themselves "Innuat" ("human beings"), inhabited a vast territory in present-day eastern and northern Québec. It stretched from the vicinity of Québec City eastward to the Gulf of St. Lawrence. The territory contained all the drainage basins north of the St. Lawrence River from Cap-Rouge to Tadoussac as well as those south of the St. Lawrence from Riviere-du-Loup to Riviere Matane. The land supplied varied animal and plant resources in diverse ecosystems consisting of coastal sites, inland rivers and lakes, and densely forested mountains. The impressive mountains of their homeland gave the Innuat their French name, that is, Montagnais or "mountaineers." Although this is the name most often used in past studies, the people now prefer their Native designation, Innu. Indigenous neighbors included Naskapis, who lived to the north, and East Crees, who inhabited territory to the west. The three peoples spoke closely related languages of the Algonkian family and developed similar cultures whose differences mainly resulted from adaptations to somewhat different environments.

The variety of natural resources in Innu territory was described by Paul LeJeune, a French Jesuit missionary who spent six months living with a nomadic band in 1633–1634:

> Among their terrestrial animals they have moose, beavers, caribou; they also have bears, badgers, porcupines, foxes, hares, martens, and three kinds of squirrels.
>
> As to birds, they have bustards, white and gray geese, several species of ducks, teals, ospreys, and several kinds of divers. These are all river birds. They also catch partridges, woodcocks, and snipe of many kinds, turtle doves, etc.
>
> As to fish, they catch, in the season, different kinds of salmon, seals, pike, carp, and sturgeon of various sorts; whitefish, goldfish, barbels, eels, lampreys, smelt, turtles, and others.
>
> They eat, besides, some small ground fruits, such as raspberries, blueberries, strawberries, nuts which have very little meat, hazelnuts, wild apples, cherries, wild grapes.
>
> They eat, besides, roots, such as bulbs of the red lily, a root which has a taste of licorice, another that … has tubers in the form of beads, and some others,

not very numerous. (*Jesuit Relations and Allied Documents 1610–1791* 6: 271–273; hereafter *JR*)

Despite diversity of resources, LeJeune described Innus with whom he travelled as "almost always hungry" due to migratory habits of the animals, birds, and fish that the people depended on for food. And he noted that animals in their territory were not very numerous, with the exception of moose and eels (*JR* 6: 273). In fact, though, the winter of 1633–1634 was an especially lean one for the people since snowfall had been light, making it difficult to track animals in the woods. Still, Native life was no doubt generally dominated by the need to seek resources. They followed an annual cycle of foraging in accord with the seasonal appearance of animals, birds, fish, and plants in their territory. According to LeJeune,

> [D]uring the months of September and October, they live for the most part upon fresh eels; in November and December and often in January, they eat smoked eels, some Porcupines, which they take during the lighter snowfalls, as also a few Beavers, if they find them. When the heavy snows come, they eat Moose meat; they dry it, to live upon the rest of the time until September; and with that they have a few birds, bears, beavers, which they take in the Spring and during the Summer. (*JR* 6: 277)

Economies

Economic production centered on hunting and fishing, while gathering wild plants provided a smaller, but significant, portion of the diet. Various strategies were used to secure different species. In early autumn, moose were hunted with bows and arrows, but before heavy snows fell it was difficult for hunters to approach close enough to kill the animals because of their keen sense of smell and swift speed. Later in the season, when the ground was covered with heavy snow impeding animals' movements, hunters could more easily track the moose and kill them with long spears. Moose meat, as well as other animal flesh, was eaten roasted or boiled in kettles of water heated by hot stones. Broth from boiled meat was taken as a drink. And grease, one of the people's most valued foods, was skimmed off the surface of the boiled liquid and eaten with wooden spoons.

Surplus meat was dried for use later in the year, a process described as follows:

> They stretch upon poles the two sides of a large Moose, the bones having been removed. If the flesh is too thick, they raise it in strips and slash it so that the smoke may penetrate and dry all parts. They pound [the meat] with stones and tramp it under foot so that no juice may remain to spoil it. At last, when it is smoked, they fold and arrange it in packages, and this forms their future store. (*JR* 6: 297)

Hunters caught beavers by different methods depending on the season. In the spring, beavers were caught in traps using baits consisting of strips of wood. During winter, they were taken in nets that were dropped through holes made in ice covering streams and lakes near the beavers' lodge. When animals entered nets seeking the bait, they were lifted to the surface and killed with clubs. A second winter method was to demolish beavers' lodges with hatchets and pursue the animals escaping into the water, catching and clubbing them (*JR* 6: 299–303). Porcupines and bears were taken in deadfall traps or snares while hares, martens, and squirrels were caught in nets or killed with bows and arrows. Birds also were killed with arrows or darts.

Most fishing was done with nets obtained through trade with Hurons who lived north of Lake Ontario to the west of Innu territory. Eels, however, were caught in wooden weirs that were placed at edges of rivers when the water was low. Rows of stones were positioned in shallow water so that eels were guided into the weirs built large enough to hold 500–600 eels. Eels were also caught with harpoons at night from canoes that were

Innu Naskapi women ca. 1908, wearing woolen and deerskin clothing. One has a Montagnais cap. The tent covering is dressed skins, smoke-blackened at the top.

lit with bark torches to attract the fish (*JR* 6: 309–311). An enormous number of eels were caught in early fall, many hundreds often killed in a single effort. Eels were dried by smoking on long racks suspended over fires. According to LeJeune, "The poles of their Cabins are all loaded with these eels" (311).

Clothing was made by women from caribou, moose, or beaver hides. Preparing hides for use was a long, arduous process. First, the hair was removed and hides were softened by soaking in water. Next, they were scraped of residual fat or tissue, stretched, and rubbed with animal brains or grease. Finally, they were smoked slowly over fire to produce a golden brown color. Hides were then cut, pieced together, and sewed with sinew. Men, women, and children wore clothing of basically similar design consisting of robes, leggings, breechcloths, and moccasins. Robes had detachable sleeves that were added in cold weather and removed in summer months. Robes were decorated with painted lines along the length of the garment and its sleeves. In warm weather, people wore their robes open or loosely tied across the chest. In winter, they were worn closed tight and belted with a sinew cord. Both men and women wore hide breechcloths or flaps hung in front from a cord around their waist. Leggings were fastened to the waist by a belt and extended the length of the leg to the foot, where they were held by a loop under the instep. Side edges of leggings were cut into a fringe to which small beads or shells were attached as decoration. Footwear consisted of moccasins made either of caribou or moose hide or of waterproof sealskin. In winter, people wore several pairs of moccasins pulled over one another and sometimes wore inner socks made of grass or hare skins. Infants were diapered with soft moss and were carried in moss-filled hide bags.

Skills required to produce traditional clothing, utensils, and other goods are still known today by a number of Native artisans. Although most craftspeople are elderly, some young Innus are learning the techniques in order both to retain their heritage and to earn an income from the sale of traditional goods. In addition to shops on the reserves that sell clothing and crafts, in 1987 CAM (Conseil des Attikamek et des Montagnais) opened a store in Québec City that sells traditional merchandise and also supplies artisans with raw materials for their work.

Settlements

Settlement size and location varied seasonally as people exploited available resources and adjusted to climatic conditions. From fall through winter, they lived in dispersed camps or "winter bands" scattered throughout their territory. Such camps contained a number of families who were usually related, although the basis of their relationship was not consistent. That is, some camps were formed through patrilateral bonds, either by father and son(s) or brothers, while other groups consisted of a couple and their daughter's family or two (or more) sisters and their husbands and children. Rather than following strict descent or locality rules, the Innus had a flexible system of affiliation that allowed people to make residence choices on the basis of age and gender composition of existing family groups.

Small camps or winter bands were nomadic, shifting their locations during the season in order to avail themselves of resources. LeJeune reported that the group with whom he lived from November 1633 through April 1634 moved twenty-three times. Winter bands generally contained no more than three or four nuclear or extended families, sometimes referred to as "lodge-groups." Lodge-groups were the basic socioeconomic units of Native society. They varied in size, averaging between ten and twenty people. A winter band therefore numbered approximately thirty to sixty individuals. But bands were subject to fissure if resources were especially scarce. Two opposing forces affected decisions to separate or remain together. Splitting up into small groups, potentially into separate family or lodge units, might allow people to survive in lean times, but the danger of possible hunting accidents or illnesses might draw people together for mutual aid. Mutual aid, though, included obligations to share food with coresidents, sometimes stretching meager supplies to the point of near or even actual starvation.

A number of winter bands, possibly two, three, or four, were informally linked into a named band that numbered from 150 to 300. Such bands shared a familiar territory whose boundaries were probably not explicitly reckoned. However, permission to use another's resources was asked, and granted, when travelling through lands known to "belong" to a particular group.

In springtime, families began to leave the woods, migrating to the shores of the St. Lawrence River or the Gulf of St. Lawrence. By summer, they congregated in large groups along the waterways, seeking seasonal resources as well as relief from huge numbers of mosquitos that infested northern woodlands at that time. Summer communities sometimes numbered 1,000 or more, although settlements of 200 or 300 were more common. People remained near the rivers, hunting and fishing until the start of autumn when they returned to the woods.

Although most Innus today do not follow aboriginal economic cycles of their ancestors, a significant minority do continue to engage in traditional hunting activities. During spring and summer months, they live in permanent communities on the reserves, but in the fall, they head "into the bush" to hunt and trap animals in the forests of their ancestral territory. Modern hunters employ the same basic methods as did their forebears except, of course, that they have replaced wooden and stone hunting equipment with guns and steel traps. And while subsistence hunting remains important, the economic focus has shifted to trapping animals, especially beaver, for Canadian and international markets. In addition, the composition of hunting groups today differs from that of the past. In some cases, entire families spend fall and winter months in the woods, whereas in others, only men engage in hunting activities while wives and children remain in reserve communities. Even when families accompany the hunters, they do not necessarily stay together throughout the season. Hunters, or rather trappers, have trapping lines that may extend for many miles through the woods. When they check their lines, they typically travel alone or in teams of two or three, stopping overnight along the trail, sheltered in small tents that they take with them. The excursion may last from several days to several weeks.

In contrast to tents used today in the woods, the Innus traditionally lived in cone-shaped lodges made of birch bark spread over a light wooden frame consisting of twenty or thirty thin poles. Constructing a lodge was cooperative labor of women and men. When a camp site was chosen, women went into the forest and cut the necessary poles while men cleared the ground and dug holes in a circular pattern for insertion of the frame. Once the poles were in place and joined together at the top, rolls of birch bark that had been sewn together were fitted over them, allowing an opening for exit of smoke from a central fire. The floor and walls were covered with fir branches. Flooring was then covered with mats or sealskins that, according to the Jesuit missionary Pierre Biard, were "as soft as velvet." Biard, writing in 1616, noted that the Montagnais "stretch themselves [on the flooring] around the fire with their heads resting upon their baggage. And, what no one would believe, they are very warm in there, even in the greatest rigors of the winter" (*JR* 3: 77). Although most dwellings were conical lodges, some were elliptical or rectangular in shape. They had a central row of three or four hearths that were each used by separate families who had quarters within the lodge. Such houses were more common in summer settlements, when large groups of people congregated in villages that were relatively stable during the season.

The Innus developed means of transportation that were critical to their nomadic lifestyle. In summer, they travelled on rivers and lakes in canoes made of birch bark. They also crossed small lakes and streams on rafts made by tying logs together. When summer ended and people prepared to head into the woods for fall and winter hunting, they cached their canoes along riverbanks and retrieved them the following spring. Once heavy snows began to fall, people wore snowshoes made of a birch frame laced with strands of animal hide. They were fashioned in a variety of styles, some long and narrow or oval in shape. During winter, people piled their belongings on toboggans made of two thin birch boards that were connected by crossbars. Toboggans were turned up in front to maneuver over snow. They were dragged by means of a cord slung across a person's chest.

Families and Social Groups

Aboriginal society was organized around kinship relationships and household units ("lodge-groups") whose membership was flexible, adapted to local resource supplies and population densities. People reckoned their kin bilaterally but formal kinship groups did not exist. Responsibilities to relatives were strong, including obligations to share food, equipment, and other goods. People depended on their kin for aid and support in times of need.

Marriages were most often contracted by the man and woman themselves, although parental guidance was common and arranged marriages also occurred. Prospective mates usually had sexual experience before their formal union, either with each other or with other partners. Marriage between cross-cousins was preferred since it solidified kinship networks and underscored obligations that already existed between relatives. Although cross-cousin marriage has been largely abandoned today under pressure from the Catholic Church in Québec, a linguistic reflection of its import remains in the use of the word "ni: timus" ("my cross-cousin of the opposite sex") to mean "my sweetheart" (Hallowell 1932; Rogers and Leacock 1981: 183–184). Additional examples of the solidarity of families were preferences for sororate and levirate marriages in the event of the death of a spouse.

Polygynous marriages were possible, usually limited to two or at the most three wives. Polygyny was a means of ensuring marriage for all women since the mortality rate among men exceeded that among women, resulting in a proportional scarcity of husbands. For this reason, when the missionary LeJeune lectured the people about the evils of plural marriage, women resisted any change in their system: "Since I have been preaching among them that a man should not have more than one wife, I have not been well received by the women; for, since they are more numerous than the men, if a man can only marry one of them, the others will have to suffer. Therefore this doctrine is not to their liking" (*JR* 12: 165)

Marital relations were characterized by respect and affection between wife and husband and by mutual cooperation in economic and social life. Marriages lasted as long as these conditions existed, but when friction or incompatibility developed, people were free to divorce and seek other mates. In LeJeune's words: "The young people do not think they can persevere in the state of matrimony with a bad wife or a bad husband. They wish to be free and to be able to divorce the consort if they do not love each other" (*JR* 16: 41).

Choice of residence after marriage was responsive to familial circumstances, available resources, and personality preferences. Since marriages tended to take place between people belonging to different, but nearby, local bands, couples had to decide with which group to reside. Although there were no absolute rules of matrilocal or patrilocal residence, early accounts record tendencies toward matrilocality. For example, when a young man (a prospective husband) "saw that he was well received, he went to lodge in the cabin of his future spouse, according to the former custom of the Savages" (*JR* 30: 169). And "[Montagnais men] prefer to take the children of their sisters as heirs, rather than their own, or than those of their brothers" (*JR* 6: 255). Residence with the wife's kin was the norm during early years of marriage, but thereafter couples might change their living arrangements.

Aboriginal marital and residence patterns continued to exist among modern Innus through the middle of the twentieth century. In the 1940s, Leacock reported for Southeastern nomadic groups that band exogamy and bilocal residence were the norm. Quoting a Native man, "Ask'em woman, 'You marry, come back Natashquan.' Woman say 'No. You go to Mingan!'" (quoted in Leacock 1981: 69). However, within a decade, band endogamy became common, a result of more stabilized and settled communities, itself a result of territorial constriction and shifts away from subsistence economies. Again quoting Leacock, "As one man [from Natashquan] put it, 'Just now young men stay Natashquan. Long ago not same. Going to hunt Mingan, Romaine,' meaning a man would marry, move, and hunt in a different band territory" (69).

Social Norms

Traditional social ethics stressed generosity, hospitality, cooperation, and loyalty. People were expected to share resources and aid each other in household and community work. Coupled with responsibilities to kin and coresidents, individual autonomy and the rights of all men and women to make decisions and act independently were valued. Coercion of others either within households or camps was not tolerated and, given the strong negative reactions against such behavior, it was rarely attempted. In accord with Native ethics, group leadership was diffuse, flexible, and dependent on personal qualities and subsistence skills. People looked for advice to those who were intelligent and successful in the particular endeavor requiring assistance or consultation, for example, skilled hunters were consulted regarding hunting. However, a man's or woman's influence was temporary, fitted to a given occasion. Advice, therefore, was sought among local "experts," but such people could not exert authority or control. Decisions were made jointly by all those who were affected. Although European observers of Innu society referred to some men as "chiefs" or "captains," no formal leadership actually existed. Indeed, the people "imagine that they ought to enjoy liberty, rendering no homage to any one except when they like … All the authority of their chief is in his tongue's end; for he is powerful in so far as he is eloquent; and, even if he kills himself talking and haranguing, he will not be obeyed unless he pleases the Savages" (*JR* 6: 243).

Innu social and political systems rendered the people difficult to control. And since Europeans (in this case the French) wished to control Native people in order to better exploit their resources, they tried to alter traditional leadership patterns. As LeJeune complained, "if someone could stop the wanderings of the Savages, and give authority to one of them to rule the others, we would see them converted and civilized in a short time" (*JR* 12: 169). However, it took hundreds of years to fundamentally alter indigenous behavior and values. And, although changes did result from religious and political intervention, of greater significance was Native involvement in the fur trade and the transformation of indigenous economies from community subsistence to trapping for external markets.

The egalitarian nature of Innu society was reflected in their values regarding personality and behavior. They shunned and ridiculed people who tried to assume superiority over others or who were haughty or boastful. Instead, they "place all virtue in a certain gentleness or apathy" (*JR* 16: 165). And the absence of social, economic, or political hierarchy in their society meant that "As they have neither political organization, nor offices, nor dignities, nor any authority, they never kill each other to acquire these honors. Also, as they are contented with a mere living, not one of them gives himself to the Devil to acquire wealth" (*JR* 6: 231). The Innus approved of people who were even tempered and in good spirits. Laughter was considered the best response to misfortune. Cheerfulness was thought to be not only a social virtue but a remedy for discomfort and illness. Patience and tolerance were highly valued behavioral traits. And social interactions were characterized by camaraderie and lively joking. In contrast, open displays of anger were met with strong disapproval. In the Native view, "anger brings on sadness, and sadness brings sickness" (*JR* 7: 83). Anger was thought to be a precursor of interpersonal friction, bitterness, and dangerous antisocial acts such as violence and witchcraft. However, anger was properly displayed toward enemies or others who had given insult or injury.

Principles of equality and individual autonomy were manifested in traditional gender relations. Women and men were considered independent, autonomous beings whose subsistence skills and intelligence were equally valued. Although the division of labor within households was theoretically based on gender, in actual practice most tasks could be performed by anyone given the necessity or convenience of doing so. Only craft production seems to have been an exception to the flexibility of work: men produced objects made of wood (e.g., canoes, snowshoes) while women worked with hides (e.g., clothing, bedding, containers) (Leacock 1981: 37).

Both women and men were consulted concerning areas of their expertise. And all people contributed to making group decisions. According to Jesuit missionaries, women had "great power" and "the choice of plans, of undertakings, of journeys, of winterings, lies in nearly every instance in the hands of the housewife" (*JR* 68: 93). While this observation is undoubtedly an exaggeration since no one had power to the exclusion of others, it does reflect the important contributions of women to decision-making in their households and communities.

Gender equality was also demonstrated in marital relationships, characterized as they were by mutual respect shown between husbands and wives and by the lack of violence within households. In addition, women and men were similarly free to engage in sexual behavior before, or even outside, marriage. And either wife or husband could initiate divorce if they were unhappy with their mate.

As Leacock (1980) has ably demonstrated, gender relations began to change as the result of a combination of economic shifts and pressure from Jesuit missionaries in the seventeenth century. In the early sixteenth century, the people were becoming involved in trading furs to Europeans in exchange for manufactured goods. At first, these activities were marginal to Native economies, but as years passed, people were increasingly dependent on metal tools, utensils, and weapons that could only be obtained from European sources. As their desire and dependence grew, trapping took a larger share of people's energy and attention. And with a shift to trapping and trading, economic relations between women and men were altered toward a greater reliance on male labor since men were the key players in commerce with Europeans. In addition, Native social relations came under intense ideological pressure when Jesuits began to visit the people, established missions, and embarked on a concerted effort to convert Indians and replace indigenous customs and values with those consistent with European mores.

In contrast to egalitarian marital relations characteristic of the Innus, Jesuits preached that "the man was the master and in France women do not rule their husbands" (*JR* 5: 179). In fact, Innu women did not rule their husbands either, but the existence of genuine gender equality where women were not obedient and submissive struck the European eye as female dominance. Another Jesuit observation was actually more accurate than the one just quoted, that is, that harmonious Native household life resulted from "the order which they maintain in their occupations; the women know what they are to do, and the men also; and one never meddles with the work of the other" (*JR* 5: 133).

Missionaries attempted to instill in their converts, and in the Innus generally, the notion that premarital and extramarital sexual relations were evil. Proscriptions against what priests saw as promiscuity, however, violated Native norms about personal freedom and the naturalness of sexual activity. In addition, Jesuit preachings against polygyny not only contradicted aboriginal custom but also ignored practical needs and wishes of women to marry in a society where they outnumbered men.

Although most of the people ignored the Jesuits' teachings and resisted conversion (at least in the seventeenth century), a minority did adopt Christianity and slowly absorbed moral and interpersonal messages imparted by missionaries. Among them, monogamy, marital fidelity, and absence of divorce gained acceptance. The Jesuits' records do not attest to the "profound social disruption [caused] for the group as a whole and deep psychological turmoil for these individuals who made an often agonizing decision to give up traditional beliefs and practices and adhere to new codes of conduct" (Leacock 1980: 35–36), but such disruption and turmoil must have been present as some people adopted, and others resisted, fundamental changes in their culture.

In contrast to Innu beliefs in personal independence and autonomy, Jesuits favored a moral order based on obedience, both within communities and households. They successfully urged converts to elect "captains" who were responsible for actions of their "subjects" and who, by their position, implicitly deserved obedience from the public. In addition, interpersonal hierarchies of authority were created in families as women were told to obey their husbands and children were told to obey their parents. And since people often found it difficult or impossible to accept domination by others, corporal punishment was introduced. That many people were appalled by the punishment of others is clear from Jesuits' own accounts. Although writings on the subject were meant to praise the zealous behavior of converts, they can just as well shed light on the attempts of the unconverted to maintain their own moral dignity. In one case, a married woman convert left her husband and refused to "return to her duty" as the "captains" had urged her to do. In the face of her resistance, the captains decided to have her taken to Québec (City) to be imprisoned. As they were tying her up and placing her in a canoe, a number of young "pagan" men threatened the captains, "declaring that they would kill any one who laid a hand on the woman." The woman, however, agreed to return to her husband in order to avoid imprisonment, thus defusing a potential conflict between believers and nonbelievers (JR 22: 81–85). In another case, a young woman was publicly beaten by her relatives because she had spoken to a suitor against her parents' wishes. When the suitor and his father threatened the converts, only direct intervention by the French governor muted their protest. The governor summoned the young man to Québec and told him that any attack on Christians would be taken as an attack against him (JR 22: 115–127).

Recognizing the acute differences between traditional Innu and European cultures, Indians were often critical of French ethics and behavior. They derided Europeans for acting submissive toward officials and reproached them for inflicting corporal punishment on wrongdoers, including children, and for executing criminals, wondering why relatives of the accused did not seek revenge against the authorities (JR 22: 81–85). Some also criticized the missionaries for bringing new forms of disease. For example, a woman whose Christian husband urged her to convert answered by saying, "Dost thou not see that we are all dying since they told us to pray to God? Where are thy relatives? Where are mine? The most of them are dead. It is no longer a time to believe" (JR 20: 195–197). As she observed, Innu communities were struck by epidemic diseases of European origin shortly after contact with the foreigners. Until Jesuits began to visit Native settlements in the 1630s, contact was sporadic and of short duration. But the priests lived and travelled with the people, entering their lodges, sharing food and clothing, and thus facilitating the spread of disease-causing organisms. Although many people connected the Jesuits' presence with the origin of epidemic diseases, a crisis of faith emerged in their communities because traditional methods of healing, based in large part on ritual, failed to cure the new ailments. Of course, baptisms offered by missionaries were no more effective, but some people hoped that by adopting the Christian religion they would be protected, since they saw that the priests were healthy and therefore assumed to be spiritually powerful. Divisions soon developed in Native communities between those who accepted conversion and those who retained faith in aboriginal beliefs and practices.

Religious Beliefs and Practices

Innu religion centered on beliefs in spirit forces that affected human life and that could be controlled or at least influenced by human action. Care was taken to avoid offending spirit beings by not violating religious taboos and by showing respect through prayers and rituals. If people acted properly, spirits responded by granting requests, offering protection through songs and charms, and imparting secret and powerful knowledge and abilities. All people could acquire spiritual knowledge but some were more powerful than others. These men and women used their skills to cure illness, foretell the future, and communicate with the spirit world.

The Innus believed that all living creatures as well as inanimate objects had immortal souls that appear as shadows or dark images. After death, souls proceed along the Milky Way to a large village "very far away, situated where the sun sets" (JR 6: 177). Their existence in the village is similar to life on earth except that day and night are reversed. "During the day time [souls] are seated with their elbows upon their knees, and their heads between their hands, the usual position of the sick; during the night they go and come, they work, they go to the chase." According to the people, "souls are not like us, they do not see at all during the day, and see very clearly at night; their day is in the darkness of the night, and their night in the light of day" (JR 6: 179).

Each animal species was believed to have a spirit protector, expressed through kinship metaphors as an "elder brother," who was "the source and origin of all individuals." Animal elders allowed members of their species to be caught by humans provided that people showed respect, for example, by keeping animal bones away from dogs and by taking care not to spill beaver blood on the ground (JR 5: 165, 179; 6: 211). Dreams often foretold what animals would be caught; for example, if a dreamer saw the Beaver elder, then beavers would be found. Concern with success in hunting was also ritualized by throwing spoonfuls of grease, the Innus' most valued food, into a fire after feasting and repeating the prayer, "Make us find something to eat, make us find something to eat" (JR 6: 173). And children, coming out of their lodges in the morning, prayed, "Come, Porcupines; come, Beavers; come Elk" (JR 6: 203).

Prayers and songs were recited on other occasions as well. Indeed, singing was a primary means of conveying wishes to the spirit world. People sang for good weather, successful hunting, easy labor, healthy births, and cure from illness. In times of hardship, scarcity, and suffering, people sang to spirits for aid and protection. Drumming often accompanied singing, especially at night when ritual sessions could last until dawn. A myth, as recorded by LeJeune, explained the connection between singing and good fortune: "Two Savages, being once in great distress, seeing themselves within two finger lengths of death for want of food, were advised to sing; and when they had sung, they found something to eat" (JR 6: 185). This myth further

expressed the people's pragmatic attitude toward ritual. They did not view the spirit world with awe but rather with a practical, experiential understanding of cause and effect. Ritual acts and prayers were meant to produce results.

The spirit world was inhabited by numerous deities including a creator spirit called Atachocam and a world-transformer named Messou who figured prominently in Innu mythology. A principal transforming myth relates that one day while Messou was out hunting, the Lynxes that accompanied him fell into a lake and disappeared under the water. After searching for the Lynxes, Messou was told by a bird that they had vanished in the middle of the lake. When Messou entered the lake to find the Lynxes, the water overflowed, covering the earth and swallowing up the world. Messou then sent Raven to retrieve a piece of dry earth so that he could rebuild the world, but Raven returned unsuccessful. Messou next sent Otter into the lake, but Otter also failed. Finally, Muskrat tried, and succeeded, in bringing back a small bit of earth that Messou used to remake the world as we know it. After the world was restored, Messou married a Muskrat; their children repeopled the earth. This central myth, in addition to explaining the creation or transformation of the physical world, dramatizes a primordial spiritual bond between animals and humans through the metaphor of human descent from a spirit/animal pair.

Many spirits associated with nature and natural phenomena also were believed to exist. For instance, seasons were personified as two deities: Nipinoukhe (spring and summer) and Pipounoukhe (winter). The two deities live on opposite sides of the world, changing places as the seasons alternate. "When Nipinoukhe returns, he brings back the heat, the birds, the verdure, and restores life and beauty to the world; but Pipounoukhe lays waste everything. [The Montagnais] call this succession of one to the other, 'they pass reciprocally to each other's places'" (JR 6: 163). The Moon and Sun were wife and husband, each having her/his own dominion during phases of night and day. Thunderers were another prominent group of nature spirits. And there were numerous spirits of light and air who had knowledge of the future and were therefore consulted by shamans.

Shamans had greater spiritual power than ordinary people. In the Innu language, they are called "kakushapitak," meaning a "person who can see through, who can foretell, who has authority, power" (Mathieu Andre, an

Innu elder, in *Rencontre*, March 1989: 5). In the seventeenth century when LeJeune described Innu culture, both men and women could be shamans, but by the twentieth century, women had been excluded as practitioners. With the aid of supernatural helpers, shamans had insight into the future and could cure illness and other misfortunes. They acquired their abilities through prayer, song, and drumming, in some cases learning from other shamans, in some cases obtaining their skills independently. In addition, aspiring shamans had to select animal spirits that would be their helpers. As described by Mathieu Andre, a novice

> must stand before a pond with no outlet. Then a small female white-billed scoter runs on the water as if she were trying to fly. The scoter circles the pond and as she does so, the water runs out and the pond dries up. The outlines of animals can be seen, some of them misshapen. The shaman chooses the animals he thinks he may need during his life. He may choose the misshapen animals if he wishes to acquire their evil power to kill human beings. (5)

Shamans selected their animal helpers by touching their outlines with a stick and then wiping the stick with a cloth, thus acquiring their power. Shamanic powers were also encapsulated in objects that were kept in sacred bags. Such objects typically included "bones and skin of a newborn caribou, the meat of a young caribou, and the skin of an adult caribou" (5). Shamanic bags further held tools and equipment needed to perform rituals. They, and the power they contained, were inherited through family descent from parent to child or grandchild.

Shamans helped their communities by predicting the location of game using techniques of scapulimancy, that is, reading marks on a caribou's charred shoulder bone. They might also gain extraordinary knowledge through dreams, songs, and drumming.

A shaman's most dramatic ritual was called the "shaking-tent rite," used to foretell the future, locate animals, and communicate with absent families. The rite was always held at night in a tent totally darkened "because the shaman is looking for the light in the animals' eyes" (6). All community members were present and seated in the tent before the shaman entered. As soon as s/he did so, the tent began to shake, the tentpoles bending and flattening all around. Soon whistling sounds and the buzzing of black flies could be heard. Then cries of birds and animals could be distinguished.

All of these creatures communicated with the shaman in a sacred language not understood by ordinary people. They imparted knowledge of the future and transmitted messages from spirits and from distant people.

The public nature of the "shaking-tent rite" validated a shaman's ability to communicate with the spirit world and solidified the respect s/he received from community members. A shaman's powers were also demonstrated by the ability to heal the sick. Along with their medical ministrations, they conducted healing rituals consisting mainly of prayers and songs accompanied by drumming. Patients were expected to participate in their own treatment as well by remaining cheerful and optimistic. Their mental attitude was deemed critical to recovery since the Innus believed that if a sick person were sad, her/his illness would worsen, eventually resulting in death. As one Indian told LeJeune when the priest was ill: "Do not be sad. See what a beautiful country this is; love it; if thou lovest it, thou wilt take pleasure in it, and if thou takest pleasure in it thou wilt become cheerful, and if thou art cheerful thou wilt recover" (*JR* 7: 191).

THE FUR TRADE AND THE TRANSFORMATION OF INNU CULTURE

Because of their location in eastern Québec, the Innus were among the first indigenous people to meet European fishermen, traders, and missionaries. In fact, it is likely that they had contact with French and Basque fishermen in the fifteenth century before the voyages of Columbus brought ever-increasing numbers of foreigners to their shores. Trade between Indians and Europeans was at first sporadic, but by 1534 when Cartier met Innus along the St. Lawrence River, they were already familiar with European goods as well as with Europeans' interest in obtaining fur, especially beaver skins, at that time used in the manufacture of hats. By mid-century, the French had established a permanent post in Innu territory at Tadoussac, situated at the juncture of the Saguenay and St. Lawrence Rivers. And a half-century later, in 1608, the town of Tadoussac was founded by Champlain as the headquarters of New France.

As French presence grew in the region, the Innus' involvement in trade grew as well. Indians were especially interested in obtaining kettles, needles, awls, axes, knives, scissors, and points for arrows and spears. They also acquired cloth, beads, and a few items of food. In order to obtain European products, they trapped the animals whose skins were the medium of exchange. As reported by LeJeune, "The [Montagnais] say that the Beaver is the animal well-loved by the French, English, and Basques. I heard my host say one day, 'The Beaver does everything perfectly well, it makes Kettles, hatchets, swords, knives, bread; in short, it makes everything'" (JR 6: 297).

At first, Innu trappers did not receive fair value for the furs they brought to European merchants, but by the seventeenth century, competition among traders reduced prices for manufactured goods, in effect raising the value of beaver skins. Champlain complained that Indians did not offer the skins they had procured "until several ships had arrived in order to get our wares more cheaply. Thus those people are mistaken who think that by coming first they can do better business; for these Indians are now too sharp" (1922, II: 171). Marc Lescarbot, a Jesuit missionary in New France, similarly noted that the proliferation of traders raised prices for furs, adding "every beaver skin [is] worth here today ten livres, when they might have been sold for one half that price if the traffic herein had been limited to one person" (JR 2: 127).

The Innus' role in the fur trade expanded as they came to function as intermediaries between French merchants and Native people living further distant from trading posts. Since traditional Innu territory included land along the Saguenay and St. Lawrence Rivers as well as along other routes of travel, they were positioned to exert regional influence. In 1603, Champlain reported that they were supplying European goods to Indians in exchange for beaver and marten skins (1922, I: 123–124). The Indians' need to control trade increased as their dependence on manufactured products deepened. As early as 1632, some foreign imports, such as copper kettles and iron tools, had completely replaced indigenous equipment (JR 5: 25, 97). But since the Innus, along with their Algonkin allies, were not able to establish hegemony by purely peaceful means, they often resorted to violence in order to achieve their economic goals.

As the Innus widened their sphere of influence, they directly confronted the Five-Nations Iroquois who were waging war for both social and economic reasons. Iroquois pursued "mourning wars" to seek captives to replace their deceased kin and also attempted to set themselves up as intermediaries and exert control over

trade further to the west along the Hudson and St. Lawrence Rivers. The Innus had an important ally in the French, who opposed the Iroquois because they were allies of France's European rivals. Champlain and his troops supported Innu, Algonkin, and Huron warriors in several raids against Iroquois towns in the early 1600s. Among other warfare techniques, Champlain taught his Native allies to set fire to palisaded Iroquois villages and urged them to destroy outlying cornfields (Champlain 1907: 293). But Champlain derided what he thought was Native failure to obey orders during warfare, noting,

> they are not warriors, and will have no discipline nor correction, and will do only as they please … The chiefs have no absolute control over their men, who are governed by their own will and follow their own fancy … for having determined upon anything with their leaders, [they may] break it off and form a new plan. (293–294)

However, he did remark on the Indians' well-organized retreats, "placing all the wounded and aged in their centre, being well armed on the wings and in the rear, and continuing this order without interruption until they reach a place of security" (296). Without realizing it, Champlain was commenting on expressions of Innu social ethics as they were translated into military action. No one had the right, by position or authority, to control the behavior of others. Instead, all members of a group jointly made decisions that could be altered as conditions or sentiments changed. And, when leaving the battle scene, Innus responded with compassion and concern for colleagues who could not survive without aid.

At first, Innus were successful against the Iroquois because they were well armed with European guns, but when the Iroquois began to acquire guns from their own Dutch allies, the Innu military advantage evaporated. Once both groups were similarly armed, the Iroquois' cultural advantages grew in importance. First, since Iroquois subsistence was based primarily on women's farm labor, men were able to depart on warfare expeditions supplied with dried cornbread and other provisions without having to divert time and energy to hunting. And second, their formally structured kinship and leadership systems made military organization and discipline more dependable. Still, although the Innus were not able to penetrate the area of Iroquois dominance, they did maintain control in the eastern St. Lawrence and Saguenay basins.

As European traders increased their activities in the Northeast, missionaries came to the region as well. Jesuit priests accompanied Champlain and other explorer/traders in the early seventeenth century, establishing a permanent presence in the Northeast after 1632. Several priests were sent to Innu camps where they learned the Native language and lived in a manner that approximated that of their hosts but their scattered camps and nomadic movements made them difficult to contact and contain. Indeed, Paul LeJeune, head of the Jesuit mission in New France, often complained that the people's "wanderings" rendered them uncontrollable. Still, missionary activities continued among the Innus throughout the seventeenth century and until the expulsion of the French from eastern Canada in the middle of the eighteenth century (Vecsey 1997: 55).

In order to more easily alter Native habits and values, Jesuits sought to remove some converts from their home communities. Accordingly, a small settlement for Christian Innus was established in 1637 just outside Québec, called both "St. Joseph" and "Sillery," beginning with just two families but soon growing to about thirty-five or forty Innu and Algonkin households whose lives were structured around an annual cycle that combined activities of traditional Indian hunters and settled French farmers. They remained at Sillery most of the year, leaving to hunt moose toward the end of January, returning to Sillery in the spring and, after preparing hides taken in the winter hunt, planted crops in gardens near their lodges. Then they awaited the arrival of French ships in the summer and early fall to obtain manufactured products and foods that they had come to depend on. Sillery became a center for Jesuit activity among the Innus, enabling the priests to contact families coming to the settlement to trade and returning with them in the fall to preach among the hunting groups.

Jesuits hoped to alter traditional behavior by educating children in Christian beliefs and French mores. As LeJeune described, the children "will be permitted during the first few years to have a great deal of liberty [so that] they will become so accustomed to our food and our clothes, that they will have a horror of the Savages and their filth" (*JR* 9: 103). To accomplish this goal, Jesuits opened a school for Native children in Québec in 1635, desiring to remove the youngsters from their families because parents "will not tolerate the chastisement of their children, whatever they may do" (*JR* 5: 197). Despite their plans, however, only a small number of families agreed to part with their children. Some people expressed misgivings, especially since the French did not reciprocate by sending their own children to live among the Indians.

Although Jesuits' impact on Innu culture was significant, major transformations of Native society resulted from people's dependence on the fur trade to supply them with products that they considered necessities. The degree of dependence varied among different Innu bands. Those living closest to Tadoussac, Québec, and other French trading centers came to rely on European goods as early as the middle of the seventeenth century. However, bands whose territories were more remote continued aboriginal economic and social patterns for many decades, in some cases even for centuries. Several factors contributed to their isolation. First, their geographic location kept them insulated from European influences. Second, the founding of the Hudson's Bay Company in 1670 and rapid growth in French and British commercial interests in resources to the west soon led to comparable loss of interest in eastern regions, in part because the supply of beaver had been seriously depleted in the east. Even though the land around Hudson's Bay was formally ceded to the British in 1713 by terms of the Treaty of Utrecht, French traders continued their operations in the area, bypassing the eastern posts and people who had originally developed trading networks. Third, when the British gained possession of all of Canada in 1762 following Britain's victory in the French and Indian War, economic interest in eastern Québec waned even more, thus ensuring the isolation of many Innu bands.

In the early nineteenth century, commercial control of the Native market by Canadian and British merchants was solidified by a nearly complete monopoly achieved by the Hudson's Bay Company after its merger with competitors in 1821. Thereafter, Company traders determined fixed prices for furs exchanged at a growing number of posts throughout the country, including eastern Québec. Major transformations of Innu economy and social practice date from that period, including fundamental changes in concepts of property, ownership, and cooperation within families and communities.

In contrast to aboriginal patterns where resources were consumed either immediately or within a short period of time, participation in the fur trade required people to keep animal skins on hand for many months until they could visit trading posts and exchange their catch for goods that they wanted. Whereas in the past all resources and goods were shared among community residents, some possessions became the restricted property of individuals (or families) and were withdrawn from redistributive networks. This process had an additional consequence, namely a development of differences in wealth among families.

Again in contrast to aboriginal patterns, the people gradually expanded the concept of individual property from objects to territory. As Leacock (1954) has shown, family "hunting territories" were outgrowths of changes in the purposes to which land was used. Among the Innus, access to land and therefore to the products of land were traditionally considered common to all members of a band, a flexibly defined social and economic group inhabiting a vaguely defined territory. But a system of land and resource management evolved that assigned use and extraction rights to bands and then to families within the band.

As with other cultural changes, the process of individualizing property was uneven, some Southeastern bands not fully adopting the system until the middle of the twentieth century (20). Differences in the development of private property in land correlate with temporal differences in various bands' shifts from subsistence hunting to trapping and dependence on the fur trade to supply a majority of their needs. Some bands, especially those living closest to trading centers of Québec and Tadoussac, developed at least seasonal recognition of family rights to hunting and trapping territories by the beginning of the eighteenth century. According to Bacqueville de la Potherie, a French observer of the period, the Innus assigned "pieces of land about two leagues square for each group to hunt exclusively" (Leacock 1954: 15–16). Families owned the beaver houses located within their territory, but, in accordance with aboriginal ethics of communal interdependence, if a member of another group were starving, they could kill and eat the beaver, leaving the fur and tail for the proper "owners" (16).

The system of group or family ownership initially operated only during the trapping season. There is some evidence that an entire band, or even several bands, discussed seasonal allocations of land, assigning a parcel or lot to each group. But by the second half of the eighteenth century, family allotments were becoming stable, passed on through inheritance from parents to children, probably most often through patrilineal inheritance.

Although Innus were spending more time and energy trapping fur-bearing animals than had been their aboriginal custom, they continued to depend on hunting deer, moose, and caribou in order to supply most of their food. Reports from employees of the Hudson's Bay Company posts located near Lac-St.-Jean in the middle of the nineteenth century attest to people's reliance on hunting, much to the chagrin of traders who wanted them to focus instead on trapping beaver and marten. Traders tried to encourage trapping by providing Indians with a wide assortment of goods that could only be obtained in exchange for furs. As one trader in the region commented, "I doubt not but artificial wants will, in time, be created. They may become as indispensable to their comfort as their present real wants. All the arts of the trader are exercised to produce such a result, and those arts never fail of ultimate success" (Leacock 1954: 37). As predicted, Native families came to depend on an ever-greater number of European products, eventually including foods as well as equipment and clothing. Their need for food increased in the late nineteenth century when caribou populations decreased sharply. And as their reliance on traders for food grew, families concentrated their labor on trapping.

Innu bands in southeastern Québec maintained traditional (or nearly traditional) hunting patterns into the twentieth century. Leacock's consultants in the 1940s and 1950s remembered times when families remained "in the bush" for most of the year, visiting trading posts briefly in the summer to replenish supplies and purchase new equipment. They hunted deer and occasionally caribou, still the mainstays of their diet, supplemented by a small amount of flour and salt purchased at the posts (24–25). Small groups (similar to aboriginal "winter bands") hunted together and shared resources. Privately owned territories were unknown. But changes came when material needs grew, flour replacing meat in the basic diet and canvas and cloth replacing caribou skins to make canoes, tents, and clothing. Hunting became unnecessary and even detrimental since it interfered with the pursuit of trapping. And, as had occurred earlier among more westerly bands, emphasis on trapping led to the development of private or family control of territory and resources.

In tandem with increasing dependence on trade, Innu bands began to alter traditional nomadic patterns, gravitating to areas near trading posts. As in the case of other changes, the development of "trading-post bands" reflected aboriginal location; that is, those groups situated closer to the posts tended to settle in their vicinity earlier than did those groups whose lands were more distant. During the summer, people remained near the posts, focussing their activities on preparing and trading the furs they trapped during the fall and winter. Gradually, trappers' families were less likely to accompany the men on expeditions, remaining at "home" camps for most of the year. Bands located near trading posts also tended to become more stabilized social units and to develop more structured sociopolitical functions than did the more remote groups who, in contrast, maintained traditional cultural practices well into the twentieth century. According to Leacock's ethnographic research among Southeastern peoples in the 1940s and 1950s, "band boundaries are not yet completely established [in the region]" (19). Of course, by the late twentieth century, boundaries did become firmly demarcated, assigned to reserves that were established in the 1950s, 1960s, and 1970s.

CONTEMPORARY INNU COMMUNITIES

The Innus currently reside on nine reserves in Québec. Three of the reserves (Mashteuiastsh, Betsiamites, and Les Escoumins, now called Essipit) were established in the middle and late nineteenth century as Innu territories north of the St. Lawrence River were invaded by companies seeking to exploit the rich forestry resources of the region. Then the people obtained reserves whose boundaries were guaranteed by the Canadian government. In the early twentieth century, resources lying under Native land in Québec became targets of Canadian and American companies. Mining, especially of iron ore, brought renewed pressures on Innu communities. And, later in the century, construction of hydroelectric dams on rivers in their territory further compelled the people to seek secure reserves. The communities of Maliotenam, Mingan, Natashquan, La Romaine, Pakuashipi, and Matimekosh were then founded.

Of the nine Innu reserves, the largest by population is Mashteuiatsh, located on the southern shores of Lac-St-Jean. Its Native name means "see you at the point," referring to the land that juts out into the lake. In 2015, Mashteuiatsh had a Band membership of 6,562, but less than half that number (2,058) lived on the reserve (Aboriginal Affairs and Northern Development Canada 2016). Members have left Mashteuiatsh

in order to seek higher education and/or employment in cities and towns in Québec and elsewhere in Canada. Although out-migration is usually a symptom of lack of opportunities at home, economic conditions at Mashteuiatsh are actually better than in other Innu communities. A critical difference, however, between Mashteuiatsh and the more isolated reserves, is that it is situated amidst prosperous Canadian towns along the south shore of Lac-St-Jean and to the east along the Saguenay River. The comparative disadvantage of Mashteuiatsh therefore becomes apparent. In addition, its location near major highways links the reserve to Québec City and Montreal to the south.

Mashteuiatsh has made improvements in the standard of living including construction of new modern homes and streets. The central town contains grocery stores, gas stations, and numerous retail shops selling crafts, clothing, and other goods as well as a community-run elementary school, secondary school, band offices, senior citizens' home, church, and headquarters of the Native police force of Québec. There is also a residence for teenagers from other reserves who come to Mashteuiatsh for secondary education. And the reserve contains a large community center that includes a health clinic, library, gymnasium, community hall, theatre, indoor skating rink, and several offices.

Employment is available in public and private sectors. Local businesses, both on the reserve and in nearby towns such as Roberval, provide some 200 jobs while nearly 50 people work at a sawmill that is owned by the reserve and 300 are employees of the Band Council. Some 40 families continue the hunting and trapping traditions of their ancestors, heading into the dense woods every autumn (*Rencontre*, March 1989: 4–8). There are around 130 buisnesses on the reserve as of 2010. Band economy received a boost in 2000 with compensation for land ceded to Canada in the nineteenth century, an amount of about $7 million (*Rencontre*, May 2000: 19). Consistent with assertion of aboriginal identity, in 1986 the community re-adopted its Native name, Mashteuiatsh, that had been replaced by the French "Pointe-Bleue" in the nineteenth century. And the people focussed efforts on revamping their educational system to include Innu history, traditional skills, arts, and language. There are two schools on the Innu reserve, an elementary and a secondary, which are commited to passing on their culture to the next generation. Additionally, history classes are taught in the Native language, nehlueun, to encourage fluency (Amishk de Mashteuiatsh 2016).

The governing council has authority over activities within the reserve as well as in their hunting lands located to the north. Indeed, protection of land and resources is central to the council's mission. They promote creation of new businesses, and help existing businesses expand through grants from a fund of $900,000, part of a settlement they won from the power company Hydro-Quebec for allowing electricity transmission lines to cross their territory (Amishk de Mashteuiatsh 2016).

In addition to the communities of Mashteuiatsh and Matimekosh, there are seven other Innu reserves in Québec. Second in band membership to Mashteuiatsh, but outranking it in actual number of residents, is Betsiamites, situated on the northern shore of the St. Lawrence River about 30 mi. southwest of the town of Baie-Comeau. Betsiamites has 2,830 residents (2011 figures) and a total of 3,925 Band members. It is the largest Innu reserve in size, consisting of 63,100 acres. The Uashat-Maliotenam similarly have only 4,532 members but 2,456 residents. The remaining communities have populations of fewer than 1,000 and encompass much smaller areas. Four reserves range in acreage from just over 1,000 acres to slightly less than 7,000 while three have fewer than 100 acres of land. These figures indicate a growing population with total increases of about 4,000 in the decades since 1990. More than twice as many Innus live on their reserves than have moved elsewhere, a further sign of confidence. And according to statistics gathered in the 1996 census, about 10,965 Innus reported knowledge of Montagnais or another Innu dialect, and 9,870 said that Montagnais was their "home language" (Statistics Canada 2011). These numbers have been steadily increasing since the 1990s. In fact, in all communities except Masheuiatsh, nearly all residents have knowledge of their Native language and the great majority speak it at home.

To facilitate resource development in northern Québec, the provincial government negotiated with Innu leaders from the community at Uashat Mak Mani-Utenam, located near Sept-Iles on the north shore of the St. Lawrence River, to allow construction of a hydroelectric project in their territory. In return for permitting the La Romaine project to proceed, the Innu people, numbering about 4000, receive a payment of $80 million spread over fifty years. These funds are allocated for economic development plans. An additional $45 million is earmarked for construction contracts and jobs given to Innu companies and workers. The government of Québec also agreed to negotiate discussions between Innu representatives and officials from mining or forestry companies interested in resource development in the Innu region. Protection of their environment and equitable compensation for their resources are critical concerns of the Innu community.

Some members of the Innu reserve are opposed to the agreement, claiming that it infringes on their sovereignty and jeopardizes their ability to continue traditional foraging practices. Indeed, Innu voters rejected the deal in a referendum held in their community. However, the project persists as of 2015, and has started with the construction of a dam, despite strong opposition from individuals (Curtis 2015). The community is also pursuing a land claims suit against the Québec and federal Canadian governments, claiming that hydro, mining, and forestry companies exploited resources in their territories without their consent and without appropriate oversight by federal and provincial authorities. They are seeking some $2 billion in compensation for damages.

Although most Innu territory is located within the province of Québec, there are some Innu whose lands are in Newfoundland. Living in remote regions poses challenges in terms of ecological and social adaptations. In addition, some nomadic groups are vulnerable to pressure from the Canadian government to settle in year-round villages but adjustments are difficult without the infrastructure and services that might make these moves beneficial. For example, in 1967, Canadian officials persuaded a group of Innu to settle in a newly built village called Utshimassits (or Davis Inlet) in Newfoundland, promising to provide housing, schools, and other services. However, the houses in the village did not have heating or internal plumbing, making life there difficult in the cold northern environment. And the change in location resulted in the abandonment of the Innus' traditional hunting and fishing economy, rendering them reliant on storebought food and manufactured items. But without much money due to the lack of jobs, many people became dependent on government payments. As a response to these problems, in 2002 the Canadian government again stepped in with a plan to move the people elsewhere, to a village called Natuashish, about 9 mi. inland, once again promising programs and social services to help people adjust and seek employment. These pledges have also not been meaningfully fulfilled. Economic difficulties have led to social problems within families and to alcohol and drug abuse. High rates of suicide, especially among young people, are also reported. Officials suggest the solution of moving the Innu to another larger village where there would be more jobs available. Some community members favor such a move while others fear that the same pattern of empty promises will be played out. And some Innu advocate a return, at least partially, to their traditional hunting lifestyle, one that in the past gave them some greater sense of accomplishment and security, allowing them to express their values and identities.

The government's proposals and actions in this case seem to be the modern manifestation of policies initiated in the seventeenth century by French and British officials, later to be followed in the nineteenth century by US and Canadian authorities. These policies attempted to control the lives of indigenous peoples, settling them in permanent villages, altering their economic systems, and affecting their family and community structures. Such policies have evidently not been completely abandoned in the twenty-first century.

In addition to these problems, the Innu are involved in negotiation with the Canadian government over land rights. Because of their remote location, the federal government was not concerned about delineating First Nation's territories but discussions have begun in order to set boundaries and establish people's rights in their lands to the territory itself and to its mineral resources.

Current employment and income data reveal continuing serious economic problems on all Innu reserves. The composite labor force participation rate stood at 50.7 percent, with an employment rate of 38.0 percent and an unemployment rate of 25.1 percent; note that "participation rate" refers to percent of population aged sixteen or older in the workforce, "employment rate" refers to percent of the entire population aged sixteen or older that is employed, and "unemployment rate" documents the percentage of the population aged sixteen or older that is actively seeking work). Innu figures are near the norm for on-reserve Indian populations in Canada, although some bands are above the average and others fall below. However, employment data for Innu communities contrast sharply with figures for the general

lation: labor force participation rate of 64.6 percent, employment rate of 59.9 percent, and unemployment rate of 7.2 percent. Specific band data compiled from the 2011 census are displayed in tables 24.1 and 24.2.

Consistent with employment data, individual incomes for most people are low. For Innus on all reserves, the average income of men who receive income from employment was $25,873 in 2011,

TABLE 24.1 — Populations for Selected Innu Reserves

Reserve Name (founded)	Total Population
Betsiamites (1853)	3,925
La Romaine (1955)	1,161
Essipit (1892)	729
Uashat-Maliotenam (1949)	4,532
Mashteuiatsh (1853)	6,562
Matimekosh (1960)	7,324
Mingan (1963)	622
Natashquan (1952)	1,097
Pakuashipi (1971)	363*
Totals	26,315

* 2006 value; 2011 data unavailable.

TABLE 24.2 — Employment Rates for Selected Innu Reserves

	Participation (%)	Employment (%)	Unemployment (%)
Betsiamites	39.9	27.4	31.4
La Romaine	32.6	26.4	17.0
Uashat-Maliotenam	51.4	39.5	23.2
Mashteuiatsh	57.7	43.5	24.1
Matimekosh	57.5	41.2	28.3
Mingan	54.7	34.4	34.3
Natashquan	46.2	37.0	18.2
Pakuashipi*	66.1	50.0	22.7

Source: Statistics Canada 2006: Custom tabulations.
* 2006 values; data for 2011 unavailable.
Note: "Participation rate" refers to percent of population aged sixteen or older in the workforce, "employment to population ratio" refers to percent of the entire population aged sixteen or older that is employed, and "unemployment rate" documents the percentage of the population aged sixteen or older that is actively seeking work.

TABLE 24.3	Average Incomes for Selected Innu Reserves	
	Average Income ($)	
	Men	**Women**
Betsiamites	20,064	18,379
La Romaine	12,009	14,834
Uashat-Maliotenam	29,287	20,431
Mashteuiatsh	31,739	24,567
Matimekosh	22,054	26,553
Mingan	16,376	21,721
Natashquan	16,014	17,879
Pakuashipi*	18,487	19,030

* 2006 values; 2011 data unavailable.

while women's average earnings (for women receiving income from employment) were even lower, that is, $21,429. These figures are substantially below the Québec norms of $42,343 and $30,523 for women and men respectively, and also lower than the Canada-wide Native on-reserve averages. Specific band income data are given in Table 24.3.

Data compiled from the 2006 census on educational achievement document another source of disadvantage for members of Innu bands. On all reserves, the proportion of people with less than ninth-grade educations far exceed that general Canadian norm of 7.1 percent. Indeed, the proportion range from 11.5 percent (for Mashteuiatsh) to as much as 49.1 percent (for La Romaine). Table 24.4 presents data for Innu bands.

TABLE 24.4	Education Levels for Selected Innu Reserves		
	No Certificate, Diploma, or Degree	**High School Certificate or Equivalent**	**Some College or Higher**
Betsiamites	940	195	130
La Romaine	570	30	35
Uashat-Maliotenam	ua	ua	ua
Mashteuiatsh	870	255	260
Matimekosh	260	60	0
Mingan	235	10	15
Pakuashipi	145	10	10

Note: 2006 values; 2011 data unavailable. ua, unavailable.

All of the Innu reserves joined together in 1975, along with the nearby nation of Attikamekw, to form the "Conseil des Attikamekw et des Montagnais" or CAM (Council of the Attikamekw and the Montagnais) in order to pursue discussions with Québec's government concerning proposals for aboriginal self-government and settlement of Native land claims in the province. Priorities of CAM include recovery of full ownership rights to much of their ancestral lands, control of surface and subsurface resources, establishment of autonomous governments in Native communities with jurisdiction over social and economic development, complete control of traditional hunting, fishing, and gathering activities, and establishment of equal government-to-government relations with Québec and the federal Canadian nation.

CAM and other organizations representing Native people in the region signed an agreement with the Québec and federal governments in 1975, called the "James Bay and Northern Québec Agreement," that effectively delineated boundaries of Native territory as well as set forth responsibilities of the governments toward Canada's First Nations. Indeed, land and the authority to decide future territorial development are central. As stated by Remy Kurtness, chief of the Mashteuiatsh Band:

Self-government is impossible without land, without access to natural resources. We don't want Québecers to go back to Europe. But we do expect compensation for occupied land. We are looking at various forms of co-ownership, co-jurisdiction, co-management with national or local governments and, in some cases, sole jurisdiction on our part. Without economic power, there can be no social, cultural, or human development … Once you've decided to keep this sacred visceral link with the land, you will never lose your identity. (Quoted in *Rencontre*, Spring 1994: 5–6)

In 1995, the Québec government made a proposal to CAM that they said combined "autonomy and partnership.and created several kinds of territorial entities with varying rights. The plan establishes twelve districts that encompass the twelve existing Innu and Attikamekw communities, totalling some 1,500 sq. mi., where self-government is complete. A number of additional zones, comprising approximately 15,000 sq. mi., are created where traditional activities and resources are under the control of indigenous people, although non-Indians may also use the land and resources based on agreements worked out between the Native nations and Québec. In addition, exclusive hunting and trapping rights are given to Native families in lots and trapping lines that they have used for generations. Finally, conservation areas of some 4,000 sq. mi. are under joint jurisdiction of the Native nations and the government of Québec (*Rencontre* Spring 1995: 10–11).

Financing of economic, social, and administrative activities in Innu and Attikamekw communities come from three sources: taxes levied by indigenous governments, income from resources in Native territories, and a fund of $342 million provided by Québec and Canada in recognition of past inadequacies in government aid to Native communities (10–11).

Although external and material conditions have been forever altered, many people remember and continue to reproduce the kinds of social relations that bind kin and community together. Recalling the time of his youth, Daniel Vachon, an elder from the reserve of Maliotenam (located 10 mi. east of the city of Sept-Iles), commented:

> At that time when government aid didn't exist, if a hunter came upon several caribou, he killed them; not only for himself and his family, but to feed all the families. What was important was that everyone could eat. If a hunter was less lucky, there was always another ready to share his catch with him and his family. People shared with other bands as well. They exchanged canoes, snowshoes, and clothing too. (*Rencontre*, Spring 1995: 4–5)

But poverty and insecurity also existed during that period because bad weather, bad luck, and illness could push families and entire bands to the brink of starvation. Such dire circumstances have been largely eliminated today due to governmental support in the form of family aid, healthcare, and other social services. Wagework and a cash economy have also contributed to the atomization of families and individuals. Still, as Louisa Rock, another resident of Maliotenam, explained, "some traditional forms of sharing remain in the community." When she and her family return from their months "in the bush," they share the fish and meat caught in the woods with people in need. "My sons or my daughter make an announcement over the community radio station so that old people who can't go hunting anymore can profit from it. They take the food to whoever asks for it" (6).

Communal sharing at Maliotenam takes other forms as well, translated from aboriginal custom into modern contexts. In the springtime, the entire community gathers along the banks of the Moisie River, sharing a feast of salmon and meat, reminiscent of traditional "first fruits" celebrations. In addition, when couples get married, the occasion is celebrated at a community center where everyone is welcome to share food and good times. Deaths, too, are noted by reserve residents at the center. People meet together after the burial, bringing food and comfort for the deceased's family, demonstrating in word and deed their remembrance of the deceased and the continuing solidarity of the community.

REFERENCES

Aboriginal Affairs and Northern Development Canada. 2016a. *Aboriginal Community Profiles*. Ottawa, Canada.

Aboriginal Affairs and Northern Development Canada. 2016b. *First Nation Profiles*. Ottawa, Canada.

Amishk de Mashteuiatsh. 2016.

Champlain, Samuel de. 1907. *Voyages of Samuel de Champlain, 1604–1618*. (ed. W. L. Grant). New York: Charles Scribner's Sons.

Champlain, Samuel de. 1922–1936. *The Works of Samuel de Champlain*, 6 vols. (ed. H. Biggar). Toronto: The Champlain Society.

Curtis, Christopher. 2015. "Québec Agrees to Meet with Innu to Discuss Hydro Dam." *Montreal Gazette*. Online.

Department of Indian Affairs and Northern Development. 2000. *Registered Indian Population by Sex and Residence, 1990*. Ottawa, Canada.

Hallowell, A. I. 1932. "Kinship Terms and Cross-Cousin Marriage of the Montagnais-Naskapi and the Cree." *American Anthropologist* 34, no. 2: 171–199.

Jesuit Relations and Allied Documents 1610–1791 (JR). 1896–1901. 73 vols. (ed. R. G. Thwaites). Cleveland, OH: The Burrows Brothers.

Leacock, Eleanor. 1954. *The Montagnais "Hunting Territory" and the Fur Trade*. Washington, DC: American Anthropological Association 56.5, Part 2, Memoir No. 78.

Leacock, Eleanor. 1980. "Montagnais Women and the Jesuit Program for Colonization." *Women and Colonization* (ed. M. Etienne and E. Leacock). New York: Praeger, pp. 25–42.

Leacock, Eleanor. 1981. "Matrilocality among the Montagnais- Naskapi." Reprinted in *Myths of Male Dominance*. New York: Monthly Review Press, pp. 63–81.

Rencontre. March 1989 Québec: Secretariat aux Affaires Autochtones.

Rencontre. June 1989. Québec: Secretariat aux Affaires Autochtones.

Rencontre. Spring 1994. Québec: Secretariat aux Affaires Autochtones.

Rencontre. Spring 1995. Québec: Secretariat aux Affaires Autochtones.

Rencontre. May 2000. Québec: Secretariat aux Affaires Autochtones.

Rogers, Edward, and Eleanor Leacock. 1981. "Montagnais-Naskapi." *Subarctic* (ed. J. Helm), Vol. 6 of *Handbook of North American Indians*. Washington, DC: Smithsonian Institution, pp. 169–189.

Statistics Canada. 2006. Ottawa, CA.

Statistics Canada. 2011. "Language Highlight Tables." *2011 Census*. Ottawa, CA.

Vecsey, Christopher. 1997. *The Paths of Kateri's Kin*. Notre Dame, IN: University of Notre Dame Press.

The Inuit

Things have improved since they [Inuit] began to realize that their culture has been upset too much. That upset was part of our lives, everything was new, everything was being tested. We were told it was for the best. We believed that. We lived through all that, and now we're making our own assessment.

Mitiarjuk; *Rencontre*, Fall 1994: 6–7

THE INUIT (IN-U-IT) LIVE IN a unique and forbidding environment, located throughout the Arctic from the western Pacific Coast of Alaska to the eastern Atlantic shores of Canada. Theirs is a vast territory, spreading more than 4,000 mi. through six time zones. Today numbering at least 125,000 in Alaska and Canada, Inuit are united by similarities in culture and history. Their languages belong to two different but related linguistic families. One, called Yupik, consists of five languages spoken in coastal Alaska and Siberia. The other, called Inuit-Inupiaq or Inuktitut, is a grouping of closely related dialects spoken from coastal Alaska through Arctic Canada and along the eastern coasts of Québec, Labrador, and Greenland. According to Canadian data from the 2011 census, 34,110 people reported Inuktitut as their mother tongue, making it the third most widely spoken aboriginal language in Canada (Statistics Canada 2011). In Alaska, the 2010 US census reported 7,203 speakers of Inupik and 18,950 speakers of Yupik (Siebens and Julian 2011). In local dialects, the words for the people themselves vary but in 1977 delegates to the Inuit Circumpolar Conference held in Barrow, Alaska, adopted the name Inuit ("the people") as a standard designation for all communities regardless of local usages (Damas 1984: 7). The formerly used term "Eskimo" was a European modification of a word from the Montagnais language with no currently certain meaning although many have been suggested (6).

Temperatures in the Arctic vary across the enormous expanse of land. Daily temperatures in the coldest month of January range from a low of ⊠30° or ⊠35°F in central and eastern Canada to a high of 0° or 10°F in western Alaska. Average temperatures in the warmest summer month of July range from a low of 35° or 40°F in central and eastern Canada to a high of 50° or 55°F in western Alaska. Despite some warming in the summer, however, Arctic ground remains frozen throughout the year because of long, intensely cold winters. Annual rates of snowfall are relatively light considering the region's northern location, averaging from 40–65 in. in the west up to 45–125 in. in the east. But since the ground is frozen and the air continuously cold, little or no snow melts or seeps into the earth to drain underground. Ice begins to form on lakes and rivers early in autumn, and by the middle of October many inland waterways are completely frozen. The ice does not usually begin to clear until early June and is often not completely melted until the end of June or beginning of July. However, due to global warming, snowfall levels are falling and temperatures rising. Over the last few decades, Alaska has gotten 6° warmer, on average. It is still unknown how global warming will affect traditional Inuit societies (Romm 2015).

ADAPTATIONS TO THE ARCTIC ENVIRONMENT

Living in the Arctic environment has led to physiological and biochemical adaptations over the many centuries that Inuit and their ancestors have resided in the region. Their bodies have adapted to extreme cold by mechanisms that protect against heat loss and by others that provide for digestion of high animal protein and fat content in their diet. The major problem presented by living in the Arctic is the need to preserve body heat, particularly to protect the central core of the body, that is, the outer skin of the chest and back and the internal organs. Hypothermia or loss of body heat can be fatal while prolonged cold in the arms and legs can lead to frostbite, which can also cause death. Inuit's metabolism produces a greater amount of body heat than does that of other people, reflected by a measure known as "basal metabolic rate" or the minimum amount of heat produced by a body at rest when not engaged in any activity, including digestion. Comparisons of basal metabolic rates of Inuit with those of other groups indicate that the Inuit's rate is some 13 percent to 33 percent higher (Itoh 1980). In addition, Inuit have fewer sweat glands on the chest and abdomen and in the legs and feet than do other people. Since the production of sweat is the body's means of cooling, people who have fewer sweat glands can retain more body heat.

In general, Inuit demonstrate a better physiological response to exposure to the cold than do other groups. Blood vessels in their hands dilate faster when exposed to the cold, thus enabling them to carry fresh warm blood rapidly to body extremities and avoid dangers of frostbite. Furthermore, Inuit's hands and fingers stay warmer, rewarm faster, and tolerate the pain and stress of cold better than do those of other people.

Another important physiological adaptation is Inuit's ability to digest the high proportion of animal protein and fat typical of a diet rich in fish and marine and land animals. Although Inuit's foods contain high amounts of fats and oils, the people have very low rates of ailments such as diabetes and cardiovascular disease. Most of the sources of fat in the Native diet, such as sea mammals, fish, and caribou, contain polyunsaturated rather than saturated fats and therefore do not contribute high levels of cholesterol in the blood. In fact, oils from fish may actually help reduce serum cholesterol. Moreover, even when eating the same diet as other people in Canada and the United States, Inuit absorb cholesterol from foods in a more efficient manner, avoiding the buildup of cholesterol in the blood that can lead to heart ailments and strokes.

In addition to physiological adaptations, Inuit have survived in the Arctic because of unique cultural developments such as specialized technology to make clothing and build houses that retain as much heat as possible. People have coped with a scarcity of resources by living in small communities and gaining a broad knowledge of the habits of animals that they depended upon for food. The bulk of the traditional diet centered on marine animals such as seals, walrus, and whales; freshwater fish such as Arctic char, salmon, lake trout, whitefish, and pike; and a number of species of land animals that enter inland Arctic territory during seasonal migrations, including caribou, bear, wolf, musk ox, fox, weasel, and squirrel. Ravens, snowy owls, and some water and shore birds also make their appearance in the region during summer migrations. However, despite a variety of food sources, most of the animals, fish, and birds that Inuit depended upon appeared in limited supply and only during short seasons of the year. Because of these limitations, Inuit were attentive to the migration cycles and the behavior of marine and land animals. Due to the mobility of their food sources, the Inuit lifestyle was correspondingly highly mobile. Resources were utilized intensively whenever available, but seasonal changes in the movements and supplies of animals led to relocations of settlements. Given the conditions of the land and scarcity of resources, the people required a vast hunting territory and needed to know local weather conditions, thickness of ice, and habits of the animals in order to survive. But despite the people's best efforts to exploit all the resources in their region, periods of hunger or even starvation were not unknown and in fact were common in certain areas, especially toward the end of the long winter when scarcity was most pronounced. Episodes of hunger and starvation were part of many families' histories. For example, Graburn recorded an elderly consultant's account of her family's ordeal in northern Québec at the turn of the twentieth century. After many days of searching for food, the family of mother, two daughters, and two sons killed their own dogs and ate them. Then,

We were very hungry, going on day after day. My older brother and his wife got a caribou at their place. So he brought us some small pieces of meat.

Even then, it was not enough. My married older sister and her husband also brought us some food, eating little themselves. They moved off again to another place to get some food. We kept on moving again. We used a polar bear skin dragging it along as a sled with no dogs left. Other people were abandoning their own children. Then we got one ptarmingan. Eating one ptarmingan—that was hardly enough for everyone. My mother was cutting up her clothes to eat, hats, hoods, and all. We kept on having this for food every time we stopped. We nearly didn't have any clothes left, just enough to keep us warm.

My brother kept on falling down because he was so weak. Then they caught one caribou, but we could still hardly walk from being so thin. We started running out of food again, we left my older sister behind and then our older brother left us behind.

Finally we arrived in Sugluk [a village on the Québec coast] as the snows were beginning to melt, and we were not starved again. (Graburn 1969: 37–38)

In order to utilize resources, Inuit settlements were temporary and seasonal, changing location depending upon the availability of animals. Major changes occurred in the winter and summer months, although even during these seasons, small camps were set up on a temporary basis, some lasting for only a few weeks or even a few days. Throughout most of the arctic, Inuit set up winter camps on the ice formed over the seas, remaining in this general vicinity from October or November until sometime in May. Winter camps were the larger of the seasonal settlements, with populations numbering from fifty to one hundred. During the winter, the people lived in two types of dwellings. One, a house made of sod, was oval in shape and varied in size but could accommodate several related families. Sod houses were entered through a long passageway that could be as much as 20 ft. in length, ending with a small doorway covered with sealskin or caribou hide. The house and passageway were lined with stone, driftwood, or whalebone in order to protect inhabitants against the cold. Along the passageways, storage areas were set aside to keep tools, utensils, hunting equipment, and surplus food, the latter buried in "ice cellars" dug into the frozen ground. People slept on raised platforms or benches built in the rear section of the house and covered with warm animal skins. In the center of the house, a fire was used for cooking and heating. Lamps, usually made of soapstone, provided heat during the long dark winters.

Igloos, dwellings made of blocks of snow, were similar in design to sod houses although they were generally smaller, accommodating one or two families. Igloos were sometimes built close to each other and joined together with dome passages so that people could visit without having to expose themselves to the frigid air.

As the ice began to melt in May or June, winter settlements dispersed. Small groups, consisting of at most several related families, moved inland to catch fish and birds, hunt land animals, and gather wild plants and berries that grew briefly during the summer months. During this season, Inuit lived in tents made of sealskin or caribou hide. Summer tents, either conical or rounded on the top, were smaller than winter houses and accommodated one or at most two families. Tents were portable and could easily be dismantled and carried by teams of dogs on the frequent moves that people made staying close to herds of migrating animals.

When moving from place to place, Inuit relied on dogs to help carry or pull their belongings on sleds made of whalebone and driftwood. Five or six dogs were harnessed to sleds in a fan formation with ropes of different lengths. Sleds were packed with utensils, hunting equipment, heavy clothing, and animal skins used for bedding and housing. During the spring and summer when the ice melted, dogs carried some of the peoples' possessions on their backs.

INUIT SOCIETY

Economies

Since nearly all of the food that Inuit ate came from animals, men performed most of the direct subsistence work, using different methods to hunt the various species that they depended on. When hunting on the sea, they used boats, called kayaks, made of driftwood and whalebone, wrapped with a waterproof sealskin cover. The top of the cover had a hole large enough for one person to sit inside. Lances or harpoons were used to catch seals or walrus in the ocean. When hunting seals on land, men positioned themselves near seals' breathing holes on the sea ice where the animals came periodically to breathe fresh air. Once hunters located breathing holes, often with the help of their dogs, they

The seal-hunter, Noatak, in a kayak, ca. 1929.

waited for a seal to return. This type of hunting technique was most successful if several men cooperated and positioned themselves at various breathing holes within a relatively small area. Even so, hunters often had to wait many hours and might still be unsuccessful. But, if a seal came to the breathing hole the hunter snared it with a harpoon and then other men nearby came to help drag the animal onto the ice surface.

Hunting whales was always a cooperative task given the large size of the animal and the danger involved. Groups of men formed whaling crews under the leadership of an "umialik" or owner of hunting equipment and a whaling boat called an umiak. Umiaks were open boats made of driftwood and whalebone, measuring 15–20 ft. in length and covered on the sides and bottom with sealskins to keep water from seeping inside. They were steered and propelled with paddles. Whaling crews, consisting of seven to ten men, were recruited by umialiks from among their relatives. At the start of the whaling season in early spring, they were given a new set of clothing made by the umialik's wife. When whales were sighted, the crew embarked, and as they approached a whale, they threw harpoons into its flesh, all helping to pull the animal close to the boat and finally killing it with lances. The importance of whaling is symbolized by rituals that are associated with it. Hunters must abide by many taboos before departing on whaling expeditions, including abstaining from sexual activity, refraining from eating certain foods, or building cooking fires. The umialik's wife is critically responsible for carrying out rituals surrounding whaling. Once the men are out on the hunt, she must "move slowly, think peaceful thoughts

and act generously" (Bodenhorn 1993: 192). These actions attract the whales and persuade them to give themselves up to be caught. Recognition of a woman's role was expressed by a skilled Alaskan hunter who said, "I am not a great hunter, my wife is" (Bodenhorn 1988: 5). When a crew returns with a whale, the umialik's wife, dressed in her best clothing, greets the whale, offers it fresh water from a special wooden pot, thanks it for allowing itself to be caught, and later gives her husband water from the same pot.

Meat from whales and other sea mammals was distributed to members of the community according to specific rules of etiquette. If a single hunter caught an animal, it was his right to distribute meat, but if several men cooperated in hunting, the man who first harpooned the animal took charge of the distribution and allocated meat to various members of the community. For example, seal meat was distributed in the following manner: the head, eyes, forelimbs, thoracic vertebrae, and heart were given to women; the cervical and lumbar vertebrae were given to men; the hunter who killed the animals received the ribs, sternum, and attached meat; the lumbar meat went to all the men in the hunting party; and the sacral and caudal vertebrae and hind flippers were cooked in broth and eaten by all (Graburn 1969: 69). Whales were also butchered and their meat distributed according to formal procedures. In Alaska, the whaling captain directs the butchering and then allocates shares of meat. The hunter who killed the animal receives the hide. He and other members of the crew and any man or woman who contributed labor or equipment to the communal effort are entitled to meat. The captain generally receives extra shares, but these are later distributed at public gatherings and ceremonials, not consumed by his household. Once the meat destined for sharing has been cut from the whale, any woman in the community is entitled to carve away what she wants (Bodenhorn 1988: 6–7).

Land animals were hunted along the coast and in interior regions. Polar bears were caught on the ice by first approaching the animal, usually when it was asleep, and having dogs surround it and hold it a bay while the hunter shot it with bows and arrows or lances. Caribou hunting was done singly or cooperatively. Often an entire community took part in caribou drives, especially in the fall when the animals were most numerous and most valuable, having fattened over the spring and summer. Stones and boulders were placed in two lines forming a path leading to a pit where hunters awaited the caribou. Then, women and children chased after the animals, keeping them between the rows of boulders and, as the animals neared the end of the drive, they were shot with bows and arrows or were attacked with lances.

Products of sea and land animals were valued for many purposes in addition to their use as food. Seal and caribou skins were made into clothing, bedding, boat covers, and containers. Sealskins were used as doorways and windows in winter houses, while caribou skins were used to make tents for summer shelters. Caribou bones and antlers were made into tools and utensils such as spades, scrapers, handles, arrowheads, blades, knives, hooks, and needles. Caribou and seal guts were used for thread and rope. Whalebone was used extensively to make the frame of kayaks, umiaks, and sleds, and whale oil was used for cooking and for lighting lamps. In addition to sea and land animals, men and women fished in coastal waters and inland lakes and rivers for salmon, Arctic char, and whitefish. Some fish were caught by using hooks and lines or spears, while other fish, especially salmon and char, were caught in traps or nets spread across streams. Women and men also caught seagulls, ducks, and geese, with bows and arrows, darts, and traps. Bird's eggs were collected from nests along the coast and inland rookeries. Finally, women gathered several kinds of roots such as young willow root and knotweed as well as blueberries and cranberries when these were available during the summer, but due to the short season, these foods made only a small contribution to the annual diet.

In addition to women's participation in hunting, fishing, and food collecting, they prepared daily meals, almost always consisting of meat or fish. One large meal was eaten each day, usually in the late afternoon or evening, while leftovers were eaten as small snacks the next day. Meat from sea or land animals was boiled in oil, roasted, or allowed to partially decay before eating. Fish were eaten either raw or frozen first in ice or snow. Berries were eaten fresh or frozen, while roots were boiled in oil and then combined with meat or fish. Surplus foods were preserved for later use. The simplest preservation technique was to bury the food in "ice cellars," but fish and meat were also cut into strips and cured over small fires.

In preparing animal skins for use as clothing, women first cut the skins off the carcass, taking great care not to make tears or holes in the skins. If any tears occurred, they had to be sewn securely so that no air or water could seep through. Then the fat attached to the inner side of the skin was scraped off and the skin was washed with snow or rubbed with pebbles to render it smooth. Next, the skin was spread on pegs about an inch from the ground to allow air to circulate underneath. In the summer or early fall when most clothing was made, sealskins were dried in the sun so that they would remain soft and pliable, but in winter they were dried over lamps. When the skins were dry, they were cleaned again with a sharp scraper to eliminate any remaining fat or residues. They were then soaked in cold water, washed again, dried, and scraped one last time.

Clothing worn by women and men differed somewhat although the basic garments were similar in function and styling. Undershirts, underpants, and stockings were made with the hair-side turned inward, while outer pants and hooded parkas had the hair-side turned outward. Women's parkas had a hood large enough to provide room for a baby because Inuit mothers carried their babies on their backs inside their garments.

Inuit salmon fishers, killing salmon with spears, Canada.

Men wore long outer pants while women wore a wider style similar to culottes. Both women and men wore knee-high boots, stockings, and mittens. When inside their houses and during the summer, people omitted outer garments and wore their underclothing with the hair-side turned out.

Families and Social Systems

Inuit communities were united by strong bonds of kinship. Relatives depended upon one another for help in daily living and for assistance in times of trouble. Two or more related families often lived together in the same house, travelled together, worked cooperatively, and shared food and other resources. When winter villages dispersed in the spring and summer, small groups of related people separated and established temporary camps where they hunted, fished, and gathered plant food. Although Inuit followed patterns of bilateral descent reckoning and residential groups could be composed of relatives related either through men or women, camps usually consisted of an older couple and the families of their grown sons. After parents' deaths, brothers formed the basis of such settlements. Affiliation of men was common since a hunting economy emphasized the cooperative work of men.

The complexity of the Inuit concept of kinship is expressed by the term "ila":

> In its most general sense, ila means "part." It is most commonly used for something that has a separable identity yet is a necessary or functioning part of a larger whole, such as a part of a motor or harpoon. In referring to persons, ila has the general meaning of "partner" or "companion." It is used for someone who accompanies one on a trip; for any co-participant in some activity. In talking about these uses of the term, informants emphasized not simply the physical proximity of the individuals but the cooperation and assistance involved.
>
> The use of ila to designate genealogical relatives shares much of the meaning of the more general uses of the term. In discussing these terms informants emphasized the importance of helping, love, being "mindful" and concerned, and not being afraid or uneasy. The concept of ila involves attitudinal and behavioral criteria as well as genealogical ones. Informants spoke of love, aid, and lack of fear not simply as things that "ilait" [relatives] normally and ideally felt and did for one another, but as characteristics that were incorporated in the

definition of the term, and that determined whether or not someone was "really" one's ila. (Maxwell 1994: 36–37)

Relatives are expected to reciprocate economic and social aid and support. If they fail to act appropriately, kin bonds may be "deactivated; it is not unusual to hear someone say, 'he used to be my cousin'" (Bodenhorn 1988: 3).

When deciding upon marriage, people usually followed their own preferences, although in some communities in central Canada, parents arranged marriages for their sons and daughters when the children were infants. Marriages were not formalized through ceremony but rather were socially recognized when a couple began to live together. Parents of the couple might exchange gifts in recognition of the new bond between them. After marriage, a couple often resided with or near the wife's family for some period during which the husband assisted his parents-in-law and provided food and other services for them. The couple remained with the wife's family at least until the birth of their first child and then might move near the husband's relatives if they desired.

Children were treated with great affection and indulgence. In most Inuit communities, the birth of boys and girls was equally welcomed, although in some areas of central Canada, there was a marked preference for boys. In some families, in addition to learning duties associated with their own gender, daughters and sons might also be taught the tasks associated with the other. If a father especially preferred his daughter or if he had no son, he might take the girl on hunting expeditions and teach her the skills of tracking and hunting. If a family had no daughters, parents might teach a son to cook and sew. People who knew the full range of duties were later valued as spouses since they had a double set of subsistence skills (Saladin d'Aglure 1984: 492). In Alaska, families sometimes adopt children in order to balance the size and gender composition of their households (Bodenhorn 1988: 14).

Community Integration

Inuit communities did not have formal leadership but rather people sought the advice of able and gifted members of their settlements. In small camps of related families, the eldest man might be recognized as an informal leader, but in addition to seniority, he had to be a successful hunter and conform to the desired personality traits of generosity, cooperativeness, and even temper. In larger settlements, more than one such "leader" might be recognized. Except for areas of their expertise, leaders did not have authority to control other people. Instead, communities most often exerted informal control by teasing, ridiculing, or insulting people who violated social norms of hospitality, generosity, and cooperation. If conflicts developed between men, they were sometimes settled by public contests or "song duels" in which two rivals composed insulting songs about each other, taking turns and competing to outdo their adversary while others in the village witnessed the contest and responded with laughter. Song duels might lead to resolution of underlying conflicts although they might exacerbate the dislike of one man toward another.

Assaults or murders could lead to revenge killings and feuds since families of victims might seek to avenge the death of their kin. A person who committed murder or repeatedly assaulted others might be exiled or executed when the group reached a consensus favoring such action after tolerating antisocial behavior for a period of time, hoping to avoid trouble. The family of an executed murderer was unlikely to avenge their relative since they understood that "the situation was better for all concerned" (Spencer 1967: 161). Reminders of the difficulties caused by the person executed would usually lead members of his family to ignore his execution and not seek revenge. In any case, blood feuds seldom continued for a great length of time but were instead settled quickly and forgotten. The dispersal of villages in the summer months aided the process of dissolving feuds as families separated into small hunting groups.

Gender Relations

Gender relations among Inuit were characterized by some degree of male dominance although the nature and extent of this dominance varied in different regions. It was most marked in the central Arctic where female infanticide was evidently not infrequent, resulting in population imbalances favoring men (Balikci 1967, 1970). Among the Netsilik, for example, numerical preponderance of males was noted by Rasmussen in 1923, recording a Netsilik population of 150 males and 109 females (1931: 141). If one assumes an equal number of male and female births, approximately one-third of the girls may have been victims of infanticide. Not coincidentally, central Inuit parents often

arranged marriages for their infant children. Given lowered numbers of available women in central Arctic communities because of female infanticide, infant betrothal can be interpreted as an attempt by parents of a boy to ensure a wife for their son. However, this strategy did not actually lead to future stability, since there was no guarantee that a couple would remain together given the ease and frequency of divorce.

Some anthropologists rationalize female infanticide as a reflection of the need to limit population growth given dire survival circumstances and the fact that men perform primary subsistence activities. According to this theory, whereas men as hunters are essential to survival of a family and community, women are expendable. However, there are a number of problems with this argument. Among the groups in the central Arctic who practiced female infanticide, gender roles were not as rigid as in the west where the practice seems to have been rare. Central Inuit women engage with men in cooperative hunting during caribou drives, independently catch birds and fish, and make and repair clothing that are essential to everyone's survival. Women's skills in sewing and repairing clothing were socially recognized. Just as a successful hunter was desired as a potential husband, so an expert sewer was a valued wife (Briggs 1974: 275). Women's labor was therefore neither expendable nor socially invisible. Rather than solving societal problems, female infanticide contributed to discord within settlements because the gender imbalances it created led to competition and conflict among men over available women. Netsilik men often attempted to steal another man's wife, sometimes killing the husband in the process. Resulting suspicions and jealousies frequently led to fighting between men. Retaliatory beating of wives was even more frequent. Community cohesion, presumably a societal imperative, was thus undermined by conditions resulting from female infanticide.

Since infanticide among the Inuit was practiced almost exclusively against females, except in cases of physical deformity where a male infant was killed, it was likely a reflection of male dominance. Male dominance was also manifested in violence against women in the form of wife-beating for real or suspected adultery or as an outgrowth of conflicts derived from other sources and tensions. In addition, rape was not uncommon.

Male dominance, however, was tempered by several practices. First, while residence patterns tended to favor patrilateral bonds, couples typically began married life residing with the wife's kin, thus enabling a woman to establish a cooperative relationship with her husband. Second, attitudes toward premarital sexuality were equally permissive concerning girls and boys. Although there was some pressure for an unwed mother to marry the father of her child, it was not intense. Third, flexibility in subsistence activities publicly recognized that tasks could be performed equally well by either women or men. Fourth, decision-making tended to involve people who were directly concerned in the focal activity. Men made decisions regarding their tasks while women did likewise. Knowledgeable people, whether male or female, were well respected and their advice was sought. Fifth, ritual activity tied to economic endeavors symbolized the "gendered interdependence" (Bodenhorn 1993: 198) that is pervasive in Inuit worldview and ethics. And sixth, absence of warfare limited male dominance. Without much intercommunity violence, the kind of warrior ideologies that often enhance men's prestige at the expense of women did not develop.

Religious Beliefs and Practices

The Inuit believe that at the beginning of existence, the earth was covered with a great flood, but then the waters gradually receded, exposing dry earth and creating vast oceans. The sky is thought of as a rigid dome resting on the flat earth. After the earth emerged and seas were formed, human beings were created out of nothingness. Some animals have always existed while others were created by spirit beings. The world is inhabited by many kinds of spirits, some associated with natural forms and forces such as the sun, moon, stars, winds, and air. Thunder and lightning are two sisters who create rain by pouring water from their pails. Spirits associated with seas, lakes, mountains, and other natural locations guard their domains and can help or harm people travelling nearby.

One of the central deities is a being who resides in the bottom of the ocean and controls the yearly supply of sea mammals. She has different names among different Inuit groups but is often called Sedna or "the one from below" (Boas 1964). Myths concerning Sedna are focal explanations for the resources on which Inuit depend. Sedna was once a human being who lived with her father in a small camp. She repeatedly rejected marriage proposals from various young men, finding fault with each one. She finally accepted the proposal of a handsome young stranger who promised to take her to his distant land where life was easy and pleasurable. However, when they got to his island home, Sedna found that it was barren, damp, and lonely. Her husband was not a real person but instead turned into a large bird. After a long period of time, her constant wailing and moaning brought her father from shore to rescue her, but as they were retreating across the ocean, Sedna's husband flew overhead with his companions, flapping their wings to create a storm. In danger of death from drowning, Sedna's father threw her overboard in order to save his own life. Then, as she clung to the boat for safety, he cut off her fingers beginning at the first joint, then at the second joint and finally at the last joint. As each part of her fingers fell into the sea, they turned into sea mammals: the smallest into seals, the middle section into walruses, and the largest into whales. Sedna then sank to the ocean's floor, where she became immortal and dispatched a spirit helper to kill her father as punishment for what he had done to her. But Sedna is also a giver of life since she continues to be responsible for the yearly abundance of sea mammals.

Inuit believe that all living beings have souls. People have two souls residing in their bodies when alive: one, called the "breath of life," disappears when a person dies; the other, called "soul," separates from the body at death and continues to exist in an afterworld. Souls of most people go to a place inside the earth, but souls of women who died in childbirth and of people who died a violent death or committed suicide go instead to an afterworld in the sky.

Animals also have souls and spirit guardians who must be respected. When an animal is killed by a hunter, its soul leaves the body and takes over the body of another animal. Since animals show kindness to humans by allowing themselves to be caught, hunters thank them with prayers. The hunter's wife also thanks the animal's soul by placing cold fresh water in the mouth of a sea mammal or giving a land animal a small present such as a knife, needle case, or container. If these rituals are neglected, spirits who protect animals grow angry and do not allow their kind to be caught, whereas the proper performance of rituals and recitation of prayers and songs helps ensure a successful catch. Because of its prominence in the economy, coastal Alaskan Inupiat follow many ritual prescriptions surrounding whale-hunting. It is believed that whales give themselves to be caught by the ritual preparations and generosity shown by the whaling-captain's wife. Once the whaling crew is out hunting, she has to "move slowly, think peaceful thoughts and act generously" (Bodenhorn 1993: 192). The couple's generosity in providing feasts of whale meat for the entire community further honors the animal.

Out of respect for animals and for the order of the universe, Inuit were careful to keep separate the products of sea and land. Meat from land and sea animals was never cooked in the same pot at the same time; seal meat and caribou meat were never placed next to each other; seal blood was not used to coat arrows used for hunting caribou; and caribou skins were not made into clothing once the seal-hunting season began in early winter.

These and other rules of behavior are consistent with the Inuit concept of "sila," or the order of the universe (Merkur 1989: 19). Inuit believed that all of nature is coordinated through balance, reciprocity, and order. Violating rules of order creates an imbalance in the natural scheme and can lead to disaster if not corrected. People help maintain the order of the universe by ritual, prayer, and song. Such acts also help protect people from the potential danger caused by any unforeseen or inadvertent disturbance of balance. In addition, carrying amulets or charms brings good luck, success, and protection against potentially harmful forces that may create failure and illness.

People sought ritual protection when engaging in dangerous activities. Pregnancy too was surrounded with ritual prohibitions on the behavior of both the expectant mother and her husband. Pregnant women were expected to remain as active as possible in order to have an easy delivery and a healthy birth. Parents also made sure to keep knots out of their laces and belts because they believed that otherwise the umbilical cord might strangle the baby as it was born. In addition, if parents hoped to have a daughter, they might face their tent in an inland direction while if they wanted a son, they faced their tent toward the sea.

When a woman knew that her baby was about to be born, she went alone to a separate shelter and awaited the birth, delivering alone and cutting the umbilical cord herself. The mother then cleansed the baby with the soft skin of a bird. Babies were given their names immediately after birth, usually receiving the name of a recently deceased relative of either gender. Children were cared for and attended to by their parents and other members of the household and community. According to Inuit beliefs, a child's mind was thought of as "unformed at birth," developing gradually during the first years of life (Maxwell 1994: 41). Bonds between parents and children were the primary means by which a child's mind and personality were formed. Naming a child was an important event. In Alaska, children were often named after a respected, recently deceased relative regardless of gender. The name carried with it the personality attributes or knowledge accumulated by the deceased. The "fit" between the child and her/his namesake was critical since an unsuitable name might cause the child to be cranky or even ill (Bodenhorn 1988: 11). If a child were frequently ill, a new name would be given. Linguistic evidence of this practice is revealed by the fact that the Yup'ik word for curing literally means "to rename" (11). In the central Arctic, when a child is about to be born, an elderly woman calls out as many appropriate names as she knows. When the baby hears its name being called, it emerges from its mother.

The only lifecycle event that was consistently ritualized by Inuit was death. When death occurred, the deceased's body was wrapped in animal skins and taken outside. If someone died inside a house, the body was removed through a hole made in a wall rather than through the door normally used by the living. This precaution protected people from the potential harm of contact with the dead. In winter, the body was put in a separate snow house, but in warmer weather it was placed on the ground and covered with rocks or driftwood. Possessions of the deceased, such as kayaks, sleds, utensils, and tools, were piled inside or on top of the grave to aid the deceased's soul in the afterlife. The remainder of the deceased's property was distributed to his/her children. A woman's possessions were given to an eldest daughter while a son received goods owned by his father.

When misfortune struck, people sought the aid of a shaman who could diagnose and treat illnesses, protect people from harmful spirits, predict the future, control the weather, find lost objects, and know the location of sea and land animals. In addition, they journeyed to the spirit realm, conversed with spirit beings, and brought back messages from the dead. Some Inuit also believed that shamans could return to life after they had died.

Shamans were usually recruited through a calling from a spirit, who appeared in a vision or dream and instructed the novice that s/he had special powers that must be used to help others. Once having received a calling, the man or woman sought training from an established shaman in order to learn rituals, prayers, songs, and other skills that would later be used in his/her role as healer and intermediary between ordinary people and spirit beings and forces. A shaman learned how to acquire spirit helpers to assist in rituals and in journeys to the spirit realm. Shamans acted on behalf of their community in contacting spirits and transmitting messages between the spirits and the people. For example, shamans made annual journeys to Sedna in order to obtain sea animals. A shaman's journeys took place during rituals that were intensely dramatic. According to Knud Rasmussen, the journey proceeded as follows:

> The shaman sits for awhile in silence, breathing deeply, and then, he begins to call upon his helping spirits, repeating over and over again: "the way is made ready for me; the way opens before me!"
>
> When the helping spirits have arrived, the earth opens under the shaman. And now one hears at first under the sleeping place: "Halala-he-he-he, ha-la-la-he-he-he!" And afterwards under the passage, below the ground, the same cry. And the sound can be distinctly heard to recede farther and farther until it is lost altogether. Then all know that he is on his way to the ruler of the sea beasts.
>
> Then one hears only sighing and groaning. This sighing and puffing sounds as if the spirits were down under water, in the sea, and in between all the noises one hears the blowing and splashing of creatures coming up to breathe. (Rasmussen 1929; repr. 1975: 14–15)

When the shaman finally arrives at Sedna's dwelling place, the deity responds with anger because of people's misdeeds during the previous year, but after the shaman pleads with her, she relents and releases a sufficient supply of sea animals for the coming season.

In addition to aiding their communities through rituals and prayers, a shaman specialized in treating illnesses that were thought to have spirit causes. For example, when a patient was nervous, agitated, or prone to emotional outbursts, a shaman was likely to conclude that the patient's problem had resulted from violation of a ritual rule or offense that angered a spirit. Shamans began treating patients by prompting them to recall their wrongdoings, followed by a community gathering where the patient made a public confession and received the people's forgiveness. Both the confession and the community's forgiving response helped the patient by relieving guilt and anxiety. Disease could also be caused by the intrusion of foreign objects into a patient's body. Objects such as small pebbles, animal teeth, or pieces of bone might be shot into someone's body by an angry spirit or a human witch to retaliate for some wrongdoing or simply out of malice. When a patient had a localized pain, stiffness, or a burning sensation, the presence of a foreign object was usually suspected. In these cases, the shaman located the object and extracted it by massaging and sucking on the inflamed or hardened part of the body where the object was lodged. Finally, illness could be caused by "soul loss," a process connected to ideas about sleep and dreams. Inuit believe that a person's soul leaves the body during sleep and has adventures that are recalled as dreams. The soul normally returns to the sleeper's body before awakening, but in some cases it is unable to return, either because it has gotten lost and cannot find its way back or because a malevolent spirit, monster, or witch has captured it and blocked its return. Patients who are listless, lack energy and appetite, suffer from insomnia, or lose interest in their normal activities were likely to be victims of soul loss. Such cases are extremely serious because without a soul, a person will die. A shaman must therefore find the soul and return it to the patient's body with the aid of spirit helpers. The search takes place during a ritual performed in a darkened tent or house at night. The shaman stands at the front of the room, the patient lies on the floor nearby, and the rest of the community makes up an apprehensive audience. The shaman enters a trance state and calls on spirit helpers to guide and protect him/her during fierce battles with evil creatures trying to block their path. During this dramatic journey, the audience hears groans and shouts from spirits and monsters in contest over the missing soul. And when the shaman brings the soul back to safety, the patient is enormously relieved and generally recovers and resumes a normal life. Psychological relief results not only from the knowledge that one's soul has been returned but additionally from the heightened emotional experience created by the drama of the ritual itself. A patient is understandably terrified at the prospect of dying because their soul is lost, a terror made more intense during the ritual by hearing the battle between the shaman and the malevolent adversaries. The emotional catharsis that comes at the end of a successful cure helps relieve the tension caused by many kinds of illnesses.

CONSEQUENCES OF EUROPEAN TRADE AND COMMERCIAL ACTIVITY

In the middle of the sixteenth century, Inuit living along the eastern coast of Canada encountered fishermen from France, Portugal, and Spain who sailed to North America in the summer months and caught cod and herring in the North Atlantic ocean near Newfoundland, Labrador, and Québec. Relations between Inuit, who fished and hunted seals in coastal waters, and Europeans were usually friendly although in some cases conflicts erupted, perhaps because the two groups competed over resources.

Toward the end of the sixteenth century, explorers began to venture north into the seas and waterways of the eastern Arctic, searching in vain for a northwest passage to China. Traders joined the expeditions, hoping to establish commercial relations with Native people. The British and French competed in the eastern Arctic for access to the developing fur trade, exchanging the beaver, mink, fox, and seal skins supplied by Inuit for manufactured goods, particularly metal tools and utensils. At the same time, Russian interest in trade with western Arctic people for sea otters, seals, and beavers also intensified.

After 1763, when the "French and Indian War" ended with France's defeat by Great Britain and the expulsion of the French from Labrador, British merchants had an advantage in the region, one that they exploited to the full. They built trading posts in the eastern arctic, tending their stores in the early summer when the sea ice melted and the Inuit came to the posts to exchange their goods for European products. An English explorer, Captain Davidson, who navigated the north coast of Hudson Strait in 1786, noted: "It should be observed that the arrival of the ships is considered by the Inuit as a sort of annual fair; their manufacture of dresses, spears, etc. are reserved for the expected jubilee" (Chappell 1817: 57–58).

When the Hudson Bay Company began commercial operations in the arctic in the mid-seventeenth century, traders usually remained at their stores, exchanging goods with Inuit who came to them, but in the later years of the next century, merchants began to send agents into interior regions to establish trading networks with inland communities. Relations between Inuit and Britons were generally friendly as attested by Moses Norton, governor of Fort Churchill on the western coast of Hudson Bay:

> I have the vanity to think that if any accident was to happen to the English, I have reasons to believe that the Natives would rather assist a man in distress than to do otherwise by him. (Morton 1973: 146)

British merchants also opened trading posts along the Labrador coast to trade with Inuit who brought whale bone and blubber in exchange for manufactured products and a few foods such as flour, tea, and sugar. In addition to trade carried out with merchants, Inuit exchanged their goods with sailors aboard ships, informally bargaining over terms of trade (Chappell 1817: 63–64).

In response to conditions stimulated by trade, Inuit began to alter their economic activities and settlement patterns. To obtain the goods that they wanted, people shifted some of their time and energy to trapping in order to procure the animals skins that traders demanded. At first, the shift away from traditional economic activities toward trapping was gradual and had little impact on Native life and culture, but it was the beginning of a trend that deepened throughout the nineteenth and twentieth centuries. Once traders and sailors remained in the Arctic during the winter as well as summer months, Inuit had prolonged contact with them and, as a result, trading activities assumed greater importance. The Hudson Bay Company enlarged its number of stores, strengthened its control over Inuit activities, monopolized trade, and set prices and standardized terms of exchange (Erlandson [1834]1963: 259). Since the worth of the Inuit's labor and of the products brought in for trade were undervalued, men had to spend more time trapping animals while women prepared the skins for market, intensifying a process of economic transformation that had begun decades earlier. In addition, some people gradually shifted their residence patterns to be closer to trading posts during most, if not all, of the year.

In some cases, Inuit living near the stores acted as intermediaries between traders and indigenous people in more remote regions, collecting furs from interior groups, exchanging them for goods at the stores, and distributing the goods to the original trappers. This system was in effect by the late nineteenth century, as noted by a Canadian observer, F. F. Payne: "It is remarkable that, although the Inuit traders carry as many as 30 or 40 parcels of furs owned by different families, they seemed quite able to remember on their return, to whom the goods they obtained in exchange belong, apparently the only note being made by a few marks with their teeth upon some of the articles" (Payne 1888–1889: 221).

By the middle of the nineteenth century, European, Canadian, and American whaling operations rapidly expanded in the eastern Arctic in search of whale blubber to be used for oiling tools and machinery as well as for lighting lamps and street lights in American and European cities. They also sought whale bone or baleen, extracted from the upper jaw of bowhead whales, for use in corset stays, hoop skirts, buggy whips, umbrella ribs, fishing rods, chair seats, and mattresses. At first, whaling vessels operated in the Arctic only during the summer, but in the 1840s, whalers began to stay over during the winter, constructing harbors on the Atlantic coast of Labrador and Québec and along the shores of Hudson Strait and Hudson Bay. Inuit supplied the Europeans with food during the long winter months and worked as whalers and boatmen aboard the ships. In most cases, relations between Inuit and Europeans were friendly, as noted by an English captain, M'Clintock, in 1859: "The Inuit men were stout, hardy fellows, and the women were arrant thieves, but all were good humored and friendly. There was not a trace of fear, every countenance was lighted up with joy; even the children were not shy, nor backward either, in crowding about us, poking in everywhere" (M'Clintock 1859: 212, 236). In contrast to this favorable portrayal, though, some observers described negative aspects of encounters between Inuit and Europeans. A German scientist, Bernhard Hantzch, traveling with a Canadian fleet in the early twentieth century, noted that whaling crews took advantage of the people: "[They] treated the Natives in shameless fashion, betraying the men with a little tobacco, and the women with Branntwein … the poor Eskimos yielded themselves to degrading influences, not from badness of character, but from frivolity, good humored compliance, and heathenish ignorance" (Hantzsch 1977: 98–99).

Despite reports of the "good humored compliance" of the Inuit, indigenous people were threatened by the intruders' presence. Observing that Europeans were able to catch a large number of fish with their nets and kill many sea and land animals with their guns, Inuit sometimes attacked and killed foreign whalers, fishers, and hunters who were taking scarce resources. In addition, several epidemics of measles and influenza struck Inuit communities in the nineteenth century, resulting in many deaths and spreading fear among survivors, who saw the destructive effects of these previously unknown ailments.

In the early nineteenth century, Russian merchants turned their attention northward and inland from their original bases along the southwestern coast of Alaska. Since the supply of sea otters, hunted by Aleuts, declined considerably because of overkill, Russian traders contacted Inuit who lived along the northern coast and in the Alaskan interior in their search for beaver and mink furs. The Russian-American company established its first trading post in Inuit territory in 1818. Russian merchants also travelled to Native settlements to make direct contact with the people. The Inuit supplied beaver pelts in return for iron tools, copper bracelets, glass beads, and some items of clothing. As in the eastern Arctic, trading activities affected Native culture as people gradually became dependent on traders for manufactured goods.

After 1850, European and American whaling ships expanded their operations from the eastern Arctic into the waters near Alaska, trading with and employing Inuit aboard whaling ships and at coastal whaling stations. But cultural conflict sometimes arose between Native employees and foreign whalers. According to Inuit custom, hunters needed to follow ritual rules to ensure a successful catch, but foreign whalers refused to comply, as attested by recollections of Charles Brower, the first American hunter in the region:

> In everything we [Americans] did the Inuit found fault with, saying if we did thus and so the whales would never come along the ice. First they objected to our hammering after the sun came up, the whales would hear us, whales could hear a long distance. Our gear was wrong; they had never used that kind, it was forbidden. Tents were out of the question, as for cooking on the ice, that was not to be thought of. When they found out we were getting extra footgear to take with us, that was the limit, then they knew we would never get a whale. (Blackman 1989: 16)

Commercial whaling increased in the late nineteenth century when American whalers began to winter over in Alaska, founding two major whaling stations, one at Barrow in 1884 and the second at Point Hope in 1887. In addition to Inuit's participation in whaling and trapping, they worked in the commercial salmon industry that developed in Alaska in the 1880s.

Missionaries came to the Arctic as well, in the late eighteenth century. Moravians were the first to arrive, working among Inuit along the eastern coast of Labrador and Québec. Although their earliest attempts met with little success, Moravian missions increased in the nineteenth century as ministers traveled into the interior of the Canadian Arctic. Moravians also operated stores and thus competed with commercial trading companies. As they became involved in trade, they gained influence in the Native communities. At roughly the same time, Russian Orthodox priests began missionary activities in Alaska, with policies set forth by church officials in Russia, who instructed the priests to respect the customs and cultures of indigenous people, learning Native languages and translating the Bible and other religious texts. They also opened schools in some coastal communities and established a seminary in the town of Sitka to train Aleut and Inuit converts to become clergy so that they could work among their own people. In addition, they operated health clinics, providing medical care and attempting to improve health and sanitary conditions. After 1867 when the territory of Alaska was sold by Russia to the United States, many Orthodox clergy returned to their home country, but some remained among the Inuit and continued their missionary, educational, and medical activities.

Once Alaska became a possession of the United States, American missionaries from several Protestant sects began efforts to convert the Inuit to their own religions, competing for influence among the indigenous population. In 1884, the US Congress passed the Alaska Organic Act that, among other provisions, affirmed that the territorial government should not interfere with indigenous people's traditional uses of land and sea resources, but it did allow interference with aboriginal cultural practices and mandated education for Inuit and Aleut children. After a Presbyterian minister, Sheldon Jackson, was appointed superintendent of education for Alaska, the territory was divided into regional sections, each under the control of a specific Protestant church. Although Russian Orthodox clergy were omitted from the scheme, they continued to run private church schools in some Inuit communities and defended people against abuse by traders and government agents. For example, in 1897, Bishop Nikolai of Alaska sent a letter of protest to US President McKinley detailing fraudulent actions by merchants of the Alaska Commercial Company and criticizing educational policies of Superintendent Jackson. Although the Russian priests were dedicated to converting the Inuit, they opposed forced "westernization," recognizing that traditional subsistence activities and some social institutions were beneficial to Native survival (Kan 1985; Smith 1980).

Changes in the Twentieth Century

The twentieth century brought an acceleration of changes in Inuit economy and social life as people became dependent on manufactured goods and as traditional subsistence activities were replaced by trapping and wage work. In Alaska, the commercial whaling industry declined because the demand for whale oil disappeared after the discovery of petroleum in Pennsylvania in the 1860s. The market for baleen also sharply diminished because of rising prices due to the overkill of whales. Baleen was then replaced with cheaper substitutes, principally rubber molded over a thin piece of steel. When whalers abandoned the arctic, Inuit who had traded with them or worked for them found themselves in a difficult economic situation, but as whaling declined, another economic opportunity arose, namely the hunting and trapping of Arctic animals (especially fox and mink) destined for Canadian, American, and European markets. It was fortunate that trapping appeared as a replacement for whaling since people were still able to obtain manufactured goods that they wanted, but the rapid shift to trapping covered up a deeper problem in the new Inuit economy, namely its continued reliance on industries that were unstable and unpredictable. Just as prices for whale products had risen and fallen due to factors outside Inuit control, prices for animal furs also reacted to external market forces. Native economic security therefore remained uncertain since people were not able to affect or control the markets on which they depended.

The shift to trapping for external markets had a series of effects on community life. Since the new technology made it more likely for a hunter to be successful than in the past, he no longer needed cooperation and assistance from other men. Traditional patterns of food distribution therefore weakened. Rather than share one's catch with other members of the settlement, people kept what they had caught or distributed it within a small network of relatives. Trapping also became an individual endeavor since men worked trap lines by themselves and kept the products received from traders for their own or their family's use.

Whale hunting, of course, continued to be a collective effort, but even this activity changed from previous times. In the past, members of a whaling crew usually remained together year after year, forming a stable social network even when the whaling season ended. But such communal bonds gradually weakened as whaling crews were recruited only on a limited seasonal basis. The decline in cooperative labor and in sharing resources with all members of one's community led to shifts in family relations. The nuclear family became more important than the wider extended family that had previously been the norm for reciprocal economic and household tasks.

Due to changes in economic activities, people tended to remain in more permanent settlements, altering patterns of seasonal movement. Villages sprang up around trading posts and administrative centers that were much larger than Native settlements of the past, numbering as many as 300 people. Although the new pattern of permanent residence made life more secure for the Inuit, who no longer had to endure difficult and dangerous journeys from place to place, the growth of larger settlements posed some new problems for Native society (Graburn 1969). In the past, social order and cooperation were easily maintained within a small camp. Community leaders had informal influence, ensuring cooperation among their own family members and among others in the settlement as well, most of whom were related in some way. But in the new system, many people living in a community were strangers to one another, having no traditional basis for cooperation. Family leaders could not automatically use their influence when disputes or social tensions arose.

In the early years of the century, the American government turned its attention to the schooling of children in Alaska. Until that time, Inuit, Aleut, and American children attended schools together in their local district, but as American settlements grew, the newcomers complained that they did not want their children attending school with Native youngsters and pressured the government to segregate the schools. Educational policy was clearly set forth in a statement issued by the Alaska Bureau of Education in 1911: "The work of the Bureau of Education, which is conducted for the benefit of adults as well as children, is practical in character, emphasis being placed on the development of domestic industries, household arts, personal hygiene, village sanitation, and the elementary English

subjects" (Blackman 1989: 20–21). According to the recollections of an Inuit man, John Tetton:

I'll never forget my first day at school. I had waited for this day for years—to enter the white framed building where my two older brothers read books and learned to write their names. I was 6 years old and didn't know a word of English. Excited, I jabbered away to all my friends in Inupiaq.

From the front of the room, the teacher studied us closely. He was a big man with giant hands, dressed in a white shirt and tie. He walked slowly around the room and suddenly, out of nowhere, his great big hand grabbed me around the neck. He shoved a big bar of soap into my mouth. "No one here will speak Inupiaq," he ordered. (Chance 1990: 7)

The economic situation of Inuit both in Alaska and Canada vacillated in the early decades of the twentieth century as prices for fox and mink first rose and then fell. During rising times, a greater number of people shifted from subsistence hunting to commercial trapping and trading, but when fur prices fell sharply in the 1930s during the worldwide economic depression, Inuit suffered severely. By that time, Inuit in Canada had become dependent on the Hudson Bay Company, whose policies bound Native trappers and hunters in a non-cash system of exchange (Innis 1930: 362). Since the Company paid trappers in goods and tokens rather than in cash and since Inuit could redeem tokens only at Company stores, people's dependency was secured. Furthermore, Inuit were unable to hunt caribou for their subsistence because the herds had greatly diminished, partly from overkill and partly from diseases affecting the animals. In Labrador, Québec, and the Northwest territories, many people suffered periods of starvation and many died as a result. The Canadian government and the Hudson Bay Company responded by offering temporary financial assistance and food supplies. By that time, the government had begun to assert its control over the vast Arctic regions, sending members of the Royal Canadian Mounted Police (RCMP) to establish stations throughout Inuit territory. Actual control exerted by the RCMP was minimal, but they did establish contact with some groups who had previously been influenced very little by the Anglo world. The government also acted to improve health conditions, opening nursing stations that provided basic medical care services. Epidemic diseases such as measles, influenza, and tuberculosis were devastating to the Inuit. In Labrador, for example, during the worldwide influenza epidemic of 1918 and 1919, one-third of the Inuit population died in a period of only three months.

After World War II as the "Cold War" developed, a new source of income emerged for some Inuit as the governments of the United States and Canada began to build the Distant Early Warning (DEW) defense system consisting of approximately fifty radar stations spread from Alaska to Labrador at a total cost of $600 million. Inuit were employed in construction and maintenance of the DEW line, but since their employment was related to national foreign policy, it proved temporary in nature. However, the scope of government policies and operations in the Arctic increased during that period. In Canada, the government took over the educational system that had previously been operated by missions, building additional schools and mandating compulsory primary education. They opened additional nursing stations to offer basic medical treatment and also provided family allowances for needy people.

In the United States, governmental regulations affected traditional hunting and fishing activities by setting quotas for several species of animals and birds. Extension of the Migratory Bird Act of 1916 to the Arctic outlawed the hunting of migratory waterfowl from May through September, although that was the only period when ducks and geese inhabit the region. The Act therefore denied Inuit the right to hunt waterfowl at the very time that the birds are abundant in their territory. The application of the Migratory Bird Act to the Inuit was repealed after people in Barrow, Alaska, staged a protest in 1961, supported by some public sentiment in the state: "As it is now the federal government won't let the Natives take ducks and geese while ducks and geese are in the Arctic, but after the birds go south, where they are killed by the thousands by white sportsmen, the government says to the hungry Native, 'Now you can hunt'" (Rev. John Chambers, *Fairbanks Daily News Miner*, May 31,1961; in Blackman 1989: 181).

After 1959, when Alaska was granted statehood, the new state government took over educational services, ending the system of segregated schooling for Inuit children. However, other federal programs continued to affect the Native way of life. BIA officials encouraged the formation of village councils, but the councils were not fully independent, operating instead under the supervision of BIA agents. In Canada, similar local councils were established as intermediaries between Native communities and federal bureaucracies, but they too were not consistent with indigenous patterns of leadership, rather imposing Anglo norms of authority and decision-making (Graburn 1969: 212).

CONTEMPORARY INUIT COMMUNITIES

Inuit in the United States and Canada number at least 125,000 according to census statistics from the two countries. The 2011 Census of Canada recorded 59,445 Inuit, almost three-quarters living in the Inuit-majority territory of Nunavut and Nunavik. In addition to the 27,070 Inuit in Nunavut and 10,750 in Nunavik, 12,575 reside in Québec, 6,265 in Newfoundland (Labrador), 3,360 in Ontario, and smaller numbers in other provinces. Their population has increased some 18 percent between 2006 and 2011, due to a high birthrate. The US Census of 2000 reported 44,381 Inuit shareholders in Alaskan regional corporations set up pursuant to the Alaskan Natives Claims Settlement Act of 1971 (US Bureau of the Census 2000: 23, 29). Ryan Madden's 2005 book claims that 80,000 Inuits have been enrolled in the program (Madden 2005).

Inuit communities in Alaska and Canada are mixtures of old traditions and new ways of living. A recent description of the northernmost Alaskan town of Barrow can stand for many Arctic communities:

> Barrow's three well stocked grocery stores notwithstanding, fish and bearded seal meat hang to dry in the summer sun from racks beside the houses. A Native student participating in a summer archeology dig misses a day of work to go walrus hunting with his father; an umiak rests upside down next to a Plexiglas bus stop. The sleek city buses take shotgun toting Inuit six miles north of town where enormous flocks of ducks fly to and from their summer feeding grounds. The mayor of Barrow has been a whaling captain, and the former magistrate found time to sew new clothing for members of her husband's whaling crew. The cabs in town may not run in the spring because their drivers are out on the ice, hunting whales. (Blackman 1989: 4)

Since the 1960s, important developments have taken place in Inuit communities. Economic cooperatives have been formed in Canada and Alaska to market sculpture, paintings, prints, calendars, and embroidered clothing to galleries and shops in Canada, the United States, and Europe. In fact, craft production is a major source of income for many Inuit, continuing a style of artwork dating back thousands of years. Cooperatives also organize local businesses such as lumber mills, bakeries, house and boat construction firms, and canneries for Native foods.

Wage work has become a primary means of livelihood in the north. The shift to wage work is perhaps more significant in Alaska than in the Canadian Arctic. Jobs are available in construction, lumbering, oil fields, and salmon canneries in addition to service sector occupations in local businesses, restaurants, and shops. But the shift to working for wages has altered a traditional community orientation once prevalent in Native society. As people now often say, "You cannot share money the way you can share food" (Bodenhorn 1988: 8). In the Canadian Arctic, most available jobs are connected to government agencies providing health, educational, social welfare, and police services. But despite the growth of employment, many Inuit, especially those living in small communities with few job opportunities, continue to face poverty and hunger. Conditions were noted by a report issued in 1968 by the US Federal Field Committee for Development Planning in Alaska:

> A great contrast exists today between the high income, moderate standard of living and existence of reasonable opportunity of most Alaskans and the appallingly low income and standard of living and virtual absence of opportunity for most Eskimos, Indians, and Aleuts of Alaska … The economic position of Alaskan Natives, and of the communities in which they live, is steadily falling further behind state wide averages. (1968: 3, 528)

And in the words of an Alaskan man in 1990:

> Again spring is here with us, and work and jobs are pretty dim in our area. Last year, all the men were without work all summer long. It is tough with our work and hunting only does not meet our needs. Sometimes we have bad luck even though we hunt. We have to worry where our next meal will be. (Chance 1990: 134)

Statistics compiled by the Canadian Census Bureau in 2006 reveal continuing high rates of unemployment in Inuit communities. The average unemployment rate stood at 19.0 percent but many villages had rates exceeding that. This rate is almost four times the 5.2 percent unemployment rate in Canada in 2006. Data past 1989 is not available for Inuit in Alaska, but analysis of several smaller communities suggests Inuit in the United States have a similar unemployment rate to their Canadian counterparts (Inuit Tapiriit Kanatami 2011).

In Alaska and Canada, the growth of mining and resource industries has provided jobs for some people but has also roused controversy involving claims over rights to land, land-management decisions, and economic and political self-determination. The first major governmental agreement stimulated by resource development in the Arctic occurred in Alaska after the discovery of oil in 1968 motivated American energy companies to submit bids for exploration and extraction. In order to first settle Native claims, the US government negotiated with members of the Alaska Federation of Natives, representatives of Inuit and other indigenous people, to resolve territorial issues. Their negotiations culminated in 1971 in passage of the Alaskan Natives Claims Settlement Act that provides for Inuit and Indians to select 44 million acres of land, relinquish legal claim to the remainder of the state, and receive payment of $962.5 million distributed over a period of eleven years (Arnold et al. 1978; see Chapter 23 for discussion of the Claims and Settlement Act). The Act created thirteen regional corporations and over 200 village corporations, granting shares to Native residents. Corporations receive cash payments awarded under the Settlement Act and can either invest the money or distribute it to shareholders. Corporations must also operate businesses, some for profit.

In 1993, Inuit residing in the Northwest territories reached a historic agreement with the Canadian government after a plebiscite showed overwhelming support for creation of a new territory to be administered entirely by indigenous residents. The governmental agreement, called the Nunavut Final Land Claim Agreement, divides the Northwest territories into two regions. The majority-Inuit territory now called Nunavut or "Our Land" came into existence on April 1, 1999 (see Chapter 23 for discussion of the founding of Nunavut).

In Arctic Québec, changes toward self-government have also advanced since 1989 when, an election was held in the fourteen villages making up Québec's north, now called Nunavik, for six members to a constituent

A traditional qamutik (sled) in the Inuit village of Cape Dorset, Nunavut, in 1999.

more than $1.4 billion million annually ("Québec's Budget Sets Millions Aside for Nunavik's Plan Nord" 2015). However, despite these efforts, unemployment rates remain high due to the lack of jobs and to the lack of training for the few skilled, technical, and managerial positions that are available. Many jobs require a higher level of education and training than the local population have achieved and therefore are held by people from outside the region. Although education has improved in Inuit communities, only 51 percent of Canadian Inuit held a high school (or equivalent) diploma in 2006, and less than 36 percent had completed some form of postsecondary education, including college, trade school, and other certification programs (Statistics Canada 2006).

In many Canadian Inuit communities, concerns over the social integration of communities has led to the development of programs not only to train young people in new skills but also to encourage them to appreciate their traditional culture. Instruction in schools is done in the Native language, Inuktitut, from kindergarten through the third grade. Thereafter, children are instructed in Inuktitut and in either French or English. The schools are managed by local school boards and thus provide a comprehensive education stressing traditional values and culture as well as skills and techniques needed to improve standards of living. The curriculum differs considerably from that in the past where, according to an Inuit commissioner of education, "In federal schools, I learned about the existence of countries far away in Asia and Africa. I didn't learn until recently where the countries were where Inuit lived, my people: Greenland, NorthWest Territories, Alaska. How I would have liked to learn what they teach today in our schools!" (Annie Tertiluk, in *Rencontre*, Winter 1994–1995: 10).

The administration of social service programs and of local policing and judicial functions has similarly been taken over by Inuit communities. Health

assembly or Parnaitiit to draft a constitution establishing regional government. Although Nunavik is not separate from the province of Québec, it is a region of functional self-government with powers to prepare legislation, organize and administer funds provided through the James Bay and Northern Québec Agreement, and develop and pursue programs in education, social welfare, health, local policing, and administration (see Chapter 23).

The villages in Nunavik, with an aggregate population of more than 6,000, have expanded considerably from small temporary camps to settled villages. Although most are quite small by Canadian standards, their large size compared to villages of traditional times presents problems of adjustment. The largest village, Inukjuak, on the coast of Hudson Bay, has a population of more than 800. Inukjuak, like many other villages in the territory, has a school, dispensary, and new housing built under programs sponsored by the federal government. In addition, an airport was recently opened that provides the only means of contact with the Canadian south. A serious problem in Inukjuak, though, is the lack of employment, leading most people to rely on traditional hunting or income from production of soapstone sculpture. Under agreements with the Québec government, Nunavut manages local programs for job creation and training, administering a budget of programs, nursing stations, field nursing personnel, and health maintenance education are also in the hands of local authorities and employees.. The availability of traditional foods such as sea mammals and fish aids in the survival of Inuit who do not have access to jobs and therefore do not have cash for the purchase of processed foods. Such a traditional diet rich in protein and a diet to which Inuit have adapted biochemically over the past millennia is enormously beneficial. However, recent findings of contamination in the food supply from PCBs, lead, and mercury point to the dangers inherent in exploiting traditional sources of food. The harmful chemicals and minerals found in the food have resulted from industrial waste that has been emitted into rivers and oceans by industries in southern Canada and brought to the arctic by ocean currents and winds. Since many industrial wastes, particularly PCBs, do not biodegrade, they remain in the environment for many years and still present a problem of contamination today, even though they have been banned since 1977. PCBs are absorbed by animal and human fat and have been found to accumulate in the fatty tissues of fish, seals, walruses, whales, and other marine animals as well as in the stomachs and livers of polar bears. Inuit are particularly vulnerable to these contaminants because a large part of their diet comes from fish and sea mammals. In humans, exposure to PCBs affects the skin, liver, kidneys, and reproductive systems and may be carcinogenic. They accumulate and are found in blood and especially in breast milk of nursing women (*Rencontre*, June 1989: 5). And since most Inuit babies are breastfed for a year or more, they are particularly at risk for developing both short-term and long-term health problems. However, despite drawbacks associated with traditional foods, processed imported foods also present difficulties, particularly lack of overall nutritional content and excess sugars and salts.

Studies of Inuit's health today reveal both positive and negative trends. Blood pressure levels and cholesterol and sugar rates indicate that heart disease is virtually absent in Nunavik, but tuberculosis and other respiratory ailments are prevalent. Hearing loss is also common, a result of modern equipment such as snowmobiles, motor boats, and motor bikes that are used by many Inuit, particularly men. Dental problems are widespread as well, due to diet and

to lack of preventive care (*Rencontre*, June 1996: 9). A report issued by health researchers assessed data on mental health, including stress and suicide attempts And concluded that these problems are "indications that the social, cultural and technological upheaval that Inuit have experienced since the late 1950s have left wounds that also need to be healed" (6).

As an Inuit elder, Mitiarjuk, commented while recalling differences between her community today and those of the past:

> The Inuit now know how much that [cultural change, drugs, alcohol] can change the life. They're getting a grip on themselves. Things have improved since they began to realize that their culture has been upset too much. That upset was part of our lives, everything was new, everything was being tested. We were told it was for the best. We believed that. We lived through all that, and now we're making our own assessment. Things can only get better. (*Rencontre*, Fall 1994: 6–7)

Another, named Naalak, recalled,

> Inuit used to help one another every way they could. By sharing food, when a man got a seal, it would be distributed to every family. Women who hadn't learned to sew would be taught by other women. When one camp was short of food, some men from other camps would bring food to that camp. If someone went shopping in a community that had a trading post or a small store, they would share what they bought with their neighbors. Nowadays, we don't seem to know who needs help anymore. (*Rencontre*, Winter 1995–1996: 15)

And, finally, an Alaskan teenager, just graduated from high school, looked both toward the past and the future:

> I see myself getting an education and growing up in a modern town. Because of my heritage and culture, I spend a lot of time thinking about that. I try to mix both together and take the best of the two, and try to be myself too. I don't want to forget about my past culture because of whom I am. But I can't go back 10,000 years ago. I've got to go to school and find a job—try to relate it to who I am and what I want to be. (Chance 1990: 91)

REFERENCES

Arnold, Robert *et al.* 1978. *Alaska Native Land Claims.* Anchorage: Alaska Native Foundation.

Balikci, Asen. 1967. "Female Infanticide on the Arctic Coast." *Man* 2, no. 4: 615–625.

Balikci, Asen. 1970. *The Netsilik Eskimo.* Garden City, NY: Natural History Press.

Blackman, Margaret. 1989. *Sadie Brower Neakok, An Inupiaq Woman.* Seattle, WA: University of Washington Press.

Boas, Franz. [1888]1964. *The Central Eskimo.* Lincoln, NE: University of Nebraska Press.

Bodenhorn, Barbara. *1988.* "Whales, Souls, Children, and Other Things that Are 'Good to Share': Core Metaphors in a Contemporary Whaling Society." *Cambridge Anthropology* 13, no. 1: 1–19.

Bodenhorn, Barbara. 1993. "Gendered Spaces, Public Places: Public and Private Revisited on the North Slope of Alaska." *Landscape: Politics and Perspectives* (ed. B. Bender). Providence, RI: Berg, pp. 169–203.

Briggs, Jean. 1974. "Eskimo Women: Makers of Men." *Many Sisters* (ed. C. Matthiason). New York: Free Press, pp. 261–304.

Chance, Norman. 1990. *The Inupiat and Arctic Alaska.* New York: Holt, Rinehart, and Winston.

Chappell, W. 1817. *Narrative of a Voyage to Hudson's Bay in His Majesty's Ship Rosamund.* London.

Damas, David. *1984.* "Introduction." *Arctic* (ed. D. Damas), Vol. 5 of *Handbook of North American Indians.* Washington, DC: Smithsonian Institution Press, pp. 1–7.

Erlandson, Erland. [1834]1963. "Journal and Correspondence." *Northern Québec and Labrador Journals and Correspondence 1819–1835* (ed. K. G. Davies). Vol. 24 of Hudson's Bay Record Society.

Graburn, Nelson. 1969. *Eskimos without Igloos: Social and Economic Development in Sugluk.* Boston, MA: Little, Brown.

Hantzsch, Bernard. 1977. *My Life among the Eskimos* (ed. L. H. Neatby). Saskatoon: University of Saskatchewan Press.

Innis, Harold. 1930. *The Fur Trade in Canada.* New Haven, CT: Yale University Press.

Inuit Tapiriit Kanatami. 2011. *Inuit Population.* Ottawa, Canada.

Itoh, Shinji. 1980. "Physiology of Circumpolar People." *The Human Biology of Circumpolar Populations* (ed. F. A. Milan). Cambridge: Cambridge University Press.

Kan, Sergei. 1985. "Russian Orthodox Brotherhoods among the Tlingit: Missionary Goals and Native Response." *Ethnohistory* 32, no. 3: 196–222.

Madden, Ryan. 2005. *Alaska: On-the-Road Histories.* Northampton, MA: Interlink Books.

M'Clintock, Francis. 1859. *The Voyage of the "Fox" in the Arctic Seas.* London: J. Murray.

Merkur, Daniel. 1989. "Arctic: Inuit." *Witchcraft and Sorcery of the American Native Peoples.* (ed. D. Walker, and D. Carrasco). Moscow, ID: University of Idaho Press, pp. 11–22.

"Québec's Budget Sets Millions Aside for Nunavik's Plan Nord." 2015. *Nunatsiaq News.* Online.

Payne, F. F. 1888–1889. "Eskimo of Hudson's Strait." *Proceedings of the Canadian Institute,* 3rd ser., 6: 213–230.

Rasmussen, Knud. 1929. *Intellectual Culture of the Iglulik Eskimo.* Report of the Fifth Thule Expedition 1921–1924, 7.1. Copenhagen: Cyldendalske Boghandel.

Rasmussen, Knud. 1931. *The Netsilik Eskimos: Social Life and Spiritual Culture.* Copenhagen: Report of the Fifth Thule Expedition 1921–1924, 8.1–2.

Rencontre. June 1989. Québec: Secretariat Aux Affaires Autochtones.

Rencontre. Fall 1994. Québec: Secretariat Aux Affaires Autochtones.

Rencontre. Winter 1994–1995. Québec: Secretariat Aux Affaires Autochtones.

Rencontre. June 1996. Québec: Secretariat Aux Affaires Autochtones.

Romm, Joe. 2015. *Rate of Climate Change to Soar by 2020s, with Artic Warming 1F Per Decade.* Center for American Progress Action Fund. Online.

Saladin d'Aglure, Bernard. "Inuit of Québec." *Arctic* (ed. D. Damas), Vol. 5 of *Handbook of North American Indians.* Washington, DC: Smithsonian Institution Press, pp. 476–507.

Siebens, Julie, and Tiffany Julian. 2011. "Native North American Languages Spoken at Home in the United States and Puerto Rico." American Community Survey Briefs. US Bureau of the Census.

Smith, Barbara. 1980. *Russian Orthodoxy in Alaska: A History, Inventory, and Analysis of the Church Archives in Alaska.* Anchorage, AK: Alaska Historical Commission.

Spencer, Robert. 1967. "Eskimo Customary Law." *North American Indians: A Sourcebook* (ed. R. Owen *et al.*). New York: Macmillan, pp. 160–169.

Statistics Canada. 2011. "Language Highlight Tables." *2011 Census.* Ottawa, Canada.

US Bureau of the Census. 2000. Washington, DC.

US Federal Field Committee for Development Planning in Alaska. 1968. *Alaska Natives and the Land.* Washington, DC: US Government Printing Office.

WEBSITES FOR NATIVE NATIONS IN THE UNITED STATES AND CANADA

As noted at the outset, the Native nations of North America are a tremendously diverse group. The following list provides links to available websites for many individual Native American tribes and First Nations. In addition to these resources, a list of all US federally recognized tribes and Canadian First Nations peoples is available via the book's webpage at www.rowman.com.

CHAPTER 4: THE NORTHEAST

Ojibwa/Chippewa: http://www.mnchippewatribe.org (Minnesota Chippewa Tribe official website)

http://www.saulttribe.com (Sault Tribe of Chippewa Indians official website)

http://tmbci.kkbold.com (Turtle Mountain Band of Chippewa Indians official website)

http://www.sagchip.org (Saginaw Chippewa Indian Tribe official website)

http://www.boisforte.com (Bois Forte Band of Chippewa official website)

http://www.fdlrez.com (Fond du Lac Band of Lake Superior Chippewa official website)

http://www.llojibwe.com (Leech Lake Band of Ojibwe official website)

http://millelacsband.com (Mille Lacs Band of Ojibwe official website)

http://www.whiteearth.com (White Earth Nation Band of Ojibwe official website)

CHAPTER 5: THE MOHAWKS

Mohawk: http://www.kahnawake.com (Mohawk Council of Kahnawà:ke official website)

http://www.akwesasne.ca (Mohawk Council of Akwesasne official website)

http://www.srmt-nsn.gov (Saint Regis Mohawk Tribe official website)

CHAPTER 6: THE MI'KMAQS

Mi'kmaq: http://www.micmac-nsn.gov (Aroostook Band of Micmacs official website)

http://www.abegweit.ca (Abegweit First Nation official website)

http://www.acadiafirstnation.ca (Acadia First Nation official website)

http://www.bearriverfirstnation.ca/Bear_River_First_Nation/Welcome.html (Bear River First Nation official website)

http://www.esgenoopetitjfirstnation.org (Esgenoopetitj First Nation official website)

http://www.potlotek.ca (Potlotek (Chapel Island First Nation) official website)

http://www.eelgroundfirstnation.ca (Eel Ground First Nation official website)

https://www.elsipogtog.ca (Elsipogtog First Nation official website)

http://www.eskasoni.ca/home/ (Eskasoni Mi'Kmaw Nation official website)

http://www.fortfolly.nb.ca/firstpg6.html (Fort Folly First Nation official website)

http://www.gespeg.ca/english.html (Micmac Nation of Gespeg official website)

http://www.glooscapfirstnation.com (Glooscap First Nation official website)

http://indianisland.ca (Indian Island First Nation official website)

http://www.lennoxisland.com (Lennox Island First Nation official website)

http://www.listuguj.ca (Listuguj Mi'gmaq Government official website)

http://www.membertou.ca (Membertou First Nation official website)

http://www.mfngov.ca (Miawpukek First Nation official website)

http://qalipu.ca (Qalipu Mi'kmaq First Nation Band official website)

http://millbrookfirstnation.net (Millbrook First Nation official website)

http://www.pabineaufirstnation.ca (Pabineau First Nation official website)

http://paqtnkek.ca (Paqtnkek Mi'kmaw Nation official website)

http://www.plfn.ca (Pictou Landing First Nation official website)

http://sipeknekatik.ca (Sipekne'katik (Indian Brook First Nation) official website)

http://www.wagmatcook.com (Wagmatcook First Nation official website)

http://www.waycobah.ca (Waycobah First Nation official website)

CHAPTER 7: THE SOUTHEAST

Cherokee: http://www.cherokee.org (Cherokee Nation official website)

http://nc-cherokee.com (Eastern Band of Cherokee official website)

http://www.keetoowahcherokee.org (United Keetoowah Band of Cherokee Indians in Oklahoma official website)

Seminole: http://www.semtribe.com (Seminole Tribe of Florida official website)

http://sno-nsn.gov (Great Seminole Nation of Oklahoma official website)

http://www.miccosukeeseminolenation.com (Sovereign Miccosukee Seminole Nation official website)

CHAPTER 8: THE CHOCTAWS

Choctaw: http://www.choctawnation.com (Choctaw Nation of Oklahoma official website)

http://www.jenachoctaw.org (Jena Band of Choctaw Indians official website)

http://www.unitedhoumanation.org (United Houma Nation official website)

http://www.choctaw-apache.org (Choctaw Apache Tribe of Ebarb official website)

http://www.chahta.org (Mount Tabor Indian Community official website, currently under construction)

http://www.choctaw.org (Mississippi Band of Choctaw Indians)

CHAPTER 9: THE PLAINS

Cheyenne: http://www.cheyennenation.com (Northern Cheyenne Tribe official site) http://www.c-a-tribes.org (Cheyenne and Arapaho Tribes official website)

Crow: http://www.crow-nsn.gov (Crow Nation official website)

Comanche: http://www.comanchenation.com (Comanche Nation of Oklahoma official website)

CHAPTER 10: THE TETON LAKOTAS

Teton Lakota: http://www.oglalalakotanation.org/oln/Home.html (Oglala Lakota Nation official website)

http://www.rosebudsiouxtribe-nsn.gov (Rosebud Sioux Tribe official website)

http://www.standingrock.org (Standing Rock Sioux Tribe official website)

http://www.sioux.org (Cheyenne River Sioux Tribe official website)

CHAPTER 11: THE HIDATSAS

Hidatsas: http://www.mhanation.com (MHA (Mandan, Hidatsa, and Arikara) Nation official website)

CHAPTER 12: THE GREAT BASIN

Paiute: [NOTE: The Warm Springs reservation and Klamath Tribe official pages also fall under this category]

http://www.burnspaiute-nsn.gov (Burns Paiute Tribe official website)

http://www.shoshonebannocktribes.com (Shoshone-Bannock Tribes official websites)

http://www.lovelockpaiutetribe.com (Lovelock Paiute Tribe official website)

http://www.fpst.org (Fallon Paiute-Shoshone Tribe official website)

http://plpt.nsn.us (Pyramid Lake Paiute Tribe official website)

http://www.rsic.org (Reno-Sparks Indian Colony official website, includes the Paiute, Shoshone, and Washo tribes)

http://shopaitribes.org/spt-15/ (Shoshone Paiute Tribes of the Duck Valley Indian Reservation official website)

http://www.summitlaketribe.org (Summit Lake Paiute Tribe official website)

http://www.wrpt.us (Walker River Paiute Tribe official website)

http://winnemuccaindiancolony.weebly.com (Western Band of the Western Shoshone official website)

http://www.ypt-nsn.gov/joomla/ (Yerington Paiute Tribe official website)

http://www.citlink.net/cedranch/Cedarville_Rancheria/Welcome.html (Cedarville Rancheria Northern Paiute Tribe official website)

http://www.sir-nsn.gov (Susanville Indian Rancheria official website)

http://www.bigpinepaiute.org (Big Pine Paiute Tribe of the Owens Valley official website)

http://www.bishoppaiutetribe.com (Bishop Paiute Tribe official website)

http://lppsr.org (Lone Pine Paiute-Shoshone Reservation)

CHAPTER 13: THE SHOSHONES

Shoshone: [NOTE: The Reno-Sparks Indian Colony, Fallon Paiute-Shoshone Tribe, Shoshone Paiute Tribes of the Duck Valley Indian Reservation, Shoshone-Bannock Tribes, Big Pine Paiute Tribe of the Owens Valley, Bishop Paiute Tribe, Lone Pine Paiute-Shoshone Reservation, and Western Band of the Western Shoshone pages also fall under this category]

http://easternshoshonetribe.org (Eastern Shoshone Tribe official website)

http://www.nwbshoshone.com/culture/history/index.htm (Northwestern Band of the Shoshone Nation official website)

http://shoshone-arapaho-tribal-court.org (Shoshone and Arapaho Tribal Court of the Wind River Reservation official website)

http://www.lemhi-shoshone.com (Lemhi-Shoshone Tribes official website)

http://www.goshutetribe.com (Confederate Tribes of the Goshute Indian Reservation official website)

http://www.temoaktribe.com (Te-Moak Tribe of Western Shoshone official website)

http://timbisha.com (Timbisha Shoshone Tribe official website)

http://www.duckwatertribe.org (Duckwater Shoshone Tribe official website)

http://www.elyshoshonetribe-nsn.gov (Ely Shoshone Tribe official website)

http://yombatribe.org (Yomba Shoshone Tribe official website)

CHAPTER 14: THE SOUTHWEST

Hopi: http://www.hopi-nsn.gov (The Hopi Tribe official website)

http://www.crit-nsn.gov (Colorado River Indian Tribes official website, includes Mohave, Chemehuevi, Hopi, and Navajo tribes)

Tewa: http://indianpueblo.org (Indian Pueblo Cultural Center, includes Acoma, Cochiti Isleta, Jemez, Laguna, Nambé, Ohkay Owingeh, Picuris, Pojoaque, Sandia, San Felipe, San Ildefonso, Santa Ana, Santa Clara, Santo Domingo, Taos, Tesuque, Zia, and Zuni)

http://nambepueblo.org (Nambé Pueblo official website)

http://pojoaque.org (Pueblo of Pojoaque official website)

http://www.sanipueblo.org (Pueblo de San Ildefonso official website)

http://ohkayowingeh-nsn.gov (Ohkay Owingeh Development Committee official website)

Apache: http://www.wmat.nsn.us (White Mountain Apache Tribe official website)

http://www.sancarlosapache.com/home.htm (San Carlos Apache official website)

http://itcaonline.com/?page_id=1183 (InterTribal Council of Arizona, Tonto Apache Tribe page)

http://www.chiricahuaapache.org (Chiricahua Apache Nde Nation official website)

http://mescaleroapachetribe.com (Mescalero Apache Tribe official website)

http://www.jicarillaonline.com (Jicarilla Apache Nation official website)

http://www.lipanapache.org (Lipan Apache Tribe of Texas official website)

http://www.apachetribe.org (Apache Tribe of Oklahoma (Plains Apache) official website)

Pima: http://www.srpmic-nsn.gov (Salt River Pima-Maricopa Indian Community official website)

http://www.gilariver.org (Gila River Indian Community official website)

Tohono O'odham: http://www.tonation-nsn.gov (Tohono O'odham Nation official website)

Mohave: http://mojaveindiantribe.com (Fort Mojave Indian Tribe official website)

http://www.crit-nsn.gov (Colorado River Indian Tribes official website, includes Mohave, Chemehuevi, Hopi, and Navajo tribes)

CHAPTER 15: THE ZUNIS

Zuni: http://www.ashiwi.org (Pueblo of Zuni official website)

CHAPTER 16: THE DINE (OR NAVAJOS)

Diné (Navajo): http://www.navajo-nsn.gov (Navajo Nation official website)

CHAPTER 17: CALIFORNIA

Karok: http://www.qvir.com (Quartz Valley Indian Reservation official website)

http://www.karuk.us (Karuk Tribe official website)

http://trinidad-rancheria.org (Cher-Ae Heights Indian Community of the Trinidad Rancheria official website)

Chumash: http://www.santaynezchumash.org (Santa Ynez Band of Chumash Indians official website)

http://coastalbandofthechumashnation.weebly.com (Coastal Band of the Chumash Nation official website)

http://www.barbarenochumashcouncil.com (Barbareno Chumash Council official website)

Yurok: http://trinidad-rancheria.org (Cher-Ae Heights Indian Community of the Trinidad Rancheria official website)

http://www.yuroktribe.org (Yurok Tribe official website)

http://www.bluelakerancheria-nsn.gov (Blue Lake Rancheria Tribe official website)

http://www.elk-valley.com (Elk Valley Rancheria official website)

http://resighinirancheria.com (Resighini Rancheria)

http://www.tolowa-nsn.gov (Smith River Rancheria official website)

CHAPTER 18: THE POMOS

http://www.cloverdalerancheria.com (Cloverdale Rancheria of Pomo Indians official website)

https://www.facebook.com/CoyoteValleyTribe (Coyote Valley Band of Pomo Indians official Facebook page)

http://drycreekrancheria.com (Dry Creek Rancheria Band of Pomo Indians official website)

http://www.elemindiancolony.org (Elem Indian Colony Pomo Tribe official website)

http://www.gratonrancheria.com (Federated Indians of Graton Rancheria official website, includes Coast Miwok and Southern Pomo)

http://www.upperlakepomo.com (Habematolel Pomo of Upper Lake official website)

http://stewartspoint.org/wp/ (Kashia Band of Pomo Indians official website)

http://www.hoplandtribe.com (Hopland Band of Pomo Indians official website, website currently unavailable (servers are down))

http://www.koination.com (Koi Nation of Northern California official website)

http://pottervalleytribe.com (Potter Valley Tribe of Pomo Indians official website)

http://www.robinsonrancheria.org (Robinson Rancheria of Pomo Indians official website)

http://www.rvit.org (Round Valley Indian Tribes official website, includes Yuki, Pit River, Pomo, Nomlacki, Concow, and Wailacki)

https://www.facebook.com/pages/Official-Scotts-Valley-Band-of-Pomo-Indians/162007124009441 (Scotts Valley Band of Pomo Indians official Facebook page)

http://sherwoodvalleyband.com (Sherwood Valley Rancheria Band of Pomo Indians official website)

CHAPTER 19: THE PLATEAU

Coeur d'Alene: http://www.cdatribe-nsn.gov (Coeur d'Alene official website)

http://cdatribalschool.org (tribal school official website)

Klamath: http://klamathtribes.org (Klamath Tribes (Klamath, Modoc, and Yahooskin) official website)

http://www.qvir.com (Quartz Valley Indian Reservation official website)

Sahaptin:

- **Nez Perce:** (see above)
- **Umatilla:** http://ctuir.org (Confederated Tribes of the Umatilla Indian Reserve - includes Cayuse, Umatilla, and Walla Walla), http://www.critfc.org/member_tribes_overview/the-confederated-tribes-of-the-umatilla-indian-reservation/ (Columbia River Inter-Tribal Fish Commission, Umatilla member page)
- **Tenino:** http://www.native-languages.org/tenino_culture.htm (overview of Tenino culture and history, with links), http://www.warmsprings.com (Official website of Warm Springs reservation, home of the Tenino, Wasco, and Paiute tribes)
- **Yakama:** http://www.yakamanation-nsn.gov (Yakama official website)

CHAPTER 20: THE NEZ PERCE

Nez Perce: http://www.nezperce.org (Nez Perce official website)

CHAPTER 21: THE NORTHWEST COAST

Tlingit: http://ccthita.org (Central Council of the Tlingit and Haida Indian Tribes of Alaska official website)

Haida: http://ccthita.org (Central Council of the Tlingit and Haida Indian Tribes of Alaska official website)

http://www.haidanation.ca (Council of the Haida Nation official website)

Coast Salish: http://www.twnation.ca (Tsleil-Waututh Nation official website)

http://www.musqueam.bc.ca (Musqueam official website)

http://www.komoks.ca (K'ómoks First Nation official website)

http://klahoose.org (Klahoose First Nation official website)

http://www.lummi-nsn.org (Lummi Nation official website)

http://www.nisqually-nsn.gov (Nisqually Indian Tribe official website)

http://www.duwamishtribe.org (Duwamish Tribe official website)

http://www.nooksacktribe.org (Nooksack Indian Tribe)

http://www.chehalistribe.org (Chehalis Tribe official website)

http://www.malahatnation.ca (Málexeł Nation official website)

http://www.elwha.org (Lower Elwha Klallam Tribe official website)

http://www.jamestowntribe.org (Jamestown S'Klallam Tribe official website)

https://www.pgst.nsn.us (Port Gamble S'Klallam Tribe official website)

http://www.tsoukenation.com (T'Sou-ke Nation official website)

http://halalt.org (Halalt First Nation official website)

http://lyackson.bc.ca (Lyackson First Nation official website)

http://www.penelakut.ca (Penelakut Tribe official website)

http://www.cowichantribes.com (Cowichan Tribes official website)

http://www.stzuminus.com (Stz'uminus First Nation official website)

http://www.snuneymuxw.ca (Snuneymuxw First Nation official website)

http://www.nanoose.org (Nanoose First Nation (Snaw-Naw-As) official website)

http://sliammonfirstnation.com (Tla'amin First Nation official website)

http://www.saanich.ca (Saanich official website)

http://www.samishtribe.nsn.us (Samish Indian Nation official website)

http://www.shishalh.com (Shíshálh Nation official website)

http://ctsi.nsn.us (Confederated Tribes of Siletz Indians)

http://www.swinomish-nsn.gov (Swinomish Indian Tribal Community official website)

http://www.skokomish.org (Skokomish Indian Tribe official website) http://www.snohomishtribe.com (Snohomish Tribe of Indians official website)

http://www.snoqualmienation.com (Snoqualmie Tribe official website)

http://songheesnation.ca (Songhees Nation official website, under construction)

http://www.squamish.net (Squamish Nation official website)

http://squaxinisland.org (Squaxin Island Tribe official website)

http://www.stillaguamish.com (Stillaguamish Tribe of Indians official website)

http://www.stolonation.bc.ca (Stó:lō Nation official website)http://www.stolotribalcouncil.ca (Stó:lō Tribal Council official website)

http://www.suquamish.nsn.us (Suquamish Tribe official website)

http://tsawwassenfirstnation.com (Tsawwassen First Nation official website)

http://www.tulaliptribes-nsn.gov (Tulalip Tribes official website)

Makah: http://makah.com (Makah Tribe/Neah Bay official website)

CHAPTER 22: THE KWAKWAKA'WAKW (OR KWAKIUTL)

Kwakwaka'wakw: http://kwakiutl.bc.ca (Kwakiutl Indian Band official website)

CHAPTER 23: THE SUBARCTIC AND THE ARCTIC

Cree: http://www.naskapi.ca (Naskapi Community official website)

http://www.innu.ca (Innu Nation official website)

http://www.atikamekwsipi.com (Atikamekw Sipi official website (in French))

http://www.gcc.ca (Grand Council of the Crees official website)

http://www.creeculture.ca (Cree Culture and Language Department of the Cree Nation Government (link above) official website)

http://www.moosecree.com (Moose Cree First Nation official website)

Métis: http://www.omaa.org (Woodland Métis Tribe official website)

http://www.usmetis.com (United States Métis Nation official website)

http://www.albertametis.com/MNAHome/Home.aspx (Métis Nation of Alberta official website)

CHAPTER 24: THE INNUS (OR MONTAGNAIS)

Innu (Montagnais): http://www.innu.ca (Innu Nation official website)

CHAPTER 25: THE INUIT

Inuit: http://www.inupiatheritage.org (Iñupiat Heritage Center official website)

http://www.inupiatgov.com (Iñupiat Community of the Arctic Slope official website)

http://www.nunatsiavut.com (Nunatsiavut official website)

http://www.nunatukavut.ca/home/ (Nunatukavut official website)

CHAPTER 2

20 Library of Congress, LC-USZ62-51802; **21** Beinecke Rare Book & Manuscript Library, Yale University

CHAPTER 4

61 Courtesy of the Connecticut State Library; **65** SF photo/Thinkstock; **69** Library of Congress, LC-DIG-ggbain-00160

CHAPTER 5

88 Courtesy of the Iroquois Indian Museum; **99** AP Photo/Heather Ainsworth

CHAPTER 6

106 Nova Scotia Archives & Records Management; **124** AP Photo/Andrew Vaughan/The Canadian Press

CHAPTER 7

137 Library of Congress, LC-USZ62-100257; **141** David Lyons/Alamy Stock Photo; **144** AP Photo/Luis M. Alvarez

CHAPTER 8

158 Library of Congress, LC-USZC4-4810; **168** AP Photo/Sun Herald, John Fitzhugh

CHAPTER 9

178 National Archives, American Indian Select List #84; **190** National Archives, American Indian Select List #38; **193** ThinkStock

CHAPTER 10

203 Library of Congress, LC-USZ62-46735; **211** Library of Congress, LC-USZC4-7160; **216** Allen Russell/Alamy Stock Photo

CHAPTER 11

231 Library of Congress, LC-DIG-pga-03543

CHAPTER 12

246 From The New York Public Library; **254** AP Photo/Las Vegas Sun, Steve Marcus

CHAPTER 13

263 Library of Congress, LC-DIG-npcc-19666; **269** National Archives, American West Photographs, #73; **273** Momastiuk & Eastcott/Science Source

CHAPTER 14

280 Library of Congress, LC-USZ62-105863/Edward S. Curtis; **282** AP Photo/Jacquelyn Martin

CHAPTER 15

301 Library of Congress, LC-USZ62-102037/Edward S. Curtis; **305** Library of Congress, LC-USZ62-117706/Edward S. Curtis; **313** AP Photo/Benjamin Chrisman

CHAPTER 16

320 Library of Congress, LC-DIG-ppmsc-00135; **334** AP Photo/USDOJ

CHAPTER 17

346 Lawrence Migdale/Science Source; **348** Library of Congress, LC-USZ62-111286; **356** Harrington papers, National Anthropological Archives, Smithsonian Institution

CHAPTER 18

365 Library of Congress, LC-USZ62-116525; **380** Inga Spence/Photo Researchers, Inc.

CHAPTER 19

388 Library of Congress, LC-USZ62-105859/Edward S. Curtis; **397** AP Photo/Yakima Herald-Republic/TJ Mullinax

CHAPTER 20

409 Library of Congress, LC-USZ62-101259/Edward S. Curtis; **413** Library of Congress, LC-USZC4-5785; **416** William H. Mullins/Science Source

CHAPTER 21

426 Miles Brothers/National Archives; **437** Library of Congress, LC-USZ62-107820/Asahel Curtis

CHAPTER 22

443 Library of Congress, LC-USZ62-47016/Edward S. Curtis; **458** AP Photo/The Canadian Press, Darryl Dyck

CHAPTER 23

467 Library of Congress, LC-USZC4-8295/Edward S. Curtis; **473** Bryan and Cherry Alexander/Science Source

CHAPTER 24

482 Mina Benson Hubbard/Wikipedia Commons

CHAPTER 25

502 Library of Congress, LC-USZ62-107282; **503** Library of Congress, LC-USZ62-112765/Canadian Geological Survey; **515** Ansgar Walk/Wikipedia Commons